Place-of-Service Codes for Professional (

Listed below are place-of-service codes and descriptions. These codes should b
entity where service(s) were rendered. Check with individual payers (eg, Medi
reimbursement policies regarding these codes. If you would like to comment
your request to posinfo@cms.hhs.gov.

Place of Service Code(s)	Place of Service Name	Place of Service Description
01	Pharmacy	A facility or location where drugs and other medically related items and services are sold, dispensed, or otherwise provided directly to patients.
02	Unassigned	N/A
03	School	A facility whose primary purpose is education.
04	Homeless shelter	A facility or location whose primary purpose is to provide temporary housing to homeless individuals (eg, emergency shelters, individual or family shelters).
05	Indian Health Service freestanding facility	A facility or location, owned and operated by the Indian Health Service, that provides diagnostic, therapeutic (surgical and nonsurgical), and rehabilitation services to American Indians and Alaska Natives who do not require hospitalization.
06	Indian Health Service provider-based facility	A facility or location, owned and operated by the Indian Health Service, that provides diagnostic, therapeutic (surgical and nonsurgical), and rehabilitation services rendered by, or under the supervision of, physicians to American Indians and Alaska Natives admitted as inpatients or outpatients.
07	Tribal 638 freestanding facility	A facility or location owned and operated by a federally recognized American Indian or Alaska Native tribe or tribal organization under a 638 agreement that provides diagnostic, therapeutic (surgical and nonsurgical), and rehabilitation services to tribal members who do not require hospitalization.
08	Tribal 638 provider-based facility	A facility or location owned and operated by a federally recognized American Indian or Alaska Native tribe or tribal organization under a 638 agreement that provides diagnostic, therapeutic (surgical and nonsurgical), and rehabilitation services to tribal members admitted as inpatients or outpatients.
09	Prison-Correctional Facility	A prison, jail, reformatory, work farm, detention center, or any other similar facility maintained by either Federal, State, or local authorities for the purpose of confinement or rehabilitation of adult or juvenile criminal offenders. (effective 7/1/06)
10	Unassigned	N/A
11	Office	Location, other than a hospital, skilled nursing facility (SNF), military treatment facility, community health center, state or local public health clinic, or intermediate care facility (ICF), where the health professional routinely provides health examinations, diagnosis, and treatment of illness or injury on an ambulatory basis.
12	Home	Location, other than a hospital or other facility, where the patient receives care in a private residence.
13	Assisted living facility	Congregate residential facility with self-contained living units providing assessment of each resident's needs and on-site support 24 hours a day, seven days a week, with the capacity to deliver or arrange for services including some health care and other services. (effective 10/1/03)
14	Group home	A residence, with shared living areas, where clients receive supervision and other services such as social and/or behavioral services, custodial service, and minimal services (eg, medication administration)
15	Mobile unit	A facility or unit that moves from place to place and is equipped to provide preventive, screening, diagnostic, and/or treatment services.
16	Temporary Lodging	A short-term accommodation such as a hotel, camp ground, hostel, cruise ship or resort where the patient receives care, and which is not identified by any other POS code. (effective 04/01/08)
17-19	Unassigned	N/A
20	Urgent care facility	Location, distinct from a hospital emergency department, an office, or a clinic, whose purpose is to diagnose and treat illness or injury for unscheduled, ambulatory patients seeking immediate medical attention.
21	Inpatient hospital	A facility, other than psychiatric, that primarily provides diagnostic, therapeutic (both surgical and nonsurgical), and rehabilitation services by, or under, the supervision of physicians to patients admitted for a variety of medical conditions.
22	Outpatient hospital	A portion of a hospital that provides diagnostic, therapeutic (both surgical and nonsurgical), and rehabilitation services to sick or injured persons who do not require hospitalization or institutionalization.
23	Emergency room—hospital	A portion of a hospital where emergency diagnosis and treatment of illness or injury is provided.
24	Ambulatory surgical center	A freestanding facility, other than a physician's office, where surgical and diagnostic services are provided on an ambulatory basis.
25	Birthing center	A facility, other than a hospital's maternity facilities or a physician's office, that provides a setting for labor, delivery, and immediate postpartum care as well as immediate care of newborn infants.
26	Military treatment facility	A medical facility operated by one or more of the uniformed services. Military treatment facility also refers to certain former US Public Health Service facilities now designated as uniformed service treatment facilities.
27-30	Unassigned	N/A
31	Skilled nursing facility	A facility that primarily provides inpatient skilled nursing care and related services to patients who require medical, nursing, or rehabilitative services but does not provide the level of care or treatment available in a hospital.

32	Nursing facility	A facility that primarily provides to residents skilled nursing care and related services for the rehabilitation of injured, disabled, or sick persons, or, on a regular basis, health-related care services above the level of custodial care to other than mentally retarded individuals.
33	Custodial care facility	A facility that provides room, board, and other personal assistance services, generally on a long-term basis, and does not include a medical component.
34	Hospice	A facility, other than a patient's home, in which palliative and supportive care for terminally ill patients and their families are provided.
35-40	Unassigned	N/A
41	Ambulance—land	A land vehicle specifically designed, equipped, and staffed for lifesaving and transporting the sick or injured.
42	Ambulance—air or water	An air or water vehicle specifically designed, equipped, and staffed for lifesaving and transporting the sick or injured.
43-48	Unassigned	N/A
49	Independent clinic	A location, not part of a hospital and not described by any other place-of-service code, that is organized and operated to provide preventive, diagnostic, therapeutic, rehabilitative, or palliative services to outpatients only. (effective 10/1/03)
50	Federally qualified health center	A facility located in a medically underserved area that provides Medicare beneficiaries preventive primary medical care under the general direction of a physician.
51	Inpatient psychiatric facility	A facility that provides inpatient psychiatric services for the diagnosis and treatment of mental illness on a 24-hour basis, by or under the supervision of a physician.
52	Psychiatric facility—partial hospitalization	A facility for the diagnosis and treatment of mental illness that provides a planned therapeutic program for patients who do not require full-time hospitalization but who need broader programs than are possible from outpatient visits to a hospital-based or hospital-affiliated facility.
53	Community mental health center	A facility that provides the following services: outpatient services, including specialized outpatient services for children, the elderly, individuals who are chronically ill, and residents of the community mental health center's mental health services area who have been discharged from inpatient treatment at a mental health facility; 24-hour-a-day emergency care services; day treatment, other partial hospitalization services, or psychosocial rehabilitation services; screening for patients being considered for admission to state mental health facilities to determine the appropriateness of such admission; and consultation and education services.
54	Intermediate care facility/mentally retarded	A facility that primarily provides health-related care and services above the level of custodial care to mentally retarded individuals but does not provide the level of care or treatment available in a hospital or skilled nursing facility.
55	Residential substance abuse treatment facility	A facility that provides treatment for substance (alcohol and drug) abuse to live-in residents who do not require acute medical care. Services include individual and group therapy and counseling, family counseling, laboratory tests, drugs and supplies, psychological testing, and room and board.
56	Psychiatric residential treatment center	A facility or distinct part of a facility for psychiatric care that provides a total 24-hour therapeutically planned and professionally staffed group living and learning environment.
57	Nonresidential substance abuse treatment facility	A location that provides treatment for substance (alcohol and drug) abuse on an ambulatory basis. Services include individual and group therapy and counseling, family counseling, laboratory tests, drugs and supplies, and psychological testing. (effective 10/1/03)
58-59	Unassigned	N/A
60	Mass immunization center	A location where providers administer pneumococcal pneumonia and influenza virus vaccinations and submit these services as electronic media claims or paper claims or by using the roster billing method. This generally takes place in a mass immunization setting, such as a public health center, pharmacy, or mall but may include a physician office setting.
61	Comprehensive inpatient rehabilitation facility	A facility that provides comprehensive rehabilitation services under the supervision of a physician to inpatients with physical disabilities. Services include physical therapy, occupational therapy, speech pathology, social or psychological services, and orthotics and prosthetics services.
62	Comprehensive outpatient rehabilitation facility	A facility that provides comprehensive rehabilitation services under the supervision of a physician to outpatients with physical disabilities. Services include physical therapy, occupational therapy, and speech pathology services.
63-64	Unassigned	N/A
65	End-stage renal disease treatment facility	A facility, other than a hospital, that provides dialysis treatment, maintenance, and/or training to patients or caregivers on an ambulatory or home-care basis.
66-70	Unassigned	N/A
71	Public health clinic	A facility maintained by either state or local health departments that provides ambulatory primary medical care under the general direction of a physician. (effective 10/1/03)
72	Rural health clinic	A certified facility located in a rural, medically underserved area that provides ambulatory primary medical care under the general direction of a physician.
73-80	Unassigned	N/A
81	Independent laboratory	A laboratory certified to perform diagnostic and/or clinical tests independent of an institution or a physician's office.
82-98	Unassigned	N/A
99	Other place of service	Other place of service not identified above.

current procedural terminology

cpt® 2009

Standard Edition

Michael Beebe
Joyce A. Dalton
Martha Espronceda, AAS
Desiree D. Evans, AAS
Rejina L. Glenn
Gloria Green, BA
DeHandro Hayden, BS
Anita Majerowicz, MS, RHIA
Janette Meggs, RHIA
Marie L. Mindeman, BA, RHIT
Karen E. O'Hara, BS, CCS-P
Mary R. O'Heron, RHIA, CCS-P
Danielle Pavloski, BS, RHIT, CCS-P
Dan Reyes
Desiree Rozell, MPA
Lianne Stancik, RHIT
Peggy Thompson, MS, RHIA, CCS
Susan Tracy, MA, RHIT
Jennifer Trajkovski, MJ, RHIT
Ada Walker, CCA

AMA
AMERICAN MEDICAL ASSOCIATION

Executive Vice President, Chief Executive Officer: Michael D. Maves, MD, MBA
Chief Operating Officer: Bernard L. Hengesbaugh
Senior Vice President, Publishing and Business Services: Robert A. Musacchio, PhD
Vice President and General Manager, Publishing: Frank J. Krause
Publisher, Physician Practice Solutions: Jay T. Ahlman
Vice President, Business Operations: Vanessa Hayden
Senior Acquisitions Editor: Elise Schumacher
Director of Marketing, Business Marketing and Communication: Pam Palmersheim
Director of Sales, Business Products: J.D. Kinney
Director, Production and Manufacturing: Jean Roberts
Manager, Marketing and Strategic Planning: Erin Kalitowski
Developmental Editor: Elizabeth A. Kennedy
Production Manager: Rosalyn Carlton
Senior Production Coordinator: Boon Ai Tan
Senior Print Coordinator: Ronnie Summers
Marketing Manager: Leigh Adams

Standard ISBN: 978-1-60359-063-1
ISSN: 0276-8283

1st Edition printed 1966
2nd Edition printed 1970
3rd Edition printed 1973
4th Edition printed 1977
Revised: 1978, 1979, 1980, 1981, 1982, 1984, 1985, 1986,
1987, 1988, 1989, 1990, 1991, 1992, 1993, 1994, 1995, 1996,
1997, 1998, 1999, 2000, 2001, 2002, 2003, 2004, 2005, 2006, 2007, 2008

To purchase additional CPT products, contact the American Medical Association Customer Service at 800 621-8335.

To request a license for distribution of products containing or reprinting CPT codes and/or guidelines, please see our Web site at *www.ama-assn.org/go/cpt* or contact the American Medical Association CPT Intellectual Property Services, 515 N. State Street, Chicago, Illinois 60654, 312 464-5022.

AC35:OP054109:11/08

Foreword

Current Procedural Terminology, (CPT®) Fourth Edition, is a listing of descriptive terms and identifying codes for reporting medical services and procedures performed by physicians. The purpose of the terminology is to provide a uniform language that will accurately describe medical, surgical, and diagnostic services, and will thereby provide an effective means for reliable nationwide communication among physicians, patients, and third parties. *CPT 2009* is the most recent revision of a work that first appeared in 1966.

CPT descriptive terms and identifying codes currently serve a wide variety of important functions in the field of medical nomenclature. The CPT codebook is useful for administrative management purposes such as claims processing and for the development of guidelines for medical care review. The uniform language is also applicable to medical education and outcomes, health services, and quality research by providing a useful basis for local, regional, and national utilization comparisons. The CPT codebook is the most widely accepted nomenclature for the reporting of physician procedures and services under government and private health insurance programs. In 2000, the CPT code set was designated by the Department of Health and Human Services as the national coding standard for physician and other health care professional services and procedures under the Health Insurance Portability and Accountability Act (HIPAA). This means that for all financial and administrative health care transactions sent electronically, the CPT code set will need to be used.

The changes that appear in this revision have been prepared by the CPT Editorial Panel with the assistance of physicians representing all specialties of medicine, and with important contributions from many third-party payers and governmental agencies.

The American Medical Association trusts that this revision will continue the usefulness of its predecessors in identifying, describing, and coding medical, surgical, and diagnostic services.

Michael D. Maves, MD, MBA
Executive Vice President, CEO

Acknowledgments

Publication of the annual CPT codebook represents many challenges and opportunities. From reconciling the many differences of opinion about the best way to describe a procedure, to the last details on placement of a semicolon, many individuals and organizations devote their energies and expertise to the preparation of this revision.

The editorial staff wishes to express sincere thanks to the many national medical specialty societies, health insurance organizations and agencies, and individual physicians and other health professionals who have made contributions.

Thanks are due to Robert A. Musacchio, PhD, Sr VP, American Medical Association; Claudia Bonnell, Blue Cross and Blue Shield Association; Nelly Leon-Chisen, American Hospital Association; Jeannette Thornton, America's Health Insurance Plans; and Sue Bowman, RHIA, American Health Information Management Association, Deborah J. Grider, CPC, American Academy of Professional Coders, for their invaluable assistance for enhancing the CPT code set.

For their assistance in development of the CPT Category II codes:

Ronald A. Gabel, MD	Sylvia Publ, RHIA, MBA
Darryl T. Gray, MD, ScD	Phil Renner, MBA
Robert S. Haskey, MD	Sam J. W. Romeo, MD, MBA
Peter A. Hollmann, MD	Paul M. Schyve, MD
Susan M. Nedza, MD	Sharon Sprenger, RHIA, PHQ, MPA
Gregory Pawlson, MD, MPH	Sally Turbyville, MA

We recognize the following people for efforts in working with the Physician Consortium for Performance Improvement® (PCPI) and other quality measurement organizations:

Mark Antman, DDS, MBA	Karen S. Kmetik, PhD
Heidi Bossley, MSN, MBA	Shannon Sims, MD, PhD
Joseph Gave, MPH	Beth Tapper, MA, MPH
Kendra Hanley, MS, CHE	Sheila Teasdale, MMed Sci FBCS
Erin Kaleba, MPH	Samantha Tierney, MPH

Dedication

We dedicate *CPT 2009* to Tracy R. Gordy, MD for his devoted service following his retirement from the chair of the CPT Editorial Panel for eight memorable and successful years. His position as chair was preceded by nine years service as a Panel member, beginning in 1990, and two years as an interim chair. His trademarks through almost two decades of continuous service as a volunteer for the American Medical Association included outstanding professionalism, consideration, and perseverance. Under his guidance, the CPT-5 recommendations were implemented, and two new code categories were added, steering the CPT code set toward an enhanced structure to meet the demands of today's dynamic healthcare system. His retirement allows him to pursue other activities in health care policy, while remaining a lifetime ambassador for CPT.

Farewell to our Panel member and friend, Samuel Hassenbusch III, MD, PhD, a devoted researcher, physician, patient, husband, and father. You showed us the importance of passion in life, work, and play. February 6, 1954–February 25, 2008

AMA CPT Editorial Panel

AMA CPT Advisory Committee

American Society for Aesthetic Plastic Surgery, Inc.
Paul R. Weiss, MD
American Society for Clinical Pathology
Mark S. Synovec, MD
Lee H. Hilborne, MD, MPH, FASCP
American Society for Dermatologic Surgery
Pamela K. Phillips, MD
American Society for Gastrointestinal Endoscopy
Glenn D. Littenberg, MD
American Society for Reproductive Medicine
John T. Queenan, Jr, MD
American Society for Surgery of the Hand
Daniel J. Nagle, MD
American Society for Therapeutic Radiology and Oncology
Michael L. Steinberg, MD, FACR
American Society of Abdominal Surgeons
Louis F. Alfano, Jr, MD
American Society of Anesthesiologists
Douglas G. Merrill, MD
American Society of Bariatric Physicians
Mary C. Vernon, MD
American Society of Cataract and Refractive Surgery
Stephen S. Lane, MD
American Society of Clinical Oncology
William C. Penley, MD
American Society of Colon and Rectal Surgeons
Guy R. Orangio, MD, FACS, FASCRS
American Society of Cytopathology
Patricia A. Gregg, MD, FCAP
American Society of General Surgeons
Charles Drueck III, MD, FACS
American Society of Hematology
Samuel M. Silver, MD, PhD, FACP, FAHA
American Society of Neuroimaging
Mircea A. Morariu, Jr, MD
American Society of Neuroradiology
C. Douglas Phillips, MD, FACR
American Society of Ophthalmic Plastic and Reconstructive Surgery
L. Neal Freeman, MD, MBA, CCS-P, FACS
American Society of Plastic Surgeons
Raymond V. Janevicius, MD
American Thoracic Society
Stephen P. Hoffmann, MD
American Urological Association
Jeffrey A. Dann, MD, MBA
Association of University Radiologists
Bob W. Gayler, MD
College of American Pathologists
James P. Almas, MD, FCAP
Congress of Neurological Surgeons
R. Patrick Jacob, MD
Contact Lens Association of Ophthalmologists
Charles B. Slonim, MD, FACS
Infectious Disease Society of America
Lawrence P. Martinelli, MD
International Society for Cardiovascular Surgery
Sean Roddy, MD‡
International Spinal Injection Society
Claire Tibiletti, MD
National Association of Medical Examiners
Paul A. Raslavicus, MD, MHA, CPE
North American Spine Society
William Mitchell, MD
Radiological Society of North America
Richard E. Fulton, MD
Timothy A. Crummy, MD‡
Renal Physicians Association
Richard J. Hamburger, MD
Society for Investigative Dermatology
Stephen P. Stone, MD
Society of American Gastrointestinal Endoscopic Surgeons
Paresh C. Shah, MD
Society of Critical Care Medicine
George A. Sample, MD, FCCP
Society of Nuclear Medicine
Kenneth A. McKusick, MD
Society of Thoracic Surgeons
Cameron D. Wright, MD
The Academy of Pharamaceutical Physicians and Investigators
Grant P. Bagley, MD
The Endocrine Society
Richard A. Guthrie, MD
The Society of Interventional Radiology
Katharine L. Krol, MD
United States and Canadian Academy of Pathology
David S. Wilkinson, MD, PhD

AMA Health Care Professionals Advisory Committee (HCPAC)

Tracy R. Gordy, MD, Co-Chair
William T. Thorwarth, Jr, MD
AMA CPT Editorial Panel
Helene Fearon, PT, Co-Chair
AMA CPT Editorial Panel
American Academy of Physician Assistants
Terry E. Carlisle, PA-C, MPAS
American Association of Naturopathic Physicians
Wendell B. Milliman, ND
American Association for Respiratory Care
Susan Rinaldo-Gallo, Med, RRT
American Chiropractic Association
Craig S. Little, DC, FACO
American Dietetic Association
Keith Thomas-Ayoob, EdD, RD, FADA, CSP
American Massage Therapy Association
Susan B. Rosen
American Nurses Association
David Keepnews, PhD, JD, RN
American Occupational Therapy Association
Leslie F. Davidson, MS, Ed, OTR/L
American Optometric Association
Douglas C. Morrow, OD
Pharmacist Services Technical Advisory Coalition
Daniel E. Buffington, PharmD, MBA
American Physical Therapy Association
Paul A. Rockar, Jr, DPT, MS
American Podiatric Medical Association
Michael J. King, DPM, FACFAS
American Psychological Association
Antonio E. Puente, PhD
American Speech-Language Hearing Association
R. Wayne Holland, EdD, CCC-SLP
National Athletic Trainers' Association
J. David Jones, MSHA, MS, ATC
National Association of Social Workers
Nelda Spyres, ACSW, LCSW
National Society of Genetic Counselors
Debra L. Doyle, MS, CGC

Contents

► ◄=Contains new or revised text

Introduction

Current Procedural Terminology (CPT®), Fourth Edition, is a set of codes, descriptions, and guidelines intended to describe procedures and services performed by physicians and other health care providers. Each procedure or service is identified with a five-digit code. The use of CPT codes simplifies the reporting of services.

Inclusion of a descriptor and its associated five-digit code number in the CPT codebook is based on whether the procedure is consistent with contemporary medical practice and is performed by many practitioners in clinical practice in multiple locations. Inclusion in the CPT codebook does not represent endorsement by the American Medical Association (AMA) of any particular diagnostic or therapeutic procedure. Inclusion or exclusion of a procedure does not imply any health insurance coverage or reimbursement policy.

►The CPT code set is published annually in the late summer or early fall as both electronic data files and books. The release of CPT data files on the Internet typically precedes the book by several weeks. In any case, January 1 is the effective date for use of the update of the CPT code set. The interval between the release of the update and the effective date is considered the implementation period and is intended to allow physicians and other providers, payers, and vendors to incorporate CPT changes into their systems. The exceptions to this schedule of release and effective dates are CPT Category III and vaccine product codes, which are released twice a year on January 1 or July 1 with effective dates for use six months later, and CPT Category II codes. Changes to the CPT code set are meant to be applied prospectively from the effective date.◄

The main body of the material is listed in six sections. Each section is divided into subsections with anatomic, procedural, condition, or descriptor subheadings. The procedures and services with their identifying codes are presented in numeric order with one exception—the entire **Evaluation and Management** section (99201-99499) appears at the beginning of the listed procedures. These items are used by most physicians in reporting a significant portion of their services.

Section Numbers and Their Sequences

Category I

Evaluation and Management 99201-99499
Anesthesiology 00100-01999, 99100-99140
Surgery 10021-69990
Radiology (Including Nuclear Medicine and Diagnostic Ultrasound) 70010-79999
Pathology and Laboratory 80047-89356
Medicine (except Anesthesiology) 90281-99199, 99500-99607

Category II 0001F-7025F

Category III 0016T-0196T

The first and last code numbers and the subsection name of the items appear at the top margin of most pages (eg, "11010-11306 Surgery/Integumentary System"). The continuous pagination of the CPT codebook is found on the lower margin of each page along with explanation of any code symbols that are found on that page.

Instructions for Use of the CPT Codebook

Select the name of the procedure or service that accurately identifies the service performed. Do not select a CPT code that merely approximates the service provided. If no such specific code exists, then report the service using the appropriate unlisted procedure or service code. In surgery, it may be an operation; in medicine, a diagnostic or therapeutic procedure; in radiology, a radiograph. Other additional procedures performed or pertinent special services are also listed. When necessary, any modifying or extenuating circumstances are added. Any service or procedure should be adequately documented in the medical record.

It is important to recognize that the listing of a service or procedure and its code number in a specific section of this book does not restrict its use to a specific specialty group. Any procedure or service in any section of this book may be used to designate the services rendered by any qualified physician or other qualified health care professional.

Instructions, typically included as parenthetical notes with selected codes, indicate that a code should not be reported with another code or codes. These instructions are intended to prevent errors of significant probability and are not all inclusive. For example, the code with such instructions may be a component of another code and therefore it would be incorrect to report both codes even when the component service is performed. These instructions are not intended as a listing of all possible code combinations that should not be reported, nor to indicate all possible code combinations that are appropriately reported. When reporting codes for services provided, it is important to assure the accuracy and quality of coding through verification of the intent of the code by use of the related guidelines, parenthetical instructions, and coding resources, including *CPT Assistant* and other publications resulting from collaborative efforts of the AMA with medical specialty societies (ie, *Clinical Examples in Radiology*).

Format of the Terminology

The CPT code set has been developed as stand-alone descriptions of medical procedures. However, some of the procedures in the CPT codebook are not printed in their entirety but refer back to a common portion of the procedure listed in a preceding entry. This is evident when an entry is followed by one or more indentations. This is done in an effort to conserve space.

Example

25100 Arthrotomy, wrist joint; with biopsy

25105 with synovectomy

Note that the common part of code 25100 (the part before the semicolon) should be considered part of code 25105. Therefore, the full procedure represented by code 25105 should read:

25105 Arthrotomy, wrist joint; with synovectomy

Requests to Update the CPT Nomenclature

The effectiveness of the CPT nomenclature depends on constant updating to reflect changes in medical practice. This can only be accomplished through the interest and timely suggestions of practicing physicians, medical specialty societies, state medical associations, and other organizations and agencies. Accordingly, the AMA welcomes correspondence, inquiries, and suggestions concerning old and new procedures, as well as other matters such as codes and indices.

To submit a suggestion to add, delete, or revise procedures contained in the CPT codebook, please contact:

CPT Editorial Research & Development
American Medical Association
515 North State Street
Chicago, Illinois 60654

Coding change request forms are available at the AMA's CPT Web site: www.ama-assn.org/ama/pub/category/3866.html.

All proposed changes of the CPT codebook will be considered by the CPT Editorial Panel with consultation of appropriate medical specialty societies.

Guidelines

Specific guidelines are presented at the beginning of each of the six sections. These guidelines define items that are necessary to appropriately interpret and report the procedures and services contained in that section. For example, in the **Medicine** section, specific instructions are provided for handling unlisted services or procedures, special reports, and supplies and materials provided. Guidelines also provide explanations regarding terms that apply only to a particular section. For instance, **Radiology Guidelines** provide a definition of the unique term, "radiological supervision and interpretation." While in **Anesthesia,** a discussion of reporting time is included.

Add-on Codes

Some of the listed procedures are commonly carried out in addition to the primary procedure performed. These additional or supplemental procedures are designated as add-on codes with the symbol ✚ and they are listed in **Appendix D** of the CPT codebook. Add-on codes in *CPT 2009* can be readily identified by specific descriptor nomenclature that includes phrases such as "each additional" or "(List separately in addition to primary procedure)."

The add-on code concept in *CPT 2009* applies only to add-on procedures or services performed by the same physician. Add-on codes describe additional intra-service work associated with the primary procedure (eg, additional digit[s], lesion[s], neurorrhaphy[s], vertebral segment[s], tendon[s], joint[s]).

Add-on codes are always performed in addition to the primary service or procedure and must never be reported as a stand-alone code. All add-on codes found in the CPT codebook are exempt from the multiple procedure concept (see the modifier 51 definition in **Appendix A**).

Modifiers

A modifier provides the means to report or indicate that a service or procedure that has been performed has been altered by some specific circumstance but not changed in its definition or code. Modifiers also enable health care professionals to effectively respond to payment policy requirements established by other entities. The judicious application of modifiers obviates the necessity for separate procedure listings that may describe the modifying circumstance. Modifiers may be used to indicate to the recipient of a report that:

- A service or procedure had both a professional and technical component.
- A service or procedure was performed by more than one physician and/or in more than one location.
- A service or procedure was increased or reduced.
- Only part of a service was performed.
- An adjunctive service was performed.
- A bilateral procedure was performed.
- A service or procedure was provided more than once.
- Unusual events occurred.

Example

A physician providing diagnostic or therapeutic radiology services, ultrasound, or nuclear medicine services in a hospital would add modifier 26 to report the professional component.

73090 with modifier 26 = Professional component only for an X ray of the forearm

Example

Two surgeons may be required to manage a specific surgical problem. When two surgeons work together as primary surgeons performing distinct part(s) of a procedure, each surgeon should report his/her distinct operative work by adding modifier 62 to the procedure code and any associated code(s) for that procedure as long as both surgeons continue to work together as primary surgeons. Each surgeon should report the co-surgery once using the same procedure code. Modifier 62 would be applicable. For instance, a neurological surgeon and an otolaryngologist are working as co-surgeons in performing transphenoidal excision of a pituitary neoplasm.

The first surgeon would report:

61548 62 = Hypophysectomy or excision of pituitary tumor, transnasal or transseptal approach, nonstereotactic + two surgeons modifier

AND the second surgeon would report:

61548 62 = Hypophysectomy or excision of pituitary tumor, transnasal or transseptal approach, nonstereotactic + two surgeons modifier

If additional procedure(s) (including add-on procedure[s]) are performed during the same surgical session, separate code(s) may also be reported with modifier 62 added. It should be noted that if a co-surgeon acts as an assistant in the performance of additional procedure(s) during the same surgical session, those services may be reported using separate procedure code(s) with modifier 80 or modifier 82 added, as appropriate. A complete listing of modifiers is found in **Appendix A.**

Place of Service and Facility Reporting

Some codes have specified places of service (eg, evaluation and management codes are specific to a setting). Other services and procedures may have instructions specific to the place of service (eg, therapeutic, prophylactic, and diagnostic injections and infusions). The CPT code set is designated for reporting physician and qualified health care professional services. It is also the designated code set for reporting services by organizational or facility providers (eg, hospitals) in specific circumstances. Facilities are entities that may report services in addition to the physician or qualified health care professional for the same service. For example, a physician may report a procedure performed in the outpatient department of the hospital and the hospital may report the same procedure. The CPT codebook uses the term *facility* to describe such providers and the term *nonfacility* to describe services where no facility reporting may occur. Services provided in the home by an agency are facility services. Services provided in the home by a physician or qualified health care professional who is not a representative of the agency are nonfacility services.

Unlisted Procedure or Service

It is recognized that there may be services or procedures performed by physicians that are not found in the CPT codebook. Therefore, a number of specific code numbers have been designated for reporting unlisted procedures. When an unlisted procedure number is used, the service or procedure should be described. Each of these unlisted procedural code numbers (with the appropriate accompanying topical entry) relates to a specific section of the book and is presented in the guidelines of that section.

Results, Testing, Interpretation, and Report

Results are the technical component of a service. Testing leads to results; results lead to interpretation. Reports are the work product of the interpretation of test results. Certain procedures or services described in the CPT codebook involve a technical component (eg, tests), which produce results (eg, data, images, slides). For clinical use, some of these results require interpretation. Some CPT descriptors specifically require interpretation and reporting to report that code.

Special Report

A service that is rarely provided, unusual, variable, or new may require a special report in determining medical appropriateness of the service. Pertinent information should include an adequate definition or description of the nature, extent, and need for the procedure and the time, effort, and equipment necessary to provide the service. Additional items may include complexity of symptoms, final diagnosis, pertinent physical findings, diagnostic and therapeutic procedures, concurrent problems, and follow-up care.

Code Symbols

A summary listing of additions, deletions, and revisions applicable to the CPT codebook is found in **Appendix B.** New procedure numbers added to the CPT codebook are identified throughout the text with the symbol ● placed before the code number. In instances where a code revision has resulted in a substantially altered procedure descriptor, the symbol ▲ is placed before the code number. The symbol ○ is used to identify codes that are reinstated or recycled. The symbols ►◄ are used to indicate new and revised text other than the procedure descriptors. These symbols indicate CPT Editorial Panel actions. The AMA reserves the right to correct typographical errors and make stylistic improvements. CPT add-on codes are annotated by the symbol ✚ and are listed in **Appendix D**. The symbol ⊘ is used to identify codes that are exempt from the use of modifier 51 but have not been designated as CPT add-on procedures or services. A list of codes exempt from modifier 51 usage is included in **Appendix E.** The symbol ⊙ is used to identify codes that include moderate sedation (see **Appendix G**). The symbol ⚡ is used to identify codes for vaccines that are pending FDA approval (see **Appendix K**).

Alphabetical Reference Index

This codebook features an expanded alphabetical index that includes listings by procedure and anatomic site. Procedures and services commonly known by their eponyms or other designations are also included.

CPT 2009 in Electronic Formats

CPT 2009 procedure codes and descriptions are available on CD-ROM as data files and electronic software. Data files are available in ASCII and EBCDIC formats and can be imported into any billing and claims reporting software that accepts a text (.TXT) file format.

CPT 2009 Electronic Professional software, now with *Netter's Atlas of Human Anatomy for CPT Coding,* provides access to the entire *CPT 2009 Professional Edition* codebook on your desktop. Easy-to-use and fully searchable, this invaluable software contains all of the favorite *CPT Professional* features plus CPT codes and quick linking access between CPT codes, guidelines, modifiers, appendices, index, and more. For more information call (800) 621-8335 or visit *www.amabookstore.com.*

Additional CPT Resources

The AMA publishes additional CPT coding books and software to ensure your practice has current, complete, and compliant coding resources.

CPT® Assistant Newsletter

As the AMA's official communication tool for circulating accurate information and guidance on CPT codes and issues, this insightful monthly newsletter should be part of every compliance program. Each issue features articles used for answering day-to-day coding questions, appealing insurance denials, and validating coding to auditors. *CPT® Assistant* keeps you informed on critical code changes, enhances your coding proficiency through case studies and clinical examples, and provides a coding consultation section featuring questions and answers drawn from the *CPT® Information Services.*

Subscriptions to *CPT® Assistant* can be purchased by calling the AMA's Unified Services Center at (800) 621-8335. Individual back issues are available for purchase and immediate download at *www.amabookstore.com.*

CPT® Assistant Archives 1990–2008

Enjoy convenient access to 18 years of *CPT® Assistant* newsletter articles on your computer desktop. Search past issues of the AMA's authoritative coding newsletter by keyword, phrase, CPT code number, newsletter issue, article index, or codebook table of contents. The new edition of this product offers simple search capabilities, menu screens, a cumulative index of article titles, and a complete historical CPT code list from 1990-2008 that references when a code was added, deleted, and/or revised. Call (800) 621-8335 or visit *www.amabookstore.com* for more information.

CPT® Network

Your resource for CPT® coding answers straight from the source!

CPT® Network provides the tools to quickly research a database of commonly asked coding questions and clinical examples. Subscribers can submit electronic inquiries directly to a CPT expert for a quick, accurate solution to their coding question.

For complete details, and to choose the subscription service or special AMA member pricing that best fits your needs, visit *www.cptnetwork.com* today.

CPT® Changes 2009: An Insider's View

An indispensable guide for CPT codebook users. This book provides the official AMA interpretations and rationales for every new, revised, and deleted CPT code and guideline change. This valuable resource provides useful clinical examples and procedural descriptions to help explain the practical application for each new CPT code, and an "at-a-glance" tabular review of 2009 changes helps you easily determine the level to which your particular field has been affected by the changes. Call (800) 621-8335 or visit *www.amabookstore.com* for more information.

CPT® Changes Archives 2000–2009

Access current and historical CPT code and guideline changes on your computer desktop. An invaluable electronic library, use it to search the AMA's best-selling *CPT® Changes: An Insider's View* by keyword, phrase, CPT code number, edition, and CPT codebook table of contents. This product offers simple, intuitive search capabilities and a complete historical CPT code list from 1990-2009 that references when a code was added, deleted, and/or revised. Call (800) 621-8335 or visit *www.amabookstore.com* for more information.

More AMA Coding Resources

Check out these additional AMA coding resources at *www.amabookstore.com*:

- *CPT Handbook for Office Based Coding*
- *CPT® Reference of Clinical Examples: Official Coding Scenarios for Correct Coding, Second Edition*
- *Practical E/M: Documentation and Coding Solutions for Quality Patient Care, Second Edition*
- *Coding with Modifiers: A Guide to Correct CPT® and HCPCS Level II Modifier Usage*
- *Principles of CPT® Coding*
- *Principles of CPT® Coding Workbook: Coding Challenges and Exercises for Instructors and Students*
- *CodeManager®* software

Additional References

For best coding results, you will need to use other reference materials in addition to your coding books. These references include a medical dictionary and one or more anatomy books that can be purchased from the American Medical Association by calling 800 621-8335.

Medical Dictionaries

Merriam-Webster's Medical Desk Dictionary.
Springfield, Mass: Merriam Webster.
OP941493

Stedman's CPT® Dictionary.
Chicago, Ill: American Medical Association, 2007.
OP300607

Stedman's Medical Dictionary, 27th ed.
Baltimore, Md: Williams & Wilkins; 2000.
OP982900

Anatomy References

Kirschner, CG. *Netter's Atlas of Anatomy for CPT® and ICD-9-CM Coding Series: Musculoskeletal.*
Chicago, Ill: American Medical Association; *Coming Soon.*
OP492206

Kirschner, CG. *Netter's Atlas of Human Anatomy for CPT® Coding.*
Chicago, Ill: American Medical Association; 2005.
OP490605

Netter, FH. *Atlas of Human Anatomy.* 3rd ed.
East Hanover, NJ: Novartis; 2003.
OP936798

Evaluation and Management (E/M) Services Guidelines

In addition to the information presented in the Introduction, several other items unique to this section are defined or identified here.

Classification of Evaluation and Management (E/M) Services

The E/M section is divided into broad categories such as office visits, hospital visits, and consultations. Most of the categories are further divided into two or more subcategories of E/M services. For example, there are two subcategories of office visits (new patient and established patient) and there are two subcategories of hospital visits (initial and subsequent). The subcategories of E/M services are further classified into levels of E/M services that are identified by specific codes. This classification is important because the nature of physician work varies by type of service, place of service, and the patient's status.

The basic format of the levels of E/M services is the same for most categories. First, a unique code number is listed. Second, the place and/or type of service is specified, eg, office consultation. Third, the content of the service is defined, eg, comprehensive history and comprehensive examination. (See "Levels of E/M Services," page 3, for details on the content of E/M services.) Fourth, the nature of the presenting problem(s) usually associated with a given level is described. Fifth, the time typically required to provide the service is specified. (A detailed discussion of time is provided on page 4.)

Definitions of Commonly Used Terms

►Certain key words and phrases are used throughout the E/M section. The following definitions are intended to reduce the potential for differing interpretations and to increase the consistency of reporting by physicians in differing specialties. E/M services may also be reported by other qualified health care professionals who are authorized to perform such services within the scope of their practice.◄

New and Established Patient

Solely for the purposes of distinguishing between new and established patients, **professional services** are those face-to-face services rendered by a physician and reported by a specific CPT code(s). A new patient is one who has not received any professional services from the physician or another physician of the same specialty who belongs to the same group practice, within the past three years.

An established patient is one who has received professional services from the physician or another physician of the same specialty who belongs to the same group practice, within the past three years.

In the instance where a physician is on call for or covering for another physician, the patient's encounter will be classified as it would have been by the physician who is not available.

No distinction is made between new and established patients in the emergency department. E/M services in the emergency department category may be reported for any new or established patient who presents for treatment in the emergency department.

The decision tree on page 2 is provided to aid in determining whether to report the E/M service provided as a new or an established patient encounter.

Chief Complaint

A chief complaint is a concise statement describing the symptom, problem, condition, diagnosis, or other factor that is the reason for the encounter, usually stated in the patient's words.

Concurrent Care

Concurrent care is the provision of similar services (eg, hospital visits) to the same patient by more than one physician on the same day. When concurrent care is provided, no special reporting is required.

Counseling

Counseling is a discussion with a patient and/or family concerning one or more of the following areas:

- Diagnostic results, impressions, and/or recommended diagnostic studies
- Prognosis
- Risks and benefits of management (treatment) options
- Instructions for management (treatment) and/or follow-up
- Importance of compliance with chosen management (treatment) options
- Risk factor reduction
- Patient and family education

(For psychotherapy, see 90804-90857)

Decision Tree for New vs Established Patients

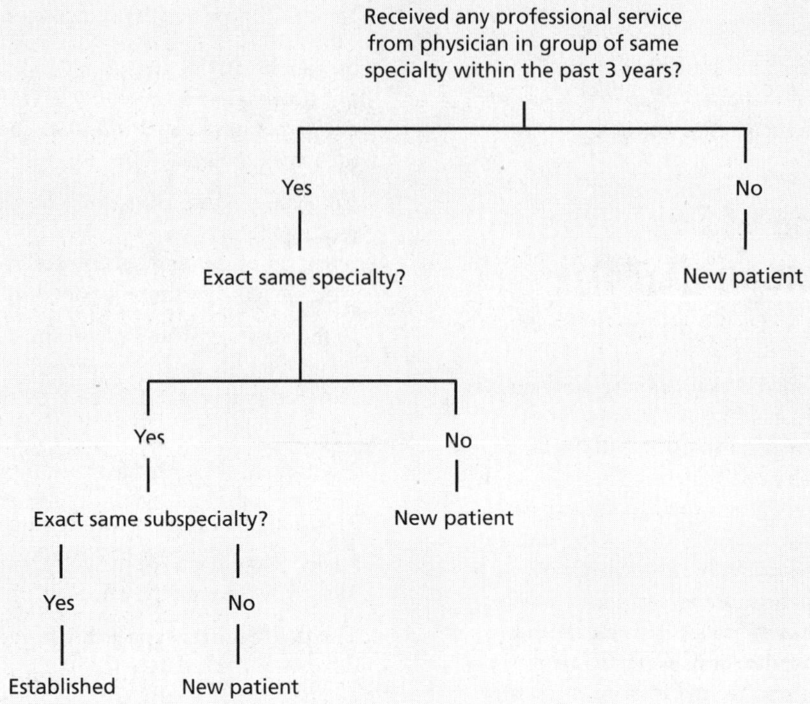

Family History

A review of medical events in the patient's family that includes significant information about:

- The health status or cause of death of parents, siblings, and children
- Specific diseases related to problems identified in the Chief Complaint or History of the Present Illness, and/or System Review
- Diseases of family members that may be hereditary or place the patient at risk

History of Present Illness

A chronological description of the development of the patient's present illness from the first sign and/or symptom to the present. This includes a description of location, quality, severity, timing, context, modifying factors, and associated signs and symptoms significantly related to the presenting problem(s).

Levels of E/M Services

Within each category or subcategory of E/M service, there are three to five levels of E/M services available for reporting purposes. Levels of E/M services are **not** interchangeable among the different categories or subcategories of service. For example, the first level of E/M services in the subcategory of office visit, new patient, does not have the same definition as the first level of E/M services in the subcategory of office visit, established patient.

The levels of E/M services include examinations, evaluations, treatments, conferences with or concerning patients, preventive pediatric and adult health supervision, and similar medical services, such as the determination of the need and/or location for appropriate care. Medical screening includes the history, examination, and medical decision-making required to determine the need and/or location for appropriate care and treatment of the patient (eg, office and other outpatient setting, emergency department, nursing facility). The levels of E/M services encompass the wide variations in skill, effort, time, responsibility, and medical knowledge required for the prevention or diagnosis and treatment of illness or injury and the promotion of optimal health. Each level of E/M services may be used by all physicians.

The descriptors for the levels of E/M services recognize seven components, six of which are used in defining the levels of E/M services. These components are:

- History
- Examination
- Medical decision making
- Counseling
- Coordination of care
- Nature of presenting problem
- Time

The first three of these components (history, examination, and medical decision making) are considered the **key** components in selecting a level of E/M services. (See "Determine the Extent of History Obtained," page 7.)

The next three components (counseling, coordination of care, and the nature of the presenting problem) are considered **contributory** factors in the majority of encounters. Although the first two of these contributory factors are important E/M services, it is not required that these services be provided at every patient encounter.

Coordination of care with other providers or agencies without a patient encounter on that day is reported using the case management codes.

The final component, time, is discussed in detail on page 4.

Any specifically identifiable procedure (ie, identified with a specific CPT code) performed on or subsequent to the date of initial or subsequent E/M services should be reported separately.

The actual performance and/or interpretation of diagnostic tests/studies ordered during a patient encounter are not included in the levels of E/M services. Physician performance of diagnostic tests/studies for which specific CPT codes are available may be reported separately, in addition to the appropriate E/M code. The physician's interpretation of the results of diagnostic tests/studies (ie, professional component) with preparation of a separate distinctly identifiable signed written report may also be reported separately, using the appropriate CPT code with modifier 26 appended.

The physician may need to indicate that on the day a procedure or service identified by a CPT code was performed, the patient's condition required a significant separately identifiable E/M service above and beyond other services provided or beyond the usual preservice and postservice care associated with the procedure that was performed. The E/M service may be caused or prompted by the symptoms or condition for which the procedure and/or service was provided. This circumstance may be reported by adding modifier 25 to the appropriate level of E/M service. As such, different diagnoses are not required for reporting of the procedure and the E/M services on the same date.

Nature of Presenting Problem

A presenting problem is a disease, condition, illness, injury, symptom, sign, finding, complaint, or other reason for encounter, with or without a diagnosis being established at the time of the encounter. The E/M codes recognize five types of presenting problems that are defined as follows:

Minimal: A problem that may not require the presence of the physician, but service is provided under the physician's supervision.

Self-limited or minor: A problem that runs a definite and prescribed course, is transient in nature, and is not likely to permanently alter health status OR has a good prognosis with management/compliance.

Low severity: A problem where the risk of morbidity without treatment is low; there is little to no risk of mortality without treatment; full recovery without functional impairment is expected.

Moderate severity: A problem where the risk of morbidity without treatment is moderate; there is moderate risk of mortality without treatment; uncertain prognosis OR increased probability of prolonged functional impairment.

High severity: A problem where the risk of morbidity without treatment is high to extreme; there is a moderate to high risk of mortality without treatment OR high probability of severe, prolonged functional impairment.

Past History

A review of the patient's past experiences with illnesses, injuries, and treatments that includes significant information about:

- Prior major illnesses and injuries
- Prior operations
- Prior hospitalizations
- Current medications
- Allergies (eg, drug, food)
- Age appropriate immunization status
- Age appropriate feeding/dietary status

Social History

An age appropriate review of past and current activities that includes significant information about:

- Marital status and/or living arrangements
- Current employment
- Occupational history
- Use of drugs, alcohol, and tobacco
- Level of education
- Sexual history
- Other relevant social factors

System Review (Review of Systems)

An inventory of body systems obtained through a series of questions seeking to identify signs and/or symptoms that the patient may be experiencing or has experienced. For the purposes of the CPT codebook the following elements of a system review have been identified:

- Constitutional symptoms (fever, weight loss, etc)
- Eyes
- Ears, nose, mouth, throat
- Cardiovascular
- Respiratory
- Gastrointestinal
- Genitourinary
- Musculoskeletal
- Integumentary (skin and/or breast)
- Neurological
- Psychiatric
- Endocrine
- Hematologic/lymphatic
- Allergic/immunologic

The review of systems helps define the problem, clarify the differential diagnosis, identify needed testing, or serves as baseline data on other systems that might be affected by any possible management options.

Time

The inclusion of time in the definitions of levels of E/M services has been implicit in prior editions of the CPT codebook. The inclusion of time as an explicit factor beginning in *CPT 1992* is done to assist physicians in selecting the most appropriate level of E/M services. It should be recognized that the specific times expressed in the visit code descriptors are averages and, therefore, represent a range of times that may be higher or lower depending on actual clinical circumstances.

Time is **not** a descriptive component for the emergency department levels of E/M services because emergency department services are typically provided on a variable intensity basis, often involving multiple encounters with several patients over an extended period of time. Therefore, it is often difficult for physicians to provide accurate estimates of the time spent face-to-face with the patient.

Studies to establish levels of E/M services employed surveys of practicing physicians to obtain data on the amount of time and work associated with typical E/M services. Since "work" is not easily quantifiable, the codes must rely on other objective, verifiable measures that correlate with physicians' estimates of their "work." It has been demonstrated that physicians' estimations of **intraservice** time (as explained on the next page), both within and across specialties, is a variable that is predictive of the "work" of E/M services. This same research has shown there is a strong relationship between intraservice time and total time for E/M services. Intraservice time, rather than total time, was chosen for inclusion with the codes because of its relative ease of measurement and because of its direct correlation with measurements of the total amount of time and work associated with typical E/M services.

Intraservice times are defined as **face-to-face** time for office and other outpatient visits and as **unit/floor** time for hospital and other inpatient visits. This distinction is necessary because most of the work of typical office visits takes place during the face-to-face time with the patient, while most of the work of typical hospital visits takes place during the time spent on the patient's floor or unit.

Face-to-face time (office and other outpatient visits and office consultations): For coding purposes, face-to-face time for these services is defined as only that time that the physician spends face-to-face with the patient and/or family. This includes the time in which the physician performs such tasks as obtaining a history, performing an examination, and counseling the patient.

Physicians also spend time doing work before or after the face-to-face time with the patient, performing such tasks as reviewing records and tests, arranging for further services, and communicating further with other professionals and the patient through written reports and telephone contact.

This **non-face-to-face** time for office services—also called pre- and postencounter time—is not included in the time component described in the E/M codes. However, the pre- and post-face-to-face work associated with an encounter was included in calculating the total work of typical services in physician surveys.

Thus, the face-to-face time associated with the services described by any E/M code is a valid proxy for the total work done before, during, and after the visit.

Unit/floor time (hospital observation services, inpatient hospital care, initial and follow-up hospital consultations, nursing facility): For reporting purposes, intraservice time for these services is defined as unit/floor time, which includes the time that the physician is present on the patient's hospital unit and at the bedside rendering services for that patient. This includes the time in which the physician establishes and/or reviews the patient's chart, examines the patient, writes notes, and communicates with other professionals and the patient's family.

In the hospital, pre- and post-time includes time spent off the patient's floor performing such tasks as reviewing pathology and radiology findings in another part of the hospital.

This pre- and postvisit time is not included in the time component described in these codes. However, the pre- and postwork performed during the time spent off the floor or unit was included in calculating the total work of typical services in physician surveys.

Thus, the unit/floor time associated with the services described by any code is a valid proxy for the total work done before, during, and after the visit.

Unlisted Service

An E/M service may be provided that is not listed in this section of the CPT codebook. When reporting such a service, the appropriate unlisted code may be used to indicate the service, identifying it by "Special Report," as discussed in the following paragraph. The "Unlisted Services" and accompanying codes for the E/M section are as follows:

99429 **Unlisted preventive** medicine service

99499 **Unlisted evaluation and management** service

Special Report

An unlisted service or one that is unusual, variable, or new may require a special report demonstrating the medical appropriateness of the service. Pertinent information should include an adequate definition or description of the nature, extent, and need for the procedure and the time, effort, and equipment necessary to provide the service. Additional items that may be included are complexity of symptoms, final diagnosis, pertinent physical findings, diagnostic and therapeutic procedures, concurrent problems, and follow-up care.

Clinical Examples

Clinical examples of the codes for E/M services are provided to assist physicians in understanding the meaning of the descriptors and selecting the correct code. The clinical examples are listed in Appendix C. Each example was developed by physicians in the specialties shown.

The same problem, when seen by physicians in different specialties, may involve different amounts of work. Therefore, the appropriate level of encounter should be reported using the descriptors rather than the examples.

The examples have been tested for validity and approved by the CPT Editorial Panel. Physicians were given the examples and asked to assign a code or assess the amount of time and work involved. Only examples that were rated consistently have been included in Appendix C.

Instructions for Selecting a Level of E/M Service

Identify the Category and Subcategory of Service

The categories and subcategories of codes available for reporting E/M services are shown in Table 1.

Table 1

Categories and Subcategories of Service

Category/Subcategory	Code Numbers
Office or Other Outpatient Services	
New Patient	99201-99205
Established Patient	99211-99215
Hospital Observation Services	
Hospital Observation Discharge Services	99217
Initial Hospital Observation Services	99218-99220
Hospital Observation or Inpatient Care Services (Including Admission and Discharge Services)	99234-99236
Hospital Inpatient Services	
Initial Hospital Care	99221-99223
Subsequent Hospital Care	99231-99233
Hospital Discharge Services	99238-99239
Consultations	
Office Consultations	99241-99245
Inpatient Consultations	99251-99255
Emergency Department Services	99281-99288
Critical Care Services	
Adult (over 24 months of age)	99291-99292
Nursing Facility Services	
Initial Nursing Facility Care	99304-99306
Subsequent Nursing Facility Care	99307-99310
Other Nursing Facility Services	99318
Nursing Facility Discharge Services	99315-99316
Domiciliary, Rest Home or Custodial Care Services	
New Patient	99324-99328
Established Patient	99334-99337
Domiciliary, Rest Home (eg, Assisted Living Facility), or Home Care Plan Oversight Services	99339-99340
Home Services	
New Patient	99341-99345
Established Patient	99347-99350
Prolonged Services	
With Direct Patient Contact	99354-99357
Without Direct Patient Contact	99358-99359
Standby Services	99360
Case Management Services	
Anticoagulant Management	99363-99364
Care Plan Oversight Services	99374-99380
Medical Team Conferences	99366-99368
Preventive Medicine Services	
New Patient	99381-99387
Established Patient	99391-99397
Individual Counseling	99401-99404
Group Counseling	99411-99412
Other	99420-99429
Non-Face-to-Face Physician Services	
Telephone Services	99441-99443
Online Medical Evaluation	99444
Special E/M Services	99450-99456
►Newborn Care	99460-99463
Delivery/Birthing Room Attendance	99464-99465
Neonatal and Pediatric Critical Care Services	
Pediatric Patient Transport	99466-99467
Inpatient Neonatal Critical Care Services	99468-99469
Inpatient Pediatric Critical Care Services	99471-99476
Initial and Continuing Intensive Care Services	99477-99480
Other E/M Services	99499◄

Review the Reporting Instructions for the Selected Category or Subcategory

Most of the categories and many of the subcategories of service have special guidelines or instructions unique to that category or subcategory. Where these are indicated, eg, "Inpatient Hospital Care," special instructions will be presented preceding the levels of E/M services.

Review the Level of E/M Service Descriptors and Examples in the Selected Category or Subcategory

The descriptors for the levels of E/M services recognize seven components, six of which are used in defining the levels of E/M services. These components are:

- History
- Examination
- Medical decision making
- Counseling
- Coordination of care
- Nature of presenting problem
- Time

The first three of these components (ie, history, examination, and medical decision making) should be considered the **key** components in selecting the level of E/M services. An exception to this rule is in the case of visits that consist predominantly of counseling or coordination of care (see numbered paragraph 3, page 8).

The nature of the presenting problem and time are provided in some levels to assist the physician in determining the appropriate level of E/M service.

Determine the Extent of History Obtained

The extent of the history is dependent upon clinical judgment and on the nature of the presenting problems(s). The levels of E/M services recognize four types of history that are defined as follows:

Problem focused: Chief complaint; brief history of present illness or problem.

Expanded problem focused: Chief complaint; brief history of present illness; problem pertinent system review.

Detailed: Chief complaint; extended history of present illness; problem pertinent system review extended to include a review of a limited number of additional systems; **pertinent** past, family, and/or social history **directly related to the patient's problems.**

Comprehensive: Chief complaint; extended history of present illness; review of systems that is directly related to the problem(s) identified in the history of the present illness plus a review of all additional body systems; **complete** past, family, and social history.

The comprehensive history obtained as part of the preventive medicine E/M service is not problem-oriented and does not involve a chief complaint or present illness. It does, however, include a comprehensive system review and comprehensive or interval past, family, and social history as well as a comprehensive assessment/history of pertinent risk factors.

Determine the Extent of Examination Performed

The extent of the examination performed is dependent on clinical judgment and on the nature of the presenting problem(s). The levels of E/M services recognize four types of examination that are defined as follows:

Problem focused: A limited examination of the affected body area or organ system.

Expanded problem focused: A limited examination of the affected body area or organ system and other symptomatic or related organ system(s).

Detailed: An extended examination of the affected body area(s) and other symptomatic or related organ system(s).

Comprehensive: A general multisystem examination or a complete examination of a single organ system. **Note:** The comprehensive examination performed as part of the preventive medicine E/M service is multisystem, but its extent is based on age and risk factors identified.

For the purposes of these CPT definitions, the following body areas are recognized:

- Head, including the face
- Neck
- Chest, including breasts and axilla
- Abdomen
- Genitalia, groin, buttocks
- Back
- Each extremity

For the purposes of these CPT definitions, the following organ systems are recognized:

- Eyes
- Ears, nose, mouth, and throat
- Cardiovascular
- Respiratory
- Gastrointestinal
- Genitourinary
- Musculoskeletal
- Skin
- Neurologic
- Psychiatric
- Hematologic/lymphatic/immunologic

Determine the Complexity of Medical Decision Making

Medical decision making refers to the complexity of establishing a diagnosis and/or selecting a management option as measured by:

- The number of possible diagnoses and/or the number of management options that must be considered
- The amount and/or complexity of medical records, diagnostic tests, and/or other information that must be obtained, reviewed, and analyzed
- The risk of significant complications, morbidity, and/or mortality, as well as comorbidities, associated with the patient's presenting problems(s), the diagnostic procedure(s), and/or the possible management options

Four types of medical decision making are recognized: straightforward, low complexity, moderate complexity, and high complexity. To qualify for a given type of decision making, two of the three elements in Table 2 must be met or exceeded.

Comorbidities/underlying diseases, in and of themselves, are not considered in selecting a level of E/M services *unless* their presence significantly increases the complexity of the medical decision making.

Select the Appropriate Level of E/M Services Based on the Following

1. For the following categories/subcategories, **all of the key components,** ie, history, examination, and medical decision making, must meet or exceed the stated requirements to qualify for a particular level of E/M service: office, new patient; hospital observation services; initial hospital care; office consultations; initial inpatient consultations; emergency department services; initial nursing facility care; domiciliary care, new patient; and home, new patient.

Table 2
Complexity of Medical Decision Making

Number of Diagnoses or Management Options	Amount and/or Complexity of Data to be Reviewed	Risk of Complications and/or Morbidity or Mortality	Type of Decision Making
minimal	minimal or none	minimal	**straightforward**
limited	limited	low	**low complexity**
multiple	moderate	moderate	**moderate complexity**
extensive	extensive	high	**high complexity**

2. For the following categories/subcategories, **two of the three key components** (ie, history, examination, and medical decision making) must meet or exceed the stated requirements to qualify for a particular level of E/M services: office, established patient; subsequent hospital care; subsequent nursing facility care; domiciliary care, established patient; and home, established patient.

3. When counseling and/or coordination of care dominates (more than 50%) the physician/patient and/or family encounter (face-to-face time in the office or other outpatient setting or floor/unit time in the hospital or nursing facility), then **time** may be considered the key or controlling factor to qualify for a particular level of E/M services. This includes time spent with parties who have assumed responsibility for the care of the patient or decision making whether or not they are family members (eg, foster parents, person acting in loco parentis, legal guardian). The extent of counseling and/or coordination of care must be documented in the medical record.

Evaluation and Management

Office or Other Outpatient Services

The following codes are used to report evaluation and management services provided in the physician's office or in an outpatient or other ambulatory facility. A patient is considered an outpatient until inpatient admission to a health care facility occurs.

To report services provided to a patient who is admitted to a hospital or nursing facility in the course of an encounter in the office or other ambulatory facility, see the notes for initial hospital inpatient care (page 11) or initial nursing facility care (page 19).

For services provided by physicians in the emergency department, see 99281-99285.

For observation care, see 99217-99220.

For observation or inpatient care services (including admission and discharge services), see 99234-99236.

New Patient

99201 **Office or other outpatient visit** for the evaluation and management of a new patient, which requires these 3 key components:

- **A problem focused history;**
- **A problem focused examination;**
- **Straightforward medical decision making.**

Counseling and/or coordination of care with other providers or agencies are provided consistent with the nature of the problem(s) and the patient's and/or family's needs.

Usually, the presenting problem(s) are self limited or minor. Physicians typically spend 10 minutes face-to-face with the patient and/or family.

99202 **Office or other outpatient visit** for the evaluation and management of a new patient, which requires these 3 key components:

- **An expanded problem focused history;**
- **An expanded problem focused examination;**
- **Straightforward medical decision making.**

Counseling and/or coordination of care with other providers or agencies are provided consistent with the nature of the problem(s) and the patient's and/or family's needs.

Usually, the presenting problem(s) are of low to moderate severity. Physicians typically spend 20 minutes face-to-face with the patient and/or family.

99203 **Office or other outpatient visit** for the evaluation and management of a new patient, which requires these 3 key components:

- **A detailed history;**
- **A detailed examination;**
- **Medical decision making of low complexity.**

Counseling and/or coordination of care with other providers or agencies are provided consistent with the nature of the problem(s) and the patient's and/or family's needs.

Usually, the presenting problem(s) are of moderate severity. Physicians typically spend 30 minutes face-to-face with the patient and/or family.

99204 **Office or other outpatient visit** for the evaluation and management of a new patient, which requires these 3 key components:

- **A comprehensive history;**
- **A comprehensive examination;**
- **Medical decision making of moderate complexity.**

Counseling and/or coordination of care with other providers or agencies are provided consistent with the nature of the problem(s) and the patient's and/or family's needs.

Usually, the presenting problem(s) are of moderate to high severity. Physicians typically spend 45 minutes face-to-face with the patient and/or family.

99205 **Office or other outpatient visit** for the evaluation and management of a new patient, which requires these 3 key components:

- **A comprehensive history;**
- **A comprehensive examination;**
- **Medical decision making of high complexity.**

Counseling and/or coordination of care with other providers or agencies are provided consistent with the nature of the problem(s) and the patient's and/or family's needs.

Usually, the presenting problem(s) are of moderate to high severity. Physicians typically spend 60 minutes face-to-face with the patient and/or family.

Established Patient

99211 **Office or other outpatient visit** for the evaluation and management of an established patient, that may not require the presence of a physician. Usually, the presenting problem(s) are minimal. Typically, 5 minutes are spent performing or supervising these services.

99212 **Office or other outpatient visit** for the evaluation and management of an established patient, which requires at least 2 of these 3 key components:

- **A problem focused history;**
- **A problem focused examination;**
- **Straightforward medical decision making.**

Counseling and/or coordination of care with other providers or agencies are provided consistent with the nature of the problem(s) and the patient's and/or family's needs.

Usually, the presenting problem(s) are self limited or minor. Physicians typically spend 10 minutes face-to-face with the patient and/or family.

99213 **Office or other outpatient visit** for the evaluation and management of an established patient, which requires at least 2 of these 3 key components:

- **An expanded problem focused history;**
- **An expanded problem focused examination;**
- **Medical decision making of low complexity.**

Counseling and/or coordination of care with other providers or agencies are provided consistent with the nature of the problem(s) and the patient's and/or family's needs.

Usually, the presenting problem(s) are of low to moderate severity. Physicians typically spend 15 minutes face-to-face with the patient and/or family.

99214 **Office or other outpatient visit** for the evaluation and management of an established patient, which requires at least 2 of these 3 key components:

- **A detailed history;**
- **A detailed examination;**
- **Medical decision making of moderate complexity.**

Counseling and/or coordination of care with other providers or agencies are provided consistent with the nature of the problem(s) and the patient's and/or family's needs.

Usually, the presenting problem(s) are of moderate to high severity. Physicians typically spend 25 minutes face-to-face with the patient and/or family.

99215 **Office or other outpatient visit** for the evaluation and management of an established patient, which requires at least 2 of these 3 key components:

- **A comprehensive history;**
- **A comprehensive examination;**
- **Medical decision making of high complexity.**

Counseling and/or coordination of care with other providers or agencies are provided consistent with the nature of the problem(s) and the patient's and/or family's needs.

Usually, the presenting problem(s) are of moderate to high severity. Physicians typically spend 40 minutes face-to-face with the patient and/or family.

Hospital Observation Services

The following codes are used to report evaluation and management services provided to patients designated/admitted as "observation status" in a hospital. It is not necessary that the patient be located in an observation area designated by the hospital.

If such an area does exist in a hospital (as a separate unit in the hospital, in the emergency department, etc.), these codes are to be utilized if the patient is placed in such an area.

For definitions of key components and commonly used terms, please see **Evaluation and Management Services Guidelines.**

Typical times have not yet been established for this category of services.

Observation Care Discharge Services

Observation care discharge of a patient from "observation status" includes final examination of the patient, discussion of the hospital stay, instructions for continuing care, and preparation of discharge records. For observation or inpatient hospital care including the admission and discharge of the patient on the same date, see codes 99234-99236 as appropriate.

99217 **Observation care discharge** day management (This code is to be utilized by the physician to report all services provided to a patient on discharge from "observation status" if the discharge is on other than the initial date of "observation status." To report services to a patient designated as "observation status" or "inpatient status" and discharged on the same date, use the codes for Observation or Inpatient Care Services [including Admission and Discharge Services, 99234-99236 as appropriate.])

Initial Observation Care

New or Established Patient

The following codes are used to report the encounter(s) by the supervising physician with the patient when designated as "observation status." This refers to the initiation of observation status, supervision of the care plan for observation and performance of periodic reassessments. For observation encounters by other physicians, see Office or Other Outpatient Consultation codes (99241-99245).

To report services provided to a patient who is admitted to the hospital after receiving hospital observation care services on the same date, see the notes for initial hospital inpatient care (page 11). For a patient admitted to the hospital on a date subsequent to the date of observation status, the hospital admission would be reported with the appropriate Initial Hospital Care code (99221-99223). For a patient admitted and discharged from observation or inpatient status on the same date, the services should be reported with codes 99234-99236 as appropriate. Do not report observation discharge (99217) in conjunction with a hospital admission.

When "observation status" is initiated in the course of an encounter in another site of service (eg, hospital emergency department, physician's office, nursing facility) all evaluation and management services provided by the supervising physician in conjunction with initiating "observation status" are considered part of the initial observation care when performed on the same date. The observation care level of service reported by the supervising physician should include the services related to initiating "observation status" provided in the other sites of service as well as in the observation setting.

Evaluation and management services on the same date provided in sites that are related to initiating "observation status" should **not** be reported separately.

These codes may not be utilized for post-operative recovery if the procedure is considered part of the surgical "package." These codes apply to all evaluation and management services that are provided on the same date of initiating "observation status."

99218 **Initial observation care,** per day, for the evaluation and management of a patient which requires these 3 key components:

- **A detailed or comprehensive history;**
- **A detailed or comprehensive examination; and**
- **Medical decision making that is straightforward or of low complexity.**

Counseling and/or coordination of care with other providers or agencies are provided consistent with the nature of the problem(s) and the patient's and/or family's needs.

Usually, the problem(s) requiring admission to "observation status" are of low severity.

99219 **Initial observation care,** per day, for the evaluation and management of a patient, which requires these 3 key components:

- **A comprehensive history;**
- **A comprehensive examination; and**
- **Medical decision making of moderate complexity.**

Counseling and/or coordination of care with other providers or agencies are provided consistent with the nature of the problem(s) and the patient's and/or family's needs.

Usually, the problem(s) requiring admission to "observation status" are of moderate severity.

99220 **Initial observation care,** per day, for the evaluation and management of a patient, which requires these 3 key components:

- **A comprehensive history;**
- **A comprehensive examination; and**
- **Medical decision making of high complexity.**

Counseling and/or coordination of care with other providers or agencies are provided consistent with the nature of the problem(s) and the patient's and/or family's needs.

Usually, the problem(s) requiring admission to "observation status" are of high severity.

Hospital Inpatient Services

The following codes are used to report evaluation and management services provided to hospital inpatients. Hospital inpatient services include those services provided to patients in a "partial hospital" setting. These codes are to be used to report these partial hospitalization services. See also psychiatry notes in the full text of the CPT codebook.

For definitions of key components and commonly used terms, please see **Evaluation and Management Services Guidelines.** For Hospital Observation Services, see 99218-99220. For a patient admitted and discharged from observation or inpatient status on the same date, the services should be reported with codes 99234-99236 as appropriate.

Initial Hospital Care

New or Established Patient

The following codes are used to report the first hospital inpatient encounter with the patient by the admitting physician.

For initial inpatient encounters by physicians other than the admitting physician, see initial inpatient consultation codes (99251-99255) or subsequent hospital care codes (99231-99233) as appropriate.

For admission services for the neonate (28 days of age or less) requiring intensive observation, frequent interventions, and other intensive care services, see 99477.

When the patient is admitted to the hospital as an inpatient in the course of an encounter in another site of service (eg, hospital emergency department, observation status in a hospital, physician's office, nursing facility) all evaluation and management services provided by that physician in conjunction with that admission are considered part of the initial hospital care when performed on the same date as the admission. The inpatient care level of service reported by the admitting physician should include the services related to the admission he/she provided in the other sites of service as well as in the inpatient setting.

Evaluation and management services on the same date provided in sites that are related to the admission "observation status" should **not** be reported separately. For a patient admitted and discharged from observation or inpatient status on the same date, the services should be reported with codes 99234-99236 as appropriate.

99221 **Initial hospital care,** per day, for the evaluation and management of a patient, which requires these 3 key components:

- **A detailed or comprehensive history;**
- **A detailed or comprehensive examination; and**
- **Medical decision making that is straightforward or of low complexity.**

Counseling and/or coordination of care with other providers or agencies are provided consistent with the nature of the problem(s) and the patient's and/or family's needs.

Usually, the problem(s) requiring admission are of low severity. Physicians typically spend 30 minutes at the bedside and on the patient's hospital floor or unit.

99222 **Initial hospital care,** per day, for the evaluation and management of a patient, which requires these 3 key components:

- **A comprehensive history;**
- **A comprehensive examination; and**
- **Medical decision making of moderate complexity.**

Counseling and/or coordination of care with other providers or agencies are provided consistent with the nature of the problem(s) and the patient's and/or family's needs.

Usually, the problem(s) requiring admission are of moderate severity. Physicians typically spend 50 minutes at the bedside and on the patient's hospital floor or unit.

99223 **Initial hospital care,** per day, for the evaluation and management of a patient, which requires these 3 key components:

- **A comprehensive history;**
- **A comprehensive examination; and**
- **Medical decision making of high complexity.**

Counseling and/or coordination of care with other providers or agencies are provided consistent with the nature of the problem(s) and the patient's and/or family's needs.

Usually, the problem(s) requiring admission are of high severity. Physicians typically spend 70 minutes at the bedside and on the patient's hospital floor or unit.

Subsequent Hospital Care

All levels of subsequent hospital care include reviewing the medical record and reviewing the results of diagnostic studies and changes in the patient's status (ie, changes in history, physical condition and response to management) since the last assessment by the physician.

99231 **Subsequent hospital care,** per day, for the evaluation and management of a patient, which requires at least 2 of these 3 key components:

- **A problem focused interval history;**
- **A problem focused examination;**
- **Medical decision making that is straightforward or of low complexity.**

Counseling and/or coordination of care with other providers or agencies are provided consistent with the nature of the problem(s) and the patient's and/or family's needs.

Usually, the patient is stable, recovering or improving. Physicians typically spend 15 minutes at the bedside and on the patient's hospital floor or unit.

99232 **Subsequent hospital care,** per day, for the evaluation and management of a patient, which requires at least 2 of these 3 key components:

- **An expanded problem focused interval history;**
- **An expanded problem focused examination;**
- **Medical decision making of moderate complexity.**

Counseling and/or coordination of care with other providers or agencies are provided consistent with the nature of the problem(s) and the patient's and/or family's needs.

Usually, the patient is responding inadequately to therapy or has developed a minor complication. Physicians typically spend 25 minutes at the bedside and on the patient's hospital floor or unit.

99233 **Subsequent hospital care,** per day, for the evaluation and management of a patient, which requires at least 2 of these 3 key components:

- **A detailed interval history;**
- **A detailed examination;**
- **Medical decision making of high complexity.**

Counseling and/or coordination of care with other providers or agencies are provided consistent with the nature of the problem(s) and the patient's and/or family's needs.

Usually, the patient is unstable or has developed a significant complication or a significant new problem. Physicians typically spend 35 minutes at the bedside and on the patient's hospital floor or unit.

Observation or Inpatient Care Services (Including Admission and Discharge Services)

The following codes are used to report observation or inpatient hospital care services provided to patients admitted and discharged on the same date of service. When a patient is admitted to the hospital from observation status on the same date, the physician should report only the initial hospital care code. The initial hospital care code reported by the admitting physician should include the services related to the observation status services he/she provided on the same date of inpatient admission.

When "observation status" is initiated in the course of an encounter in another site of service (eg, hospital emergency department, physician's office, nursing facility) all evaluation and management services provided by the supervising physician in conjunction with initiating "observation status" are considered part of the initial observation care when performed on the same date. The observation care level of service should include the services related to initiating "observation status" provided in the other sites of service as well as in the observation setting when provided by the same physician.

For patients admitted to observation or inpatient care and discharged on a different date, see codes 99218-99220 and 99217, or 99221-99223 and 99238, 99239.

99234 **Observation or inpatient hospital care,** for the evaluation and management of a patient including admission and discharge on the same date, which requires these 3 key components:

- **A detailed or comprehensive history;**
- **A detailed or comprehensive examination; and**
- **Medical decision making that is straightforward or of low complexity.**

Counseling and/or coordination of care with other providers or agencies are provided consistent with the nature of the problem(s) and the patient's and/or family's needs.

Usually the presenting problem(s) requiring admission are of low severity.

99235 **Observation or inpatient hospital care,** for the evaluation and management of a patient including admission and discharge on the same date, which requires these 3 key components:

- **A comprehensive history;**
- **A comprehensive examination; and**
- **Medical decision making of moderate complexity.**

Counseling and/or coordination of care with other providers or agencies are provided consistent with the nature of the problem(s) and the patient's and/or family's needs.

Usually the presenting problem(s) requiring admission are of moderate severity.

99236 **Observation or inpatient hospital care,** for the evaluation and management of a patient including admission and discharge on the same date, which requires these 3 key components:

- **A comprehensive history;**
- **A comprehensive examination; and**
- **Medical decision making of high complexity.**

Counseling and/or coordination of care with other providers or agencies are provided consistent with the nature of the problem(s) and the patient's and/or family's needs.

Usually the presenting problem(s) requiring admission are of high severity.

Hospital Discharge Services

The hospital discharge day management codes are to be used to report the total duration of time spent by a physician for final hospital discharge of a patient. The codes include, as appropriate, final examination of the patient, discussion of the hospital stay, even if the time spent by the physician on that date is not continuous, instructions for continuing care to all relevant caregivers, and preparation of discharge records, prescriptions and referral forms. For a patient admitted and discharged from observation or inpatient status on the same date, the services should be reported with codes 99234-99236 as appropriate.

99238 **Hospital discharge day management;** 30 minutes or less

99239 more than 30 minutes

(These codes are to be utilized by the physician to report all services provided to a patient on the date of discharge, if other than the initial date of inpatient status. To report services to a patient who is admitted as an inpatient and discharged on the same date, see codes 99234-99236 for observation or inpatient hospital care including the admission and discharge of the patient on the same date. To report concurrent care services provided by a physician[s] other than the attending physician, use subsequent hospital care codes [99231-99233] on the day of discharge.)

(For Observation Care Discharge, use 99217)

(For observation or inpatient hospital care including the admission and discharge of the patient on the same date, see 99234-99236)

(For Nursing Facility Care Discharge, see 99315, 99316)

►(For discharge services provided to newborns admitted and discharged on the same date, use 99463)◄

Evaluation and Management

Consultations

A consultation is a type of service provided by a physician whose opinion or advice regarding evaluation and/or management of a specific problem is requested by another physician or other appropriate source.

A physician consultant may initiate diagnostic and/or therapeutic services at the same or subsequent visit.

The written or verbal request for a consult may be made by a physician or other appropriate source and documented in the patient's medical record. The consultant's opinion and any services that were ordered or performed must also be documented in the patient's medical record and communicated by written report to the requesting physician or other appropriate source.

A "consultation" initiated by a patient and/or family, and not requested by a physician or other appropriate source (eg, physician assistant, nurse practitioner, doctor of chiropractic, physical therapist, occupational therapist, speech-language pathologist, psychologist, social worker, lawyer, or insurance company), is not reported using the consultation codes but may be reported using the office visit, home service, or domiciliary/rest home care codes.

If a consultation is mandated (eg, by a third-party payer) modifier 32 should also be reported.

Any specifically identifiable procedure (ie, identified with a specific CPT code) performed on or subsequent to the date of the initial consultation should be reported separately.

If subsequent to the completion of a consultation the consultant assumes responsibility for management of a portion or all of the patient's condition(s), the appropriate **Evaluation and Management** services code for the site of service should be reported. In the hospital or nursing facility setting, the consulting physician should use the appropriate inpatient consultation code for the initial encounter and then subsequent hospital or nursing facility care codes. In the office setting, the physician should use the appropriate office or other outpatient consultation codes and then the established patient office or other outpatient services codes.

For definitions of key components and commonly used terms, please see **Evaluation and Management Services Guidelines.**

Office or Other Outpatient Consultations

New or Established Patient

The following codes are used to report consultations provided in the physician's office or in an outpatient or other ambulatory facility, including hospital observation services, home services, domiciliary, rest home, or emergency department (see the preceding consultation definition above). Follow-up visits in the consultant's office or other outpatient facility that are initiated by the physician consultant or patient are reported using the appropriate codes for established patients, office visits (99211-99215), domiciliary, rest home (99334-99337), or home (99347-99350). If an additional request for an opinion or advice regarding the same or a new problem is received from another physician or other appropriate source and documented in the medical record, the office consultation codes may be used again.

99241 **Office consultation** for a new or established patient, which requires these 3 key components:

- **A problem focused history;**
- **A problem focused examination; and**
- **Straightforward medical decision making.**

Counseling and/or coordination of care with other providers or agencies are provided consistent with the nature of the problem(s) and the patient's and/or family's needs.

Usually, the presenting problem(s) are self limited or minor. Physicians typically spend 15 minutes face-to-face with the patient and/or family.

99242 **Office consultation** for a new or established patient, which requires these 3 key components:

- **An expanded problem focused history;**
- **An expanded problem focused examination; and**
- **Straightforward medical decision making.**

Counseling and/or coordination of care with other providers or agencies are provided consistent with the nature of the problem(s) and the patient's and/or family's needs.

Usually, the presenting problem(s) are of low severity. Physicians typically spend 30 minutes face-to-face with the patient and/or family.

99243 **Office consultation** for a new or established patient, which requires these 3 key components:

- **A detailed history;**
- **A detailed examination; and**
- **Medical decision making of low complexity.**

Counseling and/or coordination of care with other providers or agencies are provided consistent with the nature of the problem(s) and the patient's and/or family's needs.

Usually, the presenting problem(s) are of moderate severity. Physicians typically spend 40 minutes face-to-face with the patient and/or family.

99244 **Office consultation** for a new or established patient, which requires these 3 key components:

- **A comprehensive history;**
- **A comprehensive examination; and**
- **Medical decision making of moderate complexity.**

Counseling and/or coordination of care with other providers or agencies are provided consistent with the nature of the problem(s) and the patient's and/or family's needs.

Usually, the presenting problem(s) are of moderate to high severity. Physicians typically spend 60 minutes face-to-face with the patient and/or family.

99245 **Office consultation** for a new or established patient, which requires these 3 key components:

- **A comprehensive history;**
- **A comprehensive examination; and**
- **Medical decision making of high complexity.**

Counseling and/or coordination of care with other providers or agencies are provided consistent with the nature of the problem(s) and the patient's and/or family's needs.

Usually, the presenting problem(s) are of moderate to high severity. Physicians typically spend 80 minutes face-to-face with the patient and/or family.

Inpatient Consultations

New or Established Patient

The following codes are used to report physician consultations provided to hospital inpatients, residents of nursing facilities, or patients in a partial hospital setting. Only one consultation should be reported by a consultant per admission. Subsequent services during the same admission are reported using Subsequent Hospital Care codes (99231-99233) or Subsequent Nursing Facility Care codes (99307-99310), including services to complete the initial consultation, monitor progress, revise recommendations, or address a new problem.

99251 **Inpatient consultation** for a new or established patient, which requires these 3 key components:

- **A problem focused history;**
- **A problem focused examination; and**
- **Straightforward medical decision making.**

Counseling and/or coordination of care with other providers or agencies are provided consistent with the nature of the problem(s) and the patient's and/or family's needs.

Usually, the presenting problem(s) are self limited or minor. Physicians typically spend 20 minutes at the bedside and on the patient's hospital floor or unit.

99252 **Inpatient consultation** for a new or established patient, which requires these 3 key components:

- **An expanded problem focused history;**
- **An expanded problem focused examination; and**
- **Straightforward medical decision making.**

Counseling and/or coordination of care with other providers or agencies are provided consistent with the nature of the problem(s) and the patient's and/or family's needs.

Usually, the presenting problem(s) are of low severity. Physicians typically spend 40 minutes at the bedside and on the patient's hospital floor or unit.

99253 **Inpatient consultation** for a new or established patient, which requires these 3 key components:

- **A detailed history;**
- **A detailed examination; and**
- **Medical decision making of low complexity.**

Counseling and/or coordination of care with other providers or agencies are provided consistent with the nature of the problem(s) and the patient's and/or family's needs.

Usually, the presenting problem(s) are of moderate severity. Physicians typically spend 55 minutes at the bedside and on the patient's hospital floor or unit.

99254 **Inpatient consultation** for a new or established patient, which requires these 3 key components:

- **A comprehensive history;**
- **A comprehensive examination; and**
- **Medical decision making of moderate complexity.**

Counseling and/or coordination of care with other providers or agencies are provided consistent with the nature of the problem(s) and the patient's and/or family's needs.

Usually, the presenting problem(s) are of moderate to high severity. Physicians typically spend 80 minutes at the bedside and on the patient's hospital floor or unit.

99255 **Inpatient consultation** for a new or established patient, which requires these 3 key components:

- **A comprehensive history;**
- **A comprehensive examination; and**
- **Medical decision making of high complexity.**

Counseling and/or coordination of care with other providers or agencies are provided consistent with the nature of the problem(s) and the patient's and/or family's needs.

Usually, the presenting problem(s) are of moderate to high severity. Physicians typically spend 110 minutes at the bedside and on the patient's hospital floor or unit.

Emergency Department Services

New or Established Patient

The following codes are used to report evaluation and management services provided in the emergency department. No distinction is made between new and established patients in the emergency department.

An emergency department is defined as an organized hospital-based facility for the provision of unscheduled episodic services to patients who present for immediate medical attention. The facility must be available 24 hours a day.

For critical care services provided in the emergency department, see Critical Care notes and 99291, 99292.

For evaluation and management services provided to a patient in an observation area of a hospital, see 99217-99220.

For observation or inpatient care services (including admission and discharge services), see 99234-99236.

99281 **Emergency department visit** for the evaluation and management of a patient, which requires these 3 key components:

- **A problem focused history;**
- **A problem focused examination; and**
- **Straightforward medical decision making.**

Counseling and/or coordination of care with other providers or agencies are provided consistent with the nature of the problem(s) and the patient's and/or family's needs.

Usually, the presenting problem(s) are self limited or minor.

99282 **Emergency department visit** for the evaluation and management of a patient, which requires these 3 key components:

- **An expanded problem focused history;**
- **An expanded problem focused examination; and**
- **Medical decision making of low complexity.**

Counseling and/or coordination of care with other providers or agencies are provided consistent with the nature of the problem(s) and the patient's and/or family's needs.

Usually, the presenting problem(s) are of low to moderate severity.

99283 **Emergency department visit** for the evaluation and management of a patient, which requires these 3 key components:

- **An expanded problem focused history;**
- **An expanded problem focused examination; and**
- **Medical decision making of moderate complexity.**

Counseling and/or coordination of care with other providers or agencies are provided consistent with the nature of the problem(s) and the patient's and/or family's needs.

Usually, the presenting problem(s) are of moderate severity.

99284 **Emergency department visit** for the evaluation and management of a patient, which requires these 3 key components:

- **A detailed history;**
- **A detailed examination; and**
- **Medical decision making of moderate complexity.**

Counseling and/or coordination of care with other providers or agencies are provided consistent with the nature of the problem(s) and the patient's and/or family's needs.

Usually, the presenting problem(s) are of high severity, and require urgent evaluation by the physician but do not pose an immediate significant threat to life or physiologic function.

99285 **Emergency department visit** for the evaluation and management of a patient, which requires these 3 key components within the constraints imposed by the urgency of the patient's clinical condition and/or mental status:

- **A comprehensive history;**
- **A comprehensive examination; and**
- **Medical decision making of high complexity.**

Counseling and/or coordination of care with other providers or agencies are provided consistent with the nature of the problem(s) and the patient's and/or family's needs.

Usually, the presenting problem(s) are of high severity and pose an immediate significant threat to life or physiologic function.

Other Emergency Services

In physician directed emergency care, advanced life support, the physician is located in a hospital emergency or critical care department, and is in two-way voice communication with ambulance or rescue personnel outside the hospital. The physician directs the performance of necessary medical procedures, including but not limited to: telemetry of cardiac rhythm; cardiac and/or pulmonary resuscitation; endotracheal or esophageal obturator airway intubation; administration of intravenous fluids and/or administration of intramuscular, intratracheal or subcutaneous drugs; and/or electrical conversion of arrhythmia.

99288 **Physician direction of** emergency medical systems (EMS) emergency care, advanced life support

►(99289 has been deleted. To report, use 99466)◄

►(99290 has been deleted. To report, use 99467)◄

Critical Care Services

Critical care is the direct delivery by a physician(s) of medical care for a critically ill or critically injured patient. A critical illness or injury acutely impairs one or more vital organ systems such that there is a high probability of imminent or life threatening deterioration in the patient's condition. Critical care involves high complexity decision making to assess, manipulate, and support vital system function(s) to treat single or multiple vital organ system failure and/or to prevent further life threatening deterioration of the patient's condition. Examples of vital organ system failure include, but are not limited to: central nervous system failure, circulatory failure, shock, renal, hepatic, metabolic, and/or respiratory failure. Although critical care typically requires interpretation of multiple physiologic parameters and/or application of advanced technology(s), critical care may be provided in life threatening situations when these elements are not present. Critical care may be provided on multiple days, even if no changes are made in the treatment rendered to the patient, provided that the patient's condition continues to require the level of physician attention described above.

Providing medical care to a critically ill, injured, or post-operative patient qualifies as a critical care service only if both the illness or injury and the treatment being provided meet the above requirements. Critical care is usually, but not always, given in a critical care area, such as the coronary care unit, intensive care unit, pediatric intensive care unit, respiratory care unit, or the emergency care facility.

►Inpatient critical care services provided to infants 29 days through 71 months of age are reported with pediatric critical care codes 99471-99476. The pediatric critical care codes are reported as long as the infant/young child qualifies for critical care services during the hospital stay through 71 months of age. Inpatient critical care services provided to neonates (28 days of age or less) are reported with the neonatal critical care codes 99468 and 99469. The neonatal critical care codes are reported as long as the neonate qualifies for critical care services during the hospital stay through the 28th postnatal day. The reporting of the pediatric and neonatal critical care services is not based on time or the type of unit (eg, pediatric or neonatal critical care unit) and it is not dependent upon the type of provider delivering the care. To report critical care services provided in the outpatient setting (eg, emergency department or office), for neonates and pediatric patients up through 71 months of age, see the critical care codes 99291, 99292. If the same physician provides critical care services for a neonatal or pediatric patient in both the outpatient and inpatient settings on the same day, report only the appropriate neonatal or pediatric critical care code 99468-99472 for all critical care services provided on that day. Also report 99291-99292 for neonatal or pediatric critical care services provided by the physician providing critical care at one facility but transferring the patient to another facility. Critical care services provided by a second physician of a different specialty not reporting a per day neonatal or pediatric critical care code can be reported with codes 99291-99292. For additional instructions on reporting these services, see the Neonatal and Pediatric Critical Care section and codes 99468-99476.◄

Services for a patient who is not critically ill but happens to be in a critical care unit are reported using other appropriate E/M codes.

Critical care and other E/M services may be provided to the same patient on the same date by the same physician.

The following services are included in reporting critical care when performed during the critical period by the physician(s) providing critical care: the interpretation of cardiac output measurements (93561, 93562), chest X-rays (71010, 71015, 71020), pulse oximetry (94760, 94761, 94762), blood gases, and information data stored in computers (eg, ECGs, blood pressures, hematologic data [99090]); gastric intubation (43752, 91105); temporary transcutaneous pacing (92953); ventilatory management (94002-94004, 94660, 94662); and vascular access procedures (36000, 36410, 36415, 36591, 36600). Any services performed that are not listed above should be reported separately.

►Codes 99291, 99292 should be reported for the physician's attendance during the transport of critically ill or critically injured patients over 24 months of age to or from a facility or hospital. For physician transport services of critically ill or critically injured pediatric patients 24 months of age or less, see 99466, 99467.◄

The critical care codes 99291 and 99292 are used to report the total duration of time spent by a physician providing critical care services to a critically ill or critically injured patient, even if the time spent by the physician on that date is not continuous. For any given period of time spent providing critical care services, the physician must devote his or her full attention to the patient and, therefore, cannot provide services to any other patient during the same period of time.

Time spent with the individual patient should be recorded in the patient's record. The time that can be reported as critical care is the time spent engaged in work directly related to the individual patient's care whether that time was spent at the immediate bedside or elsewhere on the floor or unit. For example, time spent on the unit or at the nursing station on the floor reviewing test results or imaging studies, discussing the critically ill patient's care with other medical staff or documenting critical care services in the medical record would be reported as critical care, even though it does not occur at the bedside. Also, when the patient is unable or lacks capacity to participate in discussions, time spent on the floor or unit with family members or surrogate decision makers obtaining a medical history, reviewing the patient's condition or prognosis, or discussing treatment or limitation(s) of treatment may be reported as critical care, provided that the conversation bears directly on the management of the patient.

►Time spent in activities that occur outside of the unit or off the floor (eg, telephone calls whether taken at home, in the office, or elsewhere in the hospital) may not be reported as critical care since the physician is not immediately available to the patient. Time spent in activities that do not directly contribute to the treatment of the patient may not be reported as critical care, even if they are performed in the critical care unit (eg, participation in administrative meetings or telephone calls to discuss other patients). Time spent performing separately reportable procedures or services should not be included in the time reported as critical care time. No physician may report remote real-time interactive video-conferenced critical care services (0188T, 0189T) for the period in which any physician reports 99291-99292.◄

Code 99291 is used to report the first 30-74 minutes of critical care on a given date. It should be used only once per date even if the time spent by the physician is not continuous on that date. Critical care of less than 30 minutes total duration on a given date should be reported with the appropriate E/M code.

Code 99292 is used to report additional block(s) of time, of up to 30 minutes each beyond the first 74 minutes. (See table below.)

The following examples illustrate the correct reporting of critical care services:

Total Duration of Critical Care	Codes
less than 30 minutes	appropriate E/M codes
30-74 minutes (30 minutes - 1 hr. 14 min.)	99291 X 1
75-104 minutes (1 hr. 15 min. - 1 hr. 44 min.)	99291 X 1 AND 99292 X 1
105-134 minutes (1 hr. 45 min. - 2 hr. 14 min.)	99291 X 1 AND 99292 X 2
135-164 minutes (2 hr. 15 min. - 2 hr. 44 min.)	99291 X 1 AND 99292 X 3
165-194 minutes (2 hr. 45 min. - 3 hr. 14 min.)	99291 X 1 AND 99292 X 4
194 minutes or longer (3 hr. 14 min. - etc.)	99291 and 99292 as appropriate (see illustrated reporting examples above)

99291 **Critical care, evaluation and management** of the critically ill or critically injured patient; first 30-74 minutes

+ 99292 each additional 30 minutes (List separately in addition to code for primary service)

(Use 99292 in conjunction with 99291)

►(99293 has been deleted. To report, use 99471)◄

►(99294 has been deleted. To report, use 99472)◄

►(99295 has been deleted. To report, use 99468)◄

►(99296 has been deleted. To report, use 99469)◄

►(99298 has been deleted. To report, use 99478)◄

►(99299 has been deleted. To report, use 99479)◄

►(99300 has been deleted. To report, use 99480)◄

Nursing Facility Services

The following codes are used to report evaluation and management services to patients in nursing facilities (formerly called skilled nursing facilities [SNFs], intermediate care facilities [ICFs], or long-term care facilities [LTCFs]).

These codes should also be used to report evaluation and management services provided to a patient in a psychiatric residential treatment center (a facility or a distinct part of a facility for psychiatric care, which provides a 24-hour therapeutically planned and professionally staffed group living and learning environment). If procedures such as medical psychotherapy are provided in addition to evaluation and management services, these should be reported in addition to the evaluation and management services provided.

Nursing facilities that provide convalescent, rehabilitative, or long term care are required to conduct comprehensive, accurate, standardized, and reproducible assessments of each resident's functional capacity using a Resident Assessment Instrument (RAI). All RAIs include the Minimum Data Set (MDS), Resident Assessment Protocols (RAPs), and utilization guidelines. The MDS is the primary screening and assessment tool; the RAPs trigger the identification of potential problems and provide guidelines for follow-up assessments.

Physicians have a central role in assuring that all residents receive thorough assessments and that medical plans of care are instituted or revised to enhance or maintain the residents' physical and psychosocial functioning. This role includes providing input in the development of the MDS and a multi-disciplinary plan of care, as required by regulations pertaining to the care of nursing facility residents.

Two major subcategories of nursing facility services are recognized: Initial Nursing Facility Care and Subsequent Nursing Facility Care. Both subcategories apply to new or established patients.

For definitions of key components and commonly used terms, please see **Evaluation and Management Services Guidelines.**

(For care plan oversight services provided to nursing facility residents, see 99379-99380)

Initial Nursing Facility Care

New or Established Patient

When the patient is admitted to the nursing facility in the course of an encounter in another site of service (eg, hospital emergency department, physician's office), all evaluation and management services provided by that physician in conjunction with that admission are considered part of the initial nursing facility care when performed on the same date as the admission or readmission. The nursing facility care level of service reported by the admitting physician should include the services related to the admission he/she provided in the other sites of service as well as in the nursing facility setting.

Hospital discharge or observation discharge services performed on the same date of nursing facility admission or readmission may be reported separately. For a patient discharged from inpatient status on the same date of nursing facility admission or readmission, the hospital discharge services should be reported with codes 99238, 99239 as appropriate. For a patient discharged from observation status on the same date of nursing facility admission or readmission, the observation care discharge services should be reported with code 99217. For a patient admitted and discharged from observation or inpatient status on the same date, see codes 99234-99236.

(For nursing facility care discharge, see 99315, 99316)

99304 Initial nursing facility care, per day, for the evaluation and management of a patient, which requires these 3 key components:

- **A detailed or comprehensive history;**
- **A detailed or comprehensive examination; and**
- **Medical decision making that is straightforward or of low complexity.**

Counseling and/or coordination of care with other providers or agencies are provided consistent with the nature of the problem(s) and the patient's and/or family's needs.

Usually, the problem(s) requiring admission are of low severity. Physicians typically spend 25 minutes with the patient and/or family or caregiver.

99305 Initial nursing facility care, per day, for the evaluation and management of a patient, which requires these 3 key components:

- **A comprehensive history;**
- **A comprehensive examination; and**
- **Medical decision making of moderate complexity.**

Counseling and/or coordination of care with other providers or agencies are provided consistent with the nature of the problem(s) and the patient's and/or family's needs.

Usually, the problem(s) requiring admission are of moderate severity. Physicians typically spend 35 minutes with the patient and/or family or caregiver.

99306 Initial nursing facility care, per day, for the evaluation and management of a patient, which requires these 3 key components:

- **A comprehensive history;**
- **A comprehensive examination; and**
- **Medical decision making of high complexity.**

Counseling and/or coordination of care with other providers or agencies are provided consistent with the nature of the problem(s) and the patient's and/or family's needs.

Usually, the problem(s) requiring admission are of high severity. Physicians typically spend 45 minutes with the patient and/or family or caregiver.

Subsequent Nursing Facility Care

All levels of subsequent nursing facility care include reviewing the medical record and reviewing the results of diagnostic studies and changes in the patient's status (ie, changes in history, physical condition, and response to management) since the last assessment by the physician.

99307 Subsequent nursing facility care, per day, for the evaluation and management of a patient, which requires at least 2 of these 3 key components:

- **A problem focused interval history;**
- **A problem focused examination;**
- **Straightforward medical decision making.**

Counseling and/or coordination of care with other providers or agencies are provided consistent with the nature of the problem(s) and the patient's and/or family's needs.

Usually, the patient is stable, recovering, or improving. Physicians typically spend 10 minutes with the patient and/or family or caregiver.

99308 Subsequent nursing facility care, per day, for the evaluation and management of a patient, which requires at least 2 of these 3 key components:

- **An expanded problem focused interval history;**
- **An expanded problem focused examination;**
- **Medical decision making of low complexity.**

Counseling and/or coordination of care with other providers or agencies are provided consistent with the nature of the problem(s) and the patient's and/or family's needs.

Usually, the patient is responding inadequately to therapy or has developed a minor complication. Physicians typically spend 15 minutes with the patient and/or family or caregiver.

99309 Subsequent nursing facility care, per day, for the evaluation and management of a patient, which requires at least 2 of these 3 key components:

- **A detailed interval history;**
- **A detailed examination;**
- **Medical decision making of moderate complexity.**

Counseling and/or coordination of care with other providers or agencies are provided consistent with the nature of the problem(s) and the patient's and/or family's needs.

Usually, the patient has developed a significant complication or a significant new problem. Physicians typically spend 25 minutes with the patient and/or family or caregiver.

99310 Subsequent nursing facility care, per day, for the evaluation and management of a patient, which requires at least 2 of these 3 key components:

- **A comprehensive interval history;**
- **A comprehensive examination;**
- **Medical decision making of high complexity.**

Counseling and/or coordination of care with other providers or agencies are provided consistent with the nature of the problem(s) and the patient's and/or family's needs.

The patient may be unstable or may have developed a significant new problem requiring immediate physician attention. Physicians typically spend 35 minutes with the patient and/or family or caregiver.

Nursing Facility Discharge Services

The nursing facility discharge day management codes are to be used to report the total duration of time spent by a physician for the final nursing facility discharge of a patient. The codes include, as appropriate, final examination of the patient, discussion of the nursing facility stay, even if the time spent by the physician on that date is not continuous. Instructions are given for continuing care to all relevant caregivers, and preparation of discharge records, prescriptions and referral forms.

99315 Nursing facility discharge day management; 30 minutes or less

99316 more than 30 minutes

Other Nursing Facility Services

99318 Evaluation and management of a patient involving an annual nursing facility assessment, which requires these 3 key components:

- **A detailed interval history;**
- **A comprehensive examination; and**
- **Medical decision making that is of low to moderate complexity.**

Counseling and/or coordination of care with other providers or agencies are provided consistent with the nature of the problem(s) and the patient's and/or family's needs.

Usually, the patient is stable, recovering, or improving. Physicians typically spend 30 minutes with the patient and/or family or caregiver.

(Do not report 99318 on the same date of service as nursing facility services codes 99304-99316)

Domiciliary, Rest Home (eg, Boarding Home), or Custodial Care Services

The following codes are used to report evaluation and management services in a facility which provides room, board and other personal assistance services, generally on a long-term basis. They also are used to report evaluation and management services in an assisted living facility.

The facility's services do not include a medical component.

For definitions of key components and commonly used terms, please see **Evaluation and Management Services Guidelines.**

(For care plan oversight services provided to a patient in a domiciliary facility under the care of a home health agency, see 99374-99375)

(For care plan oversight services provided to a patient in a domiciliary facility under the individual supervision of a physician, see 99339, 99340)

New Patient

99324 Domiciliary or rest home visit for the evaluation and management of a new patient, which requires these 3 key components:

- **A problem focused history;**
- **A problem focused examination; and**
- **Straightforward medical decision making.**

Counseling and/or coordination of care with other providers or agencies are provided consistent with the nature of the problem(s) and the patient's and/or family's needs.

Usually, the presenting problem(s) are of low severity. Physicians typically spend 20 minutes with the patient and/or family or caregiver.

99325 Domiciliary or rest home visit for the evaluation and management of a new patient, which requires these 3 key components:

- **An expanded problem focused history;**
- **An expanded problem focused examination; and**
- **Medical decision making of low complexity.**

Counseling and/or coordination of care with other providers or agencies are provided consistent with the nature of the problem(s) and the patient's and/or family's needs.

Usually, the presenting problem(s) are of moderate severity. Physicians typically spend 30 minutes with the patient and/or family or caregiver.

99326 Domiciliary or rest home visit for the evaluation and management of a new patient, which requires these 3 key components:

- **A detailed history;**
- **A detailed examination; and**
- **Medical decision making of moderate complexity.**

Counseling and/or coordination of care with other providers or agencies are provided consistent with the nature of the problem(s) and the patient's and/or family's needs.

Usually, the presenting problem(s) are of moderate to high severity. Physicians typically spend 45 minutes with the patient and/or family or caregiver.

99327 Domiciliary or rest home visit for the evaluation and management of a new patient, which requires these 3 key components:

- **A comprehensive history;**
- **A comprehensive examination; and**
- **Medical decision making of moderate complexity.**

Counseling and/or coordination of care with other providers or agencies are provided consistent with the nature of the problem(s) and the patient's and/or family's needs.

Usually, the presenting problem(s) are of high severity. Physicians typically spend 60 minutes with the patient and/or family or caregiver.

99328 Domiciliary or rest home visit for the evaluation and management of a new patient, which requires these 3 key components:

- **A comprehensive history;**
- **A comprehensive examination; and**
- **Medical decision making of high complexity.**

Counseling and/or coordination of care with other providers or agencies are provided consistent with the nature of the problem(s) and the patient's and/or family's needs.

Usually, the patient is unstable or has developed a significant new problem requiring immediate physician attention. Physicians typically spend 75 minutes with the patient and/or family or caregiver.

Established Patient

99334 Domiciliary or rest home visit for the evaluation and management of an established patient, which requires at least 2 of these 3 key components:

- **A problem focused interval history;**
- **A problem focused examination;**
- **Straightforward medical decision making.**

Counseling and/or coordination of care with other providers or agencies are provided consistent with the nature of the problem(s) and the patient's and/or family's needs.

Usually, the presenting problem(s) are self-limited or minor. Physicians typically spend 15 minutes with the patient and/or family or caregiver.

99335 Domiciliary or rest home visit for the evaluation and management of an established patient, which requires at least 2 of these 3 key components:

- **An expanded problem focused interval history;**
- **An expanded problem focused examination;**
- **Medical decision making of low complexity.**

Counseling and/or coordination of care with other providers or agencies are provided consistent with the nature of the problem(s) and the patient's and/or family's needs.

Usually, the presenting problem(s) are of low to moderate severity. Physicians typically spend 25 minutes with the patient and/or family or caregiver.

99336 Domiciliary or rest home visit for the evaluation and management of an established patient, which requires at least 2 of these 3 key components:

- **A detailed interval history;**
- **A detailed examination;**
- **Medical decision making of moderate complexity.**

Counseling and/or coordination of care with other providers or agencies are provided consistent with the nature of the problem(s) and the patient's and/or family's needs.

Usually, the presenting problem(s) are of moderate to high severity. Physicians typically spend 40 minutes with the patient and/or family or caregiver.

99337 Domiciliary or rest home visit for the evaluation and management of an established patient, which requires at least 2 of these 3 key components:

- **A comprehensive interval history;**
- **A comprehensive examination;**
- **Medical decision making of moderate to high complexity.**

Counseling and/or coordination of care with other providers or agencies are provided consistent with the nature of the problem(s) and the patient's and/or family's needs.

Usually, the presenting problem(s) are of moderate to high severity. The patient may be unstable or may have developed a significant new problem requiring immediate physician attention. Physicians typically spend 60 minutes with the patient and/or family or caregiver.

Domiciliary, Rest Home (eg, Assisted Living Facility), or Home Care Plan Oversight Services

(For instructions on the use of 99339, 99340, see introductory notes for 99374-99380)

(For care plan oversight services for patients under the care of a home health agency, hospice, or nursing facility, see 99374-99380)

(Do not report 99339, 99340 for time reported with 98966-98969, 99441-99444)

99339 Individual physician supervision of a patient (patient not present) in home, domiciliary or rest home (eg, assisted living facility) requiring complex and multidisciplinary care modalities involving regular physician development and/or revision of care plans, review of subsequent reports of patient status, review of related laboratory and other studies, communication (including telephone calls) for purposes of assessment or care decisions with health care professional(s), family member(s), surrogate decision maker(s) (eg, legal guardian) and/or key caregiver(s) involved in patient's care, integration of new information into the medical treatment plan and/or adjustment of medical therapy, within a calendar month; 15-29 minutes

99340 30 minutes or more

(Do not report 99339, 99340 for patients under the care of a home health agency, enrolled in a hospice program, or for nursing facility residents)

Home Services

The following codes are used to report evaluation and management services provided in a private residence.

For definitions of key components and commonly used terms, please see **Evaluation and Management Services Guidelines.**

(For care plan oversight services provided to a patient in the home under the care of a home health agency, see 99374-99375)

(For care plan oversight services provided to a patient in the home under the individual supervision of a physician, see 99339, 99340)

New Patient

99341 **Home visit** for the evaluation and management of a new patient, which requires these 3 key components:

- **A problem focused history;**
- **A problem focused examination; and**
- **Straightforward medical decision making.**

Counseling and/or coordination of care with other providers or agencies are provided consistent with the nature of the problem(s) and the patient's and/or family's needs.

Usually, the presenting problem(s) are of low severity. Physicians typically spend 20 minutes face-to-face with the patient and/or family.

99342 **Home visit** for the evaluation and management of a new patient, which requires these 3 key components:

- **An expanded problem focused history;**
- **An expanded problem focused examination; and**
- **Medical decision making of low complexity.**

Counseling and/or coordination of care with other providers or agencies are provided consistent with the nature of the problem(s) and the patient's and/or family's needs.

Usually, the presenting problem(s) are of moderate severity. Physicians typically spend 30 minutes face-to-face with the patient and/or family.

99343 **Home visit** for the evaluation and management of a new patient, which requires these 3 key components:

- **A detailed history;**
- **A detailed examination; and**
- **Medical decision making of moderate complexity.**

Counseling and/or coordination of care with other providers or agencies are provided consistent with the nature of the problem(s) and the patient's and/or family's needs.

Usually, the presenting problem(s) are of moderate to high severity. Physicians typically spend 45 minutes face-to-face with the patient and/or family.

99344 **Home visit** for the evaluation and management of a new patient, which requires these 3 key components:

- **A comprehensive history;**
- **A comprehensive examination; and**
- **Medical decision making of moderate complexity.**

Counseling and/or coordination of care with other providers or agencies are provided consistent with the nature of the problem(s) and the patient's and/or family's needs.

Usually, the presenting problem(s) are of high severity. Physicians typically spend 60 minutes face-to-face with the patient and/or family.

99345 **Home visit** for the evaluation and management of a new patient, which requires these 3 key components:

- **A comprehensive history;**
- **A comprehensive examination; and**
- **Medical decision making of high complexity.**

Counseling and/or coordination of care with other providers or agencies are provided consistent with the nature of the problem(s) and the patient's and/or family's needs.

Usually, the patient is unstable or has developed a significant new problem requiring immediate physician attention. Physicians typically spend 75 minutes face-to-face with the patient and/or family.

Established Patient

99347 **Home visit** for the evaluation and management of an established patient, which requires at least 2 of these 3 key components:

- **A problem focused interval history;**
- **A problem focused examination;**
- **Straightforward medical decision making.**

Counseling and/or coordination of care with other providers or agencies are provided consistent with the nature of the problem(s) and the patient's and/or family's needs.

Usually, the presenting problem(s) are self limited or minor. Physicians typically spend 15 minutes face-to-face with the patient and/or family.

99348 **Home visit** for the evaluation and management of an established patient, which requires at least 2 of these 3 key components:

- **An expanded problem focused interval history;**
- **An expanded problem focused examination;**
- **Medical decision making of low complexity.**

Counseling and/or coordination of care with other providers or agencies are provided consistent with the nature of the problem(s) and the patient's and/or family's needs.

Usually, the presenting problem(s) are of low to moderate severity. Physicians typically spend 25 minutes face-to-face with the patient and/or family.

99349 **Home visit** for the evaluation and management of an established patient, which requires at least 2 of these 3 key components:

- **A detailed interval history;**
- **A detailed examination;**
- **Medical decision making of moderate complexity.**

Counseling and/or coordination of care with other providers or agencies are provided consistent with the nature of the problem(s) and the patient's and/or family's needs.

Usually, the presenting problem(s) are moderate to high severity. Physicians typically spend 40 minutes face-to-face with the patient and/or family.

99350 **Home visit** for the evaluation and management of an established patient, which requires at least 2 of these 3 key components:

- **A comprehensive interval history;**
- **A comprehensive examination;**
- **Medical decision making of moderate to high complexity.**

Counseling and/or coordination of care with other providers or agencies are provided consistent with the nature of the problem(s) and the patient's and/or family's needs.

Usually, the presenting problem(s) are of moderate to high severity. The patient may be unstable or may have developed a significant new problem requiring immediate physician attention. Physicians typically spend 60 minutes face-to-face with the patient and/or family.

Prolonged Services

Prolonged Physician Service With Direct (Face-To-Face) Patient Contact

►Codes 99354-99357 are used when a physician provides prolonged service involving direct (face-to-face) patient contact that is beyond the usual service in either the inpatient or outpatient setting. This service is reported in addition to the designated evaluation and management services at any level and any other physician services provided at the same session as evaluation and management services. Appropriate codes should be selected for supplies provided or procedures performed in the care of the patient during this period.

Codes 99354-99355 are used to report the total duration of face-to-face time spent by a physician on a given date providing prolonged service, even if the time spent by the physician on that date is not continuous. Codes 99356-99357 are used to report the total duration of unit time spent by a physician on a given date providing prolonged service to a patient, even if the time spent by the physician on that date is not continuous.◄

Code 99354 or 99356 is used to report the first hour of prolonged service on a given date, depending on the place of service.

►Either code should be used only once per date, even if the time spent by the physician is not continuous on that date. Prolonged service of less than 30 minutes total duration on a given date is not separately reported because the work involved is included in the total work of the evaluation and management codes.◄

Code 99355 or 99357 is used to report each additional 30 minutes beyond the first hour, depending on the place of service. Either code may also be used to report the final 15-30 minutes of prolonged service on a given date. Prolonged service of less than 15 minutes beyond the first hour or less than 15 minutes beyond the final 30 minutes is not reported separately.

►The use of the time based add-on codes requires that the primary evaluation and management service have a typical or specified time published in the CPT codebook.◄

The following examples illustrate the correct reporting of prolonged physician service with direct patient contact in the office setting:

Total Duration of Prolonged Services	Code(s)
less than 30 minutes (less than 30 minutes)	Not reported separately
30-74 minutes (30 minutes - 1 hr. 14 min.)	99354 X 1
75-104 minutes (1 hr. 15 min. - 1 hr. 44 min.)	99354 X 1 AND 99355 X 1
►105 or more (1 hr. 45 min. or more)	99354 X 1 AND 99355 X 2 or more for each additional 30 minutes◄

+▲ 99354 Prolonged physician service in the office or other outpatient setting requiring direct (face-to-face) patient contact beyond the usual service; first hour (List separately in addition to code for office or other outpatient **Evaluation and Management** service)

►(Use 99354 in conjunction with 99201-99215, 99241-99245, 99324-99337, 99341-99350, 90809, 90815)◄

+▲ 99355 each additional 30 minutes (List separately in addition to code for prolonged physician service)

(Use 99355 in conjunction with 99354)

+▲ 99356 Prolonged physician service in the inpatient setting, requiring unit/floor time beyond the usual service; first hour (List separately in addition to code for inpatient Evaluation and Management service)

►(Use 99356 in conjunction with 99221-99233, 99251-99255, 99304-99310, 90822, 90829)◄

+▲ 99357 each additional 30 minutes (List separately in addition to code for prolonged physician service)

(Use 99357 in conjunction with 99356)

Prolonged Physician Service Without Direct (Face-To-Face) Patient Contact

Codes 99358 and 99359 are used when a physician provides prolonged service not involving direct (face-to-face) care that is beyond the usual service in either the inpatient or outpatient setting.

This service is to be reported in addition to other physician service, including evaluation and management services at any level.

Codes 99358 and 99359 are used to report the total duration of non-face-to-face time spent by a physician on a given date providing prolonged service, even if the time spent by the physician on that date is not continuous. Code 99358 is used to report the first hour of prolonged service on a given date regardless of the place of service.

It may also be used to report a total duration of prolonged service of 30 to 60 minutes on a given date. It should be used only once per date even if the time spent by the physician is not continuous on that date.

Prolonged service of less than 30 minutes total duration on a given date is not separately reported.

Code 99359 is used to report each additional 30 minutes beyond the first hour regardless of the place of service. It may also be used to report the final 15 to 30 minutes of prolonged service on a given date.

Prolonged service of less than 15 minutes beyond the first hour or less than 15 minutes beyond the final 30 minutes is not reported separately.

+ 99358 **Prolonged evaluation and management service** before and/or after direct (face-to-face) patient care (eg, review of extensive records and tests, communication with other professionals and/or the patient/family); first hour (List separately in addition to code(s) for other physician service(s) and/or inpatient or outpatient Evaluation and Management service)

+ 99359 each additional 30 minutes (List separately in addition to code for prolonged physician service)

(Use 99359 in conjunction with 99358)

(To report telephone evaluation and management services, see 99441-99443)

Physician Standby Services

Code 99360 is used to report physician standby service that is requested by another physician and that involves prolonged physician attendance without direct (face-to-face) patient contact. The physician may not be providing care or services to other patients during this period. This code is not used to report time spent proctoring another physician. It is also not used if the period of standby ends with the performance of a procedure subject to a "surgical" package by the physician who was on standby.

Code 99360 is used to report the total duration of time spent by a physician on a given date on standby. Standby service of less than 30 minutes total duration on a given date is not reported separately.

Second and subsequent periods of standby beyond the first 30 minutes may be reported only if a full 30 minutes of standby was provided for each unit of service reported.

99360 **Physician standby service,** requiring prolonged physician attendance, each 30 minutes (eg, operative standby, standby for frozen section, for cesarean/high risk delivery, for monitoring EEG)

(For hospital mandated on call services, see 99026, 99027)

►(99360 may be reported in addition to 99460, 99465 as appropriate)◄

►(Do not report 99360 in conjunction with 99464)◄

Case Management Services

Case management is a process in which a physician or another qualified health care professional is responsible for direct care of a patient and, additionally, for coordinating, managing access to, initiating, and/or supervising other health care services needed by the patient.

(99361, 99362 have been deleted. To report, see 99366-99368)

Anticoagulant Management

Anticoagulant services are intended to describe the outpatient management of warfarin therapy, including ordering, review, and interpretation of International Normalized Ratio (INR) testing, communication with patient, and dosage adjustments as appropriate.

When reporting these services, the work of anticoagulant management may not be used as a basis for reporting an evaluation and management (E/M) service or care plan oversight time during the reporting period. Do not report these services with 98966-98969, 99441-99444 when telephone or on-line services address anticoagulation with warfarin management. If a significant, separately identifiable E/M service is performed, report the appropriate E/M service code using modifier 25.

►These services are outpatient services only. When anticoagulation therapy is initiated or continued in the inpatient or observation setting, a new period begins after discharge and is reported with 99364. Do not report 99363-99364 with 99217-99239, 99291-99292, 99304-99318, 99471-99480 or other code(s) for physician review, interpretation, and patient management of home INR testing for a patient with mechanical heart valve(s).◄

Any period less than 60 continuous outpatient days is not reported. If less than the specified minimum number of services per period are performed, do not report the anticoagulant management services (99363-99364).

99363 Anticoagulant management for an outpatient taking warfarin, physician review and interpretation of International Normalized Ratio (INR) testing, patient instructions, dosage adjustment (as needed), and ordering of additional tests; initial 90 days of therapy (must include a minimum of 8 INR measurements)

99364 each subsequent 90 days of therapy (must include a minimum of 3 INR measurements)

Medical Team Conferences

Medical team conferences include face-to-face participation by a minimum of three qualified health care professionals from different specialties or disciplines (each of whom provide direct care to the patient), with or without the presence of the patient, family member(s), community agencies, surrogate decision maker(s) (eg, legal guardian), and/or caregiver(s). The participants are actively involved in the development, revision, coordination, and implementation of health care services needed by the patient. Reporting participants shall have performed face-to-face evaluations or treatments of the patient, independent of any team conference, within the previous 60 days.

Physicians may report their time spent in a team conference with the patient and/or family present using evaluation and management (E/M) codes (and time as the key controlling factor for code selection when counseling and/or coordination of care dominates the service). These introductory guidelines do not apply to services reported using E/M codes (see E/M services guidelines). However, the physician must be directly involved with the patient, providing face-to-face services outside of the conference visit with other providers or agencies.

Reporting participants shall document their participation in the team conference as well as their contributed information and subsequent treatment recommendations.

No more than one individual from the same specialty may report 99366-99368 at the same encounter.

Individuals should not report 99366-99368 when their participation in the medical team conference is part of a facility or organizational service contractually provided by the organizational or facility provider.

The team conference starts at the beginning of the review of an individual patient and ends at the conclusion of the review. Time related to record keeping and report generation is not reported. The reporting participant shall be present for all time reported. The time reported is not limited to the time that the participant is communicating to the other team members or patient and/or family. Time reported for medical team conferences may not be used in the determination of time for other services such as care plan oversight (99374-99380), home, domiciliary, or rest home care plan oversight (99339-99340), prolonged services (99354-99359), psychotherapy, or any E/M service. For team conferences where the patient is present for any part of the duration of the conference, nonphysician qualified health care professionals report the team conference face-to-face code 99366.

Medical Team Conference, Direct (Face-to-Face) Contact With Patient and/or Family

99366 **Medical team conference** with interdisciplinary team of health care professionals, face-to-face with patient and/or family, 30 minutes or more, participation by nonphysician qualified health care professional

(Team conference services of less than 30 minutes duration are not reported separately)

(For team conference services by a physician with patient and/or family present, see Evaluation and Management services)

Medical Team Conference, Without Direct (Face-to-Face) Contact With Patient and/or Family

99367 **Medical team conference** with interdisciplinary team of health care professionals, patient and/or family not present, 30 minutes or more; participation by physician

99368 participation by nonphysician qualified health care professional

(Team conference services of less than 30 minutes duration are not reported separately)

(99371-99373 have been deleted. To report telephone evaluation and management services, see 99441-99443)

Care Plan Oversight Services

Care plan oversight services are reported separately from codes for office/outpatient, hospital, home, nursing facility or domiciliary, or non-face-to-face services. The complexity and approximate physician time of the care plan oversight services provided within a 30-day period determine code selection. Only one physician may report services for a given period of time, to reflect that physician's sole or predominant supervisory role with a particular patient. These codes should not be reported for supervision of patients in nursing facilities or under the care of home health agencies unless they require recurrent supervision of therapy.

The work involved in providing very low intensity or infrequent supervision services is included in the pre- and post-encounter work for home, office/outpatient and nursing facility or domiciliary visit codes.

(For care plan oversight services of patients in the home, domiciliary, or rest home (eg, assisted living facility) under the individual supervision of a physician, see 99339, 99340)

(Do not report 99374-99380 for time reported with 98966-98969, 99441-99444)

99374 **Physician supervision** of a patient under care of home health agency (patient not present) in home, domiciliary or equivalent environment (eg, Alzheimer's facility) requiring complex and multidisciplinary care modalities involving regular physician development and/or revision of care plans, review of subsequent reports of patient status, review of related laboratory and other studies, communication (including telephone calls) for purposes of assessment or care decisions with health care professional(s), family member(s), surrogate decision maker(s) (eg, legal guardian) and/or key caregiver(s) involved in patient's care, integration of new information into the medical treatment plan and/or adjustment of medical therapy, within a calendar month; 15-29 minutes

99375 30 minutes or more

99377 **Physician supervision** of a hospice patient (patient not present) requiring complex and multidisciplinary care modalities involving regular physician development and/or revision of care plans, review of subsequent reports of patient status, review of related laboratory and other studies, communication (including telephone calls) for purposes of assessment or care decisions with health care professional(s), family member(s), surrogate decision maker(s) (eg, legal guardian) and/or key caregiver(s) involved in patient's care, integration of new information into the medical treatment plan and/or adjustment of medical therapy, within a calendar month; 15-29 minutes

99378 30 minutes or more

99379 **Physician supervision** of a nursing facility patient (patient not present) requiring complex and multidisciplinary care modalities involving regular physician development and/or revision of care plans, review of subsequent reports of patient status, review of related laboratory and other studies, communication (including telephone calls) for purposes of assessment or care decisions with health care professional(s), family member(s), surrogate decision maker(s) (eg, legal guardian) and/or key caregiver(s) involved in patient's care, integration of new information into the medical treatment plan and/or adjustment of medical therapy, within a calendar month; 15-29 minutes

99380 30 minutes or more

Preventive Medicine Services

The following codes are used to report the preventive medicine evaluation and management of infants, children, adolescents and adults.

The extent and focus of the services will largely depend on the age of the patient.

If an abnormality/ies is encountered or a preexisting problem is addressed in the process of performing this preventive medicine evaluation and management service, and if the problem/abnormality is significant enough to require additional work to perform the key components of a problem-oriented E/M service, then the appropriate Office/Outpatient code 99201-99215 should also be reported. Modifier 25 should be added to the Office/Outpatient code to indicate that a significant, separately identifiable Evaluation and Management service was provided by the same physician on the same day as the preventive medicine service. The appropriate preventive medicine service is additionally reported.

An insignificant or trivial problem/abnormality that is encountered in the process of performing the preventive medicine evaluation and management service and which does not require additional work and the performance of the key components of a problem-oriented E/M service should not be reported.

The "comprehensive" nature of the Preventive Medicine Services codes 99381-99397 reflects an age and gender appropriate history/exam and is NOT synonymous with the "comprehensive" examination required in Evaluation and Management codes 99201-99350.

Codes 99381-99397 include counseling/anticipatory guidance/risk factor reduction interventions which are provided at the time of the initial or periodic comprehensive preventive medicine examination. (Refer to codes 99401-99412 for reporting those counseling/anticipatory guidance/risk factor reduction interventions that are provided at an encounter separate from the preventive medicine examination.)

►Vaccine/toxoid products, immunization administrations, ancillary studies involving laboratory, radiology, other procedures, or screening tests (eg, vision, hearing, developmental) identified with a specific CPT code are reported separately. For immunization administration and vaccine risk/benefit counseling, see 90465-90474. For vaccine/toxoid products, see 90476-90749.◄

New Patient

▲ 99381 **Initial comprehensive preventive medicine** evaluation and management of an individual including an age and gender appropriate history, examination, counseling/anticipatory guidance/risk factor reduction interventions, and the ordering of laboratory/diagnostic procedures, new patient; infant (age younger than 1 year)

▲ 99382 early childhood (age 1 through 4 years)

▲ 99383 late childhood (age 5 through 11 years)

▲ 99384 adolescent (age 12 through 17 years)

▲ 99385 18-39 years

▲ 99386 40-64 years

▲ 99387 65 years and older

Established Patient

▲ 99391 **Periodic comprehensive preventive medicine** reevaluation and management of an individual including an age and gender appropriate history, examination, counseling/anticipatory guidance/risk factor reduction interventions, and the ordering of laboratory/diagnostic procedures, established patient; infant (age younger than 1 year)

▲ 99392 early childhood (age 1 through 4 years)

▲ 99393 late childhood (age 5 through 11 years)

▲ 99394 adolescent (age 12 through 17 years)

▲ 99395 18-39 years

▲ 99396 40-64 years

▲ 99397 65 years and older

Counseling Risk Factor Reduction and Behavior Change Intervention

New or Established Patient

These codes are used to report services provided face-to-face by a physician or other qualified health care professional for the purpose of promoting health and preventing illness or injury. They are distinct from evaluation and management (E/M) services that may be reported separately when performed. Risk factor reduction services are used for persons without a specific illness for which the counseling might otherwise be used as part of treatment.

Preventive medicine counseling and risk factor reduction interventions will vary with age and should address such issues as family problems, diet and exercise, substance use, sexual practices, injury prevention, dental health, and diagnostic and laboratory test results available at the time of the encounter.

Behavior change interventions are for persons who have a behavior that is often considered an illness itself, such as tobacco use and addiction, substance abuse/misuse, or obesity. Behavior change services may be reported when performed as part of the treatment of condition(s) related to or potentially exacerbated by the behavior or when performed to change the harmful behavior that has not yet resulted in illness. Any E/M services reported on the same day must be distinct, and time spent providing these services may not be used as a basis for the E/M code selection. Behavior change services involve specific validated interventions of assessing readiness for change and barriers to change, advising a change in behavior, assisting by providing specific suggested actions and motivational counseling, and arranging for services and follow-up.

For counseling groups of patients with symptoms or established illness, use 99078.

►Health and Behavior Assessment/Intervention services (96150-96155) should not be reported on the same day.◄

Preventive Medicine, Individual Counseling

99401 **Preventive medicine counseling** and/or risk factor reduction intervention(s) provided to an individual (separate procedure); approximately 15 minutes

99402 approximately 30 minutes

99403 approximately 45 minutes

99404 approximately 60 minutes

Behavior Change Interventions, Individual

99406 Smoking and tobacco use cessation counseling visit; intermediate, greater than 3 minutes up to 10 minutes

99407 intensive, greater than 10 minutes

(Do not report 99407 in conjunction with 99406)

99408 Alcohol and/or substance (other than tobacco) abuse structured screening (eg, AUDIT, DAST), and brief intervention (SBI) services; 15 to 30 minutes

(Do not report services of less than 15 minutes with 99408)

99409 greater than 30 minutes

(Do not report 99409 in conjunction with 99408)

(Do not report 99408, 99409 in conjunction with 99420)

(Use 99408, 99409 only for initial screening and brief intervention)

Preventive Medicine, Group Counseling

99411 **Preventive medicine counseling** and/or risk factor reduction intervention(s) provided to individuals in a group setting (separate procedure); approximately 30 minutes

99412 approximately 60 minutes

Other Preventive Medicine Services

99420 **Administration and interpretation** of health risk assessment instrument (eg, health hazard appraisal)

99429 **Unlisted preventive** medicine service

►(99431 has been deleted. To report, use 99460)◄

►(99432 has been deleted. To report, use 99461)◄

►(99433 has been deleted. To report, use 99462)◄

►(99435 has been deleted. To report, use 99463)◄

►(99436 has been deleted. To report, use 99464)◄

►(99440 has been deleted. To report, use 99465)◄

Non-Face-to-Face Physician Services

Telephone Services

Telephone services are non-face-to-face evaluation and management (E/M) services provided by a physician to a patient using the telephone. These codes are used to report episodes of care by the physician initiated by an established patient or guardian of an established patient. If the telephone service ends with a decision to see the patient within 24 hours or next available urgent visit appointment, the code is not reported; rather the encounter is considered part of the preservice work of the subsequent E/M service, procedure, and visit. Likewise if the telephone call refers to an E/M service performed and reported by the physician within the previous seven days (either physician requested or unsolicited patient follow-up) or within the postoperative period of the previously completed procedure, then the service(s) are considered part of that previous E/M service or procedure. (Do not report 99441-99443 if reporting 99441-99444 performed in the previous seven days.)

(For telephone services provided by a qualified nonphysician health care professional, see 98966-98968)

99441 Telephone evaluation and management service provided by a physician to an established patient, parent, or guardian not originating from a related E/M service provided within the previous 7 days nor leading to an E/M service or procedure within the next 24 hours or soonest available appointment; 5-10 minutes of medical discussion

99442 11-20 minutes of medical discussion

99443 21-30 minutes of medical discussion

(Do not report 99441-99443 when using 99339-99340, 99374-99380 for the same call[s])

(Do not report 99441-99443 for anticoagulation management when reporting 99363-99364)

On-Line Medical Evaluation

An on-line electronic medical evaluation is a non-face-to-face evaluation and management (E/M) service by a physician to a patient using Internet resources in response to a patient's on-line inquiry. Reportable services involve the physician's personal timely response to the patient's inquiry and must involve permanent storage (electronic or hard copy) of the encounter. This service is reported only once for the same episode of care during a seven-day period, although multiple physicians could report their exchange with the same patient. If the on-line medical evaluation refers to an E/M service previously performed and reported by the physician within the previous seven days (either physician requested or unsolicited patient follow-up) or within the postoperative period of the previously completed procedure, then the service(s) are considered covered by the previous E/M service or procedure. A reportable service encompasses the sum of communication (eg, related telephone calls, prescription provision, laboratory orders) pertaining to the on-line patient encounter.

(For an on-line medical evaluation provided by a qualified nonphysician health care professional, use 98969)

99444 Online evaluation and management service provided by a physician to an established patient, guardian, or health care provider not originating from a related E/M service provided within the previous 7 days, using the Internet or similar electronic communications network

(Do not report 99444 when using 99339-99340, 99374-99380 for the same communication[s])

(Do not report 99444 for anticoagulation management when reporting 99363, 99364)

Special Evaluation and Management Services

The following codes are used to report evaluations performed to establish baseline information prior to life or disability insurance certificates being issued. This service is performed in the office or other setting, and applies to both new and established patients. When using these codes, no active management of the problem(s) is undertaken during the encounter.

If other evaluation and management services and/or procedures are performed on the same date, the appropriate E/M or procedure code(s) should be reported in addition to these codes.

Basic Life and/or Disability Evaluation Services

99450 **Basic life** and/or disability examination that includes:

- **Measurement of height, weight, and blood pressure;**
- **Completion of a medical history following a life insurance pro forma;**
- **Collection of blood sample and/or urinalysis complying with "chain of custody" protocols; and**
- **Completion of necessary documentation/certificates.**

Work Related or Medical Disability Evaluation Services

99455 **Work related** or medical disability examination by the treating physician that includes:

- **Completion of a medical history commensurate with the patient's condition;**
- **Performance of an examination commensurate with the patient's condition;**
- **Formulation of a diagnosis, assessment of capabilities and stability, and calculation of impairment;**
- **Development of future medical treatment plan; and**
- **Completion of necessary documentation/certificates and report.**

99456 **Work related** or medical disability examination by other than the treating physician that includes:

- **Completion of a medical history commensurate with the patient's condition;**
- **Performance of an examination commensurate with the patient's condition;**
- **Formulation of a diagnosis, assessment of capabilities and stability, and calculation of impairment;**
- **Development of future medical treatment plan; and**
- **Completion of necessary documentation/certificates and report.**

(Do not report 99455, 99456 in conjunction with 99080 for the completion of Workman's Compensation forms)

►Newborn Care Services◄

►The following codes are used to report the services provided to newborns (birth through the first 28 days) in several different settings. Use of the normal newborn codes is limited to the initial care of the newborn in the first days after birth prior to home discharge.

Evaluation and Management (E/M) services for the newborn include maternal and/or fetal and newborn history, newborn physical examination(s), ordering of diagnostic tests and treatments, meetings with the family, and documentation in the medical record.

When delivery room attendance services (99464) or delivery room resuscitation services (99465) are required, report these in addition to normal newborn services Evaluation and Management codes.

For E/M services provided to newborns who are other than normal, see codes for hospital inpatient services (99221-99233) and neonatal intensive and critical care services (99466-99469, 99477-99480). When normal newborn services are provided by the same physician on the same date that the newborn later becomes ill and receives additional intensive or critical care services, report the appropriate E/M code with modifier 25 for these services in addition to the normal newborn code.

Procedures (eg, 54150, newborn circumcision) are not included with the normal newborn codes, and when performed, should be reported in addition to the newborn services.

When newborns are seen in follow-up after the date of discharge in the office or outpatient setting, see 99201-99215, 99381, 99391 as appropriate.◄

● **99460** Initial hospital or birthing center care, per day, for evaluation and management of normal newborn infant

● **99461** Initial care, per day, for evaluation and management of normal newborn infant seen in other than hospital or birthing center

● **99462** Subsequent hospital care, per day, for evaluation and management of normal newborn

● **99463** Initial hospital or birthing center care, per day, for evaluation and management of normal newborn infant admitted and discharged on the same date

►(For newborn hospital discharge services provided on a date subsequent to the admission date, see 99238, 99239)◄

►Delivery/Birthing Room Attendance and Resuscitation Services◄

● **99464** Attendance at delivery (when requested by the delivering physician) and initial stabilization of newborn

►(99464 may be reported in conjunction with 99460, 99468, 99477)◄

►(Do not report 99464 in conjunction with 99465)◄

● **99465** Delivery/birthing room resuscitation, provision of positive pressure ventilation and/or chest compressions in the presence of acute inadequate ventilation and/or cardiac output

►(Do not report 99465 in conjunction with 99460, 99468, 99477)◄

►(Do not report 99465 in conjunction with 99464)◄

►(Procedures that are performed as a necessary part of the resuscitation [eg, intubation, vascular lines] are reported separately in addition to 99465. In order to report these procedures, they must be performed as a necessary component of the resuscitation and not as a convenience before admission to the neonatal intensive care unit)◄

►Inpatient Neonatal Intensive Care Services and Pediatric and Neonatal Critical Care Services◄

►Pediatric Critical Care Patient Transport◄

►The following codes (99466, 99467) are used to report the physical attendance and direct face-to-face care by a physician during the interfacility transport of a critically ill or critically injured pediatric patient 24 months of age or less. For the purpose of reporting codes 99466 and 99467, face-to-face care begins when the physician assumes primary responsibility of the pediatric patient at the referring hospital/facility, and ends when the receiving hospital/facility accepts responsibility for the pediatric patient's care. Only the time the physician spends in direct face-to-face contact with the patient during the transport should be reported. Pediatric patient transport services involving less than 30 minutes of face-to-face physician care should not be reported using codes 99466, 99467. Procedure(s) or service(s) performed by other members of the transporting team may not be reported by the supervising physician.

For the definition of the critically ill or critically injured pediatric patient and the list of services included in critical care, see the **Neonatal and Pediatric Critical Care Services** section. Any services performed, which are not listed, may be reported separately.

The direction of emergency care to transporting staff by a physician located in a hospital or other facility by two-way communication is not considered direct face-to-face care and should not be reported with 99466, 99467. Physician-directed emergency care through outside voice communication to transporting staff personnel is reported with 99288.

Emergency department services (99281-99285), initial hospital care (99221-99223), critical care (99291, 99292), initial date neonatal intensive (99477) or critical care (99468) are only reported after the patient has been admitted to the emergency department, the inpatient floor, or the critical care unit of the receiving facility. If inpatient critical care services are reported in the referring facility prior to transfer to the receiving hospital, use the critical care codes (99291, 99292).

Code 99466 is used to report the first 30 to 74 minutes of direct face-to-face time with the transport pediatric patient and should be reported only once on a given date. Code 99467 is used to report each additional 30 minutes provided on a given date. Face-to-face services of less than 30 minutes should not be reported with these codes.◄

● **99466** **Critical care** services delivered by a physician, face-to-face, during an interfacility transport of critically ill or critically injured pediatric patient, 24 months of age or less; first 30-74 minutes of hands-on care during transport

+● **99467** each additional 30 minutes (List separately in addition to code for primary service)

►(Use 99467 in conjunction with 99466)◄

►(Critical care of less than 30 minutes total duration should be reported with the appropriate E/M code)◄

►Inpatient Neonatal and Pediatric Critical Care◄

►The same definitions for critical care services apply for the adult, child, and neonate.

Codes 99468, 99469 are used to report services provided by a physician directing the inpatient care of a critically ill neonate or infant 28 days of age or less. They represent care starting with the date of admission (99468) and subsequent day(s) (99469) that the neonate remains critical. These codes may be reported only by a single physician and only once per day, per patient.

The initial day neonatal critical care code (99468) can be used in addition to 99464 or 99465 as appropriate, when the physician is present for the delivery (99464) or resuscitation (99465) is required. Other procedures performed as a necessary part of the resuscitation (eg, endotracheal intubation [31500]) are also reported separately when performed as part of the pre-admission delivery room care. In order to report these procedures separately, they must be performed as a necessary component of the resuscitation and not simply as a convenience before admission to the neonatal intensive care unit.

Codes 99471-99476 are used to report services provided by a physician directing the inpatient care of a critically ill infant or young child from 29 days of postnatal age through 5 years of age. They represent care starting with the date of admission (99471, 99475) and subsequent day(s) (99472, 99476) the infant or child remains critical. These codes may be reported only by a single physician and only once per day, per patient in a given setting. Service for the critically ill or critically injured child older than 5 years of age would be reported with critical care codes (99291, 99292).

The pediatric and neonatal critical care codes include those procedures listed for the critical care codes (99291, 99292). In addition, the following procedures are also included (and not separately reported) in the pediatric and neonatal critical care service codes (99468-99472, 99475, 99476), the intensive care services codes (99477-99480), and the pediatric critical care patient transport codes (99466, 99467):

Invasive or non-invasive electronic monitoring of vital signs

Vascular access procedures

- Peripheral vessel catheterization (36000)
- Other arterial catheters (36140, 36620)
- Umbilical venous catheters (36510)
- Central vessel catheterization (36555)
- Vascular access procedures (36400, 36405, 36406)
- Vascular punctures oral (36420, 36600)
- Umbilical arterial catheters (36660)

Airway and ventilation management

- Endotracheal intubation (31500)
- Ventilatory management (94002-94004)
- Bedside pulmonary function testing (94375)
- Surfactant administration (94610)
- Continuous positive airway pressure (CPAP) (94660)

Monitoring or interpretation of blood gases or oxygen saturation (94760-94762)

Transfusion of blood components (36430, 36440)

Oral or nasogastric tube placement (43752)

Suprapubic bladder aspiration (51100)

Bladder catheterization (51701, 51702)

Lumbar puncture (62270)

Any services performed which are not listed above may be reported separately.

When a neonate or infant is not critically ill, but requires intensive observation, frequent interventions, and other intensive care services, the Continuing Intensive Care Services codes (99477-99480) should be used to report these services.

To report critical care services provided in the outpatient setting (eg, emergency department or office) for neonates and pediatric patients of any age, see the Critical Care codes 99291, 99292. If the same physician provides critical care services for a neonatal or pediatric patient in both the outpatient and inpatient settings on the same day, report only the appropriate Neonatal or Pediatric Critical Care codes 99468-99476 for all critical care services provided on that day. Critical care services provided by a second physician of a different specialty not reporting a per-day neonatal or pediatric critical care code can be reported with 99291, 99292.

When critical care services are provided to neonates or pediatric patients less than 5 years of age at two separate institutions by a physician from a different group on the same date of service, the physician from the referring institution should report their critical care services with the critical care codes (99291, 99292) and the receiving institution should report the appropriate global admission code (99468, 99471, 99475, 99476) for the same date of service.

Critical care services to a pediatric patient 6 years of age or older are reported with the critical care codes 99291, 99292.

Critical care services to a neonate or pediatric patient provided in an outpatient environment are reported with the critical care codes 99291, 99292.

Critical care services provided by a second physician of a different specialty not reporting a 24-hour global code can be reported with the critical care codes 99291, 99292.

No physician may report remote real-time videoconferenced critical care (0188T, 0189T) when neonatal or pediatric intensive or critical care services (99468-99476) are reported.◄

● 99468 **Initial inpatient neonatal critical care,** per day, for the evaluation and management of a critically ill neonate, 28 days of age or less

● 99469 **Subsequent inpatient neonatal critical care,** per day, for the evaluation and management of a critically ill neonate, 28 days of age or less

● 99471 **Initial inpatient pediatric critical care,** per day, for the evaluation and management of a critically ill infant or young child, 29 days through 24 months of age

● 99472 **Subsequent inpatient pediatric critical care,** per day, for the evaluation and management of a critically ill infant or young child, 29 days through 24 months of age

● 99475 **Initial inpatient pediatric critical care,** per day, for the evaluation and management of a critically ill infant or young child, 2 through 5 years of age

● 99476 **Subsequent inpatient pediatric critical care,** per day, for the evaluation and management of a critically ill infant or young child, 2 through 5 years of age

►Initial and Continuing Intensive Care Services◄

►Code 99477 represents the initial day of inpatient care for the child who is not critically ill but requires intensive observation, frequent interventions, and other intensive care services. Codes 99478-99480 are used to report subsequent day services provided by a physician directing the continuing intensive care of the low birth weight (LBW 1500-2500 grams) present body weight infant, very low birth weight (VLBW less than 1500 grams) present body weight infant, or normal (2501-5000 grams) present body weight newborn who does not meet the definition of critically ill but continues to require intensive observation, frequent interventions, and other intensive care services. These services are for infants and neonates who are not critically ill but continue to require intensive cardiac and respiratory monitoring, continuous and/or frequent vital sign monitoring, heat maintenance, enteral and/or parenteral nutritional adjustments, laboratory and oxygen monitoring, and constant observation by the health care team under direct physician supervision. Codes 99477-99480 may be reported by only one physician and only once per day, per patient. These codes include the same procedures that are outlined in the **Pediatric Critical Care Services** section and these services should not be separately reported.◄

►For the subsequent care of the sick neonate less than 28 days of age but more than 5000 grams who does not require intensive or critical care services, use codes 99231-99233.◄

99477 **Initial hospital care,** per day, for the evaluation and management of the neonate, 28 days of age or less, who requires intensive observation, frequent interventions, and other intensive care services

►(For the initiation of inpatient care of the normal newborn, use 99460)◄

►(For the initiation of care of the critically ill neonate, use 99468)◄

►(For initiation of inpatient hospital care of the ill neonate not requiring intensive observation, frequent interventions, and other intensive care services, see 99221-99223)◄

● 99478 **Subsequent intensive care,** per day, for the evaluation and management of the recovering very low birth weight infant (present body weight less than 1500 grams)

● 99479 **Subsequent intensive care,** per day, for the evaluation and management of the recovering low birth weight infant (present body weight of 1500-2500 grams)

● 99480 **Subsequent intensive care,** per day, for the evaluation and management of the recovering infant (present body weight of 2501-5000 grams)

Other Evaluation and Management Services

99499 **Unlisted evaluation and management** service

Anesthesia Guidelines

Services involving administration of anesthesia are reported by the use of the anesthesia five-digit procedure code (00100-01999) plus modifier codes (defined under "Anesthesia Modifiers" later in these Guidelines).

The reporting of anesthesia services is appropriate by or under the responsible supervision of a physician. These services may include but are not limited to general, regional, supplementation of local anesthesia, or other supportive services in order to afford the patient the anesthesia care deemed optimal by the anesthesiologist during any procedure. These services include the usual preoperative and postoperative visits, the anesthesia care during the procedure, the administration of fluids and/or blood and the usual monitoring services (eg, ECG, temperature, blood pressure, oximetry, capnography, and mass spectrometry). Unusual forms of monitoring (eg, intra-arterial, central venous, and Swan-Ganz) are not included.

Items used by all physicians in reporting their services are presented in the **Introduction.** Some of the commonalities are repeated in this section for the convenience of those physicians referring to this section on **Anesthesia.** Other definitions and items unique to anesthesia are also listed.

To report moderate (conscious) sedation provided by a physician also performing the service for which conscious sedation is being provided, see codes 99143-99145.

For the procedures listed in Appendix G, when a second physician other than the health care professional performing the diagnostic or therapeutic services provides moderate (conscious) sedation in the facility setting (eg, hospital, outpatient hospital/ambulatory surgery center, skilled nursing facility), the second physician reports the associated moderate sedation procedure/service 99148-99150; when these services are performed by the second physician in the nonfacility setting (eg, physician office, freestanding imaging center), codes 99148-99150 would not be reported. Moderate sedation does not include minimal sedation (anxiolysis), deep sedation, or monitored anesthesia care (00100-01999).

To report regional or general anesthesia provided by a physician also performing the services for which the anesthesia is being provided, see modifier 47 in Appendix A.

Time Reporting

Time for anesthesia procedures may be reported as is customary in the local area. Anesthesia time begins when the anesthesiologist begins to prepare the patient for the induction of anesthesia in the operating room (or in an equivalent area) and ends when the anesthesiologist is no longer in personal attendance, that is, when the patient may be safely placed under postoperative supervision.

Physician's Services

Physician's services rendered in the office, home, or hospital; consultation; and other medical services are listed in the section titled **Evaluation and Management Services** (99201-99499 series) found on page 1. "Special Services and Reporting" (99000-99091 series) are listed in the **Medicine** section.

Materials Supplied by Physician

Supplies and materials provided by the physician (eg, sterile trays, drugs) over and above those usually included with the office visit or other services rendered may be listed separately. Drugs, tray supplies, and materials provided should be listed and identified with 99070 or the appropriate supply code.

Separate or Multiple Procedures

When multiple surgical procedures are performed during a single anesthetic administration, the anesthesia code representing the most complex procedure is reported. The time reported is the combined total for all procedures.

Special Report

A service that is rarely provided, unusual, variable, or new may require a special report in determining medical appropriateness of the service. Pertinent information should include an adequate definition or description of the nature, extent, and need for the procedure and the time, effort, and equipment necessary to provide the service. Additional items may include:

- Complexity of symptoms
- Final diagnosis
- Pertinent physical findings
- Diagnostic and therapeutic procedures
- Concurrent problems
- Follow-up care

Anesthesia Modifiers

All anesthesia services are reported by use of the anesthesia five-digit procedure code (00100-01999) plus the addition of a physical status modifier. The use of other optional modifiers may be appropriate.

Physical Status Modifiers

Physical Status modifiers are represented by the initial letter 'P' followed by a single digit from 1 to 6 as defined in the following list:

P1: A normal healthy patient

P2: A patient with mild systemic disease

P3: A patient with severe systemic disease

P4: A patient with severe systemic disease that is a constant threat to life

P5: A moribund patient who is not expected to survive without the operation

P6: A declared brain-dead patient whose organs are being removed for donor purposes

These six levels are consistent with the American Society of Anesthesiologists (ASA) ranking of patient physical status. Physical status is included in the CPT codebook to distinguish among various levels of complexity of the anesthesia service provided.

Example: 00100-P1

Qualifying Circumstances

More than one qualifying circumstance may be selected.

Many anesthesia services are provided under particularly difficult circumstances, depending on factors such as extraordinary condition of patient, notable operative conditions, and/or unusual risk factors. This section includes a list of important qualifying circumstances that significantly affect the character of the anesthesia service provided. These procedures would not be reported alone but would be reported as additional procedure numbers qualifying an anesthesia procedure or service.

+ 99100 Anesthesia for patient of extreme age, younger than 1 year and older than 70 (List separately in addition to code for primary anesthesia procedure)

(For procedure performed on infants younger than 1 year of age at time of surgery, see 00326, 00561, 00834, 00836)

+ 99116 Anesthesia complicated by utilization of total body hypothermia (List separately in addition to code for primary anesthesia procedure)

+ 99135 Anesthesia complicated by utilization of controlled hypotension (List separately in addition to code for primary anesthesia procedure)

+ 99140 Anesthesia complicated by emergency conditions (specify) (List separately in addition to code for primary anesthesia procedure)

(An emergency is defined as existing when delay in treatment of the patient would lead to a significant increase in the threat to life or body part.)

Anesthesia

Head

00100 Anesthesia for procedures on salivary glands, including biopsy

00102 Anesthesia for procedures involving plastic repair of cleft lip

00103 Anesthesia for reconstructive procedures of eyelid (eg, blepharoplasty, ptosis surgery)

00104 Anesthesia for electroconvulsive therapy

00120 Anesthesia for procedures on external, middle, and inner ear including biopsy; not otherwise specified

00124 otoscopy

00126 tympanotomy

00140 Anesthesia for procedures on eye; not otherwise specified

00142 lens surgery

00144 corneal transplant

00145 vitreoretinal surgery

00147 iridectomy

00148 ophthalmoscopy

00160 Anesthesia for procedures on nose and accessory sinuses; not otherwise specified

00162 radical surgery

00164 biopsy, soft tissue

00170 Anesthesia for intraoral procedures, including biopsy; not otherwise specified

00172 repair of cleft palate

00174 excision of retropharyngeal tumor

00176 radical surgery

00190 Anesthesia for procedures on facial bones or skull; not otherwise specified

00192 radical surgery (including prognathism)

00210 Anesthesia for intracranial procedures; not otherwise specified

● **00211** craniotomy or craniectomy for evacuation of hematoma

00212 subdural taps

00214 burr holes, including ventriculography

00215 cranioplasty or elevation of depressed skull fracture, extradural (simple or compound)

00216 vascular procedures

00218 procedures in sitting position

00220 cerebrospinal fluid shunting procedures

00222 electrocoagulation of intracranial nerve

Neck

00300 Anesthesia for all procedures on the integumentary system, muscles and nerves of head, neck, and posterior trunk, not otherwise specified

00320 Anesthesia for all procedures on esophagus, thyroid, larynx, trachea and lymphatic system of neck; not otherwise specified, age 1 year or older

00322 needle biopsy of thyroid

(For procedures on cervical spine and cord, see 00600, 00604, 00670)

00326 Anesthesia for all procedures on the larynx and trachea in children younger than 1 year of age

(Do not report 00326 in conjunction with 99100)

00350 Anesthesia for procedures on major vessels of neck; not otherwise specified

00352 simple ligation

(For arteriography, use 01916)

Thorax (Chest Wall and Shoulder Girdle)

00400 Anesthesia for procedures on the integumentary system on the extremities, anterior trunk and perineum; not otherwise specified

00402 reconstructive procedures on breast (eg, reduction or augmentation mammoplasty, muscle flaps)

00404 radical or modified radical procedures on breast

00406 radical or modified radical procedures on breast with internal mammary node dissection

00410 electrical conversion of arrhythmias

00450 Anesthesia for procedures on clavicle and scapula; not otherwise specified

00452 radical surgery

00454 biopsy of clavicle

00470 Anesthesia for partial rib resection; not otherwise specified

00472 thoracoplasty (any type)

00474 radical procedures (eg, pectus excavatum)

Anesthesia

Intrathoracic

00500 Anesthesia for all procedures on esophagus

00520 Anesthesia for closed chest procedures; (including bronchoscopy) not otherwise specified

00522 needle biopsy of pleura

00524 pneumocentesis

00528 mediastinoscopy and diagnostic thoracoscopy not utilizing one lung ventilation

(For tracheobronchial reconstruction, use 00539)

00529 mediastinoscopy and diagnostic thoracoscopy utilizing one lung ventilation

00530 Anesthesia for permanent transvenous pacemaker insertion

00532 Anesthesia for access to central venous circulation

00534 Anesthesia for transvenous insertion or replacement of pacing cardioverter-defibrillator

(For transthoracic approach, use 00560)

00537 Anesthesia for cardiac electrophysiologic procedures including radiofrequency ablation

00539 Anesthesia for tracheobronchial reconstruction

00540 Anesthesia for thoracotomy procedures involving lungs, pleura, diaphragm, and mediastinum (including surgical thoracoscopy); not otherwise specified

00541 utilizing one lung ventilation

(For thoracic spine and cord anesthesia procedures via an anterior transthoracic approach, see 00625-00626)

00542 decortication

00546 pulmonary resection with thoracoplasty

00548 intrathoracic procedures on the trachea and bronchi

00550 Anesthesia for sternal debridement

00560 Anesthesia for procedures on heart, pericardial sac, and great vessels of chest; without pump oxygenator

00561 with pump oxygenator, younger than 1 year of age

(Do not report 00561 in conjunction with 99100, 99116, and 99135)

▲ **00562** with pump oxygenator, age 1 year or older, for all non-coronary bypass procedures (eg, valve procedures) or for re-operation for coronary bypass more than 1 month after original operation

00563 with pump oxygenator with hypothermic circulatory arrest

▲ **00566** Anesthesia for direct coronary artery bypass grafting; without pump oxygenator

● **00567** with pump oxygenator

00580 Anesthesia for heart transplant or heart/lung transplant

Spine and Spinal Cord

00600 Anesthesia for procedures on cervical spine and cord; not otherwise specified

(For percutaneous image-guided spine and spinal cord anesthesia procedures, see 01935, 01936)

00604 procedures with patient in the sitting position

00620 Anesthesia for procedures on thoracic spine and cord; not otherwise specified

00622 thoracolumbar sympathectomy

00625 Anesthesia for procedures on the thoracic spine and cord, via an anterior transthoracic approach; not utilizing one lung ventilation

00626 utilizing one lung ventilation

(For anesthesia for thoracotomy procedures other than spinal, see 00540-00541)

00630 Anesthesia for procedures in lumbar region; not otherwise specified

00632 lumbar sympathectomy

00634 chemonucleolysis

00635 diagnostic or therapeutic lumbar puncture

00640 Anesthesia for manipulation of the spine or for closed procedures on the cervical, thoracic or lumbar spine

00670 Anesthesia for extensive spine and spinal cord procedures (eg, spinal instrumentation or vascular procedures)

Upper Abdomen

00700 Anesthesia for procedures on upper anterior abdominal wall; not otherwise specified

00702 percutaneous liver biopsy

00730 Anesthesia for procedures on upper posterior abdominal wall

00740 Anesthesia for upper gastrointestinal endoscopic procedures, endoscope introduced proximal to duodenum

00750 Anesthesia for hernia repairs in upper abdomen; not otherwise specified

00752 lumbar and ventral (incisional) hernias and/or wound dehiscence

00754 omphalocele

00756 transabdominal repair of diaphragmatic hernia

00770 Anesthesia for all procedures on major abdominal blood vessels

00790 Anesthesia for intraperitoneal procedures in upper abdomen including laparoscopy; not otherwise specified

00792 partial hepatectomy or management of liver hemorrhage (excluding liver biopsy)

00794 pancreatectomy, partial or total (eg, Whipple procedure)

00796 liver transplant (recipient)

(For harvesting of liver, use 01990)

00797 gastric restrictive procedure for morbid obesity

Lower Abdomen

00800 Anesthesia for procedures on lower anterior abdominal wall; not otherwise specified

00802 panniculectomy

00810 Anesthesia for lower intestinal endoscopic procedures, endoscope introduced distal to duodenum

00820 Anesthesia for procedures on lower posterior abdominal wall

00830 Anesthesia for hernia repairs in lower abdomen; not otherwise specified

00832 ventral and incisional hernias

(For hernia repairs in the infant 1 year of age or younger, see 00834, 00836)

00834 Anesthesia for hernia repairs in the lower abdomen not otherwise specified, younger than 1 year of age

(Do not report 00834 in conjunction with 99100)

00836 Anesthesia for hernia repairs in the lower abdomen not otherwise specified, infants younger than 37 weeks gestational age at birth and younger than 50 weeks gestational age at time of surgery

(Do not report 00836 in conjunction with 99100)

00840 Anesthesia for intraperitoneal procedures in lower abdomen including laparoscopy; not otherwise specified

00842 amniocentesis

00844 abdominoperineal resection

00846 radical hysterectomy

00848 pelvic exenteration

00851 tubal ligation/transection

00860 Anesthesia for extraperitoneal procedures in lower abdomen, including urinary tract; not otherwise specified

00862 renal procedures, including upper one-third of ureter, or donor nephrectomy

00864 total cystectomy

00865 radical prostatectomy (suprapubic, retropubic)

00866 adrenalectomy

00868 renal transplant (recipient)

(For donor nephrectomy, use 00862)

(For harvesting kidney from brain-dead patient, use 01990)

00870 cystolithotomy

00872 Anesthesia for lithotripsy, extracorporeal shock wave; with water bath

00873 without water bath

00880 Anesthesia for procedures on major lower abdominal vessels; not otherwise specified

00882 inferior vena cava ligation

Perineum

(For perineal procedures on integumentary system, muscles and nerves, see 00300, 00400)

00902 Anesthesia for; anorectal procedure

00904 radical perineal procedure

00906 vulvectomy

00908 perineal prostatectomy

00910 Anesthesia for transurethral procedures (including urethrocystoscopy); not otherwise specified

00912 transurethral resection of bladder tumor(s)

00914 transurethral resection of prostate

00916 post-transurethral resection bleeding

00918 with fragmentation, manipulation and/or removal of ureteral calculus

00920 Anesthesia for procedures on male genitalia (including open urethral procedures); not otherwise specified

00921 vasectomy, unilateral or bilateral

00922 seminal vesicles

00924 undescended testis, unilateral or bilateral

00926 radical orchiectomy, inguinal

00928 radical orchiectomy, abdominal

00930 orchiopexy, unilateral or bilateral

00932 complete amputation of penis

00934 radical amputation of penis with bilateral inguinal lymphadenectomy

00936 radical amputation of penis with bilateral inguinal and iliac lymphadenectomy

00938 insertion of penile prosthesis (perineal approach)

00940 Anesthesia for vaginal procedures (including biopsy of labia, vagina, cervix or endometrium); not otherwise specified

00942 colpotomy, vaginectomy, colporrhaphy, and open urethral procedures

00944 vaginal hysterectomy

00948 cervical cerclage

00950 culdoscopy

00952 hysteroscopy and/or hysterosalpingography

Pelvis (Except Hip)

01112 Anesthesia for bone marrow aspiration and/or biopsy, anterior or posterior iliac crest

01120 Anesthesia for procedures on bony pelvis

01130 Anesthesia for body cast application or revision

01140 Anesthesia for interpelviabdominal (hindquarter) amputation

01150 Anesthesia for radical procedures for tumor of pelvis, except hindquarter amputation

01160 Anesthesia for closed procedures involving symphysis pubis or sacroiliac joint

01170 Anesthesia for open procedures involving symphysis pubis or sacroiliac joint

01173 Anesthesia for open repair of fracture disruption of pelvis or column fracture involving acetabulum

01180 Anesthesia for obturator neurectomy; extrapelvic

01190 intrapelvic

Upper Leg (Except Knee)

01200 Anesthesia for all closed procedures involving hip joint

01202 Anesthesia for arthroscopic procedures of hip joint

01210 Anesthesia for open procedures involving hip joint; not otherwise specified

01212 hip disarticulation

01214 total hip arthroplasty

01215 revision of total hip arthroplasty

01220 Anesthesia for all closed procedures involving upper two-thirds of femur

01230 Anesthesia for open procedures involving upper two-thirds of femur; not otherwise specified

01232 amputation

01234 radical resection

01250 Anesthesia for all procedures on nerves, muscles, tendons, fascia, and bursae of upper leg

01260 Anesthesia for all procedures involving veins of upper leg, including exploration

01270 Anesthesia for procedures involving arteries of upper leg, including bypass graft; not otherwise specified

01272 femoral artery ligation

01274 femoral artery embolectomy

Knee and Popliteal Area

01320 Anesthesia for all procedures on nerves, muscles, tendons, fascia, and bursae of knee and/or popliteal area

01340 Anesthesia for all closed procedures on lower one-third of femur

01360 Anesthesia for all open procedures on lower one-third of femur

01380 Anesthesia for all closed procedures on knee joint

01382 Anesthesia for diagnostic arthroscopic procedures of knee joint

01390 Anesthesia for all closed procedures on upper ends of tibia, fibula, and/or patella

01392 Anesthesia for all open procedures on upper ends of tibia, fibula, and/or patella

01400 Anesthesia for open or surgical arthroscopic procedures on knee joint; not otherwise specified

01402 total knee arthroplasty

01404 disarticulation at knee

01420 Anesthesia for all cast applications, removal, or repair involving knee joint

01430 Anesthesia for procedures on veins of knee and popliteal area; not otherwise specified

01432 arteriovenous fistula

01440 Anesthesia for procedures on arteries of knee and popliteal area; not otherwise specified

01442 popliteal thromboendarterectomy, with or without patch graft

01444 popliteal excision and graft or repair for occlusion or aneurysm

Lower Leg (Below Knee, Includes Ankle and Foot)

01462 Anesthesia for all closed procedures on lower leg, ankle, and foot

01464 Anesthesia for arthroscopic procedures of ankle and/or foot

01470 Anesthesia for procedures on nerves, muscles, tendons, and fascia of lower leg, ankle, and foot; not otherwise specified

01472 repair of ruptured Achilles tendon, with or without graft

01474 gastrocnemius recession (eg, Strayer procedure)

01480 Anesthesia for open procedures on bones of lower leg, ankle, and foot; not otherwise specified

01482 radical resection (including below knee amputation)

01484 osteotomy or osteoplasty of tibia and/or fibula

01486 total ankle replacement

01490 Anesthesia for lower leg cast application, removal, or repair

01500 Anesthesia for procedures on arteries of lower leg, including bypass graft; not otherwise specified

01502 embolectomy, direct or with catheter

01520 Anesthesia for procedures on veins of lower leg; not otherwise specified

01522 venous thrombectomy, direct or with catheter

Shoulder and Axilla

Includes humeral head and neck, sternoclavicular joint, acromioclavicular joint, and shoulder joint.

01610 Anesthesia for all procedures on nerves, muscles, tendons, fascia, and bursae of shoulder and axilla

01620 Anesthesia for all closed procedures on humeral head and neck, sternoclavicular joint, acromioclavicular joint, and shoulder joint

01622 Anesthesia for diagnostic arthroscopic procedures of shoulder joint

01630 Anesthesia for open or surgical arthroscopic procedures on humeral head and neck, sternoclavicular joint, acromioclavicular joint, and shoulder joint; not otherwise specified

01632 radical resection

01634 shoulder disarticulation

01636 interthoracoscapular (forequarter) amputation

01638 total shoulder replacement

01650 Anesthesia for procedures on arteries of shoulder and axilla; not otherwise specified

01652 axillary-brachial aneurysm

01654 bypass graft

01656 axillary-femoral bypass graft

01670 Anesthesia for all procedures on veins of shoulder and axilla

01680 Anesthesia for shoulder cast application, removal or repair; not otherwise specified

01682 shoulder spica

Upper Arm and Elbow

01710 Anesthesia for procedures on nerves, muscles, tendons, fascia, and bursae of upper arm and elbow; not otherwise specified

01712 tenotomy, elbow to shoulder, open

01714 tenoplasty, elbow to shoulder

01716 tenodesis, rupture of long tendon of biceps

01730 Anesthesia for all closed procedures on humerus and elbow

01732 Anesthesia for diagnostic arthroscopic procedures of elbow joint

01740 Anesthesia for open or surgical arthroscopic procedures of the elbow; not otherwise specified

01742 osteotomy of humerus

01744 repair of nonunion or malunion of humerus

01756 radical procedures

01758 excision of cyst or tumor of humerus

01760 total elbow replacement

01770 Anesthesia for procedures on arteries of upper arm and elbow; not otherwise specified

01772 embolectomy

01780 Anesthesia for procedures on veins of upper arm and elbow; not otherwise specified

01782 phleborrhaphy

Forearm, Wrist, and Hand

01810 Anesthesia for all procedures on nerves, muscles, tendons, fascia, and bursae of forearm, wrist, and hand

01820 Anesthesia for all closed procedures on radius, ulna, wrist, or hand bones

01829 Anesthesia for diagnostic arthroscopic procedures on the wrist

01830 Anesthesia for open or surgical arthroscopic/endoscopic procedures on distal radius, distal ulna, wrist, or hand joints; not otherwise specified

01832 total wrist replacement

01840 Anesthesia for procedures on arteries of forearm, wrist, and hand; not otherwise specified

01842 embolectomy

01844 Anesthesia for vascular shunt, or shunt revision, any type (eg, dialysis)

01850 Anesthesia for procedures on veins of forearm, wrist, and hand; not otherwise specified

01852 phleborrhaphy

01860 Anesthesia for forearm, wrist, or hand cast application, removal, or repair

Radiological Procedures

(01905 has been deleted. To report, see 01935, 01936)

01916 Anesthesia for diagnostic arteriography/venography

(Do not report 01916 in conjunction with therapeutic codes 01924-01926, 01930-01933)

01920 Anesthesia for cardiac catheterization including coronary angiography and ventriculography (not to include Swan-Ganz catheter)

01922 Anesthesia for non-invasive imaging or radiation therapy

01924 Anesthesia for therapeutic interventional radiological procedures involving the arterial system; not otherwise specified

01925 carotid or coronary

01926 intracranial, intracardiac, or aortic

01930 Anesthesia for therapeutic interventional radiological procedures involving the venous/lymphatic system (not to include access to the central circulation); not otherwise specified

01931 intrahepatic or portal circulation (eg, transvenous intrahepatic portosystemic shunt[s] [TIPS])

01932 intrathoracic or jugular

01933 intracranial

01935 Anesthesia for percutaneous image guided procedures on the spine and spinal cord; diagnostic

01936 therapeutic

Burn Excisions or Debridement

01951 Anesthesia for second- and third-degree burn excision or debridement with or without skin grafting, any site, for total body surface area (TBSA) treated during anesthesia and surgery; less than 4% total body surface area

01952 between 4% and 9% of total body surface area

+ 01953 each additional 9% total body surface area or part thereof (List separately in addition to code for primary procedure)

(Use 01953 in conjunction with 01952)

Obstetric

01958 Anesthesia for external cephalic version procedure

01960 Anesthesia for vaginal delivery only

01961 Anesthesia for cesarean delivery only

01962 Anesthesia for urgent hysterectomy following delivery

01963 Anesthesia for cesarean hysterectomy without any labor analgesia/anesthesia care

01965 Anesthesia for incomplete or missed abortion procedures

01966 Anesthesia for induced abortion procedures

01967 Neuraxial labor analgesia/anesthesia for planned vaginal delivery (this includes any repeat subarachnoid needle placement and drug injection and/or any necessary replacement of an epidural catheter during labor)

+ 01968 Anesthesia for cesarean delivery following neuraxial labor analgesia/anesthesia (List separately in addition to code for primary procedure performed)

(Use 01968 in conjunction with 01967)

+ 01969 Anesthesia for cesarean hysterectomy following neuraxial labor analgesia/anesthesia (List separately in addition to code for primary procedure performed)

(Use 01969 in conjunction with 01967)

Other Procedures

01990 Physiological support for harvesting of organ(s) from brain-dead patient

01991 Anesthesia for diagnostic or therapeutic nerve blocks and injections (when block or injection is performed by a different provider); other than the prone position

01992 prone position

(Do not report 01991 or 01992 in conjunction with 99143-99150)

(When regional intravenous administration of local anesthetic agent or other medication in the upper or lower extremity is used as the anesthetic for a surgical procedure, report the appropriate anesthesia code. To report a Bier block for pain management, use 64999. For intra-arterial or intravenous injections, see 90773, 90774)

►(For intra-arterial or intravenous therapy for pain management, see 96373, 96374)◄

(01995 has been deleted)

01996 Daily hospital management of epidural or subarachnoid continuous drug administration

(Report code 01996 for daily hospital management of continuous epidural or subarachnoid drug administration performed after insertion of an epidural or subarachnoid catheter)

01999 Unlisted anesthesia procedure(s)

Surgery Guidelines

Items used by all physicians in reporting their services are presented in the **Introduction.** Some of the commonalities are repeated here for the convenience of those physicians referring to this section on **Surgery.** Other definitions and items unique to Surgery are also listed.

Physicians' Services

Physicians' services rendered in the office, home, or hospital, consultations, and other medical services are listed in the section entitled **Evaluation and Management Services** (99201-99499) found in the front of the book, beginning on page 9. "Special Services and Reports" (99000 series) is presented in the **Medicine** section.

CPT Surgical Package Definition

The services provided by the physician to any patient by their very nature are variable. The CPT codes that represent a readily identifiable surgical procedure thereby include, on a procedure-by-procedure basis, a variety of services. In defining the specific services "included" in a given CPT surgical code, the following services are always included in addition to the operation per se:

- Local infiltration, metacarpal/metatarsal/digital block or topical anesthesia
- Subsequent to the decision for surgery, one related Evaluation and Management (E/M) encounter on the date immediately prior to or on the date of procedure (including history and physical)
- Immediate postoperative care, including dictating operative notes, talking with the family and other physicians
- Writing orders
- Evaluating the patient in the postanesthesia recovery area
- Typical postoperative follow-up care

Follow-Up Care for Diagnostic Procedures

Follow-up care for diagnostic procedures (eg, endoscopy, arthroscopy, injection procedures for radiography) includes only that care related to recovery from the diagnostic procedure itself. Care of the condition for which the diagnostic procedure was performed or of other concomitant conditions is not included and may be listed separately.

Follow-Up Care for Therapeutic Surgical Procedures

Follow-up care for therapeutic surgical procedures includes only that care which is usually a part of the surgical service. Complications, exacerbations, recurrence, or the presence of other diseases or injuries requiring additional services should be separately reported.

Materials Supplied by Physician

Supplies and materials provided by the physician (eg, sterile trays/drugs), over and above those usually included with the procedure(s) rendered are reported separately. List drugs, trays, supplies, and materials provided. Identify as 99070 or specific supply code.

Reporting More Than One Procedure/Service

When a physician performs more than one procedure/service on the same date, same session or during a post-operative period (subject to the "surgical package" concept), several CPT modifiers may apply (see Appendix A for definition).

Separate Procedure

Some of the procedures or services listed in the CPT codebook that are commonly carried out as an integral component of a total service or procedure have been identified by the inclusion of the term "separate procedure." The codes designated as "separate procedure" should not be reported in addition to the code for the total procedure or service of which it is considered an integral component.

However, when a procedure or service that is designated as a "separate procedure" is carried out independently or considered to be unrelated or distinct from other procedures/services provided at that time, it may be reported by itself, or in addition to other procedures/services by appending modifier 59 to the specific "separate procedure" code to indicate that the procedure is not considered to be a component of another procedure, but is a distinct, independent procedure. This may represent a different session, different procedure or surgery, different site or organ system, separate incision/excision, separate lesion, or separate injury (or area of injury in extensive injuries).

Subsection Information

Several of the subheadings or subsections have special needs or instructions unique to that section. Where these are indicated (eg, "Maternity Care and Delivery"), special **"Notes"** will be presented preceding those procedural terminology listings, referring to that subsection specifically. If there is an "Unlisted Procedure" code number (see below) for the individual subsection, it will also be shown. Those subsections within the **Surgery** section that have **"Notes"** are as follows:

Biopsy 11100-11101

Removal of Skin Tags. 11200-11201

Shaving of Lesions. 11300-11313

Excision—Benign Lesions 11400-11471

Excision—Malignant Lesions 11600-11646

Repair (Closure) 12001-13160

Adjacent Tissue Transfer or Rearrangement 14000-14350

Skin Replacement Surgery and Skin Substitutes. 15002-15431

Allograft and Tissue Cultured Allogeneic Skin Substitutes. 15300-15366

Xenograft. 15400-15431

Flaps (Skin and/or Deep Tissue) 15570-15999

Burns, Local Treatment 16000-16036

Destruction 17000-17286

Mohs Micrographic Surgery 17311-17315

Breast—Excision 19100-19272

Musculoskeletal. 20000-29999

Wound Exploration—Trauma. 20100-20103

Grafts (or Implants). 20900-20938

Head Prosthesis. 21076-21088

Spine: (Vertebral Column). 22100-22855

Spine: Excision 22100-22208

Spine: Osteotomy 22206-22226

Spine: Fracture/Dislocation. 22305-22328

Spine: Arthrodesis 22532-22812

Spine: Exploration 22830

Spinal Instrumentation 22840-22865

Casting and Strapping. 29000-29750

Musculoskeletal: Endoscopy/Arthroscopy 29800-29999

Respiratory: Endoscopy 31231-31294, 31505-31579, 31615-31656, 32601-32665

Lung Transplantation 32850-32856

Cardiovascular System. 33010-37799

Pacing Cardioverter-Pacemaker or Defibrillator 33202-33249

Electrophysiologic Procedures. 33250-33266

CABG

- **Venous** 33510-33516
- **Combined** 33517-33530
- **Arterial**. 33533-33548

Endovascular Repair of Descending Thoracic Aorta. 33880-33891

Heart/Lung Transplantation 33930-33945

Arteries and Veins 34001-37790

Endovascular Repair of Abdominal Aortic Aneurysm 34800-34826

Endovascular Repair of Illiac Aneurysm 34900

Transluminal Angioplasty 35450-35476

Transluminal Atherectomy 35480-35495

Bypass Graft, Vein 35500-35572

Composite Grafts. 35681-35683

Adjuvant Techniques 35685-35686

Vascular Injection Procedures: Intravenous 36000-36015

Central Venous Access Procedures . . . 36555-36597

Transcatheter Procedures. 37184-37216

Intravascular Ultrasound. 37250-37251

Bone Marrow or Stem Cell Services/Procedures 38204-38242

Hemic and Lymphatic Systems: Laparoscopy 38570-38589

Digestive:
Endoscopy/Laparoscopy 43200-43272, 43280-43289, 43651-43659, 43770-43774, 44180-44238, 44360-44397, 44970-44979, 45300-45387, 45395-45397, 45400-45402, 46600-46615, 47370-47379, 47550-47556, 47560-47562, 49320-49329, 49650-49659

Pancreas Transplantation 48550-48556

Herniotomy 49491-49611

Renal Transplantation 50300-50380

Urodynamics 51725-51798

Endoscopy/Laparoscopy

Urinary 50541-50545, 50945-50980, 51990-52648

Male Genital 54690-54699, 55550-55559, 55866

Female Genital 58541-58579, 58660-58679

Endocrine 60650-60659

Maternity Care and Delivery 59000-59899

Nervous System:
Surgery of Skull Base 61580-61619

Neurostimulators (Intracranial) 61850-61888, 62160-62319

Neurostimulators (Spinal) 63650-63688

Neurostimulators (Peripheral Nerve). 64553-64595

Secondary Implants(s) 65125-65175

Removal Cataract 66830-66999

Prophylaxis 67141-67229

Eyelid:
Excision, Destruction 67800-67840

Reconstruction 67930-67975

Operating Microscope 69990

Unlisted Service or Procedure

A service or procedure may be provided that is not listed in this edition of the CPT codebook. When reporting such a service, the appropriate "Unlisted Procedure" code may be used to indicate the service, identifying it by "Special Report" as discussed in the section below. The "Unlisted Procedures" and accompanying codes for **Surgery** are as follows:

15999	Unlisted procedure, excision pressure ulcer
17999	Unlisted procedure, skin, mucous membrane and subcutaneous tissue
19499	Unlisted procedure, breast
20999	Unlisted procedure, musculoskeletal system, general
21089	Unlisted maxillofacial prosthetic procedure
21299	Unlisted craniofacial and maxillofacial procedure
21499	Unlisted musculoskeletal procedure, head
21899	Unlisted procedure, neck or thorax
22899	Unlisted procedure, spine
22999	Unlisted procedure, abdomen, musculoskeletal system
23929	Unlisted procedure, shoulder
24999	Unlisted procedure, humerus or elbow
25999	Unlisted procedure, forearm or wrist
26989	Unlisted procedure, hands or fingers
27299	Unlisted procedure, pelvis or hip joint
27599	Unlisted procedure, femur or knee
27899	Unlisted procedure, leg or ankle
28899	Unlisted procedure, foot or toes
29799	Unlisted procedure, casting or strapping
29999	Unlisted procedure, arthroscopy
30999	Unlisted procedure, nose
31299	Unlisted procedure, accessory sinuses
31599	Unlisted procedure, larynx
31899	Unlisted procedure, trachea, bronchi
32999	Unlisted procedure, lungs and pleura
33999	Unlisted procedure, cardiac surgery
36299	Unlisted procedure, vascular injection
37501	Unlisted vascular endoscopy procedure
37799	Unlisted procedure, vascular surgery
38129	Unlisted laparoscopy procedure, spleen
38589	Unlisted laparoscopy procedure, lymphatic system
38999	Unlisted procedure, hemic or lymphatic system
39499	Unlisted procedure, mediastinum
39599	Unlisted procedure, diaphragm
40799	Unlisted procedure, lips
40899	Unlisted procedure, vestibule of mouth
41599	Unlisted procedure, tongue, floor of mouth
41899	Unlisted procedure, dentoalveolar structures
42299	Unlisted procedure, palate, uvula
42699	Unlisted procedure, salivary glands or ducts
42999	Unlisted procedure, pharynx, adenoids, or tonsils
43289	Unlisted laparoscopy procedure, esophagus
43499	Unlisted procedure, esophagus
43659	Unlisted laparoscopy procedure, stomach
43999	Unlisted procedure, stomach
44238	Unlisted laparoscopy procedure, intestine (except rectum)

44799	Unlisted procedure, intestine
44899	Unlisted procedure, Meckel's diverticulum and the mesentery
44979	Unlisted laparoscopy procedure, appendix
45499	Unlisted laparoscopy procedure, rectum
45999	Unlisted procedure, rectum
46999	Unlisted procedure, anus
47379	Unlisted laparoscopic procedure, liver
47399	Unlisted procedure, liver
47579	Unlisted laparoscopy procedure, biliary tract
47999	Unlisted procedure, biliary tract
48999	Unlisted procedure, pancreas
49329	Unlisted laparoscopy procedure, abdomen, peritoneum and omentum
49659	Unlisted laparoscopy procedure, hernioplasty, herniorrhaphy, herniotomy
49999	Unlisted procedure, abdomen, peritoneum and omentum
50549	Unlisted laparoscopy procedure, renal
50949	Unlisted laparoscopy procedure, ureter
51999	Unlisted laparoscopy procedure, bladder
53899	Unlisted procedure, urinary system
54699	Unlisted laparoscopy procedure, testis
55559	Unlisted laparoscopy procedure, spermatic cord
55899	Unlisted procedure, male genital system
58578	Unlisted laparoscopy procedure, uterus
58579	Unlisted hysteroscopy procedure, uterus
58679	Unlisted laparoscopy procedure, oviduct, ovary
58999	Unlisted procedure, female genital system (nonobstetrical)
59897	Unlisted fetal invasive procedure, including ultrasound guidance
59898	Unlisted laparoscopy procedure, maternity care and delivery
59899	Unlisted procedure, maternity care and delivery
60659	Unlisted laparoscopy procedure, endocrine system
60699	Unlisted procedure, endocrine system
64999	Unlisted procedure, nervous system
66999	Unlisted procedure, anterior segment of eye
67299	Unlisted procedure, posterior segment
67399	Unlisted procedure, ocular muscle
67599	Unlisted procedure, orbit
67999	Unlisted procedure, eyelids
68399	Unlisted procedure, conjunctiva
68899	Unlisted procedure, lacrimal system
69399	Unlisted procedure, external ear
69799	Unlisted procedure, middle ear
69949	Unlisted procedure, inner ear
69979	Unlisted procedure, temporal bone, middle fossa approach

Special Report

A service that is rarely provided, unusual, variable, or new may require a special report in determining medical appropriateness of the service. Pertinent information should include an adequate definition or description of the nature, extent, and need for the procedure, and the time, effort, and equipment necessary to provide the service. Additional items which may be included are:

- Complexity of symptoms
- Final diagnosis
- Pertinent physical findings (such as size, locations, and number of lesion[s], if appropriate)
- Diagnostic and therapeutic procedures (including major and supplementary surgical procedures, if appropriate)
- Concurrent problems
- Follow-up care

Surgical Destruction

Surgical destruction is a part of a surgical procedure and different methods of destruction are not ordinarily listed separately unless the technique substantially alters the standard management of a problem or condition. Exceptions under special circumstances are provided for by separate code numbers.

Surgery

General

10021 Fine needle aspiration; without imaging guidance

10022 with imaging guidance

(For radiological supervision and interpretation, see 76942, 77002, 77012, 77021)

►(For percutaneous needle biopsy other than fine needle aspiration, see 20206 for muscle, 32400 for pleura, 32405 for lung or mediastinum, 42400 for salivary gland, 47000, 47001 for liver, 48102 for pancreas, 49180 for abdominal or retroperitoneal mass, 60100 for thyroid, 62267 for nucleus pulposus, intervertebral disc, or paravertebral tissue, 62269 for spinal cord)◄

(For evaluation of fine needle aspirate, see 88172, 88173)

Integumentary System

Skin, Subcutaneous and Accessory Structures

Incision and Drainage

(For excision, see 11400, et seq)

10040 Acne surgery (eg, marsupialization, opening or removal of multiple milia, comedones, cysts, pustules)

10060 Incision and drainage of abscess (eg, carbuncle, suppurative hidradenitis, cutaneous or subcutaneous abscess, cyst, furuncle, or paronychia); simple or single

10061 complicated or multiple

10080 Incision and drainage of pilonidal cyst; simple

10081 complicated

(For excision of pilonidal cyst, see 11770-11772)

10120 Incision and removal of foreign body, subcutaneous tissues; simple

10121 complicated

(To report wound exploration due to penetrating trauma without laparotomy or thoracotomy, see 20100-20103, as appropriate)

(To report debridement associated with open fracture(s) and/or dislocation(s), use 11010-11012, as appropriate)

10140 Incision and drainage of hematoma, seroma or fluid collection

(If imaging guidance is performed, see 76942, 77012, 77021)

10160 Puncture aspiration of abscess, hematoma, bulla, or cyst

(If imaging guidance is performed, see 76942, 77012, 77021)

10180 Incision and drainage, complex, postoperative wound infection

(For secondary closure of surgical wound, see 12020, 12021, 13160)

Excision—Debridement

(For dermabrasions, see 15780-15783)

(For nail debridement, see 11720-11721)

(For burn(s), see 16000-16035)

11000 Debridement of extensive eczematous or infected skin; up to 10% of body surface

(For abdominal wall or genitalia debridement for necrotizing soft tissue infection, see 11004-11006)

+▲ 11001 each additional 10% of the body surface, or part thereof (List separately in addition to code for primary procedure)

(Use 11001 in conjunction with 11000)

11004 Debridement of skin, subcutaneous tissue, muscle and fascia for necrotizing soft tissue infection; external genitalia and perineum

11005 abdominal wall, with or without fascial closure

11006 external genitalia, perineum and abdominal wall, with or without fascial closure

+ 11008 Removal of prosthetic material or mesh, abdominal wall for infection (eg, for chronic or recurrent mesh infection or necrotizing soft tissue infection) (List separately in addition to code for primary procedure)

(Use 11008 in conjunction with 10180, 11004-11006)

(Do not report 11008 in conjunction with 11000-11001, 11010-11044)

(Report skin grafts or flaps separately when performed for closure at the same session as 11004-11008)

(When insertion of mesh is used for closure, use 49568)

(If orchiectomy is performed, use 54520)

(If testicular transplantation is performed, use 54680)

11010 Debridement including removal of foreign material associated with open fracture(s) and/or dislocation(s); skin and subcutaneous tissues

11011 skin, subcutaneous tissue, muscle fascia, and muscle

11012 skin, subcutaneous tissue, muscle fascia, muscle, and bone

11040 Debridement; skin, partial thickness

11041 skin, full thickness

11042 skin, and subcutaneous tissue

11043 skin, subcutaneous tissue, and muscle

11044 skin, subcutaneous tissue, muscle, and bone

(Do not report 11040-11044 in conjunction with 97597-97602)

Paring or Cutting

(To report destruction, see 17000-17004)

11055 Paring or cutting of benign hyperkeratotic lesion (eg, corn or callus); single lesion

11056 2 to 4 lesions

11057 more than 4 lesions

Biopsy

During certain surgical procedures in the integumentary system, such as excision, destruction, or shave removals, the removed tissue is often submitted for pathologic examination. The obtaining of tissue for pathology during the course of these procedures is a routine component of such procedures. This obtaining of tissue is not considered a separate biopsy procedure and is not separately reported. The use of a biopsy procedure code (eg, 11100, 11101) indicates that the procedure to obtain tissue for pathologic examination was performed independently, or was unrelated or distinct from other procedures/services provided at that time. Such biopsies are not considered components of other procedures when performed on different lesions or different sites on the same date, and are to be reported separately.

(For biopsy of conjunctiva, use 68100; eyelid, use 67810)

11100 Biopsy of skin, subcutaneous tissue and/or mucous membrane (including simple closure), unless otherwise listed; single lesion

✚ **11101** each separate/additional lesion (List separately in addition to code for primary procedure)

(Use 11101 in conjunction with 11100)

Removal of Skin Tags

Removal by scissoring or any sharp method, ligature strangulation, electrosurgical destruction or combination of treatment modalities, including chemical destruction or electrocauterization of wound, with or without local anesthesia.

11200 Removal of skin tags, multiple fibrocutaneous tags, any area; up to and including 15 lesions

✚▲ **11201** each additional 10 lesions, or part thereof (List separately in addition to code for primary procedure)

(Use 11201 in conjunction with 11200)

Shaving of Epidermal or Dermal Lesions

Shaving is the sharp removal by transverse incision or horizontal slicing to remove epidermal and dermal lesions without a full-thickness dermal excision. This includes local anesthesia, chemical or electrocauterization of the wound. The wound does not require suture closure.

11300 Shaving of epidermal or dermal lesion, single lesion, trunk, arms or legs; lesion diameter 0.5 cm or less

11301 lesion diameter 0.6 to 1.0 cm

11302 lesion diameter 1.1 to 2.0 cm

11303 lesion diameter over 2.0 cm

11305 Shaving of epidermal or dermal lesion, single lesion, scalp, neck, hands, feet, genitalia; lesion diameter 0.5 cm or less

11306 lesion diameter 0.6 to 1.0 cm

11307 lesion diameter 1.1 to 2.0 cm

11308 lesion diameter over 2.0 cm

11310 Shaving of epidermal or dermal lesion, single lesion, face, ears, eyelids, nose, lips, mucous membrane; lesion diameter 0.5 cm or less

11311 lesion diameter 0.6 to 1.0 cm

11312 lesion diameter 1.1 to 2.0 cm

11313 lesion diameter over 2.0 cm

Excision—Benign Lesions

Excision (including simple closure) of benign lesions of skin (eg, neoplasm, cicatricial, fibrous, inflammatory, congenital, cystic lesions), includes local anesthesia. See appropriate size and area below. For shave removal, see 11300 et seq, and for electrosurgical and other methods see 17000 et seq.

Excision is defined as full-thickness (through the dermis) removal of a lesion, including margins, and includes simple (non-layered) closure when performed. Report separately each benign lesion excised. Code selection is determined by measuring the greatest clinical diameter of the apparent lesion plus that margin required for complete excision (lesion diameter plus the most narrow margins required equals the excised diameter). The margins refer to the most narrow margin required to adequately excise the lesion, based on the physician's judgment. The measurement of lesion plus margin is made prior to excision. The excised diameter is the same whether the surgical defect is repaired in a linear fashion, or reconstructed (eg, with a skin graft).

The closure of defects created by incision, excision, or trauma may require intermediate or complex closure. Repair by intermediate or complex closure should be reported separately. For excision of benign lesions requiring more than simple closure, ie, requiring intermediate or complex closure, report 11400-11446 in addition to appropriate intermediate (12031-12057) or complex closure (13100-13153) codes. For reconstructive closure, see 15002-15261, 15570-15770. For excision performed in conjunction with adjacent tissue transfer, report only the adjacent tissue transfer code (14000-14300). Excision of lesion (11400–11446) is not separately reportable with adjacent tissue transfer. See page 49 for the definition of *intermediate* or *complex* closure.

11400 Excision, benign lesion including margins, except skin tag (unless listed elsewhere), trunk, arms or legs; excised diameter 0.5 cm or less

11401 excised diameter 0.6 to 1.0 cm

11402 excised diameter 1.1 to 2.0 cm

11403 excised diameter 2.1 to 3.0 cm

11404 excised diameter 3.1 to 4.0 cm

11406 excised diameter over 4.0 cm

(For unusual or complicated excision, add modifier 22)

11420 Excision, benign lesion including margins, except skin tag (unless listed elsewhere), scalp, neck, hands, feet, genitalia; excised diameter 0.5 cm or less

11421 excised diameter 0.6 to 1.0 cm

11422 excised diameter 1.1 to 2.0 cm

11423 excised diameter 2.1 to 3.0 cm

11424 excised diameter 3.1 to 4.0 cm

11426 excised diameter over 4.0 cm

(For unusual or complicated excision, add modifier 22)

11440 Excision, other benign lesion including margins, except skin tag (unless listed elsewhere), face, ears, eyelids, nose, lips, mucous membrane; excised diameter 0.5 cm or less

11441 excised diameter 0.6 to 1.0 cm

11442 excised diameter 1.1 to 2.0 cm

11443 excised diameter 2.1 to 3.0 cm

11444 excised diameter 3.1 to 4.0 cm

11446 excised diameter over 4.0 cm

(For unusual or complicated excision, add modifier 22)

(For eyelids involving more than skin, see also 67800 et seq)

11450 Excision of skin and subcutaneous tissue for hidradenitis, axillary; with simple or intermediate repair

11451 with complex repair

11462 Excision of skin and subcutaneous tissue for hidradenitis, inguinal; with simple or intermediate repair

11463 with complex repair

11470 Excision of skin and subcutaneous tissue for hidradenitis, perianal, perineal, or umbilical; with simple or intermediate repair

11471 with complex repair

(When skin graft or flap is used for closure, use appropriate procedure code in addition)

(For bilateral procedure, add modifier 50)

Excision—Malignant Lesions

Excision (including simple closure) of malignant lesions of skin (eg, basal cell carcinoma, squamous cell carcinoma, melanoma) includes local anesthesia. (See appropriate size and body area below.) For destruction of malignant lesions of skin, see destruction codes 17260-17286.

Excision is defined as full-thickness (through the dermis) removal of a lesion including margins, and includes simple (non-layered) closure when performed. Report separately each malignant lesion excised. Code selection is determined by measuring the greatest clinical diameter of the apparent lesion plus that margin required for complete excision (lesion diameter plus the most narrow margins required equals the excised diameter). The margins refer to the most narrow margin required to adequately excise the lesion, based on the physician's judgment. The measurement of lesion plus margin is made prior to excision. The excised diameter is the same whether the surgical defect is repaired in a linear fashion, or reconstructed (eg, with a skin graft).

The closure of defects created by incision, excision, or trauma may require intermediate or complex closure. Repair by intermediate or complex closure should be reported separately. For excision of malignant lesions requiring more than simple closure, ie, requiring intermediate or complex closure, report 11600-11646 in addition to appropriate intermediate (12031-12057) or complex closure (13100-13153) codes. For reconstructive closure, see 15002-15261, 15570-15770. For excision performed in conjunction with adjacent tissue transfer, report only the adjacent tissue transfer code (14000-14300). Excision of lesion (11600–11646) is not separately reportable with adjacent tissue transfer. See page 49 for the definition of *intermediate* or *complex* closure.

When frozen section pathology shows the margins of excision were not adequate, an additional excision may be necessary for complete tumor removal. Use only one code to report the additional excision and re-excision(s) based on the final widest excised diameter required for complete tumor removal at the same operative session. To report a re-excision procedure performed to widen margins at a subsequent operative session, see codes 11600-11646, as appropriate. Append modifier 58 if the re-excision procedure is performed during the postoperative period of the primary excision procedure.

11600 Excision, malignant lesion including margins, trunk, arms, or legs; excised diameter 0.5 cm or less

11601 excised diameter 0.6 to 1.0 cm

11602 excised diameter 1.1 to 2.0 cm

11603 excised diameter 2.1 to 3.0 cm

11604 excised diameter 3.1 to 4.0 cm

11606 excised diameter over 4.0 cm

11620 Excision, malignant lesion including margins, scalp, neck, hands, feet, genitalia; excised diameter 0.5 cm or less

11621 excised diameter 0.6 to 1.0 cm

11622 excised diameter 1.1 to 2.0 cm

11623 excised diameter 2.1 to 3.0 cm

11624 excised diameter 3.1 to 4.0 cm

11626 excised diameter over 4.0 cm

11640 Excision, malignant lesion including margins, face, ears, eyelids, nose, lips; excised diameter 0.5 cm or less

11641 excised diameter 0.6 to 1.0 cm

11642 excised diameter 1.1 to 2.0 cm

11643 excised diameter 2.1 to 3.0 cm

11644 excised diameter 3.1 to 4.0 cm

11646 excised diameter over 4.0 cm

(For eyelids involving more than skin, see also 67800 et seq)

Nails

(For drainage of paronychia or onychia, see 10060, 10061)

11719 Trimming of nondystrophic nails, any number

11720 Debridement of nail(s) by any method(s); 1 to 5

11721 6 or more

11730 Avulsion of nail plate, partial or complete, simple; single

+ **11732** each additional nail plate (List separately in addition to code for primary procedure)

(Use 11732 in conjunction with 11730)

11740 Evacuation of subungual hematoma

11750 Excision of nail and nail matrix, partial or complete (eg, ingrown or deformed nail), for permanent removal;

11752 with amputation of tuft of distal phalanx

(For skin graft, if used, use 15050)

11755 Biopsy of nail unit (eg, plate, bed, matrix, hyponychium, proximal and lateral nail folds) (separate procedure)

11760 Repair of nail bed

11762 Reconstruction of nail bed with graft

11765 Wedge excision of skin of nail fold (eg, for ingrown toenail)

Pilonidal Cyst

11770 Excision of pilonidal cyst or sinus; simple

11771 extensive

11772 complicated

(For incision of pilonidal cyst, see 10080, 10081)

Introduction

11900 Injection, intralesional; up to and including 7 lesions

11901 more than 7 lesions

(11900, 11901 are not to be used for preoperative local anesthetic injection)

(For veins, see 36470, 36471)

(For intralesional chemotherapy administration, see 96405, 96406)

11920 Tattooing, intradermal introduction of insoluble opaque pigments to correct color defects of skin, including micropigmentation; 6.0 sq cm or less

11921 6.1 to 20.0 sq cm

+▲ **11922** each additional 20.0 sq cm, or part thereof (List separately in addition to code for primary procedure)

(Use 11922 in conjunction with 11921)

11950 Subcutaneous injection of filling material (eg, collagen); 1 cc or less

11951 1.1 to 5.0 cc

11952 5.1 to 10.0 cc

11954 over 10.0 cc

11960 Insertion of tissue expander(s) for other than breast, including subsequent expansion

(For breast reconstruction with tissue expander(s), use 19357)

11970 Replacement of tissue expander with permanent prosthesis

11971 Removal of tissue expander(s) without insertion of prosthesis

11975 Insertion, implantable contraceptive capsules

11976 Removal, implantable contraceptive capsules

11977 Removal with reinsertion, implantable contraceptive capsules

11980 Subcutaneous hormone pellet implantation (implantation of estradiol and/or testosterone pellets beneath the skin)

11981 Insertion, non-biodegradable drug delivery implant

11982 Removal, non-biodegradable drug delivery implant

11983 Removal with reinsertion, non-biodegradable drug delivery implant

Repair (Closure)

Use the codes in this section to designate wound closure utilizing sutures, staples, or tissue adhesives (eg, 2-cyanoacrylate), either singly or in combination with each other, or in combination with adhesive strips. Wound closure utilizing adhesive strips as the sole repair material should be coded using the appropriate E/M code.

Definitions

The repair of wounds may be classified as Simple, Intermediate, or Complex.

Simple repair is used when the wound is superficial; eg, involving primarily epidermis or dermis, or subcutaneous tissues without significant involvement of deeper structures, and requires simple one layer closure. This includes local anesthesia and chemical or electrocauterization of wounds not closed.

Intermediate repair includes the repair of wounds that, in addition to the above, require layered closure of one or more of the deeper layers of subcutaneous tissue and superficial (non-muscle) fascia, in addition to the skin (epidermal and dermal) closure. Single-layer closure of heavily contaminated wounds that have required extensive cleaning or removal of particulate matter also constitutes intermediate repair.

Complex repair includes the repair of wounds requiring more than layered closure, viz., scar revision, debridement (eg, traumatic lacerations or avulsions), extensive undermining, stents or retention sutures. Necessary preparation includes creation of a defect for repairs (eg, excision of a scar requiring a complex repair) or the debridement of complicated lacerations or avulsions. Complex repair does not include excision of benign (11400-11446) or malignant (11600-11646) lesions.

Instructions for listing services at time of wound repair:

1. The repaired wound(s) should be measured and recorded in centimeters, whether curved, angular, or stellate.

2. When multiple wounds are repaired, add together the lengths of those in the same classification (see above) and from all anatomic sites that are grouped together into the same code descriptor. For example, add together the lengths of intermediate repairs to the trunk and extremities. Do not add lengths of repairs from different groupings of anatomic sites (eg, face and extremities). Also, do not add together lengths of different classifications (eg, intermediate and complex repairs).

When more than one classification of wounds is repaired, list the more complicated as the primary procedure and the less complicated as the secondary procedure, using modifier 51.

3. Decontamination and/or debridement: Debridement is considered a separate procedure only when gross contamination requires prolonged cleansing, when appreciable amounts of devitalized or contaminated tissue are removed, or when debridement is carried out separately without immediate primary closure. (For extensive debridement of soft tissue and/or bone, see 11040-11044.)

(For extensive debridement of soft tissue and/or bone, not associated with open fracture(s) and/or dislocation(s) resulting from penetrating and/or blunt trauma, see 11040-11044.)

(For extensive debridement of subcutaneous tissue, muscle fascia, muscle, and/or bone associated with open fracture(s) and/or dislocation(s), see 11010-11012.)

4. Involvement of nerves, blood vessels and tendons: Report under appropriate system (Nervous, Cardiovascular, Musculoskeletal) for repair of these structures. The repair of these associated wounds is included in the primary procedure unless it qualifies as a complex wound, in which case modifier 51 applies.

Simple ligation of vessels in an open wound is considered as part of any wound closure.

Simple "exploration" of nerves, blood vessels or tendons exposed in an open wound is also considered part of the essential treatment of the wound and is not a separate procedure unless appreciable dissection is required. If the wound requires enlargement, extension of dissection (to determine penetration), debridement, removal of foreign body(s), ligation or coagulation of minor subcutaneous and/or muscular blood vessel(s) of the subcutaneous tissue, muscle fascia, and/or muscle, not requiring thoracotomy or laparotomy, use codes 20100-20103, as appropriate.

Repair—Simple

Sum of lengths of repairs for each group of anatomic sites.

12001 Simple repair of superficial wounds of scalp, neck, axillae, external genitalia, trunk and/or extremities (including hands and feet); 2.5 cm or less

12002 2.6 cm to 7.5 cm

12004 7.6 cm to 12.5 cm

12005 12.6 cm to 20.0 cm

12006 20.1 cm to 30.0 cm

12007 over 30.0 cm

12011 Simple repair of superficial wounds of face, ears, eyelids, nose, lips and/or mucous membranes; 2.5 cm or less

12013 2.6 cm to 5.0 cm

12014 5.1 cm to 7.5 cm

Surgery: Integumentary System

12015 7.6 cm to 12.5 cm

12016 12.6 cm to 20.0 cm

12017 20.1 cm to 30.0 cm

12018 over 30.0 cm

12020 Treatment of superficial wound dehiscence; simple closure

12021 with packing

(For extensive or complicated secondary wound closure, use 13160)

Repair—Intermediate

Sum of lengths of repairs for each group of anatomic sites.

▲ **12031** Repair, intermediate, wounds of scalp, axillae, trunk and/or extremities (excluding hands and feet); 2.5 cm or less

▲ **12032** 2.6 cm to 7.5 cm

▲ **12034** 7.6 cm to 12.5 cm

▲ **12035** 12.6 cm to 20.0 cm

▲ **12036** 20.1 cm to 30.0 cm

▲ **12037** over 30.0 cm

▲ **12041** Repair, intermediate, wounds of neck, hands, feet and/or external genitalia; 2.5 cm or less

▲ **12042** 2.6 cm to 7.5 cm

▲ **12044** 7.6 cm to 12.5 cm

▲ **12045** 12.6 cm to 20.0 cm

▲ **12046** 20.1 cm to 30.0 cm

▲ **12047** over 30.0 cm

▲ **12051** Repair, intermediate, wounds of face, ears, eyelids, nose, lips and/or mucous membranes; 2.5 cm or less

▲ **12052** 2.6 cm to 5.0 cm

▲ **12053** 5.1 cm to 7.5 cm

▲ **12054** 7.6 cm to 12.5 cm

▲ **12055** 12.6 cm to 20.0 cm

▲ **12056** 20.1 cm to 30.0 cm

▲ **12057** over 30.0 cm

Repair—Complex

Reconstructive procedures, complicated wound closure.

Sum of lengths of repairs for each group of anatomic sites.

(For full thickness repair of lip or eyelid, see respective anatomical subsections)

13100 Repair, complex, trunk; 1.1 cm to 2.5 cm

(For 1.0 cm or less, see simple or intermediate repairs)

13101 2.6 cm to 7.5 cm

✚ **13102** each additional 5 cm or less (List separately in addition to code for primary procedure)

(Use 13102 in conjunction with 13101)

13120 Repair, complex, scalp, arms, and/or legs; 1.1 cm to 2.5 cm

(For 1.0 cm or less, see simple or intermediate repairs)

13121 2.6 cm to 7.5 cm

✚ **13122** each additional 5 cm or less (List separately in addition to code for primary procedure)

(Use 13122 in conjunction with 13121)

13131 Repair, complex, forehead, cheeks, chin, mouth, neck, axillae, genitalia, hands and/or feet; 1.1 cm to 2.5 cm

(For 1.0 cm or less, see simple or intermediate repairs)

13132 2.6 cm to 7.5 cm

✚ **13133** each additional 5 cm or less (List separately in addition to code for primary procedure)

(Use 13133 in conjunction with 13132)

13150 Repair, complex, eyelids, nose, ears and/or lips; 1.0 cm or less

(See also 40650-40654, 67961-67975)

13151 1.1 cm to 2.5 cm

13152 2.6 cm to 7.5 cm

✚ **13153** each additional 5 cm or less (List separately in addition to code for primary procedure)

(Use 13153 in conjunction with 13152)

13160 Secondary closure of surgical wound or dehiscence, extensive or complicated

(For packing or simple secondary wound closure, see 12020, 12021)

Adjacent Tissue Transfer or Rearrangement

For full thickness repair of lip or eyelid, see respective anatomical subsections.

Codes 14000-14300 are used for excision (including lesion) and/or repair by adjacent tissue transfer or rearrangement (eg, Z-plasty, W-plasty, V-Y plasty, rotation flap, advancement flap, double pedicle flap). When applied in repairing lacerations, the procedures listed must be performed by the surgeon to accomplish the repair. They do not apply to direct closure or rearrangement of traumatic wounds incidentally resulting in these configurations. The excision of a benign lesion (11400-11446) or a malignant lesion (11600-11646) is not separately reportable with codes 14000-14300.

Skin graft necessary to close secondary defect is considered an additional procedure. For purposes of code selection, the term "defect" includes the primary and secondary defects. The primary defect resulting from the excision and the secondary defect resulting from flap design to perform the reconstruction are measured together to determine the code.

14000 Adjacent tissue transfer or rearrangement, trunk; defect 10 sq cm or less

14001 defect 10.1 sq cm to 30.0 sq cm

14020 Adjacent tissue transfer or rearrangement, scalp, arms and/or legs; defect 10 sq cm or less

14021 defect 10.1 sq cm to 30.0 sq cm

14040 Adjacent tissue transfer or rearrangement, forehead, cheeks, chin, mouth, neck, axillae, genitalia, hands and/or feet; defect 10 sq cm or less

14041 defect 10.1 sq cm to 30.0 sq cm

14060 Adjacent tissue transfer or rearrangement, eyelids, nose, ears and/or lips; defect 10 sq cm or less

14061 defect 10.1 sq cm to 30.0 sq cm

(For eyelid, full thickness, see 67961 et seq)

14300 Adjacent tissue transfer or rearrangement, more than 30 sq cm, unusual or complicated, any area

14350 Filleted finger or toe flap, including preparation of recipient site

Skin Replacement Surgery and Skin Substitutes

Identify by size and location of the defect (recipient area) and the type of graft or skin substitute; includes simple debridement of granulation tissue or recent avulsion.

When a primary procedure such as orbitectomy, radical mastectomy, or deep tumor removal requires skin graft for definitive closure, see appropriate anatomical subsection for primary procedure and this section for skin graft or skin substitute.

Use codes 15002-15005 for initial wound recipient site preparation.

►Use codes 15100-15261 for autologous skin grafts. For autologous tissue-cultured epidermal grafts, use codes 15150-15157. For harvesting of autologous keratinocytes and dermal tissue for tissue-cultured skin grafts, use code 15040. Procedures are coded by recipient site. Use codes 15170-15176 for acellular dermal replacement. ◄

Repair of donor site requiring skin graft or local flaps is to be added as an additional procedure.

Codes 15002-15005 describe burn and wound preparation or incisional or excisional release of scar contracture resulting in an open wound requiring a skin graft. Codes 15100-15431 describe the application of skin replacements and skin substitutes. The following definition should be applied to those codes that reference "100 sq cm or 1% of body area of infants and children" when determining the involvement of body size: The measurement of 100 sq cm is applicable to adults and children age 10 and older; percentages of body surface area apply to infants and children younger than the age of 10.

►These codes are not intended to be reported for simple graft application alone or application stabilized with dressings (eg, by simple gauze wrap). The skin substitute/graft is anchored using the surgeon's choice of fixation. When services are performed in the office, the supply of the skin substitute/graft should be reported separately. Routine dressing supplies are not reported separately. When square centimeters are indicated, this refers to 1 sq cm up to the stated amount. Add-on codes begin with the next sq cm (eg, 130 sq cm would be coded using a code for the first 100 sq cm and an add-on code for the next 30 sq cm). Use modifier 58 for staged application procedure(s).◄

(For microvascular flaps, see 15756-15758)

Surgical Preparation

(15000, 15001 have been deleted. To report, see 15002-15005)

15002 Surgical preparation or creation of recipient site by excision of open wounds, burn eschar, or scar (including subcutaneous tissues), or incisional release of scar contracture, trunk, arms, legs; first 100 sq cm or 1% of body area of infants and children

+▲ 15003 each additional 100 sq cm, or part thereof, or each additional 1% of body area of infants and children (List separately in addition to code for primary procedure)

(Use 15003 in conjunction with 15002)

15004 Surgical preparation or creation of recipient site by excision of open wounds, burn eschar, or scar (including subcutaneous tissues), or incisional release of scar contracture, face, scalp, eyelids, mouth, neck, ears, orbits, genitalia, hands, feet and/or multiple digits; first 100 sq cm or 1% of body area of infants and children

+▲ 15005 each additional 100 sq cm, or part thereof, or each additional 1% of body area of infants and children (List separately in addition to code for primary procedure)

(Use 15005 in conjunction with 15004)

(Report 15002-15005 in conjunction with code for appropriate skin grafts or replacements [15050-15261, 15330-15336]. List the graft or replacement separately by its procedure number when the graft, immediate or delayed, is applied)

(For excision of benign lesions, see 11400-11471)

(For excision of malignant lesions, see 11600-11646)

(For excision to prepare or create recipient site with dressings or materials not listed in 15040-15431, use 15002-15005 only)

(For excision with immediate skin grafting, use 15002-15005 in conjunction with 15050-15261)

(For excision with immediate allograft skin placement, use 15002-15005 in conjunction with 15300-15336 and 15360-15366)

(For excision with immediate xenogeneic dermis placement, use 15002-15005 in conjunction with 15400-15421)

Grafts

Autograft/Tissue Cultured Autograft

15040 Harvest of skin for tissue cultured skin autograft, 100 sq cm or less

15050 Pinch graft, single or multiple, to cover small ulcer, tip of digit, or other minimal open area (except on face), up to defect size 2 cm diameter

15100 Split-thickness autograft, trunk, arms, legs; first 100 sq cm or less, or 1% of body area of infants and children (except 15050)

+ 15101 each additional 100 sq cm, or each additional 1% of body area of infants and children, or part thereof (List separately in addition to code for primary procedure)

(Use 15101 in conjunction with 15100)

15110 Epidermal autograft, trunk, arms, legs; first 100 sq cm or less, or 1% of body area of infants and children

+ 15111 each additional 100 sq cm, or each additional 1% of body area of infants and children, or part thereof (List separately in addition to code for primary procedure)

(Use 15111 in conjunction with 15110)

15115 Epidermal autograft, face, scalp, eyelids, mouth, neck, ears, orbits, genitalia, hands, feet, and/or multiple digits; first 100 sq cm or less, or 1% of body area of infants and children

+ 15116 each additional 100 sq cm, or each additional 1% of body area of infants and children, or part thereof (List separately in addition to code for primary procedure)

(Use 15116 in conjunction with 15115)

15120 Split-thickness autograft, face, scalp, eyelids, mouth, neck, ears, orbits, genitalia, hands, feet, and/or multiple digits; first 100 sq cm or less, or 1% of body area of infants and children (except 15050)

+ 15121 each additional 100 sq cm, or each additional 1% of body area of infants and children, or part thereof (List separately in addition to code for primary procedure)

(Use 15121 in conjunction with 15120)

(For eyelids, see also 67961 et seq)

15130 Dermal autograft, trunk, arms, legs; first 100 sq cm or less, or 1% of body area of infants and children

+ 15131 each additional 100 sq cm, or each additional 1% of body area of infants and children, or part thereof (List separately in addition to code for primary procedure)

(Use 15131 in conjunction with 15130)

15135 Dermal autograft, face, scalp, eyelids, mouth, neck, ears, orbits, genitalia, hands, feet, and/or multiple digits; first 100 sq cm or less, or 1% of body area of infants and children

+ 15136 each additional 100 sq cm, or each additional 1% of body area of infants and children, or part thereof (List separately in addition to code for primary procedure)

(Use 15136 in conjunction with 15135)

15150 Tissue cultured epidermal autograft, trunk, arms, legs; first 25 sq cm or less

+ 15151 additional 1 sq cm to 75 sq cm (List separately in addition to code for primary procedure)

(Do not report 15151 more than once per session)

(Use 15151 in conjunction with 15150)

+ 15152 each additional 100 sq cm, or each additional 1% of body area of infants and children, or part thereof (List separately in addition to code for primary procedure)

(Use 15152 in conjunction with 15151)

15155 Tissue cultured epidermal autograft, face, scalp, eyelids, mouth, neck, ears, orbits, genitalia, hands, feet, and/or multiple digits; first 25 sq cm or less

+ 15156 additional 1 sq cm to 75 sq cm (List separately in addition to code for primary procedure)

(Do not report 15156 more than once per session)

(Use 15156 in conjunction with 15155)

+ 15157 each additional 100 sq cm, or each additional 1% of body area of infants and children, or part thereof (List separately in addition to code for primary procedure)

(Use 15157 in conjunction with 15156)

Acellular Dermal Replacement

15170 Acellular dermal replacement, trunk, arms, legs; first 100 sq cm or less, or 1% of body area of infants and children

+ 15171 each additional 100 sq cm, or each additional 1% of body area of infants and children, or part thereof (List separately in addition to code for primary procedure)

(Use 15171 in conjunction with 15170)

15175 Acellular dermal replacement, face, scalp, eyelids, mouth, neck, ears, orbits, genitalia, hands, feet, and/or multiple digits; first 100 sq cm or less, or 1% of body area of infants and children

+ 15176 each additional 100 sq cm, or each additional 1% of body area of infants and children, or part thereof (List separately in addition to code for primary procedure)

(Use 15176 in conjunction with 15175)

15200 Full thickness graft, free, including direct closure of donor site, trunk; 20 sq cm or less

+▲ 15201 each additional 20 sq cm, or part thereof (List separately in addition to code for primary procedure)

(Use 15201 in conjunction with 15200)

15220 Full thickness graft, free, including direct closure of donor site, scalp, arms, and/or legs; 20 sq cm or less

+▲ 15221 each additional 20 sq cm, or part thereof (List separately in addition to code for primary procedure)

(Use 15221 in conjunction with 15220)

15240 Full thickness graft, free, including direct closure of donor site, forehead, cheeks, chin, mouth, neck, axillae, genitalia, hands, and/or feet; 20 sq cm or less

(For finger tip graft, use 15050)

(For repair of syndactyly, fingers, see 26560-26562)

+▲ 15241 each additional 20 sq cm, or part thereof (List separately in addition to code for primary procedure)

(Use 15241 in conjunction with 15240)

15260 Full thickness graft, free, including direct closure of donor site, nose, ears, eyelids, and/or lips; 20 sq cm or less

+▲ 15261 each additional 20 sq cm, or part thereof (List separately in addition to code for primary procedure)

(Use 15261 in conjunction with 15260)

(For eyelids, see also 67961 et seq)

(Repair of donor site requiring skin graft or local flaps, to be added as additional separate procedure)

Allograft/Tissue Cultured Allogeneic Skin Substitute

Application of a non-autologous human skin graft (ie, homograft) from a donor to a part of the recipient's body to resurface an area damaged by burns, traumatic injury, soft tissue infection and/or tissue necrosis or surgery.

15300 Allograft skin for temporary wound closure, trunk, arms, legs; first 100 sq cm or less, or 1% of body area of infants and children

+ 15301 each additional 100 sq cm, or each additional 1% of body area of infants and children, or part thereof (List separately in addition to code for primary procedure)

(Use 15301 in conjunction with 15300)

15320 Allograft skin for temporary wound closure, face, scalp, eyelids, mouth, neck, ears, orbits, genitalia, hands, feet, and/or multiple digits; first 100 sq cm or less, or 1% of body area of infants and children

+ 15321 each additional 100 sq cm, or each additional 1% of body area of infants and children, or part thereof (List separately in addition to code for primary procedure)

(Use 15321 in conjunction with 15320)

15330 Acellular dermal allograft, trunk, arms, legs; first 100 sq cm or less, or 1% of body area of infants and children

+ 15331 each additional 100 sq cm, or each additional 1% of body area of infants and children, or part thereof (List separately in addition to code for primary procedure)

(Use 15331 in conjunction with 15330)

15335 Acellular dermal allograft, face, scalp, eyelids, mouth, neck, ears, orbits, genitalia, hands, feet, and/or multiple digits; first 100 sq cm or less, or 1% of body area of infants and children

+ 15336 each additional 100 sq cm, or each additional 1% of body area of infants and children, or part thereof (List separately in addition to code for primary procedure)

(Use 15336 in conjunction with 15335)

15340 Tissue cultured allogeneic skin substitute; first 25 sq cm or less

+▲ 15341 each additional 25 sq cm, or part thereof (List separately in addition to code for primary procedure)

(Use 15341 in conjunction with 15340)

(Do not report 15340, 15341 in conjunction with 11040-11042, 15002-15005)

15360 Tissue cultured allogeneic dermal substitute, trunk, arms, legs; first 100 sq cm or less, or 1% of body area of infants and children

+ 15361 each additional 100 sq cm, or each additional 1% of body area of infants and children, or part thereof (List separately in addition to code for primary procedure)

(Use 15361 in conjunction with 15360)

15365 Tissue cultured allogeneic dermal substitute, face, scalp, eyelids, mouth, neck, ears, orbits, genitalia, hands, feet, and/or multiple digits; first 100 sq cm or less, or 1% of body area of infants and children

+ 15366 each additional 100 sq cm, or each additional 1% of body area of infants and children, or part thereof (List separately in addition to code for primary procedure)

(Use 15366 in conjunction with 15365)

Xenograft

Application of a non-human skin graft or biologic wound dressing (eg, porcine tissue or pigskin) to a part of the recipient's body following debridement of the burn wound or area of traumatic injury, soft tissue infection and/or tissue necrosis, or surgery.

15400 Xenograft, skin (dermal), for temporary wound closure, trunk, arms, legs; first 100 sq cm or less, or 1% of body area of infants and children

+ 15401 each additional 100 sq cm, or each additional 1% of body area of infants and children, or part thereof (List separately in addition to code for primary procedure)

(Use 15401 in conjunction with 15400)

15420 Xenograft skin (dermal), for temporary wound closure, face, scalp, eyelids, mouth, neck, ears, orbits, genitalia, hands, feet, and/or multiple digits; first 100 sq cm or less, or 1% of body area of infants and children

+ 15421 each additional 100 sq cm, or each additional 1% of body area of infants and children, or part thereof (List separately in addition to code for primary procedure)

(Use 15421 in conjunction with 15420)

15430 Acellular xenograft implant; first 100 sq cm or less, or 1% of body area of infants and children

+ 15431 each additional 100 sq cm, or each additional 1% of body area of infants and children, or part thereof (List separately in addition to code for primary procedure)

(Use 15431 in conjunction with 15430)

(Do not report 15430, 15431 in conjunction with 11040-11042, 15002-15005, 0170T)

Flaps (Skin and/or Deep Tissues)

The regions listed refer to the recipient area (not the donor site) when a flap is being attached in a transfer or to a final site.

►The regions listed refer to a donor site when a tube is formed for later transfer or when a "delay" of flap occurs prior to the transfer.◄

Procedures 15570-15738 do not include extensive immobilization (eg, large plaster casts and other immobilizing devices are considered additional separate procedures).

A repair of a donor site requiring a skin graft or local flaps is considered an additional separate procedure.

(For microvascular flaps, see 15756-15758)

(For flaps without inclusion of a vascular pedicle, see 15570-15576)

(For adjacent tissue transfer flaps, see 14000-14300)

15570 Formation of direct or tubed pedicle, with or without transfer; trunk

15572 scalp, arms, or legs

15574 forehead, cheeks, chin, mouth, neck, axillae, genitalia, hands or feet

15576 eyelids, nose, ears, lips, or intraoral

15600 Delay of flap or sectioning of flap (division and inset); at trunk

15610 at scalp, arms, or legs

15620 at forehead, cheeks, chin, neck, axillae, genitalia, hands, or feet

15630 at eyelids, nose, ears, or lips

15650 Transfer, intermediate, of any pedicle flap (eg, abdomen to wrist, Walking tube), any location

(For eyelids, nose, ears, or lips, see also anatomical area)

(For revision, defatting or rearranging of transferred pedicle flap or skin graft, see 13100-14300)

(Procedures 15732-15738 are described by donor site of the muscle, myocutaneous, or fasciocutaneous flap)

15731 Forehead flap with preservation of vascular pedicle (eg, axial pattern flap, paramedian forehead flap)

(For muscle, myocutaneous, or fasciocutaneous flap of the head or neck, use 15732)

15732 Muscle, myocutaneous, or fasciocutaneous flap; head and neck (eg, temporalis, masseter muscle, sternocleidomastoid, levator scapulae)

(For forehead flap with preservation of vascular pedicle, use 15731)

15734 trunk

15736 upper extremity

15738 lower extremity

Other Flaps and Grafts

Repair of donor site requiring skin graft or local flaps should be reported as an additional procedure.

15740 Flap; island pedicle

15750 neurovascular pedicle

15756 Free muscle or myocutaneous flap with microvascular anastomosis

(Do not report code 69990 in addition to code 15756)

15757 Free skin flap with microvascular anastomosis

(Do not report code 69990 in addition to code 15757)

15758 Free fascial flap with microvascular anastomosis

(Do not report code 69990 in addition to code 15758)

15760 Graft; composite (eg, full thickness of external ear or nasal ala), including primary closure, donor area

15770 derma-fat-fascia

15775 Punch graft for hair transplant; 1 to 15 punch grafts

15776 more than 15 punch grafts

(For strip transplant, use 15220)

Other Procedures

15780 Dermabrasion; total face (eg, for acne scarring, fine wrinkling, rhytids, general keratosis)

15781 segmental, face

15782 regional, other than face

15783 superficial, any site (eg, tattoo removal)

15786 Abrasion; single lesion (eg, keratosis, scar)

+ **15787** each additional four lesions or less (List separately in addition to code for primary procedure)

(Use 15787 in conjunction with 15786)

15788 Chemical peel, facial; epidermal

15789 dermal

15792 Chemical peel, nonfacial; epidermal

15793 dermal

15819 Cervicoplasty

15820 Blepharoplasty, lower eyelid;

15821 with extensive herniated fat pad

15822 Blepharoplasty, upper eyelid;

15823 with excessive skin weighting down lid

(For bilateral blepharoplasty, add modifier 50)

15824 Rhytidectomy; forehead

(For repair of brow ptosis, use 67900)

15825 neck with platysmal tightening (platysmal flap, P-flap)

15826 glabellar frown lines

15828 cheek, chin, and neck

15829 superficial musculoaponeurotic system (SMAS) flap

(For bilateral rhytidectomy, add modifier 50)

15830 Excision, excessive skin and subcutaneous tissue (includes lipectomy); abdomen, infraumbilical panniculectomy

(Do not report 15830 in conjunction with 12031, 12032, 12034, 12035, 12036, 12037, 13100, 13101, 13102, 14000-14001, 14300)

(15831 has been deleted. To report abdominoplasty with panniculectomy, use 15830 in conjunction with 15847. To report other abdominoplasty, use 17999)

15832 thigh

15833 leg

15834 hip

15835 buttock

15836 arm

15837 forearm or hand

15838 submental fat pad

15839 other area

(For bilateral procedure, add modifier 50)

15840 Graft for facial nerve paralysis; free fascia graft (including obtaining fascia)

(For bilateral procedure, add modifier 50)

15841 free muscle graft (including obtaining graft)

15842 free muscle flap by microsurgical technique

(Do not report code 69990 in addition to code 15842)

15845 regional muscle transfer

(For intravenous fluorescein examination of blood flow in graft or flap, use 15860)

(For nerve transfers, decompression, or repair, see 64831-64876, 64905, 64907, 69720, 69725, 69740, 69745, 69955)

+ **15847** Excision, excessive skin and subcutaneous tissue (includes lipectomy), abdomen (eg, abdominoplasty) (includes umbilical transposition and fascial plication) (List separately in addition to code for primary procedure)

(Use 15847 in conjunction with 15830)

(For abdominal wall hernia repair, see 49491-49587)

(To report other abdominoplasty, use 17999)

15850 Removal of sutures under anesthesia (other than local), same surgeon

15851 Removal of sutures under anesthesia (other than local), other surgeon

15852 Dressing change (for other than burns) under anesthesia (other than local)

15860 Intravenous injection of agent (eg, fluorescein) to test vascular flow in flap or graft

15876 Suction assisted lipectomy; head and neck

15877 trunk

15878 upper extremity

15879 lower extremity

Pressure Ulcers (Decubitus Ulcers)

15920 Excision, coccygeal pressure ulcer, with coccygectomy; with primary suture

15922 with flap closure

15931 Excision, sacral pressure ulcer, with primary suture;

15933 with ostectomy

15934 Excision, sacral pressure ulcer, with skin flap closure;

15935 with ostectomy

15936 Excision, sacral pressure ulcer, in preparation for muscle or myocutaneous flap or skin graft closure;

15937 with ostectomy

(For repair of defect using muscle or myocutaneous flap, use code(s) 15734 and/or 15738 in addition to 15936, 15937. For repair of defect using split skin graft, use codes 15100 and/or 15101 in addition to 15936, 15937)

15940 Excision, ischial pressure ulcer, with primary suture;

15941 with ostectomy (ischiectomy)

15944 Excision, ischial pressure ulcer, with skin flap closure;

15945 with ostectomy

15946 Excision, ischial pressure ulcer, with ostectomy, in preparation for muscle or myocutaneous flap or skin graft closure

(For repair of defect using muscle or myocutaneous flap, use code(s) 15734 and/or 15738 in addition to 15946. For repair of defect using split skin graft, use codes 15100 and/or 15101 in addition to 15946)

15950 Excision, trochanteric pressure ulcer, with primary suture;

15951 with ostectomy

15952 Excision, trochanteric pressure ulcer, with skin flap closure;

15953 with ostectomy

15956 Excision, trochanteric pressure ulcer, in preparation for muscle or myocutaneous flap or skin graft closure;

15958 with ostectomy

(For repair of defect using muscle or myocutaneous flap, use code(s) 15734 and/or 15738 in addition to 15956, 15958. For repair of defect using split skin graft, use codes 15100 and/or 15101 in addition to 15956, 15958)

15999 Unlisted procedure, excision pressure ulcer

(For free skin graft to close ulcer or donor site, see 15002 et seq)

Burns, Local Treatment

Procedures 16000-16036 refer to local treatment of burned surface only. Codes 16020-16030 include the application of materials (eg, dressings) not described in codes 15100-15431.

List percentage of body surface involved and depth of burn.

For necessary related medical services (eg, hospital visits, detention) in management of burned patients, see appropriate services in **Evaluation and Management** and **Medicine** sections.

For the application of skin grafts or skin substitutes, see codes 15100-15650.

16000 Initial treatment, first degree burn, when no more than local treatment is required

16020 Dressings and/or debridement of partial-thickness burns, initial or subsequent; small (less than 5% total body surface area)

16025 medium (eg, whole face or whole extremity, or 5% to 10% total body surface area)

16030 large (eg, more than one extremity, or greater than 10% total body surface area)

16035 Escharotomy; initial incision

+ 16036 each additional incision (List separately in addition to code for primary procedure)

(Use 16036 in conjunction with 16035)

(For debridement, curettement of burn wound, see 16020-16030)

Destruction

Destruction means the ablation of benign, premalignant or malignant tissues by any method, with or without curettement, including local anesthesia, and not usually requiring closure.

Any method includes electrosurgery, cryosurgery, laser and chemical treatment. Lesions include condylomata, papillomata, molluscum contagiosum, herpetic lesions, warts (ie, common, plantar, flat), milia, or other benign, premalignant (eg, actinic keratoses), or malignant lesions.

(For destruction of lesion(s) in specific anatomic sites, see 40820, 46900-46917, 46924, 54050-54057, 54065, 56501, 56515, 57061, 57065, 67850, 68135)

(For paring or cutting of benign hyperkeratotic lesions (eg, corns or calluses), see 11055-11057)

(For sharp removal or electrosurgical destruction of skin tags and fibrocutaneous tags, see 11200, 11201)

(For cryotherapy of acne, use 17340)

(For initiation or follow-up care of topical chemotherapy (eg, 5-FU or similar agents), see appropriate office visits)

(For shaving of epidermal or dermal lesions, see 11300-11313)

Destruction, Benign or Premalignant Lesions

17000 Destruction (eg, laser surgery, electrosurgery, cryosurgery, chemosurgery, surgical curettement), premalignant lesions (eg, actinic keratoses); first lesion

+ 17003 second through 14 lesions, each (List separately in addition to code for first lesion)

(Use 17003 in conjunction with 17000)

(For destruction of common or plantar warts, see 17110, 17111)

⊘ 17004 Destruction (eg, laser surgery, electrosurgery, cryosurgery, chemosurgery, surgical curettement), premalignant lesions (eg, actinic keratoses), 15 or more lesions

(Do not report 17004 in conjunction with 17000-17003)

17106 Destruction of cutaneous vascular proliferative lesions (eg, laser technique); less than 10 sq cm

17107 10.0 to 50.0 sq cm

17108 over 50.0 sq cm

17110 Destruction (eg, laser surgery, electrosurgery, cryosurgery, chemosurgery, surgical curettement), of benign lesions other than skin tags or cutaneous vascular proliferative lesions; up to 14 lesions

17111 15 or more lesions

17250 Chemical cauterization of granulation tissue (proud flesh, sinus or fistula)

(17250 is not to be used with removal or excision codes for the same lesion)

Destruction, Malignant Lesions, Any Method

17260 Destruction, malignant lesion (eg, laser surgery, electrosurgery, cryosurgery, chemosurgery, surgical curettement), trunk, arms or legs; lesion diameter 0.5 cm or less

17261 lesion diameter 0.6 to 1.0 cm

17262 lesion diameter 1.1 to 2.0 cm

17263 lesion diameter 2.1 to 3.0 cm

17264 lesion diameter 3.1 to 4.0 cm

17266 lesion diameter over 4.0 cm

17270 Destruction, malignant lesion (eg, laser surgery, electrosurgery, cryosurgery, chemosurgery, surgical curettement), scalp, neck, hands, feet, genitalia; lesion diameter 0.5 cm or less

17271 lesion diameter 0.6 to 1.0 cm

17272 lesion diameter 1.1 to 2.0 cm

17273 lesion diameter 2.1 to 3.0 cm

17274 lesion diameter 3.1 to 4.0 cm

17276 lesion diameter over 4.0 cm

17280 Destruction, malignant lesion (eg, laser surgery, electrosurgery, cryosurgery, chemosurgery, surgical curettement), face, ears, eyelids, nose, lips, mucous membrane; lesion diameter 0.5 cm or less

17281 lesion diameter 0.6 to 1.0 cm

17282 lesion diameter 1.1 to 2.0 cm

17283 lesion diameter 2.1 to 3.0 cm

17284 lesion diameter 3.1 to 4.0 cm

17286 lesion diameter over 4.0 cm

Mohs Micrographic Surgery

Mohs micrographic surgery is a technique for the removal of complex or ill-defined skin cancer with histologic examination of 100% of the surgical margins. It requires a single physician to act in two integrated but separate and distinct capacities: surgeon and pathologist. If either of these responsibilities is delegated to another physician who reports the services separately, these codes should not be reported. The Mohs surgeon removes the tumor tissue and maps and divides the tumor specimen into pieces, and each piece is embedded into an individual tissue block for histopathologic examination. Thus a tissue block in Mohs surgery is defined as an individual tissue piece embedded in a mounting medium for sectioning.

If repair is performed, use separate repair, flap, or graft codes. If a biopsy of a suspected skin cancer is performed on the same day as Mohs surgery because there was no prior pathology confirmation of a diagnosis, then report diagnostic skin biopsy (11100, 11101) and frozen section pathology (88331) with modifier 59 to distinguish from the subsequent definitive surgical procedure of Mohs surgery.

(17304-17310 have been deleted. To report, see 17311-17315)

(If additional special pathology procedures, stains or immunostains are required, use 88311-88314, 88342)

(Do not report 88314 in conjunction with 17311-17315 for routine frozen section stain (eg, hematoxylin and eosin, toluidine blue) performed during Mohs surgery. When a nonroutine histochemical stain on frozen tissue is utilized, report 88314 with modifier 59)

(Do not report 88302-88309 on the same specimen as part of the Mohs surgery)

17311 Mohs micrographic technique, including removal of all gross tumor, surgical excision of tissue specimens, mapping, color coding of specimens, microscopic examination of specimens by the surgeon, and histopathologic preparation including routine stain(s) (eg, hematoxylin and eosin, toluidine blue), head, neck, hands, feet, genitalia, or any location with surgery directly involving muscle, cartilage, bone, tendon, major nerves, or vessels; first stage, up to 5 tissue blocks

+ 17312 each additional stage after the first stage, up to 5 tissue blocks (List separately in addition to code for primary procedure)

(Use 17312 in conjunction with 17311)

17313 Mohs micrographic technique, including removal of all gross tumor, surgical excision of tissue specimens, mapping, color coding of specimens, microscopic examination of specimens by the surgeon, and histopathologic preparation including routine stain(s) (eg, hematoxylin and eosin, toluidine blue), of the trunk, arms, or legs; first stage, up to 5 tissue blocks

+ 17314 each additional stage after the first stage, up to 5 tissue blocks (List separately in addition to code for primary procedure)

(Use 17314 in conjunction with 17313)

+ 17315 Mohs micrographic technique, including removal of all gross tumor, surgical excision of tissue specimens, mapping, color coding of specimens, microscopic examination of specimens by the surgeon, and histopathologic preparation including routine stain(s) (eg, hematoxylin and eosin, toluidine blue), each additional block after the first 5 tissue blocks, any stage (List separately in addition to code for primary procedure)

(Use 17315 in conjunction with 17311-17314)

Other Procedures

17340 Cryotherapy (CO_2 slush, liquid N_2) for acne

17360 Chemical exfoliation for acne (eg, acne paste, acid)

17380 Electrolysis epilation, each 30 minutes

(For actinotherapy, use 96900)

17999 Unlisted procedure, skin, mucous membrane and subcutaneous tissue

Breast

Incision

19000 Puncture aspiration of cyst of breast;

+ 19001 each additional cyst (List separately in addition to code for primary procedure)

(Use 19001 in conjunction with 19000)

(If imaging guidance is performed, see 76942, 77021, 77031, 77032)

19020 Mastotomy with exploration or drainage of abscess, deep

19030 Injection procedure only for mammary ductogram or galactogram

(For radiological supervision and interpretation, see 77053, 77054)

Excision

Excisional breast surgery includes certain biopsy procedures, the removal of cysts or other benign or malignant tumors or lesions, and the surgical treatment of breast and chest wall malignancies. Biopsy procedures may be percutaneous or open, and they involve the removal of differing amounts of tissue for diagnosis.

Breast biopsies are reported using codes 19100-19103. The open excision of breast lesions (eg, lesions of the breast ducts, cysts, benign or malignant tumors), without specific attention to adequate surgical margins, with or without the preoperative placement of radiological markers, is reported using codes 19110-19126. Partial mastectomy procedures (eg, lumpectomy, tylectomy, quadrantectomy, or segmentectomy) describe open excisions of breast tissue with specific attention to adequate surgical margins.

Partial mastectomy procedures are reported using codes 19301 or 19302 as appropriate. Documentation for partial mastectomy procedures includes attention to the removal of adequate surgical margins surrounding the breast mass or lesion.

Total mastectomy procedures include simple mastectomy, complete mastectomy, subcutaneous mastectomy, modified radical mastectomy, radical mastectomy, and more extended procedures (eg, Urban type operation). Total mastectomy procedures are reported using codes 19303-19307 as appropriate.

Excisions or resections of chest wall tumors including ribs, with or without reconstruction, with or without mediastinal lymphadenectomy, are reported using codes 19260, 19271, or 19272. Codes 19260-19272 are not restricted to breast tumors and are used to report resections of chest wall tumors originating from any chest wall component. (For excision of lung or pleura, see 32310 et seq)

(To report bilateral procedure, report modifier 50 with the procedure code)

19100 Biopsy of breast; percutaneous, needle core, not using imaging guidance (separate procedure)

(For fine needle aspiration, use 10021)

(For image guided breast biopsy, see 19102, 19103, 10022)

19101 open, incisional

19102 percutaneous, needle core, using imaging guidance

(For placement of percutaneous localization clip, use 19295)

19103 percutaneous, automated vacuum assisted or rotating biopsy device, using imaging guidance

(For imaging guidance performed in conjunction with 19102, 19103, see 76942, 77012, 77021, 77031, 77032)

(For placement of percutaneous localization clip, use 19295)

19105 Ablation, cryosurgical, of fibroadenoma, including ultrasound guidance, each fibroadenoma

(Do not report 19105 in conjunction with 76940, 76942)

(For adjacent lesions treated with one cryoprobe insertion, report once)

19110 Nipple exploration, with or without excision of a solitary lactiferous duct or a papilloma lactiferous duct

19112 Excision of lactiferous duct fistula

19120 Excision of cyst, fibroadenoma, or other benign or malignant tumor, aberrant breast tissue, duct lesion, nipple or areolar lesion (except 19300), open, male or female, one or more lesions

19125 Excision of breast lesion identified by preoperative placement of radiological marker, open; single lesion

+ 19126 each additional lesion separately identified by a preoperative radiological marker (List separately in addition to code for primary procedure)

(Use 19126 in conjunction with 19125)

(19140-19240 have been deleted. To report, see 19300-19307)

19260 Excision of chest wall tumor including ribs

19271 Excision of chest wall tumor involving ribs, with plastic reconstruction; without mediastinal lymphadenectomy

19272 with mediastinal lymphadenectomy

(Do not report 19260, 19271, 19272 in conjunction with 32100, 32422, 32503, 32504, 32551)

Introduction

19290 Preoperative placement of needle localization wire, breast;

+ 19291 each additional lesion (List separately in addition to code for primary procedure)

(Use 19291 in conjunction with 19290)

(For radiological supervision and interpretation, see 76942, 77031, 77032)

+ 19295 Image guided placement, metallic localization clip, percutaneous, during breast biopsy (List separately in addition to code for primary procedure)

(Use 19295 in conjunction with 19102, 19103)

▲ 19296 Placement of radiotherapy afterloading expandable catheter (single or multichannel) into the breast for interstitial radioelement application following partial mastectomy, includes imaging guidance; on date separate from partial mastectomy

+▲ 19297 concurrent with partial mastectomy (List separately in addition to code for primary procedure)

(Use 19297 in conjunction with 19301 or 19302)

⊙ 19298 Placement of radiotherapy afterloading brachytherapy catheters (multiple tube and button type) into the breast for interstitial radioelement application following (at the time of or subsequent to) partial mastectomy, includes imaging guidance

Mastectomy Procedures

19300 Mastectomy for gynecomastia

19301 Mastectomy, partial (eg, lumpectomy, tylectomy, quadrantectomy, segmentectomy);

19302 with axillary lymphadenectomy

(For placement of radiotherapy afterloading balloon/brachytherapy catheters, see 19296-19298)

19303 Mastectomy, simple, complete

(For immediate or delayed insertion of implant, see 19340, 19342)

(For gynecomastia, use 19300)

19304 Mastectomy, subcutaneous

(For immediate or delayed insertion of implant, see 19340, 19342)

19305 Mastectomy, radical, including pectoral muscles, axillary lymph nodes

(For immediate or delayed insertion of implant, see 19340, 19342)

19306 Mastectomy, radical, including pectoral muscles, axillary and internal mammary lymph nodes (Urban type operation)

(For immediate or delayed insertion of implant, see 19340, 19342)

19307 Mastectomy, modified radical, including axillary lymph nodes, with or without pectoralis minor muscle, but excluding pectoralis major muscle

(For immediate or delayed insertion of implant, see 19340, 19342)

Repair and/or Reconstruction

(To report bilateral procedure, report modifier 50 with the procedure code)

19316 Mastopexy

19318 Reduction mammaplasty

19324 Mammaplasty, augmentation; without prosthetic implant

19325 with prosthetic implant

(For flap or graft, use also appropriate number)

19328 Removal of intact mammary implant

19330 Removal of mammary implant material

19340 Immediate insertion of breast prosthesis following mastopexy, mastectomy or in reconstruction

19342 Delayed insertion of breast prosthesis following mastopexy, mastectomy or in reconstruction

(For supply of implant, use 99070)

(For preparation of custom breast implant, use 19396)

19350 Nipple/areola reconstruction

19355 Correction of inverted nipples

19357 Breast reconstruction, immediate or delayed, with tissue expander, including subsequent expansion

19361 Breast reconstruction with latissimus dorsi flap, without prosthetic implant

(For insertion of prosthesis, use also 19340)

19364 Breast reconstruction with free flap

(Do not report code 69990 in addition to code 19364)

(19364 includes harvesting of the flap, microvascular transfer, closure of the donor site, and inset shaping the flap into a breast)

19366 Breast reconstruction with other technique

(For operating microscope, use 69990)

(For insertion of prosthesis, use also 19340 or 19342)

19367 Breast reconstruction with transverse rectus abdominis myocutaneous flap (TRAM), single pedicle, including closure of donor site;

19368 with microvascular anastomosis (supercharging)

(Do not report code 69990 in addition to code 19368)

19369 Breast reconstruction with transverse rectus abdominis myocutaneous flap (TRAM), double pedicle, including closure of donor site

19370 Open periprosthetic capsulotomy, breast

19371 Periprosthetic capsulectomy, breast

19380 Revision of reconstructed breast

19396 Preparation of moulage for custom breast implant

Other Procedures

19499 Unlisted procedure, breast

Musculoskeletal System

Cast and strapping procedures appear at the end of this section.

The services listed below include the application and removal of the first cast or traction device only. Subsequent replacement of cast and/or traction device may require an additional listing.

Definitions

The terms "closed treatment," "open treatment," and "percutaneous skeletal fixation" have been carefully chosen to accurately reflect current orthopaedic procedural treatments.

Closed treatment specifically means that the fracture site is not surgically opened (exposed to the external environment and directly visualized). This terminology is used to describe procedures that treat fractures by three methods: 1) without manipulation; 2) with manipulation; or 3) with or without traction.

Open treatment is used when the fractured bone is either: 1) surgically opened (exposed to the external environment) and the fracture (bone ends) visualized and internal fixation may be used; or 2) the fractured bone is opened remote from the fracture site in order to insert an intramedullary nail across the fracture site (the fracture site is not opened and visualized).

Percutaneous skeletal fixation describes fracture treatment which is neither open nor closed. In this procedure, the fracture fragments are not visualized, but fixation (eg, pins) is placed across the fracture site, usually under X-ray imaging.

The type of fracture (eg, open, compound, closed) does not have any coding correlation with the type of treatment (eg, closed, open, or percutaneous) provided.

The codes for treatment of fractures and joint injuries (dislocations) are categorized by the type of manipulation (reduction) and stabilization (fixation or immobilization). These codes can apply to either open (compound) or closed fractures or joint injuries.

Skeletal traction is the application of a force (distracting or traction force) to a limb segment through a wire, pin, screw, or clamp that is attached (eg, penetrates) to bone.

Skin traction is the application of a force (longitudinal) to a limb using felt or strapping applied directly to skin only.

External fixation is the usage of skeletal pins plus an attaching mechanism/device used for temporary or definitive treatment of acute or chronic bony deformity.

Codes for obtaining autogenous bone grafts, cartilage, tendon, fascia lata grafts or other tissues through separate incisions are to be used only when the graft is not already listed as part of the basic procedure.

Re-reduction of a fracture and/or dislocation performed by the primary physician may be identified by the addition of the modifier 76 to the usual procedure number to indicate "Repeat Procedure or Service by Same Physician." (See Appendix A guidelines.)

Codes for external fixation are to be used only when external fixation is not already listed as part of the basic procedure.

All codes for suction irrigation have been deleted. To report, list only the primary surgical procedure performed (eg, sequestrectomy, deep incision).

Manipulation is used throughout the musculoskeletal fracture and dislocation subsections to specifically mean the attempted reduction or restoration of a fracture or joint dislocation to its normal anatomic alignment by the application of manually applied forces.

General

Incision

20000 Incision of soft tissue abscess (eg, secondary to osteomyelitis); superficial

20005 deep or complicated

Wound Exploration—Trauma (eg, Penetrating Gunshot, Stab Wound)

20100-20103 relate to wound(s) resulting from penetrating trauma. These codes describe surgical exploration and enlargement of the wound, extension of dissection (to determine penetration), debridement, removal of foreign body(s), ligation or coagulation of minor subcutaneous and/or muscular blood vessel(s), of the subcutaneous tissue, muscle fascia, and/or muscle, not requiring thoracotomy or laparotomy. If a repair is done to major structure(s) or major blood vessel(s) requiring thoracotomy or laparotomy, then those specific code(s) would supersede the use of codes 20100-20103. To report simple, intermediate, or complex repair of wound(s) that do not require enlargement of the wound, extension of dissection, etc, as stated above, use specific Repair code(s) in the **Integumentary System** section.

20100 Exploration of penetrating wound (separate procedure); neck

20101 chest

20102 abdomen/flank/back

20103 extremity

Excision

20150 Excision of epiphyseal bar, with or without autogenous soft tissue graft obtained through same fascial incision

(For aspiration of bone marrow, use 38220)

20200 Biopsy, muscle; superficial

20205 deep

20206 Biopsy, muscle, percutaneous needle

(If imaging guidance is performed, see 76942, 77012, 77021)

(For fine needle aspiration, use 10021 or 10022)

(For evaluation of fine needle aspirate, see 88172-88173)

(For excision of muscle tumor, deep, see specific anatomic section)

20220 Biopsy, bone, trocar, or needle; superficial (eg, ilium, sternum, spinous process, ribs)

20225 deep (eg, vertebral body, femur)

(For bone marrow biopsy, use 38221)

(For radiologic supervision and interpretation, see 77002, 77012, 77021)

20240 Biopsy, bone, open; superficial (eg, ilium, sternum, spinous process, ribs, trochanter of femur)

20245 deep (eg, humerus, ischium, femur)

20250 Biopsy, vertebral body, open; thoracic

20251 lumbar or cervical

(For sequestrectomy, osteomyelitis or drainage of bone abscess, see anatomical area)

Introduction or Removal

(For injection procedure for arthrography, see anatomical area)

20500 Injection of sinus tract; therapeutic (separate procedure)

20501 diagnostic (sinogram)

(For radiological supervision and interpretation, use 76080)

(For contrast injection[s] and radiological assessment of gastrostomy, duodenostomy, jejunostomy, gastro-jejunostomy, or cecostomy [or other colonic] tube including fluoroscopic imaging guidance, use 49465)

20520 Removal of foreign body in muscle or tendon sheath; simple

20525 deep or complicated

20526 Injection, therapeutic (eg, local anesthetic, corticosteroid), carpal tunnel

20550 Injection(s); single tendon sheath, or ligament, aponeurosis (eg, plantar "fascia")

►(For injection of Morton's neuroma, see 64455, 64632)◄

20551 single tendon origin/insertion

20552 Injection(s); single or multiple trigger point(s), 1 or 2 muscle(s)

20553 single or multiple trigger point(s), 3 or more muscle(s)

(If imaging guidance is performed, see 76942, 77002, 77021)

20555 Placement of needles or catheters into muscle and/or soft tissue for subsequent interstitial radioelement application (at the time of or subsequent to the procedure)

(For placement of devices into the breast for interstitial radioelement application, see 19296-19298)

(For placement of needles, catheters, or devices into muscle or soft tissue of the head and neck, for interstitial radioelement application, use 41019)

(For placement of needles or catheters for interstitial radioelement application into prostate, use 55875)

(For placement of needles or catheters into the pelvic organs or genitalia [except prostate] for interstitial radioelement application, use 55920)

(For interstitial radioelement application, see 77776-77784)

(For imaging guidance, see 76942, 77002, 77012, 77021)

20600 Arthrocentesis, aspiration and/or injection; small joint or bursa (eg, fingers, toes)

20605 intermediate joint or bursa (eg, temporomandibular, acromioclavicular, wrist, elbow or ankle, olecranon bursa)

20610 major joint or bursa (eg, shoulder, hip, knee joint, subacromial bursa)

(If imaging guidance is performed, see 76942, 77002, 77012, 77021)

20612 Aspiration and/or injection of ganglion cyst(s) any location

(To report multiple ganglion cyst aspirations/injections, use 20612 and append modifier 59)

20615 Aspiration and injection for treatment of bone cyst

20650 Insertion of wire or pin with application of skeletal traction, including removal (separate procedure)

20660 Application of cranial tongs, caliper, or stereotactic frame, including removal (separate procedure)

20661 Application of halo, including removal; cranial

20662 pelvic

20663 femoral

20664 Application of halo, including removal, cranial, 6 or more pins placed, for thin skull osteology (eg, pediatric patients, hydrocephalus, osteogenesis imperfecta), requiring general anesthesia

20665 Removal of tongs or halo applied by another physician

20670 Removal of implant; superficial (eg, buried wire, pin or rod) (separate procedure)

20680 deep (eg, buried wire, pin, screw, metal band, nail, rod or plate)

20690 Application of a uniplane (pins or wires in one plane), unilateral, external fixation system

20692 Application of a multiplane (pins or wires in more than one plane), unilateral, external fixation system (eg, Ilizarov, Monticelli type)

20693 Adjustment or revision of external fixation system requiring anesthesia (eg, new pin[s] or wire[s] and/or new ring[s] or bar[s])

20694 Removal, under anesthesia, of external fixation system

● **20696** Application of multiplane (pins or wires in more than one plane), unilateral, external fixation with stereotactic computer-assisted adjustment (eg, spatial frame), including imaging; initial and subsequent alignment(s), assessment(s), and computation(s) of adjustment schedule(s)

►(Do not report 20696 in conjunction with 20692, 20697)◄

⊘● **20697** exchange (ie, removal and replacement) of strut, each

►(Do not report 20697 in conjunction with 20692, 20696)◄

Replantation

20802 Replantation, arm (includes surgical neck of humerus through elbow joint), complete amputation

(To report replantation of incomplete arm amputation, see specific code[s] for repair of bone[s], ligament[s], tendon[s], nerve[s], or blood vessel[s] with modifier 52)

20805 Replantation, forearm (includes radius and ulna to radial carpal joint), complete amputation

(To report replantation of incomplete forearm amputation, see specific code[s] for repair of bone[s], ligament[s], tendon[s], nerve[s], or blood vessel[s] with modifier 52)

20808 Replantation, hand (includes hand through metacarpophalangeal joints), complete amputation

(To report replantation of incomplete hand amputation, see specific code[s] for repair of bone[s], ligament[s], tendon[s], nerve[s], or blood vessel[s] with modifier 52)

20816 Replantation, digit, excluding thumb (includes metacarpophalangeal joint to insertion of flexor sublimis tendon), complete amputation

(To report replantation of incomplete digit amputation, excluding thumb, see specific code[s] for repair of bone[s], ligament[s], tendon[s], nerve[s], or blood vessel[s] with modifier 52)

20822 Replantation, digit, excluding thumb (includes distal tip to sublimis tendon insertion), complete amputation

(To report replantation of incomplete digit amputation, excluding thumb, see specific code[s] for repair of bone[s], ligament[s], tendon[s], nerve[s], or blood vessel[s] with modifier 52)

20824 Replantation, thumb (includes carpometacarpal joint to MP joint), complete amputation

(To report replantation of incomplete thumb amputation, see specific code[s] for repair of bone[s], ligament[s], tendon[s], nerve[s], or blood vessel[s] with modifier 52)

20827 Replantation, thumb (includes distal tip to MP joint), complete amputation

(To report replantation of incomplete thumb amputation, see specific code[s] for repair of bone[s], ligament[s], tendon[s], nerve[s], or blood vessel[s] with modifier 52)

(To report replantation of complete leg amputation, see specific code[s] for repair of bone[s], ligament[s], tendon[s], nerve[s], or blood vessel[s] with modifier 52)

(To report replantation of incomplete leg amputation, see specific code[s] for repair of bone[s], ligament[s], tendon[s], nerve[s], or blood vessel[s] with modifier 52)

20838 Replantation, foot, complete amputation

(To report replantation of incomplete foot amputation, see specific code[s] for repair of bone[s], ligament[s], tendon[s], nerve[s], or blood vessel[s] with modifier 52)

Grafts (or Implants)

Codes for obtaining autogenous bone, cartilage, tendon, fascia lata grafts, or other tissues through separate skin/fascial incisions should be reported separately unless the code descriptor references the harvesting of the graft or implant (eg, includes obtaining graft).

Do not append modifier 62 to bone graft codes 20900-20938.

(For spinal surgery bone graft[s] see codes 20930-20938)

20900 Bone graft, any donor area; minor or small (eg, dowel or button)

20902 major or large

20910 Cartilage graft; costochondral

20912 nasal septum

(For ear cartilage, use 21235)

20920 Fascia lata graft; by stripper

20922 by incision and area exposure, complex or sheet

20924 Tendon graft, from a distance (eg, palmaris, toe extensor, plantaris)

20926 Tissue grafts, other (eg, paratenon, fat, dermis)

+ **20930** Allograft for spine surgery only; morselized (List separately in addition to code for primary procedure)

►(Use 20930 in conjunction with 22319, 22532, 22533, 22548-22558, 22590-22612, 22630, 22800-22812, 0195T, 0196T)◄

+ **20931** structural (List separately in addition to code for primary procedure)

(Use 20931 in conjunction with 22319, 22532-22533, 22548-22558, 22590-22612, 22630, 22800-22812)

+ **20936** Autograft for spine surgery only (includes harvesting the graft); local (eg, ribs, spinous process, or laminar fragments) obtained from same incision (List separately in addition to code for primary procedure)

►(Use 20936 in conjunction with 22319, 22532, 22533, 22548-22558, 22590-22612, 22630, 22800-22812, 0195T, 0196T)◄

+ **20937** morselized (through separate skin or fascial incision) (List separately in addition to code for primary procedure)

►(Use 20937 in conjunction with 22319, 22532, 22533, 22548-22558, 22590-22612, 22630, 22800-22812, 0195T, 0196T)◄

+ **20938** structural, bicortical or tricortical (through separate skin or fascial incision) (List separately in addition to code for primary procedure)

(Use 20938 in conjunction with 22319, 22532, 22533, 22548-22558, 22590-22612, 22630, 22800-22812)

(For needle aspiration of bone marrow for the purpose of bone grafting, use 38220)

Other Procedures

20950 Monitoring of interstitial fluid pressure (includes insertion of device, eg, wick catheter technique, needle manometer technique) in detection of muscle compartment syndrome

20955 Bone graft with microvascular anastomosis; fibula

20956 iliac crest

20957 metatarsal

20962 other than fibula, iliac crest, or metatarsal

(Do not report code 69990 in addition to codes 20955-20962)

20969 Free osteocutaneous flap with microvascular anastomosis; other than iliac crest, metatarsal, or great toe

20970 iliac crest

20972 metatarsal

20973 great toe with web space

(Do not report code 69990 in addition to codes 20969-20973)

(For great toe, wrap-around procedure, use 26551)

⊘ **20974** Electrical stimulation to aid bone healing; noninvasive (nonoperative)

⊘ **20975** invasive (operative)

20979 Low intensity ultrasound stimulation to aid bone healing, noninvasive (nonoperative)

⊙ **20982** Ablation, bone tumor(s) (eg, osteoid osteoma, metastasis) radiofrequency, percutaneous, including computed tomographic guidance

(Do not report 20982 in conjunction with 77013)

+▲ **20985** Computer-assisted surgical navigational procedure for musculoskeletal procedures, image-less (List separately in addition to code for primary procedure)

►(Do not report 20985 in conjunction with 61795)◄

►(20986, 20987 have been deleted)◄

►(For computer-assisted navigational procedures with image guidance based on pre-operative and intraoperatively obtained images, see 0054T, 0055T)◄

20999 Unlisted procedure, musculoskeletal system, general

Head

Skull, facial bones, and temporomandibular joint.

Incision

(For drainage of superficial abscess and hematoma, use 20000)

(For removal of embedded foreign body from dentoalveolar structure, see 41805, 41806)

21010 Arthrotomy, temporomandibular joint

(To report bilateral procedure, report 21010 with modifier 50)

Excision

21015 Radical resection of tumor (eg, malignant neoplasm), soft tissue of face or scalp

(To report excision of skull tumor for osteomyelitis, use 61501)

21025 Excision of bone (eg, for osteomyelitis or bone abscess); mandible

21026 facial bone(s)

21029 Removal by contouring of benign tumor of facial bone (eg, fibrous dysplasia)

21030 Excision of benign tumor or cyst of maxilla or zygoma by enucleation and curettage

21031 Excision of torus mandibularis

21032 Excision of maxillary torus palatinus

21034 Excision of malignant tumor of maxilla or zygoma

21040 Excision of benign tumor or cyst of mandible, by enucleation and/or curettage

(For enucleation and/or curettage of benign cysts or tumors of mandible not requiring osteotomy, use 21040)

(For excision of benign tumor or cyst of mandible requiring osteotomy, see 21046-21047)

21044 Excision of malignant tumor of mandible;

21045 radical resection

(For bone graft, use 21215)

21046 Excision of benign tumor or cyst of mandible; requiring intra-oral osteotomy (eg, locally aggressive or destructive lesion(s))

21047 requiring extra-oral osteotomy and partial mandibulectomy (eg, locally aggressive or destructive lesion(s))

21048 Excision of benign tumor or cyst of maxilla; requiring intra-oral osteotomy (eg, locally aggressive or destructive lesion(s))

21049 requiring extra-oral osteotomy and partial maxillectomy (eg, locally aggressive or destructive lesion(s))

21050 Condylectomy, temporomandibular joint (separate procedure)

(For bilateral procedures, report 21050 with modifier 50)

21060 Meniscectomy, partial or complete, temporomandibular joint (separate procedure)

(For bilateral procedures, report 21060 with modifier 50)

21070 Coronoidectomy (separate procedure)

(For bilateral procedures, report 21070 with modifier 50)

Manipulation

21073 Manipulation of temporomandibular joint(s) (TMJ), therapeutic, requiring an anesthesia service (ie, general or monitored anesthesia care)

(For TMJ manipulation without an anesthesia service [ie, general or monitored anesthesia care], see 97140, 98925-98929, 98943)

(For closed treatment of temporomandibular dislocation, see 21480, 21485)

Head Prosthesis

Codes 21076-21089 describe professional services for the rehabilitation of patients with oral, facial, or other anatomical deficiencies by means of prostheses such as an artificial eye, ear, or nose or intraoral obturator to close a cleft. Codes 21076-21089 should only be used when the physician actually designs and prepares the prosthesis (ie, not prepared by an outside laboratory).

(For application or removal of caliper or tongs, see 20660, 20665)

21076 Impression and custom preparation; surgical obturator prosthesis

21077 orbital prosthesis

21079 interim obturator prosthesis

21080 definitive obturator prosthesis

21081 mandibular resection prosthesis

21082 palatal augmentation prosthesis

21083 palatal lift prosthesis

21084 speech aid prosthesis

21085 oral surgical splint

21086 auricular prosthesis

21087 nasal prosthesis

21088 facial prosthesis

Other Procedures

21089 Unlisted maxillofacial prosthetic procedure

Introduction or Removal

21100 Application of halo type appliance for maxillofacial fixation, includes removal (separate procedure)

21110 Application of interdental fixation device for conditions other than fracture or dislocation, includes removal

(For removal of interdental fixation by another physician, see 20670-20680)

21116 Injection procedure for temporomandibular joint arthrography

(For radiological supervision and interpretation, use 70332. Do not report 77002 in conjunction with 70332)

Repair, Revision, and/or Reconstruction

(For cranioplasty, see 21179, 21180 and 62116, 62120, 62140-62147)

21120 Genioplasty; augmentation (autograft, allograft, prosthetic material)

21121 sliding osteotomy, single piece

21122 sliding osteotomies, 2 or more osteotomies (eg, wedge excision or bone wedge reversal for asymmetrical chin)

21123 sliding, augmentation with interpositional bone grafts (includes obtaining autografts)

21125 Augmentation, mandibular body or angle; prosthetic material

21127 with bone graft, onlay or interpositional (includes obtaining autograft)

21137 Reduction forehead; contouring only

21138 contouring and application of prosthetic material or bone graft (includes obtaining autograft)

21139 contouring and setback of anterior frontal sinus wall

21141 Reconstruction midface, LeFort I; single piece, segment movement in any direction (eg, for Long Face Syndrome), without bone graft

21142 2 pieces, segment movement in any direction, without bone graft

21143 3 or more pieces, segment movement in any direction, without bone graft

21145 single piece, segment movement in any direction, requiring bone grafts (includes obtaining autografts)

21146 2 pieces, segment movement in any direction, requiring bone grafts (includes obtaining autografts) (eg, ungrafted unilateral alveolar cleft)

21147 3 or more pieces, segment movement in any direction, requiring bone grafts (includes obtaining autografts) (eg, ungrafted bilateral alveolar cleft or multiple osteotomies)

21150 Reconstruction midface, LeFort II; anterior intrusion (eg, Treacher-Collins Syndrome)

21151 any direction, requiring bone grafts (includes obtaining autografts)

21154 Reconstruction midface, LeFort III (extracranial), any type, requiring bone grafts (includes obtaining autografts); without LeFort I

21155 with LeFort I

21159 Reconstruction midface, LeFort III (extra and intracranial) with forehead advancement (eg, mono bloc), requiring bone grafts (includes obtaining autografts); without LeFort I

21160 with LeFort I

21172 Reconstruction superior-lateral orbital rim and lower forehead, advancement or alteration, with or without grafts (includes obtaining autografts)

(For frontal or parietal craniotomy performed for craniosynostosis, use 61556)

21175 Reconstruction, bifrontal, superior-lateral orbital rims and lower forehead, advancement or alteration (eg, plagiocephaly, trigonocephaly, brachycephaly), with or without grafts (includes obtaining autografts)

(For bifrontal craniotomy performed for craniosynostosis, use 61557)

21179 Reconstruction, entire or majority of forehead and/or supraorbital rims; with grafts (allograft or prosthetic material)

21180 with autograft (includes obtaining grafts)

(For extensive craniectomy for multiple suture craniosynostosis, use only 61558 or 61559)

21181 Reconstruction by contouring of benign tumor of cranial bones (eg, fibrous dysplasia), extracranial

21182 Reconstruction of orbital walls, rims, forehead, nasoethmoid complex following intra- and extracranial excision of benign tumor of cranial bone (eg, fibrous dysplasia), with multiple autografts (includes obtaining grafts); total area of bone grafting less than 40 sq cm

21183 total area of bone grafting greater than 40 sq cm but less than 80 sq cm

21184 total area of bone grafting greater than 80 sq cm

(For excision of benign tumor of cranial bones, see 61563, 61564)

21188 Reconstruction midface, osteotomies (other than LeFort type) and bone grafts (includes obtaining autografts)

21193 Reconstruction of mandibular rami, horizontal, vertical, C, or L osteotomy; without bone graft

21194 with bone graft (includes obtaining graft)

21195 Reconstruction of mandibular rami and/or body, sagittal split; without internal rigid fixation

21196 with internal rigid fixation

21198 Osteotomy, mandible, segmental;

21199 with genioglossus advancement

(To report total osteotomy of the maxilla, see 21141-21160)

21206 Osteotomy, maxilla, segmental (eg, Wassmund or Schuchard)

21208 Osteoplasty, facial bones; augmentation (autograft, allograft, or prosthetic implant)

21209 reduction

21210 Graft, bone; nasal, maxillary or malar areas (includes obtaining graft)

(For cleft palate repair, see 42200-42225)

21215 mandible (includes obtaining graft)

21230 Graft; rib cartilage, autogenous, to face, chin, nose or ear (includes obtaining graft)

21235 ear cartilage, autogenous, to nose or ear (includes obtaining graft)

(To report graft augmentation of facial bones, use 21208)

21240 Arthroplasty, temporomandibular joint, with or without autograft (includes obtaining graft)

21242 Arthroplasty, temporomandibular joint, with allograft

21243 Arthroplasty, temporomandibular joint, with prosthetic joint replacement

21244 Reconstruction of mandible, extraoral, with transosteal bone plate (eg, mandibular staple bone plate)

21245 Reconstruction of mandible or maxilla, subperiosteal implant; partial

21246 complete

21247 Reconstruction of mandibular condyle with bone and cartilage autografts (includes obtaining grafts) (eg, for hemifacial microsomia)

21248 Reconstruction of mandible or maxilla, endosteal implant (eg, blade, cylinder); partial

21249 complete

(To report midface reconstruction, see 21141-21160)

21255 Reconstruction of zygomatic arch and glenoid fossa with bone and cartilage (includes obtaining autografts)

21256 Reconstruction of orbit with osteotomies (extracranial) and with bone grafts (includes obtaining autografts) (eg, micro-ophthalmia)

21260 Periorbital osteotomies for orbital hypertelorism, with bone grafts; extracranial approach

21261 combined intra- and extracranial approach

21263 with forehead advancement

21267 Orbital repositioning, periorbital osteotomies, unilateral, with bone grafts; extracranial approach

21268 combined intra- and extracranial approach

21270 Malar augmentation, prosthetic material

(For malar augmentation with bone graft, use 21210)

21275 Secondary revision of orbitocraniofacial reconstruction

21280 Medial canthopexy (separate procedure)

(For medial canthoplasty, use 67950)

21282 Lateral canthopexy

21295 Reduction of masseter muscle and bone (eg, for treatment of benign masseteric hypertrophy); extraoral approach

21296 intraoral approach

Other Procedures

21299 Unlisted craniofacial and maxillofacial procedure

Fracture and/or Dislocation

(For operative repair of skull fracture, see 62000-62010)

(21300 has been deleted)

(To report closed treatment of skull fracture, use the appropriate Evaluation and Management code)

21310 Closed treatment of nasal bone fracture without manipulation

21315 Closed treatment of nasal bone fracture; without stabilization

21320 with stabilization

21325 Open treatment of nasal fracture; uncomplicated

21330 complicated, with internal and/or external skeletal fixation

21335 with concomitant open treatment of fractured septum

21336 Open treatment of nasal septal fracture, with or without stabilization

21337 Closed treatment of nasal septal fracture, with or without stabilization

21338 Open treatment of nasoethmoid fracture; without external fixation

21339 with external fixation

21340 Percutaneous treatment of nasoethmoid complex fracture, with splint, wire or headcap fixation, including repair of canthal ligaments and/or the nasolacrimal apparatus

21343 Open treatment of depressed frontal sinus fracture

21344 Open treatment of complicated (eg, comminuted or involving posterior wall) frontal sinus fracture, via coronal or multiple approaches

21345 Closed treatment of nasomaxillary complex fracture (LeFort II type), with interdental wire fixation or fixation of denture or splint

21346 Open treatment of nasomaxillary complex fracture (LeFort II type); with wiring and/or local fixation

21347 requiring multiple open approaches

21348 with bone grafting (includes obtaining graft)

21355 Percutaneous treatment of fracture of malar area, including zygomatic arch and malar tripod, with manipulation

21356 Open treatment of depressed zygomatic arch fracture (eg, Gillies approach)

21360 Open treatment of depressed malar fracture, including zygomatic arch and malar tripod

21365 Open treatment of complicated (eg, comminuted or involving cranial nerve foramina) fracture(s) of malar area, including zygomatic arch and malar tripod; with internal fixation and multiple surgical approaches

21366 with bone grafting (includes obtaining graft)

21385 Open treatment of orbital floor blowout fracture; transantral approach (Caldwell-Luc type operation)

21386 periorbital approach

21387 combined approach

21390 periorbital approach, with alloplastic or other implant

21395 periorbital approach with bone graft (includes obtaining graft)

21400 Closed treatment of fracture of orbit, except blowout; without manipulation

21401 with manipulation

21406 Open treatment of fracture of orbit, except blowout; without implant

21407 with implant

21408 with bone grafting (includes obtaining graft)

21421 Closed treatment of palatal or maxillary fracture (LeFort I type), with interdental wire fixation or fixation of denture or splint

21422 Open treatment of palatal or maxillary fracture (LeFort I type);

21423 complicated (comminuted or involving cranial nerve foramina), multiple approaches

21431 Closed treatment of craniofacial separation (LeFort III type) using interdental wire fixation of denture or splint

21432 Open treatment of craniofacial separation (LeFort III type); with wiring and/or internal fixation

21433 complicated (eg, comminuted or involving cranial nerve foramina), multiple surgical approaches

21435 complicated, utilizing internal and/or external fixation techniques (eg, head cap, halo device, and/or intermaxillary fixation)

(For removal of internal or external fixation device, use 20670)

21436 complicated, multiple surgical approaches, internal fixation, with bone grafting (includes obtaining graft)

21440 Closed treatment of mandibular or maxillary alveolar ridge fracture (separate procedure)

21445 Open treatment of mandibular or maxillary alveolar ridge fracture (separate procedure)

21450 Closed treatment of mandibular fracture; without manipulation

21451 with manipulation

21452 Percutaneous treatment of mandibular fracture, with external fixation

21453 Closed treatment of mandibular fracture with interdental fixation

21454 Open treatment of mandibular fracture with external fixation

21461 Open treatment of mandibular fracture; without interdental fixation

21462 with interdental fixation

21465 Open treatment of mandibular condylar fracture

21470 Open treatment of complicated mandibular fracture by multiple surgical approaches including internal fixation, interdental fixation, and/or wiring of dentures or splints

21480 Closed treatment of temporomandibular dislocation; initial or subsequent

21485 complicated (eg, recurrent requiring intermaxillary fixation or splinting), initial or subsequent

21490 Open treatment of temporomandibular dislocation

(For interdental wire fixation, use 21497)

21495 Open treatment of hyoid fracture

(For laryngoplasty with open reduction of fracture, use 31584)

(To report treatment of closed fracture of larynx, use the applicable Evaluation and Management codes)

21497 Interdental wiring, for condition other than fracture

Other Procedures

21499 Unlisted musculoskeletal procedure, head

(For unlisted craniofacial or maxillofacial procedure, use 21299)

Neck (Soft Tissues) and Thorax

(For cervical spine and back, see 21920 et seq)

(For injection of fracture site or trigger point, use 20550)

Incision

(For incision and drainage of abscess or hematoma, superficial, see 10060, 10140)

21501 Incision and drainage, deep abscess or hematoma, soft tissues of neck or thorax;

(For posterior spine subfascial incision and drainage, see 22010-22015)

21502 with partial rib ostectomy

21510 Incision, deep, with opening of bone cortex (eg, for osteomyelitis or bone abscess), thorax

Excision

(For bone biopsy, see 20220-20251)

21550 Biopsy, soft tissue of neck or thorax

(For needle biopsy of soft tissue, use 20206)

21555 Excision tumor, soft tissue of neck or thorax; subcutaneous

21556 deep, subfascial, intramuscular

21557 Radical resection of tumor (eg, malignant neoplasm), soft tissue of neck or thorax

21600 Excision of rib, partial

(For radical resection of chest wall and rib cage for tumor, use 19260)

(For radical debridement of chest wall and rib cage for injury, see 11040-11044)

21610 Costotransversectomy (separate procedure)

21615 Excision first and/or cervical rib;

21616 with sympathectomy

21620 Ostectomy of sternum, partial

21627 Sternal debridement

(For debridement and closure, use 21750)

21630 Radical resection of sternum;

21632 with mediastinal lymphadenectomy

Repair, Revision, and/or Reconstruction

(For superficial wound, see **Integumentary System** section under Repair—Simple)

21685 Hyoid myotomy and suspension

21700 Division of scalenus anticus; without resection of cervical rib

21705 with resection of cervical rib

21720 Division of sternocleidomastoid for torticollis, open operation; without cast application

(For transection of spinal accessory and cervical nerves, see 63191, 64722)

21725 with cast application

21740 Reconstructive repair of pectus excavatum or carinatum; open

21742 minimally invasive approach (Nuss procedure), without thoracoscopy

21743 minimally invasive approach (Nuss procedure), with thoracoscopy

21750 Closure of median sternotomy separation with or without debridement (separate procedure)

Fracture and/or Dislocation

21800 Closed treatment of rib fracture, uncomplicated, each

21805 Open treatment of rib fracture without fixation, each

21810 Treatment of rib fracture requiring external fixation (flail chest)

21820 Closed treatment of sternum fracture

21825 Open treatment of sternum fracture with or without skeletal fixation

(For sternoclavicular dislocation, see 23520-23532)

Other Procedures

21899 Unlisted procedure, neck or thorax

Back and Flank

Excision

21920 Biopsy, soft tissue of back or flank; superficial

21925 deep

(For needle biopsy of soft tissue, use 20206)

21930 Excision, tumor, soft tissue of back or flank

21935 Radical resection of tumor (eg, malignant neoplasm), soft tissue of back or flank

Spine (Vertebral Column)

Cervical, thoracic, and lumbar spine.

Within the spine section, bone grafting procedures are reported separately and in addition to arthrodesis. For bone grafts in other Musculoskeletal sections, see specific code(s) descriptor(s) and/or accompanying guidelines.

To report bone grafts performed after arthrodesis, see 20930-20938. Do not append modifier 62 to bone graft codes 20900-20938.

Example:

Posterior arthrodesis of L5-S1 for degenerative disc disease utilizing morselized autogenous iliac bone graft harvested through a separate fascial incision.

Report as 22612 and 20937.

Within the spine section, instrumentation is reported separately and in addition to arthrodesis. To report instrumentation procedures performed with definitive vertebral procedure(s), see 22840-22855. Instrumentation procedure codes 22840-22848 and 22851 are reported in addition to the definitive procedure(s). Modifier 62 may not be appended to the definitive or add-on spinal instrumentation procedure code(s) 22840-22848 and 22850-22852.

Example:

Posterior arthrodesis of L4-S1, utilizing morselized autogenous iliac bone graft harvested through separate fascial incision, and pedicle screw fixation.

Report as 22612, 22614, 22842, and 20937.

Vertebral procedures are sometimes followed by arthrodesis and in addition may include bone grafts and instrumentation.

When arthrodesis is performed in addition to another procedure, the arthrodesis should be reported in addition to the original procedure with modifier 51 (multiple procedures). Examples are after osteotomy, fracture care, vertebral corpectomy, and laminectomy. Bone grafts and instrumentation are never performed without arthrodesis.

Example:

Treatment of a burst fracture of L2 by corpectomy followed by arthrodesis of L1-L3, utilizing anterior instrumentation L1-L3 and structural allograft.

Report as 63090, 22558-51, 22585, 22845, and 20931.

When two surgeons work together as primary surgeons performing distinct part(s) of a single reportable procedure, each surgeon should report his/her distinct operative work by appending modifier 62 to the single definitive procedure code. If additional procedure(s) (including add-on procedure[s]) are performed during the same surgical session, separate code(s) may be reported by each co-surgeon, with modifier 62 appended (see Appendix A).

Example:

A 42-year-old male with a history of posttraumatic degenerative disc disease at L3-4 and L4-5 (internal disc disruption) underwent surgical repair. Surgeon A performed an anterior exposure of the spine with mobilization of the great vessels. Surgeon B performed anterior (minimal) discectomy and fusion at L3-4 and L4-5 using anterior interbody technique.

Report surgeon A: 22558 append modifier 62, 22585 append modifier 62
Report surgeon B: 22558 append modifier 62, 22585 append modifier 62, 20931

(Do not append modifier 62 to bone graft code 20931)

(For injection procedure for myelography, use 62284)

(For injection procedure for discography, see 62290, 62291)

(For injection procedure, chemonucleolysis, single or multiple levels, use 62292)

(For injection procedure for facet joints, see 64470-64476, 64622-64627)

(For needle or trocar biopsy, see 20220-20225)

Incision

22010 Incision and drainage, open, of deep abscess (subfascial), posterior spine; cervical, thoracic, or cervicothoracic

22015 lumbar, sacral, or lumbosacral

(Do not report 22015 in conjunction with 22010)

(Do not report 22015 in conjunction with instrumentation removal, 10180, 22850, 22852)

(For incision and drainage of abscess or hematoma, superficial, see 10060, 10140)

Excision

For the following codes, when two surgeons work together as primary surgeons performing distinct part(s) of partial vertebral body excision, each surgeon should report his/her distinct operative work by appending modifier 62 to the procedure code. In this situation, modifier 62 may be appended to the procedure code(s) 22100-22102, 22110-22114 and, as appropriate, to the associated additional vertebral segment add-on code(s) 22103, 22116 as long as both surgeons continue to work together as primary surgeons.

(For bone biopsy, see 20220-20251)

(To report soft tissue biopsy of back or flank, see 21920-21925)

(For needle biopsy of soft tissue, use 20206)

(To report excision of soft tissue tumor of back or flank, use 21930)

22100 Partial excision of posterior vertebral component (eg, spinous process, lamina or facet) for intrinsic bony lesion, single vertebral segment; cervical

22101 thoracic

22102 lumbar

(For insertion of posterior spinous process distraction devices, see 0171T, 0172T)

+ 22103 each additional segment (List separately in addition to code for primary procedure)

(Use 22103 in conjunction with 22100, 22101, 22102)

22110 Partial excision of vertebral body, for intrinsic bony lesion, without decompression of spinal cord or nerve root(s), single vertebral segment; cervical

22112 thoracic

22114 lumbar

+ 22116 each additional vertebral segment (List separately in addition to code for primary procedure)

(Use 22116 in conjunction with 22110, 22112, 22114)

(For complete or near complete resection of vertebral body, see vertebral corpectomy, 63081-63091)

(For spinal reconstruction with bone graft (autograft, allograft) and/or methylmethacrylate of cervical vertebral body, use 63081 and 22554 and 20931 or 20938)

(For spinal reconstruction with bone graft (autograft, allograft) and/or methylmethacrylate of thoracic vertebral body, use 63085 or 63087 and 22556 and 20931 or 20938)

(For spinal reconstruction with bone graft (autograft, allograft) and/or methylmethacrylate of lumbar vertebral body, use 63087 or 63090 and 22558 and 20931 or 20938)

(For spinal reconstruction following vertebral body resection, use 63082 or 63086 or 63088 or 63091, and 22585)

(For harvest of bone autograft for vertebral reconstruction, see 20931 or 20938)

(For cervical spinal reconstruction with prosthetic replacement of resected vertebral bodies, see codes 63081 and 22554 and 20931 or 20938 and 22851)

(For thoracic spinal reconstruction with prosthetic replacement of resected vertebral bodies, see codes 63085 or 63087 and 22556 and 20931 or 20938 and 22851)

(For lumbar spinal reconstruction with prosthetic replacement of resected vertebral bodies, see codes 63087 or 63090 and 22558, and 20931 or 20938 and 22851)

(For osteotomy of spine, see 22210-22226)

Osteotomy

To report arthrodesis, see codes 22590-22632. (Report in addition to code[s] for the definitive procedure with modifier 51.)

To report instrumentation procedures, see 22840-22855. (Report in addition to code[s] for the definitive procedure[s].) Do not append modifier 62 to spinal instrumentation codes 22840-22848 and 22850-22852.

To report bone graft procedures, see 20930-20938. (Report in addition to code[s] for the definitive procedure[s].) Do not append modifier 62 to bone graft codes 20900-20938.

For the following codes, when two surgeons work together as primary surgeons performing distinct part(s) of an anterior spine osteotomy, each surgeon should report his/her distinct operative work by appending modifier 62 to the procedure code. In this situation, modifier 62 may be appended to the procedure code(s) 22210-22214, 22220-22224 and, as appropriate, to associated additional segment add-on code(s) 22216, 22226 as long as both surgeons continue to work together as primary surgeons.

Spinal osteotomy procedures are reported when a portion(s) of the vertebral segment(s) is cut and removed in preparation for re-aligning the spine as part of a spinal deformity correction. For excision of an intrinsic lesion of the vertebra without deformity correction, see 22100-22116. For decompression of the spinal cord and/or nerve roots, see 63001-63308.

The three columns are defined as anterior (anterior two-thirds of the vertebral body), middle (posterior third of the vertebral body and the pedicle), and posterior (articular facets, lamina, and spinous process).

22206 Osteotomy of spine, posterior or posterolateral approach, three columns, one vertebral segment (eg, pedicle/vertebral body subtraction); thoracic

(Do not report 22206 in conjunction with 22207)

22207 lumbar

(Do not report 22207 in conjunction with 22206)

+ 22208 each additional vertebral segment (List separately in addition to code for primary procedure)

(Use 22208 in conjunction with 22206, 22207)

(Do not report 22206, 22207, 22208 in conjunction with 22210-22226, 22830, 63001-63048, 63055-63066, 63075-63091, 63101-63103, when performed at the same level)

22210 Osteotomy of spine, posterior or posterolateral approach, one vertebral segment; cervical

22212 thoracic

22214 lumbar

+ 22216 each additional vertebral segment (List separately in addition to primary procedure)

(Use 22216 in conjunction with 22210, 22212, 22214)

22220 Osteotomy of spine, including discectomy, anterior approach, single vertebral segment; cervical

22222 thoracic

22224 lumbar

+ 22226 each additional vertebral segment (List separately in addition to code for primary procedure)

(Use 22226 in conjunction with 22220, 22222, 22224)

(For vertebral corpectomy, see 63081-63091)

Fracture and/or Dislocation

To report arthrodesis, see codes 22590-22632. (Report in addition to code[s] for the definitive procedure with modifier 51.)

To report instrumentation procedures, see 22840-22855. (Report in addition to code[s] for the definitive procedure[s].) Do not append modifier 62 to spinal instrumentation codes 22840-22848 and 22850-22852.

To report bone graft procedures, see 20930-20938. (Report in addition to code[s] for the definitive procedure[s].) Do not append modifier 62 to bone graft codes 20900-20938.

For the following codes, when two surgeons work together as primary surgeons performing distinct part(s) of open fracture and/or dislocation procedure(s), each surgeon should report his/her distinct operative work by appending modifier 62 to the procedure code. In this situation, modifier 62 may be appended to the procedure code(s) 22318-22327 and, as appropriate, the associated additional fracture vertebrae or dislocated segment add-on code 22328 as long as both surgeons continue to work together as primary surgeons.

22305 Closed treatment of vertebral process fracture(s)

22310 Closed treatment of vertebral body fracture(s), without manipulation, requiring and including casting or bracing

22315 Closed treatment of vertebral fracture(s) and/or dislocation(s) requiring casting or bracing, with and including casting and/or bracing, with or without anesthesia, by manipulation or traction

(For spinal subluxation, use 97140)

22318 Open treatment and/or reduction of odontoid fracture(s) and or dislocation(s) (including os odontoideum), anterior approach, including placement of internal fixation; without grafting

22319 with grafting

22325 Open treatment and/or reduction of vertebral fracture(s) and/or dislocation(s), posterior approach, one fractured vertebra or dislocated segment; lumbar

22326 cervical

22327 thoracic

+ 22328 each additional fractured vertebra or dislocated segment (List separately in addition to code for primary procedure)

(Use 22328 in conjunction with 22325-22327)

(For treatment of vertebral fracture by the anterior approach, see corpectomy 63081-63091, and appropriate arthrodesis, bone graft and instrument codes)

(For decompression of spine following fracture, see 63001-63091; for arthrodesis of spine following fracture, see 22548-22632)

Manipulation

(For spinal manipulation without anesthesia, use 97140)

22505 Manipulation of spine requiring anesthesia, any region

Vertebral Body, Embolization or Injection

22520 Percutaneous vertebroplasty, one vertebral body, unilateral or bilateral injection; thoracic

22521 lumbar

+ 22522 each additional thoracic or lumbar vertebral body (List separately in addition to code for primary procedure)

(Use 22522 in conjunction with 22520, 22521 as appropriate)

(For radiological supervision and interpretation, see 72291, 72292)

22523 Percutaneous vertebral augmentation, including cavity creation (fracture reduction and bone biopsy included when performed) using mechanical device, one vertebral body, unilateral or bilateral cannulation (eg, kyphoplasty); thoracic

22524 lumbar

+ 22525 each additional thoracic or lumbar vertebral body (List separately in addition to code for primary procedure)

(Do not report 22525 in conjunction with 20225 when performed at the same level as 22523-22525)

(Use 22525 in conjunction with 22523, 22524)

(For radiological supervision and interpretation, see 72291, 72292)

⊙ 22526 Percutaneous intradiscal electrothermal annuloplasty, unilateral or bilateral including fluoroscopic guidance; single level

⊙+ 22527 one or more additional levels (List separately in addition to code for primary procedure)

(Do not report codes 22526, 22527 in conjunction with 77002, 77003)

(For percutaneous intradiscal annuloplasty using method other than electrothermal, see 0062T, 0063T)

Arthrodesis

Arthrodesis may be performed in the absence of other procedures and therefore when it is combined with another definitive procedure (eg, osteotomy, fracture care, vertebral corpectomy or laminectomy), modifier 51 is appropriate. However, arthrodesis codes 22585, 22614, and 22632 are considered add-on procedure codes and should not be used with modifier 51.

To report instrumentation procedures, see 22840-22855. (Codes 22840-22848, 22851 are reported in conjunction with code[s] for the definitive procedure[s]. When instrumentation reinsertion or removal is reported in conjunction with other definitive procedures including arthrodesis, decompression, and exploration of fusion, append modifier 51 to 22849, 22850, 22852, and 22855.) To report exploration of fusion, use 22830. (When exploration is reported in conjunction with other definitive procedures, including arthrodesis and decompression, append modifier 51 to 22830.) Do not append modifier 62 to spinal instrumentation codes 22840-22848 and 22850-22852.

To report bone graft procedures, see 20930-20938. (Report in addition to code[s] for the definitive procedure[s].) Do not append modifier 62 to bone graft codes 20900-20938.

Lateral Extracavitary Approach Technique

22532 Arthrodesis, lateral extracavitary technique, including minimal discectomy to prepare interspace (other than for decompression); thoracic

22533 lumbar

+ 22534 thoracic or lumbar, each additional vertebral segment (List separately in addition to code for primary procedure)

(Use 22534 in conjunction with 22532 and 22533)

Anterior or Anterolateral Approach Technique

Procedure codes 22554-22558 are for SINGLE interspace; for additional interspaces, use 22585. A vertebral interspace is the non-bony compartment between two adjacent vertebral bodies, which contains the intervertebral disc, and includes the nucleus pulposus, annulus fibrosus, and two cartilagenous endplates.

For the following codes, when two surgeons work together as primary surgeons performing distinct part(s) of an anterior interbody arthrodesis, each surgeon should report his/her distinct operative work by appending modifier 62 to the procedure code. In this situation, modifier 62 may be appended to the procedure code(s) 22548-22558 and, as appropriate, to the associated additional interspace add-on code 22585 as long as both surgeons continue to work together as primary surgeons.

22548 Arthrodesis, anterior transoral or extraoral technique, clivus-C1-C2 (atlas-axis), with or without excision of odontoid process

(For intervertebral disc excision by laminotomy or laminectomy, see 63020-63042)

22554 Arthrodesis, anterior interbody technique, including minimal discectomy to prepare interspace (other than for decompression); cervical below C2

22556 thoracic

22558 lumbar

+ 22585 each additional interspace (List separately in addition to code for primary procedure)

(Use 22585 in conjunction with 22554, 22556, 22558)

Posterior, Posterolateral or Lateral Transverse Process Technique

To report instrumentation procedures, see 22840-22855. (Report in addition to code[s] for the definitive procedure[s].) Do not append modifier 62 to spinal instrumentation codes 22840-22848 and 22850-22852.

To report bone graft procedures, see 20930-20938. (Report in addition to code[s] for the definitive procedure[s].) Do not append modifier 62 to bone graft codes 20900-20938.

A vertebral segment describes the basic constituent part into which the spine may be divided. It represents a single complete vertebral bone with its associated articular processes and laminae. A vertebral interspace is the non-bony compartment between two adjacent vertebral bodies which contains the intervertebral disc, and includes the nucleus pulposus, annulus fibrosus, and two cartilagenous endplates.

22590 Arthrodesis, posterior technique, craniocervical (occiput-C2)

22595 Arthrodesis, posterior technique, atlas-axis (C1-C2)

22600 Arthrodesis, posterior or posterolateral technique, single level; cervical below C2 segment

22610 thoracic (with or without lateral transverse technique)

22612 lumbar (with or without lateral transverse technique)

+ 22614 each additional vertebral segment (List separately in addition to code for primary procedure)

(Use 22614 in conjunction with 22600, 22610, 22612)

22630 Arthrodesis, posterior interbody technique, including laminectomy and/or discectomy to prepare interspace (other than for decompression), single interspace; lumbar

+ 22632 each additional interspace (List separately in addition to code for primary procedure)

(Use 22632 in conjunction with 22630)

Spine Deformity (eg, Scoliosis, Kyphosis)

To report instrumentation procedures, see 22840-22855. (Report in addition to code[s] for the definitive procedure[s].) Do not append modifier 62 to spinal instrumentation codes 22840-22848 and 22850-22852.

To report bone graft procedures, see 20930-20938. (Report in addition to code[s] for the definitive procedure[s].) Do not append modifier 62 to bone graft codes 20900-20938.

A vertebral segment describes the basic constituent part into which the spine may be divided. It represents a single complete vertebral bone with its associated articular processes and laminae.

For the following codes, when two surgeons work together as primary surgeons performing distinct part(s) of an arthrodesis for spinal deformity, each surgeon should report his/her distinct operative work by appending modifier 62 to the procedure code. In this situation, modifier 62 may be appended to procedure code(s) 22800-22819 as long as both surgeons continue to work together as primary surgeons.

22800 Arthrodesis, posterior, for spinal deformity, with or without cast; up to 6 vertebral segments

22802 7 to 12 vertebral segments

22804 13 or more vertebral segments

22808 Arthrodesis, anterior, for spinal deformity, with or without cast; 2 to 3 vertebral segments

22810 4 to 7 vertebral segments

22812 8 or more vertebral segments

22818 Kyphectomy, circumferential exposure of spine and resection of vertebral segment(s) (including body and posterior elements); single or 2 segments

22819 3 or more segments

(To report arthrodesis, see 22800-22804 and add modifier 51)

Exploration

To report instrumentation procedures, see 22840-22855. (Codes 22840-22848 and 22851 are reported in conjunction with code[s] for the definitive procedure[s]. When instrumentation reinsertion or removal is reported in conjunction with other definitive procedures including arthrodesis, decompression, and exploration of fusion, append modifier 51 to 22849, 22850, 22852 and 22855.) Code 22849 should not be reported with 22850, 22852, and 22855 at the same spinal levels. To report exploration of fusion, see 22830. (When exploration is reported in conjunction with other definitive procedures, including arthrodesis and decompression, append modifier 51 to 22830.)

(To report bone graft procedures, see 20930-20938)

22830 Exploration of spinal fusion

Spinal Instrumentation

Segmental instrumentation is defined as fixation at each end of the construct and at least one additional interposed bony attachment.

Non-segmental instrumentation is defined as fixation at each end of the construct and may span several vertebral segments without attachment to the intervening segments.

Insertion of spinal instrumentation is reported separately and in addition to arthrodesis. Instrumentation procedure codes 22840-22848 and 22851 are reported in addition to the definitive procedure(s). Do not append modifier 62 to spinal instrumentation codes 22840-22848 and 22850-22852.

To report bone graft procedures, see 20930-20938. (Report in addition to code[s] for definitive procedure[s].) Do not append modifier 62 to bone graft codes 20900-20938.

A vertebral segment describes the basic constituent part into which the spine may be divided. It represents a single complete vertebral bone with its associated articular processes and laminae. A vertebral interspace is the non-bony compartment between two adjacent vertebral bodies, which contains the intervertebral disc, and includes the nucleus pulposus, annulus fibrosus, and two cartilagenous endplates.

Codes 22849, 22850, 22852, and 22855 are subject to modifier 51 if reported with other definitive procedure(s), including arthrodesis, decompression, and exploration of fusion. Code 22849 should not be reported with 22850, 22852, and 22855 at the same spinal levels.

+ 22840 Posterior non-segmental instrumentation (eg, Harrington rod technique, pedicle fixation across one interspace, atlantoaxial transarticular screw fixation, sublaminar wiring at C1, facet screw fixation) (List separately in addition to code for primary procedure)

►(Use 22840 in conjunction with 22100-22102, 22110-22114, 22206, 22207, 22210-22214, 22220-22224, 22305-22327, 22532, 22533, 22548-22558, 22590-22612, 22630, 22800-22812, 63001-63030, 63040-63042, 63045-63047, 63050-63056, 63064, 63075, 63077, 63081, 63085, 63087, 63090, 63101, 63102, 63170-63290, 63300-63307)◄

(For insertion of posterior spinous process distraction devices, see 0171T, 0172T)

+ 22841 Internal spinal fixation by wiring of spinous processes (List separately in addition to code for primary procedure)

►(Use 22841 in conjunction with 22100-22102, 22110-22114, 22206, 22207, 22210-22214, 22220-22224, 22305-22327, 22532, 22533, 22548-22558, 22590-22612, 22630, 22800-22812, 63001-63030, 63040-63042, 63045-63047, 63050-63056, 63064, 63075, 63077, 63081, 63085, 63087, 63090, 63101, 63102, 63170-63290, 63300-63307)◄

+ 22842 Posterior segmental instrumentation (eg, pedicle fixation, dual rods with multiple hooks and sublaminar wires); 3 to 6 vertebral segments (List separately in addition to code for primary procedure)

►(Use 22842 in conjunction with 22100-22102, 22110-22114, 22206, 22207, 22210-22214, 22220-22224, 22305-22327, 22532, 22533, 22548-22558, 22590-22612, 22630, 22800-22812, 63001-63030, 63040-63042, 63045-63047, 63050-63056, 63064, 63075, 63077, 63081, 63085, 63087, 63090, 63101, 63102, 63170-63290, 63300-63307)◄

+ 22843 7 to 12 vertebral segments (List separately in addition to code for primary procedure)

►(Use 22843 in conjunction with 22100-22102, 22110-22114, 22206, 22207, 22210-22214, 22220-22224, 22305-22327, 22532, 22533, 22548-22558, 22590-22612, 22630, 22800-22812, 63001-63030, 63040-63042, 63045-63047, 63050-63056, 63064, 63075, 63077, 63081, 63085, 63087, 63090, 63101, 63102, 63170-63290, 63300-63307)◄

+ 22844 13 or more vertebral segments (List separately in addition to code for primary procedure)

►(Use 22844 in conjunction with 22100-22102, 22110-22114, 22206, 22207, 22210-22214, 22220-22224, 22305-22327, 22532, 22533, 22548-22558, 22590-22612, 22630, 22800-22812, 63001-63030, 63040-63042, 63045-63047, 63050-63056, 63064, 63075, 63077, 63081, 63085, 63087, 63090, 63101, 63102, 63170-63290, 63300-63307)◄

+ 22845 Anterior instrumentation; 2 to 3 vertebral segments (List separately in addition to code for primary procedure)

►(Use 22845 in conjunction with 22100-22102, 22110-22114, 22206, 22207, 22210-22214, 22220-22224, 22305-22327, 22532, 22533, 22548-22558, 22590-22612, 22630, 22800-22812, 63001-63030, 63040-63042, 63045-63047, 63050-63056, 63064, 63075, 63077, 63081, 63085, 63087, 63090, 63101, 63102, 63170-63290, 63300-63307)◄

+ 22846 4 to 7 vertebral segments (List separately in addition to code for primary procedure)

►(Use 22846 in conjunction with 22100-22102, 22110-22114, 22206, 22207, 22210-22214, 22220-22224, 22305-22327, 22532, 22533, 22548-22558, 22590-22612, 22630, 22800-22812, 63001-63030, 63040-63042, 63045-63047, 63050-63056, 63064, 63075, 63077, 63081, 63085, 63087, 63090, 63101, 63102, 63170-63290, 63300-63307)◄

+ 22847 8 or more vertebral segments (List separately in addition to code for primary procedure)

►(Use 22847 in conjunction with 22100-22102, 22110-22114, 22206, 22207, 22210-22214, 22220-22224, 22305-22327, 22532, 22533, 22548-22558, 22590-22612, 22630, 22800-22812, 63001-63030, 63040-63042, 63045-63047, 63050-63056, 63064, 63075, 63077, 63081, 63085, 63087, 63090, 63101, 63102, 63170-63290, 63300-63307)◄

+ 22848 Pelvic fixation (attachment of caudal end of instrumentation to pelvic bony structures) other than sacrum (List separately in addition to code for primary procedure)

►(Use 22848 in conjunction with 22100-22102, 22110-22114, 22206, 22207, 22210-22214, 22220-22224, 22305-22327, 22532, 22533, 22548-22558, 22590-22612, 22630, 22800-22812, 63001-63030, 63040-63042, 63045-63047, 63050-63056, 63064, 63075, 63077, 63081, 63085, 63087, 63090, 63101, 63102, 63170-63290, 63300-63307)◄

22849 Reinsertion of spinal fixation device

22850 Removal of posterior nonsegmental instrumentation (eg, Harrington rod)

+ 22851 Application of intervertebral biomechanical device(s) (eg, synthetic cage(s), threaded bone dowel(s), methylmethacrylate) to vertebral defect or interspace (List separately in addition to code for primary procedure)

►(Use 22851 in conjunction with 22100-22102, 22110-22114, 22206, 22207, 22210-22214, 22220-22224, 22305-22327, 22532, 22533, 22548-22558, 22590-22612, 22630, 22800-22812, 63001-63030, 63040-63042, 63045-63047, 63050-63056, 63064, 63075, 63077, 63081, 63085, 63087, 63090, 63101, 63102, 63170-63290, 63300-63307)◄

(For insertion of posterior spinous process distraction devices, see 0171T, 0172T)

22852 Removal of posterior segmental instrumentation

22855 Removal of anterior instrumentation

● 22856 Total disc arthroplasty (artificial disc), anterior approach, including discectomy with end plate preparation (includes osteophytectomy for nerve root or spinal cord decompression and microdissection), single interspace, cervical

►(Do not report 22856 in conjunction with 22554, 22845, 22851, 63075 when performed at the same level)◄

►(Do not report 22856 in conjunction with 69990)◄

►(For additional interspace cervical total disc arthroplasty, use 0092T)◄

▲ 22857 Total disc arthroplasty (artificial disc), anterior approach, including discectomy to prepare interspace (other than for decompression), single interspace, lumbar

(Do not report 22857 in conjunction with 22558, 22845, 22851, 49010 when performed at the same level)

(For additional interspace, use Category III code 0163T)

● 22861 Revision including replacement of total disc arthroplasty (artificial disc), anterior approach, single interspace; cervical

►(Do not report 22861 in conjunction with 22845, 22851, 22864, 63075 when performed at the same level)◄

►(Do not report 22861 in conjunction with 69990)◄

►(For additional interspace revision of cervical total disc arthroplasty, use 0098T)◄

▲ 22862 lumbar

(Do not report 22862 in conjunction with 22558, 22845, 22851, 22865, 49010 when performed at the same level)

(For additional interspace, use Category III code 0165T)

● 22864 Removal of total disc arthroplasty (artificial disc), anterior approach, single interspace; cervical

►(Do not report 22864 in conjunction with 22861, 69990)◄

►(For additional interspace removal of cervical total disc arthroplasty, use 0095T)◄

▲ 22865 lumbar

(Do not report 22865 in conjunction with 49010)

(For additional interspace, see Category III code 0164T)

►(22856-22865 include fluoroscopy when performed)◄

(For decompression, see 63001-63048)

Other Procedures

22899 Unlisted procedure, spine

Abdomen

Excision

22900 Excision, abdominal wall tumor, subfascial (eg, desmoid)

Other Procedures

22999 Unlisted procedure, abdomen, musculoskeletal system

Shoulder

The area known as the shoulder is made up of the clavicle, scapula, humerus head and neck, sterno-clavicular joint, acromioclavicular joint, and shoulder joint.

Incision

23000 Removal of subdeltoid calcareous deposits, open

(For arthroscopic removal of bursal deposits, use 29999)

23020 Capsular contracture release (eg, Sever type procedure)

(For incision and drainage procedures, superficial, see 10040-10160)

23030 Incision and drainage, shoulder area; deep abscess or hematoma

23031 infected bursa

23035 Incision, bone cortex (eg, osteomyelitis or bone abscess), shoulder area

23040 Arthrotomy, glenohumeral joint, including exploration, drainage, or removal of foreign body

23044 Arthrotomy, acromioclavicular, sternoclavicular joint, including exploration, drainage, or removal of foreign body

Excision

23065 Biopsy, soft tissue of shoulder area; superficial

23066 deep

(For needle biopsy of soft tissue, use 20206)

23075 Excision, soft tissue tumor, shoulder area; subcutaneous

23076 deep, subfascial, or intramuscular

23077 Radical resection of tumor (eg, malignant neoplasm), soft tissue of shoulder area

23100 Arthrotomy, glenohumeral joint, including biopsy

23101 Arthrotomy, acromioclavicular joint or sternoclavicular joint, including biopsy and/or excision of torn cartilage

23105 Arthrotomy; glenohumeral joint, with synovectomy, with or without biopsy

23106 sternoclavicular joint, with synovectomy, with or without biopsy

23107 Arthrotomy, glenohumeral joint, with joint exploration, with or without removal of loose or foreign body

23120 Claviculectomy; partial

(For arthroscopic procedure, use 29824)

23125 total

23130 Acromioplasty or acromionectomy, partial, with or without coracoacromial ligament release

23140 Excision or curettage of bone cyst or benign tumor of clavicle or scapula;

23145 with autograft (includes obtaining graft)

23146 with allograft

23150 Excision or curettage of bone cyst or benign tumor of proximal humerus;

23155 with autograft (includes obtaining graft)

23156 with allograft

23170 Sequestrectomy (eg, for osteomyelitis or bone abscess), clavicle

23172 Sequestrectomy (eg, for osteomyelitis or bone abscess), scapula

23174 Sequestrectomy (eg, for osteomyelitis or bone abscess), humeral head to surgical neck

23180 Partial excision (craterization, saucerization, or diaphysectomy) bone (eg, osteomyelitis), clavicle

23182 Partial excision (craterization, saucerization, or diaphysectomy) bone (eg, osteomyelitis), scapula

23184 Partial excision (craterization, saucerization, or diaphysectomy) bone (eg, osteomyelitis), proximal humerus

23190 Ostectomy of scapula, partial (eg, superior medial angle)

23195 Resection, humeral head

(For replacement with implant, use 23470)

23200 Radical resection for tumor; clavicle

23210 scapula

23220 Radical resection of bone tumor, proximal humerus;

23221 with autograft (includes obtaining graft)

23222 with prosthetic replacement

Introduction or Removal

(For arthrocentesis or needling of bursa, use 20610)

(For K-wire or pin insertion or removal, see 20650, 20670, 20680)

23330 Removal of foreign body, shoulder; subcutaneous

23331 deep (eg, Neer hemiarthroplasty removal)

23332 complicated (eg, total shoulder)

23350 Injection procedure for shoulder arthrography or enhanced CT/MRI shoulder arthrography

(For radiographic arthrography, radiological supervision and interpretation, use 73040. Fluoroscopy [77002] is inclusive of radiographic arthrography)

(When fluoroscopic guided injection is performed for enhanced CT arthrography, use 23350, 77002, and 73201 or 73202)

(When fluoroscopic guided injection is performed for enhanced MR arthrography, use 23350, 77002, and 73222 or 73223)

(For enhanced CT or enhanced MRI arthrography, use 77002 and either 73201, 73202, 73222, or 73223)

(To report biopsy of the shoulder and joint, see 29805-29826)

Repair, Revision, and/or Reconstruction

23395 Muscle transfer, any type, shoulder or upper arm; single

23397 multiple

23400 Scapulopexy (eg, Sprengels deformity or for paralysis)

23405 Tenotomy, shoulder area; single tendon

23406 multiple tendons through same incision

23410 Repair of ruptured musculotendinous cuff (eg, rotator cuff) open; acute

23412 chronic

(For arthroscopic procedure, use 29827)

23415 Coracoacromial ligament release, with or without acromioplasty

(For arthroscopic procedure, use 29826)

23420 Reconstruction of complete shoulder (rotator) cuff avulsion, chronic (includes acromioplasty)

23430 Tenodesis of long tendon of biceps

(For arthroscopic biceps tenodesis, use 29828)

23440 Resection or transplantation of long tendon of biceps

23450 Capsulorrhaphy, anterior; Putti-Platt procedure or Magnuson type operation

(To report arthroscopic thermal capsulorrhaphy, use 29999)

23455 with labral repair (eg, Bankart procedure)

(For arthroscopic procedure, use 29806)

23460 Capsulorrhaphy, anterior, any type; with bone block

23462 with coracoid process transfer

(To report open thermal capsulorrhaphy, use 23929)

23465 Capsulorrhaphy, glenohumeral joint, posterior, with or without bone block

(For sternoclavicular and acromioclavicular reconstruction, see 23530, 23550)

23466 Capsulorrhaphy, glenohumeral joint, any type multi-directional instability

23470 Arthroplasty, glenohumeral joint; hemiarthroplasty

23472 total shoulder (glenoid and proximal humeral replacement (eg, total shoulder))

(For removal of total shoulder implants, see 23331, 23332)

(For osteotomy, proximal humerus, use 24400)

23480 Osteotomy, clavicle, with or without internal fixation;

23485 with bone graft for nonunion or malunion (includes obtaining graft and/or necessary fixation)

23490 Prophylactic treatment (nailing, pinning, plating or wiring) with or without methylmethacrylate; clavicle

23491 proximal humerus

Fracture and/or Dislocation

23500 Closed treatment of clavicular fracture; without manipulation

23505 with manipulation

23515 Open treatment of clavicular fracture, includes internal fixation, when performed

23520 Closed treatment of sternoclavicular dislocation; without manipulation

23525 with manipulation

23530 Open treatment of sternoclavicular dislocation, acute or chronic;

23532 with fascial graft (includes obtaining graft)

23540 Closed treatment of acromioclavicular dislocation; without manipulation

23545 with manipulation

23550 Open treatment of acromioclavicular dislocation, acute or chronic;

23552 with fascial graft (includes obtaining graft)

23570 Closed treatment of scapular fracture; without manipulation

23575 with manipulation, with or without skeletal traction (with or without shoulder joint involvement)

▲ **23585** Open treatment of scapular fracture (body, glenoid or acromion) includes internal fixation, when performed

23600 Closed treatment of proximal humeral (surgical or anatomical neck) fracture; without manipulation

23605 with manipulation, with or without skeletal traction

23615 Open treatment of proximal humeral (surgical or anatomical neck) fracture, includes internal fixation, when performed, includes repair of tuberosity(s), when performed;

23616 with proximal humeral prosthetic replacement

23620 Closed treatment of greater humeral tuberosity fracture; without manipulation

23625 with manipulation

23630 Open treatment of greater humeral tuberosity fracture, includes internal fixation, when performed

23650 Closed treatment of shoulder dislocation, with manipulation; without anesthesia

23655 requiring anesthesia

23660 Open treatment of acute shoulder dislocation

(Repairs for recurrent dislocations, see 23450-23466)

23665 Closed treatment of shoulder dislocation, with fracture of greater humeral tuberosity, with manipulation

23670 Open treatment of shoulder dislocation, with fracture of greater humeral tuberosity, includes internal fixation, when performed

23675 Closed treatment of shoulder dislocation, with surgical or anatomical neck fracture, with manipulation

23680 Open treatment of shoulder dislocation, with surgical or anatomical neck fracture, includes internal fixation, when performed

Manipulation

23700 Manipulation under anesthesia, shoulder joint, including application of fixation apparatus (dislocation excluded)

Arthrodesis

23800 Arthrodesis, glenohumeral joint;

23802 with autogenous graft (includes obtaining graft)

Amputation

23900 Interthoracoscapular amputation (forequarter)

23920 Disarticulation of shoulder;

23921 secondary closure or scar revision

Other Procedures

23929 Unlisted procedure, shoulder

Humerus (Upper Arm) and Elbow

The elbow area includes the head and neck of the radius and olecranon process.

Incision

(For incision and drainage procedures, superficial, see 10040-10160)

23930 Incision and drainage, upper arm or elbow area; deep abscess or hematoma

23931 bursa

23935 Incision, deep, with opening of bone cortex (eg, for osteomyelitis or bone abscess), humerus or elbow

24000 Arthrotomy, elbow, including exploration, drainage, or removal of foreign body

24006 Arthrotomy of the elbow, with capsular excision for capsular release (separate procedure)

Excision

24065 Biopsy, soft tissue of upper arm or elbow area; superficial

24066 deep (subfascial or intramuscular)

(For needle biopsy of soft tissue, use 20206)

24075 Excision, tumor, soft tissue of upper arm or elbow area; subcutaneous

24076 deep (subfascial or intramuscular)

24077 Radical resection of tumor (eg, malignant neoplasm), soft tissue of upper arm or elbow area

24100 Arthrotomy, elbow; with synovial biopsy only

24101 with joint exploration, with or without biopsy, with or without removal of loose or foreign body

24102 with synovectomy

24105 Excision, olecranon bursa

24110 Excision or curettage of bone cyst or benign tumor, humerus;

24115 with autograft (includes obtaining graft)

24116 with allograft

24120 Excision or curettage of bone cyst or benign tumor of head or neck of radius or olecranon process;

24125 with autograft (includes obtaining graft)

24126 with allograft

24130 Excision, radial head

(For replacement with implant, use 24366)

24134 Sequestrectomy (eg, for osteomyelitis or bone abscess), shaft or distal humerus

24136 Sequestrectomy (eg, for osteomyelitis or bone abscess), radial head or neck

24138 Sequestrectomy (eg, for osteomyelitis or bone abscess), olecranon process

24140 Partial excision (craterization, saucerization, or diaphysectomy) bone (eg, osteomyelitis), humerus

24145 Partial excision (craterization, saucerization, or diaphysectomy) bone (eg, osteomyelitis), radial head or neck

24147 Partial excision (craterization, saucerization, or diaphysectomy) bone (eg, osteomyelitis), olecranon process

24149 Radical resection of capsule, soft tissue, and heterotopic bone, elbow, with contracture release (separate procedure)

(For capsular and soft tissue release only, use 24006)

24150 Radical resection for tumor, shaft or distal humerus;

24151 with autograft (includes obtaining graft)

24152 Radical resection for tumor, radial head or neck;

24153 with autograft (includes obtaining graft)

24155 Resection of elbow joint (arthrectomy)

Introduction or Removal

(For K-wire or pin insertion or removal, see 20650, 20670, 20680)

(For arthrocentesis or needling of bursa or joint, use 20605)

24160 Implant removal; elbow joint

24164 radial head

24200 Removal of foreign body, upper arm or elbow area; subcutaneous

24201 deep (subfascial or intramuscular)

24220 Injection procedure for elbow arthrography

(For radiological supervision and interpretation, use 73085. Do not report 77002 in conjunction with 73085)

(For injection for tennis elbow, use 20550)

Repair, Revision, and/or Reconstruction

24300 Manipulation, elbow, under anesthesia

(For application of external fixation, see 20690 or 20692)

24301 Muscle or tendon transfer, any type, upper arm or elbow, single (excluding 24320-24331)

24305 Tendon lengthening, upper arm or elbow, each tendon

24310 Tenotomy, open, elbow to shoulder, each tendon

24320 Tenoplasty, with muscle transfer, with or without free graft, elbow to shoulder, single (Seddon-Brookes type procedure)

24330 Flexor-plasty, elbow (eg, Steindler type advancement);

24331 with extensor advancement

24332 Tenolysis, triceps

24340 Tenodesis of biceps tendon at elbow (separate procedure)

24341 Repair, tendon or muscle, upper arm or elbow, each tendon or muscle, primary or secondary (excludes rotator cuff)

24342 Reinsertion of ruptured biceps or triceps tendon, distal, with or without tendon graft

24343 Repair lateral collateral ligament, elbow, with local tissue

24344 Reconstruction lateral collateral ligament, elbow, with tendon graft (includes harvesting of graft)

24345 Repair medial collateral ligament, elbow, with local tissue

24346 Reconstruction medial collateral ligament, elbow, with tendon graft (includes harvesting of graft)

(24350-24356 have been deleted. To report, see 24357-24359)

24357 Tenotomy, elbow, lateral or medial (eg, epicondylitis, tennis elbow, golfer's elbow); percutaneous

24358 debridement, soft tissue and/or bone, open

24359 debridement, soft tissue and/or bone, open with tendon repair or reattachment

(Do not report 24357-24359 in conjunction with 29837, 29838)

24360 Arthroplasty, elbow; with membrane (eg, fascial)

24361 with distal humeral prosthetic replacement

24362 with implant and fascia lata ligament reconstruction

24363 with distal humerus and proximal ulnar prosthetic replacement (eg, total elbow)

24365 Arthroplasty, radial head;

24366 with implant

24400 Osteotomy, humerus, with or without internal fixation

24410 Multiple osteotomies with realignment on intramedullary rod, humeral shaft (Sofield type procedure)

24420 Osteoplasty, humerus (eg, shortening or lengthening) (excluding 64876)

24430 Repair of nonunion or malunion, humerus; without graft (eg, compression technique)

24435 with iliac or other autograft (includes obtaining graft)

(For proximal radius and/or ulna, see 25400-25420)

24470 Hemiepiphyseal arrest (eg, cubitus varus or valgus, distal humerus)

24495 Decompression fasciotomy, forearm, with brachial artery exploration

24498 Prophylactic treatment (nailing, pinning, plating or wiring), with or without methylmethacrylate, humeral shaft

Fracture and/or Dislocation

24500 Closed treatment of humeral shaft fracture; without manipulation

24505 with manipulation, with or without skeletal traction

24515 Open treatment of humeral shaft fracture with plate/screws, with or without cerclage

24516 Treatment of humeral shaft fracture, with insertion of intramedullary implant, with or without cerclage and/or locking screws

24530 Closed treatment of supracondylar or transcondylar humeral fracture, with or without intercondylar extension; without manipulation

24535 with manipulation, with or without skin or skeletal traction

24538 Percutaneous skeletal fixation of supracondylar or transcondylar humeral fracture, with or without intercondylar extension

24545 Open treatment of humeral supracondylar or transcondylar fracture, includes internal fixation, when performed; without intercondylar extension

24546 with intercondylar extension

24560 Closed treatment of humeral epicondylar fracture, medial or lateral; without manipulation

24565 with manipulation

24566 Percutaneous skeletal fixation of humeral epicondylar fracture, medial or lateral, with manipulation

24575 Open treatment of humeral epicondylar fracture, medial or lateral, includes internal fixation, when performed

24576 Closed treatment of humeral condylar fracture, medial or lateral; without manipulation

24577 with manipulation

24579 Open treatment of humeral condylar fracture, medial or lateral, includes internal fixation, when performed

(To report closed treatment of fractures without manipulation, see 24530, 24560, 24576, 24650, 24670)

(To report closed treatment of fractures with manipulation, see 24535, 24565, 24577, 24675)

24582 Percutaneous skeletal fixation of humeral condylar fracture, medial or lateral, with manipulation

24586 Open treatment of periarticular fracture and/or dislocation of the elbow (fracture distal humerus and proximal ulna and/or proximal radius);

24587 with implant arthroplasty

(See also 24361)

24600 Treatment of closed elbow dislocation; without anesthesia

24605 requiring anesthesia

24615 Open treatment of acute or chronic elbow dislocation

24620 Closed treatment of Monteggia type of fracture dislocation at elbow (fracture proximal end of ulna with dislocation of radial head), with manipulation

24635 Open treatment of Monteggia type of fracture dislocation at elbow (fracture proximal end of ulna with dislocation of radial head), includes internal fixation, when performed

24640 Closed treatment of radial head subluxation in child, nursemaid elbow, with manipulation

24650 Closed treatment of radial head or neck fracture; without manipulation

24655 with manipulation

24665 Open treatment of radial head or neck fracture, includes internal fixation or radial head excision, when performed;

24666 with radial head prosthetic replacement

24670 Closed treatment of ulnar fracture, proximal end (eg, olecranon or coronoid process[es]); without manipulation

24675 with manipulation

24685 Open treatment of ulnar fracture, proximal end (eg, olecranon or coronoid process[es]), includes internal fixation, when performed

(Do not report 24685 in conjunction with 24100-24102)

Arthrodesis

24800 Arthrodesis, elbow joint; local

24802 with autogenous graft (includes obtaining graft)

Amputation

24900 Amputation, arm through humerus; with primary closure

24920 open, circular (guillotine)

24925 secondary closure or scar revision

24930 re-amputation

24931 with implant

24935 Stump elongation, upper extremity

24940 Cineplasty, upper extremity, complete procedure

Other Procedures

24999 Unlisted procedure, humerus or elbow

Forearm and Wrist

Radius, ulna, carpal bones, and joints.

Incision

25000 Incision, extensor tendon sheath, wrist (eg, deQuervains disease)

(For decompression median nerve or for carpal tunnel syndrome, use 64721)

25001 Incision, flexor tendon sheath, wrist (eg, flexor carpi radialis)

25020 Decompression fasciotomy, forearm and/or wrist, flexor OR extensor compartment; without debridement of nonviable muscle and/or nerve

25023 with debridement of nonviable muscle and/or nerve

(For decompression fasciotomy with brachial artery exploration, use 24495)

(For incision and drainage procedures, superficial, see 10060-10160)

(For debridement, see also 11000-11044)

25024 Decompression fasciotomy, forearm and/or wrist, flexor AND extensor compartment; without debridement of nonviable muscle and/or nerve

25025 with debridement of nonviable muscle and/or nerve

25028 Incision and drainage, forearm and/or wrist; deep abscess or hematoma

25031 bursa

25035 Incision, deep, bone cortex, forearm and/or wrist (eg, osteomyelitis or bone abscess)

25040 Arthrotomy, radiocarpal or midcarpal joint, with exploration, drainage, or removal of foreign body

Excision

25065 Biopsy, soft tissue of forearm and/or wrist; superficial

25066 deep (subfascial or intramuscular)

(For needle biopsy of soft tissue, use 20206)

25075 Excision, tumor, soft tissue of forearm and/or wrist area; subcutaneous

25076 deep (subfascial or intramuscular)

25077 Radical resection of tumor (eg, malignant neoplasm), soft tissue of forearm and/or wrist area

25085 Capsulotomy, wrist (eg, contracture)

25100 Arthrotomy, wrist joint; with biopsy

25101 with joint exploration, with or without biopsy, with or without removal of loose or foreign body

25105 with synovectomy

25107 Arthrotomy, distal radioulnar joint including repair of triangular cartilage, complex

25109 Excision of tendon, forearm and/or wrist, flexor or extensor, each

25110 Excision, lesion of tendon sheath, forearm and/or wrist

25111 Excision of ganglion, wrist (dorsal or volar); primary

25112 recurrent

(For hand or finger, use 26160)

25115 Radical excision of bursa, synovia of wrist, or forearm tendon sheaths (eg, tenosynovitis, fungus, Tbc, or other granulomas, rheumatoid arthritis); flexors

25116 extensors, with or without transposition of dorsal retinaculum

(For finger synovectomies, use 26145)

25118 Synovectomy, extensor tendon sheath, wrist, single compartment;

25119 with resection of distal ulna

25120 Excision or curettage of bone cyst or benign tumor of radius or ulna (excluding head or neck of radius and olecranon process);

(For head or neck of radius or olecranon process, see 24120-24126)

25125 with autograft (includes obtaining graft)

25126 with allograft

25130 Excision or curettage of bone cyst or benign tumor of carpal bones;

25135 with autograft (includes obtaining graft)

25136 with allograft

25145 Sequestrectomy (eg, for osteomyelitis or bone abscess), forearm and/or wrist

25150 Partial excision (craterization, saucerization, or diaphysectomy) of bone (eg, for osteomyelitis); ulna

25151 radius

(For head or neck of radius or olecranon process, see 24145, 24147)

25170 Radical resection for tumor, radius or ulna

25210 Carpectomy; one bone

(For carpectomy with implant, see 25441-25445)

25215 all bones of proximal row

25230 Radial styloidectomy (separate procedure)

25240 Excision distal ulna partial or complete (eg, Darrach type or matched resection)

(For implant replacement, distal ulna, use 25442)

(For obtaining fascia for interposition, see 20920, 20922)

Introduction or Removal

(For K-wire, pin or rod insertion or removal, see 20650, 20670, 20680)

25246 Injection procedure for wrist arthrography

(For radiological supervision and interpretation, use 73115. Do not report 77002 in conjunction with 73115)

(For foreign body removal, superficial use 20520)

25248 Exploration with removal of deep foreign body, forearm or wrist

25250 Removal of wrist prosthesis; (separate procedure)

25251 complicated, including total wrist

25259 Manipulation, wrist, under anesthesia

(For application of external fixation, see 20690 or 20692)

Repair, Revision, and/or Reconstruction

25260 Repair, tendon or muscle, flexor, forearm and/or wrist; primary, single, each tendon or muscle

25263 secondary, single, each tendon or muscle

25265 secondary, with free graft (includes obtaining graft), each tendon or muscle

25270 Repair, tendon or muscle, extensor, forearm and/or wrist; primary, single, each tendon or muscle

25272 secondary, single, each tendon or muscle

25274 secondary, with free graft (includes obtaining graft), each tendon or muscle

25275 Repair, tendon sheath, extensor, forearm and/or wrist, with free graft (includes obtaining graft) (eg, for extensor carpi ulnaris subluxation)

25280 Lengthening or shortening of flexor or extensor tendon, forearm and/or wrist, single, each tendon

25290 Tenotomy, open, flexor or extensor tendon, forearm and/or wrist, single, each tendon

25295 Tenolysis, flexor or extensor tendon, forearm and/or wrist, single, each tendon

25300 Tenodesis at wrist; flexors of fingers

25301 extensors of fingers

25310 Tendon transplantation or transfer, flexor or extensor, forearm and/or wrist, single; each tendon

25312 with tendon graft(s) (includes obtaining graft), each tendon

25315 Flexor origin slide (eg, for cerebral palsy, Volkmann contracture), forearm and/or wrist;

25316 with tendon(s) transfer

25320 Capsulorrhaphy or reconstruction, wrist, open (eg, capsulodesis, ligament repair, tendon transfer or graft) (includes synovectomy, capsulotomy and open reduction) for carpal instability

25332 Arthroplasty, wrist, with or without interposition, with or without external or internal fixation

(For obtaining fascia for interposition, see 20920, 20922)

(For prosthetic replacement arthroplasty, see 25441-25446)

25335 Centralization of wrist on ulna (eg, radial club hand)

25337 Reconstruction for stabilization of unstable distal ulna or distal radioulnar joint, secondary by soft tissue stabilization (eg, tendon transfer, tendon graft or weave, or tenodesis) with or without open reduction of distal radioulnar joint

(For harvesting of fascia lata graft, see 20920, 20922)

25350 Osteotomy, radius; distal third

25355 middle or proximal third

25360 Osteotomy; ulna

25365 radius AND ulna

25370 Multiple osteotomies, with realignment on intramedullary rod (Sofield type procedure); radius OR ulna

25375 radius AND ulna

25390 Osteoplasty, radius OR ulna; shortening

25391 lengthening with autograft

25392 Osteoplasty, radius AND ulna; shortening (excluding 64876)

25393 lengthening with autograft

25394 Osteoplasty, carpal bone, shortening

25400 Repair of nonunion or malunion, radius OR ulna; without graft (eg, compression technique)

25405 with autograft (includes obtaining graft)

25415 Repair of nonunion or malunion, radius AND ulna; without graft (eg, compression technique)

25420 with autograft (includes obtaining graft)

25425 Repair of defect with autograft; radius OR ulna

25426 radius AND ulna

25430 Insertion of vascular pedicle into carpal bone (eg, Hori procedure)

25431 Repair of nonunion of carpal bone (excluding carpal scaphoid (navicular)) (includes obtaining graft and necessary fixation), each bone

25440 Repair of nonunion, scaphoid carpal (navicular) bone, with or without radial styloidectomy (includes obtaining graft and necessary fixation)

25441 Arthroplasty with prosthetic replacement; distal radius

25442 distal ulna

25443 scaphoid carpal (navicular)

25444 lunate

25445 trapezium

25446 distal radius and partial or entire carpus (total wrist)

25447 Arthroplasty, interposition, intercarpal or carpometacarpal joints

(For wrist arthroplasty, use 25332)

25449 Revision of arthroplasty, including removal of implant, wrist joint

25450 Epiphyseal arrest by epiphysiodesis or stapling; distal radius OR ulna

25455 distal radius AND ulna

25490 Prophylactic treatment (nailing, pinning, plating or wiring) with or without methylmethacrylate; radius

25491 ulna

25492 radius AND ulna

Fracture and/or Dislocation

(For application of external fixation in addition to internal fixation, use 20690 and the appropriate internal fixation code)

25500 Closed treatment of radial shaft fracture; without manipulation

25505 with manipulation

25515 Open treatment of radial shaft fracture, includes internal fixation, when performed

25520 Closed treatment of radial shaft fracture and closed treatment of dislocation of distal radioulnar joint (Galeazzi fracture/dislocation)

25525 Open treatment of radial shaft fracture, includes internal fixation, when performed, and closed treatment of distal radioulnar joint dislocation (Galeazzi fracture/dislocation), includes percutaneous skeletal fixation, when performed

25526 Open treatment of radial shaft fracture, includes internal fixation, when performed, and open treatment of distal radioulnar joint dislocation (Galeazzi fracture/dislocation), includes internal fixation, when performed, includes repair of triangular fibrocartilage complex

25530 Closed treatment of ulnar shaft fracture; without manipulation

25535 with manipulation

25545 Open treatment of ulnar shaft fracture, includes internal fixation, when performed

25560 Closed treatment of radial and ulnar shaft fractures; without manipulation

25565 with manipulation

25574 Open treatment of radial AND ulnar shaft fractures, with internal fixation, when performed; of radius OR ulna

25575 of radius AND ulna

25600 Closed treatment of distal radial fracture (eg, Colles or Smith type) or epiphyseal separation, includes closed treatment of fracture of ulnar styloid, when performed; without manipulation

25605 with manipulation

(Do not report 25600, 25605 in conjunction with 25650)

25606 Percutaneous skeletal fixation of distal radial fracture or epiphyseal separation

(Do not report 25606 in conjunction with 25650)

(For percutaneous treatment of ulnar styloid fracture, use 25651)

(For open treatment of ulnar styloid fracture, use 25652)

25607 Open treatment of distal radial extra-articular fracture or epiphyseal separation, with internal fixation

(Do not report 25607 in conjunction with 25650)

(For percutaneous treatment of ulnar styloid fracture, use 25651)

(For open treatment of ulnar styloid fracture, use 25652)

25608 Open treatment of distal radial intra-articular fracture or epiphyseal separation; with internal fixation of 2 fragments

(Do not report 25608 in conjunction with 25609)

25609 with internal fixation of 3 or more fragments

(Do not report 25608, 25609 in conjunction with 25650)

(For percutaneous treatment of ulnar styloid fracture, use 25651)

(For open treatment of ulnar styloid fracture, use 25652)

(25611 has been deleted. To report, use 25606)

(25620 has been deleted. To report, see 25607-25609)

25622 Closed treatment of carpal scaphoid (navicular) fracture; without manipulation

25624 with manipulation

25628 Open treatment of carpal scaphoid (navicular) fracture, includes internal fixation, when performed

25630 Closed treatment of carpal bone fracture (excluding carpal scaphoid [navicular]); without manipulation, each bone

25635 with manipulation, each bone

25645 Open treatment of carpal bone fracture (other than carpal scaphoid [navicular]), each bone

25650 Closed treatment of ulnar styloid fracture

(Do not report 25650 in conjunction with 25600, 25605, 25607-25609)

25651 Percutaneous skeletal fixation of ulnar styloid fracture

25652 Open treatment of ulnar styloid fracture

25660 Closed treatment of radiocarpal or intercarpal dislocation, one or more bones, with manipulation

25670 Open treatment of radiocarpal or intercarpal dislocation, one or more bones

25671 Percutaneous skeletal fixation of distal radioulnar dislocation

25675 Closed treatment of distal radioulnar dislocation with manipulation

25676 Open treatment of distal radioulnar dislocation, acute or chronic

25680 Closed treatment of trans-scaphoperilunar type of fracture dislocation, with manipulation

25685 Open treatment of trans-scaphoperilunar type of fracture dislocation

25690 Closed treatment of lunate dislocation, with manipulation

25695 Open treatment of lunate dislocation

Arthrodesis

25800 Arthrodesis, wrist; complete, without bone graft (includes radiocarpal and/or intercarpal and/or carpometacarpal joints)

25805 with sliding graft

25810 with iliac or other autograft (includes obtaining graft)

25820 Arthrodesis, wrist; limited, without bone graft (eg, intercarpal or radiocarpal)

25825 with autograft (includes obtaining graft)

25830 Arthrodesis, distal radioulnar joint with segmental resection of ulna, with or without bone graft (eg, Sauve-Kapandji procedure)

Amputation

25900 Amputation, forearm, through radius and ulna;

25905 open, circular (guillotine)

25907 secondary closure or scar revision

25909 re-amputation

25915 Krukenberg procedure

25920 Disarticulation through wrist;

25922 secondary closure or scar revision

25924 re-amputation

25927 Transmetacarpal amputation;

25929 secondary closure or scar revision

25931 re-amputation

Other Procedures

25999 Unlisted procedure, forearm or wrist

Hand and Fingers

Incision

26010 Drainage of finger abscess; simple

26011 complicated (eg, felon)

26020 Drainage of tendon sheath, digit and/or palm, each

26025 Drainage of palmar bursa; single, bursa

26030 multiple bursa

26034 Incision, bone cortex, hand or finger (eg, osteomyelitis or bone abscess)

26035 Decompression fingers and/or hand, injection injury (eg, grease gun)

26037 Decompressive fasciotomy, hand (excludes 26035)

(For injection injury, use 26035)

26040 Fasciotomy, palmar (eg, Dupuytren's contracture); percutaneous

26045 open, partial

(For fasciectomy, see 26121-26125)

26055 Tendon sheath incision (eg, for trigger finger)

26060 Tenotomy, percutaneous, single, each digit

26070 Arthrotomy, with exploration, drainage, or removal of loose or foreign body; carpometacarpal joint

26075 metacarpophalangeal joint, each

26080 interphalangeal joint, each

Excision

26100 Arthrotomy with biopsy; carpometacarpal joint, each

26105 metacarpophalangeal joint, each

26110 interphalangeal joint, each

26115 Excision, tumor or vascular malformation, soft tissue of hand or finger; subcutaneous

26116 deep (subfascial or intramuscular)

26117 Radical resection of tumor (eg, malignant neoplasm), soft tissue of hand or finger

26121 Fasciectomy, palm only, with or without Z-plasty, other local tissue rearrangement, or skin grafting (includes obtaining graft)

26123 Fasciectomy, partial palmar with release of single digit including proximal interphalangeal joint, with or without Z-plasty, other local tissue rearrangement, or skin grafting (includes obtaining graft);

✚ 26125 each additional digit (List separately in addition to code for primary procedure)

(Use 26125 in conjunction with 26123)

(For fasciotomy, see 26040, 26045)

26130 Synovectomy, carpometacarpal joint

26135 Synovectomy, metacarpophalangeal joint including intrinsic release and extensor hood reconstruction, each digit

26140 Synovectomy, proximal interphalangeal joint, including extensor reconstruction, each interphalangeal joint

26145 Synovectomy, tendon sheath, radical (tenosynovectomy), flexor tendon, palm and/or finger, each tendon

(For tendon sheath synovectomies at wrist, see 25115, 25116)

26160 Excision of lesion of tendon sheath or joint capsule (eg, cyst, mucous cyst, or ganglion), hand or finger

(For wrist ganglion, see 25111, 25112)

(For trigger digit, use 26055)

26170 Excision of tendon, palm, flexor or extensor, single, each tendon

(Do not report 26170 in conjunction with 26390, 26415)

26180 Excision of tendon, finger, flexor or extensor, each tendon

(Do not report 26180 in conjunction with 26390, 26415)

26185 Sesamoidectomy, thumb or finger (separate procedure)

26200 Excision or curettage of bone cyst or benign tumor of metacarpal;

26205 with autograft (includes obtaining graft)

26210 Excision or curettage of bone cyst or benign tumor of proximal, middle, or distal phalanx of finger;

26215 with autograft (includes obtaining graft)

26230 Partial excision (craterization, saucerization, or diaphysectomy) bone (eg, osteomyelitis); metacarpal

26235 proximal or middle phalanx of finger

26236 distal phalanx of finger

26250 Radical resection, metacarpal (eg, tumor);

26255 with autograft (includes obtaining graft)

26260 Radical resection, proximal or middle phalanx of finger (eg, tumor);

26261 with autograft (includes obtaining graft)

26262 Radical resection, distal phalanx of finger (eg, tumor)

Introduction or Removal

26320 Removal of implant from finger or hand

(For removal of foreign body in hand or finger, see 20520, 20525)

Repair, Revision, and/or Reconstruction

26340 Manipulation, finger joint, under anesthesia, each joint

(For application of external fixation, see 20690 or 20692)

26350 Repair or advancement, flexor tendon, not in zone 2 digital flexor tendon sheath (eg, no man's land); primary or secondary without free graft, each tendon

26352 secondary with free graft (includes obtaining graft), each tendon

26356 Repair or advancement, flexor tendon, in zone 2 digital flexor tendon sheath (eg, no man's land); primary, without free graft, each tendon

26357 secondary, without free graft, each tendon

26358 secondary, with free graft (includes obtaining graft), each tendon

26370 Repair or advancement of profundus tendon, with intact superficialis tendon; primary, each tendon

26372 secondary with free graft (includes obtaining graft), each tendon

26373 secondary without free graft, each tendon

26390 Excision flexor tendon, with implantation of synthetic rod for delayed tendon graft, hand or finger, each rod

26392 Removal of synthetic rod and insertion of flexor tendon graft, hand or finger (includes obtaining graft), each rod

26410 Repair, extensor tendon, hand, primary or secondary; without free graft, each tendon

26412 with free graft (includes obtaining graft), each tendon

26415 Excision of extensor tendon, with implantation of synthetic rod for delayed tendon graft, hand or finger, each rod

26416 Removal of synthetic rod and insertion of extensor tendon graft (includes obtaining graft), hand or finger, each rod

26418 Repair, extensor tendon, finger, primary or secondary; without free graft, each tendon

26420 with free graft (includes obtaining graft) each tendon

26426 Repair of extensor tendon, central slip, secondary (eg, boutonniere deformity); using local tissue(s), including lateral band(s), each finger

26428 with free graft (includes obtaining graft), each finger

26432 Closed treatment of distal extensor tendon insertion, with or without percutaneous pinning (eg, mallet finger)

26433 Repair of extensor tendon, distal insertion, primary or secondary; without graft (eg, mallet finger)

26434 with free graft (includes obtaining graft)

(For tenovaginotomy for trigger finger, use 26055)

26437 Realignment of extensor tendon, hand, each tendon

26440 Tenolysis, flexor tendon; palm OR finger, each tendon

26442 palm AND finger, each tendon

26445 Tenolysis, extensor tendon, hand OR finger, each tendon

26449 Tenolysis, complex, extensor tendon, finger, including forearm, each tendon

26450 Tenotomy, flexor, palm, open, each tendon

26455 Tenotomy, flexor, finger, open, each tendon

26460 Tenotomy, extensor, hand or finger, open, each tendon

26471 Tenodesis; of proximal interphalangeal joint, each joint

26474 of distal joint, each joint

26476 Lengthening of tendon, extensor, hand or finger, each tendon

26477 Shortening of tendon, extensor, hand or finger, each tendon

26478 Lengthening of tendon, flexor, hand or finger, each tendon

26479 Shortening of tendon, flexor, hand or finger, each tendon

26480 Transfer or transplant of tendon, carpometacarpal area or dorsum of hand; without free graft, each tendon

26483 with free tendon graft (includes obtaining graft), each tendon

26485 Transfer or transplant of tendon, palmar; without free tendon graft, each tendon

26489 with free tendon graft (includes obtaining graft), each tendon

26490 Opponensplasty; superficialis tendon transfer type, each tendon

26492 tendon transfer with graft (includes obtaining graft), each tendon

26494 hypothenar muscle transfer

26496 other methods

(For thumb fusion in opposition, use 26820)

26497 Transfer of tendon to restore intrinsic function; ring and small finger

26498 all four fingers

26499 Correction claw finger, other methods

26500 Reconstruction of tendon pulley, each tendon; with local tissues (separate procedure)

26502 with tendon or fascial graft (includes obtaining graft) (separate procedure)

(26504 has been deleted. To report, use 26390)

26508 Release of thenar muscle(s) (eg, thumb contracture)

26510 Cross intrinsic transfer, each tendon

26516 Capsulodesis, metacarpophalangeal joint; single digit

26517 2 digits

26518 3 or 4 digits

26520 Capsulectomy or capsulotomy; metacarpophalangeal joint, each joint

26525 interphalangeal joint, each joint

(To report carpometacarpal joint arthroplasty, use 25447)

26530 Arthroplasty, metacarpophalangeal joint; each joint

26531 with prosthetic implant, each joint

26535 Arthroplasty, interphalangeal joint; each joint

26536 with prosthetic implant, each joint

26540 Repair of collateral ligament, metacarpophalangeal or interphalangeal joint

26541 Reconstruction, collateral ligament, metacarpophalangeal joint, single; with tendon or fascial graft (includes obtaining graft)

26542 with local tissue (eg, adductor advancement)

26545 Reconstruction, collateral ligament, interphalangeal joint, single, including graft, each joint

26546 Repair non-union, metacarpal or phalanx (includes obtaining bone graft with or without external or internal fixation)

26548 Repair and reconstruction, finger, volar plate, interphalangeal joint

26550 Pollicization of a digit

26551 Transfer, toe-to-hand with microvascular anastomosis; great toe wrap-around with bone graft

(For great toe with web space, use 20973)

26553 other than great toe, single

26554 other than great toe, double

(Do not report code 69990 in addition to codes 26551-26554)

26555 Transfer, finger to another position without microvascular anastomosis

26556 Transfer, free toe joint, with microvascular anastomosis

(Do not report code 69990 in addition to code 26556)

(To report great toe-to-hand transfer, use 20973)

26560 Repair of syndactyly (web finger) each web space; with skin flaps

26561 with skin flaps and grafts

26562 complex (eg, involving bone, nails)

26565 Osteotomy; metacarpal, each

26567 phalanx of finger, each

26568 Osteoplasty, lengthening, metacarpal or phalanx

26580 Repair cleft hand

26587 Reconstruction of polydactylous digit, soft tissue and bone

(For excision of polydactylous digit, soft tissue only, use 11200)

26590 Repair macrodactylia, each digit

26591 Repair, intrinsic muscles of hand, each muscle

26593 Release, intrinsic muscles of hand, each muscle

26596 Excision of constricting ring of finger, with multiple Z-plasties

(To report release of scar contracture or graft repairs see 11041-11042, 14040-14041, or 15120, 15240)

Fracture and/or Dislocation

26600 Closed treatment of metacarpal fracture, single; without manipulation, each bone

26605 with manipulation, each bone

26607 Closed treatment of metacarpal fracture, with manipulation, with external fixation, each bone

26608 Percutaneous skeletal fixation of metacarpal fracture, each bone

26615 Open treatment of metacarpal fracture, single, includes internal fixation, when performed, each bone

26641 Closed treatment of carpometacarpal dislocation, thumb, with manipulation

26645 Closed treatment of carpometacarpal fracture dislocation, thumb (Bennett fracture), with manipulation

26650 Percutaneous skeletal fixation of carpometacarpal fracture dislocation, thumb (Bennett fracture), with manipulation

26665 Open treatment of carpometacarpal fracture dislocation, thumb (Bennett fracture), includes internal fixation, when performed

26670 Closed treatment of carpometacarpal dislocation, other than thumb, with manipulation, each joint; without anesthesia

26675 requiring anesthesia

26676 Percutaneous skeletal fixation of carpometacarpal dislocation, other than thumb, with manipulation, each joint

26685 Open treatment of carpometacarpal dislocation, other than thumb; includes internal fixation, when performed, each joint

26686 complex, multiple, or delayed reduction

26700 Closed treatment of metacarpophalangeal dislocation, single, with manipulation; without anesthesia

26705 requiring anesthesia

26706 Percutaneous skeletal fixation of metacarpophalangeal dislocation, single, with manipulation

26715 Open treatment of metacarpophalangeal dislocation, single, includes internal fixation, when performed

26720 Closed treatment of phalangeal shaft fracture, proximal or middle phalanx, finger or thumb; without manipulation, each

26725 with manipulation, with or without skin or skeletal traction, each

26727 Percutaneous skeletal fixation of unstable phalangeal shaft fracture, proximal or middle phalanx, finger or thumb, with manipulation, each

26735 Open treatment of phalangeal shaft fracture, proximal or middle phalanx, finger or thumb, includes internal fixation, when performed, each

26740 Closed treatment of articular fracture, involving metacarpophalangeal or interphalangeal joint; without manipulation, each

26742 with manipulation, each

26746 Open treatment of articular fracture, involving metacarpophalangeal or interphalangeal joint, includes internal fixation, when performed, each

26750 Closed treatment of distal phalangeal fracture, finger or thumb; without manipulation, each

26755 with manipulation, each

26756 Percutaneous skeletal fixation of distal phalangeal fracture, finger or thumb, each

26765 Open treatment of distal phalangeal fracture, finger or thumb, includes internal fixation, when performed, each

26770 Closed treatment of interphalangeal joint dislocation, single, with manipulation; without anesthesia

26775 requiring anesthesia

26776 Percutaneous skeletal fixation of interphalangeal joint dislocation, single, with manipulation

26785 Open treatment of interphalangeal joint dislocation, includes internal fixation, when performed, single

Arthrodesis

26820 Fusion in opposition, thumb, with autogenous graft (includes obtaining graft)

26841 Arthrodesis, carpometacarpal joint, thumb, with or without internal fixation;

26842 with autograft (includes obtaining graft)

26843 Arthrodesis, carpometacarpal joint, digit, other than thumb, each;

26844 with autograft (includes obtaining graft)

26850 Arthrodesis, metacarpophalangeal joint, with or without internal fixation;

26852 with autograft (includes obtaining graft)

26860 Arthrodesis, interphalangeal joint, with or without internal fixation;

+ 26861 each additional interphalangeal joint (List separately in addition to code for primary procedure)

(Use 26861 in conjunction with 26860)

26862 with autograft (includes obtaining graft)

+ 26863 with autograft (includes obtaining graft), each additional joint (List separately in addition to code for primary procedure)

(Use 26863 in conjunction with 26862)

Amputation

(For hand through metacarpal bones, use 25927)

26910 Amputation, metacarpal, with finger or thumb (ray amputation), single, with or without interosseous transfer

(For repositioning, see 26550, 26555)

Surgery: Musculoskeletal System

26951 Amputation, finger or thumb, primary or secondary, any joint or phalanx, single, including neurectomies; with direct closure

26952 with local advancement flaps (V-Y, hood)

(For repair of soft tissue defect requiring split or full thickness graft or other pedicle flaps, see 15050-15758)

Other Procedures

26989 Unlisted procedure, hands or fingers

Pelvis and Hip Joint

Including head and neck of femur.

Incision

(For incision and drainage procedures, superficial, see 10040-10160)

26990 Incision and drainage, pelvis or hip joint area; deep abscess or hematoma

26991 infected bursa

26992 Incision, bone cortex, pelvis and/or hip joint (eg, osteomyelitis or bone abscess)

27000 Tenotomy, adductor of hip, percutaneous (separate procedure)

27001 Tenotomy, adductor of hip, open

(To report bilateral procedure, report 27001 with modifier 50)

27003 Tenotomy, adductor, subcutaneous, open, with obturator neurectomy

(To report bilateral procedure, report 27003 with modifier 50)

27005 Tenotomy, hip flexor(s), open (separate procedure)

27006 Tenotomy, abductors and/or extensor(s) of hip, open (separate procedure)

27025 Fasciotomy, hip or thigh, any type

(To report bilateral procedure, report 27025 with modifier 50)

● **27027** Decompression fasciotomy(ies), pelvic (buttock) compartment(s) (eg, gluteus medius-minimus, gluteus maximus, iliopsoas, and/or tensor fascia lata muscle), unilateral

►(To report bilateral procedure, report 27027 with modifier 50)◄

27030 Arthrotomy, hip, with drainage (eg, infection)

27033 Arthrotomy, hip, including exploration or removal of loose or foreign body

27035 Denervation, hip joint, intrapelvic or extrapelvic intra-articular branches of sciatic, femoral, or obturator nerves

(For obturator neurectomy, see 64763, 64766)

27036 Capsulectomy or capsulotomy, hip, with or without excision of heterotopic bone, with release of hip flexor muscles (ie, gluteus medius, gluteus minimus, tensor fascia latae, rectus femoris, sartorius, iliopsoas)

Excision

27040 Biopsy, soft tissue of pelvis and hip area; superficial

27041 deep, subfascial or intramuscular

(For needle biopsy of soft tissue, use 20206)

27047 Excision, tumor, pelvis and hip area; subcutaneous tissue

27048 deep, subfascial, intramuscular

27049 Radical resection of tumor, soft tissue of pelvis and hip area (eg, malignant neoplasm)

27050 Arthrotomy, with biopsy; sacroiliac joint

27052 hip joint

27054 Arthrotomy with synovectomy, hip joint

● **27057** Decompression fasciotomy(ies), pelvic (buttock) compartment(s) (eg, gluteus medius-minimus, gluteus maximus, iliopsoas, and/or tensor fascia lata muscle) with debridement of nonviable muscle, unilateral

►(To report bilateral procedure, report 27057 with modifier 50)◄

27060 Excision; ischial bursa

27062 trochanteric bursa or calcification

(For arthrocentesis or needling of bursa, use 20610)

27065 Excision of bone cyst or benign tumor; superficial (wing of ilium, symphysis pubis, or greater trochanter of femur) with or without autograft

27066 deep, with or without autograft

27067 with autograft requiring separate incision

27070 Partial excision (craterization, saucerization) (eg, osteomyelitis or bone abscess); superficial (eg, wing of ilium, symphysis pubis, or greater trochanter of femur)

27071 deep (subfascial or intramuscular)

27075 Radical resection of tumor or infection; wing of ilium, one pubic or ischial ramus or symphysis pubis

27076 ilium, including acetabulum, both pubic rami, or ischium and acetabulum

27077 innominate bone, total

27078 ischial tuberosity and greater trochanter of femur

27079 ischial tuberosity and greater trochanter of femur, with skin flaps

27080 Coccygectomy, primary

(For pressure (decubitus) ulcer, see 15920, 15922 and 15931-15958)

Introduction or Removal

27086 Removal of foreign body, pelvis or hip; subcutaneous tissue

27087 deep (subfascial or intramuscular)

27090 Removal of hip prosthesis; (separate procedure)

27091 complicated, including total hip prosthesis, methylmethacrylate with or without insertion of spacer

27093 Injection procedure for hip arthrography; without anesthesia

(For radiological supervision and interpretation, use 73525. Do not report 77002 in conjunction with 73525)

27095 with anesthesia

(For radiological supervision and interpretation, use 73525. Do not report 77002 in conjunction with 73525)

27096 Injection procedure for sacroiliac joint, arthrography and/or anesthetic/steroid

(27096 is to be used only with imaging confirmation of intra-articular needle positioning)

(For radiological supervision and interpretation of sacroiliac joint arthrography, use 73542)

(For fluoroscopic guidance without formal arthrography, use 77003)

(Code 27096 is a unilateral procedure. For bilateral procedure, use modifier 50)

Repair, Revision, and/or Reconstruction

27097 Release or recession, hamstring, proximal

27098 Transfer, adductor to ischium

27100 Transfer external oblique muscle to greater trochanter including fascial or tendon extension (graft)

27105 Transfer paraspinal muscle to hip (includes fascial or tendon extension graft)

27110 Transfer iliopsoas; to greater trochanter of femur

27111 to femoral neck

27120 Acetabuloplasty; (eg, Whitman, Colonna, Haygroves, or cup type)

27122 resection, femoral head (eg, Girdlestone procedure)

27125 Hemiarthroplasty, hip, partial (eg, femoral stem prosthesis, bipolar arthroplasty)

(For prosthetic replacement following fracture of the hip, use 27236)

27130 Arthroplasty, acetabular and proximal femoral prosthetic replacement (total hip arthroplasty), with or without autograft or allograft

27132 Conversion of previous hip surgery to total hip arthroplasty, with or without autograft or allograft

27134 Revision of total hip arthroplasty; both components, with or without autograft or allograft

27137 acetabular component only, with or without autograft or allograft

27138 femoral component only, with or without allograft

27140 Osteotomy and transfer of greater trochanter of femur (separate procedure)

27146 Osteotomy, iliac, acetabular or innominate bone;

27147 with open reduction of hip

27151 with femoral osteotomy

27156 with femoral osteotomy and with open reduction of hip

27158 Osteotomy, pelvis, bilateral (eg, congenital malformation)

27161 Osteotomy, femoral neck (separate procedure)

27165 Osteotomy, intertrochanteric or subtrochanteric including internal or external fixation and/or cast

27170 Bone graft, femoral head, neck, intertrochanteric or subtrochanteric area (includes obtaining bone graft)

27175 Treatment of slipped femoral epiphysis; by traction, without reduction

27176 by single or multiple pinning, in situ

27177 Open treatment of slipped femoral epiphysis; single or multiple pinning or bone graft (includes obtaining graft)

27178 closed manipulation with single or multiple pinning

27179 osteoplasty of femoral neck (Heyman type procedure)

27181 osteotomy and internal fixation

27185 Epiphyseal arrest by epiphysiodesis or stapling, greater trochanter of femur

27187 Prophylactic treatment (nailing, pinning, plating or wiring) with or without methylmethacrylate, femoral neck and proximal femur

Fracture and/or Dislocation

27193 Closed treatment of pelvic ring fracture, dislocation, diastasis or subluxation; without manipulation

27194 with manipulation, requiring more than local anesthesia

27200 Closed treatment of coccygeal fracture

27202 Open treatment of coccygeal fracture

▲ **27215** Open treatment of iliac spine(s), tuberosity avulsion, or iliac wing fracture(s), unilateral, for pelvic bone fracture patterns that do not disrupt the pelvic ring, includes internal fixation, when performed

►(To report bilateral procedure, report 27215 with modifier 50)◄

Surgery: Musculoskeletal System

▲ **27216** Percutaneous skeletal fixation of posterior pelvic bone fracture and/or dislocation, for fracture patterns that disrupt the pelvic ring, unilateral (includes ipsilateral ilium, sacroiliac joint and/or sacrum)

►(To report bilateral procedure, report 27216 with modifier 50)◄

▲ **27217** Open treatment of anterior pelvic bone fracture and/or dislocation for fracture patterns that disrupt the pelvic ring, unilateral, includes internal fixation, when performed (includes pubic symphysis and/or ipsilateral superior/inferior rami)

►(To report bilateral procedure, report 27217 with modifier 50)◄

▲ **27218** Open treatment of posterior pelvic bone fracture and/or dislocation, for fracture patterns that disrupt the pelvic ring, unilateral, includes internal fixation, when performed (includes ipsilateral ilium, sacroiliac joint and/or sacrum)

►(To report bilateral procedure, report 27218 with modifier 50)◄

27220 Closed treatment of acetabulum (hip socket) fracture(s); without manipulation

27222 with manipulation, with or without skeletal traction

27226 Open treatment of posterior or anterior acetabular wall fracture, with internal fixation

27227 Open treatment of acetabular fracture(s) involving anterior or posterior (one) column, or a fracture running transversely across the acetabulum, with internal fixation

27228 Open treatment of acetabular fracture(s) involving anterior and posterior (two) columns, includes T-fracture and both column fracture with complete articular detachment, or single column or transverse fracture with associated acetabular wall fracture, with internal fixation

27230 Closed treatment of femoral fracture, proximal end, neck; without manipulation

27232 with manipulation, with or without skeletal traction

27235 Percutaneous skeletal fixation of femoral fracture, proximal end, neck

27236 Open treatment of femoral fracture, proximal end, neck, internal fixation or prosthetic replacement

27238 Closed treatment of intertrochanteric, peritrochanteric, or subtrochanteric femoral fracture; without manipulation

27240 with manipulation, with or without skin or skeletal traction

27244 Treatment of intertrochanteric, peritrochanteric, or subtrochanteric femoral fracture; with plate/screw type implant, with or without cerclage

27245 with intramedullary implant, with or without interlocking screws and/or cerclage

27246 Closed treatment of greater trochanteric fracture, without manipulation

27248 Open treatment of greater trochanteric fracture, includes internal fixation, when performed

27250 Closed treatment of hip dislocation, traumatic; without anesthesia

27252 requiring anesthesia

27253 Open treatment of hip dislocation, traumatic, without internal fixation

27254 Open treatment of hip dislocation, traumatic, with acetabular wall and femoral head fracture, with or without internal or external fixation

(For treatment of acetabular fracture with fixation, see 27226, 27227)

27256 Treatment of spontaneous hip dislocation (developmental, including congenital or pathological), by abduction, splint or traction; without anesthesia, without manipulation

27257 with manipulation, requiring anesthesia

27258 Open treatment of spontaneous hip dislocation (developmental, including congenital or pathological), replacement of femoral head in acetabulum (including tenotomy, etc);

27259 with femoral shaft shortening

27265 Closed treatment of post hip arthroplasty dislocation; without anesthesia

27266 requiring regional or general anesthesia

27267 Closed treatment of femoral fracture, proximal end, head; without manipulation

27268 with manipulation

27269 Open treatment of femoral fracture, proximal end, head, includes internal fixation, when performed

(Do not report 27269 in conjunction with 27033, 27253)

Manipulation

27275 Manipulation, hip joint, requiring general anesthesia

Arthrodesis

27280 Arthrodesis, sacroiliac joint (including obtaining graft)

(To report bilateral procedure, report 27280 with modifier 50)

27282 Arthrodesis, symphysis pubis (including obtaining graft)

27284 Arthrodesis, hip joint (including obtaining graft);

27286 with subtrochanteric osteotomy

Amputation

27290 Interpelviabdominal amputation (hindquarter amputation)

27295 Disarticulation of hip

Other Procedures

27299 Unlisted procedure, pelvis or hip joint

Femur (Thigh Region) and Knee Joint

Including tibial plateaus.

Incision

(For incision and drainage of abscess or hematoma, superficial, see 10040-10160)

27301 Incision and drainage, deep abscess, bursa, or hematoma, thigh or knee region

27303 Incision, deep, with opening of bone cortex, femur or knee (eg, osteomyelitis or bone abscess)

27305 Fasciotomy, iliotibial (tenotomy), open

(For combined Ober-Yount fasciotomy, use 27025)

27306 Tenotomy, percutaneous, adductor or hamstring; single tendon (separate procedure)

27307 multiple tendons

27310 Arthrotomy, knee, with exploration, drainage, or removal of foreign body (eg, infection)

(27315 has been deleted. To report, use 27325)

(27320 has been deleted. To report, use 27326)

Excision

27323 Biopsy, soft tissue of thigh or knee area; superficial

27324 deep (subfascial or intramuscular)

(For needle biopsy of soft tissue, use 20206)

27325 Neurectomy, hamstring muscle

27326 Neurectomy, popliteal (gastrocnemius)

27327 Excision, tumor, thigh or knee area; subcutaneous

27328 deep, subfascial, or intramuscular

27329 Radical resection of tumor (eg, malignant neoplasm), soft tissue of thigh or knee area

27330 Arthrotomy, knee; with synovial biopsy only

27331 including joint exploration, biopsy, or removal of loose or foreign bodies

27332 Arthrotomy, with excision of semilunar cartilage (meniscectomy) knee; medial OR lateral

27333 medial AND lateral

27334 Arthrotomy, with synovectomy, knee; anterior OR posterior

27335 anterior AND posterior including popliteal area

27340 Excision, prepatellar bursa

27345 Excision of synovial cyst of popliteal space (eg, Baker's cyst)

27347 Excision of lesion of meniscus or capsule (eg, cyst, ganglion), knee

27350 Patellectomy or hemipatellectomy

27355 Excision or curettage of bone cyst or benign tumor of femur;

27356 with allograft

27357 with autograft (includes obtaining graft)

+ 27358 with internal fixation (List in addition to code for primary procedure)

(Use 27358 in conjunction with 27355, 27356, or 27357)

27360 Partial excision (craterization, saucerization, or diaphysectomy) bone, femur, proximal tibia and/or fibula (eg, osteomyelitis or bone abscess)

27365 Radical resection of tumor, bone, femur or knee

(For radical resection of tumor, soft tissue, use 27329)

Introduction or Removal

27370 Injection procedure for knee arthrography

(For radiological supervision and interpretation, use 73580. Do not report 77002 in conjunction with 73580)

27372 Removal of foreign body, deep, thigh region or knee area

(For removal of knee prosthesis including "total knee," use 27488)

(For surgical arthroscopic knee procedures, see 29870-29887)

Repair, Revision, and/or Reconstruction

27380 Suture of infrapatellar tendon; primary

27381 secondary reconstruction, including fascial or tendon graft

27385 Suture of quadriceps or hamstring muscle rupture; primary

27386 secondary reconstruction, including fascial or tendon graft

27390 Tenotomy, open, hamstring, knee to hip; single tendon

27391 multiple tendons, one leg

27392 multiple tendons, bilateral

27393 Lengthening of hamstring tendon; single tendon

27394 multiple tendons, one leg

27395 multiple tendons, bilateral

▲ 27396 Transplant or transfer (with muscle redirection or rerouting), thigh (eg, extensor to flexor); single tendon

▲ 27397 multiple tendons

27400 Transfer, tendon or muscle, hamstrings to femur (eg, Egger's type procedure)

27403 Arthrotomy with meniscus repair, knee

(For arthroscopic repair, use 29882)

27405 Repair, primary, torn ligament and/or capsule, knee; collateral

27407 cruciate

(For cruciate ligament reconstruction, use 27427)

27409 collateral and cruciate ligaments

(For ligament reconstruction, see 27427-27429)

27412 Autologous chondrocyte implantation, knee

(Do not report 27412 in conjunction with 20926, 27331, 27570)

(For harvesting of chondrocytes, use 29870)

27415 Osteochondral allograft, knee, open

(For arthroscopic implant of osteochondral allograft, use 29867)

(Do not report 27415 in conjunction with 27416)

27416 Osteochondral autograft(s), knee, open (eg, mosaicplasty) (includes harvesting of autograft[s])

(Do not report 27416 in conjunction with 27415, 29870, 29871, 29875, 29884 when performed at the same session and/or 29874, 29877, 29879, 29885-29887 when performed in the same compartment)

(For arthroscopic osteochondral autograft of knee, use 29866)

27418 Anterior tibial tubercleplasty (eg, Maquet type procedure)

27420 Reconstruction of dislocating patella; (eg, Hauser type procedure)

27422 with extensor realignment and/or muscle advancement or release (eg, Campbell, Goldwaite type procedure)

27424 with patellectomy

27425 Lateral retinacular release, open

(For arthroscopic lateral release, use 29873)

27427 Ligamentous reconstruction (augmentation), knee; extra-articular

27428 intra-articular (open)

27429 intra-articular (open) and extra-articular

(For primary repair of ligament(s) performed in conjunction with reconstruction, report 27405, 27407 or 27409 in conjunction with 27427, 27428 or 27429)

27430 Quadricepsplasty (eg, Bennett or Thompson type)

27435 Capsulotomy, posterior capsular release, knee

27437 Arthroplasty, patella; without prosthesis

27438 with prosthesis

27440 Arthroplasty, knee, tibial plateau;

27441 with debridement and partial synovectomy

27442 Arthroplasty, femoral condyles or tibial plateau(s), knee;

27443 with debridement and partial synovectomy

27445 Arthroplasty, knee, hinge prosthesis (eg, Walldius type)

27446 Arthroplasty, knee, condyle and plateau; medial OR lateral compartment

27447 medial AND lateral compartments with or without patella resurfacing (total knee arthroplasty)

(For revision of total knee arthroplasty, use 27487)

(For removal of total knee prosthesis, use 27488)

27448 Osteotomy, femur, shaft or supracondylar; without fixation

(To report bilateral procedure, report 27448 with modifier 50)

27450 with fixation

(To report bilateral procedure, report 27450 with modifier 50)

27454 Osteotomy, multiple, with realignment on intramedullary rod, femoral shaft (eg, Sofield type procedure)

27455 Osteotomy, proximal tibia, including fibular excision or osteotomy (includes correction of genu varus [bowleg] or genu valgus [knock-knee]); before epiphyseal closure

(To report bilateral procedure, report 27455 with modifier 50)

27457 after epiphyseal closure

(To report bilateral procedure, report 27457 with modifier 50)

27465 Osteoplasty, femur; shortening (excluding 64876)

27466 lengthening

27468 combined, lengthening and shortening with femoral segment transfer

27470 Repair, nonunion or malunion, femur, distal to head and neck; without graft (eg, compression technique)

27472 with iliac or other autogenous bone graft (includes obtaining graft)

27475 Arrest, epiphyseal, any method (eg, epiphysiodesis); distal femur

27477 tibia and fibula, proximal

27479 combined distal femur, proximal tibia and fibula

27485 Arrest, hemiepiphyseal, distal femur or proximal tibia or fibula (eg, genu varus or valgus)

27486 Revision of total knee arthroplasty, with or without allograft; one component

27487 femoral and entire tibial component

27488 Removal of prosthesis, including total knee prosthesis, methylmethacrylate with or without insertion of spacer, knee

27495 Prophylactic treatment (nailing, pinning, plating, or wiring) with or without methylmethacrylate, femur

27496 Decompression fasciotomy, thigh and/or knee, one compartment (flexor or extensor or adductor);

27497 with debridement of nonviable muscle and/or nerve

27498 Decompression fasciotomy, thigh and/or knee, multiple compartments;

27499 with debridement of nonviable muscle and/or nerve

Fracture and/or Dislocation

(For arthroscopic treatment of intercondylar spine[s] and tuberosity fracture[s] of the knee, see 29850, 29851)

(For arthroscopic treatment of tibial fracture, see 29855, 29856)

27500 Closed treatment of femoral shaft fracture, without manipulation

27501 Closed treatment of supracondylar or transcondylar femoral fracture with or without intercondylar extension, without manipulation

27502 Closed treatment of femoral shaft fracture, with manipulation, with or without skin or skeletal traction

27503 Closed treatment of supracondylar or transcondylar femoral fracture with or without intercondylar extension, with manipulation, with or without skin or skeletal traction

27506 Open treatment of femoral shaft fracture, with or without external fixation, with insertion of intramedullary implant, with or without cerclage and/or locking screws

27507 Open treatment of femoral shaft fracture with plate/screws, with or without cerclage

27508 Closed treatment of femoral fracture, distal end, medial or lateral condyle, without manipulation

27509 Percutaneous skeletal fixation of femoral fracture, distal end, medial or lateral condyle, or supracondylar or transcondylar, with or without intercondylar extension, or distal femoral epiphyseal separation

27510 Closed treatment of femoral fracture, distal end, medial or lateral condyle, with manipulation

27511 Open treatment of femoral supracondylar or transcondylar fracture without intercondylar extension, includes internal fixation, when performed

27513 Open treatment of femoral supracondylar or transcondylar fracture with intercondylar extension, includes internal fixation, when performed

27514 Open treatment of femoral fracture, distal end, medial or lateral condyle, includes internal fixation, when performed

27516 Closed treatment of distal femoral epiphyseal separation; without manipulation

27517 with manipulation, with or without skin or skeletal traction

27519 Open treatment of distal femoral epiphyseal separation, includes internal fixation, when performed

27520 Closed treatment of patellar fracture, without manipulation

27524 Open treatment of patellar fracture, with internal fixation and/or partial or complete patellectomy and soft tissue repair

27530 Closed treatment of tibial fracture, proximal (plateau); without manipulation

27532 with or without manipulation, with skeletal traction

(For arthroscopic treatment, see 29855, 29856)

27535 Open treatment of tibial fracture, proximal (plateau); unicondylar, includes internal fixation, when performed

27536 bicondylar, with or without internal fixation

(For arthroscopic treatment, see 29855, 29856)

27538 Closed treatment of intercondylar spine(s) and/or tuberosity fracture(s) of knee, with or without manipulation

(For arthroscopic treatment, see 29850, 29851)

27540 Open treatment of intercondylar spine(s) and/or tuberosity fracture(s) of the knee, includes internal fixation, when performed

27550 Closed treatment of knee dislocation; without anesthesia

27552 requiring anesthesia

27556 Open treatment of knee dislocation, includes internal fixation, when performed; without primary ligamentous repair or augmentation/reconstruction

27557 with primary ligamentous repair

27558 with primary ligamentous repair, with augmentation/reconstruction

27560 Closed treatment of patellar dislocation; without anesthesia

(For recurrent dislocation, see 27420-27424)

27562 requiring anesthesia

27566 Open treatment of patellar dislocation, with or without partial or total patellectomy

Manipulation

27570 Manipulation of knee joint under general anesthesia (includes application of traction or other fixation devices)

Arthrodesis

27580 Arthrodesis, knee, any technique

Amputation

27590 Amputation, thigh, through femur, any level;

27591 immediate fitting technique including first cast

27592 open, circular (guillotine)

27594 secondary closure or scar revision

27596 re-amputation

27598 Disarticulation at knee

Other Procedures

27599 Unlisted procedure, femur or knee

Leg (Tibia and Fibula) and Ankle Joint

Incision

27600 Decompression fasciotomy, leg; anterior and/or lateral compartments only

27601 posterior compartment(s) only

27602 anterior and/or lateral, and posterior compartment(s)

(For incision and drainage procedures, superficial, see 10040-10160)

(For decompression fasciotomy with debridement, see 27892-27894)

27603 Incision and drainage, leg or ankle; deep abscess or hematoma

27604 infected bursa

27605 Tenotomy, percutaneous, Achilles tendon (separate procedure); local anesthesia

27606 general anesthesia

27607 Incision (eg, osteomyelitis or bone abscess), leg or ankle

27610 Arthrotomy, ankle, including exploration, drainage, or removal of foreign body

27612 Arthrotomy, posterior capsular release, ankle, with or without Achilles tendon lengthening

(See also 27685)

Excision

27613 Biopsy, soft tissue of leg or ankle area; superficial

27614 deep (subfascial or intramuscular)

(For needle biopsy of soft tissue, use 20206)

27615 Radical resection of tumor (eg, malignant neoplasm), soft tissue of leg or ankle area

27618 Excision, tumor, leg or ankle area; subcutaneous tissue

27619 deep (subfascial or intramuscular)

27620 Arthrotomy, ankle, with joint exploration, with or without biopsy, with or without removal of loose or foreign body

27625 Arthrotomy, with synovectomy, ankle;

27626 including tenosynovectomy

27630 Excision of lesion of tendon sheath or capsule (eg, cyst or ganglion), leg and/or ankle

27635 Excision or curettage of bone cyst or benign tumor, tibia or fibula;

27637 with autograft (includes obtaining graft)

27638 with allograft

27640 Partial excision (craterization, saucerization, or diaphysectomy) bone (eg, osteomyelitis or exostosis); tibia

27641 fibula

27645 Radical resection of tumor, bone; tibia

27646 fibula

27647 talus or calcaneus

Introduction or Removal

27648 Injection procedure for ankle arthrography

(For radiological supervision and interpretation, use 73615. Do not report 77002 in conjunction with 73615)

(For ankle arthroscopy, see 29894-29898)

Repair, Revision, and/or Reconstruction

27650 Repair, primary, open or percutaneous, ruptured Achilles tendon;

27652 with graft (includes obtaining graft)

27654 Repair, secondary, Achilles tendon, with or without graft

27656 Repair, fascial defect of leg

27658 Repair, flexor tendon, leg; primary, without graft, each tendon

27659 secondary, with or without graft, each tendon

27664 Repair, extensor tendon, leg; primary, without graft, each tendon

27665 secondary, with or without graft, each tendon

27675 Repair, dislocating peroneal tendons; without fibular osteotomy

27676 with fibular osteotomy

27680 Tenolysis, flexor or extensor tendon, leg and/or ankle; single, each tendon

27681 multiple tendons (through separate incision(s))

27685 Lengthening or shortening of tendon, leg or ankle; single tendon (separate procedure)

27686 multiple tendons (through same incision), each

27687 Gastrocnemius recession (eg, Strayer procedure)

(Toe extensors are considered as a group to be a single tendon when transplanted into midfoot)

27690 Transfer or transplant of single tendon (with muscle redirection or rerouting); superficial (eg, anterior tibial extensors into midfoot)

27691 deep (eg, anterior tibial or posterior tibial through interosseous space, flexor digitorum longus, flexor hallucis longus, or peroneal tendon to midfoot or hindfoot)

+ 27692 each additional tendon (List separately in addition to code for primary procedure)

(Use 27692 in conjunction with 27690, 27691)

27695 Repair, primary, disrupted ligament, ankle; collateral

27696 both collateral ligaments

27698 Repair, secondary, disrupted ligament, ankle, collateral (eg, Watson-Jones procedure)

27700 Arthroplasty, ankle;

27702 with implant (total ankle)

27703 revision, total ankle

27704 Removal of ankle implant

27705 Osteotomy; tibia

27707 fibula

27709 tibia and fibula

27712 multiple, with realignment on intramedullary rod (eg, Sofield type procedure)

(For osteotomy to correct genu varus [bowleg] or genu valgus [knock-knee], see 27455-27457)

27715 Osteoplasty, tibia and fibula, lengthening or shortening

27720 Repair of nonunion or malunion, tibia; without graft, (eg, compression technique)

27722 with sliding graft

27724 with iliac or other autograft (includes obtaining graft)

27725 by synostosis, with fibula, any method

27726 Repair of fibula nonunion and/or malunion with internal fixation

(Do not report 27726 in conjunction with 27707)

27727 Repair of congenital pseudarthrosis, tibia

27730 Arrest, epiphyseal (epiphysiodesis), open; distal tibia

27732 distal fibula

27734 distal tibia and fibula

27740 Arrest, epiphyseal (epiphysiodesis), any method, combined, proximal and distal tibia and fibula;

27742 and distal femur

(For epiphyseal arrest of proximal tibia and fibula, use 27477)

27745 Prophylactic treatment (nailing, pinning, plating or wiring) with or without methylmethacrylate, tibia

Fracture and/or Dislocation

27750 Closed treatment of tibial shaft fracture (with or without fibular fracture); without manipulation

27752 with manipulation, with or without skeletal traction

27756 Percutaneous skeletal fixation of tibial shaft fracture (with or without fibular fracture) (eg, pins or screws)

27758 Open treatment of tibial shaft fracture (with or without fibular fracture), with plate/screws, with or without cerclage

27759 Treatment of tibial shaft fracture (with or without fibular fracture) by intramedullary implant, with or without interlocking screws and/or cerclage

27760 Closed treatment of medial malleolus fracture; without manipulation

27762 with manipulation, with or without skin or skeletal traction

27766 Open treatment of medial malleolus fracture, includes internal fixation, when performed

27767 Closed treatment of posterior malleolus fracture; without manipulation

27768 with manipulation

27769 Open treatment of posterior malleolus fracture, includes internal fixation, when performed

(Do not report 27767-27769 in conjunction with 27808-27823)

27780 Closed treatment of proximal fibula or shaft fracture; without manipulation

27781 with manipulation

27784 Open treatment of proximal fibula or shaft fracture, includes internal fixation, when performed

27786 Closed treatment of distal fibular fracture (lateral malleolus); without manipulation

27788 with manipulation

27792 Open treatment of distal fibular fracture (lateral malleolus), includes internal fixation, when performed

(For treatment of tibia and fibula shaft fractures, see 27750-27759)

27808 Closed treatment of bimalleolar ankle fracture (eg, lateral and medial malleoli, or lateral and posterior malleoli or medial and posterior malleoli); without manipulation

27810 with manipulation

27814 Open treatment of bimalleolar ankle fracture (eg, lateral and medial malleoli, or lateral and posterior malleoli, or medial and posterior malleoli), includes internal fixation, when performed

27816 Closed treatment of trimalleolar ankle fracture; without manipulation

27818 with manipulation

27822 Open treatment of trimalleolar ankle fracture, includes internal fixation, when performed, medial and/or lateral malleolus; without fixation of posterior lip

27823 with fixation of posterior lip

27824 Closed treatment of fracture of weight bearing articular portion of distal tibia (eg, pilon or tibial plafond), with or without anesthesia; without manipulation

27825 with skeletal traction and/or requiring manipulation

27826 Open treatment of fracture of weight bearing articular surface/portion of distal tibia (eg, pilon or tibial plafond), with internal fixation, when performed; of fibula only

27827 of tibia only

27828 of both tibia and fibula

27829 Open treatment of distal tibiofibular joint (syndesmosis) disruption, includes internal fixation, when performed

27830 Closed treatment of proximal tibiofibular joint dislocation; without anesthesia

27831 requiring anesthesia

27832 Open treatment of proximal tibiofibular joint dislocation, includes internal fixation, when performed, or with excision of proximal fibula

27840 Closed treatment of ankle dislocation; without anesthesia

27842 requiring anesthesia, with or without percutaneous skeletal fixation

27846 Open treatment of ankle dislocation, with or without percutaneous skeletal fixation; without repair or internal fixation

27848 with repair or internal or external fixation

(For surgical or diagnostic arthroscopic procedures, see 29894-29898)

Manipulation

27860 Manipulation of ankle under general anesthesia (includes application of traction or other fixation apparatus)

Arthrodesis

27870 Arthrodesis, ankle, open

(For arthroscopic ankle arthrodesis, use 29899)

27871 Arthrodesis, tibiofibular joint, proximal or distal

Amputation

27880 Amputation, leg, through tibia and fibula;

27881 with immediate fitting technique including application of first cast

27882 open, circular (guillotine)

27884 secondary closure or scar revision

27886 re-amputation

27888 Amputation, ankle, through malleoli of tibia and fibula (eg, Syme, Pirogoff type procedures), with plastic closure and resection of nerves

27889 Ankle disarticulation

Other Procedures

27892 Decompression fasciotomy, leg; anterior and/or lateral compartments only, with debridement of nonviable muscle and/or nerve

(For decompression fasciotomy of the leg without debridement, use 27600)

27893 posterior compartment(s) only, with debridement of nonviable muscle and/or nerve

(For decompression fasciotomy of the leg without debridement, use 27601)

27894 anterior and/or lateral, and posterior compartment(s), with debridement of nonviable muscle and/or nerve

(For decompression fasciotomy of the leg without debridement, use 27602)

27899 Unlisted procedure, leg or ankle

Foot and Toes

Incision

(For incision and drainage procedures, superficial, see 10040-10160)

28001 Incision and drainage, bursa, foot

28002 Incision and drainage below fascia, with or without tendon sheath involvement, foot; single bursal space

28003 multiple areas

28005 Incision, bone cortex (eg, osteomyelitis or bone abscess), foot

28008 Fasciotomy, foot and/or toe

(See also 28060, 28062, 28250)

28010 Tenotomy, percutaneous, toe; single tendon

28011 multiple tendons

(For open tenotomy, see 28230-28234)

28020 Arthrotomy, including exploration, drainage, or removal of loose or foreign body; intertarsal or tarsometatarsal joint

28022 metatarsophalangeal joint

28024 interphalangeal joint

(28030 has been deleted. To report, use 28055)

28035 Release, tarsal tunnel (posterior tibial nerve decompression)

(For other nerve entrapments, see 64704, 64722)

Excision

28043 Excision, tumor, foot; subcutaneous tissue

28045 deep, subfascial, intramuscular

28046 Radical resection of tumor (eg, malignant neoplasm), soft tissue of foot

28050 Arthrotomy with biopsy; intertarsal or tarsometatarsal joint

28052 metatarsophalangeal joint

28054 interphalangeal joint

28055 Neurectomy, intrinsic musculature of foot

28060 Fasciectomy, plantar fascia; partial (separate procedure)

28062 radical (separate procedure)

(For plantar fasciotomy, see 28008, 28250)

28070 Synovectomy; intertarsal or tarsometatarsal joint, each

28072 metatarsophalangeal joint, each

28080 Excision, interdigital (Morton) neuroma, single, each

28086 Synovectomy, tendon sheath, foot; flexor

28088 extensor

28090 Excision of lesion, tendon, tendon sheath, or capsule (including synovectomy) (eg, cyst or ganglion); foot

28092 toe(s), each

28100 Excision or curettage of bone cyst or benign tumor, talus or calcaneus;

28102 with iliac or other autograft (includes obtaining graft)

28103 with allograft

28104 Excision or curettage of bone cyst or benign tumor, tarsal or metatarsal, except talus or calcaneus;

28106 with iliac or other autograft (includes obtaining graft)

28107 with allograft

28108 Excision or curettage of bone cyst or benign tumor, phalanges of foot

(For ostectomy, partial (eg, hallux valgus, Silver type procedure), use 28290)

28110 Ostectomy, partial excision, fifth metatarsal head (bunionette) (separate procedure)

28111 Ostectomy, complete excision; first metatarsal head

28112 other metatarsal head (second, third or fourth)

28113 fifth metatarsal head

28114 all metatarsal heads, with partial proximal phalangectomy, excluding first metatarsal (eg, Clayton type procedure)

28116 Ostectomy, excision of tarsal coalition

28118 Ostectomy, calcaneus;

28119 for spur, with or without plantar fascial release

28120 Partial excision (craterization, saucerization, sequestrectomy, or diaphysectomy) bone (eg, osteomyelitis or bossing); talus or calcaneus

28122 tarsal or metatarsal bone, except talus or calcaneus

(For partial excision of talus or calcaneus, use 28120)

(For cheilectomy for hallux rigidus, use 28289)

28124 phalanx of toe

28126 Resection, partial or complete, phalangeal base, each toe

28130 Talectomy (astragalectomy)

(For calcanectomy, use 28118)

28140 Metatarsectomy

28150 Phalangectomy, toe, each toe

28153 Resection, condyle(s), distal end of phalanx, each toe

28160 Hemiphalangectomy or interphalangeal joint excision, toe, proximal end of phalanx, each

28171 Radical resection of tumor, bone; tarsal (except talus or calcaneus)

28173 metatarsal

28175 phalanx of toe

(For talus or calcaneus, use 27647)

Introduction or Removal

28190 Removal of foreign body, foot; subcutaneous

28192 deep

28193 complicated

Repair, Revision, and/or Reconstruction

28200 Repair, tendon, flexor, foot; primary or secondary, without free graft, each tendon

28202 secondary with free graft, each tendon (includes obtaining graft)

28208 Repair, tendon, extensor, foot; primary or secondary, each tendon

28210 secondary with free graft, each tendon (includes obtaining graft)

28220 Tenolysis, flexor, foot; single tendon

28222 multiple tendons

28225 Tenolysis, extensor, foot; single tendon

28226 multiple tendons

28230 Tenotomy, open, tendon flexor; foot, single or multiple tendon(s) (separate procedure)

28232 toe, single tendon (separate procedure)

28234 Tenotomy, open, extensor, foot or toe, each tendon

(For tendon transfer to midfoot or hindfoot, see 27690, 27691)

28238 Reconstruction (advancement), posterior tibial tendon with excision of accessory tarsal navicular bone (eg, Kidner type procedure)

(For subcutaneous tenotomy, see 28010, 28011)

(For transfer or transplant of tendon with muscle redirection or rerouting, see 27690-27692)

(For extensor hallucis longus transfer with great toe IP fusion (Jones procedure), use 28760)

28240 Tenotomy, lengthening, or release, abductor hallucis muscle

28250 Division of plantar fascia and muscle (eg, Steindler stripping) (separate procedure)

28260 Capsulotomy, midfoot; medial release only (separate procedure)

28261 with tendon lengthening

28262 extensive, including posterior talotibial capsulotomy and tendon(s) lengthening (eg, resistant clubfoot deformity)

28264 Capsulotomy, midtarsal (eg, Heyman type procedure)

28270 Capsulotomy; metatarsophalangeal joint, with or without tenorrhaphy, each joint (separate procedure)

28272 interphalangeal joint, each joint (separate procedure)

28280 Syndactylization, toes (eg, webbing or Kelikian type procedure)

28285 Correction, hammertoe (eg, interphalangeal fusion, partial or total phalangectomy)

28286 Correction, cock-up fifth toe, with plastic skin closure (eg, Ruiz-Mora type procedure)

28288 Ostectomy, partial, exostectomy or condylectomy, metatarsal head, each metatarsal head

28289 Hallux rigidus correction with cheilectomy, debridement and capsular release of the first metatarsophalangeal joint

28290 Correction, hallux valgus (bunion), with or without sesamoidectomy; simple exostectomy (eg, Silver type procedure)

28292 Keller, McBride, or Mayo type procedure

28293 resection of joint with implant

28294 with tendon transplants (eg, Joplin type procedure)

28296 with metatarsal osteotomy (eg, Mitchell, Chevron, or concentric type procedures)

28297 Lapidus-type procedure

28298 by phalanx osteotomy

28299 by double osteotomy

28300 Osteotomy; calcaneus (eg, Dwyer or Chambers type procedure), with or without internal fixation

28302 talus

28304 Osteotomy, tarsal bones, other than calcaneus or talus;

28305 with autograft (includes obtaining graft) (eg, Fowler type)

28306 Osteotomy, with or without lengthening, shortening or angular correction, metatarsal; first metatarsal

28307 first metatarsal with autograft (other than first toe)

28308 other than first metatarsal, each

28309 multiple (eg, Swanson type cavus foot procedure)

28310 Osteotomy, shortening, angular or rotational correction; proximal phalanx, first toe (separate procedure)

28312 other phalanges, any toe

28313 Reconstruction, angular deformity of toe, soft tissue procedures only (eg, overlapping second toe, fifth toe, curly toes)

28315 Sesamoidectomy, first toe (separate procedure)

28320 Repair, nonunion or malunion; tarsal bones

28322 metatarsal, with or without bone graft (includes obtaining graft)

28340 Reconstruction, toe, macrodactyly; soft tissue resection

28341 requiring bone resection

28344 Reconstruction, toe(s); polydactyly

28345 syndactyly, with or without skin graft(s), each web

28360 Reconstruction, cleft foot

Fracture and/or Dislocation

28400 Closed treatment of calcaneal fracture; without manipulation

28405 with manipulation

28406 Percutaneous skeletal fixation of calcaneal fracture, with manipulation

28415 Open treatment of calcaneal fracture, includes internal fixation, when performed;

28420 with primary iliac or other autogenous bone graft (includes obtaining graft)

28430 Closed treatment of talus fracture; without manipulation

28435 with manipulation

28436 Percutaneous skeletal fixation of talus fracture, with manipulation

28445 Open treatment of talus fracture, includes internal fixation, when performed

28446 Open osteochondral autograft, talus (includes obtaining graft[s])

(Do not report 28446 in conjunction with 27705, 27707)

(For arthroscopic osteochondral talus graft, use 29892)

►(For open osteochondral allograft or repairs with industrial grafts, use 28899)◄

28450 Treatment of tarsal bone fracture (except talus and calcaneus); without manipulation, each

28455 with manipulation, each

28456 Percutaneous skeletal fixation of tarsal bone fracture (except talus and calcaneus), with manipulation, each

28465 Open treatment of tarsal bone fracture (except talus and calcaneus), includes internal fixation, when performed, each

28470 Closed treatment of metatarsal fracture; without manipulation, each

28475 with manipulation, each

28476 Percutaneous skeletal fixation of metatarsal fracture, with manipulation, each

28485 Open treatment of metatarsal fracture, includes internal fixation, when performed, each

28490 Closed treatment of fracture great toe, phalanx or phalanges; without manipulation

28495 with manipulation

28496 Percutaneous skeletal fixation of fracture great toe, phalanx or phalanges, with manipulation

28505 Open treatment of fracture, great toe, phalanx or phalanges, includes internal fixation, when performed

28510 Closed treatment of fracture, phalanx or phalanges, other than great toe; without manipulation, each

28515 with manipulation, each

28525 Open treatment of fracture, phalanx or phalanges, other than great toe, includes internal fixation, when performed, each

28530 Closed treatment of sesamoid fracture

28531 Open treatment of sesamoid fracture, with or without internal fixation

28540 Closed treatment of tarsal bone dislocation, other than talotarsal; without anesthesia

28545 requiring anesthesia

28546 Percutaneous skeletal fixation of tarsal bone dislocation, other than talotarsal, with manipulation

28555 Open treatment of tarsal bone dislocation, includes internal fixation, when performed

28570 Closed treatment of talotarsal joint dislocation; without anesthesia

28575 requiring anesthesia

28576 Percutaneous skeletal fixation of talotarsal joint dislocation, with manipulation

28585 Open treatment of talotarsal joint dislocation, includes internal fixation, when performed

28600 Closed treatment of tarsometatarsal joint dislocation; without anesthesia

28605 requiring anesthesia

28606 Percutaneous skeletal fixation of tarsometatarsal joint dislocation, with manipulation

28615 Open treatment of tarsometatarsal joint dislocation, includes internal fixation, when performed

28630 Closed treatment of metatarsophalangeal joint dislocation; without anesthesia

28635 requiring anesthesia

28636 Percutaneous skeletal fixation of metatarsophalangeal joint dislocation, with manipulation

28645 Open treatment of metatarsophalangeal joint dislocation, includes internal fixation, when performed

28660 Closed treatment of interphalangeal joint dislocation; without anesthesia

28665 requiring anesthesia

28666 Percutaneous skeletal fixation of interphalangeal joint dislocation, with manipulation

28675 Open treatment of interphalangeal joint dislocation, includes internal fixation, when performed

Arthrodesis

28705 Arthrodesis; pantalar

28715 triple

28725 subtalar

28730 Arthrodesis, midtarsal or tarsometatarsal, multiple or transverse;

28735 with osteotomy (eg, flatfoot correction)

28737 Arthrodesis, with tendon lengthening and advancement, midtarsal, tarsal navicular-cuneiform (eg, Miller type procedure)

28740 Arthrodesis, midtarsal or tarsometatarsal, single joint

28750 Arthrodesis, great toe; metatarsophalangeal joint

28755 interphalangeal joint

28760 Arthrodesis, with extensor hallucis longus transfer to first metatarsal neck, great toe, interphalangeal joint (eg, Jones type procedure)

(For hammertoe operation or interphalangeal fusion, use 28285)

Amputation

28800 Amputation, foot; midtarsal (eg, Chopart type procedure)

28805 transmetatarsal

28810 Amputation, metatarsal, with toe, single

28820 Amputation, toe; metatarsophalangeal joint

28825 interphalangeal joint

(For amputation of tuft of distal phalanx, use 11752)

Other Procedures

28890 Extracorporeal shock wave, high energy, performed by a physician, requiring anesthesia other than local, including ultrasound guidance, involving the plantar fascia

(For extracorporeal shock wave therapy involving musculoskeletal system not otherwise specified, see Category III codes 0019T, 0101T, 0102T)

28899 Unlisted procedure, foot or toes

Application of Casts and Strapping

The listed procedures apply when the cast application or strapping is a replacement procedure used during or after the period of follow-up care, or when the cast application or strapping is an initial service performed without a restorative treatment or procedure(s) to stabilize or protect a fracture, injury, or dislocation and/or to afford comfort to a patient. Restorative treatment or procedure(s) rendered by another physician following the application of the initial cast/splint/strap may be reported with a treatment of fracture and/or dislocation code.

A physician who applies the initial cast, strap or splint and also assumes all of the subsequent fracture, dislocation, or injury care cannot use the application of casts and strapping codes as an initial service, since the first cast/splint or strap application is included in the treatment of fracture and/or dislocation codes. (See notes under Musculoskeletal System, page 61.) A temporary cast/splint/strap is not considered to be part of the preoperative care, and the use of the modifier 56 is not applicable. Additional evaluation and management services are reportable only if significant identifiable further services are provided at the time of the cast application or strapping.

If cast application or strapping is provided as an initial service (eg, casting of a sprained ankle or knee) in which no other procedure or treatment (eg, surgical repair, reduction of a fracture, or joint dislocation) is performed or is expected to be performed by a physician rendering the initial care only, use the casting, strapping and/or supply code (99070) in addition to an evaluation and management code as appropriate.

Listed procedures include removal of cast or strapping.

(For orthotics management and training, see 97760-97762)

Body and Upper Extremity

Casts

29000 Application of halo type body cast (see 20661-20663 for insertion)

29010 Application of Risser jacket, localizer, body; only

29015 including head

29020 Application of turnbuckle jacket, body; only

29025 including head

29035 Application of body cast, shoulder to hips;

29040 including head, Minerva type

29044 including one thigh

29046 including both thighs

29049 Application, cast; figure-of-eight

29055 shoulder spica

29058 plaster Velpeau

29065 shoulder to hand (long arm)

29075 elbow to finger (short arm)

29085 hand and lower forearm (gauntlet)

29086 finger (eg, contracture)

Splints

29105 Application of long arm splint (shoulder to hand)

29125 Application of short arm splint (forearm to hand); static

29126 dynamic

29130 Application of finger splint; static

29131 dynamic

Strapping—Any Age

29200 Strapping; thorax

29220 low back

29240 shoulder (eg, Velpeau)

29260 elbow or wrist

29280 hand or finger

Lower Extremity

Casts

29305 Application of hip spica cast; one leg

29325 one and one-half spica or both legs

(For hip spica (body) cast, including thighs only, use 29046)

29345 Application of long leg cast (thigh to toes);

29355 walker or ambulatory type

29358 Application of long leg cast brace

29365 Application of cylinder cast (thigh to ankle)

29405 Application of short leg cast (below knee to toes);

29425 walking or ambulatory type

29435 Application of patellar tendon bearing (PTB) cast

29440 Adding walker to previously applied cast

29445 Application of rigid total contact leg cast

29450 Application of clubfoot cast with molding or manipulation, long or short leg

(To report bilateral procedure, use 29450 with modifier 50)

Splints

29505 Application of long leg splint (thigh to ankle or toes)

29515 Application of short leg splint (calf to foot)

Strapping—Any Age

29520 Strapping; hip

29530 knee

29540 ankle and/or foot

29550 toes

29580 Unna boot

29590 Denis-Browne splint strapping

Removal or Repair

Codes for cast removals should be employed only for casts applied by another physician.

29700 Removal or bivalving; gauntlet, boot or body cast

29705 full arm or full leg cast

29710 shoulder or hip spica, Minerva, or Risser jacket, etc.

29715 turnbuckle jacket

29720 Repair of spica, body cast or jacket

29730 Windowing of cast

29740 Wedging of cast (except clubfoot casts)

29750 Wedging of clubfoot cast

(To report bilateral procedure, use 29750 with modifier 50)

Other Procedures

29799 Unlisted procedure, casting or strapping

Endoscopy/Arthroscopy

Surgical endoscopy/arthroscopy always includes a diagnostic endoscopy/arthroscopy.

When arthroscopy is performed in conjunction with arthrotomy, add modifier 51.

29800 Arthroscopy, temporomandibular joint, diagnostic, with or without synovial biopsy (separate procedure)

29804 Arthroscopy, temporomandibular joint, surgical

(For open procedure, use 21010)

29805 Arthroscopy, shoulder, diagnostic, with or without synovial biopsy (separate procedure)

(For open procedure, see 23065-23066, 23100-23101)

29806 Arthroscopy, shoulder, surgical; capsulorrhaphy

(For open procedure, see 23450-23466)

(To report thermal capsulorrhaphy, use 29999)

29807 repair of SLAP lesion

29819 with removal of loose body or foreign body

(For open procedure, see 23040-23044, 23107)

29820 synovectomy, partial

(For open procedure, see 23105)

29821 synovectomy, complete

(For open procedure, see 23105)

29822 debridement, limited

(For open procedure, see specific open shoulder procedure performed)

29823 debridement, extensive

(For open procedure, see specific open shoulder procedure performed)

29824 distal claviculectomy including distal articular surface (Mumford procedure)

(For open procedure, use 23120)

29825 with lysis and resection of adhesions, with or without manipulation

(For open procedure, see specific open shoulder procedure performed)

29826 decompression of subacromial space with partial acromioplasty, with or without coracoacromial release

(For open procedure, use 23130 or 23415)

29827 with rotator cuff repair

(For open or mini-open rotator cuff repair, use 23412)

(When arthroscopic subacromial decompression is performed at the same setting, use 29826 and append modifier 51)

(When arthroscopic distal clavicle resection is performed at the same setting, use 29824 and append modifier 51)

29828 biceps tenodesis

(Do not report 29828 in conjunction with 29805, 29820, 29822)

(For open biceps tenodesis, use 23430)

29830 Arthroscopy, elbow, diagnostic, with or without synovial biopsy (separate procedure)

29834 Arthroscopy, elbow, surgical; with removal of loose body or foreign body

29835 synovectomy, partial

29836 synovectomy, complete

29837 debridement, limited

29838 debridement, extensive

29840 Arthroscopy, wrist, diagnostic, with or without synovial biopsy (separate procedure)

29843 Arthroscopy, wrist, surgical; for infection, lavage and drainage

29844 synovectomy, partial

29845 synovectomy, complete

29846 excision and/or repair of triangular fibrocartilage and/or joint debridement

29847 internal fixation for fracture or instability

29848 Endoscopy, wrist, surgical, with release of transverse carpal ligament

(For open procedure, use 64721)

29850 Arthroscopically aided treatment of intercondylar spine(s) and/or tuberosity fracture(s) of the knee, with or without manipulation; without internal or external fixation (includes arthroscopy)

29851 with internal or external fixation (includes arthroscopy)

(For bone graft, use 20900, 20902)

29855 Arthroscopically aided treatment of tibial fracture, proximal (plateau); unicondylar, includes internal fixation, when performed (includes arthroscopy)

29856 bicondylar, includes internal fixation, when performed (includes arthroscopy)

(For bone graft, use 20900, 20902)

29860 Arthroscopy, hip, diagnostic with or without synovial biopsy (separate procedure)

29861 Arthroscopy, hip, surgical; with removal of loose body or foreign body

29862 with debridement/shaving of articular cartilage (chondroplasty), abrasion arthroplasty, and/or resection of labrum

29863 with synovectomy

29866 Arthroscopy, knee, surgical; osteochondral autograft(s) (eg, mosaicplasty) (includes harvesting of the autograft[s])

(Do not report 29866 in conjunction with 29870, 29871, 29875, 29884 when performed at the same session and/or 29874, 29877, 29879, 29885-29887 when performed in the same compartment)

(For open osteochondral autograft of knee, use 27416)

29867 osteochondral allograft (eg, mosaicplasty)

(Do not report 29867 in conjunction with 27570, 29870, 29871, 29875, 29884 when performed at the same session and/or 29874, 29877, 29879, 29885-29887 when performed in the same compartment)

(Do not report 29867 in conjunction with 27415)

29868 meniscal transplantation (includes arthrotomy for meniscal insertion), medial or lateral

(Do not report 29868 in conjunction with 29870, 29871, 29875, 29880, 29883, 29884 when performed at the same session or 29874, 29877, 29881, 29882 when performed in the same compartment)

29870 Arthroscopy, knee, diagnostic, with or without synovial biopsy (separate procedure)

(For open autologous chondrocyte implantation of the knee, use 27412)

29871 Arthroscopy, knee, surgical; for infection, lavage and drainage

(For implantation of osteochondral graft for treatment of articular surface defect, see 27412, 27415, 29866, 29867)

29873 with lateral release

(For open lateral release, use 27425)

29874 for removal of loose body or foreign body (eg, osteochondritis dissecans fragmentation, chondral fragmentation)

29875 synovectomy, limited (eg, plica or shelf resection) (separate procedure)

29876 synovectomy, major, two or more compartments (eg, medial or lateral)

29877 debridement/shaving of articular cartilage (chondroplasty)

29879 abrasion arthroplasty (includes chondroplasty where necessary) or multiple drilling or microfracture

29880 with meniscectomy (medial AND lateral, including any meniscal shaving)

29881 with meniscectomy (medial OR lateral, including any meniscal shaving)

29882 with meniscus repair (medial OR lateral)

29883 with meniscus repair (medial AND lateral)

(For meniscal transplantation, medial or lateral, knee, use 29868)

29884 with lysis of adhesions, with or without manipulation (separate procedure)

29885 drilling for osteochondritis dissecans with bone grafting, with or without internal fixation (including debridement of base of lesion)

29886 drilling for intact osteochondritis dissecans lesion

29887 drilling for intact osteochondritis dissecans lesion with internal fixation

29888 Arthroscopically aided anterior cruciate ligament repair/augmentation or reconstruction

29889 Arthroscopically aided posterior cruciate ligament repair/augmentation or reconstruction

(Procedures 29888 and 29889 should not be used with reconstruction procedures 27427-27429)

29891 Arthroscopy, ankle, surgical, excision of osteochondral defect of talus and/or tibia, including drilling of the defect

29892 Arthroscopically aided repair of large osteochondritis dissecans lesion, talar dome fracture, or tibial plafond fracture, with or without internal fixation (includes arthroscopy)

29893 Endoscopic plantar fasciotomy

29894 Arthroscopy, ankle (tibiotalar and fibulotalar joints), surgical; with removal of loose body or foreign body

29895 synovectomy, partial

29897 debridement, limited

29898 debridement, extensive

29899 with ankle arthrodesis

(For open ankle arthrodesis, use 27870)

29900 Arthroscopy, metacarpophalangeal joint, diagnostic, includes synovial biopsy

(Do not report 29900 with 29901, 29902)

29901 Arthroscopy, metacarpophalangeal joint, surgical; with debridement

29902 with reduction of displaced ulnar collateral ligament (eg, Stenar lesion)

29904 Arthroscopy, subtalar joint, surgical; with removal of loose body or foreign body

29905 with synovectomy

29906 with debridement

29907 with subtalar arthrodesis

29999 Unlisted procedure, arthroscopy

Notes

Respiratory System

Nose

Incision

30000 Drainage abscess or hematoma, nasal, internal approach

(For external approach, see 10060, 10140)

30020 Drainage abscess or hematoma, nasal septum

(For lateral rhinotomy, see specific application (eg, 30118, 30320))

Excision

30100 Biopsy, intranasal

(For biopsy skin of nose, see 11100, 11101)

30110 Excision, nasal polyp(s), simple

(30110 would normally be completed in an office setting)

(To report bilateral procedure, use 30110 with modifier 50)

30115 Excision, nasal polyp(s), extensive

(30115 would normally require the facilities available in a hospital setting)

(To report bilateral procedure, use 30115 with modifier 50)

30117 Excision or destruction (eg, laser), intranasal lesion; internal approach

30118 external approach (lateral rhinotomy)

30120 Excision or surgical planing of skin of nose for rhinophyma

30124 Excision dermoid cyst, nose; simple, skin, subcutaneous

30125 complex, under bone or cartilage

30130 Excision inferior turbinate, partial or complete, any method

(For excision of superior or middle turbinate, use 30999)

30140 Submucous resection inferior turbinate, partial or complete, any method

(Do not report 30130 or 30140 in conjunction with 30801, 30802, 30930)

(For submucous resection of superior or middle turbinate, use 30999)

(For endoscopic resection of concha bullosa of middle turbinate, use 31240)

(For submucous resection of nasal septum, use 30520)

(For reduction of turbinates, use 30140 with modifier 52)

30150 Rhinectomy; partial

30160 total

(For closure and/or reconstruction, primary or delayed, see **Integumentary System,** 13150-13160, 14060-14300, 15120, 15121, 15260, 15261, 15760, 20900-20912)

Introduction

30200 Injection into turbinate(s), therapeutic

30210 Displacement therapy (Proetz type)

30220 Insertion, nasal septal prosthesis (button)

Removal of Foreign Body

30300 Removal foreign body, intranasal; office type procedure

30310 requiring general anesthesia

30320 by lateral rhinotomy

Repair

(For obtaining tissues for graft, see 20900-20926, 21210)

30400 Rhinoplasty, primary; lateral and alar cartilages and/or elevation of nasal tip

(For columellar reconstruction, see 13150 et seq)

30410 complete, external parts including bony pyramid, lateral and alar cartilages, and/or elevation of nasal tip

30420 including major septal repair

30430 Rhinoplasty, secondary; minor revision (small amount of nasal tip work)

30435 intermediate revision (bony work with osteotomies)

30450 major revision (nasal tip work and osteotomies)

30460 Rhinoplasty for nasal deformity secondary to congenital cleft lip and/or palate, including columellar lengthening; tip only

30462 tip, septum, osteotomies

30465 Repair of nasal vestibular stenosis (eg, spreader grafting, lateral nasal wall reconstruction)

(30465 excludes obtaining graft. For graft procedure, see 20900-20926, 21210)

(30465 is used to report a bilateral procedure. For unilateral procedure, use modifier 52)

30520 Septoplasty or submucous resection, with or without cartilage scoring, contouring or replacement with graft

(For submucous resection of turbinates, use 30140)

30540 Repair choanal atresia; intranasal

30545 transpalatine

(Do not report modifier 63 in conjunction with 30540, 30545)

30560 Lysis intranasal synechia

30580 Repair fistula; oromaxillary (combine with 31030 if antrotomy is included)

30600 oronasal

30620 Septal or other intranasal dermatoplasty (does not include obtaining graft)

30630 Repair nasal septal perforations

Destruction

30801 Cautery and/or ablation, mucosa of inferior turbinates, unilateral or bilateral, any method; superficial

(For cautery and ablation of superior or middle turbinates, use 30999)

30802 intramural

(Do not report 30801, 30802, 30930 in conjunction with 30130 or 30140)

(For cautery performed for control of nasal hemorrhage, see 30901-30906)

Other Procedures

30901 Control nasal hemorrhage, anterior, simple (limited cautery and/or packing) any method

(To report bilateral procedure, use 30901 with modifier 50)

30903 Control nasal hemorrhage, anterior, complex (extensive cautery and/or packing) any method

(To report bilateral procedure, use 30903 with modifier 50)

30905 Control nasal hemorrhage, posterior, with posterior nasal packs and/or cautery, any method; initial

30906 subsequent

30915 Ligation arteries; ethmoidal

30920 internal maxillary artery, transantral

(For ligation external carotid artery, use 37600)

30930 Fracture nasal inferior turbinate(s), therapeutic

(Do not report 30801, 30802, 30930 in conjunction with 30130 or 30140)

(For fracture of superior or middle turbinate(s), use 30999)

30999 Unlisted procedure, nose

Accessory Sinuses

Incision

31000 Lavage by cannulation; maxillary sinus (antrum puncture or natural ostium)

(To report bilateral procedure, use 31000 with modifier 50)

31002 sphenoid sinus

31020 Sinusotomy, maxillary (antrotomy); intranasal

(To report bilateral procedure, use 31020 with modifier 50)

31030 radical (Caldwell-Luc) without removal of antrochoanal polyps

(To report bilateral procedure, use 31030 with modifier 50)

31032 radical (Caldwell-Luc) with removal of antrochoanal polyps

(To report bilateral procedure, use 31032 with modifier 50)

31040 Pterygomaxillary fossa surgery, any approach

(For transantral ligation of internal maxillary artery, use 30920)

31050 Sinusotomy, sphenoid, with or without biopsy;

31051 with mucosal stripping or removal of polyp(s)

31070 Sinusotomy frontal; external, simple (trephine operation)

(For frontal intranasal sinusotomy, use 31276)

31075 transorbital, unilateral (for mucocele or osteoma, Lynch type)

31080 obliterative without osteoplastic flap, brow incision (includes ablation)

31081 obliterative, without osteoplastic flap, coronal incision (includes ablation)

31084 obliterative, with osteoplastic flap, brow incision

31085 obliterative, with osteoplastic flap, coronal incision

31086 nonobliterative, with osteoplastic flap, brow incision

31087 nonobliterative, with osteoplastic flap, coronal incision

31090 Sinusotomy, unilateral, three or more paranasal sinuses (frontal, maxillary, ethmoid, sphenoid)

Excision

31200 Ethmoidectomy; intranasal, anterior

31201 intranasal, total

31205 extranasal, total

31225 Maxillectomy; without orbital exenteration

31230 with orbital exenteration (en bloc)

(For orbital exenteration only, see 65110 et seq)

(For skin grafts, see 15120 et seq)

Endoscopy

A surgical sinus endoscopy includes a sinusotomy (when appropriate) and diagnostic endoscopy.

Codes 31231-31294 are used to report unilateral procedures unless otherwise specified.

The codes 31231-31235 for diagnostic evaluation refer to employing a nasal/sinus endoscope to inspect the interior of the nasal cavity and the middle and superior meatus, the turbinates, and the spheno-ethmoid recess. Any time a diagnostic evaluation is performed all these areas would be inspected and a separate code is not reported for each area.

31231 Nasal endoscopy, diagnostic, unilateral or bilateral (separate procedure)

31233 Nasal/sinus endoscopy, diagnostic with maxillary sinusoscopy (via inferior meatus or canine fossa puncture)

31235 Nasal/sinus endoscopy, diagnostic with sphenoid sinusoscopy (via puncture of sphenoidal face or cannulation of ostium)

31237 Nasal/sinus endoscopy, surgical; with biopsy, polypectomy or debridement (separate procedure)

31238 with control of nasal hemorrhage

31239 with dacryocystorhinostomy

31240 with concha bullosa resection

(For endoscopic osteomeatal complex [OMC] resection with antrostomy and/or anterior ethmoidectomy, with or without removal of polyp[s], use 31254 and 31256)

(For endoscopic osteomeatal complex [OMC] resection with antrostomy, removal of antral mucosal disease, and/or anterior ethmoidectomy, with or without removal of polyp[s], use 31254 and 31267)

(For endoscopic frontal sinus exploration, osteomeatal complex [OMC] resection and/or anterior ethmoidectomy, with or without removal of polyp[s], use 31254 and 31276)

(For endoscopic frontal sinus exploration, osteomeatal complex [OMC] resection, antrostomy, and/or anterior ethmoidectomy, with or without removal of polyp[s], use 31254, 31256, and 31276)

(For endoscopic nasal diagnostic endoscopy, see 31231-31235)

(For endoscopic osteomeatal complex [OMC] resection, frontal sinus exploration, antrostomy, removal of antral mucosal disease, and/or anterior ethmoidectomy, with or without removal of polyp[s], use 31254, 31267, and 31276)

31254 Nasal/sinus endoscopy, surgical; with ethmoidectomy, partial (anterior)

31255 with ethmoidectomy, total (anterior and posterior)

31256 Nasal/sinus endoscopy, surgical, with maxillary antrostomy;

(For endoscopic anterior and posterior ethmoidectomy [APE] and antrostomy, with or without removal of polyp[s], use 31255 and 31256)

(For endoscopic anterior and posterior ethmoidectomy [APE], antrostomy and removal of antral mucosal disease, with or without removal of polyp[s], use 31255 and 31267)

(For endoscopic anterior and posterior ethmoidectomy [APE], and frontal sinus exploration, with or without removal of polyp[s], use 31255 and 31276)

31267 with removal of tissue from maxillary sinus

(For endoscopic anterior and posterior ethmoidectomy [APE], and frontal sinus exploration and antrostomy, with or without removal of polyp[s], use 31255, 31256, and 31276)

(For endoscopic anterior and posterior ethmoidectomy [APE], frontal sinus exploration, antrostomy, and removal of antral mucosal disease, with or without removal of polyp[s], use 31255, 31267, and 31276)

31276 Nasal/sinus endoscopy, surgical with frontal sinus exploration, with or without removal of tissue from frontal sinus

(For endoscopic anterior and posterior ethmoidectomy and sphenoidotomy [APS], with or without removal of polyp[s], use 31255, 31287 or 31288)

(For endoscopic anterior and posterior ethmoidectomy and sphenoidotomy [APS], and antrostomy, with or without removal of polyp[s], use 31255, 31256, and 31287 or 31288)

(For endoscopic anterior and posterior ethmoidectomy and sphenoidotomy [APS], antrostomy and removal of antral mucosal disease, with or without removal of polyp[s], use 31255, 31267, and 31287 or 31288)

(For endoscopic anterior and posterior ethmoidectomy and sphenoidotomy [APS], and frontal sinus exploration with or without removal of polyp[s], use 31255, 31287 or 31288, and 31276)

(For endoscopic anterior and posterior ethmoidectomy and sphenoidotomy [APS], with or without removal of polyp[s], with frontal sinus exploration and antrostomy, use 31255, 31256, 31287 or 31288, and 31276)

(For unilateral endoscopy of two or more sinuses, see 31231-31235)

(For endoscopic anterior and posterior ethmoidectomy and sphenoidotomy [APS], frontal sinus exploration, antrostomy and removal of antral mucosal disease, with or without removal of polyp[s], see 31255, 31267, 31287 or 31288 and 31276)

Surgery: Respiratory System

31287 Nasal/sinus endoscopy, surgical, with sphenoidotomy;

31288 with removal of tissue from the sphenoid sinus

31290 Nasal/sinus endoscopy, surgical, with repair of cerebrospinal fluid leak; ethmoid region

31291 sphenoid region

31292 Nasal/sinus endoscopy, surgical; with medial or inferior orbital wall decompression

31293 with medial orbital wall and inferior orbital wall decompression

31294 with optic nerve decompression

Other Procedures

(For hypophysectomy, transantral or transeptal approach, use 61548)

(For transcranial hypophysectomy, use 61546)

31299 Unlisted procedure, accessory sinuses

Larynx

Excision

31300 Laryngotomy (thyrotomy, laryngofissure); with removal of tumor or laryngocele, cordectomy

31320 diagnostic

31360 Laryngectomy; total, without radical neck dissection

31365 total, with radical neck dissection

31367 subtotal supraglottic, without radical neck dissection

31368 subtotal supraglottic, with radical neck dissection

31370 Partial laryngectomy (hemilaryngectomy); horizontal

31375 laterovertical

31380 anterovertical

31382 antero-latero-vertical

31390 Pharyngolaryngectomy, with radical neck dissection; without reconstruction

31395 with reconstruction

31400 Arytenoidectomy or arytenoidopexy, external approach

(For endoscopic arytenoidectomy, use 31560)

31420 Epiglottidectomy

Introduction

⊘ **31500** Intubation, endotracheal, emergency procedure

(For injection procedure for segmental bronchography, use 31656)

31502 Tracheotomy tube change prior to establishment of fistula tract

Endoscopy

For endoscopic procedures, code appropriate endoscopy of each anatomic site examined. If using operating microscope, telescope, or both, use the applicable code only once per operative session.

31505 Laryngoscopy, indirect; diagnostic (separate procedure)

31510 with biopsy

31511 with removal of foreign body

31512 with removal of lesion

31513 with vocal cord injection

31515 Laryngoscopy direct, with or without tracheoscopy; for aspiration

31520 diagnostic, newborn

(Do not report modifier 63 in conjunction with 31520)

31525 diagnostic, except newborn

31526 diagnostic, with operating microscope or telescope

(Do not report code 69990 in addition to code 31526)

31527 with insertion of obturator

31528 with dilation, initial

31529 with dilation, subsequent

31530 Laryngoscopy, direct, operative, with foreign body removal;

31531 with operating microscope or telescope

(Do not report code 69990 in addition to code 31531)

31535 Laryngoscopy, direct, operative, with biopsy;

31536 with operating microscope or telescope

(Do not report code 69990 in addition to code 31536)

31540 Laryngoscopy, direct, operative, with excision of tumor and/or stripping of vocal cords or epiglottis;

31541 with operating microscope or telescope

(Do not report code 69990 in addition to code 31541)

31545 Laryngoscopy, direct, operative, with operating microscope or telescope, with submucosal removal of non-neoplastic lesion(s) of vocal cord; reconstruction with local tissue flap(s)

31546 reconstruction with graft(s) (includes obtaining autograft)

(Do not report 31546 in addition to 20926 for graft harvest)

(For reconstruction of vocal cord with allograft, use 31599)

(Do not report 31545 or 31546 in conjunction with 31540, 31541, 69990)

31560 Laryngoscopy, direct, operative, with arytenoidectomy;

31561 with operating microscope or telescope

(Do not report code 69990 in addition to code 31561)

31570 Laryngoscopy, direct, with injection into vocal cord(s), therapeutic;

31571 with operating microscope or telescope

(Do not report code 69990 in addition to code 31571)

31575 Laryngoscopy, flexible fiberoptic; diagnostic

31576 with biopsy

31577 with removal of foreign body

31578 with removal of lesion

(To report flexible fiberoptic endoscopic evaluation of swallowing, see 92612-92613)

(To report flexible fiberoptic endoscopic evaluation with sensory testing, see 92614-92615)

(To report flexible fiberoptic endoscopic evaluation of swallowing with sensory testing, see 92616-92617)

(For flexible fiberoptic laryngoscopy as part of flexible fiberoptic endoscopic evaluation of swallowing and/or laryngeal sensory testing by cine or video recording, see 92612-92617)

31579 Laryngoscopy, flexible or rigid fiberoptic, with stroboscopy

Repair

31580 Laryngoplasty; for laryngeal web, two stage, with keel insertion and removal

31582 for laryngeal stenosis, with graft or core mold, including tracheotomy

31584 with open reduction of fracture

31587 Laryngoplasty, cricoid split

31588 Laryngoplasty, not otherwise specified (eg, for burns, reconstruction after partial laryngectomy)

31590 Laryngeal reinnervation by neuromuscular pedicle

Destruction

31595 Section recurrent laryngeal nerve, therapeutic (separate procedure), unilateral

Other Procedures

31599 Unlisted procedure, larynx

Trachea and Bronchi

Incision

31600 Tracheostomy, planned (separate procedure);

31601 younger than two years

31603 Tracheostomy, emergency procedure; transtracheal

31605 cricothyroid membrane

31610 Tracheostomy, fenestration procedure with skin flaps

(For endotracheal intubation, use 31500)

(For tracheal aspiration under direct vision, use 31515)

31611 Construction of tracheoesophageal fistula and subsequent insertion of an alaryngeal speech prosthesis (eg, voice button, Blom-Singer prosthesis)

31612 Tracheal puncture, percutaneous with transtracheal aspiration and/or injection

31613 Tracheostoma revision; simple, without flap rotation

31614 complex, with flap rotation

Endoscopy

For endoscopy procedures, code appropriate endoscopy of each anatomic site examined. Surgical bronchoscopy always includes diagnostic bronchoscopy when performed by the same physician. Codes 31622-31646 include fluoroscopic guidance, when performed.

(For tracheoscopy, see laryngoscopy codes 31515-31578)

⊙ **31615** Tracheobronchoscopy through established tracheostomy incision

⊙+ **31620** Endobronchial ultrasound (EBUS) during bronchoscopic diagnostic or therapeutic intervention(s) (List separately in addition to code for primary procedure[s])

(Use 31620 in conjunction with 31622-31646)

⊙ **31622** Bronchoscopy, rigid or flexible, with or without fluoroscopic guidance; diagnostic, with or without cell washing (separate procedure)

⊙ **31623** with brushing or protected brushings

⊙ **31624** with bronchial alveolar lavage

⊙ **31625** with bronchial or endobronchial biopsy(s), single or multiple sites

⊙ **31628** with transbronchial lung biopsy(s), single lobe

(31628 should be reported only once regardless of how many transbronchial lung biopsies are performed in a lobe)

(To report transbronchial lung biopsies performed on additional lobe, use 31632)

Surgery: Respiratory System

⊙ **31629** with transbronchial needle aspiration biopsy(s), trachea, main stem and/or lobar bronchus(i)

(31629 should be reported only once for upper airway biopsies regardless of how many transbronchial needle aspiration biopsies are performed in the upper airway or in a lobe)

(To report transbronchial needle aspiration biopsies performed on additional lobe(s), use 31633)

31630 with tracheal/bronchial dilation or closed reduction of fracture

31631 with placement of tracheal stent(s) (includes tracheal/bronchial dilation as required)

(For placement of bronchial stent, see 31636, 31637)

(For revision of tracheal/bronchial stent, use 31638)

✚ **31632** with transbronchial lung biopsy(s), each additional lobe (List separately in addition to code for primary procedure)

(Use 31632 in conjunction with 31628)

(31632 should be reported only once regardless of how many transbronchial lung biopsies are performed in a lobe)

✚ **31633** with transbronchial needle aspiration biopsy(s), each additional lobe (List separately in addition to code for primary procedure)

(Use 31633 in conjunction with 31629)

(31633 should be reported only once regardless of how many transbronchial needle aspiration biopsies are performed in the trachea or the additional lobe)

⊙ **31635** with removal of foreign body

31636 with placement of bronchial stent(s) (includes tracheal/bronchial dilation as required), initial bronchus

✚ **31637** each additional major bronchus stented (List separately in addition to code for primary procedure)

(Use 31637 in conjunction with 31636)

31638 with revision of tracheal or bronchial stent inserted at previous session (includes tracheal/bronchial dilation as required)

31640 with excision of tumor

31641 Bronchoscopy (rigid or flexible); with destruction of tumor or relief of stenosis by any method other than excision (eg, laser therapy, cryotherapy)

(For bronchoscopic photodynamic therapy, report 31641 in addition to 96570, 96571 as appropriate)

31643 with placement of catheter(s) for intracavitary radioelement application

►(For intracavitary radioelement application, see 77761-77763, 77785-77787)◄

⊙ **31645** with therapeutic aspiration of tracheobronchial tree, initial (eg, drainage of lung abscess)

⊙ **31646** with therapeutic aspiration of tracheobronchial tree, subsequent

(For catheter aspiration of tracheobronchial tree at bedside, use 31725)

⊙ **31656** with injection of contrast material for segmental bronchography (fiberscope only)

(For radiological supervision and interpretation, see 71040, 71060)

Introduction

(For endotracheal intubation, use 31500)

(For tracheal aspiration under direct vision, see 31515)

(31700, 31708, 31710 have been deleted)

31715 Transtracheal injection for bronchography

(For radiological supervision and interpretation, see 71040, 71060)

(For prolonged services, see 99354-99360)

31717 Catheterization with bronchial brush biopsy

31720 Catheter aspiration (separate procedure); nasotracheal

⊙ **31725** tracheobronchial with fiberscope, bedside

31730 Transtracheal (percutaneous) introduction of needle wire dilator/stent or indwelling tube for oxygen therapy

Excision, Repair

31750 Tracheoplasty; cervical

31755 tracheopharyngeal fistulization, each stage

31760 intrathoracic

31766 Carinal reconstruction

31770 Bronchoplasty; graft repair

31775 excision stenosis and anastomosis

(For lobectomy and bronchoplasty, use 32501)

31780 Excision tracheal stenosis and anastomosis; cervical

31781 cervicothoracic

31785 Excision of tracheal tumor or carcinoma; cervical

31786 thoracic

31800 Suture of tracheal wound or injury; cervical

31805 intrathoracic

31820 Surgical closure tracheostomy or fistula; without plastic repair

31825 with plastic repair

(For repair tracheoesophageal fistula, see 43305, 43312)

31830 Revision of tracheostomy scar

Other Procedures

31899 Unlisted procedure, trachea, bronchi

Lungs and Pleura

Incision

(32000 has been deleted. To report, use 32421)

(32002 has been deleted. To report, use 32422)

(32005 has been deleted. To report, use 32560)

(32019 has been deleted. To report, use 32550)

(32020 has been deleted. To report, use 32551)

32035 Thoracostomy; with rib resection for empyema

32036 with open flap drainage for empyema

32095 Thoracotomy, limited, for biopsy of lung or pleura

(To report wound exploration due to penetrating trauma without thoractomy, use 20102)

32100 Thoracotomy, major; with exploration and biopsy

(Do not report 32100 in conjunction with 19260, 19271, 19272, 32503, 32504)

32110 with control of traumatic hemorrhage and/or repair of lung tear

32120 for postoperative complications

32124 with open intrapleural pneumonolysis

32140 with cyst(s) removal, with or without a pleural procedure

32141 with excision-plication of bullae, with or without any pleural procedure

(For lung volume reduction, use 32491)

32150 with removal of intrapleural foreign body or fibrin deposit

32151 with removal of intrapulmonary foreign body

32160 with cardiac massage

(For segmental or other resections of lung, see 32480-32504)

32200 Pneumonostomy; with open drainage of abscess or cyst

⊙ **32201** with percutaneous drainage of abscess or cyst

(For radiological supervision and interpretation, use 75989)

32215 Pleural scarification for repeat pneumothorax

32220 Decortication, pulmonary (separate procedure); total

32225 partial

Excision

32310 Pleurectomy, parietal (separate procedure)

32320 Decortication and parietal pleurectomy

32400 Biopsy, pleura; percutaneous needle

(If imaging guidance is performed, see 76942, 77002, 77012, 77021)

(For fine needle aspiration, use 10021 or 10022)

(For evaluation of fine needle aspirate, see 88172, 88173)

32402 open

32405 Biopsy, lung or mediastinum, percutaneous needle

(For radiological supervision and interpretation, see 76942, 77002, 77012, 77021)

(For fine needle aspiration, use 10022)

(For evaluation of fine needle aspirate, see 88172, 88173)

Removal

32420 Pneumocentesis, puncture of lung for aspiration

32421 Thoracentesis, puncture of pleural cavity for aspiration, initial or subsequent

(If imaging guidance is performed, see 76942, 77002, 77012)

(For total lung lavage, use 32997)

32422 Thoracentesis with insertion of tube, includes water seal (eg, for pneumothorax), when performed (separate procedure)

(Do not report 32422 in conjunction with 19260, 19271, 19272, 32503, 32504)

(If imaging guidance is performed, see 76942, 77002, 77012)

32440 Removal of lung, total pneumonectomy;

32442 with resection of segment of trachea followed by broncho-tracheal anastomosis (sleeve pneumonectomy)

32445 extrapleural

(For extrapleural pneumonectomy, with empyemectomy, use 32445 and 32540)

(If lung resection is performed with chest wall tumor resection, report the appropriate chest wall tumor resection code, 19260-19272, in addition to lung resection code 32440-32445)

32480 Removal of lung, other than total pneumonectomy; single lobe (lobectomy)

32482 two lobes (bilobectomy)

32484 single segment (segmentectomy)

(For removal of lung with bronchoplasty, use 32501)

32486 with circumferential resection of segment of bronchus followed by broncho-bronchial anastomosis (sleeve lobectomy)

32488 all remaining lung following previous removal of a portion of lung (completion pneumonectomy)

(For total or segmental lobectomy, with concomitant decortication, use 32320 and the appropriate removal of lung code)

32491 excision-plication of emphysematous lung(s) (bullous or non-bullous) for lung volume reduction, sternal split or transthoracic approach, with or without any pleural procedure

32500 wedge resection, single or multiple

(If lung resection is performed with chest wall tumor resection, report the appropriate chest wall tumor resection code, 19260-19272, in addition to lung resection code 32480-32500)

+ **32501** Resection and repair of portion of bronchus (bronchoplasty) when performed at time of lobectomy or segmentectomy (List separately in addition to code for primary procedure)

(Use 32501 in conjunction with 32480, 32482, 32484)

(32501 is to be used when a portion of the bronchus to preserved lung is removed and requires plastic closure to preserve function of that preserved lung. It is not to be used for closure for the proximal end of a resected bronchus)

32503 Resection of apical lung tumor (eg, Pancoast tumor), including chest wall resection, rib(s) resection(s), neurovascular dissection, when performed; without chest wall reconstruction(s)

32504 with chest wall reconstruction

(Do not report 32503, 32504 in conjunction with 19260, 19271, 19272, 32100, 32422, 32551)

(For performance of lung resection in conjunction with chest wall resection, see 19260, 19271, 19272 and 32480-32500, 32503, 32504)

32540 Extrapleural enucleation of empyema (empyemectomy)

(For extrapleural enucleation of empyema (empyemectomy) with lobectomy, use 32540 and the appropriate removal of lung code)

Introduction

⊙ **32550** Insertion of indwelling tunneled pleural catheter with cuff

►(Do not report 32550 in conjunction with 32421, 32422)◄

(If imaging guidance is performed, use 75989)

⊙ **32551** Tube thoracostomy, includes water seal (eg, for abscess, hemothorax, empyema), when performed (separate procedure)

(Do not report 32551 in conjunction with 19260, 19271, 19272, 32503, 32504)

(If imaging guidance is performed, use 75989)

Destruction

32560 Chemical pleurodesis (eg, for recurrent or persistent pneumothorax)

Endoscopy

Surgical thoracoscopy always includes diagnostic thoracoscopy.

For endoscopic procedures, code appropriate endoscopy of each anatomic site examined.

32601 Thoracoscopy, diagnostic (separate procedure); lungs and pleural space, without biopsy

32602 lungs and pleural space, with biopsy

32603 pericardial sac, without biopsy

32604 pericardial sac, with biopsy

32605 mediastinal space, without biopsy

32606 mediastinal space, with biopsy

(Surgical thoracoscopy always includes diagnostic thoracoscopy)

32650 Thoracoscopy, surgical; with pleurodesis (eg, mechanical or chemical)

32651 with partial pulmonary decortication

32652 with total pulmonary decortication, including intrapleural pneumonolysis

32653 with removal of intrapleural foreign body or fibrin deposit

32654 with control of traumatic hemorrhage

32655 with excision-plication of bullae, including any pleural procedure

32656 with parietal pleurectomy

32657 with wedge resection of lung, single or multiple

32658 with removal of clot or foreign body from pericardial sac

32659 with creation of pericardial window or partial resection of pericardial sac for drainage

32660 with total pericardiectomy

32661 with excision of pericardial cyst, tumor, or mass

32662 with excision of mediastinal cyst, tumor, or mass

32663 with lobectomy, total or segmental

32664 with thoracic sympathectomy

32665 with esophagomyotomy (Heller type)

(For exploratory thoracoscopy, and exploratory thoracoscopy with biopsy, see 32601-32606)

Repair

32800 Repair lung hernia through chest wall

32810 Closure of chest wall following open flap drainage for empyema (Clagett type procedure)

32815 Open closure of major bronchial fistula

32820 Major reconstruction, chest wall (posttraumatic)

Lung Transplantation

Lung allotransplantation involves three distinct components of physician work:

1. ***Cadaver donor pneumonectomy(s)***, which include(s) harvesting the allograft and cold preservation of the allograft (perfusing with cold preservation solution and cold maintenance) (use 32850).
2. ***Backbench work***:

   Preparation of a cadaver donor single lung allograft prior to transplantation, including dissection of the allograft from surrounding soft tissues to prepare the pulmonary venous/atrial cuff, pulmonary artery, and bronchus unilaterally (use 32855).

   Preparation of a cadaver donor double lung allograft prior to transplantation, including dissection of the allograft from surrounding soft tissues to prepare the pulmonary venous/atrial cuff, pulmonary artery, and bronchus bilaterally (use 32856).
3. ***Recipient lung allotransplantation***, which includes transplantation of a single or double lung allograft and care of the recipient (see 32851-32854).

32850 Donor pneumonectomy(s) (including cold preservation), from cadaver donor

32851 Lung transplant, single; without cardiopulmonary bypass

32852 with cardiopulmonary bypass

32853 Lung transplant, double (bilateral sequential or en bloc); without cardiopulmonary bypass

32854 with cardiopulmonary bypass

32855 Backbench standard preparation of cadaver donor lung allograft prior to transplantation, including dissection of allograft from surrounding soft tissues to prepare pulmonary venous/atrial cuff, pulmonary artery, and bronchus; unilateral

32856 bilateral

(For repair or resection procedures on the donor lung, see 32491, 32500, 35216, or 35276)

Surgical Collapse Therapy; Thoracoplasty

(See also 32503, 32504)

32900 Resection of ribs, extrapleural, all stages

32905 Thoracoplasty, Schede type or extrapleural (all stages);

32906 with closure of bronchopleural fistula

(For open closure of major bronchial fistula, use 32815)

(For resection of first rib for thoracic outlet compression, see 21615, 21616)

32940 Pneumonolysis, extraperiosteal, including filling or packing procedures

32960 Pneumothorax, therapeutic, intrapleural injection of air

Other Procedures

32997 Total lung lavage (unilateral)

(For bronchoscopic bronchial alveolar lavage, use 31624)

32998 Ablation therapy for reduction or eradication of one or more pulmonary tumor(s) including pleura or chest wall when involved by tumor extension, percutaneous, radiofrequency, unilateral

(For imaging guidance and monitoring, see 76940, 77013, 77022)

32999 Unlisted procedure, lungs and pleura

Notes

Cardiovascular System

Selective vascular catheterizations should be coded to include introduction and all lesser order selective catheterizations used in the approach (eg, the description for a selective right middle cerebral artery catheterization includes the introduction and placement catheterization of the right common and internal carotid arteries).

Additional second and/or third order arterial catheterizations within the same family of arteries supplied by a single first order artery should be expressed by 36218 or 36248. Additional first order or higher catheterizations in vascular families supplied by a first order vessel different from a previously selected and coded family should be separately coded using the conventions described above.

(For monitoring, operation of pump and other nonsurgical services, see 99190-99192, 99291, 99292, 99354-99360)

(For other medical or laboratory related services, see appropriate section)

(For radiological supervision and interpretation, see 75600-75978)

Heart and Pericardium

Pericardium

⊙ **33010** Pericardiocentesis; initial

(For radiological supervision and interpretation, use 76930)

⊙ **33011** subsequent

(For radiological supervision and interpretation, use 76930)

33015 Tube pericardiostomy

33020 Pericardiotomy for removal of clot or foreign body (primary procedure)

33025 Creation of pericardial window or partial resection for drainage

33030 Pericardiectomy, subtotal or complete; without cardiopulmonary bypass

33031 with cardiopulmonary bypass

33050 Excision of pericardial cyst or tumor

Cardiac Tumor

33120 Excision of intracardiac tumor, resection with cardiopulmonary bypass

33130 Resection of external cardiac tumor

Transmyocardial Revascularization

33140 Transmyocardial laser revascularization, by thoracotomy; (separate procedure)

✚ **33141** performed at the time of other open cardiac procedure(s) (List separately in addition to code for primary procedure)

(Use 33141 in conjunction with 33400-33496, 33510-33536, 33542)

Pacemaker or Pacing Cardioverter-Defibrillator

A pacemaker system includes a pulse generator containing electronics, a battery, and one or more electrodes (leads). Pulse generators are placed in a subcutaneous "pocket" created in either a subclavicular site or underneath the abdominal muscles just below the ribcage. Electrodes may be inserted through a vein (transvenous) or they may be placed on the surface of the heart (epicardial). The epicardial location of electrodes requires a thoracotomy for electrode insertion.

A single chamber pacemaker system includes a pulse generator and one electrode inserted in either the atrium or ventricle. A dual chamber pacemaker system includes a pulse generator and one electrode inserted in the right atrium and one electrode inserted in the right ventricle. In certain circumstances, an additional electrode may be required to achieve pacing of the left ventricle (bi-ventricular pacing). In this event, transvenous (cardiac vein) placement of the electrode should be separately reported using code 33224 or 33225. Epicardial placement of the electrode should be separately reported using 33202-33203.

Like a pacemaker system, a pacing cardioverter-defibrillator system includes a pulse generator and electrodes, although pacing cardioverter-defibrillators may require multiple leads, even when only a single chamber is being paced. A pacing cardioverter-defibrillator system may be inserted in a single chamber (pacing in the ventricle) or in dual chambers (pacing in atrium and ventricle). These devices use a combination of antitachycardia pacing, low-energy cardioversion or defibrillating shocks to treat ventricular tachycardia or ventricular fibrillation.

Pacing cardioverter-defibrillator pulse generators may be implanted in a subcutaneous infraclavicular pocket or in an abdominal pocket. Removal of a pacing cardioverter-defibrillator pulse generator requires opening of the existing subcutaneous pocket and disconnection of the pulse generator from its electrode(s). A thoracotomy (or laparotomy in the case of abdominally placed pulse generators) is not required to remove the pulse generator.

The electrodes (leads) of a pacing cardioverter-defibrillator system are positioned in the heart via the venous system (transvenously), in most circumstances. In certain circumstances, an additional electrode may be required to achieve pacing of the left ventricle (bi-ventricular pacing). In this event, transvenous (cardiac vein) placement of the electrode should be separately reported using code 33224 or 33225. Epicardial placement of the electrode should be separately reported using 33202-33203.

Electrode positioning on the epicardial surface of the heart requires thoracotomy, or thoracoscopic placement of the leads. Removal of electrode(s) may first be attempted by transvenous extraction (code 33244). However, if transvenous extraction is unsuccessful, a thoracotomy may be required to remove the electrodes (code 33243). Use codes 33212, 33213, 33240 as appropriate in addition to the thoracotomy or endoscopic epicardial lead placement codes to report the insertion of the generator if done by the same physician during thc same session.

When the "battery" of a pacemaker or pacing cardioverter-defibrillator is changed, it is actually the pulse generator that is changed. Replacement of a pulse generator should be reported with a code for removal of the pulse generator and another code for insertion of a pulse generator.

Repositioning of a pacemaker electrode, pacing cardioverter-defibrillator electrode(s), or a left ventricular pacing electrode is reported using 33215 or 33226, as appropriate. Replacement of a pacemaker electrode, pacing cardioverter-defibrillator electrode(s), or a left ventricular pacing electrode is reported using 33206-33208, 33210-33213, or 33224, as appropriate.

►(For electronic, telephonic analysis of internal pacemaker system, see 93279, 93280, 93288, 93293, 93294)◄

(For radiological supervision and interpretation with insertion of pacemaker, use 71090)

(33200, 33201 have been deleted)

33202 Insertion of epicardial electrode(s); open incision (eg, thoracotomy, median sternotomy, subxiphoid approach)

33203 endoscopic approach (eg, thoracoscopy, pericardioscopy)

(When epicardial lead placement is performed by the same physician at the same session as insertion of the generator, report 33202, 33203 in conjunction with 33212, 33213, as appropriate)

⊙ **33206** Insertion or replacement of permanent pacemaker with transvenous electrode(s); atrial

⊙ **33207** ventricular

⊙ **33208** atrial and ventricular

(Codes 33206-33208 include subcutaneous insertion of the pulse generator and transvenous placement of electrode[s])

⊙ **33210** Insertion or replacement of temporary transvenous single chamber cardiac electrode or pacemaker catheter (separate procedure)

⊙ **33211** Insertion or replacement of temporary transvenous dual chamber pacing electrodes (separate procedure)

⊙ **33212** Insertion or replacement of pacemaker pulse generator only; single chamber, atrial or ventricular

⊙ **33213** dual chamber

(Use 33212, 33213, as appropriate, in conjunction with the epicardial lead placement codes 33202, 33203 to report the insertion of the generator when done by the same physician during the same session)

⊙ **33214** Upgrade of implanted pacemaker system, conversion of single chamber system to dual chamber system (includes removal of previously placed pulse generator, testing of existing lead, insertion of new lead, insertion of new pulse generator)

(When epicardial electrode placement is performed, report 33214 in conjunction with 33202, 33203)

33215 Repositioning of previously implanted transvenous pacemaker or pacing cardioverter-defibrillator (right atrial or right ventricular) electrode

⊙ **33216** Insertion of a transvenous electrode; single chamber (one electrode) permanent pacemaker or single chamber pacing cardioverter-defibrillator

⊙ **33217** dual chamber (two electrodes) permanent pacemaker or dual chamber pacing cardioverter-defibrillator

(Do not report 33216-33217 in conjunction with 33214)

⊙ **33218** Repair of single transvenous electrode for a single chamber, permanent pacemaker or single chamber pacing cardioverter-defibrillator

(For atrial or ventricular single chamber repair of pacemaker electrode[s] with replacement of pulse generator, see 33212 or 33213 and 33218 or 33220)

⊙ **33220** Repair of two transvenous electrodes for a dual chamber permanent pacemaker or dual chamber pacing cardioverter-defibrillator

⊙ **33222** Revision or relocation of skin pocket for pacemaker

⊙ **33223** Revision of skin pocket for single or dual chamber pacing cardioverter-defibrillator

33224 Insertion of pacing electrode, cardiac venous system, for left ventricular pacing, with attachment to previously placed pacemaker or pacing cardioverter-defibrillator pulse generator (including revision of pocket, removal, insertion, and/or replacement of generator)

(When epicardial electrode placement is performed, report 33224 in conjunction with 33202, 33203)

+ 33225 Insertion of pacing electrode, cardiac venous system, for left ventricular pacing, at time of insertion of pacing cardioverter-defibrillator or pacemaker pulse generator (including upgrade to dual chamber system) (List separately in addition to code for primary procedure)

(Use 33225 in conjunction with 33206, 33207, 33208, 33212, 33213, 33214, 33216, 33217, 33222, 33233, 33234, 33235, 33240, 33249)

33226 Repositioning of previously implanted cardiac venous system (left ventricular) electrode (including removal, insertion and/or replacement of generator)

⊙ 33233 Removal of permanent pacemaker pulse generator

⊙ 33234 Removal of transvenous pacemaker electrode(s); single lead system, atrial or ventricular

⊙ 33235 dual lead system

33236 Removal of permanent epicardial pacemaker and electrodes by thoracotomy; single lead system, atrial or ventricular

33237 dual lead system

33238 Removal of permanent transvenous electrode(s) by thoracotomy

⊙ 33240 Insertion of single or dual chamber pacing cardioverter-defibrillator pulse generator

(Use 33240, as appropriate, in addition to the epicardial lead placement codes to report the insertion of the generator when done by the same physician during the same session)

⊙ 33241 Subcutaneous removal of single or dual chamber pacing cardioverter-defibrillator pulse generator

(For removal of electrode[s] by thoracotomy, use 33243 in conjunction with 33241)

(For removal of electrode[s] by transvenous extraction, use 33244 in conjunction with 33241)

(For removal and reinsertion of a pacing cardioverter-defibrillator system (pulse generator and electrodes), report 33241 and 33243 or 33244 and 33249)

(For repair of implantable cardioverter-defibrillator pulse generator and/or leads, see 33218, 33220)

33243 Removal of single or dual chamber pacing cardioverter-defibrillator electrode(s); by thoracotomy

⊙ 33244 by transvenous extraction

(For subcutaneous removal of the pulse generator, use 33241 in conjunction with 33243 or 33244)

(33245, 33246 have been deleted)

⊙ 33249 Insertion or repositioning of electrode lead(s) for single or dual chamber pacing cardioverter-defibrillator and insertion of pulse generator

(For removal and reinsertion of a pacing cardioverter-defibrillator system (pulse generator and electrodes), report 33241 and 33243 or 33244 and 33249)

(For insertion of implantable cardioverter-defibrillator lead(s), without thoracotomy, use 33216)

Electrophysiologic Operative Procedures

This family of codes describes the surgical treatment of supraventricular dysrhythmias. Tissue ablation, disruption, and reconstruction can be accomplished by many methods including surgical incision or through the use of a variety of energy sources (eg, radiofrequency, cryotherapy, microwave, ultrasound, laser). If excision or isolation of the left atrial appendage by any method, including stapling, oversewing, ligation, or plication, is performed in conjunction with any of the atrial tissue ablation and reconstruction (maze) procedures (33254-33259, 33265-33266), it is considered part of the procedure. Codes 33254-33256 are only to be reported when there is no concurrently performed procedure that requires median sternotomy or cardiopulmonary bypass. The appropriate atrial tissue ablation add-on code, 33257, 33258, 33259 should be reported in addition to an open cardiac procedure requiring sternotomy or cardiopulmonary bypass if performed concurrently.

Definitions

Limited operative ablation and reconstruction includes:

Surgical isolation of triggers of supraventricular dysrhythmias by operative ablation that isolates the pulmonary veins or other anatomically defined triggers in the left or right atrium.

Extensive operative ablation and reconstruction includes:

1. The services included in "*limited*"
2. Additional ablation of atrial tissue to eliminate sustained supraventricular dysrhythmias. This must include operative ablation that involves either the right atrium, the atrial septum, or left atrium in continuity with the atrioventricular annulus.

Incision

33250 Operative ablation of supraventricular arrhythmogenic focus or pathway (eg, Wolff-Parkinson-White, atrioventricular node re-entry), tract(s) and/or focus (foci); without cardiopulmonary bypass

►(For intraoperative pacing and mapping by a separate provider, use 93631)◄

33251 with cardiopulmonary bypass

(33253 has been deleted. To report, use 33254–33256)

Surgery: Cardiovascular System

33254 Operative tissue ablation and reconstruction of atria, limited (eg, modified maze procedure)

33255 Operative tissue ablation and reconstruction of atria, extensive (eg, maze procedure); without cardiopulmonary bypass

33256 with cardiopulmonary bypass

►(Do not report 33254-33256 in conjunction with 32100, 32551, 33120, 33130, 33210, 33211, 33400-33507, 33510-33523, 33533-33548, 33600-33853, 33860-33864, 33910-33920)◄

+ 33257 Operative tissue ablation and reconstruction of atria, performed at the time of other cardiac procedure(s), limited (eg, modified maze procedure) (List separately in addition to code for primary procedure)

(Use 33257 in conjunction with 33120-33130, 33250-33251, 33261, 33300-33335, 33400-33496, 33500-33507, 33510-33516, 33533-33548, 33600-33619, 33641-33697, 33702-33732, 33735-33767, 33770-33814, 33840-33877, 33910-33922, 33925-33926, 33935, 33945, 33975-33980)

+ 33258 Operative tissue ablation and reconstruction of atria, performed at the time of other cardiac procedure(s), extensive (eg, maze procedure), without cardiopulmonary bypass (List separately in addition to code for primary procedure)

(Use 33258 in conjunction with 33130, 33250, 33300, 33310, 33320, 33321, 33330, 33332, 33401, 33414-33417, 33420, 33470-33472, 33501-33503, 33510-33516, 33533-33536, 33690, 33735, 33737, 33800-33813, 33840-33852, 33915, 33925 when the procedure is performed without cardiopulmonary bypass)

+ 33259 Operative tissue ablation and reconstruction of atria, performed at the time of other cardiac procedure(s), extensive (eg, maze procedure), with cardiopulmonary bypass (List separately in addition to code for primary procedure)

(Use 33259 in conjunction with 33120, 33251, 33261, 33305, 33315, 33322, 33335, 33400, 33403-33413, 33422-33468, 33474-33478, 33496, 33500, 33504-33507, 33510-33516, 33533-33548, 33600-33688, 33692-33722, 33730, 33732, 33736, 33750-33767, 33770-33781, 33786-33788, 33814, 33853, 33860-33877, 33910, 33916-33922, 33926, 33935, 33945, 33975-33980 when the procedure is performed with cardiopulmonary bypass)

(Do not report 33257, 33258 and 33259 in conjunction with 32551, 33210, 33211, 33254-33256, 33265, 33266)

33261 Operative ablation of ventricular arrhythmogenic focus with cardiopulmonary bypass

Endoscopy

33265 Endoscopy, surgical; operative tissue ablation and reconstruction of atria, limited (eg, modified maze procedure), without cardiopulmonary bypass

33266 operative tissue ablation and reconstruction of atria, extensive (eg, maze procedure), without cardiopulmonary bypass

(Do not report 33265-33266 in conjunction with 32551, 33210, 33211)

Patient-Activated Event Recorder

33282 Implantation of patient-activated cardiac event recorder

►(Initial implantation includes programming. For subsequent electronic analysis and/or reprogramming, use 93285, 93291, 93298)◄

33284 Removal of an implantable, patient-activated cardiac event recorder

Wounds of the Heart and Great Vessels

33300 Repair of cardiac wound; without bypass

33305 with cardiopulmonary bypass

33310 Cardiotomy, exploratory (includes removal of foreign body, atrial or ventricular thrombus); without bypass

33315 with cardiopulmonary bypass

(Do not report removal of thrombus [33310-33315] in conjunction with other cardiac procedures unless a separate incision in the heart is required to remove the atrial or ventricular thrombus)

(If removal of thrombus with cardiopulmonary bypass [33315] is reported in conjunction with 33120, 33130, 33420-33430, 33460-33468, 33496, 33542, 33545, 33641-33647, 33670, 33681, 33975-33980 which requires a separate heart incision, report 33315 with modifier 59)

33320 Suture repair of aorta or great vessels; without shunt or cardiopulmonary bypass

33321 with shunt bypass

33322 with cardiopulmonary bypass

33330 Insertion of graft, aorta or great vessels; without shunt, or cardiopulmonary bypass

33332 with shunt bypass

33335 with cardiopulmonary bypass

Cardiac Valves

(For multiple valve procedures, see 33400-33478 and add modifier 51 to the secondary valve procedure code)

Aortic Valve

33400 Valvuloplasty, aortic valve; open, with cardiopulmonary bypass

33401 open, with inflow occlusion

33403 using transventricular dilation, with cardiopulmonary bypass

(Do not report modifier 63 in conjunction with 33401, 33403)

33404 Construction of apical-aortic conduit

33405 Replacement, aortic valve, with cardiopulmonary bypass; with prosthetic valve other than homograft or stentless valve

33406 with allograft valve (freehand)

(For aortic valve valvotomy, [commissurotomy] with inflow occlusion, use 33401)

(For aortic valve valvotomy, [commissurotomy] with cardiopulmonary bypass, use 33403)

33410 with stentless tissue valve

33411 Replacement, aortic valve; with aortic annulus enlargement, noncoronary cusp

33412 with transventricular aortic annulus enlargement (Konno procedure)

33413 by translocation of autologous pulmonary valve with allograft replacement of pulmonary valve (Ross procedure)

33414 Repair of left ventricular outflow tract obstruction by patch enlargement of the outflow tract

33415 Resection or incision of subvalvular tissue for discrete subvalvular aortic stenosis

33416 Ventriculomyotomy (-myectomy) for idiopathic hypertrophic subaortic stenosis (eg, asymmetric septal hypertrophy)

33417 Aortoplasty (gusset) for supravalvular stenosis

Mitral Valve

33420 Valvotomy, mitral valve; closed heart

33422 open heart, with cardiopulmonary bypass

33425 Valvuloplasty, mitral valve, with cardiopulmonary bypass;

33426 with prosthetic ring

33427 radical reconstruction, with or without ring

33430 Replacement, mitral valve, with cardiopulmonary bypass

Tricuspid Valve

33460 Valvectomy, tricuspid valve, with cardiopulmonary bypass

33463 Valvuloplasty, tricuspid valve; without ring insertion

33464 with ring insertion

33465 Replacement, tricuspid valve, with cardiopulmonary bypass

33468 Tricuspid valve repositioning and plication for Ebstein anomaly

Pulmonary Valve

33470 Valvotomy, pulmonary valve, closed heart; transventricular

(Do not report modifier 63 in conjunction with 33470)

33471 via pulmonary artery

(To report percutaneous valvuloplasty of pulmonary valve, use 92990)

33472 Valvotomy, pulmonary valve, open heart; with inflow occlusion

(Do not report modifier 63 in conjunction with 33472)

33474 with cardiopulmonary bypass

33475 Replacement, pulmonary valve

33476 Right ventricular resection for infundibular stenosis, with or without commissurotomy

33478 Outflow tract augmentation (gusset), with or without commissurotomy or infundibular resection

(Use 33478 in conjunction with 33768 when a cavopulmonary anastomosis to a second superior vena cava is performed)

Other Valvular Procedures

33496 Repair of non-structural prosthetic valve dysfunction with cardiopulmonary bypass (separate procedure)

(For reoperation, use 33530 in addition to 33496)

Coronary Artery Anomalies

Basic procedures include endarterectomy or angioplasty.

33500 Repair of coronary arteriovenous or arteriocardiac chamber fistula; with cardiopulmonary bypass

33501 without cardiopulmonary bypass

33502 Repair of anomalous coronary artery from pulmonary artery origin; by ligation

33503 by graft, without cardiopulmonary bypass

(Do not report modifier 63 in conjunction with 33502, 33503)

33504 by graft, with cardiopulmonary bypass

33505 with construction of intrapulmonary artery tunnel (Takeuchi procedure)

33506 by translocation from pulmonary artery to aorta

(Do not report modifier 63 in conjunction with 33505, 33506)

33507 Repair of anomalous (eg, intramural) aortic origin of coronary artery by unroofing or translocation

Endoscopy

Surgical vascular endoscopy always includes diagnostic endoscopy.

+ 33508 Endoscopy, surgical, including video-assisted harvest of vein(s) for coronary artery bypass procedure (List separately in addition to code for primary procedure)

(Use 33508 in conjunction with 33510-33523)

(For open harvest of upper extremity vein procedure, use 35500)

Venous Grafting Only for Coronary Artery Bypass

The following codes are used to report coronary artery bypass procedures using venous grafts only. These codes should NOT be used to report the performance of coronary artery bypass procedures using arterial grafts and venous grafts during the same procedure. See 33517-33523 and 33533-33536 for reporting combined arterial-venous grafts.

Procurement of the saphenous vein graft is included in the description of the work for 33510-33516 and should not be reported as a separate service or co-surgery. To report harvesting of an upper extremity vein, use 35500 in addition to the bypass procedure. To report harvesting of a femoropopliteal vein segment, report 35572 in addition to the bypass procedure. When surgical assistant performs graft procurement, add modifier 80 to 33510-33516.

33510 Coronary artery bypass, vein only; single coronary venous graft

33511 two coronary venous grafts

33512 three coronary venous grafts

33513 four coronary venous grafts

33514 five coronary venous grafts

33516 six or more coronary venous grafts

Combined Arterial-Venous Grafting for Coronary Bypass

The following codes are used to report coronary artery bypass procedures using venous grafts and arterial grafts during the same procedure. These codes may NOT be used alone.

To report combined arterial-venous grafts it is necessary to report two codes: 1) the appropriate combined arterial-venous graft code (33517-33523); and 2) the appropriate arterial graft code (33533-33536).

Procurement of the saphenous vein graft is included in the description of the work for 33517-33523 and should not be reported as a separate service or co-surgery. Procurement of the artery for grafting is included in the description of the work for 33533-33536 and should not be reported as a separate service or co-surgery, except when an upper extremity artery (eg, radial artery) is procured. To report harvesting of an upper extremity artery, use 35600 in addition to the bypass procedure. To report harvesting of an upper extremity vein, use 35500 in addition to the bypass procedure. To report harvesting of a femoropopliteal vein segment, report 35572 in addition to the bypass procedure. When surgical assistant performs arterial and/or venous graft procurement, add modifier 80 to 33517-33523, 33533-33536, as appropriate.

+ 33517 Coronary artery bypass, using venous graft(s) and arterial graft(s); single vein graft (List separately in addition to code for primary procedure)

(Use 33517 in conjunction with 33533-33536)

+ 33518 two venous grafts (List separately in addition to code for primary procedure)

(Use 33518 in conjunction with 33533-33536)

+ 33519 three venous grafts (List separately in addition to code for primary procedure)

(Use 33519 in conjunction with 33533-33536)

+ 33521 four venous grafts (List separately in addition to code for primary procedure)

(Use 33521 in conjunction with 33533-33536)

+ 33522 five venous grafts (List separately in addition to code for primary procedure)

(Use 33522 in conjunction with 33533-33536)

+ 33523 six or more venous grafts (List separately in addition to code for primary procedure)

(Use 33523 in conjunction with 33533-33536)

+ 33530 Reoperation, coronary artery bypass procedure or valve procedure, more than one month after original operation (List separately in addition to code for primary procedure)

(Use 33530 in conjunction with 33400-33496; 33510-33536, 33863)

Surgery: Cardiovascular System

Arterial Grafting for Coronary Artery Bypass

The following codes are used to report coronary artery bypass procedures using either arterial grafts only or a combination of arterial-venous grafts. The codes include the use of the internal mammary artery, gastroepiploic artery, epigastric artery, radial artery, and arterial conduits procured from other sites.

To report combined arterial-venous grafts it is necessary to report two codes: 1) the appropriate arterial graft code (33533-33536); and 2) the appropriate combined arterial-venous graft code (33517-33523).

Procurement of the artery for grafting is included in the description of the work for 33533-33536 and should not be reported as a separate service or co-surgery, except when an upper extremity artery (eg, radial artery) is procured. To report harvesting of an upper extremity artery, use 35600 in addition to the bypass procedure. To report harvesting of an upper extremity vein, use 35500 in addition to the bypass procedure. To report harvesting of a femoropopliteal vein segment, report 35572 in addition to the bypass procedure. When surgical assistant performs arterial and/or venous graft procurement, add modifier 80 to 33517-33523, 33533-33536, as appropriate.

33533 Coronary artery bypass, using arterial graft(s); single arterial graft

33534 two coronary arterial grafts

33535 three coronary arterial grafts

33536 four or more coronary arterial grafts

33542 Myocardial resection (eg, ventricular aneurysmectomy)

33545 Repair of postinfarction ventricular septal defect, with or without myocardial resection

33548 Surgical ventricular restoration procedure, includes prosthetic patch, when performed (eg, ventricular remodeling, SVR, SAVER, Dor procedures)

(Do not report 33548 in conjunction with 32551, 33210, 33211, 33310, 33315)

(For Batista procedure or pachopexy, use 33999)

Coronary Endarterectomy

+ 33572 Coronary endarterectomy, open, any method, of left anterior descending, circumflex, or right coronary artery performed in conjunction with coronary artery bypass graft procedure, each vessel (List separately in addition to primary procedure)

(Use 33572 in conjunction with 33510-33516, 33533-33536)

Single Ventricle and Other Complex Cardiac Anomalies

33600 Closure of atrioventricular valve (mitral or tricuspid) by suture or patch

33602 Closure of semilunar valve (aortic or pulmonary) by suture or patch

33606 Anastomosis of pulmonary artery to aorta (Damus-Kaye-Stansel procedure)

33608 Repair of complex cardiac anomaly other than pulmonary atresia with ventricular septal defect by construction or replacement of conduit from right or left ventricle to pulmonary artery

(For repair of pulmonary artery arborization anomalies by unifocalization, see 33925-33926)

33610 Repair of complex cardiac anomalies (eg, single ventricle with subaortic obstruction) by surgical enlargement of ventricular septal defect

(Do not report modifier 63 in conjunction with 33610)

33611 Repair of double outlet right ventricle with intraventricular tunnel repair;

(Do not report modifier 63 in conjunction with 33611)

33612 with repair of right ventricular outflow tract obstruction

33615 Repair of complex cardiac anomalies (eg, tricuspid atresia) by closure of atrial septal defect and anastomosis of atria or vena cava to pulmonary artery (simple Fontan procedure)

33617 Repair of complex cardiac anomalies (eg, single ventricle) by modified Fontan procedure

(Use 33617 in conjunction with 33768 when a cavopulmonary anastomosis to a second superior vena cava is performed)

33619 Repair of single ventricle with aortic outflow obstruction and aortic arch hypoplasia (hypoplastic left heart syndrome) (eg, Norwood procedure)

(Do not report modifier 63 in conjunction with 33619)

Septal Defect

33641 Repair atrial septal defect, secundum, with cardiopulmonary bypass, with or without patch

33645 Direct or patch closure, sinus venosus, with or without anomalous pulmonary venous drainage

(Do not report 33645 in conjunction with 33724, 33726)

33647 Repair of atrial septal defect and ventricular septal defect, with direct or patch closure

(Do not report modifier 63 in conjunction with 33647)

(For repair of tricuspid atresia (eg, Fontan, Gago procedures), use 33615)

33660 Repair of incomplete or partial atrioventricular canal (ostium primum atrial septal defect), with or without atrioventricular valve repair

33665 Repair of intermediate or transitional atrioventricular canal, with or without atrioventricular valve repair

33670 Repair of complete atrioventricular canal, with or without prosthetic valve

(Do not report modifier 63 in conjunction with 33670)

33675 Closure of multiple ventricular septal defects;

33676 with pulmonary valvotomy or infundibular resection (acyanotic)

33677 with removal of pulmonary artery band, with or without gusset

(Do not report 33675-33677 in conjunction with 32100, 32422, 32551, 33210, 33681, 33684, 33688)

(For transmyocardial closure, see Category III codes 0166T and 0167T)

(For percutaneous closure, use 93581)

33681 Closure of single ventricular septal defect, with or without patch;

33684 with pulmonary valvotomy or infundibular resection (acyanotic)

33688 with removal of pulmonary artery band, with or without gusset

(For pulmonary vein repair requiring creation of atrial septal defect, use 33724)

33690 Banding of pulmonary artery

(Do not report modifier 63 in conjunction with 33690)

33692 Complete repair tetralogy of Fallot without pulmonary atresia;

33694 with transannular patch

(Do not report modifier 63 in conjunction with 33694)

(For ligation and takedown of a systemic-to-pulmonary artery shunt, performed in conjunction with a congenital heart procedure; see 33924)

33697 Complete repair tetralogy of Fallot with pulmonary atresia including construction of conduit from right ventricle to pulmonary artery and closure of ventricular septal defect

(For ligation and takedown of a systemic-to-pulmonary artery shunt, performed in conjunction with a congenital heart procedure; see 33924)

Sinus of Valsalva

33702 Repair sinus of Valsalva fistula, with cardiopulmonary bypass;

33710 with repair of ventricular septal defect

33720 Repair sinus of Valsalva aneurysm, with cardiopulmonary bypass

33722 Closure of aortico-left ventricular tunnel

Venous Anomalies

33724 Repair of isolated partial anomalous pulmonary venous return (eg, Scimitar Syndrome)

(Do not report 33724 in conjunction with 32551, 33210, 33211)

33726 Repair of pulmonary venous stenosis

(Do not report 33726 in conjunction with 32551, 33210, 33211)

33730 Complete repair of anomalous pulmonary venous return (supracardiac, intracardiac, or infracardiac types)

(Do not report modifier 63 in conjunction with 33730)

(For partial anomalous pulmonary venous return, use 33724; for repair of pulmonary venous stenosis, use 33726)

33732 Repair of cor triatriatum or supravalvular mitral ring by resection of left atrial membrane

(Do not report modifier 63 in conjunction with 33732)

Shunting Procedures

33735 Atrial septectomy or septostomy; closed heart (Blalock-Hanlon type operation)

33736 open heart with cardiopulmonary bypass

(Do not report modifier 63 in conjunction with 33735, 33736)

33737 open heart, with inflow occlusion

(For transvenous method cardiac catheterization balloon atrial septectomy or septostomy (Rashkind type), use 92992)

(For blade method cardiac catheterization atrial septectomy or septostomy (Sang-Park septostomy), use 92993)

33750 Shunt; subclavian to pulmonary artery (Blalock-Taussig type operation)

33755 ascending aorta to pulmonary artery (Waterston type operation)

33762 descending aorta to pulmonary artery (Potts-Smith type operation)

(Do not report modifier 63 in conjunction with 33750, 33755, 33762)

33764 central, with prosthetic graft

33766 superior vena cava to pulmonary artery for flow to one lung (classical Glenn procedure)

33767 superior vena cava to pulmonary artery for flow to both lungs (bidirectional Glenn procedure)

+ 33768 Anastomosis, cavopulmonary, second superior vena cava (List separately in addition to primary procedure)

(Use 33768 in conjunction with 33478, 33617, 33767)

(Do not report 33768 in conjunction with 32551, 33210, 33211)

Transposition of the Great Vessels

33770 Repair of transposition of the great arteries with ventricular septal defect and subpulmonary stenosis; without surgical enlargement of ventricular septal defect

33771 with surgical enlargement of ventricular septal defect

33774 Repair of transposition of the great arteries, atrial baffle procedure (eg, Mustard or Senning type) with cardiopulmonary bypass;

33775 with removal of pulmonary band

33776 with closure of ventricular septal defect

33777 with repair of subpulmonic obstruction

33778 Repair of transposition of the great arteries, aortic pulmonary artery reconstruction (eg, Jatene type);

(Do not report modifier 63 in conjunction with 33778)

33779 with removal of pulmonary band

33780 with closure of ventricular septal defect

33781 with repair of subpulmonic obstruction

Truncus Arteriosus

33786 Total repair, truncus arteriosus (Rastelli type operation)

(Do not report modifier 63 in conjunction with 33786)

33788 Reimplantation of an anomalous pulmonary artery

(For pulmonary artery band, use 33690)

Aortic Anomalies

33800 Aortic suspension (aortopexy) for tracheal decompression (eg, for tracheomalacia) (separate procedure)

33802 Division of aberrant vessel (vascular ring);

33803 with reanastomosis

33813 Obliteration of aortopulmonary septal defect; without cardiopulmonary bypass

33814 with cardiopulmonary bypass

33820 Repair of patent ductus arteriosus; by ligation

33822 by division, younger than 18 years

33824 by division, 18 years and older

33840 Excision of coarctation of aorta, with or without associated patent ductus arteriosus; with direct anastomosis

33845 with graft

33851 repair using either left subclavian artery or prosthetic material as gusset for enlargement

33852 Repair of hypoplastic or interrupted aortic arch using autogenous or prosthetic material; without cardiopulmonary bypass

33853 with cardiopulmonary bypass

(For repair of hypoplastic left heart syndrome (eg, Norwood type), via excision of coarctation of aorta, use 33619)

Thoracic Aortic Aneurysm

33860 Ascending aorta graft, with cardiopulmonary bypass, with or without valve suspension;

33861 with coronary reconstruction

33863 with aortic root replacement using composite prosthesis and coronary reconstruction

(For graft of ascending aorta, with cardiopulmonary bypass and valve replacement, with or without coronary implant or valve suspension; use 33860 or 33861 and 33405 or 33406)

33864 Ascending aorta graft, with cardiopulmonary bypass with valve suspension, with coronary reconstruction and valve-sparing aortic annulus remodeling (eg, David Procedure, Yacoub Procedure)

►(Do not report 33864 in conjunction with 32551, 33210, 33211, 33400, 33860-33863)◄

33870 Transverse arch graft, with cardiopulmonary bypass

33875 Descending thoracic aorta graft, with or without bypass

33877 Repair of thoracoabdominal aortic aneurysm with graft, with or without cardiopulmonary bypass

Endovascular Repair of Descending Thoracic Aorta

Codes 33880-33891 represent a family of procedures to report placement of an endovascular graft for repair of the descending thoracic aorta. These codes include all device introduction, manipulation, positioning, and deployment. All balloon angioplasty and/or stent deployment within the target treatment zone for the endoprosthesis, either before or after endograft deployment, are not separately reportable. Open arterial exposure and associated closure of the arteriotomy sites (eg, 34812, 34820, 34833, 34834), introduction of guidewires and catheters (eg, 36140, 36200-36218), and extensive repair or replacement of an artery (eg, 35226, 35286) should be additionally reported. Transposition of subclavian artery to carotid, and carotid-carotid bypass performed in conjunction with endovascular repair of the descending thoracic aorta (eg, 33889, 33891) should be separately reported. The primary codes, 33880 and 33881, include placement of all distal extensions, if required, in the distal thoracic aorta, while proximal extensions, if needed, are reported separately.

For fluoroscopic guidance in conjunction with endovascular repair of the thoracic aorta, see codes 75956-75959 as appropriate. Codes 75956 and 75957 include all angiography of the thoracic aorta and its branches for diagnostic imaging prior to deployment of the primary endovascular devices (including all routine components of modular devices), fluoroscopic guidance in the delivery of the endovascular components, and intraprocedural arterial angiography (eg, confirm position, detect endoleak, evaluate runoff). Code 75958 includes the analogous services for placement of each proximal thoracic endovascular extension. Code 75959 includes the analogous services for placement of a distal thoracic endovascular extension(s) placed during a procedure after the primary repair.

Other interventional procedures performed at the time of endovascular repair of the descending thoracic aorta should be additionally reported (eg, innominate, carotid, subclavian, visceral, or iliac artery transluminal angioplasty or stenting, arterial embolization, intravascular ultrasound) when performed before or after deployment of the aortic prostheses.

(For transcatheter placement of wireless physiologic sensor in aneurysmal sac, use 34806)

(For analysis, interpretation, and report of implanted wireless pressure sensor in aneurysmal sac, use 93982)

33880 Endovascular repair of descending thoracic aorta (eg, aneurysm, pseudoaneurysm, dissection, penetrating ulcer, intramural hematoma, or traumatic disruption); involving coverage of left subclavian artery origin, initial endoprosthesis plus descending thoracic aortic extension(s), if required, to level of celiac artery origin

(For radiological supervision and interpretation, use 75956 in conjunction with 33880)

33881 not involving coverage of left subclavian artery origin, initial endoprosthesis plus descending thoracic aortic extension(s), if required, to level of celiac artery origin

(For radiological supervision and interpretation, use 75957 in conjunction with 33881)

33883 Placement of proximal extension prosthesis for endovascular repair of descending thoracic aorta (eg, aneurysm, pseudoaneurysm, dissection, penetrating ulcer, intramural hematoma, or traumatic disruption); initial extension

(For radiological supervision and interpretation, use 75958 in conjunction with 33883)

(Do not report 33881, 33883 when extension placement converts repair to cover left subclavian origin. Use only 33880)

+ 33884 each additional proximal extension (List separately in addition to code for primary procedure)

(Use 33884 in conjunction with 33883)

(For radiological supervision and interpretation, use 75958 in conjunction with 33884)

33886 Placement of distal extension prosthesis(s) delayed after endovascular repair of descending thoracic aorta

(Do not report 33886 in conjunction with 33880, 33881)

(Report 33886 once, regardless of number of modules deployed)

(For radiological supervision and interpretation, use 75959 in conjunction with 33886)

33889 Open subclavian to carotid artery transposition performed in conjunction with endovascular repair of descending thoracic aorta, by neck incision, unilateral

(Do not report 33889 in conjunction with 35694)

33891 Bypass graft, with other than vein, transcervical retropharyngeal carotid-carotid, performed in conjunction with endovascular repair of descending thoracic aorta, by neck incision

(Do not report 33891 in conjunction with 35509, 35601)

Pulmonary Artery

33910 Pulmonary artery embolectomy; with cardiopulmonary bypass

33915 without cardiopulmonary bypass

33916 Pulmonary endarterectomy, with or without embolectomy, with cardiopulmonary bypass

33917 Repair of pulmonary artery stenosis by reconstruction with patch or graft

33920 Repair of pulmonary atresia with ventricular septal defect, by construction or replacement of conduit from right or left ventricle to pulmonary artery

(For repair of other complex cardiac anomalies by construction or replacement of right or left ventricle to pulmonary artery conduit, use 33608)

33922 Transection of pulmonary artery with cardiopulmonary bypass

(Do not report modifier 63 in conjunction with 33922)

+ 33924 Ligation and takedown of a systemic-to-pulmonary artery shunt, performed in conjunction with a congenital heart procedure (List separately in addition to code for primary procedure)

(Use 33924 in conjunction with 33470-33475, 33600-33619, 33684-33688, 33692-33697, 33735-33767, 33770-33781, 33786, 33920-33922)

Surgery: Cardiovascular System

33925 Repair of pulmonary artery arborization anomalies by unifocalization; without cardiopulmonary bypass

33926 with cardiopulmonary bypass

Heart/Lung Transplantation

Heart with or without lung allotransplantation involves three distinct components of physician work:

1. ***Cadaver donor cardiectomy with or without pneumonectomy***, which includes harvesting the allograft and cold preservation of the allograft (perfusing with cold preservation solution and cold maintenance) (see 33930, 33940).
2. ***Backbench work***:

   Preparation of a cadaver donor heart and lung allograft prior to transplantation, including dissection of the allograft from surrounding soft tissues to prepare the aorta, superior vena cava, inferior vena cava, and trachea for implantation (use 33933).

   Preparation of a cadaver donor heart allograft prior to transplantation, including dissection of the allograft from surrounding soft tissues to prepare aorta, superior vena cava, inferior vena cava, pulmonary artery, and left atrium for implantation (use 33944).
3. ***Recipient heart with or without lung allotransplantation***, which includes transplantation of allograft and care of the recipient (see 33935, 33945).

(For implantation of a total replacement heart system (artificial heart) with recipient cardiectomy or heart replacement system components, see Category III codes 0051T-0053T)

33930 Donor cardiectomy-pneumonectomy (including cold preservation)

33933 Backbench standard preparation of cadaver donor heart/lung allograft prior to transplantation, including dissection of allograft from surrounding soft tissues to prepare aorta, superior vena cava, inferior vena cava, and trachea for implantation

33935 Heart-lung transplant with recipient cardiectomy-pneumonectomy

33940 Donor cardiectomy (including cold preservation)

33944 Backbench standard preparation of cadaver donor heart allograft prior to transplantation, including dissection of allograft from surrounding soft tissues to prepare aorta, superior vena cava, inferior vena cava, pulmonary artery, and left atrium for implantation

(For repair or resection procedures on the donor heart, see 33300, 33310, 33320, 33400, 33463, 33464, 33510, 33641, 35216, 35276 or 35685)

33945 Heart transplant, with or without recipient cardiectomy

Cardiac Assist

►(For percutaneous implantation of extracorporeal ventricular assist device or for removal of percutaneously implanted extracorporeal ventricular assist device, see Category III codes 0048T, 0050T)◄

33960 Prolonged extracorporeal circulation for cardiopulmonary insufficiency; initial 24 hours

+ 33961 each additional 24 hours (List separately in addition to code for primary procedure)

(Do not report modifier 63 in conjunction with 33960, 33961)

(Use 33961 in conjunction with 33960)

(For insertion of cannula for prolonged extracorporeal circulation, use 36822)

33967 Insertion of intra-aortic balloon assist device, percutaneous

33968 Removal of intra-aortic balloon assist device, percutaneous

33970 Insertion of intra-aortic balloon assist device through the femoral artery, open approach

33971 Removal of intra-aortic balloon assist device including repair of femoral artery, with or without graft

33973 Insertion of intra-aortic balloon assist device through the ascending aorta

33974 Removal of intra-aortic balloon assist device from the ascending aorta, including repair of the ascending aorta, with or without graft

33975 Insertion of ventricular assist device; extracorporeal, single ventricle

33976 extracorporeal, biventricular

33977 Removal of ventricular assist device; extracorporeal, single ventricle

33978 extracorporeal, biventricular

33979 Insertion of ventricular assist device, implantable intracorporeal, single ventricle

33980 Removal of ventricular assist device, implantable intracorporeal, single ventricle

Other Procedures

33999 Unlisted procedure, cardiac surgery

Arteries and Veins

Primary vascular procedure listings include establishing both inflow and outflow by whatever procedures necessary. Also included is that portion of the operative arteriogram performed by the surgeon, as indicated. Sympathectomy, when done, is included in the listed aortic procedures. For unlisted vascular procedure, use 37799.

Embolectomy/Thrombectomy

Arterial, With or Without Catheter

34001 Embolectomy or thrombectomy, with or without catheter; carotid, subclavian or innominate artery, by neck incision

34051 innominate, subclavian artery, by thoracic incision

34101 axillary, brachial, innominate, subclavian artery, by arm incision

34111 radial or ulnar artery, by arm incision

34151 renal, celiac, mesentery, aortoiliac artery, by abdominal incision

34201 femoropopliteal, aortoiliac artery, by leg incision

34203 popliteal-tibio-peroneal artery, by leg incision

Venous, Direct or With Catheter

34401 Thrombectomy, direct or with catheter; vena cava, iliac vein, by abdominal incision

34421 vena cava, iliac, femoropopliteal vein, by leg incision

34451 vena cava, iliac, femoropopliteal vein, by abdominal and leg incision

34471 subclavian vein, by neck incision

34490 axillary and subclavian vein, by arm incision

Venous Reconstruction

34501 Valvuloplasty, femoral vein

34502 Reconstruction of vena cava, any method

34510 Venous valve transposition, any vein donor

34520 Cross-over vein graft to venous system

34530 Saphenopopliteal vein anastomosis

Endovascular Repair of Abdominal Aortic Aneurysm

Codes 34800-34826 represent a family of component procedures to report placement of an endovascular graft for abdominal aortic aneurysm repair. These codes describe open femoral or iliac artery exposure, device manipulation and deployment, and closure of the arteriotomy sites. Balloon angioplasty and/or stent deployment within the target treatment zone for the endoprosthesis, either before or after endograft deployment, are not separately reportable. Introduction of guidewires and catheters should be reported separately (eg, 36200, 36245-36248, 36140). Extensive repair or replacement of an artery should be additionally reported (eg, 35226 or 35286).

For fluoroscopic guidance in conjunction with endovascular aneurysm repair, see code 75952 or 75953, as appropriate. Code 75952 includes angiography of the aorta and its branches for diagnostic imaging prior to deployment of the endovascular device (including all routine components of modular devices), fluoroscopic guidance in the delivery of the endovascular components, and intraprocedural arterial angiography (eg, confirm position, detect endoleak, evaluate runoff). Code 75953 includes the analogous services for placement of additional extension prostheses (not for routine components of modular devices).

Other interventional procedures performed at the time of endovascular abdominal aortic aneurysm repair should be additionally reported (eg, renal transluminal angioplasty, arterial embolization, intravascular ultrasound, balloon angioplasty or stenting of native artery[s] outside the endoprosthesis target zone, when done before or after deployment of graft).

(For transcatheter placement of wireless physiologic sensor in aneurysmal sac, use 34806)

(For analysis, interpretation and report of implanted wireless pressure sensor in aneurysmal sac, use 93982)

34800 Endovascular repair of infrarenal abdominal aortic aneurysm or dissection; using aorto-aortic tube prosthesis

34802 using modular bifurcated prosthesis (one docking limb)

34803 using modular bifurcated prosthesis (two docking limbs)

(For endovascular repair of abdominal aortic aneurysm or dissection involving visceral vessels using a fenestrated modular bifurcated prosthesis (two docking limbs), use Category III codes 0078T, 0079T)

34804 using unibody bifurcated prosthesis

34805 using aorto-uniiliac or aorto-unifemoral prosthesis

+▲ 34806 Transcatheter placement of wireless physiologic sensor in aneurysmal sac during endovascular repair, including radiological supervision and interpretation, instrument calibration, and collection of pressure data (List separately in addition to code for primary procedure)

(Use 34806 in conjunction with 33880, 33881, 33886, 34800-34805, 34825, 34900)

(Do not report 34806 in conjunction with 93982)

+ 34808 Endovascular placement of iliac artery occlusion device (List separately in addition to code for primary procedure)

(Use 34808 in conjunction with 34800, 34805, 34813, 34825, 34826)

(For radiological supervision and interpretation, use 75952 in conjunction with 34800-34808)

(For open arterial exposure, report 34812, 34820, 34833, 34834 as appropriate, in addition to 34800-34808)

34812 Open femoral artery exposure for delivery of endovascular prosthesis, by groin incision, unilateral

(For bilateral procedure, use modifier 50)

+ 34813 Placement of femoral-femoral prosthetic graft during endovascular aortic aneurysm repair (List separately in addition to code for primary procedure)

(Use 34813 in conjunction with 34812)

(For femoral artery grafting, see 35521, 35533, 35539, 35540, 35551-35558, 35566, 35621, 35646, 35651-35661, 35666, 35700)

34820 Open iliac artery exposure for delivery of endovascular prosthesis or iliac occlusion during endovascular therapy, by abdominal or retroperitoneal incision, unilateral

(For bilateral procedure, use modifier 50)

34825 Placement of proximal or distal extension prosthesis for endovascular repair of infrarenal abdominal aortic or iliac aneurysm, false aneurysm, or dissection; initial vessel

+ 34826 each additional vessel (List separately in addition to code for primary procedure)

(Use 34826 in conjunction with 34825)

(Use 34825, 34826 in addition to 34800-34808, 34900 as appropriate)

(For staged procedure, use modifier 58)

(For radiological supervision and interpretation, use 75953)

34830 Open repair of infrarenal aortic aneurysm or dissection, plus repair of associated arterial trauma, following unsuccessful endovascular repair; tube prosthesis

34831 aorto-bi-iliac prosthesis

34832 aorto-bifemoral prosthesis

34833 Open iliac artery exposure with creation of conduit for delivery of aortic or iliac endovascular prosthesis, by abdominal or retroperitoneal incision, unilateral

(For bilateral procedure, use modifier 50)

(Do not report 34833 in addition to 34820)

34834 Open brachial artery exposure to assist in the deployment of aortic or iliac endovascular prosthesis by arm incision, unilateral

(For bilateral procedure, use modifier 50)

Endovascular Repair of Iliac Aneurysm

Code 34900 represents a procedure to report introduction, positioning, and deployment of an endovascular graft for treatment of aneurysm, pseudoaneurysm, or arteriovenous malformation or trauma of the iliac artery (common, hypogastric, external). All balloon angioplasty and/or stent deployments within the target treatment zone for the endoprosthesis, either before or after endograft deployment, are included in the work of 34900 and are not separately reportable. Open femoral or iliac artery exposure (eg, 34812, 34820), introduction of guidewires and catheters (eg, 36200, 36215-36218), and extensive repair or replacement of an artery (eg, 35206-35286) should be additionally reported.

For fluoroscopic guidance in conjunction with endovascular iliac aneurysm repair, see code 75954. Code 75954 includes angiography of the aorta and iliac arteries for diagnostic imaging prior to deployment of the endovascular device (including all routine components), fluoroscopic guidance in the delivery of the endovascular components, and intraprocedural arterial angiography to confirm appropriate position of the graft, detect endoleaks, and evaluate the status of the runoff vessels (eg, evaluation for dissection, stenosis, thrombosis, distal embolization, or iatrogenic injury).

Other interventional procedures performed at the time of endovascular iliac aneurysm repair should be additionally reported (eg, transluminal angioplasty outside the aneurysm target zone, arterial embolization, intravascular ultrasound).

34900 Endovascular graft placement for repair of iliac artery (eg, aneurysm, pseudoaneurysm, arteriovenous malformation, trauma)

(For radiological supervision and interpretation, use 75954)

(For placement of extension prosthesis during endovascular iliac artery repair, use 34825)

(For bilateral procedure, use modifier 50)

Direct Repair of Aneurysm or Excision (Partial or Total) and Graft Insertion for Aneurysm, Pseudoaneurysm, Ruptured Aneurysm, and Associated Occlusive Disease

Procedures 35001-35152 include preparation of artery for anastomosis including endarterectomy.

(For direct repairs associated with occlusive disease only, see 35201-35286)

(For intracranial aneurysm, see 61700 et seq)

(For endovascular repair of abdominal aortic aneurysm, see 34800-34826)

(For endovascular repair of iliac artery aneurysm, see 34900)

(For thoracic aortic aneurysm, see 33860-33875)

(For endovascular repair of descending thoracic aorta, involving coverage of left subclavian artery origin, use 33880)

35001 Direct repair of aneurysm, pseudoaneurysm, or excision (partial or total) and graft insertion, with or without patch graft; for aneurysm and associated occlusive disease, carotid, subclavian artery, by neck incision

35002 for ruptured aneurysm, carotid, subclavian artery, by neck incision

35005 for aneurysm, pseudoaneurysm, and associated occlusive disease, vertebral artery

35011 for aneurysm and associated occlusive disease, axillary-brachial artery, by arm incision

35013 for ruptured aneurysm, axillary-brachial artery, by arm incision

35021 for aneurysm, pseudoaneurysm, and associated occlusive disease, innominate, subclavian artery, by thoracic incision

35022 for ruptured aneurysm, innominate, subclavian artery, by thoracic incision

35045 for aneurysm, pseudoaneurysm, and associated occlusive disease, radial or ulnar artery

35081 for aneurysm, pseudoaneurysm, and associated occlusive disease, abdominal aorta

35082 for ruptured aneurysm, abdominal aorta

35091 for aneurysm, pseudoaneurysm, and associated occlusive disease, abdominal aorta involving visceral vessels (mesenteric, celiac, renal)

35092 for ruptured aneurysm, abdominal aorta involving visceral vessels (mesenteric, celiac, renal)

35102 for aneurysm, pseudoaneurysm, and associated occlusive disease, abdominal aorta involving iliac vessels (common, hypogastric, external)

35103 for ruptured aneurysm, abdominal aorta involving iliac vessels (common, hypogastric, external)

35111 for aneurysm, pseudoaneurysm, and associated occlusive disease, splenic artery

35112 for ruptured aneurysm, splenic artery

35121 for aneurysm, pseudoaneurysm, and associated occlusive disease, hepatic, celiac, renal, or mesenteric artery

35122 for ruptured aneurysm, hepatic, celiac, renal, or mesenteric artery

35131 for aneurysm, pseudoaneurysm, and associated occlusive disease, iliac artery (common, hypogastric, external)

35132 for ruptured aneurysm, iliac artery (common, hypogastric, external)

35141 for aneurysm, pseudoaneurysm, and associated occlusive disease, common femoral artery (profunda femoris, superficial femoral)

35142 for ruptured aneurysm, common femoral artery (profunda femoris, superficial femoral)

35151 for aneurysm, pseudoaneurysm, and associated occlusive disease, popliteal artery

35152 for ruptured aneurysm, popliteal artery

Repair Arteriovenous Fistula

35180 Repair, congenital arteriovenous fistula; head and neck

35182 thorax and abdomen

35184 extremities

35188 Repair, acquired or traumatic arteriovenous fistula; head and neck

35189 thorax and abdomen

35190 extremities

Repair Blood Vessel Other Than for Fistula, With or Without Patch Angioplasty

(For AV fistula repair, see 35180-35190)

35201 Repair blood vessel, direct; neck

35206 upper extremity

35207 hand, finger

35211 intrathoracic, with bypass

35216 intrathoracic, without bypass

35221 intra-abdominal

35226 lower extremity

35231 Repair blood vessel with vein graft; neck

35236 upper extremity

35241 intrathoracic, with bypass

35246 intrathoracic, without bypass

35251 intra-abdominal

35256 lower extremity

35261 Repair blood vessel with graft other than vein; neck

35266 upper extremity

35271 intrathoracic, with bypass

35276 intrathoracic, without bypass

35281 intra-abdominal

35286 lower extremity

Thromboendarterectomy

(For coronary artery, see 33510-33536 and 33572)

(35301-35372 include harvest of saphenous or upper extremity vein when performed)

35301 Thromboendarterectomy, including patch graft, if performed; carotid, vertebral, subclavian, by neck incision

35302 superficial femoral artery

35303 popliteal artery

(Do not report 35302, 35303 in conjunction with 35483, 35500)

35304 tibioperoneal trunk artery

35305 tibial or peroneal artery, initial vessel

+ 35306 each additional tibial or peroneal artery (List separately in addition to code for primary procedure)

(Use 35306 in conjunction with 35305)

(Do not report 35304, 35305, 35306 in conjunction with 35485, 35500)

35311 subclavian, innominate, by thoracic incision

35321 axillary-brachial

35331 abdominal aorta

35341 mesenteric, celiac, or renal

35351 iliac

35355 iliofemoral

35361 combined aortoiliac

35363 combined aortoiliofemoral

35371 common femoral

35372 deep (profunda) femoral

(35381 has been deleted. For thromboendarterectomy of the superficial femoral artery, use 35302; of the popliteal artery, use 35303; of the tibioperoneal trunk, use 35304; of the tibial or peroneal artery, see 35305, 35306)

+ 35390 Reoperation, carotid, thromboendarterectomy, more than one month after original operation (List separately in addition to code for primary procedure)

(Use 35390 in conjunction with 35301)

Angioscopy

+ 35400 Angioscopy (non-coronary vessels or grafts) during therapeutic intervention (List separately in addition to code for primary procedure)

Transluminal Angioplasty

If done as part of another operation, use modifier 51 or use modifier 52.

(For radiological supervision and interpretation, see 75962-75968 and 75978)

Open

35450 Transluminal balloon angioplasty, open; renal or other visceral artery

35452 aortic

35454 iliac

35456 femoral-popliteal

35458 brachiocephalic trunk or branches, each vessel

35459 tibioperoneal trunk and branches

35460 venous

Percutaneous

Codes for catheter placement and the radiologic supervision and interpretation should also be reported, in addition to the code(s) for the therapeutic aspect of the procedure.

⊙ 35470 Transluminal balloon angioplasty, percutaneous; tibioperoneal trunk or branches, each vessel

⊙ 35471 renal or visceral artery

⊙ 35472 aortic

⊙ 35473 iliac

⊙ 35474 femoral-popliteal

⊙ 35475 brachiocephalic trunk or branches, each vessel

⊙ 35476 venous

(For radiological supervision and interpretation, use 75978)

Transluminal Atherectomy

If done as part of another operation, use modifier 51 or use modifier 52.

(For radiological supervision and interpretation, see 75992-75996)

Open

35480 Transluminal peripheral atherectomy, open; renal or other visceral artery

35481 aortic

35482 iliac

35483 femoral-popliteal

35484 brachiocephalic trunk or branches, each vessel

35485 tibioperoneal trunk and branches

Percutaneous

Codes for catheter placement and the radiologic supervision and interpretation should also be reported, in addition to the code(s) for the therapeutic aspect of the procedure.

35490 Transluminal peripheral atherectomy, percutaneous; renal or other visceral artery

35491 aortic

35492 iliac

35493 femoral-popliteal

35494 brachiocephalic trunk or branches, each vessel

35495 tibioperoneal trunk and branches

Bypass Graft

Vein

Procurement of the saphenous vein graft is included in the description of the work for 35501-35587 and should not be reported as a separate service or co-surgery. To report harvesting of an upper extremity vein, use 35500 in addition to the bypass procedure. To report harvesting of a femoropopliteal vein segment, use 35572 in addition to the bypass procedure. To report harvesting and construction of an autogenous composite graft of two segments from two distant locations, report 35682 in addition to the bypass procedure, for autogenous composite of three or more segments from distant sites, report 35683.

✚ **35500** Harvest of upper extremity vein, one segment, for lower extremity or coronary artery bypass procedure (List separately in addition to code for primary procedure)

(Use 35500 in conjunction with 33510-33536, 35556, 35566, 35571, 35583-35587)

(For harvest of more than one vein segment, see 35682, 35683)

(For endoscopic procedure, use 33508)

35501 Bypass graft, with vein; common carotid-ipsilateral internal carotid

35506 carotid-subclavian or subclavian-carotid

(35507 has been deleted. For subclavian-carotid bypass with vein, use 35506)

35508 carotid vertebral

35509 carotid-contralateral carotid

35510 carotid-brachial

35511 subclavian-subclavian

35512 subclavian-brachial

35515 subclavian-vertebral

35516 subclavian-axillary

35518 axillary-axillary

35521 axillary-femoral

(For bypass graft performed with synthetic graft, use 35621)

35522 axillary-brachial

35523 brachial-ulnar or -radial

(Do not report 35523 in conjunction with 35206, 35500, 35525, 36838)

(For bypass graft performed with synthetic conduit, use 37799)

35525 brachial-brachial

35526 aortosubclavian or carotid

(For bypass graft performed with synthetic graft, use 35626)

35531 aortoceliac or aortomesenteric

35533 axillary-femoral-femoral

(For bypass graft performed with synthetic graft, use 35654)

● **35535** hepatorenal

►(Do not report 35535 in conjunction with 35221, 35251, 35281, 35500, 35536, 35560, 35631, 35636)◄

35536 splenorenal

35537 aortoiliac

(For bypass graft performed with synthetic graft, use 35637)

(Do not report 35537 in conjunction with 35538)

35538 aortobi-iliac

(For bypass graft performed with synthetic graft, use 35638)

(Do not report 35538 in conjunction with 35537)

35539 aortofemoral

(For bypass graft performed with synthetic graft, use 35647)

(Do not report 35539 in conjunction with 35540)

35540 aortobifemoral

(For bypass graft performed with synthetic graft, use 35646)

(Do not report 35540 in conjunction with 35539)

(35541 has been deleted. For aortoiliac graft with vein, use 35537. For aortobi-iliac graft with vein, use 35538)

(35546 has been deleted. For aortofemoral graft with vein use 35539. For aortobifemoral graft with vein, use 35540)

35548 aortoiliofemoral, unilateral

(For bypass graft performed with synthetic graft, use 37799)

35549 aortoiliofemoral, bilateral

(For bypass graft performed with synthetic graft, use 37799)

35551 aortofemoral-popliteal

35556 femoral-popliteal

35558 femoral-femoral

35560 aortorenal

35563 ilioiliac

35565 iliofemoral

35566 femoral-anterior tibial, posterior tibial, peroneal artery or other distal vessels

● **35570** tibial-tibial, peroneal-tibial, or tibial/peroneal trunk-tibial

►(Do not report 35570 in conjunction with 35256, 35286)◄

35571 popliteal-tibial, -peroneal artery or other distal vessels

✚ **35572** Harvest of femoropopliteal vein, one segment, for vascular reconstruction procedure (eg, aortic, vena caval, coronary, peripheral artery) (List separately in addition to code for primary procedure)

(Use 35572 in conjunction with 33510-33516, 33517-33523, 33533-33536, 34502, 34520, 35001, 35002, 35011-35022, 35102, 35103, 35121-35152, 35231-35256, 35501-35587, 35879-35907)

(For bilateral procedure, use modifier 50)

In-Situ Vein

(To report aortobifemoral bypass using synthetic conduit, and femoral-popliteal bypass with vein conduit in-situ, use 35646 and 35583. To report aorto[uni]femoral bypass with synthetic conduit, and femoral-popliteal bypass with vein conduit in-situ, use 35647 and 35583. To report aortofemoral bypass using vein conduit, and femoral-popliteal bypass with vein conduit in-situ, use 35539 and 35583)

35583 In-situ vein bypass; femoral-popliteal

35585 femoral-anterior tibial, posterior tibial, or peroneal artery

35587 popliteal-tibial, peroneal

Other Than Vein

(For arterial transposition and/or reimplantation, see 35691-35695)

✚ **35600** Harvest of upper extremity artery, one segment, for coronary artery bypass procedure (List separately in addition to code for primary procedure)

(Use 35600 in conjunction with 33533–33536)

35601 Bypass graft, with other than vein; common carotid-ipsilateral internal carotid

35606 carotid-subclavian

(For open transcervical common carotid-common carotid bypass performed in conjunction with endovascular repair of descending thoracic aorta, use 33891)

(For open subclavian to carotid artery transposition performed in conjunction with endovascular thoracic aneurysm repair by neck incision, use 33889)

35612 subclavian-subclavian

35616 subclavian-axillary

35621 axillary-femoral

35623 axillary-popliteal or -tibial

35626 aortosubclavian or carotid

35631 aortoceliac, aortomesenteric, aortorenal

● **35632** ilio-celiac

►(Do not report 35632 in conjunction with 35221, 35251, 35281, 35531, 35631)◄

● **35633** ilio-mesenteric

►(Do not report 35633 in conjunction with 35221, 35251, 35281, 35531, 35631)◄

● **35634** iliorenal

►(Do not report 35634 in conjunction with 35221, 35251, 35281, 35560, 35536, 35631)◄

35636 splenorenal (splenic to renal arterial anastomosis)

35637 aortoiliac

(Do not report 35637 in conjunction with 35638, 35646)

35638 aortobi-iliac

(Do not report 35638 in conjunction with 35637, 35646)

(35641 has been deleted. For aortoiliac graft constructed with conduit other than vein, use 35637. For aortobi-iliac graft with other than vein, use 35638)

(For open placement of aortobi-iliac prosthesis following unsuccessful endovascular repair, use 34831)

35642 carotid-vertebral

35645 subclavian-vertebral

35646 aortobifemoral

(For bypass graft performed with vein graft, use 35540)

(For open placement of aortobifemoral prosthesis following unsuccessful endovascular repair, use 34832)

35647 aortofemoral

(For bypass graft performed with vein graft, use 35539)

35650 axillary-axillary

35651 aortofemoral-popliteal

35654 axillary-femoral-femoral

35656 femoral-popliteal

35661 femoral-femoral

35663 ilioiliac

35665 iliofemoral

35666 femoral-anterior tibial, posterior tibial, or peroneal artery

35671 popliteal-tibial or -peroneal artery

Composite Grafts

Codes 35682-35683 are used to report harvest and anastomosis of multiple vein segments from distant sites for use as arterial bypass graft conduits. These codes are intended for use when the two or more vein segments are harvested from a limb other than that undergoing bypass. Add-on codes 35682 and 35683 may be reported in addition to codes 35556, 35566, 35571, 35583-35587, as appropriate.

+ **35681** Bypass graft; composite, prosthetic and vein (List separately in addition to code for primary procedure)

(Do not report 35681 in addition to 35682, 35683)

+ **35682** autogenous composite, two segments of veins from two locations (List separately in addition to code for primary procedure)

(Do not report 35682 in addition to 35681, 35683)

+ **35683** autogenous composite, three or more segments of vein from two or more locations (List separately in addition to code for primary procedure)

(Do not report 35683 in addition to 35681, 35682)

Adjuvant Techniques

Adjuvant (additional) technique(s) may be required at the time a bypass graft is created to improve patency of the lower extremity autogenous or synthetic bypass graft (eg, femoral-popliteal, femoral-tibial, or popliteal-tibial arteries). Code 35685 should be reported in addition to the primary synthetic bypass graft procedure, when an interposition of venous tissue (vein patch or cuff) is placed at the anastomosis between the synthetic bypass conduit and the involved artery (includes harvest).

Code 35686 should be reported in addition to the primary bypass graft procedure, when autogenous vein is used to create a fistula between the tibial or peroneal artery and vein at or beyond the distal bypass anastomosis site of the involved artery.

(For composite graft(s), see 35681-35683)

+ **35685** Placement of vein patch or cuff at distal anastomosis of bypass graft, synthetic conduit (List separately in addition to code for primary procedure)

(Use 35685 in conjunction with 35656, 35666, or 35671)

+ **35686** Creation of distal arteriovenous fistula during lower extremity bypass surgery (non-hemodialysis) (List separately in addition to code for primary procedure)

(Use 35686 in conjunction with 35556, 35566, 35571, 35583-35587, 35623, 35656, 35666, 35671)

Arterial Transposition

35691 Transposition and/or reimplantation; vertebral to carotid artery

35693 vertebral to subclavian artery

35694 subclavian to carotid artery

(For open subclavian to carotid artery transposition performed in conjunction with endovascular repair of descending thoracic aorta, use 33889)

35695 carotid to subclavian artery

+ **35697** Reimplantation, visceral artery to infrarenal aortic prosthesis, each artery (List separately in addition to code for primary procedure)

(Do not report 35697 in conjunction with 33877)

Excision, Exploration, Repair, Revision

+ **35700** Reoperation, femoral-popliteal or femoral (popliteal)-anterior tibial, posterior tibial, peroneal artery, or other distal vessels, more than one month after original operation (List separately in addition to code for primary procedure)

(Use 35700 in conjunction with 35556, 35566, 35571, 35583, 35585, 35587, 35656, 35666, 35671)

35701 Exploration (not followed by surgical repair), with or without lysis of artery; carotid artery

35721 femoral artery

35741 popliteal artery

35761 other vessels

35800 Exploration for postoperative hemorrhage, thrombosis or infection; neck

35820 chest

35840 abdomen

35860 extremity

35870 Repair of graft-enteric fistula

35875 Thrombectomy of arterial or venous graft (other than hemodialysis graft or fistula);

35876 with revision of arterial or venous graft

(For thrombectomy of hemodialysis graft or fistula, see 36831, 36833)

Codes 35879 and 35881 describe open revision of graft-threatening stenoses of lower extremity arterial bypass graft(s) (previously constructed with autogenous vein conduit) using vein patch angioplasty or segmental vein interposition techniques. For thrombectomy with revision of any non-coronary arterial or venous graft, including those of the lower extremity, (other than hemodialysis graft or fistula), use 35876. For direct repair (other than for fistula) of a lower extremity blood vessel (with or without patch angioplasty), use 35226. For repair (other than for fistula) of a lower extremity blood vessel using a vein graft, use 35256.

35879 Revision, lower extremity arterial bypass, without thrombectomy, open; with vein patch angioplasty

35881 with segmental vein interposition

(For revision of femoral anastomosis of synthetic arterial bypass graft, see 35883, 35884)

(For excision of infected graft, see 35901-35907 and appropriate revascularization code)

35883 Revision, femoral anastomosis of synthetic arterial bypass graft in groin, open; with nonautogenous patch graft (eg, Dacron, ePTFE, bovine pericardium)

(For bilateral procedure, use modifier 50)

(Do not report 35883 in conjunction with 35700, 35875, 35876, 35884)

35884 with autogenous vein patch graft

(For bilateral procedure, use modifier 50)

(Do not report 35884 in conjunction with 35700, 35875, 35876, 35883)

35901 Excision of infected graft; neck

35903 extremity

35905 thorax

35907 abdomen

Vascular Injection Procedures

Listed services for injection procedures include necessary local anesthesia, introduction of needles or catheter, injection of contrast media with or without automatic power injection, and/or necessary pre- and postinjection care specifically related to the injection procedure.

Catheters, drugs, and contrast media are not included in the listed service for the injection procedures.

Selective vascular catheterization should be coded to include introduction and all lesser order selective catheterization used in the approach (eg, the description for a selective right middle cerebral artery catheterization includes the introduction and placement catheterization of the right common and internal carotid arteries).

Additional second and/or third order arterial catheterization within the same family of arteries or veins supplied by a single first order vessel should be expressed by 36012, 36218, or 36248.

Additional first order or higher catheterization in vascular families supplied by a first order vessel different from a previously selected and coded family should be separately coded using the conventions described above.

(For radiological supervision and interpretation, see **Radiology**)

(For injection procedures in conjunction with cardiac catheterization, see 93541-93545)

(For chemotherapy of malignant disease, see 96401-96549)

Intravenous

An intracatheter is a sheathed combination of needle and short catheter.

36000 Introduction of needle or intracatheter, vein

36002 Injection procedures (eg, thrombin) for percutaneous treatment of extremity pseudoaneurysm

(For imaging guidance, see 76942, 77002, 77012, 77021)

(For ultrasound guided compression repair of pseudoaneurysms, use 76936)

(Do not report 36002 for vascular sealant of an arteriotomy site)

36005 Injection procedure for extremity venography (including introduction of needle or intracatheter)

(For radiological supervision and interpretation, see 75820, 75822)

36010 Introduction of catheter, superior or inferior vena cava

36011 Selective catheter placement, venous system; first order branch (eg, renal vein, jugular vein)

36012 second order, or more selective, branch (eg, left adrenal vein, petrosal sinus)

36013 Introduction of catheter, right heart or main pulmonary artery

36014 Selective catheter placement, left or right pulmonary artery

36015 Selective catheter placement, segmental or subsegmental pulmonary artery

(For insertion of flow directed catheter (eg, Swan-Ganz), use 93503)

(For venous catheterization for selective organ blood sampling, use 36500)

Intra-Arterial—Intra-Aortic

(For radiological supervision and interpretation, see **Radiology**)

36100 Introduction of needle or intracatheter, carotid or vertebral artery

(For bilateral procedure, report 36100 with modifier 50)

36120 Introduction of needle or intracatheter; retrograde brachial artery

36140 extremity artery

36145 arteriovenous shunt created for dialysis (cannula, fistula, or graft)

(For insertion of arteriovenous cannula, see 36810-36821)

36160 Introduction of needle or intracatheter, aortic, translumbar

36200 Introduction of catheter, aorta

36215 Selective catheter placement, arterial system; each first order thoracic or brachiocephalic branch, within a vascular family

(For catheter placement for coronary angiography, use 93508)

36216 initial second order thoracic or brachiocephalic branch, within a vascular family

36217 initial third order or more selective thoracic or brachiocephalic branch, within a vascular family

+ 36218 additional second order, third order, and beyond, thoracic or brachiocephalic branch, within a vascular family (List in addition to code for initial second or third order vessel as appropriate)

(Use 36218 in conjunction with 36216, 36217)

(For angiography, see 75600-75790)

(For angioplasty, see 35470-35475)

(For transcatheter therapies, see 37200-37208, 61624, 61626)

(When coronary artery, arterial conduit (eg, internal mammary, inferior epigastric or free radical artery) or venous bypass graft angiography is performed in conjunction with cardiac catheterization, see the appropriate cardiac catheterization, injection procedure, and imaging supervision code(s) (93501-93556) in the **Medicine** section of the CPT codebook. When coronary artery, arterial coronary conduit or venous bypass graft angiography is performed without concomitant left heart cardiac catheterization, use 93508. When internal mammary artery angiography only is performed without a concomitant left heart cardiac catheterization, use 36216 or 36217 as appropriate.)

36245 Selective catheter placement, arterial system; each first order abdominal, pelvic, or lower extremity artery branch, within a vascular family

36246 initial second order abdominal, pelvic, or lower extremity artery branch, within a vascular family

36247 initial third order or more selective abdominal, pelvic, or lower extremity artery branch, within a vascular family

+ 36248 additional second order, third order, and beyond, abdominal, pelvic, or lower extremity artery branch, within a vascular family (List in addition to code for initial second or third order vessel as appropriate)

(Use 36248 in conjunction with 36246, 36247)

36260 Insertion of implantable intra-arterial infusion pump (eg, for chemotherapy of liver)

36261 Revision of implanted intra-arterial infusion pump

36262 Removal of implanted intra-arterial infusion pump

36299 Unlisted procedure, vascular injection

Venous

Venipuncture, needle or catheter for diagnostic study or intravenous therapy, percutaneous. These codes are also used to report the therapy as specified. For collection of a specimen from an established catheter, use 36592. For collection of a specimen from a completely implantable venous access device, use 36591.

36400 Venipuncture, younger than age 3 years, necessitating physician's skill, not to be used for routine venipuncture; femoral or jugular vein

36405 scalp vein

36406 other vein

36410 Venipuncture, age 3 years or older, necessitating physician's skill (separate procedure), for diagnostic or therapeutic purposes (not to be used for routine venipuncture)

36415 Collection of venous blood by venipuncture

(Do not report modifier 63 in conjunction with 36415)

36416 Collection of capillary blood specimen (eg, finger, heel, ear stick)

36420 Venipuncture, cutdown; younger than age 1 year

(Do not report modifier 63 in conjunction with 36420)

36425 age 1 or over

36430 Transfusion, blood or blood components

36440 Push transfusion, blood, 2 years or younger

36450 Exchange transfusion, blood; newborn

(Do not report modifier 63 in conjunction with 36450)

36455 other than newborn

36460 Transfusion, intrauterine, fetal

(Do not report modifier 63 in conjunction with 36460)

(For radiological supervision and interpretation, use 76941)

36468 Single or multiple injections of sclerosing solutions, spider veins (telangiectasia); limb or trunk

36469 face

36470 Injection of sclerosing solution; single vein

36471 multiple veins, same leg

36475 Endovenous ablation therapy of incompetent vein, extremity, inclusive of all imaging guidance and monitoring, percutaneous, radiofrequency; first vein treated

+ 36476 second and subsequent veins treated in a single extremity, each through separate access sites (List separately in addition to code for primary procedure)

(Use 36476 in conjunction with 36475)

►(Do not report 36475, 36476 in conjunction with 36000-36005, 36410, 36425, 36478, 36479, 37204, 75894, 76000, 76001, 76937, 76942, 76998, 77022, 93970, 93971)◄

36478 Endovenous ablation therapy of incompetent vein, extremity, inclusive of all imaging guidance and monitoring, percutaneous, laser; first vein treated

+ 36479 second and subsequent veins treated in a single extremity, each through separate access sites (List separately in addition to code for primary procedure)

(Use 36479 in conjunction with 36478)

►(Do not report 36478, 36479 in conjunction with 36000-36005, 36410, 36425, 36475, 36476, 37204, 75894, 76000, 76001, 76937, 76942, 76998, 77022, 93970, 93971)◄

36481 Percutaneous portal vein catheterization by any method

(For radiological supervision and interpretation, see 75885, 75887)

36500 Venous catheterization for selective organ blood sampling

(For catheterization in superior or inferior vena cava, use 36010)

(For radiological supervision and interpretation, use 75893)

36510 Catheterization of umbilical vein for diagnosis or therapy, newborn

(Do not report modifier 63 in conjunction with 36510)

36511 Therapeutic apheresis; for white blood cells

36512 for red blood cells

36513 for platelets

36514 for plasma pheresis

36515 with extracorporeal immunoadsorption and plasma reinfusion

36516 with extracorporeal selective adsorption or selective filtration and plasma reinfusion

(For physician evaluation, use modifier 26)

36522 Photopheresis, extracorporeal

(36540 has been deleted. To report, use 36591)

(36550 has been deleted. To report, use 36593)

Central Venous Access Procedures

To qualify as a central venous access catheter or device, the tip of the catheter/device must terminate in the subclavian, brachiocephalic (innominate) or iliac veins, the superior or inferior vena cava, or the right atrium. The venous access device may be either centrally inserted (jugular, subclavian, femoral vein or inferior vena cava catheter entry site) or peripherally inserted (eg, basilic or cephalic vein). The device may be accessed for use either via exposed catheter (external to the skin), via a subcutaneous port or via a subcutaneous pump.

The procedures involving these types of devices fall into five categories:

1. ***Insertion*** (placement of catheter through a newly established venous access)
2. ***Repair*** (fixing device without replacement of either catheter or port/pump, other than pharmacologic or mechanical correction of intracatheter or pericatheter occlusion [see 36595 or 36596])
3. ***Partial replacement*** of only the catheter component associated with a port/pump device, but not entire device
4. ***Complete replacement*** of entire device via same venous access site (complete exchange)
5. ***Removal*** of entire device.

There is no coding distinction between venous access achieved percutaneously versus by cutdown or based on catheter size.

For the repair, partial (catheter only) replacement, complete replacement, or removal of both catheters (placed from separate venous access sites) of a multi-catheter device, with or without subcutaneous ports/pumps, use the appropriate code describing the service with a frequency of two.

If an existing central venous access device is removed and a new one placed via a separate venous access site, appropriate codes for both procedures (removal of old, if code exists, and insertion of new device) should be reported.

When imaging is used for these procedures, either for gaining access to the venous entry site or for manipulating the catheter into final central position, use 76937, 77001.

(For refilling and maintenance of an implantable pump or reservoir for intravenous or intra-arterial drug delivery, use 96522)

Insertion of Central Venous Access Device

⊙ 36555 Insertion of non-tunneled centrally inserted central venous catheter; younger than 5 years of age

(For peripherally inserted non-tunneled central venous catheter, younger than 5 years of age, use 36568)

36556 age 5 years or older

(For peripherally inserted non-tunneled central venous catheter, age 5 years or older, use 36569)

⊙ 36557 Insertion of tunneled centrally inserted central venous catheter, without subcutaneous port or pump; younger than 5 years of age

⊙ 36558 age 5 years or older

(For peripherally inserted central venous catheter with port, 5 years or older, use 36571)

Surgery: Cardiovascular System

⊙ **36560** Insertion of tunneled centrally inserted central venous access device, with subcutaneous port; younger than 5 years of age

(For peripherally inserted central venous access device with subcutaneous port, younger than 5 years of age, use 36570)

⊙ **36561** age 5 years or older

(For peripherally inserted central venous catheter with subcutaneous port, 5 years or older, use 36571)

⊙ **36563** Insertion of tunneled centrally inserted central venous access device with subcutaneous pump

⊙ **36565** Insertion of tunneled centrally inserted central venous access device, requiring two catheters via two separate venous access sites; without subcutaneous port or pump (eg, Tesio type catheter)

⊙ **36566** with subcutaneous port(s)

⊙ **36568** Insertion of peripherally inserted central venous catheter (PICC), without subcutaneous port or pump; younger than 5 years of age

(For placement of centrally inserted non-tunneled central venous catheter, without subcutaneous port or pump, younger than 5 years of age, use 36555)

36569 age 5 years or older

(For placement of centrally inserted non-tunneled central venous catheter, without subcutaneous port or pump, age 5 years or older, use 36556)

⊙ **36570** Insertion of peripherally inserted central venous access device, with subcutaneous port; younger than 5 years of age

(For insertion of tunneled centrally inserted central venous access device with subcutaneous port, younger than 5 years of age, use 36560)

⊙ **36571** age 5 years or older

(For insertion of tunneled centrally inserted central venous access device with subcutaneous port, age 5 years or older, use 36561)

Repair of Central Venous Access Device

(For mechanical removal of pericatheter obstructive material, use 36595)

(For mechanical removal of intracatheter obstructive material, use 36596)

36575 Repair of tunneled or non-tunneled central venous access catheter, without subcutaneous port or pump, central or peripheral insertion site

⊙ **36576** Repair of central venous access device, with subcutaneous port or pump, central or peripheral insertion site

Partial Replacement of Central Venous Access Device (Catheter Only)

⊙ **36578** Replacement, catheter only, of central venous access device, with subcutaneous port or pump, central or peripheral insertion site

(For complete replacement of entire device through same venous access, use 36582 or 36583)

Complete Replacement of Central Venous Access Device Through Same Venous Access Site

36580 Replacement, complete, of a non-tunneled centrally inserted central venous catheter, without subcutaneous port or pump, through same venous access

⊙ **36581** Replacement, complete, of a tunneled centrally inserted central venous catheter, without subcutaneous port or pump, through same venous access

⊙ **36582** Replacement, complete, of a tunneled centrally inserted central venous access device, with subcutaneous port, through same venous access

⊙ **36583** Replacement, complete, of a tunneled centrally inserted central venous access device, with subcutaneous pump, through same venous access

36584 Replacement, complete, of a peripherally inserted central venous catheter (PICC), without subcutaneous port or pump, through same venous access

⊙ **36585** Replacement, complete, of a peripherally inserted central venous access device, with subcutaneous port, through same venous access

Removal of Central Venous Access Device

36589 Removal of tunneled central venous catheter, without subcutaneous port or pump

⊙ **36590** Removal of tunneled central venous access device, with subcutaneous port or pump, central or peripheral insertion

(Do not report 36589 or 36590 for removal of non-tunneled central venous catheters)

Other Central Venous Access Procedures

36591 Collection of blood specimen from a completely implantable venous access device

(Do not report 36591 in conjunction with any other service)

(For collection of venous blood specimen by venipuncture, use 36415)

(For collection of capillary blood specimen, use 36416)

36592 Collection of blood specimen using established central or peripheral catheter, venous, not otherwise specified

(For blood collection from an established arterial catheter, use 37799)

(Do not report 36592 in conjunction with any other service)

36593 Declotting by thrombolytic agent of implanted vascular access device or catheter

36595 Mechanical removal of pericatheter obstructive material (eg, fibrin sheath) from central venous device via separate venous access

(Do not report 36595 in conjunction with 36593)

(For venous catheterization, see 36010-36012)

(For radiological supervision and interpretation, use 75901)

36596 Mechanical removal of intraluminal (intracatheter) obstructive material from central venous device through device lumen

(Do not report 36596 in conjunction with 36593)

(For venous catheterization, see 36010-36012)

(For radiological supervision and interpretation, use 75902)

36597 Repositioning of previously placed central venous catheter under fluoroscopic guidance

(For fluoroscopic guidance, use 76000)

36598 Contrast injection(s) for radiologic evaluation of existing central venous access device, including fluoroscopy, image documentation and report

(Do not report 36598 in conjunction with 76000)

(Do not report 36598 in conjunction with 36595, 36596)

(For complete diagnostic studies, see 75820, 75825, 75827)

Arterial

36600 Arterial puncture, withdrawal of blood for diagnosis

⊘ **36620** Arterial catheterization or cannulation for sampling, monitoring or transfusion (separate procedure); percutaneous

36625 cutdown

36640 Arterial catheterization for prolonged infusion therapy (chemotherapy), cutdown

(See also 96420-96425)

(For arterial catheterization for occlusion therapy, see 75894)

36660 Catheterization, umbilical artery, newborn, for diagnosis or therapy

(Do not report modifier 63 in conjunction with 36660)

Intraosseous

36680 Placement of needle for intraosseous infusion

Hemodialysis Access, Intervascular Cannulation for Extracorporeal Circulation, or Shunt Insertion

36800 Insertion of cannula for hemodialysis, other purpose (separate procedure); vein to vein

36810 arteriovenous, external (Scribner type)

36815 arteriovenous, external revision, or closure

36818 Arteriovenous anastomosis, open; by upper arm cephalic vein transposition

(Do not report 36818 in conjunction with 36819, 36820, 36821, 36830 during a unilateral upper extremity procedure. For bilateral upper extremity open arteriovenous anastomoses performed at the same operative session, use modifier 50 or 59 as appropriate)

36819 by upper arm basilic vein transposition

(Do not report 36819 in conjunction with 36818, 36820, 36821, 36830 during a unilateral upper extremity procedure. For bilateral upper extremity open arteriovenous anastomoses performed at the same operative session, use modifier 50 or 59 as appropriate)

36820 by forearm vein transposition

36821 direct, any site (eg, Cimino type) (separate procedure)

36822 Insertion of cannula(s) for prolonged extracorporeal circulation for cardiopulmonary insufficiency (ECMO) (separate procedure)

(For maintenance of prolonged extracorporeal circulation, see 33960, 33961)

36823 Insertion of arterial and venous cannula(s) for isolated extracorporeal circulation including regional chemotherapy perfusion to an extremity, with or without hyperthermia, with removal of cannula(s) and repair of arteriotomy and venotomy sites

(36823 includes chemotherapy perfusion supported by a membrane oxygenator/perfusion pump. Do not report 96409-96425 in conjunction with 36823)

36825 Creation of arteriovenous fistula by other than direct arteriovenous anastomosis (separate procedure); autogenous graft

(For direct arteriovenous anastomosis, use 36821)

36830 nonautogenous graft (eg, biological collagen, thermoplastic graft)

(For direct arteriovenous anastomosis, use 36821)

36831 Thrombectomy, open, arteriovenous fistula without revision, autogenous or nonautogenous dialysis graft (separate procedure)

36832 Revision, open, arteriovenous fistula; without thrombectomy, autogenous or nonautogenous dialysis graft (separate procedure)

36833 with thrombectomy, autogenous or nonautogenous dialysis graft (separate procedure)

36834 Plastic repair of arteriovenous aneurysm (separate procedure)

36835 Insertion of Thomas shunt (separate procedure)

36838 Distal revascularization and interval ligation (DRIL), upper extremity hemodialysis access (steal syndrome)

(Do not report 36838 in conjunction with 35512, 35522, 35523, 36832, 37607, 37618)

36860 External cannula declotting (separate procedure); without balloon catheter

36861 with balloon catheter

(If imaging guidance is performed, use 76000)

⊙ **36870** Thrombectomy, percutaneous, arteriovenous fistula, autogenous or nonautogenous graft (includes mechanical thrombus extraction and intra-graft thrombolysis)

(Do not report 36870 in conjunction with 36593)

(For catheterization, use 36145)

(For radiological supervision and interpretation, use 75790)

Portal Decompression Procedures

37140 Venous anastomosis, open; portocaval

(For peritoneal-venous shunt, use 49425)

37145 renoportal

37160 caval-mesenteric

37180 splenorenal, proximal

37181 splenorenal, distal (selective decompression of esophagogastric varices, any technique)

(For percutaneous procedure, use 37182)

37182 Insertion of transvenous intrahepatic portosystemic shunt(s) (TIPS) (includes venous access, hepatic and portal vein catheterization, portography with hemodynamic evaluation, intrahepatic tract formation/dilatation, stent placement and all associated imaging guidance and documentation)

(Do not report 75885 or 75887 in conjunction with 37182)

(For open procedure, use 37140)

37183 Revision of transvenous intrahepatic portosystemic shunt(s) (TIPS) (includes venous access, hepatic and portal vein catheterization, portography with hemodynamic evaluation, intrahepatic tract recanulization/dilatation, stent placement and all associated imaging guidance and documentation)

(Do not report 75885 or 75887 in conjunction with 37183)

(For repair of arteriovenous aneurysm, use 36834)

Transcatheter Procedures

Codes for catheter placement and the radiologic supervision and interpretation should also be reported, in addition to the code(s) for the therapeutic aspect of the procedure.

Mechanical Thrombectomy

Code(s) for catheter placement(s), diagnostic studies, and other percutaneous interventions (eg, transluminal balloon angioplasty, stent placement) provided are separately reportable.

Codes 37184-37188 specifically include intraprocedural fluoroscopic radiological supervision and interpretation services for guidance of the procedure.

Intraprocedural injection(s) of a thrombolytic agent is an included service and not separately reportable in conjunction with mechanical thrombectomy. However, subsequent or prior continuous infusion of a thrombolytic is not an included service and is separately reportable (see 37201, 75896, 75898).

For coronary mechanical thrombectomy, use 92973.

For mechanical thrombectomy for dialysis fistula, use 36870.

Arterial Mechanical Thrombectomy

Arterial mechanical thrombectomy may be performed as a "primary" transcatheter procedure with pretreatment planning, performance of the procedure, and postprocedure evaluation focused on providing this service. Typically, the diagnosis of thrombus has been made prior to the procedure, and a mechanical thrombectomy is planned preoperatively. Primary mechanical thrombectomy is reported per vascular family using 37184 for the initial vessel treated and 37185 for second or all subsequent vessel(s) within the same vascular family. To report mechanical thrombectomy of an additional vascular family treated through a separate access site, use modifier 51 in conjunction with 37184-37185.

Primary mechanical thrombectomy may precede or follow another percutaneous intervention. Most commonly primary mechanical thrombectomy will precede another percutaneous intervention with the decision regarding the need for other services not made until after mechanical thrombectomy has been performed. Occasionally, the performance of primary mechanical thrombectomy may follow another percutaneous intervention.

Do **NOT** report 37184-37185 for mechanical thrombectomy performed for the retrieval of short segments of thrombus or embolus evident during other percutaneous interventional procedures. See 37186 for these procedures.

Arterial mechanical thrombectomy is considered a "secondary" transcatheter procedure for removal or retrieval of short segments of thrombus or embolus when performed either before or after another percutaneous intervention (eg, percutaneous transluminal balloon angioplasty, stent placement). Secondary mechanical thrombectomy is reported using 37186. Do **NOT** report 37186 in conjunction with 37184-37185.

Venous Mechanical Thrombectomy

Use 37187 to report the initial application of venous mechanical thrombectomy. To report bilateral venous mechanical thrombectomy performed through a separate access site(s), use modifier 50 in conjunction with 37187. For repeat treatment on a subsequent day during a course of thrombolytic therapy, use 37188.

Arterial Mechanical Thrombectomy

⊙ **37184** Primary percutaneous transluminal mechanical thrombectomy, noncoronary, arterial or arterial bypass graft, including fluoroscopic guidance and intraprocedural pharmacological thrombolytic injection(s); initial vessel

►(Do not report 37184 in conjunction with 76000, 76001, 96374, 99143-99150)◄

⊙+ **37185** second and all subsequent vessel(s) within the same vascular family (List separately in addition to code for primary mechanical thrombectomy procedure)

►(Do not report 37185 in conjunction with 76000, 76001, 96375)◄

⊙+ **37186** Secondary percutaneous transluminal thrombectomy (eg, nonprimary mechanical, snare basket, suction technique), noncoronary, arterial or arterial bypass graft, including fluoroscopic guidance and intraprocedural pharmacological thrombolytic injections, provided in conjunction with another percutaneous intervention other than primary mechanical thrombectomy (List separately in addition to code for primary procedure)

►(Do not report 37186 in conjunction with 76000, 76001, 96375)◄

Venous Mechanical Thrombectomy

⊙ **37187** Percutaneous transluminal mechanical thrombectomy, vein(s), including intraprocedural pharmacological thrombolytic injections and fluoroscopic guidance

►(Do not report 37187 in conjunction with 76000, 76001, 96375)◄

⊙ **37188** Percutaneous transluminal mechanical thrombectomy, vein(s), including intraprocedural pharmacological thrombolytic injections and fluoroscopic guidance, repeat treatment on subsequent day during course of thrombolytic therapy

►(Do not report 37188 in conjunction with 76000, 76001, 96375)◄

Other Procedures

37195 Thrombolysis, cerebral, by intravenous infusion

37200 Transcatheter biopsy

(For radiological supervision and interpretation, use 75970)

37201 Transcatheter therapy, infusion for thrombolysis other than coronary

(For radiological supervision and interpretation, use 75896)

37202 Transcatheter therapy, infusion other than for thrombolysis, any type (eg, spasmolytic, vasoconstrictive)

(For thrombolysis of coronary vessels, see 92975, 92977)

(For radiological supervision and interpretation, use 75896)

⊙ **37203** Transcatheter retrieval, percutaneous, of intravascular foreign body (eg, fractured venous or arterial catheter)

(For radiological supervision and interpretation, use 75961)

37204 Transcatheter occlusion or embolization (eg, for tumor destruction, to achieve hemostasis, to occlude a vascular malformation), percutaneous, any method, non-central nervous system, non-head or neck

(See also 61624, 61626)

(For radiological supervision and interpretation, use 75894)

(For uterine fibroid embolization [uterine artery embolization performed to treat uterine fibroids], use 37210)

(For obstetrical and gynecologic embolization procedures other than uterine fibroid embolization [eg, embolization to treat obstetrical or postpartum hemorrhage], use 37204)

37205 Transcatheter placement of an intravascular stent(s) (except coronary, carotid, and vertebral vessel), percutaneous; initial vessel

(For radiological supervision and interpretation, use 75960)

(For coronary stent placement, see 92980, 92981; intracranial, use 61635)

+ **37206** each additional vessel (List separately in addition to code for primary procedure)

(Use 37206 in conjunction with 37205)

(For transcatheter placement of intravascular cervical carotid artery stent(s), see 37215, 37216)

(For transcatheter placement of extracranial vertebral or intrathoracic carotid artery stent(s), see Category III codes 0075T, 0076T)

(For radiological supervision and interpretation, use 75960)

37207 Transcatheter placement of an intravascular stent(s) (non-coronary vessel), open; initial vessel

+ 37208 each additional vessel (List separately in addition to code for primary procedure)

(Use 37208 in conjunction with 37207)

(For radiological supervision and interpretation, use 75960)

(For catheterizations, see 36215-36248)

(For transcatheter placement of intracoronary stent(s), see 92980, 92981)

37209 Exchange of a previously placed intravascular catheter during thrombolytic therapy

(For radiological supervision and interpretation, use 75900)

⊙ 37210 Uterine fibroid embolization (UFE, embolization of the uterine arteries to treat uterine fibroids, leiomyomata), percutaneous approach inclusive of vascular access, vessel selection, embolization, and all radiological supervision and interpretation, intraprocedural roadmapping, and imaging guidance necessary to complete the procedure

(37210 includes all catheterizations and intraprocedural imaging required for a UFE procedure to confirm the presence of previously known fibroids and to roadmap vascular anatomy to enable appropriate therapy)

(Do not report 37210 in conjunction with 36200, 36245-36248, 37204, 75894, 75898)

(For all other non-central nervous system (CNS) embolization procedures, use 37204)

⊙ 37215 Transcatheter placement of intravascular stent(s), cervical carotid artery, percutaneous; with distal embolic protection

⊙ 37216 without distal embolic protection

(37215 and 37216 include all ipsilateral selective carotid catheterization, all diagnostic imaging for ipsilateral, cervical and cerebral carotid arteriography, and all related radiological supervision and interpretation. When ipsilateral carotid arteriogram (including imaging and selective catheterization) confirms the need for carotid stenting, 37215 and 37216 are inclusive of these services. If carotid stenting is not indicated, then the appropriate codes for carotid catheterization and imaging should be reported in lieu of 37215 and 37216)

(Do not report 37215, 37216 in conjunction with 75671, 75680)

(For transcatheter placement of extracranial vertebral or intrathoracic carotid artery stent(s), see Category III codes 0075T, 0076T)

(For percutaneous transcatheter placement of intravascular stents other than coronary, carotid, or vertebral, see 37205, 37206)

Intravascular Ultrasound Services

Intravascular ultrasound services include all transducer manipulations and repositioning within the specific vessel being examined, both before and after therapeutic intervention (eg, stent placement).

Vascular access for intravascular ultrasound performed during a therapeutic intervention is not reported separately.

+ 37250 Intravascular ultrasound (non-coronary vessel) during diagnostic evaluation and/or therapeutic intervention; initial vessel (List separately in addition to code for primary procedure)

+ 37251 each additional vessel (List separately in addition to code for primary procedure)

(Use 37251 in conjunction with 37250)

(For catheterizations, see 36215-36248)

(For transcatheter therapies, see 37200-37208, 61624, 61626)

(For radiological supervision and interpretation see 75945, 75946)

Endoscopy

Surgical vascular endoscopy always includes diagnostic endoscopy.

37500 Vascular endoscopy, surgical, with ligation of perforator veins, subfascial (SEPS)

(For open procedure, use 37760)

37501 Unlisted vascular endoscopy procedure

Ligation

(For phleborraphy and arteriorraphy, see 35201-35286)

37565 Ligation, internal jugular vein

37600 Ligation; external carotid artery

37605 internal or common carotid artery

37606 internal or common carotid artery, with gradual occlusion, as with Selverstone or Crutchfield clamp

(For transcatheter permanent arterial occlusion or embolization, see 61624-61626)

(For endovascular temporary arterial balloon occlusion, use 61623)

(For ligation treatment of intracranial aneurysm, use 61703)

37607 Ligation or banding of angioaccess arteriovenous fistula

37609 Ligation or biopsy, temporal artery

37615 Ligation, major artery (eg, post-traumatic, rupture); neck

37616 chest

37617 abdomen

37618 extremity

37620 Interruption, partial or complete, of inferior vena cava by suture, ligation, plication, clip, extravascular, intravascular (umbrella device)

(For radiological supervision and interpretation, use 75940)

37650 Ligation of femoral vein

(For bilateral procedure, report 37650 with modifier 50)

37660 Ligation of common iliac vein

37700 Ligation and division of long saphenous vein at saphenofemoral junction, or distal interruptions

(Do not report 37700 in conjunction with 37718, 37722)

(For bilateral procedure, report 37700 with modifier 50)

37718 Ligation, division, and stripping, short saphenous vein

(For bilateral procedure, use modifier 50)

(Do not report 37718 in conjunction with 37735, 37780)

37722 Ligation, division, and stripping, long (greater) saphenous veins from saphenofemoral junction to knee or below

(For ligation and stripping of the short saphenous vein, use 37718)

(For bilateral procedure, report 37722 with modifier 50)

(Do not report 37722 in conjunction with 37700, 37735)

►(For ligation, division, and stripping of the greater saphenous vein, use 37722. For ligation, division, and stripping of the short saphenous vein, use 37718)◄

37735 Ligation and division and complete stripping of long or short saphenous veins with radical excision of ulcer and skin graft and/or interruption of communicating veins of lower leg, with excision of deep fascia

(Do not report 37735 in conjunction with 37700, 37718, 37722, 37780)

(For bilateral procedure, report 37735 with modifier 50)

37760 Ligation of perforator veins, subfascial, radical (Linton type), with or without skin graft, open

(For endoscopic procedure, use 37500)

37765 Stab phlebectomy of varicose veins, one extremity; 10-20 stab incisions

(For less than 10 incisions, use 37799)

(For more than 20 incisions, use 37766)

37766 more than 20 incisions

37780 Ligation and division of short saphenous vein at saphenopopliteal junction (separate procedure)

(For bilateral procedure, report 37780 with modifier 50)

37785 Ligation, division, and/or excision of varicose vein cluster(s), one leg

(For bilateral procedure, report 37785 with modifier 50)

Other Procedures

37788 Penile revascularization, artery, with or without vein graft

37790 Penile venous occlusive procedure

37799 Unlisted procedure, vascular surgery

Hemic and Lymphatic Systems

Spleen

Excision

38100 Splenectomy; total (separate procedure)

38101 partial (separate procedure)

+ **38102** total, en bloc for extensive disease, in conjunction with other procedure (List in addition to code for primary procedure)

Repair

38115 Repair of ruptured spleen (splenorrhaphy) with or without partial splenectomy

Laparoscopy

Surgical laparoscopy always includes diagnostic laparoscopy. To report a diagnostic laparoscopy (peritoneoscopy) (separate procedure), use 49320.

38120 Laparoscopy, surgical, splenectomy

38129 Unlisted laparoscopy procedure, spleen

Introduction

38200 Injection procedure for splenoportography

(For radiological supervision and interpretation, use 75810)

General

Bone Marrow or Stem Cell Services/Procedures

Codes 38207-38215 describe various steps used to preserve, prepare and purify bone marrow/stem cells prior to transplantation or reinfusion. Each code may be reported only once per day regardless of the quantity of bone marrow/stem cells manipulated.

38204 Management of recipient hematopoietic progenitor cell donor search and cell acquisition

38205 Blood-derived hematopoietic progenitor cell harvesting for transplantation, per collection; allogenic

38206 autologous

38207 Transplant preparation of hematopoietic progenitor cells; cryopreservation and storage

(For diagnostic cryopreservation and storage, see 88240)

38208 thawing of previously frozen harvest, without washing

(For diagnostic thawing and expansion of frozen cells, see 88241)

38209 thawing of previously frozen harvest, with washing

38210 specific cell depletion within harvest, T-cell depletion

38211 tumor cell depletion

38212 red blood cell removal

38213 platelet depletion

38214 plasma (volume) depletion

38215 cell concentration in plasma, mononuclear, or buffy coat layer

(Do not report 38207-38215 in conjunction with 88182, 88184-88189)

38220 Bone marrow; aspiration only

38221 biopsy, needle or trocar

(For bone marrow biopsy interpretation, use 88305)

38230 Bone marrow harvesting for transplantation

(For autologous and allogenic blood-derived peripheral stem cell harvesting for transplantation, see 38205-38206)

38240 Bone marrow or blood-derived peripheral stem cell transplantation; allogenic

38241 autologous

38242 allogeneic donor lymphocyte infusions

(For bone marrow aspiration, use 38220)

(For modification, treatment, and processing of bone marrow or blood-derived stem cell specimens for transplantation, use 38210-38213)

(For cryopreservation, freezing and storage of blood-derived stem cells for transplantation, use 88240)

(For thawing and expansion of blood-derived stem cells for transplantation, use 88241)

(For compatibility studies, see 86812-86822)

Lymph Nodes and Lymphatic Channels

Incision

38300 Drainage of lymph node abscess or lymphadenitis; simple

38305 extensive

38308 Lymphangiotomy or other operations on lymphatic channels

38380 Suture and/or ligation of thoracic duct; cervical approach

38381 thoracic approach

38382 abdominal approach

Excision

(For injection for sentinel node identification, use 38792)

38500 Biopsy or excision of lymph node(s); open, superficial

(Do not report 38500 with 38700-38780)

38505 by needle, superficial (eg, cervical, inguinal, axillary)

(If imaging guidance is performed, see 76942, 77012, 77021)

(For fine needle aspiration, use 10021 or 10022)

(For evaluation of fine needle aspirate, see 88172, 88173)

38510 open, deep cervical node(s)

38520 open, deep cervical node(s) with excision scalene fat pad

38525 open, deep axillary node(s)

38530 open, internal mammary node(s)

(Do not report 38530 with 38720-38746)

(For percutaneous needle biopsy, retroperitoneal lymph node or mass, use 49180. For fine needle aspiration, use 10022)

38542 Dissection, deep jugular node(s)

(For radical cervical neck dissection, use 38720)

38550 Excision of cystic hygroma, axillary or cervical; without deep neurovascular dissection

38555 with deep neurovascular dissection

Limited Lymphadenectomy for Staging

38562 Limited lymphadenectomy for staging (separate procedure); pelvic and para-aortic

(When combined with prostatectomy, use 55812 or 55842)

(When combined with insertion of radioactive substance into prostate, use 55862)

38564 retroperitoneal (aortic and/or splenic)

Laparoscopy

Surgical laparoscopy always includes diagnostic laparoscopy. To report a diagnostic laparoscopy (peritoneoscopy) (separate procedure), use 49320.

38570 Laparoscopy, surgical; with retroperitoneal lymph node sampling (biopsy), single or multiple

38571 with bilateral total pelvic lymphadenectomy

38572 with bilateral total pelvic lymphadenectomy and peri-aortic lymph node sampling (biopsy), single or multiple

(For drainage of lymphocele to peritoneal cavity, use 49323)

38589 Unlisted laparoscopy procedure, lymphatic system

Radical Lymphadenectomy (Radical Resection of Lymph Nodes)

(For limited pelvic and retroperitoneal lymphadenectomies, see 38562, 38564)

38700 Suprahyoid lymphadenectomy

(For bilateral procedure, report 38700 with modifier 50)

38720 Cervical lymphadenectomy (complete)

(For bilateral procedure, report 38720 with modifier 50)

38724 Cervical lymphadenectomy (modified radical neck dissection)

38740 Axillary lymphadenectomy; superficial

38745 complete

+ 38746 Thoracic lymphadenectomy, regional, including mediastinal and peritracheal nodes (List separately in addition to code for primary procedure)

+ 38747 Abdominal lymphadenectomy, regional, including celiac, gastric, portal, peripancreatic, with or without para-aortic and vena caval nodes (List separately in addition to code for primary procedure)

38760 Inguinofemoral lymphadenectomy, superficial, including Cloquets node (separate procedure)

(For bilateral procedure, report 38760 with modifier 50)

38765 Inguinofemoral lymphadenectomy, superficial, in continuity with pelvic lymphadenectomy, including external iliac, hypogastric, and obturator nodes (separate procedure)

(For bilateral procedure, report 38765 with modifier 50)

38770 Pelvic lymphadenectomy, including external iliac, hypogastric, and obturator nodes (separate procedure)

(For bilateral procedure, report 38770 with modifier 50)

38780 Retroperitoneal transabdominal lymphadenectomy, extensive, including pelvic, aortic, and renal nodes (separate procedure)

(For excision and repair of lymphedematous skin and subcutaneous tissue, see 15004-15005, 15570-15650)

Introduction

38790 Injection procedure; lymphangiography

(For bilateral procedure, report 38790 with modifier 50)

(For radiological supervision and interpretation, see 75801-75807)

38792 for identification of sentinel node

(For excision of sentinel node, see 38500-38542)

(For nuclear medicine lymphatics and lymph gland imaging, use 78195)

38794 Cannulation, thoracic duct

Other Procedures

38999 Unlisted procedure, hemic or lymphatic system

Mediastinum and Diaphragm

Mediastinum

Incision

39000 Mediastinotomy with exploration, drainage, removal of foreign body, or biopsy; cervical approach

39010 transthoracic approach, including either transthoracic or median sternotomy

Excision

39200 Excision of mediastinal cyst

39220 Excision of mediastinal tumor

(For substernal thyroidectomy, use 60270)

(For thymectomy, use 60520)

Endoscopy

39400 Mediastinoscopy, with or without biopsy

Other Procedures

39499 Unlisted procedure, mediastinum

Diaphragm

Repair

(For transabdominal repair of diaphragmatic [esophageal hiatal] hernia, see 43324, 43325)

39501 Repair, laceration of diaphragm, any approach

39502 Repair, paraesophageal hiatus hernia, transabdominal, with or without fundoplasty, vagotomy, and/or pyloroplasty, except neonatal

39503 Rcpair, neonatal diaphragmatic hernia, with or without chest tube insertion and with or without creation of ventral hernia

(Do not report modifier 63 in conjunction with 39503)

39520 Repair, diaphragmatic hernia (esophageal hiatal); transthoracic

39530 combined, thoracoabdominal

39531 combined, thoracoabdominal, with dilation of stricture (with or without gastroplasty)

39540 Repair, diaphragmatic hernia (other than neonatal), traumatic; acute

39541 chronic

39545 Imbrication of diaphragm for eventration, transthoracic or transabdominal, paralytic or nonparalytic

39560 Resection, diaphragm; with simple repair (eg, primary suture)

39561 with complex repair (eg, prosthetic material, local muscle flap)

Other Procedures

39599 Unlisted procedure, diaphragm

Digestive System

Lips

(For procedures on skin of lips, see 10040 et seq)

Excision

40490 Biopsy of lip

40500 Vermilionectomy (lip shave), with mucosal advancement

40510 Excision of lip; transverse wedge excision with primary closure

40520 V-excision with primary direct linear closure

(For excision of mucous lesions, see 40810-40816)

40525 full thickness, reconstruction with local flap (eg, Estlander or fan)

40527 full thickness, reconstruction with cross lip flap (Abbe-Estlander)

40530 Resection of lip, more than one-fourth, without reconstruction

(For reconstruction, see 13131 et seq)

Repair (Cheiloplasty)

40650 Repair lip, full thickness; vermilion only

40652 up to half vertical height

40654 over one-half vertical height, or complex

40700 Plastic repair of cleft lip/nasal deformity; primary, partial or complete, unilateral

40701 primary bilateral, one stage procedure

40702 primary bilateral, one of two stages

40720 secondary, by recreation of defect and reclosure

(For bilateral procedure, report 40720 with modifier 50)

(To report rhinoplasty only for nasal deformity secondary to congenital cleft lip, see 30460, 30462)

(For repair of cleft lip, with cross lip pedicle flap (Abbe-Estlander type), use 40527)

40761 with cross lip pedicle flap (Abbe-Estlander type), including sectioning and inserting of pedicle

(For repair cleft palate, see 42200 et seq)

(For other reconstructive procedures, see 14060, 14061, 15120-15261, 15574, 15576, 15630)

Other Procedures

40799 Unlisted procedure, lips

Vestibule of Mouth

The vestibule is the part of the oral cavity outside the dentoalveolar structures; it includes the mucosal and submucosal tissue of lips and cheeks.

Incision

40800 Drainage of abscess, cyst, hematoma, vestibule of mouth; simple

40801 complicated

40804 Removal of embedded foreign body, vestibule of mouth; simple

40805 complicated

40806 Incision of labial frenum (frenotomy)

Excision, Destruction

40808 Biopsy, vestibule of mouth

40810 Excision of lesion of mucosa and submucosa, vestibule of mouth; without repair

40812 with simple repair

40814 with complex repair

40816 complex, with excision of underlying muscle

40818 Excision of mucosa of vestibule of mouth as donor graft

40819 Excision of frenum, labial or buccal (frenumectomy, frenulectomy, frenectomy)

40820 Destruction of lesion or scar of vestibule of mouth by physical methods (eg, laser, thermal, cryo, chemical)

Repair

40830 Closure of laceration, vestibule of mouth; 2.5 cm or less

40831 over 2.5 cm or complex

40840 Vestibuloplasty; anterior

40842 posterior, unilateral

40843 posterior, bilateral

40844 entire arch

40845 complex (including ridge extension, muscle repositioning)

(For skin grafts, see 15002 et seq)

Other Procedures

40899 Unlisted procedure, vestibule of mouth

Tongue and Floor of Mouth

Incision

41000 Intraoral incision and drainage of abscess, cyst, or hematoma of tongue or floor of mouth; lingual

41005 sublingual, superficial

41006 sublingual, deep, supramylohyoid

41007 submental space

41008 submandibular space

41009 masticator space

41010 Incision of lingual frenum (frenotomy)

41015 Extraoral incision and drainage of abscess, cyst, or hematoma of floor of mouth; sublingual

41016 submental

41017 submandibular

41018 masticator space

(For frenoplasty, use 41520)

41019 Placement of needles, catheters, or other device(s) into the head and/or neck region (percutaneous, transoral, or transnasal) for subsequent interstitial radioelement application

(For imaging guidance, see 76942, 77002, 77012, 77021)

(For stereotactic insertion of intracranial brachytherapy radiation sources, use 61770)

►(For interstitial radioelement application, see 77776-77787)◄

Excision

41100 Biopsy of tongue; anterior two-thirds

41105 posterior one-third

41108 Biopsy of floor of mouth

41110 Excision of lesion of tongue without closure

41112 Excision of lesion of tongue with closure; anterior two-thirds

41113 posterior one-third

41114 with local tongue flap

(List 41114 in addition to code 41112 or 41113)

41115 Excision of lingual frenum (frenectomy)

41116 Excision, lesion of floor of mouth

41120 Glossectomy; less than one-half tongue

41130 hemiglossectomy

41135 partial, with unilateral radical neck dissection

41140 complete or total, with or without tracheostomy, without radical neck dissection

41145 complete or total, with or without tracheostomy, with unilateral radical neck dissection

41150 composite procedure with resection floor of mouth and mandibular resection, without radical neck dissection

41153 composite procedure with resection floor of mouth, with suprahyoid neck dissection

41155 composite procedure with resection floor of mouth, mandibular resection, and radical neck dissection (Commando type)

Repair

41250 Repair of laceration 2.5 cm or less; floor of mouth and/or anterior two-thirds of tongue

41251 posterior one-third of tongue

41252 Repair of laceration of tongue, floor of mouth, over 2.6 cm or complex

Other Procedures

41500 Fixation of tongue, mechanical, other than suture (eg, K-wire)

41510 Suture of tongue to lip for micrognathia (Douglas type procedure)

● **41512** Tongue base suspension, permanent suture technique

►(For fixation of tongue, mechanical, other than suture, use 41500)◄

►(For suture of tongue to lip for micrognathia, use 41510)◄

41520 Frenoplasty (surgical revision of frenum, eg, with Z-plasty)

(For frcnotomy, see 40806, 41010)

● **41530** Submucosal ablation of the tongue base, radiofrequency, one or more sites, per session

41599 Unlisted procedure, tongue, floor of mouth

Dentoalveolar Structures

Incision

41800 Drainage of abscess, cyst, hematoma from dentoalveolar structures

41805 Removal of embedded foreign body from dentoalveolar structures; soft tissues

41806 bone

Excision, Destruction

41820 Gingivectomy, excision gingiva, each quadrant

41821 Operculectomy, excision pericoronal tissues

41822 Excision of fibrous tuberosities, dentoalveolar structures

41823 Excision of osseous tuberosities, dentoalveolar structures

41825 Excision of lesion or tumor (except listed above), dentoalveolar structures; without repair

41826 with simple repair

41827 with complex repair

(For nonexcisional destruction, use 41850)

41828 Excision of hyperplastic alveolar mucosa, each quadrant (specify)

41830 Alveolectomy, including curettage of osteitis or sequestrectomy

41850 Destruction of lesion (except excision), dentoalveolar structures

Other Procedures

41870 Periodontal mucosal grafting

41872 Gingivoplasty, each quadrant (specify)

41874 Alveoloplasty, each quadrant (specify)

(For closure of lacerations, see 40830, 40831)

(For segmental osteotomy, use 21206)

(For reduction of fractures, see 21421-21490)

41899 Unlisted procedure, dentoalveolar structures

Palate and Uvula

Incision

42000 Drainage of abscess of palate, uvula

Excision, Destruction

42100 Biopsy of palate, uvula

42104 Excision, lesion of palate, uvula; without closure

42106 with simple primary closure

42107 with local flap closure

(For skin graft, see 14040-14300)

(For mucosal graft, use 40818)

42120 Resection of palate or extensive resection of lesion

(For reconstruction of palate with extraoral tissue, see 14040-14300, 15050, 15120, 15240, 15576)

42140 Uvulectomy, excision of uvula

42145 Palatopharyngoplasty (eg, uvulopalatopharyngoplasty, uvulopharyngoplasty)

(For removal of exostosis of the bony palate, see 21031, 21032)

42160 Destruction of lesion, palate or uvula (thermal, cryo or chemical)

Repair

42180 Repair, laceration of palate; up to 2 cm

42182 over 2 cm or complex

42200 Palatoplasty for cleft palate, soft and/or hard palate only

42205 Palatoplasty for cleft palate, with closure of alveolar ridge; soft tissue only

42210 with bone graft to alveolar ridge (includes obtaining graft)

42215 Palatoplasty for cleft palate; major revision

42220 secondary lengthening procedure

42225 attachment pharyngeal flap

42226 Lengthening of palate, and pharyngeal flap

42227 Lengthening of palate, with island flap

42235 Repair of anterior palate, including vomer flap

(For repair of oronasal fistula, use 30600)

42260 Repair of nasolabial fistula

(For repair of cleft lip, see 40700 et seq)

42280 Maxillary impression for palatal prosthesis

42281 Insertion of pin-retained palatal prosthesis

Other Procedures

42299 Unlisted procedure, palate, uvula

Salivary Gland and Ducts

Incision

42300 Drainage of abscess; parotid, simple

42305 parotid, complicated

42310 Drainage of abscess; submaxillary or sublingual, intraoral

42320 submaxillary, external

42330 Sialolithotomy; submandibular (submaxillary), sublingual or parotid, uncomplicated, intraoral

42335 submandibular (submaxillary), complicated, intraoral

42340 parotid, extraoral or complicated intraoral

Excision

42400 Biopsy of salivary gland; needle

(For fine needle aspiration, see 10021, 10022)

(For evaluation of fine needle aspirate, see 88172, 88173)

(If imaging guidance is performed, see 76942, 77002, 77012, 77021)

42405 incisional

(If imaging guidance is performed, see 76942, 77002, 77012, 77021)

42408 Excision of sublingual salivary cyst (ranula)

42409 Marsupialization of sublingual salivary cyst (ranula)

42410 Excision of parotid tumor or parotid gland; lateral lobe, without nerve dissection

42415 lateral lobe, with dissection and preservation of facial nerve

42420 total, with dissection and preservation of facial nerve

42425 total, en bloc removal with sacrifice of facial nerve

42426 total, with unilateral radical neck dissection

(For suture or grafting of facial nerve, see 64864, 64865, 69740, 69745)

42440 Excision of submandibular (submaxillary) gland

42450 Excision of sublingual gland

Repair

42500 Plastic repair of salivary duct, sialodochoplasty; primary or simple

42505 secondary or complicated

42507 Parotid duct diversion, bilateral (Wilke type procedure);

42508 with excision of one submandibular gland

42509 with excision of both submandibular glands

42510 with ligation of both submandibular (Wharton's) ducts

Other Procedures

42550 Injection procedure for sialography

(For radiological supervision and interpretation, use 70390)

42600 Closure salivary fistula

42650 Dilation salivary duct

42660 Dilation and catheterization of salivary duct, with or without injection

42665 Ligation salivary duct, intraoral

42699 Unlisted procedure, salivary glands or ducts

Pharynx, Adenoids, and Tonsils

Incision

42700 Incision and drainage abscess; peritonsillar

42720 retropharyngeal or parapharyngeal, intraoral approach

42725 retropharyngeal or parapharyngeal, external approach

Excision, Destruction

42800 Biopsy; oropharynx

42802 hypopharynx

42804 nasopharynx, visible lesion, simple

42806 nasopharynx, survey for unknown primary lesion

(For laryngoscopic biopsy, see 31510, 31535, 31536)

42808 Excision or destruction of lesion of pharynx, any method

42809 Removal of foreign body from pharynx

42810 Excision branchial cleft cyst or vestige, confined to skin and subcutaneous tissues

42815 Excision branchial cleft cyst, vestige, or fistula, extending beneath subcutaneous tissues and/or into pharynx

42820 Tonsillectomy and adenoidectomy; younger than age 12

42821 age 12 or over

42825 Tonsillectomy, primary or secondary; younger than age 12

42826 age 12 or over

42830 Adenoidectomy, primary; younger than age 12

42831 age 12 or over

42835 Adenoidectomy, secondary; younger than age 12

42836 age 12 or over

42842 Radical resection of tonsil, tonsillar pillars, and/or retromolar trigone; without closure

42844 closure with local flap (eg, tongue, buccal)

42845 closure with other flap

(For closure with other flap(s), use appropriate number for flap(s))

(When combined with radical neck dissection, use also 38720)

42860 Excision of tonsil tags

42870 Excision or destruction lingual tonsil, any method (separate procedure)

(For resection of the nasopharynx [eg, juvenile angiofibroma] by bicoronal and/or transzygomatic approach, see 61586 and 61600)

42890 Limited pharyngectomy

42892 Resection of lateral pharyngeal wall or pyriform sinus, direct closure by advancement of lateral and posterior pharyngeal walls

(When combined with radical neck dissection, use also 38720)

42894 Resection of pharyngeal wall requiring closure with myocutaneous flap

(When combined with radical neck dissection, use also 38720)

(For limited pharyngectomy with radical neck dissection, use 38720 with 42890)

Repair

42900 Suture pharynx for wound or injury

42950 Pharyngoplasty (plastic or reconstructive operation on pharynx)

(For pharyngeal flap, use 42225)

42953 Pharyngoesophageal repair

(For closure with myocutaneous or other flap, use appropriate number in addition)

Other Procedures

42955 Pharyngostomy (fistulization of pharynx, external for feeding)

42960 Control oropharyngeal hemorrhage, primary or secondary (eg, post-tonsillectomy); simple

42961 complicated, requiring hospitalization

42962 with secondary surgical intervention

42970 Control of nasopharyngeal hemorrhage, primary or secondary (eg, postadenoidectomy); simple, with posterior nasal packs, with or without anterior packs and/or cautery

42971 complicated, requiring hospitalization

42972 with secondary surgical intervention

42999 Unlisted procedure, pharynx, adenoids, or tonsils

Esophagus

Incision

(For esophageal intubation with laparotomy, use 43510)

43020 Esophagotomy, cervical approach, with removal of foreign body

43030 Cricopharyngeal myotomy

43045 Esophagotomy, thoracic approach, with removal of foreign body

Excision

(For gastrointestinal reconstruction for previous esophagectomy, see 43360, 43361)

43100 Excision of lesion, esophagus, with primary repair; cervical approach

43101 thoracic or abdominal approach

(For wide excision of malignant lesion of cervical esophagus, with total laryngectomy without radical neck dissection, see 43107, 43116, 43124, and 31360)

(For wide excision of malignant lesion of cervical esophagus, with total laryngectomy with radical neck dissection, see 43107, 43116, 43124, and 31365)

43107 Total or near total esophagectomy, without thoracotomy; with pharyngogastrostomy or cervical esophagogastrostomy, with or without pyloroplasty (transhiatal)

43108 with colon interposition or small intestine reconstruction, including intestine mobilization, preparation and anastomosis(es)

43112 Total or near total esophagectomy, with thoracotomy; with pharyngogastrostomy or cervical esophagogastrostomy, with or without pyloroplasty

43113 with colon interposition or small intestine reconstruction, including intestine mobilization, preparation, and anastomosis(es)

43116 Partial esophagectomy, cervical, with free intestinal graft, including microvascular anastomosis, obtaining the graft and intestinal reconstruction

(Do not report 43116 in conjunction with 69990)

(Report 43116 with the modifier 52 appended if intestinal or free jejunal graft with microvascular anastomosis is performed by another physician)

(For free jejunal graft with microvascular anastomosis performed by another physician, use 43496)

43117 Partial esophagectomy, distal two-thirds, with thoracotomy and separate abdominal incision, with or without proximal gastrectomy; with thoracic esophagogastrostomy, with or without pyloroplasty (Ivor Lewis)

43118 with colon interposition or small intestine reconstruction, including intestine mobilization, preparation, and anastomosis(es)

(For total esophagectomy with gastropharyngostomy, see 43107, 43124)

(For esophagogastrectomy (lower third) and vagotomy, use 43122)

43121 Partial esophagectomy, distal two-thirds, with thoracotomy only, with or without proximal gastrectomy, with thoracic esophagogastrostomy, with or without pyloroplasty

43122 Partial esophagectomy, thoracoabdominal or abdominal approach, with or without proximal gastrectomy; with esophagogastrostomy, with or without pyloroplasty

43123 with colon interposition or small intestine reconstruction, including intestine mobilization, preparation, and anastomosis(es)

43124 Total or partial esophagectomy, without reconstruction (any approach), with cervical esophagostomy

43130 Diverticulectomy of hypopharynx or esophagus, with or without myotomy; cervical approach

43135 thoracic approach

Endoscopy

For endoscopic procedures, code appropriate endoscopy of each anatomic site examined.

Surgical endoscopy always includes diagnostic endoscopy.

⊙ 43200 Esophagoscopy, rigid or flexible; diagnostic, with or without collection of specimen(s) by brushing or washing (separate procedure)

⊙ 43201 with directed submucosal injection(s), any substance

(For injection sclerosis of esophageal varices, use 43204)

⊙ 43202 with biopsy, single or multiple

⊙ 43204 with injection sclerosis of esophageal varices

⊙ 43205 with band ligation of esophageal varices

⊙ 43215 with removal of foreign body

(For radiological supervision and interpretation, use 74235)

⊙ 43216 with removal of tumor(s), polyp(s), or other lesion(s) by hot biopsy forceps or bipolar cautery

⊙ 43217 with removal of tumor(s), polyp(s), or other lesion(s) by snare technique

⊙ 43219 with insertion of plastic tube or stent

⊙ 43220 with balloon dilation (less than 30 mm diameter)

(If imaging guidance is performed, use 74360)

(For endoscopic dilation with balloon 30 mm diameter or larger, use 43458)

(For dilation without visualization, use 43450-43453)

(For diagnostic fiberoptic esophagogastroscopy, use 43200, 43235)

(For fiberoptic esophagogastroscopy with biopsy or collection of specimen, use 43200, 43202, 43235, 43239)

(For fiberoptic esophagogastroscopy with removal of foreign body, use 43215, 43247)

(For fiberoptic esophagogastroscopy with removal of polyp(s), use 43217, 43251)

⊙ 43226 with insertion of guide wire followed by dilation over guide wire

(For radiological supervision and interpretation, use 74360)

⊙ 43227 with control of bleeding (eg, injection, bipolar cautery, unipolar cautery, laser, heater probe, stapler, plasma coagulator)

⊙ 43228 with ablation of tumor(s), polyp(s), or other lesion(s), not amenable to removal by hot biopsy forceps, bipolar cautery or snare technique

(For esophagoscopic photodynamic therapy, report 43228 in addition to 96570, 96571 as appropriate)

⊙ 43231 with endoscopic ultrasound examination

(Do not report 43231 in conjunction with 76975)

⊙ 43232 with transendoscopic ultrasound-guided intramural or transmural fine needle aspiration/biopsy(s)

(Do not report 43232 in conjunction with 76942, 76975)

(For interpretation of specimen, see 88172-88173)

⊙ 43234 Upper gastrointestinal endoscopy, simple primary examination (eg, with small diameter flexible endoscope) (separate procedure)

⊙ 43235 Upper gastrointestinal endoscopy including esophagus, stomach, and either the duodenum and/or jejunum as appropriate; diagnostic, with or without collection of specimen(s) by brushing or washing (separate procedure)

⊙ 43236 with directed submucosal injection(s), any substance

(For injection sclerosis of esophageal and/or gastric varices, use 43243)

⊙ 43237 with endoscopic ultrasound examination limited to the esophagus

(Do not report 43237 in conjunction with 76942, 76975)

⊙ 43238 with transendoscopic ultrasound-guided intramural or transmural fine needle aspiration/biopsy(s), esophagus (includes endoscopic ultrasound examination limited to the esophagus)

(Do not report 43238 in conjunction with 76942 or 76975)

⊙ 43239 with biopsy, single or multiple

⊙ 43240 with transmural drainage of pseudocyst

⊙ 43241 with transendoscopic intraluminal tube or catheter placement

⊙ 43242 with transendoscopic ultrasound-guided intramural or transmural fine needle aspiration/biopsy(s) (includes endoscopic ultrasound examination of the esophagus, stomach, and either the duodenum and/or jejunum as appropriate)

(Do not report 43242 in conjunction with 76942, 76975)

(For transendoscopic fine needle aspiration/biopsy limited to esophagus, use 43238)

(For interpretation of specimen, see 88172-88173)

⊙ 43243 with injection sclerosis of esophageal and/or gastric varices

⊙ 43244 with band ligation of esophageal and/or gastric varices

⊙ 43245 with dilation of gastric outlet for obstruction (eg, balloon, guide wire, bougie)

(Do not report 43245 in conjunction with 43256)

⊙ 43246 with directed placement of percutaneous gastrostomy tube

(For nonendoscopic percutaneous placement of gastrostomy tube, see 49440)

⊙ 43247 with removal of foreign body

(For radiological supervision and interpretation, use 74235)

⊙ **43248** with insertion of guide wire followed by dilation of esophagus over guide wire

⊙ **43249** with balloon dilation of esophagus (less than 30 mm diameter)

⊙ **43250** with removal of tumor(s), polyp(s), or other lesion(s) by hot biopsy forceps or bipolar cautery

⊙ **43251** with removal of tumor(s), polyp(s), or other lesion(s) by snare technique

⊙ **43255** with control of bleeding, any method

⊙ **43256** with transendoscopic stent placement (includes predilation)

⊙ **43257** with delivery of thermal energy to the muscle of lower esophageal sphincter and/or gastric cardia, for treatment of gastroesophageal reflux disease

⊙ **43258** with ablation of tumor(s), polyp(s), or other lesion(s) not amenable to removal by hot biopsy forceps, bipolar cautery or snare technique

(For injection sclerosis of esophageal varices, use 43204, 43243)

⊙ **43259** with endoscopic ultrasound examination, including the esophagus, stomach, and either the duodenum and/or jejunum as appropriate

(Do not report 43259 in conjunction with 76975)

⊙ **43260** Endoscopic retrograde cholangiopancreatography (ERCP); diagnostic, with or without collection of specimen(s) by brushing or washing (separate procedure)

(For radiological supervision and interpretation, see 74328, 74329, 74330)

⊙ **43261** with biopsy, single or multiple

(For radiological supervision and interpretation, see 74328, 74329, 74330)

⊙ **43262** with sphincterotomy/papillotomy

(For radiological supervision and interpretation, see 74328, 74329, 74330)

⊙ **43263** with pressure measurement of sphincter of Oddi (pancreatic duct or common bile duct)

(For radiological supervision and interpretation, see 74328, 74329, 74330)

⊙ **43264** with endoscopic retrograde removal of calculus/calculi from biliary and/or pancreatic ducts

(When done with sphincterotomy, also use 43262)

(For radiological supervision and interpretation, see 74328, 74329, 74330)

⊙ **43265** with endoscopic retrograde destruction, lithotripsy of calculus/calculi, any method

(When done with sphincterotomy, also use 43262)

(For radiological supervision and interpretation, see 74328, 74329, 74330)

⊙ **43267** with endoscopic retrograde insertion of nasobiliary or nasopancreatic drainage tube

(When done with sphincterotomy, also use 43262)

(For radiological supervision and interpretation, see 74328, 74329, 74330)

⊙ **43268** with endoscopic retrograde insertion of tube or stent into bile or pancreatic duct

(When done with sphincterotomy, also use 43262)

(For radiological supervision and interpretation, see 74328, 74329, 74330)

⊙ **43269** with endoscopic retrograde removal of foreign body and/or change of tube or stent

(When done with sphincterotomy, also use 43262)

(For radiological supervision and interpretation, see 74328, 74329, 74330)

⊙ **43271** with endoscopic retrograde balloon dilation of ampulla, biliary and/or pancreatic duct(s)

(When done with sphincterotomy, also use 43262)

(For radiological supervision and interpretation, see 74328, 74329, 74330)

⊙ **43272** with ablation of tumor(s), polyp(s), or other lesion(s) not amenable to removal by hot biopsy forceps, bipolar cautery or snare technique

(For radiological supervision and interpretation, see 74328, 74329, 74330)

⊙+● **43273** Endoscopic cannulation of papilla with direct visualization of common bile duct(s) and/or pancreatic duct(s) (List separately in addition to code(s) for primary procedure)

►(Use 43273 in conjunction with 43260, 43261, 43263-43265, 43267-43272)◄

Laparoscopy

Surgical laparoscopy always includes diagnostic laparoscopy. To report a diagnostic laparoscopy (peritoneoscopy) (separate procedure), use 49320.

● **43279** Laparoscopy, surgical, esophagomyotomy (Heller type), with fundoplasty, when performed

►(For open approach, see 43330, 43331)◄

►(Do not report 43279 in conjunction with 43280)◄

43280 Laparoscopy, surgical, esophagogastric fundoplasty (eg, Nissen, Toupet procedures)

►(Do not report 43280 in conjunction with 43279)◄

(For open approach, use 43324)

43289 Unlisted laparoscopy procedure, esophagus

Surgery: Digestive System

Repair

43300 Esophagoplasty (plastic repair or reconstruction), cervical approach; without repair of tracheoesophageal fistula

43305 with repair of tracheoesophageal fistula

43310 Esophagoplasty (plastic repair or reconstruction), thoracic approach; without repair of tracheoesophageal fistula

43312 with repair of tracheoesophageal fistula

43313 Esophagoplasty for congenital defect (plastic repair or reconstruction), thoracic approach; without repair of congenital tracheoesophageal fistula

43314 with repair of congenital tracheoesophageal fistula

(Do not report modifier 63 in conjunction with 43313, 43314)

43320 Esophagogastrostomy (cardioplasty), with or without vagotomy and pyloroplasty, transabdominal or transthoracic approach

43324 Esophagogastric fundoplasty (eg, Nissen, Belsey IV, Hill procedures)

(For laparoscopic procedure, use 43280)

43325 Esophagogastric fundoplasty; with fundic patch (Thal-Nissen procedure)

(For cricopharyngeal myotomy, use 43030)

43326 with gastroplasty (eg, Collis)

43330 Esophagomyotomy (Heller type); abdominal approach

►(For laparoscopic esophagomyotomy procedure, use 43279)◄

43331 thoracic approach

(For thoracoscopic esophagomyotomy, use 32665)

43340 Esophagojejunostomy (without total gastrectomy); abdominal approach

43341 thoracic approach

43350 Esophagostomy, fistulization of esophagus, external; abdominal approach

43351 thoracic approach

43352 cervical approach

43360 Gastrointestinal reconstruction for previous esophagectomy, for obstructing esophageal lesion or fistula, or for previous esophageal exclusion; with stomach, with or without pyloroplasty

43361 with colon interposition or small intestine reconstruction, including intestine mobilization, preparation, and anastomosis(es)

43400 Ligation, direct, esophageal varices

43401 Transection of esophagus with repair, for esophageal varices

43405 Ligation or stapling at gastroesophageal junction for pre-existing esophageal perforation

43410 Suture of esophageal wound or injury; cervical approach

43415 transthoracic or transabdominal approach

43420 Closure of esophagostomy or fistula; cervical approach

43425 transthoracic or transabdominal approach

(For repair of esophageal hiatal hernia, see 39520 et seq)

Manipulation

(For associated esophagogram, use 74220)

43450 Dilation of esophagus, by unguided sound or bougie, single or multiple passes

(For radiological supervision and interpretation, use 74360)

⊙ **43453** Dilation of esophagus, over guide wire

(For dilation with direct visualization, use 43220)

(For dilation of esophagus, by balloon or dilator, scc 43220, 43458, and 74360)

(For radiological supervision and interpretation, use 74360)

⊙ **43456** Dilation of esophagus, by balloon or dilator, retrograde

(For radiological supervision and interpretation, use 74360)

⊙ **43458** Dilation of esophagus with balloon (30 mm diameter or larger) for achalasia

(For dilation with balloon less than 30 mm diameter, use 43220)

(For radiological supervision and interpretation, use 74360)

▲ **43460** Esophagogastric tamponade, with balloon (Sengstaken type)

(For removal of esophageal foreign body by balloon catheter, see 43215, 43247, 74235)

Other Procedures

43496 Free jejunum transfer with microvascular anastomosis

(Do not report code 69990 in addition to code 43496)

43499 Unlisted procedure, esophagus

Stomach

Incision

43500 Gastrotomy; with exploration or foreign body removal

43501 with suture repair of bleeding ulcer

43502 with suture repair of pre-existing esophagogastric laceration (eg, Mallory-Weiss)

43510 with esophageal dilation and insertion of permanent intraluminal tube (eg, Celestin or Mousseaux-Barbin)

43520 Pyloromyotomy, cutting of pyloric muscle (Fredet-Ramstedt type operation)

(Do not report modifier 63 in conjunction with 43520)

Excision

43600 Biopsy of stomach; by capsule, tube, peroral (one or more specimens)

43605 by laparotomy

43610 Excision, local; ulcer or benign tumor of stomach

43611 malignant tumor of stomach

43620 Gastrectomy, total; with esophagoenterostomy

43621 with Roux-en-Y reconstruction

43622 with formation of intestinal pouch, any type

43631 Gastrectomy, partial, distal; with gastroduodenostomy

43632 with gastrojejunostomy

43633 with Roux-en-Y reconstruction

43634 with formation of intestinal pouch

+ 43635 Vagotomy when performed with partial distal gastrectomy (List separately in addition to code[s] for primary procedure)

(Use 43635 in conjunction with 43631, 43632, 43633, 43634)

43640 Vagotomy including pyloroplasty, with or without gastrostomy; truncal or selective

(For pyloroplasty, use 43800)

(For vagotomy, see 64752-64760)

43641 parietal cell (highly selective)

(For upper gastrointestinal endoscopy, see 43234-43259)

Laparoscopy

Surgical laparoscopy always includes diagnostic laparoscopy. To report a diagnostic laparoscopy (peritoneoscopy) (separate procedure), use 49320.

(For upper gastrointestinal endoscopy including esophagus, stomach, and either the duodenum and/or jejunum, see 43235-43259)

43644 Laparoscopy, surgical, gastric restrictive procedure; with gastric bypass and Roux-en-Y gastroenterostomy (roux limb 150 cm or less)

(Do not report 43644 in conjunction with 43846, 49320)

(Esophagogastroduodenoscopy [EGD] performed for a separate condition should be reported with modifier 59)

(For greater than 150 cm, use 43645)

(For open procedure, use 43846)

43645 with gastric bypass and small intestine reconstruction to limit absorption

(Do not report 43645 in conjunction with 49320, 43847)

43647 Laparoscopy, surgical; implantation or replacement of gastric neurostimulator electrodes, antrum

43648 revision or removal of gastric neurostimulator electrodes, antrum

(For open approach, see 43881, 43882)

(For insertion of gastric neurostimulator pulse generator, use 64590)

(For revision or removal of gastric neurostimulator pulse generator, use 64595)

(For electronic analysis and programming of gastric neurostimulator pulse generator, see 95980-95982)

(For laparoscopic implantation, revision, or removal of gastric neurostimulator electrodes, lesser curvature [morbid obesity], see Category III codes 0155T, 0156T)

(For electronic analysis and programming of gastric neurostimulator, lesser curvature, use Category III code 0162T)

43651 Laparoscopy, surgical; transection of vagus nerves, truncal

43652 transection of vagus nerves, selective or highly selective

43653 gastrostomy, without construction of gastric tube (eg, Stamm procedure) (separate procedure)

43659 Unlisted laparoscopy procedure, stomach

Introduction

(43750 has been deleted. To report percutaneous gastrostomy tube insertion, use 43246)

43752 Naso- or oro-gastric tube placement, requiring physician's skill and fluoroscopic guidance (includes fluoroscopy, image documentation and report)

(For percutaneous placement of gastrostomy tube, use 49440)

(For enteric tube placement, see 44500, 74340)

►(Do not report 43752 in conjunction with critical care codes 99291-99292, neonatal critical care codes 99468, 99469, pediatric critical care codes 99471, 99472 or low birth weight intensive care service codes 99478, 99479)◄

43760 Change of gastrostomy tube, percutaneous, without imaging or endoscopic guidance

(To report fluoroscopically guided gastrostomy, use 49450)

(For endoscopic placement of gastrostomy tube, use 43246)

43761 Repositioning of the gastric feeding tube, through the duodenum for enteric nutrition

(If imaging guidance is performed, use 76000)

(For endoscopic conversion of a gastrostomy tube to jejunostomy tube, use 44373)

(For placement of a long gastrointestinal tube into the duodenum, use 44500)

(Do not report 43761 in conjunction with 44500, 49446)

Bariatric Surgery

Bariatric surgical procedures may involve the stomach, duodenum, jejunum, and/or the ileum.

Laparoscopy

Surgical laparoscopy always includes diagnostic laparoscopy. To report a diagnostic laparoscopy (separate procedure), use 49320.

Typical postoperative follow-up care (see Surgery Guidelines, CPT Surgical Package Definition) after gastric restriction using the adjustable gastric restrictive device includes subsequent restrictive device adjustment(s) through the postoperative period for the typical patient. Adjustment consists of changing the gastric restrictive device component diameter by injection or aspiration of fluid through the subcutaneous port component.

43770 Laparoscopy, surgical, gastric restrictive procedure; placement of adjustable gastric restrictive device (eg, gastric band and subcutaneous port components)

(For individual component placement, report 43770 with modifier 52)

43771 revision of adjustable gastric restrictive device component only

43772 removal of adjustable gastric restrictive device component only

43773 removal and replacement of adjustable gastric restrictive device component only

(Do not report 43773 in conjunction with 43772)

43774 removal of adjustable gastric restrictive device and subcutaneous port components

(For removal and replacement of both gastric band and subcutaneous port components, use 43659)

Other Procedures

43800 Pyloroplasty

(For pyloroplasty and vagotomy, use 43640)

43810 Gastroduodenostomy

43820 Gastrojejunostomy; without vagotomy

43825 with vagotomy, any type

43830 Gastrostomy, open; without construction of gastric tube (eg, Stamm procedure) (separate procedure)

43831 neonatal, for feeding

(For change of gastrostomy tube, use 43760)

(Do not report modifier 63 in conjunction with 43831)

43832 with construction of gastric tube (eg, Janeway procedure)

(For percutaneous endoscopic gastrostomy, use 43246)

43840 Gastrorrhaphy, suture of perforated duodenal or gastric ulcer, wound, or injury

43842 Gastric restrictive procedure, without gastric bypass, for morbid obesity; vertical-banded gastroplasty

43843 other than vertical-banded gastroplasty

43845 Gastric restrictive procedure with partial gastrectomy, pylorus-preserving duodenoileostomy and ileoileostomy (50 to 100 cm common channel) to limit absorption (biliopancreatic diversion with duodenal switch)

(Do not report 43845 in conjunction with 43633, 43847, 44130, 49000)

43846 Gastric restrictive procedure, with gastric bypass for morbid obesity; with short limb (150 cm or less) Roux-en-Y gastroenterostomy

(For greater than 150 cm, use 43847)

(For laparoscopic procedure, use 43644)

43847 with small intestine reconstruction to limit absorption

43848 Revision, open, of gastric restrictive procedure for morbid obesity, other than adjustable gastric restrictive device (separate procedure)

(For laparoscopic adjustable gastric restrictive procedures, see 43770-43774)

(For gastric restrictive port procedures, see 43886-43888)

43850 Revision of gastroduodenal anastomosis (gastroduodenostomy) with reconstruction; without vagotomy

43855 with vagotomy

43860 Revision of gastrojejunal anastomosis (gastrojejunostomy) with reconstruction, with or without partial gastrectomy or intestine resection; without vagotomy

43865 with vagotomy

43870 Closure of gastrostomy, surgical

43880 Closure of gastrocolic fistula

43881 Implantation or replacement of gastric neurostimulator electrodes, antrum, open

43882 Revision or removal of gastric neurostimulator electrodes, antrum, open

(For laparoscopic approach, see 43647, 43648)

(For insertion of gastric neurostimulator pulse generator, use 64590)

(For revision or removal of gastric neurostimulator pulse generator, use 64595)

►(For electronic analysis and programming of gastric neurostimulator pulse generator, see 95980-95982)◄

(For open implantation, revision, or removal of gastric neurostimulator electrodes, lesser curvature [morbid obesity], see Category III codes 0157T, 0158T)

(For electronic analysis and programming of gastric neurostimulator, lesser curvature, use Category III code 0162T)

43886 Gastric restrictive procedure, open; revision of subcutaneous port component only

43887 removal of subcutaneous port component only

43888 removal and replacement of subcutaneous port component only

(Do not report 43888 in conjunction with 43774, 43887)

(For laparoscopic removal of both gastric restrictive device and subcutaneous port components, use 43774)

(For removal and replacement of both gastric restrictive device and subcutaneous port components, use 43659)

43999 Unlisted procedure, stomach

Intestines (Except Rectum)

Incision

44005 Enterolysis (freeing of intestinal adhesion) (separate procedure)

(Do not report 44005 in addition to 45136)

(For laparoscopic approach, use 44180)

44010 Duodenotomy, for exploration, biopsy(s), or foreign body removal

+ 44015 Tube or needle catheter jejunostomy for enteral alimentation, intraoperative, any method (List separately in addition to primary procedure)

44020 Enterotomy, small intestine, other than duodenum; for exploration, biopsy(s), or foreign body removal

44021 for decompression (eg, Baker tube)

44025 Colotomy, for exploration, biopsy(s), or foreign body removal

(For exteriorization of intestine (Mikulicz resection with crushing of spur), see 44602-44605)

44050 Reduction of volvulus, intussusception, internal hernia, by laparotomy

44055 Correction of malrotation by lysis of duodenal bands and/or reduction of midgut volvulus (eg, Ladd procedure)

(Do not report modifier 63 in conjunction with 44055)

Excision

Intestinal allotransplantation involves three distinct components of physician work:

1. ***Cadaver donor enterectomy***, which includes harvesting the intestine graft and cold preservation of the graft (perfusing with cold preservation solution and cold maintenance) (use 44132). ***Living donor enterectomy***, which includes harvesting the intestine graft, cold preservation of the graft (perfusing with cold preservation solution and cold maintenance), and care of the donor (use 44133).
2. ***Backbench work***:

   Standard preparation of an intestine allograft prior to transplantation includes mobilization and fashioning of the superior mesenteric artery and vein (see 44715).

   Additional reconstruction of an intestine allograft prior to transplantation may include venous and/or arterial anastomosis(es) (see 44720-44721).
3. ***Recipient intestinal allotransplantation with or without recipient enterectomy***, which includes transplantation of allograft and care of the recipient (see 44135, 44136).

44100 Biopsy of intestine by capsule, tube, peroral (one or more specimens)

44110 Excision of one or more lesions of small or large intestine not requiring anastomosis, exteriorization, or fistulization; single enterotomy

44111 multiple enterotomies

44120 Enterectomy, resection of small intestine; single resection and anastomosis

(Do not report 44120 in addition to 45136)

+ 44121 each additional resection and anastomosis (List separately in addition to code for primary procedure)

(Use 44121 in conjunction with 44120)

44125 with enterostomy

44126 Enterectomy, resection of small intestine for congenital atresia, single resection and anastomosis of proximal segment of intestine; without tapering

44127 with tapering

+ 44128 each additional resection and anastomosis (List separately in addition to code for primary procedure)

(Use 44128 in conjunction with 44126, 44127)

(Do not report modifier 63 in conjunction with 44126, 44127, 44128)

44130 Enteroenterostomy, anastomosis of intestine, with or without cutaneous enterostomy (separate procedure)

44132 Donor enterectomy (including cold preservation), open; from cadaver donor

44133 partial, from living donor

(For backbench intestinal graft preparation or reconstruction, see 44715, 44720, 44721)

44135 Intestinal allotransplantation; from cadaver donor

44136 from living donor

44137 Removal of transplanted intestinal allograft, complete

(For partial removal of transplant allograft, see 44120, 44121, 44140)

+ 44139 Mobilization (take-down) of splenic flexure performed in conjunction with partial colectomy (List separately in addition to primary procedure)

(Use 44139 in conjunction with 44140-44147)

44140 Colectomy, partial; with anastomosis

(For laparoscopic procedure, use 44204)

44141 with skin level cecostomy or colostomy

44143 with end colostomy and closure of distal segment (Hartmann type procedure)

(For laparoscopic procedure, use 44206)

44144 with resection, with colostomy or ileostomy and creation of mucofistula

44145 with coloproctostomy (low pelvic anastomosis)

(For laparoscopic procedure, use 44207)

44146 with coloproctostomy (low pelvic anastomosis), with colostomy

(For laparoscopic procedure, use 44208)

44147 abdominal and transanal approach

44150 Colectomy, total, abdominal, without proctectomy; with ileostomy or ileoproctostomy

(For laparoscopic procedure, use 44210)

44151 with continent ileostomy

(44152 and 44153 have been deleted. To report, use 44799)

44155 Colectomy, total, abdominal, with proctectomy; with ileostomy

(For laparoscopic procedure, use 44212)

44156 with continent ileostomy

44157 with ileoanal anastomosis, includes loop ileostomy, and rectal mucosectomy, when performed

44158 with ileoanal anastomosis, creation of ileal reservoir (S or J), includes loop ileostomy, and rectal mucosectomy, when performed

(For laparoscopic procedure, use 44211)

44160 Colectomy, partial, with removal of terminal ileum with ileocolostomy

(For laparoscopic procedure, use 44205)

Laparoscopy

Surgical laparoscopy always includes diagnostic laparoscopy. To report a diagnostic laparoscopy (peritoneoscopy) (separate procedure), use 49320.

Incision

44180 Laparoscopy, surgical, enterolysis (freeing of intestinal adhesion) (separate procedure)

(For laparoscopy with salpingolysis, ovariolysis, use 58660)

Enterostomy—External Fistulization of Intestines

44186 Laparoscopy, surgical; jejunostomy (eg, for decompression or feeding)

44187 ileostomy or jejunostomy, non-tube

(For open procedure, use 44310)

44188 Laparoscopy, surgical, colostomy or skin level cecostomy

(For open procedure, use 44320)

(Do not report 44188 in conjunction with 44970)

Excision

44202 Laparoscopy, surgical; enterectomy, resection of small intestine, single resection and anastomosis

+ 44203 each additional small intestine resection and anastomosis (List separately in addition to code for primary procedure)

(Use 44203 in conjunction with 44202)

(For open procedure, see 44120, 44121)

44204 colectomy, partial, with anastomosis

(For open procedure, use 44140)

44205 colectomy, partial, with removal of terminal ileum with ileocolostomy

(For open procedure, use 44160)

44206 colectomy, partial, with end colostomy and closure of distal segment (Hartmann type procedure)

(For open procedure, use 44143)

44207 colectomy, partial, with anastomosis, with coloproctostomy (low pelvic anastomosis)

(For open procedure, use 44145)

44208 colectomy, partial, with anastomosis, with coloproctostomy (low pelvic anastomosis) with colostomy

(For open procedure, use 44146)

44210 colectomy, total, abdominal, without proctectomy, with ileostomy or ileoproctostomy

(For open procedure, use 44150)

44211 colectomy, total, abdominal, with proctectomy, with ileoanal anastomosis, creation of ileal reservoir (S or J), with loop ileostomy, includes rectal mucosectomy, when performed

(For open procedure, see 44157, 44158)

44212 colectomy, total, abdominal, with proctectomy, with ileostomy

(For open procedure, use 44155)

+ 44213 Laparoscopy, surgical, mobilization (take-down) of splenic flexure performed in conjunction with partial colectomy (List separately in addition to primary procedure)

(Use 44213 in conjunction with 44204-44208)

(For open procedure, use 44139)

Repair

44227 Laparoscopy, surgical, closure of enterostomy, large or small intestine, with resection and anastomosis

(For open procedure, see 44625, 44626)

Other Procedures

44238 Unlisted laparoscopy procedure, intestine (except rectum)

Enterostomy—External Fistulization of Intestines

44300 Placement, enterostomy or cecostomy, tube open (eg, for feeding or decompression) (separate procedure)

(For percutaneous placement of duodenostomy, jejunostomy, gastro-jejunostomy or cecostomy [or other colonic] tube including fluoroscopic imaging guidance, see 49441-49442)

44310 Ileostomy or jejunostomy, non-tube

(For laparoscopic procedure, use 44187)

(Do not report 44310 in conjunction with 44144, 44150-44151, 44155, 44156, 45113, 45119, 45136)

44312 Revision of ileostomy; simple (release of superficial scar) (separate procedure)

44314 complicated (reconstruction in-depth) (separate procedure)

44316 Continent ileostomy (Kock procedure) (separate procedure)

(For fiberoptic evaluation, use 44385)

44320 Colostomy or skin level cecostomy;

(For laparoscopic procedure, use 44188)

(Do not report 44320 in conjunction with 44141, 44144, 44146, 44605, 45110, 45119, 45126, 45563, 45805, 45825, 50810, 51597, 57307, or 58240)

44322 with multiple biopsies (eg, for congenital megacolon) (separate procedure)

44340 Revision of colostomy; simple (release of superficial scar) (separate procedure)

44345 complicated (reconstruction in-depth) (separate procedure)

44346 with repair of paracolostomy hernia (separate procedure)

Endoscopy, Small Intestine and Stomal

Surgical endoscopy always includes diagnostic endoscopy.

(For upper gastrointestinal endoscopy, see 43234-43258)

⊙ **44360** Small intestinal endoscopy, enteroscopy beyond second portion of duodenum, not including ileum; diagnostic, with or without collection of specimen(s) by brushing or washing (separate procedure)

⊙ **44361** with biopsy, single or multiple

⊙ **44363** with removal of foreign body

⊙ **44364** with removal of tumor(s), polyp(s), or other lesion(s) by snare technique

⊙ **44365** with removal of tumor(s), polyp(s), or other lesion(s) by hot biopsy forceps or bipolar cautery

⊙ **44366** with control of bleeding (eg, injection, bipolar cautery, unipolar cautery, laser, heater probe, stapler, plasma coagulator)

⊙ **44369** with ablation of tumor(s), polyp(s), or other lesion(s) not amenable to removal by hot biopsy forceps, bipolar cautery or snare technique

⊙ **44370** with transendoscopic stent placement (includes predilation)

⊙ **44372** with placement of percutaneous jejunostomy tube

⊙ **44373** with conversion of percutaneous gastrostomy tube to percutaneous jejunostomy tube

(For fiberoptic jejunostomy through stoma, use 43235)

⊙ **44376** Small intestinal endoscopy, enteroscopy beyond second portion of duodenum, including ileum; diagnostic, with or without collection of specimen(s) by brushing or washing (separate procedure)

⊙ **44377** with biopsy, single or multiple

⊙ **44378** with control of bleeding (eg, injection, bipolar cautery, unipolar cautery, laser, heater probe, stapler, plasma coagulator)

⊙ **44379** with transendoscopic stent placement (includes predilation)

⊙ **44380** Ileoscopy, through stoma; diagnostic, with or without collection of specimen(s) by brushing or washing (separate procedure)

⊙ **44382** with biopsy, single or multiple

⊙ **44383** with transendoscopic stent placement (includes predilation)

⊙ **44385** Endoscopic evaluation of small intestinal (abdominal or pelvic) pouch; diagnostic, with or without collection of specimen(s) by brushing or washing (separate procedure)

⊙ **44386** with biopsy, single or multiple

⊙ **44388** Colonoscopy through stoma; diagnostic, with or without collection of specimen(s) by brushing or washing (separate procedure)

⊙ **44389** with biopsy, single or multiple

⊙ **44390** with removal of foreign body

⊙ **44391** with control of bleeding (eg, injection, bipolar cautery, unipolar cautery, laser, heater probe, stapler, plasma coagulator)

⊙ **44392** with removal of tumor(s), polyp(s), or other lesion(s) by hot biopsy forceps or bipolar cautery

⊙ **44393** with ablation of tumor(s), polyp(s), or other lesion(s) not amenable to removal by hot biopsy forceps, bipolar cautery or snare technique

⊙ **44394** with removal of tumor(s), polyp(s), or other lesion(s) by snare technique

(For colonoscopy per rectum, see 45330-45385)

⊙ **44397** with transendoscopic stent placement (includes predilation)

Introduction

⊙⊘ **44500** Introduction of long gastrointestinal tube (eg, Miller-Abbott) (separate procedure)

(For radiological supervision and interpretation, use 74340)

(For naso- or oro-gastric tube placement, use 43752)

Repair

44602 Suture of small intestine (enterorrhaphy) for perforated ulcer, diverticulum, wound, injury or rupture; single perforation

44603 multiple perforations

44604 Suture of large intestine (colorrhaphy) for perforated ulcer, diverticulum, wound, injury or rupture (single or multiple perforations); without colostomy

44605 with colostomy

44615 Intestinal stricturoplasty (enterotomy and enterorrhaphy) with or without dilation, for intestinal obstruction

44620 Closure of enterostomy, large or small intestine;

44625 with resection and anastomosis other than colorectal

44626 with resection and colorectal anastomosis (eg, closure of Hartmann type procedure)

(For laparoscopic procedure, use 44227)

44640 Closure of intestinal cutaneous fistula

44650 Closure of enteroenteric or enterocolic fistula

44660 Closure of enterovesical fistula; without intestinal or bladder resection

44661 with intestine and/or bladder resection

(For closure of renocolic fistula, see 50525, 50526)

(For closure of gastrocolic fistula, use 43880)

(For closure of rectovesical fistula, see 45800, 45805)

44680 Intestinal plication (separate procedure)

Other Procedures

44700 Exclusion of small intestine from pelvis by mesh or other prosthesis, or native tissue (eg, bladder or omentum)

(For therapeutic radiation clinical treatment, see **Radiation Oncology** section)

✚ **44701** Intraoperative colonic lavage (List separately in addition to code for primary procedure)

(Use 44701 in conjunction with 44140, 44145, 44150, or 44604 as appropriate)

(Do not report 44701 in conjunction with 44300, 44950-44960)

44715 Backbench standard preparation of cadaver or living donor intestine allograft prior to transplantation, including mobilization and fashioning of the superior mesenteric artery and vein

44720 Backbench reconstruction of cadaver or living donor intestine allograft prior to transplantation; venous anastomosis, each

44721 arterial anastomosis, each

44799 Unlisted procedure, intestine

(For unlisted laparoscopic procedure, intestine except rectum, use 44238)

Meckel's Diverticulum and the Mesentery

Excision

44800 Excision of Meckel's diverticulum (diverticulectomy) or omphalomesenteric duct

44820 Excision of lesion of mesentery (separate procedure)

(With intestine resection, see 44120 or 44140 et seq)

Suture

44850 Suture of mesentery (separate procedure)

(For reduction and repair of internal hernia, use 44050)

Other Procedures

44899 Unlisted procedure, Meckel's diverticulum and the mesentery

Appendix

Incision

44900 Incision and drainage of appendiceal abscess; open

⊙ **44901** percutaneous

(For radiological supervision and interpretation, use 75989)

Excision

44950 Appendectomy;

(Incidental appendectomy during intra-abdominal surgery does not usually warrant a separate identification. If necessary to report, add modifier 52)

+ **44955** when done for indicated purpose at time of other major procedure (not as separate procedure) (List separately in addition to code for primary procedure)

44960 for ruptured appendix with abscess or generalized peritonitis

Laparoscopy

Surgical laparoscopy always includes diagnostic laparoscopy. To report a diagnostic laparoscopy (peritoneoscopy) (separate procedure), use 49320.

44970 Laparoscopy, surgical, appendectomy

44979 Unlisted laparoscopy procedure, appendix

Rectum

Incision

45000 Transrectal drainage of pelvic abscess

45005 Incision and drainage of submucosal abscess, rectum

45020 Incision and drainage of deep supralevator, pelvirectal, or retrorectal abscess

(See also 46050, 46060)

Excision

45100 Biopsy of anorectal wall, anal approach (eg, congenital megacolon)

(For endoscopic biopsy, use 45305)

45108 Anorectal myomectomy

45110 Proctectomy; complete, combined abdominoperineal, with colostomy

(For laparoscopic procedure, use 45395)

45111 partial resection of rectum, transabdominal approach

45112 Proctectomy, combined abdominoperineal, pull-through procedure (eg, colo-anal anastomosis)

(For colo-anal anastomosis with colonic reservoir or pouch, use 45119)

45113 Proctectomy, partial, with rectal mucosectomy, ileoanal anastomosis, creation of ileal reservoir (S or J), with or without loop ileostomy

45114 Proctectomy, partial, with anastomosis; abdominal and transsacral approach

45116 transsacral approach only (Kraske type)

45119 Proctectomy, combined abdominoperineal pull-through procedure (eg, colo-anal anastomosis), with creation of colonic reservoir (eg, J-pouch), with diverting enterostomy when performed

(For laparoscopic procedure, use 45397)

45120 Proctectomy, complete (for congenital megacolon), abdominal and perineal approach; with pull-through procedure and anastomosis (eg, Swenson, Duhamel, or Soave type operation)

45121 with subtotal or total colectomy, with multiple biopsies

45123 Proctectomy, partial, without anastomosis, perineal approach

45126 Pelvic exenteration for colorectal malignancy, with proctectomy (with or without colostomy), with removal of bladder and ureteral transplantations, and/or hysterectomy, or cervicectomy, with or without removal of tube(s), with or without removal of ovary(s), or any combination thereof

45130 Excision of rectal procidentia, with anastomosis; perineal approach

45135 abdominal and perineal approach

45136 Excision of ileoanal reservoir with ileostomy

(Do not report 45136 in addition to 44005, 44120, 44310)

45150 Division of stricture of rectum

45160 Excision of rectal tumor by proctotomy, transsacral or transcoccygeal approach

45170 Excision of rectal tumor, transanal approach

►(For transanal endoscopic microsurgical [ie, TEMS] excision of rectal tumor, use 0184T)◄

Destruction

45190 Destruction of rectal tumor (eg, electrodesiccation, electrosurgery, laser ablation, laser resection, cryosurgery) transanal approach

Endoscopy

Definitions

Proctosigmoidoscopy is the examination of the rectum and sigmoid colon.

Sigmoidoscopy is the examination of the entire rectum, sigmoid colon and may include examination of a portion of the descending colon.

Colonoscopy is the examination of the entire colon, from the rectum to the cecum, and may include the examination of the terminal ileum.

For an incomplete colonoscopy, with full preparation for a colonoscopy, use a colonoscopy code with the modifier 52 and provide documentation.

Surgical endoscopy always includes diagnostic endoscopy.

45300 Proctosigmoidoscopy, rigid; diagnostic, with or without collection of specimen(s) by brushing or washing (separate procedure)

⊙ **45303** with dilation (eg, balloon, guide wire, bougie)

(For radiological supervision and interpretation, use 74360)

⊙ **45305** with biopsy, single or multiple

⊙ **45307** with removal of foreign body

⊙ **45308** with removal of single tumor, polyp, or other lesion by hot biopsy forceps or bipolar cautery

⊙ **45309** with removal of single tumor, polyp, or other lesion by snare technique

⊙ **45315** with removal of multiple tumors, polyps, or other lesions by hot biopsy forceps, bipolar cautery or snare technique

⊙ **45317** with control of bleeding (eg, injection, bipolar cautery, unipolar cautery, laser, heater probe, stapler, plasma coagulator)

⊙ **45320** with ablation of tumor(s), polyp(s), or other lesion(s) not amenable to removal by hot biopsy forceps, bipolar cautery or snare technique (eg, laser)

⊙ **45321** with decompression of volvulus

⊙ **45327** with transendoscopic stent placement (includes predilation)

45330 Sigmoidoscopy, flexible; diagnostic, with or without collection of specimen(s) by brushing or washing (separate procedure)

45331 with biopsy, single or multiple

⊙ **45332** with removal of foreign body

⊙ **45333** with removal of tumor(s), polyp(s), or other lesion(s) by hot biopsy forceps or bipolar cautery

⊙ **45334** with control of bleeding (eg, injection, bipolar cautery, unipolar cautery, laser, heater probe, stapler, plasma coagulator)

⊙ **45335** with directed submucosal injection(s), any substance

⊙ **45337** with decompression of volvulus, any method

⊙ **45338** with removal of tumor(s), polyp(s), or other lesion(s) by snare technique

⊙ **45339** with ablation of tumor(s), polyp(s), or other lesion(s) not amenable to removal by hot biopsy forceps, bipolar cautery or snare technique

⊙ **45340** with dilation by balloon, 1 or more strictures

(Do not report 45340 in conjunction with 45345)

⊙ **45341** with endoscopic ultrasound examination

⊙ **45342** with transendoscopic ultrasound guided intramural or transmural fine needle aspiration/biopsy(s)

(Do not report 45341, 45342 in conjunction with 76942, 76975)

(For interpretation of specimen, see 88172-88173)

(For transrectal ultrasound utilizing rigid probe device, use 76872)

⊙ **45345** with transendoscopic stent placement (includes predilation)

⊙ **45355** Colonoscopy, rigid or flexible, transabdominal via colotomy, single or multiple

(For fiberoptic colonoscopy beyond 25cm to splenic flexure, see 45330-45345)

⊙ **45378** Colonoscopy, flexible, proximal to splenic flexure; diagnostic, with or without collection of specimen(s) by brushing or washing, with or without colon decompression (separate procedure)

⊙ **45379** with removal of foreign body

⊙ **45380** with biopsy, single or multiple

⊙ **45381** with directed submucosal injection(s), any substance

⊙ **45382** with control of bleeding (eg, injection, bipolar cautery, unipolar cautery, laser, heater probe, stapler, plasma coagulator)

⊙ **45383** with ablation of tumor(s), polyp(s), or other lesion(s) not amenable to removal by hot biopsy forceps, bipolar cautery or snare technique

⊙ **45384** with removal of tumor(s), polyp(s), or other lesion(s) by hot biopsy forceps or bipolar cautery

⊙ **45385** with removal of tumor(s), polyp(s), or other lesion(s) by snare technique

(For small intestine and stomal endoscopy, see 44360-44393)

⊙ **45386** with dilation by balloon, 1 or more strictures

(Do not report 45386 in conjunction with 45387)

⊙ **45387** with transendoscopic stent placement (includes predilation)

⊙ **45391** with endoscopic ultrasound examination

(Do not report 45391 in conjunction with 45330, 45341, 45342, 45378, 76872)

⊙ **45392** with transendoscopic ultrasound guided intramural or transmural fine needle aspiration/biopsy(s)

(Do not report 45392 in conjunction with 45330, 45341, 45342, 45378, 76872)

Laparoscopy

Surgical laparoscopy always includes diagnostic laparoscopy. To report a diagnostic laparoscopy (peritoneoscopy) (separate procedure), use 49320.

Excision

45395 Laparoscopy, surgical; proctectomy, complete, combined abdominoperineal, with colostomy

(For open procedure, use 45110)

45397 proctectomy, combined abdominoperineal pull-through procedure (eg, colo-anal anastomosis), with creation of colonic reservoir (eg, J-pouch), with diverting enterostomy, when performed

(For open procedure, use 45119)

Repair

45400 Laparoscopy, surgical; proctopexy (for prolapse)

(For open procedure, use 45540, 45541)

45402 proctopexy (for prolapse), with sigmoid resection

(For open procedure, use 45550)

45499 Unlisted laparoscopy procedure, rectum

Repair

45500 Proctoplasty; for stenosis

45505 for prolapse of mucous membrane

45520 Perirectal injection of sclerosing solution for prolapse

45540 Proctopexy (eg, for prolapse); abdominal approach

(For laparoscopic procedure, use 45400)

45541 perineal approach

45550 with sigmoid resection, abdominal approach

(For laparoscopic procedure, use 45402)

45560 Repair of rectocele (separate procedure)

(For repair of rectocele with posterior colporrhaphy, use 57250)

45562 Exploration, repair, and presacral drainage for rectal injury;

45563 with colostomy

45800 Closure of rectovesical fistula;

45805 with colostomy

45820 Closure of rectourethral fistula;

45825 with colostomy

(For rectovaginal fistula closure, see 57300-57308)

Manipulation

45900 Reduction of procidentia (separate procedure) under anesthesia

45905 Dilation of anal sphincter (separate procedure) under anesthesia other than local

45910 Dilation of rectal stricture (separate procedure) under anesthesia other than local

45915 Removal of fecal impaction or foreign body (separate procedure) under anesthesia

Other Procedures

Surgical diagnostic anorectal exam (45990) includes the following elements: external perineal exam, digital rectal exam, pelvic exam (when performed), diagnostic anoscopy, and diagnostic rigid proctoscopy.

45990 Anorectal exam, surgical, requiring anesthesia (general, spinal, or epidural), diagnostic

(Do not report 45990 in conjunction with 45300-45327, 46600, 57410, 99170)

45999 Unlisted procedure, rectum

(For unlisted laparoscopic procedure, rectum, use 45499)

Anus

Incision

(For subcutaneous fistulotomy, use 46270)

46020 Placement of seton

(Do not report 46020 in addition to 46060, 46280, 46600)

46030 Removal of anal seton, other marker

46040 Incision and drainage of ischiorectal and/or perirectal abscess (separate procedure)

46045 Incision and drainage of intramural, intramuscular, or submucosal abscess, transanal, under anesthesia

46050 Incision and drainage, perianal abscess, superficial

(See also 45020, 46060)

46060 Incision and drainage of ischiorectal or intramural abscess, with fistulectomy or fistulotomy, submuscular, with or without placement of seton

(Do not report 46060 in addition to 46020)

(See also 45020)

46070 Incision, anal septum (infant)

(For anoplasty, see 46700-46705)

(Do not report modifier 63 in conjunction with 46070)

46080 Sphincterotomy, anal, division of sphincter (separate procedure)

46083 Incision of thrombosed hemorrhoid, external

Excision

46200 Fissurectomy, with or without sphincterotomy

46210 Cryptectomy; single

46211 multiple (separate procedure)

46220 Papillectomy or excision of single tag, anus (separate procedure)

46221 Hemorrhoidectomy, by simple ligature (eg, rubber band)

46230 Excision of external hemorrhoid tags and/or multiple papillae

46250 Hemorrhoidectomy, external, complete

46255 Hemorrhoidectomy, internal and external, simple;

46257 with fissurectomy

46258 with fistulectomy, with or without fissurectomy

46260 Hemorrhoidectomy, internal and external, complex or extensive;

46261 with fissurectomy

46262 with fistulectomy, with or without fissurectomy

►(For injection of hemorrhoids, use 46500; for destruction, use 46930; for ligation, see 46945, 46946; for hemorrhoidopexy, use 46947)◄

46270 Surgical treatment of anal fistula (fistulectomy/fistulotomy); subcutaneous

46275 submuscular

46280 complex or multiple, with or without placement of seton

(Do not report 46280 in addition to 46020)

46285 second stage

46288 Closure of anal fistula with rectal advancement flap

46320 Enucleation or excision of external thrombotic hemorrhoid

Introduction

46500 Injection of sclerosing solution, hemorrhoids

►(For excision of hemorrhoids, see 46250-46262; for destruction, use 46930; for ligation, see 46945, 46946; for hemorrhoidopexy, use 46947)◄

46505 Chemodenervation of internal anal sphincter

(For chemodenervation of other muscles, see 64612-64614, 64640)

(Report the specific service in conjunction with the specific substance(s) or drug(s) provided)

Endoscopy

Surgical endoscopy always includes diagnostic endoscopy.

46600 Anoscopy; diagnostic, with or without collection of specimen(s) by brushing or washing (separate procedure)

(Do not report 46600 in addition to 46020)

46604 with dilation (eg, balloon, guide wire, bougie)

46606 with biopsy, single or multiple

46608 with removal of foreign body

46610 with removal of single tumor, polyp, or other lesion by hot biopsy forceps or bipolar cautery

46611 with removal of single tumor, polyp, or other lesion by snare technique

46612 with removal of multiple tumors, polyps, or other lesions by hot biopsy forceps, bipolar cautery or snare technique

46614 with control of bleeding (eg, injection, bipolar cautery, unipolar cautery, laser, heater probe, stapler, plasma coagulator)

46615 with ablation of tumor(s), polyp(s), or other lesion(s) not amenable to removal by hot biopsy forceps, bipolar cautery or snare technique

Repair

46700 Anoplasty, plastic operation for stricture; adult

46705 infant

(For simple incision of anal septum, use 46070)

(Do not report modifier 63 in conjunction with 46705)

46706 Repair of anal fistula with fibrin glue

46710 Repair of ileoanal pouch fistula/sinus (eg, perineal or vaginal), pouch advancement; transperineal approach

46712 combined transperineal and transabdominal approach

46715 Repair of low imperforate anus; with anoperineal fistula (cut-back procedure)

46716 with transposition of anoperineal or anovestibular fistula

(Do not report modifier 63 in conjunction with 46715, 46716)

46730 Repair of high imperforate anus without fistula; perineal or sacroperineal approach

46735 combined transabdominal and sacroperineal approaches

(Do not report modifier 63 in conjunction with 46730, 46735)

46740 Repair of high imperforate anus with rectourethral or rectovaginal fistula; perineal or sacroperineal approach

46742 combined transabdominal and sacroperineal approaches

(Do not report modifier 63 in conjunction with 46740, 46742)

46744 Repair of cloacal anomaly by anorectovaginoplasty and urethroplasty, sacroperineal approach

(Do not report modifier 63 in conjunction with 46744)

46746 Repair of cloacal anomaly by anorectovaginoplasty and urethroplasty, combined abdominal and sacroperineal approach;

46748 with vaginal lengthening by intestinal graft or pedicle flaps

46750 Sphincteroplasty, anal, for incontinence or prolapse; adult

46751 child

46753 Graft (Thiersch operation) for rectal incontinence and/or prolapse

46754 Removal of Thiersch wire or suture, anal canal

46760 Sphincteroplasty, anal, for incontinence, adult; muscle transplant

46761 levator muscle imbrication (Park posterior anal repair)

46762 implantation artificial sphincter

Destruction

46900 Destruction of lesion(s), anus (eg, condyloma, papilloma, molluscum contagiosum, herpetic vesicle), simple; chemical

46910 electrodesiccation

46916 cryosurgery

46917 laser surgery

46922 surgical excision

46924 Destruction of lesion(s), anus (eg, condyloma, papilloma, molluscum contagiosum, herpetic vesicle), extensive (eg, laser surgery, electrosurgery, cryosurgery, chemosurgery)

● **46930** Destruction of internal hemorrhoid(s) by thermal energy (eg, infrared coagulation, cautery, radiofrequency)

►(Codes 46934-46936 have been deleted. For incision of external thrombosed hemorrhoid(s), use 46083; for destruction of internal hemorrhoid(s) by thermal energy, use 46930; for destruction of hemorrhoid(s) by cryosurgery, use 46999; for excision of hemorrhoid(s), see 46250-46262, 46320; for injection, use 46500; for ligation, see 46221, 46945, 46946; for hemorrhoidopexy, use 46947)◄

46937 Cryosurgery of rectal tumor; benign

46938 malignant

46940 Curettage or cautery of anal fissure, including dilation of anal sphincter (separate procedure); initial

46942 subsequent

Suture

46945 Ligation of internal hemorrhoids; single procedure

46946 multiple procedures

46947 Hemorrhoidopexy (eg, for prolapsing internal hemorrhoids) by stapling

►(For excision of hemorrhoids, see 46250-46262; for injection, use 46500; for destruction, use 46930)◄

Other Procedures

46999 Unlisted procedure, anus

Liver

Incision

47000 Biopsy of liver, needle; percutaneous

(If imaging guidance is performed, see 76942, 77002, 77012, 77021)

+ **47001** when done for indicated purpose at time of other major procedure (List separately in addition to code for primary procedure)

(If imaging guidance is performed, see 76942, 77002)

(For fine needle aspiration in conjunction with 47000, 47001, see 10021, 10022)

(For evaluation of fine needle aspirate in conjunction with 47000, 47001, see 88172, 88173)

47010 Hepatotomy; for open drainage of abscess or cyst, one or two stages

⊙ **47011** for percutaneous drainage of abscess or cyst, one or two stages

(For radiological supervision and interpretation, use 75989)

47015 Laparotomy, with aspiration and/or injection of hepatic parasitic (eg, amoebic or echinococcal) cyst(s) or abscess(es)

Excision

47100 Biopsy of liver, wedge

47120 Hepatectomy, resection of liver; partial lobectomy

47122 trisegmentectomy

47125 total left lobectomy

47130 total right lobectomy

Liver Transplantation

Liver allotransplantation involves three distinct components of physician work:

1. ***Cadaver donor hepatectomy***, which includes harvesting the graft and cold preservation of the graft (perfusing with cold preservation solution and cold maintenance) (use 47133). ***Living donor hepatectomy***, which includes harvesting the graft, cold preservation of the graft (perfusing with cold preservation solution and cold maintenance), and care of the donor (see 47140-47142).
2. ***Backbench work***:

   Standard preparation of the whole liver graft will include one of the following:

   Preparation of whole liver graft (including cholecystectomy, if necessary, and dissection and removal of surrounding soft tissues to prepare vena cava, portal vein, hepatic artery, and common bile duct for implantation) (use 47143).

   Preparation as described for whole liver graft, plus trisegment split into two partial grafts (use 47144).

   Preparation as described for whole liver graft, plus lobe split into two partial grafts (use 47145).

   Additional reconstruction of the liver graft may include venous and/or arterial anastomosis(es) (see 47146, 47147).
3. ***Recipient liver allotransplantation***, which includes recipient hepatectomy (partial or whole), transplantation of the allograft (partial or whole), and care of the recipient (see 47135, 47136).

47133 Donor hepatectomy (including cold preservation), from cadaver donor

47135 Liver allotransplantation; orthotopic, partial or whole, from cadaver or living donor, any age

47136 heterotopic, partial or whole, from cadaver or living donor, any age

47140 Donor hepatectomy (including cold preservation), from living donor; left lateral segment only (segments II and III)

47141 total left lobectomy (segments II, III and IV)

47142 total right lobectomy (segments V, VI, VII and VIII)

47143 Backbench standard preparation of cadaver donor whole liver graft prior to allotransplantation, including cholecystectomy, if necessary, and dissection and removal of surrounding soft tissues to prepare the vena cava, portal vein, hepatic artery, and common bile duct for implantation; without trisegment or lobe split

47144 with trisegment split of whole liver graft into two partial liver grafts (ie, left lateral segment [segments II and III] and right trisegment [segments I and IV through VIII])

47145 with lobe split of whole liver graft into two partial liver grafts (ie, left lobe [segments II, III, and IV] and right lobe [segments I and V through VIII])

47146 Backbench reconstruction of cadaver or living donor liver graft prior to allotransplantation; venous anastomosis, each

47147 arterial anastomosis, each

(Do not report 47143-47147 in conjunction with 47120-47125, 47600, 47610)

Repair

47300 Marsupialization of cyst or abscess of liver

47350 Management of liver hemorrhage; simple suture of liver wound or injury

47360 complex suture of liver wound or injury, with or without hepatic artery ligation

47361 exploration of hepatic wound, extensive debridement, coagulation and/or suture, with or without packing of liver

47362 re-exploration of hepatic wound for removal of packing

Laparoscopy

Surgical laparoscopy always includes diagnostic laparoscopy. To report a diagnostic laparoscopy (peritoneoscopy) (separate procedure), use 49320.

47370 Laparoscopy, surgical, ablation of one or more liver tumor(s); radiofrequency

(For imaging guidance, use 76940)

47371 cryosurgical

(For imaging guidance, use 76940)

47379 Unlisted laparoscopic procedure, liver

Other Procedures

47380 Ablation, open, of one or more liver tumor(s); radiofrequency

(For imaging guidance, use 76940)

47381 cryosurgical

(For imaging guidance, use 76940)

47382 Ablation, one or more liver tumor(s), percutaneous, radiofrequency

(For imaging guidance and monitoring, see 76940, 77013, 77022)

47399 Unlisted procedure, liver

Biliary Tract

Incision

47400 Hepaticotomy or hepaticostomy with exploration, drainage, or removal of calculus

47420 Choledochotomy or choledochostomy with exploration, drainage, or removal of calculus, with or without cholecystotomy; without transduodenal sphincterotomy or sphincteroplasty

47425 with transduodenal sphincterotomy or sphincteroplasty

47460 Transduodenal sphincterotomy or sphincteroplasty, with or without transduodenal extraction of calculus (separate procedure)

47480 Cholecystotomy or cholecystostomy with exploration, drainage, or removal of calculus (separate procedure)

47490 Percutaneous cholecystostomy

(For radiological supervision and interpretation, use 75989)

Introduction

47500 Injection procedure for percutaneous transhepatic cholangiography

(For radiological supervision and interpretation, use 74320)

47505 Injection procedure for cholangiography through an existing catheter (eg, percutaneous transhepatic or T-tube)

(For radiological supervision and interpretation, use 74305)

47510 Introduction of percutaneous transhepatic catheter for biliary drainage

(For radiological supervision and interpretation, use 75980)

47511 Introduction of percutaneous transhepatic stent for internal and external biliary drainage

(For radiological supervision and interpretation, use 75982)

47525 Change of percutaneous biliary drainage catheter

(For radiological supervision and interpretation, use 75984)

47530 Revision and/or reinsertion of transhepatic tube

(For radiological supervision and interpretation, use 75984)

Endoscopy

Surgical endoscopy always includes diagnostic endoscopy.

+ 47550 Biliary endoscopy, intraoperative (choledochoscopy) (List separately in addition to code for primary procedure)

47552 Biliary endoscopy, percutaneous via T-tube or other tract; diagnostic, with or without collection of specimen(s) by brushing and/or washing (separate procedure)

47553 with biopsy, single or multiple

47554 with removal of calculus/calculi

47555 with dilation of biliary duct stricture(s) without stent

47556 with dilation of biliary duct stricture(s) with stent

(For ERCP, see 43260-43272, 74363)

(If imaging guidance is performed, see 74363, 75982)

Laparoscopy

Surgical laparoscopy always includes diagnostic laparoscopy. To report a diagnostic laparoscopy (peritoneoscopy) (separate procedure), use 49320.

47560 Laparoscopy, surgical; with guided transhepatic cholangiography, without biopsy

47561 with guided transhepatic cholangiography with biopsy

47562 cholecystectomy

47563 cholecystectomy with cholangiography

47564 cholecystectomy with exploration of common duct

47570 cholecystoenterostomy

47579 Unlisted laparoscopy procedure, biliary tract

Excision

47600 Cholecystectomy;

47605 with cholangiography

(For laparoscopic approach, see 47562-47564)

47610 Cholecystectomy with exploration of common duct;

(For cholecystectomy with exploration of common duct with biliary endoscopy, use 47610 with 47550)

47612 with choledochoenterostomy

47620 with transduodenal sphincterotomy or sphincteroplasty, with or without cholangiography

47630 Biliary duct stone extraction, percutaneous via T-tube tract, basket, or snare (eg, Burhenne technique)

(For radiological supervision and interpretation, use 74327)

47700 Exploration for congenital atresia of bile ducts, without repair, with or without liver biopsy, with or without cholangiography

(Do not report modifier 63 in conjunction with 47700)

47701 Portoenterostomy (eg, Kasai procedure)

(Do not report modifier 63 in conjunction with 47701)

47711 Excision of bile duct tumor, with or without primary repair of bile duct; extrahepatic

47712 intrahepatic

(For anastomosis, see 47760-47800)

47715 Excision of choledochal cyst

Repair

(47719 has been deleted)

47720 Cholecystoenterostomy; direct

(For laparoscopic approach, use 47570)

47721 with gastroenterostomy

47740 Roux-en-Y

47741 Roux-en-Y with gastroenterostomy

47760 Anastomosis, of extrahepatic biliary ducts and gastrointestinal tract

47765 Anastomosis, of intrahepatic ducts and gastrointestinal tract

47780 Anastomosis, Roux-en-Y, of extrahepatic biliary ducts and gastrointestinal tract

47785 Anastomosis, Roux-en-Y, of intrahepatic biliary ducts and gastrointestinal tract

47800 Reconstruction, plastic, of extrahepatic biliary ducts with end-to-end anastomosis

47801 Placement of choledochal stent

47802 U-tube hepaticoenterostomy

47900 Suture of extrahepatic biliary duct for pre-existing injury (separate procedure)

Other Procedures

47999 Unlisted procedure, biliary tract

Pancreas

(For peroral pancreatic endoscopic procedures, see 43260-43272)

Incision

48000 Placement of drains, peripancreatic, for acute pancreatitis;

48001 with cholecystostomy, gastrostomy, and jejunostomy

(48005 has been deleted. To report, see 48105)

48020 Removal of pancreatic calculus

Excision

48100 Biopsy of pancreas, open (eg, fine needle aspiration, needle core biopsy, wedge biopsy)

48102 Biopsy of pancreas, percutaneous needle

(For radiological supervision and interpretation, see 76942, 77002, 77012, 77021)

(For fine needle aspiration, use 10022)

(For evaluation of fine needle aspirate, see 88172, 88173)

48105 Resection or debridement of pancreas and peripancreatic tissue for acute necrotizing pancreatitis

48120 Excision of lesion of pancreas (eg, cyst, adenoma)

48140 Pancreatectomy, distal subtotal, with or without splenectomy; without pancreaticojejunostomy

48145 with pancreaticojejunostomy

48146 Pancreatectomy, distal, near-total with preservation of duodenum (Child-type procedure)

48148 Excision of ampulla of Vater

48150 Pancreatectomy, proximal subtotal with total duodenectomy, partial gastrectomy, choledochoenterostomy and gastrojejunostomy (Whipple-type procedure); with pancreatojejunostomy

48152 without pancreatojejunostomy

48153 Pancreatectomy, proximal subtotal with near-total duodenectomy, choledochoenterostomy and duodenojejunostomy (pylorus-sparing, Whipple-type procedure); with pancreatojejunostomy

48154 without pancreatojejunostomy

48155 Pancreatectomy, total

48160 Pancreatectomy, total or subtotal, with autologous transplantation of pancreas or pancreatic islet cells

(48180 has been deleted. To report, see 48548)

Introduction

✚ **48400** Injection procedure for intraoperative pancreatography (List separately in addition to code for primary procedure)

(For radiological supervision and interpretation, see 74300-74305)

Repair

48500 Marsupialization of pancreatic cyst

48510 External drainage, pseudocyst of pancreas; open

⊙ **48511** percutaneous

(For radiological supervision and interpretation, use 75989)

48520 Internal anastomosis of pancreatic cyst to gastrointestinal tract; direct

48540 Roux-en-Y

48545 Pancreatorrhaphy for injury

48547 Duodenal exclusion with gastrojejunostomy for pancreatic injury

48548 Pancreaticojejunostomy, side-to-side anastomosis (Puestow-type operation)

Pancreas Transplantation

Pancreas allotransplantation involves three distinct components of physician work:

1. ***Cadaver donor pancreatectomy***, which includes harvesting the pancreas graft, with or without duodenal segment, and cold preservation of the graft (perfusing with cold preservation solution and cold maintenance) (use 48550).
2. ***Backbench work***:

   Standard preparation of a cadaver donor pancreas allograft prior to transplantation includes dissection of the allograft from surrounding soft tissues, splenectomy, duodenotomy, ligation of bile duct, ligation of mesenteric vessels, and Y-graft arterial anastomoses from the iliac artery to the superior mesenteric artery and to the splenic artery (use 48551).

   Additional reconstruction of a cadaver donor pancreas allograft prior to transplantation may include venous anastomosis(es) (use 48552).
3. ***Recipient pancreas allotransplantation***, which includes transplantation of allograft, and care of the recipient (use 48554).

48550 Donor pancreatectomy (including cold preservation), with or without duodenal segment for transplantation

48551 Backbench standard preparation of cadaver donor pancreas allograft prior to transplantation, including dissection of allograft from surrounding soft tissues, splenectomy, duodenotomy, ligation of bile duct, ligation of mesenteric vessels, and Y-graft arterial anastomoses from iliac artery to superior mesenteric artery and to splenic artery

48552 Backbench reconstruction of cadaver donor pancreas allograft prior to transplantation, venous anastomosis, each

(Do not report 48551 and 48552 in conjunction with 35531, 35563, 35685, 38100-38102, 44010, 44820, 44850, 47460, 47505-47525, 47550-47556, 48100-48120, 48545)

48554 Transplantation of pancreatic allograft

48556 Removal of transplanted pancreatic allograft

Other Procedures

48999 Unlisted procedure, pancreas

Abdomen, Peritoneum, and Omentum

Incision

49000 Exploratory laparotomy, exploratory celiotomy with or without biopsy(s) (separate procedure)

(To report wound exploration due to penetrating trauma without laparotomy, use 20102)

49002 Reopening of recent laparotomy

(To report re-exploration of hepatic wound for removal of packing, use 47362)

49010 Exploration, retroperitoneal area with or without biopsy(s) (separate procedure)

(To report wound exploration due to penetrating trauma without laparotomy, use 20102)

49020 Drainage of peritoneal abscess or localized peritonitis, exclusive of appendiceal abscess; open

(For appendiceal abscess, use 44900)

⊙ **49021** percutaneous

(For radiological supervision and interpretation, use 75989)

49040 Drainage of subdiaphragmatic or subphrenic abscess; open

⊙ **49041** percutaneous

(For radiological supervision and interpretation, use 75989)

49060 Drainage of retroperitoneal abscess; open

⊙ **49061** percutaneous

(For laparoscopic drainage, use 49323)

(For radiological supervision and interpretation, use 75989)

49062 Drainage of extraperitoneal lymphocele to peritoneal cavity, open

49080 Peritoneocentesis, abdominal paracentesis, or peritoneal lavage (diagnostic or therapeutic); initial

49081 subsequent

(If imaging guidance is performed, see 76942, 77012)

(49085 has been deleted. To report, see 49402)

Excision, Destruction

(For lysis of intestinal adhesions, use 44005)

49180 Biopsy, abdominal or retroperitoneal mass, percutaneous needle

(If imaging guidance is performed, see 76942, 77002, 77012, 77021)

(For fine needle aspiration, use 10021 or 10022)

(For evaluation of fine needle aspirate, see 88172, 88173)

(49200, 49201 have been deleted. To report, see 49203-49205, 58957, 58958)

49203 Excision or destruction, open, intra-abdominal tumors, cysts or endometriomas, 1 or more peritoneal, mesenteric, or retroperitoneal primary or secondary tumors; largest tumor 5 cm diameter or less

49204 largest tumor 5.1-10.0 cm diameter

49205 largest tumor greater than 10.0 cm diameter

(Do not report 49203-49205 in conjunction with 38770, 38780, 49000, 49010, 49215, 50010, 50205, 50225, 50236, 50250, 50290, 58900-58960)

(For partial or total nephrectomy, use 50220 or 50240 in conjunction with 49203-49205)

(For colectomy, use 44140 in conjunction with 49203-49205)

(For small bowel resection, use 44120 in conjunction with 49203-49205)

(For vena caval resection with reconstruction, use 49203-49205 in conjunction with 37799)

(For resection of recurrent ovarian, tubal, primary peritoneal, or uterine malignancy, see 58957, 58958)

(For cryoablation of renal tumors, see 50250, 50593)

49215 Excision of presacral or sacrococcygeal tumor

(Do not report modifier 63 in conjunction with 49215)

49220 Staging laparotomy for Hodgkins disease or lymphoma (includes splenectomy, needle or open biopsies of both liver lobes, possibly also removal of abdominal nodes, abdominal node and/or bone marrow biopsies, ovarian repositioning)

49250 Umbilectomy, omphalectomy, excision of umbilicus (separate procedure)

49255 Omentectomy, epiploectomy, resection of omentum (separate procedure)

Laparoscopy

Surgical laparoscopy always includes diagnostic laparoscopy. To report a diagnostic laparoscopy (peritoneoscopy), (separate procedure), use 49320.

For laparoscopic fulguration or excision of lesions of the ovary, pelvic viscera, or peritoneal surface use 58662.

49320 Laparoscopy, abdomen, peritoneum, and omentum, diagnostic, with or without collection of specimen(s) by brushing or washing (separate procedure)

49321 Laparoscopy, surgical; with biopsy (single or multiple)

49322 with aspiration of cavity or cyst (eg, ovarian cyst) (single or multiple)

49323 with drainage of lymphocele to peritoneal cavity

(For percutaneous or open drainage, see 49060, 49061)

49324 with insertion of intraperitoneal cannula or catheter, permanent

(For subcutaneous extension of intraperitoneal catheter with remote chest exit site, use 49435 in conjunction with 49324)

(For open insertion of permanent intraperitoneal cannula or catheter, use 49421)

49325 with revision of previously placed intraperitoneal cannula or catheter, with removal of intraluminal obstructive material if performed

✚ **49326** with omentopexy (omental tacking procedure) (List separately in addition to code for primary procedure)

(Use 49326 in conjunction with 49324, 49325)

49329 Unlisted laparoscopy procedure, abdomen, peritoneum and omentum

Introduction, Revision, Removal

49400 Injection of air or contrast into peritoneal cavity (separate procedure)

(For radiological supervision and interpretation, use 74190)

49402 Removal of peritoneal foreign body from peritoneal cavity

(For lysis of intestinal adhesions, use 44005)

49419 Insertion of intraperitoneal cannula or catheter, with subcutaneous reservoir, permanent (ie, totally implantable)

(For removal, use 49422)

49420 Insertion of intraperitoneal cannula or catheter for drainage or dialysis; temporary

49421 permanent

(For laparoscopic insertion of permanent intraperitoneal cannula or catheter, use 49324)

(For subcutaneous extension of intraperitoneal catheter with remote chest exit site, use 49435 in conjunction with 49421)

49422 Removal of permanent intraperitoneal cannula or catheter

(For removal of a temporary catheter/cannula, use appropriate E/M code)

49423 Exchange of previously placed abscess or cyst drainage catheter under radiological guidance (separate procedure)

(For radiological supervision and interpretation, use 75984)

49424 Contrast injection for assessment of abscess or cyst via previously placed drainage catheter or tube (separate procedure)

(For radiological supervision and interpretation, use 76080)

49425 Insertion of peritoneal-venous shunt

49426 Revision of peritoneal-venous shunt

(For shunt patency test, use 78291)

49427 Injection procedure (eg, contrast media) for evaluation of previously placed peritoneal-venous shunt

(For radiological supervision and interpretation, see 75809, 78291)

49428 Ligation of peritoneal-venous shunt

49429 Removal of peritoneal-venous shunt

+ 49435 Insertion of subcutaneous extension to intraperitoneal cannula or catheter with remote chest exit site (List separately in addition to code for primary procedure)

(Use 49435 in conjunction with 49324, 49421)

49436 Delayed creation of exit site from embedded subcutaneous segment of intraperitoneal cannula or catheter

Initial Placement

Do not additionally report 43752 for placement of a nasogastric (NG) or orogastric (OG) tube to insufflate the stomach prior to percutaneous gastrointestinal tube placement. NG or OG tube placement is considered part of the procedure in this family of codes.

⊙ **49440** Insertion of gastrostomy tube, percutaneous, under fluoroscopic guidance including contrast injection(s), image documentation and report

(For conversion to a gastro-jejunostomy tube at the time of initial gastrostomy tube placement, use 49440 in conjunction with 49446)

⊙ **49441** Insertion of duodenostomy or jejunostomy tube, percutaneous, under fluoroscopic guidance including contrast injection(s), image documentation and report

(For conversion of gastrostomy tube to gastro-jejunostomy tube, use 49446)

⊙ **49442** Insertion of cecostomy or other colonic tube, percutaneous, under fluoroscopic guidance including contrast injection(s), image documentation and report

Conversion

⊙ **49446** Conversion of gastrostomy tube to gastro-jejunostomy tube, percutaneous, under fluoroscopic guidance including contrast injection(s), image documentation and report

(For conversion to a gastro-jejunostomy tube at the time of initial gastrostomy tube placement, use 49446 in conjunction with 49440)

Replacement

If an existing gastrostomy, duodenostomy, jejunostomy, gastro-jejunostomy, or cecostomy (or other colonic) tube is removed and a new tube is placed via a separate percutaneous access site, the placement of the new tube is not considered a replacement and would be reported using the appropriate initial placement codes 49440-49442.

49450 Replacement of gastrostomy or cecostomy (or other colonic) tube, percutaneous, under fluoroscopic guidance including contrast injection(s), image documentation and report

49451 Replacement of duodenostomy or jejunostomy tube, percutaneous, under fluoroscopic guidance including contrast injection(s), image documentation and report

49452 Replacement of gastro-jejunostomy tube, percutaneous, under fluoroscopic guidance including contrast injection(s), image documentation and report

Mechanical Removal of Obstructive Material

49460 Mechanical removal of obstructive material from gastrostomy, duodenostomy, jejunostomy, gastro-jejunostomy, or cecostomy (or other colonic) tube, any method, under fluoroscopic guidance including contrast injection(s), if performed, image documentation and report

(Do not report 49460 in conjunction with 49450-49452, 49465)

Other

49465 Contrast injection(s) for radiological evaluation of existing gastrostomy, duodenostomy, jejunostomy, gastro-jejunostomy, or cecostomy (or other colonic) tube, from a percutaneous approach including image documentation and report

(Do not report 49465 in conjunction with 49450-49460)

Repair

Hernioplasty, Herniorrhaphy, Herniotomy

The hernia repair codes in this section are categorized primarily by the type of hernia (inguinal, femoral, incisional, etc).

Some types of hernias are further categorized as "initial" or "recurrent" based on whether or not the hernia has required previous repair(s).

Additional variables accounted for by some of the codes include patient age and clinical presentation (reducible vs. incarcerated or strangulated).

With the exception of the incisional hernia repairs (see 49560-49566) the use of mesh or other prostheses is not separately reported.

The excision/repair of strangulated organs or structures such as testicle(s), intestine, ovaries are reported by using the appropriate code for the excision/repair (eg, 44120, 54520, and 58940) in addition to the appropriate code for the repair of the strangulated hernia.

(For reduction and repair of intra-abdominal hernia, use 44050)

(For debridement of abdominal wall, see 11042, 11043)

(Codes 49491-49651 are unilateral procedures. To report bilateral procedure, report modifier 50 with the appropriate procedure code)

49491 Repair, initial inguinal hernia, preterm infant (younger than 37 weeks gestation at birth), performed from birth up to 50 weeks postconception age, with or without hydrocelectomy; reducible

49492 incarcerated or strangulated

(Do not report modifier 63 in conjunction with 49491, 49492)

(Postconception age equals gestational age at birth plus age of infant in weeks at the time of the hernia repair. Initial inguinal hernia repairs that are performed on preterm infants who are older than 50 weeks postconception age and younger than age 6 months at the time of surgery, should be reported using codes 49495, 49496)

49495 Repair, initial inguinal hernia, full term infant younger than age 6 months, or preterm infant older than 50 weeks postconception age and younger than age 6 months at the time of surgery, with or without hydrocelectomy; reducible

49496 incarcerated or strangulated

(Do not report modifier 63 in conjunction with 49495, 49496)

(Postconception age equals gestational age at birth plus age in weeks at the time of the hernia repair. Initial inguinal hernia repairs that are performed on preterm infants who are younger than or up to 50 weeks postconception age but younger than 6 months of age since birth, should be reported using codes 49491, 49492. Inguinal hernia repairs on infants age 6 months to younger than 5 years should be reported using codes 49500-49501)

49500 Repair initial inguinal hernia, age 6 months to younger than 5 years, with or without hydrocelectomy; reducible

49501 incarcerated or strangulated

49505 Repair initial inguinal hernia, age 5 years or older; reducible

49507 incarcerated or strangulated

(For inguinal hernia repair, with simple orchiectomy, see 49505 or 49507 and 54520)

(For inguinal hernia repair, with excision of hydrocele or spermatocele, see 49505 or 49507 and 54840 or 55040)

49520 Repair recurrent inguinal hernia, any age; reducible

49521 incarcerated or strangulated

49525 Repair inguinal hernia, sliding, any age

(For incarcerated or strangulated inguinal hernia repair, see 49496, 49501, 49507, 49521)

49540 Repair lumbar hernia

49550 Repair initial femoral hernia, any age; reducible

49553 incarcerated or strangulated

49555 Repair recurrent femoral hernia; reducible

49557 incarcerated or strangulated

49560 Repair initial incisional or ventral hernia; reducible

49561 incarcerated or strangulated

49565 Repair recurrent incisional or ventral hernia; reducible

49566 incarcerated or strangulated

+▲ 49568 Implantation of mesh or other prosthesis for open incisional or ventral hernia repair or mesh for closure of debridement for necrotizing soft tissue infection (List separately in addition to code for the incisional or ventral hernia repair)

(Use 49568 in conjunction with 11004-11006, 49560-49566)

49570 Repair epigastric hernia (eg, preperitoneal fat); reducible (separate procedure)

49572 incarcerated or strangulated

49580 Repair umbilical hernia, younger than age 5 years; reducible

49582 incarcerated or strangulated

49585 Repair umbilical hernia, age 5 years or older; reducible

49587 incarcerated or strangulated

49590 Repair spigelian hernia

49600 Repair of small omphalocele, with primary closure

(Do not report modifier 63 in conjunction with 49600)

49605 Repair of large omphalocele or gastroschisis; with or without prosthesis

49606 with removal of prosthesis, final reduction and closure, in operating room

(Do not report modifier 63 in conjunction with 49605, 49606)

49610 Repair of omphalocele (Gross type operation); first stage

49611 second stage

(Do not report modifier 63 in conjunction with 49610, 49611)

(For diaphragmatic or hiatal hernia repair, see 39502-39541)

(For surgical repair of omentum, use 49999)

Laparoscopy

Surgical laparoscopy always includes diagnostic laparoscopy. To report a diagnostic laparoscopy (peritoneoscopy) (separate procedure), use 49320.

49650 Laparoscopy, surgical; repair initial inguinal hernia

49651 repair recurrent inguinal hernia

● 49652 Laparoscopy, surgical, repair, ventral, umbilical, spigelian or epigastric hernia (includes mesh insertion, when performed); reducible

►(Do not report 49652 in conjunction with 44180, 49568)◄

● 49653 incarcerated or strangulated

►(Do not report 49653 in conjunction with 44180, 49568)◄

● 49654 Laparoscopy, surgical, repair, incisional hernia (includes mesh insertion, when performed); reducible

►(Do not report 49654 in conjunction with 44180, 49568)◄

● 49655 incarcerated or strangulated

►(Do not report 49655 in conjunction with 44180, 49568)◄

● 49656 Laparoscopy, surgical, repair, recurrent incisional hernia (includes mesh insertion, when performed); reducible

►(Do not report 49656 in conjunction with 44180, 49568)◄

● 49657 incarcerated or strangulated

►(Do not report 49657 in conjunction with 44180, 49568)◄

49659 Unlisted laparoscopy procedure, hernioplasty, herniorrhaphy, herniotomy

Suture

49900 Suture, secondary, of abdominal wall for evisceration or dehiscence

(For suture of ruptured diaphragm, see 39540, 39541)

(For debridement of abdominal wall, see 11042, 11043)

Other Procedures

49904 Omental flap, extra-abdominal (eg, for reconstruction of sternal and chest wall defects)

(Code 49904 includes harvest and transfer. If a second surgeon harvests the omental flap, then the two surgeons should code 49904 as co-surgeons, using modifier 62)

+ 49905 Omental flap, intra-abdominal (List separately in addition to code for primary procedure)

(Do not report 49905 in conjunction with 44700)

49906 Free omental flap with microvascular anastomosis

(Do not report code 69990 in addition to 49906)

49999 Unlisted procedure, abdomen, peritoneum and omentum

Notes

Urinary System

(For provision of chemotherapeutic agents, report both the specific service in addition to code(s) for the specific substance(s) or drug(s) provided)

Kidney

Incision

(For retroperitoneal exploration, abscess, tumor, or cyst, see 49010, 49060, 49203-49205)

50010 Renal exploration, not necessitating other specific procedures

(For laparoscopic ablation of renal mass lesion(s), use 50542)

50020 Drainage of perirenal or renal abscess; open

⊙ **50021** percutaneous

(For radiological supervision and interpretation, use 75989)

50040 Nephrostomy, nephrotomy with drainage

50045 Nephrotomy, with exploration

(For renal endoscopy performed in conjunction with this procedure, see 50570-50580)

50060 Nephrolithotomy; removal of calculus

50065 secondary surgical operation for calculus

50070 complicated by congenital kidney abnormality

50075 removal of large staghorn calculus filling renal pelvis and calyces (including anatrophic pyelolithotomy)

50080 Percutaneous nephrostolithotomy or pyelostolithotomy, with or without dilation, endoscopy, lithotripsy, stenting, or basket extraction; up to 2 cm

50081 over 2 cm

(For establishment of nephrostomy without nephrostolithotomy, see 50040, 50395, 52334)

(For fluoroscopic guidance, see 76000, 76001)

50100 Transection or repositioning of aberrant renal vessels (separate procedure)

50120 Pyelotomy; with exploration

(For renal endoscopy performed in conjunction with this procedure, see 50570-50580)

50125 with drainage, pyelostomy

50130 with removal of calculus (pyelolithotomy, pelviolithotomy, including coagulum pyelolithotomy)

50135 complicated (eg, secondary operation, congenital kidney abnormality)

(For supply of anticarcinogenic agents, use 99070 in addition to code for primary procedure)

Excision

(For excision of retroperitoneal tumor or cyst, see 49203-49205)

(For laparoscopic ablation of renal mass lesion(s), use 50542)

50200 Renal biopsy; percutaneous, by trocar or needle

(For radiological supervision and interpretation, see 76942, 77002, 77012, 77021)

(For fine needle aspiration, use 10022)

(For evaluation of fine needle aspirate, see 88172, 88173)

50205 by surgical exposure of kidney

50220 Nephrectomy, including partial ureterectomy, any open approach including rib resection;

50225 complicated because of previous surgery on same kidney

50230 radical, with regional lymphadenectomy and/or vena caval thrombectomy

(When vena caval resection with reconstruction is necessary, use 37799)

50234 Nephrectomy with total ureterectomy and bladder cuff; through same incision

50236 through separate incision

50240 Nephrectomy, partial

(For laparoscopic partial nephrectomy, use 50543)

50250 Ablation, open, 1 or more renal mass lesion(s), cryosurgical, including intraoperative ultrasound, if performed

(For laparoscopic ablation of renal mass lesions, use 50542)

(For cryoablation of renal tumors, use 50593)

50280 Excision or unroofing of cyst(s) of kidney

(For laparoscopic ablation of renal cysts, use 50541)

50290 Excision of perinephric cyst

Renal Transplantation

Renal *auto*transplantation includes reimplantation of the autograft as the primary procedure, along with secondary extra-corporeal procedure(s) (eg, partial nephrectomy, nephrolithotomy) reported with modifier 51 (see 50380 and applicable secondary procedure(s)).

Renal *allo*transplantation involves three distinct components of physician work:

1. ***Cadaver donor nephrectomy, unilateral or bilateral,*** which includes harvesting the graft(s) and cold preservation of the graft(s) (perfusing with cold preservation solution and cold maintenance) (use

50300). ***Living donor nephrectomy***, which includes harvesting the graft, cold preservation of the graft (perfusing with cold preservation solution and cold maintenance), and care of the donor (see 50320, 50547).

2. ***Backbench work***:

   Standard preparation of a cadaver donor renal allograft prior to transplantation including dissection and removal of perinephric fat, diaphragmatic and retroperitoneal attachments; excision of adrenal gland; and preparation of ureter(s), renal vein(s), and renal artery(s), ligating branches, as necessary (use 50323).

   Standard preparation of a living donor renal allograft (open or laparoscopic) prior to transplantation including dissection and removal of perinephric fat and preparation of ureter(s), renal vein(s), and renal artery(s), ligating branches, as necessary (use 50325).

   Additional reconstruction of a cadaver or living donor renal allograft prior to transplantation may include venous, arterial, and/or ureteral anastomosis(es) necessary for implantation (see 50327-50329).

3. ***Recipient renal allotransplantation***, which includes transplantation of the allograft (with or without recipient nephrectomy) and care of the recipient (see 50360, 50365).

(For dialysis, see 90935-90999)

(For laparoscopic donor nephrectomy, use 50547)

(For laparoscopic drainage of lymphocele to peritoneal cavity, use 49323)

50300 Donor nephrectomy (including cold preservation); from cadaver donor, unilateral or bilateral

50320 open, from living donor

50323 Backbench standard preparation of cadaver donor renal allograft prior to transplantation, including dissection and removal of perinephric fat, diaphragmatic and retroperitoneal attachments, excision of adrenal gland, and preparation of ureter(s), renal vein(s), and renal artery(s), ligating branches, as necessary

(Do not report 50323 in conjunction with 60540, 60545)

50325 Backbench standard preparation of living donor renal allograft (open or laparoscopic) prior to transplantation, including dissection and removal of perinephric fat and preparation of ureter(s), renal vein(s), and renal artery(s), ligating branches, as necessary

50327 Backbench reconstruction of cadaver or living donor renal allograft prior to transplantation; venous anastomosis, each

50328 arterial anastomosis, each

50329 ureteral anastomosis, each

50340 Recipient nephrectomy (separate procedure)

(For bilateral procedure, report 50340 with modifier 50)

50360 Renal allotransplantation, implantation of graft; without recipient nephrectomy

50365 with recipient nephrectomy

(For bilateral procedure, report 50365 with modifier 50)

50370 Removal of transplanted renal allograft

50380 Renal autotransplantation, reimplantation of kidney

(For renal autotransplantation extra-corporeal [bench] surgery, use autotransplantation as the primary procedure and report secondary procedure[s] [eg, partial nephrectomy, nephrolithotomy] with modifier 51)

Introduction

Renal Pelvis Catheter Procedures

Internally Dwelling

⊙ **50382** Removal (via snare/capture) and replacement of internally dwelling ureteral stent via percutaneous approach, including radiological supervision and interpretation

(For bilateral procedure, use modifier 50)

(For removal and replacement of an internally dwelling ureteral stent via a transurethral approach, use 50385)

⊙ **50384** Removal (via snare/capture) of internally dwelling ureteral stent via percutaneous approach, including radiological supervision and interpretation

(For bilateral procedure, use modifier 50)

(Do not report 50382, 50384 in conjunction with 50395)

(For removal of an internally dwelling ureteral stent via a transurethral approach, use 50386)

⊙ **50385** Removal (via snare/capture) and replacement of internally dwelling ureteral stent via transurethral approach, without use of cystoscopy, including radiological supervision and interpretation

⊙ **50386** Removal (via snare/capture) of internally dwelling ureteral stent via transurethral approach, without use of cystoscopy, including radiological supervision and interpretation

Externally Accessible

⊙ **50387** Removal and replacement of externally accessible transnephric ureteral stent (eg, external/internal stent) requiring fluoroscopic guidance, including radiological supervision and interpretation

(For bilateral procedure, use modifier 50)

(For removal and replacement of externally accessible ureteral stent via ureterostomy or ilieal conduit, use 50688)

(For removal without replacement of an externally accessible ureteral stent not requiring fluoroscopic guidance, see **Evaluation and Management** services codes)

50389 Removal of nephrostomy tube, requiring fluoroscopic guidance (eg, with concurrent indwelling ureteral stent)

(Removal of nephrostomy tube not requiring fluoroscopic guidance is considered inherent to E/M services. Report the appropriate level of E/M service provided)

Other Introduction Procedures

50390 Aspiration and/or injection of renal cyst or pelvis by needle, percutaneous

(For radiological supervision and interpretation, see 74425, 74470, 76942, 77002, 77012, 77021)

(For evaluation of fine needle aspirate, see 88172, 88173)

50391 Instillation(s) of therapeutic agent into renal pelvis and/or ureter through established nephrostomy, pyelostomy or ureterostomy tube (eg, anticarcinogenic or antifungal agent)

50392 Introduction of intracatheter or catheter into renal pelvis for drainage and/or injection, percutaneous

(For radiological supervision and interpretation, see 74475, 76942, 77012)

50393 Introduction of ureteral catheter or stent into ureter through renal pelvis for drainage and/or injection, percutaneous

(For radiological supervision and interpretation, see 74480, 76942, 77002, 77012)

50394 Injection procedure for pyelography (as nephrostogram, pyelostogram, antegrade pyeloureterograms) through nephrostomy or pyelostomy tube, or indwelling ureteral catheter

(For radiological supervision and interpretation, use 74425)

50395 Introduction of guide into renal pelvis and/or ureter with dilation to establish nephrostomy tract, percutaneous

(For radiological supervision and interpretation, see 74475, 74480, 74485)

(For nephrostolithotomy, see 50080, 50081)

(For retrograde percutaneous nephrostomy, use 52334)

(For endoscopic surgery, see 50551-50561)

50396 Manometric studies through nephrostomy or pyelostomy tube, or indwelling ureteral catheter

(For radiological supervision and interpretation, see 74425, 74475, 74480)

50398 Change of nephrostomy or pyelostomy tube

(For radiological supervision and interpretation, use 75984)

Repair

50400 Pyeloplasty (Foley Y-pyeloplasty), plastic operation on renal pelvis, with or without plastic operation on ureter, nephropexy, nephrostomy, pyelostomy, or ureteral splinting; simple

50405 complicated (congenital kidney abnormality, secondary pyeloplasty, solitary kidney, calycoplasty)

(For laparoscopic approach, use 50544)

50500 Nephrorrhaphy, suture of kidney wound or injury

50520 Closure of nephrocutaneous or pyelocutaneous fistula

50525 Closure of nephrovisceral fistula (eg, renocolic), including visceral repair; abdominal approach

50526 thoracic approach

50540 Symphysiotomy for horseshoe kidney with or without pyeloplasty and/or other plastic procedure, unilateral or bilateral (one operation)

Laparoscopy

Surgical laparoscopy always includes diagnostic laparoscopy. To report a diagnostic laparoscopy (peritoneoscopy) (separate procedure), use 49320.

50541 Laparoscopy, surgical; ablation of renal cysts

50542 ablation of renal mass lesion(s)

(For open procedure, see 50220-50240)

(For cryosurgical ablation, see 50250, 50593)

50543 partial nephrectomy

(For open procedure, use 50240)

50544 pyeloplasty

50545 radical nephrectomy (includes removal of Gerota's fascia and surrounding fatty tissue, removal of regional lymph nodes, and adrenalectomy)

(For open procedure, use 50230)

50546 nephrectomy, including partial ureterectomy

50547 donor nephrectomy (including cold preservation), from living donor

(For open procedure, use 50320)

(For backbench renal allograft standard preparation prior to transplantation, use 50325)

(For backbench renal allograft reconstruction prior to transplantation, see 50327-50329)

50548 nephrectomy with total ureterectomy

(For open procedure, see 50234, 50236)

50549 Unlisted laparoscopy procedure, renal

(For laparoscopic drainage of lymphocele to peritoneal cavity, use 49323)

Endoscopy

(For supplies and materials, use 99070)

50551 Renal endoscopy through established nephrostomy or pyelostomy, with or without irrigation, instillation, or ureteropyelography, exclusive of radiologic service;

50553 with ureteral catheterization, with or without dilation of ureter

50555 with biopsy

50557 with fulguration and/or incision, with or without biopsy

50561 with removal of foreign body or calculus

50562 with resection of tumor

(When procedures 50570-50580 provide a significant identifiable service, they may be added to 50045 and 50120)

50570 Renal endoscopy through nephrotomy or pyelotomy, with or without irrigation, instillation, or ureteropyelography, exclusive of radiologic service;

(For nephrotomy, use 50045)

(For pyelotomy, use 50120)

50572 with ureteral catheterization, with or without dilation of ureter

50574 with biopsy

50575 with endopyelotomy (includes cystoscopy, ureteroscopy, dilation of ureter and ureteral pelvic junction, incision of ureteral pelvic junction and insertion of endopyelotomy stent)

50576 with fulguration and/or incision, with or without biopsy

50580 with removal of foreign body or calculus

Other Procedures

50590 Lithotripsy, extracorporeal shock wave

⊙ **50592** Ablation, 1 or more renal tumor(s), percutaneous, unilateral, radiofrequency

(50592 is a unilateral procedure. For bilateral procedure, report 50592 with modifier 50)

(For imaging guidance and monitoring, see 76940, 77013, 77022)

⊙ **50593** Ablation, renal tumor(s), unilateral, percutaneous, cryotherapy

(50593 is a unilateral procedure. For bilateral procedure, report 50593 with modifier 50)

(For imaging guidance and monitoring, see codes 76940, 77013, 77022)

Ureter

Incision

50600 Ureterotomy with exploration or drainage (separate procedure)

(For ureteral endoscopy performed in conjunction with this procedure, see 50970-50980)

50605 Ureterotomy for insertion of indwelling stent, all types

50610 Ureterolithotomy; upper one-third of ureter

50620 middle one-third of ureter

50630 lower one-third of ureter

(For laparoscopic approach, use 50945)

(For transvesical ureterolithotomy, use 51060)

(For cystotomy with stone basket extraction of ureteral calculus, use 51065)

(For endoscopic extraction or manipulation of ureteral calculus, see 50080, 50081, 50561, 50961, 50980, 52320-52330, 52352, 52353)

Excision

(For ureterocele, see 51535, 52300)

50650 Ureterectomy, with bladder cuff (separate procedure)

50660 Ureterectomy, total, ectopic ureter, combination abdominal, vaginal and/or perineal approach

Introduction

50684 Injection procedure for ureterography or ureteropyelography through ureterostomy or indwelling ureteral catheter

(For radiological supervision and interpretation, use 74425)

50686 Manometric studies through ureterostomy or indwelling ureteral catheter

50688 Change of ureterostomy tube or externally accessible ureteral stent via ileal conduit

(If imaging guidance is performed, use 75984)

50690 Injection procedure for visualization of ileal conduit and/or ureteropyelography, exclusive of radiologic service

(For radiological supervision and interpretation, use 74425)

Repair

50700 Ureteroplasty, plastic operation on ureter (eg, stricture)

50715 Ureterolysis, with or without repositioning of ureter for retroperitoneal fibrosis

(For bilateral procedure, report 50715 with modifier 50)

50722 Ureterolysis for ovarian vein syndrome

50725 Ureterolysis for retrocaval ureter, with reanastomosis of upper urinary tract or vena cava

50727 Revision of urinary-cutaneous anastomosis (any type urostomy);

50728 with repair of fascial defect and hernia

50740 Ureteropyelostomy, anastomosis of ureter and renal pelvis

50750 Ureterocalycostomy, anastomosis of ureter to renal calyx

50760 Ureteroureterostomy

50770 Transureteroureterostomy, anastomosis of ureter to contralateral ureter

(Codes 50780-50785 include minor procedures to prevent vesicoureteral reflux)

50780 Ureteroneocystostomy; anastomosis of single ureter to bladder

(For bilateral procedure, report 50780 with modifier 50)

(When combined with cystourethroplasty or vesical neck revision, use 51820)

50782 anastomosis of duplicated ureter to bladder

50783 with extensive ureteral tailoring

50785 with vesico-psoas hitch or bladder flap

(For bilateral procedure, report 50785 with modifier 50)

50800 Ureteroenterostomy, direct anastomosis of ureter to intestine

(For bilateral procedure, report 50800 with modifier 50)

50810 Ureterosigmoidostomy, with creation of sigmoid bladder and establishment of abdominal or perineal colostomy, including intestine anastomosis

50815 Ureterocolon conduit, including intestine anastomosis

(For bilateral procedure, report 50815 with modifier 50)

50820 Ureteroileal conduit (ileal bladder), including intestine anastomosis (Bricker operation)

(For bilateral procedure, report 50820 with modifier 50)

(For combination of 50800-50820 with cystectomy, see 51580-51595)

50825 Continent diversion, including intestine anastomosis using any segment of small and/or large intestine (Kock pouch or Camey enterocystoplasty)

50830 Urinary undiversion (eg, taking down of ureteroileal conduit, ureterosigmoidostomy or ureteroenterostomy with ureteroureterostomy or ureteroneocystostomy)

50840 Replacement of all or part of ureter by intestine segment, including intestine anastomosis

(For bilateral procedure, report 50840 with modifier 50)

50845 Cutaneous appendico-vesicostomy

50860 Ureterostomy, transplantation of ureter to skin

(For bilateral procedure, report 50860 with modifier 50)

50900 Ureterorrhaphy, suture of ureter (separate procedure)

50920 Closure of ureterocutaneous fistula

50930 Closure of ureterovisceral fistula (including visceral repair)

50940 Deligation of ureter

(For ureteroplasty, ureterolysis, see 50700-50860)

Laparoscopy

Surgical laparoscopy always includes diagnostic laparoscopy. To report a diagnostic laparoscopy (peritoneoscopy) (separate procedure), use 49320.

50945 Laparoscopy, surgical; ureterolithotomy

50947 ureteroneocystostomy with cystoscopy and ureteral stent placement

50948 ureteroneocystostomy without cystoscopy and ureteral stent placement

(For open ureteroneocystostomy, see 50780-50785)

50949 Unlisted laparoscopy procedure, ureter

Endoscopy

50951 Ureteral endoscopy through established ureterostomy, with or without irrigation, instillation, or ureteropyelography, exclusive of radiologic service;

50953 with ureteral catheterization, with or without dilation of ureter

50955 with biopsy

50957 with fulguration and/or incision, with or without biopsy

50961 with removal of foreign body or calculus

(When procedures 50970-50980 provide a significant identifiable service, they may be added to 50600)

50970 Ureteral endoscopy through ureterotomy, with or without irrigation, instillation, or ureteropyelography, exclusive of radiologic service;

(For ureterotomy, use 50600)

50972 with ureteral catheterization, with or without dilation of ureter

50974 with biopsy

50976 with fulguration and/or incision, with or without biopsy

50980 with removal of foreign body or calculus

Bladder

Incision

(51000 has been deleted. To report, use 51100)

(51005 has been deleted. To report, use 51101)

(51010 has been deleted. To report, use 51102)

51020 Cystotomy or cystostomy; with fulguration and/or insertion of radioactive material

51030 with cryosurgical destruction of intravesical lesion

51040 Cystostomy, cystotomy with drainage

51045 Cystotomy, with insertion of ureteral catheter or stent (separate procedure)

51050 Cystolithotomy, cystotomy with removal of calculus, without vesical neck resection

51060 Transvesical ureterolithotomy

51065 Cystotomy, with calculus basket extraction and/or ultrasonic or electrohydraulic fragmentation of ureteral calculus

51080 Drainage of perivesical or prevesical space abscess

Removal

51100 Aspiration of bladder; by needle

51101 by trocar or intracatheter

51102 with insertion of suprapubic catheter

(For imaging guidance, see 76942, 77002, 77012)

Excision

51500 Excision of urachal cyst or sinus, with or without umbilical hernia repair

51520 Cystotomy; for simple excision of vesical neck (separate procedure)

51525 for excision of bladder diverticulum, single or multiple (separate procedure)

51530 for excision of bladder tumor

(For transurethral resection, see 52234-52240, 52305)

51535 Cystotomy for excision, incision, or repair of ureterocele

(For bilateral procedure, report 51535 with modifier 50)

(For transurethral excision, use 52300)

51550 Cystectomy, partial; simple

51555 complicated (eg, postradiation, previous surgery, difficult location)

51565 Cystectomy, partial, with reimplantation of ureter(s) into bladder (ureteroneocystostomy)

51570 Cystectomy, complete; (separate procedure)

51575 with bilateral pelvic lymphadenectomy, including external iliac, hypogastric, and obturator nodes

51580 Cystectomy, complete, with ureterosigmoidostomy or ureterocutaneous transplantations;

51585 with bilateral pelvic lymphadenectomy, including external iliac, hypogastric, and obturator nodes

51590 Cystectomy, complete, with ureteroileal conduit or sigmoid bladder, including intestine anastomosis;

51595 with bilateral pelvic lymphadenectomy, including external iliac, hypogastric, and obturator nodes

51596 Cystectomy, complete, with continent diversion, any open technique, using any segment of small and/or large intestine to construct neobladder

51597 Pelvic exenteration, complete, for vesical, prostatic or urethral malignancy, with removal of bladder and ureteral transplantations, with or without hysterectomy and/or abdominoperineal resection of rectum and colon and colostomy, or any combination thereof

(For pelvic exenteration for gynecologic malignancy, use 58240)

Introduction

51600 Injection procedure for cystography or voiding urethrocystography

(For radiological supervision and interpretation, see 74430, 74455)

51605 Injection procedure and placement of chain for contrast and/or chain urethrocystography

(For radiological supervision and interpretation, use 74430)

51610 Injection procedure for retrograde urethrocystography

(For radiological supervision and interpretation, use 74450)

51700 Bladder irrigation, simple, lavage and/or instillation

(Codes 51701-51702 are reported only when performed independently. Do not report 51701-51702 when catheter insertion is an inclusive component of another procedure.)

51701 Insertion of non-indwelling bladder catheter (eg, straight catheterization for residual urine)

51702 Insertion of temporary indwelling bladder catheter; simple (eg, Foley)

51703 complicated (eg, altered anatomy, fractured catheter/balloon)

51705 Change of cystostomy tube; simple

51710 complicated

(If imaging guidance is performed, use 75984)

51715 Endoscopic injection of implant material into the submucosal tissues of the urethra and/or bladder neck

51720 Bladder instillation of anticarcinogenic agent (including retention time)

Urodynamics

The following section (51725-51797) lists procedures that may be used separately or in many and varied combinations.

When multiple procedures are performed in the same investigative session, modifier 51 should be employed.

All procedures in this section imply that these services are performed by, or are under the direct supervision of, a physician and that all instruments, equipment, fluids, gases, probes, catheters, technician's fees, medications, gloves, trays, tubing and other sterile supplies be provided by the physician. When the physician only interprets the results and/or operates the equipment, a professional component, modifier 26, should be used to identify physicians' services.

51725 Simple cystometrogram (CMG) (eg, spinal manometer)

51726 Complex cystometrogram (eg, calibrated electronic equipment)

51736 Simple uroflowmetry (UFR) (eg, stop-watch flow rate, mechanical uroflowmeter)

51741 Complex uroflowmetry (eg, calibrated electronic equipment)

51772 Urethral pressure profile studies (UPP) (urethral closure pressure profile), any technique

51784 Electromyography studies (EMG) of anal or urethral sphincter, other than needle, any technique

51785 Needle electromyography studies (EMG) of anal or urethral sphincter, any technique

51792 Stimulus evoked response (eg, measurement of bulbocavernosus reflex latency time)

51795 Voiding pressure studies (VP); bladder voiding pressure, any technique

+ 51797 intra-abdominal voiding pressure (AP) (rectal, gastric, intraperitoneal) (List separately in addition to code for primary procedure)

(Use 51797 in conjuncton with 51795)

51798 Measurement of post-voiding residual urine and/or bladder capacity by ultrasound, non-imaging

Repair

51800 Cystoplasty or cystourethroplasty, plastic operation on bladder and/or vesical neck (anterior Y-plasty, vesical fundus resection), any procedure, with or without wedge resection of posterior vesical neck

51820 Cystourethroplasty with unilateral or bilateral ureteroneocystostomy

51840 Anterior vesicourethropexy, or urethropexy (eg, Marshall-Marchetti-Krantz, Burch); simple

51841 complicated (eg, secondary repair)

(For urethropexy (Pereyra type), use 57289)

51845 Abdomino-vaginal vesical neck suspension, with or without endoscopic control (eg, Stamey, Raz, modified Pereyra)

51860 Cystorrhaphy, suture of bladder wound, injury or rupture; simple

51865 complicated

51880 Closure of cystostomy (separate procedure)

51900 Closure of vesicovaginal fistula, abdominal approach

(For vaginal approach, see 57320-57330)

51920 Closure of vesicouterine fistula;

51925 with hysterectomy

(For closure of vesicoenteric fistula, see 44660, 44661)

(For closure of rectovesical fistula, see 45800-45805)

51940 Closure, exstrophy of bladder

(See also 54390)

51960 Enterocystoplasty, including intestinal anastomosis

51980 Cutaneous vesicostomy

Laparoscopy

Surgical laparoscopy always includes diagnostic laparoscopy. To report a diagnostic laparoscopy (peritoneoscopy) (separate procedure), use 49320.

51990 Laparoscopy, surgical; urethral suspension for stress incontinence

51992 sling operation for stress incontinence (eg, fascia or synthetic)

(For open sling operation for stress incontinence, use 57288)

(For reversal or removal of sling operation for stress incontinence, use 57287)

51999 Unlisted laparoscopy procedure, bladder

Endoscopy—Cystoscopy, Urethroscopy, Cystourethroscopy

Endoscopic descriptions are listed so that the main procedure can be identified without having to list all the minor related functions performed at the same time. For example: meatotomy, urethral calibration and/or dilation, urethro-scopy, and cystoscopy prior to a transurethral resection of prostate; ureteral catheterization following extraction of ureteral calculus; internal urethrotomy and bladder neck fulguration when performing a cystourethroscopy for the female urethral syndrome. When the secondary procedure requires significant additional time and effort, it may be identified by the addition of modifier 22.

For example: urethrotomy performed for a documented pre-existing stricture or bladder neck contracture.

52000 Cystourethroscopy (separate procedure)

52001 Cystourethroscopy with irrigation and evacuation of multiple obstructing clots

(Do not report 52001 in conjunction with 52000)

52005 Cystourethroscopy, with ureteral catheterization, with or without irrigation, instillation, or ureteropyelography, exclusive of radiologic service;

52007 with brush biopsy of ureter and/or renal pelvis

52010 Cystourethroscopy, with ejaculatory duct catheterization, with or without irrigation, instillation, or duct radiography, exclusive of radiologic service

(For radiological supervision and interpretation, use 74440)

Transurethral Surgery

Urethra and Bladder

52204 Cystourethroscopy, with biopsy(s)

52214 Cystourethroscopy, with fulguration (including cryosurgery or laser surgery) of trigone, bladder neck, prostatic fossa, urethra, or periurethral glands

►(For transurethral fulguration of prostate tissue performed within the postoperative period of 52601 or 52630 performed by the same physician, append modifier 78)◄

►(For transurethral fulguration of prostate tissue performed within the postoperative period of a related procedure performed by the same physician, append modifier 78)◄

►(For transurethral fulguration of prostate for postoperative bleeding performed by the same physician, append modifier 78)◄

52224 Cystourethroscopy, with fulguration (including cryosurgery or laser surgery) or treatment of MINOR (less than 0.5 cm) lesion(s) with or without biopsy

52234 Cystourethroscopy, with fulguration (including cryosurgery or laser surgery) and/or resection of; SMALL bladder tumor(s) (0.5 up to 2.0 cm)

52235 MEDIUM bladder tumor(s) (2.0 to 5.0 cm)

52240 LARGE bladder tumor(s)

52250 Cystourethroscopy with insertion of radioactive substance, with or without biopsy or fulguration

52260 Cystourethroscopy, with dilation of bladder for interstitial cystitis; general or conduction (spinal) anesthesia

52265 local anesthesia

52270 Cystourethroscopy, with internal urethrotomy; female

52275 male

52276 Cystourethroscopy with direct vision internal urethrotomy

52277 Cystourethroscopy, with resection of external sphincter (sphincterotomy)

52281 Cystourethroscopy, with calibration and/or dilation of urethral stricture or stenosis, with or without meatotomy, with or without injection procedure for cystography, male or female

52282 Cystourethroscopy, with insertion of urethral stent

52283 Cystourethroscopy, with steroid injection into stricture

52285 Cystourethroscopy for treatment of the female urethral syndrome with any or all of the following: urethral meatotomy, urethral dilation, internal urethrotomy, lysis of urethrovaginal septal fibrosis, lateral incisions of the bladder neck, and fulguration of polyp(s) of urethra, bladder neck, and/or trigone

52290 Cystourethroscopy; with ureteral meatotomy, unilateral or bilateral

52300 with resection or fulguration of orthotopic ureterocele(s), unilateral or bilateral

52301 with resection or fulguration of ectopic ureterocele(s), unilateral or bilateral

52305 with incision or resection of orifice of bladder diverticulum, single or multiple

52310 Cystourethroscopy, with removal of foreign body, calculus, or ureteral stent from urethra or bladder (separate procedure); simple

52315 complicated

52317 Litholapaxy: crushing or fragmentation of calculus by any means in bladder and removal of fragments; simple or small (less than 2.5 cm)

52318 complicated or large (over 2.5 cm)

Ureter and Pelvis

Therapeutic cystourethroscopy always includes diagnostic cystourethroscopy. To report a diagnostic cystourethroscopy, use 52000. Therapeutic cystourethroscopy with ureteroscopy and/or pyeloscopy always includes diagnostic cystourethroscopy with ureteroscopy and/or pyeloscopy. To report a diagnostic cystourethroscopy with ureteroscopy and/or pyeloscopy, use 52351.

Do not report 52000 in conjunction with 52320-52343.

Do not report 52351 in conjunction with 52344-52346, 52352-52355.

The insertion and removal of a temporary ureteral catheter (52005) during diagnostic or therapeutic cystourethroscopic with ureteroscopy and/or pyeloscopy is included in 52320-52355 and should not be reported separately.

To report insertion of a self-retaining, indwelling stent performed during diagnostic or therapeutic cystourethroscopy with ureteroscopy and/or pyeloscopy, report 52332, in addition to primary procedure(s) performed (52320-52355), and append modifier 51. 52332 is used to report a unilateral procedure unless otherwise specified.

For bilateral insertion of self-retaining, indwelling ureteral stents, use code 52332, and append modifier 50.

To report cystourethroscopic removal of a self-retaining, indwelling ureteral stent, see 52310, 52315, and append modifier 58, if appropriate.

52320 Cystourethroscopy (including ureteral catheterization); with removal of ureteral calculus

52325 with fragmentation of ureteral calculus (eg, ultrasonic or electro-hydraulic technique)

52327 with subureteric injection of implant material

52330 with manipulation, without removal of ureteral calculus

52332 Cystourethroscopy, with insertion of indwelling ureteral stent (eg, Gibbons or double-J type)

52334 Cystourethroscopy with insertion of ureteral guide wire through kidney to establish a percutaneous nephrostomy, retrograde

(For percutaneous nephrostolithotomy, see 50080, 50081; for establishment of nephrostomy tract only, use 50395)

(For cystourethroscopy, with ureteroscopy and/or pyeloscopy, see 52351-52355)

(For cystourethroscopy with incision, fulguration, or resection of congenital posterior urethral valves or obstructive hypertrophic mucosal folds, use 52400)

52341 Cystourethroscopy; with treatment of ureteral stricture (eg, balloon dilation, laser, electrocautery, and incision)

52342 with treatment of ureteropelvic junction stricture (eg, balloon dilation, laser, electrocautery, and incision)

52343 with treatment of intra-renal stricture (eg, balloon dilation, laser, electrocautery, and incision)

52344 Cystourethroscopy with ureteroscopy; with treatment of ureteral stricture (eg, balloon dilation, laser, electrocautery, and incision)

52345 with treatment of ureteropelvic junction stricture (eg, balloon dilation, laser, electrocautery, and incision)

52346 with treatment of intra-renal stricture (eg, balloon dilation, laser, electrocautery, and incision)

(For transurethral resection or incision of ejaculatory ducts, use 52402)

52351 Cystourethroscopy, with ureteroscopy and/or pyeloscopy; diagnostic

(For radiological supervision and interpretation, use 74485)

(Do not report 52351 in conjunction with 52341-52346, 52352-52355)

52352 with removal or manipulation of calculus (ureteral catheterization is included)

52353 with lithotripsy (ureteral catheterization is included)

52354 with biopsy and/or fulguration of ureteral or renal pelvic lesion

52355 with resection of ureteral or renal pelvic tumor

Vesical Neck and Prostate

52400 Cystourethroscopy with incision, fulguration, or resection of congenital posterior urethral valves, or congenital obstructive hypertrophic mucosal folds

52402 Cystourethroscopy with transurethral resection or incision of ejaculatory ducts

52450 Transurethral incision of prostate

52500 Transurethral resection of bladder neck (separate procedure)

(52510 has been deleted)

52601 Transurethral electrosurgical resection of prostate, including control of postoperative bleeding, complete (vasectomy, meatotomy, cystourethroscopy, urethral calibration and/or dilation, and internal urethrotomy are included)

(For other approaches, see 55801-55845)

►(52606 has been deleted. For transurethral fulguration of prostate, use 52214)◄

►(52612, 52614, 52620 have been deleted. For first stage transurethral partial resection of prostate, use 52601. For second stage partial resection of prostate, use 52601 with modifier 58. For transurethral resection of residual or regrowth of obstructive prostate tissue, use 52630)◄

▲ **52630** Transurethral resection; residual or regrowth of obstructive prostate tissue including control of postoperative bleeding, complete (vasectomy, meatotomy, cystourethroscopy, urethral calibration and/or dilation, and internal urethrotomy are included)

►(For resection of residual prostate tissue performed within the postoperative period of a related procedure performed by the same physician, append modifier 78)◄

52640 of postoperative bladder neck contracture

52647 Laser coagulation of prostate, including control of postoperative bleeding, complete (vasectomy, meatotomy, cystourethroscopy, urethral calibration and/or dilation, and internal urethrotomy are included if performed)

52648 Laser vaporization of prostate, including control of postoperative bleeding, complete (vasectomy, meatotomy, cystourethroscopy, urethral calibration and/or dilation, internal urethrotomy and transurethral resection of prostate are included if performed)

52649 Laser enucleation of the prostate with morcellation, including control of postoperative bleeding, complete (vasectomy, meatotomy, cystourethroscopy, urethral calibration and/or dilation, internal urethrotomy and transurethral resection of prostate are included if performed)

(Do not report 52649 in conjunction with 52000, 52276, 52281, 52601, 52647, 52648, 53020, 55250)

52700 Transurethral drainage of prostatic abscess

(For litholapaxy, use 52317, 52318)

Urethra

(For endoscopy, see cystoscopy, urethroscopy, cystourethroscopy, 52000-52700)

(For injection procedure for urethrocystography, see 51600-51610)

Incision

53000 Urethrotomy or urethrostomy, external (separate procedure); pendulous urethra

53010 perineal urethra, external

53020 Meatotomy, cutting of meatus (separate procedure); except infant

53025 infant

(Do not report modifier 63 in conjunction with 53025)

53040 Drainage of deep periurethral abscess

(For subcutaneous abscess, see 10060, 10061)

53060 Drainage of Skene's gland abscess or cyst

53080 Drainage of perineal urinary extravasation; uncomplicated (separate procedure)

53085 complicated

Excision

53200 Biopsy of urethra

53210 Urethrectomy, total, including cystostomy; female

53215 male

53220 Excision or fulguration of carcinoma of urethra

53230 Excision of urethral diverticulum (separate procedure); female

53235 male

53240 Marsupialization of urethral diverticulum, male or female

53250 Excision of bulbourethral gland (Cowper's gland)

53260 Excision or fulguration; urethral polyp(s), distal urethra

(For endoscopic approach, see 52214, 52224)

53265 urethral caruncle

53270 Skene's glands

53275 urethral prolapse

Repair

(For hypospadias, see 54300-54352)

53400 Urethroplasty; first stage, for fistula, diverticulum, or stricture (eg, Johannsen type)

53405 second stage (formation of urethra), including urinary diversion

53410 Urethroplasty, 1-stage reconstruction of male anterior urethra

53415 Urethroplasty, transpubic or perineal, 1-stage, for reconstruction or repair of prostatic or membranous urethra

53420 Urethroplasty, 2-stage reconstruction or repair of prostatic or membranous urethra; first stage

53425 second stage

53430 Urethroplasty, reconstruction of female urethra

53431 Urethroplasty with tubularization of posterior urethra and/or lower bladder for incontinence (eg, Tenago, Leadbetter procedure)

53440 Sling operation for correction of male urinary incontinence (eg, fascia or synthetic)

53442 Removal or revision of sling for male urinary incontinence (eg, fascia or synthetic)

53444 Insertion of tandem cuff (dual cuff)

53445 Insertion of inflatable urethral/bladder neck sphincter, including placement of pump, reservoir, and cuff

53446 Removal of inflatable urethral/bladder neck sphincter, including pump, reservoir, and cuff

53447 Removal and replacement of inflatable urethral/bladder neck sphincter including pump, reservoir, and cuff at the same operative session

53448 Removal and replacement of inflatable urethral/bladder neck sphincter including pump, reservoir, and cuff through an infected field at the same operative session including irrigation and debridement of infected tissue

(Do not report 11040-11043 in addition to 53448)

53449 Repair of inflatable urethral/bladder neck sphincter, including pump, reservoir, and cuff

53450 Urethromeatoplasty, with mucosal advancement

(For meatotomy, see 53020, 53025)

53460 Urethromeatoplasty, with partial excision of distal urethral segment (Richardson type procedure)

53500 Urethrolysis, transvaginal, secondary, open, including cystourethroscopy (eg, postsurgical obstruction, scarring)

(For urethrolysis by retropubic approach, use 53899)

(Do not report 53500 in conjunction with 52000)

53502 Urethrorrhaphy, suture of urethral wound or injury, female

53505 Urethrorrhaphy, suture of urethral wound or injury; penile

53510 perineal

53515 prostatomembranous

53520 Closure of urethrostomy or urethrocutaneous fistula, male (separate procedure)

(For closure of urethrovaginal fistula, use 57310)

(For closure of urethrorectal fistula, see 45820, 45825)

Manipulation

(For radiological supervision and interpretation, use 74485)

53600 Dilation of urethral stricture by passage of sound or urethral dilator, male; initial

53601 subsequent

53605 Dilation of urethral stricture or vesical neck by passage of sound or urethral dilator, male, general or conduction (spinal) anesthesia

►(For dilation of urethral stricture, male, performed under local anesthesia, see 53600, 53601, 53620, 53621)◄

53620 Dilation of urethral stricture by passage of filiform and follower, male; initial

53621 subsequent

53660 Dilation of female urethra including suppository and/or instillation; initial

53661 subsequent

53665 Dilation of female urethra, general or conduction (spinal) anesthesia

(For urethral catheterization, see 51701-51703)

►(For dilation of urethra performed under local anesthesia, female, see 53660, 53661)◄

Other Procedures

(For two or three glass urinalysis, use 81020)

53850 Transurethral destruction of prostate tissue; by microwave thermotherapy

53852 by radiofrequency thermotherapy

►(53853 has been deleted. To report, use 55899)◄

53899 Unlisted procedure, urinary system

Notes

Male Genital System

Penis

Incision

(For abdominal perineal gangrene debridement, see 11004-11006)

54000 Slitting of prepuce, dorsal or lateral (separate procedure); newborn

(Do not report modifier 63 in conjunction with 54000)

54001 except newborn

54015 Incision and drainage of penis, deep

(For skin and subcutaneous abscess, see 10060-10160)

Destruction

54050 Destruction of lesion(s), penis (eg, condyloma, papilloma, molluscum contagiosum, herpetic vesicle), simple; chemical

54055 electrodesiccation

54056 cryosurgery

54057 laser surgery

54060 surgical excision

54065 Destruction of lesion(s), penis (eg, condyloma, papilloma, molluscum contagiosum, herpetic vesicle), extensive (eg, laser surgery, electrosurgery, cryosurgery, chemosurgery)

(For destruction or excision of other lesions, see **Integumentary System**)

Excision

54100 Biopsy of penis; (separate procedure)

54105 deep structures

54110 Excision of penile plaque (Peyronie disease);

54111 with graft to 5 cm in length

54112 with graft greater than 5 cm in length

54115 Removal foreign body from deep penile tissue (eg, plastic implant)

54120 Amputation of penis; partial

54125 complete

54130 Amputation of penis, radical; with bilateral inguinofemoral lymphadenectomy

54135 in continuity with bilateral pelvic lymphadenectomy, including external iliac, hypogastric and obturator nodes

(For lymphadenectomy (separate procedure), see 38760-38770)

54150 Circumcision, using clamp or other device with regional dorsal penile or ring block

(Do not report modifier 63 in conjunction with 54150)

(Report 54150 with modifier 52 when performed without dorsal penile or ring block)

(54152 has been deleted. To report, use 54150)

54160 Circumcision, surgical excision other than clamp, device, or dorsal slit; neonate (28 days of age or less)

(Do not report modifier 63 in conjunction with 54160)

54161 older than 28 days of age

54162 Lysis or excision of penile post-circumcision adhesions

54163 Repair incomplete circumcision

54164 Frenulotomy of penis

(Do not report 54164 with circumcision codes 54150-54161, 54162, 54163)

Introduction

54200 Injection procedure for Peyronie disease;

54205 with surgical exposure of plaque

54220 Irrigation of corpora cavernosa for priapism

54230 Injection procedure for corpora cavernosography

(For radiological supervision and interpretation, use 74445)

54231 Dynamic cavernosometry, including intracavernosal injection of vasoactive drugs (eg, papaverine, phentolamine)

54235 Injection of corpora cavernosa with pharmacologic agent(s) (eg, papaverine, phentolamine)

54240 Penile plethysmography

54250 Nocturnal penile tumescence and/or rigidity test

Repair

(For other urethroplasties, see 53400-53430)

(For penile revascularization, use 37788)

54300 Plastic operation of penis for straightening of chordee (eg, hypospadias), with or without mobilization of urethra

54304 Plastic operation on penis for correction of chordee or for first stage hypospadias repair with or without transplantation of prepuce and/or skin flaps

54308 Urethroplasty for second stage hypospadias repair (including urinary diversion); less than 3 cm

54312 greater than 3 cm

54316 Urethroplasty for second stage hypospadias repair (including urinary diversion) with free skin graft obtained from site other than genitalia

54318 Urethroplasty for third stage hypospadias repair to release penis from scrotum (eg, third stage Cecil repair)

54322 One stage distal hypospadias repair (with or without chordee or circumcision); with simple meatal advancement (eg, Magpi, V-flap)

54324 with urethroplasty by local skin flaps (eg, flip-flap, prepucial flap)

54326 with urethroplasty by local skin flaps and mobilization of urethra

54328 with extensive dissection to correct chordee and urethroplasty with local skin flaps, skin graft patch, and/or island flap

(For urethroplasty and straightening of chordee, use 54308)

54332 One stage proximal penile or penoscrotal hypospadias repair requiring extensive dissection to correct chordee and urethroplasty by use of skin graft tube and/or island flap

54336 One stage perineal hypospadias repair requiring extensive dissection to correct chordee and urethroplasty by use of skin graft tube and/or island flap

54340 Repair of hypospadias complications (ie, fistula, stricture, diverticula); by closure, incision, or excision, simple

54344 requiring mobilization of skin flaps and urethroplasty with flap or patch graft

54348 requiring extensive dissection and urethroplasty with flap, patch or tubed graft (includes urinary diversion)

54352 Repair of hypospadias cripple requiring extensive dissection and excision of previously constructed structures including re-release of chordee and reconstruction of urethra and penis by use of local skin as grafts and island flaps and skin brought in as flaps or grafts

54360 Plastic operation on penis to correct angulation

54380 Plastic operation on penis for epispadias distal to external sphincter;

54385 with incontinence

54390 with exstrophy of bladder

54400 Insertion of penile prosthesis; non-inflatable (semi-rigid)

54401 inflatable (self-contained)

(For removal or replacement of penile prosthesis, see 54415, 54416)

54405 Insertion of multi-component, inflatable penile prosthesis, including placement of pump, cylinders, and reservoir

(For reduced services, report 54405 with modifier 52)

54406 Removal of all components of a multi-component, inflatable penile prosthesis without replacement of prosthesis

(For reduced services, report 54406 with modifier 52)

54408 Repair of component(s) of a multi-component, inflatable penile prosthesis

54410 Removal and replacement of all component(s) of a multi-component, inflatable penile prosthesis at the same operative session

54411 Removal and replacement of all components of a multi-component inflatable penile prosthesis through an infected field at the same operative session, including irrigation and debridement of infected tissue

(For reduced services, report 54411 with modifier 52)

(Do not report 11040-11043 in addition to 54411)

54415 Removal of non-inflatable (semi-rigid) or inflatable (self-contained) penile prosthesis, without replacement of prosthesis

54416 Removal and replacement of non-inflatable (semi-rigid) or inflatable (self-contained) penile prosthesis at the same operative session

54417 Removal and replacement of non-inflatable (semi-rigid) or inflatable (self-contained) penile prosthesis through an infected field at the same operative session, including irrigation and debridement of infected tissue

(Do not report 11040-11043 in addition to 54417)

54420 Corpora cavernosa-saphenous vein shunt (priapism operation), unilateral or bilateral

54430 Corpora cavernosa-corpus spongiosum shunt (priapism operation), unilateral or bilateral

54435 Corpora cavernosa-glans penis fistulization (eg, biopsy needle, Winter procedure, rongeur, or punch) for priapism

54440 Plastic operation of penis for injury

Manipulation

54450 Foreskin manipulation including lysis of preputial adhesions and stretching

Testis

Excision

(For abdominal perineal gangrene debridement, see 11004-11006)

54500 Biopsy of testis, needle (separate procedure)

(For fine needle aspiration, see 10021, 10022)

(For evaluation of fine needle aspirate, see 88172, 88173)

54505 Biopsy of testis, incisional (separate procedure)

(For bilateral procedure, report 54505 with modifier 50)

(When combined with vasogram, seminal vesiculogram, or epididymogram, use 55300)

54512 Excision of extraparenchymal lesion of testis

54520 Orchiectomy, simple (including subcapsular), with or without testicular prosthesis, scrotal or inguinal approach

(For bilateral procedure, report 54520 with modifier 50)

54522 Orchiectomy, partial

54530 Orchiectomy, radical, for tumor; inguinal approach

54535 with abdominal exploration

(For orchiectomy with repair of hernia, see 49505 or 49507 and 54520)

(For radical retroperitoneal lymphadenectomy, use 38780)

Exploration

54550 Exploration for undescended testis (inguinal or scrotal area)

(For bilateral procedure, report 54550 with modifier 50)

54560 Exploration for undescended testis with abdominal exploration

(For bilateral procedure, report 54560 with modifier 50)

Repair

54600 Reduction of torsion of testis, surgical, with or without fixation of contralateral testis

54620 Fixation of contralateral testis (separate procedure)

54640 Orchiopexy, inguinal approach, with or without hernia repair

(For bilateral procedure, report 54640 with modifier 50

(For inguinal hernia repair performed in conjunction with inguinal orchiopexy, see 49495-49525)

54650 Orchiopexy, abdominal approach, for intra-abdominal testis (eg, Fowler-Stephens)

(For laparoscopic approach, use 54692)

54660 Insertion of testicular prosthesis (separate procedure)

(For bilateral procedure, report 54660 with modifier 50)

54670 Suture or repair of testicular injury

54680 Transplantation of testis(es) to thigh (because of scrotal destruction)

Laparoscopy

Surgical laparoscopy always includes diagnostic laparoscopy. To report a diagnostic laparoscopy (peritoneoscopy) (separate procedure), use 49320.

54690 Laparoscopy, surgical; orchiectomy

54692 orchiopexy for intra-abdominal testis

54699 Unlisted laparoscopy procedure, testis

Epididymis

Incision

54700 Incision and drainage of epididymis, testis and/or scrotal space (eg, abscess or hematoma)

(For debridement of necrotizing soft tissue infection of external genitalia, see 11004-11006)

Excision

54800 Biopsy of epididymis, needle

(For fine needle aspiration, see 10021, 10022)

(For evaluation of fine needle aspirate, see 88172, 88173)

(54820 has been deleted. To report, use 54865)

54830 Excision of local lesion of epididymis

54840 Excision of spermatocele, with or without epididymectomy

54860 Epididymectomy; unilateral

54861 bilateral

Exploration

54865 Exploration of epididymis, with or without biopsy

Repair

54900 Epididymovasostomy, anastomosis of epididymis to vas deferens; unilateral

54901 bilateral

(For operating microscope, use 69990)

Tunica Vaginalis

Incision

55000 Puncture aspiration of hydrocele, tunica vaginalis, with or without injection of medication

Excision

55040 Excision of hydrocele; unilateral

55041 bilateral

(With hernia repair, see 49495-49501)

Repair

55060 Repair of tunica vaginalis hydrocele (Bottle type)

Scrotum

Incision

55100 Drainage of scrotal wall abscess

(See also 54700)

(For debridement of necrotizing soft tissue infection of external genitalia, see 11004-11006)

55110 Scrotal exploration

55120 Removal of foreign body in scrotum

Excision

(For excision of local lesion of skin of scrotum, see **Integumentary System**)

55150 Resection of scrotum

Repair

55175 Scrotoplasty; simple

55180 complicated

Vas Deferens

Incision

55200 Vasotomy, cannulization with or without incision of vas, unilateral or bilateral (separate procedure)

Excision

55250 Vasectomy, unilateral or bilateral (separate procedure), including postoperative semen examination(s)

Introduction

55300 Vasotomy for vasograms, seminal vesiculograms, or epididymograms, unilateral or bilateral

(For radiological supervision and interpretation, use 74440)

(When combined with biopsy of testis, see 54505 and use modifier 51)

Repair

55400 Vasovasostomy, vasovasorrhaphy

(For bilateral procedure, report 55400 with modifier 50)

(For operating microscope, use 69990)

Suture

55450 Ligation (percutaneous) of vas deferens, unilateral or bilateral (separate procedure)

Spermatic Cord

Excision

55500 Excision of hydrocele of spermatic cord, unilateral (separate procedure)

55520 Excision of lesion of spermatic cord (separate procedure)

55530 Excision of varicocele or ligation of spermatic veins for varicocele; (separate procedure)

55535 abdominal approach

55540 with hernia repair

Laparoscopy

Surgical laparoscopy always includes diagnostic laparoscopy. To report a diagnostic laparoscopy (peritoneoscopy) (separate procedure), use 49320.

55550 Laparoscopy, surgical, with ligation of spermatic veins for varicocele

55559 Unlisted laparoscopy procedure, spermatic cord

Seminal Vesicles

Incision

55600 Vesiculotomy;

(For bilateral procedure, report 55600 with modifier 50)

55605 complicated

Excision

55650 Vesiculectomy, any approach

(For bilateral procedure, report 55650 with modifier 50)

55680 Excision of Mullerian duct cyst

(For injection procedure, see 52010, 55300)

Prostate

Incision

55700 Biopsy, prostate; needle or punch, single or multiple, any approach

(If imaging guidance is performed, use 76942)

(For fine needle aspiration, see 10021, 10022)

(For evaluation of fine needle aspirate, see 88172, 88173)

►(For transperineal stereotactic template guided saturation prostate biopsies, use 55706)◄

55705 incisional, any approach

● **55706** Biopsies, prostate, needle, transperineal, stereotactic template guided saturation sampling, including imaging guidance

►(Do not report 55706 in conjunction with 55700)◄

55720 Prostatotomy, external drainage of prostatic abscess, any approach; simple

55725 complicated

(For transurethral drainage, use 52700)

Excision

(For transurethral removal of prostate, see 52601-52640)

(For transurethral destruction of prostate, see 53850-53852)

(For limited pelvic lymphadenectomy for staging (separate procedure), use 38562)

(For independent node dissection, see 38770-38780)

55801 Prostatectomy, perineal, subtotal (including control of postoperative bleeding, vasectomy, meatotomy, urethral calibration and/or dilation, and internal urethrotomy)

55810 Prostatectomy, perineal radical;

55812 with lymph node biopsy(s) (limited pelvic lymphadenectomy)

55815 with bilateral pelvic lymphadenectomy, including external iliac, hypogastric and obturator nodes

(If 55815 is carried out on separate days, use 38770 with modifier 50 and 55810)

55821 Prostatectomy (including control of postoperative bleeding, vasectomy, meatotomy, urethral calibration and/or dilation, and internal urethrotomy); suprapubic, subtotal, 1 or 2 stages

55831 retropubic, subtotal

55840 Prostatectomy, retropubic radical, with or without nerve sparing;

55842 with lymph node biopsy(s) (limited pelvic lymphadenectomy)

55845 with bilateral pelvic lymphadenectomy, including external iliac, hypogastric, and obturator nodes

(If 55845 is carried out on separate days, use 38770 with modifier 50 and 55840)

(For laparoscopic retropubic radical prostatectomy, use 55866)

(55859 has been deleted. To report, use 55875)

55860 Exposure of prostate, any approach, for insertion of radioactive substance;

(For application of interstitial radioelement, see 77776-77778)

55862 with lymph node biopsy(s) (limited pelvic lymphadenectomy)

55865 with bilateral pelvic lymphadenectomy, including external iliac, hypogastric and obturator nodes

Laparoscopy

Surgical laparoscopy always includes diagnostic laparoscopy. To report a diagnostic laparoscopy (peritoneoscopy) (separate procedure), use 49320.

55866 Laparoscopy, surgical prostatectomy, retropubic radical, including nerve sparing

(For open procedure, use 55840)

Other Procedures

(For artificial insemination, see 58321, 58322)

55870 Electroejaculation

55873 Cryosurgical ablation of the prostate (includes ultrasonic guidance for interstitial cryosurgical probe placement)

55875 Transperineal placement of needles or catheters into prostate for interstitial radioelement application, with or without cystoscopy

(For placement of needles or catheters into pelvic organs and/or genitalia [except prostate] for interstitial radioelement application, use 55920)

►(For interstitial radioelement application, see 77776-77787)◄

(For ultrasonic guidance for interstitial radioelement application, use 76965)

55876 Placement of interstitial device(s) for radiation therapy guidance (eg, fiducial markers, dosimeter), prostate (via needle, any approach), single or multiple

(Report supply of device separately)

(For imaging guidance, see 76942, 77002, 77012, 77021)

55899 Unlisted procedure, male genital system

Reproductive System Procedures

55920 Placement of needles or catheters into pelvic organs and/or genitalia (except prostate) for subsequent interstitial radioelement application

(For placement of needles or catheters into prostate, use 55875)

(For insertion of uterine tandems and/or vaginal ovoids for clinical brachytherapy, use 57155)

(For insertion of Heyman capsules for clinical brachytherapy, use 58346)

Intersex Surgery

55970 Intersex surgery; male to female

55980 female to male

Notes

Female Genital System

(For pelvic laparotomy, use 49000)

(For excision or destruction of endometriomas, open method, see 49203-49205, 58957, 58958)

(For paracentesis, see 49080, 49081)

(For secondary closure of abdominal wall evisceration or disruption, use 49900)

(For fulguration or excision of lesions, laparoscopic approach, use 58662)

(For chemotherapy, see 96401-96549)

Vulva, Perineum, and Introitus

Definitions

The following definitions apply to the vulvectomy codes (56620-56640):

A ***simple*** procedure is the removal of skin and superficial subcutaneous tissues.

A ***radical*** procedure is the removal of skin and deep subcutaneous tissue.

A ***partial*** procedure is the removal of less than 80% of the vulvar area.

A ***complete*** procedure is the removal of greater than 80% of the vulvar area.

Incision

(For incision and drainage of sebaceous cyst, furuncle, or abscess, see 10040, 10060, 10061)

56405 Incision and drainage of vulva or perineal abscess

56420 Incision and drainage of Bartholin's gland abscess

(For incision and drainage of Skene's gland abscess or cyst, use 53060)

56440 Marsupialization of Bartholin's gland cyst

56441 Lysis of labial adhesions

56442 Hymenotomy, simple incision

Destruction

56501 Destruction of lesion(s), vulva; simple (eg, laser surgery, electrosurgery, cryosurgery, chemosurgery)

56515 extensive (eg, laser surgery, electrosurgery, cryosurgery, chemosurgery)

(For destruction of Skene's gland cyst or abscess, use 53270)

(For cautery destruction of urethral caruncle, use 53265)

Excision

56605 Biopsy of vulva or perineum (separate procedure); one lesion

+ 56606 each separate additional lesion (List separately in addition to code for primary procedure)

(Use 56606 in conjunction with 56605)

(For excision of local lesion, see 11420-11426, 11620-11626)

56620 Vulvectomy simple; partial

56625 complete

(For skin graft, see 15002 et seq)

56630 Vulvectomy, radical, partial;

(For skin graft, if used, see 15004-15005, 15120, 15121, 15240, 15241)

56631 with unilateral inguinofemoral lymphadenectomy

56632 with bilateral inguinofemoral lymphadenectomy

56633 Vulvectomy, radical, complete;

56634 with unilateral inguinofemoral lymphadenectomy

56637 with bilateral inguinofemoral lymphadenectomy

56640 Vulvectomy, radical, complete, with inguinofemoral, iliac, and pelvic lymphadenectomy

(For bilateral procedure, report 56640 with modifier 50)

(For lymphadenectomy, see 38760-38780)

56700 Partial hymenectomy or revision of hymenal ring

(56720 has been deleted. To report, use 56442)

56740 Excision of Bartholin's gland or cyst

(For excision of Skene's gland, use 53270)

(For excision of urethral caruncle, use 53265)

(For excision or fulguration of urethral carcinoma, use 53220)

(For excision or marsupialization of urethral diverticulum, see 53230, 53240)

Repair

(For repair of urethra for mucosal prolapse, use 53275)

56800 Plastic repair of introitus

56805 Clitoroplasty for intersex state

56810 Perineoplasty, repair of perineum, nonobstetrical (separate procedure)

(See also 56800)

(For repair of wounds to genitalia, see 12001-12007, 12041-12047, 13131-13133)

(For repair of recent injury of vagina and perineum, nonobstetrical, use 57210)

(For anal sphincteroplasty, see 46750, 46751)

(For episiorrhaphy, episioperineorrhaphy for recent injury of vulva and/or perineum, nonobstetrical, use 57210)

Endoscopy

56820 Colposcopy of the vulva;

56821 with biopsy(s)

(For colposcopic examinations/procedures involving the vagina, see 57420, 57421; cervix, see 57452-57461)

Vagina

Incision

57000 Colpotomy; with exploration

57010 with drainage of pelvic abscess

57020 Colpocentesis (separate procedure)

57022 Incision and drainage of vaginal hematoma; obstetrical/postpartum

57023 non-obstetrical (eg, post-trauma, spontaneous bleeding)

Destruction

57061 Destruction of vaginal lesion(s); simple (eg, laser surgery, electrosurgery, cryosurgery, chemosurgery)

57065 extensive (eg, laser surgery, electrosurgery, cryosurgery, chemosurgery)

Excision

57100 Biopsy of vaginal mucosa; simple (separate procedure)

57105 extensive, requiring suture (including cysts)

57106 Vaginectomy, partial removal of vaginal wall;

57107 with removal of paravaginal tissue (radical vaginectomy)

57109 with removal of paravaginal tissue (radical vaginectomy) with bilateral total pelvic lymphadenectomy and para-aortic lymph node sampling (biopsy)

57110 Vaginectomy, complete removal of vaginal wall;

57111 with removal of paravaginal tissue (radical vaginectomy)

57112 with removal of paravaginal tissue (radical vaginectomy) with bilateral total pelvic lymphadenectomy and para-aortic lymph node sampling (biopsy)

57120 Colpocleisis (Le Fort type)

57130 Excision of vaginal septum

57135 Excision of vaginal cyst or tumor

Introduction

57150 Irrigation of vagina and/or application of medicament for treatment of bacterial, parasitic, or fungoid disease

57155 Insertion of uterine tandems and/or vaginal ovoids for clinical brachytherapy

(For placement of needles or catheters into pelvic organs and/or genitalia [except prostate] for interstitial radioelement application, use 55920)

►(For insertion of radioelement sources or ribbons, see 77761-77763, 77785-77787)◄

57160 Fitting and insertion of pessary or other intravaginal support device

57170 Diaphragm or cervical cap fitting with instructions

57180 Introduction of any hemostatic agent or pack for spontaneous or traumatic nonobstetrical vaginal hemorrhage (separate procedure)

Repair

(For urethral suspension, Marshall-Marchetti-Krantz type, abdominal approach, see 51840, 51841)

(For laparoscopic suspension, use 51990)

57200 Colporrhaphy, suture of injury of vagina (nonobstetrical)

57210 Colpoperineorrhaphy, suture of injury of vagina and/or perineum (nonobstetrical)

57220 Plastic operation on urethral sphincter, vaginal approach (eg, Kelly urethral plication)

57230 Plastic repair of urethrocele

57240 Anterior colporrhaphy, repair of cystocele with or without repair of urethrocele

57250 Posterior colporrhaphy, repair of rectocele with or without perineorrhaphy

(For repair of rectocele (separate procedure) without posterior colporrhaphy, use 45560)

57260 Combined anteroposterior colporrhaphy;

57265 with enterocele repair

✚ **57267** Insertion of mesh or other prosthesis for repair of pelvic floor defect, each site (anterior, posterior compartment), vaginal approach (List separately in addition to code for primary procedure)

►(Use 57267 in conjunction with 45560, 57240-57265, 57285)◄

57268 Repair of enterocele, vaginal approach (separate procedure)

57270 Repair of enterocele, abdominal approach (separate procedure)

57280 Colpopexy, abdominal approach

57282 Colpopexy, vaginal; extra-peritoneal approach (sacrospinous, iliococcygeus)

57283 intra-peritoneal approach (uterosacral, levator myorrhaphy)

57284 Paravaginal defect repair (including repair of cystocele, if performed); open abdominal approach

(Do not report 57284 in conjunction with 51840, 51841, 51990, 57240, 57260, 57265, 58152, 58267)

57285 vaginal approach

(Do not report 57285 in conjunction with 51990, 57240, 57260, 57265, 58267)

57287 Removal or revision of sling for stress incontinence (eg, fascia or synthetic)

57288 Sling operation for stress incontinence (eg, fascia or synthetic)

(For laparoscopic approach, use 51992)

57289 Pereyra procedure, including anterior colporrhaphy

57291 Construction of artificial vagina; without graft

57292 with graft

57295 Revision (including removal) of prosthetic vaginal graft; vaginal approach

57296 open abdominal approach

57300 Closure of rectovaginal fistula; vaginal or transanal approach

57305 abdominal approach

57307 abdominal approach, with concomitant colostomy

57308 transperineal approach, with perineal body reconstruction, with or without levator plication

57310 Closure of urethrovaginal fistula;

57311 with bulbocavernosus transplant

57320 Closure of vesicovaginal fistula; vaginal approach

(For concomitant cystostomy, see 51020-51040, 51101, 51102)

57330 transvesical and vaginal approach

(For abdominal approach, use 51900)

57335 Vaginoplasty for intersex state

Manipulation

▲ 57400 Dilation of vagina under anesthesia (other than local)

▲ 57410 Pelvic examination under anesthesia (other than local)

▲ 57415 Removal of impacted vaginal foreign body (separate procedure) under anesthesia (other than local)

(For removal without anesthesia of an impacted vaginal foreign body, use the appropriate E/M code)

Endoscopy

57420 Colposcopy of the entire vagina, with cervix if present;

57421 with biopsy(s) of vagina/cervix

(For colposcopic visualization of cervix and adjacent upper vagina, use 57452)

(When reporting colposcopies of multiple sites, use modifier 51 as appropriate. For colposcopic examinations/procedures involving the vulva, see 56820, 56821; cervix, see 57452-57461)

(For endometrial sampling (biopsy) performed in conjunction with colposcopy, use 58110)

57423 Paravaginal defect repair (including repair of cystocele, if performed), laparoscopic approach

(Do not report 57423 in conjunction with 49320, 51840, 51841, 51990, 57240, 57260, 58152, 58267)

57425 Laparoscopy, surgical, colpopexy (suspension of vaginal apex)

Cervix Uteri

(For cervicography, see Category III code 0003T)

Endoscopy

(For colposcopic examinations/procedures involving the vulva, see 56820, 56821; vagina, see 57420, 57421)

57452 Colposcopy of the cervix including upper/adjacent vagina;

(Do not report 57452 in addition to 57454-57461)

57454 with biopsy(s) of the cervix and endocervical curettage

57455 with biopsy(s) of the cervix

57456 with endocervical curettage

57460 with loop electrode biopsy(s) of the cervix

57461 with loop electrode conization of the cervix

(Do not report 57456 in addition to 57461)

(For endometrial sampling [biopsy] performed in conjunction with colposcopy, use 58110)

Excision

(For radical surgical procedures, see 58200-58240)

57500 Biopsy of cervix, single or multiple, or local excision of lesion, with or without fulguration (separate procedure)

57505 Endocervical curettage (not done as part of a dilation and curettage)

57510 Cautery of cervix; electro or thermal

57511 cryocautery, initial or repeat

57513 laser ablation

57520 Conization of cervix, with or without fulguration, with or without dilation and curettage, with or without repair; cold knife or laser

(See also 58120)

57522 loop electrode excision

57530 Trachelectomy (cervicectomy), amputation of cervix (separate procedure)

57531 Radical trachelectomy, with bilateral total pelvic lymphadenectomy and para-aortic lymph node sampling biopsy, with or without removal of tube(s), with or without removal of ovary(s)

(For radical abdominal hysterectomy, use 58210)

57540 Excision of cervical stump, abdominal approach;

57545 with pelvic floor repair

57550 Excision of cervical stump, vaginal approach;

57555 with anterior and/or posterior repair

57556 with repair of enterocele

(For insertion of intrauterine device, use 58300)

(For insertion of any hemostatic agent or pack for control of spontaneous non-obstetrical hemorrhage, see 57180)

57558 Dilation and curettage of cervical stump

Repair

57700 Cerclage of uterine cervix, nonobstetrical

57720 Trachelorrhaphy, plastic repair of uterine cervix, vaginal approach

Manipulation

57800 Dilation of cervical canal, instrumental (separate procedure)

(57820 has been deleted. To report, use 57558)

Corpus Uteri

Excision

58100 Endometrial sampling (biopsy) with or without endocervical sampling (biopsy), without cervical dilation, any method (separate procedure)

(For endocervical curettage only, use 57505)

(For endometrial sampling (biopsy) performed in conjunction with colposcopy (57420, 57421, 57452-57461), use 58110)

+ 58110 Endometrial sampling (biopsy) performed in conjunction with colposcopy (List separately in addition to code for primary procedure)

(Use 58110 in conjunction with 57420, 57421, 57452-57461)

58120 Dilation and curettage, diagnostic and/or therapeutic (nonobstetrical)

(For postpartum hemorrhage, use 59160)

58140 Myomectomy, excision of fibroid tumor(s) of uterus, 1 to 4 intramural myoma(s) with total weight of 250 g or less and/or removal of surface myomas; abdominal approach

58145 vaginal approach

58146 Myomectomy, excision of fibroid tumor(s) of uterus, 5 or more intramural myomas and/or intramural myomas with total weight greater than 250 g, abdominal approach

(Do not report 58146 in addition to 58140-58145, 58150-58240)

Hysterectomy Procedures

58150 Total abdominal hysterectomy (corpus and cervix), with or without removal of tube(s), with or without removal of ovary(s);

58152 with colpo-urethrocystopexy (eg, Marshall-Marchetti-Krantz, Burch)

(For urethrocystopexy without hysterectomy, see 51840, 51841)

58180 Supracervical abdominal hysterectomy (subtotal hysterectomy), with or without removal of tube(s), with or without removal of ovary(s)

58200 Total abdominal hysterectomy, including partial vaginectomy, with para-aortic and pelvic lymph node sampling, with or without removal of tube(s), with or without removal of ovary(s)

58210 Radical abdominal hysterectomy, with bilateral total pelvic lymphadenectomy and para-aortic lymph node sampling (biopsy), with or without removal of tube(s), with or without removal of ovary(s)

(For radical hysterectomy with ovarian transposition, use also 58825)

58240 Pelvic exenteration for gynecologic malignancy, with total abdominal hysterectomy or cervicectomy, with or without removal of tube(s), with or without removal of ovary(s), with removal of bladder and ureteral transplantations, and/or abdominoperineal resection of rectum and colon and colostomy, or any combination thereof

(For pelvic exenteration for lower urinary tract or male genital malignancy, use 51597)

58260 Vaginal hysterectomy, for uterus 250 g or less;

58262 with removal of tube(s), and/or ovary(s)

58263 with removal of tube(s), and/or ovary(s), with repair of enterocele

(Do not report 58263 in addition to 57283)

58267 with colpo-urethrocystopexy (Marshall-Marchetti-Krantz type, Pereyra type) with or without endoscopic control

58270 with repair of enterocele

(For repair of enterocele with removal of tubes and/or ovaries, use 58263)

58275 Vaginal hysterectomy, with total or partial vaginectomy;

58280 with repair of enterocele

58285 Vaginal hysterectomy, radical (Schauta type operation)

58290 Vaginal hysterectomy, for uterus greater than 250 g;

58291 with removal of tube(s) and/or ovary(s)

58292 with removal of tube(s) and/or ovary(s), with repair of enterocele

58293 with colpo-urethrocystopexy (Marshall-Marchetti-Krantz type, Pereyra type) with or without endoscopic control

58294 with repair of enterocele

Introduction

(For insertion/removal of implantable contraceptive capsules, see 11975, 11976, 11977)

58300 Insertion of intrauterine device (IUD)

58301 Removal of intrauterine device (IUD)

58321 Artificial insemination; intra-cervical

58322 intra-uterine

58323 Sperm washing for artificial insemination

58340 Catheterization and introduction of saline or contrast material for saline infusion sonohysterography (SIS) or hysterosalpingography

(For radiological supervision and interpretation of saline infusion sonohysterography, use 76831)

(For radiological supervision and interpretation of hysterosalpingography, use 74740)

58345 Transcervical introduction of fallopian tube catheter for diagnosis and/or re-establishing patency (any method), with or without hysterosalpingography

(For radiological supervision and interpretation, use 74742)

58346 Insertion of Heyman capsules for clinical brachytherapy

(For placement of needles or catheters into pelvic organs and/or genitalia [except prostate] for interstitial radioelement application, use 55920)

►(For insertion of radioelement sources or ribbons, see 77761-77763, 77785-77787)◄

58350 Chromotubation of oviduct, including materials

(For materials supplied by physician, use 99070)

58353 Endometrial ablation, thermal, without hysteroscopic guidance

(For hysteroscopic procedure, use 58563)

58356 Endometrial cryoablation with ultrasonic guidance, including endometrial curettage, when performed

(Do not report 58356 in conjunction with 58100, 58120, 58340, 76700, 76856)

Repair

58400 Uterine suspension, with or without shortening of round ligaments, with or without shortening of sacrouterine ligaments; (separate procedure)

58410 with presacral sympathectomy

(For anastomosis of tubes to uterus, use 58752)

58520 Hysterorrhaphy, repair of ruptured uterus (nonobstetrical)

58540 Hysteroplasty, repair of uterine anomaly (Strassman type)

(For closure of vesicouterine fistula, use 51920)

Laparoscopy/Hysteroscopy

Surgical laparoscopy always includes diagnostic laparoscopy. To report a diagnostic laparoscopy (peritoneoscopy) (separate procedure), use 49320. To report a diagnostic hysteroscopy (separate procedure), use 58555.

58541 Laparoscopy, surgical, supracervical hysterectomy, for uterus 250 g or less;

58542 with removal of tube(s) and/or ovary(s)

(Do not report 58541-58542 in conjunction with 49320, 57000, 57180, 57410, 58140-58146, 58545, 58546, 58561, 58661, 58670, 58671)

58543 Laparoscopy, surgical, supracervical hysterectomy, for uterus greater than 250 g;

58544 with removal of tube(s) and/or ovary(s)

(Do not report 58543-58544 in conjunction with 49320, 57000, 57180, 57410, 58140-58146, 58545, 58546, 58561, 58661, 58670, 58671)

58545 Laparoscopy, surgical, myomectomy, excision; 1 to 4 intramural myomas with total weight of 250 g or less and/or removal of surface myomas

58546 5 or more intramural myomas and/or intramural myomas with total weight greater than 250 g

58548 Laparoscopy, surgical, with radical hysterectomy, with bilateral total pelvic lymphadenectomy and para-aortic lymph node sampling (biopsy), with removal of tube(s) and ovary(s), if performed

(Do not report 58548 in conjunction with 38570-38572, 58210, 58285, 58550-58554)

58550 Laparoscopy, surgical, with vaginal hysterectomy, for uterus 250 g or less;

58552 with removal of tube(s) and/or ovary(s)

(Do not report 58550-58552 in conjunction with 49320, 57000, 57180, 57410, 58140-58146, 58545, 58546, 58561, 58661, 58670, 58671)

58553 Laparoscopy, surgical, with vaginal hysterectomy, for uterus greater than 250 g;

58554 with removal of tube(s) and/or ovary(s)

(Do not report 58553-58554 in conjunction with 49320, 57000, 57180, 57410, 58140-58146, 58545, 58546, 58561, 58661, 58670, 58671)

58555 Hysteroscopy, diagnostic (separate procedure)

58558 Hysteroscopy, surgical; with sampling (biopsy) of endometrium and/or polypectomy, with or without D & C

58559 with lysis of intrauterine adhesions (any method)

58560 with division or resection of intrauterine septum (any method)

58561 with removal of leiomyomata

58562 with removal of impacted foreign body

58563 with endometrial ablation (eg, endometrial resection, electrosurgical ablation, thermoablation)

58565 with bilateral fallopian tube cannulation to induce occlusion by placement of permanent implants

(Do not report 58565 in conjunction with 58555 or 57800)

(For unilateral procedure, use modifier 52)

58570 Laparoscopy, surgical, with total hysterectomy, for uterus 250 g or less;

58571 with removal of tube(s) and/or ovary(s)

58572 Laparoscopy, surgical, with total hysterectomy, for uterus greater than 250 g;

58573 with removal of tube(s) and/or ovary(s)

(Do not report 58570-58573 in conjunction with 49320, 57000, 57180, 57410, 58140-58146, 58150, 58545, 58546, 58561, 58661, 58670, 58671)

58578 Unlisted laparoscopy procedure, uterus

58579 Unlisted hysteroscopy procedure, uterus

Oviduct/Ovary

Incision

58600 Ligation or transection of fallopian tube(s), abdominal or vaginal approach, unilateral or bilateral

58605 Ligation or transection of fallopian tube(s), abdominal or vaginal approach, postpartum, unilateral or bilateral, during same hospitalization (separate procedure)

(For laparoscopic procedures, use 58670, 58671)

✚ **58611** Ligation or transection of fallopian tube(s) when done at the time of cesarean delivery or intra-abdominal surgery (not a separate procedure) (List separately in addition to code for primary procedure)

58615 Occlusion of fallopian tube(s) by device (eg, band, clip, Falope ring) vaginal or suprapubic approach

(For laparoscopic approach, use 58671)

(For lysis of adnexal adhesions, use 58740)

Laparoscopy

Surgical laparoscopy always includes diagnostic laparoscopy. To report a diagnostic laparoscopy (peritoneoscopy) (separate procedure), use 49320.

58660 Laparoscopy, surgical; with lysis of adhesions (salpingolysis, ovariolysis) (separate procedure)

58661 with removal of adnexal structures (partial or total oophorectomy and/or salpingectomy)

58662 with fulguration or excision of lesions of the ovary, pelvic viscera, or peritoneal surface by any method

58670 with fulguration of oviducts (with or without transection)

58671 with occlusion of oviducts by device (eg, band, clip, or Falope ring)

58672 with fimbrioplasty

58673 with salpingostomy (salpingoneostomy)

(Codes 58672 and 58673 are used to report unilateral procedures. For bilateral procedure, use modifier 50)

58679 Unlisted laparoscopy procedure, oviduct, ovary

(For laparoscopic aspiration of ovarian cyst, use 49322)

(For laparoscopic biopsy of the ovary or fallopian tube, use 49321)

Excision

58700 Salpingectomy, complete or partial, unilateral or bilateral (separate procedure)

58720 Salpingo-oophorectomy, complete or partial, unilateral or bilateral (separate procedure)

Repair

58740 Lysis of adhesions (salpingolysis, ovariolysis)

(For laparoscopic approach, use 58660)

(For excision or destruction of endometriomas, open method, see 49203-49205, 58957, 58958)

(For fulguration or excision of lesions, laparoscopic approach, use 58662)

58750 Tubotubal anastomosis

58752 Tubouterine implantation

58760 Fimbrioplasty

(For laparoscopic approach, use 58672)

58770 Salpingostomy (salpingoneostomy)

(For laparoscopic approach, use 58673)

Ovary

Incision

58800 Drainage of ovarian cyst(s), unilateral or bilateral (separate procedure); vaginal approach

58805 abdominal approach

58820 Drainage of ovarian abscess; vaginal approach, open

58822 abdominal approach

⊙ **58823** Drainage of pelvic abscess, transvaginal or transrectal approach, percutaneous (eg, ovarian, pericolic)

(For radiological supervision and interpretation, use 75989)

58825 Transposition, ovary(s)

Excision

58900 Biopsy of ovary, unilateral or bilateral (separate procedure)

(For laparoscopic biopsy of the ovary or fallopian tube, use 49321)

58920 Wedge resection or bisection of ovary, unilateral or bilateral

58925 Ovarian cystectomy, unilateral or bilateral

58940 Oophorectomy, partial or total, unilateral or bilateral;

(For oophorectomy with concomitant debulking for ovarian malignancy, use 58952)

58943 for ovarian, tubal or primary peritoneal malignancy, with para-aortic and pelvic lymph node biopsies, peritoneal washings, peritoneal biopsies, diaphragmatic assessments, with or without salpingectomy(s), with or without omentectomy

58950 Resection (initial) of ovarian, tubal or primary peritoneal malignancy with bilateral salpingo-oophorectomy and omentectomy;

58951 with total abdominal hysterectomy, pelvic and limited para-aortic lymphadenectomy

58952 with radical dissection for debulking (ie, radical excision or destruction, intra-abdominal or retroperitoneal tumors)

(For resection of recurrent ovarian, tubal, primary peritoneal, or uterine malignancy, see 58957, 58958)

58953 Bilateral salpingo-oophorectomy with omentectomy, total abdominal hysterectomy and radical dissection for debulking;

58954 with pelvic lymphadenectomy and limited para-aortic lymphadenectomy

58956 Bilateral salpingo-oophorectomy with total omentectomy, total abdominal hysterectomy for malignancy

(Do not report 58956 in conjunction with 49255, 58150, 58180, 58262, 58263, 58550, 58661, 58700, 58720, 58900, 58925, 58940, 58957, 58958)

58957 Resection (tumor debulking) of recurrent ovarian, tubal, primary peritoneal, uterine malignancy (intra-abdominal, retroperitoneal tumors), with omentectomy, if performed;

58958 with pelvic lymphadenectomy and limited para-aortic lymphadenectomy

(Do not report 58957, 58958 in conjunction with 38770, 38780, 44005, 49000, 49203-49215, 49255, 58900-58960)

58960 Laparotomy, for staging or restaging of ovarian, tubal, or primary peritoneal malignancy (second look), with or without omentectomy, peritoneal washing, biopsy of abdominal and pelvic peritoneum, diaphragmatic assessment with pelvic and limited para-aortic lymphadenectomy

(Do not report 58960 in conjunction with 58957, 58958)

In Vitro Fertilization

58970 Follicle puncture for oocyte retrieval, any method

(For radiological supervision and interpretation, use 76948)

58974 Embryo transfer, intrauterine

58976 Gamete, zygote, or embryo intrafallopian transfer, any method

(For laparoscopic adnexal procedures, see 58660-58673)

Other Procedures

58999 Unlisted procedure, female genital system (nonobstetrical)

Maternity Care and Delivery

The services normally provided in uncomplicated maternity cases include antepartum care, delivery, and postpartum care.

Antepartum care includes the initial and subsequent history, physical examinations, recording of weight, blood pressures, fetal heart tones, routine chemical urinalysis, and monthly visits up to 28 weeks gestation, biweekly visits to 36 weeks gestation, and weekly visits until delivery. Any other visits or services within this time period should be coded separately.

Delivery services include admission to the hospital, the admission history and physical examination, management of uncomplicated labor, vaginal delivery (with or without episiotomy, with or without forceps), or cesarean delivery. Medical problems complicating labor and delivery management may require additional resources and should be identified by utilizing the codes in the **Medicine** and **Evaluation and Management Services** section in addition to codes for maternity care.

Postpartum care includes hospital and office visits following vaginal or cesarean section delivery.

For medical complications of pregnancy (eg, cardiac problems, neurological problems, diabetes, hypertension, toxemia, hyperemesis, pre-term labor, premature rupture of membranes), see services in the **Medicine** and **Evaluation and Management Services** section.

For surgical complications of pregnancy (eg, appendectomy, hernia, ovarian cyst, Bartholin cyst), see services in the **Surgery** section.

If a physician provides all or part of the antepartum and/or postpartum patient care but does not perform delivery due to termination of pregnancy by abortion or referral to another physician for delivery, see the antepartum and postpartum care codes 59425-59426 and 59430.

(For circumcision of newborn, see 54150, 54160)

Antepartum Services

59000 Amniocentesis; diagnostic

(For radiological supervision and interpretation, use 76946)

59001 therapeutic amniotic fluid reduction (includes ultrasound guidance)

59012 Cordocentesis (intrauterine), any method

(For radiological supervision and interpretation, use 76941)

59015 Chorionic villus sampling, any method

(For radiological supervision and interpretation, use 76945)

59020 Fetal contraction stress test

59025 Fetal non-stress test

59030 Fetal scalp blood sampling

(For repeat fetal scalp blood sampling, use 59030 and see modifiers 76 and 77)

59050 Fetal monitoring during labor by consulting physician (ie, non-attending physician) with written report; supervision and interpretation

59051 interpretation only

59070 Transabdominal amnioinfusion, including ultrasound guidance

59072 Fetal umbilical cord occlusion, including ultrasound guidance

59074 Fetal fluid drainage (eg, vesicocentesis, thoracocentesis, paracentesis), including ultrasound guidance

59076 Fetal shunt placement, including ultrasound guidance

(For unlisted fetal invasive procedure, use 59897)

Excision

59100 Hysterotomy, abdominal (eg, for hydatidiform mole, abortion)

(When tubal ligation is performed at the same time as hysterotomy, use 58611 in addition to 59100)

59120 Surgical treatment of ectopic pregnancy; tubal or ovarian, requiring salpingectomy and/or oophorectomy, abdominal or vaginal approach

59121 tubal or ovarian, without salpingectomy and/or oophorectomy

59130 abdominal pregnancy

59135 interstitial, uterine pregnancy requiring total hysterectomy

59136 interstitial, uterine pregnancy with partial resection of uterus

59140 cervical, with evacuation

59150 Laparoscopic treatment of ectopic pregnancy; without salpingectomy and/or oophorectomy

59151 with salpingectomy and/or oophorectomy

59160 Curettage, postpartum

Introduction

(For intrauterine fetal transfusion, use 36460)

(For introduction of hypertonic solution and/or prostaglandins to initiate labor, see 59850-59857)

59200 Insertion of cervical dilator (eg, laminaria, prostaglandin) (separate procedure)

Repair

(For tracheloplasty, use 57700)

59300 Episiotomy or vaginal repair, by other than attending physician

59320 Cerclage of cervix, during pregnancy; vaginal

59325 abdominal

59350 Hysterorrhaphy of ruptured uterus

Vaginal Delivery, Antepartum and Postpartum Care

59400 Routine obstetric care including antepartum care, vaginal delivery (with or without episiotomy, and/or forceps) and postpartum care

59409 Vaginal delivery only (with or without episiotomy and/or forceps);

59410 including postpartum care

59412 External cephalic version, with or without tocolysis

(Use 59412 in addition to code[s] for delivery)

59414 Delivery of placenta (separate procedure)

(For antepartum care only, see 59425, 59426 or appropriate E/M code(s))

(For 1-3 antepartum care visits, see appropriate E/M code(s))

59425 Antepartum care only; 4-6 visits

59426 7 or more visits

59430 Postpartum care only (separate procedure)

Cesarean Delivery

(For standby attendance for infant, use 99360)

(For low cervical cesarean section, see 59510, 59515, 59525)

59510 Routine obstetric care including antepartum care, cesarean delivery, and postpartum care

59514 Cesarean delivery only;

59515 including postpartum care

(For classic cesarean section, see 59510, 59515, 59525)

+ 59525 Subtotal or total hysterectomy after cesarean delivery (List separately in addition to code for primary procedure)

(Use 59525 in conjunction with 59510, 59514, 59515, 59618, 59620, 59622)

(For extraperitoneal cesarean section, or cesarean section with subtotal or total hysterectomy, see 59510, 59515, 59525)

Delivery After Previous Cesarean Delivery

Patients who have had a previous cesarean delivery and now present with the expectation of a vaginal delivery are coded using codes 59610-59622. If the patient has a successful vaginal delivery after a previous cesarean delivery (VBAC), use codes 59610-59614. If the attempt is unsuccessful and another cesarean delivery is carried out, use codes 59618-59622. To report elective cesarean deliveries use code 59510, 59514 or 59515.

59610 Routine obstetric care including antepartum care, vaginal delivery (with or without episiotomy, and/or forceps) and postpartum care, after previous cesarean delivery

59612 Vaginal delivery only, after previous cesarean delivery (with or without episiotomy and/or forceps);

59614 including postpartum care

59618 Routine obstetric care including antepartum care, cesarean delivery, and postpartum care, following attempted vaginal delivery after previous cesarean delivery

59620 Cesarean delivery only, following attempted vaginal delivery after previous cesarean delivery;

59622 including postpartum care

Abortion

(For medical treatment of spontaneous complete abortion, any trimester, use E/M codes 99201-99233)

(For surgical treatment of spontaneous abortion, use 59812)

59812 Treatment of incomplete abortion, any trimester, completed surgically

59820 Treatment of missed abortion, completed surgically; first trimester

59821 second trimester

59830 Treatment of septic abortion, completed surgically

59840 Induced abortion, by dilation and curettage

59841 Induced abortion, by dilation and evacuation

59850 Induced abortion, by one or more intra-amniotic injections (amniocentesis-injections), including hospital admission and visits, delivery of fetus and secundines;

59851 with dilation and curettage and/or evacuation

59852 with hysterotomy (failed intra-amniotic injection)

(For insertion of cervical dilator, use 59200)

59855 Induced abortion, by one or more vaginal suppositories (eg, prostaglandin) with or without cervical dilation (eg, laminaria), including hospital admission and visits, delivery of fetus and secundines;

59856 with dilation and curettage and/or evacuation

59857 with hysterotomy (failed medical evacuation)

Other Procedures

59866 Multifetal pregnancy reduction(s) (MPR)

59870 Uterine evacuation and curettage for hydatidiform mole

59871 Removal of cerclage suture under anesthesia (other than local)

59897 Unlisted fetal invasive procedure, including ultrasound guidance

59898 Unlisted laparoscopy procedure, maternity care and delivery

59899 Unlisted procedure, maternity care and delivery

Notes

Endocrine System

(For pituitary and pineal surgery, see **Nervous System**)

Thyroid Gland

Incision

60000 Incision and drainage of thyroglossal duct cyst, infected

Excision

(60001 has been deleted. To report, use 60300)

60100 Biopsy thyroid, percutaneous core needle

(If imaging guidance is performed, see 76942, 77002, 77012, 77021)

(For fine needle aspiration, use 10021 or 10022)

(For evaluation of fine needle aspirate, see 88172, 88173)

60200 Excision of cyst or adenoma of thyroid, or transection of isthmus

60210 Partial thyroid lobectomy, unilateral; with or without isthmusectomy

60212 with contralateral subtotal lobectomy, including isthmusectomy

60220 Total thyroid lobectomy, unilateral; with or without isthmusectomy

60225 with contralateral subtotal lobectomy, including isthmusectomy

60240 Thyroidectomy, total or complete

(For thyroidectomy, subtotal or partial, use 60271)

60252 Thyroidectomy, total or subtotal for malignancy; with limited neck dissection

60254 with radical neck dissection

60260 Thyroidectomy, removal of all remaining thyroid tissue following previous removal of a portion of thyroid

(For bilateral procedure, report 60260 with modifier 50)

60270 Thyroidectomy, including substernal thyroid; sternal split or transthoracic approach

60271 cervical approach

60280 Excision of thyroglossal duct cyst or sinus;

60281 recurrent

(For thyroid ultrasonography, use 76536)

Removal

60300 Aspiration and/or injection, thyroid cyst

(For fine needle aspiration, see 10021, 10022)

(If imaging guidance is performed, see 76942, 77012)

Parathyroid, Thymus, Adrenal Glands, Pancreas, and Carotid Body

Excision

(For pituitary and pineal surgery, see **Nervous System**)

60500 Parathyroidectomy or exploration of parathyroid(s);

60502 re-exploration

60505 with mediastinal exploration, sternal split or transthoracic approach

✚ **60512** Parathyroid autotransplantation (List separately in addition to code for primary procedure)

(Use 60512 in conjunction with 60500, 60502, 60505, 60212, 60225, 60240, 60252, 60254, 60260, 60270, 60271)

60520 Thymectomy, partial or total; transcervical approach (separate procedure)

60521 sternal split or transthoracic approach, without radical mediastinal dissection (separate procedure)

60522 sternal split or transthoracic approach, with radical mediastinal dissection (separate procedure)

60540 Adrenalectomy, partial or complete, or exploration of adrenal gland with or without biopsy, transabdominal, lumbar or dorsal (separate procedure);

60545 with excision of adjacent retroperitoneal tumor

(Do not report 60540, 60545 in conjunction with 50323)

(For bilateral procedure, report 60540 with modifier 50)

(For excision of remote or disseminated pheochromocytoma, see 49203-49205)

(For laparoscopic approach, use 60650)

60600 Excision of carotid body tumor; without excision of carotid artery

60605 with excision of carotid artery

Laparoscopy

Surgical laparoscopy always includes diagnostic laparoscopy. To report a diagnostic laparoscopy (peritoneoscopy) (separate procedure), use 49320.

60650 Laparoscopy, surgical, with adrenalectomy, partial or complete, or exploration of adrenal gland with or without biopsy, transabdominal, lumbar or dorsal

60659 Unlisted laparoscopy procedure, endocrine system

Other Procedures

60699 Unlisted procedure, endocrine system

Notes

Nervous System

Skull, Meninges, and Brain

(For injection procedure for cerebral angiography, see 36100-36218)

(For injection procedure for ventriculography, see 61026, 61120)

(For injection procedure for pneumoencephalography, use 61055)

Injection, Drainage, or Aspiration

61000 Subdural tap through fontanelle, or suture, infant, unilateral or bilateral; initial

61001 subsequent taps

61020 Ventricular puncture through previous burr hole, fontanelle, suture, or implanted ventricular catheter/reservoir; without injection

61026 with injection of medication or other substance for diagnosis or treatment

61050 Cisternal or lateral cervical (C1-C2) puncture; without injection (separate procedure)

61055 with injection of medication or other substance for diagnosis or treatment (eg, C1-C2)

(For radiological supervision and interpretation, see **Radiology**)

61070 Puncture of shunt tubing or reservoir for aspiration or injection procedure

(For radiological supervision and interpretation, use 75809)

Twist Drill, Burr Hole(s), or Trephine

61105 Twist drill hole for subdural or ventricular puncture

⊘ **61107** Twist drill hole(s) for subdural, intracerebral, or ventricular puncture; for implanting ventricular catheter, pressure recording device, or other intracerebral monitoring device

(For intracranial neuroendoscopic ventricular catheter placement, use 62160)

(For twist drill or burr hole performed to place thermal perfusion probe, use Category III code 0077T)

61108 for evacuation and/or drainage of subdural hematoma

61120 Burr hole(s) for ventricular puncture (including injection of gas, contrast media, dye, or radioactive material)

61140 Burr hole(s) or trephine; with biopsy of brain or intracranial lesion

61150 with drainage of brain abscess or cyst

61151 with subsequent tapping (aspiration) of intracranial abscess or cyst

61154 Burr hole(s) with evacuation and/or drainage of hematoma, extradural or subdural

(For bilateral procedure, report 61154 with modifier 50)

61156 Burr hole(s); with aspiration of hematoma or cyst, intracerebral

61210 for implanting ventricular catheter, reservoir, EEG electrode(s), pressure recording device, or other cerebral monitoring device (separate procedure)

(For intracranial neuroendoscopic ventricular catheter placement, use 62160)

61215 Insertion of subcutaneous reservoir, pump or continuous infusion system for connection to ventricular catheter

(For refilling and maintenance of an implantable infusion pump for spinal or brain drug therapy, use 95990)

(For chemotherapy, use 96450)

61250 Burr hole(s) or trephine, supratentorial, exploratory, not followed by other surgery

(For bilateral procedure, report 61250 with modifier 50)

61253 Burr hole(s) or trephine, infratentorial, unilateral or bilateral

(If burr hole[s] or trephine are followed by craniotomy at same operative session, use 61304-61321; do not use 61250 or 61253)

Craniectomy or Craniotomy

61304 Craniectomy or craniotomy, exploratory; supratentorial

61305 infratentorial (posterior fossa)

61312 Craniectomy or craniotomy for evacuation of hematoma, supratentorial; extradural or subdural

61313 intracerebral

61314 Craniectomy or craniotomy for evacuation of hematoma, infratentorial; extradural or subdural

61315 intracerebellar

+ **61316** Incision and subcutaneous placement of cranial bone graft (List separately in addition to code for primary procedure)

(Use 61316 in conjunction with 61304, 61312, 61313, 61322, 61323, 61340, 61570, 61571, 61680-61705)

61320 Craniectomy or craniotomy, drainage of intracranial abscess; supratentorial

61321 infratentorial

61322 Craniectomy or craniotomy, decompressive, with or without duraplasty, for treatment of intracranial hypertension, without evacuation of associated intraparenchymal hematoma; without lobectomy

(Do not report 61313 in addition to 61322)

(For subtemporal decompression, use 61340)

61323 with lobectomy

(Do not report 61313 in addition to 61323)

(For subtemporal decompression, use 61340)

61330 Decompression of orbit only, transcranial approach

(For bilateral procedure, report 61330 with modifier 50)

61332 Exploration of orbit (transcranial approach); with biopsy

61333 with removal of lesion

61334 with removal of foreign body

61340 Subtemporal cranial decompression (pseudotumor cerebri, slit ventricle syndrome)

(For bilateral procedure, report 61340 with modifier 50)

(For decompressive craniotomy or craniectomy for intracranial hypertension, without hematoma evacuation, see 61322, 61323)

61343 Craniectomy, suboccipital with cervical laminectomy for decompression of medulla and spinal cord, with or without dural graft (eg, Arnold-Chiari malformation)

61345 Other cranial decompression, posterior fossa

(For orbital decompression by lateral wall approach, Kroenlein type, use 67445)

61440 Craniotomy for section of tentorium cerebelli (separate procedure)

61450 Craniectomy, subtemporal, for section, compression, or decompression of sensory root of gasserian ganglion

61458 Craniectomy, suboccipital; for exploration or decompression of cranial nerves

61460 for section of one or more cranial nerves

61470 for medullary tractotomy

61480 for mesencephalic tractotomy or pedunculotomy

61490 Craniotomy for lobotomy, including cingulotomy

(For bilateral procedure, report 61490 with modifier 50)

61500 Craniectomy; with excision of tumor or other bone lesion of skull

61501 for osteomyelitis

61510 Craniectomy, trephination, bone flap craniotomy; for excision of brain tumor, supratentorial, except meningioma

61512 for excision of meningioma, supratentorial

61514 for excision of brain abscess, supratentorial

61516 for excision or fenestration of cyst, supratentorial

(For excision of pituitary tumor or craniopharyngioma, see 61545, 61546, 61548)

✚ 61517 Implantation of brain intracavitary chemotherapy agent (List separately in addition to code for primary procedure)

(Use 61517 only in conjunction with 61510 or 61518)

►(Do not report 61517 for brachytherapy insertion. For intracavitary insertion of radioelement sources or ribbons, see 77785-77787)◄

61518 Craniectomy for excision of brain tumor, infratentorial or posterior fossa; except meningioma, cerebellopontine angle tumor, or midline tumor at base of skull

61519 meningioma

61520 cerebellopontine angle tumor

61521 midline tumor at base of skull

61522 Craniectomy, infratentorial or posterior fossa; for excision of brain abscess

61524 for excision or fenestration of cyst

61526 Craniectomy, bone flap craniotomy, transtemporal (mastoid) for excision of cerebellopontine angle tumor;

61530 combined with middle/posterior fossa craniotomy/craniectomy

61531 Subdural implantation of strip electrodes through one or more burr or trephine hole(s) for long-term seizure monitoring

(For stereotactic implantation of electrodes, use 61760)

(For craniotomy for excision of intracranial arteriovenous malformation, see 61680-61692)

61533 Craniotomy with elevation of bone flap; for subdural implantation of an electrode array, for long-term seizure monitoring

(For continuous EEG monitoring, see 95950-95954)

61534 for excision of epileptogenic focus without electrocorticography during surgery

61535 for removal of epidural or subdural electrode array, without excision of cerebral tissue (separate procedure)

61536 for excision of cerebral epileptogenic focus, with electrocorticography during surgery (includes removal of electrode array)

61537 for lobectomy, temporal lobe, without electrocorticography during surgery

61538 for lobectomy, temporal lobe, with electrocorticography during surgery

61539 for lobectomy, other than temporal lobe, partial or total, with electrocorticography during surgery

61540 for lobectomy, other than temporal lobe, partial or total, without electrocorticography during surgery

61541 for transection of corpus callosum

61542 for total hemispherectomy

61543 for partial or subtotal (functional) hemispherectomy

61544 for excision or coagulation of choroid plexus

61545 for excision of craniopharyngioma

(For craniotomy for selective amygdalohippocampectomy, use 61566)

(For craniotomy for multiple subpial transections during surgery, use 61567)

61546 Craniotomy for hypophysectomy or excision of pituitary tumor, intracranial approach

61548 Hypophysectomy or excision of pituitary tumor, transnasal or transseptal approach, nonstereotactic

(Do not report code 69990 in addition to code 61548)

61550 Craniectomy for craniosynostosis; single cranial suture

61552 multiple cranial sutures

(For cranial reconstruction for orbital hypertelorism, see 21260-21263)

(For reconstruction, see 21172-21180)

61556 Craniotomy for craniosynostosis; frontal or parietal bone flap

61557 bifrontal bone flap

61558 Extensive craniectomy for multiple cranial suture craniosynostosis (eg, cloverleaf skull); not requiring bone grafts

61559 recontouring with multiple osteotomies and bone autografts (eg, barrel-stave procedure) (includes obtaining grafts)

(For reconstruction, see 21172-21180)

61563 Excision, intra and extracranial, benign tumor of cranial bone (eg, fibrous dysplasia); without optic nerve decompression

61564 with optic nerve decompression

(For reconstruction, see 21181-21183)

61566 Craniotomy with elevation of bone flap; for selective amygdalohippocampectomy

61567 for multiple subpial transections, with electrocorticography during surgery

61570 Craniectomy or craniotomy; with excision of foreign body from brain

61571 with treatment of penetrating wound of brain

(For sequestrectomy for osteomyelitis, use 61501)

61575 Transoral approach to skull base, brain stem or upper spinal cord for biopsy, decompression or excision of lesion;

61576 requiring splitting of tongue and/or mandible (including tracheostomy)

(For arthrodesis, use 22548)

Surgery of Skull Base

The surgical management of lesions involving the skull base (base of anterior, middle, and posterior cranial fossae) often requires the skills of several surgeons of different surgical specialties working together or in tandem during the operative session. These operations are usually not staged because of the need for definitive closure of dura, subcutaneous tissues, and skin to avoid serious infections such as osteomyelitis and/or meningitis.

The procedures are categorized according to (1) ***approach procedure*** necessary to obtain adequate exposure to the lesion (pathologic entity), (2) ***definitive procedure(s)*** necessary to biopsy, excise or otherwise treat the lesion, and (3) ***repair/reconstruction*** of the defect present following the definitive procedure(s).

The ***approach procedure*** is described according to anatomical area involved, ie, anterior cranial fossa, middle cranial fossa, posterior cranial fossa, and brain stem or upper spinal cord.

The ***definitive procedure(s)*** describes the repair, biopsy, resection, or excision of various lesions of the skull base and, when appropriate, primary closure of the dura, mucous membranes, and skin.

The ***repair/reconstruction procedure(s)*** is reported separately if extensive dural grafting, cranioplasty, local or regional myocutaneous pedicle flaps, or extensive skin grafts are required.

For primary closure, see the appropriate codes (ie, 15732, 15756-15758).

When one surgeon performs the approach procedure, another surgeon performs the definitive procedure, and another surgeon performs the repair/reconstruction procedure, each surgeon reports only the code for the specific procedure performed.

If one surgeon performs more than one procedure (ie, approach procedure and definitive procedure), then both codes are reported, adding modifier 51 to the secondary, additional procedure(s).

Approach Procedures

Anterior Cranial Fossa

61580 Craniofacial approach to anterior cranial fossa; extradural, including lateral rhinotomy, ethmoidectomy, sphenoidectomy, without maxillectomy or orbital exenteration

61581 extradural, including lateral rhinotomy, orbital exenteration, ethmoidectomy, sphenoidectomy and/or maxillectomy

61582 extradural, including unilateral or bifrontal craniotomy, elevation of frontal lobe(s), osteotomy of base of anterior cranial fossa

61583 intradural, including unilateral or bifrontal craniotomy, elevation or resection of frontal lobe, osteotomy of base of anterior cranial fossa

61584 Orbitocranial approach to anterior cranial fossa, extradural, including supraorbital ridge osteotomy and elevation of frontal and/or temporal lobe(s); without orbital exenteration

61585 with orbital exenteration

61586 Bicoronal, transzygomatic and/or LeFort I osteotomy approach to anterior cranial fossa with or without internal fixation, without bone graft

Middle Cranial Fossa

61590 Infratemporal pre-auricular approach to middle cranial fossa (parapharyngeal space, infratemporal and midline skull base, nasopharynx), with or without disarticulation of the mandible, including parotidectomy, craniotomy, decompression and/or mobilization of the facial nerve and/or petrous carotid artery

61591 Infratemporal post-auricular approach to middle cranial fossa (internal auditory meatus, petrous apex, tentorium, cavernous sinus, parasellar area, infratemporal fossa) including mastoidectomy, resection of sigmoid sinus, with or without decompression and/or mobilization of contents of auditory canal or petrous carotid artery

61592 Orbitocranial zygomatic approach to middle cranial fossa (cavernous sinus and carotid artery, clivus, basilar artery or petrous apex) including osteotomy of zygoma, craniotomy, extra- or intradural elevation of temporal lobe

Posterior Cranial Fossa

61595 Transtemporal approach to posterior cranial fossa, jugular foramen or midline skull base, including mastoidectomy, decompression of sigmoid sinus and/or facial nerve, with or without mobilization

61596 Transcochlear approach to posterior cranial fossa, jugular foramen or midline skull base, including labyrinthectomy, decompression, with or without mobilization of facial nerve and/or petrous carotid artery

61597 Transcondylar (far lateral) approach to posterior cranial fossa, jugular foramen or midline skull base, including occipital condylectomy, mastoidectomy, resection of C1-C3 vertebral body(s), decompression of vertebral artery, with or without mobilization

61598 Transpetrosal approach to posterior cranial fossa, clivus or foramen magnum, including ligation of superior petrosal sinus and/or sigmoid sinus

Definitive Procedures

Base of Anterior Cranial Fossa

61600 Resection or excision of neoplastic, vascular or infectious lesion of base of anterior cranial fossa; extradural

61601 intradural, including dural repair, with or without graft

Base of Middle Cranial Fossa

61605 Resection or excision of neoplastic, vascular or infectious lesion of infratemporal fossa, parapharyngeal space, petrous apex; extradural

61606 intradural, including dural repair, with or without graft

61607 Resection or excision of neoplastic, vascular or infectious lesion of parasellar area, cavernous sinus, clivus or midline skull base; extradural

61608 intradural, including dural repair, with or without graft

Codes 61609-61612 are reported in addition to code(s) for primary procedure(s) 61605-61608. Report only one transection or ligation of carotid artery code per operative session.

+ 61609 Transection or ligation, carotid artery in cavernous sinus; without repair (List separately in addition to code for primary procedure)

+ 61610 with repair by anastomosis or graft (List separately in addition to code for primary procedure)

+ 61611 Transection or ligation, carotid artery in petrous canal; without repair (List separately in addition to code for primary procedure)

+ 61612 with repair by anastomosis or graft (List separately in addition to code for primary procedure)

61613 Obliteration of carotid aneurysm, arteriovenous malformation, or carotid-cavernous fistula by dissection within cavernous sinus

Base of Posterior Cranial Fossa

61615 Resection or excision of neoplastic, vascular or infectious lesion of base of posterior cranial fossa, jugular foramen, foramen magnum, or C1-C3 vertebral bodies; extradural

61616 intradural, including dural repair, with or without graft

Repair and/or Reconstruction of Surgical Defects of Skull Base

61618 Secondary repair of dura for cerebrospinal fluid leak, anterior, middle or posterior cranial fossa following surgery of the skull base; by free tissue graft (eg, pericranium, fascia, tensor fascia lata, adipose tissue, homologous or synthetic grafts)

61619 by local or regionalized vascularized pedicle flap or myocutaneous flap (including galea, temporalis, frontalis or occipitalis muscle)

Endovascular Therapy

61623 Endovascular temporary balloon arterial occlusion, head or neck (extracranial/intracranial) including selective catheterization of vessel to be occluded, positioning and inflation of occlusion balloon, concomitant neurological monitoring, and radiologic supervision and interpretation of all angiography required for balloon occlusion and to exclude vascular injury post occlusion

(If selective catheterization and angiography of arteries other than artery to be occluded is performed, use appropriate catheterization and radiologic supervision and interpretation codes)

(If complete diagnostic angiography of the artery to be occluded is performed immediately prior to temporary occlusion, use appropriate radiologic supervision and interpretation codes only)

61624 Transcatheter permanent occlusion or embolization (eg, for tumor destruction, to achieve hemostasis, to occlude a vascular malformation), percutaneous, any method; central nervous system (intracranial, spinal cord)

(See also 37204)

(For radiological supervision and interpretation, use 75894)

61626 non-central nervous system, head or neck (extracranial, brachiocephalic branch)

(See also 37204)

(For radiological supervision and interpretation, use 75894)

61630 Balloon angioplasty, intracranial (eg, atherosclerotic stenosis), percutaneous

61635 Transcatheter placement of intravascular stent(s), intracranial (eg, atherosclerotic stenosis), including balloon angioplasty, if performed

(61630 and 61635 include all selective vascular catheterization of the target vascular family, all diagnostic imaging for arteriography of the target vascular family, and all related radiological supervision and interpretation. When diagnostic arteriogram (including imaging and selective catheterization) confirms the need for angioplasty or stent placement, 61630 and 61635 are inclusive of these services. If angioplasty or stenting are not indicated, then the appropriate codes for selective catheterization and imaging should be reported in lieu of 61630 and 61635)

61640 Balloon dilatation of intracranial vasospasm, percutaneous; initial vessel

+ 61641 each additional vessel in same vascular family (List separately in addition to code for primary procedure)

+ 61642 each additional vessel in different vascular family (List separately in addition to code for primary procedure)

(Use 61641 and 61642 in conjunction with 61640)

(61640, 61641, 61642 include all selective vascular catheterization of the target vessel, contrast injection(s), vessel measurement, roadmapping, postdilatation angiography, and fluoroscopic guidance for the balloon dilatation)

Surgery for Aneurysm, Arteriovenous Malformation or Vascular Disease

Includes craniotomy when appropriate for procedure.

61680 Surgery of intracranial arteriovenous malformation; supratentorial, simple

61682 supratentorial, complex

61684 infratentorial, simple

61686 infratentorial, complex

61690 dural, simple

61692 dural, complex

61697 Surgery of complex intracranial aneurysm, intracranial approach; carotid circulation

61698 vertebrobasilar circulation

(61697, 61698 involve aneurysms that are larger than 15 mm or with calcification of the aneurysm neck, or with incorporation of normal vessels into the aneurysm neck, or a procedure requiring temporary vessel occlusion, trapping or cardiopulmonary bypass to successfully treat the aneurysm)

61700 Surgery of simple intracranial aneurysm, intracranial approach; carotid circulation

61702 vertebrobasilar circulation

61703 Surgery of intracranial aneurysm, cervical approach by application of occluding clamp to cervical carotid artery (Selverstone-Crutchfield type)

(For cervical approach for direct ligation of carotid artery, see 37600-37606)

61705 Surgery of aneurysm, vascular malformation or carotid-cavernous fistula; by intracranial and cervical occlusion of carotid artery

61708 by intracranial electrothrombosis

(For ligation or gradual occlusion of internal/common carotid artery, see 37605, 37606)

61710 by intra-arterial embolization, injection procedure, or balloon catheter

61711 Anastomosis, arterial, extracranial-intracranial (eg, middle cerebral/cortical) arteries

(For carotid or vertebral thromboendarterectomy, use 35301)

(Use 69990 when the surgical microscope is employed for the microsurgical procedure. Do not use 69990 for visualization with magnifying loupes or corrected vision)

Stereotaxis

61720 Creation of lesion by stereotactic method, including burr hole(s) and localizing and recording techniques, single or multiple stages; globus pallidus or thalamus

61735 subcortical structure(s) other than globus pallidus or thalamus

61750 Stereotactic biopsy, aspiration, or excision, including burr hole(s), for intracranial lesion;

61751 with computed tomography and/or magnetic resonance guidance

(For radiological supervision and interpretation of computerized tomography, see 70450, 70460, or 70470 as appropriate)

(For radiological supervision and interpretation of magnetic resonance imaging, see 70551, 70552, or 70553 as appropriate)

61760 Stereotactic implantation of depth electrodes into the cerebrum for long-term seizure monitoring

61770 Stereotactic localization, including burr hole(s), with insertion of catheter(s) or probe(s) for placement of radiation source

61790 Creation of lesion by stereotactic method, percutaneous, by neurolytic agent (eg, alcohol, thermal, electrical, radiofrequency); gasserian ganglion

61791 trigeminal medullary tract

►(61793 has been deleted. To report, see 61796-61800, 63620-63621)◄

►Stereotactic Radiosurgery (Cranial)◄

►Cranial stereotactic radiosurgery is a distinct procedure that utilizes externally generated ionizing radiation to inactivate or eradicate defined target(s) in the head without the need to make an incision. The target is defined by and the treatment is delivered using high-resolution stereotactic imaging. Stereotactic radiosurgery codes and headframe application procedures are reported by the neurosurgeon. The radiation oncologist reports the appropriate code(s) for clinical treatment planning, physics and dosimetry, treatment delivery, and management from the **Radiation Oncology** section (77261-77790). Any necessary planning, dosimetry, targeting, positioning, or blocking by the neurosurgeon is included in the stereotactic radiation surgery services. The same physician should not report stereotactic radiosurgery services with radiation treatment management codes (77427-77435).

Cranial stereotactic radiosurgery is typically performed in a single planning and treatment session, using a rigidly attached stereotactic guiding device, other immobilization technology and/or a stereotactic image-guidance system, but can be performed with more than one planning session and in a limited number of treatment sessions, up to a maximum of five sessions. Do not report stereotactic radiosurgery more than once per lesion per course of treatment when the treatment requires more than one session.

Codes 61796 and 61797 involve stereotactic radiosurgery for simple cranial lesions. Simple cranial lesions are lesions less than 3.5 cm in maximum dimension that do not meet the definition of a complex lesion provided below. Report code 61796 when all lesions are simple.

Codes 61798 and 61799 involve stereotactic radiosurgery for complex cranial lesions and procedures that create therapeutic lesions (eg, thalamotomy or pallidotomy). All lesions 3.5 cm in maximum dimension or greater are complex. When performing therapeutic lesion creation procedures, report code 61798 only once regardless of the number of lesions created. Schwannomas, arterio-venous malformations, pituitary tumors, glomus tumors, pineal region tumors and cavernous sinus/parasellar/petroclival tumors are complex. Any lesion that is adjacent (5mm or less) to the optic nerve/optic chasm/optic tract or within the brainstem is complex. If treating multiple lesions, and any single lesion treated is complex, use 61798.

Do not report codes 61796-61800 in conjunction with code 20660.

Codes 61796-61799 include computer-assisted planning. Do not report codes 61796-61799 in conjunction with 61795.◄

►(For intensity modulated beam delivery plan and treatment, see 77301, 77418. For stereotactic body radiation therapy of lesions that are neither cranial nor spinal, use 77435)◄

+ 61795 Stereotactic computer-assisted volumetric (navigational) procedure, intracranial, extracranial, or spinal (List separately in addition to code for primary procedure)

● 61796 Stereotactic radiosurgery (particle beam, gamma ray, or linear accelerator); 1 simple cranial lesion

►(Do not report 61796 more than once per course of treatment)◄

►(Do not report 61796 in conjunction with 61798)◄

+● 61797 each additional cranial lesion, simple (List separately in addition to code for primary procedure)

►(Use 61797 in conjunction with 61796, 61798)◄

►(For each course of treatment, 61797 and 61799 may be reported no more than once per lesion. Do not report any combination of 61797 and 61799 more than 4 times for entire course of treatment regardless of number of lesions treated)◄

● 61798 1 complex cranial lesion

►(Do not report 61798 more than once per course of treatment)◄

►(Do not report 61798 in conjunction with 61796)◄

+● 61799 each additional cranial lesion, complex (List separately in addition to code for primary procedure)

►(Use 61799 in conjunction with 61798)◄

►(For each course of treatment, 61797 and 61799 may be reported no more than once per lesion. Do not report any combination of 61797 and 61799 more than 4 times for entire course of treatment regardless of number of lesions treated)◄

+● 61800 Application of stereotactic headframe for stereotactic radiosurgery (List separately in addition to code for primary procedure)

►(Use 61800 in conjunction with 61796, 61798)◄

Neurostimulators (Intracranial)

Codes 61850-61888 apply to both simple and complex neurostimulators. For initial or subsequent electronic analysis and programming of neurostimulator pulse generators, see codes 95970-95975.

Microelectrode recording, when performed by the operating surgeon in association with implantation of neurostimulator electrode arrays, is an inclusive service and should not be reported separately. If another physician participates in neurophysiological mapping during a deep brain stimulator implantation procedure, this service may be reported by the other physician with codes 95961-95962.

61850 Twist drill or burr hole(s) for implantation of neurostimulator electrodes, cortical

61860 Craniectomy or craniotomy for implantation of neurostimulator electrodes, cerebral, cortical

61863 Twist drill, burr hole, craniotomy, or craniectomy with stereotactic implantation of neurostimulator electrode array in subcortical site (eg, thalamus, globus pallidus, subthalamic nucleus, periventricular, periaqueductal gray), without use of intraoperative microelectrode recording; first array

+ 61864 each additional array (List separately in addition to primary procedure)

(Use 61864 in conjunction with 61863)

61867 Twist drill, burr hole, craniotomy, or craniectomy with stereotactic implantation of neurostimulator electrode array in subcortical site (eg, thalamus, globus pallidus, subthalamic nucleus, periventricular, periaqueductal gray), with use of intraoperative microelectrode recording; first array

+ 61868 each additional array (List separately in addition to primary procedure)

(Use 61868 in conjunction with 61867)

61870 Craniectomy for implantation of neurostimulator electrodes, cerebellar; cortical

61875 subcortical

61880 Revision or removal of intracranial neurostimulator electrodes

61885 Insertion or replacement of cranial neurostimulator pulse generator or receiver, direct or inductive coupling; with connection to a single electrode array

61886 with connection to two or more electrode arrays

(For open placement of cranial nerve (eg, vagal, trigeminal) neurostimulator electrode(s), use 64573)

(For percutaneous placement of cranial nerve (eg, vagal, trigeminal) neurostimulator electrode(s), use 64553)

(For revision or removal of cranial nerve (eg, vagal, trigeminal) neurostimulator electrode(s), use 64585)

61888 Revision or removal of cranial neurostimulator pulse generator or receiver

(Do not report 61888 in conjunction with 61885 or 61886 for the same pulse generator)

Repair

62000 Elevation of depressed skull fracture; simple, extradural

62005 compound or comminuted, extradural

62010 with repair of dura and/or debridement of brain

62100 Craniotomy for repair of dural/cerebrospinal fluid leak, including surgery for rhinorrhea/otorrhea

(For repair of spinal dural/CSF leak, see 63707, 63709)

62115 Reduction of craniomegalic skull (eg, treated hydrocephalus); not requiring bone grafts or cranioplasty

62116 with simple cranioplasty

62117 requiring craniotomy and reconstruction with or without bone graft (includes obtaining grafts)

62120 Repair of encephalocele, skull vault, including cranioplasty

62121 Craniotomy for repair of encephalocele, skull base

62140 Cranioplasty for skull defect; up to 5 cm diameter

62141 larger than 5 cm diameter

62142 Removal of bone flap or prosthetic plate of skull

62143 Replacement of bone flap or prosthetic plate of skull

62145 Cranioplasty for skull defect with reparative brain surgery

62146 Cranioplasty with autograft (includes obtaining bone grafts); up to 5 cm diameter

62147 larger than 5 cm diameter

✚ **62148** Incision and retrieval of subcutaneous cranial bone graft for cranioplasty (List separately in addition to code for primary procedure)

(Use 62148 in conjunction with 62140-62147)

Neuroendoscopy

Surgical endoscopy always includes diagnostic endoscopy.

✚ **62160** Neuroendoscopy, intracranial, for placement or replacement of ventricular catheter and attachment to shunt system or external drainage (List separately in addition to code for primary procedure)

(Use 62160 only in conjunction with 61107, 61210, 62220-62230, 62258)

62161 Neuroendoscopy, intracranial; with dissection of adhesions, fenestration of septum pellucidum or intraventricular cysts (including placement, replacement, or removal of ventricular catheter)

62162 with fenestration or excision of colloid cyst, including placement of external ventricular catheter for drainage

62163 with retrieval of foreign body

62164 with excision of brain tumor, including placement of external ventricular catheter for drainage

62165 with excision of pituitary tumor, transnasal or trans-sphenoidal approach

Cerebrospinal Fluid (CSF) Shunt

62180 Ventriculocisternostomy (Torkildsen type operation)

62190 Creation of shunt; subarachnoid/subdural-atrial, -jugular, -auricular

62192 subarachnoid/subdural-peritoneal, -pleural, other terminus

62194 Replacement or irrigation, subarachnoid/subdural catheter

62200 Ventriculocisternostomy, third ventricle;

62201 stereotactic, neuroendoscopic method

(For intracranial neuroendoscopic procedures, see 62161-62165)

62220 Creation of shunt; ventriculo-atrial, -jugular, -auricular

(For intracranial neuroendoscopic ventricular catheter placement, use 62160)

62223 ventriculo-peritoneal, -pleural, other terminus

(For intracranial neuroendoscopic ventricular catheter placement, use 62160)

62225 Replacement or irrigation, ventricular catheter

(For intracranial neuroendoscopic ventricular catheter placement, use 62160)

62230 Replacement or revision of cerebrospinal fluid shunt, obstructed valve, or distal catheter in shunt system

(For intracranial neuroendoscopic ventricular catheter placement, use 62160)

62252 Reprogramming of programmable cerebrospinal shunt

62256 Removal of complete cerebrospinal fluid shunt system; without replacement

62258 with replacement by similar or other shunt at same operation

(For percutaneous irrigation or aspiration of shunt reservoir, use 61070)

(For reprogramming of programmable CSF shunt, use 62252)

(For intracranial neuroendoscopic ventricular catheter placement, use 62160)

Spine and Spinal Cord

(For application of caliper or tongs, use 20660)

(For treatment of fracture or dislocation of spine, see 22305-22327)

Injection, Drainage, or Aspiration

►Injection of contrast during fluoroscopic guidance and localization is an inclusive component of 62263, 62264, 62267, 62270-62273, 62280-62282, 62310-62319. Fluoroscopic guidance and localization is reported with 77003, unless a formal contrast study (myelography, epidurography, or arthrography) is performed, in which case the use of fluoroscopy is included in the supervision and interpretation codes.◄

For radiologic supervision and interpretation of epidurography, use 72275. Code 72275 is only to be used when an epidurogram is performed, images documented, and a formal radiologic report is issued.

►Code 62263 describes a catheter-based treatment involving targeted injection of various substances (eg, hypertonic saline, steroid, anesthetic) via an indwelling

Surgery: Nervous System

epidural catheter. Code 62263 includes percutaneous insertion and removal of an epidural catheter (remaining in place over a several-day period), for the administration of multiple injections of a neurolytic agent(s) performed during serial treatment sessions (ie, spanning two or more treatment days). If required, adhesions or scarring may also be lysed by mechanical means. Code 62263 is **not** reported for each adhesiolysis treatment, but should be reported **once** to describe the entire series of injections/infusions spanning two or more treatment days. ◄

Code 62264 describes multiple adhesiolysis treatment sessions performed on the same day. Adhesions or scarring may be lysed by injections of neurolytic agent(s). If required, adhesions or scarring may also be lysed mechanically using a percutaneously-deployed catheter.

Codes 62263 and 62264 include the procedure of injections of contrast for epidurography (72275) and fluoroscopic guidance and localization (77003) during initial or subsequent sessions.

(Report 01996 for daily hospital management of continuous epidural or subarachnoid drug administration performed in conjunction with 62318-62319)

62263 Percutaneous lysis of epidural adhesions using solution injection (eg, hypertonic saline, enzyme) or mechanical means (eg, catheter) including radiologic localization (includes contrast when administered), multiple adhesiolysis sessions; 2 or more days

(62263 includes codes 72275 and 77003)

62264 1 day

(Do not report 62264 with 62263)

(62264 includes codes 72275 and 77003)

● **62267** Percutaneous aspiration within the nucleus pulposus, intervertebral disc, or paravertebral tissue for diagnostic purposes

►(For imaging, see 77003, 77012)◄

►(Do not report 62267 in conjunction with 10022, 20225, 62287, 62290, 62291)◄

62268 Percutaneous aspiration, spinal cord cyst or syrinx

(For radiological supervision and interpretation, see 76942, 77002, 77012)

62269 Biopsy of spinal cord, percutaneous needle

(For radiological supervision and interpretation, see 76942, 77002, 77012)

(For fine needle aspiration, see 10021, 10022)

(For evaluation of fine needle aspirate, see 88172, 88173)

62270 Spinal puncture, lumbar, diagnostic

62272 Spinal puncture, therapeutic, for drainage of cerebrospinal fluid (by needle or catheter)

62273 Injection, epidural, of blood or clot patch

(For injection of diagnostic or therapeutic substance(s), see 62310, 62311, 62318, 62319)

62280 Injection/infusion of neurolytic substance (eg, alcohol, phenol, iced saline solutions), with or without other therapeutic substance; subarachnoid

62281 epidural, cervical or thoracic

62282 epidural, lumbar, sacral (caudal)

62284 Injection procedure for myelography and/or computed tomography, spinal (other than C1-C2 and posterior fossa)

(For injection procedure at C1-C2, use 61055)

(For radiological supervision and interpretation, see **Radiology**)

▲ **62287** Decompression procedure, percutaneous, of nucleus pulposus of intervertebral disc, any method, single or multiple levels, lumbar (eg, manual or automated percutaneous discectomy, percutaneous laser discectomy)

►(For fluoroscopic guidance, use 77003)◄

►(Do not report 62287 in conjunction with 62267)◄

(For injection of non-neurolytic diagnostic or therapeutic substance(s), see 62310, 62311)

62290 Injection procedure for discography, each level; lumbar

62291 cervical or thoracic

(For radiological supervision and interpretation, see 72285, 72295)

62292 Injection procedure for chemonucleolysis, including discography, intervertebral disc, single or multiple levels, lumbar

62294 Injection procedure, arterial, for occlusion of arteriovenous malformation, spinal

62310 Injection, single (not via indwelling catheter), not including neurolytic substances, with or without contrast (for either localization or epidurography), of diagnostic or therapeutic substance(s) (including anesthetic, antispasmodic, opioid, steroid, other solution), epidural or subarachnoid; cervical or thoracic

62311 lumbar, sacral (caudal)

62318 Injection, including catheter placement, continuous infusion or intermittent bolus, not including neurolytic substances, with or without contrast (for either localization or epidurography), of diagnostic or therapeutic substance(s) (including anesthetic, antispasmodic, opioid, steroid, other solution), epidural or subarachnoid; cervical or thoracic

62319 lumbar, sacral (caudal)

(For transforaminal epidural injection, see 64479-64484)

(Report 01996 for daily hospital management of continuous epidural or subarachnoid drug administration performed in conjunction with 62318-62319)

Catheter Implantation

(For percutaneous placement of intrathecal or epidural catheter, see codes 62270-62273, 62280-62284, 62310-62319)

62350 Implantation, revision or repositioning of tunneled intrathecal or epidural catheter, for long-term medication administration via an external pump or implantable reservoir/infusion pump; without laminectomy

62351 with laminectomy

(For refilling and maintenance of an implantable infusion pump for spinal or brain drug therapy, see 95990, 95991)

62355 Removal of previously implanted intrathecal or epidural catheter

Reservoir/Pump Implantation

62360 Implantation or replacement of device for intrathecal or epidural drug infusion; subcutaneous reservoir

62361 nonprogrammable pump

62362 programmable pump, including preparation of pump, with or without programming

62365 Removal of subcutaneous reservoir or pump, previously implanted for intrathecal or epidural infusion

62367 Electronic analysis of programmable, implanted pump for intrathecal or epidural drug infusion (includes evaluation of reservoir status, alarm status, drug prescription status); without reprogramming

62368 with reprogramming

(For refilling and maintenance of an implantable infusion pump for spinal or brain drug therapy, use 95990-95991)

Posterior Extradural Laminotomy or Laminectomy for Exploration/ Decompression of Neural Elements or Excision of Herniated Intervertebral Discs

(When 63001-63048 are followed by arthrodesis, see 22590-22614)

63001 Laminectomy with exploration and/or decompression of spinal cord and/or cauda equina, without facetectomy, foraminotomy or discectomy (eg, spinal stenosis), 1 or 2 vertebral segments; cervical

63003 thoracic

63005 lumbar, except for spondylolisthesis

63011 sacral

63012 Laminectomy with removal of abnormal facets and/or pars inter-articularis with decompression of cauda equina and nerve roots for spondylolisthesis, lumbar (Gill type procedure)

63015 Laminectomy with exploration and/or decompression of spinal cord and/or cauda equina, without facetectomy, foraminotomy or discectomy (eg, spinal stenosis), more than 2 vertebral segments; cervical

63016 thoracic

63017 lumbar

▲ **63020** Laminotomy (hemilaminectomy), with decompression of nerve root(s), including partial facetectomy, foraminotomy and/or excision of herniated intervertebral disc, including open and endoscopically-assisted approaches; 1 interspace, cervical

(For bilateral procedure, report 63020 with modifier 50)

▲ **63030** 1 interspace, lumbar

(For bilateral procedure, report 63030 with modifier 50)

+▲ **63035** each additional interspace, cervical or lumbar (List separately in addition to code for primary procedure)

(Use 63035 in conjunction with 63020-63030)

(For bilateral procedure, report 63035 with modifier 50)

63040 Laminotomy (hemilaminectomy), with decompression of nerve root(s), including partial facetectomy, foraminotomy and/or excision of herniated intervertebral disc, reexploration, single interspace; cervical

(For bilateral procedure, report 63040 with modifier 50)

63042 lumbar

(For bilateral procedure, report 63042 with modifier 50)

+ **63043** each additional cervical interspace (List separately in addition to code for primary procedure)

(Use 63043 in conjunction with 63040)

(For bilateral procedure, report 63043 with modifier 50)

+ **63044** each additional lumbar interspace (List separately in addition to code for primary procedure)

(Use 63044 in conjunction with 63042)

(For bilateral procedure, report 63044 with modifier 50)

63045 Laminectomy, facetectomy and foraminotomy (unilateral or bilateral with decompression of spinal cord, cauda equina and/or nerve root[s], [eg, spinal or lateral recess stenosis]), single vertebral segment; cervical

63046 thoracic

63047 lumbar

+ **63048** each additional segment, cervical, thoracic, or lumbar (List separately in addition to code for primary procedure)

(Use 63048 in conjunction with 63045-63047)

63050 Laminoplasty, cervical, with decompression of the spinal cord, two or more vertebral segments;

63051 with reconstruction of the posterior bony elements (including the application of bridging bone graft and non-segmental fixation devices (eg, wire, suture, mini-plates), when performed)

(Do not report 63050 or 63051 in conjunction with 22600, 22614, 22840-22842, 63001, 63015, 63045, 63048, 63295 for the same vertebral segment(s))

Transpedicular or Costovertebral Approach for Posterolateral Extradural Exploration/Decompression

63055 Transpedicular approach with decompression of spinal cord, equina and/or nerve root(s) (eg, herniated intervertebral disc), single segment; thoracic

63056 lumbar (including transfacet, or lateral extraforaminal approach) (eg, far lateral herniated intervertebral disc)

+ 63057 each additional segment, thoracic or lumbar (List separately in addition to code for primary procedure)

(Use 63057 in conjunction with 63055, 63056)

63064 Costovertebral approach with decompression of spinal cord or nerve root(s) (eg, herniated intervertebral disc), thoracic; single segment

+ 63066 each additional segment (List separately in addition to code for primary procedure)

(Use 63066 in conjunction with 63064)

(For excision of thoracic intraspinal lesions by laminectomy, see 63266, 63271, 63276, 63281, 63286)

Anterior or Anterolateral Approach for Extradural Exploration/Decompression

For the following codes, when two surgeons work together as primary surgeons performing distinct part(s) of spinal cord exploration/decompression operation, each surgeon should report his/her distinct operative work by appending modifier 62 to the procedure code (and any associated add-on codes for that procedure code as long as both surgeons continue to work together as primary surgeons). In this situation, modifier 62 may be appended to the definitive procedure code(s) 63075, 63077, 63081, 63085, 63087, 63090 and, as appropriate, to associated additional interspace add-on code(s) 63076, 63078 or additional segment add-on code(s) 63082, 63086, 63088, 63091 as long as both surgeons continue to work together as primary surgeons.

63075 Discectomy, anterior, with decompression of spinal cord and/or nerve root(s), including osteophytectomy; cervical, single interspace

+ 63076 cervical, each additional interspace (List separately in addition to code for primary procedure)

(Use 63076 in conjunction with 63075)

63077 thoracic, single interspace

+ 63078 thoracic, each additional interspace (List separately in addition to code for primary procedure)

(Use 63078 in conjunction with 63077)

(Do not report code 69990 in addition to codes 63075-63078)

63081 Vertebral corpectomy (vertebral body resection), partial or complete, anterior approach with decompression of spinal cord and/or nerve root(s); cervical, single segment

+ 63082 cervical, each additional segment (List separately in addition to code for primary procedure)

(Use 63082 in conjunction with 63081)

(For transoral approach, see 61575, 61576)

63085 Vertebral corpectomy (vertebral body resection), partial or complete, transthoracic approach with decompression of spinal cord and/or nerve root(s); thoracic, single segment

+ 63086 thoracic, each additional segment (List separately in addition to code for primary procedure)

(Use 63086 in conjunction with 63085)

63087 Vertebral corpectomy (vertebral body resection), partial or complete, combined thoracolumbar approach with decompression of spinal cord, cauda equina or nerve root(s), lower thoracic or lumbar; single segment

+ 63088 each additional segment (List separately in addition to code for primary procedure)

(Use 63088 in conjunction with 63087)

63090 Vertebral corpectomy (vertebral body resection), partial or complete, transperitoneal or retroperitoneal approach with decompression of spinal cord, cauda equina or nerve root(s), lower thoracic, lumbar, or sacral; single segment

+ 63091 each additional segment (List separately in addition to code for primary procedure)

(Use 63091 in conjunction with 63090)

(Procedures 63081-63091 include discectomy above and/or below vertebral segment)

(If followed by arthrodesis, see 22548-22812)

(For reconstruction of spine, use appropriate vertebral corpectomy codes 63081-63091, bone graft codes 20930-20938, arthrodesis codes 22548-22812, and spinal instrumentation codes 22840-22855)

Lateral Extracavitary Approach for Extradural Exploration/Decompression

63101 Vertebral corpectomy (vertebral body resection), partial or complete, lateral extracavitary approach with decompression of spinal cord and/or nerve root(s) (eg, for tumor or retropulsed bone fragments); thoracic, single segment

63102 lumbar, single segment

+ 63103 thoracic or lumbar, each additional segment (List separately in addition to code for primary procedure)

(Use 63103 in conjunction with 63101 and 63102)

Incision

63170 Laminectomy with myelotomy (eg, Bischof or DREZ type), cervical, thoracic, or thoracolumbar

63172 Laminectomy with drainage of intramedullary cyst/syrinx; to subarachnoid space

63173 to peritoneal or pleural space

63180 Laminectomy and section of dentate ligaments, with or without dural graft, cervical; 1 or 2 segments

63182 more than 2 segments

63185 Laminectomy with rhizotomy; 1 or 2 segments

63190 more than 2 segments

63191 Laminectomy with section of spinal accessory nerve

(For bilateral procedure, report 63191 with modifier 50)

(For resection of sternocleidomastoid muscle, use 21720)

63194 Laminectomy with cordotomy, with section of 1 spinothalamic tract, 1 stage; cervical

63195 thoracic

63196 Laminectomy with cordotomy, with section of both spinothalamic tracts, 1 stage; cervical

63197 thoracic

63198 Laminectomy with cordotomy with section of both spinothalamic tracts, 2 stages within 14 days; cervical

63199 thoracic

63200 Laminectomy, with release of tethered spinal cord, lumbar

Excision by Laminectomy of Lesion Other Than Herniated Disc

63250 Laminectomy for excision or occlusion of arteriovenous malformation of spinal cord; cervical

63251 thoracic

63252 thoracolumbar

63265 Laminectomy for excision or evacuation of intraspinal lesion other than neoplasm, extradural; cervical

63266 thoracic

63267 lumbar

63268 sacral

63270 Laminectomy for excision of intraspinal lesion other than neoplasm, intradural; cervical

63271 thoracic

63272 lumbar

63273 sacral

63275 Laminectomy for biopsy/excision of intraspinal neoplasm; extradural, cervical

63276 extradural, thoracic

63277 extradural, lumbar

63278 extradural, sacral

63280 intradural, extramedullary, cervical

63281 intradural, extramedullary, thoracic

63282 intradural, extramedullary, lumbar

63283 intradural, sacral

63285 intradural, intramedullary, cervical

63286 intradural, intramedullary, thoracic

63287 intradural, intramedullary, thoracolumbar

63290 combined extradural-intradural lesion, any level

(For drainage of intramedullary cyst/syrinx, use 63172, 63173)

+ 63295 Osteoplastic reconstruction of dorsal spinal elements, following primary intraspinal procedure (List separately in addition to code for primary procedure)

(Use 63295 in conjunction with 63172, 63173, 63185, 63190, 63200-63290)

(Do not report 63295 in conjunction with 22590-22614, 22840-22844, 63050, 63051 for the same vertebral segment(s))

Excision, Anterior or Anterolateral Approach, Intraspinal Lesion

For the following codes, when two surgeons work together as primary surgeons performing distinct part(s) of an anterior approach for an intraspinal excision, each surgeon should report his/her distinct operative work by appending modifier 62 to the single definitive procedure code. In this situation, modifier 62 may be appended to the definitive procedure code(s) 63300-63307 and, as appropriate, to the associated additional segment add-on code 63308 as long as both surgeons continue to work together as primary surgeons.

(For arthrodesis, see 22548-22585)

(For reconstruction of spine, see 20930-20938)

63300 Vertebral corpectomy (vertebral body resection), partial or complete, for excision of intraspinal lesion, single segment; extradural, cervical

63301 extradural, thoracic by transthoracic approach

63302 extradural, thoracic by thoracolumbar approach

63303 extradural, lumbar or sacral by transperitoneal or retroperitoneal approach

63304 intradural, cervical

Surgery: Nervous System

63305 intradural, thoracic by transthoracic approach

63306 intradural, thoracic by thoracolumbar approach

63307 intradural, lumbar or sacral by transperitoneal or retroperitoneal approach

+ 63308 each additional segment (List separately in addition to codes for single segment)

(Use 63308 in conjunction with 63300-63307)

Stereotaxis

63600 Creation of lesion of spinal cord by stereotactic method, percutaneous, any modality (including stimulation and/or recording)

63610 Stereotactic stimulation of spinal cord, percutaneous, separate procedure not followed by other surgery

63615 Stereotactic biopsy, aspiration, or excision of lesion, spinal cord

▸Stereotactic Radiosurgery (Spinal)◂

▶Spinal stereotactic radiosurgery is a distinct procedure that utilizes externally generated ionizing radiation to inactivate or eradicate defined target(s) in the spine without the need to make an incision. The target is defined by and the treatment is delivered using high-resolution stereotactic imaging. These codes are reported by the surgeon. The radiation oncologist reports the appropriate code(s) for clinical treatment planning, physics and dosimetry, treatment delivery and management from the **Radiation Oncology** section (77261-77790). Any necessary planning, dosimetry, targeting, positioning, or blocking by the neurosurgeon is included in the stereotactic radiation surgery services. The same physician should not report stereotactic radiosurgery services with radiation treatment management codes (77427-77432).

Spinal stereotactic radiosurgery is typically performed in a single planning and treatment session using a stereotactic image-guidance system, but can be performed with a planning session and in a limited number of treatment sessions, up to a maximum of five sessions. Do not report stereotactic radiosurgery more than once per lesion per course of treatment when the treatment requires greater than one session.

Stereotactic spinal surgery is only used when the tumor being treated affects spinal neural tissue or abuts the dura mater. Arteriovenous malformations must be subdural. For other radiation services of the spine, see **Radiation Oncology** services.

Codes 63620, 63621 include computer-assisted planning. Do not report 63620, 63621 in conjunction with 61795.◀

▶(For intensity modulated beam delivery plan and treatment, see 77301, 77418. For stereotactic body radiation therapy for lesions that are neither cranial nor spinal, use 77435)◀

● 63620 Stereotactic radiosurgery (particle beam, gamma ray, or linear accelerator); 1 spinal lesion

▶(Do not report 63620 more than once per course of treatment)◀

+● 63621 each additional spinal lesion (List separately in addition to code for primary procedure)

▶(Report 63621 in conjunction with 63620)◀

▶(For each course of treatment, 63621 may be reported no more than once per lesion. Do not report 63621 more than 2 times for entire course of treatment regardless of number of lesions treated)◀

Neurostimulators (Spinal)

Codes 63650-63688 apply to both simple and complex neurostimulators. For initial or subsequent electronic analysis and programming of neurostimulator pulse generators, see codes 95970-95975.

Codes 63650, 63655, and 63660 describe the operative placement, revision, or removal of the spinal neurostimulator system components to provide spinal electrical stimulation. A neurostimulator system includes an implanted neurostimulator, external controller, extension, and collection of contacts. Multiple contacts or electrodes (4 or more) provide the actual electrical stimulation in the epidural space.

For percutaneously placed neurostimulator systems (63650, 63660), the contacts are on a catheter-like lead. An array defines the collection of contacts that are on one catheter.

For systems placed via an open surgical exposure (63655, 63660), the contacts are on a plate or paddle-shaped surface.

63650 Percutaneous implantation of neurostimulator electrode array, epidural

63655 Laminectomy for implantation of neurostimulator electrodes, plate/paddle, epidural

63660 Revision or removal of spinal neurostimulator electrode percutaneous array(s) or plate/paddle(s)

63685 Insertion or replacement of spinal neurostimulator pulse generator or receiver, direct or inductive coupling

(Do not report 63685 in conjunction with 63688 for the same pulse generator or receiver)

63688 Revision or removal of implanted spinal neurostimulator pulse generator or receiver

(For electronic analysis of implanted neurostimulator pulse generator system, see 95970-95975)

Repair

63700 Repair of meningocele; less than 5 cm diameter

63702 larger than 5 cm diameter

(Do not use modifier 63 in conjunction with 63700, 63702)

63704 Repair of myelomeningocele; less than 5 cm diameter

63706 larger than 5 cm diameter

(Do not use modifier 63 in conjunction with 63704, 63706)

(For complex skin closure, see **Integumentary System**)

63707 Repair of dural/cerebrospinal fluid leak, not requiring laminectomy

63709 Repair of dural/cerebrospinal fluid leak or pseudomeningocele, with laminectomy

63710 Dural graft, spinal

(For laminectomy and section of dentate ligaments, with or without dural graft, cervical, see 63180, 63182)

Shunt, Spinal CSF

63740 Creation of shunt, lumbar, subarachnoid-peritoneal, -pleural, or other; including laminectomy

63741 percutaneous, not requiring laminectomy

63744 Replacement, irrigation or revision of lumbosubarachnoid shunt

63746 Removal of entire lumbosubarachnoid shunt system without replacement

(For insertion of subarachnoid catheter with reservoir and/or pump for intermittent or continuous infusion of drug including laminectomy, see 62351 and 62360, 62361 or 62362)

(For insertion or replacement of subarachnoid or epidural catheter, with reservoir and/or pump for drug infusion without laminectomy, see 62350 and 62360, 62361 or 62362)

Extracranial Nerves, Peripheral Nerves, and Autonomic Nervous System

(For intracranial surgery on cranial nerves, see 61450, 61460, 61790)

Introduction/Injection of Anesthetic Agent (Nerve Block), Diagnostic or Therapeutic

Somatic Nerves

64400 Injection, anesthetic agent; trigeminal nerve, any division or branch

64402 facial nerve

64405 greater occipital nerve

64408 vagus nerve

64410 phrenic nerve

64412 spinal accessory nerve

64413 cervical plexus

64415 brachial plexus, single

▲ **64416** brachial plexus, continuous infusion by catheter (including catheter placement)

(Do not report 64416 in conjunction with 01996)

64417 axillary nerve

64418 suprascapular nerve

64420 intercostal nerve, single

64421 intercostal nerves, multiple, regional block

64425 ilioinguinal, iliohypogastric nerves

64430 pudendal nerve

64435 paracervical (uterine) nerve

64445 sciatic nerve, single

▲ **64446** sciatic nerve, continuous infusion by catheter (including catheter placement)

(Do not report 64446 in conjunction with 01996)

64447 femoral nerve, single

(Do not report 64447 in conjunction with 01996)

▲ **64448** femoral nerve, continuous infusion by catheter (including catheter placement)

(Do not report 64448 in conjunction with 01996)

▲ **64449** lumbar plexus, posterior approach, continuous infusion by catheter (including catheter placement)

(Do not report 64449 in conjunction with 01996)

64450 other peripheral nerve or branch

(For phenol destruction, see 64622-64627)

(For subarachnoid or subdural injection, see 62280, 62310-62319)

(For epidural or caudal injection, see 62273, 62281-62282, 62310-62319)

►(For injection of Morton's neuroma, see 64455, 64632)◄

● **64455** Injection(s), anesthetic agent and/or steroid, plantar common digital nerve(s) (eg, Morton's neuroma)

►(Do not report 64455 in conjunction with 64632)◄

(Codes 64470-64484 are unilateral procedures. For bilateral procedures, use modifier 50)

(For fluoroscopic guidance and localization for needle placement and injection in conjunction with 64470-64484, use 77003)

64470 Injection, anesthetic agent and/or steroid, paravertebral facet joint or facet joint nerve; cervical or thoracic, single level

+ 64472 cervical or thoracic, each additional level (List separately in addition to code for primary procedure)

(Use 64472 in conjunction with 64470)

64475 lumbar or sacral, single level

+ 64476 lumbar or sacral, each additional level (List separately in addition to code for primary procedure)

(Use 64476 in conjunction with 64475)

64479 Injection, anesthetic agent and/or steroid, transforaminal epidural; cervical or thoracic, single level

+ 64480 cervical or thoracic, each additional level (List separately in addition to code for primary procedure)

(Use 64480 in conjunction with 64479)

64483 lumbar or sacral, single level

+ 64484 lumbar or sacral, each additional level (List separately in addition to code for primary procedure)

(Use 64484 in conjunction with 64483)

Sympathetic Nerves

64505 Injection, anesthetic agent; sphenopalatine ganglion

64508 carotid sinus (separate procedure)

64510 stellate ganglion (cervical sympathetic)

64517 superior hypogastric plexus

64520 lumbar or thoracic (paravertebral sympathetic)

64530 celiac plexus, with or without radiologic monitoring

Neurostimulators (Peripheral Nerve)

Codes 64553-64595 apply to both simple and complex neurostimulators. For initial or subsequent electronic analysis and programming of neurostimulator pulse generators, see codes 95970-95975.

64550 Application of surface (transcutaneous) neurostimulator

64553 Percutaneous implantation of neurostimulator electrodes; cranial nerve

(For open placement of cranial nerve (eg, vagal, trigeminal) neurostimulator pulse generator or receiver, see 61885, 61886, as appropriate)

64555 peripheral nerve (excludes sacral nerve)

64560 autonomic nerve

64561 sacral nerve (transforaminal placement)

64565 neuromuscular

64573 Incision for implantation of neurostimulator electrodes; cranial nerve

(For open placement of cranial nerve (eg, vagal, trigeminal) neurostimulator pulse generator or receiver, see 61885, 61886, as appropriate)

(For revision or removal of cranial nerve (eg, vagal, trigeminal) neurostimulator pulse generator or receiver, use 61888)

64575 peripheral nerve (excludes sacral nerve)

64577 autonomic nerve

64580 neuromuscular

64581 sacral nerve (transforaminal placement)

64585 Revision or removal of peripheral neurostimulator electrodes

64590 Insertion or replacement of peripheral or gastric neurostimulator pulse generator or receiver, direct or inductive coupling

(Do not report 64590 in conjunction with 64595)

64595 Revision or removal of peripheral or gastric neurostimulator pulse generator or receiver

Destruction by Neurolytic Agent (eg, Chemical, Thermal, Electrical or Radiofrequency)

►Codes 64600-64681 include the injection of other therapeutic agents (eg, corticosteroids). (For therapies that are not destructive of the target nerve [eg, pulsed radiofrequency]), use 64999)◄

Somatic Nerves

64600 Destruction by neurolytic agent, trigeminal nerve; supraorbital, infraorbital, mental, or inferior alveolar branch

64605 second and third division branches at foramen ovale

64610 second and third division branches at foramen ovale under radiologic monitoring

64612 Chemodenervation of muscle(s); muscle(s) innervated by facial nerve (eg, for blepharospasm, hemifacial spasm)

64613 neck muscle(s) (eg, for spasmodic torticollis, spasmodic dysphonia)

64614 extremity(s) and/or trunk muscle(s) (eg, for dystonia, cerebral palsy, multiple sclerosis)

(For chemodenervation guided by needle electromyography or muscle electrical stimulation, see 95873, 95874)

(For chemodenervation for strabismus involving the extraocular muscles, use 67345)

(For chemodenervation of internal anal sphincter, use 46505)

64620 Destruction by neurolytic agent, intercostal nerve

(For fluoroscopic guidance and localization for needle placement and neurolysis in conjunction with 64622-64627, use 77003)

64622 Destruction by neurolytic agent, paravertebral facet joint nerve; lumbar or sacral, single level

(For bilateral procedure, report 64622 with modifier 50)

+ 64623 lumbar or sacral, each additional level (List separately in addition to code for primary procedure)

(Use 64623 in conjunction with 64622)

(For bilateral procedure, report 64623 with modifier 50)

64626 cervical or thoracic, single level

(For bilateral procedure, report 64626 with modifier 50)

+ 64627 cervical or thoracic, each additional level (List separately in addition to code for primary procedure)

(Use 64627 in conjunction with 64626)

(For bilateral procedure, report 64627 with modifier 50)

64630 Destruction by neurolytic agent; pudendal nerve

● 64632 plantar common digital nerve

►(Do not report 64632 in conjunction with 64455)◄

64640 other peripheral nerve or branch

Sympathetic Nerves

64650 Chemodenervation of eccrine glands; both axillae

64653 other area(s) (eg, scalp, face, neck), per day

(Report the specific service in conjunction with code(s) for the specific substance(s) or drug(s) provided)

(For chemodenervation of extremities (eg, hands or feet), use 64999)

64680 Destruction by neurolytic agent, with or without radiologic monitoring; celiac plexus

64681 superior hypogastric plexus

Neuroplasty (Exploration, Neurolysis or Nerve Decompression)

Neuroplasty is the decompression or freeing of intact nerve from scar tissue, including external neurolysis and/or transposition.

(For internal neurolysis requiring use of operating microscope, use 64727)

(For facial nerve decompression, use 69720)

(For neuroplasty with nerve wrapping, see 64702-64727, 64999)

64702 Neuroplasty; digital, 1 or both, same digit

64704 nerve of hand or foot

64708 Neuroplasty, major peripheral nerve, arm or leg; other than specified

64712 sciatic nerve

64713 brachial plexus

64714 lumbar plexus

64716 Neuroplasty and/or transposition; cranial nerve (specify)

64718 ulnar nerve at elbow

64719 ulnar nerve at wrist

64721 median nerve at carpal tunnel

(For arthroscopic procedure, use 29848)

64722 Decompression; unspecified nerve(s) (specify)

64726 plantar digital nerve

+ 64727 Internal neurolysis, requiring use of operating microscope (List separately in addition to code for neuroplasty) (Neuroplasty includes external neurolysis)

(Do not report code 69990 in addition to code 64727)

Transection or Avulsion

(For stereotactic lesion of gasserian ganglion, use 61790)

64732 Transection or avulsion of; supraorbital nerve

64734 infraorbital nerve

64736 mental nerve

64738 inferior alveolar nerve by osteotomy

64740 lingual nerve

64742 facial nerve, differential or complete

64744 greater occipital nerve

64746 phrenic nerve

(For section of recurrent laryngeal nerve, use 31595)

64752 vagus nerve (vagotomy), transthoracic

64755 vagus nerves limited to proximal stomach (selective proximal vagotomy, proximal gastric vagotomy, parietal cell vagotomy, supra- or highly selective vagotomy)

(For laparoscopic approach, use 43652)

64760 vagus nerve (vagotomy), abdominal

(For laparoscopic approach, use 43651)

64761 pudendal nerve

(For bilateral procedure, report 64761 with modifier 50)

64763 Transection or avulsion of obturator nerve, extrapelvic, with or without adductor tenotomy

(For bilateral procedure, report 64763 with modifier 50)

64766 Transection or avulsion of obturator nerve, intrapelvic, with or without adductor tenotomy

(For bilateral procedure, report 64766 with modifier 50)

64771 Transection or avulsion of other cranial nerve, extradural

64772 Transection or avulsion of other spinal nerve, extradural

(For excision of tender scar, skin and subcutaneous tissue, with or without tiny neuroma, see 11400-11446, 13100-13153)

Excision

Somatic Nerves

(For Morton neurectomy, use 28080)

64774 Excision of neuroma; cutaneous nerve, surgically identifiable

64776 digital nerve, 1 or both, same digit

+ 64778 digital nerve, each additional digit (List separately in addition to code for primary procedure)

(Use 64778 in conjunction with 64776)

64782 hand or foot, except digital nerve

+ 64783 hand or foot, each additional nerve, except same digit (List separately in addition to code for primary procedure)

(Use 64783 in conjunction with 64782)

64784 major peripheral nerve, except sciatic

64786 sciatic nerve

+ 64787 Implantation of nerve end into bone or muscle (List separately in addition to neuroma excision)

(Use 64787 in conjunction with 64774-64786)

64788 Excision of neurofibroma or neurolemmoma; cutaneous nerve

64790 major peripheral nerve

64792 extensive (including malignant type)

64795 Biopsy of nerve

Sympathetic Nerves

64802 Sympathectomy, cervical

(For bilateral procedure, report 64802 with modifier 50)

64804 Sympathectomy, cervicothoracic

(For bilateral procedure, report 64804 with modifier 50)

64809 Sympathectomy, thoracolumbar

(For bilateral procedure, report 64809 with modifier 50)

64818 Sympathectomy, lumbar

(For bilateral procedure, report 64818 with modifier 50)

64820 Sympathectomy; digital arteries, each digit

(Do not report 69990 in addition to code 64820)

64821 radial artery

(Do not report 69990 in addition to code 64821)

64822 ulnar artery

(Do not report 69990 in addition to code 64822)

64823 superficial palmar arch

(Do not report 69990 in addition to code 64823)

Neurorrhaphy

64831 Suture of digital nerve, hand or foot; 1 nerve

+ 64832 each additional digital nerve (List separately in addition to code for primary procedure)

(Use 64832 in conjunction with 64831)

64834 Suture of one nerve; hand or foot, common sensory nerve

64835 median motor thenar

64836 ulnar motor

+ 64837 Suture of each additional nerve, hand or foot (List separately in addition to code for primary procedure)

(Use 64837 in conjunction with 64834-64836)

64840 Suture of posterior tibial nerve

64856 Suture of major peripheral nerve, arm or leg, except sciatic; including transposition

64857 without transposition

64858 Suture of sciatic nerve

+ 64859 Suture of each additional major peripheral nerve (List separately in addition to code for primary procedure)

(Use 64859 in conjunction with 64856, 64857)

64861 Suture of; brachial plexus

64862 lumbar plexus

64864 Suture of facial nerve; extracranial

64865 infratemporal, with or without grafting

64866 Anastomosis; facial-spinal accessory

64868 facial-hypoglossal

64870 facial-phrenic

+ 64872 Suture of nerve; requiring secondary or delayed suture (List separately in addition to code for primary neurorrhaphy)

(Use 64872 in conjunction with 64831-64865)

+ 64874 requiring extensive mobilization, or transposition of nerve (List separately in addition to code for nerve suture)

(Use 64874 in conjunction with 64831-64865)

+ 64876 requiring shortening of bone of extremity (List separately in addition to code for nerve suture)

(Use 64876 in conjunction with 64831-64865)

Neurorrhaphy With Nerve Graft, Vein Graft, or Conduit

64885 Nerve graft (includes obtaining graft), head or neck; up to 4 cm in length

64886 more than 4 cm length

64890 Nerve graft (includes obtaining graft), single strand, hand or foot; up to 4 cm length

64891 more than 4 cm length

64892 Nerve graft (includes obtaining graft), single strand, arm or leg; up to 4 cm length

64893 more than 4 cm length

64895 Nerve graft (includes obtaining graft), multiple strands (cable), hand or foot; up to 4 cm length

64896 more than 4 cm length

64897 Nerve graft (includes obtaining graft), multiple strands (cable), arm or leg; up to 4 cm length

64898 more than 4 cm length

+ 64901 Nerve graft, each additional nerve; single strand (List separately in addition to code for primary procedure)

(Use 64901 in conjunction with 64885-64893)

+ 64902 multiple strands (cable) (List separately in addition to code for primary procedure)

(Use 64902 in conjunction with 64885, 64886, 64895-64898)

64905 Nerve pedicle transfer; first stage

64907 second stage

64910 Nerve repair; with synthetic conduit or vein allograft (eg, nerve tube), each nerve

64911 with autogenous vein graft (includes harvest of vein graft), each nerve

(Do not report 69990 in addition to 64910, 64911)

Other Procedures

64999 Unlisted procedure, nervous system

Eye and Ocular Adnexa

(For diagnostic and treatment ophthalmological services, see **Medicine, Ophthalmology,** and 92002 et seq)

(Do not report code 69990 in addition to codes 65091-68850)

Eyeball

Removal of Eye

65091 Evisceration of ocular contents; without implant

65093 with implant

65101 Enucleation of eye; without implant

65103 with implant, muscles not attached to implant

65105 with implant, muscles attached to implant

(For conjunctivoplasty after enucleation, see 68320 et seq)

65110 Exenteration of orbit (does not include skin graft), removal of orbital contents; only

65112 with therapeutic removal of bone

65114 with muscle or myocutaneous flap

(For skin graft to orbit (split skin), see 15120, 15121; free, full thickness, see 15260, 15261)

(For eyelid repair involving more than skin, see 67930 et seq)

Secondary Implant(s) Procedures

An ocular implant is an implant inside muscular cone; an orbital implant is an implant outside muscular cone.

65125 Modification of ocular implant with placement or replacement of pegs (eg, drilling receptacle for prosthesis appendage) (separate procedure)

65130 Insertion of ocular implant secondary; after evisceration, in scleral shell

65135 after enucleation, muscles not attached to implant

65140 after enucleation, muscles attached to implant

65150 Reinsertion of ocular implant; with or without conjunctival graft

65155 with use of foreign material for reinforcement and/or attachment of muscles to implant

65175 Removal of ocular implant

(For orbital implant (implant outside muscle cone) insertion, use 67550; removal, use 67560)

Removal of Foreign Body

(For removal of implanted material: ocular implant, use 65175; anterior segment implant, use 65920; posterior segment implant, use 67120; orbital implant, use 67560)

(For diagnostic x-ray for foreign body, use 70030)

(For diagnostic echography for foreign body, use 76529)

(For removal of foreign body from orbit: frontal approach, use 67413; lateral approach, use 67430; transcranial approach, use 61334)

(For removal of foreign body from eyelid, embedded, use 67938)

(For removal of foreign body from lacrimal system, use 68530)

65205 Removal of foreign body, external eye; conjunctival superficial

65210 conjunctival embedded (includes concretions), subconjunctival, or scleral nonperforating

65220 corneal, without slit lamp

65222 corneal, with slit lamp

(For repair of corneal laceration with foreign body, use 65275)

65235 Removal of foreign body, intraocular; from anterior chamber of eye or lens

(For removal of implanted material from anterior segment, use 65920)

65260 from posterior segment, magnetic extraction, anterior or posterior route

65265 from posterior segment, nonmagnetic extraction

(For removal of implanted material from posterior segment, use 67120)

Repair of Laceration

(For fracture of orbit, see 21385 et seq)

(For repair of wound of eyelid, skin, linear, simple, see 12011-12018; intermediate, layered closure, see 12051-12057; linear, complex, see 13150-13160; other, see 67930, 67935)

(For repair of wound of lacrimal system, use 68700)

(For repair of operative wound, use 66250)

65270 Repair of laceration; conjunctiva, with or without nonperforating laceration sclera, direct closure

65272 conjunctiva, by mobilization and rearrangement, without hospitalization

65273 conjunctiva, by mobilization and rearrangement, with hospitalization

65275 cornea, nonperforating, with or without removal foreign body

65280 cornea and/or sclera, perforating, not involving uveal tissue

65285 cornea and/or sclera, perforating, with reposition or resection of uveal tissue

65286 application of tissue glue, wounds of cornea and/or sclera

(Repair of laceration includes use of conjunctival flap and restoration of anterior chamber, by air or saline injection when indicated)

(For repair of iris or ciliary body, use 66680)

65290 Repair of wound, extraocular muscle, tendon and/or Tenon's capsule

Anterior Segment

Cornea

Excision

65400 Excision of lesion, cornea (keratectomy, lamellar, partial), except pterygium

65410 Biopsy of cornea

65420 Excision or transposition of pterygium; without graft

65426 with graft

Removal or Destruction

65430 Scraping of cornea, diagnostic, for smear and/or culture

65435 Removal of corneal epithelium; with or without chemocauterization (abrasion, curettage)

65436 with application of chelating agent (eg, EDTA)

65450 Destruction of lesion of cornea by cryotherapy, photocoagulation or thermocauterization

65600 Multiple punctures of anterior cornea (eg, for corneal erosion, tattoo)

Keratoplasty

►Corneal transplant includes use of fresh or preserved grafts. The preparation of donor material is included for penetrating or anterior lamellar keratoplasty, but reported separately for endothelial keratoplasty. Do not report 65710-65757 in conjunction with 92025.◄

(Keratoplasty excludes refractive keratoplasty procedures, 65760, 65765, and 65767)

▲ 65710 Keratoplasty (corneal transplant); anterior lamellar

▲ 65730 penetrating (except in aphakia or pseudophakia)

65750 penetrating (in aphakia)

65755 penetrating (in pseudophakia)

● 65756 endothelial

+● 65757 Backbench preparation of corneal endothelial allograft prior to transplantation (List separately in addition to code for primary procedure)

►(Use 65757 in conjunction with 65756)◄

Other Procedures

►Do not report 65760-65771 in conjunction with 92025.◄

65760 Keratomileusis

65765 Keratophakia

65767 Epikeratoplasty

65770 Keratoprosthesis

65771 Radial keratotomy

65772 Corneal relaxing incision for correction of surgically induced astigmatism

65775 Corneal wedge resection for correction of surgically induced astigmatism

(For fitting of contact lens for treatment of disease, use 92070)

(For unlisted procedures on cornea, use 66999)

65780 Ocular surface reconstruction; amniotic membrane transplantation

65781 limbal stem cell allograft (eg, cadaveric or living donor)

65782 limbal conjunctival autograft (includes obtaining graft)

(For harvesting conjunctival allograft, living donor, use 68371)

Anterior Chamber

Incision

65800 Paracentesis of anterior chamber of eye (separate procedure); with diagnostic aspiration of aqueous

65805 with therapeutic release of aqueous

65810 with removal of vitreous and/or discission of anterior hyaloid membrane, with or without air injection

65815 with removal of blood, with or without irrigation and/or air injection

(For injection, see 66020-66030)

(For removal of blood clot, use 65930)

65820 Goniotomy

(Do not report modifier 63 in conjunction with 65820)

(For use of ophthalmic endoscope with 65820, use 66990)

65850 Trabeculotomy ab externo

65855 Trabeculoplasty by laser surgery, 1 or more sessions (defined treatment series)

(If re-treatment is necessary after several months because of disease progression, a new treatment or treatment series should be reported with a modifier, if necessary, to indicate lesser or greater complexity)

(For trabeculectomy, use 66170)

65860 Severing adhesions of anterior segment, laser technique (separate procedure)

65865 Severing adhesions of anterior segment of eye, incisional technique (with or without injection of air or liquid) (separate procedure); goniosynechiae

(For trabeculoplasty by laser surgery, use 65855)

65870 anterior synechiae, except goniosynechiae

65875 posterior synechiae

(For use of ophthalmic endoscope with 65875, use 66990)

65880 corneovitreal adhesions

(For laser surgery, use 66821)

Removal

65900 Removal of epithelial downgrowth, anterior chamber of eye

65920 Removal of implanted material, anterior segment of eye

(For use of ophthalmic endoscope with 65920, use 66990)

65930 Removal of blood clot, anterior segment of eye

Introduction

66020 Injection, anterior chamber of eye (separate procedure); air or liquid

66030 medication

(For unlisted procedures on anterior segment, use 66999)

Anterior Sclera

Excision

(For removal of intraocular foreign body, use 65235)

(For operations on posterior sclera, use 67250, 67255)

66130 Excision of lesion, sclera

66150 Fistulization of sclera for glaucoma; trephination with iridectomy

66155 thermocauterization with iridectomy

66160 sclerectomy with punch or scissors, with iridectomy

66165 iridencleisis or iridotasis

66170 trabeculectomy ab externo in absence of previous surgery

(For trabeculotomy ab externo, use 65850)

(For repair of operative wound, use 66250)

(For dilation of Schlemm's Canal with or without retention of device, see 0176T, 0177T)

66172 trabeculectomy ab externo with scarring from previous ocular surgery or trauma (includes injection of antifibrotic agents)

(For transciliary body sclera fistulization, use Category III code 0123T)

Aqueous Shunt

66180 Aqueous shunt to extraocular reservoir (eg, Molteno, Schocket, Denver-Krupin)

66185 Revision of aqueous shunt to extraocular reservoir

(For removal of implanted shunt, use 67120)

Repair or Revision

(For scleral procedures in retinal surgery, see 67101 et seq)

66220 Repair of scleral staphyloma; without graft

66225 with graft

(For scleral reinforcement, see 67250, 67255)

66250 Revision or repair of operative wound of anterior segment, any type, early or late, major or minor procedure

(For unlisted procedures on anterior sclera, use 66999)

Iris, Ciliary Body

Incision

66500 Iridotomy by stab incision (separate procedure); except transfixion

66505 with transfixion as for iris bombe

(For iridotomy by photocoagulation, use 66761)

Excision

66600 Iridectomy, with corneoscleral or corneal section; for removal of lesion

66605 with cyclectomy

66625 peripheral for glaucoma (separate procedure)

66630 sector for glaucoma (separate procedure)

66635 optical (separate procedure)

(For coreoplasty by photocoagulation, use 66762)

Repair

66680 Repair of iris, ciliary body (as for iridodialysis)

(For reposition or resection of uveal tissue with perforating wound of cornea or sclera, use 65285)

66682 Suture of iris, ciliary body (separate procedure) with retrieval of suture through small incision (eg, McCannel suture)

Destruction

66700 Ciliary body destruction; diathermy

66710 cyclophotocoagulation, transscleral

66711 cyclophotocoagulation, endoscopic

(Do not report 66711 in conjunction with 66990)

⊙ **66720** cryotherapy

66740 cyclodialysis

66761 Iridotomy/iridectomy by laser surgery (eg, for glaucoma) (1 or more sessions)

66762 Iridoplasty by photocoagulation (1 or more sessions) (eg, for improvement of vision, for widening of anterior chamber angle)

66770 Destruction of cyst or lesion iris or ciliary body (nonexcisional procedure)

(For excision lesion iris, ciliary body, see 66600, 66605; for removal of epithelial downgrowth, use 65900)

(For unlisted procedures on iris, ciliary body, use 66999)

Lens

Incision

66820 Discission of secondary membranous cataract (opacified posterior lens capsule and/or anterior hyaloid); stab incision technique (Ziegler or Wheeler knife)

66821 laser surgery (eg, YAG laser) (1 or more stages)

66825 Repositioning of intraocular lens prosthesis, requiring an incision (separate procedure)

Removal

Lateral canthotomy, iridectomy, iridotomy, anterior capsulotomy, posterior capsulotomy, the use of viscoelastic agents, enzymatic zonulysis, use of other pharmacologic agents, and subconjunctival or sub-tenon injections are included as part of the code for the extraction of lens.

66830 Removal of secondary membranous cataract (opacified posterior lens capsule and/or anterior hyaloid) with corneo-scleral section, with or without iridectomy (iridocapsulotomy, iridocapsulectomy)

66840 Removal of lens material; aspiration technique, 1 or more stages

66850 phacofragmentation technique (mechanical or ultrasonic) (eg, phacoemulsification), with aspiration

66852 pars plana approach, with or without vitrectomy

66920 intracapsular

66930 intracapsular, for dislocated lens

66940 extracapsular (other than 66840, 66850, 66852)

(For removal of intralenticular foreign body without lens extraction, use 65235)

(For repair of operative wound, use 66250)

Intraocular Lens Procedures

66982 Extracapsular cataract removal with insertion of intraocular lens prosthesis (one stage procedure), manual or mechanical technique (eg, irrigation and aspiration or phacoemulsification), complex, requiring devices or techniques not generally used in routine cataract surgery (eg, iris expansion device, suture support for intraocular lens, or primary posterior capsulorrhexis) or performed on patients in the amblyogenic developmental stage

66983 Intracapsular cataract extraction with insertion of intraocular lens prosthesis (1 stage procedure)

66984 Extracapsular cataract removal with insertion of intraocular lens prosthesis (1 stage procedure), manual or mechanical technique (eg, irrigation and aspiration or phacoemulsification)

(For complex extracapsular cataract removal, use 66982)

66985 Insertion of intraocular lens prosthesis (secondary implant), not associated with concurrent cataract removal

(To code implant at time of concurrent cataract surgery, see 66982, 66983, 66984)

(For intraocular lens prosthesis supplied by physician, use 99070)

(For ultrasonic determination of intraocular lens power, use 76519)

(For removal of implanted material from anterior segment, use 65920)

(For secondary fixation (separate procedure), use 66682)

(For use of ophthalmic endoscope with 66985, use 66990)

66986 Exchange of intraocular lens

(For use of ophthalmic endoscope with 66986, use 66990)

Other Procedures

+ 66990 Use of ophthalmic endoscope (List separately in addition to code for primary procedure)

(66990 may be used only with codes 65820, 65875, 65920, 66985, 66986, 67036, 67039, 67040, 67041, 67042, 67043, 67112)

66999 Unlisted procedure, anterior segment of eye

Posterior Segment

Vitreous

67005 Removal of vitreous, anterior approach (open sky technique or limbal incision); partial removal

67010 subtotal removal with mechanical vitrectomy

(For removal of vitreous by paracentesis of anterior chamber, use 65810)

(For removal of corneovitreal adhesions, use 65880)

67015 Aspiration or release of vitreous, subretinal or choroidal fluid, pars plana approach (posterior sclerotomy)

67025 Injection of vitreous substitute, pars plana or limbal approach (fluid-gas exchange), with or without aspiration (separate procedure)

67027 Implantation of intravitreal drug delivery system (eg, ganciclovir implant), includes concomitant removal of vitreous

(For removal, use 67121)

67028 Intravitreal injection of a pharmacologic agent (separate procedure)

67030 Discission of vitreous strands (without removal), pars plana approach

67031 Severing of vitreous strands, vitreous face adhesions, sheets, membranes or opacities, laser surgery (1 or more stages)

67036 Vitrectomy, mechanical, pars plana approach;

►(For application of intraocular epiretinal radiation with 67036, use 0190T)◄

(67038 has been deleted. To report, see 67041, 67042, 67043)

67039 with focal endolaser photocoagulation

67040 with endolaser panretinal photocoagulation

67041 with removal of preretinal cellular membrane (eg, macular pucker)

67042 with removal of internal limiting membrane of retina (eg, for repair of macular hole, diabetic macular edema), includes, if performed, intraocular tamponade (ie, air, gas or silicone oil)

67043 with removal of subretinal membrane (eg, choroidal neovascularization), includes, if performed, intraocular tamponade (ie, air, gas or silicone oil) and laser photocoagulation

(For use of ophthalmic endoscope with 67036, 67039, 67040-67043, use 66990)

(For associated lensectomy, use 66850)

(For use of vitrectomy in retinal detachment surgery, see 67108, 67113)

(For associated removal of foreign body, see 65260, 65265)

(For unlisted procedures on vitreous, use 67299)

Retina or Choroid

Repair

(If diathermy, cryotherapy and/or photocoagulation are combined, report under principal modality used)

67101 Repair of retinal detachment, 1 or more sessions; cryotherapy or diathermy, with or without drainage of subretinal fluid

67105 photocoagulation, with or without drainage of subretinal fluid

67107 Repair of retinal detachment; scleral buckling (such as lamellar scleral dissection, imbrication or encircling procedure), with or without implant, with or without cryotherapy, photocoagulation, and drainage of subretinal fluid

67108 with vitrectomy, any method, with or without air or gas tamponade, focal endolaser photocoagulation, cryotherapy, drainage of subretinal fluid, scleral buckling, and/or removal of lens by same technique

67110 by injection of air or other gas (eg, pneumatic retinopexy)

67112 by scleral buckling or vitrectomy, on patient having previous ipsilateral retinal detachment repair(s) using scleral buckling or vitrectomy techniques

(For aspiration or drainage of subretinal or subchoroidal fluid, use 67015)

(For use of ophthalmic endoscope with 67112, use 66990)

67113 Repair of complex retinal detachment (eg, proliferative vitreoretinopathy, stage C-1 or greater, diabetic traction retinal detachment, retinopathy of prematurity, retinal tear of greater than 90 degrees), with vitrectomy and membrane peeling, may include air, gas, or silicone oil tamponade, cryotherapy, endolaser photocoagulation, drainage of subretinal fluid, scleral buckling, and/or removal of lens

(To report vitrectomy, pars plana approach, other than in retinal detachment surgery, see 67036-67043)

67115 Release of encircling material (posterior segment)

67120 Removal of implanted material, posterior segment; extraocular

67121 intraocular

(For removal from anterior segment, use 65920)

(For removal of foreign body, see 65260, 65265)

Prophylaxis

Codes 67141, 67145, 67208-67220, 67227, 67228, 67229 include treatment at one or more sessions that may occur at different encounters. These codes should be reported once during a defined treatment period.

Repetitive services. The services listed below are often performed in multiple sessions or groups of sessions. The methods of reporting vary.

The following descriptors are intended to include all sessions in a defined treatment period.

67141 Prophylaxis of retinal detachment (eg, retinal break, lattice degeneration) without drainage, 1 or more sessions; cryotherapy, diathermy

67145 photocoagulation (laser or xenon arc)

Destruction

67208 Destruction of localized lesion of retina (eg, macular edema, tumors), 1 or more sessions; cryotherapy, diathermy

67210 photocoagulation

67218 radiation by implantation of source (includes removal of source)

67220 Destruction of localized lesion of choroid (eg, choroidal neovascularization); photocoagulation (eg, laser), 1 or more sessions

(For destruction of macular drusen, photocoagulation, use Category III code 0017T)

(For destruction of localized lesion of choroid by transpupillary thermotherapy, use Category III code 0016T)

67221 photodynamic therapy (includes intravenous infusion)

+ 67225 photodynamic therapy, second eye, at single session (List separately in addition to code for primary eye treatment)

(Use 67225 in conjunction with 67221)

67227 Destruction of extensive or progressive retinopathy (eg, diabetic retinopathy), 1 or more sessions, cryotherapy, diathermy

67228 Treatment of extensive or progressive retinopathy, 1 or more sessions; (eg, diabetic retinopathy), photocoagulation

67229 preterm infant (less than 37 weeks gestation at birth), performed from birth up to 1 year of age (eg, retinopathy of prematurity), photocoagulation or cryotherapy

(For bilateral procedure, use modifier 50)

(For unlisted procedures on retina, use 67299)

Posterior Sclera

Repair

(For excision lesion sclera, use 66130)

67250 Scleral reinforcement (separate procedure); without graft

67255 with graft

(For repair scleral staphyloma, see 66220, 66225)

Other Procedures

67299 Unlisted procedure, posterior segment

Ocular Adnexa

Extraocular Muscles

67311 Strabismus surgery, recession or resection procedure; 1 horizontal muscle

67312 2 horizontal muscles

67314 1 vertical muscle (excluding superior oblique)

67316 2 or more vertical muscles (excluding superior oblique)

(For adjustable sutures, use 67335 in addition to codes 67311-67334 for primary procedure reflecting number of muscles operated on)

67318 Strabismus surgery, any procedure, superior oblique muscle

+ 67320 Transposition procedure (eg, for paretic extraocular muscle), any extraocular muscle (specify) (List separately in addition to code for primary procedure)

(Use 67320 in conjunction with 67311-67318)

+ 67331 Strabismus surgery on patient with previous eye surgery or injury that did not involve the extraocular muscles (List separately in addition to code for primary procedure)

(Use 67331 in conjunction with 67311-67318)

+ 67332 Strabismus surgery on patient with scarring of extraocular muscles (eg, prior ocular injury, strabismus or retinal detachment surgery) or restrictive myopathy (eg, dysthyroid ophthalmopathy) (List separately in addition to code for primary procedure)

(Use 67332 in conjunction with 67311-67318)

+ 67334 Strabismus surgery by posterior fixation suture technique, with or without muscle recession (List separately in addition to code for primary procedure)

(Use 67334 in conjunction with 67311-67318)

+ 67335 Placement of adjustable suture(s) during strabismus surgery, including postoperative adjustment(s) of suture(s) (List separately in addition to code for specific strabismus surgery)

(Use 67335 in conjunction with 67311-67334)

+ 67340 Strabismus surgery involving exploration and/or repair of detached extraocular muscle(s) (List separately in addition to code for primary procedure)

(Use 67340 in conjunction with 67311-67334)

67343 Release of extensive scar tissue without detaching extraocular muscle (separate procedure)

(Use 67343 in conjunction with 67311-67340, when such procedures are performed other than on the affected muscle)

67345 Chemodenervation of extraocular muscle

(For chemodenervation for blepharospasm and other neurological disorders, see 64612 and 64613)

67346 Biopsy of extraocular muscle

(For repair of wound, extraocular muscle, tendon or Tenon's capsule, use 65290)

Other Procedures

(67350 has been deleted. To report, use 67346)

67399 Unlisted procedure, ocular muscle

Orbit

Exploration, Excision, Decompression

67400 Orbitotomy without bone flap (frontal or transconjunctival approach); for exploration, with or without biopsy

67405 with drainage only

67412 with removal of lesion

67413 with removal of foreign body

67414 with removal of bone for decompression

67415 Fine needle aspiration of orbital contents

(For exenteration, enucleation, and repair, see 65101 et seq; for optic nerve decompression, use 67570)

67420 Orbitotomy with bone flap or window, lateral approach (eg, Kroenlein); with removal of lesion

67430 with removal of foreign body

67440 with drainage

67445 with removal of bone for decompression

(For optic nerve sheath decompression, use 67570)

67450 for exploration, with or without biopsy

(For orbitotomy, transcranial approach, see 61330-61334)

(For orbital implant, see 67550, 67560)

(For removal of eyeball or for repair after removal, see 65091-65175)

Other Procedures

67500 Retrobulbar injection; medication (separate procedure, does not include supply of medication)

67505 alcohol

67515 Injection of medication or other substance into Tenon's capsule

(For subconjunctival injection, use 68200)

67550 Orbital implant (implant outside muscle cone); insertion

67560 removal or revision

(For ocular implant (implant inside muscle cone), see 65093-65105, 65130-65175)

(For treatment of fractures of malar area, orbit, see 21355 et seq)

67570 Optic nerve decompression (eg, incision or fenestration of optic nerve sheath)

67599 Unlisted procedure, orbit

Eyelids

Incision

67700 Blepharotomy, drainage of abscess, eyelid

67710 Severing of tarsorrhaphy

67715 Canthotomy (separate procedure)

(For canthoplasty, use 67950)

(For division of symblepharon, use 68340)

Excision, Destruction

Codes for removal of lesion include more than skin (ie, involving lid margin, tarsus, and/or palpebral conjunctiva).

(For removal of lesion, involving mainly skin of eyelid, see 11310-11313; 11440-11446, 11640-11646; 17000-17004)

(For repair of wounds, blepharoplasty, grafts, reconstructive surgery, see 67930-67975)

67800 Excision of chalazion; single

67801 multiple, same lid

67805 multiple, different lids

67808 under general anesthesia and/or requiring hospitalization, single or multiple

67810 Biopsy of eyelid

67820 Correction of trichiasis; epilation, by forceps only

67825 epilation by other than forceps (eg, by electrosurgery, cryotherapy, laser surgery)

67830 incision of lid margin

67835 incision of lid margin, with free mucous membrane graft

67840 Excision of lesion of eyelid (except chalazion) without closure or with simple direct closure

(For excision and repair of eyelid by reconstructive surgery, see 67961, 67966)

67850 Destruction of lesion of lid margin (up to 1 cm)

(For Mohs micrographic surgery, see 17311-17315)

(For initiation or follow-up care of topical chemotherapy (eg, 5-FU or similar agents), see appropriate office visits)

Tarsorrhaphy

67875 Temporary closure of eyelids by suture (eg, Frost suture)

67880 Construction of intermarginal adhesions, median tarsorrhaphy, or canthorrhaphy;

67882 with transposition of tarsal plate

(For severing of tarsorrhaphy, use 67710)

(For canthoplasty, reconstruction canthus, use 67950)

(For canthotomy, use 67715)

Repair (Brow Ptosis, Blepharoptosis, Lid Retraction, Ectropion, Entropion)

67900 Repair of brow ptosis (supraciliary, mid-forehead or coronal approach)

(For forehead rhytidectomy, use 15824)

67901 Repair of blepharoptosis; frontalis muscle technique with suture or other material (eg, banked fascia)

67902 frontalis muscle technique with autologous fascial sling (includes obtaining fascia)

67903 (tarso) levator resection or advancement, internal approach

67904 (tarso) levator resection or advancement, external approach

67906 superior rectus technique with fascial sling (includes obtaining fascia)

67908 conjunctivo-tarso-Muller's muscle-levator resection (eg, Fasanella-Servat type)

67909 Reduction of overcorrection of ptosis

67911 Correction of lid retraction

(For obtaining autogenous graft materials, see 20920, 20922 or 20926)

(For correction of trichiasis by mucous membrane graft, use 67835)

67912 Correction of lagophthalmos, with implantation of upper eyelid lid load (eg, gold weight)

67914 Repair of ectropion; suture

67915 thermocauterization

67916 excision tarsal wedge

67917 extensive (eg, tarsal strip operations)

(For correction of everted punctum, use 68705)

67921 Repair of entropion; suture

67922 thermocauterization

67923 excision tarsal wedge

67924 extensive (eg, tarsal strip or capsulopalpebral fascia repairs operation)

(For repair of cicatricial ectropion or entropion requiring scar excision or skin graft, see also 67961 et seq)

Reconstruction

Codes for blepharoplasty involve more than skin (ie, involving lid margin, tarsus, and/or palpebral conjunctiva).

67930 Suture of recent wound, eyelid, involving lid margin, tarsus, and/or palpebral conjunctiva direct closure; partial thickness

67935 full thickness

67938 Removal of embedded foreign body, eyelid

(For repair of skin of eyelid, see 12011-12018; 12051-12057; 13150-13153)

(For tarsorrhaphy, canthorrhaphy, see 67880, 67882)

(For repair of blepharoptosis and lid retraction, see 67901-67911)

(For blepharoplasty for entropion, ectropion, see 67916, 67917, 67923, 67924)

(For correction of blepharochalasis (blepharorhytidectomy), see 15820-15823)

(For repair of skin of eyelid, adjacent tissue transfer, see 14060, 14061; preparation for graft, use 15004; free graft, see 15120, 15121, 15260, 15261)

(For excision of lesion of eyelid, use 67800 et seq)

(For repair of lacrimal canaliculi, use 68700)

67950 Canthoplasty (reconstruction of canthus)

67961 Excision and repair of eyelid, involving lid margin, tarsus, conjunctiva, canthus, or full thickness, may include preparation for skin graft or pedicle flap with adjacent tissue transfer or rearrangement; up to one-fourth of lid margin

67966 over one-fourth of lid margin

(For canthoplasty, use 67950)

(For free skin grafts, see 15120, 15121, 15260, 15261)

(For tubed pedicle flap preparation, use 15576; for delay, use 15630; for attachment, use 15650)

67971 Reconstruction of eyelid, full thickness by transfer of tarsoconjunctival flap from opposing eyelid; up to two-thirds of eyelid, 1 stage or first stage

67973 total eyelid, lower, 1 stage or first stage

67974 total eyelid, upper, 1 stage or first stage

67975 second stage

Other Procedures

67999 Unlisted procedure, eyelids

Conjunctiva

(For removal of foreign body, see 65205 et seq)

Incision and Drainage

68020 Incision of conjunctiva, drainage of cyst

68040 Expression of conjunctival follicles (eg, for trachoma)

Excision and/or Destruction

68100 Biopsy of conjunctiva

68110 Excision of lesion, conjunctiva; up to 1 cm

68115 over 1 cm

68130 with adjacent sclera

68135 Destruction of lesion, conjunctiva

Injection

(For injection into Tenon's capsule or retrobulbar injection, see 67500-67515)

68200 Subconjunctival injection

Conjunctivoplasty

(For wound repair, see 65270-65273)

68320 Conjunctivoplasty; with conjunctival graft or extensive rearrangement

68325 with buccal mucous membrane graft (includes obtaining graft)

68326 Conjunctivoplasty, reconstruction cul-de-sac; with conjunctival graft or extensive rearrangement

68328 with buccal mucous membrane graft (includes obtaining graft)

68330 Repair of symblepharon; conjunctivoplasty, without graft

68335 with free graft conjunctiva or buccal mucous membrane (includes obtaining graft)

68340 division of symblepharon, with or without insertion of conformer or contact lens

Other Procedures

68360 Conjunctival flap; bridge or partial (separate procedure)

68362 total (such as Gunderson thin flap or purse string flap)

(For conjunctival flap for perforating injury, see 65280, 65285)

(For repair of operative wound, use 66250)

(For removal of conjunctival foreign body, see 65205, 65210)

68371 Harvesting conjunctival allograft, living donor

68399 Unlisted procedure, conjunctiva

Lacrimal System

Incision

68400 Incision, drainage of lacrimal gland

68420 Incision, drainage of lacrimal sac (dacryocystotomy or dacryocystostomy)

68440 Snip incision of lacrimal punctum

Excision

68500 Excision of lacrimal gland (dacryoadenectomy), except for tumor; total

68505 partial

68510 Biopsy of lacrimal gland

68520 Excision of lacrimal sac (dacryocystectomy)

68525 Biopsy of lacrimal sac

68530 Removal of foreign body or dacryolith, lacrimal passages

68540 Excision of lacrimal gland tumor; frontal approach

68550 involving osteotomy

Repair

68700 Plastic repair of canaliculi

68705 Correction of everted punctum, cautery

68720 Dacryocystorhinostomy (fistulization of lacrimal sac to nasal cavity)

68745 Conjunctivorhinostomy (fistulization of conjunctiva to nasal cavity); without tube

68750 with insertion of tube or stent

68760 Closure of the lacrimal punctum; by thermocauterization, ligation, or laser surgery

68761 by plug, each

68770 Closure of lacrimal fistula (separate procedure)

Probing and/or Related Procedures

68801 Dilation of lacrimal punctum, with or without irrigation

(To report a bilateral procedure, use 68801 with modifier 50)

68810 Probing of nasolacrimal duct, with or without irrigation;

(For bilateral procedure, report 68810 with modifier 50)

68811 requiring general anesthesia

(For bilateral procedure, report 68811 with modifier 50)

68815 with insertion of tube or stent

(See also 92018)

(For bilateral procedure, report 68815 with modifier 50)

68816 with transluminal balloon catheter dilation

(Do not report 68816 in conjunction with 68810, 68811, 68815)

(For bilateral procedure, report 68816 with modifier 50)

68840 Probing of lacrimal canaliculi, with or without irrigation

68850 Injection of contrast medium for dacryocystography

(For radiological supervision and interpretation, see 70170, 78660)

Other Procedures

68899 Unlisted procedure, lacrimal system

Auditory System

(For diagnostic services (eg, audiometry, vestibular tests), see 92502 et seq)

External Ear

Incision

69000 Drainage external ear, abscess or hematoma; simple

69005 complicated

69020 Drainage external auditory canal, abscess

69090 Ear piercing

Excision

69100 Biopsy external ear

69105 Biopsy external auditory canal

69110 Excision external ear; partial, simple repair

69120 complete amputation

(For reconstruction of ear, see 15120 et seq)

69140 Excision exostosis(es), external auditory canal

69145 Excision soft tissue lesion, external auditory canal

69150 Radical excision external auditory canal lesion; without neck dissection

69155 with neck dissection

(For resection of temporal bone, use 69535)

(For skin grafting, see 15004-15261)

Removal

69200 Removal foreign body from external auditory canal; without general anesthesia

69205 with general anesthesia

69210 Removal impacted cerumen (separate procedure), 1 or both ears

69220 Debridement, mastoidectomy cavity, simple (eg, routine cleaning)

(For bilateral procedure, report 69220 with modifier 50)

69222 Debridement, mastoidectomy cavity, complex (eg, with anesthesia or more than routine cleaning)

(For bilateral procedure, report 69222 with modifier 50)

Repair

(For suture of wound or injury of external ear, see 12011-14300)

⊙ **69300** Otoplasty, protruding ear, with or without size reduction

(For bilateral procedure, report 69300 with modifier 50)

69310 Reconstruction of external auditory canal (meatoplasty) (eg, for stenosis due to injury, infection) (separate procedure)

69320 Reconstruction external auditory canal for congenital atresia, single stage

(For combination with middle ear reconstruction, see 69631, 69641)

(For other reconstructive procedures with grafts (eg, skin, cartilage, bone), see 13150-15760, 21230-21235)

Other Procedures

(For otoscopy under general anesthesia, use 92502)

69399 Unlisted procedure, external ear

Middle Ear

Introduction

69400 Eustachian tube inflation, transnasal; with catheterization

69401 without catheterization

69405 Eustachian tube catheterization, transtympanic

Incision

69420 Myringotomy including aspiration and/or eustachian tube inflation

69421 Myringotomy including aspiration and/or eustachian tube inflation requiring general anesthesia

69424 Ventilating tube removal requiring general anesthesia

(For bilateral procedure, report 69424 with modifier 50)

(Do not report code 69424 in conjunction with 69205, 69210, 69420, 69421, 69433-69676, 69710-69745, 69801-69930)

69433 Tympanostomy (requiring insertion of ventilating tube), local or topical anesthesia

(For bilateral procedure, report 69433 with modifier 50)

69436 Tympanostomy (requiring insertion of ventilating tube), general anesthesia

(For bilateral procedure, report 69436 with modifier 50)

69440 Middle ear exploration through postauricular or ear canal incision

(For atticotomy, see 69601 et seq)

69450 Tympanolysis, transcanal

Excision

69501 Transmastoid antrotomy (simple mastoidectomy)

69502 Mastoidectomy; complete

69505 modified radical

69511 radical

(For skin graft, see 15004 et seq)

(For mastoidectomy cavity debridement, see 69220, 69222)

69530 Petrous apicectomy including radical mastoidectomy

69535 Resection temporal bone, external approach

(For middle fossa approach, see 69950-69970)

69540 Excision aural polyp

69550 Excision aural glomus tumor; transcanal

69552 transmastoid

69554 extended (extratemporal)

Repair

69601 Revision mastoidectomy; resulting in complete mastoidectomy

69602 resulting in modified radical mastoidectomy

69603 resulting in radical mastoidectomy

69604 resulting in tympanoplasty

(For planned secondary tympanoplasty after mastoidectomy, see 69631, 69632)

69605 with apicectomy

(For skin graft, see 15120, 15121, 15260, 15261)

69610 Tympanic membrane repair, with or without site preparation of perforation for closure, with or without patch

69620 Myringoplasty (surgery confined to drumhead and donor area)

69631 Tympanoplasty without mastoidectomy (including canalplasty, atticotomy and/or middle ear surgery), initial or revision; without ossicular chain reconstruction

69632 with ossicular chain reconstruction (eg, postfenestration)

69633 with ossicular chain reconstruction and synthetic prosthesis (eg, partial ossicular replacement prosthesis [PORP], total ossicular replacement prosthesis [TORP])

69635 Tympanoplasty with antrotomy or mastoidotomy (including canalplasty, atticotomy, middle ear surgery, and/or tympanic membrane repair); without ossicular chain reconstruction

69636 with ossicular chain reconstruction

69637 with ossicular chain reconstruction and synthetic prosthesis (eg, partial ossicular replacement prosthesis [PORP], total ossicular replacement prosthesis [TORP])

69641 Tympanoplasty with mastoidectomy (including canalplasty, middle ear surgery, tympanic membrane repair); without ossicular chain reconstruction

69642 with ossicular chain reconstruction

69643 with intact or reconstructed wall, without ossicular chain reconstruction

69644 with intact or reconstructed canal wall, with ossicular chain reconstruction

69645 radical or complete, without ossicular chain reconstruction

69646 radical or complete, with ossicular chain reconstruction

69650 Stapes mobilization

69660 Stapedectomy or stapedotomy with reestablishment of ossicular continuity, with or without use of foreign material;

69661 with footplate drill out

69662 Revision of stapedectomy or stapedotomy

69666 Repair oval window fistula

69667 Repair round window fistula

69670 Mastoid obliteration (separate procedure)

69676 Tympanic neurectomy

(For bilateral procedure, report 69676 with modifier 50)

Other Procedures

69700 Closure postauricular fistula, mastoid (separate procedure)

69710 Implantation or replacement of electromagnetic bone conduction hearing device in temporal bone

(Replacement procedure includes removal of old device)

69711 Removal or repair of electromagnetic bone conduction hearing device in temporal bone

69714 Implantation, osseointegrated implant, temporal bone, with percutaneous attachment to external speech processor/cochlear stimulator; without mastoidectomy

69715 with mastoidectomy

69717 Replacement (including removal of existing device), osseointegrated implant, temporal bone, with percutaneous attachment to external speech processor/cochlear stimulator; without mastoidectomy

69718 with mastoidectomy

69720 Decompression facial nerve, intratemporal; lateral to geniculate ganglion

69725 including medial to geniculate ganglion

69740 Suture facial nerve, intratemporal, with or without graft or decompression; lateral to geniculate ganglion

69745 including medial to geniculate ganglion

(For extracranial suture of facial nerve, use 64864)

69799 Unlisted procedure, middle ear

Inner Ear

Incision and/or Destruction

69801 Labyrinthotomy, with or without cryosurgery including other nonexcisional destructive procedures or perfusion of vestibuloactive drugs (single or multiple perfusions); transcanal

(69801 includes all required infusions performed on initial and subsequent days of treatment)

69802 with mastoidectomy

69805 Endolymphatic sac operation; without shunt

69806 with shunt

69820 Fenestration semicircular canal

69840 Revision fenestration operation

Excision

69905 Labyrinthectomy; transcanal

69910 with mastoidectomy

69915 Vestibular nerve section, translabyrinthine approach

(For transcranial approach, use 69950)

Introduction

69930 Cochlear device implantation, with or without mastoidectomy

Other Procedures

69949 Unlisted procedure, inner ear

Temporal Bone, Middle Fossa Approach

(For external approach, use 69535)

69950 Vestibular nerve section, transcranial approach

69955 Total facial nerve decompression and/or repair (may include graft)

69960 Decompression internal auditory canal

69970 Removal of tumor, temporal bone

Other Procedures

69979 Unlisted procedure, temporal bone, middle fossa approach

Operating Microscope

►The surgical microscope is employed when the surgical services are performed using the techniques of microsurgery. Code 69990 should be reported (without modifier 51 appended) in addition to the code for the primary procedure performed. Do not use 69990 for visualization with magnifying loupes or corrected vision. Do not report 69990 in addition to procedures where use of the operating microscope is an inclusive component (15756-15758, 15842, 19364, 19368, 20955-20962, 20969-20973, 22856-22861, 26551-26554, 26556, 31526, 31531, 31536, 31541, 31545, 31546, 31561, 31571, 43116, 43496, 49906, 61548, 63075-63078, 64727, 64820-64823, 65091-68850, 0184T).◄

✚ **69990** Microsurgical techniques, requiring use of operating microscope (List separately in addition to code for primary procedure)

Notes

Radiology Guidelines (Including Nuclear Medicine and Diagnostic Ultrasound)

Items used by all physicians in reporting their services are presented in the **Introduction.** Some of the commonalities are repeated here for the convenience of those physicians referring to this section on **Radiology (Including Nuclear Medicine and Diagnostic Ultrasound).** Other definitions and items unique to Radiology are also listed.

Subject Listings

Subject listings apply when radiological services are performed by or under the responsible supervision of a physician.

Separate Procedures

Some of the procedures or services listed in the CPT codebook that are commonly carried out as an integral component of a total service or procedure have been identified by the inclusion of the term "separate procedure." The codes designated as "separate procedure" should not be reported in addition to the code for the total procedure or service of which it is considered an integral component.

However, when a procedure or service that is designated as a "separate procedure" is carried out independently or considered to be unrelated or distinct from other procedures/services provided at that time, it may be reported by itself, or in addition to other procedures/services by appending modifier 59 to the specific "separate procedure" code to indicate that the procedure is not considered to be a component of another procedure, but is a distinct, independent procedure. This may represent a different session or patient encounter, different procedure or surgery, different site or organ system, separate incision/excision, separate lesion, separate injury, or area of injury in extensive injuries.

Subsection Information

Several of the subheadings or subsections have special needs or instructions unique to that section. Where these are indicated (eg, "Radiation Oncology") special **"Notes"** will be presented preceding those procedural terminology listings, referring to that subsection specifically. If there is an "Unlisted Procedure" code number (see section below) for the individual subsection, it will be shown. Those subsections with **"Notes"** are as follows:

Functional MRI	70554-70555
Aorta and Arteries	75600-75790
Veins and Lymphatics	75801-75893
Transcatheter Procedures	75894-75989
Diagnostic Ultrasound	76506-76999
Abdomen and Retroperitoneum	76700-76776
Obstetrical	76801-76828
Non-Obstetrical	76830-76857
Radiation Oncology	77261-77799
Clinical Treatment Planning	77261-77299
Radiation Treatment Management	77427-77499
Proton Beam Treatment Delivery	77520-77525
Hyperthermia	77600-77620
Clinical Brachytherapy	77750-77799
Nuclear Medicine	78000-78299
Musculoskeletal System	78300-78399
Cardiovascular System	78414-78499
Therapeutic	79005-79999

Unlisted Service or Procedure

A service or procedure may be provided that is not listed in this edition of the CPT codebook. When reporting such a service, the appropriate "Unlisted Procedure" code may be used to indicate the service, identifying it by "Special Report" as discussed below. The "Unlisted Procedures" and accompanying codes for **Radiology (Including Nuclear Medicine and Diagnostic Ultrasound)** are as follows:

76496 Unlisted fluoroscopic procedure (eg, diagnostic, interventional)

76497 Unlisted computed tomography procedure (eg, diagnostic, interventional)

76498 Unlisted magnetic resonance procedure (eg, diagnostic, interventional)

76499 Unlisted diagnostic radiographic procedure

76999 Unlisted ultrasound procedure (eg, diagnostic, interventional)

77299 Unlisted procedure, therapeutic radiology clinical treatment planning

77399 Unlisted procedure, medical radiation physics, dosimetry and treatment devices, and special services

77499 Unlisted procedure, therapeutic radiology treatment management

77799 Unlisted procedure, clinical brachytherapy

78099 Unlisted endocrine procedure, diagnostic nuclear medicine

78199 Unlisted hematopoietic, reticuloendothelial and lymphatic procedure, diagnostic nuclear medicine

78299 Unlisted gastrointestinal procedure, diagnostic nuclear medicine

78399 Unlisted musculoskeletal procedure, diagnostic nuclear medicine

78499 Unlisted cardiovascular procedure, diagnostic nuclear medicine

78599 Unlisted respiratory procedure, diagnostic nuclear medicine

78699 Unlisted nervous system procedure, diagnostic nuclear medicine

78799 Unlisted genitourinary procedure, diagnostic nuclear medicine

78999 Unlisted miscellaneous procedure, diagnostic nuclear medicine

79999 Radiopharmaceutical therapy, unlisted procedure

Special Report

A service that is rarely provided, unusual, variable, or new may require a special report in determining medical appropriateness of the service. Pertinent information should include an adequate definition or description of the nature, extent, and need for the procedure; and the time, effort, and equipment necessary to provide the service. Additional items that may be included are:

- Complexity of symptoms
- Final diagnosis
- Pertinent physical findings
- Diagnostic and therapeutic procedures
- Concurrent problems
- Follow-up care

Supervision and Interpretation

When a procedure is performed by two physicians, the radiologic portion of the procedure is designated as "radiological supervision and interpretation." When a physician performs both the procedure and provides imaging supervision and interpretation, a combination of procedure codes outside the 70000 series and imaging supervision and interpretation codes are to be used.

(The Radiological Supervision and Interpretation codes are not applicable to the Radiation Oncology subsection.)

Administration of Contrast Material(s)

The phrase "with contrast" used in the codes for procedures performed using contrast for imaging enhancement represents contrast material administered intravascularly, intra-articularly or intrathecally.

For intra-articular injection, use the appropriate joint injection code. If radiographic arthrography is performed, also use the arthrography supervision and interpretation code for the appropriate joint (which includes fluoroscopy). If computed tomography (CT) or magnetic resonance (MR) arthrography are performed without radiographic arthrography, use the appropriate joint injection code, the appropriate CT or MR code ("with contrast" or "without followed by contrast"), and the appropriate imaging guidance code for needle placement for contrast injection.

For spine examinations using computed tomography, magnetic resonance imaging, magnetic resonance angiography, "with contrast" includes intrathecal or intravascular injection. For intrathecal injection, use also 61055 or 62284.

Injection of intravascular contrast material is part of the "with contrast" CT, computed tomographic angiography (CTA), magnetic resonance imaging (MRI), and magnetic resonance angiography (MRA) procedures.

Oral and/or rectal contrast administration alone does not qualify as a study "with contrast."

Written Report(s)

A written report signed by the interpreting physician should be considered an integral part of a radiologic procedure or interpretation.

Radiology

Diagnostic Radiology (Diagnostic Imaging)

Head and Neck

70010 Myelography, posterior fossa, radiological supervision and interpretation

70015 Cisternography, positive contrast, radiological supervision and interpretation

70030 Radiologic examination, eye, for detection of foreign body

70100 Radiologic examination, mandible; partial, less than 4 views

70110 complete, minimum of 4 views

70120 Radiologic examination, mastoids; less than 3 views per side

70130 complete, minimum of 3 views per side

70134 Radiologic examination, internal auditory meati, complete

70140 Radiologic examination, facial bones; less than 3 views

70150 complete, minimum of 3 views

70160 Radiologic examination, nasal bones, complete, minimum of three views

70170 Dacryocystography, nasolacrimal duct, radiological supervision and interpretation

70190 Radiologic examination; optic foramina

70200 orbits, complete, minimum of 4 views

70210 Radiologic examination, sinuses, paranasal, less than 3 views

70220 Radiologic examination, sinuses, paranasal, complete, minimum of 3 views

70240 Radiologic examination, sella turcica

70250 Radiologic examination, skull; less than 4 views

70260 complete, minimum of 4 views

70300 Radiologic examination, teeth; single view

70310 partial examination, less than full mouth

70320 complete, full mouth

70328 Radiologic examination, temporomandibular joint, open and closed mouth; unilateral

70330 bilateral

70332 Temporomandibular joint arthrography, radiological supervision and interpretation

(Do not report 70332 in conjunction with 77002)

70336 Magnetic resonance (eg, proton) imaging, temporomandibular joint(s)

70350 Cephalogram, orthodontic

70355 Orthopantogram

70360 Radiologic examination; neck, soft tissue

70370 pharynx or larynx, including fluoroscopy and/or magnification technique

70371 Complex dynamic pharyngeal and speech evaluation by cine or video recording

70373 Laryngography, contrast, radiological supervision and interpretation

70380 Radiologic examination, salivary gland for calculus

70390 Sialography, radiological supervision and interpretation

70450 Computed tomography, head or brain; without contrast material

70460 with contrast material(s)

70470 without contrast material, followed by contrast material(s) and further sections

(To report 3D rendering, see 76376, 76377)

70480 Computed tomography, orbit, sella, or posterior fossa or outer, middle, or inner ear; without contrast material

70481 with contrast material(s)

70482 without contrast material, followed by contrast material(s) and further sections

(To report 3D rendering, see 76376, 76377)

70486 Computed tomography, maxillofacial area; without contrast material

70487 with contrast material(s)

70488 without contrast material, followed by contrast material(s) and further sections

(To report 3D rendering, see 76376, 76377)

70490 Computed tomography, soft tissue neck; without contrast material

70491 with contrast material(s)

70492 without contrast material followed by contrast material(s) and further sections

(To report 3D rendering, see 76376, 76377)

(For cervical spine, see 72125, 72126)

70496 Computed tomographic angiography, head, with contrast material(s), including noncontrast images, if performed, and image postprocessing

70498 Computed tomographic angiography, neck, with contrast material(s), including noncontrast images, if performed, and image postprocessing

70540 Magnetic resonance (eg, proton) imaging, orbit, face, and/or neck; without contrast material(s)

(For head or neck magnetic resonance angiography studies, see 70544-70546, 70547-70549)

70542 with contrast material(s)

70543 without contrast material(s), followed by contrast material(s) and further sequences

(Report 70540-70543 once per imaging session)

70544 Magnetic resonance angiography, head; without contrast material(s)

70545 with contrast material(s)

70546 without contrast material(s), followed by contrast material(s) and further sequences

70547 Magnetic resonance angiography, neck; without contrast material(s)

70548 with contrast material(s)

70549 without contrast material(s), followed by contrast material(s) and further sequences

70551 Magnetic resonance (eg, proton) imaging, brain (including brain stem); without contrast material

70552 with contrast material(s)

70553 without contrast material, followed by contrast material(s) and further sequences

(For magnetic spectroscopy, use 76390)

Functional MRI involves identification and mapping of stimulation of brain function. When neurofunctional tests are administered by a technologist or other non-physician or non-psychologist, use 70554. When neurofunctional tests are entirely administered by a physician or psychologist, use 70555.

70554 Magnetic resonance imaging, brain, functional MRI; including test selection and administration of repetitive body part movement and/or visual stimulation, not requiring physician or psychologist administration

(Do not report 70554 in conjunction with 96020)

70555 requiring physician or psychologist administration of entire neurofunctional testing

(Do not report 70555 unless 96020 is performed)

(Do not report 70554, 70555 in conjunction with 70551-70553 unless a separate diagnostic MRI is performed)

70557 Magnetic resonance (eg, proton) imaging, brain (including brain stem and skull base), during open intracranial procedure (eg, to assess for residual tumor or residual vascular malformation); without contrast material

70558 with contrast material(s)

70559 without contrast material(s), followed by contrast material(s) and further sequences

(For stereotactic biopsy of intracranial lesion with magnetic resonance guidance, use 61751. 70557, 70558 or 70559 may be reported only if a separate report is generated. Report only one of the above codes once per operative session. Do not use these codes in conjunction with 61751, 77021, 77022)

Chest

(For fluoroscopic or ultrasonic guidance for needle placement procedures (eg, biopsy, aspiration, injection, localization device) of the thorax, see 76942, 77002)

71010 Radiologic examination, chest; single view, frontal

71015 stereo, frontal

71020 Radiologic examination, chest, 2 views, frontal and lateral;

71021 with apical lordotic procedure

71022 with oblique projections

71023 with fluoroscopy

71030 Radiologic examination, chest, complete, minimum of 4 views;

(For concurrent computer-aided detection [CAD] performed in addition to codes 71010, 71020, 71021, 71022, and 71030, use 0174T. Do not report 71010, 71020, 71021, 71022, and 71030 in conjunction with 0175T for CAD performed remotely from the primary interpretation)

71034 with fluoroscopy

(For separate chest fluoroscopy, use 76000)

71035 Radiologic examination, chest, special views (eg, lateral decubitus, Bucky studies)

71040 Bronchography, unilateral, radiological supervision and interpretation

71060 Bronchography, bilateral, radiological supervision and interpretation

71090 Insertion pacemaker, fluoroscopy and radiography, radiological supervision and interpretation

(For procedure, see appropriate organ or site)

71100 Radiologic examination, ribs, unilateral; 2 views

71101 including posteroanterior chest, minimum of 3 views

71110 Radiologic examination, ribs, bilateral; 3 views

71111 including posteroanterior chest, minimum of 4 views

71120 Radiologic examination; sternum, minimum of 2 views

71130 sternoclavicular joint or joints, minimum of 3 views

71250 Computed tomography, thorax; without contrast material

71260 with contrast material(s)

71270 without contrast material, followed by contrast material(s) and further sections

(For cardiac computed tomography of the heart, see Category III codes 0144T-0151T)

(To report 3D rendering, see 76376, 76377)

71275 Computed tomographic angiography, chest (noncoronary), with contrast material(s), including noncontrast images, if performed, and image postprocessing

(For coronary artery computed tomographic angiography including calcification score and/or cardiac morphology, see Category III codes 0146T-0149T)

71550 Magnetic resonance (eg, proton) imaging, chest (eg, for evaluation of hilar and mediastinal lymphadenopathy); without contrast material(s)

71551 with contrast material(s)

71552 without contrast material(s), followed by contrast material(s) and further sequences

(For breast MRI, see 77058, 77059)

71555 Magnetic resonance angiography, chest (excluding myocardium), with or without contrast material(s)

Spine and Pelvis

72010 Radiologic examination, spine, entire, survey study, anteroposterior and lateral

72020 Radiologic examination, spine, single view, specify level

72040 Radiologic examination, spine, cervical; 2 or 3 views

72050 minimum of 4 views

72052 complete, including oblique and flexion and/or extension studies

72069 Radiologic examination, spine, thoracolumbar, standing (scoliosis)

72070 Radiologic examination, spine; thoracic, 2 views

72072 thoracic, 3 views

72074 thoracic, minimum of 4 views

72080 thoracolumbar, 2 views

72090 scoliosis study, including supine and erect studies

72100 Radiologic examination, spine, lumbosacral; 2 or 3 views

72110 minimum of 4 views

72114 complete, including bending views

72120 Radiologic examination, spine, lumbosacral, bending views only, minimum of 4 views

(Contrast material in CT of spine is either by intrathecal or intravenous injection. For intrathecal injection, use also 61055 or 62284. IV injection of contrast material is part of the CT procedure)

72125 Computed tomography, cervical spine; without contrast material

72126 with contrast material

72127 without contrast material, followed by contrast material(s) and further sections

(For intrathecal injection procedure, see 61055, 62284)

72128 Computed tomography, thoracic spine; without contrast material

72129 with contrast material

(For intrathecal injection procedure, see 61055, 62284)

72130 without contrast material, followed by contrast material(s) and further sections

(For intrathecal injection procedure, see 61055, 62284)

72131 Computed tomography, lumbar spine; without contrast material

72132 with contrast material

72133 without contrast material, followed by contrast material(s) and further sections

(For intrathecal injection procedure, see 61055, 62284)

(To report 3D rendering, see 76376, 76377)

72141 Magnetic resonance (eg, proton) imaging, spinal canal and contents, cervical; without contrast material

72142 with contrast material(s)

(For cervical spinal canal imaging without contrast material followed by contrast material, use 72156)

72146 Magnetic resonance (eg, proton) imaging, spinal canal and contents, thoracic; without contrast material

72147 with contrast material(s)

(For thoracic spinal canal imaging without contrast material followed by contrast material, use 72157)

72148 Magnetic resonance (eg, proton) imaging, spinal canal and contents, lumbar; without contrast material

72149 with contrast material(s)

(For lumbar spinal canal imaging without contrast material followed by contrast material, use 72158)

72156 Magnetic resonance (eg, proton) imaging, spinal canal and contents, without contrast material, followed by contrast material(s) and further sequences; cervical

72157 thoracic

72158 lumbar

72159 Magnetic resonance angiography, spinal canal and contents, with or without contrast material(s)

72170 Radiologic examination, pelvis; 1 or 2 views

72190 complete, minimum of 3 views

(For pelvimetry, use 74710)

72191 Computed tomographic angiography, pelvis, with contrast material(s), including noncontrast images, if performed, and image postprocessing

(For CTA aorto-iliofemoral runoff, use 75635)

72192 Computed tomography, pelvis; without contrast material

72193 with contrast material(s)

72194 without contrast material, followed by contrast material(s) and further sections

(To report 3D rendering, see 76376, 76377)

(For computed tomographic colonography, see Category III codes 0066T, 0067T. Do not report 72192-72194 in conjunction with 0066T, 0067T)

72195 Magnetic resonance (eg, proton) imaging, pelvis; without contrast material(s)

72196 with contrast material(s)

72197 without contrast material(s), followed by contrast material(s) and further sequences

72198 Magnetic resonance angiography, pelvis, with or without contrast material(s)

72200 Radiologic examination, sacroiliac joints; less than 3 views

72202 3 or more views

72220 Radiologic examination, sacrum and coccyx, minimum of 2 views

72240 Myelography, cervical, radiological supervision and interpretation

(For complete cervical myelography, see 61055, 62284, 72240)

72255 Myelography, thoracic, radiological supervision and interpretation

(For complete thoracic myelography, see 61055, 62284, 72255)

72265 Myelography, lumbosacral, radiological supervision and interpretation

(For complete lumbosacral myelography, see 61055, 62284, 72265)

72270 Myelography, 2 or more regions (eg, lumbar/thoracic, cervical/thoracic, lumbar/cervical, lumbar/thoracic/cervical), radiological supervision and interpretation

(For complete myelography of entire spinal canal, see 61055, 62284, 72270)

72275 Epidurography, radiological supervision and interpretation

(72275 includes 77003)

►(For injection procedure, see 62280-62282, 62310-62319, 64479-64484)◄

(Use 72275 only when an epidurogram is performed, images documented, and a formal radiologic report is issued)

72285 Discography, cervical or thoracic, radiological supervision and interpretation

72291 Radiological supervision and interpretation, percutaneous vertebroplasty or vertebral augmentation including cavity creation, per vertebral body; under fluoroscopic guidance

72292 under CT guidance

(For procedure, see 22520-22525)

72295 Discography, lumbar, radiological supervision and interpretation

Upper Extremities

(For stress views, any joint, use 77071)

73000 Radiologic examination; clavicle, complete

73010 scapula, complete

73020 Radiologic examination, shoulder; 1 view

73030 complete, minimum of 2 views

73040 Radiologic examination, shoulder, arthrography, radiological supervision and interpretation

(Do not report 77002 in conjunction with 73040)

73050 Radiologic examination; acromioclavicular joints, bilateral, with or without weighted distraction

73060 humerus, minimum of 2 views

73070 Radiologic examination, elbow; 2 views

73080 complete, minimum of 3 views

73085 Radiologic examination, elbow, arthrography, radiological supervision and interpretation

(Do not report 77002 in conjunction with 73085)

73090 Radiologic examination; forearm, 2 views

73092 upper extremity, infant, minimum of 2 views

73100 Radiologic examination, wrist; 2 views

73110 complete, minimum of 3 views

73115 Radiologic examination, wrist, arthrography, radiological supervision and interpretation

(Do not report 77002 in conjunction with 73115)

73120 Radiologic examination, hand; 2 views

73130 minimum of 3 views

73140 Radiologic examination, finger(s), minimum of 2 views

73200 Computed tomography, upper extremity; without contrast material

73201 with contrast material(s)

73202 without contrast material, followed by contrast material(s) and further sections

(To report 3D rendering, see 76376, 76377)

73206 Computed tomographic angiography, upper extremity, with contrast material(s), including noncontrast images, if performed, and image postprocessing

73218 Magnetic resonance (eg, proton) imaging, upper extremity, other than joint; without contrast material(s)

73219 with contrast material(s)

73220 without contrast material(s), followed by contrast material(s) and further sequences

73221 Magnetic resonance (eg, proton) imaging, any joint of upper extremity; without contrast material(s)

73222 with contrast material(s)

73223 without contrast material(s), followed by contrast material(s) and further sequences

73225 Magnetic resonance angiography, upper extremity, with or without contrast material(s)

Lower Extremities

(For stress views, any joint, use 77071)

73500 Radiologic examination, hip, unilateral; 1 view

73510 complete, minimum of 2 views

73520 Radiologic examination, hips, bilateral, minimum of 2 views of each hip, including anteroposterior view of pelvis

73525 Radiologic examination, hip, arthrography, radiological supervision and interpretation

(Do not report 73525 in conjunction with 77002)

73530 Radiologic examination, hip, during operative procedure

73540 Radiologic examination, pelvis and hips, infant or child, minimum of 2 views

73542 Radiological examination, sacroiliac joint arthrography, radiological supervision and interpretation

(Do not report 73542 in conjunction with 77002)

(For procedure, use 27096. If formal arthrography is not performed, recorded, and a formal radiologic report is not issued, use 77003 for fluoroscopic guidance for sacroiliac joint injections)

73550 Radiologic examination, femur, 2 views

73560 Radiologic examination, knee; 1 or 2 views

73562 3 views

73564 complete, 4 or more views

73565 both knees, standing, anteroposterior

73580 Radiologic examination, knee, arthrography, radiological supervision and interpretation

(Do not report 73580 in conjunction with 77002)

73590 Radiologic examination; tibia and fibula, 2 views

73592 lower extremity, infant, minimum of 2 views

73600 Radiologic examination, ankle; 2 views

73610 complete, minimum of 3 views

73615 Radiologic examination, ankle, arthrography, radiological supervision and interpretation

(Do not report 73615 in conjunction with 77002)

73620 Radiologic examination, foot; 2 views

73630 complete, minimum of 3 views

73650 Radiologic examination; calcaneus, minimum of 2 views

73660 toe(s), minimum of 2 views

73700 Computed tomography, lower extremity; without contrast material

73701 with contrast material(s)

73702 without contrast material, followed by contrast material(s) and further sections

(To report 3D rendering, see 76376, 76377)

73706 Computed tomographic angiography, lower extremity, with contrast material(s), including noncontrast images, if performed, and image postprocessing

(For CTA aorto-iliofemoral runoff, use 75635)

73718 Magnetic resonance (eg, proton) imaging, lower extremity other than joint; without contrast material(s)

73719 with contrast material(s)

73720 without contrast material(s), followed by contrast material(s) and further sequences

73721 Magnetic resonance (eg, proton) imaging, any joint of lower extremity; without contrast material

73722 with contrast material(s)

73723 without contrast material(s), followed by contrast material(s) and further sequences

73725 Magnetic resonance angiography, lower extremity, with or without contrast material(s)

Abdomen

74000 Radiologic examination, abdomen; single anteroposterior view

74010 anteroposterior and additional oblique and cone views

74020 complete, including decubitus and/or erect views

74022 complete acute abdomen series, including supine, erect, and/or decubitus views, single view chest

74150 Computed tomography, abdomen; without contrast material

74160 with contrast material(s)

74170 without contrast material, followed by contrast material(s) and further sections

(To report 3D rendering, see 76376, 76377)

(For computed tomographic colonography, see Category III codes 0066T, 0067T. Do not report 74150-74170 in conjunction with 0066T, 0067T)

74175 Computed tomographic angiography, abdomen, with contrast material(s), including noncontrast images, if performed, and image postprocessing

(For CTA aorto-iliofemoral runoff, use 75635)

74181 Magnetic resonance (eg, proton) imaging, abdomen; without contrast material(s)

74182 with contrast material(s)

74183 without contrast material(s), followed by with contrast material(s) and further sequences

74185 Magnetic resonance angiography, abdomen, with or without contrast material(s)

74190 Peritoneogram (eg, after injection of air or contrast), radiological supervision and interpretation

(For procedure, use 49400)

(For computed tomography, see 72192 or 74150)

Gastrointestinal Tract

(For percutaneous placement of gastrostomy tube, use 43246)

74210 Radiologic examination; pharynx and/or cervical esophagus

74220 esophagus

74230 Swallowing function, with cineradiography/videoradiography

74235 Removal of foreign body(s), esophageal, with use of balloon catheter, radiological supervision and interpretation

(For procedure, see 43215, 43247)

74240 Radiologic examination, gastrointestinal tract, upper; with or without delayed films, without KUB

74241 with or without delayed films, with KUB

74245 with small intestine, includes multiple serial films

74246 Radiological examination, gastrointestinal tract, upper, air contrast, with specific high density barium, effervescent agent, with or without glucagon; with or without delayed films, without KUB

74247 with or without delayed films, with KUB

74249 with small intestine follow-through

74250 Radiologic examination, small intestine, includes multiple serial films;

74251 via enteroclysis tube

74260 Duodenography, hypotonic

▲ **74270** Radiologic examination, colon; contrast (eg, barium) enema, with or without KUB

74280 air contrast with specific high density barium, with or without glucagon

74283 Therapeutic enema, contrast or air, for reduction of intussusception or other intraluminal obstruction (eg, meconium ileus)

74290 Cholecystography, oral contrast;

74291 additional or repeat examination or multiple day examination

74300 Cholangiography and/or pancreatography; intraoperative, radiological supervision and interpretation

✚ **74301** additional set intraoperative, radiological supervision and interpretation (List separately in addition to code for primary procedure)

(Use 74301 in conjunction with 74300)

74305 through existing catheter, radiological supervision and interpretation

(For procedure, see 47505, 48400, 47560-47561, 47563)

(For biliary duct stone extraction, percutaneous, see 47630, 74327)

74320 Cholangiography, percutaneous, transhepatic, radiological supervision and interpretation

74327 Postoperative biliary duct calculus removal, percutaneous via T-tube tract, basket, or snare (eg, Burhenne technique), radiological supervision and interpretation

(For procedure, use 47630)

74328 Endoscopic catheterization of the biliary ductal system, radiological supervision and interpretation

(For procedure, see 43260-43272 as appropriate)

74329 Endoscopic catheterization of the pancreatic ductal system, radiological supervision and interpretation

(For procedure, see 43260-43272 as appropriate)

74330 Combined endoscopic catheterization of the biliary and pancreatic ductal systems, radiological supervision and interpretation

(For procedure, see 43260-43272 as appropriate)

74340 Introduction of long gastrointestinal tube (eg, Miller-Abbott), including multiple fluoroscopies and films, radiological supervision and interpretation

(For tube placement, use 44500)

(74350 has been deleted. To report gastrostomy tube placement, use 49440)

74355 Percutaneous placement of enteroclysis tube, radiological supervision and interpretation

74360 Intraluminal dilation of strictures and/or obstructions (eg, esophagus), radiological supervision and interpretation

74363 Percutaneous transhepatic dilation of biliary duct stricture with or without placement of stent, radiological supervision and interpretation

(For procedure, see 47510, 47511, 47555, 47556)

Urinary Tract

74400 Urography (pyelography), intravenous, with or without KUB, with or without tomography

74410 Urography, infusion, drip technique and/or bolus technique;

74415 with nephrotomography

74420 Urography, retrograde, with or without KUB

74425 Urography, antegrade (pyelostogram, nephrostogram, loopogram), radiological supervision and interpretation

74430 Cystography, minimum of 3 views, radiological supervision and interpretation

74440 Vasography, vesiculography, or epididymography, radiological supervision and interpretation

74445 Corpora cavernosography, radiological supervision and interpretation

74450 Urethrocystography, retrograde, radiological supervision and interpretation

74455 Urethrocystography, voiding, radiological supervision and interpretation

74470 Radiologic examination, renal cyst study, translumbar, contrast visualization, radiological supervision and interpretation

74475 Introduction of intracatheter or catheter into renal pelvis for drainage and/or injection, percutaneous, radiological supervision and interpretation

74480 Introduction of ureteral catheter or stent into ureter through renal pelvis for drainage and/or injection, percutaneous, radiological supervision and interpretation

(For transurethral surgery [ureter and pelvis], see 52320-52355)

74485 Dilation of nephrostomy, ureters, or urethra, radiological supervision and interpretation

(For dilation of ureter without radiologic guidance, use 52341, 52344)

(For change of nephrostomy or pyelostomy tube, use 50398)

Gynecological and Obstetrical

(For abdomen and pelvis, see 72170-72190, 74000-74170)

74710 Pelvimetry, with or without placental localization

74740 Hysterosalpingography, radiological supervision and interpretation

(For introduction of saline or contrast for hysterosalpingography, see 58340)

74742 Transcervical catheterization of fallopian tube, radiological supervision and interpretation

(For procedure, use 58345)

74775 Perineogram (eg, vaginogram, for sex determination or extent of anomalies)

Heart

Cardiac magnetic imaging differs from traditional magnetic resonance imaging (MRI) in its ability to provide a physiologic evaluation of cardiac function. Traditional MRI relies on static images to obtain clinical diagnoses based upon anatomic information. Improvement in spatial and temporal resolution has expanded the application from an anatomic test and includes physiologic evaluation of cardiac function. Flow and velocity assessment for valves and intracardiac shunts is performed in addition to a function and morphologic evaluation. Use 75559 and 75560 to report pharmacologic wall motion stress evaluation without contrast. Use 75563 and 75564 to report pharmacologic perfusion stress with contrast.

Listed procedures may be performed independently or in the course of overall medical care. If the physician providing these services is also responsible for diagnostic workup and/or follow-up care of the patient, see appropriate sections also. Only one procedure in the series 75557-75564 is appropriately reported per session.

Cardiac MRI studies may be performed at rest and/or during pharmacologic stress. Therefore, the appropriate stress testing code from the 93015-93018 series should be reported in addition to 75559, 75560, 75563, 75564.

(For separate injection procedures for vascular radiology, see **Surgery** section, 36000-36299)

(For cardiac catheterization procedures, see 93501-93556)

(75552-75556 have been deleted. To report, see 75557-75564)

75557 Cardiac magnetic resonance imaging for morphology and function without contrast material;

75558 with flow/velocity quantification

75559 with stress imaging

75560 with flow/velocity quantification and stress

75561 Cardiac magnetic resonance imaging for morphology and function without contrast material(s), followed by contrast material(s) and further sequences;

75562 with flow/velocity quantification

75563 with stress imaging

75564 with flow/velocity quantification and stress

(Do not report 75557-75564 in conjunction with 76376, 76377)

Vascular Procedures

Aorta and Arteries

Selective vascular catheterizations should be coded to include introduction and all lesser order selective catheterizations used in the approach (eg, the description for a selective right middle cerebral artery catheterization includes the introduction and placement catheterization of the right common and internal carotid arteries).

Additional second and/or third order arterial catheterizations within the same family of arteries supplied by a single first order artery should be expressed by 36218 or 36248. Additional first order or higher catheterizations in vascular families supplied by a first order vessel different from a previously selected and coded family should be separately coded using the conventions described above.

For angiography performed in conjunction with therapeutic transcatheter radiological supervision and interpretation services, see the **Radiology Transcatheter Procedures** guidelines.

Diagnostic angiography (radiological supervision and interpretation) codes should NOT be used with interventional procedures for:

1. Contrast injections, angiography, roadmapping, and/or fluoroscopic guidance for the intervention,
2. Vessel measurement, and
3. Post-angioplasty/stent angiography,

as this work is captured in the radiological supervision and interpretation code(s).

Diagnostic angiography performed at the time of an interventional procedure is separately reportable if:

1. No prior catheter-based angiographic study is available and a full diagnostic study is performed, and the decision to intervene is based on the diagnostic study, OR
2. A prior study is available, but as documented in the medical record:
   a. The patient's condition with respect to the clinical indication has changed since the prior study, OR
   b. There is inadequate visualization of the anatomy and/or pathology, OR
   c. There is a clinical change during the procedure that requires new evaluation outside the target area of intervention.

Diagnostic angiography performed at a separate setting from an interventional procedure is separately reported.

Diagnostic angiography performed at the time of an interventional procedure is NOT separately reportable if it is specifically included in the interventional code descriptor.

(For intravenous procedure, see 36000-36013, 36400-36425 and 36100-36248 for intra-arterial procedure)

(For radiological supervision and interpretation, see 75600-75978)

75600 Aortography, thoracic, without serialography, radiological supervision and interpretation

(For injection procedure, use 93544)

75605 Aortography, thoracic, by serialography, radiological supervision and interpretation

(For injection procedure, use 93544)

75625 Aortography, abdominal, by serialography, radiological supervision and interpretation

(For injection procedure, use 93544)

75630 Aortography, abdominal plus bilateral iliofemoral lower extremity, catheter, by serialography, radiological supervision and interpretation

75635 Computed tomographic angiography, abdominal aorta and bilateral iliofemoral lower extremity runoff, with contrast material(s), including noncontrast images, if performed, and image postprocessing

75650 Angiography, cervicocerebral, catheter, including vessel origin, radiological supervision and interpretation

75658 Angiography, brachial, retrograde, radiological supervision and interpretation

75660 Angiography, external carotid, unilateral, selective, radiological supervision and interpretation

75662 Angiography, external carotid, bilateral, selective, radiological supervision and interpretation

75665 Angiography, carotid, cerebral, unilateral, radiological supervision and interpretation

75671 Angiography, carotid, cerebral, bilateral, radiological supervision and interpretation

75676 Angiography, carotid, cervical, unilateral, radiological supervision and interpretation

75680 Angiography, carotid, cervical, bilateral, radiological supervision and interpretation

75685 Angiography, vertebral, cervical, and/or intracranial, radiological supervision and interpretation

75705 Angiography, spinal, selective, radiological supervision and interpretation

75710 Angiography, extremity, unilateral, radiological supervision and interpretation

75716 Angiography, extremity, bilateral, radiological supervision and interpretation

75722 Angiography, renal, unilateral, selective (including flush aortogram), radiological supervision and interpretation

75724 Angiography, renal, bilateral, selective (including flush aortogram), radiological supervision and interpretation

75726 Angiography, visceral, selective or supraselective (with or without flush aortogram), radiological supervision and interpretation

(For selective angiography, each additional visceral vessel studied after basic examination, use 75774)

75731 Angiography, adrenal, unilateral, selective, radiological supervision and interpretation

75733 Angiography, adrenal, bilateral, selective, radiological supervision and interpretation

75736 Angiography, pelvic, selective or supraselective, radiological supervision and interpretation

75741 Angiography, pulmonary, unilateral, selective, radiological supervision and interpretation

(For injection procedure, use 93541)

75743 Angiography, pulmonary, bilateral, selective, radiological supervision and interpretation

(For injection procedure, use 93541)

75746 Angiography, pulmonary, by nonselective catheter or venous injection, radiological supervision and interpretation

(For injection procedure, use 93541)

(For introduction of catheter, injection procedure, see 93501-93533, 93539, 93540, 93545, 93556)

75756 Angiography, internal mammary, radiological supervision and interpretation

(For introduction of catheter, injection procedure, see 93501-93533, 93545, 93556)

+ 75774 Angiography, selective, each additional vessel studied after basic examination, radiological supervision and interpretation (List separately in addition to code for primary procedure)

(Use 75774 in addition to code for specific initial vessel studied)

(For angiography, see codes 75600-75790)

(For catheterizations, see codes 36215-36248)

(For introduction of catheter, injection procedure, see 93501-93533, 93545, 93555, 93556)

75790 Angiography, arteriovenous shunt (eg, dialysis patient), radiological supervision and interpretation

(For introduction of catheter, use 36140, 36145, 36215-36217, 36245-36247)

Veins and Lymphatics

For venography performed in conjunction with therapeutic transcatheter radiological supervision and interpretation services, see the **Radiology Transcatheter Procedures** guidelines.

Diagnostic venography (radiological supervision and interpretation) codes should NOT be used with interventional procedures for:

1. Contrast injections, venography, roadmapping, and/or fluoroscopic guidance for the intervention,
2. Vessel measurement, and
3. Post-angioplasty/stent venography,

as this work is captured in the radiological supervision and interpretation code(s).

Diagnostic venography performed at the time of an interventional procedure is separately reportable if:

1. No prior catheter-based venographic study is available and a full diagnostic study is performed, and decision to intervene is based on the diagnostic study, OR
2. A prior study is available, but as documented in the medical record:
   a. The patient's condition with respect to the clinical indication has changed since the prior study, OR
   b. There is inadequate visualization of the anatomy and/or pathology, OR
   c. There is a clinical change during the procedure that requires new evaluation outside the target area of intervention.

Diagnostic venography performed at a separate setting from an interventional procedure is separately reported.

Radiology

Diagnostic venography performed at the time of an interventional procedure is NOT separately reportable if it is specifically included in the interventional code descriptor.

(For injection procedure for venous system, see 36000-36015, 36400-36510)

(For injection procedure for lymphatic system, use 38790)

75801 Lymphangiography, extremity only, unilateral, radiological supervision and interpretation

75803 Lymphangiography, extremity only, bilateral, radiological supervision and interpretation

75805 Lymphangiography, pelvic/abdominal, unilateral, radiological supervision and interpretation

75807 Lymphangiography, pelvic/abdominal, bilateral, radiological supervision and interpretation

75809 Shuntogram for investigation of previously placed indwelling nonvascular shunt (eg, LeVeen shunt, ventriculoperitoneal shunt, indwelling infusion pump), radiological supervision and interpretation

(For procedure, see 49427 or 61070)

75810 Splenoportography, radiological supervision and interpretation

75820 Venography, extremity, unilateral, radiological supervision and interpretation

75822 Venography, extremity, bilateral, radiological supervision and interpretation

75825 Venography, caval, inferior, with serialography, radiological supervision and interpretation

75827 Venography, caval, superior, with serialography, radiological supervision and interpretation

75831 Venography, renal, unilateral, selective, radiological supervision and interpretation

75833 Venography, renal, bilateral, selective, radiological supervision and interpretation

75840 Venography, adrenal, unilateral, selective, radiological supervision and interpretation

75842 Venography, adrenal, bilateral, selective, radiological supervision and interpretation

75860 Venography, venous sinus (eg, petrosal and inferior sagittal) or jugular, catheter, radiological supervision and interpretation

75870 Venography, superior sagittal sinus, radiological supervision and interpretation

75872 Venography, epidural, radiological supervision and interpretation

75880 Venography, orbital, radiological supervision and interpretation

75885 Percutaneous transhepatic portography with hemodynamic evaluation, radiological supervision and interpretation

75887 Percutaneous transhepatic portography without hemodynamic evaluation, radiological supervision and interpretation

75889 Hepatic venography, wedged or free, with hemodynamic evaluation, radiological supervision and interpretation

75891 Hepatic venography, wedged or free, without hemodynamic evaluation, radiological supervision and interpretation

75893 Venous sampling through catheter, with or without angiography (eg, for parathyroid hormone, renin), radiological supervision and interpretation

(For procedure, use 36500)

Transcatheter Procedures

Therapeutic transcatheter radiological supervision and interpretation code(s) include the following services associated with that intervention:

1. Contrast injections, angiography/venography, roadmapping, and fluoroscopic guidance for the intervention,
2. Vessel measurement, and
3. Completion angiography/venography (except for those uses permitted by 75898).

Unless specifically included in the code descriptor, diagnostic angiography/venography performed at the time of transcatheter therapeutic radiological and interpretation service(s) is separately reportable (eg, no prior catheter-based diagnostic angiography/venography study of the target vessel is available, prior diagnostic study is inadequate, patient's condition with respect to the clinical indication has changed since the prior study or during the intervention). See 75600-75893.

Codes 75956 and 75957 include all angiography of the thoracic aorta and its branches for diagnostic imaging prior to deployment of the primary endovascular devices (including all routine components of modular devices), fluoroscopic guidance in the delivery of the endovascular components, and intraprocedural arterial angiography (eg, confirm position, detect endoleak, evaluate runoff).

Code 75958 includes the analogous services for placement of each proximal thoracic endovascular extension. Code 75959 includes the analogous services for placement of a distal thoracic endovascular extension(s) placed during a procedure after the primary repair.

75894 Transcatheter therapy, embolization, any method, radiological supervision and interpretation

(For uterine fibroid embolization [uterine artery embolization performed to treat uterine fibroids], use 37210)

(For obstetrical and gynecologic embolization procedures other than uterine fibroid embolization [eg, embolization to treat obstetrical or postpartum hemorrhage], use 37204)

75896 Transcatheter therapy, infusion, any method (eg, thrombolysis other than coronary), radiological supervision and interpretation

(For infusion for coronary disease, see 92975, 92977)

75898 Angiography through existing catheter for follow-up study for transcatheter therapy, embolization or infusion

75900 Exchange of a previously placed intravascular catheter during thrombolytic therapy with contrast monitoring, radiological supervision and interpretation

(For procedure, use 37209)

75901 Mechanical removal of pericatheter obstructive material (eg, fibrin sheath) from central venous device via separate venous access, radiologic supervision and interpretation

(For procedure, use 36595)

(For venous catheterization, see 36010-36012)

75902 Mechanical removal of intraluminal (intracatheter) obstructive material from central venous device through device lumen, radiologic supervision and interpretation

(For procedure, use 36596)

(For venous catheterization, see 36010-36012)

75940 Percutaneous placement of IVC filter, radiological supervision and interpretation

75945 Intravascular ultrasound (non-coronary vessel), radiological supervision and interpretation; initial vessel

+ 75946 each additional non-coronary vessel (List separately in addition to code for primary procedure)

(Use 75946 in conjunction with 75945)

(For catheterizations, see codes 36215-36248)

(For transcatheter therapies, see codes 37200-37208, 61624, 61626)

(For procedure, see 37250, 37251)

75952 Endovascular repair of infrarenal abdominal aortic aneurysm or dissection, radiological supervision and interpretation

(For implantation of endovascular grafts, see 34800-34808)

(For radiologic supervision and interpretation of endovascular repair of abdominal aortic aneurysm involving visceral vessels, see Category III codes 0078T-0081T)

75953 Placement of proximal or distal extension prosthesis for endovascular repair of infrarenal aortic or iliac artery aneurysm, pseudoaneurysm, or dissection, radiological supervision and interpretation

(For implantation of endovascular extension prostheses, see 34825, 34826)

75954 Endovascular repair of iliac artery aneurysm, pseudoaneurysm, arteriovenous malformation, or trauma, radiological supervision and interpretation

(For implantation of endovascular graft, see 34900)

75956 Endovascular repair of descending thoracic aorta (eg, aneurysm, pseudoaneurysm, dissection, penetrating ulcer, intramural hematoma, or traumatic disruption); involving coverage of left subclavian artery origin, initial endoprosthesis plus descending thoracic aortic extension(s), if required, to level of celiac artery origin, radiological supervision and interpretation

(For implantation of endovascular graft, use 33880)

75957 not involving coverage of left subclavian artery origin, initial endoprosthesis plus descending thoracic aortic extension(s), if required, to level of celiac artery origin, radiological supervision and interpretation

(For implantation of endovascular graft, use 33881)

75958 Placement of proximal extension prosthesis for endovascular repair of descending thoracic aorta (eg, aneurysm, pseudoaneurysm, dissection, penetrating ulcer, intramural hematoma, or traumatic disruption), radiological supervision and interpretation

(Report 75958 for each proximal extension)

(For implantation of proximal endovascular extension, see 33883, 33884)

75959 Placement of distal extension prosthesis(s) (delayed) after endovascular repair of descending thoracic aorta, as needed, to level of celiac origin, radiological supervision and interpretation

(Do not report 75959 in conjunction with 75956, 75957)

(Report 75959 once, regardless of number of modules deployed)

(For implantation of distal endovascular extension, use 33886)

75960 Transcatheter introduction of intravascular stent(s) (except coronary, carotid, and vertebral vessel), percutaneous and/or open, radiological supervision and interpretation, each vessel

(For procedure, see 37205-37208)

(For radiologic supervision and interpretation for transcatheter placement of extracranial vertebral or intrathoracic carotid artery stent(s), see Category III codes 0075T, 0076T)

75961 Transcatheter retrieval, percutaneous, of intravascular foreign body (eg, fractured venous or arterial catheter), radiological supervision and interpretation

(For procedure, use 37203)

75962 Transluminal balloon angioplasty, peripheral artery, radiological supervision and interpretation

+ 75964 Transluminal balloon angioplasty, each additional peripheral artery, radiological supervision and interpretation (List separately in addition to code for primary procedure)

(Use 75964 in conjunction with 75962)

75966 Transluminal balloon angioplasty, renal or other visceral artery, radiological supervision and interpretation

+ 75968 Transluminal balloon angioplasty, each additional visceral artery, radiological supervision and interpretation (List separately in addition to code for primary procedure)

(Use 75968 in conjunction with 75966)

(For percutaneous transluminal coronary angioplasty, see 92982-92984)

75970 Transcatheter biopsy, radiological supervision and interpretation

(For injection procedure only for transcatheter therapy or biopsy, see 36100-36299)

(For transcatheter renal and ureteral biopsy, use 52007)

(For percutaneous needle biopsy of pancreas, use 48102; of retroperitoneal lymph node or mass, use 49180)

75978 Transluminal balloon angioplasty, venous (eg, subclavian stenosis), radiological supervision and interpretation

75980 Percutaneous transhepatic biliary drainage with contrast monitoring, radiological supervision and interpretation

75982 Percutaneous placement of drainage catheter for combined internal and external biliary drainage or of a drainage stent for internal biliary drainage in patients with an inoperable mechanical biliary obstruction, radiological supervision and interpretation

75984 Change of percutaneous tube or drainage catheter with contrast monitoring (eg, genitourinary system, abscess), radiological supervision and interpretation

(For percutaneous replacement of gastrostomy, duodenostomy, jejunostomy, gastro-jejunostomy, or cecostomy [or other colonic] tube including fluoroscopic imaging guidance, see 49450-49452)

(For change of nephrostomy or pyelostomy tube only, use 50398)

(For introduction procedure only for percutaneous biliary drainage, see 47510, 47511)

(For percutaneous cholecystostomy, use 47490)

(For change of percutaneous biliary drainage catheter only, use 47525)

(For percutaneous nephrostolithotomy or pyelostolithotomy, see 50080, 50081)

(For removal and/or replacement of an internally dwelling ureteral stent via a transurethral approach, see 50385-50386)

75989 Radiological guidance (ie, fluoroscopy, ultrasound, or computed tomography), for percutaneous drainage (eg, abscess, specimen collection), with placement of catheter, radiological supervision and interpretation

Transluminal Atherectomy

75992 Transluminal atherectomy, peripheral artery, radiological supervision and interpretation

(For procedure, see 35481-35485, 35491-35495)

+ 75993 Transluminal atherectomy, each additional peripheral artery, radiological supervision and interpretation (List separately in addition to code for primary procedure)

(Use 75993 in conjunction with 75992)

(For procedure, see 35481-35485, 35491-35495)

75994 Transluminal atherectomy, renal, radiological supervision and interpretation

(For procedure, see 35480, 35490)

75995 Transluminal atherectomy, visceral, radiological supervision and interpretation

(For procedure, see 35480, 35490)

+ 75996 Transluminal atherectomy, each additional visceral artery, radiological supervision and interpretation (List separately in addition to code for primary procedure)

(Use 75996 in conjunction with 75995)

(For procedure, see 35480, 35490)

Other Procedures

(For computed tomography cerebral perfusion analysis, see Category III code 0042T)

(For arthrography of shoulder, use 73040; elbow, use 73085; wrist, use 73115; hip, use 73525; knee, use 73580; ankle, use 73615)

(75998 has been deleted. To report, use 77001)

76000 Fluoroscopy (separate procedure), up to 1 hour physician time, other than 71023 or 71034 (eg, cardiac fluoroscopy)

76001 Fluoroscopy, physician time more than 1 hour, assisting a nonradiologic physician (eg, nephrostolithotomy, ERCP, bronchoscopy, transbronchial biopsy)

(76003 has been deleted. To report, use 77002)

(76005 has been deleted. To report, use 77003)

(76006 has been deleted. To report, use 77071)

76010 Radiologic examination from nose to rectum for foreign body, single view, child

(76012, 76013 have been deleted. To report, see 72291, 72292)

(76020 has been deleted. To report, use 77072)

(76040 has been deleted. To report, use 77073)

(76061, 76062 have been deleted. To report, see 77074, 77075)

(76065 has been deleted. To report, use 77076)

(76066 has been deleted. To report, use 77077)

(76070, 76071 have been deleted. To report, see 77078, 77079)

(76075-76077 have been deleted. To report, see 77080-77082)

(76078 has been deleted. To report, use 77083)

76080 Radiologic examination, abscess, fistula or sinus tract study, radiological supervision and interpretation

(For contrast injection[s] and radiological assessment of gastrostomy, duodenostomy, jejunostomy, gastro-jejunostomy, or cecostomy [or other colonic] tube including fluoroscopic imaging guidance, use 49465)

(76082, 76083 have been deleted. To report, see 77051, 77052)

(76085 has been deleted. To report, see 77051, 77052)

(76086 has been deleted. To report, use 77053)

(76088 has been deleted. To report, use 77054)

(76090, 76091 have been deleted. To report, see 77055, 77056)

(76092 has been deleted. To report, use 77057)

(76093, 76094 have been deleted. To report, see 77058, 77059)

(76095 has been deleted. To report, use 77031)

(76096 has been deleted. To report, use 77032)

76098 Radiological examination, surgical specimen

76100 Radiologic examination, single plane body section (eg, tomography), other than with urography

76101 Radiologic examination, complex motion (ie, hypercycloidal) body section (eg, mastoid polytomography), other than with urography; unilateral

76102 bilateral

(For nephrotomography, use 74415)

76120 Cineradiography/videoradiography, except where specifically included

+ 76125 Cineradiography/videoradiography to complement routine examination (List separately in addition to code for primary procedure)

76140 Consultation on X-ray examination made elsewhere, written report

76150 Xeroradiography

(76150 is to be used for non-mammographic studies only)

76350 Subtraction in conjunction with contrast studies

(76355 has been deleted. To report, use 77011)

(76360 has been deleted. To report, use 77012)

(76362 has been deleted. To report, use 77013)

(76370 has been deleted. To report, use 77014)

(2D reformatting is no longer separately reported. To report 3D rendering, see 76376, 76377)

(76376, 76377 require concurrent physician supervision of image postprocessing 3D manipulation of volumetric data set and image rendering)

76376 3D rendering with interpretation and reporting of computed tomography, magnetic resonance imaging, ultrasound, or other tomographic modality; not requiring image postprocessing on an independent workstation

(Use 76376 in conjunction with code[s] for base imaging procedure[s])

(Do not report 76376 in conjunction with 70496, 70498, 70544-70549, 71275, 71555, 72159, 72191, 72198, 73206, 73225, 73706, 73725, 74175, 74185, 75635, 75557-75564, 76377, 78000-78999, 0066T, 0067T, 0144T-0151T, 0159T)

76377 requiring image postprocessing on an independent workstation

(Use 76377 in conjunction with code[s] for base imaging procedure[s])

(Do not report 76377 in conjunction with 70496, 70498, 70544-70549, 71275, 71555, 72159, 72191, 72198, 73206, 73225, 73706, 73725, 74175, 74185, 75557-75564, 75635, 76376, 78000-78999, 0066T, 0067T, 0144T-0151T, 0159T)

(To report computer-aided detection, including computer algorithm analysis of MRI data for lesion detection/characterization, pharmacokinetic analysis, breast MRI, use Category III code 0159T)

76380 Computed tomography, limited or localized follow-up study

76390 Magnetic resonance spectroscopy

(For magnetic resonance imaging, use appropriate MRI body site code)

(76393 has been deleted. To report, use 77021)

(76394 has been deleted. To report, use 77022)

(76400 has been deleted. To report, use 77084)

76496 Unlisted fluoroscopic procedure (eg, diagnostic, interventional)

76497 Unlisted computed tomography procedure (eg, diagnostic, interventional)

76498 Unlisted magnetic resonance procedure (eg, diagnostic, interventional)

76499 Unlisted diagnostic radiographic procedure

Diagnostic Ultrasound

All diagnostic ultrasound examinations require permanently recorded images with measurements, when such measurements are clinically indicated. For those codes whose sole diagnostic goal is a biometric measure (ie, 76514, 76516, and 76519), permanently recorded images are not required. A final, written report should be issued for inclusion in the patient's medical record. The prescription form for the intraocular lens satisfies the written report requirement for 76519. For those anatomic regions that have "complete" and "limited" ultrasound codes, note the elements that comprise a "complete" exam. The report should contain a description of these elements or the reason that an element could not be visualized (eg, obscured by bowel gas, surgically absent).

If less than the required elements for a "complete" exam are reported (eg, limited number of organs or limited portion of region evaluated), the "limited" code for that anatomic region should be used once per patient exam session. A "limited" exam of an anatomic region should not be reported for the same exam session as a "complete" exam of that same region.

Evaluation of vascular structures using both color and spectral Doppler is separately reportable. To report, see **Noninvasive Vascular Diagnostic Studies** (93875-93990). However, color Doppler alone, when performed for anatomic structure identification in conjunction with a real-time ultrasound examination, is not reported separately.

Ultrasound guidance procedures also require permanently recorded images of the site to be localized, as well as a documented description of the localization process, either separately or within the report of the procedure for which the guidance is utilized.

Use of ultrasound, without thorough evaluation of organ(s) or anatomic region, image documentation, and final, written report, is not separately reportable.

Definitions

A-mode implies a one-dimensional ultrasonic measurement procedure.

M-mode implies a one-dimensional ultrasonic measurement procedure with movement of the trace to record amplitude and velocity of moving echo-producing structures.

B-scan implies a two-dimensional ultrasonic scanning procedure with a two-dimensional display.

Real-time scan implies a two-dimensional ultrasonic scanning procedure with display of both two-dimensional structure and motion with time.

(To report diagnostic vascular ultrasound studies, see 93875-93990)

(For focused ultrasound ablation treatment of uterine leiomyomata, see Category III codes 0071T, 0072T)

Radiology

Head and Neck

76506 Echoencephalography, real time with image documentation (gray scale) (for determination of ventricular size, delineation of cerebral contents, and detection of fluid masses or other intracranial abnormalities), including A-mode encephalography as secondary component where indicated

76510 Ophthalmic ultrasound, diagnostic; B-scan and quantitative A-scan performed during the same patient encounter

76511 quantitative A-scan only

76512 B-scan (with or without superimposed non-quantitative A-scan)

76513 anterior segment ultrasound, immersion (water bath) B-scan or high resolution biomicroscopy

►(For scanning computerized ophthalmic diagnostic imaging of the anterior and posterior segments using technology other than ultrasound, see 92135, 0187T)◄

76514 corneal pachymetry, unilateral or bilateral (determination of corneal thickness)

76516 Ophthalmic biometry by ultrasound echography, A-scan;

76519 with intraocular lens power calculation

(For partial coherence interferometry, use 92136)

76529 Ophthalmic ultrasonic foreign body localization

76536 Ultrasound, soft tissues of head and neck (eg, thyroid, parathyroid, parotid), real time with image documentation

Chest

76604 Ultrasound, chest (includes mediastinum), real time with image documentation

76645 Ultrasound, breast(s) (unilateral or bilateral), real time with image documentation

Abdomen and Retroperitoneum

A complete ultrasound examination of the abdomen (76700) consists of real time scans of the liver, gall bladder, common bile duct, pancreas, spleen, kidneys, and the upper abdominal aorta and inferior vena cava including any demonstrated abdominal abnormality.

A complete ultrasound examination of the retroperitoneum (76770) consists of real time scans of the kidneys, abdominal aorta, common iliac artery origins, and inferior vena cava, including any demonstrated retroperitoneal abnormality. Alternatively, if clinical history suggests urinary tract pathology, complete evaluation of the kidneys and urinary bladder also comprises a complete retroperitoneal ultrasound.

Use of ultrasound, without thorough evaluation of organ(s) or anatomic region, image documentation and final, written report, is not separately reportable.

76700 Ultrasound, abdominal, real time with image documentation; complete

76705 limited (eg, single organ, quadrant, follow-up)

76770 Ultrasound, retroperitoneal (eg, renal, aorta, nodes), real time with image documentation; complete

76775 limited

76776 Ultrasound, transplanted kidney, real time and duplex Doppler with image documentation

(For ultrasound of transplanted kidney without duplex Doppler, use 76775)

(Do not report 76776 in conjunction with 93975, 93976)

(76778 has been deleted. To report, see 76775, 76776)

Spinal Canal

76800 Ultrasound, spinal canal and contents

Pelvis

Obstetrical

Codes 76801 and 76802 include determination of the number of gestational sacs and fetuses, gestational sac/fetal measurements appropriate for gestation (younger than 14 weeks 0 days), survey of visible fetal and placental anatomic structure, qualitative assessment of amniotic fluid volume/gestational sac shape and examination of the maternal uterus and adnexa.

Codes 76805 and 76810 include determination of number of fetuses and amniotic/chorionic sacs, measurements appropriate for gestational age (older than or equal to 14 weeks 0 days), survey of intracranial/spinal/abdominal anatomy, 4 chambered heart, umbilical cord insertion site, placenta location and amniotic fluid assessment and, when visible, examination of maternal adnexa.

Codes 76811 and 76812 include all elements of codes 76805 and 76810 plus detailed anatomic evaluation of the fetal brain/ventricles, face, heart/outflow tracts and chest anatomy, abdominal organ specific anatomy, number/length/architecture of limbs and detailed evaluation of the umbilical cord and placenta and other fetal anatomy as clinically indicated.

Report should document the results of the evaluation of each element described above or the reason for non-visualization.

Code 76815 represents a focused "quick look" exam limited to the assessment of one or more of the elements listed in code 76815.

Code 76816 describes an examination designed to reassess fetal size and interval growth or reevaluate one or more anatomic abnormalities of a fetus previously demonstrated on ultrasound, and should be coded once for each fetus requiring reevaluation using modifier 59 for each fetus after the first.

Code 76817 describes a transvaginal obstetric ultrasound performed separately or in addition to one of the transabdominal examinations described above. For transvaginal examinations performed for non-obstetrical purposes, use code 76830.

76801 Ultrasound, pregnant uterus, real time with image documentation, fetal and maternal evaluation, first trimester (< 14 weeks 0 days), transabdominal approach; single or first gestation

(To report first trimester fetal nuchal translucency measurement, use 76813)

+ 76802 each additional gestation (List separately in addition to code for primary procedure)

(Use 76802 in conjunction with 76801)

(To report first trimester fetal nuchal translucency measurement, use 76814)

76805 Ultrasound, pregnant uterus, real time with image documentation, fetal and maternal evaluation, after first trimester (> or = 14 weeks 0 days), transabdominal approach; single or first gestation

+ 76810 each additional gestation (List separately in addition to code for primary procedure)

(Use 76810 in conjunction with 76805)

76811 Ultrasound, pregnant uterus, real time with image documentation, fetal and maternal evaluation plus detailed fetal anatomic examination, transabdominal approach; single or first gestation

+ 76812 each additional gestation (List separately in addition to code for primary procedure)

(Use 76812 in conjunction with 76811)

76813 Ultrasound, pregnant uterus, real time with image documentation, first trimester fetal nuchal translucency measurement, transabdominal or transvaginal approach; single or first gestation

+ 76814 each additional gestation (List separately in addition to code for primary procedure)

(Use 76814 in conjunction with 76813)

76815 Ultrasound, pregnant uterus, real time with image documentation, limited (eg, fetal heart beat, placental location, fetal position and/or qualitative amniotic fluid volume), 1 or more fetuses

(Use 76815 only once per exam and not per element)

(To report first trimester fetal nuchal translucency measurement, see 76813, 76814)

76816 Ultrasound, pregnant uterus, real time with image documentation, follow-up (eg, re-evaluation of fetal size by measuring standard growth parameters and amniotic fluid volume, re-evaluation of organ system(s) suspected or confirmed to be abnormal on a previous scan), transabdominal approach, per fetus

(Report 76816 with modifier 59 for each additional fetus examined in a multiple pregnancy)

76817 Ultrasound, pregnant uterus, real time with image documentation, transvaginal

(For non-obstetrical transvaginal ultrasound, use 76830)

(If transvaginal examination is done in addition to transabdominal obstetrical ultrasound exam, use 76817 in addition to appropriate transabdominal exam code)

76818 Fetal biophysical profile; with non-stress testing

76819 without non-stress testing

(Fetal biophysical profile assessments for the second and any additional fetuses, should be reported separately by code 76818 or 76819 with the modifier 59 appended)

(For amniotic fluid index without non-stress test, use 76815)

76820 Doppler velocimetry, fetal; umbilical artery

76821 middle cerebral artery

76825 Echocardiography, fetal, cardiovascular system, real time with image documentation (2D), with or without M-mode recording;

76826 follow-up or repeat study

76827 Doppler echocardiography, fetal, pulsed wave and/or continuous wave with spectral display; complete

76828 follow-up or repeat study

(To report the use of color mapping, use 93325)

Nonobstetrical

Code 76856 includes the complete evaluation of the female pelvic anatomy. Elements of this examination include a description and measurements of the uterus and adnexal structures, measurement of the endometrium, measurement of the bladder (when applicable), and a description of any pelvic pathology (eg, ovarian cysts, uterine leiomyomata, free pelvic fluid).

Code 76856 is also applicable to a complete evaluation of the male pelvis. Elements of the examination include evaluation and measurement (when applicable) of the urinary bladder, evaluation of the prostate and seminal vesicles to the extent that they are visualized transabdominally, and any pelvic pathology (eg, bladder tumor, enlarged prostate, free pelvic fluid, pelvic abscess).

Code 76857 represents a focused examination limited to the assessment of one or more elements listed in code 76856 and/or the reevaluation of one or more pelvic abnormalities previously demonstrated on ultrasound. Code 76857, rather than 76770, should be utilized if the urinary bladder alone (ie, not including the kidneys) is imaged, whereas code 51798 should be utilized if a bladder volume or post-void residual measurement is obtained without imaging the bladder.

Use of ultrasound, without thorough evaluation of organ(s) or anatomic region, image documentation, and final, written report, is not separately reportable.

76830 Ultrasound, transvaginal

(For obstetrical transvaginal ultrasound, use 76817)

(If transvaginal examination is done in addition to transabdominal non-obstetrical ultrasound exam, use 76830 in addition to appropriate transabdominal exam code)

76831 Saline infusion sonohysterography (SIS), including color flow Doppler, when performed

(For introduction of saline for saline infusion sonohysterography, use 58340)

76856 Ultrasound, pelvic (nonobstetric), real time with image documentation; complete

76857 limited or follow-up (eg, for follicles)

Genitalia

76870 Ultrasound, scrotum and contents

76872 Ultrasound, transrectal;

76873 prostate volume study for brachytherapy treatment planning (separate procedure)

Extremities

76880 Ultrasound, extremity, nonvascular, real time with image documentation

76885 Ultrasound, infant hips, real time with imaging documentation; dynamic (requiring physician manipulation)

76886 limited, static (not requiring physician manipulation)

Ultrasonic Guidance Procedures

76930 Ultrasonic guidance for pericardiocentesis, imaging supervision and interpretation

76932 Ultrasonic guidance for endomyocardial biopsy, imaging supervision and interpretation

76936 Ultrasound guided compression repair of arterial pseudoaneurysm or arteriovenous fistulae (includes diagnostic ultrasound evaluation, compression of lesion and imaging)

+ 76937 Ultrasound guidance for vascular access requiring ultrasound evaluation of potential access sites, documentation of selected vessel patency, concurrent realtime ultrasound visualization of vascular needle entry, with permanent recording and reporting (List separately in addition to code for primary procedure)

(Do not use 76937 in conjunction with 76942)

(If extremity venous non-invasive vascular diagnostic study is performed separate from venous access guidance, use 93965, 93970 or 93971)

76940 Ultrasound guidance for, and monitoring of, parenchymal tissue ablation

(Do not report 76940 in conjunction with 76998)

(For ablation, see 32998, 47370-47382, 50592, 50593)

76941 Ultrasonic guidance for intrauterine fetal transfusion or cordocentesis, imaging supervision and interpretation

(For procedure, see 36460, 59012)

76942 Ultrasonic guidance for needle placement (eg, biopsy, aspiration, injection, localization device), imaging supervision and interpretation

(Do not report 76942 in conjunction with 43232, 43237, 43242, 45341, 45342, or 76975)

76945 Ultrasonic guidance for chorionic villus sampling, imaging supervision and interpretation

(For procedure, use 59015)

76946 Ultrasonic guidance for amniocentesis, imaging supervision and interpretation

76948 Ultrasonic guidance for aspiration of ova, imaging supervision and interpretation

76950 Ultrasonic guidance for placement of radiation therapy fields

76965 Ultrasonic guidance for interstitial radioelement application

Other Procedures

76970 Ultrasound study follow-up (specify)

76975 Gastrointestinal endoscopic ultrasound, supervision and interpretation

(Do not report 76975 in conjunction with 43231, 43232, 43237, 43238, 43242, 43259, 45341, 45342, or 76942)

76977 Ultrasound bone density measurement and interpretation, peripheral site(s), any method

(76986 has been deleted. To report, use 76998)

76998 Ultrasonic guidance, intraoperative

►(Do not report 76998 in conjunction with 47370-47382, 36475-36479)◄

(For ultrasound guidance for open and laparoscopic radiofrequency tissue ablation, use 76940)

76999 Unlisted ultrasound procedure (eg, diagnostic, interventional)

Radiologic Guidance

Fluoroscopic Guidance

+ 77001 Fluoroscopic guidance for central venous access device placement, replacement (catheter only or complete), or removal (includes fluoroscopic guidance for vascular access and catheter manipulation, any necessary contrast injections through access site or catheter with related venography radiologic supervision and interpretation, and radiographic documentation of final catheter position) (List separately in addition to code for primary procedure)

(Do not use 77001 in conjunction with 77002)

(If formal extremity venography is performed from separate venous access and separately interpreted, use 36005 and 75820, 75822, 75825, or 75827)

77002 Fluoroscopic guidance for needle placement (eg, biopsy, aspiration, injection, localization device)

(See appropriate surgical code for procedure and anatomic location)

(77002 includes all radiographic arthrography with the exception of supervision and interpretation for CT and MR arthrography)

(Do not report 77002 in addition to 70332, 73040, 73085, 73115, 73525, 73580, 73615)

(77002 is included in the organ/anatomic specific radiological supervision and interpretation procedures 49440, 74320, 74355, 74445, 74470, 74475, 75809, 75810, 75885, 75887, 75980, 75982, 75989)

77003 Fluoroscopic guidance and localization of needle or catheter tip for spine or paraspinous diagnostic or therapeutic injection procedures (epidural, transforaminal epidural, subarachnoid, paravertebral facet joint, paravertebral facet joint nerve, or sacroiliac joint), including neurolytic agent destruction

►(Injection of contrast during fluoroscopic guidance and localization [77003] is included in 22526, 22527, 62263, 62264, 62267, 62270-62282, 62310-62319)◄

(Fluoroscopic guidance for subarachnoid puncture for diagnostic radiographic myelography is included in supervision and interpretation codes 72240-72270)

(For epidural or subarachnoid needle or catheter placement and injection, see 62270-62282, 62310-62319)

(For sacroiliac joint arthrography, see 27096, 73542. If formal arthrography is not performed and recorded, and a formal radiographic report is not issued, use 77003 for fluoroscopic guidance for sacroiliac joint injections)

(For paravertebral facet joint injection, see 64470-64476. For transforaminal epidural needle placement and injection, see 64479-64484)

(For destruction by neurolytic agent, see 64600-64680)

►(For percutaneous or endoscopic lysis of epidural adhesions, 62263, 62264 include fluoroscopic guidance and localization)◄

Computed Tomography Guidance

77011 Computed tomography guidance for stereotactic localization

77012 Computed tomography guidance for needle placement (eg, biopsy, aspiration, injection, localization device), radiological supervision and interpretation

77013 Computed tomography guidance for, and monitoring of, parenchymal tissue ablation

(Do not report 77013 in conjunction with 20982)

(For percutaneous radiofrequency ablation, see 32998, 47382, 50592, 50593)

77014 Computed tomography guidance for placement of radiation therapy fields

(For placement of interstitial device[s] for radiation therapy guidance, prostate, use 55876)

Magnetic Resonance Guidance

77021 Magnetic resonance guidance for needle placement (eg, for biopsy, needle aspiration, injection, or placement of localization device) radiological supervision and interpretation

(For procedure, see appropriate organ or site)

77022 Magnetic resonance guidance for, and monitoring of, parenchymal tissue ablation

(For percutaneous radiofrequency ablation, see 32998, 47382, 50592, 50593)

(For focused ultrasound ablation treatment of uterine leiomyomata, see Category III codes 0071T, 0072T)

Other Radiologic Guidance

77031 Stereotactic localization guidance for breast biopsy or needle placement (eg, for wire localization or for injection), each lesion, radiological supervision and interpretation

(For procedure, see 10022, 19000-19103, 19290, 19291)

(For injection for sentinel node localization without lymphoscintigraphy, use 38792)

77032 Mammographic guidance for needle placement, breast (eg, for wire localization or for injection), each lesion, radiological supervision and interpretation

(For procedure, see 10022, 19000, 19102, 19103, 19290, 19291)

(For injection for sentinel node localization without lymphoscintigraphy, use 38792)

Breast, Mammography

(For mammographic guidance for needle placement of breast lesion, use 77032)

✚ 77051 Computer-aided detection (computer algorithm analysis of digital image data for lesion detection) with further physician review for interpretation, with or without digitization of film radiographic images; diagnostic mammography (List separately in addition to code for primary procedure)

(Use 77051 in conjunction with 77055, 77056)

✚ 77052 screening mammography (List separately in addition to code for primary procedure)

(Use 77052 in conjunction with 77057)

77053 Mammary ductogram or galactogram, single duct, radiological supervision and interpretation

(For mammary ductogram or galactogram injection, use 19030)

77054 Mammary ductogram or galactogram, multiple ducts, radiological supervision and interpretation

77055 Mammography; unilateral

77056 bilateral

(Use 77055, 77056 in conjunction with 77051 for computer-aided detection applied to a diagnostic mammogram)

77057 Screening mammography, bilateral (2-view film study of each breast)

(Use 77057 in conjunction with 77052 for computer-aided detection applied to a screening mammogram)

►(For electrical impedance breast scan, use 76499)◄

77058 Magnetic resonance imaging, breast, without and/or with contrast material(s); unilateral

77059 bilateral

Bone/Joint Studies

77071 Manual application of stress performed by physician for joint radiography, including contralateral joint if indicated

(For radiographic interpretation of stressed images, see appropriate anatomic site and number of views)

77072 Bone age studies

77073 Bone length studies (orthoroentgenogram, scanogram)

77074 Radiologic examination, osseous survey; limited (eg, for metastases)

77075 complete (axial and appendicular skeleton)

77076 Radiologic examination, osseous survey, infant

77077 Joint survey, single view, 2 or more joints (specify)

77078 Computed tomography, bone mineral density study, 1 or more sites; axial skeleton (eg, hips, pelvis, spine)

77079 appendicular skeleton (peripheral) (eg, radius, wrist, heel)

77080 Dual-energy X-ray absorptiometry (DXA), bone density study, 1 or more sites; axial skeleton (eg, hips, pelvis, spine)

77081 appendicular skeleton (peripheral) (eg, radius, wrist, heel)

77082 vertebral fracture assessment

►(For dual energy x-ray absorptiometry [DEXA] body composition study, use 76499)◄

77083 Radiographic absorptiometry (eg, photodensitometry, radiogrammetry), 1 or more sites

77084 Magnetic resonance (eg, proton) imaging, bone marrow blood supply

Radiation Oncology

Listings for Radiation Oncology provide for teletherapy and brachytherapy to include initial consultation, clinical treatment planning, simulation, medical radiation physics, dosimetry, treatment devices, special services, and clinical treatment management procedures. They include normal follow-up care during course of treatment and for three months following its completion.

When a service or procedure is provided that is not listed in this edition of the CPT codebook it should be identified by a Special Report (see page 236) and one of the following unlisted procedure codes:

77299 Unlisted procedure, therapeutic radiology clinical treatment planning

77399 Unlisted procedure, medical radiation physics, dosimetry and treatment devices, and special services

77499 Unlisted procedure, therapeutic radiology treatment management

77799 Unlisted procedure, clinical brachytherapy

For treatment by injectable or ingestible isotopes, see subsection **Nuclear Medicine.**

Consultation: Clinical Management

Preliminary consultation, evaluation of patient prior to decision to treat, or full medical care (in addition to treatment management) when provided by the therapeutic radiologist may be identified by the appropriate procedure codes from **Evaluation and Management, Medicine,** or **Surgery** sections.

Clinical Treatment Planning (External and Internal Sources)

The clinical treatment planning process is a complex service including interpretation of special testing, tumor localization, treatment volume determination, treatment time/dosage determination, choice of treatment modality, determination of number and size of treatment ports, selection of appropriate treatment devices, and other procedures.

Definitions

Simple planning requires a single treatment area of interest encompassed in a single port or simple parallel opposed ports with simple or no blocking.

Intermediate planning requires three or more converging ports, two separate treatment areas, multiple blocks, or special time dose constraints.

Complex planning requires highly complex blocking, custom shielding blocks, tangential ports, special wedges or compensators, three or more separate treatment areas, rotational or special beam considerations, combination of therapeutic modalities.

77261 Therapeutic radiology treatment planning; simple

77262 intermediate

77263 complex

Definitions

Simple simulation of a single treatment area with either a single port or parallel opposed ports. Simple or no blocking.

Intermediate simulation of three or more converging ports, two separate treatment areas, multiple blocks.

Complex simulation of tangential portals, three or more treatment areas, rotation or arc therapy, complex blocking, custom shielding blocks, brachytherapy source verification, hyperthermia probe verification, any use of contrast materials.

Three-dimensional (3D) computer-generated 3D reconstruction of tumor volume and surrounding critical normal tissue structures from direct CT scans and/or MRI data in preparation for non-coplanar or coplanar therapy. The simulation uses documented 3D beam's eye view volume-dose displays of multiple or moving beams. Documentation with 3D volume reconstruction and dose distribution is required.

Simulation may be carried out on a dedicated simulator, a radiation therapy treatment unit, or diagnostic X-ray machine.

77280 Therapeutic radiology simulation-aided field setting; simple

77285 intermediate

77290 complex

77295 3-dimensional

Radiology

77299 Unlisted procedure, therapeutic radiology clinical treatment planning

Medical Radiation Physics, Dosimetry, Treatment Devices, and Special Services

77300 Basic radiation dosimetry calculation, central axis depth dose calculation, TDF, NSD, gap calculation, off axis factor, tissue inhomogeneity factors, calculation of non-ionizing radiation surface and depth dose, as required during course of treatment, only when prescribed by the treating physician

77301 Intensity modulated radiotherapy plan, including dose-volume histograms for target and critical structure partial tolerance specifications

(Dose plan is optimized using inverse or forward planning technique for modulated beam delivery [eg, binary, dynamic MLC] to create highly conformal dose distribution. Computer plan distribution must be verified for positional accuracy based on dosimetric verification of the intensity map with verification of treatment set-up and interpretation of verification methodology)

77305 Teletherapy, isodose plan (whether hand or computer calculated); simple (1 or 2 parallel opposed unmodified ports directed to a single area of interest)

77310 intermediate (3 or more treatment ports directed to a single area of interest)

77315 complex (mantle or inverted Y, tangential ports, the use of wedges, compensators, complex blocking, rotational beam, or special beam considerations)

(Only 1 teletherapy isodose plan may be reported for a given course of therapy to a specific treatment area)

77321 Special teletherapy port plan, particles, hemibody, total body

77326 Brachytherapy isodose plan; simple (calculation made from single plane, 1 to 4 sources/ribbon application, remote afterloading brachytherapy, 1 to 8 sources)

(For definition of source/ribbon, see page 258)

77327 intermediate (multiplane dosage calculations, application involving 5 to 10 sources/ribbons, remote afterloading brachytherapy, 9 to 12 sources)

77328 complex (multiplane isodose plan, volume implant calculations, over 10 sources/ribbons used, special spatial reconstruction, remote afterloading brachytherapy, over 12 sources)

77331 Special dosimetry (eg, TLD, microdosimetry) (specify), only when prescribed by the treating physician

77332 Treatment devices, design and construction; simple (simple block, simple bolus)

77333 intermediate (multiple blocks, stents, bite blocks, special bolus)

77334 complex (irregular blocks, special shields, compensators, wedges, molds or casts)

77336 Continuing medical physics consultation, including assessment of treatment parameters, quality assurance of dose delivery, and review of patient treatment documentation in support of the radiation oncologist, reported per week of therapy

77370 Special medical radiation physics consultation

Stereotactic Radiation Treatment Delivery

77371 Radiation treatment delivery, stereotactic radiosurgery (SRS), complete course of treatment of cranial lesion(s) consisting of 1 session; multi-source Cobalt 60 based

77372 linear accelerator based

(For radiation treatment management, use 77432)

77373 Stereotactic body radiation therapy, treatment delivery, per fraction to 1 or more lesions, including image guidance, entire course not to exceed 5 fractions

(Do not report 77373 in conjunction with 77401-77416, 77418)

(For single fraction cranial lesion[s], see 77371, 77372)

Other Procedures

77399 Unlisted procedure, medical radiation physics, dosimetry and treatment devices, and special services

Radiation Treatment Delivery

(Radiation treatment delivery [77401-77416] recognizes the technical component and the various energy levels)

77401 Radiation treatment delivery, superficial and/or ortho voltage

77402 Radiation treatment delivery, single treatment area, single port or parallel opposed ports, simple blocks or no blocks; up to 5 MeV

77403 6-10 MeV

77404 11-19 MeV

77406 20 MeV or greater

77407 Radiation treatment delivery, 2 separate treatment areas, 3 or more ports on a single treatment area, use of multiple blocks; up to 5 MeV

77408 6-10 MeV

77409 11-19 MeV

77411 20 MeV or greater

77412 Radiation treatment delivery, 3 or more separate treatment areas, custom blocking, tangential ports, wedges, rotational beam, compensators, electron beam; up to 5 MeV

77413 6-10 MeV

77414 11-19 MeV

77416 20 MeV or greater

77417 Therapeutic radiology port film(s)

77418 Intensity modulated treatment delivery, single or multiple fields/arcs, via narrow spatially and temporally modulated beams, binary, dynamic MLC, per treatment session

(For intensity modulated treatment planning, use 77301)

(For compensator-based beam modulation treatment delivery, use Category III code 0073T)

77421 Stereoscopic X-ray guidance for localization of target volume for the delivery of radiation therapy

(Do not report 77421 in conjunction with 77432, 77435)

(For placement of interstitial device[s] for radiation therapy guidance, prostate, use 55876)

Neutron Beam Treatment Delivery

77422 High energy neutron radiation treatment delivery; single treatment area using a single port or parallel-opposed ports with no blocks or simple blocking

77423 1 or more isocenter(s) with coplanar or non-coplanar geometry with blocking and/or wedge, and/or compensator(s)

Radiation Treatment Management

Radiation treatment management is reported in units of five fractions or treatment sessions, regardless of the actual time period in which the services are furnished. The services need not be furnished on consecutive days. Multiple fractions representing two or more treatment sessions furnished on the same day may be counted separately as long as there has been a distinct break in therapy sessions, and the fractions are of the character usually furnished on different days. Code 77427 is also reported if there are three or four fractions beyond a multiple of five at the end of a course of treatment; one or two fractions beyond a multiple of five at the end of a course of treatment are not reported separately. The professional services furnished during treatment management typically consist of:

- Review of port films;
- Review of dosimetry, dose delivery, and treatment parameters;
- Review of patient treatment set-up;
- Examination of patient for medical evaluation and management (eg, assessment of the patient's response to treatment, coordination of care and treatment, review of imaging and/or lab test results).

77427 Radiation treatment management, 5 treatments

77431 Radiation therapy management with complete course of therapy consisting of 1 or 2 fractions only

(77431 is not to be used to fill in the last week of a long course of therapy)

77432 Stereotactic radiation treatment management of cranial lesion(s) (complete course of treatment consisting of 1 session)

►(The same physician should not report both stereotactic radiosurgery services [61796-61800] and radiation treatment management [77432 or 77435] for cranial lesions)◄

(For stereotactic body radiation therapy treatment, use 77435)

77435 Stereotactic body radiation therapy, treatment management, per treatment course, to 1 or more lesions, including image guidance, entire course not to exceed 5 fractions

(Do not report 77435 in conjunction with 77427-77432)

►(The same physician should not report both stereotactic radiosurgery services [63620, 63621] and radiation treatment management [77435] for extracranial lesions)◄

77470 Special treatment procedure (eg, total body irradiation, hemibody radiation, per oral, endocavitary or intraoperative cone irradiation)

(77470 assumes that the procedure is performed 1 or more times during the course of therapy, in addition to daily or weekly patient management)

77499 Unlisted procedure, therapeutic radiology treatment management

Proton Beam Treatment Delivery

Definitions

Simple proton treatment delivery to a single treatment area utilizing a single non-tangential/oblique port, custom block with compensation (77522) and without compensation (77520).

Intermediate proton treatment delivery to one or more treatment areas utilizing two or more ports or one or more tangential/oblique ports, with custom blocks and compensators.

Complex proton treatment delivery to one or more treatment areas utilizing two or more ports per treatment area with matching or patching fields and/or multiple isocenters, with custom blocks and compensators.

77520 Proton treatment delivery; simple, without compensation

77522 simple, with compensation

77523 intermediate

77525 complex

Radiology

Hyperthermia

Hyperthermia treatments as listed in this section include external (superficial and deep), interstitial, and intracavitary.

Radiation therapy when given concurrently is listed separately.

Hyperthermia is used only as an adjunct to radiation therapy or chemotherapy. It may be induced by a variety of sources (eg, microwave, ultrasound, low energy radio-frequency conduction, or by probes).

The listed treatments include management during the course of therapy and follow-up care for three months after completion.

Preliminary consultation is not included (see **Evaluation and Management** 99241-99255).

Physics planning and interstitial insertion of temperature sensors, and use of external or interstitial heat generating sources are included.

The following descriptors are included in the treatment schedule:

⊙ **77600** Hyperthermia, externally generated; superficial (ie, heating to a depth of 4 cm or less)

⊙ **77605** deep (ie, heating to depths greater than 4 cm)

⊙ **77610** Hyperthermia generated by interstitial probe(s); 5 or fewer interstitial applicators

⊙ **77615** more than 5 interstitial applicators

Clinical Intracavitary Hyperthermia

77620 Hyperthermia generated by intracavitary probe(s)

Clinical Brachytherapy

Clinical brachytherapy requires the use of either natural or man-made radioelements applied into or around a treatment field of interest. The supervision of radioelements and dose interpretation are performed solely by the therapeutic radiologist.

Services 77750-77799 include admission to the hospital and daily visits.

For insertion of ovoids and tandems, use 57155.

For insertion of Heyman capsules, use 58346.

Definitions

(Sources refer to intracavitary placement or permanent interstitial placement; ribbons refer to temporary interstitial placement)

A simple application has one to four sources/ribbons.

An intermediate application has five to 10 sources/ribbons.

A complex application has greater than 10 sources/ribbons.

(For high dose rate electronic brachytherapy, per fraction, use Category III code 0182T)

77750 Infusion or instillation of radioelement solution (includes 3-month follow-up care)

(For administration of radiolabeled monoclonal antibodies, use 79403)

(For non-antibody radiopharmaceutical therapy by intravenous administration only, not including 3-month follow-up care, use 79101)

77761 Intracavitary radiation source application; simple

77762 intermediate

77763 complex

(Do not report 77761-77763 in conjunction with Category III code 0182T)

77776 Interstitial radiation source application; simple

77777 intermediate

77778 complex

(Do not report 77776-77778 in conjunction with Category III code 0182T)

►(77781 has been deleted. To report, see 77785, 77786)◄

►(77782-77784 have been deleted. To report, see 77785-77787)◄

● **77785** Remote afterloading high dose rate radionuclide brachytherapy; 1 channel

● **77786** 2-12 channels

● **77787** over 12 channels

77789 Surface application of radiation source

(Do not report 77789 in conjunction with Category III code 0182T)

77790 Supervision, handling, loading of radiation source

77799 Unlisted procedure, clinical brachytherapy

Nuclear Medicine

Listed procedures may be performed independently or in the course of overall medical care. If the physician providing these services is also responsible for diagnostic work-up and/or follow-up care of patient, see appropriate sections also.

Radioimmunoassay tests are found in the **Clinical Pathology** section (codes 82000-84999). These codes can be appropriately used by any specialist performing such tests in a laboratory licensed and/or certified for radioimmunoassays. The reporting of these tests is not confined to clinical pathology laboratories alone.

The services listed do not include the radiopharmaceutical or drug. Diagnostic and therapeutic radiopharmaceuticals and drugs supplied by the physician should be reported separately using the appropriate supply code(s), in addition to the procedure code.

Diagnostic

Endocrine System

78000 Thyroid uptake; single determination

78001 multiple determinations

78003 stimulation, suppression or discharge (not including initial uptake studies)

78006 Thyroid imaging, with uptake; single determination

78007 multiple determinations

78010 Thyroid imaging; only

78011 with vascular flow

78015 Thyroid carcinoma metastases imaging; limited area (eg, neck and chest only)

78016 with additional studies (eg, urinary recovery)

78018 whole body

+ 78020 Thyroid carcinoma metastases uptake (List separately in addition to code for primary procedure)

(Use 78020 in conjunction with 78018 only)

78070 Parathyroid imaging

78075 Adrenal imaging, cortex and/or medulla

78099 Unlisted endocrine procedure, diagnostic nuclear medicine

(For chemical analysis, see **Chemistry** section)

Hematopoietic, Reticuloendothelial and Lymphatic System

78102 Bone marrow imaging; limited area

78103 multiple areas

78104 whole body

78110 Plasma volume, radiopharmaceutical volume-dilution technique (separate procedure); single sampling

78111 multiple samplings

78120 Red cell volume determination (separate procedure); single sampling

78121 multiple samplings

78122 Whole blood volume determination, including separate measurement of plasma volume and red cell volume (radiopharmaceutical volume-dilution technique)

78130 Red cell survival study;

78135 differential organ/tissue kinetics (eg, splenic and/or hepatic sequestration)

78140 Labeled red cell sequestration, differential organ/tissue (eg, splenic and/or hepatic)

78185 Spleen imaging only, with or without vascular flow

(If combined with liver study, use procedures 78215 and 78216)

78190 Kinetics, study of platelet survival, with or without differential organ/tissue localization

78191 Platelet survival study

78195 Lymphatics and lymph nodes imaging

(For sentinel node identification without scintigraphy imaging, use 38792)

(For sentinel node excision, see 38500-38542)

78199 Unlisted hematopoietic, reticuloendothelial and lymphatic procedure, diagnostic nuclear medicine

(For chemical analysis, see **Chemistry** section)

Gastrointestinal System

78201 Liver imaging; static only

78202 with vascular flow

(For spleen imaging only, use 78185)

78205 Liver imaging (SPECT);

78206 with vascular flow

78215 Liver and spleen imaging; static only

78216 with vascular flow

78220 Liver function study with hepatobiliary agents, with serial images

78223 Hepatobiliary ductal system imaging, including gallbladder, with or without pharmacologic intervention, with or without quantitative measurement of gallbladder function

78230 Salivary gland imaging;

78231 with serial images

78232 Salivary gland function study

78258 Esophageal motility

78261 Gastric mucosa imaging

78262 Gastroesophageal reflux study

78264 Gastric emptying study

78267 Urea breath test, C-14 (isotopic); acquisition for analysis

78268 analysis

78270 Vitamin B-12 absorption study (eg, Schilling test); without intrinsic factor

78271 with intrinsic factor

78272 Vitamin B-12 absorption studies combined, with and without intrinsic factor

78278 Acute gastrointestinal blood loss imaging

78282 Gastrointestinal protein loss

78290 Intestine imaging (eg, ectopic gastric mucosa, Meckel's localization, volvulus)

78291 Peritoneal-venous shunt patency test (eg, for LeVeen, Denver shunt)

(For injection procedure, use 49427)

78299 Unlisted gastrointestinal procedure, diagnostic nuclear medicine

Musculoskeletal System

Bone and joint imaging can be used in the diagnosis of a variety of inflammatory processes (eg, osteomyelitis), as well as for localization of primary and/or metastatic neoplasms.

78300 Bone and/or joint imaging; limited area

78305 multiple areas

78306 whole body

78315 3 phase study

78320 tomographic (SPECT)

78350 Bone density (bone mineral content) study, 1 or more sites; single photon absorptiometry

78351 dual photon absorptiometry, 1 or more sites

(For radiographic bone density [photodensitometry], use 77083)

78399 Unlisted musculoskeletal procedure, diagnostic nuclear medicine

Cardiovascular System

Myocardial perfusion and cardiac blood pool imaging studies may be performed at rest and/or during stress. When performed during exercise and/or pharmacologic stress, the appropriate stress testing code from the 93015-93018 series should be reported in addition to 78460-78465, 78472-78492.

78414 Determination of central c-v hemodynamics (non-imaging) (eg, ejection fraction with probe technique) with or without pharmacologic intervention or exercise, single or multiple determinations

78428 Cardiac shunt detection

78445 Non-cardiac vascular flow imaging (ie, angiography, venography)

78456 Acute venous thrombosis imaging, peptide

78457 Venous thrombosis imaging, venogram; unilateral

78458 bilateral

78459 Myocardial imaging, positron emission tomography (PET), metabolic evaluation

(For myocardial perfusion study, see 78491-78492)

78460 Myocardial perfusion imaging; (planar) single study, at rest or stress (exercise and/or pharmacologic), with or without quantification

78461 multiple studies (planar), at rest and/or stress (exercise and/or pharmacologic), and redistribution and/or rest injection, with or without quantification

78464 tomographic (SPECT), single study (including attenuation correction when performed), at rest or stress (exercise and/or pharmacologic), with or without quantification

78465 tomographic (SPECT), multiple studies (including attenuation correction when performed), at rest and/or stress (exercise and/or pharmacologic) and redistribution and/or rest injection, with or without quantification

78466 Myocardial imaging, infarct avid, planar; qualitative or quantitative

78468 with ejection fraction by first pass technique

78469 tomographic SPECT with or without quantification

78472 Cardiac blood pool imaging, gated equilibrium; planar, single study at rest or stress (exercise and/or pharmacologic), wall motion study plus ejection fraction, with or without additional quantitative processing

(For assessment of right ventricular ejection fraction by first pass technique, use 78496)

78473 multiple studies, wall motion study plus ejection fraction, at rest and stress (exercise and/or pharmacologic), with or without additional quantification

+ 78478 Myocardial perfusion study with wall motion, qualitative or quantitative study (List separately in addition to code for primary procedure)

(Use 78478 in conjunction with 78460, 78461, 78464, 78465)

+ 78480 Myocardial perfusion study with ejection fraction (List separately in addition to code for primary procedure)

(Use 78480 in conjunction with 78460, 78461, 78464, 78465)

78481 Cardiac blood pool imaging (planar), first pass technique; single study, at rest or with stress (exercise and/or pharmacologic), wall motion study plus ejection fraction, with or without quantification

78483 multiple studies, at rest and with stress (exercise and/ or pharmacologic), wall motion study plus ejection fraction, with or without quantification

(For cerebral blood flow study, use 78610)

Radiology

78491 Myocardial imaging, positron emission tomography (PET), perfusion; single study at rest or stress

78492 multiple studies at rest and/or stress

78494 Cardiac blood pool imaging, gated equilibrium, SPECT, at rest, wall motion study plus ejection fraction, with or without quantitative processing

+ 78496 Cardiac blood pool imaging, gated equilibrium, single study, at rest, with right ventricular ejection fraction by first pass technique (List separately in addition to code for primary procedure)

(Use 78496 in conjunction with 78472)

78499 Unlisted cardiovascular procedure, diagnostic nuclear medicine

Respiratory System

78580 Pulmonary perfusion imaging, particulate

78584 Pulmonary perfusion imaging, particulate, with ventilation; single breath

78585 rebreathing and washout, with or without single breath

78586 Pulmonary ventilation imaging, aerosol; single projection

78587 multiple projections (eg, anterior, posterior, lateral views)

78588 Pulmonary perfusion imaging, particulate, with ventilation imaging, aerosol, 1 or multiple projections

78591 Pulmonary ventilation imaging, gaseous, single breath, single projection

78593 Pulmonary ventilation imaging, gaseous, with rebreathing and washout with or without single breath; single projection

78594 multiple projections (eg, anterior, posterior, lateral views)

78596 Pulmonary quantitative differential function (ventilation/perfusion) study

78599 Unlisted respiratory procedure, diagnostic nuclear medicine

Nervous System

78600 Brain imaging, less than 4 static views;

78601 with vascular flow

78605 Brain imaging, minimum 4 static views;

78606 with vascular flow

78607 Brain imaging, tomographic (SPECT)

78608 Brain imaging, positron emission tomography (PET); metabolic evaluation

78609 perfusion evaluation

78610 Brain imaging, vascular flow only

(78615 has been deleted. To report, use 78610)

78630 Cerebrospinal fluid flow, imaging (not including introduction of material); cisternography

(For injection procedure, see 61000-61070, 62270-62319)

78635 ventriculography

(For injection procedure, see 61000-61070, 62270-62294)

78645 shunt evaluation

(For injection procedure, see 61000-61070, 62270-62294)

78647 tomographic (SPECT)

78650 Cerebrospinal fluid leakage detection and localization

(For injection procedure, see 61000-61070, 62270-62294)

78660 Radiopharmaceutical dacryocystography

78699 Unlisted nervous system procedure, diagnostic nuclear medicine

Genitourinary System

78700 Kidney imaging morphology;

78701 with vascular flow

(78704 has been deleted. To report, see 78707-78709)

78707 with vascular flow and function, single study without pharmacological intervention

78708 with vascular flow and function, single study, with pharmacological intervention (eg, angiotensin converting enzyme inhibitor and/or diuretic)

78709 with vascular flow and function, multiple studies, with and without pharmacological intervention (eg, angiotensin converting enzyme inhibitor and/or diuretic)

(For introduction of radioactive substance in association with renal endoscopy, see 77776-77778)

78710 tomographic (SPECT)

(78715 has been deleted. To report, see 78701-78709)

78725 Kidney function study, non-imaging radioisotopic study

+ 78730 Urinary bladder residual study (List separately in addition to code for primary procedure)

(Use 78730 in conjunction with 78740)

(For measurement of postvoid residual urine and/or bladder capacity by ultrasound, nonimaging, use 51798)

(For ultrasound imaging of the bladder only, with measurement of postvoid residual urine when performed, use 76857)

78740 Ureteral reflux study (radiopharmaceutical voiding cystogram)

(Use 78740 in conjunction with 78730 for urinary bladder residual study)

(For catheterization, see 51701, 51702, 51703)

(78760 has been deleted. To report, use 78761)

78761 Testicular imaging with vascular flow

78799 Unlisted genitourinary procedure, diagnostic nuclear medicine

(For chemical analysis, see **Chemistry** section)

Other Procedures

(For specific organ, see appropriate heading)

(For radiophosphorus tumor identification, ocular, see 78800)

78800 Radiopharmaceutical localization of tumor or distribution of radiopharmaceutical agent(s); limited area

(For specific organ, see appropriate heading)

78801 multiple areas

78802 whole body, single day imaging

78803 tomographic (SPECT)

78804 whole body, requiring 2 or more days imaging

78805 Radiopharmaceutical localization of inflammatory process; limited area

78806 whole body

78807 tomographic (SPECT)

(For imaging bone infectious or inflammatory disease with a bone imaging radiopharmaceutical, see 78300, 78305, 78306)

● **78808** Injection procedure for radiopharmaceutical localization by non-imaging probe study, intravenous (eg, parathyroid adenoma)

►(For sentinel lymph node identification, use 38792)◄

(For PET of brain, see 78608, 78609)

(For PET myocardial imaging, see 78459, 78491, 78492)

78811 Positron emission tomography (PET) imaging; limited area (eg, chest, head/neck)

78812 skull base to mid-thigh

78813 whole body

78814 Positron emission tomography (PET) with concurrently acquired computed tomography (CT) for attenuation correction and anatomical localization imaging; limited area (eg, chest, head/neck)

78815 skull base to mid-thigh

78816 whole body

(Report 78811-78816 only once per imaging session)

(Computed tomography [CT] performed for other than attenuation correction and anatomical localization is reported using the appropriate site specific CT code with modifier 59)

►(78890, 78891 have been deleted)◄

78999 Unlisted miscellaneous procedure, diagnostic nuclear medicine

Therapeutic

The oral and intravenous administration codes in this section are inclusive of the mode of administration. For intra-arterial, intra-cavitary, and intra-articular administration, also use the appropriate injection and/or procedure codes, as well as imaging guidance and radiological supervision and interpretation codes, when appropriate.

79005 Radiopharmaceutical therapy, by oral administration

(For monoclonal antibody therapy, use 79403)

79101 Radiopharmaceutical therapy, by intravenous administration

(Do not report 79101 in conjunction with 36400, 36410, 79403, 90760, 90774 or 90775, 96409)

(For radiolabeled monoclonal antibody by intravenous infusion, use 79403)

(For infusion or instillation of non-antibody radioelement solution that includes 3 months follow-up care, use 77750)

79200 Radiopharmaceutical therapy, by intracavitary administration

79300 Radiopharmaceutical therapy, by interstitial radioactive colloid administration

79403 Radiopharmaceutical therapy, radiolabeled monoclonal antibody by intravenous infusion

(For pre-treatment imaging, see 78802, 78804)

(Do not report 79403 in conjunction with 79101)

79440 Radiopharmaceutical therapy, by intra-articular administration

79445 Radiopharmaceutical therapy, by intra-arterial particulate administration

(Do not report 79445 in conjunction with 90773, 96420)

(Use appropriate procedural and radiological supervision and interpretation codes for the angiographic and interventional procedures provided prerequisite to intra-arterial radiopharmaceutical therapy)

79999 Radiopharmaceutical therapy, unlisted procedure

Radiology

Pathology and Laboratory Guidelines

Items used by all physicians in reporting their services are presented in the **Introduction.** Some of the commonalities are repeated here for the convenience of those physicians referring to this section on **Pathology and Laboratory.** Other definitions and items unique to Pathology and Laboratory are also listed.

Services in Pathology and Laboratory

Services in Pathology and Laboratory are provided by a physician or by technologists under responsible supervision of a physician.

Separate or Multiple Procedures

It is appropriate to designate multiple procedures that are rendered on the same date by separate entries.

Subsection Information

Several of the subheadings or subsections have special needs or instructions unique to that section. Where these are indicated (eg, "Panel Tests"), special **"Notes"** will be presented preceding those procedural terminology listings referring to that subsection specifically. If there is an "Unlisted Procedure" code number (see the following section) for the individual subsection, it will be shown. Those subsections with **"Notes"** are as follows:

Organ or Disease Panels	80048-80076
Drug Testing	80100-80103
Therapeutic Drug Assays	80150-80299
Evocative/Suppression Testing	80400-80440
Consultations (Clinical Pathology)	80500-80502
Urinalysis	81000-81099
Chemistry	82000-84999
Molecular Diagnostics	83890-83912
Infectious Agent: Detection of Antibodies	86602-86804
Microbiology	87001-87255
Infectious Agent Detection	87260-87999
Anatomic Pathology	88000-88099
Cytopathology	88104-88199
Cytogenetic Studies	88230-88299
Surgical Pathology	88300-88399

Unlisted Service or Procedure

A service or procedure may be provided that is not listed in this edition of the CPT codebook. When reporting such a service, the appropriate "Unlisted Procedure" code may be used to indicate the service, identifying it by "Special Report" as discussed below. The "Unlisted Procedures" and accompanying codes for **Pathology and Laboratory** are as follows:

81099	Unlisted urinalysis procedure
84999	Unlisted chemistry procedure
85999	Unlisted hematology and coagulation procedure
86486	unlisted antigen, each
86849	Unlisted immunology procedure
86999	Unlisted transfusion medicine procedure
87999	Unlisted microbiology procedure
88099	Unlisted necropsy (autopsy) procedure
88199	Unlisted cytopathology procedure
88299	Unlisted cytogenetic study
88399	Unlisted surgical pathology procedure
89240	Unlisted miscellaneous pathology test

Special Report

A service that is rarely provided, unusual, variable, or new may require a special report in determining medical appropriateness of the service. Pertinent information should include an adequate definition or description of the nature, extent, and need for the procedure; and the time, effort, and equipment necessary to provide the service. Additional items that may be included are:

- Complexity of symptoms
- Final diagnosis
- Pertinent physical findings
- Diagnostic and therapeutic procedures
- Concurrent problems
- Follow-up care

Notes

Pathology and Laboratory

Organ or Disease-Oriented Panels

These panels were developed for coding purposes only and should not be interpreted as clinical parameters. The tests listed with each panel identify the defined components of that panel.

These panel components are not intended to limit the performance of other tests. If one performs tests in addition to those specifically indicated for a particular panel, those tests should be reported separately in addition to the panel code.

80047 Basic metabolic panel (Calcium, ionized)

This panel must include the following:

Calcium, ionized (82330)

Carbon dioxide (82374)

Chloride (82435)

Creatinine (82565)

Glucose (82947)

Potassium (84132)

Sodium (84295)

Urea Nitrogen (BUN) (84520)

(Do not report 80047 in conjunction with 80053)

▲ **80048** Basic metabolic panel (Calcium, total)

This panel must include the following:

Calcium, total (82310)

Carbon dioxide (82374)

Chloride (82435)

Creatinine (82565)

Glucose (82947)

Potassium (84132)

Sodium (84295)

Urea nitrogen (BUN) (84520)

(Do not use 80048 in addition to 80053)

80050 General health panel

This panel must include the following:

Comprehensive metabolic panel (80053)

Blood count, complete (CBC), automated and automated differential WBC count (85025 or 85027 and 85004)

OR

Blood count, complete (CBC), automated (85027) and appropriate manual differential WBC count (85007 or 85009)

Thyroid stimulating hormone (TSH) (84443)

80051 Electrolyte panel

This panel must include the following:

Carbon dioxide (82374)

Chloride (82435)

Potassium (84132)

Sodium (84295)

▲ **80053** Comprehensive metabolic panel

This panel must include the following:

Albumin (82040)

Bilirubin, total (82247)

Calcium, total (82310)

Carbon dioxide (bicarbonate) (82374)

Chloride (82435)

Creatinine (82565)

Glucose (82947)

Phosphatase, alkaline (84075)

Potassium (84132)

Protein, total (84155)

Sodium (84295)

Transferase, alanine amino (ALT) (SGPT) (84460)

Transferase, aspartate amino (AST) (SGOT) (84450)

Urea nitrogen (BUN) (84520)

(Do not use 80053 in addition to 80047, 80048, 80076)

80055 Obstetric panel

This panel must include the following:

Blood count, complete (CBC), automated and automated differential WBC count (85025 or 85027 and 85004)

OR

Blood count, complete (CBC), automated (85027) and appropriate manual differential WBC count (85007 or 85009)

Hepatitis B surface antigen (HBsAg) (87340)

Antibody, rubella (86762)

Syphilis test, qualitative (eg, VDRL, RPR, ART) (86592)

Antibody screen, RBC, each serum technique (86850)

Blood typing, ABO (86900) AND

Blood typing, Rh (D) (86901)

80061 Lipid panel

This panel must include the following:

Cholesterol, serum, total (82465)

Lipoprotein, direct measurement, high density cholesterol (HDL cholesterol) (83718)

Triglycerides (84478)

▲ **80069** Renal function panel

This panel must include the following:

Albumin (82040)

Calcium, total (82310)

Carbon dioxide (bicarbonate) (82374)

Chloride (82435)

Creatinine (82565)

Glucose (82947)

Phosphorus inorganic (phosphate) (84100)

Potassium (84132)

Sodium (84295)

Urea nitrogen (BUN) (84520)

80074 Acute hepatitis panel

This panel must include the following:

Hepatitis A antibody (HAAb), IgM antibody (86709)

Hepatitis B core antibody (HBcAb), IgM antibody (86705)

Hepatitis B surface antigen (HBsAg) (87340)

Hepatitis C antibody (86803)

80076 Hepatic function panel

This panel must include the following:

Albumin (82040)

Bilirubin, total (82247)

Bilirubin, direct (82248)

Phosphatase, alkaline (84075)

Protein, total (84155)

Transferase, alanine amino (ALT) (SGPT) (84460)

Transferase, aspartate amino (AST) (SGOT) (84450)

(Do not use 80076 in addition to 80053)

Drug Testing

The following list contains examples of drugs or classes of drugs that are commonly assayed by qualitative screen, followed by confirmation with a second method:

- Alcohols
- Amphetamines
- Barbiturates
- Benzodiazepines
- Cocaine and metabolites
- Methadones
- Methaqualones
- Opiates
- Phencyclidines
- Phenothiazines
- Propoxyphenes
- Tetrahydrocannabinoids
- Tricyclic antidepressants

Confirmed drugs may also be quantitated.

Use 80100 for each multiple drug class chromatographic procedure. Use 80102 for each procedure necessary for confirmation. For chromatography, each combination of stationary and mobile phase is to be counted as one procedure. For example, if detection of three drugs by chromatography requires one stationary phase with three mobile phases, use 80100 three times. However, if multiple drugs can be detected using a single analysis (eg, one stationary phase with one mobile phase), use 80100 only once.

For quantitation of drugs screened, use appropriate code in **Chemistry** section (82000-84999) or **Therapeutic Drug Assay** section (80150-80299).

80100 Drug screen, qualitative; multiple drug classes chromatographic method, each procedure

80101 single drug class method (eg, immunoassay, enzyme assay), each drug class

80102 Drug confirmation, each procedure

80103 Tissue preparation for drug analysis

Pathology and Laboratory

Therapeutic Drug Assays

The material for examination may be from any source. Examination is quantitative. For nonquantitative testing, see Drug Testing (80100-80103).

80150 Amikacin

80152 Amitriptyline

80154 Benzodiazepines

80156 Carbamazepine; total

80157 free

80158 Cyclosporine

80160 Desipramine

80162 Digoxin

80164 Dipropylacetic acid (valproic acid)

80166 Doxepin

80168 Ethosuximide

80170 Gentamicin

80172 Gold

80173 Haloperidol

80174 Imipramine

80176 Lidocaine

80178 Lithium

80182 Nortriptyline

80184 Phenobarbital

80185 Phenytoin; total

80186 free

80188 Primidone

80190 Procainamide;

80192 with metabolites (eg, n-acetyl procainamide)

80194 Quinidine

80195 Sirolimus

80196 Salicylate

80197 Tacrolimus

80198 Theophylline

80200 Tobramycin

80201 Topiramate

80202 Vancomycin

80299 Quantitation of drug, not elsewhere specified

Evocative/Suppression Testing

►The following test panels involve the administration of evocative or suppressive agents, and the baseline and subsequent measurement of their effects on chemical constituents. These codes are to be used for the reporting of the laboratory component of the overall testing protocol. For the physician's administration of the evocative or suppressive agents, see 96360, 96361, 96372-96374, 96375; for the supplies and drugs, see 99070. To report physician attendance and monitoring during the testing, use the appropriate evaluation and management code, including the prolonged physician care codes if required. Prolonged physician care codes are not separately reported when evocative/suppression testing involves prolonged infusions reported with 96360, 96361. In the code descriptors where reference is made to a particular analyte (eg, Cortisol: 82533 x 2) the "x 2" refers to the number of times the test for that particular analyte is performed.◄

80400 ACTH stimulation panel; for adrenal insufficiency

This panel must include the following:

Cortisol (82533 x 2)

80402 for 21 hydroxylase deficiency

This panel must include the following:

Cortisol (82533 x 2)

17 hydroxyprogesterone (83498 x 2)

80406 for 3 beta-hydroxydehydrogenase deficiency

This panel must include the following:

Cortisol (82533 x 2)

17 hydroxypregnenolone (84143 x 2)

80408 Aldosterone suppression evaluation panel (eg, saline infusion)

This panel must include the following:

Aldosterone (82088 x 2)

Renin (84244 x 2)

80410 Calcitonin stimulation panel (eg, calcium, pentagastrin)

This panel must include the following:

Calcitonin (82308 x 3)

80412 Corticotropic releasing hormone (CRH) stimulation panel

This panel must include the following:

Cortisol (82533 x 6)

Adrenocorticotropic hormone (ACTH) (82024 x 6)

80414 Chorionic gonadotropin stimulation panel; testosterone response

This panel must include the following:

Testosterone (84403 x 2 on 3 pooled blood samples)

80415 estradiol response

This panel must include the following:

Estradiol (82670 x 2 on 3 pooled blood samples)

80416 Renal vein renin stimulation panel (eg, captopril)

This panel must include the following:

Renin (84244 x 6)

80417 Peripheral vein renin stimulation panel (eg, captopril)

This panel must include the following:

Renin (84244 x 2)

80418 Combined rapid anterior pituitary evaluation panel

This panel must include the following:

Adrenocorticotropic hormone (ACTH) (82024 x 4)

Luteinizing hormone (LH) (83002 x 4)

Follicle stimulating hormone (FSH) (83001 x 4)

Prolactin (84146 x 4)

Human growth hormone (HGH) (83003 x 4)

Cortisol (82533 x 4)

Thyroid stimulating hormone (TSH) (84443 x 4)

80420 Dexamethasone suppression panel, 48 hour

This panel must include the following:

Free cortisol, urine (82530 x 2)

Cortisol (82533 x 2)

Volume measurement for timed collection (81050 x 2)

(For single dose dexamethasone, use 82533)

80422 Glucagon tolerance panel; for insulinoma

This panel must include the following:

Glucose (82947 x 3)

Insulin (83525 x 3)

80424 for pheochromocytoma

This panel must include the following:

Catecholamines, fractionated (82384 x 2)

80426 Gonadotropin releasing hormone stimulation panel

This panel must include the following:

Follicle stimulating hormone (FSH) (83001 x 4)

Luteinizing hormone (LH) (83002 x 4)

80428 Growth hormone stimulation panel (eg, arginine infusion, l-dopa administration)

This panel must include the following:

Human growth hormone (HGH) (83003 x 4)

80430 Growth hormone suppression panel (glucose administration)

This panel must include the following:

Glucose (82947 x 3)

Human growth hormone (HGH) (83003 x 4)

80432 Insulin-induced C-peptide suppression panel

This panel must include the following:

Insulin (83525)

C-peptide (84681 x 5)

Glucose (82947 x 5)

80434 Insulin tolerance panel; for ACTH insufficiency

This panel must include the following:

Cortisol (82533 x 5)

Glucose (82947 x 5)

80435 for growth hormone deficiency

This panel must include the following:

Glucose (82947 x 5)

Human growth hormone (HGH) (83003 x 5)

80436 Metyrapone panel

This panel must include the following:

Cortisol (82533 x 2)

11 deoxycortisol (82634 x 2)

80438 Thyrotropin releasing hormone (TRH) stimulation panel; 1 hour

This panel must include the following:

Thyroid stimulating hormone (TSH) (84443 x 3)

80439 2 hour

This panel must include the following:

Thyroid stimulating hormone (TSH) (84443 x 4)

80440 for hyperprolactinemia

This panel must include the following:

Prolactin (84146 x 3)

Consultations (Clinical Pathology)

A clinical pathology consultation is a service, including a written report, rendered by the pathologist in response to a request from an attending physician in relation to a test result(s) requiring additional medical interpretive judgment.

Reporting of a test result(s) without medical interpretive judgment is not considered a clinical pathology consultation.

80500 Clinical pathology consultation; limited, without review of patient's history and medical records

80502 comprehensive, for a complex diagnostic problem, with review of patient's history and medical records

(These codes may also be used for pharmacokinetic consultations)

(For consultations involving the examination and evaluation of the patient, see 99241-99255)

Urinalysis

For specific analyses, see appropriate section.

81000 Urinalysis, by dip stick or tablet reagent for bilirubin, glucose, hemoglobin, ketones, leukocytes, nitrite, pH, protein, specific gravity, urobilinogen, any number of these constituents; non-automated, with microscopy

81001 automated, with microscopy

81002 non-automated, without microscopy

81003 automated, without microscopy

81005 Urinalysis; qualitative or semiquantitative, except immunoassays

(For non-immunoassay reagent strip urinalysis, see 81000, 81002)

(For immunoassay, qualitative or semiquantitative, use 83518)

(For microalbumin, see 82043, 82044)

81007 bacteriuria screen, except by culture or dipstick

(For culture, see 87086-87088)

(For dipstick, use 81000 or 81002)

81015 microscopic only

(For sperm evaluation for retrograde ejaculation, use 89331)

81020 2 or 3 glass test

81025 Urine pregnancy test, by visual color comparison methods

81050 Volume measurement for timed collection, each

81099 Unlisted urinalysis procedure

Chemistry

The material for examination may be from any source unless otherwise specified in the code descriptor. When an analyte is measured in multiple specimens from different sources, or in specimens that are obtained at different times, the analyte is reported separately for each source and for each specimen. The examination is quantitative unless specified. To report an organ or disease oriented panel, see codes 80048-80076.

When a code describes a method where measurement of multiple analytes may require one or several procedures, each procedure is coded separately (eg, 82491-82492, 82541-82544). For example, if two analytes are measured using column chromatography using a single stationary or mobile phase, use 82492. If the same two analytes are measured using different stationary or mobile phase conditions, 82491 would be used twice. If a total of four analytes are measured where two analytes are measured with a single stationary and mobile phase, and the other two analytes are measured using a different stationary and mobile phase, use 82492 twice. If a total of three analytes are measured where two analytes are measured using a single stationary or mobile phase condition, and the third analyte is measured separately using a different stationary or mobile phase procedure, use 82492 once for the two analytes measured under the same condition, and use 82491 once for the third analyte measured separately.

Clinical information derived from the results of laboratory data that is mathematically calculated (eg, free thyroxine index [T7]) is considered part of the test procedure and therefore is not a separately reportable service.

82000 Acetaldehyde, blood

82003 Acetaminophen

82009 Acetone or other ketone bodies, serum; qualitative

82010 quantitative

82013 Acetylcholinesterase

(Acid, gastric, see gastric acid, 82926, 82928)

(Acid phosphatase, see 84060-84066)

82016 Acylcarnitines; qualitative, each specimen

82017 quantitative, each specimen

(For carnitine, use 82379)

82024 Adrenocorticotropic hormone (ACTH)

82030 Adenosine, 5-monophosphate, cyclic (cyclic AMP)

Pathology and Laboratory

▲ **82040** Albumin; serum, plasma or whole blood

82042 urine or other source, quantitative, each specimen

82043 urine, microalbumin, quantitative

82044 urine, microalbumin, semiquantitative (eg, reagent strip assay)

(For prealbumin, use 84134)

82045 ischemia modified

82055 Alcohol (ethanol); any specimen except breath

(For other volatiles, alcohol, use 84600)

82075 breath

82085 Aldolase

82088 Aldosterone

(Alkaline phosphatase, see 84075, 84080)

82101 Alkaloids, urine, quantitative

(Alphaketoglutarate, see 82009, 82010)

(Alpha tocopherol [Vitamin E], use 84446)

82103 Alpha-1-antitrypsin; total

82104 phenotype

82105 Alpha-fetoprotein (AFP); serum

82106 amniotic fluid

82107 AFP-L3 fraction isoform and total AFP (including ratio)

82108 Aluminum

82120 Amines, vaginal fluid, qualitative

(For combined pH and amines test for vaginitis, use 82120 and 83986)

82127 Amino acids; single, qualitative, each specimen

82128 multiple, qualitative, each specimen

82131 single, quantitative, each specimen

82135 Aminolevulinic acid, delta (ALA)

82136 Amino acids, 2 to 5 amino acids, quantitative, each specimen

82139 Amino acids, 6 or more amino acids, quantitative, each specimen

82140 Ammonia

82143 Amniotic fluid scan (spectrophotometric)

(For L/S ratio, use 83661)

(Amobarbital, see 80100-80103 for qualitative analysis, 82205 for quantitative analysis)

82145 Amphetamine or methamphetamine

(For qualitative analysis, see 80100-80103)

82150 Amylase

82154 Androstanediol glucuronide

82157 Androstenedione

82160 Androsterone

82163 Angiotensin II

82164 Angiotensin I - converting enzyme (ACE)

(Antidiuretic hormone (ADH), use 84588)

(Antimony, use 83015)

(Antitrypsin, alpha-1-, see 82103, 82104)

82172 Apolipoprotein, each

82175 Arsenic

(For heavy metal screening, use 83015)

82180 Ascorbic acid (Vitamin C), blood

(Aspirin, see acetylsalicylic acid, 80196)

(Atherogenic index, blood, ultracentrifugation, quantitative, use 83701)

82190 Atomic absorption spectroscopy, each analyte

82205 Barbiturates, not elsewhere specified

(For qualitative analysis, see 80100-80103)

(For B-Natriuretic peptide, use 83880)

82232 Beta-2 microglobulin

(Bicarbonate, use 82374)

82239 Bile acids; total

82240 cholylglycine

(For bile pigments, urine, see 81000-81005)

82247 Bilirubin; total

82248 direct

82252 feces, qualitative

82261 Biotinidase, each specimen

82270 Blood, occult, by peroxidase activity (eg, guaiac), qualitative; feces, consecutive collected specimens with single determination, for colorectal neoplasm screening (ie, patient was provided 3 cards or single triple card for consecutive collection)

82271 other sources

82272 Blood, occult, by peroxidase activity (eg, guaiac), qualitative, feces, 1-3 simultaneous determinations, performed for other than colorectal neoplasm screening

(Blood urea nitrogen [BUN], see 84520, 84525)

82274 Blood, occult, by fecal hemoglobin determination by immunoassay, qualitative, feces, 1-3 simultaneous determinations

82286 Bradykinin

82300 Cadmium

82306 Calcifediol (25-OH Vitamin D-3)

82307 Calciferol (Vitamin D)

(For 1, 25-Dihydroxyvitamin D, use 82652)

82308 Calcitonin

82310 Calcium; total

82330 ionized

82331 after calcium infusion test

82340 urine quantitative, timed specimen

82355 Calculus; qualitative analysis

82360 quantitative analysis, chemical

82365 infrared spectroscopy

82370 X-ray diffraction

(Carbamates, see individual listings)

82373 Carbohydrate deficient transferrin

82374 Carbon dioxide (bicarbonate)

(See also 82803)

▲ **82375** Carboxyhemoglobin; quantitative

▲ **82376** qualitative

►(For transcutaneous measurement of carboxyhemoglobin, use 88740)◄

82378 Carcinoembryonic antigen (CEA)

82379 Carnitine (total and free), quantitative, each specimen

(For acylcarnitine, see 82016, 82017)

82380 Carotene

82382 Catecholamines; total urine

82383 blood

82384 fractionated

(For urine metabolites, see 83835, 84585)

82387 Cathepsin-D

82390 Ceruloplasmin

82397 Chemiluminescent assay

82415 Chloramphenicol

82435 Chloride; blood

82436 urine

82438 other source

(For sweat collection by iontophoresis, use 89230)

82441 Chlorinated hydrocarbons, screen

(Chlorpromazine, use 84022)

(Cholecalciferol [Vitamin D], use 82307)

82465 Cholesterol, serum or whole blood, total

(For high density lipoprotein [HDL], use 83718)

82480 Cholinesterase; serum

82482 RBC

82485 Chondroitin B sulfate, quantitative

(Chorionic gonadotropin, see gonadotropin, 84702, 84703)

82486 Chromatography, qualitative; column (eg, gas liquid or HPLC), analyte not elsewhere specified

82487 paper, 1-dimensional, analyte not elsewhere specified

82488 paper, 2-dimensional, analyte not elsewhere specified

82489 thin layer, analyte not elsewhere specified

82491 Chromatography, quantitative, column (eg, gas liquid or HPLC); single analyte not elsewhere specified, single stationary and mobile phase

82492 multiple analytes, single stationary and mobile phase

82495 Chromium

82507 Citrate

82520 Cocaine or metabolite

(Cocaine, qualitative analysis, see 80100-80103)

(Codeine, qualitative analysis, see 80100-80103)

(Codeine, quantitative analysis, see 82101)

(Complement, see 86160-86162)

82523 Collagen cross links, any method

82525 Copper

(Coproporphyrin, see 84119, 84120)

(Corticosteroids, use 83491)

82528 Corticosterone

82530 Cortisol; free

82533 total

(C-peptide, use 84681)

82540 Creatine

82541 Column chromatography/mass spectrometry (eg, GC/MS, or HPLC/MS), analyte not elsewhere specified; qualitative, single stationary and mobile phase

82542 quantitative, single stationary and mobile phase

82543 stable isotope dilution, single analyte, quantitative, single stationary and mobile phase

82544 stable isotope dilution, multiple analytes, quantitative, single stationary and mobile phase

82550 Creatine kinase (CK), (CPK); total

82552 isoenzymes

82553 MB fraction only

82554 isoforms

82565 Creatinine; blood

82570 other source

82575 clearance

82585 Cryofibrinogen

82595 Cryoglobulin, qualitative or semi-quantitative (eg, cryocrit)

(For quantitative, cryoglobulin, see 82784, 82785)

(Crystals, pyrophosphate vs urate, use 89060)

82600 Cyanide

82607 Cyanocobalamin (Vitamin B-12);

82608 unsaturated binding capacity

(Cyclic AMP, use 82030)

(Cyclic GMP, use 83008)

(Cyclosporine, use 80158)

82610 Cystatin C

82615 Cystine and homocystine, urine, qualitative

82626 Dehydroepiandrosterone (DHEA)

82627 Dehydroepiandrosterone-sulfate (DHEA-S)

(Delta-aminolevulinic acid (ALA), use 82135)

82633 Desoxycorticosterone, 11-

82634 Deoxycortisol, 11-

(Dexamethasone suppression test, use 80420)

(Diastase, urine, use 82150)

82638 Dibucaine number

(Dichloroethane, use 84600)

(Dichloromethane, use 84600)

(Diethylether, use 84600)

82646 Dihydrocodeinone

(For qualitative analysis, see 80100-80103)

82649 Dihydromorphinone

(For qualitative analysis, see 80100-80103)

82651 Dihydrotestosterone (DHT)

82652 Dihydroxyvitamin D, 1, 25-

82654 Dimethadione

(For qualitative analysis, see 80100-80103)

(Diphenylhydantoin, use 80185)

(Dipropylacetic acid, use 80164)

(Dopamine, see 82382-82384)

(Duodenal contents, see individual enzymes; for intubation and collection, use 89100)

82656 Elastase, pancreatic (EL-1), fecal, qualitative or semi-quantitative

82657 Enzyme activity in blood cells, cultured cells, or tissue, not elsewhere specified; nonradioactive substrate, each specimen

82658 radioactive substrate, each specimen

82664 Electrophoretic technique, not elsewhere specified

(Endocrine receptor assays, see 84233-84235)

82666 Epiandrosterone

(Epinephrine, see 82382-82384)

82668 Erythropoietin

82670 Estradiol

82671 Estrogens; fractionated

82672 total

(Estrogen receptor assay, use 84233)

82677 Estriol

82679 Estrone

(Ethanol, see 82055 and 82075)

82690 Ethchlorvynol

(Ethyl alcohol, see 82055 and 82075)

82693 Ethylene glycol

82696 Etiocholanolone

(For fractionation of ketosteroids, use 83593)

82705 Fat or lipids, feces; qualitative

82710 quantitative

82715 Fat differential, feces, quantitative

82725 Fatty acids, nonesterified

82726 Very long chain fatty acids

(For long-chain [C20-22] omega-3 fatty acids in red blood cell [RBC] membranes, use Category III code 0111T)

82728 Ferritin

(Fetal hemoglobin, see hemoglobin 83030, 83033, and 85460)

(Fetoprotein, alpha-1, see 82105, 82106)

82731 Fetal fibronectin, cervicovaginal secretions, semi-quantitative

82735 Fluoride

82742 Flurazepam

(For qualitative analysis, see 80100-80103)

(Foam stability test, use 83662)

82746 Folic acid; serum

82747 RBC

(Follicle stimulating hormone [FSH], use 83001)

82757 Fructose, semen

(Fructosamine, use 82985)

(Fructose, TLC screen, use 84375)

82759 Galactokinase, RBC

82760 Galactose

82775 Galactose-1-phosphate uridyl transferase; quantitative

82776 screen

82784 Gammaglobulin; IgA, IgD, IgG, IgM, each

82785 IgE

(For allergen specific IgE, see 86003, 86005)

82787 immunoglobulin subclasses (IgG1, 2, 3, or 4), each

(Gamma-glutamyltransferase [GGT], use 82977)

82800 Gases, blood, pH only

82803 Gases, blood, any combination of pH, pCO_2, pO_2, CO_2, HCO_3 (including calculated O_2 saturation);

(Use 82803 for 2 or more of the above listed analytes)

82805 with O_2 saturation, by direct measurement, except pulse oximetry

82810 Gases, blood, O_2 saturation only, by direct measurement, except pulse oximetry

(For pulse oximetry, use 94760)

82820 Hemoglobin-oxygen affinity (pO_2 for 50% hemoglobin saturation with oxygen)

82926 Gastric acid, free and total, each specimen

82928 Gastric acid, free or total, each specimen

82938 Gastrin after secretin stimulation

82941 Gastrin

(Gentamicin, use 80170)

(GGT, use 82977)

(GLC, gas liquid chromatography, use 82486)

82943 Glucagon

82945 Glucose, body fluid, other than blood

82946 Glucagon tolerance test

82947 Glucose; quantitative, blood (except reagent strip)

82948 blood, reagent strip

82950 post glucose dose (includes glucose)

82951 tolerance test (GTT), three specimens (includes glucose)

82952 tolerance test, each additional beyond three specimens

82953 tolbutamide tolerance test

(For insulin tolerance test, see 80434, 80435)

(For leucine tolerance test, use 80428)

(For semiquantitative urine glucose, see 81000, 81002, 81005, 81099)

82955 Glucose-6-phosphate dehydrogenase (G6PD); quantitative

82960 screen

►(For glucose tolerance test with medication, use 96374 in addition)◄

82962 Glucose, blood by glucose monitoring device(s) cleared by the FDA specifically for home use

82963 Glucosidase, beta

82965 Glutamate dehydrogenase

82975 Glutamine (glutamic acid amide)

82977 Glutamyltransferase, gamma (GGT)

82978 Glutathione

82979 Glutathione reductase, RBC

82980 Glutethimide

(Glycohemoglobin, use 83036)

82985 Glycated protein

(Gonadotropin, chorionic, see 84702, 84703)

83001 Gonadotropin; follicle stimulating hormone (FSH)

83002 luteinizing hormone (LH)

(For luteinizing releasing factor [LRH], use 83727)

83003 Growth hormone, human (HGH) (somatotropin)

(For antibody to human growth hormone, use 86277)

83008 Guanosine monophosphate (GMP), cyclic

83009 Helicobacter pylori, blood test analysis for urease activity, non-radioactive isotope (eg, C-13)

(For H. pylori, breath test analysis for urease activity, see 83013, 83014)

83010 Haptoglobin; quantitative

83012 phenotypes

83013 Helicobacter pylori; breath test analysis for urease activity, non-radioactive isotope (eg, C-13)

83014 drug administration

(For H. pylori, stool, use 87338. For H. pylori, liquid scintillation counter, see 78267, 78268. For H. pylori, enzyme immunoassay, use 87339)

(For H. pylori, blood test analysis for urease activity, use 83009)

83015 Heavy metal (eg, arsenic, barium, beryllium, bismuth, antimony, mercury); screen

83018 quantitative, each

83020 Hemoglobin fractionation and quantitation; electrophoresis (eg, A2, S, C, and/or F)

83021 chromatography (eg, A2, S, C, and/or F)

(For glycosylated [A1c] hemoglobin analysis, by chromatography, in the absence of an identified hemoglobin variant, use 83036)

83026 Hemoglobin; by copper sulfate method, non-automated

83030 F (fetal), chemical

83033 F (fetal), qualitative

83036 glycosylated (A1C)

(For glycosylated [A1c] hemoglobin analysis, by chromatography, in the setting of an identified hemoglobin variant, use 83021)

(For fecal hemoglobin detection by immunoassay, use 82274)

83037 glycosylated (A1C) by device cleared by FDA for home use

83045 methemoglobin, qualitative

83050 methemoglobin, quantitative

►(For transcutaneous quantitative methemoglobin determination, use 88741)◄

83051 plasma

83055 sulfhemoglobin, qualitative

83060 sulfhemoglobin, quantitative

83065 thermolabile

83068 unstable, screen

83069 urine

83070 Hemosiderin; qualitative

83071 quantitative

(Heroin, see 80100-80103)

(HIAA, use 83497)

(High performance liquid chromatography [HPLC], use 82486)

83080 b-Hexosaminidase, each assay

83088 Histamine

(Hollander test, use 91052)

83090 Homocysteine

83150 Homovanillic acid (HVA)

(Hormones, see individual alphabetic listings in **Chemistry** section)

(Hydrogen breath test, use 91065)

83491 Hydroxycorticosteroids, 17- (17-OHCS)

(For cortisol, see 82530, 82533. For deoxycortisol, use 82634)

83497 Hydroxyindolacetic acid, 5-(HIAA)

(For urine qualitative test, use 81005)

(5-Hydroxytryptamine, use 84260)

83498 Hydroxyprogesterone, 17-d

83499 Hydroxyprogesterone, 20-

83500 Hydroxyproline; free

83505 total

83516 Immunoassay for analyte other than infectious agent antibody or infectious agent antigen, qualitative or semiquantitative; multiple step method

83518 single step method (eg, reagent strip)

83519 Immunoassay, analyte, quantitative; by radiopharmaceutical technique (eg, RIA)

83520 not otherwise specified

(For immunoassays for antibodies to infectious agent antigens, see analyte and method specific codes in the **Immunology** section)

(For immunoassay of tumor antigen not elsewhere specified, use 86316)

(Immunoglobulins, see 82784, 82785)

83525 Insulin; total

(For proinsulin, use 84206)

83527 free

83528 Intrinsic factor

(For intrinsic factor antibodies, use 86340)

83540 Iron

83550 Iron binding capacity

83570 Isocitric dehydrogenase (IDH)

(Isonicotinic acid hydrazide, INH, see code for specific method)

(Isopropyl alcohol, use 84600)

83582 Ketogenic steroids, fractionation

(Ketone bodies, for serum, see 82009, 82010; for urine, see 81000-81003)

83586 Ketosteroids, 17- (17-KS); total

83593 fractionation

83605 Lactate (lactic acid)

83615 Lactate dehydrogenase (LD), (LDH);

83625 isoenzymes, separation and quantitation

83630 Lactoferrin, fecal; qualitative

83631 quantitative

83632 Lactogen, human placental (HPL) human chorionic somatomammotropin

83633 Lactose, urine; qualitative

83634 quantitative

(For tolerance, see 82951, 82952)

(For breath hydrogen test for lactase deficiency, use 91065)

83655 Lead

83661 Fetal lung maturity assessment; lecithin sphingomyelin (L/S) ratio

83662 foam stability test

83663 fluorescence polarization

83664 lamellar body density

(For phosphatidylglycerol, use 84081)

83670 Leucine aminopeptidase (LAP)

83690 Lipase

83695 Lipoprotein (a)

83698 Lipoprotein-associated phospholipase A_2 (Lp-PLA_2)

83700 Lipoprotein, blood; electrophoretic separation and quantitation

83701 high resolution fractionation and quantitation of lipoproteins including lipoprotein subclasses when performed (eg, electrophoresis, ultracentrifugation)

83704 quantitation of lipoprotein particle numbers and lipoprotein particle subclasses (eg, by nuclear magnetic resonance spectroscopy)

83718 Lipoprotein, direct measurement; high density cholesterol (HDL cholesterol)

83719 VLDL cholesterol

83721 LDL cholesterol

(For fractionation by high resolution electrophoresis or ultracentrifugation, use 83701)

(For lipoprotein particle numbers and subclasses analysis by nuclear magnetic resonance spectroscopy, use 83704)

83727 Luteinizing releasing factor (LRH)

(Luteinizing hormone [LH], use 83002)

(For qualitative analysis, see 80100-80103)

(Macroglobulins, alpha-2, use 86329)

83735 Magnesium

83775 Malate dehydrogenase

(Maltose tolerance, see 82951, 82952)

(Mammotropin, use 84146)

83785 Manganese

(Marijuana, see 80100-80103)

83788 Mass spectrometry and tandem mass spectrometry (MS, MS/MS), analyte not elsewhere specified; qualitative, each specimen

83789 quantitative, each specimen

83805 Meprobamate

(For qualitative analysis, see 80100-80103)

83825 Mercury, quantitative

(Mercury screen, use 83015)

83835 Metanephrines

(For catecholamines, see 82382-82384)

83840 Methadone

(For methadone qualitative analysis, see 80100-80103)

(Methamphetamine, see 80100-80103, 82145)

(Methanol, use 84600)

83857 Methemalbumin

(Methemoglobin, see hemoglobin 83045, 83050)

83858 Methsuximide

(Methyl alcohol, use 84600)

(Microalbumin, see 82043 for quantitative, see 82044 for semiquantitative)

(Microglobulin, beta-2, use 82232)

83864 Mucopolysaccharides, acid; quantitative

83866 screen

83872 Mucin, synovial fluid (Ropes test)

83873 Myelin basic protein, cerebrospinal fluid

(For oligoclonal bands, use 83916)

83874 Myoglobin

(Nalorphine, use 83925)

● **83876** Myeloperoxidase (MPO)

83880 Natriuretic peptide

83883 Nephelometry, each analyte not elsewhere specified

83885 Nickel

83887 Nicotine

Codes 83890-83914 are intended for use with molecular diagnostic techniques for analysis of nucleic acids.

Codes 83890-83914 are coded by procedure rather than analyte.

Code separately for each procedure used in an analysis. For example, a procedure requiring isolation of DNA, restriction endonuclease digestion, electrophoresis, and nucleic acid probe amplification would be coded 83890, 83892, 83894, and 83898.

When molecular diagnostic procedures are performed to test for oncology, hematology, neurology or inherited disorder, use the appropriate modifier to specify probe type or condition tested. (See **Appendix I** for a listing of appropriate modifiers to report with molecular diagnostic and cytogenetic procedures.)

►Each nucleic acid preparation may include a digestate, undigested nucleic acid, or other uniquely modified nucleic acid sample (eg, newly synthesized oligonucleotide).◄

(For microbial identification, see 87470-87801)

(For array technology using more than 10 probes, see 88384-88386)

▲ **83890** Molecular diagnostics; molecular isolation or extraction, each nucleic acid type (ie, DNA or RNA)

▲ **83891** isolation or extraction of highly purified nucleic acid, each nucleic acid type (ie, DNA or RNA)

▲ **83892** enzymatic digestion, each enzyme treatment

▲ **83893** dot/slot blot production, each nucleic acid preparation

▲ **83894** separation by gel electrophoresis (eg, agarose, polyacrylamide), each nucleic acid preparation

83896 nucleic acid probe, each

▲ **83897** nucleic acid transfer (eg, Southern, Northern), each nucleic acid preparation

83898 amplification, target, each nucleic acid sequence

(For multiplex target amplification, see 83900, 83901)

(For signal amplification, use 83908)

83900 amplification, target, multiplex, first 2 nucleic acid sequences

+ **83901** amplification, target, multiplex, each additional nucleic acid sequence beyond 2 (List separately in addition to code for primary procedure)

(Use 83901 in conjunction with 83900)

83902 reverse transcription

83903 mutation scanning, by physical properties (eg, single strand conformational polymorphisms [SSCP], heteroduplex, denaturing gradient gel electrophoresis [DGGE], RNA'ase A), single segment, each

83904 mutation identification by sequencing, single segment, each segment

83905 mutation identification by allele specific transcription, single segment, each segment

83906 mutation identification by allele specific translation, single segment, each segment

▲ **83907** lysis of cells prior to nucleic acid extraction (eg, stool specimens, paraffin embedded tissue), each specimen

83908 amplification, signal, each nucleic acid sequence

(For target amplification, see 83898, 83900, 83901)

▲ **83909** separation and identification by high resolution technique (eg, capillary electrophoresis), each nucleic acid preparation

83912 interpretation and report

83913 RNA stabilization

83914 Mutation identification by enzymatic ligation or primer extension, single segment, each segment (eg, oligonucleotide ligation assay [OLA], single base chain extension [SBCE], or allele-specific primer extension [ASPE])

83915 Nucleotidase 5'-

83916 Oligoclonal immune (oligoclonal bands)

83918 Organic acids; total, quantitative, each specimen

83919 qualitative, each specimen

83921 Organic acid, single, quantitative

▲ **83925** Opiate(s), drug and metabolites, each procedure

83930 Osmolality; blood

83935 urine

83937 Osteocalcin (bone g1a protein)

83945 Oxalate

▲ **83950** Oncoprotein; HER-2/neu

(For tissue, see 88342, 88365)

● **83951** des-gamma-carboxy-prothrombin (DCP)

83970 Parathormone (parathyroid hormone)

(Pesticide, quantitative, see code for specific method. For screen for chlorinated hydrocarbons, use 82441)

83986 pH, body fluid, except blood

(For blood pH, see 82800, 82803)

83992 Phencyclidine (PCP)

(For qualitative analysis, see 80100-80103)

(Phenobarbital, use 80184)

83993 Calprotectin, fecal

84022 Phenothiazine

(For qualitative analysis, see 80100, 80101)

84030 Phenylalanine (PKU), blood

(Phenylalanine-tyrosine ratio, see 84030, 84510)

84035 Phenylketones, qualitative

84060 Phosphatase, acid; total

84061 forensic examination

84066 prostatic

84075 Phosphatase, alkaline;

84078 heat stable (total not included)

84080 isoenzymes

84081 Phosphatidylglycerol

(Phosphates inorganic, use 84100)

(Phosphates, organic, see code for specific method. For cholinesterase, see 82480, 82482)

84085 Phosphogluconate, 6-, dehydrogenase, RBC

84087 Phosphohexose isomerase

84100 Phosphorus inorganic (phosphate);

84105 urine

(Pituitary gonadotropins, see 83001-83002)

(PKU, see 84030, 84035)

84106 Porphobilinogen, urine; qualitative

84110 quantitative

84119 Porphyrins, urine; qualitative

84120 quantitation and fractionation

84126 Porphyrins, feces; quantitative

84127 qualitative

(Porphyrin precursors, see 82135, 84106, 84110)

(For protoporphyrin, RBC, see 84202, 84203)

▲ **84132** Potassium; serum, plasma or whole blood

84133 urine

84134 Prealbumin

(For microalbumin, see 82043, 82044)

84135 Pregnanediol

84138 Pregnanetriol

84140 Pregnenolone

84143 17-hydroxypregnenolone

84144 Progesterone

(Progesterone receptor assay, use 84234)

(For proinsulin, use 84206)

84146 Prolactin

84150 Prostaglandin, each

84152 Prostate specific antigen (PSA); complexed (direct measurement)

84153 total

84154 free

▲ **84155** Protein, total, except by refractometry; serum, plasma or whole blood

84156 urine

84157 other source (eg, synovial fluid, cerebrospinal fluid)

84160 Protein, total, by refractometry, any source

(For urine total protein by dipstick method, use 81000-81003)

84163 Pregnancy-associated plasma protein-A (PAPP-A)

84165 Protein; electrophoretic fractionation and quantitation, serum

84166 electrophoretic fractionation and quantitation, other fluids with concentration (eg, urine, CSF)

84181 Western Blot, with interpretation and report, blood or other body fluid

84182 Western Blot, with interpretation and report, blood or other body fluid, immunological probe for band identification, each

(For Western Blot tissue analysis, use 88371)

84202 Protoporphyrin, RBC; quantitative

84203 screen

84206 Proinsulin

(Pseudocholinesterase, use 82480)

84207 Pyridoxal phosphate (Vitamin B-6)

84210 Pyruvate

84220 Pyruvate kinase

84228 Quinine

84233 Receptor assay; estrogen

84234 progesterone

84235 endocrine, other than estrogen or progesterone (specify hormone)

84238 non-endocrine (specify receptor)

84244 Renin

84252 Riboflavin (Vitamin B-2)

(Salicylates, use 80196)

(Secretin test, see 99070, 89100 and appropriate analyses)

84255 Selenium

84260 Serotonin

(For urine metabolites (HIAA), use 83497)

84270 Sex hormone binding globulin (SHBG)

84275 Sialic acid

(Sickle hemoglobin, use 85660)

84285 Silica

▲ **84295** Sodium; serum, plasma or whole blood

84300 urine

84302 other source

(Somatomammotropin, use 83632)

(Somatotropin, use 83003)

84305 Somatomedin

84307 Somatostatin

84311 Spectrophotometry, analyte not elsewhere specified

84315 Specific gravity (except urine)

(For specific gravity, urine, see 81000-81003)

(Stone analysis, see 82355-82370)

84375 Sugars, chromatographic, TLC or paper chromatography

84376 Sugars (mono-, di-, and oligosaccharides); single qualitative, each specimen

84377 multiple qualitative, each specimen

84378 single quantitative, each specimen

84379 multiple quantitative, each specimen

84392 Sulfate, urine

(Sulfhemoglobin, see hemoglobin, 83055, 83060)

(T-3, see 84479-84481)

(T-4, see 84436-84439)

84402 Testosterone; free

84403 total

84425 Thiamine (Vitamin B-1)

84430 Thiocyanate

84432 Thyroglobulin

(Thyroglobulin, antibody, use 86800)

(Thyrotropin releasing hormone [TRH] test, see 80438, 80439)

84436 Thyroxine; total

84437 requiring elution (eg, neonatal)

84439 free

84442 Thyroxine binding globulin (TBG)

84443 Thyroid stimulating hormone (TSH)

84445 Thyroid stimulating immune globulins (TSI)

(Tobramycin, use 80200)

84446 Tocopherol alpha (Vitamin E)

(Tolbutamide tolerance, use 82953)

84449 Transcortin (cortisol binding globulin)

84450 Transferase; aspartate amino (AST) (SGOT)

84460 alanine amino (ALT) (SGPT)

84466 Transferrin

(Iron binding capacity, use 83550)

84478 Triglycerides

84479 Thyroid hormone (T3 or T4) uptake or thyroid hormone binding ratio (THBR)

84480 Triiodothyronine T3; total (TT-3)

84481 free

84482 reverse

84484 Troponin, quantitative

(For troponin, qualitative assay, use 84512)

84485 Trypsin; duodenal fluid

84488 feces, qualitative

84490 feces, quantitative, 24-hour collection

84510 Tyrosine

(Urate crystal identification, use 89060)

84512 Troponin, qualitative

(For troponin, quantitative assay, use 84484)

84520 Urea nitrogen; quantitative

84525 semiquantitative (eg, reagent strip test)

84540 Urea nitrogen, urine

84545 Urea nitrogen, clearance

84550 Uric acid; blood

84560 other source

84577 Urobilinogen, feces, quantitative

84578 Urobilinogen, urine; qualitative

84580 quantitative, timed specimen

84583 semiquantitative

(Uroporphyrins, use 84120)

(Valproic acid [dipropylacetic acid], use 80164)

84585 Vanillylmandelic acid (VMA), urine

84586 Vasoactive intestinal peptide (VIP)

84588 Vasopressin (antidiuretic hormone, ADH)

84590 Vitamin A

(Vitamin B-1, use 84425)

(Vitamin B-2, use 84252)

(Vitamin B-6, use 84207)

(Vitamin B-12, use 82607)

(Vitamin B-12, absorption (Schilling), see 78270, 78271)

(Vitamin C, use 82180)

(Vitamin D, see 82306, 82307, 82652)

(Vitamin E, use 84446)

84591 Vitamin, not otherwise specified

84597 Vitamin K

(VMA, use 84585)

84600 Volatiles (eg, acetic anhydride, carbon tetrachloride, dichloroethane, dichloromethane, diethylether, isopropyl alcohol, methanol)

(For acetaldehyde, use 82000)

(Volume, blood, RISA or Cr-51, see 78110, 78111)

84620 Xylose absorption test, blood and/or urine

(For administration, use 99070)

84630 Zinc

84681 C-peptide

84702 Gonadotropin, chorionic (hCG); quantitative

84703 qualitative

(For urine pregnancy test by visual color comparison, use 81025)

84704 free beta chain

84830 Ovulation tests, by visual color comparison methods for human luteinizing hormone

84999 Unlisted chemistry procedure

Hematology and Coagulation

(For blood banking procedures, see **Transfusion Medicine**)

(Agglutinins, see **Immunology**)

(Antiplasmin, use 85410)

(Antithrombin III, see 85300, 85301)

85002 Bleeding time

85004 Blood count; automated differential WBC count

85007 blood smear, microscopic examination with manual differential WBC count

85008 blood smear, microscopic examination without manual differential WBC count

(For other fluids [eg, CSF], see 89050, 89051)

85009 manual differential WBC count, buffy coat

(Eosinophils, nasal smear, use 89190)

85013 spun microhematocrit

85014 hematocrit (Hct)

85018 hemoglobin (Hgb)

(For other hemoglobin determination, see 83020-83069)

(For immunoassay, hemoglobin, fecal, use 82274)

85025 complete (CBC), automated (Hgb, Hct, RBC, WBC and platelet count) and automated differential WBC count

85027 complete (CBC), automated (Hgb, Hct, RBC, WBC and platelet count)

85032 manual cell count (erythrocyte, leukocyte, or platelet) each

85041 red blood cell (RBC), automated

(Do not report code 85041 in conjunction with 85025 or 85027)

85044 reticulocyte, manual

85045 reticulocyte, automated

85046 reticulocytes, automated, including one or more cellular parameters (eg, reticulocyte hemoglobin content [CHr], immature reticulocyte fraction [IRF], reticulocyte volume [MRV], RNA content), direct measurement

85048 leukocyte (WBC), automated

85049 platelet, automated

85055 Reticulated platelet assay

85060 Blood smear, peripheral, interpretation by physician with written report

85097 Bone marrow, smear interpretation

(For special stains, see 88312, 88313)

(For bone biopsy, see 20220, 20225, 20240, 20245, 20250, 20251)

85130 Chromogenic substrate assay

(Circulating anti-coagulant screen [mixing studies], see 85611, 85732)

85170 Clot retraction

85175 Clot lysis time, whole blood dilution

(Clotting factor I [fibrinogen], see 85384, 85385)

85210 Clotting; factor II, prothrombin, specific

(See also 85610-85613)

85220 factor V (AcG or proaccelerin), labile factor

85230 factor VII (proconvertin, stable factor)

85240 factor VIII (AHG), one stage

85244 factor VIII related antigen

85245 factor VIII, VW factor, ristocetin cofactor

85246 factor VIII, VW factor antigen

85247 factor VIII, von Willebrand factor, multimetric analysis

85250 factor IX (PTC or Christmas)

85260 factor X (Stuart-Prower)

85270 factor XI (PTA)

85280 factor XII (Hageman)

85290 factor XIII (fibrin stabilizing)

85291 factor XIII (fibrin stabilizing), screen solubility

85292 prekallikrein assay (Fletcher factor assay)

85293 high molecular weight kininogen assay (Fitzgerald factor assay)

85300 Clotting inhibitors or anticoagulants; antithrombin III, activity

85301 antithrombin III, antigen assay

85302 protein C, antigen

85303 protein C, activity

85305 protein S, total

85306 protein S, free

85307 Activated Protein C (APC) resistance assay

85335 Factor inhibitor test

85337 Thrombomodulin

(For mixing studies for inhibitors, use 85732)

85345 Coagulation time; Lee and White

85347 activated

85348 other methods

(Differential count, see 85007 et seq)

(Duke bleeding time, use 85002)

(Eosinophils, nasal smear, use 89190)

85360 Euglobulin lysis

(Fetal hemoglobin, see 83030, 83033, 85460)

85362 Fibrin(ogen) degradation (split) products (FDP) (FSP); agglutination slide, semiquantitative

(Immunoelectrophoresis, use 86320)

85366 paracoagulation

85370 quantitative

85378 Fibrin degradation products, D-dimer; qualitative or semiquantitative

85379 quantitative

(For ultrasensitive and standard sensitivity quantitative D-dimer, use 85379)

85380 ultrasensitive (eg, for evaluation for venous thromboembolism), qualitative or semiquantitative

85384 Fibrinogen; activity

85385 antigen

85390 Fibrinolysins or coagulopathy screen, interpretation and report

85396 Coagulation/fibrinolysis assay, whole blood (eg, viscoelastic clot assessment), including use of any pharmacologic additive(s), as indicated, including interpretation and written report, per day

● **85397** Coagulation and fibrinolysis, functional activity, not otherwise specified (eg, ADAMTS-13), each analyte

85400 Fibrinolytic factors and inhibitors; plasmin

85410 alpha-2 antiplasmin

85415 plasminogen activator

85420 plasminogen, except antigenic assay

85421 plasminogen, antigenic assay

(Fragility, red blood cell, see 85547, 85555-85557)

85441 Heinz bodies; direct

85445 induced, acetyl phenylhydrazine

(Hematocrit [PCV], see 85014, 85025, 85027)

(Hemoglobin, see 83020-83068, 85018, 85025, 85027)

85460 Hemoglobin or RBCs, fetal, for fetomaternal hemorrhage; differential lysis (Kleihauer-Betke)

(See also 83030, 83033)

(Hemolysins, see 86940, 86941)

85461 rosette

85475 Hemolysin, acid

(See also 86940, 86941)

85520 Heparin assay

85525 Heparin neutralization

85530 Heparin-protamine tolerance test

85536 Iron stain, peripheral blood

(For iron stains on bone marrow or other tissues with physician evaluation, use 88313)

85540 Leukocyte alkaline phosphatase with count

85547 Mechanical fragility, RBC

85549 Muramidase

(Nitroblue tetrazolium dye test, use 86384)

85555 Osmotic fragility, RBC; unincubated

85557 incubated

(Packed cell volume, use 85013)

(Partial thromboplastin time, see 85730, 85732)

(Parasites, blood [eg, malaria smears], use 87207)

(Plasmin, use 85400)

(Plasminogen, use 85420)

(Plasminogen activator, use 85415)

85576 Platelet, aggregation (in vitro), each agent

85597 Platelet neutralization

85610 Prothrombin time;

85611 substitution, plasma fractions, each

85612 Russell viper venom time (includes venom); undiluted

85613 diluted

(Red blood cell count, see 85025, 85027, 85041)

85635 Reptilase test

(Reticulocyte count, see 85044, 85045)

85651 Sedimentation rate, erythrocyte; non-automated

85652 automated

85660 Sickling of RBC, reduction

(Hemoglobin electrophoresis, use 83020)

(Smears [eg, for parasites, malaria], use 87207)

85670 Thrombin time; plasma

85675 titer

85705 Thromboplastin inhibition, tissue

(For individual clotting factors, see 85245-85247)

85730 Thromboplastin time, partial (PTT); plasma or whole blood

85732 substitution, plasma fractions, each

85810 Viscosity

(von Willebrand factor assay, see 85245-85247)

(WBC count, see 85025, 85027, 85048, 89050)

85999 Unlisted hematology and coagulation procedure

Immunology

(Acetylcholine receptor antibody, see 83519, 86255, 86256)

(Actinomyces, antibodies to, use 86602)

(Adrenal cortex antibodies, see 86255, 86256)

86000 Agglutinins, febrile (eg, Brucella, Francisella, Murine typhus, Q fever, Rocky Mountain spotted fever, scrub typhus), each antigen

(For antibodies to infectious agents, see 86602-86804)

86001 Allergen specific IgG quantitative or semiquantitative, each allergen

(Agglutinins and autohemolysins, see 86940, 86941)

86003 Allergen specific IgE; quantitative or semiquantitative, each allergen

(For total quantitative IgE, use 82785)

86005 qualitative, multiallergen screen (dipstick, paddle, or disk)

(For total qualitative IgE, use 83518)

(Alpha-1 antitrypsin, see 82103, 82104)

(Alpha-1 feto-protein, see 82105, 82106)

(Anti-AChR [acetylcholine receptor] antibody titer, see 86255, 86256)

(Anticardiolipin antibody, use 86147)

(Anti-DNA, use 86225)

(Anti-deoxyribonuclease titer, use 86215)

86021 Antibody identification; leukocyte antibodies

86022 platelet antibodies

86023 platelet associated immunoglobulin assay

86038 Antinuclear antibodies (ANA);

86039 titer

(Antistreptococcal antibody, ie, anti-DNAse, use 86215)

(Antistreptokinase titer, use 86590)

86060 Antistreptolysin O; titer

(For antibodies to infectious agents, see 86602-86804)

86063 screen

(For antibodies to infectious agents, see 86602-86804)

(Blastomyces, antibodies to, use 86612)

86077 Blood bank physician services; difficult cross match and/or evaluation of irregular antibody(s), interpretation and written report

86078 investigation of transfusion reaction including suspicion of transmissible disease, interpretation and written report

86079 authorization for deviation from standard blood banking procedures (eg, use of outdated blood, transfusion of Rh incompatible units), with written report

(Brucella, antibodies to, use 86622)

(Candida, antibodies to, use 86628. For skin testing, use 86485)

86140 C-reactive protein;

(Candidiasis, use 86628)

86141 high sensitivity (hsCRP)

86146 Beta 2 Glycoprotein I antibody, each

86147 Cardiolipin (phospholipid) antibody, each Ig class

86148 Anti-phosphatidylserine (phospholipid) antibody

(To report antiprothrombin [phospholipid cofactor] antibody, use Category III code 0030T)

86155 Chemotaxis assay, specify method

(Clostridium difficile toxin, use 87230)

(Coccidioides, antibodies to, see 86635. For skin testing, use 86490)

86156 Cold agglutinin; screen

86157 titer

86160 Complement; antigen, each component

86161 functional activity, each component

86162 total hemolytic (CH50)

86171 Complement fixation tests, each antigen

(Coombs test, see 86880-86886)

86185 Counterimmunoelectrophoresis, each antigen

(Cryptococcus, antibodies to, use 86641)

86200 Cyclic citrullinated peptide (CCP), antibody

Pathology and Laboratory

86215 Deoxyribonuclease, antibody

86225 Deoxyribonucleic acid (DNA) antibody; native or double stranded

(Echinococcus, antibodies to, see code for specific method)

(For HIV antibody tests, see 86701-86703)

86226 single stranded

(Anti D.S., DNA, IFA, eg, using C.Lucilae, see 86255 and 86256)

86235 Extractable nuclear antigen, antibody to, any method (eg, nRNP, SS-A, SS-B, Sm, RNP, Sc170, J01), each antibody

86243 Fc receptor

(Filaria, antibodies to, see code for specific method)

86255 Fluorescent noninfectious agent antibody; screen, each antibody

86256 titer, each antibody

(Fluorescent technique for antigen identification in tissue, use 88346; for indirect fluorescence, use 88347)

(FTA, see 86781)

(Gel [agar] diffusion tests, use 86331)

86277 Growth hormone, human (HGH), antibody

86280 Hemagglutination inhibition test (HAI)

(For rubella, use 86762)

(For antibodies to infectious agents, see 86602-86804)

86294 Immunoassay for tumor antigen, qualitative or semiquantitative (eg, bladder tumor antigen)

86300 Immunoassay for tumor antigen, quantitative; CA 15-3 (27.29)

86301 CA 19-9

86304 CA 125

(For measurement of serum HER-2/neu oncoprotein, see 83950)

(For hepatitis delta agent, antibody, use 86692)

86308 Heterophile antibodies; screening

(For antibodies to infectious agents, see 86602-86804)

86309 titer

(For antibodies to infectious agents, see 86602-86804)

86310 titers after absorption with beef cells and guinea pig kidney

(Histoplasma, antibodies to, use 86698. For skin testing, use 86510)

(For antibodies to infectious agents, see 86602-86804)

(Human growth hormone antibody, use 86277)

86316 Immunoassay for tumor antigen, other antigen, quantitative (eg, CA 50, 72-4, 549), each

86317 Immunoassay for infectious agent antibody, quantitative, not otherwise specified

(For immunoassay techniques for antigens, see 83516, 83518, 83519, 83520, 87301-87450, 87810-87899)

(For particle agglutination procedures, use 86403)

86318 Immunoassay for infectious agent antibody, qualitative or semiquantitative, single step method (eg, reagent strip)

86320 Immunoelectrophoresis; serum

86325 other fluids (eg, urine, cerebrospinal fluid) with concentration

86327 crossed (2-dimensional assay)

86329 Immunodiffusion; not elsewhere specified

86331 gel diffusion, qualitative (Ouchterlony), each antigen or antibody

86332 Immune complex assay

86334 Immunofixation electrophoresis; serum

86335 other fluids with concentration (eg, urine, CSF)

86336 Inhibin A

86337 Insulin antibodies

86340 Intrinsic factor antibodies

(Leptospira, antibodies to, use 86720)

(Leukoagglutinins, use 86021)

86341 Islet cell antibody

86343 Leukocyte histamine release test (LHR)

86344 Leukocyte phagocytosis

86353 Lymphocyte transformation, mitogen (phytomitogen) or antigen induced blastogenesis

(Malaria antibodies, use 86750)

86355 B cells, total count

86356 Mononuclear cell antigen, quantitative (eg, flow cytometry), not otherwise specified, each antigen

(Do not report 88187-88189 for interpretation of 86355, 86356, 86357, 86359, 86360, 86361, 86367)

86357 Natural killer (NK) cells, total count

86359 T cells; total count

86360 absolute CD4 and CD8 count, including ratio

86361 absolute CD4 count

86367 Stem cells (ie, CD34), total count

(For flow cytometric immunophenotyping for the assessment of potential hematolymphoid neoplasia, see 88184-88189)

86376 Microsomal antibodies (eg, thyroid or liver-kidney), each

86378 Migration inhibitory factor test (MIF)

(Mitochondrial antibody, liver, see 86255, 86256)

(Mononucleosis, see 86308-86310)

86382 Neutralization test, viral

86384 Nitroblue tetrazolium dye test (NTD)

(Ouchterlony diffusion, use 86331)

(Platelet antibodies, see 86022, 86023)

86403 Particle agglutination; screen, each antibody

86406 titer, each antibody

(Pregnancy test, see 84702, 84703)

(Rapid plasma reagin test (RPR), see 86592, 86593)

86430 Rheumatoid factor; qualitative

86431 quantitative

(Serologic test for syphilis, see 86592, 86593)

86480 Tuberculosis test, cell mediated immunity measurement of gamma interferon antigen response

86485 Skin test; candida

(For antibody, candida, use 86628)

86486 unlisted antigen, each

86490 coccidioidomycosis

86510 histoplasmosis

(For histoplasma, antibody, use 86698)

86580 tuberculosis, intradermal

(For tuberculosis test, cell mediated immunity measurement of gamma interferon antigen response, use 86480)

(For skin tests for allergy, see 95010-95199)

(Smooth muscle antibody, see 86255, 86256)

(Sporothrix, antibodies to, see code for specific method)

(86586 has been deleted. For skin testing, unlisted antigen, use 86486. For flow cytometry, quantitative, not otherwise specified, use 86356)

86590 Streptokinase, antibody

(For antibodies to infectious agents, see 86602-86804)

(Streptolysin O antibody, see antistreptolysin O, 86060, 86063)

86592 Syphilis test; qualitative (eg, VDRL, RPR, ART)

(For antibodies to infectious agents, see 86602-86804)

86593 quantitative

(For antibodies to infectious agents, see 86602-86804)

(Tetanus antibody, use 86774)

(Thyroglobulin antibody, use 86800)

(Thyroglobulin, use 84432)

(Thyroid microsomal antibody, use 86376)

(For toxoplasma antibody, see 86777-86778)

The following codes (86602-86804) are qualitative or semiquantitative immunoassays performed by multiple-step methods for the detection of antibodies to infectious agents. For immunoassays by single-step method (eg, reagent strips), use code 86318. Procedures for the identification of antibodies should be coded as precisely as possible. For example, an antibody to a virus could be coded with increasing specificity for virus, family, genus, species, or type. In some cases, further precision may be added to codes by specifying the class of immunoglobulin being detected. When multiple tests are done to detect antibodies to organisms classified more precisely than the specificity allowed by available codes, it is appropriate to code each as a separate service. For example, a test for antibody to an enterovirus is coded as 86658. Coxsackie viruses are enteroviruses, but there are no codes for the individual species of enterovirus. If assays are performed for antibodies to coxsackie A and B species, each assay should be separately coded. Similarly, if multiple assays are performed for antibodies of different immunoglobulin classes, each assay should be coded separately. When a coding option exists for reporting IgM specific antibodies (eg, 86632), the corresponding nonspecific code (eg, 86631) may be reported for performance of either an antibody analysis not specific for a particular immunoglobulin class or for an IgG analysis.

(For the detection of antibodies other than those to infectious agents, see specific antibody [eg, 86021-86023, 86376, 86800, 86850-86870] or specific method [eg, 83516, 86255, 86256]).

(For infectious agent/antigen detection, see 87260-87899)

86602 Antibody; actinomyces

86603 adenovirus

86606 Aspergillus

86609 bacterium, not elsewhere specified

86611 Bartonella

86612 Blastomyces

86615 Bordetella

86617 Borrelia burgdorferi (Lyme disease) confirmatory test (eg, Western Blot or immunoblot)

86618 Borrelia burgdorferi (Lyme disease)

86619 Borrelia (relapsing fever)

86622 Brucella

86625 Campylobacter

86628 Candida

(For skin test, candida, use 86485)

86631 Chlamydia

86632 Chlamydia, IgM

(For chlamydia antigen, see 87270, 87320. For fluorescent antibody technique, see 86255, 86256)

86635 Coccidioides

86638 Coxiella burnetii (Q fever)

86641 Cryptococcus

86644 cytomegalovirus (CMV)

86645 cytomegalovirus (CMV), IgM

86648 Diphtheria

86651 encephalitis, California (La Crosse)

86652 encephalitis, Eastern equine

86653 encephalitis, St. Louis

86654 encephalitis, Western equine

86658 enterovirus (eg, coxsackie, echo, polio)

(Trichinella, antibodies to, use 86784)

(Trypanosoma, antibodies to, see code for specific method)

(Tuberculosis, use 86580 for skin testing)

(Viral antibodies, see code for specific method)

86663 Epstein-Barr (EB) virus, early antigen (EA)

86664 Epstein-Barr (EB) virus, nuclear antigen (EBNA)

86665 Epstein-Barr (EB) virus, viral capsid (VCA)

86666 Ehrlichia

86668 Francisella tularensis

86671 fungus, not elsewhere specified

86674 Giardia lamblia

86677 Helicobacter pylori

86682 helminth, not elsewhere specified

86684 Haemophilus influenza

86687 HTLV-I

86688 HTLV-II

86689 HTLV or HIV antibody, confirmatory test (eg, Western Blot)

86692 hepatitis, delta agent

(For hepatitis delta agent, antigen, use 87380)

86694 herpes simplex, non-specific type test

86695 herpes simplex, type 1

86696 herpes simplex, type 2

86698 histoplasma

86701 HIV-1

86702 HIV-2

86703 HIV-1 and HIV-2, single assay

(When HIV antibody immunoassay [HIV testing 86701-86703] is performed using a kit or transportable instrument that wholly or in part consists of a single use, disposable analytical chamber, the service may be identified by adding modifier 92 to the usual code)

(For HIV-1 antigen, use 87390)

(For HIV-2 antigen, use 87391)

(For confirmatory test for HIV antibody (eg, Western Blot), use 86689)

86704 Hepatitis B core antibody (HBcAb); total

86705 IgM antibody

86706 Hepatitis B surface antibody (HBsAb)

86707 Hepatitis Be antibody (HBeAb)

86708 Hepatitis A antibody (HAAb); total

86709 IgM antibody

86710 Antibody; influenza virus

86713 Legionella

86717 Leishmania

86720 Leptospira

86723 Listeria monocytogenes

86727 lymphocytic choriomeningitis

86729 lymphogranuloma venereum

86732 mucormycosis

86735 mumps

86738 mycoplasma

86741 Neisseria meningitidis

86744 Nocardia

86747 parvovirus

86750 Plasmodium (malaria)

86753 protozoa, not elsewhere specified

86756 respiratory syncytial virus

86757 Rickettsia

86759 rotavirus

86762 rubella

86765 rubeola

86768 Salmonella

86771 Shigella

86774 tetanus

86777 Toxoplasma

86778 Toxoplasma, IgM

86781 Treponema pallidum, confirmatory test (eg, FTA-abs)

86784 Trichinella

86787 varicella-zoster

86788 West Nile virus, IgM

86789 West Nile virus

86790 virus, not elsewhere specified

86793 Yersinia

86800 Thyroglobulin antibody

(For thyroglobulin, use 84432)

86803 Hepatitis C antibody;

86804 confirmatory test (eg, immunoblot)

Tissue Typing

86805 Lymphocytotoxicity assay, visual crossmatch; with titration

86806 without titration

86807 Serum screening for cytotoxic percent reactive antibody (PRA); standard method

86808 quick method

86812 HLA typing; A, B, or C (eg, A10, B7, B27), single antigen

86813 A, B, or C, multiple antigens

86816 DR/DQ, single antigen

86817 DR/DQ, multiple antigens

86821 lymphocyte culture, mixed (MLC)

86822 lymphocyte culture, primed (PLC)

►(For HLA typing by molecular pathology techniques, see 83890-83914 with appropriate genetic testing modifiers 4A-4G)◄

86849 Unlisted immunology procedure

Transfusion Medicine

(For apheresis, use 36511, 36512)

(For therapeutic phlebotomy, use 99195)

86850 Antibody screen, RBC, each serum technique

86860 Antibody elution (RBC), each elution

86870 Antibody identification, RBC antibodies, each panel for each serum technique

86880 Antihuman globulin test (Coombs test); direct, each antiserum

86885 indirect, qualitative, each reagent red cell

86886 indirect, each antibody titer

(For indirect antihuman globulin [Coombs] test for RBC antibody screening, use 86850)

(For indirect antihuman globulin [Coombs] test for RBC antibody identification using reagent red cell panels, use 86870)

86890 Autologous blood or component, collection processing and storage; predeposited

86891 intra- or postoperative salvage

(For physician services to autologous donors, see 99201-99204)

86900 Blood typing; ABO

86901 Rh (D)

86903 antigen screening for compatible blood unit using reagent serum, per unit screened

86904 antigen screening for compatible unit using patient serum, per unit screened

86905 RBC antigens, other than ABO or Rh (D), each

86906 Rh phenotyping, complete

86910 Blood typing, for paternity testing, per individual; ABO, Rh and MN

86911 each additional antigen system

86920 Compatibility test each unit; immediate spin technique

86921 incubation technique

86922 antiglobulin technique

86923 electronic

(Do not use 86923 in conjunction with 86920-86922 for same unit crossmatch)

86927 Fresh frozen plasma, thawing, each unit

86930 Frozen blood, each unit; freezing (includes preparation)

86931 thawing

86932 freezing (includes preparation) and thawing

86940 Hemolysins and agglutinins; auto, screen, each

86941 incubated

86945 Irradiation of blood product, each unit

86950 Leukocyte transfusion

(For leukapheresis, use 36511)

86960 Volume reduction of blood or blood product (eg, red blood cells or platelets), each unit

86965 Pooling of platelets or other blood products

86970 Pretreatment of RBCs for use in RBC antibody detection, identification, and/or compatibility testing; incubation with chemical agents or drugs, each

86971 incubation with enzymes, each

86972 by density gradient separation

86975 Pretreatment of serum for use in RBC antibody identification; incubation with drugs, each

86976 by dilution

86977 incubation with inhibitors, each

86978 by differential red cell absorption using patient RBCs or RBCs of known phenotype, each absorption

86985 Splitting of blood or blood products, each unit

86999 Unlisted transfusion medicine procedure

Microbiology

Includes bacteriology, mycology, parasitology, and virology.

Presumptive identification of microorganisms is defined as identification by colony morphology, growth on selective media, Gram stains, or up to three tests (eg, catalase, oxidase, indole, urease). Definitive identification of microorganisms is defined as an identification to the genus or species level that requires additional tests (eg, biochemical panels, slide cultures). If additional studies involve molecular probes, chromatography, or immunologic techniques, these should be separately coded in addition to definitive identification codes (87140-87158). For multiple specimens/sites use modifier 59. For repeat laboratory tests performed on the same day, use modifier 91.

87001 Animal inoculation, small animal; with observation

87003 with observation and dissection

87015 Concentration (any type), for infectious agents

(Do not report 87015 in conjunction with 87177)

87040 Culture, bacterial; blood, aerobic, with isolation and presumptive identification of isolates (includes anaerobic culture, if appropriate)

87045 stool, aerobic, with isolation and preliminary examination (eg, KIA, LIA), Salmonella and Shigella species

87046 stool, aerobic, additional pathogens, isolation and presumptive identification of isolates, each plate

87070 any other source except urine, blood or stool, aerobic, with isolation and presumptive identification of isolates

(For urine, use 87088)

87071 quantitative, aerobic with isolation and presumptive identification of isolates, any source except urine, blood or stool

(For urine, use 87088)

87073 quantitative, anaerobic with isolation and presumptive identification of isolates, any source except urine, blood or stool

(For definitive identification of isolates, use 87076 or 87077. For typing of isolates see 87140-87158)

87075 any source, except blood, anaerobic with isolation and presumptive identification of isolates

87076 anaerobic isolate, additional methods required for definitive identification, each isolate

(For gas liquid chromatography [GLC] or high pressure liquid chromatography [HPLC], use 87143)

87077 aerobic isolate, additional methods required for definitive identification, each isolate

(For gas liquid chromatography [GLC] or high pressure liquid chromatography [HPLC], use 87143)

87081 Culture, presumptive, pathogenic organisms, screening only;

87084 with colony estimation from density chart

87086 Culture, bacterial; quantitative colony count, urine

87088 with isolation and presumptive identification of each isolate, urine

87101 Culture, fungi (mold or yeast) isolation, with presumptive identification of isolates; skin, hair, or nail

87102 other source (except blood)

87103 blood

87106 Culture, fungi, definitive identification, each organism; yeast

(Use 87106 in addition to codes 87101, 87102, or 87103 when appropriate)

87107 mold

87109 Culture, mycoplasma, any source

87110 Culture, chlamydia, any source

(For immunofluorescence staining of shell vials, use 87140)

87116 Culture, tubercle or other acid-fast bacilli (eg, TB, AFB, mycobacteria) any source, with isolation and presumptive identification of isolates

(For concentration, use 87015)

87118 Culture, mycobacterial, definitive identification, each isolate

(For nucleic acid probe identification, use 87149)

(For GLC or HPLC identification, use 87143)

87140 Culture, typing; immunofluorescent method, each antiserum

87143 gas liquid chromatography (GLC) or high pressure liquid chromatography (HPLC) method

87147 immunologic method, other than immunofluoresence (eg, agglutination grouping), per antiserum

87149 identification by nucleic acid probe

87152 identification by pulse field gel typing

87158 other methods

87164 Dark field examination, any source (eg, penile, vaginal, oral, skin); includes specimen collection

87166 without collection

87168 Macroscopic examination; arthropod

87169 parasite

87172 Pinworm exam (eg, cellophane tape prep)

87176 Homogenization, tissue, for culture

87177 Ova and parasites, direct smears, concentration and identification

(Do not report 87177 in conjunction with 87015)

(For direct smears from a primary source, use 87207)

(For coccidia or microsporidia exam, use 87207)

(For complex special stain (trichrome, iron hematoxylin), use 87209)

(For nucleic acid probes in cytologic material, use 88365)

(For molecular diagnostics, see 83890-83898, 87470-87799)

87181 Susceptibility studies, antimicrobial agent; agar dilution method, per agent (eg, antibiotic gradient strip)

87184 disk method, per plate (12 or fewer agents)

87185 enzyme detection (eg, beta lactamase), per enzyme

87186 microdilution or agar dilution (minimum inhibitory concentration [MIC] or breakpoint), each multi-antimicrobial, per plate

+ 87187 microdilution or agar dilution, minimum lethal concentration (MLC), each plate (List separately in addition to code for primary procedure)

(Use 87187 in conjunction with 87186 or 87188)

87188 macrobroth dilution method, each agent

87190 mycobacteria, proportion method, each agent

(For other mycobacterial susceptibility studies, see 87181, 87184, 87186, or 87188)

87197 Serum bactericidal titer (Schlicter test)

87205 Smear, primary source with interpretation; Gram or Giemsa stain for bacteria, fungi, or cell types

87206 fluorescent and/or acid fast stain for bacteria, fungi, parasites, viruses or cell types

87207 special stain for inclusion bodies or parasites (eg, malaria, coccidia, microsporidia, trypanosomes, herpes viruses)

(For direct smears with concentration and identification, use 87177)

(For thick smear preparation, use 87015)

(For fat, meat, fibers, nasal eosinophils, and starch, see miscellaneous section)

87209 complex special stain (eg, trichrome, iron hemotoxylin) for ova and parasites

87210 wet mount for infectious agents (eg, saline, India ink, KOH preps)

(For KOH examination of skin, hair or nails, see 87220)

87220 Tissue examination by KOH slide of samples from skin, hair, or nails for fungi or ectoparasite ova or mites (eg, scabies)

87230 Toxin or antitoxin assay, tissue culture (eg, Clostridium difficile toxin)

87250 Virus isolation; inoculation of embryonated eggs, or small animal, includes observation and dissection

87252 tissue culture inoculation, observation, and presumptive identification by cytopathic effect

87253 tissue culture, additional studies or definitive identification (eg, hemabsorption, neutralization, immunofluoresence stain), each isolate

(Electron microscopy, use 88348)

(Inclusion bodies in tissue sections, see 88304-88309; in smears, see 87207-87210; in fluids, use 88106)

87254 centrifuge enhanced (shell vial) technique, includes identification with immunofluorescence stain, each virus

(Report 87254 in addition to 87252 as appropriate)

87255 including identification by non-immunologic method, other than by cytopathic effect (eg, virus specific enzymatic activity)

►These codes are intended for primary source only. For similar studies on culture material, refer to codes 87140-87158. Infectious agents by antigen detection, immunofluorescence microscopy, or nucleic acid probe techniques should be reported as precisely as possible. The most specific code possible should be reported. If there is no specific agent code, the general methodology code (eg, 87299, 87449, 87450, 87797, 87798, 87799, 87899) should be used. For identification of antibodies to many of the listed infectious agents, see 86602-86804. When separate results are reported for different species or strain of organisms, each result should be coded separately. Use modifier 59 when separate results are reported for different species or strains that are described by the same code.◀

87260 Infectious agent antigen detection by immunofluorescent technique; adenovirus

87265 Bordetella pertussis/parapertussis

87267 Enterovirus, direct fluorescent antibody (DFA)

87269 giardia

87270 Chlamydia trachomatis

87271 Cytomegalovirus, direct fluorescent antibody (DFA)

87272 cryptosporidium

87273 Herpes simplex virus type 2

87274 Herpes simplex virus type 1

87275 influenza B virus

87276 influenza A virus

87277 Legionella micdadei

87278 Legionella pneumophila

87279 Parainfluenza virus, each type

87280 respiratory syncytial virus

87281 Pneumocystis carinii

87283 Rubeola

87285 Treponema pallidum

87290 Varicella zoster virus

87299 not otherwise specified, each organism

87300 Infectious agent antigen detection by immunofluorescent technique, polyvalent for multiple organisms, each polyvalent antiserum

(For physician evaluation of infectious disease agents by immunofluorescence, use 88346)

87301 Infectious agent antigen detection by enzyme immunoassay technique, qualitative or semiquantitative, multiple-step method; adenovirus enteric types 40/41

87305 Aspergillus

87320 Chlamydia trachomatis

87324 Clostridium difficile toxin(s)

87327 Cryptococcus neoformans

(For Cryptococcus latex agglutination, use 86403)

87328 cryptosporidium

87329 giardia

87332 cytomegalovirus

87335 Escherichia coli 0157

(For giardia antigen, use 87329)

87336 Entamoeba histolytica dispar group

87337 Entamoeba histolytica group

87338 Helicobacter pylori, stool

87339 Helicobacter pylori

(For H. pylori, stool, use 87338. For H. pylori, breath and blood by mass spectrometry, see 83013, 83014. For H. pylori, liquid scintillation counter, see 78267, 78268)

87340 hepatitis B surface antigen (HBsAg)

87341 hepatitis B surface antigen (HBsAg) neutralization

87350 hepatitis Be antigen (HBeAg)

87380 hepatitis, delta agent

87385 Histoplasma capsulatum

87390 HIV-1

87391 HIV-2

87400 Influenza, A or B, each

87420 respiratory syncytial virus

87425 rotavirus

87427 Shiga-like toxin

87430 Streptococcus, group A

87449 Infectious agent antigen detection by enzyme immunoassay technique qualitative or semiquantitative; multiple step method, not otherwise specified, each organism

87450 single step method, not otherwise specified, each organism

87451 multiple step method, polyvalent for multiple organisms, each polyvalent antiserum

87470 Infectious agent detection by nucleic acid (DNA or RNA); Bartonella henselae and Bartonella quintana, direct probe technique

87471 Bartonella henselae and Bartonella quintana, amplified probe technique

87472 Bartonella henselae and Bartonella quintana, quantification

87475 Borrelia burgdorferi, direct probe technique

87476 Borrelia burgdorferi, amplified probe technique

87477 Borrelia burgdorferi, quantification

87480 Candida species, direct probe technique

87481 Candida species, amplified probe technique

87482 Candida species, quantification

87485 Chlamydia pneumoniae, direct probe technique

87486 Chlamydia pneumoniae, amplified probe technique

87487 Chlamydia pneumoniae, quantification

87490 Chlamydia trachomatis, direct probe technique

87491 Chlamydia trachomatis, amplified probe technique

87492 Chlamydia trachomatis, quantification

87495 cytomegalovirus, direct probe technique

87496 cytomegalovirus, amplified probe technique

87497 cytomegalovirus, quantification

87498 enterovirus, amplified probe technique

87500 vancomycin resistance (eg, enterococcus species van A, van B), amplified probe technique

87510 Gardnerella vaginalis, direct probe technique

87511 Gardnerella vaginalis, amplified probe technique

87512 Gardnerella vaginalis, quantification

87515 hepatitis B virus, direct probe technique

87516 hepatitis B virus, amplified probe technique

87517 hepatitis B virus, quantification

87520 hepatitis C, direct probe technique

87521 hepatitis C, amplified probe technique

87522 hepatitis C, quantification

87525 hepatitis G, direct probe technique

87526 hepatitis G, amplified probe technique

87527 hepatitis G, quantification

87528 Herpes simplex virus, direct probe technique

87529 Herpes simplex virus, amplified probe technique

87530 Herpes simplex virus, quantification

87531 Herpes virus-6, direct probe technique

87532 Herpes virus-6, amplified probe technique

87533 Herpes virus-6, quantification

87534 HIV-1, direct probe technique

87535 HIV-1, amplified probe technique

87536 HIV-1, quantification

87537 HIV-2, direct probe technique

87538 HIV-2, amplified probe technique

87539 HIV-2, quantification

87540 Legionella pneumophila, direct probe technique

87541 Legionella pneumophila, amplified probe technique

87542 Legionella pneumophila, quantification

87550 Mycobacteria species, direct probe technique

87551 Mycobacteria species, amplified probe technique

87552 Mycobacteria species, quantification

87555 Mycobacteria tuberculosis, direct probe technique

87556 Mycobacteria tuberculosis, amplified probe technique

87557 Mycobacteria tuberculosis, quantification

87560 Mycobacteria avium-intracellulare, direct probe technique

87561 Mycobacteria avium-intracellulare, amplified probe technique

87562 Mycobacteria avium-intracellulare, quantification

87580 Mycoplasma pneumoniae, direct probe technique

87581 Mycoplasma pneumoniae, amplified probe technique

87582 Mycoplasma pneumoniae, quantification

87590 Neisseria gonorrhoeae, direct probe technique

87591 Neisseria gonorrhoeae, amplified probe technique

87592 Neisseria gonorrhoeae, quantification

87620 papillomavirus, human, direct probe technique

87621 papillomavirus, human, amplified probe technique

87622 papillomavirus, human, quantification

87640 Staphylococcus aureus, amplified probe technique

87641 Staphylococcus aureus, methicillin resistant, amplified probe technique

(For assays that detect methicillin resistance and identify Staphylococcus aureus using a single nucleic acid sequence, use 87641)

87650 Streptococcus, group A, direct probe technique

87651 Streptococcus, group A, amplified probe technique

87652 Streptococcus, group A, quantification

87653 Streptococcus, group B, amplified probe technique

87660 Trichomonas vaginalis, direct probe technique

87797 Infectious agent detection by nucleic acid (DNA or RNA), not otherwise specified; direct probe technique, each organism

87798 amplified probe technique, each organism

87799 quantification, each organism

87800 Infectious agent detection by nucleic acid (DNA or RNA), multiple organisms; direct probe(s) technique

87801 amplified probe(s) technique

(For each specific organism nucleic acid detection from a primary source, see 87470-87660. For detection of specific infectious agents not otherwise specified, see 87797, 87798, or 87799 1 time for each agent)

87802 Infectious agent antigen detection by immunoassay with direct optical observation; Streptococcus, group B

87803 Clostridium difficile toxin A

87804 Influenza

87807 respiratory syncytial virus

87808 Trichomonas vaginalis

87809 adenovirus

▲ **87810** Chlamydia trachomatis

87850 Neisseria gonorrhoeae

87880 Streptococcus, group A

87899 not otherwise specified

87900 Infectious agent drug susceptibility phenotype prediction using regularly updated genotypic bioinformatics

87901 Infectious agent genotype analysis by nucleic acid (DNA or RNA); HIV-1, reverse transcriptase and protease

(For infectious agent drug susceptibility phenotype prediction for HIV-1, use 87900)

87902 Hepatitis C virus

87903 Infectious agent phenotype analysis by nucleic acid (DNA or RNA) with drug resistance tissue culture analysis, HIV 1; first through 10 drugs tested

+ **87904** each additional drug tested (List separately in addition to code for primary procedure)

(Use 87904 in conjunction with 87903)

● **87905** Infectious agent enzymatic activity other than virus (eg, sialidase activity in vaginal fluid)

►(For virus isolation including identification by non-immunologic method, other than by cytopathic effect, use 87255)◄

87999 Unlisted microbiology procedure

Anatomic Pathology

Postmortem Examination

Procedures 88000 through 88099 represent physician services only. Use modifier 90 for outside laboratory services.

88000 Necropsy (autopsy), gross examination only; without CNS

88005 with brain

88007 with brain and spinal cord

88012 infant with brain

88014 stillborn or newborn with brain

88016 macerated stillborn

88020 Necropsy (autopsy), gross and microscopic; without CNS

88025 with brain

88027 with brain and spinal cord

88028 infant with brain

88029 stillborn or newborn with brain

88036 Necropsy (autopsy), limited, gross and/or microscopic; regional

88037 single organ

88040 Necropsy (autopsy); forensic examination

88045 coroner's call

88099 Unlisted necropsy (autopsy) procedure

Cytopathology

88104 Cytopathology, fluids, washings or brushings, except cervical or vaginal; smears with interpretation

88106 simple filter method with interpretation

88107 smears and simple filter preparation with interpretation

(For nongynecological selective cellular enhancement including filter transfer techniques, use 88112)

88108 Cytopathology, concentration technique, smears and interpretation (eg, Saccomanno technique)

(For cervical or vaginal smears, see 88150-88155)

(For gastric intubation with lavage, see 89130-89141, 91055)

(For x-ray localization, use 74340)

88112 Cytopathology, selective cellular enhancement technique with interpretation (eg, liquid based slide preparation method), except cervical or vaginal

(Do not report 88112 with 88108)

88125 Cytopathology, forensic (eg, sperm)

88130 Sex chromatin identification; Barr bodies

88140 peripheral blood smear, polymorphonuclear drumsticks

(For Guard stain, use 88313)

Codes 88141-88155, 88164-88167, 88174-88175 are used to report cervical or vaginal screening by various methods and to report physician interpretation services. Use codes 88150-88154 to report conventional Pap smears that are examined using non-Bethesda reporting. Use codes 88164-88167 to report conventional Pap smears that are examined using the Bethesda System of reporting. Use codes 88142-88143 to report liquid-based specimens processed as thin-layer preparations that are examined using any system of reporting (Bethesda or non-Bethesda). Use codes 88174-88175 to report automated screening of liquid-based specimens that are examined using any system of reporting (Bethesda or non-Bethesda). Within each of these three code families choose the one code that describes the screening method(s) used. Codes 88141 and 88155 should be reported in addition to the screening code chosen when the additional services are provided. Manual rescreening requires a complete visual reassessment of the entire slide initially screened by either an automated or manual process. Manual review represents an assessment of selected cells or regions of a slide identified by initial automated review.

88141 Cytopathology, cervical or vaginal (any reporting system), requiring interpretation by physician

(Use 88141 in conjunction with 88142-88154, 88164-88167, 88174-88175)

88142 Cytopathology, cervical or vaginal (any reporting system), collected in preservative fluid, automated thin layer preparation; manual screening under physician supervision

88143 with manual screening and rescreening under physician supervision

(For automated screening of automated thin layer preparation, see 88174, 88175)

88147 Cytopathology smears, cervical or vaginal; screening by automated system under physician supervision

88148 screening by automated system with manual rescreening under physician supervision

88150 Cytopathology, slides, cervical or vaginal; manual screening under physician supervision

88152 with manual screening and computer-assisted rescreening under physician supervision

88153 with manual screening and rescreening under physician supervision

88154 with manual screening and computer-assisted rescreening using cell selection and review under physician supervision

+ **88155** Cytopathology, slides, cervical or vaginal, definitive hormonal evaluation (eg, maturation index, karyopyknotic index, estrogenic index) (List separately in addition to code[s] for other technical and interpretation services)

(Use 88155 in conjunction with 88142-88154, 88164-88167, 88174-88175)

88160 Cytopathology, smears, any other source; screening and interpretation

88161 preparation, screening and interpretation

88162 extended study involving over 5 slides and/or multiple stains

(For aerosol collection of sputum, use 89220)

(For special stains, see 88312-88314)

88164 Cytopathology, slides, cervical or vaginal (the Bethesda System); manual screening under physician supervision

88165 with manual screening and rescreening under physician supervision

88166 with manual screening and computer-assisted rescreening under physician supervision

88167 with manual screening and computer-assisted rescreening using cell selection and review under physician supervision

(To report collection of specimen via fine needle aspiration, see 10021, 10022)

88172 Cytopathology, evaluation of fine needle aspirate; immediate cytohistologic study to determine adequacy of specimen(s)

88173 interpretation and report

(For fine needle aspirate, see 10021, 10022)

(Do not report 88172, 88173 in conjunction with 88333 and 88334 for the same specimen)

88174 Cytopathology, cervical or vaginal (any reporting system), collected in preservative fluid, automated thin layer preparation; screening by automated system, under physician supervision

88175 with screening by automated system and manual rescreening or review, under physician supervision

(For manual screening, see 88142, 88143)

88182 Flow cytometry, cell cycle or DNA analysis

(For DNA ploidy analysis by morphometric technique, use 88358)

88184 Flow cytometry, cell surface, cytoplasmic, or nuclear marker, technical component only; first marker

+ **88185** each additional marker (List separately in addition to code for first marker)

(Report 88185 in conjunction with 88184)

88187 Flow cytometry, interpretation; 2 to 8 markers

88188 9 to 15 markers

88189 16 or more markers

(Do not report 88187-88189 for interpretation of 86355, 86356, 86357, 86359, 86360, 86361, 86367)

88199 Unlisted cytopathology procedure

(For electron microscopy, see 88348, 88349)

Cytogenetic Studies

When molecular diagnostic procedures are performed to test for oncologic or inherited disorder, use the appropriate modifier to specify probe type or condition tested. (See **Appendix I** for a listing of appropriate modifiers to report with molecular diagnostic and cytogenetic procedures.)

(For acetylcholinesterase, use 82013)

(For alpha-fetoprotein, serum or amniotic fluid, see 82105, 82106)

(For laser microdissection of cells from tissue sample, see 88380)

88230 Tissue culture for non-neoplastic disorders; lymphocyte

88233 skin or other solid tissue biopsy

88235 amniotic fluid or chorionic villus cells

88237 Tissue culture for neoplastic disorders; bone marrow, blood cells

88239 solid tumor

88240 Cryopreservation, freezing and storage of cells, each cell line

(For therapeutic cryopreservation and storage, use 38207)

88241 Thawing and expansion of frozen cells, each aliquot

(For therapeutic thawing of previous harvest, use 38208)

88245 Chromosome analysis for breakage syndromes; baseline Sister Chromatid Exchange (SCE), 20-25 cells

88248 baseline breakage, score 50-100 cells, count 20 cells, 2 karyotypes (eg, for ataxia telangiectasia, Fanconi anemia, fragile X)

88249 score 100 cells, clastogen stress (eg, diepoxybutane, mitomycin C, ionizing radiation, UV radiation)

88261 Chromosome analysis; count 5 cells, 1 karyotype, with banding

88262 count 15-20 cells, 2 karyotypes, with banding

88263 count 45 cells for mosaicism, 2 karyotypes, with banding

88264 analyze 20-25 cells

88267 Chromosome analysis, amniotic fluid or chorionic villus, count 15 cells, 1 karyotype, with banding

88269 Chromosome analysis, in situ for amniotic fluid cells, count cells from 6-12 colonies, 1 karyotype, with banding

88271 Molecular cytogenetics; DNA probe, each (eg, FISH)

88272 chromosomal in situ hybridization, analyze 3-5 cells (eg, for derivatives and markers)

88273 chromosomal in situ hybridization, analyze 10-30 cells (eg, for microdeletions)

88274 interphase in situ hybridization, analyze 25-99 cells

88275 interphase in situ hybridization, analyze 100-300 cells

88280 Chromosome analysis; additional karyotypes, each study

88283 additional specialized banding technique (eg, NOR, C-banding)

88285 additional cells counted, each study

88289 additional high resolution study

88291 Cytogenetics and molecular cytogenetics, interpretation and report

88299 Unlisted cytogenetic study

Surgical Pathology

Services 88300 through 88309 include accession, examination, and reporting. They do not include the services designated in codes 88311 through 88365 and 88399, which are coded in addition when provided.

The unit of service for codes 88300 through 88309 is the specimen.

A specimen is defined as tissue or tissues that is (are) submitted for individual and separate attention, requiring individual examination and pathologic diagnosis. Two or more such specimens from the same patient (eg, separately identified endoscopic biopsies, skin lesions) are each appropriately assigned an individual code reflective of its proper level of service.

Service code 88300 is used for any specimen that in the opinion of the examining pathologist can be accurately diagnosed without microscopic examination. Service code 88302 is used when gross and microscopic examination is performed on a specimen to confirm identification and the absence of disease. Service codes 88304 through 88309 describe all other specimens requiring gross and microscopic examination, and represent additional ascending levels of physician work. Levels 88302 through 88309 are specifically defined by the assigned specimens.

Any unlisted specimen should be assigned to the code which most closely reflects the physician work involved when compared to other specimens assigned to that code.

(Do not report 88302-88309 on the same specimen as part of Mohs surgery)

88300 **Level I** - Surgical pathology, gross examination only

88302 **Level II** - Surgical pathology, gross and microscopic examination

Appendix, incidental

Fallopian tube, sterilization

Fingers/toes, amputation, traumatic

Foreskin, newborn

Hernia sac, any location

Hydrocele sac

Nerve

Skin, plastic repair

Sympathetic ganglion

Testis, castration

Vaginal mucosa, incidental

Vas deferens, sterilization

88304 **Level III** - Surgical pathology, gross and microscopic examination

Abortion, induced

Abscess

Aneurysm - arterial/ventricular

Anus, tag

Appendix, other than incidental

Artery, atheromatous plaque

Bartholin's gland cyst

Bone fragment(s), other than pathologic fracture

Bursa/synovial cyst

Carpal tunnel tissue

Cartilage, shavings

Cholesteatoma

Colon, colostomy stoma

Conjunctiva - biopsy/pterygium

Cornea

Diverticulum - esophagus/small intestine

Dupuytren's contracture tissue

Femoral head, other than fracture

Fissure/fistula

Foreskin, other than newborn

Gallbladder

Ganglion cyst

Hematoma

Hemorrhoids

Hydatid of Morgagni

Intervertebral disc

Joint, loose body

Meniscus

Mucocele, salivary

Neuroma - Morton's/traumatic

Pilonidal cyst/sinus

Polyps, inflammatory - nasal/sinusoidal

Skin - cyst/tag/debridement

Soft tissue, debridement

Soft tissue, lipoma

Spermatocele

Tendon/tendon sheath

Testicular appendage

Thrombus or embolus

Tonsil and/or adenoids

Varicocele

Vas deferens, other than sterilization

Vein, varicosity

88305 **Level IV** - Surgical pathology, gross and microscopic examination

Abortion - spontaneous/missed

Artery, biopsy

Bone marrow, biopsy

Bone exostosis

Brain/meninges, other than for tumor resection

Breast, biopsy, not requiring microscopic evaluation of surgical margins

Breast, reduction mammoplasty

Bronchus, biopsy

Cell block, any source

Cervix, biopsy

Colon, biopsy

Duodenum, biopsy

Endocervix, curettings/biopsy

Endometrium, curettings/biopsy

Esophagus, biopsy

Extremity, amputation, traumatic

Fallopian tube, biopsy

Fallopian tube, ectopic pregnancy

Femoral head, fracture

Fingers/toes, amputation, non-traumatic

Gingiva/oral mucosa, biopsy

Heart valve

Joint, resection

Kidney, biopsy

Larynx, biopsy

Leiomyoma(s), uterine myomectomy - without uterus

Lip, biopsy/wedge resection

Lung, transbronchial biopsy

Lymph node, biopsy

Muscle, biopsy

Nasal mucosa, biopsy

Nasopharynx/oropharynx, biopsy

Nerve, biopsy

Odontogenic/dental cyst

Omentum, biopsy

Ovary with or without tube, non-neoplastic

Ovary, biopsy/wedge resection

Parathyroid gland

Peritoneum, biopsy

Pituitary tumor

Placenta, other than third trimester

Pleura/pericardium - biopsy/tissue

Polyp, cervical/endometrial

Polyp, colorectal

Polyp, stomach/small intestine

Prostate, needle biopsy

Prostate, TUR

Salivary gland, biopsy

Sinus, paranasal biopsy

Skin, other than cyst/tag/debridement/plastic repair

Small intestine, biopsy

Soft tissue, other than tumor/mass/lipoma/debridement

Spleen

Stomach, biopsy

Synovium

Testis, other than tumor/biopsy/castration

Thyroglossal duct/brachial cleft cyst

Tongue, biopsy

Tonsil, biopsy

Trachea, biopsy

Ureter, biopsy

Urethra, biopsy

Urinary bladder, biopsy

Uterus, with or without tubes and ovaries, for prolapse

Vagina, biopsy

Vulva/labia, biopsy

88307 **Level V** - Surgical pathology, gross and microscopic examination

Adrenal, resection

Bone - biopsy/curettings

Bone fragment(s), pathologic fracture

Brain, biopsy

Brain/meninges, tumor resection

Breast, excision of lesion, requiring microscopic evaluation of surgical margins

Breast, mastectomy - partial/simple

Cervix, conization

Colon, segmental resection, other than for tumor

Extremity, amputation, non-traumatic

Eye, enucleation

Kidney, partial/total nephrectomy

Larynx, partial/total resection

Liver, biopsy - needle/wedge

Liver, partial resection

Lung, wedge biopsy

Lymph nodes, regional resection

Mediastinum, mass

Myocardium, biopsy

Odontogenic tumor

Ovary with or without tube, neoplastic

Pancreas, biopsy

Placenta, third trimester

Prostate, except radical resection

Salivary gland

Sentinel lymph node

Small intestine, resection, other than for tumor

Soft tissue mass (except lipoma) - biopsy/simple excision

Stomach - subtotal/total resection, other than for tumor

Testis, biopsy

Thymus, tumor

Thyroid, total/lobe

Ureter, resection

Urinary bladder, TUR

Uterus, with or without tubes and ovaries, other than neoplastic/prolapse

88309 **Level VI** - Surgical pathology, gross and microscopic examination

Bone resection

Breast, mastectomy - with regional lymph nodes

Colon, segmental resection for tumor

Colon, total resection

Esophagus, partial/total resection

Extremity, disarticulation

Fetus, with dissection

Larynx, partial/total resection - with regional lymph nodes

Lung - total/lobe/segment resection

Pancreas, total/subtotal resection

Prostate, radical resection

Small intestine, resection for tumor

Soft tissue tumor, extensive resection

Stomach - subtotal/total resection for tumor

Testis, tumor

Tongue/tonsil -resection for tumor

Urinary bladder, partial/total resection

Uterus, with or without tubes and ovaries, neoplastic

Vulva, total/subtotal resection

(For fine needle aspiration, see 10021, 10022)

(For evaluation of fine needle aspirate, see 88172-88173)

(Do not report 88302-88309 on the same specimen as part of Mohs surgery)

+ 88311 Decalcification procedure (List separately in addition to code for surgical pathology examination)

+ 88312 Special stains (List separately in addition to code for primary service); Group I for microorganisms (eg, Gridley, acid fast, methenamine silver), each

+ 88313 Group II, all other (eg, iron, trichrome), except immunocytochemistry and immunoperoxidase stains, each

(For immunocytochemistry and immunoperoxidase tissue studies, use 88342)

+ 88314 histochemical staining with frozen section(s)

(Do not report 88314 with 17311-17315 for routine frozen section stain [eg, hematoxylin and eosin, toluidine blue], performed during Mohs surgery. When a nonroutine histochemical stain on frozen tissue is utilized, report 88314 with modifier 59)

88318 Determinative histochemistry to identify chemical components (eg, copper, zinc)

88319 Determinative histochemistry or cytochemistry to identify enzyme constituents, each

88321 Consultation and report on referred slides prepared elsewhere

88323 Consultation and report on referred material requiring preparation of slides

88325 Consultation, comprehensive, with review of records and specimens, with report on referred material

88329 Pathology consultation during surgery;

88331 first tissue block, with frozen section(s), single specimen

88332 each additional tissue block with frozen section(s)

88333 cytologic examination (eg, touch prep, squash prep), initial site

88334 cytologic examination (eg, touch prep, squash prep), each additional site

(For intraoperative consultation on a specimen requiring both frozen section and cytologic evaluation, use 88331 and 88334)

(For percutaneous needle biopsy requiring intraprocedural cytologic examination, use 88333)

(Do not report 88333 and 88334 for non-intraoperative cytologic examination, see 88160-88162)

(Do not report 88333 and 88334 for intraprocedural cytologic evaluation of fine needle aspirate, see 88172)

88342 Immunohistochemistry (including tissue immunoperoxidase), each antibody

(Do not report 88342 in conjunction with 88360 or 88361 for the same antibody)

(For quantitative or semiquantitative immunohistochemistry, see 88360, 88361)

88346 Immunofluorescent study, each antibody; direct method

88347 indirect method

88348 Electron microscopy; diagnostic

88349 scanning

88355 Morphometric analysis; skeletal muscle

88356 nerve

88358 tumor (eg, DNA ploidy)

(Do not report 88358 with 88313 unless each procedure is for a different special stain)

88360 Morphometric analysis, tumor immunohistochemistry (eg, Her-2/neu, estrogen receptor/progesterone receptor), quantitative or semiquantitative, each antibody; manual

88361 using computer-assisted technology

(Do not report 88360, 88361 with 88342 unless each procedure is for a different antibody)

(For morphometric analysis using in situ hybridization techniques, see 88367, 88368)

(When semi-thin plastic-embedded sections are performed in conjunction with morphometric analysis, only the morphometric analysis should be reported; if performed as an independent procedure, see codes 88300-88309 for surgical pathology.)

88362 Nerve teasing preparations

88365 In situ hybridization (eg, FISH), each probe

(Do not report 88365 in conjunction with 88367, 88368 for the same probe)

88367 Morphometric analysis, in situ hybridization (quantitative or semi-quantitative) each probe; using computer-assisted technology

88368 manual

88371 Protein analysis of tissue by Western Blot, with interpretation and report;

88372 immunological probe for band identification, each

88380 Microdissection (ie, sample preparation of microscopically identified target); laser capture

88381 manual

(Do not report 88380 in conjunction with 88381)

88384 Array-based evaluation of multiple molecular probes; 11 through 50 probes

88385 51 through 250 probes

88386 251 through 500 probes

(For preparation of array-based evaluation, see 83890-83892, 83898-83901)

(For preparation and analyses of less than 11 probes, see 83890-83914)

88399 Unlisted surgical pathology procedure

►(88400 has been deleted. To report, use 88720)◄

►In Vivo (eg, Transcutaneous) Laboratory Procedures◄

● **88720** Bilirubin, total, transcutaneous

►(For transdermal oxygen saturation, see 94760-94762)◄

● **88740** Hemoglobin, quantitative, transcutaneous, per day; carboxyhemoglobin

►(For in vitro carboxyhemoglobin measurement, use 82375)◄

● **88741** methemoglobin

►(For in vitro quantitative methemoglobin determination, use 83050)◄

Other Procedures

89049 Caffeine halothane contracture test (CHCT) for malignant hyperthermia susceptibility, including interpretation and report

89050 Cell count, miscellaneous body fluids (eg, cerebrospinal fluid, joint fluid), except blood;

89051 with differential count

89055 Leukocyte assessment, fecal, qualitative or semiquantitative

89060 Crystal identification by light microscopy with or without polarizing lens analysis, tissue or any body fluid (except urine)

(Do not report 89060 for crystal identification on paraffin-embedded tissue)

89100 Duodenal intubation and aspiration; single specimen (eg, simple bile study or afferent loop culture) plus appropriate test procedure

89105 collection of multiple fractional specimens with pancreatic or gallbladder stimulation, single or double lumen tube

(For radiological localization, use 74340)

(For chemical analyses, see **Chemistry,** this section)

(Electrocardiogram, see 93000-93268)

(Esophagus acid perfusion test [Bernstein], see 91030)

89125 Fat stain, feces, urine, or respiratory secretions

89130 Gastric intubation and aspiration, diagnostic, each specimen, for chemical analyses or cytopathology;

89132 after stimulation

89135 Gastric intubation, aspiration, and fractional collections (eg, gastric secretory study); 1 hour

89136 2 hours

89140 2 hours including gastric stimulation (eg, histalog, pentagastrin)

89141 3 hours, including gastric stimulation

(For gastric lavage, therapeutic, use 91105)

(For radiologic localization of gastric tube, use 74340)

(For chemical analyses, see 82926, 82928)

(Joint fluid chemistry, see **Chemistry,** this section)

89160 Meat fibers, feces

89190 Nasal smear for eosinophils

(Occult blood, feces, use 82270)

(Paternity tests, use 86910)

89220 Sputum, obtaining specimen, aerosol induced technique (separate procedure)

89225 Starch granules, feces

89230 Sweat collection by iontophoresis

89235 Water load test

89240 Unlisted miscellaneous pathology test

Reproductive Medicine Procedures

89250 Culture of oocyte(s)/embryo(s), less than 4 days;

89251 with co-culture of oocyte(s)/embryos

(For extended culture of oocyte[s]/embryo[s], see 89272)

89253 Assisted embryo hatching, microtechniques (any method)

89254 Oocyte identification from follicular fluid

89255 Preparation of embryo for transfer (any method)

89257 Sperm identification from aspiration (other than seminal fluid)

(For semen analysis, see 89300-89320)

(For sperm identification from testis tissue, use 89264)

89258 Cryopreservation; embryo(s)

89259 sperm

(For cryopreservation of reproductive tissue, testicular, use 89335)

89260 Sperm isolation; simple prep (eg, sperm wash and swim-up) for insemination or diagnosis with semen analysis

89261 complex prep (eg, Percoll gradient, albumin gradient) for insemination or diagnosis with semen analysis

(For semen analysis without sperm wash or swim-up, use 89320)

89264 Sperm identification from testis tissue, fresh or cryopreserved

(For biopsy of testis, see 54500, 54505)

(For sperm identification from aspiration, use 89257)

(For semen analysis, see 89300-89320)

89268 Insemination of oocytes

89272 Extended culture of oocyte(s)/embryo(s), 4-7 days

89280 Assisted oocyte fertilization, microtechnique; less than or equal to 10 oocytes

89281 greater than 10 oocytes

89290 Biopsy, oocyte polar body or embryo blastomere, microtechnique (for pre-implantation genetic diagnosis); less than or equal to 5 embryos

89291 greater than 5 embryos

89300 Semen analysis; presence and/or motility of sperm including Huhner test (post coital)

89310 motility and count (not including Huhner test)

89320 volume, count, motility, and differential

(Skin tests, see 86485-86580 and 95010-95199)

89321 sperm presence and motility of sperm, if performed

(To report Hyaluronan binding assay [HBA], use Category III code 0087T)

89322 volume, count, motility, and differential using strict morphologic criteria (eg, Kruger)

89325 Sperm antibodies

(For medicolegal identification of sperm, use 88125)

89329 Sperm evaluation; hamster penetration test

89330 cervical mucus penetration test, with or without spinnbarkeit test

89331 Sperm evaluation, for retrograde ejaculation, urine (sperm concentration, motility, and morphology, as indicated)

(For semen analysis on concurrent semen specimen, see 89300-89322 in conjunction with 89331)

(For detection of sperm in urine, use 81015)

89335 Cryopreservation, reproductive tissue, testicular

(For cryopreservation of embryo[s], use 89258. For cryopreservation of sperm, use 89259)

(For cryopreservation of reproductive tissue, ovarian, use Category III code 0058T)

(For cryopreservation of oocyte, use Category III code 0059T)

89342 Storage (per year); embryo(s)

89343 sperm/semen

89344 reproductive tissue, testicular/ovarian

89346 oocyte(s)

89352 Thawing of cryopreserved; embryo(s)

89353 sperm/semen, each aliquot

89354 reproductive tissue, testicular/ovarian

89356 oocytes, each aliquot

Notes

Medicine Guidelines

In addition to the definitions and commonly used terms presented in the **Introduction**, several other items unique to this section on **Medicine** are defined or identified here.

Multiple Procedures

It is appropriate to designate multiple procedures that are rendered on the same date by separate entries. For example: If individual medical psychotherapy (90829) is rendered in addition to subsequent hospital care (eg, 99231), the psychotherapy would be reported separately from the hospital visit. In this instance, both 99231 and 90829 would be reported.

Add-on Codes

Some of the listed procedures are commonly carried out in addition to the primary procedure performed. All add-on codes found in the CPT codebook are exempt from the multiple procedure concept. They are exempt from the use of modifier 51, as these procedures are not reported as stand-alone codes. These additional or supplemental procedures are designated as "add-on" codes. Add-on codes in the CPT codebook can be readily identified by specific descriptor nomenclature which includes phrases such as "each additional" or "(List separately in addition to primary procedure)."

Separate Procedures

Some of the procedures or services listed in the CPT codebook that are commonly carried out as an integral component of a total service or procedure have been identified by the inclusion of the term "separate procedure." The codes designated as "separate procedure" should not be reported in addition to the code for the total procedure or service of which it is considered an integral component.

However, when a procedure or service that is designated as a "separate procedure" is carried out independently or considered to be unrelated or distinct from other procedures/services provided at that time, it may be reported by itself, or in addition to other procedures/services by appending modifier 59 to the specific "separate procedure" code to indicate that the procedure is not considered to be a component of another procedure, but is a distinct, independent procedure. This may represent a different session or patient encounter, different procedure or surgery, different site or organ system, separate incision/excision, separate lesion, or separate injury (or area of injury in extensive injuries).

Subsection Information

Several of the subheadings or subsections have special instructions unique to that section. These special instructions will be presented preceding those procedural terminology listings, referring to that subsection specifically. If there is an "Unlisted Procedure" code number (see section below) for the individual subsection, it will also be shown. Those subsections within the **Medicine** section that have special instructions are as follows:

Immune Globulins	90281-90399
Immunization Administration for Vaccines/Toxoids	90465-90474
Vaccines, Toxoids	90476-90749
Psychiatry	90801-90899
►**Dialysis**	90935-90999◄
Hemodialysis	90935-90940
►**Miscellaneous Dialysis Procedures**	90945-90947
End Stage Renal Disease Services	90951-90970◄
Ophthalmology	92002-92499
General Ophthalmological Services	92002-92014
Ophthalmoscopy	92225-92260
Contact Lens Services	92310-92326
Spectacle Services	92340-92371
Special Otorhinolaryngologic Services	92502-92700
Audiologic Function Tests	92551-92597
Evaluative and Therapeutic Services	92601-92633
Cardiography	93000-93278
►**Cardiovascular Device Monitoring-Implantable and Wearable Devices**	93279-93299◄
Echocardiography	93303-93350
Cardiac Catheterization	93501-93533
Injection Procedures	93539-93572
Intracardiac Electrophysiological Procedures/Studies	93600-93662
Peripheral Arterial Disease Rehabilitation	93668
Noninvasive Vascular Diagnostic Studies	93875-93990
Cerebrovascular Arterial Studies	93875-93893
Pulmonary	94002-94799
Allergy and Clinical Immunology	95004-95199

►**Neurology and Neuromuscular**. . . 95803-95999◄
►**Sleep Testing**. . . . . 95803-95811◄
Routine Electroencephalography (EEG) . 95812-95830
Electromyography and Nerve Conduction Tests 95860-95904
Neurostimulators, Analysis-Programming. 95970-95979
Motion Analysis. 96000-96004
Functional Brain Mapping. 96020
Medical Genetics and Genetic Counseling Services. 96040
Central Nervous System Assessments/Tests. 96101-96120
Health and Behavior Assessment/Intervention 96150-96155
►**Hydration, Therapeutic, Prophylactic, Diagnostic Injections and Infusions, and Chemotherapy and Other Highly Complex Drug or Highly Complex Biologic Agent Administration**. . 96360-96549◄
►**Hydration**. 96360-96361
Therapeutic, Prophylactic, and Diagnostic Injections and Infusions (Excludes Chemotherapy and Other Highly Complex Drug or Highly Complex Biologic Agent Administration) 96365-96379
Chemotherapy and Other Highly Complex Drug or Highly Complex Biologic Agent Administration 96401-96549
Injection and Intravenous Infusion Chemotherapy and Other Highly Complex Drug or Highly Complex Biologic Agent Administration 96401-96417
Other Injection and Infusion Servces . . . . 96440-96549◄
Special Dermatological Procedures . . 96900-96999
Physical Medicine and Rehabilitation 97001-97755
Modalities 97010-97039
Supervised 97010-97028
Constant Attendance 97032-97039
Therapeutic Procedures. 97110-97546
Active Wound Care Management 97597-97606
Tests and Measurements 97750-97755
Acupuncture 97810-97814
Osteopathic Manipulative Treatment. 98925-98929
Chiropractic Manipulative Treatment. 98940-98943
Education and Training for Patient Self-Management 98960-98962
Telephone Services. 98966-98968
Online Medical Evaluation. 98969
Special Services, Procedures and Reports 99000-99091
Moderate (Conscious) Sedation. 99143-99150
Home Health Procedures/Services 99500-99600
Medication Therapy Management Services 99605-99607

Unlisted Service or Procedure

A service or procedure may be provided that is not listed in this edition of the CPT codebook. When reporting such a service, the appropriate "Unlisted Procedure" code may be used to indicate the service, identifying it by "Special Report" as discussed on this page. The "Unlisted Procedures" and accompanying codes for **Medicine** are as follows:

90399 Unlisted immune globulin

90749 Unlisted vaccine/toxoid

90899 Unlisted psychiatric service or procedure

90999 Unlisted dialysis procedure, inpatient or outpatient

91299 Unlisted diagnostic gastroenterology procedure

92499 Unlisted ophthalmological service or procedure

92700 Unlisted otorhinolaryngological service or procedure

93799 Unlisted cardiovascular service or procedure

94799 Unlisted pulmonary service or procedure

95199 Unlisted allergy/clinical immunologic service or procedure

95999 Unlisted neurological or neuromuscular diagnostic procedure

● **96379** Unlisted therapeutic, prophylactic, or diagnostic intravenous or intra-arterial injection or infusion

96549 Unlisted chemotherapy procedure

96999 Unlisted special dermatological service or procedure

97039 Unlisted modality (specify type and time if constant attendance)

97139 Unlisted therapeutic procedure (specify)

97799 Unlisted physical medicine/rehabilitation service or procedure

99199 Unlisted special service, procedure or report

99600 Unlisted home visit service or procedure

Special Report

A service that is rarely provided, unusual, variable, or new may require a special report in determining medical appropriateness of the service. Pertinent information should include an adequate definition or description of the nature, extent, and need for the procedure; and the time, effort, and equipment necessary to provide the service. Additional items that may be included are:

- Complexity of symptoms
- Final diagnosis
- Pertinent physical findings
- Diagnostic and therapeutic procedures
- Concurrent problems
- Follow-up care

Materials Supplied by Physician

Supplies and materials provided by the physician (eg, sterile trays/drugs), over and above those usually included with the procedure(s) rendered are reported separately. List drugs, trays, supplies, and materials provided. Identify as 99070 or specific supply code.

Notes

Medicine

Immune Globulins

►Codes 90281-90399 identify the immune globulin product only and are reported in addition to the administration codes 96365-96368, 96372, 96374, 96375 as appropriate. Modifier 51 should not be reported with the immune globulin codes when performed with another procedure. Immune globulin products listed here include broad-spectrum and anti-infective immune globulins, antitoxins, and various isoantibodies.◄

90281 Immune globulin (Ig), human, for intramuscular use

90283 Immune globulin (IgIV), human, for intravenous use

90284 Immune globulin (SCIg), human, for use in subcutaneous infusions, 100 mg, each

90287 Botulinum antitoxin, equine, any route

90288 Botulism immune globulin, human, for intravenous use

90291 Cytomegalovirus immune globulin (CMV-IgIV), human, for intravenous use

90296 Diphtheria antitoxin, equine, any route

90371 Hepatitis B immune globulin (HBIg), human, for intramuscular use

90375 Rabies immune globulin (RIg), human, for intramuscular and/or subcutaneous use

90376 Rabies immune globulin, heat-treated (RIg-HT), human, for intramuscular and/or subcutaneous use

90378 Respiratory syncytial virus immune globulin (RSV-IgIM), for intramuscular use, 50 mg, each

90379 Respiratory syncytial virus immune globulin (RSV-IgIV), human, for intravenous use

90384 Rho(D) immune globulin (RhIg), human, full-dose, for intramuscular use

90385 Rho(D) immune globulin (RhIg), human, mini-dose, for intramuscular use

90386 Rho(D) immune globulin (RhIgIV), human, for intravenous use

90389 Tetanus immune globulin (TIg), human, for intramuscular use

90393 Vaccinia immune globulin, human, for intramuscular use

90396 Varicella-zoster immune globulin, human, for intramuscular use

90399 Unlisted immune globulin

Immunization Administration for Vaccines/Toxoids

Codes 90465-90474 must be reported in addition to the vaccine and toxoid code(s) 90476-90749.

Report codes 90465-90468 only when the physician provides face-to-face counseling of the patient and family during the administration of a vaccine. For immunization administration of any vaccine that is not accompanied by face-to-face physician counseling to the patient/family, report codes 90471-90474.

If a significant separately identifiable Evaluation and Management service (eg, office or other outpatient services, preventive medicine services) is performed, the appropriate E/M service code should be reported in addition to the vaccine and toxoid administration codes.

(For allergy testing, see 95004 et seq)

(For skin testing of bacterial, viral, fungal extracts, see 86485-86580)

►(For therapeutic or diagnostic injections, see 96372-96379)◄

90465 Immunization administration younger than 8 years of age (includes percutaneous, intradermal, subcutaneous, or intramuscular injections) when the physician counsels the patient/family; first injection (single or combination vaccine/toxoid), per day

(Do not report 90465 in conjunction with 90467)

+ 90466 each additional injection (single or combination vaccine/toxoid), per day (List separately in addition to code for primary procedure)

(Use 90466 in conjunction with 90465 or 90467)

90467 Immunization administration younger than age 8 years (includes intranasal or oral routes of administration) when the physician counsels the patient/family; first administration (single or combination vaccine/toxoid), per day

(Do not report 90467 in conjunction with 90465)

+ 90468 each additional administration (single or combination vaccine/toxoid), per day (List separately in addition to code for primary procedure)

(Use 90468 in conjunction with 90465 or 90467)

90471 Immunization administration (includes percutaneous, intradermal, subcutaneous, or intramuscular injections); one vaccine (single or combination vaccine/toxoid)

(Do not report 90471 in conjunction with 90473)

+ 90472 each additional vaccine (single or combination vaccine/toxoid) (List separately in addition to code for primary procedure)

(Use 90472 in conjunction with 90471 or 90473)

►(For administration of immune globulins, see 90281-90399, 96360, 96361, 96365-96368, 96374)◄

(For intravesical administration of BCG vaccine, see 51720, 90586)

90473 Immunization administration by intranasal or oral route; one vaccine (single or combination vaccine/toxoid)

(Do not report 90473 in conjunction with 90471)

+ 90474 each additional vaccine (single or combination vaccine/toxoid) (List separately in addition to code for primary procedure)

(Use 90474 in conjunction with 90471 or 90473)

Vaccines, Toxoids

To assist users to report the most recent new or revised vaccine product codes, the American Medical Association (AMA) currently uses the CPT Website, which features updates of CPT Editorial Panel actions regarding these products. Once approved by the CPT Editorial Panel, these codes will be made available for release on a semi-annual (twice a year: July 1 and January 1) basis. As part of the electronic distribution, there is a six-month implementation period from the initial release date (ie, codes released on January 1 are eligible for use on July 1 and codes released on July 1 are eligible for use January 1).

The CPT Editorial Panel, in recognition of the public health interest in vaccine products, has chosen to publish new vaccine product codes prior to approval by the Food and Drug Administration (FDA). These codes are indicated with the ⁄⁄ symbol and will be tracked by the AMA to monitor FDA approval status. Once the FDA status changes to approval, the ⁄⁄ symbol will be removed. CPT users should refer to the AMA Internet site (www.ama-assn.org/ama/pub/category/10902.html) for the most up-to-date information on codes with the ⁄⁄ symbol.

Codes 90476-90748 identify the vaccine product **only.** To report the administration of a vaccine/toxoid, the vaccine/toxoid product codes 90476-90749 must be used in addition to an immunization administration code(s) 90465-90474. Modifier 51 should not be reported for the vaccines, toxoids when performed with these administration procedures.

If a significantly separately identifiable Evaluation and Management (E/M) service (eg, office or other outpatient services, preventive medicine services) is performed, the appropriate E/M service code should be reported in addition to the vaccine and toxoid administration codes.

To meet the reporting requirements of immunization registries, vaccine distribution programs, and reporting systems (eg, Vaccine Adverse Event Reporting System) the exact vaccine product administered needs to be reported. Multiple codes for a particular vaccine are provided in the CPT codebook when the schedule (number of doses or timing) differs for two or more products of the same vaccine type (eg, hepatitis A, Hib) or the vaccine product is available in more than one chemical formulation, dosage, or route of administration.

The "age" descriptions included in CPT vaccine codes (eg, 90655-90658, 90714, 90715, 90718, 90732) are not intended to identify a product's licensed age indication. Refer to the product's prescribing information (PI) for the FDA approved age indication before administering vaccine to a patient.

Separate codes are available for combination vaccines (eg, DTP-Hib, DtaP-Hib, HepB-Hib). It is inappropriate to code each component of a combination vaccine separately. If a specific vaccine code is not available, the unlisted procedure code should be reported, until a new code becomes available.

►(For immune globulins, see codes 90281-90399, 96365-96368, 96372-96375 for administration of immune globulins)◄

90476 Adenovirus vaccine, type 4, live, for oral use

90477 Adenovirus vaccine, type 7, live, for oral use

90581 Anthrax vaccine, for subcutaneous use

90585 Bacillus Calmette-Guerin vaccine (BCG) for tuberculosis, live, for percutaneous use

90586 Bacillus Calmette-Guerin vaccine (BCG) for bladder cancer, live, for intravesical use

90632 Hepatitis A vaccine, adult dosage, for intramuscular use

90633 Hepatitis A vaccine, pediatric/adolescent dosage-2 dose schedule, for intramuscular use

90634 Hepatitis A vaccine, pediatric/adolescent dosage-3 dose schedule, for intramuscular use

90636 Hepatitis A and hepatitis B vaccine (HepA-HepB), adult dosage, for intramuscular use

90645 Hemophilus influenza b vaccine (Hib), HbOC conjugate (4 dose schedule), for intramuscular use

90646 Hemophilus influenza b vaccine (Hib), PRP-D conjugate, for booster use only, intramuscular use

90647 Hemophilus influenza b vaccine (Hib), PRP-OMP conjugate (3 dose schedule), for intramuscular use

90648 Hemophilus influenza b vaccine (Hib), PRP-T conjugate (4 dose schedule), for intramuscular use

90649 Human Papilloma virus (HPV) vaccine, types 6, 11, 16, 18 (quadrivalent), 3 dose schedule, for intramuscular use

⚡● **90650** Human Papilloma virus (HPV) vaccine, types 16, 18, bivalent, 3 dose schedule, for intramuscular use

90655 Influenza virus vaccine, split virus, preservative free, when administered to children 6-35 months of age, for intramuscular use

90656 Influenza virus vaccine, split virus, preservative free, when administered to individuals 3 years and older, for intramuscular use

90657 Influenza virus vaccine, split virus, when administered to children 6-35 months of age, for intramuscular use

90658 Influenza virus vaccine, split virus, when administered to individuals 3 years of age and older, for intramuscular use

90660 Influenza virus vaccine, live, for intranasal use

⚡ **90661** Influenza virus vaccine, derived from cell cultures, subunit, preservative and antibiotic free, for intramuscular use

⚡ **90662** Influenza virus vaccine, split virus, preservative free, enhanced immunogenicity via increased antigen content, for intramuscular use

⚡ **90663** Influenza virus vaccine, pandemic formulation

90665 Lyme disease vaccine, adult dosage, for intramuscular use

90669 Pneumococcal conjugate vaccine, polyvalent, when administered to children younger than 5 years, for intramuscular use

90675 Rabies vaccine, for intramuscular use

90676 Rabies vaccine, for intradermal use

90680 Rotavirus vaccine, pentavalent, 3 dose schedule, live, for oral use

● **90681** Rotavirus vaccine, human, attenuated, 2 dose schedule, live, for oral use

90690 Typhoid vaccine, live, oral

90691 Typhoid vaccine, Vi capsular polysaccharide (ViCPs), for intramuscular use

90692 Typhoid vaccine, heat- and phenol-inactivated (H-P), for subcutaneous or intradermal use

90693 Typhoid vaccine, acetone-killed, dried (AKD), for subcutaneous use (U.S. military)

● **90696** Diphtheria, tetanus toxoids, acellular pertussis vaccine and poliovirus vaccine, inactivated (DTaP-IPV), when administered to children 4 through 6 years of age, for intramuscular use

▲ **90698** Diphtheria, tetanus toxoids, acellular pertussis vaccine, haemophilus influenza Type B, and poliovirus vaccine, inactivated (DTaP - Hib - IPV), for intramuscular use

90700 Diphtheria, tetanus toxoids, and acellular pertussis vaccine (DTaP), when administered to individuals younger than 7 years, for intramuscular use

90701 Diphtheria, tetanus toxoids, and whole cell pertussis vaccine (DTP), for intramuscular use

90702 Diphtheria and tetanus toxoids (DT) adsorbed when administered to individuals younger than 7 years, for intramuscular use

90703 Tetanus toxoid adsorbed, for intramuscular use

90704 Mumps virus vaccine, live, for subcutaneous use

90705 Measles virus vaccine, live, for subcutaneous use

90706 Rubella virus vaccine, live, for subcutaneous use

90707 Measles, mumps and rubella virus vaccine (MMR), live, for subcutaneous use

90708 Measles and rubella virus vaccine, live, for subcutaneous use

90710 Measles, mumps, rubella, and varicella vaccine (MMRV), live, for subcutaneous use

90712 Poliovirus vaccine, (any type[s]) (OPV), live, for oral use

90713 Poliovirus vaccine, inactivated (IPV), for subcutaneous or intramuscular use

90714 Tetanus and diphtheria toxoids (Td) adsorbed, preservative free, when administered to individuals 7 years or older, for intramuscular use

90715 Tetanus, diphtheria toxoids and acellular pertussis vaccine (Tdap), when administered to individuals 7 years or older, for intramuscular use

90716 Varicella virus vaccine, live, for subcutaneous use

90717 Yellow fever vaccine, live, for subcutaneous use

90718 Tetanus and diphtheria toxoids (Td) adsorbed when administered to individuals 7 years or older, for intramuscular use

90719 Diphtheria toxoid, for intramuscular use

90720 Diphtheria, tetanus toxoids, and whole cell pertussis vaccine and Hemophilus influenza B vaccine (DTP-Hib), for intramuscular use

90721 Diphtheria, tetanus toxoids, and acellular pertussis vaccine and Hemophilus influenza B vaccine (DtaP-Hib), for intramuscular use

90723 Diphtheria, tetanus toxoids, acellular pertussis vaccine, Hepatitis B, and poliovirus vaccine, inactivated (DtaP-HepB-IPV), for intramuscular use

90725 Cholera vaccine for injectable use

90727 Plague vaccine, for intramuscular use

90732 Pneumococcal polysaccharide vaccine, 23-valent, adult or immunosuppressed patient dosage, when administered to individuals 2 years or older, for subcutaneous or intramuscular use

90733 Meningococcal polysaccharide vaccine (any group(s)), for subcutaneous use

90734 Meningococcal conjugate vaccine, serogroups A, C, Y and W-135 (tetravalent), for intramuscular use

90735 Japanese encephalitis virus vaccine, for subcutaneous use

90736 Zoster (shingles) vaccine, live, for subcutaneous injection

✓● **90738** Japanese encephalitis virus vaccine, inactivated, for intramuscular use

90740 Hepatitis B vaccine, dialysis or immunosuppressed patient dosage (3 dose schedule), for intramuscular use

90743 Hepatitis B vaccine, adolescent (2 dose schedule), for intramuscular use

90744 Hepatitis B vaccine, pediatric/adolescent dosage (3 dose schedule), for intramuscular use

90746 Hepatitis B vaccine, adult dosage, for intramuscular use

90747 Hepatitis B vaccine, dialysis or immunosuppressed patient dosage (4 dose schedule), for intramuscular use

90748 Hepatitis B and Hemophilus influenza b vaccine (HepB-Hib), for intramuscular use

90749 Unlisted vaccine/toxoid

►(90760 has been deleted. To report, use 96360)◄

►(90761 has been deleted. To report, use 96361)◄

►(90765 has been deleted. To report, use 96365)◄

►(90766 has been deleted. To report, use 96366)◄

►(90767 has been deleted. To report, use 96367)◄

►(90768 has been deleted. To report, use 96368)◄

►(90769 has been deleted. To report, use 96369)◄

►(90770 has been deleted. To report, use 96370)◄

►(90771 has been deleted. To report, use 96371)◄

►(90772 has been deleted. To report, use 96372)◄

►(90773 has been deleted. To report, use 96373)◄

►(90774 has been deleted. To report, use 96374)◄

►(90775 has been deleted. To report, use 96375)◄

►(90776 has been deleted. To report, use 96376)◄

►(90779 has been deleted. To report, use 96379)◄

Psychiatry

Hospital care by the attending physician in treating a psychiatric inpatient or partial hospitalization may be initial or subsequent in nature (see 99221-99233) and may include exchanges with nursing and ancillary personnel. Hospital care services involve a variety of responsibilities unique to the medical management of inpatients, such as physician hospital orders, interpretation of laboratory or other medical diagnostic studies and observations.

Some patients receive hospital evaluation and management services only and others receive evaluation and management services and other procedures. If other procedures such as electroconvulsive therapy or psychotherapy are rendered in addition to hospital evaluation and management services, these should be listed separately (ie, hospital care service plus electroconvulsive therapy or when psychotherapy is done, an appropriate code defining psychotherapy with medical evaluation and management services). Modifier 22 may be used to indicate a more extensive service. Modifier 52 may be used to signify a service that is reduced or less extensive than the usual procedure.

Other evaluation and management services, such as office medical service or other patient encounters, may be described as listed in the section on **Evaluation and Management,** if appropriate.

The evaluation and management services should not be reported separately, when reporting codes 90805, 90807, 90809, 90811, 90813, 90815, 90817, 90819, 90822, 90824, 90827, 90829.

Consultation for psychiatric evaluation of a patient includes examination of a patient and exchange of information with the primary physician and other informants such as nurses or family members, and preparation of a report. These consultation services (99241-99255) are limited to initial or follow-up evaluation and do not involve psychiatric treatment.

Psychiatric Diagnostic or Evaluative Interview Procedures

Psychiatric diagnostic interview examination includes a history, mental status, and a disposition, and may include communication with family or other sources, ordering and medical interpretation of laboratory or other medical diagnostic studies. In certain circumstances other informants will be seen in lieu of the patient.

Interactive psychiatric diagnostic interview examination is typically furnished to children. It involves the use of physical aids and non-verbal communication to overcome barriers to therapeutic interaction between the clinician and a patient who has not yet developed, or has lost, either the expressive language communication skills to explain his/her symptoms and response to treatment, or the receptive communication skills to understand the clinician if he/she were to use ordinary adult language for communication.

90801 Psychiatric diagnostic interview examination

90802 Interactive psychiatric diagnostic interview examination using play equipment, physical devices, language interpreter, or other mechanisms of communication

Psychiatric Therapeutic Procedures

Psychotherapy is the treatment for mental illness and behavioral disturbances in which the clinician establishes a professional contract with the patient and, through definitive therapeutic communication, attempts to alleviate the emotional disturbances, reverse or change maladaptive patterns of behavior, and encourage personality growth and development. The codes for reporting psychotherapy are divided into two broad categories: Interactive Psychotherapy; and Insight Oriented, Behavior Modifying and/or Supportive Psychotherapy.

Interactive psychotherapy is typically furnished to children. It involves the use of physical aids and non-verbal communication to overcome barriers to therapeutic interaction between the clinician and a patient who has not yet developed, or has lost, either the expressive language communication skills to explain his/her symptoms and response to treatment, or the receptive communication skills to understand the clinician if he/she were to use ordinary adult language for communication.

Insight oriented, behavior modifying and/or supportive psychotherapy refers to the development of insight or affective understanding, the use of behavior modification techniques, the use of supportive interactions, the use of cognitive discussion of reality, or any combination of the above to provide therapeutic change.

Some patients receive psychotherapy only and others receive psychotherapy and medical evaluation and management services. These evaluation and management services involve a variety of responsibilities unique to the medical management of psychiatric patients, such as medical diagnostic evaluation (eg, evaluation of comorbid medical conditions, drug interactions, and physical examinations), drug management when indicated, physician orders, interpretation of laboratory or other medical diagnostic studies and observations.

In reporting psychotherapy, the appropriate code is chosen on the basis of the type of psychotherapy (interactive using non-verbal techniques versus insight oriented, behavior modifying and/or supportive using verbal techniques), the place of service (office versus inpatient), the face-to-face time spent with the patient during psychotherapy, and whether evaluation and management services are furnished on the same date of service as psychotherapy.

To report medical evaluation and management services furnished on a day when psychotherapy is not provided, select the appropriate code from the **Evaluation and Management Services Guidelines.**

Office or Other Outpatient Facility

Insight Oriented, Behavior Modifying and/or Supportive Psychotherapy

90804 Individual psychotherapy, insight oriented, behavior modifying and/or supportive, in an office or outpatient facility, approximately 20 to 30 minutes face-to-face with the patient;

90805 with medical evaluation and management services

90806 Individual psychotherapy, insight oriented, behavior modifying and/or supportive, in an office or outpatient facility, approximately 45 to 50 minutes face-to-face with the patient;

90807 with medical evaluation and management services

90808 Individual psychotherapy, insight oriented, behavior modifying and/or supportive, in an office or outpatient facility, approximately 75 to 80 minutes face-to-face with the patient;

90809 with medical evaluation and management services

Interactive Psychotherapy

90810 Individual psychotherapy, interactive, using play equipment, physical devices, language interpreter, or other mechanisms of non-verbal communication, in an office or outpatient facility, approximately 20 to 30 minutes face-to-face with the patient;

90811 with medical evaluation and management services

90812 Individual psychotherapy, interactive, using play equipment, physical devices, language interpreter, or other mechanisms of non-verbal communication, in an office or outpatient facility, approximately 45 to 50 minutes face-to-face with the patient;

90813 with medical evaluation and management services

90814 Individual psychotherapy, interactive, using play equipment, physical devices, language interpreter, or other mechanisms of non-verbal communication, in an office or outpatient facility, approximately 75 to 80 minutes face-to-face with the patient;

90815 with medical evaluation and management services

Inpatient Hospital, Partial Hospital or Residential Care Facility

Insight Oriented, Behavior Modifying and/or Supportive Psychotherapy

90816 Individual psychotherapy, insight oriented, behavior modifying and/or supportive, in an inpatient hospital, partial hospital or residential care setting, approximately 20 to 30 minutes face-to-face with the patient;

90817 with medical evaluation and management services

90818 Individual psychotherapy, insight oriented, behavior modifying and/or supportive, in an inpatient hospital, partial hospital or residential care setting, approximately 45 to 50 minutes face-to-face with the patient;

90819 with medical evaluation and management services

90821 Individual psychotherapy, insight oriented, behavior modifying and/or supportive, in an inpatient hospital, partial hospital or residential care setting, approximately 75 to 80 minutes face-to-face with the patient;

90822 with medical evaluation and management services

Interactive Psychotherapy

90823 Individual psychotherapy, interactive, using play equipment, physical devices, language interpreter, or other mechanisms of non-verbal communication, in an inpatient hospital, partial hospital or residential care setting, approximately 20 to 30 minutes face-to-face with the patient;

90824 with medical evaluation and management services

90826 Individual psychotherapy, interactive, using play equipment, physical devices, language interpreter, or other mechanisms of non-verbal communication, in an inpatient hospital, partial hospital or residential care setting, approximately 45 to 50 minutes face-to-face with the patient;

90827 with medical evaluation and management services

90828 Individual psychotherapy, interactive, using play equipment, physical devices, language interpreter, or other mechanisms of non-verbal communication, in an inpatient hospital, partial hospital or residential care setting, approximately 75 to 80 minutes face-to-face with the patient;

90829 with medical evaluation and management services

Other Psychotherapy

90845 Psychoanalysis

90846 Family psychotherapy (without the patient present)

90847 Family psychotherapy (conjoint psychotherapy) (with patient present)

90849 Multiple-family group psychotherapy

90853 Group psychotherapy (other than of a multiple-family group)

90857 Interactive group psychotherapy

Other Psychiatric Services or Procedures

(For repetitive transcranial magnetic stimulation for treatment of clinical depression, see Category III codes 0160T, 0161T)

(For analysis/programming of neurostimulators used for vagus nerve stimulation therapy, see 95970, 95974, 95975)

90862 Pharmacologic management, including prescription, use, and review of medication with no more than minimal medical psychotherapy

90865 Narcosynthesis for psychiatric diagnostic and therapeutic purposes (eg, sodium amobarbital (Amytal) interview)

90870 Electroconvulsive therapy (includes necessary monitoring)

90875 Individual psychophysiological therapy incorporating biofeedback training by any modality (face-to-face with the patient), with psychotherapy (eg, insight oriented, behavior modifying or supportive psychotherapy); approximately 20-30 minutes

90876 approximately 45-50 minutes

90880 Hypnotherapy

90882 Environmental intervention for medical management purposes on a psychiatric patient's behalf with agencies, employers, or institutions

90885 Psychiatric evaluation of hospital records, other psychiatric reports, psychometric and/or projective tests, and other accumulated data for medical diagnostic purposes

90887 Interpretation or explanation of results of psychiatric, other medical examinations and procedures, or other accumulated data to family or other responsible persons, or advising them how to assist patient

90889 Preparation of report of patient's psychiatric status, history, treatment, or progress (other than for legal or consultative purposes) for other physicians, agencies, or insurance carriers

90899 Unlisted psychiatric service or procedure

Biofeedback

(For psychophysiological therapy incorporating biofeedback training, see 90875, 90876)

90901 Biofeedback training by any modality

90911 Biofeedback training, perineal muscles, anorectal or urethral sphincter, including EMG and/or manometry

(For testing of rectal sensation, tone and compliance, use 91120)

►(For incontinence treatment by pulsed magnetic neuromodulation, use 53899)◄

Dialysis

►(90918, 90922 have been deleted. To report ESRD-related services for patients younger than 2 years of age, see 90951-90953, 90963, 90967)◄

►(90919, 90923 have been deleted. To report ESRD-related services for patients between 2 and 11 years of age, see 90954-90956, 90964, 90968)◄

►(90920, 90924 have been deleted. To report ESRD-related services for patients between 12 and 19 years of age, see 90957-90959, 90965, 90969)◄

►(90921, 90925 have been deleted. To report ESRD-related services for patients 20 years of age and older, see 90960-90962, 90966, 90970)◄

Hemodialysis

Codes 90935, 90937 are reported to describe the hemodialysis procedure with all evaluation and management services related to the patient's renal disease on the day of the hemodialysis procedure. These codes are used for inpatient ESRD and non-ESRD procedures or for outpatient non-ESRD dialysis services. Code 90935 is reported if only one evaluation of the patient is required related to that hemodialysis procedure. Code 90937 is reported when patient re-evaluation(s) is required during a hemodialysis procedure. Use modifier 25 with Evaluation and Management codes for separately identifiable services unrelated to the dialysis procedure or renal failure which cannot be rendered during the dialysis session.

(For home visit hemodialysis services performed by a non-physician health care professional, use 99512)

(For cannula declotting, see 36831, 36833, 36860, 36861)

(For declotting of implanted vascular access device or catheter by thrombolytic agent, use 36593)

(For collection of blood specimen from a partially or completely implantable venous access device, use 36591)

(For prolonged physician attendance, see 99354-99360)

90935 Hemodialysis procedure with single physician evaluation

90937 Hemodialysis procedure requiring repeated evaluation(s) with or without substantial revision of dialysis prescription

90940 Hemodialysis access flow study to determine blood flow in grafts and arteriovenous fistulae by an indicator method

(For duplex scan of hemodialysis access, use 93990)

Miscellaneous Dialysis Procedures

Codes 90945, 90947 describe dialysis procedures other than hemodialysis (eg, peritoneal dialysis, hemofiltration or continuous renal replacement therapies), and all evaluation and management services related to the patient's renal disease on the day of the procedure. Code 90945 is reported if only one evaluation of the patient is required related to that procedure. Code 90947 is reported when patient re-evaluation(s) is required during a procedure. Utilize modifier 25 with Evaluation and Management codes for separately identifiable services unrelated to the procedure or the renal failure which cannot be rendered during the dialysis session.

(For insertion of intraperitoneal cannula or catheter, see 49420, 49421)

(For prolonged physician attendance, see 99354-99360)

90945 Dialysis procedure other than hemodialysis (eg, peritoneal dialysis, hemofiltration, or other continuous renal replacement therapies), with single physician evaluation

(For home infusion of peritoneal dialysis, use 99601, 99602)

90947 Dialysis procedure other than hemodialysis (eg, peritoneal dialysis, hemofiltration, or other continuous renal replacement therapies) requiring repeated physician evaluations, with or without substantial revision of dialysis prescription

►End-Stage Renal Disease Services◄

►Codes 90951-90962 are reported **once** per month to distinguish age-specific services related to the patient's end-stage renal disease (ESRD) performed in an outpatient setting with three levels of service based on the number of face-to-face visits. ESRD-related physician services include establishment of a dialyzing cycle, outpatient evaluation and management of the dialysis visits, telephone calls, and patient management during the dialysis provided during a full month. In the circumstances where the patient has had a complete assessment visit during the month and services are provided over a period of less than a month, 90951-90962 may be used according to the number of visits performed.

Codes 90963-90966 are reported once per month for a full month of service to distinguish age-specific services for end-stage renal disease (ESRD) services for home dialysis patients.

For ESRD and non-ESRD dialysis services performed in an inpatient setting, and for non-ESRD dialysis services performed in an outpatient setting, see 90935-90937 and 90945-90947.

Evaluation and Management services unrelated to ESRD services that cannot be performed during the dialysis session may be reported separately.

Codes 90967-90970 are reported to distinguish age-specific services for end-stage renal disease (ESRD) services for less than a full month of service, per day, for services provided under the following circumstances: home dialysis patients less than a full month, transient patients, partial month where there was one or more face-to-face visits without the complete assessment, the patient was hospitalized before a complete assessment was furnished, dialysis was stopped due to recovery or death, or the patient received a kidney transplant. For reporting purposes, each month is considered 30 days.

Examples:

ESRD-related services:

ESRD-related services are initiated on July 1 for a 57-year-old male. On July 11, he is admitted to the hospital as an inpatient and is discharged on July 27. He has had a complete assessment and the physician has performed two face-to-face visits prior to admission. Another face-to-face visit occurs after discharge during the month.

In this example, 90961 is reported for the three face-to-face outpatient visits. Report inpatient E/M services as appropriate. Dialysis procedures rendered during the hospitalization (July 11-27) should be reported as appropriate (90935-90937, 90945-90947).

If the patient did not have a complete assessment during the month or was a transient or dialysis was stopped due to recovery or death, 90970 would be used to report each day outside the inpatient hospitalization as described in the home dialysis example below.

ESRD-related services for the home dialysis patient:

Home ESRD-related services are initiated on July 1 for a 57-year-old male. On July 11, he is admitted to the hospital as an inpatient and is discharged on July 27.

In this example, 90970 should be reported for each day outside of the inpatient hospitalization (30 days/month less 17 days/hospitalization = 13 days). Report inpatient E/M services as appropriate. Dialysis procedures rendered during the hospitalization (July 11-27) should be reported as appropriate (90935-90937, 90945-90947).◄

● **90951** End-stage renal disease (ESRD) related services monthly, for patients younger than 2 years of age to include monitoring for the adequacy of nutrition, assessment of growth and development, and counseling of parents; with 4 or more face-to-face physician visits per month

● **90952** with 2-3 face-to-face physician visits per month

● **90953** with 1 face-to-face physician visit per month

● **90954** End-stage renal disease (ESRD) related services monthly, for patients 2-11 years of age to include monitoring for the adequacy of nutrition, assessment of growth and development, and counseling of parents; with 4 or more face-to-face physician visits per month

● **90955** with 2-3 face-to-face physician visits per month

● **90956** with 1 face-to-face physician visit per month

● **90957** End-stage renal disease (ESRD) related services monthly, for patients 12-19 years of age to include monitoring for the adequacy of nutrition, assessment of growth and development, and counseling of parents; with 4 or more face-to-face physician visits per month

● **90958** with 2-3 face-to-face physician visits per month

● **90959** with 1 face-to-face physician visit per month

● **90960** End-stage renal disease (ESRD) related services monthly, for patients 20 years of age and older; with 4 or more face-to-face physician visits per month

● **90961** with 2-3 face-to-face physician visits per month

● **90962** with 1 face-to-face physician visit per month

● **90963** End-stage renal disease (ESRD) related services for home dialysis per full month, for patients younger than 2 years of age to include monitoring for the adequacy of nutrition, assessment of growth and development, and counseling of parents

● **90964** End-stage renal disease (ESRD) related services for home dialysis per full month, for patients 2-11 years of age to include monitoring for the adequacy of nutrition, assessment of growth and development, and counseling of parents

● **90965** End-stage renal disease (ESRD) related services for home dialysis per full month, for patients 12-19 years of age to include monitoring for the adequacy of nutrition, assessment of growth and development, and counseling of parents

● **90966** End-stage renal disease (ESRD) related services for home dialysis per full month, for patients 20 years of age and older

● **90967** End-stage renal disease (ESRD) related services for dialysis less than a full month of service, per day; for patients younger than 2 years of age

● **90968** for patients 2-11 years of age

● **90969** for patients 12-19 years of age

● **90970** for patients 20 years of age and older

►Other Dialysis Procedures◄

90989 Dialysis training, patient, including helper where applicable, any mode, completed course

90993 Dialysis training, patient, including helper where applicable, any mode, course not completed, per training session

90997 Hemoperfusion (eg, with activated charcoal or resin)

90999 Unlisted dialysis procedure, inpatient or outpatient

Gastroenterology

(For duodenal intubation and aspiration, see 89100-89105)

(For gastrointestinal radiologic procedures, see 74210-74363)

(For esophagoscopy procedures, see 43200-43228; upper GI endoscopy 43234-43259; endoscopy, small intestine and stomal 44360-44393; proctosigmoidoscopy 45300-45321; sigmoidoscopy 45330-45339; colonoscopy 45355-45385; anoscopy 46600-46615)

91000 Esophageal intubation and collection of washings for cytology, including preparation of specimens (separate procedure)

91010 Esophageal motility (manometric study of the esophagus and/or gastroesophageal junction) study;

91011 with mecholyl or similar stimulant

91012 with acid perfusion studies

91020 Gastric motility (manometric) studies

91022 Duodenal motility (manometric) study

(If gastrointestinal endoscopy is performed, use 43235)

(If fluoroscopy is performed, use 76000)

(If gastric motility study is performed, use 91020)

91030 Esophagus, acid perfusion (Bernstein) test for esophagitis

91034 Esophagus, gastroesophageal reflux test; with nasal catheter pH electrode(s) placement, recording, analysis and interpretation

91035 with mucosal attached telemetry pH electrode placement, recording, analysis and interpretation

91037 Esophageal function test, gastroesophageal reflux test with nasal catheter intraluminal impedance electrode(s) placement, recording, analysis and interpretation;

91038 prolonged (greater than 1 hour, up to 24 hours)

91040 Esophageal balloon distension provocation study

(For balloon dilatation with endoscopy, see 43220, 43249, 43456, or 43458)

91052 Gastric analysis test with injection of stimulant of gastric secretion (eg, histamine, insulin, pentagastrin, calcium and secretin)

(For gastric biopsy by capsule, peroral, via tube, 1 or more specimens, use 43600)

(For gastric laboratory procedures, see also 89130-89141)

91055 Gastric intubation, washings, and preparing slides for cytology (separate procedure)

(For gastric lavage, therapeutic, use 91105)

(91060 has been deleted)

(For biopsy by capsule, small intestine, per oral, via tube [one or more specimens], use 44100)

91065 Breath hydrogen test (eg, for detection of lactase deficiency, fructose intolerance, bacterial overgrowth, or oro-cecal gastrointestinal transit)

(For H. pylori breath test analysis, use 83013 for non-radioactive (C-13) isotope or 78268 for radioactive (C-14) isotope)

►(91100 has been deleted)◄

►(To report placement of an esophageal tamponade tube for management of variceal bleeding, use 43460. To report placement of a long intestinal Miller-Abbott tube, use 44500)◄

91105 Gastric intubation, and aspiration or lavage for treatment (eg, for ingested poisons)

(For cholangiography, see 47500, 74320)

(For abdominal paracentesis, see 49080, 49081; with instillation of medication, see 96440, 96445)

(For peritoneoscopy, use 49320; with biopsy, use 49321)

(For peritoneoscopy and guided transhepatic cholangiography, use 47560; with biopsy, use 47561)

(For splenoportography, see 38200, 75810)

91110 Gastrointestinal tract imaging, intraluminal (eg, capsule endoscopy), esophagus through ileum, with physician interpretation and report

(Visualization of the colon is not reported separately)

(Append modifier 52 if the ileum is not visualized)

91111 Gastrointestinal tract imaging, intraluminal (eg, capsule endoscopy), esophagus with physician interpretation and report

(Do not report 91111 in conjunction with 91110)

91120 Rectal sensation, tone, and compliance test (ie, response to graded balloon distention)

(For biofeedback training, use 90911)

(For anorectal manometry, use 91122)

91122 Anorectal manometry

91123 Pulsed irrigation of fecal impaction

Gastric Physiology

91132 Electrogastrography, diagnostic, transcutaneous;

91133 with provocative testing

Other Procedures

91299 Unlisted diagnostic gastroenterology procedure

Ophthalmology

(For surgical procedures, see **Surgery,** Eye and Ocular Adnexa, 65091 et seq)

Definitions

Intermediate ophthalmological services describes an evaluation of a new or existing condition complicated with a new diagnostic or management problem not necessarily relating to the primary diagnosis, including history, general medical observation, external ocular and adnexal examination and other diagnostic procedures as indicated; may include the use of mydriasis for ophthalmoscopy.

Medicine

For example:

a. Review of history, external examination, ophthalmoscopy, biomicroscopy for an acute complicated condition (eg, iritis) not requiring comprehensive ophthalmological services.

b. Review of interval history, external examination, ophthalmoscopy, biomicroscopy and tonometry in established patient with known cataract not requiring comprehensive ophthalmological services.

Comprehensive ophthalmological services describes a general evaluation of the complete visual system. The comprehensive services constitute a single service entity but need not be performed at one session. The service includes history, general medical observation, external and ophthalmoscopic examinations, gross visual fields and basic sensorimotor examination. It often includes, as indicated: biomicroscopy, examination with cycloplegia or mydriasis and tonometry. It always includes initiation of diagnostic and treatment programs.

Intermediate and comprehensive ophthalmological services constitute integrated services in which medical decision making cannot be separated from the examining techniques used. Itemization of service components, such as slit lamp examination, keratometry, routine ophthalmoscopy, retinoscopy, tonometry, or motor evaluation is not applicable.

For example:

The comprehensive services required for diagnosis and treatment of a patient with symptoms indicating possible disease of the visual system, such as glaucoma, cataract or retinal disease, or to rule out disease of the visual system, new or established patient.

Initiation of diagnostic and treatment program includes the prescription of medication, and arranging for special ophthalmological diagnostic or treatment services, consultations, laboratory procedures and radiological services.

Special ophthalmological services describes services in which a special evaluation of part of the visual system is made, which goes beyond the services included under general ophthalmological services, or in which special treatment is given. Special ophthalmological services may be reported in addition to the general ophthalmological services or evaluation and management services.

For example:

Fluorescein angioscopy, quantitative visual field examination, refraction or extended color vision examination (such as Nagel's anomaloscope) should be separately reported.

Prescription of lenses, when required, is included in 92015. It includes specification of lens type (monofocal, bifocal, other), lens power, axis, prism, absorptive factor, impact resistance, and other factors.

Interpretation and report by the physician is an integral part of special ophthalmological services where indicated. Technical procedures (which may or may not be performed by the physician personally) are often part of the service, but should not be mistaken to constitute the service itself.

General Ophthalmological Services

New Patient

Solely for the purposes of distinguishing between new and established patients, **professional services** are those face-to-face services rendered by a physician and reported by a specific code(s). A new patient is one who has not received any professional services from the physician or another physician of the same specialty who belongs to the same group practice within the past three years.

92002 Ophthalmological services: medical examination and evaluation with initiation of diagnostic and treatment program; intermediate, new patient

92004 comprehensive, new patient, 1 or more visits

Established Patient

Solely for the purposes of distinguishing between new and established patients, **professional services** are those face-to-face services rendered by a physician and reported by a specific code(s). An established patient is one who has received professional services from the physician or another physician of the same specialty who belongs to the same group practice within the past three years.

92012 Ophthalmological services: medical examination and evaluation, with initiation or continuation of diagnostic and treatment program; intermediate, established patient

92014 comprehensive, established patient, 1 or more visits

(For surgical procedures, see **Surgery,** Eye and Ocular Adnexa, 65091 et seq)

Special Ophthalmological Services

92015 Determination of refractive state

92018 Ophthalmological examination and evaluation, under general anesthesia, with or without manipulation of globe for passive range of motion or other manipulation to facilitate diagnostic examination; complete

92019 limited

92020 Gonioscopy (separate procedure)

(For gonioscopy under general anesthesia, use 92018)

Medicine

92025 Computerized corneal topography, unilateral or bilateral, with interpretation and report

►(Do not report 92025 in conjunction with 65710-65771)◄

(92025 is not used for manual keratoscopy, which is part of a single system Evaluation and Management or ophthalmological service)

92060 Sensorimotor examination with multiple measurements of ocular deviation (eg, restrictive or paretic muscle with diplopia) with interpretation and report (separate procedure)

92065 Orthoptic and/or pleoptic training, with continuing medical direction and evaluation

92070 Fitting of contact lens for treatment of disease, including supply of lens

92081 Visual field examination, unilateral or bilateral, with interpretation and report; limited examination (eg, tangent screen, Autoplot, arc perimeter, or single stimulus level automated test, such as Octopus 3 or 7 equivalent)

92082 intermediate examination (eg, at least 2 isopters on Goldmann perimeter, or semiquantitative, automated suprathreshold screening program, Humphrey suprathreshold automatic diagnostic test, Octopus program 33)

92083 extended examination (eg, Goldmann visual fields with at least 3 isopters plotted and static determination within the central 30°, or quantitative, automated threshold perimetry, Octopus program G-1, 32 or 42, Humphrey visual field analyzer full threshold programs 30-2, 24-2, or 30/60-2)

(Gross visual field testing (eg, confrontation testing) is a part of general ophthalmological services and is not reported separately)

92100 Serial tonometry (separate procedure) with multiple measurements of intraocular pressure over an extended time period with interpretation and report, same day (eg, diurnal curve or medical treatment of acute elevation of intraocular pressure)

92120 Tonography with interpretation and report, recording indentation tonometer method or perilimbal suction method

92130 Tonography with water provocation

92135 Scanning computerized ophthalmic diagnostic imaging, posterior segment, (eg, scanning laser) with interpretation and report, unilateral

92136 Ophthalmic biometry by partial coherence interferometry with intraocular lens power calculation

92140 Provocative tests for glaucoma, with interpretation and report, without tonography

Ophthalmoscopy

Routine ophthalmoscopy is part of general and special ophthalmologic services whenever indicated. It is a non-itemized service and is not reported separately.

92225 Ophthalmoscopy, extended, with retinal drawing (eg, for retinal detachment, melanoma), with interpretation and report; initial

92226 subsequent

92230 Fluorescein angioscopy with interpretation and report

92235 Fluorescein angiography (includes multiframe imaging) with interpretation and report

92240 Indocyanine-green angiography (includes multiframe imaging) with interpretation and report

92250 Fundus photography with interpretation and report

92260 Ophthalmodynamometry

(For ophthalmoscopy under general anesthesia, use 92018)

Other Specialized Services

92265 Needle oculoelectromyography, 1 or more extraocular muscles, 1 or both eyes, with interpretation and report

92270 Electro-oculography with interpretation and report

92275 Electroretinography with interpretation and report

(For electronystagmography for vestibular function studies, see 92541 et seq)

(For ophthalmic echography (diagnostic ultrasound), see 76511-76529)

92283 Color vision examination, extended, eg, anomaloscope or equivalent

(Color vision testing with pseudoisochromatic plates [such as HRR or Ishihara] is not reported separately. It is included in the appropriate general or ophthalmological service, or 99172)

92284 Dark adaptation examination with interpretation and report

92285 External ocular photography with interpretation and report for documentation of medical progress (eg, close-up photography, slit lamp photography, goniophotography, stereo-photography)

92286 Special anterior segment photography with interpretation and report; with specular endothelial microscopy and cell count

92287 with fluorescein angiography

Contact Lens Services

The prescription of contact lens includes specification of optical and physical characteristics (such as power, size, curvature, flexibility, gas-permeability). It is NOT a part of the general ophthalmological services.

The fitting of contact lens includes instruction and training of the wearer and incidental revision of the lens during the training period.

Follow-up of successfully fitted extended wear lenses is reported as part of a general ophthalmological service (92012 et seq).

The supply of contact lenses may be reported as part of the service of fitting. It may also be reported separately by using the appropriate supply codes.

(For therapeutic or surgical use of contact lens, see 68340, 92070)

92310 Prescription of optical and physical characteristics of and fitting of contact lens, with medical supervision of adaptation; corneal lens, both eyes, except for aphakia

(For prescription and fitting of 1 eye, add modifier 52)

92311 corneal lens for aphakia, 1 eye

92312 corneal lens for aphakia, both eyes

92313 corneoscleral lens

92314 Prescription of optical and physical characteristics of contact lens, with medical supervision of adaptation and direction of fitting by independent technician; corneal lens, both eyes except for aphakia

(For prescription and fitting of 1 eye, add modifier 52)

92315 corneal lens for aphakia, 1 eye

92316 corneal lens for aphakia, both eyes

92317 corneoscleral lens

92325 Modification of contact lens (separate procedure), with medical supervision of adaptation

92326 Replacement of contact lens

(For prescription, fitting, and/or medical supervision of ocular prosthetic adaptation by a physician, see Evaluation and Management services or General Ophthalmological service codes 92002-92014)

Spectacle Services (Including Prosthesis for Aphakia)

Prescription of lenses, when required, is included in 92015 Determination of refractive state. It includes specification of lens type (monofocal, bifocal, other), lens power, axis, prism, absorptive factor, impact resistance, and other factors.

Fitting of spectacles is a separate service; when provided by the physician, it is reported as indicated by 92340-92371.

Fitting includes measurement of anatomical facial characteristics, the writing of laboratory specifications, and the final adjustment of the spectacles to the visual axes and anatomical topography. Presence of physician is not required.

Supply of materials is a separate service component; it is not part of the service of fitting spectacles.

92340 Fitting of spectacles, except for aphakia; monofocal

92341 bifocal

92342 multifocal, other than bifocal

92352 Fitting of spectacle prosthesis for aphakia; monofocal

92353 multifocal

92354 Fitting of spectacle mounted low vision aid; single element system

92355 telescopic or other compound lens system

92358 Prosthesis service for aphakia, temporary (disposable or loan, including materials)

92370 Repair and refitting spectacles; except for aphakia

92371 spectacle prosthesis for aphakia

Other Procedures

92499 Unlisted ophthalmological service or procedure

Special Otorhinolaryngologic Services

►Diagnostic or treatment procedures that are reported as evaluation and management services (eg, otoscopy, anterior rhinoscopy, tuning fork test, removal of non-impacted cerumen) are not reported separately.

Special otorhinolaryngologic services are those diagnostic and treatment services not included in an Evaluation and Management service. These services are reported separately, using codes 92502-92700.◄

Code 92506 is used to report evaluation of speech production, receptive language, and expressive language abilities. Tests may examine speech sound production, articulatory movements of oral musculature, the patient's ability to understand the meaning and intent of written and verbal expressions, and the appropriate formulation and utterance of expressive thought. In contrast, 92626 and 92627 are reported for an evaluation of auditory rehabilitation status determining the patient's ability to use residual hearing in order to identify the acoustic characteristics of sounds associated with speech communication.

(For laryngoscopy with stroboscopy, use 31579)

92502 Otolaryngologic examination under general anesthesia

92504 Binocular microscopy (separate diagnostic procedure)

92506 Evaluation of speech, language, voice, communication, and/or auditory processing

92507 Treatment of speech, language, voice, communication, and/or auditory processing disorder; individual

92508 group, 2 or more individuals

(For auditory rehabilitation, prelingual hearing loss, use 92630)

(For auditory rehabilitation, postlingual hearing loss, use 92633)

(For cochlear implant programming, see 92601-92604)

92511 Nasopharyngoscopy with endoscope (separate procedure)

92512 Nasal function studies (eg, rhinomanometry)

92516 Facial nerve function studies (eg, electroneuronography)

92520 Laryngeal function studies (ie, aerodynamic testing and acoustic testing)

(For performance of a single test, use modifier 52)

(To report flexible fiberoptic laryngeal evaluation of swallowing and laryngeal sensory testing, see 92611-92617)

(To report other testing of laryngeal function (eg, electroglottography), use 92700)

92526 Treatment of swallowing dysfunction and/or oral function for feeding

▸Vestibular Function Tests, Without Electrical Recording◂

92531 Spontaneous nystagmus, including gaze

92532 Positional nystagmus test

▶(Do not report 92531, 92532 with evaluation and management services)◀

92533 Caloric vestibular test, each irrigation (binaural, bithermal stimulation constitutes four tests)

92534 Optokinetic nystagmus test

▸Vestibular Function Tests, With Recording (eg, ENG) ◂

92541 Spontaneous nystagmus test, including gaze and fixation nystagmus, with recording

92542 Positional nystagmus test, minimum of 4 positions, with recording

92543 Caloric vestibular test, each irrigation (binaural, bithermal stimulation constitutes four tests), with recording

92544 Optokinetic nystagmus test, bidirectional, foveal or peripheral stimulation, with recording

92545 Oscillating tracking test, with recording

92546 Sinusoidal vertical axis rotational testing

+ 92547 Use of vertical electrodes (List separately in addition to code for primary procedure)

(Use 92547 in conjunction with 92541-92546)

(For unlisted vestibular tests, use 92700)

92548 Computerized dynamic posturography

▸Audiologic Function Tests◂

▶The audiometric tests listed below require the use of calibrated electronic equipment, recording of results and a report with interpretation. Hearing tests (such as whispered voice, tuning fork) that are otorhinolaryngologic Evaluation and Management services are not reported separately. All services include testing of both ears. Use modifier 52 if a test is applied to one ear instead of two ears. All codes (except 92559) apply to testing of individuals. For testing of groups, use 92559 and specify test(s) used.◀

(For evaluation of speech, language and/or hearing problems through observation and assessment of performance, use 92506)

92551 Screening test, pure tone, air only

92552 Pure tone audiometry (threshold); air only

92553 air and bone

92555 Speech audiometry threshold;

92556 with speech recognition

92557 Comprehensive audiometry threshold evaluation and speech recognition (92553 and 92556 combined)

(For hearing aid evaluation and selection, see 92590-92595)

92559 Audiometric testing of groups

92560 Bekesy audiometry; screening

92561 diagnostic

92562 Loudness balance test, alternate binaural or monaural

92563 Tone decay test

92564 Short increment sensitivity index (SISI)

92565 Stenger test, pure tone

92567 Tympanometry (impedance testing)

92568 Acoustic reflex testing; threshold

92569 decay

92571 Filtered speech test

92572 Staggered spondaic word test

(92573 has been deleted. To report the Lombard test, use 92700)

92575 Sensorineural acuity level test

92576 Synthetic sentence identification test

92577 Stenger test, speech

92579 Visual reinforcement audiometry (VRA)

92582 Conditioning play audiometry

92583 Select picture audiometry

92584 Electrocochleography

92585 Auditory evoked potentials for evoked response audiometry and/or testing of the central nervous system; comprehensive

92586 limited

92587 Evoked otoacoustic emissions; limited (single stimulus level, either transient or distortion products)

92588 comprehensive or diagnostic evaluation (comparison of transient and/or distortion product otoacoustic emissions at multiple levels and frequencies)

(For central auditory function evaluation, see 92620, 92621)

92590 Hearing aid examination and selection; monaural

92591 binaural

92592 Hearing aid check; monaural

92593 binaural

92594 Electroacoustic evaluation for hearing aid; monaural

92595 binaural

92596 Ear protector attenuation measurements

92597 Evaluation for use and/or fitting of voice prosthetic device to supplement oral speech

(To report augmentative and alternative communication device services, see 92605, 92607, 92608)

Evaluative and Therapeutic Services

Codes 92601 and 92603 describe post-operative analysis and fitting of previously placed external devices, connection to the cochlear implant, and programming of the stimulator. Codes 92602 and 92604 describe subsequent sessions for measurements and adjustment of the external transmitter and re-programming of the internal stimulator.

(For placement of cochlear implant, use 69930)

92601 Diagnostic analysis of cochlear implant, patient younger than 7 years of age; with programming

92602 subsequent reprogramming

(Do not report 92602 in addition to 92601)

(For aural rehabilitation services following cochlear implant, including evaluation of rehabilitation status, see 92626-92627, 92630-92633)

92603 Diagnostic analysis of cochlear implant, age 7 years or older; with programming

92604 subsequent reprogramming

(Do not report 92604 in addition to 92603)

92605 Evaluation for prescription of non-speech-generating augmentative and alternative communication device

92606 Therapeutic service(s) for the use of non-speech-generating device, including programming and modification

92607 Evaluation for prescription for speech-generating augmentative and alternative communication device, face-to-face with the patient; first hour

(For evaluation for prescription of a non-speech-generating device, use 92605)

+ 92608 each additional 30 minutes (List separately in addition to code for primary procedure)

(Use 92608 in conjunction with 92607)

92609 Therapeutic services for the use of speech-generating device, including programming and modification

(For therapeutic service(s) for the use of a non-speech-generating device, use 92606)

92610 Evaluation of oral and pharyngeal swallowing function

(For motion fluoroscopic evaluation of swallowing function, use 92611)

(For flexible endoscopic examination, use 92612-92617)

92611 Motion fluoroscopic evaluation of swallowing function by cine or video recording

(For radiological supervision and interpretation, use 74230)

(For evaluation of oral and pharyngeal swallowing function, use 92610)

(For flexible fiberoptic diagnostic laryngoscopy, use 31575. Do not report 31575 in conjunction with 92612-92617)

92612 Flexible fiberoptic endoscopic evaluation of swallowing by cine or video recording;

(If flexible fiberoptic or endoscopic evaluation of swallowing is performed without cine or video recording, use 92700)

92613 physician interpretation and report only

(To report an evaluation of oral and pharyngeal swallowing function, use 92610)

(To report motion fluoroscopic evaluation of swallowing function, use 92611)

92614 Flexible fiberoptic endoscopic evaluation, laryngeal sensory testing by cine or video recording;

(If flexible fiberoptic or endoscopic evaluation of swallowing is performed without cine or video recording, use 92700)

92615 physician interpretation and report only

92616 Flexible fiberoptic endoscopic evaluation of swallowing and laryngeal sensory testing by cine or video recording;

(If flexible fiberoptic or endoscopic evaluation of swallowing is performed without cine or video recording, use 92700)

92617 physician interpretation and report only

92620 Evaluation of central auditory function, with report; initial 60 minutes

92621 each additional 15 minutes

(Do not report 92620, 92621 in conjunction with 92506)

92625 Assessment of tinnitus (includes pitch, loudness matching, and masking)

(Do not report 92625 in conjunction with 92562)

(For unilateral assessment, use modifier 52)

92626 Evaluation of auditory rehabilitation status; first hour

+ 92627 each additional 15 minutes (List separately in addition to code for primary procedure)

(Use 92627 in conjunction with 92626)

(When reporting 92626, 92627, use the face-to-face time with the patient or family)

92630 Auditory rehabilitation; prelingual hearing loss

92633 postlingual hearing loss

Special Diagnostic Procedures

92640 Diagnostic analysis with programming of auditory brainstem implant, per hour

(Report nonprogramming services separately [eg, cardiac monitoring])

Other Procedures

92700 Unlisted otorhinolaryngological service or procedure

Cardiovascular

Therapeutic Services and Procedures

►(For nonsurgical septal reduction therapy [eg, alcohol ablation], use 93799)◄

92950 Cardiopulmonary resuscitation (eg, in cardiac arrest)

(See also critical care services, 99291, 99292)

⊙ 92953 Temporary transcutaneous pacing

(For physician direction of ambulance or rescue personnel outside the hospital, use 99288)

⊙ 92960 Cardioversion, elective, electrical conversion of arrhythmia; external

⊙ 92961 internal (separate procedure)

►(Do not report 92961 in addition to codes 93282, 93283, 93289, 93292, 93295, 93662, 93618-93624, 93631, 93640-93642, 93650-93652)◄

92970 Cardioassist-method of circulatory assist; internal

92971 external

(For balloon atrial-septostomy, use 92992)

(For placement of catheters for use in circulatory assist devices such as intra-aortic balloon pump, use 33970)

⊙+ 92973 Percutaneous transluminal coronary thrombectomy (List separately in addition to code for primary procedure)

(Use 92973 in conjunction with 92980, 92982)

⊙+ 92974 Transcatheter placement of radiation delivery device for subsequent coronary intravascular brachytherapy (List separately in addition to code for primary procedure)

(Use 92974 in conjunction with 92980, 92982, 92995, 93508)

(For intravascular radioelement application, see 77781-77784)

⊙ 92975 Thrombolysis, coronary; by intracoronary infusion, including selective coronary angiography

92977 by intravenous infusion

(For thrombolysis of vessels other than coronary, see 37201, 75896)

(For cerebral thrombolysis, use 37195)

⊙+ 92978 Intravascular ultrasound (coronary vessel or graft) during diagnostic evaluation and/or therapeutic intervention including imaging supervision, interpretation and report; initial vessel (List separately in addition to code for primary procedure)

⊙+ 92979 each additional vessel (List separately in addition to code for primary procedure)

(Use 92979 in conjunction with 92978)

(Intravascular ultrasound services include all transducer manipulations and repositioning within the specific vessel being examined, both before and after therapeutic intervention [eg, stent placement])

⊙ 92980 Transcatheter placement of an intracoronary stent(s), percutaneous, with or without other therapeutic intervention, any method; single vessel

⊙+ 92981 each additional vessel (List separately in addition to code for primary procedure)

(Use 92981 in conjunction with 92980)

(Codes 92980, 92981 are used to report coronary artery stenting. Coronary angioplasty [92982, 92984] or atherectomy [92995, 92996], in the same artery, is considered part of the stenting procedure and is not reported separately. Codes 92973 [percutaneous transluminal coronary thombectomy], 92974 [coronary brachytherapy] and 92978, 92979 [intravascular ultrasound] are add-on codes for reporting procedures performed in addition to coronary stenting, atherectomy, and angioplasty and are not included in the "therapeutic interventions" in 92980)

(To report additional vessels treated by angioplasty or atherectomy only during the same session, see 92984, 92996)

(To report transcatheter placement of radiation delivery device for coronary intravascular brachytherapy, use 92974)

(For intravascular radioelement application, see 77781-77784)

⊙ **92982** Percutaneous transluminal coronary balloon angioplasty; single vessel

⊙+ **92984** each additional vessel (List separately in addition to code for primary procedure)

(Use 92984 in conjunction with 92980, 92982, 92995)

(For stent placement following completion of angioplasty or atherectomy, see 92980, 92981)

(To report transcatheter placement of radiation delivery device for coronary intravascular brachytherapy, use 92974)

(For intravascular radioelement application, see 77781-77784)

⊙ **92986** Percutaneous balloon valvuloplasty; aortic valve

⊙ **92987** mitral valve

92990 pulmonary valve

92992 Atrial septectomy or septostomy; transvenous method, balloon (eg, Rashkind type) (includes cardiac catheterization)

92993 blade method (Park septostomy) (includes cardiac catheterization)

⊙ **92995** Percutaneous transluminal coronary atherectomy, by mechanical or other method, with or without balloon angioplasty; single vessel

⊙+ **92996** each additional vessel (List separately in addition to code for primary procedure)

(Use 92996 in conjunction with 92980, 92982, 92995)

(For stent placement following completion of angioplasty or atherectomy, see 92980, 92981)

(To report additional vessels treated by angioplasty only during the same session, use 92984)

92997 Percutaneous transluminal pulmonary artery balloon angioplasty; single vessel

+ **92998** each additional vessel (List separately in addition to code for primary procedure)

(Use 92998 in conjunction with 92997)

Cardiography

Codes 93040-93042 are appropriate when an order for the test is triggered by an event, the rhythm strip is used to help diagnose the presence or absence of an arrhythmia, and a report is generated. There must be a specific order for an electrocardiogram or rhythm strip followed by a separate, signed, written, and retrievable report. It is not appropriate to use these codes for reviewing the telemetry monitor strips taken from a monitoring system. The need for an electrocardiogram or rhythm strip should be supported by documentation in the patient medical record.

►Cardiovascular monitoring services are diagnostic medical procedures using in-person and remote technology to assess cardiovascular rhythm (ECG) data.

Attended surveillance is the immediate availability of a remote technician to respond to rhythm or device alert transmissions from a patient, either from an implanted or wearable monitoring or therapy device, as they are generated and transmitted to the remote surveillance location or center.

Mobile cardiovascular telemetry (MCT) continuously records the electrocardiographic rhythm from external electrodes placed on the patient's body. Segments of the ECG data are automatically (without patient intervention) transmitted to a remote surveillance location by cellular or landline telephone signal. The segments of the rhythm, selected for transmission, are triggered automatically (MCT device algorithm) by rapid and slow heart rates or by the patient during a symptomatic episode. There is continuous real time data analysis by preprogrammed algorithms in the device and attended surveillance of the transmitted rhythm segments by a surveillance center technician to evaluate any arrhythmias and to determine signal quality. The surveillance center technician reviews the data and notifies the physician depending on the prescribed criteria.

ECG rhythm derived elements are distinct from physiologic data, even when the same device is capable of producing both. Implantable cardiovascular monitor (ICM) device services are always separately reported from Implantable cardioverter-defibrillator (ICD) service.

For other services related to a wearable defibrillator, see 93745.◄

(For echocardiography, see 93303-93350)

(For electrocardiogram, 64 leads or greater, with graphic presentation and analysis, see 0178T-0180T)

93000 Electrocardiogram, routine ECG with at least 12 leads; with interpretation and report

93005 tracing only, without interpretation and report

93010 interpretation and report only

(For acoustic heart sound recording, see Category III codes 0068T-0070T)

(For ECG monitoring, see 99354-99360)

93012 Telephonic transmission of post-symptom electrocardiogram rhythm strip(s), 24-hour attended monitoring, per 30 day period of time; tracing only

93014 physician review with interpretation and report only

►(Do not report 93014 in conjunction with 93228, 93229)◄

93015 Cardiovascular stress test using maximal or submaximal treadmill or bicycle exercise, continuous electrocardiographic monitoring, and/or pharmacological stress; with physician supervision, with interpretation and report

93016 physician supervision only, without interpretation and report

93017 tracing only, without interpretation and report

93018 interpretation and report only

(For inert gas rebreathing measurement, see Category III codes 0104T, 0105T)

93024 Ergonovine provocation test

93025 Microvolt T-wave alternans for assessment of ventricular arrhythmias

93040 Rhythm ECG, 1-3 leads; with interpretation and report

93041 tracing only without interpretation and report

93042 interpretation and report only

▲ **93224** Wearable electrocardiographic rhythm derived monitoring for 24 hours by continuous original waveform recording and storage, with visual superimposition scanning; includes recording, scanning analysis with report, physician review and interpretation

▲ **93225** recording (includes connection, recording, and disconnection)

▲ **93226** scanning analysis with report

▲ **93227** physician review and interpretation

● **93228** Wearable mobile cardiovascular telemetry with electrocardiographic recording, concurrent computerized real time data analysis and greater than 24 hours of accessible ECG data storage (retrievable with query) with ECG triggered and patient selected events transmitted to a remote attended surveillance center for up to 30 days; physician review and interpretation with report

►(Report 93228 only once per 30 days)◄

►(Do not report 93228 in conjunction with 93014)◄

● **93229** technical support for connection and patient instructions for use, attended surveillance, analysis and physician prescribed transmission of daily and emergent data reports

►(Report 93229 only once per 30 days)◄

►(Do no report 93229 in conjunction with 93014)◄

►(For wearable cardiovascular monitors that do not perform automatic ECG triggered transmissions to an attended surveillance center, see 93224-93227, 93230-93272)◄

▲ **93230** Wearable electrocardiographic rhythm derived monitoring for 24 hours by continuous original waveform recording and storage without superimposition scanning utilizing a device capable of producing a full miniaturized printout; includes recording, microprocessor-based analysis with report, physician review and interpretation

▲ **93231** recording (includes connection, recording, and disconnection)

▲ **93232** microprocessor-based analysis with report

▲ **93233** physician review and interpretation

▲ **93235** Wearable electrocardiographic rhythm derived monitoring for 24 hours by continuous computerized monitoring and non-continuous recording, and real-time data analysis utilizing a device capable of producing intermittent full-sized waveform tracings, possibly patient activated; includes monitoring and real-time data analysis with report, physician review and interpretation

▲ **93236** monitoring and real-time data analysis with report

▲ **93237** physician review and interpretation

►(For wearable mobile telemetry with ECG triggered transmissions to an attended surveillance center, see 93228, 93229)◄

▲ **93268** Wearable patient activated electrocardiographic rhythm derived event recording with presymptom memory loop, 24-hour attended monitoring, per 30 day period of time; includes transmission, physician review and interpretation

▲ **93270** recording (includes connection, recording, and disconnection)

▲ **93271** monitoring, receipt of transmissions, and analysis

▲ **93272** physician review and interpretation

(For postsymptom recording, see 93012, 93014)

►(For implanted patient activated cardiac event recording, see 33282, 93285, 93291, 93298)◄

93278 Signal-averaged electrocardiography (SAECG), with or without ECG

(For interpretation and report only, use 93278 with modifier 26)

(For unlisted cardiographic procedure, use 93799)

►Cardiovascular Device Monitoring—Implantable and Wearable Devices◄

►Cardiovascular monitoring services are diagnostic medical procedures using in-person and remote technology to assess device therapy and cardiovascular physiologic data. Codes 93279-93299 describe this technology and technical/professional physician and service center practice. Codes 93279-93292 are reported per procedure. Codes 93293-93296 are reported no more than **once** every 90 days. Do not report 93293-93296 if the monitoring period is less than 30 days. Codes 93297, 93298 are reported no more than **once** up to every 30 days. Do not report 93297-93299 if the monitoring period is less than 10 days.

A service center may report 93296 or 93299 during a period in which a physician performs an in-person interrogation device evaluation. A physician may not report an in-person and remote interrogation of the same device during the same period. Report only remote services when an in-person interrogation device evaluation is performed during a period of remote interrogation device evaluation. A period is established by the initiation of the remote monitoring or the 91st day of a pacemaker or implantable cardioverter-defibrillator (ICD) monitoring or the 31st day of an implantable loop recorder (ILR) or implantable cardiovascular monitor (ICM) monitoring and extends for the subsequent 30 or 90 days, respectively, for which remote monitoring is occurring. Programming device evaluations and in-person interrogation device evaluations may not be reported on the same date by the same physician. Programming device evaluations and remote interrogation device evaluations may both be reported during the remote interrogation device evaluation period.

ECG rhythm derived elements are distinct from physiologic data, even when the same device is capable of producing both. ICM device services are always separately reported from ICD services. When ILR data is derived from an ICD or pacemaker, do not report ILR services with pacemaker or ICD services.

For monitoring by wearable devices, see 93224-93272, 93228, 93229.

For other services related to a wearable defibrillator, use 93745.

Do not report 93012, 93014 when performing 93279-93289, 93291-93296 or 93298-93299. Do not report 93040-93042 when performing 93279-93289, 93291-93296, or 93298-93299.

The pacemaker and ICD interrogation device evaluations, peri-procedural device evaluations and programming, and programming device evaluations may not be reported in conjunction with pacemaker or ICD device and/or lead insertion or revision services by the same physician.

The following definitions and instructions apply to codes 93279-93299:

Attended surveillance: the immediate availability of a remote technician to respond to rhythm or device alert transmissions from a patient, either from an implanted or wearable monitoring or therapy device, as they are generated and transmitted to the remote surveillance location or center.

Device, single lead: a pacemaker or implantable cardioverter-defibrillator with pacing and sensing function in only one chamber of the heart.

Device, dual lead: a pacemaker or implantable cardioverter-defibrillator with pacing and sensing function in only two chambers of the heart.

Device, multiple lead: a pacemaker or implantable cardioverter-defibrillator with pacing and sensing function in three or more chambers of the heart.

Electrocardiographic rhythm derived: data analysis derived from recordings of the electrical activation of the heart including, but not limited to heart rhythm, rate, ST analysis, heart rate variability, T-wave alternans.

Implantable cardiovascular monitor (ICM): an implantable cardiovascular device used to assist the physician in the management of non-rhythm related cardiac conditions such as heart failure. The device collects longitudinal physiologic cardiovascular data elements from one or more internal sensors (such as right ventricular pressure, left atrial pressure or an index of lung water) and/or external sensors (such as blood pressure or body weight) for patient assessment and management. The data are stored and transmitted to the physician by either local telemetry or remotely to an Internet based file server or surveillance technician. The function of the ICM may be an additional function of an implantable cardiac device (eg, implantable cardioverter defibrillator) or a function of a stand-alone device. When ICM functionality is included in an ICD device, the ICM data and the ICD heart rhythm data such as sensing, pacing and tachycardia detection therapy are distinct and therefore, the monitoring processes are distinct.

Implantable cardioverter-defibrillator (ICD): an implantable device that provides high-energy and low-energy stimulation to one or more chambers of the heart to terminate rapid heart rhythms called tachycardia or fibrillation. ICDs also have pacemaker functions to treat slow heart rhythms called bradycardia. In addition to the tachycardia and bradycardia functions, the ICD may or may not include the functionality of an implantable cardiovascular monitor or an implantable loop recorder.

Implantable loop recorder (ILR): an implantable device that continuously records the electrocardiographic rhythm triggered automatically by rapid and slow heart rates or by the patient during a symptomatic episode. The ILR function may be the only function of the device or it may be part of a pacemaker or implantable cardioverter-defibrillator device. The data are stored and transmitted to the physician by either local telemetry or remotely to an Internet based file server or surveillance technician.

Interrogation device evaluation (in person): a face-to-face evaluation of an implantable device such as a cardiac pacemaker, implantable cardioverter-defibrillator, implantable cardiovascular monitor, or implantable loop recorder. Using an office, hospital, or emergency room instrument, stored and measured information about the lead(s) when present, sensor(s) when present, battery and the implanted pulse generator function, as well as data collected about the patient's heart rhythm and heart rate is retrieved. The retrieved information is evaluated to determine the current programming of the device and to evaluate certain aspects of the device function such as battery voltage, lead impedance, tachycardia detection settings, and rhythm treatment settings.

The components that must be evaluated for the various types of implantable cardiac devices are listed below. (The required components for both remote and in-person interrogations are the same.)

Pacemaker: Programmed parameters, lead(s), battery, capture and sensing function and heart rhythm.

Implantable cardioverter-defibrillator: Programmed parameters, lead(s), battery, capture and sensing function, presence or absence of therapy for ventricular tachyarrhythmias and underlying heart rhythm.

Implantable cardiovascular monitor: Programmed parameters and analysis of at least one recorded physiologic cardiovascular data element from either internal or external sensors.

Implantable loop recorder: Programmed parameters and the heart rate and rhythm during recorded episodes from both patient initiated and device algorithm detected events, when present.

Pacemaker is an implantable device that provides low energy localized stimulation to one or more chambers of the heart to initiate contraction in that chamber.◄

►***Peri-procedural device evaluation and programming:*** an evaluation of an implantable device system (either a pacemaker or implantable cardioverter defibrillator) to adjust the device to settings appropriate for the patient prior to a surgery, procedure, or test. The device system data are interrogated to evaluate the lead(s), sensor(s), and battery in addition to review of stored information, including patient and system measurements. The device is programmed to settings appropriate for the surgery, procedure, or test, as required. A second evaluation and programming are performed after the surgery, procedure, or test to provide settings appropriate to the post procedural situation, as required. If one provider performs both the pre- and post-evaluation and programming service, the appropriate code, either 93286 or 93287, would be reported two times. If one provider performs the pre-surgical service and a separate provider performs the post-surgical service, each reports either 93286 or 93287 only one time.

Physiologic cardiovascular data elements: data elements from one or more internal sensors (such as right ventricular pressure, left atrial pressure or an index of lung water) and/or external sensors (such as blood pressure or body weight) for patient assessement and management. It does not include ECG rhythm derived data elements.

Programming device evaluation: a procedure performed for patients with a pacemaker, implantable cardioverter-defibrillator, or implantable loop recorder. All device functions, including the battery, programmable settings and lead(s), when present, are evaluated. To assess capture thresholds, iterative adjustments (eg, progressive changes in pacing output of a pacing lead) of the programmable parameters are conducted. The iterative adjustments provide information that permits the operator to assess and select the most appropriate final program parameters to provide for consistent delivery of the appropriate therapy and to verify the function of the device. The final program parameters may or may not change after evaluation.

The programming device evaluation includes all of the components of the interrogation device evaluation (remote) or the interrogation device evaluation (in person), and it includes the selection of patient specific programmed parameters depending on the type of device.

The components that must be evaluated for the various types of programming device evaluations are listed below. (See also required interrogation device evaluation [remote and in person] components above.)

Pacemaker: Programmed parameters, lead(s), battery, capture and sensing function, and heart rhythm. Often, but not always, the sensor rate response, lower and upper heart rates, AV intervals, pacing voltage and pulse duration, sensing value, and diagnostics will be adjusted during a programming evaluation.

Implantable cardioverter-defibrillator: Programmed parameters, lead(s), battery, capture and sensing function, presence or absence of therapy for ventricular tachyarrhythmias and underlying heart rhythm. Often, but not always, the sensor rate response, lower and upper heart rates, AV intervals, pacing voltage and pulse duration, sensing value, and diagnostics will be adjusted during a programming evaluation. In addition, ventricular tachycardia detection and therapies are sometimes altered depending on the interrogated data, patient's rhythm, symptoms, and condition.

Implantable loop recorder: Programmed parameters and the heart rhythm during recorded episodes from both patient initiated and device algorithm detected events. Often, but not always, the tachycardia and bradycardia detection criteria will be adjusted during a programming evaluation.

Transtelephonic rhythm strip pacemaker evaluation: service of transmission of an electrocardiographic rhythm strip over the telephone by the patient using a transmitter and recorded by a receiving location using a receiver/recorder (also commonly known as transtelephonic pacemaker monitoring). The electrocardiographic rhythm strip is recorded both with and without a magnet applied over the pacemaker. The rhythm strip is evaluated for heart rate and rhythm, atrial and ventricular capture (if observed) and atrial and ventricular sensing (if observed). In addition, the battery status of the pacemaker is determined by measurement of the paced rate on the electrocardiographic rhythm strip recorded with the magnet applied.◄

● **93279** Programming device evaluation with iterative adjustment of the implantable device to test the function of the device and select optimal permanent programmed values with physician analysis, review and report; single lead pacemaker system

►(Do not report 93279 in conjunction with 93286, 93288)◄

● **93280** dual lead pacemaker system

►(Do not report 93280 in conjunction with 93286, 93288)◄

● **93281** multiple lead pacemaker system

►(Do not report 93281 in conjunction with 93286, 93288)◄

● **93282** single lead implantable cardioverter-defibrillator system

►(Do not report 93282 in conjunction with 93287, 93289, 93745)◄

● **93283** dual lead implantable cardioverter-defibrillator system

►(Do not report 93283 in conjunction with 93287, 93289)◄

● **93284** multiple lead implantable cardioverter-defibrillator system

►(Do not report 93284 in conjunction with 93287, 93289)◄

● **93285** implantable loop recorder system

►(Do not report 93285 in conjunction with 33282, 93279, 93284, 93291)◄

● **93286** Peri-procedural device evaluation and programming of device system parameters before or after a surgery, procedure, or test with physician analysis, review and report; single, dual, or multiple lead pacemaker system

►(Report 93286 once before and once after surgery, procedure, or test, when device evaluation and programming is performed before and after surgery, procedure, or test)◄

►(Do not report 93286 in conjunction with 93279-93281, 93288)◄

● **93287** single, dual, or multiple lead implantable cardioverter-defibrillator system

►(Report 93287 once before and once after surgery, procedure, or test, when device evaluation and programming is performed before and after surgery, procedure, or test)◄

►(Do not report 93287 in conjunction with 93282-93284, 93289)◄

● **93288** Interrogation device evaluation (in person) with physician analysis, review and report, includes connection, recording and disconnection per patient encounter; single, dual, or multiple lead pacemaker system

►(Do not report 93288 in conjunction with 93279-93281, 93286, 93294, 93296)◄

● **93289** single, dual, or multiple lead implantable cardioverter-defibrillator system, including analysis of heart rhythm derived data elements

►(For monitoring physiologic cardiovascular data elements derived from an ICD, use 93290)◄

►(Do not report 93289 in conjunction with 93282-93284, 93287, 93295, 93296)◄

● **93290** implantable cardiovascular monitor system, including analysis of 1 or more recorded physiologic cardiovascular data elements from all internal and external sensors

►(For heart rhythm derived data elements, use 93289)◄

►(Do not report 93290 in conjunction with 93297, 93299)◄

● **93291** implantable loop recorder system, including heart rhythm derived data analysis

►(Do not report 93291 in conjunction with 33282, 93288-93290, 93298, 93299)◄

● **93292** wearable defibrillator system

►(Do not report 93292 in conjunction with 93745)◄

● **93293** Transtelephonic rhythm strip pacemaker evaluation(s) single, dual, or multiple lead pacemaker system, includes recording with and without magnet application with physician analysis, review and report(s), up to 90 days

►(Do not report 93293 in conjunction with 93294)◄

►(For in person evaluation, see 93040, 93041, 93042)◄

►(Report 93293 only once per 90 days)◄

● **93294** Interrogation device evaluation(s) (remote), up to 90 days; single, dual, or multiple lead pacemaker system with interim physician analysis, review(s) and report(s)

►(Do not report 93294 in conjunction with 93288, 93293)◄

►(Report 93294 only once per 90 days)◄

● **93295** single, dual, or multiple lead implantable cardioverter-defibrillator system with interim physician analysis, review(s) and report(s)

►(For remote monitoring of physiologic cardiovascular data elements derived from an ICD, use 93297)◄

►(Do not report 93295 in conjunction with 93289)◄

►(Report 93295 only once per 90 days)◄

● **93296** single, dual, or multiple lead pacemaker system or implantable cardioverter-defibrillator system, remote data acquisition(s), receipt of transmissions and technician review, technical support and distribution of results

►(Do not report 93296 in conjunction with 93288, 93289, 93299)◄

►(Report 93296 only once per 90 days)◄

● **93297** Interrogation device evaluation(s), (remote) up to 30 days; implantable cardiovascular monitor system, including analysis of 1 or more recorded physiologic cardiovascular data elements from all internal and external sensors, physician analysis, review(s) and report(s)

►(For heart rhythm derived data elements, use 93295)◄

►(Do not report 93297 in conjunction with 93290, 93298)◄

►(Report 93297 only once per 30 days)◄

● **93298** implantable loop recorder system, including analysis of recorded heart rhythm data, physician analysis, review(s) and report(s)

►(Do not report 93298 in conjunction with 93291, 93297)◄

►(Report 93298 only once per 30 days)◄

● **93299** implantable cardiovascular monitor system or implantable loop recorder system, remote data acquisition(s), receipt of transmissions and technician review, technical support and distribution of results

►(Do not report 93299 in conjunction with 93290, 93291, 93296)◄

►(Report 93299 only once per 30 days)◄

Echocardiography

►Echocardiography includes obtaining ultrasonic signals from the heart and great vessels, with real time image and/or Doppler ultrasonic signal documentation, with interpretation and report. When interpretation is performed separately, use modifier 26.

A complete transthoracic echocardiogram without spectral or color flow Doppler (93307) is a comprehensive procedure that includes 2-dimensional and selected M-mode examination of the left and right atria, left and right ventricles, the aortic, mitral, and tricuspid valves, the pericardium, and adjacent portions of the aorta. Multiple views are required to obtain a complete functional and anatomic evaluation, and appropriate measurements are obtained and recorded. Despite significant effort, identification and measurement of some structures may not always be possible. In such instances, the reason that an element could not be visualized must be documented. Additional structures that may be visualized (eg, pulmonary veins, pulmonary artery, pulmonic valve, inferior vena cava) would be included as part of the service.

A complete transthoracic echocardiogram with spectral and color flow Doppler (93306) is a comprehensive procedure that includes spectral Doppler and color flow Doppler in addition to the 2-dimensional and selected M-mode examinations. Spectral Doppler (93320, 93321) and color flow Doppler (93325) provide information regarding intracardiac blood flow and hemodynamics.

A follow-up or limited echocardiographic study (93308) is an examination that does not evaluate or document the attempt to evaluate all the structures that comprise the complete echocardiographic exam. This is typically limited to, or performed in follow-up of a focused clinical concern.

In stress echocardiography, echocardiographic images are recorded from multiple cardiac windows before, after, and in some protocols, during stress. The stress is achieved by (1) walking on a treadmill; (2) using a bicycle (supine or upright); or (3) the administration of pharmacological agents that either simulate exercise (by increasing heart rate, blood pressure, or myocardial contractility) or alter coronary flow (vasodilation). The patient's ECG, heart rate, and blood pressure are monitored at baseline, throughout the procedure and during recovery. Reports are prepared to evaluate (1) the duration of stress, the reason for stopping, and the hemodynamic response to stress; (2) the electrocardiographic response to stress; and (3) the echocardiographic response to stress.

When a stress echocardiogram is performed with a complete cardiovascular stress test (continuous electrocardiographic monitoring, physician supervision, interpretation and report), use 93351. Code 93350 is used to report the performance and interpretation of a stress echocardiogram only, with the components of the cardiovascular stress test reported separately using the appropriate codes (93016–93018).

When left ventricular endocardial borders cannot be adequately identified by standard echocardiographic imaging, echocardiographic contrast may be infused intravenously both at rest and with stress to achieve that purpose. Code 93352 is used to report the administration of echocardiographic contrast agent in conjunction with the stress echocardiography codes (93350 or 93351). Supply of contrast agent and/or drugs used for pharmacological stress are reported separately in addition to the procedure code.◄

Report of an echocardiographic study, whether complete or limited, includes an interpretation of all obtained information, documentation of all clinically relevant findings including quantitative measurements obtained, plus a description of any recognized abnormalities. Pertinent images, videotape, and/or digital data are archived for permanent storage and are available for subsequent review. Use of echocardiography not meeting these criteria is not separately reportable.

Use of ultrasound, without thorough evaluation of organ(s) or anatomic region, image documentation and final, written report, is not separately reportable.

(For fetal echocardiography, see 76825-76828)

93303 Transthoracic echocardiography for congenital cardiac anomalies; complete

93304 follow-up or limited study

● **93306** Echocardiography, transthoracic, real-time with image documentation (2D), includes M-mode recording, when performed, complete, with spectral Doppler echocardiography, and with color flow Doppler echocardiography

►(For transthoracic echocardiography without spectral and color Doppler, use 93307)◄

▲ **93307** Echocardiography, transthoracic, real-time with image documentation (2D), includes M-mode recording, when performed, complete, without spectral or color Doppler echocardiography

►(Do not report 93307 in conjunction with 93320, 93321, 93325)◄

▲ **93308** Echocardiography, transthoracic, real-time with image documentation (2D), includes M-mode recording, when performed, follow-up or limited study

⊙ **93312** Echocardiography, transesophageal, real-time with image documentation (2D) (with or without M-mode recording); including probe placement, image acquisition, interpretation and report

⊙ **93313** placement of transesophageal probe only

⊙ **93314** image acquisition, interpretation and report only

⊙ **93315** Transesophageal echocardiography for congenital cardiac anomalies; including probe placement, image acquisition, interpretation and report

⊙ **93316** placement of transesophageal probe only

⊙ **93317** image acquisition, interpretation and report only

⊙ **93318** Echocardiography, transesophageal (TEE) for monitoring purposes, including probe placement, real time 2-dimensional image acquisition and interpretation leading to ongoing (continuous) assessment of (dynamically changing) cardiac pumping function and to therapeutic measures on an immediate time basis

✚ **93320** Doppler echocardiography, pulsed wave and/or continuous wave with spectral display (List separately in addition to codes for echocardiographic imaging); complete

►(Use 93320 in conjunction with 93303, 93304, 93312, 93314, 93315, 93317, 93350, 93351)◄

✚ **93321** follow-up or limited study (List separately in addition to codes for echocardiographic imaging)

►(Use 93321 in conjunction with 93303, 93304, 93308, 93312, 93314, 93315, 93317, 93350, 93351)◄

✚ **93325** Doppler echocardiography color flow velocity mapping (List separately in addition to codes for echocardiography)

►(Use 93325 in conjunction with 76825, 76826, 76827, 76828, 93303, 93304, 93308, 93312, 93314, 93315, 93317, 93350, 93351)◄

▲ **93350** Echocardiography, transthoracic, real-time with image documentation (2D), includes M-mode recording, when performed, during rest and cardiovascular stress test using treadmill, bicycle exercise and/or pharmacologically induced stress, with interpretation and report;

►(The appropriate stress testing code(s) from the 93016-93018 series should be reported in addition to 93350 to capture the exercise stress portion of the study)◄

● **93351** including performance of continuous electrocardiographic monitoring, with physician supervision

►(Do not report 93351 in conjunction with 93015-93018, 93350)◄

✚● **93352** Use of echocardiographic contrast agent during stress echocardiography (List separately in addition to code for primary procedure)

►(Do not report 93352 more than once per stress echocardiogram)◄

►(Use 93352 in conjunction with 93350, 93351)◄

Cardiac Catheterization

Cardiac catheterization is a diagnostic medical procedure which includes introduction, positioning and repositioning of catheter(s), when necessary, recording of intracardiac and intravascular pressure, obtaining blood samples for measurement of blood gases or dilution curves and cardiac output measurements (Fick or other method, with or without rest and exercise and/or studies) with or without electrode catheter placement, final evaluation and report of procedure. When selective injection procedures are performed without a preceding cardiac catheterization, these services should be reported using codes in the Vascular Injection Procedures section, 36011-36015 and 36215-36218.

When coronary artery, arterial coronary conduit or venous bypass graft angiography is performed without concomitant left heart cardiac catheterization, use 93508. Injection procedures 93539, 93540, 93544, and 93545 represent separate identifiable services and may be reported in conjunction with one another in addition to 93508, as appropriate. To report imaging supervision, interpretation and report in conjunction with 93508, use 93556.

►Modifier 51 should not be appended to 93503, 93539, 93540, 93544-93556.◄

⊙ **93501** Right heart catheterization

(For bundle of His recording, use 93600)

⊘ **93503** Insertion and placement of flow directed catheter (eg, Swan-Ganz) for monitoring purposes

(For subsequent monitoring, see 99356-99357)

⊙ **93505** Endomyocardial biopsy

⊙ **93508** Catheter placement in coronary artery(s), arterial coronary conduit(s), and/or venous coronary bypass graft(s) for coronary angiography without concomitant left heart catheterization

(93508 is to be used only when left heart catheterization 93510, 93511, 93524, 93526 is not performed)

(93508 is to be used only once per procedure)

(To report transcatheter placement of radiation delivery device for coronary intravascular brachytherapy, use 92974)

(For intravascular radioelement application, see 77781-77784)

⊙ **93510** Left heart catheterization, retrograde, from the brachial artery, axillary artery or femoral artery; percutaneous

⊙ **93511** by cutdown

⊙ **93514** Left heart catheterization by left ventricular puncture

⊙ **93524** Combined transseptal and retrograde left heart catheterization

⊙ **93526** Combined right heart catheterization and retrograde left heart catheterization

⊙ **93527** Combined right heart catheterization and transseptal left heart catheterization through intact septum (with or without retrograde left heart catheterization)

⊙ **93528** Combined right heart catheterization with left ventricular puncture (with or without retrograde left heart catheterization)

⊙ **93529** Combined right heart catheterization and left heart catheterization through existing septal opening (with or without retrograde left heart catheterization)

⊙ **93530** Right heart catheterization, for congenital cardiac anomalies

93531 Combined right heart catheterization and retrograde left heart catheterization, for congenital cardiac anomalies

93532 Combined right heart catheterization and transseptal left heart catheterization through intact septum with or without retrograde left heart catheterization, for congenital cardiac anomalies

93533 Combined right heart catheterization and transseptal left heart catheterization through existing septal opening, with or without retrograde left heart catheterization, for congenital cardiac anomalies

Injection Procedures

►When injection procedures are performed in conjunction with cardiac catheterization, these services do not include introduction of catheters but do include repositioning of catheters when necessary and use of automatic power injectors. Injection procedures 93539-93545 represent separate identifiable services and may be coded in conjunction with one another when appropriate. The technical details of angiography, supervision of filming and processing, interpretation, and report are not included. To report radiological supervision, interpretation, and report for 93542 or 93543, use 93555. To report radiological supervision, interpretation, and report for 93539, 93540, 93541, 93544, or 93545, use 93556. Modifier 51 should not be appended to 93539, 93540, 93544-93556.◄

⊙⊘ **93539** Injection procedure during cardiac catheterization; for selective opacification of arterial conduits (eg, internal mammary), whether native or used for bypass

⊙⊘ **93540** for selective opacification of aortocoronary venous bypass grafts, one or more coronary arteries

⊙ **93541** for pulmonary angiography

⊙ **93542** for selective right ventricular or right atrial angiography

⊙ **93543** for selective left ventricular or left atrial angiography

⊙⊘ **93544** for aortography

⊙⊘ **93545** for selective coronary angiography (injection of radiopaque material may be by hand)

⊙⊘ **93555** Imaging supervision, interpretation and report for injection procedure(s) during cardiac catheterization; ventricular and/or atrial angiography

⊙⊘ **93556** pulmonary angiography, aortography, and/or selective coronary angiography including venous bypass grafts and arterial conduits (whether native or used in bypass)

⊙ **93561** Indicator dilution studies such as dye or thermal dilution, including arterial and/or venous catheterization; with cardiac output measurement (separate procedure)

⊙ **93562** subsequent measurement of cardiac output

(93561, 93562 are not to be used with cardiac catheterization codes)

(For radioisotope method of cardiac output, see 78472, 78473, or 78481)

Medicine

⊙✚ **93571** Intravascular Doppler velocity and/or pressure derived coronary flow reserve measurement (coronary vessel or graft) during coronary angiography including pharmacologically induced stress; initial vessel (List separately in addition to code for primary procedure)

⊙✚ **93572** each additional vessel (List separately in addition to code for primary procedure)

(Intravascular distal coronary blood flow velocity measurements include all Doppler transducer manipulations and repositioning within the specific vessel being examined, during coronary angiography or therapeutic intervention [eg, angioplasty])

(For unlisted cardiac catheterization procedure, use 93799)

Repair of Septal Defect

93580 Percutaneous transcatheter closure of congenital interatrial communication (ie, Fontan fenestration, atrial septal defect) with implant

(Percutaneous transcatheter closure of atrial septal defect includes a right heart catheterization procedure. Code 93580 includes injection of contrast for atrial and ventricular angiograms. Codes 93501, 93529-93533, 93539, 93543, 93555 should not be reported separately in addition to code 93580)

93581 Percutaneous transcatheter closure of a congenital ventricular septal defect with implant

(Percutaneous transcatheter closure of ventricular septal defect includes a right heart catheterization procedure. Code 93581 includes injection of contrast for atrial and ventricular angiograms. Codes 93501, 93529-93533, 93539, 93543, 93555 should not be reported separately in addition to code 93581)

(For ventricular septal defect closure via transmyocardial implant delivery, see 0166T, 0167T)

(For echocardiographic services performed in addition to 93580, 93581, see 93303-93317, 93662 as appropriate)

Intracardiac Electrophysiological Procedures/Studies

Intracardiac electrophysiologic studies (EPS) are an invasive diagnostic medical procedure which include the insertion and repositioning of electrode catheters, recording of electrograms before and during pacing or programmed stimulation of multiple locations in the heart, analysis of recorded information, and report of the procedure. Electrophysiologic studies are most often performed with two or more electrode catheters. In many circumstances, patients with arrhythmias are evaluated and treated at the same encounter. In this situation, a diagnostic *electrophysiologic study* is performed, induced tachycardia(s) are *mapped*, and on the basis of the diagnostic and mapping information, the tissue is *ablated*. Electrophysiologic study(ies), mapping, and ablation represent distinctly different procedures, requiring individual reporting whether performed on the same or subsequent dates.

Definitions

***Arrhythmia Induction*:** In most electrophysiologic studies, an attempt is made to induce arrhythmia(s) from single or multiple sites within the heart. Arrhythmia induction is achieved by performing pacing at different rates, programmed stimulation (introduction of critically timed electrical impulses), and other techniques. Because arrhythmia induction occurs via the same catheter(s) inserted for the electrophysiologic study(ies), catheter insertion and temporary pacemaker codes are not additionally reported. Codes 93600-93603, 93610-93612 and 93618 are used to describe unusual situations where there may be recording, pacing or an attempt at arrhythmia induction from only one site in the heart. Code 93619 describes only evaluation of the sinus node, atrioventricular node and His-Purkinje conduction system, without arrhythmia induction. Codes 93620-93624 and 93640-93642 all include recording, pacing and attempted arrhythmia induction from one or more site(s) in the heart.

***Mapping*:** Mapping is a distinct procedure performed in addition to a diagnostic electrophysiologic procedure and should be separately reported using 93609 or 93613. Do not report standard mapping (93609) in addition to 3D mapping (93613). When a tachycardia is induced, the site of tachycardia origination or its electrical path through the heart is often defined by mapping. Mapping creates a multidimensional depiction of a tachycardia by recording multiple electrograms obtained sequentially or simultaneously from multiple catheter sites in the heart. Depending upon the technique, certain types of mapping catheters may be repositioned from point-to-point within the heart, allowing sequential recording from the various sites to construct maps. Other types of mapping catheters allow mapping without a point-to-point technique by allowing simultaneous recording from many electrodes on the same catheter and computer-assisted three dimensional reconstruction of the tachycardia activation sequence.

***Ablation*:** Once the part of the heart involved in the tachycardia is localized, the tachycardia may be treated by ablation (the delivery of a radiofrequency energy to the area to selectively destroy cardiac tissue). Ablation procedures (93651-93652) may be performed: independently on a date subsequent to a diagnostic electrophysiologic study and mapping; or, at the time a diagnostic electrophysiologic study, tachycardia(s) induction and mapping is performed. When an electrophysiologic study, mapping, and ablation are performed on the same date, each procedure should be separately reported. In reporting catheter ablation, 93651 and/or 93652 should be reported once to describe ablation of cardiac arrhythmias, regardless of the number of arrhythmias ablated.

►Modifier 51 should not be appended to 93600-93603, 93610, 93612, 93615-93618, 93631.◄

⊘ **93600** Bundle of His recording

⊘ **93602** Intra-atrial recording

⊘ **93603** Right ventricular recording

⊙✚ **93609** Intraventricular and/or intra-atrial mapping of tachycardia site(s) with catheter manipulation to record from multiple sites to identify origin of tachycardia (List separately in addition to code for primary procedure)

(Use 93609 in conjunction with 93620, 93651, 93652)

(Do not report 93609 in addition to 93613)

⊘ **93610** Intra-atrial pacing

⊘ **93612** Intraventricular pacing

(Do not report 93612 in conjunction with 93620-93622)

⊙✚ **93613** Intracardiac electrophysiologic 3-dimensional mapping (List separately in addition to code for primary procedure)

(Use 93613 in conjunction with 93620, 93651, 93652)

(Do not report 93613 in addition to 93609)

⊙⊘ **93615** Esophageal recording of atrial electrogram with or without ventricular electrogram(s);

⊙⊘ **93616** with pacing

⊙⊘ **93618** Induction of arrhythmia by electrical pacing

(For intracardiac phonocardiogram, use 93799)

⊙ **93619** Comprehensive electrophysiologic evaluation with right atrial pacing and recording, right ventricular pacing and recording, His bundle recording, including insertion and repositioning of multiple electrode catheters, without induction or attempted induction of arrhythmia

(Do not report 93619 in conjunction with 93600, 93602, 93610, 93612, 93618, or 93620-93622)

⊙ **93620** Comprehensive electrophysiologic evaluation including insertion and repositioning of multiple electrode catheters with induction or attempted induction of arrhythmia; with right atrial pacing and recording, right ventricular pacing and recording, His bundle recording

(Do not report 93620 in conjunction with 93600, 93602, 93610, 93612, 93618 or 93619)

⊙✚ **93621** with left atrial pacing and recording from coronary sinus or left atrium (List separately in addition to code for primary procedure)

(Use 93621 in conjunction with 93620)

⊙✚ **93622** with left ventricular pacing and recording (List separately in addition to code for primary procedure)

(Use 93622 in conjunction with 93620)

✚ **93623** Programmed stimulation and pacing after intravenous drug infusion (List separately in addition to code for primary procedure)

(Use 93623 in conjunction with 93619, 93620)

⊙ **93624** Electrophysiologic follow-up study with pacing and recording to test effectiveness of therapy, including induction or attempted induction of arrhythmia

⊘ **93631** Intra-operative epicardial and endocardial pacing and mapping to localize the site of tachycardia or zone of slow conduction for surgical correction

►(For operative ablation of an arrhythmogenic focus or pathway by a separate provider, see 33250-33261)◄

⊙ **93640** Electrophysiologic evaluation of single or dual chamber pacing cardioverter-defibrillator leads including defibrillation threshold evaluation (induction of arrhythmia, evaluation of sensing and pacing for arrhythmia termination) at time of initial implantation or replacement;

⊙ **93641** with testing of single or dual chamber pacing cardioverter-defibrillator pulse generator

(For subsequent or periodic electronic analysis and/or reprogramming of single or dual chamber pacing cardioverter-defibrillators, see 93642, 93741-93744)

⊙ **93642** Electrophysiologic evaluation of single or dual chamber pacing cardioverter-defibrillator (includes defibrillation threshold evaluation, induction of arrhythmia, evaluation of sensing and pacing for arrhythmia termination, and programming or reprogramming of sensing or therapeutic parameters)

⊙ **93650** Intracardiac catheter ablation of atrioventricular node function, atrioventricular conduction for creation of complete heart block, with or without temporary pacemaker placement

⊙ **93651** Intracardiac catheter ablation of arrhythmogenic focus; for treatment of supraventricular tachycardia by ablation of fast or slow atrioventricular pathways, accessory atrioventricular connections or other atrial foci, singly or in combination

⊙ **93652** for treatment of ventricular tachycardia

93660 Evaluation of cardiovascular function with tilt table evaluation, with continuous ECG monitoring and intermittent blood pressure monitoring, with or without pharmacological intervention

(For testing of autonomic nervous system function, see 95921-95923)

✚ **93662** Intracardiac echocardiography during therapeutic/diagnostic intervention, including imaging supervision and interpretation (List separately in addition to code for primary procedure)

(Use 93662 in conjunction with 92987, 93527, 93532, 93580, 93581, 93621, 93622, 93651, or 93652, as appropriate)

(Do not report 92961 in addition to 93662)

Peripheral Arterial Disease Rehabilitation

Peripheral arterial disease (PAD) rehabilitative physical exercise consists of a series of sessions, lasting 45-60 minutes per session, involving use of either a motorized treadmill or a track to permit each patient to achieve symptom-limited claudication. Each session is supervised by an exercise physiologist or nurse. The supervising provider monitors the individual patient's claudication threshold and other cardiovascular limitations for adjustment of workload. During this supervised rehabilitation program, the development of new arrhythmias, symptoms that might suggest angina or the continued inability of the patient to progress to an adequate level of exercise may require physician review and examination of the patient. These physician services would be separately reported with an appropriate level E/M service code.

93668 Peripheral arterial disease (PAD) rehabilitation, per session

Noninvasive Physiologic Studies and Procedures

(For arterial cannulization and recording of direct arterial pressure, use 36620)

(For radiographic injection procedures, see 36000-36299)

(For vascular cannulization for hemodialysis, see 36800-36821)

(For chemotherapy for malignant disease, see 96409-96549)

(For penile plethysmography, use 54240)

93701 Bioimpedance, thoracic, electrical

93720 Plethysmography, total body; with interpretation and report

93721 tracing only, without interpretation and report

93722 interpretation and report only

(For regional plethysmography, see 93875-93931)

93724 Electronic analysis of antitachycardia pacemaker system (includes electrocardiographic recording, programming of device, induction and termination of tachycardia via implanted pacemaker, and interpretation of recordings)

►(93727 has been deleted. For programming of implantable loop recorder, use 93285. For interrogation of implantable loop recorder, see 93291, 93298)◄

►(93731, 93732 have been deleted. For interrogation of dual lead pacemaker, see 93288, 93294. For programming of dual chamber pacemaker, use 93280)◄

►(93733 has been deleted. For transtelephonic rhythm strip pacemaker, single and dual, or multiple lead pacemaker evaluation, use 93293)◄

►(93734, 93735 have been deleted. For interrogation of single lead pacemaker, see 93288, 93294. For programming of single lead pacemaker, use 93279)◄

►(93736 has been deleted. For transtelephonic rhythm strip pacemaker, single and dual, or multiple lead pacemaker evaluation, use 93293)◄

93740 Temperature gradient studies

►(93741, 93742 have been deleted. For interrogation of single implantable cardioverter-defibrillator [ICD], see 93289, 93295. For programming of single ICD, use 93282. For interrogation of wearable cardioverter-defibrillator, use 93292)◄

►(93743, 93744 have been deleted. For interrogation of dual implantable cardioverter-defibrillator [ICD], see 93289, 93295. For programming of dual ICD, use 93283)◄

93745 Initial set-up and programming by a physician of wearable cardioverter-defibrillator includes initial programming of system, establishing baseline electronic ECG, transmission of data to data repository, patient instruction in wearing system and patient reporting of problems or events

►(Do not report 93745 in conjunction with 93282, 93292)◄

►(93760, 93762 have been deleted)◄

93770 Determination of venous pressure

(For central venous cannulization see 36555-36556, 36500)

93784 Ambulatory blood pressure monitoring, utilizing a system such as magnetic tape and/or computer disk, for 24 hours or longer; including recording, scanning analysis, interpretation and report

93786 recording only

93788 scanning analysis with report

93790 physician review with interpretation and report

Other Procedures

93797 Physician services for outpatient cardiac rehabilitation; without continuous ECG monitoring (per session)

93798 with continuous ECG monitoring (per session)

93799 Unlisted cardiovascular service or procedure

Noninvasive Vascular Diagnostic Studies

Vascular studies include patient care required to perform the studies, supervision of the studies and interpretation of study results with copies for patient records of hard copy output with analysis of all data, including bidirectional vascular flow or imaging when provided.

The use of a simple hand-held or other Doppler device that does not produce hard copy output, or that produces a record that does not permit analysis of bidirectional vascular flow, is considered to be part of the physical examination of the vascular system and is not separately reported.

Duplex scan (eg, 93880, 93882) describes an ultrasonic scanning procedure for characterizing the pattern and direction of blood flow in arteries or veins with the production of real-time images integrating B-mode two-dimensional vascular structure, Doppler spectral analysis, and color flow Doppler imaging.

Noninvasive physiologic studies are performed using equipment separate and distinct from the duplex scanner. Codes 93875, 93965, 93922, 93923, and 93924 describe the evaluation of non-imaging physiologic recordings of pressures, Doppler analysis of bi-directional blood flow, plethysmography, and/or oxygen tension measurements appropriate for the anatomic area studied.

Cerebrovascular Arterial Studies

A complete transcranial Doppler (TCD) study (93886) includes ultrasound evaluation of the right and left anterior circulation territories and the posterior circulation territory (to include vertebral arteries and basilar artery). In a limited TCD study (93888) there is ultrasound evaluation of two or fewer of these territories. For TCD, ultrasound evaluation is a reasonable and concerted attempt to identify arterial signals through an acoustic window.

93875 Noninvasive physiologic studies of extracranial arteries, complete bilateral study (eg, periorbital flow direction with arterial compression, ocular pneumoplethysmography, Doppler ultrasound spectral analysis)

93880 Duplex scan of extracranial arteries; complete bilateral study

93882 unilateral or limited study

(To report common carotid intima-media thickness (IMT) study for evaluation of atherosclerotic burden or coronary heart disease risk factor assessment, use Category III code 0126T)

93886 Transcranial Doppler study of the intracranial arteries; complete study

93888 limited study

93890 vasoreactivity study

93892 emboli detection without intravenous microbubble injection

93893 emboli detection with intravenous microbubble injection

(Do not report 93890-93893 in conjunction with 93888)

Extremity Arterial Studies (Including Digits)

93922 Noninvasive physiologic studies of upper or lower extremity arteries, single level, bilateral (eg, ankle/brachial indices, Doppler waveform analysis, volume plethysmography, transcutaneous oxygen tension measurement)

93923 Noninvasive physiologic studies of upper or lower extremity arteries, multiple levels or with provocative functional maneuvers, complete bilateral study (eg, segmental blood pressure measurements, segmental Doppler waveform analysis, segmental volume plethysmography, segmental transcutaneous oxygen tension measurements, measurements with postural provocative tests, measurements with reactive hyperemia)

93924 Noninvasive physiologic studies of lower extremity arteries, at rest and following treadmill stress testing, complete bilateral study

93925 Duplex scan of lower extremity arteries or arterial bypass grafts; complete bilateral study

93926 unilateral or limited study

93930 Duplex scan of upper extremity arteries or arterial bypass grafts; complete bilateral study

93931 unilateral or limited study

Extremity Venous Studies (Including Digits)

93965 Noninvasive physiologic studies of extremity veins, complete bilateral study (eg, Doppler waveform analysis with responses to compression and other maneuvers, phleborheography, impedance plethysmography)

93970 Duplex scan of extremity veins including responses to compression and other maneuvers; complete bilateral study

93971 unilateral or limited study

Visceral and Penile Vascular Studies

93975 Duplex scan of arterial inflow and venous outflow of abdominal, pelvic, scrotal contents and/or retroperitoneal organs; complete study

93976 limited study

93978 Duplex scan of aorta, inferior vena cava, iliac vasculature, or bypass grafts; complete study

93979 unilateral or limited study

93980 Duplex scan of arterial inflow and venous outflow of penile vessels; complete study

93981 follow-up or limited study

93982 Noninvasive physiologic study of implanted wireless pressure sensor in aneurysmal sac following endovascular repair, complete study including recording, analysis of pressure and waveform tracings, interpretation and report

(Do not report 93982 in conjunction with 34806)

Extremity Arterial-Venous Studies

93990 Duplex scan of hemodialysis access (including arterial inflow, body of access and venous outflow)

(For measurement of hemodialysis access flow using indicator dilution methods, use 90940)

Pulmonary

Ventilator Management

94002 Ventilation assist and management, initiation of pressure or volume preset ventilators for assisted or controlled breathing; hospital inpatient/observation, initial day

94003 hospital inpatient/observation, each subsequent day

94004 nursing facility, per day

(Do not report 94002-94004 in conjunction with Evaluation and Management services 99201-99499)

94005 Home ventilator management care plan oversight of a patient (patient not present) in home, domiciliary or rest home (eg, assisted living) requiring review of status, review of laboratories and other studies and revision of orders and respiratory care plan (as appropriate), within a calendar month, 30 minutes or more

(Do not report 94005 in conjunction with 99339, 99340, 99374-99378)

(Ventilator management care plan oversight is reported separately from home or domiciliary, rest home [eg, assisted living] services. A physician may report 94005, when performed, including when a different physician reports 99339, 99340, 99374-99378 for the same 30 days)

Other Procedures

Codes 94010-94799 include laboratory procedure(s) and interpretation of test results. If a separate identifiable Evaluation and Management service is performed, the appropriate E/M service code should be reported in addition to 94010-94799.

94010 Spirometry, including graphic record, total and timed vital capacity, expiratory flow rate measurement(s), with or without maximal voluntary ventilation

94014 Patient-initiated spirometric recording per 30-day period of time; includes reinforced education, transmission of spirometric tracing, data capture, analysis of transmitted data, periodic recalibration and physician review and interpretation

94015 recording (includes hook-up, reinforced education, data transmission, data capture, trend analysis, and periodic recalibration)

94016 physician review and interpretation only

94060 Bronchodilation responsiveness, spirometry as in 94010, pre- and post-bronchodilator administration

(Report bronchodilator supply separately with 99070 or appropriate supply code)

(For prolonged exercise test for bronchospasm with pre- and post-spirometry, use 94620)

94070 Bronchospasm provocation evaluation, multiple spirometric determinations as in 94010, with administered agents (eg, antigen[s], cold air, methacholine)

(Report antigen[s] administration separately with 99070 or appropriate supply code)

94150 Vital capacity, total (separate procedure)

94200 Maximum breathing capacity, maximal voluntary ventilation

94240 Functional residual capacity or residual volume: helium method, nitrogen open circuit method, or other method

94250 Expired gas collection, quantitative, single procedure (separate procedure)

94260 Thoracic gas volume

(For plethysmography, see 93720-93722)

94350 Determination of maldistribution of inspired gas: multiple breath nitrogen washout curve including alveolar nitrogen or helium equilibration time

94360 Determination of resistance to airflow, oscillatory or plethysmographic methods

94370 Determination of airway closing volume, single breath tests

94375 Respiratory flow volume loop

94400 Breathing response to CO_2 (CO_2 response curve)

94450 Breathing response to hypoxia (hypoxia response curve)

(For high altitude simulation test [HAST], see 94452, 94453)

94452 High altitude simulation test (HAST), with physician interpretation and report;

(For obtaining arterial blood gases, use 36600)

(Do not report 94452 in conjunction with 94453, 94760, 94761)

94453 with supplemental oxygen titration

(For obtaining arterial blood gases, use 36600)

(Do not report 94453 in conjunction with 94452, 94760, 94761)

⊘ **94610** Intrapulmonary surfactant administration by a physician through endotracheal tube

(Do not report 94610 in conjunction with 99293-99296)

(For endotracheal intubation, use 31500)

(Report 94610 once per dosing episode)

94620 Pulmonary stress testing; simple (eg, 6-minute walk test, prolonged exercise test for bronchospasm with pre- and post-spirometry and oximetry)

94621 complex (including measurements of CO_2 production, O_2 uptake, and electrocardiographic recordings)

94640 Pressurized or nonpressurized inhalation treatment for acute airway obstruction or for sputum induction for diagnostic purposes (eg, with an aerosol generator, nebulizer, metered dose inhaler or intermittent positive pressure breathing [IPPB] device)

(For more than 1 inhalation treatment performed on the same date, append modifier 76)

(For continuous inhalation treatment of 1 hour or more, see 94644, 94645)

94642 Aerosol inhalation of pentamidine for pneumocystis carinii pneumonia treatment or prophylaxis

94644 Continuous inhalation treatment with aerosol medication for acute airway obstruction; first hour

(For services of less than 1 hour, use 94640)

✚ **94645** each additional hour (List separately in addition to code for primary procedure)

(Use 94645 in conjunction with 94644)

(94656, 94657 have been deleted. To report, see 94002-94005)

94660 Continuous positive airway pressure ventilation (CPAP), initiation and management

94662 Continuous negative pressure ventilation (CNP), initiation and management

94664 Demonstration and/or evaluation of patient utilization of an aerosol generator, nebulizer, metered dose inhaler or IPPB device

(94664 can be reported one time only per day of service)

94667 Manipulation chest wall, such as cupping, percussing, and vibration to facilitate lung function; initial demonstration and/or evaluation

94668 subsequent

94680 Oxygen uptake, expired gas analysis; rest and exercise, direct, simple

94681 including CO_2 output, percentage oxygen extracted

94690 rest, indirect (separate procedure)

(For single arterial puncture, use 36600)

94720 Carbon monoxide diffusing capacity (eg, single breath, steady state)

94725 Membrane diffusion capacity

94750 Pulmonary compliance study (eg, plethysmography, volume and pressure measurements)

94760 Noninvasive ear or pulse oximetry for oxygen saturation; single determination

(For blood gases, see 82803-82810)

94761 multiple determinations (eg, during exercise)

94762 by continuous overnight monitoring (separate procedure)

►(For other in vivo laboratory procedures, see 88720-88741)◄

94770 Carbon dioxide, expired gas determination by infrared analyzer

(For bronchoscopy, see 31622-31656)

(For placement of flow directed catheter, use 93503)

(For venipuncture, use 36410)

(For central venous catheter placement, see 36555-36556)

(For arterial puncture, use 36600)

(For arterial catheterization, use 36620)

(For thoracentesis, use 32421)

(For phlebotomy, therapeutic, use 99195)

(For lung biopsy, needle, use 32405)

(For intubation, orotracheal or nasotracheal, use 31500)

94772 Circadian respiratory pattern recording (pediatric pneumogram), 12-24 hour continuous recording, infant

(Separate procedure codes for electromyograms, EEG, ECG, and recordings of respiration are excluded when 94772 is reported)

94774 Pediatric home apnea monitoring event recording including respiratory rate, pattern and heart rate per 30-day period of time; includes monitor attachment, download of data, physician review, interpretation, and preparation of a report

(Do not report 94774 in conjunction with 94775-94777 during the same reporting period)

94775 monitor attachment only (includes hook-up, initiation of recording and disconnection)

94776 monitoring, download of information, receipt of transmission(s) and analyses by computer only

94777 physician review, interpretation and preparation of report only

(When oxygen saturation monitoring is used in addition to heart rate and respiratory monitoring, it is not reported separately)

(Do not report 94774-94777 in conjunction with 93224-93272)

(Do not report apnea recording device separately)

(For sleep study, see 95805-95811)

94799 Unlisted pulmonary service or procedure

Allergy and Clinical Immunology

Definitions

Immunotherapy (desensitization, hyposensitization) is the parenteral administration of allergenic extracts as antigens at periodic intervals, usually on an increasing dosage scale to a dosage which is maintained as maintenance therapy. Indications for immunotherapy are determined by appropriate diagnostic procedures coordinated with clinical judgment and knowledge of the natural history of allergic diseases.

Other therapy: for medical conferences on the use of mechanical and electronic devices (precipitators, air conditioners, air filters, humidifiers, dehumidifiers), climatotherapy, physical therapy, occupational and recreational therapy, see **Evaluation and Management** section.

Do not report Evaluation and Management (E/M) services for test interpretation and report. If a significant separately identifiable E/M service is performed, the appropriate E/M service code should be reported using modifier 25.

Allergy Testing

(For allergy laboratory tests, see 86000-86999)

►(For therapy for severe or intractable allergic disease, see 96365-96368, 96372, 96374, 96375)◄

95004 Percutaneous tests (scratch, puncture, prick) with allergenic extracts, immediate type reaction, including test interpretation and report by a physician, specify number of tests

▲ 95010 Percutaneous tests (scratch, puncture, prick) sequential and incremental, with drugs, biologicals or venoms, immediate type reaction, including test interpretation and report by a physician, specify number of tests

95012 Nitric oxide expired gas determination

(For nitric oxide determination by spectroscopy, use Category III code 0064T)

▲ 95015 Intracutaneous (intradermal) tests, sequential and incremental, with drugs, biologicals, or venoms, immediate type reaction, including test interpretation and report by a physician, specify number of tests

95024 Intracutaneous (intradermal) tests with allergenic extracts, immediate type reaction, including test interpretation and report by a physician, specify number of tests

95027 Intracutaneous (intradermal) tests, sequential and incremental, with allergenic extracts for airborne allergens, immediate type reaction, including test interpretation and report by a physician, specify number of tests

95028 Intracutaneous (intradermal) tests with allergenic extracts, delayed type reaction, including reading, specify number of tests

95044 Patch or application test(s) (specify number of tests)

95052 Photo patch test(s) (specify number of tests)

95056 Photo tests

95060 Ophthalmic mucous membrane tests

95065 Direct nasal mucous membrane test

95070 Inhalation bronchial challenge testing (not including necessary pulmonary function tests); with histamine, methacholine, or similar compounds

95071 with antigens or gases, specify

(For pulmonary function tests, see 94060, 94070)

95075 Ingestion challenge test (sequential and incremental ingestion of test items, eg, food, drug or other substance such as metabisulfite)

(95078 has been deleted)

Allergen Immunotherapy

Codes 95115-95199 include the professional services necessary for allergen immunotherapy. Office visit codes may be used in addition to allergen immunotherapy if other identifiable services are provided at that time.

95115 Professional services for allergen immunotherapy not including provision of allergenic extracts; single injection

95117 2 or more injections

95120 Professional services for allergen immunotherapy in prescribing physicians office or institution, including provision of allergenic extract; single injection

95125 2 or more injections

95130 single stinging insect venom

95131 2 stinging insect venoms

95132 3 stinging insect venoms

95133 4 stinging insect venoms

95134 5 stinging insect venoms

95144 Professional services for the supervision of preparation and provision of antigens for allergen immunotherapy, single dose vial(s) (specify number of vials)

(A single dose vial contains a single dose of antigen administered in 1 injection)

95145 Professional services for the supervision of preparation and provision of antigens for allergen immunotherapy (specify number of doses); single stinging insect venom

95146 2 single stinging insect venoms

95147 3 single stinging insect venoms

95148 4 single stinging insect venoms

95149 5 single stinging insect venoms

95165 Professional services for the supervision of preparation and provision of antigens for allergen immunotherapy; single or multiple antigens (specify number of doses)

95170 whole body extract of biting insect or other arthropod (specify number of doses)

(For allergy immunotherapy reporting, a dose is the amount of antigen[s] administered in a single injection from a multiple dose vial)

95180 Rapid desensitization procedure, each hour (eg, insulin, penicillin, equine serum)

95199 Unlisted allergy/clinical immunologic service or procedure

(For skin testing of bacterial, viral, fungal extracts, see 86485-86580, 95028)

(For special reports on allergy patients, use 99080)

(For testing procedures such as radioallergosorbent testing [RAST], rat mast cell technique [RMCT], mast cell degranulation test [MCDT], lymphocytic transformation test [LTT], leukocyte histamine release [LHR], migration inhibitory factor test [MIF], transfer factor test [TFT], nitroblue tetrazolium dye test [NTD], see Immunology section in **Pathology** or use 95199)

Endocrinology

▲ **95250** Ambulatory continuous glucose monitoring of interstitial tissue fluid via a subcutaneous sensor for a minimum of 72 hours; sensor placement, hook-up, calibration of monitor, patient training, removal of sensor, and printout of recording

►(Do not report 95250 more than once per month)◄

(Do not report 95250 in conjunction with 99091)

▲ **95251** interpretation and report

►(Do not report 95251 more than once per month)◄

►(Do not report 95251 in conjunction with 99091)◄

Neurology and Neuromuscular Procedures

Neurologic services are typically consultative, and any of the levels of consultation (99241-99255) may be appropriate.

In addition, services and skills outlined under **Evaluation and Management** levels of service appropriate to neurologic illnesses should be reported similarly.

The EEG, autonomic function, evoked potential, reflex tests, EMG, NCV, and MEG services (95812-95829 and 95860-95967) include recording, interpretation by a physician, and report. For interpretation only, use modifier 26. For EMG guidance, see 95873, 95874.

(For repetitive transcranial magnetic stimulation for treatment of clinical depression, see Category III codes 0160T, 0161T)

(Do not report codes 95860-95875 in addition to 96000-96004)

Sleep Testing

Sleep studies and polysomnography refer to the continuous and simultaneous monitoring and recording of various physiological and pathophysiological parameters of sleep for 6 or more hours with physician review, interpretation and report. The studies are performed to diagnose a variety of sleep disorders and to evaluate a patient's response to therapies such as nasal continuous positive airway pressure (NCPAP). Polysomnography is distinguished from sleep studies by the inclusion of sleep staging which is defined to include a 1-4 lead electroencephalogram (EEG), an electro-oculogram (EOG), and a submental electromyogram (EMG). Additional parameters of sleep include (1) ECG; (2) airflow; (3) ventilation and respiratory effort; (4) gas exchange by oximetry, transcutaneous monitoring, or end tidal gas analysis; (5) extremity muscle activity, motor activity-movement; (6) extended EEG monitoring;
(7) penile tumescence; (8) gastroesophageal reflux; (9) continuous blood pressure monitoring; (10) snoring; (11) body positions; etc.

The sleep services (95805-95811) include recording, interpretation and report. For interpretation only, use modifier 26.

For a study to be reported as polysomnography, sleep must be recorded and staged.

● **95803** Actigraphy testing, recording, analysis, interpretation, and report (minimum of 72 hours to 14 consecutive days of recording)

►(Do not report 95803 more than once in any 14 day period)◄

►(Do not report 95803 in conjunction with 95806-95811)◄

(Report with modifier 52 if less than 6 hours of recording or in other cases of reduced services as appropriate)

(For unattended sleep study, use 95806)

95805 Multiple sleep latency or maintenance of wakefulness testing, recording, analysis and interpretation of physiological measurements of sleep during multiple trials to assess sleepiness

95806 Sleep study, simultaneous recording of ventilation, respiratory effort, ECG or heart rate, and oxygen saturation, unattended by a technologist

95807 Sleep study, simultaneous recording of ventilation, respiratory effort, ECG or heart rate, and oxygen saturation, attended by a technologist

95808 Polysomnography; sleep staging with 1-3 additional parameters of sleep, attended by a technologist

95810 sleep staging with 4 or more additional parameters of sleep, attended by a technologist

95811 sleep staging with 4 or more additional parameters of sleep, with initiation of continuous positive airway pressure therapy or bilevel ventilation, attended by a technologist

Routine Electroencephalography (EEG)

EEG codes 95812-95822 include hyperventilation and/or photic stimulation when appropriate. Routine EEG codes 95816-95822 include 20 to 40 minutes of recording. Extended EEG codes 95812-95813 include reporting times longer than 40 minutes.

95812 Electroencephalogram (EEG) extended monitoring; 41-60 minutes

95813 greater than 1 hour

95816 Electroencephalogram (EEG); including recording awake and drowsy

95819 including recording awake and asleep

95822 recording in coma or sleep only

95824 cerebral death evaluation only

95827 all night recording

(For 24-hour EEG monitoring, see 95950-95953 or 95956)

(For EEG during nonintracranial surgery, use 95955)

(For Wada test, use 95958)

(For digital analysis of EEG, use 95957)

95829 Electrocorticogram at surgery (separate procedure)

95830 Insertion by physician of sphenoidal electrodes for electroencephalographic (EEG) recording

Muscle and Range of Motion Testing

95831 Muscle testing, manual (separate procedure) with report; extremity (excluding hand) or trunk

95832 hand, with or without comparison with normal side

95833 total evaluation of body, excluding hands

95834 total evaluation of body, including hands

95851 Range of motion measurements and report (separate procedure); each extremity (excluding hand) or each trunk section (spine)

95852 hand, with or without comparison with normal side

95857 Tensilon test for myasthenia gravis

►Electromyography◄

Needle electromyographic procedures include the interpretation of electrical waveforms measured by equipment that produces both visible and audible components of electrical signals recorded from the muscle(s) studied by the needle electrode.

95860 Needle electromyography; one extremity with or without related paraspinal areas

95861 2 extremities with or without related paraspinal areas

(For dynamic electromyography performed during motion analysis studies, see 96002-96003)

95863 3 extremities with or without related paraspinal areas

95864 4 extremities with or without related paraspinal areas

95865 larynx

(Do not report modifier 50 in conjunction with 95865)

(For unilateral procedure, report modifier 52 in conjunction with 95865)

95866 hemidiaphragm

95867 cranial nerve supplied muscle(s), unilateral

95868 cranial nerve supplied muscles, bilateral

95869 thoracic paraspinal muscles (excluding T1 or T12)

95870 limited study of muscles in one extremity or non-limb (axial) muscles (unilateral or bilateral), other than thoracic paraspinal, cranial nerve supplied muscles, or sphincters

(To report a complete study of the extremities, see 95860-95864)

(For anal or urethral sphincter, detrusor, urethra, perineum musculature, see 51785-51792)

(For eye muscles, use 92265)

95872 Needle electromyography using single fiber electrode, with quantitative measurement of jitter, blocking and/or fiber density, any/all sites of each muscle studied

►Guidance for Chemodenervation and Ischemic Muscle Testing◄

+ 95873 Electrical stimulation for guidance in conjunction with chemodenervation (List separately in addition to code for primary procedure)

+ 95874 Needle electromyography for guidance in conjunction with chemodenervation (List separately in addition to code for primary procedure)

(Use 95873, 95874 in conjunction with 64612-64614)

(Do not report 95874 in conjunction with 95873)

(Do not report 95873, 95874 in conjunction with 95860-95870)

95875 Ischemic limb exercise test with serial specimen(s) acquisition for muscle(s) metabolite(s)

(For listing of nerves considered for separate study, see **Appendix J**)

►Nerve Conduction Tests◄

⃠ **95900** Nerve conduction, amplitude and latency/velocity study, each nerve; motor, without F-wave study

⃠ **95903** motor, with F-wave study

⃠ **95904** sensory

(Report 95900, 95903, and/or 95904 only once when multiple sites on the same nerve are stimulated or recorded)

Intraoperative Neurophysiology

+ 95920 Intraoperative neurophysiology testing, per hour (List separately in addition to code for primary procedure)

(Use 95920 in conjunction with the study performed, 92585, 95822, 95860, 95861, 95867, 95868, 95870, 95900, 95904, 95925-95937)

(Code 95920 describes ongoing electrophysiologic testing and monitoring performed during surgical procedures. Code 95920 is reported per hour of service, and includes only the ongoing electrophysiologic monitoring time distinct from performance of specific type(s) of baseline electrophysiologic study(s) (95860, 95861, 95867, 95868, 95870, 95900, 95904, 95928, 95929, 95933-95937) or interpretation of specific type(s) of baseline electrophysiologic study(s) (92585, 95822, 95870, 95925-95928, 95929, 95930). The time spent performing or interpreting the baseline electrophysiologic study(s) should not be counted as intraoperative monitoring, but represents separately reportable procedures. Code 95920 should be used once per hour even if multiple electrophysiologic studies are performed. The baseline electrophysiologic study(s) should be used once per operative session.)

(For electrocorticography, use 95829)

(For intraoperative EEG during nonintracranial surgery, use 95955)

(For intraoperative functional cortical or subcortical mapping, see 95961-95962)

(For intraoperative neurostimulator programming and analysis, see 95970-95975)

Autonomic Function Tests

95921 Testing of autonomic nervous system function; cardiovagal innervation (parasympathetic function), including two or more of the following: heart rate response to deep breathing with recorded R-R interval, Valsalva ratio, and 30:15 ratio

95922 vasomotor adrenergic innervation (sympathetic adrenergic function), including beat-to-beat blood pressure and R-R interval changes during Valsalva maneuver and at least 5 minutes of passive tilt

95923 sudomotor, including one or more of the following: quantitative sudomotor axon reflex test (QSART), silastic sweat imprint, thermoregulatory sweat test, and changes in sympathetic skin potential

Evoked Potentials and Reflex Tests

95925 Short-latency somatosensory evoked potential study, stimulation of any/all peripheral nerves or skin sites, recording from the central nervous system; in upper limbs

95926 in lower limbs

95927 in the trunk or head

(To report a unilateral study, use modifier 52)

(For auditory evoked potentials, use 92585)

95928 Central motor evoked potential study (transcranial motor stimulation); upper limbs

95929 lower limbs

95930 Visual evoked potential (VEP) testing central nervous system, checkerboard or flash

95933 Orbicularis oculi (blink) reflex, by electrodiagnostic testing

95934 H-reflex, amplitude and latency study; record gastrocnemius/soleus muscle

95936 record muscle other than gastrocnemius/soleus muscle

(To report a bilateral study, use modifier 50)

95937 Neuromuscular junction testing (repetitive stimulation, paired stimuli), each nerve, any one method

Special EEG Tests

95950 Monitoring for identification and lateralization of cerebral seizure focus, electroencephalographic (eg, 8 channel EEG) recording and interpretation, each 24 hours

95951 Monitoring for localization of cerebral seizure focus by cable or radio, 16 or more channel telemetry, combined electroencephalographic (EEG) and video recording and interpretation (eg, for presurgical localization), each 24 hours

95953 Monitoring for localization of cerebral seizure focus by computerized portable 16 or more channel EEG, electroencephalographic (EEG) recording and interpretation, each 24 hours

95954 Pharmacological or physical activation requiring physician attendance during EEG recording of activation phase (eg, thiopental activation test)

95955 Electroencephalogram (EEG) during nonintracranial surgery (eg, carotid surgery)

95956 Monitoring for localization of cerebral seizure focus by cable or radio, 16 or more channel telemetry, electroencephalographic (EEG) recording and interpretation, each 24 hours

95957 Digital analysis of electroencephalogram (EEG) (eg, for epileptic spike analysis)

95958 Wada activation test for hemispheric function, including electroencephalographic (EEG) monitoring

95961 Functional cortical and subcortical mapping by stimulation and/or recording of electrodes on brain surface, or of depth electrodes, to provoke seizures or identify vital brain structures; initial hour of physician attendance

+ 95962 each additional hour of physician attendance (List separately in addition to code for primary procedure)

(Use 95962 in conjunction with 95961)

95965 Magnetoencephalography (MEG), recording and analysis; for spontaneous brain magnetic activity (eg, epileptic cerebral cortex localization)

95966 for evoked magnetic fields, single modality (eg, sensory, motor, language, or visual cortex localization)

+ 95967 for evoked magnetic fields, each additional modality (eg, sensory, motor, language, or visual cortex localization) (List separately in addition to code for primary procedure)

(Use 95967 in conjunction with 95966)

(For electroencephalography performed in addition to magnetoencephalography, see 95812-95827)

(For somatosensory evoked potentials, auditory evoked potentials, and visual evoked potentials performed in addition to magnetic evoked field responses, see 92585, 95925, 95926, and/or 95930)

(For computerized tomography performed in addition to magnetoencephalography, see 70450-70470, 70496)

(For magnetic resonance imaging performed in addition to magnetoencephalography, see 70551-70553)

Neurostimulators, Analysis-Programming

A simple neurostimulator pulse generator/transmitter (95970, 95971) is one capable of affecting three or fewer of the following: pulse amplitude, pulse duration, pulse frequency, eight or more electrode contacts, cycling, stimulation train duration, train spacing, number of programs, number of channels, alternating electrode polarities, dose time (stimulation parameters changing in time periods of minutes including dose lockout times), more than one clinical feature (eg, rigidity, dyskinesia, tremor). A complex neurostimulator pulse generator/transmitter (95970, 95972- 95975) is one capable of affecting more than three of the above.

Code 95970 describes subsequent electronic analysis of a previously-implanted simple or complex brain, spinal cord, or peripheral neurostimulator pulse generator system, without reprogramming. Code 95971 describes intraoperative or subsequent electronic analysis of an implanted simple spinal cord, or peripheral (ie, peripheral nerve, autonomic nerve, neuromuscular) neurostimulator pulse generator system, with programming. Codes 95972 and 95973 describe intraoperative (at initial insertion/revision) or subsequent electronic analysis of an implanted complex spinal cord or peripheral (except cranial nerve) neurostimulator pulse generator system, with programming. Codes 95974 and 95975 describe intraoperative (at initial insertion/revision) or subsequent electronic analysis of an implanted complex cranial nerve neurostimulator pulse generator system, with programming. Codes 95978 and 95979 describe initial or subsequent electronic analysis of an implanted brain neurostimulator pulse generator system, with programming.

►Code 95980 describes intraoperative electronic analysis of an implanted gastric neurostimulator pulse generator system, with programming; code 95981 describes subsequent analysis of the device; code 95982 describes subsequent analysis and reprogramming. For electronic analysis and reprogramming of gastric neurostimulator, lesser curvature, see 95980-95982.◄

(For insertion of neurostimulator pulse generator, see 61885, 63685, 64590)

(For revision or removal of neurostimulator pulse generator or receiver, see 61888, 63688, 64595)

(For implantation of neurostimulator electrodes, see 43647, 43881, 61850-61875, 63650-63655, 64553-64580, 0155T, 0157T. For revision or removal of neurostimulator electrodes, see 43648, 43882, 61880, 63660, 64585, 0156T, 0158T)

95970 Electronic analysis of implanted neurostimulator pulse generator system (eg, rate, pulse amplitude and duration, configuration of wave form, battery status, electrode selectability, output modulation, cycling, impedance and patient compliance measurements); simple or complex brain, spinal cord, or peripheral (ie, cranial nerve, peripheral nerve, autonomic nerve, neuromuscular) neurostimulator pulse generator/transmitter, without reprogramming

95971 simple spinal cord, or peripheral (ie, peripheral nerve, autonomic nerve, neuromuscular) neurostimulator pulse generator/transmitter, with intraoperative or subsequent programming

95972 complex spinal cord, or peripheral (except cranial nerve) neurostimulator pulse generator/transmitter, with intraoperative or subsequent programming, first hour

+ 95973 complex spinal cord, or peripheral (except cranial nerve) neurostimulator pulse generator/transmitter, with intraoperative or subsequent programming, each additional 30 minutes after first hour (List separately in addition to code for primary procedure)

(Use 95973 in conjunction with 95972)

95974 complex cranial nerve neurostimulator pulse generator/transmitter, with intraoperative or subsequent programming, with or without nerve interface testing, first hour

+ 95975 complex cranial nerve neurostimulator pulse generator/transmitter, with intraoperative or subsequent programming, each additional 30 minutes after first hour (List separately in addition to code for primary procedure)

(Use 95975 in conjunction with 95974)

(For electronic analysis programming of gastric neurostimulator, lesser curvature, use Category III code 0162T)

95978 Electronic analysis of implanted neurostimulator pulse generator system (eg, rate, pulse amplitude and duration, battery status, electrode selectability and polarity, impedance and patient compliance measurements), complex deep brain neurostimulator pulse generator/transmitter, with initial or subsequent programming; first hour

+ 95979 each additional 30 minutes after first hour (List separately in addition to code for primary procedure)

(Use 95979 in conjunction with 95978)

95980 Electronic analysis of implanted neurostimulator pulse generator system (eg, rate, pulse amplitude and duration, configuration of wave form, battery status, electrode selectability, output modulation, cycling, impedance and patient measurements) gastric neurostimulator pulse generator/transmitter; intraoperative, with programming

95981 subsequent, without reprogramming

95982 subsequent, with reprogramming

Other Procedures

95990 Refilling and maintenance of implantable pump or reservoir for drug delivery, spinal (intrathecal, epidural) or brain (intraventricular);

(For analysis and/or reprogramming of implantable infusion pump, see 62367-62368)

(For refill and maintenance of implanted infusion pump or reservoir for systemic drug therapy [eg, chemotherapy or insulin], use 96522)

95991 administered by physician

⊘● **95992** Canalith repositioning procedure(s) (eg, Epley maneuver, Semont maneuver), per day

►(Do not report 95992 in conjunction with 92531, 92532)◄

95999 Unlisted neurological or neuromuscular diagnostic procedure

Motion Analysis

Codes 96000-96004 describe services performed as part of a major therapeutic or diagnostic decision making process. Motion analysis is performed in a dedicated motion analysis laboratory (ie, a facility capable of performing videotaping from the front, back and both sides, computerized 3D kinematics, 3D kinetics, and dynamic electromyography). Code 96000 may include 3D kinetics and stride characteristics. Codes 96002-96003 describe dynamic electromyography.

Code 96004 should only be reported once regardless of the number of study(ies) reviewed/interpreted.

(For performance of needle electromyography procedures, see 95860-95875)

(For gait training, use 97116)

96000 Comprehensive computer-based motion analysis by video-taping and 3D kinematics;

96001 with dynamic plantar pressure measurements during walking

96002 Dynamic surface electromyography, during walking or other functional activities, 1-12 muscles

96003 Dynamic fine wire electromyography, during walking or other functional activities, 1 muscle

(Do not report 96002, 96003 in conjunction with 95860-95864, 95869-95872)

96004 Physician review and interpretation of comprehensive computer-based motion analysis, dynamic plantar pressure measurements, dynamic surface electromyography during walking or other functional activities, and dynamic fine wire electromyography, with written report

Functional Brain Mapping

Code 96020 includes selection and administration of testing of language, memory, cognition, movement, sensation, and other neurological functions when conducted in association with functional neuroimaging, monitoring of performance of this testing, and determination of validity of neurofunctional testing relative to separately interpreted functional magnetic resonance images.

96020 Neurofunctional testing selection and administration during noninvasive imaging functional brain mapping, with test administered entirely by a physician or psychologist, with review of test results and report

(For functional magnetic resonance imaging [fMRI], brain, use 70555)

(Do not report 96020 in conjunction with 96101-96103, 96116-96120)

(Do not report 96020 in conjunction with 70554)

(Evaluation and Management services codes should not be reported on the same day as 96020)

Medical Genetics and Genetic Counseling Services

These services are provided by trained genetic counselors and may include obtaining a structured family genetic history, pedigree construction, analysis for genetic risk assessment, and counseling of the patient and family. These activities may be provided during one or more sessions and may include review of medical data and family information, face-to-face interviews, and counseling services.

96040 Medical genetics and genetic counseling services, each 30 minutes face-to-face with patient/family

(For genetic counseling and education provided by a physician to an individual, see the appropriate Evaluation and Management codes)

(For genetic counseling and education provided by a physician to a group, use 99078)

(For education regarding genetic risks by a nonphysician to a group, see 98961, 98962)

(For genetic counseling and/or risk factor reduction intervention provided by a physician to patient(s) without symptoms or established disease, see 99401-99412)

Central Nervous System Assessments/Tests (eg, Neuro-Cognitive, Mental Status, Speech Testing)

The following codes are used to report the services provided during testing of the cognitive function of the central nervous system. The testing of cognitive processes, visual motor responses, and abstractive abilities is accomplished by the combination of several types of testing procedures. It is expected that the administration of these tests will generate material that will be formulated into a report.

(For development of cognitive skills, see 97532, 97533)

(For mini-mental status examination performed by a physician, see **Evaluation and Management** services codes)

96101 Psychological testing (includes psychodiagnostic assessment of emotionality, intellectual abilities, personality and psychopathology, eg, MMPI, Rorschach, WAIS), per hour of the psychologist's or physician's time, both face-to-face time administering tests to the patient and time interpreting these test results and preparing the report

(96101 is also used in those circumstances when additional time is necessary to integrate other sources of clinical data, including previously completed and reported technician- and computer-administered tests)

(Do not report 96101 for the interpretation and report of 96102, 96103)

96102 Psychological testing (includes psychodiagnostic assessment of emotionality, intellectual abilities, personality and psychopathology, eg, MMPI and WAIS), with qualified health care professional interpretation and report, administered by technician, per hour of technician time, face-to-face

96103 Psychological testing (includes psychodiagnostic assessment of emotionality, intellectual abilities, personality and psychopathology, eg, MMPI), administered by a computer, with qualified health care professional interpretation and report

96105 Assessment of aphasia (includes assessment of expressive and receptive speech and language function, language comprehension, speech production ability, reading, spelling, writing, eg, by Boston Diagnostic Aphasia Examination) with interpretation and report, per hour

96110 Developmental testing; limited (eg, Developmental Screening Test II, Early Language Milestone Screen), with interpretation and report

96111 extended (includes assessment of motor, language, social, adaptive and/or cognitive functioning by standardized developmental instruments) with interpretation and report

96116 Neurobehavioral status exam (clinical assessment of thinking, reasoning and judgment, eg, acquired knowledge, attention, language, memory, planning and problem solving, and visual spatial abilities), per hour of the psychologist's or physician's time, both face-to-face time with the patient and time interpreting test results and preparing the report

96118 Neuropsychological testing (eg, Halstead-Reitan Neuropsychological Battery, Wechsler Memory Scales and Wisconsin Card Sorting Test), per hour of the psychologist's or physician's time, both face-to-face time administering tests to the patient and time interpreting these test results and preparing the report

(96118 is also used in those circumstances when additional time is necessary to integrate other sources of clinical data, including previously completed and reported technician- and computer-administered tests)

(Do not report 96118 for the interpretation and report of 96119 or 96120)

96119 Neuropsychological testing (eg, Halstead-Reitan Neuropsychological Battery, Wechsler Memory Scales and Wisconsin Card Sorting Test), with qualified health care professional interpretation and report, administered by technician, per hour of technician time, face-to-face

96120 Neuropsychological testing (eg, Wisconsin Card Sorting Test), administered by a computer, with qualified health care professional interpretation and report

96125 Standardized cognitive performance testing (eg, Ross Information Processing Assessment) per hour of a qualified health care professional's time, both face-to-face time administering tests to the patient and time interpreting these test results and preparing the report

(For psychological and neuropsychological testing by a physician or psychologist, see 96101-96103, 96118-96120)

Health and Behavior Assessment/Intervention

Health and behavior assessment procedures are used to identify the psychological, behavioral, emotional, cognitive, and social factors important to the prevention, treatment, or management of physical health problems.

The focus of the assessment is not on mental health but on the biopsychosocial factors important to physical health problems and treatments. The focus of the intervention is to improve the patient's health and well-being utilizing cognitive, behavioral, social, and/or psychophysiological procedures designed to ameliorate specific disease-related problems.

Codes 96150-96155 describe services offered to patients who present with primary physical illnesses, diagnoses, or symptoms and may benefit from assessments and interventions that focus on the biopsychosocial factors related to the patient's health status. These services do not represent preventive medicine counseling and risk factor reduction interventions.

For patients that require psychiatric services (90801-90899) as well as health and behavior assessment/intervention (96150-96155), report the predominant service performed. Do not report 96150-96155 in conjunction with 90801-90899 on the same date.

►Evaluation and Management services codes (including Counseling Risk Factor Reduction and Behavior Change Intervention [99401-99412]), should not be reported on the same day.◄

(For health and behavior assessment and/or intervention performed by a physician, see **Evaluation and Management** or **Preventive Medicine** services codes)

96150 Health and behavior assessment (eg, health-focused clinical interview, behavioral observations, psychophysiological monitoring, health-oriented questionnaires), each 15 minutes face-to-face with the patient; initial assessment

96151 re-assessment

96152 Health and behavior intervention, each 15 minutes, face-to-face; individual

96153 group (2 or more patients)

96154 family (with the patient present)

96155 family (without the patient present)

►Hydration, Therapeutic, Prophylactic, Diagnostic Injections and Infusions, and Chemotherapy and Other Highly Complex Drug or Highly Complex Biologic Agent Administration◄

►Physician work related to hydration, injection, and infusion services predominantly involves affirmation of treatment plan and direct supervision of staff.◄

►If a significant, separately identifiable Evaluation and Management service is performed, the appropriate E/M service code should be reported using modifier 25 in addition to 96360-96549. For same day E/M service, a different diagnosis is not required.

If performed to facilitate the infusion or injection, the following services are included and are not reported separately:

a. Use of local anesthesia

b. IV start

c. Access to indwelling IV, subcutaneous catheter or port

d. Flush at conclusion of infusion

e. Standard tubing, syringes, and supplies◄

►(For declotting a catheter or port, use 36593)◄

►When multiple drugs are administered, report the service(s) and the specific materials or drugs for each.

When administering multiple infusions, injections or combinations, only one "initial" service code should be reported, unless protocol requires that two separate IV sites must be used. If an injection or infusion is of a subsequent or concurrent nature, even if it is the first such service within that group of services, then a subsequent or concurrent code from the appropriate section should be reported (eg, the first IV push given subsequent to an initial one-hour infusion is reported using a subsequent IV push code).

When these codes are reported by the physician, the "initial" code that best describes the key or primary reason for the encounter should always be reported irrespective of the order in which the infusions or injections occur.

When these codes are reported *by the facility*, the following instructions apply. The initial code should be selected using a hierarchy whereby chemotherapy services are primary to therapeutic, prophylactic, and diagnostic services which are primary to hydration services. Infusions are primary to pushes, which are primary to injections.

When reporting codes for which infusion time is a factor, use the actual time over which the infusion is administered. Intravenous or intra-arterial push is defined as: (a) an injection in which the health care professional who administers the substance/drug is continuously present to administer the injection and observe the patient, or (b) an infusion of 15 minutes or less.◄

►Hydration◄

►Codes 96360-96361 are intended to report a hydration IV infusion to consist of a pre-packaged fluid and electrolytes (eg, normal saline, D5-1/2 normal saline+30mEq KCl/liter), but are not used to report infusion of drugs or other substances. Hydration IV infusions typically require direct physician supervision for purposes of consent, safety oversight, or intraservice supervision of staff. Typically such infusions require little special handling to prepare or dispose of, and staff that administer these do not typically require advanced practice training. After initial set-up, infusion typically entails little patient risk and thus little monitoring. These codes are not intended to be reported by the physician in the facility setting.◄

● **96360** Intravenous infusion, hydration; initial, 31 minutes to 1 hour

►(Do not report 96360 if performed as a concurrent infusion service)◄

►(Do not report intravenous infusion for hydration of 30 minutes or less)◄

+● **96361** each additional hour (List separately in addition to code for primary procedure)

►(Use 96361 in conjunction with 96360)◄

►(Report 96361 for hydration infusion intervals of greater than 30 minutes beyond 1 hour increments)◄

►(Report 96361 to identify hydration if provided as a secondary or subsequent service after a different initial service [96360, 96365, 96374, 96409, 96413] is administered through the same IV access)◄

►Therapeutic, Prophylactic, and Diagnostic Injections and Infusions (Excludes Chemotherapy and Other Highly Complex Drug or Highly Complex Biologic Agent Administration)◄

►A therapeutic, prophylactic, or diagnostic IV infusion or injection (other than hydration) is for the administration of substances/drugs. When fluids are used to administer the drug(s), the administration of the fluid is considered incidental hydration and is not separately reportable. These services typically require direct physician supervision for any or all purposes of patient assessment, provision of consent, safety oversight, and intra-service supervision of staff. Typically, such infusions require special consideration to prepare, dose or dispose of, require practice training and competency for staff who administer the infusions, and require periodic patient assessment with vital sign monitoring during the infusion. These codes are not intended to be reported by the physician in the facility setting.

See codes 96401-96549 for the administration of chemotherapy or other highly complex drug or highly complex biologic agent services. These highly complex services require advanced practice training and competency for staff who provide these services; special considerations for preparation, dosage or disposal; and commonly, these services entail significant patient risk and frequent monitoring. Examples are frequent changes in the infusion rate, prolonged presence of nurse administering the solution for patient monitoring and infusion adjustments, and frequent conferring with the physician about these issues.◄

►(Do not report 96365-96379 with codes for which IV push or infusion is an inherent part of the procedure [eg, administration of contrast material for a diagnostic imaging study])◄

● **96365** Intravenous infusion, for therapy, prophylaxis, or diagnosis (specify substance or drug); initial, up to 1 hour

+● **96366** each additional hour (List separately in addition to code for primary procedure)

►(Report 96366 in conjunction with 96365, 96367)◄

►(Report 96366 for additional hour[s] of sequential infusion)◄

►(Report 96366 for infusion intervals of greater than 30 minutes beyond 1 hour increments)◄

+● **96367** additional sequential infusion, up to 1 hour (List separately in addition to code for primary procedure)

►(Report 96367 in conjunction with 96365, 96374, 96409, 96413 if provided as a secondary or subsequent service after a different initial service is administered through the same IV access. Report 96367 only once per sequential infusion of same infusate mix)◄

+● **96368** concurrent infusion (List separately in addition to code for primary procedure)

►(Report 96368 only once per encounter)◄

►(Report 96368 in conjunction with 96365, 96366, 96413, 96415, 96416)◄

● **96369** Subcutaneous infusion for therapy or prophylaxis (specify substance or drug); initial, up to 1 hour, including pump set-up and establishment of subcutaneous infusion site(s)

►(For infusions of 15 minutes or less, use 96372)◄

+● **96370** each additional hour (List separately in addition to code for primary procedure)

►(Use 96370 in conjunction with 96369)◄

►(Use 96370 for infusion intervals of greater than 30 minutes beyond 1 hour increments)◄

+● **96371** additional pump set-up with establishment of new subcutaneous infusion site(s) (List separately in addition to code for primary procedure)

►(Use 96371 in conjunction with 96369)◄

►(Use 96369, 96371 only once per encounter)◄

● **96372** Therapeutic, prophylactic, or diagnostic injection (specify substance or drug); subcutaneous or intramuscular

►(For administration of vaccines/toxoids, see 90465, 90466, 90471, 90472)◄

►(Report 96372 for non-antineoplastic hormonal therapy injections)◄

►(Report 96401 for anti-neoplastic nonhormonal injection therapy)◄

►(Report 96402 for anti-neoplastic hormonal injection therapy)◄

►(Physicians do not report 96372 for injections given without direct physician supervision. To report, use 99211. Hospitals may report 96372 when the physician is not present)◄

►(96372 does not include injections for allergen immunotherapy. For allergen immunotherapy injections, see 95115-95117)◄

● **96373** intra-arterial

● **96374** intravenous push, single or initial substance/drug

+● **96375** each additional sequential intravenous push of a new substance/drug (List separately in addition to code for primary procedure)

►(Use 96375 in conjunction with 96365, 96374, 96409, 96413)◄

►(Report 96375 to identify intravenous push of a new substance/drug if provided as a secondary or subsequent service after a different initial service is administered through the same IV access)◄

+● **96376** each additional sequential intravenous push of the same substance/drug provided in a facility (List separately in addition to code for primary procedure)

►(Do not report 96376 for a push performed within 30 minutes of a reported push of the same substance or drug)◄

►(96376 may be reported by facilities only)◄

● **96379** Unlisted therapeutic, prophylactic, or diagnostic intravenous or intra-arterial injection or infusion

►(For allergy immunology, see 95004 et seq)◄

►Chemotherapy and Other Highly Complex Drug or Highly Complex Biologic Agent Administration◄

►Chemotherapy administration codes 96401-96549 apply to parenteral administration of non-radionuclide anti-neoplastic drugs; and also to anti-neoplastic agents provided for treatment of noncancer diagnoses (eg, cyclophosphamide for auto-immune conditions) or to substances such as certain monoclonal antibody agents, and other biologic response modifiers. The highly complex infusion of chemotherapy or other drug or biologic agents requires physician work and/or clinical staff monitoring well beyond that of therapeutic drug agents (96360-96379) because the incidence of severe adverse patient reactions are typically greater. These services can be provided by any physician. Chemotherapy services are typically highly complex and require direct physician supervision for any or all purposes of patient assessment, provision of consent, safety oversight, and intraservice supervision of staff. Typically, such chemotherapy services require advanced practice training and competency for staff who provide these services; special considerations for preparation, dosage, or disposal;

Medicine

and commonly, these services entail significant patient risk and frequent monitoring. Examples are frequent changes in the infusion rate, prolonged presence of the nurse administering the solution for patient monitoring and infusion adjustments, and frequent conferring with the physician about these issues. When performed to facilitate the infusion of injection, preparation of chemotherapy agent(s), highly complex agent(s), or other highly complex drugs is included and is not reported separately. To report infusions that do not require this level of complexity, see 96360-96379. Codes 96401-96402, 96409-96425, 96521-96523 are not intended to be reported by the physician in the facility setting.

The term "chemotherapy" in 96401-96549 includes other highly complex drugs or highly complex biologic agents.

Report separate codes for each parenteral method of administration employed when chemotherapy is administered by different techniques. The administration of medications (eg, antibiotics, steroidal agents, antiemetics, narcotics, analgesics) administered independently or sequentially as supportive management of chemotherapy administration, should be separately reported using 96360, 96361, 96365, 96379 as appropriate.◄

Report both the specific service as well as code(s) for the specific substance(s) or drug(s) provided. The fluid used to administer the drug(s) is considered incidental hydration and is not separately reportable.

Regional (isolation) chemotherapy perfusion should be reported using the codes for arterial infusion (96420-96425). Placement of the intra-arterial catheter should be reported using the appropriate code from the **Cardiovascular Surgery** section. Placement of arterial and venous cannula(s) for extracorporeal circulation via a membrane oxygenator perfusion pump should be reported using 36823. Code 36823 includes dose calculation and administration of the chemotherapy agent by injection into the perfusate. Do not report 96409-96425 in conjunction with 36823.

(For home infusion services, see 99601-99602)

►Injection and Intravenous Infusion Chemotherapy and Other Highly Complex Drug or Highly Complex Biologic Agent Administration◄

Intravenous or intra-arterial push is defined as: (a) an injection in which the healthcare professional who administers the substance/drug is continuously present to administer the injection and observe the patient, or (b) an infusion of 15 minutes or less.

96401 Chemotherapy administration, subcutaneous or intramuscular; non-hormonal anti-neoplastic

96402 hormonal anti-neoplastic

96405 Chemotherapy administration; intralesional, up to and including 7 lesions

96406 intralesional, more than 7 lesions

96409 intravenous, push technique, single or initial substance/drug

+ 96411 intravenous, push technique, each additional substance/drug (List separately in addition to code for primary procedure)

(Use 96411 in conjunction with 96409, 96413)

96413 Chemotherapy administration, intravenous infusion technique; up to 1 hour, single or initial substance/drug

►(Report 96361 to identify hydration if administered as a secondary or subsequent service in association with 96413 through the same IV access)◄

►(Report 96366, 96367, 96375 to identify therapeutic, prophylactic, or diagnostic drug infusion or injection, if administered as a secondary or subsequent service in association with 96413 through the same IV access)◄

+ 96415 each additional hour (List separately in addition to code for primary procedure)

(Use 96415 in conjunction with 96413)

(Report 96415 for infusion intervals of greater than 30 minutes beyond 1-hour increments)

96416 initiation of prolonged chemotherapy infusion (more than 8 hours), requiring use of a portable or implantable pump

(For refilling and maintenance of a portabie pump or an implantable infusion pump or reservoir for drug delivery, see 96521-96523)

+ 96417 each additional sequential infusion (different substance/drug), up to 1 hour (List separately in addition to code for primary procedure)

(Use 96417 in conjunction with 96413)

(Report only once per sequential infusion. Report 96415 for additional hour(s) of sequential infusion)

►Intra-Arterial Chemotherapy and Other Highly Complex Drug or Highly Complex Biologic Agent Administration◄

96420 Chemotherapy administration, intra-arterial; push technique

96422 infusion technique, up to 1 hour

+ 96423 infusion technique, each additional hour (List separately in addition to code for primary procedure)

(Use 96423 in conjunction with 96422)

(Report 96423 for infusion intervals of greater than 30 minutes beyond 1-hour increments)

(For regional chemotherapy perfusion via membrane oxygenator perfusion pump to an extremity, use 36823)

96425 infusion technique, initiation of prolonged infusion (more than 8 hours), requiring the use of a portable or implantable pump

(For refilling and maintenance of a portable pump or an implantable infusion pump or reservoir for drug delivery, see 96521-96523)

►Other Injection and Infusion Services◄

Code 96523 does not require direct physician supervision. Codes 96521-96523 may be reported when these devices are used for therapeutic drugs other than chemotherapy.

(For collection of blood specimen from a completely implantable venous access device, use 36591)

96440 Chemotherapy administration into pleural cavity, requiring and including thoracentesis

96445 Chemotherapy administration into peritoneal cavity, requiring and including peritoneocentesis

96450 Chemotherapy administration, into CNS (eg, intrathecal), requiring and including spinal puncture

(For intravesical (bladder) chemotherapy administration, use 51720)

(For insertion of subarachnoid catheter and reservoir for infusion of drug, see 62350, 62351, 62360-62362; for insertion of intraventricular catheter and reservoir, see 61210, 61215)

96521 Refilling and maintenance of portable pump

96522 Refilling and maintenance of implantable pump or reservoir for drug delivery, systemic (eg, intravenous, intra-arterial)

(For refilling and maintenance of an implantable infusion pump for spinal or brain drug infusion, use 95990-95991)

96523 Irrigation of implanted venous access device for drug delivery systems

(Do not report 96523 if any other services are provided on the same day)

96542 Chemotherapy injection, subarachnoid or intraventricular via subcutaneous reservoir, single or multiple agents

(For radioactive isotope therapy, use 79005)

96549 Unlisted chemotherapy procedure

Photodynamic Therapy

(To report ocular photodynamic therapy, use 67221)

96567 Photodynamic therapy by external application of light to destroy premalignant and/or malignant lesions of the skin and adjacent mucosa (eg, lip) by activation of photosensitive drug(s), each phototherapy exposure session

+ 96570 Photodynamic therapy by endoscopic application of light to ablate abnormal tissue via activation of photosensitive drug(s); first 30 minutes (List separately in addition to code for endoscopy or bronchoscopy procedures of lung and esophagus)

+ 96571 each additional 15 minutes (List separately in addition to code for endoscopy or bronchoscopy procedures of lung and esophagus)

(96570, 96571 are to be used in addition to bronchoscopy, endoscopy codes)

(Use 96570, 96571 in conjunction with 31641, 43228 as appropriate)

Special Dermatological Procedures

Dermatologic services are typically consultative, and any of the five levels of consultation (99241-99255) may be appropriate.

In addition, services and skills outlined under **Evaluation and Management** levels of service appropriate to dermatologic illnesses should be coded similarly.

(For intralesional injections, see 11900, 11901)

(For Tzanck smear, see 88160-88161)

96900 Actinotherapy (ultraviolet light)

96902 Microscopic examination of hairs plucked or clipped by the examiner (excluding hair collected by the patient) to determine telogen and anagen counts, or structural hair shaft abnormality

96904 Whole body integumentary photography, for monitoring of high risk patients with dysplastic nevus syndrome or a history of dysplastic nevi, or patients with a personal or familial history of melanoma

96910 Photochemotherapy; tar and ultraviolet B (Goeckerman treatment) or petrolatum and ultraviolet B

96912 psoralens and ultraviolet A (PUVA)

96913 Photochemotherapy (Goeckerman and/or PUVA) for severe photoresponsive dermatoses requiring at least four to eight hours of care under direct supervision of the physician (includes application of medication and dressings)

96920 Laser treatment for inflammatory skin disease (psoriasis); total area less than 250 sq cm

96921 250 sq cm to 500 sq cm

96922 over 500 sq cm

96999 Unlisted special dermatological service or procedure

Physical Medicine and Rehabilitation

Codes 97001-97755 should be used to report each distinct procedure performed. Do not append modifier 51 to 97001-97755.

(For muscle testing, range of joint motion, electromyography, see 95831 et seq)

(For biofeedback training by EMG, use 90901)

(For transcutaneous nerve stimulation (TNS), use 64550)

97001 Physical therapy evaluation

97002 Physical therapy re-evaluation

97003 Occupational therapy evaluation

97004 Occupational therapy re-evaluation

97005 Athletic training evaluation

97006 Athletic training re-evaluation

Modalities

Any physical agent applied to produce therapeutic changes to biologic tissue; includes but not limited to thermal, acoustic, light, mechanical, or electric energy.

Supervised

The application of a modality that does not require direct (one-on-one) patient contact by the provider.

97010 Application of a modality to 1 or more areas; hot or cold packs

97012 traction, mechanical

97014 electrical stimulation (unattended)

(For acupuncture with electrical stimulation, see 97813, 97814)

97016 vasopneumatic devices

97018 paraffin bath

97022 whirlpool

97024 diathermy (eg, microwave)

97026 infrared

97028 ultraviolet

Constant Attendance

The application of a modality that requires direct (one-on-one) patient contact by the provider.

97032 Application of a modality to one or more areas; electrical stimulation (manual), each 15 minutes

97033 iontophoresis, each 15 minutes

97034 contrast baths, each 15 minutes

97035 ultrasound, each 15 minutes

97036 Hubbard tank, each 15 minutes

97039 Unlisted modality (specify type and time if constant attendance)

Therapeutic Procedures

A manner of effecting change through the application of clinical skills and/or services that attempt to improve function.

Physician or therapist required to have direct (one-on-one) patient contact.

97110 Therapeutic procedure, one or more areas, each 15 minutes; therapeutic exercises to develop strength and endurance, range of motion and flexibility

97112 neuromuscular reeducation of movement, balance, coordination, kinesthetic sense, posture, and/or proprioception for sitting and/or standing activities

97113 aquatic therapy with therapeutic exercises

97116 gait training (includes stair climbing)

(Use 96000-96003 to report comprehensive gait and motion analysis procedures)

97124 massage, including effleurage, petrissage and/or tapotement (stroking, compression, percussion)

(For myofascial release, use 97140)

97139 Unlisted therapeutic procedure (specify)

97140 Manual therapy techniques (eg, mobilization/ manipulation, manual lymphatic drainage, manual traction), one or more regions, each 15 minutes

97150 Therapeutic procedure(s), group (2 or more individuals)

(Report 97150 for each member of group)

(Group therapy procedures involve constant attendance of the physician or therapist, but by definition do not require one-on-one patient contact by the physician or therapist)

(For manipulation under general anesthesia, see appropriate anatomic section in **Musculoskeletal System**)

(For osteopathic manipulative treatment [OMT], see 98925-98929)

97530 Therapeutic activities, direct (one-on-one) patient contact by the provider (use of dynamic activities to improve functional performance), each 15 minutes

97532 Development of cognitive skills to improve attention, memory, problem solving (includes compensatory training), direct (one-on-one) patient contact by the provider, each 15 minutes

97533 Sensory integrative techniques to enhance sensory processing and promote adaptive responses to environmental demands, direct (one-on-one) patient contact by the provider, each 15 minutes

97535 Self-care/home management training (eg, activities of daily living (ADL) and compensatory training, meal preparation, safety procedures, and instructions in use of assistive technology devices/adaptive equipment) direct one-on-one contact by provider, each 15 minutes

97537 Community/work reintegration training (eg, shopping, transportation, money management, avocational activities and/or work environment/modification analysis, work task analysis, use of assistive technology device/adaptive equipment), direct one-on-one contact by provider, each 15 minutes

(For wheelchair management/propulsion training, use 97542)

97542 Wheelchair management (eg, assessment, fitting, training), each 15 minutes

97545 Work hardening/conditioning; initial 2 hours

+ 97546 each additional hour (List separately in addition to code for primary procedure)

(Use 97546 in conjunction with 97545)

Active Wound Care Management

Active wound care procedures are performed to remove devitalized and/or necrotic tissue and promote healing. Provider is required to have direct (one-on-one) patient contact.

(Do not report 97597-97602 in conjunction with 11040-11044)

97597 Removal of devitalized tissue from wound(s), selective debridement, without anesthesia (eg, high pressure waterjet with/without suction, sharp selective debridement with scissors, scalpel and forceps), with or without topical application(s), wound assessment, and instruction(s) for ongoing care, may include use of a whirlpool, per session; total wound(s) surface area less than or equal to 20 square centimeters

97598 total wound(s) surface area greater than 20 square centimeters

97602 Removal of devitalized tissue from wound(s), non-selective debridement, without anesthesia (eg, wet-to-moist dressings, enzymatic, abrasion), including topical application(s), wound assessment, and instruction(s) for ongoing care, per session

97605 Negative pressure wound therapy (eg, vacuum assisted drainage collection), including topical application(s), wound assessment, and instruction(s) for ongoing care, per session; total wound(s) surface area less than or equal to 50 square centimeters

97606 total wound(s) surface area greater than 50 square centimeters

Tests and Measurements

Requires direct one-on-one patient contact.

(For muscle testing, manual or electrical, joint range of motion, electromyography or nerve velocity determination, see 95831-95904)

97750 Physical performance test or measurement (eg, musculoskeletal, functional capacity), with written report, each 15 minutes

97755 Assistive technology assessment (eg, to restore, augment or compensate for existing function, optimize functional tasks and/or maximize environmental accessibility), direct one-on-one contact by provider, with written report, each 15 minutes

(To report augmentative and alternative communication devices, see 92605, 92607)

Orthotic Management and Prosthetic Management

97760 Orthotic(s) management and training (including assessment and fitting when not otherwise reported), upper extremity(s), lower extremity(s) and/or trunk, each 15 minutes

(Code 97760 should not be reported with 97116 for the same extremity)

97761 Prosthetic training, upper and/or lower extremity(s), each 15 minutes

97762 Checkout for orthotic/prosthetic use, established patient, each 15 minutes

Other Procedures

(For extracorporeal shock wave musculoskeletal therapy, see Category III codes 0019T, 0101T, 0102T)

97799 Unlisted physical medicine/rehabilitation service or procedure

Medical Nutrition Therapy

97802 Medical nutrition therapy; initial assessment and intervention, individual, face-to-face with the patient, each 15 minutes

97803 re-assessment and intervention, individual, face-to-face with the patient, each 15 minutes

97804 group (2 or more individual(s)), each 30 minutes

(For medical nutrition therapy assessment and/or intervention performed by a physician, see **Evaluation and Management** or **Preventive Medicine** service codes)

Acupuncture

Acupuncture is reported based on 15-minute increments of personal (face-to-face) contact with the patient, not the duration of acupuncture needle(s) placement.

If no electrical stimulation is used during a 15-minute increment, use 97810, 97811. If electrical stimulation of any needle is used during a 15-minute increment, use 97813, 97814.

Only one code may be reported for each 15-minute increment. Use either 97810 or 97813 for the initial 15-minute increment. Only one initial code is reported per day.

Evaluation and Management services may be reported separately, using modifier 25, if the patient's condition requires a significant separately identifiable E/M service, above and beyond the usual preservice and postservice work associated with the acupuncture services. The time of the E/M service is not included in the time of the acupuncture service.

97810 Acupuncture, 1 or more needles; without electrical stimulation, initial 15 minutes of personal one-on-one contact with the patient

(Do not report 97810 in conjunction with 97813)

+ 97811 without electrical stimulation, each additional 15 minutes of personal one-on-one contact with the patient, with re-insertion of needle(s) (List separately in addition to code for primary procedure)

(Use 97811 in conjunction with 97810, 97813)

97813 with electrical stimulation, initial 15 minutes of personal one-on-one contact with the patient

(Do not report 97813 in conjunction with 97810)

+ 97814 with electrical stimulation, each additional 15 minutes of personal one-on-one contact with the patient, with re-insertion of needle(s) (List separately in addition to code for primary procedure)

(Use 97814 in conjunction with 97810, 97813)

Osteopathic Manipulative Treatment

Osteopathic manipulative treatment (OMT) is a form of manual treatment applied by a physician to eliminate or alleviate somatic dysfunction and related disorders. This treatment may be accomplished by a variety of techniques.

Evaluation and Management services may be reported separately if, using modifier 25, the patient's condition requires a significant separately identifiable E/M service, above and beyond the usual preservice and postservice work associated with the procedure. The E/M service may be caused or prompted by the same symptoms or condition for which the OMT service was provided. As such, different diagnoses are not required for the reporting of the OMT and E/M service on the same date.

Body regions referred to are: head region; cervical region; thoracic region; lumbar region; sacral region; pelvic region; lower extremities; upper extremities; rib cage region; abdomen and viscera region.

98925 Osteopathic manipulative treatment (OMT); 1-2 body regions involved

98926 3-4 body regions involved

98927 5-6 body regions involved

98928 7-8 body regions involved

98929 9-10 body regions involved

Chiropractic Manipulative Treatment

Chiropractic manipulative treatment (CMT) is a form of manual treatment to influence joint and neurophysiological function. This treatment may be accomplished using a variety of techniques.

The chiropractic manipulative treatment codes include a pre-manipulation patient assessment. Additional Evaluation and Management services may be reported separately using modifier 25, if the patient's condition requires a significant separately identifiable E/M service, above and beyond the usual preservice and postservice work associated with the procedure. The E/M service may be caused or prompted by the same symptoms or condition for which the CMT service was provided. As such, different diagnoses are not required for the reporting of the CMT and E/M service on the same date.

For purposes of CMT, the five spinal regions referred to are: cervical region (includes atlanto-occipital joint); thoracic region (includes costovertebral and costotransverse joints); lumbar region; sacral region; and pelvic (sacro-iliac joint) region. The five extraspinal regions referred to are: head (including temporomandibular joint, excluding atlanto-occipital) region; lower extremities; upper extremities; rib cage (excluding costotransverse and costovertebral joints) and abdomen.

98940 Chiropractic manipulative treatment (CMT); spinal, 1-2 regions

98941 spinal, 3-4 regions

98942 spinal, 5 regions

98943 extraspinal, 1 or more regions

Education and Training for Patient Self-Management

The following codes are used to report educational and training services prescribed by a physician and provided by a qualified, nonphysician healthcare professional using a standardized curriculum to an individual or a group of patients for the treatment of established illness(s)/disease(s) or to delay comorbidity(s). Education and training for patient self-management may be reported with these codes only when using a standardized curriculum as described below. This curriculum may be modified as necessary for the clinical needs, cultural norms and health literacy of the individual patient(s).

The purpose of the educational and training services is to teach the patient (may include caregiver[s]) how to effectively self-manage the patient's illness(s)/disease(s) or delay disease comorbidity(s) in conjunction with the patient's professional healthcare team. Education and training related to subsequent reinforcement or due to changes in the patient's condition or treatment plan are reported in the same manner as the original education and training. The type of education and training provided for the patient's clinical condition will be identified by the appropriate diagnosis code(s) reported.

The qualifications of the nonphysician healthcare professionals and the content of the educational and training program must be consistent with guidelines or standards established or recognized by a physician society, nonphysician healthcare professional society/association, or other appropriate source.

(For counseling and education provided by a physician to an individual, see the appropriate Evaluation and Management codes)

(For counseling and education provided by a physician to a group, use 99078)

(For counseling and/or risk factor reduction intervention provided by a physician to patient(s) without symptoms or established disease, see 99401-99412)

(For medical nutrition therapy, see 97802-97804)

(For health and behavior assessment/intervention that is not part of a standardized curriculum, see 96150-96155)

(For education provided as genetic counseling services, use 96040. For education to a group regarding genetic risks, see 98961, 98962)

98960 Education and training for patient self-management by a qualified, nonphysician health care professional using a standardized curriculum, face-to-face with the patient (could include caregiver/family) each 30 minutes; individual patient

98961 2-4 patients

98962 5-8 patients

Non-Face-to-Face Nonphysician Services

Telephone Services

Telephone services are non-face-to-face assessment and management services provided by a qualified health care professional to a patient using the telephone. These codes are used to report episodes of care by the qualified health care professional initiated by an established patient or guardian of an established patient. If the telephone service ends with a decision to see the patient within 24 hours or the next available urgent visit appointment, the code is not reported; rather the encounter is considered part of the preservice work of the subsequent assessment and management service, procedure and visit. Likewise, if the telephone call refers to a service performed and reported by the qualified health care professional within the previous seven days (either qualified health care professional requested or unsolicited patient follow-up) or within the postoperative period of the previously completed procedure, then the service(s) are considered part of that previous service or procedure. (Do not report 98966-98969 if reporting 98966-98969 performed in the previous seven days.)

(For telephone services provided by a physician, see 99441-99443)

98966 Telephone assessment and management service provided by a qualified nonphysician health care professional to an established patient, parent, or guardian not originating from a related assessment and management service provided within the previous 7 days nor leading to an assessment and management service or procedure within the next 24 hours or soonest available appointment; 5-10 minutes of medical discussion

98967 11-20 minutes of medical discussion

98968 21-30 minutes of medical discussion

On-line Medical Evaluation

An on-line electronic medical evaluation is a non-face-to-face assessment and management service by a qualified health care professional to a patient using Internet resources in response to a patient's on-line inquiry. Reportable services involve the qualified health care professional's personal timely response to the patient's inquiry and must involve permanent storage (electronic or hard copy) of the encounter. This service is reported only once for the same episode of care during a seven-day period, although multiple qualified healthcare professionals could report their exchange with the same patient. If the on-line medical evaluation refers to an assessment and management service previously performed and reported by the qualified health care professional within the previous seven days (either qualified health care professional requested or unsolicited patient follow-up) or within the postoperative period of the previously completed procedure, then the service(s) are considered covered by the previous assessment and management office service or procedure. A reportable service encompasses the sum of communication (eg, related telephone calls, prescription provision, laboratory orders) pertaining to the on-line patient encounter.

(For an on-line medical evaluation provided by a physician, use 99444)

98969 Online assessment and management service provided by a qualified nonphysician health care professional to an established patient, guardian, or health care provider not originating from a related assessment and management service provided within the previous 7 days, using the Internet or similar electronic communications network

(Do not report 98969 when using 99339-99340, 99374-99380 for the same communication[s])

(Do not report 98969 for anticoagulation management when reporting 99363, 99364)

Special Services, Procedures and Reports

The procedures with code numbers 99000 through 99091 provide the reporting physician or other qualified healthcare professional with the means of identifying the completion of special reports and services that are an adjunct to the basic services rendered. The specific number assigned indicates the special circumstances under which a basic procedure is performed.

Code 99091 should be reported no more than once in a 30-day period to include the physician or health care provider time involved with data accession, review and interpretation, modification of care plan as necessary (including communication to patient and/or caregiver), and associated documentation.

If the services described by 99091 are provided on the same day the patient presents for an E/M service, these services should be considered part of the E/M service and not separately reported.

Do not report 99091 if it occurs within 30 days of care plan oversight services 99374-99380. Do not report 99091 if other more specific CPT codes exist (eg, 93014, 93227, 93233, 93272 for cardiographic services; 95250 for continuous glucose monitoring). Do not report 99091 for transfer and interpretation of data from hospital or clinical laboratory computers.

Codes 99050-99060 are reported in addition to an associated basic service. Typically only a single adjunct code from among 99050-99060 would be reported per patient encounter. However, there may be circumstances in which reporting multiple adjunct codes per patient encounter may be appropriate.

Miscellaneous Services

99000 Handling and/or conveyance of specimen for transfer from the physician's office to a laboratory

99001 Handling and/or conveyance of specimen for transfer from the patient in other than a physician's office to a laboratory (distance may be indicated)

99002 Handling, conveyance, and/or any other service in connection with the implementation of an order involving devices (eg, designing, fitting, packaging, handling, delivery or mailing) when devices such as orthotics, protectives, prosthetics are fabricated by an outside laboratory or shop but which items have been designed, and are to be fitted and adjusted by the attending physician

(For routine collection of venous blood, use 36415)

99024 Postoperative follow-up visit, normally included in the surgical package, to indicate that an evaluation and management service was performed during a postoperative period for a reason(s) related to the original procedure

(As a component of a surgical "package," see **Surgery Guidelines**)

99026 Hospital mandated on call service; in-hospital, each hour

99027 out-of-hospital, each hour

(For physician standby services requiring prolonged physician attendance, use 99360, as appropriate. Time spent performing separately reportable procedure(s) or service(s) should not be included in the time reported as mandated on call service)

99050 Services provided in the office at times other than regularly scheduled office hours, or days when the office is normally closed (eg, holidays, Saturday or Sunday), in addition to basic service

99051 Service(s) provided in the office during regularly scheduled evening, weekend, or holiday office hours, in addition to basic service

99053 Service(s) provided between 10:00 PM and 8:00 AM at 24-hour facility, in addition to basic service

99056 Service(s) typically provided in the office, provided out of the office at request of patient, in addition to basic service

99058 Service(s) provided on an emergency basis in the office, which disrupts other scheduled office services, in addition to basic service

99060 Service(s) provided on an emergency basis, out of the office, which disrupts other scheduled office services, in addition to basic service

Medicine

99070 Supplies and materials (except spectacles), provided by the physician over and above those usually included with the office visit or other services rendered (list drugs, trays, supplies, or materials provided)

(For supply of spectacles, use the appropriate supply codes)

99071 Educational supplies, such as books, tapes, and pamphlets, provided by the physician for the patient's education at cost to physician

99075 Medical testimony

99078 Physician educational services rendered to patients in a group setting (eg, prenatal, obesity, or diabetic instructions)

99080 Special reports such as insurance forms, more than the information conveyed in the usual medical communications or standard reporting form

(Do not report 99080 in conjunction with 99455, 99456 for the completion of Workmen's Compensation forms)

99082 Unusual travel (eg, transportation and escort of patient)

99090 Analysis of clinical data stored in computers (eg, ECGs, blood pressures, hematologic data)

(For physician/health care professional collection and interpretation of physiologic data stored/transmitted by patient/caregiver, see 99091)

(Do not report 99090 if other more specific CPT codes exist, eg, 93227, 93233, 93272 for cardiographic services; 95250 for continuous glucose monitoring, 97750 for musculoskeletal function testing)

99091 Collection and interpretation of physiologic data (eg, ECG, blood pressure, glucose monitoring) digitally stored and/or transmitted by the patient and/or caregiver to the physician or other qualified health care professional, requiring a minimum of 30 minutes of time

Qualifying Circumstances for Anesthesia

(For explanation of these services, see **Anesthesia Guidelines**)

+ 99100 Anesthesia for patient of extreme age, younger than 1 year and older than 70 (List separately in addition to code for primary anesthesia procedure)

(For procedure performed on infants younger than 1 year of age at time of surgery, see 00326, 00561, 00834, 00836)

+ 99116 Anesthesia complicated by utilization of total body hypothermia (List separately in addition to code for primary anesthesia procedure)

+ 99135 Anesthesia complicated by utilization of controlled hypotension (List separately in addition to code for primary anesthesia procedure)

+ 99140 Anesthesia complicated by emergency conditions (specify) (List separately in addition to code for primary anesthesia procedure)

(An emergency is defined as existing when delay in treatment of the patient would lead to a significant increase in the threat to life or body part.)

Moderate (Conscious) Sedation

Moderate (conscious) sedation is a drug induced depression of consciousness during which patients respond purposefully to verbal commands, either alone or accompanied by light tactile stimulation. No interventions are required to maintain a patent airway, and spontaneous ventilation is adequate. Cardiovascular function is usually maintained.

Moderate sedation does not include minimal sedation (anxiolysis), deep sedation or monitored anesthesia care (00100-01999).

When providing moderate sedation, the following services are included and NOT reported separately:

- Assessment of the patient (not included in intraservice time);
- Establishment of IV access and fluids to maintain patency, when performed;
- Administration of agent(s);
- Maintenance of sedation;
- Monitoring of oxygen saturation, heart rate and blood pressure; and
- Recovery (not included in intraservice time).

Intraservice time starts with the administration of the sedation agent(s), requires continuous face-to-face attendance, and ends at the conclusion of personal contact by the physician providing the sedation.

Do not report 99143-99150 in conjunction with 94760-94762.

Do not report 99143-99145 in conjunction with codes listed in Appendix G. Do not report 99148-99150 in conjunction with codes listed in Appendix G when performed in the nonfacility setting.

When a second physician other than the healthcare professional performing the diagnostic or therapeutic services provides moderate sedation in the facility setting (eg, hospital, outpatient hospital/ambulatory surgery center, skilled nursing facility) for the procedures listed in

Appendix G, the second physician reports 99148-99150. However, for the circumstance in which these services are performed by the second physician in the nonfacility setting (eg, physician office, freestanding imaging center), codes 99148-99150 are not reported.

⊘ **99143** Moderate sedation services (other than those services described by codes 00100-01999) provided by the same physician performing the diagnostic or therapeutic service that the sedation supports, requiring the presence of an independent trained observer to assist in the monitoring of the patient's level of consciousness and physiological status; younger than 5 years of age, first 30 minutes intra-service time

⊘ **99144** age 5 years or older, first 30 minutes intra-service time

✚ **99145** each additional 15 minutes intra-service time (List separately in addition to code for primary service)

(Use 99145 in conjunction with 99143, 99144)

99148 Moderate sedation services (other than those services described by codes 00100-01999), provided by a physician other than the health care professional performing the diagnostic or therapeutic service that the sedation supports; younger than 5 years of age, first 30 minutes intra-service time

99149 age 5 years or older, first 30 minutes intra-service time

✚ **99150** each additional 15 minutes intra-service time (List separately in addition to code for primary service)

(Use 99150 in conjunction with 99148, 99149)

Other Services and Procedures

99170 Anogenital examination with colposcopic magnification in childhood for suspected trauma

(For conscious sedation, use 99143-99150)

99172 Visual function screening, automated or semi-automated bilateral quantitative determination of visual acuity, ocular alignment, color vision by pseudoisochromatic plates, and field of vision (may include all or some screening of the determination[s] for contrast sensitivity, vision under glare)

(This service must employ graduated visual acuity stimuli that allow a quantitative determination of visual acuity [eg, Snellen chart]. This service may not be used in addition to a general ophthalmological service or an E/M service)

(Do not report 99172 in conjunction with 99173)

99173 Screening test of visual acuity, quantitative, bilateral

(The screening test used must employ graduated visual acuity stimuli that allow a quantitative estimate of visual acuity [eg, Snellen chart]. Other identifiable services unrelated to this screening test provided at the same time may be reported separately [eg, preventive medicine services]. When acuity is measured as part of a general ophthalmological service or of an E/M service of the eye, it is a diagnostic examination and not a screening test.)

(Do not report 99173 in conjunction with 99172)

99174 Ocular photoscreening with interpretation and report, bilateral

(Do not report 99174 in conjunction with 92002-92014, 99172, 99173)

99175 Ipecac or similar administration for individual emesis and continued observation until stomach adequately emptied of poison

(For diagnostic intubation, see 82926-82928, 89130-89141)

(For gastric lavage for diagnostic purposes, see 91055)

99183 Physician attendance and supervision of hyperbaric oxygen therapy, per session

(Evaluation and Management services and/or procedures [eg, wound debridement] provided in a hyperbaric oxygen treatment facility in conjunction with a hyperbaric oxygen therapy session should be reported separately)

99185 Hypothermia; regional

99186 total body

99190 Assembly and operation of pump with oxygenator or heat exchanger (with or without ECG and/or pressure monitoring); each hour

99191 45 minutes

99192 30 minutes

99195 Phlebotomy, therapeutic (separate procedure)

99199 Unlisted special service, procedure or report

Home Health Procedures/Services

These codes are used by non-physician health care professionals. Physicians should utilize the home visit codes 99341-99350 and utilize CPT codes other than 99500-99600 for any additional procedure/service provided to a patient living in a residence.

The following codes are used to report services provided in a patient's residence (including assisted living apartments, group homes, nontraditional private homes, custodial care facilities, or schools).

Health care professionals who are authorized to use Evaluation and Management (E/M) Home Visit codes (99341-99350) may report 99500-99600 in addition to 99341-99350 if both services are performed. E/M services may be reported separately, using modifier 25, if the patient's condition requires a significant separately identifiable E/M service, above and beyond the home health service(s)/procedure(s) codes 99500-99600.

99500 Home visit for prenatal monitoring and assessment to include fetal heart rate, non-stress test, uterine monitoring, and gestational diabetes monitoring

99501 Home visit for postnatal assessment and follow-up care

99502 Home visit for newborn care and assessment

99503 Home visit for respiratory therapy care (eg, bronchodilator, oxygen therapy, respiratory assessment, apnea evaluation)

99504 Home visit for mechanical ventilation care

99505 Home visit for stoma care and maintenance including colostomy and cystostomy

99506 Home visit for intramuscular injections

99507 Home visit for care and maintenance of catheter(s) (eg, urinary, drainage, and enteral)

99509 Home visit for assistance with activities of daily living and personal care

(To report self-care/home management training, see 97535)

(To report home medical nutrition assessment and intervention services, see 97802-97804)

(To report home speech therapy services, see 92507-92508)

99510 Home visit for individual, family, or marriage counseling

99511 Home visit for fecal impaction management and enema administration

99512 Home visit for hemodialysis

(For home infusion of peritoneal dialysis, use 99601, 99602)

99600 Unlisted home visit service or procedure

Home Infusion Procedures/Services

99601 Home infusion/specialty drug administration, per visit (up to 2 hours);

+ 99602 each additional hour (List separately in addition to code for primary procedure)

(Use 99602 in conjunction with 99601)

Medication Therapy Management Services

Medication therapy management service(s) (MTMS) describe face-to-face patient assessment and intervention as appropriate, by a pharmacist, upon request. MTMS is provided to optimize the response to medications or to manage treatment-related medication interactions or complications.

MTMS includes the following documented elements: review of the pertinent patient history, medication profile (prescription and nonprescription), and recommendations for improving health outcomes and treatment compliance. These codes are not to be used to describe the provision of product-specific information at the point of dispensing or any other routine dispensing-related activities.

99605 Medication therapy management service(s) provided by a pharmacist, individual, face-to-face with patient, with assessment and intervention if provided; initial 15 minutes, new patient

99606 initial 15 minutes, established patient

+ 99607 each additional 15 minutes (List separately in addition to code for primary service)

(Use 99607 in conjunction with 99605, 99606)

Notes

Medicine

Category II Codes

The following section of *Current Procedural Terminology* (CPT) contains a set of supplemental tracking codes that can be used for performance measurement. It is anticipated that the use of Category II codes for performance measurement will decrease the need for record abstraction and chart review, and thereby minimize administrative burden on physicians, other health care professionals, hospitals, and entities seeking to measure the quality of patient care. These codes are intended to facilitate data collection about the quality of care rendered by coding certain services and test results that support nationally established performance measures and that have an evidence base as contributing to quality patient care.

The use of these codes is optional. The codes are not required for correct coding and may not be used as a substitute for Category I codes.

These codes describe clinical components that may be typically included in evaluation and management services or clinical services and, therefore, do not have a relative value associated with them. Category II codes may also describe results from clinical laboratory or radiology tests and other procedures, identified processes intended to address patient safety practices, or services reflecting compliance with state or federal law.

Category II codes described in this section make use of alphabetical characters as the 5th character in the string (ie, 4 digits followed by the letter **F**). These digits are not intended to reflect the placement of the code in the regular (Category I) part of the CPT codebook. To promote understanding of these codes and their associated measures, users are referred to Appendix H, which contains information about performance measurement exclusion modifiers, measures, and the measure's source.

CPT Category II codes are arranged according to the following categories derived from standard clinical documentation format:

Composite Measures 0001F-0015F

Patient Management 0500F-0526F

Patient History.................. 1000F-1137F

Physical Examination.............. 2000F-2044F

Diagnostic/Screening Processes or Results....................... 3006F-3354F

Therapeutic, Preventive or Other Interventions 4000F-4250F

Follow-up or Other Outcomes 5005F-5062F

Patient Safety 6005F-6045F

►Structural Measures .... 7010F-7025F◄

Cross-references to the measures associated with each Category II code and their source are included for reference in Appendix H. In addition, acronyms for the related diseases or clinical condition(s) have been added at the end of each code descriptor to identify the topic or clinical category in which that code is included. A complete listing of the diseases/clinical conditions, and their acronyms are provided in alphabetical order in Appendix H. Users should review the complete measure(s) associated with each code prior to implementation.

Category II codes are reviewed by the Performance Measures Advisory Group (PMAG), an advisory body to the CPT Editorial Panel and the CPT/HCPAC Advisory Committee. The PMAG is comprised of performance measurement experts representing the Agency for Healthcare Research and Quality (AHRQ), the American Medical Association (AMA), the Centers for Medicare and Medicaid Services (CMS), the Joint Commission on Accreditation of Healthcare Organizations (JCAHO), the National Committee for Quality Assurance (NCQA), and the Physician Consortium for Performance Improvement (PCPI). The PMAG may seek additional expertise and/or input from other national health care organizations, as necessary, for the development of tracking codes. These may include national medical specialty societies, other national health care professional associations, accrediting bodies, and federal regulatory agencies.

The most current listing of Category II codes, including guidelines, Code Change Proposal forms, and release and implementation dates for Category II codes may be accessed at http://www.ama-assn.org/go/cpt.

(For blood pressure measured, use 2000F)

(0003F has been deleted. To report, see 1034F-1036F)

(For tobacco use cessation intervention, pharmacologic therapy, use 4001F)

Modifiers

The following performance measurement modifiers may be used for Category II codes to indicate that a service specified in the associated measure(s) was considered but, due to either medical, patient, or system circumstance(s) documented in the medical record, the service was not provided. These modifiers serve as denominator exclusions from the performance measure. The user should note that not all listed measures provide for exclusions (see Appendix H for more discussion regarding exclusion criteria).

Category II modifiers should only be reported with Category II codes—they should not be reported with Category I or Category III codes. In addition, the modifiers in the Category II section should only be used where specified in the guidelines, reporting instructions, parenthetic notes, or code descriptor language listed in the Category II section (code listing and Appendix H).

1P Performance Measure Exclusion Modifier due to Medical Reasons

Reasons include:

- Not indicated (absence of organ/limb, already received/performed, other)
- Contraindicated (patient allergic history, potential adverse drug interaction, other)

Other medical reasons

2P Performance Measure Exclusion Modifier due to Patient Reasons

Reasons include:

- Patient declined
- Economic, social, or religious reasons
- Other patient reasons

3P Performance Measure Exclusion Modifier due to System Reasons

Reasons include:

- Resources to perform the services not available
- Insurance coverage/payor-related limitations
- Other reasons attributable to health care delivery system

Modifier 8P is intended to be used as a "reporting modifier" to allow the reporting of circumstances when an action described in a measure's numerator is not performed and the reason is not otherwise specified.

8P Performance measure reporting modifier — action not performed, reason not otherwise specified

Composite Codes

Composite codes combine several measures grouped within a single code descriptor to facilitate reporting for a clinical condition when all components are met. If only some of the components are met or if services are provided in addition to those included in the composite code, they may be reported individually using the corresponding CPT Category II codes for those services.

0001F Heart failure assessed (includes assessment of all the following components) (CAD, HF)[1]:

Blood pressure measured (2000F)[1]

Level of activity assessed (1003F)[1]

Clinical symptoms of volume overload (excess) assessed (1004F)[1]

Weight, recorded (2001F)[1]

Clinical signs of volume overload (excess) assessed (2002F)[1]

(To report blood pressure measured, use 2000F)

0005F Osteoarthritis assessed (OA)[1]

Includes assessment of all the following components:

Osteoarthritis symptoms and functional status assessed (1006F)[1]

Use of anti-inflammatory or over-the-counter (OTC) analgesic medications assessed (1007F)[1]

Initial examination of the involved joint(s) (includes visual inspection, palpation, range of motion) (2004F)[1]

(To report tobacco use cessation intervention, use 4001F)

0012F Community-acquired bacterial pneumonia assessment (includes all of the following components) (CAP)[1]:

Co-morbid conditions assessed (1026F)[1]

Vital signs recorded (2010F)[1]

Mental status assessed (2014F)[1]

Hydration status assessed (2018F)[1]

Footnotes

[1] Physician Consortium for Performance Improvement® (PCPI), www.physicianconsortium.org

[2] National Committee on Quality Assurance (NCQA), Health Employer Data Information Set (HEDIS®), www.ncqa.org

[3] Joint Commission on Accreditation of Healthcare Organizations (JCAHO), ORYX Initiative Performance Measures, www.jcaho.org/pms

[4] National Diabetes Quality Improvement Alliance (NDQIA), www.nationaldiabetesalliance.org

[5] Joint measure from the Physician Consortium for Performance Improvement, www.physicianconsortium.org and National Committee on Quality Assurance (NCQA), www.ncqa.org

[6] The Society of Thoracic Surgeons, www.sts.org, National Quality Forum, www.qualityforum.org

● **0014F** Comprehensive preoperative assessment performed for cataract surgery with intraocular lens (IOL) placement (includes assessment of all of the following components) (EC)[5]:

Dilated fundus evaluation performed within 12 months prior to cataract surgery (2020F)[5]

Pre-surgical (cataract) axial length, corneal power measurement and method of intraocular lens power calculation documented (must be performed within 12 months prior to surgery) (3073F)[5]

Preoperative assessment of functional or medical indication(s) for surgery prior to the cataract surgery with intraocular lens placement (must be performed within 12 months prior to cataract surgery) (3325F)[5]

● **0015F** Melanoma follow up completed (includes assessment of all of the following components) (ML)[5]:

History obtained regarding new or changing moles (1050F)[5]

Complete physical skin exam performed (2029F)[5]

Patient counseled to perform a monthly self skin examination (5005F)[5]

Patient Management

Patient management codes describe utilization measures or measures of patient care provided for specific clinical purposes (eg, prenatal care, pre- and post-surgical care).

0500F Initial prenatal care visit (report at first prenatal encounter with health care professional providing obstetrical care. Report also date of visit and, in a separate field, the date of the last menstrual period - LMP) (Prenatal)[2]

0501F Prenatal flow sheet documented in medical record by first prenatal visit (documentation includes at minimum blood pressure, weight, urine protein, uterine size, fetal heart tones, and estimated date of delivery). Report also: date of visit and, in a separate field, the date of the last menstrual period - LMP (Note: If reporting 0501F Prenatal flow sheet, it is not necessary to report 0500F Initial prenatal care visit) (Prenatal)[1]

0502F Subsequent prenatal care visit (Prenatal)[2]

[Excludes: patients who are seen for a condition unrelated to pregnancy or prenatal care (eg, an upper respiratory infection; patients seen for consultation only, not for continuing care)]

0503F Postpartum care visit (Prenatal)[2]

0505F Hemodialysis plan of care documented (ESRD)[1]

0507F Peritoneal dialysis plan of care documented (ESRD)[1]

0509F Urinary incontinence plan of care documented (GER)[5]

● **0513F** Elevated blood pressure plan of care documented (CKD)[1]

● **0514F** Plan of care for elevated hemoglobin level documented for patient receiving Erythropoiesis-Stimulating Agent therapy (ESA) (CKD)[1]

● **0516F** Anemia plan of care documented (ESRD)[1]

● **0517F** Glaucoma plan of care documented (EC)[5]

● **0518F** Falls plan of care documented (GER)[5]

● **0519F** Planned chemotherapy regimen, including at a minimum: drug(s) prescribed, dose, and duration, documented prior to initiation of course of treatment (ONC)[1]

● **0520F** Normal tissue dose constraints established within 5 treatment days from the initiation of a course of 3D conformal radiation for a minimum of one tissue/organ (ONC)[1]

● **0521F** Plan of care to address pain documented (ONC)[1]

● **0525F** Initial visit for episode (BkP)[2]

● **0526F** Subsequent visit for episode (BkP)[2]

Patient History

Patient history codes describe measures for select aspects of patient history or review of systems.

1000F Tobacco use assessed (CAD, CAP, COPD, PV)[1] (DM)[4]

(1001F has been deleted. To report smoking use, tobacco use, or non-use of tobacco products, see 1034F-1036F)

1002F Anginal symptoms and level of activity assessed (CAD)[1]

Footnotes

[1] Physician Consortium for Performance Improvement® (PCPI), www.physicianconsortium.org

[2] National Committee on Quality Assurance (NCQA), Health Employer Data Information Set (HEDIS®), www.ncqa.org

[3] Joint Commission on Accreditation of Healthcare Organizations (JCAHO), ORYX Initiative Performance Measures, www.jcaho.org/pms

[4] National Diabetes Quality Improvement Alliance (NDQIA), www.nationaldiabetesalliance.org

[5] Joint measure from the Physician Consortium for Performance Improvement, www.physicianconsortium.org and National Committee on Quality Assurance (NCQA), www.ncqa.org

[6] The Society of Thoracic Surgeons, www.sts.org, National Quality Forum, www.qualityforum.org

1003F Level of activity assessed (HF)[1]

1004F Clinical symptoms of volume overload (excess) assessed (HF)[1]

1005F Asthma symptoms evaluated (includes physician documentation of numeric frequency of symptoms or patient completion of an asthma assessment tool/survey/questionnaire) (Asthma)[1]

1006F Osteoarthritis symptoms and functional status assessed (may include the use of a standardized scale or the completion of an assessment questionnaire, such as the SF-36, AAOS Hip & Knee Questionnaire) (OA)[1]

[Instructions: Report when osteoarthritis is addressed during the patient encounter]

1007F Use of anti-inflammatory or analgesic over-the-counter (OTC) medications for symptom relief assessed (OA)[1]

1008F Gastrointestinal and renal risk factors assessed for patients on prescribed or OTC non-steroidal anti-inflammatory drug (NSAID) (OA)[1]

1015F Chronic obstructive pulmonary disease (COPD) symptoms assessed (Includes assessment of at least 1 of the following: dyspnea, cough/sputum, wheezing), or respiratory symptom assessment tool completed (COPD)[1]

1018F Dyspnea assessed, not present (COPD)[1]

1019F Dyspnea assessed, present (COPD)[1]

1022F Pneumococcus immunization status assessed (CAP, COPD)[1]

1026F Co-morbid conditions assessed (eg, includes assessment for presence or absence of: malignancy, liver disease, congestive heart failure, cerebrovascular disease, renal disease, chronic obstructive pulmonary disease, asthma, diabetes, other co-morbid conditions) (CAP)[1]

1030F Influenza immunization status assessed (CAP)[1]

1034F Current tobacco smoker (CAD, CAP, COPD, PV)[1] (DM)[4]

1035F Current smokeless tobacco user (eg, chew, snuff) (PV)[1]

1036F Current tobacco non-user (CAD, CAP, COPD, PV)[1] (DM)[4]

1038F Persistent asthma (mild, moderate or severe) (Asthma)[1]

1039F Intermittent asthma (Asthma)[1]

▲ **1040F** DSM-IV™ criteria for major depressive disorder documented at the initial evaluation (MDD)[1]

1050F History obtained regarding new or changing moles (ML)[5]

1055F Visual functional status assessed (EC)[5]

1060F Documentation of permanent OR persistent OR paroxysmal atrial fibrillation (STR)[5]

1061F Documentation of absence of permanent AND persistent AND paroxysmal atrial fibrillation (STR)[5]

1065F Ischemic stroke symptom onset of less than 3 hours prior to arrival (STR)[5]

1066F Ischemic stroke symptom onset greater than or equal to 3 hours prior to arrival (STR)[5]

1070F Alarm symptoms (involuntary weight loss, dysphagia, or gastrointestinal bleeding) assessed; none present (GERD)[5]

1071F 1 or more present (GERD)[5]

►(1080F has been deleted. To report surrogate decision maker or advance care plan documented in the medical record, report 1123F or 1124F)◄

1090F Presence or absence of urinary incontinence assessed (GER)[5]

1091F Urinary incontinence characterized (eg frequency, volume, timing, type of symptoms, how bothersome) (GER)[5]

1100F Patient screened for future fall risk; documentation of 2 or more falls in the past year or any fall with injury in the past year (GER)[5]

1101F documentation of no falls in the past year or only 1 fall without injury in the past year (GER)[5]

1110F Patient discharged from an inpatient facility (eg hospital, skilled nursing facility, or rehabilitation facility) within the last 60 days (GER)[5]

1111F Discharge medications reconciled with the current medication list in outpatient medical record (GER)[5]

● **1116F** Auricular or periauricular pain assessed (AOE)[1]

● **1118F** GERD symptoms assessed after 12 months of therapy (GERD)[5]

● **1119F** Initial evaluation for condition (HEP C)[1]

● **1121F** Subsequent evaluation for condition (HEP C)[1]

Footnotes

[1] Physician Consortium for Performance Improvement® (PCPI), www.physicianconsortium.org

[2] National Committee on Quality Assurance (NCQA), Health Employer Data Information Set (HEDIS®), www.ncqa.org

[3] Joint Commission on Accreditation of Healthcare Organizations (JCAHO), ORYX Initiative Performance Measures, www.jcaho.org/pms

[4] National Diabetes Quality Improvement Alliance (NDQIA), www .nationaldiabetesalliance.org

[5] Joint measure from the Physician Consortium for Performance Improvement, www.physicianconsortium.org and National Committee on Quality Assurance (NCQA), www.ncqa.org

[6] The Society of Thoracic Surgeons, www.sts.org, National Quality Forum, www.qualityforum.org

● **1123F** Advance care planning discussed and documented advance care plan or surrogate decision maker documented in the medical record (GER)[5]

● **1124F** Advance care planning discussed and documented in the medical record patient did not wish or was not able to name a surrogate decision maker or provide an advance care plan (GER)[5]

● **1125F** Pain severity quantified; pain present (ONC)[1]

● **1126F** no pain present (ONC)[1]

● **1127F** New episode for condition (ML)[5]

● **1128F** Subsequent episode for condition (ML)[5]

● **1130F** Back pain and function assessed, including all of the following: Pain assessment AND functional status AND patient history, including notation of presence or absence of "red flags" (warning signs) AND assessment of prior treatment and response, AND employment status (BkP)[2]

● **1134F** Episode of back pain lasting 6 weeks or less (BkP)[2]

● **1135F** Episode of back pain lasting longer than 6 weeks (BkP)[2]

● **1136F** Episode of back pain lasting 12 weeks or less (BkP)[2]

● **1137F** Episode of back pain lasting longer than 12 weeks (BkP)[2]

Physical Examination

Physical examination codes describe aspects of physical examination or clinical assessment.

2000F Blood pressure measured (CAD, CKD, HF, HTN)[1](DM)[2,4]

2001F Weight recorded (HF, PAG)[1]

2002F Clinical signs of volume overload (excess) assessed (HF)[1]

(Code 2003F has been deleted. For performance measurement coding information regarding heart failure, see the Heart Failure Clinical Topic listing in Appendix H)

2004F Initial examination of the involved joint(s) (includes visual inspection, palpation, range of motion) (OA)[1]

[Instructions: Report only for initial osteoarthritis visit or for visits for new joint involvement]

2010F Vital signs (temperature, pulse, respiratory rate, and blood pressure) documented and reviewed (CAP)[1] (EM)[5]

2014F Mental status assessed (CAP)[1] (EM)[5]

2018F Hydration status assessed (normal/mildly dehydrated/severely dehydrated) (CAP)[1]

2019F Dilated macular exam performed, including documentation of the presence or absence of macular thickening or hemorrhage AND the level of macular degeneration severity (EC)[5]

▲ **2020F** Dilated fundus evaluation performed within 12 months prior to cataract surgery (EC)[5]

2021F Dilated macular or fundus exam performed, including documentation of the presence or absence of macular edema AND level of severity of retinopathy (EC)[5]

2022F Dilated retinal eye exam with interpretation by an ophthalmologist or optometrist documented and reviewed (DM)[2, 4]

2024F Seven standard field stereoscopic photos with interpretation by an ophthalmologist or optometrist documented and reviewed (DM)[2,4]

2026F Eye imaging validated to match diagnosis from 7 standard field stereoscopic photos results documented and reviewed (DM)[2,4]

2027F Optic nerve head evaluation performed (EC)[5]

2028F Foot examination performed (includes examination through visual inspection, sensory exam with monofilament, and pulse exam – report when any of the 3 components are completed) (DM)[4]

2029F Complete physical skin exam performed (ML)[5]

2030F Hydration status documented, normally hydrated (PAG)[1]

2031F Hydration status documented, dehydrated (PAG)[1]

● **2035F** Tympanic membrane mobility assessed with pneumatic otoscopy or tympanometry (OME)[1]

● **2040F** Physical examination on the date of the initial visit for low back pain performed, in accordance with specifications (BkP)[2]

● **2044F** Documentation of mental health assessment prior to intervention (back surgery or epidural steroid injection) or for back pain episode lasting longer than 6 weeks (BkP)[2]

Footnotes

[1] Physician Consortium for Performance Improvement® (PCPI), www.physicianconsortium.org

[2] National Committee on Quality Assurance (NCQA), Health Employer Data Information Set (HEDIS®), www.ncqa.org

[3] Joint Commission on Accreditation of Healthcare Organizations (JCAHO), ORYX Initiative Performance Measures, www.jcaho.org/pms

[4] National Diabetes Quality Improvement Alliance (NDQIA), www.nationaldiabetesalliance.org

[5] Joint measure from the Physician Consortium for Performance Improvement, www.physicianconsortium.org and National Committee on Quality Assurance (NCQA), www.ncqa.org

[6] The Society of Thoracic Surgeons, www.sts.org, National Quality Forum, www.qualityforum.org

Diagnostic/Screening Processes or Results

►Diagnostic/screening processes or results codes describe results of tests ordered (clinical laboratory tests, radiological or other procedural examinations, and conclusions of medical decision making).◄

(Code 3000F has been deleted. To report blood pressure use the corresponding systolic codes (3074F, 3075F, 3077F) and diastolic codes (3078F, 3079F, 3080F)

(Code 3002F has been deleted. To report blood pressure use the corresponding systolic codes (3074F, 3075F, 3077F) and diastolic codes (3078F, 3079F, 3080F)

3006F Chest X-ray results documented and reviewed (CAP)[1]

3011F Lipid panel results documented and reviewed (must include total cholesterol, HDL-C, triglycerides and calculated LDL-C) (CAD)[1]

3014F Screening mammography results documented and reviewed (PV)[1, 2]

▲ **3017F** Colorectal cancer screening results documented and reviewed (PV)[1, 2]

3020F Left ventricular function (LVF) assessment (eg, echocardiography, nuclear test, or ventriculography) documented in the medical record (Includes quantitative or qualitative assessment results) (HF)[1]

3021F Left ventricular ejection fraction (LVEF) less than 40% or documentation of moderately or severely depressed left ventricular systolic function (CAD, HF)[1]

3022F Left ventricular ejection fraction (LVEF) greater than or equal to 40% or documentation as normal or mildly depressed left ventricular systolic function (CAD, HF)[1]

3023F Spirometry results documented and reviewed (COPD)[1]

3025F Spirometry test results demonstrate FEV_1/FVC less than 70% with COPD symptoms (eg, dyspnea, cough/sputum, wheezing) (CAP, COPD)[1]

3027F Spirometry test results demonstrate FEV_1/FVC greater than or equal to 70% or patient does not have COPD symptoms (COPD)[1]

3028F Oxygen saturation results documented and reviewed (includes assessment through pulse oximetry or arterial blood gas measurement) (CAP, COPD)[1] (EM)[5]

3035F Oxygen saturation less than or equal to 88 % or a PaO_2 less than or equal to 55 mm Hg (COPD)[1].

3037F Oxygen saturation greater than 88% or PaO_2 greater than 55 mmHg (COPD)[1]

3040F Functional expiratory volume (FEV_1) less than 40% of predicted value (COPD)[1]

3042F Functional expiratory volume (FEV_1) greater than or equal to 40% of predicted value (COPD)[1]

3044F Most recent hemoglobin A1c (HbA1c) level less than 7.0% (DM)[2,4]

3045F Most recent hemoglobin A1c (HbA1c) level 7.0 – 9.0 % (DM)[2,4]

3046F Most recent hemoglobin A1c level greater than 9.0% (DM)[4]

(Code 3047F has been deleted. To report most recent hemoglobin A1c level less than or equal to 9.0%, see codes 3044F-3045F)

3048F Most recent LDL-C less than 100 mg/dL (DM)[4]

3049F Most recent LDL-C 100-129 mg/dL (DM)[4]

3050F Most recent LDL-C greater than or equal to 130 mg/dL (DM)[4]

3060F Positive microalbuminuria test result documented and reviewed (DM)[2,4]

3061F Negative microalbuminuria test result documented and reviewed (DM)[2, 4]

3062F Positive macroalbuminuria test result documented and reviewed (DM)[2,4]

3066F Documentation of treatment for nephropathy (eg, patient receiving dialysis, patient being treated for ESRD, CRF, ARF, or renal insufficiency, any visit to a nephrologist) (DM)[2,4]

3072F Low risk for retinopathy (no evidence of retinopathy in the prior year) (DM)[2,4]

▲ **3073F** Pre-surgical (cataract) axial length, corneal power measurement and method of intraocular lens power calculation documented within 12 months prior to surgery (EC)[5]

3074F Most recent systolic blood pressure less than 130 mm Hg (DM)[2,4] (HTN, CKD)[1]

Footnotes

[1] Physician Consortium for Performance Improvement® (PCPI), www.physicianconsortium.org

[2] National Committee on Quality Assurance (NCQA), Health Employer Data Information Set (HEDIS®), www.ncqa.org

[3] Joint Commission on Accreditation of Healthcare Organizations (JCAHO), ORYX Initiative Performance Measures, www.jcaho.org/pms

[4] National Diabetes Quality Improvement Alliance (NDQIA), www .nationaldiabetesalliance.org

[5] Joint measure from the Physician Consortium for Performance Improvement, www.physicianconsortium.org and National Committee on Quality Assurance (NCQA), www.ncqa.org

[6] The Society of Thoracic Surgeons, www.sts.org, National Quality Forum, www.qualityforum.org

3075F Most recent systolic blood pressure 130 - 139 mm Hg (DM)[2,4] (HTN, CKD)[1]

(Code 3076F has been deleted. To report most recent systolic blood pressure less than 140 mm Hg, see codes 3074F-3075F)

3077F Most recent systolic blood pressure greater than or equal to 140 mm Hg (HTN, CKD)[1] (DM)[2, 4]

3078F Most recent diastolic blood pressure less than 80 mm Hg (HTN, CKD)[1] (DM)[2, 4]

3079F Most recent diastolic blood pressure 80-89 mm Hg (HTN, CKD)[1] (DM)[2, 4]

3080F Most recent diastolic blood pressure greater than or equal to 90 mm Hg (HTN, CKD)[1] (DM)[2, 4]

3082F Kt/V less than 1.2 (Clearance of urea [Kt]/volume [V]) (ESRD)[1]

3083F Kt/V equal to or greater than 1.2 and less than 1.7 (Clearance of urea [Kt]/volume [V]) (ESRD)[1]

3084F Kt/V greater than or equal to 1.7 (Clearance of urea [Kt]/volume [V]) (ESRD)[1]

3085F Suicide risk assessed (MDD)[1]

3088F Major depressive disorder, mild (MDD)[1]

3089F Major depressive disorder, moderate (MDD)[1]

3090F Major depressive disorder, severe without psychotic features (MDD)[1]

3091F Major depressive disorder, severe with psychotic features (MDD)[1]

3092F Major depressive disorder, in remission (MDD)[1]

3093F Documentation of new diagnosis of initial or recurrent episode of major depressive disorder (MDD)[1]

3095F Central dual-energy x-ray absorptiometry (DXA) results documented (OP)[5]

3096F Central dual-energy x-ray absorptiometry (DXA) ordered (OP)[5]

3100F Carotid imaging study report (includes direct or indirect reference to measurements of distal internal carotid diameter as the denominator for stenosis measurement) (STR, RAD)[5]

(Code 3101F has been deleted)

(Code 3102F has been deleted)

3110F Presence or absence of hemorrhage and mass lesion and acute infarction documented in final CT or MRI report (STR)[5]

3111F CT or MRI of the brain performed within 24 hours of arrival to the hospital (STR)[5]

3112F CT or MRI of the brain performed greater than 24 hours after arrival to the hospital (STR)[5]

3120F 12-Lead ECG Performed (EM)[5]

3130F Upper gastrointestinal endoscopy performed (GERD)[5]

3132F Documentation of referral for upper gastrointestinal endoscopy (GERD)[5]

3140F Upper gastrointestinal endoscopy report indicates suspicion of Barrett's esophagus (GERD)[5]

3141F Upper gastrointestinal endoscopy report indicates no suspicion of Barrett's esophagus (GERD)[5]

3142F Barium swallow test ordered (GERD)[1]

(3143F has been deleted. To report documentation of barium swallow study, use code 3142F)

3150F Forceps esophageal biopsy performed (GERD)[5]

3155F Cytogenetic testing performed on bone marrow at time of diagnosis or prior to initiating treatment (HEM)[1]

3160F Documentation of iron stores prior to initiating erythropoietin therapy (HEM)[1]

3170F Flow cytometry studies performed at time of diagnosis or prior to initiating treatment (HEM)[1]

3200F Barium swallow test not ordered (GERD)[5]

3210F Group A Strep Test Performed (PHAR)[2]

● **3215F** Patient has documented immunity to Hepatitis A (HEP-C)[1]

● **3216F** Patient has documented immunity to Hepatitis B (HEP-C)[1]

►(3217F has been deleted)◄

● **3218F** RNA testing for Hepatitis C documented as performed within 6 months prior to initiation of antiviral treatment for Hepatitis C (HEP-C)[1]

►(3219F has been deleted)◄

● **3220F** Hepatitis C quantitative RNA testing documented as performed at 12 weeks from initiation of antiviral treatment (HEP-C)[1]

Footnotes

[1] Physician Consortium for Performance Improvement® (PCPI), www.physicianconsortium.org

[2] National Committee on Quality Assurance (NCQA), Health Employer Data Information Set (HEDIS®), www.ncqa.org

[3] Joint Commission on Accreditation of Healthcare Organizations (JCAHO), ORYX Initiative Performance Measures, www.jcaho.org/pms

[4] National Diabetes Quality Improvement Alliance (NDQIA), www .nationaldiabetesalliance.org

[5] Joint measure from the Physician Consortium for Performance Improvement, www.physicianconsortium.org and National Committee on Quality Assurance (NCQA), www.ncqa.org

[6] The Society of Thoracic Surgeons, www.sts.org, National Quality Forum, www.qualityforum.org

● **3230F** Documentation that hearing test was performed within 6 months prior to tympanostomy tube insertion (OME)[1]

● **3260F** pT category (primary tumor), pN category (regional lymph nodes), and histologic grade documented in pathology report (PATH) [1]

● **3265F** Ribonucleic acid (RNA) testing for Hepatitis C viremia ordered or results documented (HEP C)[1]

● **3266F** Hepatitis C genotype testing documented as performed prior to initiation of antiviral treatment for Hepatitis C (HEP C)[1]

● **3268F** Prostate-specific antigen (PSA), AND primary tumor (T) stage, AND Gleason score documented prior to initiation of treatment (PRCA)[1]

● **3269F** Bone scan performed prior to initiation of treatment or at any time since diagnosis of prostate cancer (PRCA)[1]

● **3270F** Bone scan not performed prior to initiation of treatment nor at any time since diagnosis of prostate cancer (PRCA)[1]

● **3271F** Low risk of recurrence, prostate cancer (PRCA)[1]

● **3272F** Intermediate risk of recurrence, prostate cancer (PRCA)[1]

● **3273F** High risk of recurrence, prostate cancer (PRCA)[1]

● **3274F** Prostate cancer risk of recurrence not determined or neither low, intermediate nor high (PRCA)[1]

● **3278F** Serum levels of calcium, phosphorus, intact Parathyroid Hormone (PTH) and lipid profile ordered (CKD)[1]

● **3279F** Hemoglobin level greater than or equal to 13 g/dL (CKD, ESRD)[1]

● **3280F** Hemoglobin level 11 g/dL to 12.9 g/dL (CKD, ESRD)[1]

● **3281F** Hemoglobin level less than 11 g/dL (CKD, ESRD)[1]

● **3284F** Intraocular pressure (IOP) reduced by a value of greater than or equal to 15% from the pre-intervention level (EC)[5]

● **3285F** Intraocular pressure (IOP) reduced by a value less than 15% from the pre-intervention level (EC)[5]

● **3288F** Falls risk assessment documented (GER)[5]

● **3290F** Patient is D (Rh) negative and unsensitized (PRENATAL)[1]

● **3291F** Patient is D (Rh) positive or sensitized (PRENATAL)[1]

● **3292F** HIV testing ordered or documented and reviewed during the first or second prenatal visit (PRENATAL)[1]

● **3300F** American Joint Committee on Cancer (AJCC) stage documented and reviewed (ONC)[1]

● **3301F** Cancer stage documented in medical record as metastatic and reviewed (ONC)[1]

● **3302F** AJCC Cancer Stage 0, documented (ONC)1, (ML)[5]

● **3303F** AJCC Cancer Stage IA, documented (ONC)1, (ML)[5]

● **3304F** AJCC Cancer Stage IB, documented (ONC)1, (ML)[5]

● **3305F** AJCC Cancer Stage IC, documented (ONC)1, (ML)[5]

● **3306F** AJCC Cancer Stage IIA, documented (ONC)1, (ML)[5]

● **3307F** AJCC Cancer Stage IIB, documented (ONC)1, (ML)[5]

● **3308F** AJCC Cancer Stage IIC, documented (ONC)1, (ML)[5]

● **3309F** AJCC Cancer Stage IIIA, documented (ONC)[1], (ML)[5]

● **3310F** AJCC Cancer Stage IIIB, documented (ONC)1, (ML)[5]

● **3311F** AJCC Cancer Stage IIIC, documented (ONC)[1], (ML)[5]

● **3312F** AJCC Cancer Stage IV, documented (ONC)[1], (ML)[5]

►(3313F and 3314F have been deleted)◄

● **3315F** Estrogen receptor (ER) or progesterone receptor (PR) positive breast cancer (ONC)[1]

● **3316F** Estrogen receptor (ER) and progesterone receptor (PR) negative breast cancer (ONC)[1]

● **3317F** Pathology report confirming malignancy documented in the medical record and reviewed prior to the initiation of chemotherapy (ONC)[1]

● **3318F** Pathology report confirming malignancy documented in the medical record and reviewed prior to the initiation of radiation therapy (ONC)[1]

● **3319F** One of the following diagnostic imaging studies ordered: chest X-ray, CT, ultrasound, MRI, PET, or nuclear medicine scans (ML)[5]

● **3320F** None of the following diagnostic imaging studies ordered: chest X-ray, CT, ultrasound, MRI, PET, or nuclear medicine scans (ML)[5]

● **3325F** Preoperative assessment of functional or medical indication(s) for surgery prior to the cataract surgery with intraocular lens placement (must be performed within twelve months prior to cataract surgery) (EC)[5]

Footnotes

[1] Physician Consortium for Performance Improvement® (PCPI), www.physicianconsortium.org

[2] National Committee on Quality Assurance (NCQA), Health Employer Data Information Set (HEDIS®), www.ncqa.org

[3] Joint Commission on Accreditation of Healthcare Organizations (JCAHO), ORYX Initiative Performance Measures, www.jcaho.org/pms

[4] National Diabetes Quality Improvement Alliance (NDQIA), www.nationaldiabetesalliance.org

[5] Joint measure from the Physician Consortium for Performance Improvement, www.physicianconsortium.org and National Committee on Quality Assurance (NCQA), www.ncqa.org

[6] The Society of Thoracic Surgeons, www.sts.org, National Quality Forum, www.qualityforum.org

● **3330F** Imaging study ordered (BkP)[2]

● **3331F** Imaging study not ordered (BkP)[2]

● **3340F** Mammogram assessment category of "incomplete: need additional imaging evaluation", documented (RAD)[5]

● **3341F** Mammogram assessment category of "negative", documented(RAD)[5]

● **3342F** Mammogram assessment category of "benign", documented (RAD)[5]

● **3343F** Mammogram assessment category of "probably benign", documented (RAD)[5]

● **3344F** Mammogram assessment category of "suspicious", documented (RAD)[5]

● **3345F** Mammogram assessment category of "highly suggestive of malignancy", documented (RAD)[5]

● **3350F** Mammogram assessment category of "known biopsy proven malignancy", documented (RAD)[5]

● **3351F** Negative screen for depressive symptoms as categorized by using a standardized depression screening/assessment tool (MDD)[2]

● **3352F** No significant depressive symptoms as categorized by using a standardized depression assessment tool (MDD)[2]

● **3353F** Mild to moderate depressive symptoms as categorized by using a standardized depression screening/assessment tool (MDD)[2]

● **3354F** Clinically significant depressive symptoms as categorized by using a standardized depression screening/assessment tool (MDD)[2]

Therapeutic, Preventive, or Other Interventions

Therapeutic, preventive, or other interventions codes describe pharmacologic, procedural, or behavioral therapies, including preventive services such as patient education and counseling.

4000F Tobacco use cessation intervention, counseling (COPD, CAP, CAD)[1](DM)[4](PV)[2]

4001F Tobacco use cessation intervention, pharmacologic therapy (COPD, CAD, CAP, PV)[1] (DM)[4](PV)[2]

4002F Statin therapy, prescribed (CAD)[1]

4003F Patient education, written/oral, appropriate for patients with heart failure, performed (HF)[1]

4005F Pharmacologic therapy (other than minerals/vitamins) for osteoporosis prescribed (OP)[5]

4006F Beta-blocker therapy, prescribed (CAD, HF)[1]

►(4007F has been deleted. To report age related eye disease study [AREDS] formulation prescribed or recommended, use code 4177F)◄

4009F Angiotensin converting enzyme (ACE) inhibitor or angiotensin receptor blocker (ARB) therapy, prescribed (HF, CAD, CKD)[1],(DM)[2]

4011F Oral antiplatelet therapy prescribed (eg, aspirin, clopidogrel/Plavix, or combination of aspirin and dipyridamole/Aggrenox) (CAD)[1]

4012F Warfarin therapy prescribed (HF)[1]

4014F Written discharge instructions provided to heart failure patients discharged home (Instructions include all of the following components: activity level, diet, discharge medications, follow-up appointment, weight monitoring, what to do if symptoms worsen)[3](HF)

(Excludes patients less than 18 years of age)

4015F Persistent asthma, preferred long term control medication or an acceptable alternative treatment, prescribed (Asthma)[1]

(Note: There are no medical exclusion criteria)

(Do not report modifier 1P with 4015F)

(To report patient reasons for not prescribing, use modifier 2P)

4016F Anti-inflammatory/analgesic agent prescribed (OA)[1]

(Use for prescribed or continued medication[s], including over-the-counter medication[s])

4017F Gastrointestinal prophylaxis for NSAID use prescribed (OA)[1]

4018F Therapeutic exercise for the involved joint(s) instructed or physical or occupational therapy prescribed (OA)[1]

Footnotes

[1] Physician Consortium for Performance Improvement® (PCPI), www.physicianconsortium.org

[2] National Committee on Quality Assurance (NCQA), Health Employer Data Information Set (HEDIS®), www.ncqa.org

[3] Joint Commission on Accreditation of Healthcare Organizations (JCAHO), ORYX Initiative Performance Measures, www.jcaho.org/pms

[4] National Diabetes Quality Improvement Alliance (NDQIA), www.nationaldiabetesalliance.org

[5] Joint measure from the Physician Consortium for Performance Improvement, www.physicianconsortium.org and National Committee on Quality Assurance (NCQA), www.ncqa.org

[6] The Society of Thoracic Surgeons, www.sts.org, National Quality Forum, www.qualityforum.org

4019F Documentation of receipt of counseling on exercise AND either both calcium and vitamin D use or counseling regarding both calcium and vitamin D use (OP)[5]

4025F Inhaled bronchodilator prescribed (COPD)[1]

4030F Long-term oxygen therapy prescribed (more than 15 hours per day) (COPD)[1]

4033F Pulmonary rehabilitation exercise training recommended (COPD)[1]

(Report 4033F with 1019F)

4035F Influenza immunization recommended (COPD)[1]

4037F Influenza immunization ordered or administered (COPD, PV, CKD, ESRD)[1]

▲ **4040F** Pneumococcal vaccine administered or previously received (COPD)[1],(PV)[2]

4041F Documentation of order for cefazolin OR cefuroxime for antimicrobial prophylaxis (PERI 2)[5]

4042F Documentation that prophylactic antibiotics were neither given within 4 hours prior to surgical incision nor given intraoperatively (PERI 2)[5]

4043F Documentation that an order was given to discontinue prophylactic antibiotics within 48 hours of surgical end time, cardiac procedures (PERI 2)[5]

4044F Documentation that an order was given for venous thromboembolism (VTE) prophylaxis to be given within 24 hours prior to incision time or 24 hours after surgery end time (PERI 2)[5]

4045F Appropriate empiric antibiotic prescribed (CAP)[1], (EM)[5]

4046F Documentation that prophylactic antibiotics were given within 4 hours prior to surgical incision or given intraoperatively (PERI 2)[5]

4047F Documentation of order for prophylactic antibiotics to be given within 1 hour (if fluoroquinolone or vancomycin, 2 hours) prior to surgical incision (or start of procedure when no incision is required) (PERI 2)[5]

4048F Documentation that prophylactic antibiotic was given within 1 hour (if fluoroquinolone or vancomycin, 2 hours) prior to surgical incision (or start of procedure when no incision is required) (PERI 2)[5]

4049F Documentation that order was given to discontinue prophylactic antibiotics within 24 hours of surgical end time, non-cardiac procedure (PERI 2)[5]

4050F Hypertension plan of care documented as appropriate (HTN)[1]

4051F Referred for an arteriovenous (AV) fistula (ESRD, CKD)[1]

4052F Hemodialysis via functioning arteriovenous (AV) fistula (ESRD)[1]

4053F Hemodialysis via functioning arteriovenous (AV) graft (ESRD)[1]

4054F Hemodialysis via catheter (ESRD)[1]

4055F Patient receiving peritoneal dialysis (ESRD)[1]

4056F Appropriate oral rehydration solution recommended (PAG)[1]

4058F Pediatric gastroenteritis education provided to caregiver (PAG)[1]

4060F Psychotherapy services provided (MDD)[1]

4062F Patient referral for psychotherapy documented (MDD)[1]

4064F Antidepressant pharmacotherapy prescribed (MDD)[1]

4065F Antipsychotic pharmacotherapy prescribed (MDD)[1]

4066F Electroconvulsive therapy (ECT) provided (MDD)[1]

4067F Patient referral for electroconvulsive therapy (ECT) documented (MDD)[1]

4070F Deep vein thrombosis (DVT) prophylaxis received by end of hospital day 2 (STR)[5]

4073F Oral antiplatelet therapy prescribed at discharge (STR)[5]

4075F Anticoagulant therapy prescribed at discharge (STR)[5]

4077F Documentation that tissue plasminogen activator (t-PA) administration was considered (STR)[5]

4079F Documentation that rehabilitation services were considered (STR)[5]

4084F Aspirin received within 24 hours before emergency department arrival or during emergency department stay (EM)[5]

4090F Patient receiving erythropoietin therapy (HEM)[1]

4095F Patient not receiving erythropoietin therapy (HEM)[1]

4100F Bisphosphonate therapy, intravenous, ordered or received (HEM)[1]

4110F Internal mammary artery graft performed for primary, isolated coronary artery bypass graft procedure (CABG)[6]

4115F Beta blocker administered within 24 hours prior to surgical incision (CABG)[6]

Footnotes

[1] Physician Consortium for Performance Improvement® (PCPI), www.physicianconsortium.org

[2] National Committee on Quality Assurance (NCQA), Health Employer Data Information Set (HEDIS®), www.ncqa.org

[3] Joint Commission on Accreditation of Healthcare Organizations (JCAHO), ORYX Initiative Performance Measures, www.jcaho.org/pms

[4] National Diabetes Quality Improvement Alliance (NDQIA), www.nationaldiabetesalliance.org

[5] Joint measure from the Physician Consortium for Performance Improvement, www.physicianconsortium.org and National Committee on Quality Assurance (NCQA), www.ncqa.org

[6] The Society of Thoracic Surgeons, www.sts.org, National Quality Forum, www.qualityforum.org

4120F Antibiotic prescribed or dispensed (URI, PHAR)[2], (A-BRONCH)[2]

4124F Antibiotic neither prescribed nor dispensed (URI, PHAR)[2], (A-BRONCH)[2]

● **4130F** Topical preparations (including OTC) prescribed for acute otitis externa (AOE)[1]

● **4131F** Systemic antimicrobial therapy prescribed (AOE)[1]

● **4132F** Systemic antimicrobial therapy not prescribed (AOE)[1]

● **4133F** Antihistamines or decongestants prescribed or recommended (OME)[1]

● **4134F** Antihistamines or decongestants neither prescribed nor recommended (OME)[1]

● **4135F** Systemic corticosteroids prescribed (OME)[1]

● **4136F** Systemic corticosteroids not prescribed (OME)[1]

● **4150F** Patient receiving antiviral treatment for Hepatitis C (HEP-C)[1]

● **4151F** Patient not receiving antiviral treatment for Hepatitis C (HEP-C)[1]

● **4152F** Documentation that combination peginterferon and ribavirin therapy considered (HEP-C) [1]

● **4153F** Combination peginterferon and ribavirin therapy prescribed (HEP-C)[1]

● **4154F** Hepatitis A vaccine series recommended (HEP-C)[1]

● **4155F** Hepatitis A vaccine series previously received (HEP-C)[1]

● **4156F** Hepatitis B vaccine series recommended (HEP-C)[1]

● **4157F** Hepatitis B vaccine series previously received (HEP-C)[1]

● **4158F** Patient education regarding risk of alcohol consumption performed (HEP-C)[1]

● **4159F** Counseling regarding contraception received prior to initiation of antiviral treatment (HEP-C)[1]

● **4163F** Patient counseling at a minimum on all of the following treatment options for clinically localized prostate cancer: active surveillance, AND interstitial prostate brachytherapy, AND external beam radiotherapy, AND radical prostatectomy, provided prior to initiation of treatment (PRCA)[1]

● **4164F** Adjuvant (ie, in combination with external beam radiotherapy to the prostate for prostate cancer) hormonal therapy (gonadotropin-releasing hormone [GnRH] agonist or antagonist) prescribed/administered (PRCA)[1]

● **4165F** 3-dimensional conformal radiotherapy (3D-CRT) or intensity modulated radiation therapy (IMRT) received (PRCA)[1]

● **4167F** Head of bed elevation (30-45 degrees) on first ventilator day ordered (CRIT)[1]

● **4168F** Patient receiving care in the intensive care unit (ICU) and receiving mechanical ventilation, 24 hours or less (CRIT)[1]

● **4169F** Patient either not receiving care in the intensive care unit (ICU) OR not receiving mechanical ventilation OR receiving mechanical ventilation greater than 24 hours (CRIT)[1]

● **4171F** Patient receiving erythropoiesis-stimulating agents (ESA) therapy (CKD)[1]

● **4172F** Patient not receiving erythropoiesis-stimulating agents (ESA) therapy (CKD)[1]

● **4174F** Counseling about the potential impact of glaucoma on visual functioning and quality of life, and importance of treatment adherence provided to patient and/or caregiver(s) (EC)[5]

● **4175F** Best-corrected visual acuity of 20/40 or better (distance or near) achieved within the 90 days following cataract surgery (EC)[5]

● **4176F** Counseling about value of protection from UV light and lack of proven efficacy of nutritional supplements in prevention or progression of cataract development provided to patient and/or caregiver(s) (NMA-No Measure Associated)

● **4177F** Counseling about the benefits and/or risks of the Age-Related Eye Disease Study (AREDS) formulation for preventing progression of age-related macular degeneration (AMD) provided to patient and/or caregiver(s) (EC)[5]

● **4178F** Anti-D immune globulin received between 26 and 30 weeks gestation (PRENATAL)[1]

● **4179F** Tamoxifen or aromatase inhibitor (AI) prescribed (ONC)[1]

● **4180F** Adjuvant chemotherapy prescribed or previously received for Stage IIIA through Stage IIIC colon cancer (ONC)[1]

● **4181F** Conformal radiation therapy received (NMA-No Measure Assoc.)

● **4182F** Conformal radiation therapy not received (NMA-No Measure Assoc.)

Footnotes

[1] Physician Consortium for Performance Improvement® (PCPI), www.physicianconsortium.org

[2] National Committee on Quality Assurance (NCQA), Health Employer Data Information Set (HEDIS®), www.ncqa.org

[3] Joint Commission on Accreditation of Healthcare Organizations (JCAHO), ORYX Initiative Performance Measures, www.jcaho.org/pms

[4] National Diabetes Quality Improvement Alliance (NDQIA), www .nationaldiabetesalliance.org

[5] Joint measure from the Physician Consortium for Performance Improvement, www.physicianconsortium.org and National Committee on Quality Assurance (NCQA), www.ncqa.org

[6] The Society of Thoracic Surgeons, www.sts.org, National Quality Forum, www.qualityforum.org

● **4185F** Continuous (12-months) therapy with proton pump inhibitor (PPI) or histamine H2 receptor antagonist (H2RA) received (GERD)[5]

● **4186F** No continuous (12-months) therapy with either proton pump inhibitor (PPI) or histamine H2 receptor antagonist (H2RA) received (GERD)[5]

● **4187F** Disease modifying anti-rheumatic drug therapy prescribed or dispensed (RA)[2]

● **4188F** Appropriate angiotensin converting enzyme (ACE)/angiotensin receptor blockers (ARB) therapeutic monitoring test ordered or performed (AM)[2]

● **4189F** Appropriate digoxin therapeutic monitoring test ordered or performed (AM)[2]

● **4190F** Appropriate diuretic therapeutic monitoring test ordered or performed (AM)[2]

● **4191F** Appropriate anticonvulsant therapeutic monitoring test ordered or performed (AM)[2]

● **4200F** External beam radiotherapy to prostate only (PRCA)[1]

● **4201F** External beam radiotherapy for prostate cancer to region(s) other than prostate only (PRCA)[1]

● **4210F** Angiotensin converting enzyme (ACE) or angiotensin receptor blockers (ARB) medication therapy for 6 months or more (MM)[2]

● **4220F** Digoxin medication therapy for 6 months or more (MM)[2]

● **4221F** Diuretic medication therapy for 6 months or more (MM)[2]

● **4230F** Anticonvulsant medication therapy for 6 months or more (MM)[2]

● **4240F** Instruction in therapeutic exercise with follow-up by the physician provided to patients during episode of back pain lasting longer than 12 weeks (BkP)[2]

● **4242F** Counseling for supervised exercise program provided to patients during episode of back pain lasting longer than 12 weeks (BkP)[2]

● **4245F** Patient counseled during the initial visit to maintain or resume normal activities (BkP)[2]

● **4248F** Patient counseled during the initial visit for an episode of back pain against bed rest lasting 4 days or longer (BkP)[2]

● **4250F** Active warming used intraoperatively for the purpose of maintaining normothermia, OR at least one body temperature equal to or greater than 36 degrees Centigrade (or 96.8 degrees Fahrenheit) recorded within the 30 minutes immediately before or the 30 minutes immediately after anesthesia end time (CRIT)[1]

Follow-up or Other Outcomes

Follow-up or other outcomes codes describe review and communication of test results to patients, patient satisfaction or experience with care, patient functional status, and patient morbidity and mortality.

5005F Patient counseled on self-examination for new or changing moles (ML)[5]

5010F Findings of dilated macular or fundus exam communicated to the physician managing the diabetes care (EC)[5]

5015F Documentation of communication that a fracture occurred and that the patient was or should be tested or treated for osteoporosis (OP)[5]

● **5020F** Treatment summary report communicated to physician(s) managing continuing care within 1 month of completing treatment (ONC)[1]

● **5050F** Treatment plan communicated to provider(s) managing continuing care within 1 month of diagnosis (ML)[5]

● **5060F** Findings from diagnostic mammogram communicated to practice managing patient's ongoing care within 3 business days of exam interpretation (RAD)[5]

● **5062F** Findings from diagnostic mammogram communicated to the patient within 5 business days of exam interpretation (RAD)[5]

Patient Safety

Patient safety codes that describe patient safety practices.

6005F Rationale (eg, severity of illness and safety) for level of care (eg, home, hospital) documented (CAP)[1]

6010F Dysphagia screening conducted prior to order for or receipt of any foods, fluids, or medication by mouth (STR)[5]

6015F Patient receiving or eligible to receive foods, fluids, or medication by mouth (STR)[5]

6020F NPO (nothing by mouth) ordered (STR)[5]

Footnotes

[1] Physician Consortium for Performance Improvement® (PCPI), www.physicianconsortium.org

[2] National Committee on Quality Assurance (NCQA), Health Employer Data Information Set (HEDIS®), www.ncqa.org

[3] Joint Commission on Accreditation of Healthcare Organizations (JCAHO), ORYX Initiative Performance Measures, www.jcaho.org/pms

[4] National Diabetes Quality Improvement Alliance (NDQIA), www .nationaldiabetesalliance.org

[5] Joint measure from the Physician Consortium for Performance Improvement, www.physicianconsortium.org and National Committee on Quality Assurance (NCQA), www.ncqa.org

[6] The Society of Thoracic Surgeons, www.sts.org, National Quality Forum, www.qualityforum.org

● **6030F** All elements of maximal sterile barrier technique including: cap AND mask AND sterile gown AND sterile gloves AND a large sterile sheet AND hand hygiene AND 2% chlorhexidine for cutaneous antisepsis, followed (CRIT)[1]

● **6040F** Use of appropriate radiation dose reduction devices OR manual techniques for appropriate moderation of exposure, documented (RAD)[5]

● **6045F** Radiation exposure or exposure time in final report for procedure using fluoroscopy, documented (RAD)[5]

▸Structural Measures◂

►Structural measures codes are used to identify measures that address the setting or system of the delivered care. These codes also address aspects of the capabilities of the organization or health care professional providing the care.◄

● **7010F** Patient information entered into a recall system with the target date for the next exam specified (ML)[5]

● **7020F** Mammogram assessment category (eg, Mammography Quality Standards Act [MQSA], Breast Imaging Reporting and Data System [BI-RADS®], or FDA approved equivalent categories) entered into an internal database to allow for analysis of abnormal interpretation (recall) rate (RAD)[5]

● **7025F** Patient information entered into a reminder system with a target due date for the next mammogram (RAD)[5]

Category II Codes

Footnotes

[1] Physician Consortium for Performance Improvement® (PCPI), www.physicianconsortium.org

[2] National Committee on Quality Assurance (NCQA), Health Employer Data Information Set (HEDIS®), www.ncqa.org

[3] Joint Commission on Accreditation of Healthcare Organizations (JCAHO), ORYX Initiative Performance Measures, www.jcaho.org/pms

[4] National Diabetes Quality Improvement Alliance (NDQIA), www.nationaldiabetesalliance.org

[5] Joint measure from the Physician Consortium for Performance Improvement, www.physicianconsortium.org and National Committee on Quality Assurance (NCQA), www.ncqa.org

[6] The Society of Thoracic Surgeons, www.sts.org, National Quality Forum, www.qualityforum.org

Notes

Category III Codes

The following section contains a set of temporary codes for emerging technology, services, and procedures. Category III codes allow data collection for these services/procedures. Use of unlisted codes does not offer the opportunity for the collection of specific data. If a Category III code is available, this code must be reported instead of a Category I unlisted code. This is an activity that is critically important in the evaluation of health care delivery and the formation of public and private policy. The use of the codes in this section allow physicians and other qualified health care professionals, insurers, health services researchers, and health policy experts to identify emerging technology, services, and procedures for clinical efficacy, utilization and outcomes.

The inclusion of a service or procedure in this section neither implies nor endorses clinical efficacy, safety or the applicability to clinical practice. The codes in this section may not conform to the usual requirements for CPT Category I codes established by the Editorial Panel. For Category I codes, the Panel requires that the service/procedure be performed by many health care professionals in clinical practice in multiple locations and that FDA approval, as appropriate, has already been received. The nature of emerging technology, services, and procedures is such that these requirements may not be met. For these reasons, temporary codes for emerging technology, services, and procedures have been placed in a separate section of the CPT codebook and the codes are differentiated from Category I CPT codes by the use of alphanumeric characters.

►Services/procedures described in this section make use of alphanumeric characters. These codes have an alpha character as the 5th character in the string, preceded by four digits. The digits are not intended to reflect the placement of the code in the Category I section of CPT nomenclature. Codes in this section may or may not eventually receive a Category I CPT code. In either case, a given Category III code will be archived five years from its date of publication or revision in the CPT code book unless it is demonstrated that a temporary code is still needed. Services/procedures described by Category III codes which have been archived after five years, without conversion, may be reported using the Category I unlisted code. New codes in this section are released semi-annually via the AMA/CPT Web site, to expedite dissemination for reporting. The full set of temporary codes for emerging technology, services, and procedures are published annually in the CPT codebook. Go to www.ama-assn.org/go/cpt for the most current listing.◄

(0003T has been deleted)

(0008T has been deleted)

0016T Destruction of localized lesion of choroid (eg, choroidal neovascularization), transpupillary thermotherapy

0017T Destruction of macular drusen, photocoagulation

(0018T has been deleted. To report, see 0160T, 0161T)

0019T Extracorporeal shock wave involving musculoskeletal system, not otherwise specified, low energy

(For application of high energy extracorporeal shock wave involving musculoskeletal system not otherwise specified, use 0101T)

(For application of high energy extracorporeal shock wave involving lateral humeral epicondyle, use 0102T)

(0021T has been deleted)

►(0024T has been deleted)◄

►(For non-surgical septal reduction therapy, use 93799)◄

►(0026T has been deleted)◄

►(For lipoprotein, direct measurement, intermediate density lipoproteins [IDL] [remnant lipoprotein], use 84999)◄

►(0027T has been deleted)◄

►(For endoscopic lysis of epidural adhesions with direct visualization using mechnical means or solution injection [eg, normal saline], use 64999)◄

►(0028T has been deleted)◄

►(For dual energy x-ray absorptiometry [DEXA] body composition study, use 76499)◄

►(0029T has been deleted)◄

►(For pulsed magnetic neuromodulation incontinence treatment, use 53899)◄

0030T Antiprothrombin (phospholipid cofactor) antibody, each Ig class

►(0031T, 0032T have been deleted)◄

►(For speculoscopy, including sampling, use 58999)◄

►(0041T has been deleted)◄

►(For urinalysis infectious agent detection, semi-quantitative analysis of volatile compounds, use 81099)◄

0042T Cerebral perfusion analysis using computed tomography with contrast administration, including post-processing of parametric maps with determination of cerebral blood flow, cerebral blood volume, and mean transit time

►(0043T has been deleted)◄

►(For carbon monoxide, expired gas analysis [eg, $ETCO_c$/hemolysis breath test], use 84999)◄

(0044T and 0045T have been deleted. To report, use 96904)

►(0046T, 0047T have been deleted)◄

►(For mammary duct[s] catheter lavage, use 19499)◄

0048T Implantation of a ventricular assist device, extracorporeal, percutaneous transseptal access, single or dual cannulation

►(0049T has been deleted)◄

►(For prolonged extracorporeal percutaneous transseptal ventricular assist device, use 33999)◄

0050T Removal of a ventricular assist device, extracorporeal, percutaneous transseptal access, single or dual cannulation

0051T Implantation of a total replacement heart system (artificial heart) with recipient cardiectomy

(For implantation of heart assist or ventricular assist device, see 33975, 33976)

0052T Replacement or repair of thoracic unit of a total replacement heart system (artificial heart)

(For replacement or repair of other implantable components in a total replacement heart system (artificial heart), use 0053T)

0053T Replacement or repair of implantable component or components of total replacement heart system (artificial heart), excluding thoracic unit

(For replacement or repair of a thoracic unit of a total replacement heart system (artificial heart), use 0052T)

+○ **0054T** Computer-assisted musculoskeletal surgical navigational orthopedic procedure, with image-guidance based on fluoroscopic images (List separately in addition to code for primary procedure)

+○ **0055T** Computer-assisted musculoskeletal surgical navigational orthopedic procedure, with image-guidance based on CT/MRI images (List separately in addition to code for primary procedure)

►(When CT and MRI are both performed, report 0055T only once)◄

►(0056T has been deleted. To report, use 20985)◄

►(0058T, 0059T have been deleted)◄

►(For cryopreservation, ovarian reproductive tissue, oocytes, use 89240)◄

►(0060T has been deleted)◄

►(For electrical impedance breast scan, use 76499)◄

►(0061T has been deleted)◄

►(For destruction/reduction of malignant breast tumor, microwave phased array thermotherapy, use 19499)◄

0062T Percutaneous intradiscal annuloplasty, any method except electrothermal, unilateral or bilateral including fluoroscopic guidance; single level

+ **0063T** 1 or more additional levels (List separately in addition to 0062T for primary procedure)

(For CT or MRI guidance and localization for needle placement and annuloplasty in conjunction with 0062T, 0063T, see 77012, 77021)

(For intradiscal electrothermal annuloplasty, see 22526-22527)

0064T Spectroscopy, expired gas analysis (eg, nitric oxide/carbon dioxide test)

(0065T has been deleted. To report, use 99174)

0066T Computed tomographic (CT) colonography (ie, virtual colonoscopy); screening

0067T diagnostic

(Do not report 0066T or 0067T in conjunction with 72192-72194, 74150-74170)

0068T Acoustic heart sound recording and computer analysis; with interpretation and report

0069T acoustic heart sound recording and computer analysis only

0070T interpretation and report only

0071T Focused ultrasound ablation of uterine leiomyomata, including MR guidance; total leiomyomata volume less than 200 cc of tissue

0072T total leiomyomata volume greater or equal to 200 cc of tissue

(Do not report 0071T, 0072T in conjunction with 51702 or 77022)

0073T Compensator-based beam modulation treatment delivery of inverse planned treatment using 3 or more high resolution (milled or cast) compensator convergent beam modulated fields, per treatment session

(For treatment planning, use 77301)

(Do not report 0073T in conjunction with 77401-77416, 77418)

(0074T has been deleted. To report, see 98969, 99444)

0075T Transcatheter placement of extracranial vertebral or intrathoracic carotid artery stent(s), including radiologic supervision and interpretation, percutaneous; initial vessel

+ **0076T** each additional vessel (List separately in addition to code for primary procedure)

(Use 0076T in conjunction with 0075T)

(When the ipsilateral extracranial vertebral or intrathoracic carotid arteriogram (including imaging and selective catheterization) confirms the need for stenting, then 0075T and 0076T include all ipsilateral extracranial vertebral or intrathoracic selective carotid catheterization, all diagnostic imaging for ipsilateral extracranial vertebral or intrathoracic carotid artery stenting, and all related radiologic supervision and interpretation. If stenting is not indicated, then the appropriate codes for selective catheterization and imaging should be reported in lieu of code 0075T or 0076T.)

0077T Implanting and securing cerebral thermal perfusion probe, including twist drill or burr hole, to measure absolute cerebral tissue perfusion

(0078T-0081T should be reported in accordance with the Endovascular Abdominal Aneurysm Repair guidelines established for 34800-34826)

0078T Endovascular repair using prosthesis of abdominal aortic aneurysm, pseudoaneurysm or dissection, abdominal aorta involving visceral branches (superior mesenteric, celiac and/or renal artery[s])

(Do not report 0078T in conjunction with 34800-34805, 35081, 35102, 35452, 35454, 35472, 37205-37208)

(Report 0078T in conjunction with 35454, 37205-37208 when these procedures are performed outside the target zone of the endoprosthesis)

+ 0079T Placement of visceral extension prosthesis for endovascular repair of abdominal aortic aneurysm involving visceral vessels, each visceral branch (List separately in addition to code for primary procedure)

(Use 0079T in conjunction with 0078T)

(Do not report 0079T in conjunction with 34800-34805, 35081, 35102, 35452, 35454, 35472, 37205-37208)

(Report 0079T in conjunction with 35454, 37205-37208 when these procedures are performed outside the target zone of the endoprosthesis)

0080T Endovascular repair of abdominal aortic aneurysm, pseudoaneurysm or dissection, abdominal aorta involving visceral vessels (superior mesenteric, celiac or renal), using fenestrated modular bifurcated prosthesis (2 docking limbs), radiological supervision and interpretation

(Do not report 0080T in conjunction with 34800-34805, 35081, 35102, 35452, 35454, 35472, 37205-37208)

(Report 0080T in conjunction with 35454, 37205-37208 when these procedures are performed outside the target zone of the endoprosthesis)

+ 0081T Placement of visceral extension prosthesis for endovascular repair of abdominal aortic aneurysm involving visceral vessels, each visceral branch, radiological supervision and interpretation (List separately in addition to code for primary procedure)

(Use 0081T in conjunction with 0080T)

(Do not report 0081T in conjunction with 34800-34805, 35081, 35102, 35452, 35454, 35472, 37205-37208)

(Report 0081T in conjunction with 35454, 37205-37208 when these procedures are performed outside the target zone of the endoprosthesis)

(0082T, 0083T have been deleted. To report, see 77373, 77435)

0084T Insertion of a temporary prostatic urethral stent

0085T Breath test for heart transplant rejection

0086T Left ventricular filling pressure indirect measurement by computerized calibration of the arterial waveform response to Valsalva maneuver

0087T Sperm evaluation, Hyaluronan sperm binding test

►(0088T has been deleted. To report, use 41530)◄

►(0089T has been deleted. For actigraphy testing, use 95803)◄

►(0090T has been deleted. To report total disc cervical arthroplasty, use 22856)◄

(0091T has been deleted)

(To report total disc lumbar arthroplasty, use 22857)

+▲ 0092T Total disc arthroplasty (artificial disc), anterior approach, including discectomy with end plate preparation (includes osteophytectomy for nerve root or spinal cord decompression and microdissection), each additional interspace, cervical (List separately in addition to code for primary procedure)

►(Use 0092T in conjunction with 22856)◄

►(Do not report 0092T in conjunction with 22851 when performed at the same level)◄

►(0093T has been deleted. To report removal of total disc cervical arthroplasty, use 22864)◄

(0094T has been deleted)

(To report removal of total disc lumbar arthroplasty, use 22865)

+▲ 0095T Removal of total disc arthroplasty (artificial disc), anterior approach, each additional interspace, cervical (List separately in addition to code for primary procedure)

►(Use 0095T in conjunction with 22864)◄

►(0096T has been deleted. To report revision of total disc cervical arthroplasty, use 22861)◄

(0097T has been deleted)

(To report revision of total disc lumbar arthroplasty, use 22862)

+▲ **0098T** Revision including replacement of total disc arthroplasty (artificial disc), anterior approach, each additional interspace, cervical (List separately in addition to code for primary procedure)

►(Use 0098T in conjunction with 22861)◄

►(Do not report 0098T in conjunction with 0095T)◄

►(Do not report 0098T in conjunction with 22851 when performed at the same level)◄

(For decompression, see 63001-63048)

0099T Implantation of intrastromal corneal ring segments

0100T Placement of a subconjunctival retinal prosthesis receiver and pulse generator, and implantation of intra-ocular retinal electrode array, with vitrectomy

0101T Extracorporeal shock wave involving musculoskeletal system, not otherwise specified, high energy

(For application of low energy musculoskeletal system extracorporeal shock wave, use 0019T)

0102T Extracorporeal shock wave, high energy, performed by a physician, requiring anesthesia other than local, involving lateral humeral epicondyle

(For application of low energy musculoskeletal system extracorporeal shock wave, use 0019T)

0103T Holotranscobalamin, quantitative

0104T Inert gas rebreathing for cardiac output measurement; during rest

0105T during exercise

0106T Quantitative sensory testing (QST), testing and interpretation per extremity; using touch pressure stimuli to assess large diameter sensation

0107T using vibration stimuli to assess large diameter fiber sensation

0108T using cooling stimuli to assess small nerve fiber sensation and hyperalgesia

0109T using heat-pain stimuli to assess small nerve fiber sensation and hyperalgesia

0110T using other stimuli to assess sensation

0111T Long-chain (C20-22) omega-3 fatty acids in red blood cell (RBC) membranes

(For very long chain fatty acids, use 82726)

(0115T-0117T have been deleted. To report, see 99605-99607)

(0120T has been deleted. To report, use 19105)

0123T Fistulization of sclera for glaucoma, through ciliary body

▲ **0124T** Conjunctival incision with posterior extrascleral placement of pharmacological agent (does not include supply of medication)

►(For suprachoroidal delivery of pharmacologic agent, use 0186T)◄

0126T Common carotid intima-media thickness (IMT) study for evaluation of atherosclerotic burden or coronary heart disease risk factor assessment

0130T Validated, statistically reliable, randomized, controlled, single-patient clinical investigation of FDA approved chronic care drugs, provided by a pharmacist, interpretation and report to the prescribing health care professional

(0133T has been deleted)

(0135T has been deleted. To report, use 50593)

►(0137T has been deleted. For transperineal stereotactic template guided saturation prostate biopsies, use 55706)◄

0140T Exhaled breath condensate pH

Pancreatic islet cells are transplanted by infusion into the portal vein. The portal vein may be cannulated percutaneously with imaging guidance, by laparoscopy, or by laparotomy. Codes 0141T-0143T include infusion of islet cells with monitoring and management of portal and systemic hemodynamics, monitoring and management of blood glucose and insulin therapy, immunotherapy infusion, antibiotic infusion, analgesic and sedative administration and monitoring, and all other therapeutic injections and infusions administered during the islet infusion. Codes 0141T-0143T also include typical postprocedural care. When reporting 0141T, percutaneous portal vein catheterization is reported separately (see codes 36481, 75887). Code 0142T includes diagnostic laparotomy (49000, 49002). Code 0143T includes diagnostic laparoscopy (49320).

0141T Pancreatic islet cell transplantation through portal vein, percutaneous

(For open approach, use 0142T)

(For laparoscopic approach, use 0143T)

(For percutaneous portal vein catheterization, use 36481)

(For radiological supervision and interpretation, use 75887)

0142T Pancreatic islet cell transplantation through portal vein, open

(For percutaneous approach, use 0141T)

(For laparoscopic approach, use 0143T)

(Do not report 0142T in conjunction with 49000, 49002)

0143T Laparoscopy, surgical, pancreatic islet cell transplantation through portal vein

(For percutaneous approach, use 0141T)

(For open approach, use 0142T)

(Do not report 0143T in conjunction with 49320)

0144T Computed tomography, heart, without contrast material, including image postprocessing and quantitative evaluation of coronary calcium

(Do not report 0144T in conjunction with 0145T-0151T)

0145T Computed tomography, heart, with contrast material(s), including noncontrast images, if performed, cardiac gating and 3D image postprocessing; cardiac structure and morphology

(For cardiac structure and morphology in congenital heart disease, use 0150T)

0146T computed tomographic angiography of coronary arteries (including native and anomalous coronary arteries, coronary bypass grafts), without quantitative evaluation of coronary calcium

0147T computed tomographic angiography of coronary arteries (including native and anomalous coronary arteries, coronary bypass grafts), with quantitative evaluation of coronary calcium

(Do not report 0147T in conjunction with 0144T)

0148T cardiac structure and morphology and computed tomographic angiography of coronary arteries (including native and anomalous coronary arteries, coronary bypass grafts), without quantitative evaluation of coronary calcium

0149T cardiac structure and morphology and computed tomographic angiography of coronary arteries (including native and anomalous coronary arteries, coronary bypass grafts), with quantitative evaluation of coronary calcium

(Do not report 0149T in conjunction with 0144T)

0150T cardiac structure and morphology in congenital heart disease

+ 0151T Computed tomography, heart, with contrast material(s), including noncontrast images, if performed, cardiac gating and 3D image postprocessing, function evaluation (left and right ventricular function, ejection-fraction and segmental wall motion) (List separately in addition to code for primary procedure)

(Use 0151T in conjunction with 0145T-0150T)

(0152T has been deleted. To report, see 0174T, 0175T)

(0153T has been deleted. To report, use 34806)

(0154T has been deleted. To report, use 93982)

0155T Laparoscopy, surgical; implantation or replacement of gastric stimulation electrodes, lesser curvature (ie, morbid obesity)

0156T revision or removal of gastric stimulation electrodes, lesser curvature (ie, morbid obesity)

(For open approach, see 0157T, 0158T)

(For laparoscopic or open insertion, revision or removal of antral gastric neurostimulator electrodes, see 43647, 43648, 43881, 43882)

(For insertion, revision or removal of gastric neurostimulator pulse generator, see 64590, 64595)

(For electronic analysis and programming of antral gastric neurostimulator pulse generator, see 95980-95982)

(For electronic analysis and programming of a gastric neurostimulator, lesser curvature, use 0162T)

0157T Laparotomy, implantation or replacement of gastric stimulation electrodes, lesser curvature (ie, morbid obesity)

0158T Laparotomy, revision or removal of gastric stimulation electrodes, lesser curvature (ie, morbid obesity)

(For laparoscopic approach, see 0155T, 0156T)

(For insertion of gastric neurostimulator pulse generator, use 64590)

(For revision or removal of gastric neurostimulator pulse generator, use 64595)

(For electronic analysis and programming of antral gastric neurostimulator pulse generator, see 95980-95982)

(For electronic analysis and programming of a gastric neurostimulator, lesser curvature, use 0162T)

+ 0159T Computer-aided detection, including computer algorithm analysis of MRI image data for lesion detection/characterization, pharmacokinetic analysis, with further physician review for interpretation, breast MRI (List separately in addition to code for primary procedure)

(Use 0159T in conjunction with 77058, 77059)

(Do not report 0159T in conjunction with 76376, 76377)

0160T Therapeutic repetitive transcranial magnetic stimulation treatment planning

(Pre-treatment determination of optimal magnetic field strength via titration, treatment location determination and stimulation parameter and protocol programming in the therapeutic use of high power, focal magnetic pulses for the direct, noninvasive modulation of cortical neurons)

0161T Therapeutic repetitive transcranial magnetic stimulation treatment delivery and management, per session

(Treatment session using high power, focal magnetic pulses for the direct, noninvasive modulation of cortical neurons. Clinical evaluation, safety monitoring and treatment parameter review in the therapeutic use of high power, focal magnetic pulses for the direct, noninvasive modulation of cortical neurons)

►(0162T has been deleted. To report, see 95980–95982)◄

+▲ 0163T Total disc arthroplasty (artificial disc), anterior approach, including discectomy to prepare interspace (other than for decompression), each additional interspace, lumbar (List separately in addition to code for primary procedure)

(Use 0163T in conjunction with 22857)

+▲ **0164T** Removal of total disc arthroplasty, (artificial disc), anterior approach, each additional interspace, lumbar (List separately in addition to code for primary procedure)

(Use 0164T in conjunction with 22865)

+▲ **0165T** Revision including replacement of total disc arthroplasty (artificial disc), anterior approach, each additional interspace, lumbar (List separately in addition to code for primary procedure)

(Use 0165T in conjunction with 22862)

(Do not report 0163T-0165T in conjunction with 22851, 49010, when performed at the same level)

(For decompression, see 63001-63048)

0166T Transmyocardial transcatheter closure of ventricular septal defect, with implant; without cardiopulmonary bypass

0167T with cardiopulmonary bypass

(Do not report 0166T, 0167T in conjunction with 32551, 33210, 33211)

(For ventricular septal defect closure via percutaneous transcatheter implant delivery, use 93581)

0168T Rhinophototherapy, intranasal application of ultraviolet and visible light, bilateral

0169T Stereotactic placement of infusion catheter(s) in the brain for delivery of therapeutic agent(s), including computerized stereotactic planning and burr hole(s)

(Do not report code 0169T in conjunction with 20660, 61107, 61795)

0170T Repair of anorectal fistula with plug (eg, porcine small intestine submucosa [SIS])

(For repair of anal fistula using fibrin glue, use 46706)

(Do not report 0170T in conjunction with 15430, 15431)

0171T Insertion of posterior spinous process distraction device (including necessary removal of bone or ligament for insertion and imaging guidance), lumbar; single level

+ **0172T** each additional level (List separately in addition to code for primary procedure)

(Use 0172T in conjunction with 0171T)

+ **0173T** Monitoring of intraocular pressure during vitrectomy surgery (List separately in addition to code for primary procedure)

(Use 0173T in conjunction with 67036, 67039-67043, 67108, 67112)

+ **0174T** Computer-aided detection (CAD) (computer algorithm analysis of digital image data for lesion detection) with further physician review for interpretation and report, with or without digitization of film radiographic images, chest radiograph(s), performed concurrent with primary interpretation (List separately in addition to code for primary procedure)

(Use 0174T in conjunction with 71010, 71020, 71021, 71022, 71030)

0175T Computer-aided detection (CAD) (computer algorithm analysis of digital image data for lesion detection) with further physician review for interpretation and report, with or without digitization of film radiographic images, chest radiograph(s), performed remote from primary interpretation

(Do not report 0175T in conjunction with 71010, 71020, 71021, 71022, 71030)

0176T Transluminal dilation of aqueous outflow canal; without retention of device or stent

0177T with retention of device or stent

0178T Electrocardiogram, 64 leads or greater, with graphic presentation and analysis; with interpretation and report

0179T tracing and graphics only, without interpretation and report

0180T interpretation and report only

(For electrocardiogram, routine, with at least 12 leads separately performed, see 93000-93010)

0181T Corneal hysteresis determination, by air impulse stimulation, bilateral, with interpretation and report

0182T High dose rate electronic brachytherapy, per fraction

(Do not report 0182T in conjunction with 77761-77763, 77776-77778, 77781-77784, 77789)

0183T Low frequency, non-contact, non-thermal ultrasound, including topical application(s), when performed, wound assessment, and instruction(s) for ongoing care, per day

● **0184T** Excision of rectal tumor, transanal endoscopic microsurgical approach (ie, TEMS)

►(For non-endoscopic excision of rectal tumor, see 45160, 45170)◄

►(Do not report 0184T in conjunction with 45300-45327, 69990)◄

● **0185T** Multivariate analysis of patient-specific findings with quantifiable computer probability assessment, including report

►(Do not report 0185T in conjunction with 99090)◄

● **0186T** Suprachoroidal delivery of pharmacologic agent (does not include supply of medication)

● **0187T** Scanning computerized ophthalmic diagnostic imaging, anterior segment, with interpretation and report, unilateral

►Remote Real-Time Interactive Videoconferenced Critical Care Services◄

►Remote real-time interactive video-conferenced critical care is the direct delivery by a physician(s) of medical care for a critically ill or critically injured patient from an off-site location. Remote real-time interactive video-conferenced critical care is intended to supplement on-site critical care services at times when a critically ill or injured patient requires additional critical care resources than are available on-site. (For definitions of critical illness or injury and critical care services, see **Critical Care Services** section).

In order to report remote real-time interactive video-conferenced critical care, the physician(s) in the remote location must have real-time access to the patient's medical record including progress notes, nursing notes, current medications, vital signs, clinical laboratory test results, other diagnostic test results, and radiographic images. The physician must have real-time capability to enter electronic orders; document the remote care services provided in the hospital medical record; videoconference with the on-site health care team in the patient room; assess patients in their individual rooms, using high fidelity audio and video capabilities, including clear observation of the patient, monitors, ventilators, and infusion pumps; and speak to patients and family members.

The review and/or interpretation of all diagnostic information is included in reporting remote real-time interactive video-conferenced critical care when performed during the critical period by the physician(s) providing remote real-time interactive video-conferenced critical care and should not be reported separately.

The remote real-time interactive video-conferenced critical care codes 0188T and 0189T are used to report the total duration of time spent by a physician providing remote real-time interactive video-conferenced critical care services to a critically ill or critically injured patient, even if the time spent by the physician on that date is not continuous. For any given period of time spent providing remote real-time interactive video-conferenced critical care services, the physician must devote his or her full attention to the patient and, therefore, cannot provide services to any other patient during the same period of time.

Time spent with the individual patient should be recorded in the patient's record. The time that can be reported as remote real-time interactive video-conferenced critical care is the time spent engaged in work directly related to the individual patient's care. For example, time spent reviewing test results or imaging studies, discussing the critically ill patient's care with other medical staff or documenting remote real-time interactive video-conferenced critical care services in the medical record would be reported as remote real-time interactive video-conferenced critical care, even though it does not occur at the bedside. Also, when the patient is unable or lacks capacity to participate in discussions, time spent from the remote site with family members or surrogate decision makers obtaining a medical history, reviewing the patient's condition or prognosis, or discussing treatment or limitation(s) of treatment may be reported as remote real-time interactive video-conferenced critical care, provided that the conversation bears directly on the management of the patient.

Time spent in activities that occur away from the bedside when the physician does not have the real-time capabilities described above may not be reported as remote real-time interactive video-conferenced critical care because the physician is not immediately available to the patient. Time spent in activities that do not directly contribute to the treatment of the patient may not be reported as remote real-time interactive video-conferenced critical care, even if they are performed in the remote site (eg, participation in administrative meetings or telephone calls to discuss other patients). Only one physician may report either Critical Care Services (99291, 99292) or remote real-time interactive video-conferenced Critical Care for the same period of time. Do not report remote real-time interactive video-conferenced critical care if another physician reports Pediatric or Neonatal Critical Care or Intensive Care services (99468-99476).

Code 0188T is used to report the first 30 to 74 minutes of remote real-time interactive video-conferenced, critical care on a given date. It should be used only once per date even if the time spent by the physician is not continuous on that date. Remote real-time interactive video-conferenced, critical care of less than 30 minutes total duration on a given date should not be reported.

Code 0189T is used to report additional block(s) of time, of up to 30 minutes each, beyond the first 74 minutes (see table below).

The following examples illustrate the correct reporting of remote critical care services:◄

►Total Duration of Critical Care	Codes◄
►less than 30 minutes (less than 1/2 hour)	Do not report
30-74 minutes (1/2 hr. - 1 hr. 14 min.)	0188T X 1
75-104 minutes (1 hr. 15 min. - 1 hr. 44 min.)	0188T X 1 AND 0189T X 1
105-134 minutes (1 hr. 45 min. - 2 hr. 14 min.)	0188T X 1 AND 0189T X 2◄

● **0188T** Remote real-time interactive video-conferenced critical care, evaluation and management of the critically ill or critically injured patient; first 30- 74 minutes

+● **0189T** each additional 30 minutes (List separately in addition to code for primary service)

►(Use 0189T in conjunction with 0188T)◄

+● **0190T** Placement of intraocular radiation source applicator (List separately in addition to primary procedure)

►(Use 0190T in conjunction with 67036)◄

►(For application of the source by radiation oncologist, see Clinical Brachytherapy section)◄

● **0191T** Insertion of anterior segment aqueous drainage device, without extraocular reservoir; internal approach

● **0192T** external approach

● **0193T** Transurethral, radiofrequency micro-remodeling of the female bladder neck and proximal urethra for stress urinary incontinence

►(Do not report 0193T in conjunction with 51701)◄

● **0194T** Procalcitonin (PCT)

● **0195T** Arthrodesis, pre-sacral interbody technique, including instrumentation, imaging (when performed), and discectomy to prepare interspace, lumbar; single interspace

+● **0196T** each additional interspace (List separately in addition to code for primary procedure)

►(Use 0196T in conjunction with 0195T)◄

►(Do not report 0195T, 0196T in conjunction with 22558, 22845, 22851, 76000, 76380, 76496, 76497)◄

Appendix A

Modifiers

This list includes all of the modifiers applicable to *CPT 2009* codes.

A modifier provides the means to report or indicate that a service or procedure that has been performed has been altered by some specific circumstance but not changed in its definition or code. Modifiers also enable health care professionals to effectively respond to payment policy requirements established by other entities.

►(Modifier 21 has been deleted. To report prolonged physician services, see 99354-99357)◄

22 **Increased Procedural Services:** When the work required to provide a service is substantially greater than typically required, it may be identified by adding modifier 22 to the usual procedure code. Documentation must support the substantial additional work and the reason for the additional work (ie, increased intensity, time, technical difficulty of procedure, severity of patient's condition, physical and mental effort required). **Note:** This modifier should not be appended to an E/M service.

23 **Unusual Anesthesia:** Occasionally, a procedure, which usually requires either no anesthesia or local anesthesia, because of unusual circumstances must be done under general anesthesia. This circumstance may be reported by adding modifier 23 to the procedure code of the basic service.

24 **Unrelated Evaluation and Management Service by the Same Physician During a Postoperative Period:** The physician may need to indicate that an evaluation and management service was performed during a postoperative period for a reason(s) unrelated to the original procedure. This circumstance may be reported by adding modifier 24 to the appropriate level of E/M service.

25 **Significant, Separately Identifiable Evaluation and Management Service by the Same Physician on the Same Day of the Procedure or Other Service:** It may be necessary to indicate that on the day a procedure or service identified by a CPT code was performed, the patient's condition required a significant, separately identifiable E/M service above and beyond the other service provided or beyond the usual preoperative and postoperative care associated with the procedure that was performed. A significant, separately identifiable E/M service is defined or substantiated by documentation that satisfies the relevant criteria for the respective E/M service to be reported (see **Evaluation and Management Services Guidelines** for instructions on determining level of E/M service). The E/M service may be prompted by the symptom or condition for which the procedure and/or service was provided. As such, different diagnoses are not required for reporting of the E/M services on the same date. This circumstance may be reported by adding modifier 25 to the appropriate level of E/M service. **Note:** This modifier is not used to report an E/M service that resulted in a decision to perform surgery. See modifier 57. For significant, separately identifiable non-E/M services, see modifier 59.

26 **Professional Component:** Certain procedures are a combination of a physician component and a technical component. When the physician component is reported separately, the service may be identified by adding modifier 26 to the usual procedure number.

32 **Mandated Services:** Services related to *mandated* consultation and/or related services (eg, third party payer, governmental, legislative or regulatory requirement) may be identified by adding modifier 32 to the basic procedure.

47 **Anesthesia by Surgeon:** Regional or general anesthesia provided by the surgeon may be reported by adding modifier 47 to the basic service. (This does not include local anesthesia.) **Note:** Modifier 47 would not be used as a modifier for the anesthesia procedures.

50 **Bilateral Procedure:** Unless otherwise identified in the listings, bilateral procedures that are performed at the same operative session, should be identified by adding modifier 50 to the appropriate five digit code.

51 **Multiple Procedures:** When multiple procedures, other than E/M services, Physical Medicine and Rehabilitation services or provision of supplies (eg, vaccines), are performed at the same session by the same provider, the primary procedure or service may be reported as listed. The additional procedure(s) or service(s) may be identified by appending modifier 51 to the additional procedure or service code(s). **Note:** This modifier should not be appended to designated "add-on" codes (see Appendix D).

52 **Reduced Services:** Under certain circumstances a service or procedure is partially reduced or eliminated at the physician's discretion. Under these circumstances the service provided can be identified by its usual procedure number and the addition of modifier 52, signifying that the service is reduced. This provides a means of reporting reduced services without disturbing the identification of the basic service. **Note:** For hospital outpatient reporting of a previously scheduled procedure/service that is partially reduced or cancelled as a result of extenuating circumstances or those that threaten the well-being of the patient prior to or after administration of anesthesia, see modifiers 73 and 74 (see modifiers approved for ASC hospital outpatient use).

53 **Discontinued Procedure:** Under certain circumstances, the physician may elect to terminate a surgical or diagnostic procedure. Due to extenuating circumstances or those that threaten the well being of the patient, it may be necessary to indicate that a surgical or diagnostic procedure was started but discontinued. This circumstance may be reported by adding modifier 53 to the code reported by the

physician for the discontinued procedure. **Note:** This modifier is not used to report the elective cancellation of a procedure prior to the patient's anesthesia induction and/or surgical preparation in the operating suite. For outpatient hospital/ambulatory surgery center (ASC) reporting of a previously scheduled procedure/service that is partially reduced or cancelled as a result of extenuating circumstances or those that threaten the well being of the patient prior to or after administration of anesthesia, see modifiers 73 and 74 (see modifiers approved for ASC hospital outpatient use).

54 Surgical Care Only: When one physician performs a surgical procedure and another provides preoperative and/or postoperative management, surgical services may be identified by adding modifier 54 to the usual procedure number.

55 Postoperative Management Only: When one physician performed the postoperative management and another physician performed the surgical procedure, the postoperative component may be identified by adding modifier 55 to the usual procedure number.

56 Preoperative Management Only: When one physician performed the preoperative care and evaluation and another physician performed the surgical procedure, the preoperative component may be identified by adding modifier 56 to the usual procedure number.

57 Decision for Surgery: An evaluation and management service that resulted in the initial decision to perform the surgery may be identified by adding modifier 57 to the appropriate level of E/M service.

58 Staged or Related Procedure or Service by the Same Physician During the Postoperative Period: It may be necessary to indicate that the performance of a procedure or service during the postoperative period was: a) planned or anticipated (staged); b) more extensive than the original procedure; or c) for therapy following a surgical procedure. This circumstance may be reported by adding modifier 58 to the staged or related procedure. **Note:** For treatment of a problem that requires a return to the operating/procedure room (eg, unanticipated clinical condition), see modifier 78.

59 Distinct Procedural Service: Under certain circumstances, it may be necessary to indicate that a procedure or service was distinct or independent from other non-E/M services performed on the same day. Modifier 59 is used to identify procedures/services, other than E/M services, that are not normally reported together, but are appropriate under the circumstances. Documentation must support a different session, different procedure or surgery, different site or organ system, separate incision/excision, separate lesion, or separate injury (or area of injury in extensive injuries) not ordinarily encountered or performed on the same day by the same individual. However, when another already established modifier is appropriate it should be used rather than modifier 59. Only if no more descriptive modifier is available, and the use of modifier 59 best explains the circumstances, should modifier 59 be used. **Note:** Modifier 59 should not be appended to an E/M service. To report a separate and distinct E/M service with a non-E/M service performed on the same date, see modifier 25.

62 Two Surgeons: When two surgeons work together as primary surgeons performing distinct part(s) of a procedure, each surgeon should report his/her distinct operative work by adding modifier 62 to the procedure code and any associated add-on code(s) for that procedure as long as both surgeons continue to work together as primary surgeons. Each surgeon should report the co-surgery once using the same procedure code. If additional procedure(s) (including add-on procedure(s) are performed during the same surgical session, separate code(s) may also be reported with modifier 62 added. **Note:** If a co-surgeon acts as an assistant in the performance of additional procedure(s) during the same surgical session, those services may be reported using separate procedure code(s) with modifier 80 or modifier 82 added, as appropriate.

63 Procedure Performed on Infants less than 4 kg: Procedures performed on neonates and infants up to a present body weight of 4 kg may involve significantly increased complexity and physician work commonly associated with these patients. This circumstance may be reported by adding modifier 63 to the procedure number. **Note:** Unless otherwise designated, this modifier may only be appended to procedures/services listed in the 20000-69990 code series. Modifier 63 should not be appended to any CPT codes listed in the **Evaluation and Management Services, Anesthesia, Radiology, Pathology/Laboratory, or Medicine** sections.

66 Surgical Team: Under some circumstances, highly complex procedures (requiring the concomitant services of several physicians, often of different specialties, plus other highly skilled, specially trained personnel, various types of complex equipment) are carried out under the "surgical team" concept. Such circumstances may be identified by each participating physician with the addition of modifier 66 to the basic procedure number used for reporting services.

76 Repeat Procedure or Service by Same Physician: It may be necessary to indicate that a procedure or service was repeated subsequent to the original procedure or service. This circumstance may be reported by adding modifier 76 to the repeated procedure/service.

77 Repeat Procedure by Another Physician: The physician may need to indicate that a basic procedure or service performed by another physician had to be repeated. This situation may be reported by adding modifier 77 to the repeated procedure/service.

78 Unplanned Return to the Operating/Procedure Room by the Same Physician Following Initial Procedure for a Related Procedure During the Postoperative Period: It may be necessary to indicate that another procedure was performed during the postoperative period of the initial procedure (unplanned procedure following initial procedure). When this procedure is related to the first, and requires the use of an operating/procedure room, it may be reported by adding modifier 78 to the related procedure. (For repeat procedures, see modifier 76.)

79 **Unrelated Procedure or Service by the Same Physician During the Postoperative Period:** The physician may need to indicate that the performance of a procedure or service during the postoperative period was unrelated to the original procedure. This circumstance may be reported by using modifier 79. (For repeat procedures on the same day, see modifier 76.)

80 **Assistant Surgeon:** Surgical assistant services may be identified by adding modifier 80 to the usual procedure number(s).

81 **Minimum Assistant Surgeon:** Minimum surgical assistant services are identified by adding modifier 81 to the usual procedure number.

82 **Assistant Surgeon (when qualified resident surgeon not available):** The unavailability of a qualified resident surgeon is a prerequisite for use of modifier 82 appended to the usual procedure code number(s).

90 **Reference (Outside) Laboratory:** When laboratory procedures are performed by a party other than the treating or reporting physician, the procedure may be identified by adding modifier 90 to the usual procedure number.

91 **Repeat Clinical Diagnostic Laboratory Test:** In the course of treatment of the patient, it may be necessary to repeat the same laboratory test on the same day to obtain subsequent (multiple) test results. Under these circumstances, the laboratory test performed can be identified by its usual procedure number and the addition of modifier 91. **Note:** This modifier may not be used when tests are rerun to confirm initial results; due to testing problems with specimens or equipment; or for any other reason when a normal, one-time, reportable result is all that is required. This modifier may not be used when other code(s) describe a series of test results (eg, glucose tolerance tests, evocative/suppression testing). This modifier may only be used for laboratory test(s) performed more than once on the same day on the same patient.

92 **Alternative Laboratory Platform Testing:** When laboratory testing is being performed using a kit or transportable instrument that wholly or in part consists of a single use, disposable analytical chamber, the service may be identified by adding modifier 92 to the usual laboratory procedure code (HIV testing 86701-86703). The test does not require permanent dedicated space, hence by its design may be hand carried or transported to the vicinity of the patient for immediate testing at that site, although location of the testing is not in itself determinative of the use of this modifier.

99 **Multiple Modifiers:** Under certain circumstances two or more modifiers may be necessary to completely delineate a service. In such situations modifier 99 should be added to the basic procedure, and other applicable modifiers may be listed as part of the description of the service.

Anesthesia Physical Status Modifiers

The Physical Status modifiers are consistent with the American Society of Anesthesiologists ranking of patient physical status, and distinguishing various levels of complexity of the anesthesia service provided. All anesthesia services are reported by use of the anesthesia five-digit procedure code (00100-01999) with the appropriate physical status modifier appended.

Example: 00100-P1

Under certain circumstances, when another established modifier(s) is appropriate, it should be used in addition to the physical status modifier.

Example: 00100-P4-53

Physical Status Modifier P1: A normal healthy patient

Physical Status Modifier P2: A patient with mild systemic disease

Physical Status Modifier P3: A patient with severe systemic disease

Physical Status Modifier P4: A patient with severe systemic disease that is a constant threat to life

Physical Status Modifier P5: A moribund patient who is not expected to survive without the operation

Physical Status Modifier P6: A declared brain-dead patient whose organs are being removed for donor purposes

Modifiers Approved for Ambulatory Surgery Center (ASC) Hospital Outpatient Use

CPT Level I Modifiers

25 **Significant, Separately Identifiable Evaluation and Management Service by the Same Physician on the Same Day of the Procedure or Other Service:** It may be necessary to indicate that on the day a procedure or service identified by a CPT code was performed, the patient's condition required a significant, separately identifiable E/M service above and beyond the other service provided or beyond the usual preoperative and postoperative care associated with the procedure that was performed. A significant, separately identifiable E/M service is defined or substantiated by documentation that satisfies the relevant criteria for the respective E/M service to be reported (see **Evaluation and Management Services Guidelines** for instructions on determining level of E/M service). The E/M service may be prompted by the symptom or condition for which the procedure and/or service was provided. As such, different diagnoses are not required for reporting of the E/M services on the same date. This circumstance may be reported by adding modifier 25 to the appropriate level of E/M service. **Note:** This modifier is not used to report an E/M service that resulted in a decision to perform surgery. See modifier 57. For significant, separately identifiable non-E/M services, see modifier 59.

27 Multiple Outpatient Hospital E/M Encounters on the Same Date: For hospital outpatient reporting purposes, utilization of hospital resources related to separate and distinct E/M encounters performed in multiple outpatient hospital settings on the same date may be reported by adding modifier 27 to each appropriate level outpatient and/or emergency department E/M code(s). This modifier provides a means of reporting circumstances involving evaluation and management services provided by physician(s) in more than one (multiple) outpatient hospital setting(s) (eg, hospital emergency department, clinic). **Note:** This modifier is not to be used for physician reporting of multiple E/M services performed by the same physician on the same date. For physician reporting of all outpatient evaluation and management services provided by the same physician on the same date and performed in multiple outpatient setting(s) (eg, hospital emergency department, clinic), see **Evaluation and Management, Emergency Department, or Preventive Medicine Services** codes.

50 Bilateral Procedure: Unless otherwise identified in the listings, bilateral procedures that are performed at the same operative session should be identified by adding modifier 50 to the appropriate five digit code.

52 Reduced Services: Under certain circumstances a service or procedure is partially reduced or eliminated at the physician's discretion. Under these circumstances the service provided can be identified by its usual procedure number and the addition of modifier 52, signifying that the service is reduced. This provides a means of reporting reduced services without disturbing the identification of the basic service. **Note:** For hospital outpatient reporting of a previously scheduled procedure/service that is partially reduced or cancelled as a result of extenuating circumstances or those that threaten the well-being of the patient prior to or after administration of anesthesia, see modifiers 73 and 74.

58 Staged or Related Procedure or Service by the Same Physician During the Postoperative Period: It may be necessary to indicate that the performance of a procedure or service during the postoperative period was: a) planned or anticipated (staged); b) more extensive than the original procedure; or c) for therapy following a surgical procedure. This circumstance may be reported by adding modifier 58 to the staged or related procedure. **Note:** For treatment of a problem that requires a return to the operating/procedure room (eg, unanticipated clinical condition), see modifier 78.

59 Distinct Procedural Service: Under certain circumstances, it may be necessary to indicate that a procedure or service was distinct or independent from other non-E/M services performed on the same day. Modifier 59 is used to identify procedures/services, other than E/M services, that are not normally reported together, but are appropriate under the circumstances. Documentation must support a different session, different procedure or surgery, different site or organ system, separate incision/excision, separate lesion, or separate injury (or area of injury in extensive injuries) not ordinarily encountered or performed on the same day by the same individual. However, when another already established modifier is appropriate it should be used rather than modifier 59. Only if no more descriptive modifier is available, and the use of modifier 59 best explains the circumstances, should modifier 59 be used. **Note:** Modifier 59 should not be appended to an E/M service. To report a separate and distinct E/M service with a non-E/M service performed on the same date, see modifier 25.

73 Discontinued Outpatient Hospital/Ambulatory Surgery Center (ASC) Procedure Prior to the Administration of Anesthesia: Due to extenuating circumstances or those that threaten the well being of the patient, the physician may cancel a surgical or diagnostic procedure subsequent to the patient's surgical preparation (including sedation when provided, and being taken to the room where the procedure is to be performed), but prior to the administration of anesthesia (local, regional block(s) or general). Under these circumstances, the intended service that is prepared for but cancelled can be reported by its usual procedure number and the addition of modifier 73. **Note:** The elective cancellation of a service prior to the administration of anesthesia and/or surgical preparation of the patient should not be reported. For physician reporting of a discontinued procedure, see modifier 53.

74 Discontinued Outpatient Hospital/Ambulatory Surgery Center (ASC) Procedure After Administration of Anesthesia: Due to extenuating circumstances or those that threaten the well being of the patient, the physician may terminate a surgical or diagnostic procedure after the administration of anesthesia (local, regional block(s), general) or after the procedure was started (incision made, intubation started, scope inserted, etc). Under these circumstances, the procedure started but terminated can be reported by its usual procedure number and the addition of modifier 74. **Note:** The elective cancellation of a service prior to the administration of anesthesia and/or surgical preparation of the patient should not be reported. For physician reporting of a discontinued procedure, see modifier 53.

76 Repeat Procedure or Service by Same Physician: It may be necessary to indicate that a procedure or service was repeated subsequent to the original procedure or service. This circumstance may be reported by adding modifier 76 to the repeated procedure/service.

77 Repeat Procedure by Another Physician: The physician may need to indicate that a basic procedure or service performed by another physician had to be repeated. This situation may be reported by adding modifier 77 to the repeated procedure/service.

78 Unplanned Return to the Operating/Procedure Room by the Same Physician Following Initial Procedure for a Related Procedure During the Postoperative Period: It may be necessary to indicate that another procedure was performed during the postoperative period of the initial procedure (unplanned procedure following initial procedure). When this procedure is related to the first, and requires the use of an operating/procedure room, it may be reported by adding modifier 78 to the related procedure. (For repeat procedures, see modifier 76.)

79 Unrelated Procedure or Service by the Same Physician During the Postoperative Period: The physician may need to indicate that the performance of a procedure or service during the postoperative period was unrelated to the original procedure. This circumstance may be reported by using modifier 79. (For repeat procedures on the same day, see 76.)

91 Repeat Clinical Diagnostic Laboratory Test: In the course of treatment of the patient, it may be necessary to repeat the same laboratory test on the same day to obtain subsequent (multiple) test results. Under these circumstances, the laboratory test performed can be identified by its usual procedure number and the addition of modifier 91. **Note:** This modifier may not be used when tests are rerun to confirm initial results; due to testing problems with specimens or equipment; or for any other reason when a normal, one-time, reportable result is all that is required. This modifier may not be used when other code(s) describe a series of test results (eg, glucose tolerance tests, evocative/suppression testing). This modifier may only be used for laboratory test(s) performed more than once on the same day on the same patient.

Level II (HCPCS/National) Modifiers

E1 Upper left, eyelid

E2 Lower left, eyelid

E3 Upper right, eyelid

E4 Lower right, eyelid

F1 Left hand, second digit

F2 Left hand, third digit

F3 Left hand, fourth digit

F4 Left hand, fifth digit

F5 Right hand, thumb

F6 Right hand, second digit

F7 Right hand, third digit

F8 Right hand, fourth digit

F9 Right hand, fifth digit

FA Left hand, thumb

GG Performance and payment of a screening mammogram and diagnostic mammogram on the same patient, same day

GH Diagnostic mammogram converted from screening mammogram on same day

LC Left circumflex coronary artery (Hospitals use with codes 92980-92984, 92995, 92996)

LD Left anterior descending coronary artery (Hospitals use with codes 92980-92984, 92995, 92996)

LT Left side (used to identify procedures performed on the left side of the body)

QM Ambulance service provided under arrangement by a provider of services

QN Ambulance service furnished directly by a provider of services

RC Right coronary artery (Hospitals use with codes 92980-92984, 92995, 92996)

RT Right side (used to identify procedures performed on the right side of the body)

T1 Left foot, second digit

T2 Left foot, third digit

T3 Left foot, fourth digit

T4 Left foot, fifth digit

T5 Right foot, great toe

T6 Right foot, second digit

T7 Right foot, third digit

T8 Right foot, fourth digit

T9 Right foot, fifth digit

TA Left foot, great toe

Appendix B

Summary of Additions, Deletions, and Revisions

►Appendix B shows the actual changes that were made to the code descriptors. New codes appear with a bullet (●) and are indicated as "Code Added." Revised codes are preceded with a triangle (▲). The symbol ○ precedes codes that are recycled or reinstated. Within revised codes, the deleted language appears with a ~~strikethrough~~, while new text appears underlined. Codes with which conscious sedation would not be separately reported when performed at the same session by the same provider are denoted with the bullseye (⦿). The symbol ⁄⁄ is used to identify codes for vaccines that are pending FDA approval (see **Appendix K**).◄

Revisions to the headings, notes, introductory paragraphs, and cross-references are not included in this Appendix, but are identified in the main text of the book with the "► ◄" symbols and presented in green.

Evaluation and Management

~~**99289**~~ ~~Critical care services delivered by a physician, face-to-face, during an interfacility transport of critically ill or critically injured pediatric patient, 24 months of age or less; first 30-74 minutes of hands-on care during transport~~

~~**99290**~~ ~~each additional 30 minutes (List separately in addition to code for primary service)~~

~~**99293**~~ ~~**Initial inpatient pediatric critical care,** per day, for the evaluation and management of a critically ill infant or young child, 29 days through 24 months of age~~

~~**99294**~~ ~~**Subsequent inpatient pediatric critical care,** per day, for the evaluation and management of a critically ill infant or young child, 29 days through 24 months of age~~

~~**99295**~~ ~~**Initial inpatient neonatal critical care,** per day, for the evaluation and management of a critically ill neonate, 28 days of age or less~~

~~**99296**~~ ~~**Subsequent inpatient neonatal critical care,** per day, for the evaluation and management of a critically ill neonate, 28 days of age or less~~

~~**99298**~~ ~~**Subsequent intensive care,** per day, for the evaluation and management of the recovering very low birth weight infant (present body weight less than 1500 g)~~

~~**99299**~~ ~~**Subsequent intensive care,** per day, for the evaluation and management of the recovering low birth weight infant (present body weight of 1500-2500 g)~~

~~**99300**~~ ~~**Subsequent intensive care,** per day, for the evaluation and management of the recovering infant (present body weight of 2501-5000 g)~~

+▲ 99354 Prolonged physician service in the office or other outpatient setting requiring direct (face-to-face) patient contact beyond the usual service~~(eg, prolonged care and treatment of an acute asthmatic patient in an outpatient setting)~~; first hour (List separately in addition to code for office or other outpatient **Evaluation and Management** service)

+▲ 99355 each additional 30 minutes (List separately in addition to code for prolonged physician service)

+▲ 99356 Prolonged physician service in the inpatient setting, requiring unit/floor time~~ direct (face-to-face) patient contact~~ beyond the usual service~~ (eg, maternal fetal monitoring for high risk delivery or other physiological monitoring, prolonged care of an acutely ill inpatient)~~; first hour (List separately in addition to code for inpatient Evaluation and Management service)

+▲ 99357 each additional 30 minutes (List separately in addition to code for prolonged physician service)

▲ 99381 **Initial comprehensive preventive medicine** evaluation and management of an individual including an age and gender appropriate history, examination, counseling/anticipatory guidance/risk factor reduction interventions, and the ordering of ~~appropriate immunization(s),~~ laboratory/diagnostic procedures, new patient; infant (age younger than 1 year)

▲ 99382 early childhood (age 1 through 4 years)

▲ 99383 late childhood (age 5 through 11 years)

▲ 99384 adolescent (age 12 through 17 years)

▲ 99385 18-39 years

▲ 99386 40-64 years

▲ 99387 65 years and older

▲ 99391 **Periodic comprehensive preventive medicine** reevaluation and management of an individual including an age and gender appropriate history, examination, counseling/anticipatory guidance/risk factor reduction interventions, and the ordering of ~~appropriate immunization(s),~~ laboratory/diagnostic procedures, established patient; infant (age younger than 1 year)

▲ 99392 early childhood (age 1 through 4 years)

▲ 99393 late childhood (age 5 through 11 years)

▲ 99394 adolescent (age 12 through 17 years)

▲ 99395 18-39 years

▲ 99396 40-64 years

▲ 99397 65 years and older

~~**99431**~~ ~~**History and examination** of the normal newborn infant, initiation of diagnostic and treatment programs and preparation of hospital records. (This code should also be used for birthing room deliveries.)~~

~~**99432**~~ ~~**Normal newborn care** in other than hospital or birthing room setting, including physical examination of baby and conference(s) with parent(s)~~

~~**99433**~~ ~~**Subsequent hospital care,** for the evaluation and management of a normal newborn, per day~~

~~**99435**~~ ~~**History and examination** of the normal newborn infant, including the preparation of medical records. (This code should only be used for newborns assessed and discharged from the hospital or birthing room on the same date.)~~

~~**99436**~~ ~~**Attendance** at delivery (when requested by delivering physician) and initial stabilization of newborn~~

~~99440~~ ~~**Newborn resuscitation**: provision of positive pressure ventilation and/or chest compressions in the presence of acute inadequate ventilation and/or cardiac output~~

● 99460 Code added

● 99461 Code added

● 99462 Code added

● 99463 Code added

● 99464 Code added

● 99465 Code added

● 99466 Code added

+● 99467 Code added

● 99468 Code added

● 99469 Code added

● 99471 Code added

● 99472 Code added

● 99475 Code added

● 99476 Code added

● 99478 Code added

● 99479 Code added

● 99480 Code added

Anesthesia

● 00211 Code added

00561 Grammatical Change

▲ 00562 with pump oxygenator, age 1 year or older, for all non-coronary bypass procedures (eg, valve procedures) or for re-operation for coronary bypass more than 1 month after original operation

▲ 00566 Anesthesia for direct coronary artery bypass grafting; without pump oxygenator

● 00567 Code added

Surgery

+▲ 11001 each additional 10% of the body surface, or part thereof (List separately in addition to code for primary procedure)

+▲ 11201 each additional 10 lesions, or part thereof (List separately in addition to code for primary procedure)

11720 Grammatical Change

11721 Grammatical Change

+▲ 11922 each additional 20.0 sq cm, or part thereof (List separately in addition to code for primary procedure)

▲ 12031 Repair, intermediate, ~~Layer closure of~~ wounds of scalp, axillae, trunk and/or extremities (excluding hands and feet); 2.5 cm or less

▲ 12032 2.6 cm to 7.5 cm

▲ 12034 7.6 cm to 12.5 cm

▲ 12035 12.6 cm to 20.0 cm

▲ 12036 20.1 cm to 30.0 cm

▲ 12037 over 30.0 cm

▲ 12041 Repair, intermediate, ~~Layer closure of~~ wounds of neck, hands, feet and/or external genitalia; 2.5 cm or less

▲ 12042 2.6 cm to 7.5 cm

▲ 12044 7.6 cm to 12.5 cm

▲ 12045 12.6 cm to 20.0 cm

▲ 12046 20.1 cm to 30.0 cm

▲ 12047 over 30.0 cm

▲ 12051 Repair, intermediate, ~~Layer closure of~~ wounds of face, ears, eyelids, nose, lips and/or mucous membranes; 2.5 cm or less

▲ 12052 2.6 cm to 5.0 cm

▲ 12053 5.1 cm to 7.5 cm

▲ 12054 7.6 cm to 12.5 cm

▲ 12055 12.6 cm to 20.0 cm

▲ 12056 20.1 cm to 30.0 cm

▲ 12057 over 30.0 cm

+▲ 15003 each additional 100 sq cm, or part thereof, or each additional 1% of body area of infants and children (List separately in addition to code for primary procedure)

+▲ 15005 each additional 100 sq cm, or part thereof, or each additional 1% of body area of infants and children (List separately in addition to code for primary procedure)

+▲ 15201 each additional 20 sq cm, or part thereof (List separately in addition to code for primary procedure)

+▲ 15221 each additional 20 sq cm, or part thereof (List separately in addition to code for primary procedure)

+▲ 15241 each additional 20 sq cm, or part thereof (List separately in addition to code for primary procedure)

+▲ 15261 each additional 20 sq cm, or part thereof (List separately in addition to code for primary procedure)

+▲ 15341 each additional 25 sq cm, or part thereof (List separately in addition to code for primary procedure)

▲ 19296 Placement of radiotherapy afterloading ~~balloon~~ expandable catheter (single or multichannel) into the breast for interstitial radioelement application following partial mastectomy, includes imaging guidance; on date separate from partial mastectomy

+▲ 19297 concurrent with partial mastectomy (List separately in addition to code for primary procedure)

20552 Grammatical Change

20553 Grammatical Change

20693 Grammatical Change

● 20696 Code added

⊘● 20697 Code added

+▲ 20985 Computer-assisted surgical navigational procedure for musculoskeletal procedures, ~~;~~ image-less (List separately in addition to code for primary procedure)

~~20986~~ ~~with image guidance based on intraoperatively obtained images (eg, fluoroscopy, ultrasound) (List separately in addition to code for primary procedure)~~

~~20987~~ ~~with image guidance based on preoperative images (List separately in addition to code for primary procedure)~~

21122 Grammatical Change

21142 Grammatical Change

21143	Grammatical Change
21146	Grammatical Change
21147	Grammatical Change
● 22856	Code added
▲ 22857	Total disc arthroplasty (artificial disc), anterior approach, including discectomy to prepare interspace (other than for decompression), single interspace, lumbar~~, single interspace~~
● 22861	Code added
▲ 22862	~~Revision including replacement of total disc arthroplasty (artificial disc) anterior approach, single interspace,~~ lumbar~~, single interspace~~
● 22864	Code added
▲ 22865	~~Removal of total disc arthroplasty (artificial disc), anterior approach,~~lumbar~~, single interspace~~
▲ 23585	Open treatment of scapular fracture (body, glenoid or acromion) ~~with or without~~includes internal fixation, when performed
25630	Grammatical Change
25645	Grammatical Change
26517	Grammatical Change
26518	Grammatical Change
● 27027	Code added
● 27057	Code added
▲ 27215	Open treatment of iliac spine(s), tuberosity avulsion, or iliac wing fracture(s), ~~(eg,~~ unilateral, for pelvic bone fracture~~(s)~~ patterns that do not disrupt the pelvic ring~~)~~, ~~with~~ includes internal fixation, when performed
▲ 27216	Percutaneous skeletal fixation of posterior pelvic ~~ring~~bone fracture and/or dislocation, for fracture patterns that disrupt the pelvic ring, unilateral (includes ipsilateral ilium, sacroiliac joint and/or sacrum)
▲ 27217	Open treatment of anterior ~~ring~~pelvic bone fracture and/or dislocation for fracture patterns that disrupt the pelvic ring, unilateral, ~~with~~includes internal fixation, when performed (includes pubic symphysis and/or ipsilateral superior/inferior rami)
▲ 27218	Open treatment of posterior pelvic bone ~~ring~~ fracture and/or dislocation, for fracture patterns that disrupt the pelvic ring, unilateral, ~~with~~includes internal fixation, when performed (includes ipsilateral ilium, sacroiliac joint and/or sacrum)
▲ 27396	Transplant or transfer (with muscle redirection or rerouting), ~~hamstring tendon to patella~~thigh (eg, extensor to flexor); single tendon
▲ 27397	multiple tendons
27455	Grammatical Change
+⊙ 31620	Grammatical Change
+▲ 34806	Transcatheter placement of wireless physiologic sensor in aneurysmal sac during endovascular repair, including radiological supervision and interpretation, instrument calibration, and collection of pressure data (List separately in addition to code for primary procedure)
● 35535	Code added
● 35570	Code added
● 35632	Code added
● 35633	Code added
● 35634	Code added
● 41512	Code added
● 41530	Code added
+⊙● 43273	Code added
● 43279	Code added
▲ 43460	Esophagogastric tamponade, with balloon (~~Sengstaaken~~Sengstaken type)
● 46930	Code added
~~46934~~	~~Destruction of hemorrhoids, any method; internal~~
~~46935~~	~~external~~
~~46936~~	~~internal and external~~
47144	Grammatical Change
+▲ 49568	Implantation of mesh or other prosthesis for open incisional or ventral hernia repair or mesh for closure of debridement for necrotizing soft tissue infection (List separately in addition to code for the incisional or ventral hernia repair)
● 49652	Code added
● 49653	Code added
● 49654	Code added
● 49655	Code added
● 49656	Code added
● 49657	Code added
~~52606~~	~~Transurethral fulguration for postoperative bleeding occurring after the usual follow-up time~~
~~52612~~	~~Transurethral resection of prostate; first stage of two-stage resection (partial resection)~~
~~52614~~	~~second stage of two-stage resection (resection completed)~~
~~52620~~	~~Transurethral resection; of residual obstructive tissue after 90 days postoperative~~
▲ 52630	Transurethral resection; residual or~~of~~ regrowth of obstructive prostate tissue ~~longer than one year postoperative~~including control of postoperative bleeding, complete (vasectomy, meatotomy, cystourethroscopy, urethral calibration and/or dilation, and internal urethrotomy are included)
53410	Grammatical Change
53420	Grammatical Change
~~53853~~	~~by water-induced thermotherapy~~
● 55706	Code added
▲ 57400	Dilation of vagina under anesthesia (other than local)
▲ 57410	Pelvic examination under anesthesia (other than local)
▲ 57415	Removal of impacted vaginal foreign body (separate procedure) under anesthesia (other than local)
~~61793~~	~~Stereotactic radiosurgery (particle beam, gamma ray or linear accelerator), one or more sessions~~
● 61796	Code added
+● 61797	Code added
● 61798	Code added
+● 61799	Code added

+● **61800** Code added

● **62267** Code added

▲ **62287** ~~Aspiration or d~~Decompression procedure, percutaneous, of nucleus pulposus of intervertebral disc, any method, single or multiple levels, lumbar (eg, manual or automated percutaneous discectomy, percutaneous laser discectomy)

▲ **63020** Laminotomy (hemilaminectomy), with decompression of nerve root(s), including partial facetectomy, foraminotomy and/or excision of herniated intervertebral disc~~;~~, including open and endoscopically-assisted approaches; 1 interspace, cervical

▲ **63030** 1 interspace, lumbar ~~(including open or endoscopically assisted approach)~~

+▲ **63035** each additional interspace, cervical or lumbar (List separately in addition to code for primary procedure)

63180 Grammatical Change

63182 Grammatical Change

63185 Grammatical Change

63190 Grammatical Change

63194 Grammatical Change

63196 Grammatical Change

63198 Grammatical Change

● **63620** Code added

+● **63621** Code added

▲ **64416** brachial plexus, continuous infusion by catheter (including catheter placement)~~including daily management for anesthetic agent administration~~

▲ **64446** sciatic nerve, continuous infusion by catheter (including catheter placement)~~, including daily management for anesthetic agent administration~~

▲ **64448** femoral nerve, continuous infusion by catheter (including catheter placement) ~~including daily management for anesthetic agent administration~~

▲ **64449** lumbar plexus, posterior approach, continuous infusion by catheter (including catheter placement) ~~including daily management for anesthetic agent administration~~

● **64455** Code added

● **64632** Code added

64702 Grammatical Change

64776 Grammatical Change

64831 Grammatical Change

▲ **65710** Keratoplasty (corneal transplant); anterior lamellar

▲ **65730** penetrating (except in aphakia or pseudophakia)

● **65756** Code added

+● **65757** Code added

65855 Grammatical Change

66761 Grammatical Change

66762 Grammatical Change

66821 Grammatical Change

66840 Grammatical Change

66983 Grammatical Change

66984 Grammatical Change

67031 Grammatical Change

67101 Grammatical Change

67141 Grammatical Change

67208 Grammatical Change

67220 Grammatical Change

67227 Grammatical Change

67228 Grammatical Change

67311 Grammatical Change

67312 Grammatical Change

67314 Grammatical Change

67316 Grammatical Change

67971 Grammatical Change

67973 Grammatical Change

67974 Grammatical Change

69210 Grammatical Change

69633 Grammatical Change

69637 Grammatical Change

Radiology

70100 Grammatical Change

70110 Grammatical Change

70120 Grammatical Change

70130 Grammatical Change

70140 Grammatical Change

70150 Grammatical Change

70200 Grammatical Change

70210 Grammatical Change

70220 Grammatical Change

70250 Grammatical Change

70260 Grammatical Change

71020 Grammatical Change

71030 Grammatical Change

71100 Grammatical Change

71101 Grammatical Change

71110 Grammatical Change

71111 Grammatical Change

71120 Grammatical Change

71130 Grammatical Change

72040 Grammatical Change

72050 Grammatical Change

72070 Grammatical Change

72072 Grammatical Change

72074 Grammatical Change

72080 Grammatical Change

72100 Grammatical Change

72110 Grammatical Change

72120 Grammatical Change

72170 Grammatical Change

72190 Grammatical Change

72200 Grammatical Change

72202 Grammatical Change

72220 Grammatical Change

72270 Grammatical Change

73020 Grammatical Change

73030 Grammatical Change

73060 Grammatical Change

73070 Grammatical Change

73080 Grammatical Change

73090 Grammatical Change

73092 Grammatical Change

73100 Grammatical Change

73110 Grammatical Change

73120 Grammatical Change

73130 Grammatical Change

73140 Grammatical Change

73500 Grammatical Change

73510 Grammatical Change

73520 Grammatical Change

73540 Grammatical Change

73550 Grammatical Change

73560 Grammatical Change

73562 Grammatical Change

73564 Grammatical Change

73590 Grammatical Change

73592 Grammatical Change

73600 Grammatical Change

73610 Grammatical Change

73620 Grammatical Change

73630 Grammatical Change

73650 Grammatical Change

73660 Grammatical Change

▲ **74270** Radiologic examination, colon; contrast (eg, barium) enema, with or without KUB

76815 Grammatical Change

77305 Grammatical Change

77310 Grammatical Change

77326 Grammatical Change

77407 Grammatical Change

77412 Grammatical Change

77427 Grammatical Change

77431 Grammatical Change

77432 Grammatical Change

77435 Grammatical Change

77750 Grammatical Change

~~**77781** Remote afterloading high intensity brachytherapy; 1-4 source positions or catheters~~

~~**77782** 5-8 source positions or catheters~~

~~**77783** 9-12 source positions or catheters~~

~~**77784** over 12 source positions or catheters~~

● **77785** Code added

● **77786** Code added

● **77787** Code added

78315 Grammatical Change

78350 Grammatical Change

78351 Grammatical Change

78588 Grammatical Change

78804 Grammatical Change

● **78808** Code added

~~**78890** Generation of automated data: interactive process involving nuclear physician and/or allied health professional personnel; simple manipulations and interpretation, not to exceed 30 minutes~~

~~**78891** complex manipulations and interpretation, exceeding 30 minutes~~

Pathology and Laboratory

▲ **80048** Basic metabolic panel (Calcium, total)

This panel must include the following:

Calcium, total (82310)

Carbon dioxide (82374)

Chloride (82435)

Creatinine (82565)

Glucose (82947)

Potassium (84132)

Sodium (84295)

Urea nitrogen (BUN) (84520)

▲ **80053** Comprehensive metabolic panel

This panel must include the following:

Albumin (82040)

Bilirubin, total (82247)

Calcium, total (82310)

Carbon dioxide (bicarbonate) (82374)

Chloride (82435)

Creatinine (82565)

Glucose (82947)

Phosphatase, alkaline (84075)

Potassium (84132)

Protein, total (84155)

Sodium (84295)

	Transferase, alanine amino (ALT) (SGPT) (84460)
	Transferase, aspartate amino (AST) (SGOT) (84450)
	Urea nitrogen (BUN) (84520)
▲ 80069	Renal function panel
	This panel must include the following:
	Albumin (82040)
	Calcium, total (82310)
	Carbon dioxide (bicarbonate) (82374)
	Chloride (82435)
	Creatinine (82565)
	Glucose (82947)
	Phosphorus inorganic (phosphate) (84100)
	Potassium (84132)
	Sodium (84295)
	Urea nitrogen (BUN) (84520)
80438	Grammatical Change
80439	Grammatical Change
81020	Grammatical Change
▲ 82040	Albumin; serum, plasma or whole blood
▲ 82375	~~Carbon monoxide (c~~Carboxyhemoglobin~~)~~; quantitative
▲ 82376	qualitative
82652	Grammatical Change
● 83876	Code added
▲ 83890	Molecular diagnostics; molecular isolation or extraction, each nucleic acid type (ie, DNA or RNA)
▲ 83891	isolation or extraction of highly purified nucleic acid, each nucleic acid type (ie, DNA or RNA)
▲ 83892	enzymatic digestion, each enzyme treatment
▲ 83893	dot/slot blot production, each nucleic acid preparation
▲ 83894	separation by gel electrophoresis (eg, agarose, polyacrylamide), each nucleic acid preparation
▲ 83897	nucleic acid transfer (eg, Southern, Northern), each nucleic acid preparation
83900	Grammatical Change
83903	Grammatical Change
▲ 83907	lysis of cells prior to nucleic acid extraction (eg, stool specimens, paraffin embedded tissue), each specimen
▲ 83909	separation and identification by high resolution technique (eg, capillary electrophoresis), each nucleic acid preparation
83914	Grammatical Change
▲ 83925	Opiate(s), ~~(eg, morphine, meperidine)~~drug and metabolites, each procedure
▲ 83950	Oncoprotein~~,~~; HER-2/neu
● 83951	Code added
▲ 84132	Potassium; serum, plasma or whole blood
▲ 84155	Protein, total, except by refractometry; serum, plasma or whole blood
▲ 84295	Sodium; serum, plasma or whole blood
85046	Grammatical Change
● 85397	Code added
87186	Grammatical Change
▲ 87810	~~Infectious agent detection by immunoassay with direct optical observation;~~ Chlamydia trachomatis
87901	Grammatical Change
● 87905	Code added
✚ 88155	Grammatical Change
~~88400~~	~~Bilirubin, total, transcutaneous~~
● 88720	Code added
● 88740	Code added
● 88741	Code added
89135	Grammatical Change

Medicine

✗● 90650	Code added
● 90681	Code added
● 90696	Code added
90698	Diphtheria, tetanus toxoids, acellular pertussis vaccine, haemophilus influenza Type B, and poliovirus vaccine, inactivated (DTaP - Hib - IPV), for intramuscular use
✗● 90738	Code added
~~90760~~	~~Intravenous infusion, hydration; initial, 31 minutes to 1 hour~~
~~90761~~	~~each additional hour (List separately in addition to code for primary procedure)~~
~~90765~~	~~Intravenous infusion, for therapy, prophylaxis, or diagnosis (specify substance or drug); initial, up to 1 hour~~
~~90766~~	~~each additional hour (List separately in addition to code for primary procedure)~~
~~90767~~	~~additional sequential infusion, up to 1 hour (List separately in addition to code for primary procedure)~~
~~90768~~	~~concurrent infusion (List separately in addition to code for primary procedure)~~
~~90769~~	~~Subcutaneous infusion for therapy or prophylaxis (specify substance or drug); initial, up to one hour, including pump set-up and establishment of subcutaneous infusion site(s)~~
~~90770~~	~~each additional hour (List separately in addition to code for primary procedure)~~
~~90771~~	~~additional pump set-up with establishment of new subcutaneous infusion site(s) (List separately in addition to code for primary procedure)~~
~~90772~~	~~Therapeutic, prophylactic or diagnostic injection (specify substance or drug); subcutaneous or intramuscular~~
~~90773~~	~~intra-arterial~~
~~90774~~	~~intravenous push, single or initial substance/drug~~
~~90775~~	~~each additional sequential intravenous push of a new substance/drug (List separately in addition to code for primary procedure)~~
~~90776~~	~~each additional sequential intravenous push of the same substance/drug provided in a facility (List separately in addition to code for primary procedure)~~

~~**90779**~~ ~~Unlisted therapeutic, prophylactic or diagnostic intravenous or intra-arterial injection or infusion~~

~~**90918**~~ ~~End stage renal disease (ESRD) related services per full month; for patients younger than two years of age to include monitoring for the adequacy of nutrition, assessment of growth and development, and counseling of parents~~

~~**90919**~~ ~~for patients between two and eleven years of age to include monitoring for the adequacy of nutrition, assessment of growth and development, and counseling of parents~~

~~**90920**~~ ~~for patients between twelve and nineteen years of age to include monitoring for the adequacy of nutrition, assessment of growth and development, and counseling of parents~~

~~**90921**~~ ~~for patients twenty years of age and older~~

~~**90922**~~ ~~End stage renal disease (ESRD) related services (less than full month), per day; for patients younger than two years of age~~

~~**90923**~~ ~~for patients between two and eleven years of age~~

~~**90924**~~ ~~for patients between twelve and nineteen years of age~~

~~**90925**~~ ~~for patients twenty years of age and older~~

● **90951** Code added

● **90952** Code added

● **90953** Code added

● **90954** Code added

● **90955** Code added

● **90956** Code added

● **90957** Code added

● **90958** Code added

● **90959** Code added

● **90960** Code added

● **90961** Code added

● **90962** Code added

● **90963** Code added

● **90964** Code added

● **90965** Code added

● **90966** Code added

● **90967** Code added

● **90968** Code added

● **90969** Code added

● **90970** Code added

~~**91100**~~ ~~Intestinal bleeding tube, passage, positioning and monitoring~~

92004 Grammatical Change

92014 Grammatical Change

92265 Grammatical Change

92311 Grammatical Change

92315 Grammatical Change

93040 Grammatical Change

▲ **93224** Wearable ~~E~~electrocardiographic rhythm derived monitoring for 24 hours by continuous original ~~ECG~~ waveform recording and storage, with visual superimposition scanning; includes recording, scanning analysis with report, physician review and interpretation

▲ **93225** recording (includes connection ~~hook up~~, recording, and disconnection)

▲ **93226** scanning analysis with report

▲ **93227** physician review and interpretation

● **93228** Code added

● **93229** Code added

▲ **93230** Wearable ~~E~~electrocardiographic rhythm derived monitoring for 24 hours by continuous original ~~ECG~~ waveform recording and storage without superimposition scanning utilizing a device capable of producing a full miniaturized printout; includes recording, microprocessor-based analysis with report, physician review and interpretation

▲ **93231** recording (includes connection ~~hook up~~, recording, and disconnection)

▲ **93232** microprocessor-based analysis with report

▲ **93233** physician review and interpretation

▲ **93235** Wearable ~~E~~electrocardiographic rhythm derived monitoring for 24 hours by continuous computerized monitoring and non-continuous recording, and real-time data analysis utilizing a device capable of producing intermittent full-sized waveform tracings, possibly patient activated; includes monitoring and real-time data analysis with report, physician review and interpretation

▲ **93236** monitoring and real-time data analysis with report

▲ **93237** physician review and interpretation

▲ **93268** Wearable ~~P~~patient activated ~~demand single or multiple~~ electrocardiographic rhythm derived event recording with presymptom memory loop, 24-hour attended monitoring, per 30 day period of time; includes transmission, physician review and interpretation

▲ **93270** recording (includes ~~hook up~~ connection, recording, and disconnection)

▲ **93271** monitoring, receipt of transmissions, and analysis

▲ **93272** physician review and interpretation

● **93279** Code added

● **93280** Code added

● **93281** Code added

● **93282** Code added

● **93283** Code added

● **93284** Code added

● **93285** Code added

● **93286** Code added

● **93287** Code added

● **93288** Code added

● **93289** Code added

● **93290** Code added

● **93291** Code added

● **93292** Code added

● **93293** Code added

● **93294** Code added

● **93295** Code added

●	93296	Code added
●	93297	Code added
●	93298	Code added
●	93299	Code added
●	93306	Code added
▲	93307	Echocardiography, transthoracic, real-time with image documentation (2D), includes ~~with or without~~ M-mode recording, when performed, complete, without spectral or color Doppler echocardiography
▲	93308	Echocardiography, transthoracic, real-time with image documentation (2D), includes M-mode recording, when performed, follow-up or limited study
⊙	93312	Grammatical Change
▲	93350	Echocardiography, transthoracic, real-time with image documentation (2D), includes ~~with or without~~ M-mode recording, when performed, during rest and cardiovascular stress test using treadmill, bicycle exercise and/or pharmacologically induced stress, with interpretation and report;
●	93351	Code added
+●	93352	Code added
	~~93727~~	~~Electronic analysis of implantable loop recorder (ILR) system (includes retrieval of recorded and stored ECG data, physician review and interpretation of retrieved ECG data and reprogramming)~~
	~~93731~~	~~Electronic analysis of dual-chamber pacemaker system (includes evaluation of programmable parameters at rest and during activity where applicable, using electrocardiographic recording and interpretation of recordings at rest and during exercise, analysis of event markers and device response); without reprogramming~~
	~~93732~~	~~with reprogramming~~
	~~93733~~	~~Electronic analysis of dual chamber internal pacemaker system (may include rate, pulse amplitude and duration, configuration of wave form, and/or testing of sensory function of pacemaker), telephonic analysis~~
	~~93734~~	~~Electronic analysis of single chamber pacemaker system (includes evaluation of programmable parameters at rest and during activity where applicable, using electrocardiographic recording and interpretation of recordings at rest and during exercise, analysis of event markers and device response); without reprogramming~~
	~~93735~~	~~with reprogramming~~
	~~93736~~	~~Electronic analysis of single chamber internal pacemaker system (may include rate, pulse amplitude and duration, configuration of wave form, and/or testing of sensory function of pacemaker), telephonic analysis~~
	~~93741~~	~~Electronic analysis of pacing cardioverter-defibrillator (includes interrogation, evaluation of pulse generator status, evaluation of programmable parameters at rest and during activity where applicable, using electrocardiographic recording and interpretation of recordings at rest and during exercise, analysis of event markers and device response); single chamber or wearable cardioverter-defibrillator system, without reprogramming~~
	~~93742~~	~~single chamber or wearable cardioverter-defibrillator system, with reprogramming~~
	~~93743~~	~~dual chamber, without reprogramming~~
	~~93744~~	~~dual chamber, with reprogramming~~
	~~93760~~	~~Thermogram; cephalic~~
	~~93762~~	~~peripheral~~
▲	95010	Percutaneous tests (scratch, puncture, prick) sequential and incremental, with drugs, biologicals or venoms, immediate type reaction, including test interpretation and report by a physician, specify number of tests
▲	95015	Intracutaneous (intradermal) tests, sequential and incremental, with drugs, biologicals, or venoms, immediate type reaction, including test interpretation and report by a physician, specify number of tests
	95117	Grammatical Change
	95125	Grammatical Change
	95131	Grammatical Change
	95132	Grammatical Change
	95133	Grammatical Change
	95134	Grammatical Change
	95146	Grammatical Change
	95147	Grammatical Change
	95148	Grammatical Change
	95149	Grammatical Change
▲	95250	Ambulatory continuous glucose monitoring of interstitial tissue fluid via a subcutaneous sensor for ~~up to~~a minimum of 72 hours; sensor placement, hook-up, calibration of monitor, patient training, removal of sensor, and printout of recording
▲	95251	~~physician~~interpretation and report
●	95803	Code added
	95813	Grammatical Change
	95861	Grammatical Change
	95863	Grammatical Change
	95864	Grammatical Change
	95922	Grammatical Change
⊘●	95992	Code added
	96000	Grammatical Change
●	96360	Code added
+●	96361	Code added
●	96365	Code added
+●	96366	Code added
+●	96367	Code added
+●	96368	Code added
●	96369	Code added
+●	96370	Code added
+●	96371	Code added
●	96372	Code added
●	96373	Code added
●	96374	Code added
+●	96375	Code added
+●	96376	Code added

● **96379**	Code added
96422	Grammatical Change
97010	Grammatical Change
98925	Grammatical Change
98926	Grammatical Change
98927	Grammatical Change
98928	Grammatical Change
98929	Grammatical Change
98940	Grammatical Change
98941	Grammatical Change
98942	Grammatical Change
98943	Grammatical Change
98966	Grammatical Change
✚ **99100**	Grammatical Change

Category II Codes

● **0014F**	Code added
● **0015F**	Code added
● **0513F**	Code added
● **0514F**	Code added
● **0516F**	Code added
● **0517F**	Code added
● **0518F**	Code added
● **0519F**	Code added
● **0520F**	Code added
● **0521F**	Code added
● **0525F**	Code added
● **0526F**	Code added
▲ **1040F**	DSM-IV™ criteria for major depressive disorder documented at the initial evaluation (MDD)[1]
~~**1080F**~~	~~Surrogate decision maker or advance care plan documented in the medical record (GER)[5]~~
● **1116F**	Code added
● **1118F**	Code added
● **1119F**	Code added
● **1121F**	Code added
● **1123F**	Code added
● **1124F**	Code added
● **1125F**	Code added
● **1126F**	Code added
● **1127F**	Code added
● **1128F**	Code added
● **1130F**	Code added
● **1134F**	Code added
● **1135F**	Code added
● **1136F**	Code added
● **1137F**	Code added
2000F	Grammatical Change
2010F	Grammatical Change
2022F	Grammatical Change
2024F	Grammatical Change
2026F	Grammatical Change
2028F	Grammatical Change
● **2035F**	Code added
● **2040F**	Code added
● **2044F**	Code added
3014F	Grammatical Change
▲ **3017F**	Colorectal cancer screening results documented and reviewed (PV)[1, 2] ~~(Includes: fecal occult blood testing annually, flexible sigmoidoscopy every 5 years, annual fecal occult blood testing plus flexible sigmoidoscopy every 5 years, double contrast barium enema every 5 years, or colonoscopy every 10 years)~~
3027F	Grammatical Change
3035F	Grammatical Change
3037F	Grammatical Change
3042F	Grammatical Change
3046F	Grammatical Change
3060F	Grammatical Change
3061F	Grammatical Change
3062F	Grammatical Change
3066F	Grammatical Change
3072F	Grammatical Change
▲ **3073F**	Pre-surgical (cataract) axial length, corneal power measurement and method of intraocular lens power calculation documented within ~~six~~ 12 months prior to surgery (EC)[5]
3075F	Grammatical Change
3077F	Grammatical Change
3078F	Grammatical Change
3079F	Grammatical Change
3080F	Grammatical Change
3082F	Grammatical Change
3083F	Grammatical Change
3084F	Grammatical Change
3095F	Grammatical Change
3096F	Grammatical Change
● **3215F**	Code added
● **3216F**	Code added
3217F	~~RNA testing for Hepatitis C viremia ordered at initial evaluation or previously performed (HEP C)[1]~~
● **3218F**	Code added
3219F	~~Hepatitis C genotype testing documented as performed prior to initiation of antiviral treatment for Hepatitis C (HEP C)[1]~~

● **3220F** Code added

● **3230F** Code added

● **3260F** Code added

● **3265F** Code added

● **3266F** Code added

● **3268F** Code added

● **3269F** Code added

● **3270F** Code added

● **3271F** Code added

● **3272F** Code added

● **3273F** Code added

● **3274F** Code added

● **3278F** Code added

● **3279F** Code added

● **3280F** Code added

● **3281F** Code added

● **3284F** Code added

● **3285F** Code added

● **3288F** Code added

● **3290F** Code added

● **3291F** Code added

● **3292F** Code added

● **3300F** Code added

● **3301F** Code added

● **3302F** Code added

● **3303F** Code added

● **3304F** Code added

● **3305F** Code added

● **3306F** Code added

● **3307F** Code added

● **3308F** Code added

● **3309F** Code added

● **3310F** Code added

● **3311F** Code added

● **3312F** Code added

3313F ~~AJCC Cancer Stage IVB, documented (ONC)[1], (ML)[5]~~

3314F ~~AJCC Cancer Stage IVC, documented (ONC)[1], (ML)[5]~~

● **3315F** Code added

● **3316F** Code added

● **3317F** Code added

● **3318F** Code added

● **3319F** Code added

● **3320F** Code added

● **3325F** Code added

● **3330F** Code added

● **3331F** Code added

● **3340F** Code added

● **3341F** Code added

● **3342F** Code added

● **3343F** Code added

● **3344F** Code added

● **3345F** Code added

● **3350F** Code added

● **3351F** Code added

● **3352F** Code added

● **3353F** Code added

● **3354F** Code added

4000F Grammatical Change

4001F Grammatical Change

4006F Grammatical Change

~~**4007F**~~ ~~Age Related Eye Disease Study (AREDS) formulation prescribed or recommended (EC)[5]~~

4009F Grammatical Change

4012F Grammatical Change

4014F Grammatical Change

4037F Grammatical Change

▲ **4040F** Pneumococcal vaccine~~immunization ordered or~~ administered or previously received (COPD)[1],(PV)[2]

4044F Grammatical Change

4047F Grammatical Change

4048F Grammatical Change

4052F Grammatical Change

4053F Grammatical Change

4058F Grammatical Change

4066F Grammatical Change

4070F Grammatical Change

4120F Grammatical Change

4124F Grammatical Change

● **4130F** Code added

● **4131F** Code added

● **4132F** Code added

● **4133F** Code added

● **4134F** Code added

● **4135F** Code added

● **4136F** Code added

● **4150F** Code added

● **4151F** Code added

● **4152F** Code added

● **4153F** Code added

● **4154F** Code added

● **4155F**	Code added
● **4156F**	Code added
● **4157F**	Code added
● **4158F**	Code added
● **4159F**	Code added
● **4163F**	Code added
● **4164F**	Code added
● **4165F**	Code added
● **4167F**	Code added
● **4168F**	Code added
● **4169F**	Code added
● **4171F**	Code added
● **4172F**	Code added
● **4174F**	Code added
● **4175F**	Code added
▲ **4176F**	Counseling about value of protection from UV light and lack of proven efficacy of nutritional supplements in prevention of progression of cataract development provided to patient and/or caregiver(s) (EC)[5]
● **4177F**	Code added
● **4178F**	Code added
● **4179F**	Code added
● **4180F**	Code added
● **4181F**	Code added
● **4182F**	Code added
● **4185F**	Code added
● **4186F**	Code added
● **4187F**	Code added
● **4188F**	Code added
● **4189F**	Code added
● **4190F**	Code added
● **4191F**	Code added
● **4200F**	Code added
● **4201F**	Code added
● **4210F**	Code added
● **4220F**	Code added
● **4221F**	Code added
● **4230F**	Code added
● **4240F**	Code added
● **4242F**	Code added
● **4245F**	Code added
● **4248F**	Code added
● **4250F**	Code added
● **5020F**	Code added
● **5050F**	Code added
● **5060F**	Code added
● **5062F**	Code added
● **6030F**	Code added
● **6040F**	Code added
● **6045F**	Code added
● **7010F**	Code added
● **7020F**	Code added
● **7025F**	Code added

Category III Codes

~~**0026T**~~	~~Lipoprotein, direct measurement, intermediate density lipoproteins (IDL) (remnant lipoproteins)~~
~~**0027T**~~	~~Endoscopic lysis of epidural adhesions with direct visualization using mechanical means (eg, spinal endoscopic catheter system) or solution injection (eg, normal saline) including radiologic localization and epidurography~~
~~**0028T**~~	~~Dual energy x-ray absorptiometry (DEXA) body composition study, one or more sites~~
~~**0029T**~~	~~Treatment(s) for incontinence, pulsed magnetic neuromodulation, per day~~
~~**0031T**~~	~~Speculoscopy;~~
~~**0032T**~~	~~with directed sampling~~
~~**0041T**~~	~~Urinalysis infectious agent detection, semi-quantitative analysis of volatile compounds~~
~~**0043T**~~	~~Carbon monoxide, expired gas analysis (eg, ETCO$_2$/hemolysis breath test)~~
~~**0046T**~~	~~Catheter lavage of a mammary duct(s) for collection of cytology specimen(s), in high risk individuals (GAIL risk scoring or prior personal history of breast cancer), each breast; single duct~~
~~**0047T**~~	~~each additional duct~~
✚ ~~**0049T**~~	~~Prolonged extracorporeal percutaneous transseptal ventricular assist device, greater than 24 hours, each subsequent 24 hour period (List separately in addition to code for primary procedure)~~
✚○ **0054T**	Code Reinstated/Recycled
✚○ **0055T**	Code Reinstated/Recycled
~~**0058T**~~	~~Cryopreservation; reproductive tissue, ovarian~~
~~**0059T**~~	~~oocyte(s)~~
~~**0060T**~~	~~Electrical impedance scan of the breast, bilateral (risk assessment device for breast cancer)~~
~~**0061T**~~	~~Destruction/reduction of malignant breast tumor including breast carcinoma cells in the margins, microwave phased array thermotherapy, disposable catheter with combined temperature monitoring probe and microwave sensor, externally applied microwave energy, including interstitial placement of sensor~~
0073T	Grammatical Change
0078T	Grammatical Change
0080T	Grammatical Change
~~**0088T**~~	~~Submucosal radiofrequency tissue volume reduction of tongue base, one or more sites, per session (ie, for treatment of obstructive sleep apnea syndrome)~~
~~**0089T**~~	~~Actigraphy testing, recording, analysis and interpretation (minimum of three-day recording)~~

~~0090T~~ ~~Total disc arthroplasty (artificial disc), anterior approach, including discectomy to prepare interspace (other than for decompression), cervical; single interspace~~

+▲ 0092T Total disc arthroplasty (artificial disc), anterior approach, including discectomy with end plate preparation (includes osteophytectomy for nerve root or spinal cord decompression and microdissection), ~~to prepare interspace (other than for decompression), cervical;~~ each additional interspace, cervical (List separately in addition to code for primary procedure)

~~0093T~~ ~~Removal of total disc arthroplasty, anterior approach cervical; single interspace~~

+▲ 0095T Removal of total disc arthroplasty (artificial disc), anterior approach, ~~cervical;~~ each additional interspace, cervical (List separately in addition to code for primary procedure)

~~0096T~~ ~~Revision of total disc arthroplasty, anterior approach cervical; single interspace~~

+▲ 0098T Revision including replacement of total disc arthroplasty (artificial disc), anterior approach, ~~cervical;~~each additional interspace, cervical (List separately in addition to code for primary procedure)

▲ 0124T Conjunctival incision with posterior ~~juxtascleral~~ extrascleral placement of pharmacological agent (does not include supply of medication)

~~0137T~~ ~~Biopsy, prostate, needle, saturation sampling for prostate mapping~~

~~0162T~~ ~~Electronic analysis and programming, reprogramming of gastric neurostimulator (ie, morbid obesity)~~

+▲ 0163T Total disc arthroplasty (artificial disc), anterior approach, including discectomy to prepare interspace (other than for decompression), ~~lumbar,~~ each additional interspace, lumbar (List separately in addition to code for primary procedure)

+▲ 0164T Removal of total disc arthroplasty, (artificial disc), anterior approach, ~~lumbar,~~ each additional interspace, lumbar (List separately in addition to code for primary procedure)

+▲ 0165T Revision including replacement of total disc arthroplasty (artificial disc), anterior approach, ~~lumbar,~~ each additional interspace, lumbar (List separately in addition to code for primary procedure)

● 0184T Code added

● 0185T Code added

● 0186T Code added

● 0187T Code added

● 0188T Code added

+● 0189T Code added

+● 0190T Code added

● 0191T Code added

● 0192T Code added

● 0193T Code added

● 0194T Code added

● 0195T Code added

+● 0196T Code added

Appendix C

Clinical Examples

As described in *CPT 2009*, clinical examples of the CPT codes for Evaluation and Management (E/M) services are intended to be an important element of the coding system. The clinical examples, when used with the E/M descriptors contained in the full text of *CPT*, provide a comprehensive and powerful tool for physicians to report the services provided to their patients.

The American Medical Association is pleased to provide you with these clinical examples for *CPT 2009*. The clinical examples that are provided in this supplement are limited to Office or Other Outpatient Services, Hospital Inpatient Services, Consultations, Critical Care, Prolonged Services and Care Plan Oversight.

These clinical examples do not encompass the entire scope of medical practice. Inclusion or exclusion of any particular specialty group does not infer any judgment of importance or lack thereof; nor does it limit the applicability of the example to any particular specialty.

Of utmost importance is that these clinical examples are just that: examples. A particular patient encounter, depending on the specific circumstances, must be judged by the services provided by the physician for that particular patient. Simply because the patient's complaints, symptoms, or diagnoses match those of a particular clinical example, does not automatically assign that patient encounter to that particular level of service. The three components (history, examination, and medical decision making) must be met and documented in the medical record to report a particular level of service.

New Patient

Office or Other Outpatient Service

99201 Initial office visit for a 50-year-old male from out-of-town who needs a prescription refill for a nonsteroidal anti-inflammatory drug. (Anesthesiology)

Initial office visit for a 40-year-old female, new patient, requesting information about local pain clinics. (Anesthesiology/Pain Medicine)

Initial office visit for a 10-year-old girl for determination of visual acuity as part of a summer camp physical (does not include determination of refractive error). (Ophthalmology)

Initial office visit for an out-of-town patient requiring topical refill. (Dermatology)

Initial office visit for a 65-year-old male for reassurance about an isolated seborrheic keratosis on upper back. (Plastic Surgery)

Initial office visit for an out-of-state visitor who needs refill of topical steroid to treat lichen planus. (Dermatology)

Initial office visit for an 86-year-old male, out-of-town visitor, who needs prescription refilled for an anal skin preparation that he forgot. (General Surgery/Colon & Rectal Surgery)

Initial office visit for a patient with alveolar osteitis for repacking. (Oral & Maxillofacial Surgery)

Initial office visit for a patient with a pedunculated lesion of the neck which is unsightly. (Dermatology)

Initial office visit for a 10-year-old male, for limited subungual hematoma not requiring drainage. (Internal Medicine)

Initial office visit with an out-of-town visitor who needs a prescription refilled because she forgot her hay fever medication. (Allergy & Immunology/Internal Medicine)

Initial office visit with a 9-month-old female with diaper rash. (Pediatrics)

Initial office visit with a 10-year-old male with severe rash and itching for the past 24 hours, positive history for contact with poison oak 48 hours prior to the visit. (Family Medicine)

Initial office visit with a 5-year-old female to remove sutures from simple wound placed by another physician. (Plastic Surgery)

Initial office visit for a 22-year-old male with a small area of sunburn requiring first aid. (Dermatology/Family Medicine/Internal Medicine)

Initial office visit for the evaluation and management of a contusion of a finger. (Orthopaedic Surgery)

99202 Initial office visit for a 13-year-old patient with comedopapular acne of the face unresponsive to over-the-counter medications. (Family Medicine)

Initial office visit for a patient with a clinically benign lesion or nodule of the lower leg which has been present for many years. (Dermatology)

Initial office visit for a patient with a circumscribed patch of dermatitis of the leg. (Dermatology)

Initial office visit for a patient with papulosquamous eruption of elbows. (Dermatology)

Initial office visit for a 9-year-old patient with erythematous grouped, vesicular eruption of the lip of three day's duration. (Pediatrics)

Initial office visit for an 18-year-old male referred by an orthodontist for advice regarding removal of four wisdom teeth. (Oral & Maxillofacial Surgery)

Initial office visit for a 14-year-old male, who was referred by his orthodontist, for advice on the exposure of impacted maxillary cuspids. (Oral & Maxillofacial Surgery)

Initial office visit for a patient presenting with itching patches on the wrists and ankles. (Dermatology)

Initial office visit for a 30-year-old male for evaluation and discussion of treatment of rhinophyma. (Plastic Surgery)

Initial office visit for a 16-year-old male with severe cystic acne, new patient. (Dermatology)

Initial office evaluation for gradual hearing loss, 58-year-old male, history and physical examination, with interpretation of complete audiogram, air bone, etc. (Otolaryngology)

Initial evaluation and management of recurrent urinary infection in female. (Internal Medicine)

Initial office visit with a 10-year-old girl with history of chronic otitis media and a draining ear. (Pediatrics)

Initial office visit for a 10-year-old female with acute maxillary sinusitis. (Family Medicine)

Initial office visit for a patient with recurring episodes of herpes simplex who has developed a clustering of vesicles on the upper lip. (Internal Medicine)

Initial office visit for a 25-year-old patient with a single season allergic rhinitis. (Allergy & Immunology)

99203 Initial office visit of a 76-year-old male with a stasis ulcer of three month's duration. (Dermatology)

Initial office visit for a 30-year-old female with pain in the lateral aspect of the forearm. (Physical Medicine & Rehabilitation)

Initial office visit for a 15-year-old patient with a four-year history of moderate comedopapular acne of the face, chest, and back with early scarring. Discussion of use of systemic medication. (Dermatology)

Initial office visit for a patient with papulosquamous eruption of the elbow with pitting of nails and itchy scalp. (Dermatology)

Initial office visit for a 57-year-old female who complains of painful parotid swelling for one week's duration. (Oral & Maxillofacial Surgery)

Initial office visit for a patient with an ulcerated non-healing lesion or nodule on the tip of the nose. (Dermatology)

Initial office visit for a patient with dermatitis of the antecubital and popliteal fossae. (Dermatology)

Initial office visit for a 22-year-old female with irregular menses. (Family Medicine)

Initial office visit for a 50-year-old female with dyspepsia and nausea. (Family Medicine)

Initial office visit for a 53-year-old laborer with degenerative joint disease of the knee with no prior treatment. (Orthopaedic Surgery)

Initial office visit for a 60-year-old male with Dupuytren's contracture of one hand with multiple digit involvement. (Orthopaedic Surgery)

Initial office visit for a 33-year-old male with painless gross hematuria without cystoscopy. (Internal Medicine)

Initial office visit for a 55-year-old female with chronic blepharitis. There is a history of use of many medications. (Ophthalmology)

Initial office visit for an 18-year-old female with a two-day history of acute conjunctivitis. Extensive history of possible exposures, prior normal ocular history, and medication use is obtained. (Ophthalmology)

Initial office visit for a 14-year-old male with unilateral anterior knee pain. (Physical Medicine & Rehabilitation)

Initial office visit of an adult who presents with symptoms of an upper-respiratory infection that has progressed to unilateral purulent nasal discharge and discomfort in the right maxillary teeth. (Otolaryngology, Head & Neck Surgery)

Initial office visit of a 40-year-old female with symptoms of atopic allergies including eye and sinus congestion, often associated with infections. She would like to be tested for allergies. (Otolaryngology, Head & Neck Surgery)

Initial office visit of a 65-year-old with nasal stuffiness. (Otolaryngology, Head & Neck Surgery)

Initial office visit for initial evaluation of a 48-year-old man with recurrent low back pain radiating to the leg. (General Surgery)

Initial office visit for evaluation, diagnosis, and management of painless gross hematuria in a new patient, without cystoscopy. (Internal Medicine)

Initial office visit with couple for counseling concerning voluntary vasectomy for sterility. Spent 30 minutes discussing procedure, risks and benefits, and answering questions. (Urology)

Initial office visit of a 49-year-old male with nasal obstruction. Detailed exam with topical anesthesia. (Plastic Surgery)

Initial office visit for evaluation of a 13-year-old female with progressive scoliosis. (Physical Medicine & Rehabilitation)

Initial office visit for a 21-year-old female desiring counseling and evaluation of initiation of contraception. (Family Practice/Internal Medicine/Obstetrics & Gynecology)

Initial office visit for a 49-year-old male presenting with painless blood per rectum associated with bowel movement. (Colon & Rectal Surgery)

Initial office visit for a 19-year-old football player with three-day-old acute knee injury; now with swelling and pain. (Orthopaedic Surgery)

99204 Initial office visit for a 13-year-old female with progressive scoliosis. (Orthopaedic Surgery)

Initial office visit for a 34-year-old female with primary infertility for evaluation and counseling. (Obstetrics & Gynecology)

Initial office visit for a 6-year-old male with multiple upper respiratory infections. (Allergy & Immunology)

Initial office visit for a patient with generalized dermatitis of 80 percent of the body surface area. (Dermatology)

Initial office visit for an adolescent who was referred by school counselor because of repeated skipping school. (Psychiatry)

Initial office visit for a 50-year-old machinist with a generalized eruption. (Dermatology)

Initial office visit for a 45-year-old female who has been abstinent from alcohol and benzodiazepines for three months but complains of headaches, insomnia, and anxiety. (Psychiatry)

Initial office visit for a 60-year-old male with recent change in bowel habits, weight loss, and abdominal pain. (Abdominal Surgery/General Surgery)

Initial office visit for a 50-year-old male with an aortic aneurysm who is considering surgery. (General Surgery)

Initial office visit for a 17-year-old female with depression. (Internal Medicine)

Initial office visit of a 40-year-old with chronic draining ear, imbalance, and probable cholesteatoma. (Otolaryngology, Head & Neck Surgery)

Initial office visit for initial evaluation of a 63-year-old male with chest pain on exertion. (Cardiology/Internal Medicine)

Initial office visit for evaluation of a 70-year-old patient with recent onset of episodic confusion. (Internal Medicine)

Initial office visit for a 7-year-old female with juvenile diabetes mellitus, new to area, past history of hospitalization times three. (Pediatrics)

Initial office visit of a 50-year-old female with progressive solid food dysphagia. (Gastroenterology)

Initial office visit for a 34-year-old patient with primary infertility, including counseling. (Obstetrics & Gynecology)

Initial office visit for evaluation of a 70-year-old female with polyarthralgia. (Rheumatology)

Initial office visit for a patient with papulosquamous eruption involving 60 percent of the cutaneous surface with joint pain. Combinations of topical and systemic treatments discussed. (Dermatology)

99205 Initial office visit for a patient with disseminated lupus erythematosus with kidney disease, edema, purpura, and scarring lesions on the extremities plus cardiac symptoms. (Dermatology/General Surgery/Internal Medicine)

Initial office visit for a 25-year-old female with systemic lupus erythematosus, fever, seizures, and profound thrombocytopenia. (Rheumatology/Allergy & Immunology)

Initial office visit for an adult with multiple cutaneous blisters, denuded secondarily infected ulcerations, oral lesions, weight loss, and increasing weakness refractory to high dose corticosteroid. Initiation of new immunosuppressive therapy. (Dermatology)

Initial office visit for a 28-year-old male with systemic vasculitis and compromised circulation to the limbs. (Rheumatology)

Initial office visit for a 41-year-old female new to the area requesting rheumatologic care, on disability due to scleroderma and recent hospitalization for malignant hypertension. (Rheumatology)

Initial office visit for a 52-year-old female with acute four extremity weakness and shortness of breath one week post-flu vaccination. (Physical Medicine & Rehabilitation)

Initial office visit for a 60-year-old male with previous back surgery; now presents with back and pelvic pain, two-month history of bilateral progressive calf and thigh tightness and weakness when walking, causing several falls. (Orthopaedic Surgery)

Initial office visit for an adolescent referred from emergency department after making suicide gesture. (Psychiatry)

Initial office visit for a 49-year-old female with a history of headaches and dependence on opioids. She reports weight loss, progressive headache, and depression. (Psychiatry)

Initial office visit for a 50-year-old female with symptoms of rash, swellings, recurrent arthritic complaints, and diarrhea and lymphadenopathy. Patient has had a 25 lb weight loss and was recently camping in the Amazon. (Allergy & Immunology)

Initial office visit for a 34-year-old uremic Type I diabetic patient referred for ESRD modality assessment and planning. (Nephrology)

Initial office visit for a 75-year-old female with neck and bilateral shoulder pain, brisk deep tendon reflexes, and stress incontinence. (Physical Medicine & Rehabilitation)

Initial office visit for an 8-year-old male with cerebral palsy and spastic quadriparesis. (Physical Medicine & Rehabilitation)

Initial office visit for a 73-year-old male with known prostate malignancy, who presents with severe back pain and a recent onset of lower extremity weakness. (Physical Medicine & Rehabilitation)

Initial office visit for a 38-year-old male with paranoid delusions and a history of alcohol abuse. (Psychiatry)

Initial office visit for a 12-week-old with bilateral hip dislocations and bilateral club feet. (Orthopaedic Surgery)

Initial office visit for a 29-year-old female with acute orbital congestion, eyelid retraction, and bilateral visual loss from optic neuropathy. (Ophthalmology)

Initial office visit for a 70-year-old diabetic patient with progressive visual field loss, advanced optic disc cupping and neovascularization of retina. (Ophthalmology)

Initial office visit for a newly diagnosed Type I diabetic patient. (Endocrinology)

Initial office evaluation of a 65-year-old female with exertional chest pain, intermittent claudication, syncope and a murmur of aortic stenosis. (Cardiology)

Initial office visit for a 73-year-old male with an unexplained 20 lb weight loss. (Hematology/Oncology)

Initial office evaluation, patient with systemic lupus erythematosus, fever, seizures and profound thrombocytopenia. (Allergy & Immunology/Internal Medicine/Rheumatology)

Initial office evaluation and management of patient with systemic vasculitis and compromised circulation to the limbs. (Rheumatology)

Initial office visit for a 24-year-old homosexual male who has a fever, a cough, and shortness of breath. (Infectious Disease)

Initial outpatient evaluation of a 69-year-old male with severe chronic obstructive pulmonary disease, congestive heart failure, and hypertension. (Family Medicine)

Initial office visit for a 17-year-old female, who is having school problems and has told a friend that she is considering suicide. The patient and her family are consulted in regard to treatment options. (Psychiatry)

Initial office visit for a female with severe hirsutism, amenorrhea, weight loss and a desire to have children. (Endocrinology/Obstetrics & Gynecology)

Initial office visit for a 42-year-old male on hypertensive medication, newly arrived to the area, with diastolic blood pressure of 110, history of recurrent calculi, episodic headaches, intermittent chest pain and orthopnea. (Internal Medicine)

Established Patient

99211 Office visit for an 82-year-old female, established patient, for a monthly B12 injection with documented Vitamin B12 deficiency. (Geriatrics/Internal Medicine/Family Medicine)

Office visit for a 50-year-old male, established patient, for removal of uncomplicated facial sutures. (Plastic Surgery)

Office visit for an established patient who lost prescription for lichen planus. Returned for new copy. (Dermatology)

Office visit for an established patient undergoing orthodontics who complains of a wire which is irritating his/her cheek and asks you to check it. (Oral & Maxillofacial Surgery)

Office visit for a 50-year-old female, established patient, seen for her gold injection by the nurse. (Rheumatology)

Office visit for a 73-year-old female, established patient, with pernicious anemia for weekly B12 injection. (Gastroenterology)

Office visit for an established patient for dressing change on a skin biopsy. (Dermatology)

Office visit for a 19-year-old, established patient, for removal of sutures from a two-cm laceration of forehead, which you placed four days ago in ER. (Plastic Surgery)

Office visit of a 20-year-old female, established patient, who receives an allergy vaccine injection and is observed for a reaction by the nurse. (Otolaryngology, Head & Neck Surgery)

Office visit for a 45-year-old male, established patient, with chronic renal failure for the administration of erythropoietin. (Nephrology)

Office visit for an established patient, a Peace Corps enlistee, who requests documentation that third molars have been removed. (Oral & Maxillofacial Surgery)

Office visit for a 69-year-old female, established patient, for partial removal of antibiotic gauze from an infected wound site. (Plastic Surgery)

Office visit for a 9-year-old, established patient, successfully treated for impetigo, requiring release to return to school. (Dermatology/Pediatrics)

Office visit for an established patient requesting a return-to-work certificate for resolving contact dermatitis. (Dermatology)

Office visit for an established patient who is performing glucose monitoring and wants to check accuracy of machine with lab blood glucose by technician who checks accuracy and function of patient machine. (Endocrinology)

Follow-up office visit for a 65-year-old female with a chronic indwelling percutaneous nephrostomy catheter seen for routine pericatheter skin care and dressing change. (Interventional Radiology)

Outpatient visit with 19-year-old male, established patient, for supervised drug screen. (Addiction Medicine)

Office visit with 12-year-old male, established patient, for cursory check of hematoma one day after venipuncture. (Internal Medicine)

Office visit with 31-year-old female, established patient, for return to work certificate. (Anesthesiology)

Office visit for a 42-year-old, established patient, to read tuberculin test results. (Allergy & Immunology)

Office visit for 14-year-old, established patient, to re-dress an abrasion. (Orthopaedic Surgery)

Office visit for a 45-year-old female, established patient, for a blood pressure check. (Obstetrics & Gynecology)

Office visit for a 23-year-old, established patient, for instruction in use of peak flow meter. (Allergy & Immunology)

Office visit for prescription refill for a 35-year-old female, established patient, with schizophrenia who is stable but has run out of neuroleptic and is scheduled to be seen in a week. (Psychiatry)

99212 Office visit for an 11-year-old, established patient, seen in follow-up for mild comedonal acne of the cheeks on topical desquamating agents. (Dermatology/Family Medicine/Pediatrics)

Office visit for a 10-year-old female, established patient, who has been swimming in a lake, now presents with a one-day history of left ear pain with purulent drainage. (Family Medicine)

Office visit for a child, established patient, with chronic secretory otitis media. (Otolaryngology, Head & Neck Surgery)

Office visit for an established patient seen in follow-up of clearing patch of localized contact dermatitis. (Family Medicine/Dermatology)

Office visit for an established patient returning for evaluation of response to treatment of lichen planus on wrists and ankles. (Dermatology)

Office visit for an established patient with tinea pedis being treated with topical therapy. (Dermatology)

Office visit for an established patient with localized erythematous plaque of psoriasis with topical hydration. (Dermatology)

Office visit for a 50-year-old male, established patient, recently seen for acute neck pain, diagnosis of spondylosis, responding to physical therapy and intermittent cervical traction. Returns for evaluation for return to work. (Neurology)

Office visit for an established patient with recurring episodes of herpes simplex who has developed a clustering of vesicles on the upper lip. (Oral & Maxillofacial Surgery)

Evaluation of a 50-year-old male, established patient, who has experienced a recurrence of knee pain after he discontinued NSAID. (Anesthesiology/Pain Medicine)

Office visit for an established patient with an irritated skin tag for reassurance. (Dermatology)

Office visit for a 40-year-old, established patient, who has experienced a systemic allergic reaction following administration of immunotherapy. The dose must be readjusted. (Allergy & Immunology)

Office visit for a 33-year-old, established patient, for contusion and abrasion of lower extremity. (Orthopaedic Surgery)

Office visit for a 22-year-old male, established patient, one month after I & D of "wrestler's ear." (Plastic Surgery)

Office visit for a 21-year-old, established patient, who is seen in follow-up after antibiotic therapy for acute bacterial tonsillitis. (Otolaryngology, Head & Neck Surgery)

Office visit for a 4-year-old, established patient, with tympanostomy tubes, check-up. (Otolaryngology, Head & Neck Surgery)

Office visit for an established patient who has had needle aspiration of a peritonsillar abscess. (Otolaryngology, Head & Neck Surgery)

Follow-up office examination for evaluation and treatment of acute draining ear in a 5-year-old with tympanotomy tubes. (Otolaryngology, Head & Neck Surgery)

Office visit, established patient, 6-year-old with sore throat and headache. (Family Medicine/Pediatrics)

Office evaluation for possible purulent bacterial conjunctivitis with one- to two-day history of redness and discharge, 16-year-old female, established patient. (Pediatrics/Internal Medicine/Family Medicine)

Office visit for a 65-year-old female, established patient, returns for three-week follow-up for resolving severe ankle sprain. (Orthopaedic Surgery)

Office visit, sore throat, fever, and fatigue in a 19-year-old college student, established patient. (Internal Medicine)

Office visit with a 33-year-old female, established patient, recently started on treatment for hemorrhoidal complaints, for re-evaluation. (Colon & Rectal Surgery)

Office visit with a 36-year-old male, established patient, for follow-up on effectiveness of medicine management of oral candidiasis. (Oral & Maxillofacial Surgery)

Office visit for a 27-year-old female, established patient, with complaints of vaginal itching. (Obstetrics & Gynecology)

Office visit for a 65-year-old, established patient, with eruptions on both arms from poison oak exposure. (Allergy & Immunology/Internal Medicine)

99213 Office visit for an established patient with new lesions of lichen planus in spite of topical therapies. (Dermatology)

Office visit for the quarterly follow-up of a 45-year-old male with stable chronic asthma requiring regular drug therapy. (Allergy & Immunology)

Office visit for a 13-year-old, established patient, with comedopapular acne of the face which has shown poor response to topical medication. Discussion of use of systemic medication. (Dermatology)

Office visit for a 62-year-old female, established patient, for follow-up for stable cirrhosis of the liver. (Internal Medicine/Family Medicine)

Office visit for a 3-year-old, established patient, with atopic dermatitis and food hypersensitivity for quarterly follow-up evaluation. The patient is on topical lotions and steroid creams as well as oral antihistamines. (Allergy & Immunology)

Office visit for an 80-year-old female, established patient, to evaluate medical management of osteoarthritis of the temporomandibular joint. (Rheumatology)

Office visit for a 70-year-old female, established patient, one year post excision of basal cell carcinoma of nose with nasolabial flap. Now presents with new suspicious recurrent lesion and suspicious lesion of the back. (Plastic Surgery)

Office visit for a 68-year-old female, established patient, with polymyalgia rheumatic, maintained on chronic low-dose corticosteroid, with no new complaints. (Rheumatology)

Office visit for a 3-year-old female, established patient, for earache and dyshidrosis of feet. (Pediatrics/Family Medicine)

Office visit for an established patient for 18-months post-operative follow-up of TMJ repair. (Oral & Maxillofacial Surgery)

Office visit for a 45-year-old male, established patient, being re-evaluated for recurrent acute prostatitis. (Urology)

Office visit for a 43-year-old male, established patient, with known reflex sympathetic dystrophy. (Anesthesiology)

Office visit for an established patient with an evenly pigmented superficial nodule of leg which is symptomatic. (Dermatology)

Office visit for an established patient with psoriasis involvement of the elbows, pitting of the nails, and itchy scalp. (Dermatology)

Office visit for a 27-year-old male, established patient, with deep follicular and perifollicular inflammation unable to tolerate systemic antibiotics due to GI upset, requires change of systemic medication. (Dermatology)

Office visit for a 16-year-old male, established patient, who is on medication for exercise-induced bronchospasm. (Allergy & Immunology)

Office visit for a 60-year-old, established patient, with chronic essential hypertension on multiple drug regimen, for blood pressure check. (Family Medicine)

Office visit for a 20-year-old male, established patient, for removal of sutures in hand. (Family Medicine)

Office visit for a 58-year-old female, established patient, with unilateral painful bunion. (Orthopaedic Surgery)

Office visit for a 45-year-old female, established patient, with known osteoarthritis and painful swollen knees. (Rheumatology)

Office visit for a 25-year-old female, established patient, complaining of bleeding and heavy menses. (Obstetrics & Gynecology)

Office visit for a 55-year-old male, established patient, with hypertension managed by a beta blocker/thiazide regime; now experiencing mild fatigue. (Nephrology)

Office visit for a 65-year-old female, established patient, with primary glaucoma for interval determination of intraocular pressure and possible adjustment of medication. (Ophthalmology)

Office visit for a 56-year-old male, established patient, with stable exertional angina who complains of new onset of calf pain while walking. (Cardiology)

Office visit for a 63-year-old female, established patient, with rheumatoid arthritis on auranofin and ibuprofen, seen for routine follow-up visit. (Rheumatology)

Office visit for an established patient with Graves' disease, three months post I-131 therapy, who presents with lassitude and malaise. (Endocrinology)

Office visit for the quarterly follow-up of a 63-year-old male, established patient, with chronic myofascial pain syndrome, effectively managed by doxepin, who presents with new onset urinary hesitancy. (Pain Medicine)

Office visit for the biannual follow-up of an established patient with migraine variant having infrequent, intermittent, moderate to severe headaches with nausea and vomiting, which are sometimes effectively managed by ergotamine tartrate and an antiemetic, but occasionally requiring visits to an emergency department. (Pain Medicine)

Office visit for an established patient after discharge from a pain rehabilitation program to review and adjust medication dosage. (Pain Medicine)

Office visit with 55-year-old male, established patient, for management of hypertension, mild fatigue, on beta blocker/thiazide regimen. (Family Medicine/Internal Medicine)

Outpatient visit with 37-year-old male, established patient, who is three years post total colectomy for chronic ulcerative colitis, presents for increased irritation at his stoma. (General Surgery)

Office visit for a 70-year-old diabetic hypertensive established patient with recent change in insulin requirement. (Internal Medicine/Nephrology)

Office visit with 80-year-old female, established patient, for follow-up osteoporosis, status-post compression fractures. (Rheumatology)

Office visit for an established patient with stable cirrhosis of the liver. (Gastroenterology)

Routine, follow-up office evaluation at a three-month interval for a 77-year-old female, established patient, with nodular small cleaved-cell lymphoma. (Hematology/Oncology)

Quarterly follow-up office visit for a 45-year-old male, established patient, with stable chronic asthma, on steroid and bronchodilator therapy. (Pulmonary Medicine)

Office visit for a 50-year-old female, established patient, with insulin-dependent diabetes mellitus and stable coronary artery disease, for monitoring. (Family Medicine/Internal Medicine)

99214 Office visit for an established patient now presenting with generalized dermatitis of 80% of the body surface area. (Dermatology)

Office visit for a 32-year-old female, established patient, with new onset right lower quadrant pain. (Family Medicine)

Office visit for reassessment and reassurance/counseling of a 40-year-old female, established patient, who is experiencing increased symptoms while on a pain management treatment program. (Pain Medicine)

Office visit for a 30-year-old, established patient, under management for intractable low back pain, who now presents with new onset right posterior thigh pain. (Pain Medicine)

Office visit for an established patient with frequent intermittent, moderate to severe headaches requiring beta blocker or tricyclic antidepressant prophylaxis, as well as four symptomatic treatments, but who is still experiencing headaches at a frequency of several times a month that are unresponsive to treatment. (Pain Medicine)

Office visit for an established patient with psoriasis with extensive involvement of scalp, trunk, palms, and soles with joint pain. Combinations of topical and systemic treatments discussed and instituted. (Dermatology)

Office visit for a 55-year-old male, established patient, with increasing night pain, limp, and progressive varus of both knees. (Orthopaedic Surgery)

Follow-up visit for a 15-year-old withdrawn patient with four-year history of papulocystic acne of the face, chest, and back with early scarring and poor response to past treatment. Discussion of use of systemic medication. (Dermatology)

Office visit for a 28-year-old male, established patient, with regional enteritis, diarrhea, and low-grade fever. (Internal Medicine)

Office visit for a 25-year-old female, established patient, following recent arthrogram and MR imaging for TMJ pain. (Oral & Maxillofacial Surgery)

Office visit for a 32-year-old female, established patient, with large obstructing stone in left mid-ureter, to discuss management options including urethroscopy with extraction or ESWL. (Urology)

Evaluation for a 28-year-old male, established patient, with new onset of low back pain. (Anesthesiology/Pain Medicine)

Office visit for a 28-year-old female, established patient, with right lower quadrant abdominal pain, fever, and anorexia. (Internal Medicine/Family Medicine)

Office visit for a 45-year-old male, established patient, four months follow-up of L4-5 discectomy, with persistent incapacitating low back and leg pain. (Orthopaedic Surgery)

Outpatient visit for a 77-year-old male, established patient, with hypertension, presenting with a three-month history of episodic substernal chest pain on exertion. (Cardiology)

Office visit for a 25-year-old female, established patient, for evaluation of progressive saddle nose deformity of unknown etiology. (Plastic Surgery)

Office visit for a 65-year-old male, established patient, with BPH and severe bladder outlet obstruction, to discuss management options such as TURP. (Urology)

Office visit for an adult diabetic established patient with a past history of recurrent sinusitis who presents with a one-week history of double vision. (Otolaryngology, Head & Neck Surgery)

Office visit for an established patient with lichen planus and 60% of the cutaneous surface involved, not responsive to systemic steroids, as well as developing symptoms of progressive heartburn and paranoid ideation. (Dermatology)

Office visit for a 52-year-old male, established patient, with a 12-year history of bipolar disorder responding to lithium carbonate and brief psychotherapy. Psychotherapy and prescription provided. (Psychiatry)

Office visit for a 63-year-old female, established patient, with a history of familial polyposis, status post-colectomy with sphincter sparing procedure, who now presents with rectal bleeding and increase in stooling frequency. (General Surgery)

Office visit for a 68-year-old male, established patient, with the sudden onset of multiple flashes and floaters in the right eye due to a posterior vitreous detachment. (Ophthalmology)

Office visit for a 55-year-old female, established patient, on cyclosporin for treatment of resistant, small vessel vasculitis. (Rheumatology)

Follow-up office visit for a 55-year-old male, two months after iliac angioplasty with new onset of contralateral extremity claudication. (Interventional Radiology)

Office visit for a 68-year-old male, established patient, with stable angina, two months post myocardial infarction, who is not tolerating one of his medications. (Cardiology)

Weekly office visit for 5FU therapy for an ambulatory established patient with metastatic colon cancer and increasing shortness of breath. (Hematology/Oncology)

Follow-up office visit for a 60-year-old male, established patient, whose post-traumatic seizures have disappeared on medication and who now raises the question of stopping the medication. (Neurology)

Office evaluation on new onset RLQ pain in a 32-year-old female, established patient. (Urology/General Surgery/Internal Medicine/Family Medicine)

Office evaluation of 28-year-old, established patient, with regional enteritis, diarrhea, and low-grade fever. (Family Medicine/Internal Medicine)

Office visit with 50-year-old female, established patient, diabetic, blood sugar controlled by diet. She now complains of frequency of urination and weight loss, blood sugar of 320, and negative ketones on dipstick. (Internal Medicine)

Follow-up office visit for a 45-year-old, established patient, with rheumatoid arthritis on gold, methotrexate, or immunosuppressive therapy. (Rheumatology)

Office visit for a 60-year-old male, established patient, two years post-removal of intracranial meningioma, now with new headaches and visual disturbance. (Neurosurgery)

Office visit for a 68-year-old female, established patient, for routine review and follow-up of non-insulin dependent diabetes, obesity, hypertension, and congestive heart failure. Complains of vision difficulties and admits dietary noncompliance. Patient is counseled concerning diet and current medications adjusted. (Family Medicine)

99215 Office visit for an established patient who developed persistent cough, rectal bleeding, weakness, and diarrhea plus pustular infection on skin. Patient on immunosuppressive therapy. (Dermatology)

Office visit for an established patient with disseminated lupus erythematosus, extensive edema of extremities, kidney disease, and weakness requiring monitored course on azathioprene, corticosteroid and complicated by acute depression. (Dermatology/Internal Medicine/Rheumatology)

Office visit for an established patient with progressive dermatomyositis and recent onset of fever, nasal speech, and regurgitation of fluids through the nose. (Dermatology)

Office visit for a 28-year-old female, established patient, who is abstinent from previous cocaine dependence, but reports progressive panic attacks and chest pains. (Psychiatry)

Office visit for an established adolescent patient with history of bipolar disorder treated with lithium; seen on urgent basis at family's request because of severe depressive symptoms. (Psychiatry)

Office visit for an established patient having acute migraine with new onset neurological symptoms and whose headaches are unresponsive to previous attempts at management with a combination of preventive and abortive medication. (Pain Medicine)

Office visit for an established patient with exfoliative lichen planus with daily fever spikes, disorientation, and shortness of breath. (Dermatology)

Office visit for a 25-year-old, established patient, two years post-burn with bilateral ectropion, hypertrophic facial burn scars, near absence of left breast, and burn syndactyly of both hands. Discussion of treatment options following examination. (Plastic Surgery)

Office visit for a 6-year-old, established patient, to review newly diagnosed immune deficiency with recommendations for therapy including IV immunoglobulin and chronic antibiotics. (Allergy & Immunology)

Office visit for a 36-year-old, established patient, three months status post-transplant, with new onset of peripheral edema, increased blood pressure, and progressive fatigue. (Nephrology)

Office visit for an established patient with Kaposi's sarcoma who presents with fever and widespread vesicles. (Dermatology)

Office visit for a 27-year-old female, established patient, with bipolar disorder who was stable on lithium carbonate and monthly supportive psychotherapy but now has developed symptoms of hypomania. (Psychiatry)

Office visit for a 25-year-old male, established patient with a history of schizophrenia who has been seen bi-monthly but is complaining of auditory hallucinations. (Psychiatry)

Office visit for a 62-year-old male, established patient, three years postoperative abdominal perineal resection, now with a rising carcinoembryonic antigen, weight loss, and pelvic pain. (Abdominal Surgery)

Office visit for a 42-year-old male, established patient, nine months postoperative emergency vena cava shunt for variceal bleeding, now presents with complaints of one episode of "dark" bowel movement, weight gain, tightness in abdomen, whites of eyes seem "yellow" and occasional drowsiness after eating hamburgers. (Abdominal Surgery)

Office visit for a 68-year-old male, established patient, with biopsy-proven rectal carcinoma, for evaluation and discussion of treatment options. (General Surgery)

Office visit for a 60-year-old, established patient, with diabetic nephropathy with increasing edema and dyspnea. (Endocrinology)

Office visit with 30-year-old male, established patient for three-month history of fatigue, weight loss, intermittent fever, and presenting with diffuse adenopathy and splenomegaly. (Family Medicine)

Office visit for restaging of an established patient with new lymphadenopathy one year post-therapy for lymphoma. (Hematology/Oncology)

Office visit for evaluation of recent onset syncopal attacks in a 70-year-old female, established patient. (Internal Medicine)

Follow-up visit, 40-year-old mother of three, established patient, with acute rheumatoid arthritis, anatomical Stage 3, ARA function Class 3 rheumatoid arthritis, and deteriorating function. (Rheumatology)

Follow-up office visit for a 65-year-old male, established patient, with a fever of recent onset while on outpatient antibiotic therapy for endocarditis. (Infectious Disease)

Office visit for a 75-year-old, established patient, with ALS (amyotrophic lateral sclerosis), who is no longer able to swallow. (Neurology)

Office visit for a 70-year-old female, established patient, with diabetes mellitus and hypertension, presenting with a two-month history of increasing confusion, agitation and short-term memory loss. (Family Medicine/Internal Medicine)

Hospital Inpatient Services

Initial Hospital Care

New or Established Patient

99221 Initial hospital visit following admission for a 42-year-old male for observation following an uncomplicated mandible fracture. (Plastic Surgery/Oral & Maxillofacial Surgery)

Initial hospital visit for a 40-year-old patient with a thrombosed synthetic arteriovenous conduit. (Nephrology)

Initial hospital visit for a healthy 24-year-old male with an acute onset of low back pain following a lifting injury. (Internal Medicine/Anesthesiology/Pain Medicine)

Initial hospital visit for a 69-year-old female with controlled hypertension, scheduled for surgery. (Internal Medicine/Cardiology)

Initial hospital visit for a 24-year-old healthy female with benign tumor of palate. (Oral & Maxillofacial Surgery)

Initial hospital visit for a 14-year-old female with infectious mononucleosis and dehydration. (Internal Medicine)

Initial hospital visit for a 62-year-old female with stable rheumatoid arthritis, admitted for total joint replacement. (Rheumatology)

Initial hospital visit for a 12-year-old patient with a laceration of the upper eyelid, involving the lid margin and superior canaliculus, admitted prior to surgery for IV antibiotic therapy. (Plastic Surgery)

Initial hospital visit for a 69-year-old female with controlled hypertension, scheduled for surgery. (Cardiology)

Hospital admission, examination, and initiation of treatment program for a 67-year-old male with uncomplicated pneumonia who requires IV antibiotic therapy. (Internal Medicine)

Hospital admission for an 18-month-old with 10% dehydration. (Pediatrics)

Hospital admission for a 12-year-old with a laceration of the upper eyelid involving the lid margin and superior canaliculus, admitted prior to surgery for IV antibiotic therapy. (Ophthalmology)

Hospital admission for a 32-year-old female with severe flank pain, hematuria and presumed diagnosis of ureteral calculus as determined by Emergency Department physician. (Urology)

Initial hospital visit for a patient with several large venous stasis ulcers not responding to outpatient therapy. (Dermatology)

Initial hospital visit for 21-year-old pregnant patient (nine-weeks gestation) with hyperemesis gravidarum. (Obstetrics & Gynecology)

Initial hospital visit for a 73-year-old female with acute pyelonephritis who is otherwise generally healthy. (Geriatrics)

Initial hospital visit for 62-year-old patient with cellulitis of the foot requiring bedrest and intravenous antibiotics. (Orthopaedic Surgery)

99222 Initial hospital visit for a 50-year-old patient with lower quadrant abdominal pain and increased temperature, but without septic picture. (General Surgery/Abdominal Surgery/Colon & Rectal Surgery)

Initial hospital visit for airway management, due to a benign laryngeal mass. (Otolaryngology, Head & Neck Surgery)

Initial hospital visit for a 66-year-old female with an L-2 vertebral compression fracture with acute onset of paralytic ileus; seen in the office two days previously. (Orthopaedic Surgery)

Initial hospital visit and evaluation of a 15-year-old male admitted with peritonsillar abscess or cellulitis requiring intravenous antibiotic therapy. (Otolaryngology, Head & Neck Surgery)

Initial hospital visit for a 42-year-old male with vertebral compression fracture following a motor vehicle accident. (Orthopaedic Surgery)

Initial hospital visit for a patient with generalized atopic dermatitis and secondary infection. (Dermatology)

Initial hospital visit for a 3-year-old patient with high temperature, limp, and painful hip motion of 18 hours' duration. (Pediatrics/Orthopaedic Surgery)

Initial hospital visit for a young adult, presenting with an acute asthma attack unresponsive to outpatient therapy. (Allergy & Immunology)

Initial hospital visit for an 18-year-old male who has suppurative sialoadenitis and dehydration. (Oral & Maxillofacial Surgery)

Initial hospital visit for a 65-year-old female for acute onset of thrombotic cerebrovascular accident with contralateral paralysis and aphasia. (Neurology)

Initial hospital visit for a 50-year-old male chronic paraplegic patient with pain and spasm below the lesion. (Anesthesiology)

Partial hospital admission for an adolescent patient from chaotic blended family, transferred from inpatient setting, for continued treatment to control symptomatic expressions of hostility and depression. (Psychiatry)

Initial hospital visit for a 15-year-old male with acute status asthmaticus, unresponsive to outpatient therapy. (Internal Medicine)

Initial hospital visit for a 61-year-old male with history of previous myocardial infarction, who now complains of chest pain. (Internal Medicine)

Initial hospital visit of a 15-year-old on medications for a sore throat over the last two weeks. The sore throat has worsened and patient now has dysphagia. The exam shows large necrotic tonsils with an adequate airway and small palpable nodes. The initial mono test was negative. (Otolaryngology, Head & Neck Surgery)

Initial hospital evaluation of a 23-year-old allergy patient admitted with eyelid edema and pain on fifth day of oral antibiotic therapy. (Otolaryngology, Head & Neck Surgery)

Hospital admission, young adult patient, failed previous therapy and now presents in acute asthmatic attack. (Family Medicine/Allergy & Immunology)

Hospital admission of a 62-year-old smoker, established patient, with bronchitis in acute respiratory distress. (Internal Medicine/Pulmonary Medicine)

Hospital admission, examination, and initiation of a treatment program for a 65-year-old female with new onset of right-sided paralysis and aphasia. (Neurology)

Hospital admission, examination, and initiation of treatment program for a 66-year-old chronic hemodialysis patient with fever and a new pulmonary infiltrate. (Nephrology)

Hospital admission for an 8-year-old febrile patient with chronic sinusitis and severe headache, unresponsive to oral antibiotics. (Allergy & Immunology)

Hospital admission for a 40-year-old male with submaxillary cellulitis and trismus from infected lower molar. (Oral & Maxillofacial Surgery)

99223 Initial hospital visit for a 45-year-old female, who has a history of rheumatic fever as a child and now has anemia, fever, and congestive heart failure. (Cardiology)

Initial hospital visit for a 50-year-old male with acute chest pain and diagnostic electrocardiographic changes of an acute anterior myocardial infarction. (Cardiology/Family Medicine/Internal Medicine)

Initial hospital visit of a 75-year-old with progressive stridor and dysphagia with history of cancer of the larynx treated by radiation therapy in the past. Exam shows a large recurrent tumor of the glottis with a mass in the neck. (Otolaryngology, Head & Neck Surgery)

Initial hospital visit for a 70-year-old male admitted with chest pain, complete heart block, and congestive heart failure. (Cardiology)

Initial hospital visit for an 82-year-old male who presents with syncope, chest pain, and ventricular arrhythmias. (Cardiology)

Initial hospital visit for a 75-year-old male with history of arteriosclerotic coronary vascular disease, who is severely dehydrated, disoriented, and experiencing auditory hallucinations. (Psychiatry)

Initial hospital visit for a 70-year-old male with alcohol and sedative-hypnotic dependence, admitted by family for severe withdrawal, hypertension, and diabetes mellitus. (Psychiatry)

Initial hospital visit for a persistently suicidal latency-aged child whose parents have requested admission to provide safety during evaluation, but are anxious about separation from her. (Psychiatry)

Initial psychiatric visit for an adolescent patient without previous psychiatric history, who was transferred from the medical ICU after a significant overdose. (Psychiatry)

Initial hospital visit for a 35-year-old female with severe systemic lupus erythematosus on corticosteroid and cyclophosphamide, with new onset of fever, chills, rash, and chest pain. (Rheumatology)

Initial hospital visit for a 52-year-old male with known rheumatic heart disease who presents with anasarca, hypertension, and history of alcohol abuse. (Cardiology)

Initial hospital visit for a 55-year-old female with a history of congenital heart disease; now presents with cyanosis. (Cardiology)

Initial hospital visit for a psychotic, hostile, violently combative adolescent, involuntarily committed, for seclusion and restraint in order to provide for safety on unit. (Psychiatry)

Initial hospital visit for a now subdued and sullen teenage male with six-month history of declining school performance, increasing self-endangerment, and resistance of parental expectations, including running away past weekend after physical fight with father. (Psychiatry)

Initial partial hospital admission for a 17-year-old female with history of borderline mental retardation who has developed auditory hallucinations. Parents are known to abuse alcohol, and Child Protective Services is investigating allegations of sexual abuse of a younger sibling. (Psychiatry)

Initial hospital visit of a 67-year-old male admitted with a large neck mass, dysphagia, and history of myocardial infarction three months before. (Otolaryngology, Head & Neck Surgery)

Initial hospital visit for a patient with suspected cerebrospinal fluid rhinorrhea which developed two weeks after head injury. (Otolaryngology, Head & Neck Surgery)

Initial hospital visit for a 25-year-old female with history of poly-substance abuse and psychiatric disorder. The patient appears to be psychotic with markedly elevated vital signs. (Psychiatry)

Initial hospital visit for a 70-year-old male with cutaneous T-cell lymphoma who has developed fever and lymphadenopathy. (Internal Medicine)

Initial hospital visit for a 62-year-old female with known coronary artery disease, for evaluation of increasing edema, dyspnea on exertion, confusion, and sudden onset of fever with productive cough. (Internal Medicine)

Initial hospital visit for a 3-year-old female with 36-hour history of sore throat and high fever; now with sudden onset of lethargy, irritability, photophobia, and nuchal rigidity. (Pediatrics)

Initial hospital visit for a 26-year-old female for evaluation of severe facial fractures (LeFort's II/III). (Plastic Surgery)

Initial hospital visit for a 55-year-old female for bilateral mandibular fractures resulting in flail mandible and airway obstruction. (Plastic Surgery)

Initial hospital visit for a 71-year-old patient with a red painful eye four days following uncomplicated cataract surgery due to endophthalmitis. (Ophthalmology)

Initial hospital visit for a 45-year-old patient involved in a motor vehicle accident who suffered a perforating corneoscleral laceration with loss of vision. (Ophthalmology)

Initial hospital visit for a 58-year-old male who has Ludwig's angina and progressive airway compromise. (Oral & Maxillofacial Surgery)

Initial hospital visit for a patient with generalized systemic sclerosis, receiving immunosuppressive therapy because of recent onset of cough, fever, and inability to swallow. (Dermatology)

Initial hospital visit for an 82-year-old male who presents with syncope, chest pain, and ventricular arrhythmias. (Cardiology)

Initial hospital visit for a 62-year-old male with history of previous myocardial infarction, comes in with recurrent, sustained ventricular tachycardia. (Cardiology)

Initial hospital visit for a chronic dialysis patient with infected PTFE fistula, septicemia, and shock. (Nephrology)

Initial hospital visit for a 1-year-old male, victim of child abuse, with central nervous system depression, skull fracture, and retinal hemorrhage. (Family Medicine/Neurology)

Initial hospital visit for a 25-year-old female with recent C4-5 quadriplegia, admitted for rehabilitation. (Physical Medicine & Rehabilitation)

Initial hospital visit for an 18-year-old male, post-traumatic brain injury with multiple impairment. (Physical Medicine & Rehabilitation)

Initial partial hospital admission for 16-year-old male, sullen and subdued, with six-month history of declining school performance, increasing self-endangerment, and resistance to parental expectations. (Psychiatry)

Initial hospital visit for a 16-year-old primigravida at 32-weeks gestation with severe hypertension (200/110), thrombocytopenia, and headache. (Obstetrics & Gynecology)

Initial hospital visit for a 49-year-old male with cirrhosis of liver with hematemesis, hepatic encephalopathy, and fever. (Gastroenterology)

Initial hospital visit for a 55-year-old female in chronic pain who has attempted suicide. (Psychiatry)

Initial hospital visit for a 70-year-old male, with multiple organ system disease, admitted with history of being aneuric and septic for 24 hours prior to admission. (Urology)

Initial hospital visit for a 3-year-old female with 36-hour history of sore throat and high fever, now with sudden onset of lethargy, irritability, photophobia, and nuchal rigidity. (Internal Medicine)

Initial hospital visit for a 78-year-old male, transfers from nursing home with dysuria and pyuria, increasing confusion, and high fever. (Internal Medicine)

Initial hospital visit for a 1-day-old male with cyanosis, respiratory distress, and tachypnea. (Cardiology)

Initial hospital visit for a 3-year-old female with recurrent tachycardia and syncope. (Cardiology)

Initial hospital visit for a thyrotoxic patient who presents with fever, atrial fibrillation, and delirium. (Endocrinology)

Initial hospital visit for a 50-year-old Type I diabetic who presents with diabetic ketoacidosis with fever and obtundation. (Endocrinology)

Initial hospital visit for a 40-year-old female with anatomical stage 3, ARA functional class 3 rheumatoid arthritis on methotrexate, corticosteroid, and nonsteroidal anti-inflammatory drugs. Patient presents with severe arthritis flare, new oral ulcers, abdominal pain, and leukopenia. (Rheumatology)

Initial hospital exam of a pediatric patient with high fever and proptosis. (Otolaryngology, Head & Neck Surgery)

Initial hospital visit for a 25-year-old patient admitted for the first time to the rehab unit, with recent C4-C5 quadriplegia. (Physical Medicine & Rehabilitation)

Hospital admission, examination, and initiation of treatment program for a previously unknown 58-year-old male who presents with acute chest pain. (Cardiology)

Hospital admission, examination, and initiation of induction chemotherapy for a 42-year-old patient with newly diagnosed acute myelogenous leukemia. (Hematology/Oncology)

Hospital admission following a motor vehicle accident of a 24-year-old male with fracture dislocation of C5-C6; neurologically intact. (Neurosurgery)

Hospital admission for a 78-year-old female with left lower lobe pneumonia and a history of coronary artery disease, congestive heart failure, osteoarthritis and gout. (Family Medicine)

Hospital admission, examination, and initiation of treatment program for a 65-year-old immunosuppressed male with confusion, fever, and a headache. (Infectious Disease)

Hospital admission for a 9-year-old with vomiting, dehydration, fever, tachypnea, and an admitting diagnosis of diabetic ketoacidosis. (Pediatrics)

Initial hospital visit for a 65-year-old male who presents with acute myocardial infarction, oliguria, hypotension, and altered state of consciousness. (Cardiology)

Initial hospital visit for a hostile/resistant adolescent patient who is severely depressed and involved in poly-substance abuse. Patient is experiencing significant conflict in his chaotic family situation and was suspended from school following an attack on a teacher with a baseball bat. (Psychiatry)

Initial hospital visit for 89-year-old female with fulminant hepatic failure and encephalopathy. (Gastroenterology)

Initial hospital visit for a 42-year-old female with rapidly progressing scleroderma, malignant hypertension, digital infarcts, and oligurea. (Rheumatology)

Subsequent Hospital Care

99231 Subsequent hospital visit for a 65-year-old female, post-open reduction and internal fixation of a fracture. (Physical Medicine & Rehabilitation)

Subsequent hospital visit for a 33-year-old patient with pelvic pain who is responding to pain medication and observation. (Obstetrics & Gynecology)

Subsequent hospital visit for a 21-year-old female with hyperemesis who has responded well to intravenous fluids. (Obstetrics & Gynecology)

Subsequent hospital visit to re-evaluate postoperative pain and titrate patient-controlled analgesia for a 27-year-old female. (Anesthesiology)

Follow-up hospital visit for a 35-year-old female, status post-epidural analgesia. (Anesthesiology/Pain Medicine)

Subsequent hospital visit for a 56-year-old male, post-gastrectomy, for maintenance of analgesia using an intravenous dilaudid infusion. (Anesthesiology)

Subsequent hospital visit for a 4-year-old on day three receiving medication for uncomplicated pneumonia. (Allergy & Immunology)

Subsequent hospital visit for a 30-year-old female with urticaria which has stabilized with medication. (Allergy & Immunology)

Subsequent hospital visit for a 76-year-old male with venous stasis ulcers. (Dermatology)

Subsequent hospital visit for a 24-year-old female with otitis externa, seen two days before in consultation, now to have otic wick removal. (Otolaryngology, Head & Neck Surgery)

Subsequent hospital visit for a 27-year-old with acute labyrinthitis. (Otolaryngology, Head & Neck Surgery)

Subsequent hospital visit for a 10-year-old male admitted for lobar pneumonia with vomiting and dehydration; is becoming afebrile and tolerating oral fluids. (Family Medicine/Pediatrics)

Subsequent hospital visit for a 62-year-old patient with resolving cellulitis of the foot. (Orthopaedic Surgery)

Subsequent hospital visit for a 25-year-old male admitted for supra-ventricular tachycardia and converted on medical therapy. (Cardiology)

Subsequent hospital visit for a 27-year-old male two days after open reduction and internal fixation for malar complex fracture. (Plastic Surgery)

Subsequent hospital visit for a 76-year-old male with venous stasis ulcers. (Geriatrics)

Subsequent hospital visit for a 67-year-old female admitted three days ago with bleeding gastric ulcer; now stable. (Gastroenterology)

Subsequent hospital visit for stable 33-year-old male, status post-lower gastrointestinal bleeding. (General Surgery/Gastroenterology)

Subsequent hospital visit for a 29-year-old auto mechanic with effort thrombosis of left upper extremity. (General Surgery)

Subsequent hospital visit for a 14-year-old female in middle phase of inpatient treatment, who is now behaviorally stable and making satisfactory progress in treatment. (Psychiatry)

Subsequent hospital visit for an 18-year-old male with uncomplicated asthma who is clinically stable. (Allergy & Immunology)

Subsequent hospital visit for a 55-year-old male with rheumatoid arthritis, two days following an uncomplicated total joint replacement. (Rheumatology)

Subsequent hospital visit for a 60-year-old dialysis patient with an access infection, now afebrile on antibiotic. (Nephrology)

Subsequent hospital visit for a 36-year-old female with stable post-rhinoplasty epistaxis. (Plastic Surgery)

Subsequent hospital visit for a 66-year-old female with L-2 vertebral compression fracture with resolving ileus. (Orthopaedic Surgery)

Subsequent hospital visit for a patient with peritonsillar abscess. (Otolaryngology, Head & Neck Surgery)

Subsequent hospital visit for an 18-year-old female responding to intravenous antibiotic therapy for ear or sinus infection. (Otolaryngology, Head & Neck Surgery)

Subsequent hospital visit for a 70-year-old male admitted with congestive heart failure who has responded to therapy. (Cardiology)

Follow-up hospital visit for a 32-year-old female with left ureteral calculus; being followed in anticipation of spontaneous passage. (Urology)

Subsequent hospital visit for a 4-year-old female, admitted for acute gastroenteritis and dehydration, requiring IV hydration; now stable. (Family Medicine)

Subsequent hospital visit for a 50-year-old Type II diabetic who is clinically stable and without complications requiring regulation of a single dose of insulin daily. (Endocrinology)

Subsequent hospital visit to reassesses the status of a 65-year-old patient post-open reduction and internal fixation of hip fracture, on the rehab unit. (Physical Medicine & Rehabilitation)

Subsequent hospital visit for a 78-year-old male with cholangiocarcinoma managed by biliary drainage. (Interventional Radiology)

Subsequent hospital visit for a 50-year-old male with uncomplicated myocardial infarction who is clinically stable and without chest pain. (Family Medicine/Cardiology/Internal Medicine)

Subsequent hospital visit for a stable 72-year-old lung cancer patient undergoing a five-day course of infusion chemotherapy. (Hematology/Oncology)

Subsequent hospital visit, two days post admission for a 65-year-old male with a CVA (cerebral vascular accident) and left hemiparesis, who is clinically stable. (Neurology/Physical Medicine and Rehabilitation)

Subsequent hospital visit for now stable, 33-year-old male, status post lower gastrointestinal bleeding. (General Surgery)

Subsequent visit on third day of hospitalization for a 60-year-old female recovering from an uncomplicated pneumonia. (Infectious Disease/Internal Medicine/Pulmonary Medicine)

Subsequent hospital visit for a 3-year-old patient in traction for a congenital dislocation of the hip. (Orthopaedic Surgery)

Subsequent hospital visit for a 4-year-old female, admitted for acute gastroenteritis and dehydration, requiring IV hydration; now stable. (Family Medicine/Internal Medicine)

Subsequent hospital visit for 50-year-old female with resolving uncomplicated acute pancreatitis. (Gastroenterology)

99232 Subsequent hospital visit for a patient with venous stasis ulcers who developed fever and red streaks adjacent to the ulcer. (Dermatology/Internal Medicine/Family Medicine)

Subsequent hospital visit for a 66-year-old male for dressing changes and observation. Patient has had a myocutaneous flap to close a pharyngeal fistula and now has a low-grade fever. (Plastic Surgery)

Subsequent hospital visit for a 54-year-old female admitted for myocardial infarction, but who is now having frequent premature ventricular contractions. (Internal Medicine)

Subsequent hospital visit for an 80-year-old patient with a pelvic rim fracture, inability to walk, and severe pain; now 36 hours post-injury, experiencing urinary retention. (Orthopaedic Surgery)

Subsequent hospital visit for a 17-year-old female with fever, pharyngitis, and airway obstruction, who after 48 hours develops a maculopapular rash. (Pediatrics/Family Medicine)

Follow-up hospital visit for a 32-year-old patient admitted the previous day for corneal ulcer. (Dermatology)

Follow-up visit for a 67-year-old male with congestive heart failure who has responded to antibiotics and diuretics, and has now developed a monoarthropathy. (Internal Medicine)

Follow-up hospital visit for a 58-year-old male receiving continuous opioids who is experiencing severe nausea and vomiting. (Pain Medicine)

Subsequent hospital visit for a patient after an auto accident who is slow to respond to ambulation training. (Physical Medicine & Rehabilitation)

Subsequent hospital visit for a 14-year-old with unstable bronchial asthma complicated by pneumonia. (Allergy & Immunology)

Subsequent hospital visit for a 50-year-old diabetic, hypertensive male with back pain not responding to conservative inpatient management with continued radiation of pain to the lower left extremity. (Orthopaedic Surgery)

Subsequent hospital visit for a 37-year-old female on day five of antibiotics for bacterial endocarditis, who still has low-grade fever. (Cardiology)

Subsequent hospital visit for a 54-year-old patient, post MI (myocardial infarction), who is out of the CCU (coronary care unit) but is now having frequent premature ventricular contractions on telemetry. (Cardiology/Internal Medicine)

Subsequent hospital visit for a patient with neutropenia, a fever responding to antibiotics, and continued slow gastrointestinal bleeding on platelet support. (Hematology/Oncology)

Subsequent hospital visit for a 50-year-old male admitted two days ago for sub-acute renal allograft rejection. (Nephrology)

Subsequent hospital visit for a 35-year-old drug addict, not responding to initial antibiotic therapy for pyelonephritis. (Urology)

Subsequent hospital visit of an 81-year-old male with abdominal distention, nausea, and vomiting. (General Surgery)

Subsequent hospital care for a 62-year-old female with congestive heart failure, who remains dyspneic and febrile. (Internal Medicine)

Subsequent hospital visit for a 73-year-old female with recently diagnosed lung cancer, who complains of unsteady gait. (Pulmonary Medicine)

Subsequent hospital visit for a 20-month-old male with bacterial meningitis treated one week with antibiotic therapy; has now developed a temperature of 101.0 degrees. (Pediatrics)

Subsequent hospital visit for 13-year-old male admitted with left lower quadrant abdominal pain and fever, not responding to therapy. (General Surgery)

Subsequent hospital visit for a 65-year-old male with hemiplegia and painful paretic shoulder. (Physical Medicine & Rehabilitation)

99233 Subsequent hospital visit for a 38-year-old male, quadriplegic with acute autonomic hyperreflexia, who is not responsive to initial care. (Physical Medicine & Rehabilitation)

Follow-up hospital visit for a teenage female who continues to experience severely disruptive, violent and life-threatening symptoms in a complicated multi-system illness. Family/social circumstances also a contributing factor. (Psychiatry)

Subsequent hospital visit for a 42-year-old female with progressive systemic sclerosis (scleroderma), renal failure on dialysis, congestive heart failure, cardiac arrhythmias, and digital ulcers. (Allergy & Immunology)

Subsequent hospital visit for a 50-year-old diabetic, hypertensive male with nonresponding back pain and radiating pain to the lower left extremity, who develops chest pain, cough, and bloody sputum. (Orthopaedic Surgery)

Subsequent hospital visit for a 64-year-old female, status post-abdominal aortic aneurysm resection, with non-responsive coagulopathy, who has now developed lower GI bleeding. (Abdominal Surgery/Colon & Rectal Surgery/General Surgery)

Follow-up hospital care of a patient with pansinusitis infection complicated by a brain abscess and asthma; no response to current treatment. (Otolaryngology, Head & Neck Surgery)

Subsequent hospital visit for a patient with a laryngeal neoplasm who develops airway compromise, suspected metastasis. (Otolaryngology, Head & Neck Surgery)

Subsequent hospital visit for a 49-year-old male with significant rectal bleeding, etiology undetermined, not responding to treatment. (Abdominal Surgery/General Surgery/Colon & Rectal Surgery)

Subsequent hospital visit for a 50-year-old male, post-aortocoronary bypass surgery; now develops hypotension and oliguria. (Cardiology)

Subsequent hospital visit for an adolescent patient who is violent, unsafe, and noncompliant, with multiple expectations for participation in treatment plan and behavior on the treatment unit. (Psychiatry)

Subsequent hospital visit for an 18-year-old male being treated for presumed PCP psychosis. Patient is still moderately symptomatic with auditory hallucinations and is insisting on signing out against medical advice. (Psychiatry)

Subsequent hospital visit for an 8-year-old female with caustic ingestion, who now has fever, dyspnea, and dropping hemoglobin. (Gastroenterology)

Follow-up hospital visit for a chronic renal failure patient on dialysis who develops chest pain and shortness of breath and a new onset pericardial friction rub. (Nephrology)

Subsequent hospital visit for a 44-year-old patient with electrical burns to the left arm with ascending infection. (Orthopaedic Surgery)

Subsequent hospital visit for a patient with systemic sclerosis who has aspirated and is short of breath. (Dermatology)

Subsequent hospital visit for a 65-year-old female, status post-op resection of abdominal aortic aneurysm, with suspected ischemic bowel. (General Surgery)

Subsequent hospital visit for a 50-year-old male, post-aortocoronary bypass surgery, now develops hypotension and oliguria. (Cardiology)

Subsequent hospital visit for a 65-year-old male, following an acute myocardial infarction, who complains of shortness of breath and new chest pain. (Cardiology)

Subsequent hospital visit for a 65-year-old female with rheumatoid arthritis (stage 3, class 3) admitted for urosepsis. On the third hospital day, chest pain, dyspnea and fever develop. (Rheumatology)

Follow-up hospital care of a pediatric case with stridor, laryngomalacia, established tracheostomy, complicated by multiple medical problems in PICU. (Otolaryngology, Head & Neck Surgery)

Subsequent hospital visit for a 60-year-old female, four days post uncomplicated inferior myocardial infarction who has developed severe chest pain, dyspnea, diaphoresis and nausea. (Family Medicine)

Subsequent hospital visit for a patient with AML (acute myelogenous leukemia), fever, elevated white count and uric acid undergoing induction chemotherapy. (Hematology/Oncology)

Subsequent hospital visit for a 38-year-old quadriplegic male with acute autonomic hyperreflexia, who is not responsive to initial care. (Physical Medicine & Rehabilitation)

Subsequent hospital visit for a 65-year-old female postoperative resection of abdominal aortic aneurysm, with suspected ischemic bowel. (General Surgery)

Subsequent hospital visit for a 60-year-old female with persistent leukocytosis and a fever seven days after a sigmoid colon resection for carcinoma. (Infectious Disease)

Subsequent hospital visit for a chronic renal failure patient on dialysis, who develops chest pain, shortness of breath and new onset of pericardial friction rub. (Nephrology)

Subsequent hospital visit for a 65-year-old male with acute myocardial infarction who now demonstrates complete heart block and congestive heart failure. (Cardiology)

Subsequent hospital visit for a 25-year-old female with hypertension and systemic lupus erythematosus, admitted for fever and respiratory distress. On the third hospital day, the patient presented with purpuric skin lesions and acute renal failure. (Allergy & Immunology)

Subsequent hospital visit for a 55-year-old male with severe chronic obstructive pulmonary disease and bronchospasm; initially admitted for acute respiratory distress requiring ventilatory support in the ICU. The patient was stabilized, extubated and transferred to the floor, but has now developed acute fever, dyspnea, left lower lobe rhonchi and laboratory evidence of carbon dioxide retention and hypoxemia. (Family Medicine/Internal Medicine)

Subsequent hospital visit for 46-year-old female, known liver cirrhosis patient, with recent upper gastrointestinal hemorrhage from varices; now with worsening ascites and encephalopathy. (Gastroenterology)

Subsequent hospital visit for 62-year-old female admitted with acute subarachnoid hemorrhage, negative cerebral arteriogram, increased lethargy and hemiparesis with fever. (Neurosurgery)

Consultations

Office or Other Outpatient Consultations

New or Established Patient

99241 Initial office consultation for a 40-year-old female in pain from blister on lip following a cold. (Oral & Maxillofacial Surgery)

Initial office consultation for a 62-year-old construction worker with olecranon bursitis. (Orthopaedic Surgery)

Office consultation with 25-year-old postpartum female with severe symptomatic hemorrhoids. (Colon & Rectal Surgery)

Office consultation with 58-year-old male, referred for follow-up of creatinine level and evaluation of obstructive uropathy, relieved two months ago. (Nephrology)

Office consultation for 30-year-old female tennis player with sprain or contusion of the forearm. (Orthopaedic Surgery)

Office consultation for a 45-year-old male, requested by his internist, with asymptomatic torus palatinus requiring no further treatment. (Oral & Maxillofacial Surgery)

99242 Initial office consultation for a 20-year-old male with acute upper respiratory tract symptoms. (Allergy & Immunology)

Initial office consultation for a 29-year-old soccer player with painful proximal thigh/groin injury. (Orthopaedic Surgery)

Initial office consultation for a 66-year-old female with wrist and hand pain, numbness of finger tips, suspected median nerve compression by carpal tunnel syndrome. (Plastic Surgery)

Initial office consultation for a patient with a solitary lesion of discoid lupus erythematosus on left cheek to rule out malignancy or self-induced lesion. (Dermatology)

Office consultation for management of systolic hypertension in a 70-year-old male scheduled for elective prostate resection. (Geriatrics)

Office consultation with 27-year-old female, with old amputation, for evaluation of existing above-knee prosthesis. (Physical Medicine & Rehabilitation)

Office consultation with 66-year-old female with wrist and hand pain, and finger numbness, secondary to suspected carpal tunnel syndrome. (Orthopaedic Surgery)

Office consultation for 61-year-old female, recently on antibiotic therapy, now with diarrhea and leukocytosis. (Abdominal Surgery)

Office consultation for a patient with papulosquamous eruption of elbow with pitting of nails and itchy scalp. (Dermatology)

Office consultation for a 30-year-old female with single season allergic rhinitis. (Allergy & Immunology)

99243 Initial office consultation for a 60-year-old male with avascular necrosis of the left femoral head with increasing pain. (Orthopaedic Surgery)

Office consultation for a 31-year-old woman complaining of palpitations and chest pains. Her internist had described a mild systolic click. (Cardiology)

Office consultation for a 65-year-old female with persistent bronchitis. (Infectious Disease)

Office consultation for a 65-year-old man with chronic low-back pain radiating to the leg. (Neurosurgery)

Office consultation for 23-year-old female with Crohn's disease not responding to therapy. (Abdominal Surgery/Colon & Rectal Surgery)

Office consultation for 25-year-old patient with symptomatic knee pain and swelling, with torn anterior cruciate ligament and/or torn meniscus. (Orthopaedic Surgery)

Office consultation for a 67-year-old patient with osteoporosis and mandibular atrophy with regard to reconstructive alternatives. (Oral & Maxillofacial Surgery)

Office consultation for 39-year-old patient referred at a perimenopausal age for irregular menses and menopausal symptoms. (Obstetrics & Gynecology)

99244 Initial office consultation for a 28-year-old male, HIV+, with a recent change in visual acuity. (Ophthalmology)

Initial office consultation for a 15-year-old male with failing grades, suspected drug abuse. (Pediatrics)

Initial office consultation for a 36-year-old factory worker, status four months post-occupational low back injury and requires management of intractable low back pain. (Pain Medicine)

Initial office consultation for a 45-year-old female with a history of chronic arthralgia of TMJ and associated myalgia and sudden progressive symptomatology over last two to three months. (Oral & Maxillofacial Surgery)

Initial office consultation for evaluation of a 70-year-old male with appetite loss and diminished energy. (Psychiatry)

Initial office consultation for an elementary school-aged patient, referred by pediatrician, with multiple systematic complaints and recent onset of behavioral discontrol. (Psychiatry)

Initial office consultation for a 23-year-old female with developmental facial skeletal anomaly and subsequent abnormal relationship of jaw(s) to cranial base. (Oral & Maxillofacial Surgery)

Initial office consultation for a 45-year-old myopic patient with a one-week history of floaters and a partial retinal detachment. (Ophthalmology)

Initial office consultation for a 65-year-old female with moderate dementia, mild unsteadiness, back pain fatigue on ambulation, intermittent urinary incontinence. (Neurosurgery)

Initial office consultation for a 33-year-old female referred by endocrinologist with amenorrhea and galactorrhea, for evaluation of pituitary tumor. (Neurosurgery)

Initial office consultation for a 34-year-old male with new onset nephrotic syndrome. (Nephrology)

Initial office consultation for a 39-year-old female with intractable chest wall pain secondary to metastatic breast cancer. (Anesthesiology/Pain Medicine)

Initial office consultation for a patient with multiple giant tumors of jaws. (Oral & Maxillofacial Surgery)

Initial office consultation for a patient with a failed total hip replacement with loosening and pain upon walking. (Orthopaedic Surgery)

Initial office consultation for a 60-year-old female with three-year history of intermittent tic-like unilateral facial pain; now constant pain for six weeks without relief by adequate carbamazepine dosage. (Neurosurgery)

Initial office consultation for a 45-year-old male heavy construction worker with prior lumbar disc surgery two years earlier; now gradually recurring low back and unilateral leg pain for three months, unable to work for two weeks. (Neurosurgery)

Initial office consultation of a patient who presents with a 30-year history of smoking and right neck mass. (Otolaryngology, Head & Neck Surgery)

Office consultation with 38-year-old female, with inflammatory bowel disease, who now presents with right lower quadrant pain and suspected intra-abdominal abscess. (General Surgery/Colon & Rectal Surgery)

Office consultation with 72-year-old male with esophageal carcinoma, symptoms of dysphagia, and reflux. (Thoracic Surgery)

Office consultation for discussion of treatment options for a 40-year-old female with a 2-cm adenocarcinoma of the breast. (Radiation Oncology)

Office consultation for young patient referred by pediatrician because of patient's short attention span, easy distractibility and hyperactivity. (Psychiatry)

Office consultation for 66-year-old female, history of colon resection for adenocarcinoma six years earlier, now with severe mid-back pain; X rays showing osteoporosis and multiple vertebral compression fractures. (Neurosurgery)

Office consultation for a patient with chronic pelvic inflammatory disease who now has left lower quadrant pain with a palpable pelvic mass. (Obstetrics & Gynecology)

Office consultation for a patient with long-standing psoriasis with acute onset of erythroderma, pustular lesions, chills, and fever. Combinations of topical and systemic treatments discussed and instituted. (Dermatology)

99245 Initial office consultation for a 35-year-old multiple-trauma male patient with complex pelvic fractures, for evaluation and formulation of management plan. (Orthopaedic Surgery)

Initial emergency room consultation for 10-year-old male in status epilepticus, recent closed head injury, information about medication not available. (Neurosurgery)

Initial emergency room consultation for a 23-year-old patient with severe abdominal pain, guarding, febrile, and unstable vital signs. (Obstetrics & Gynecology)

Office consultation for a 67-year-old female longstanding uncontrolled diabetic who presents with retinopathy, nephropathy, and a foot ulcer. (Endocrinology)

Office consultation for a 37-year-old male for initial evaluation and management of Cushing's disease. (Endocrinology)

Office consultation for a 60-year-old male who presents with thyrotoxicosis, exophthalmos, frequent premature ventricular contractions and congestive heart failure. (Endocrinology)

Initial office consultation for a 36-year-old patient, one year status post occupational herniated cervical disk treated by laminectomy, requiring management of multiple sites of intractable pain, depression, and narcotic dependence. (Pain Medicine)

Office consultation for a 58-year-old man with a history of MI and CHF who complains of the recent onset of rest angina and shortness of breath. The patient has a systolic blood pressure of 90 mmHG and is in Class IV heart failure. (Cardiology)

Emergency department consultation for a 1-year-old with a three-day history of fever with increasing respiratory distress who is thought to have cardiac tamponade by the ER physician. (Cardiology)

Office consultation in the emergency department for a 25-year-old male with severe, acute, closed head injury. (Neurosurgery)

Office consultation for a 23-year-old female with Stage II A Hodgkins disease with positive supraclavicular and mediastinal nodes. (Radiation Oncology)

Office consultation for a 27-year-old juvenile diabetic patient with severe diabetic retinopathy, gastric atony, nephrotic syndrome and progressive renal failure, now with a serum creatinine of 2.7, and a blood pressure of 170/114. (Nephrology)

Office consultation for independent medical evaluation of a patient with a history of complicated low back and neck problems with previous multiple failed back surgeries. (Orthopaedic Surgery)

Office consultation for an adolescent referred by pediatrician for recent onset of violent and self-injurious behavior. (Psychiatry)

Office consultation for a 6-year-old male for evaluation of severe muscle and joint pain and a diffuse rash. Patient was feeling well until 4 to 6 weeks earlier, when he developed arthralgia, myalgias, and a fever of 102 degrees for one week. (Rheumatology)

Inpatient Consultations

New or Established Patient

99251 Initial hospital consultation for a 27-year-old female with fractured incisor post-intubation. (Oral & Maxillofacial Surgery)

Initial hospital consultation for an orthopaedic patient on IV antibiotics who has developed an apparent candida infection of the oral cavity. (Oral & Maxillofacial Surgery)

Initial inpatient consultation for a 30-year-old female complaining of vaginal itching, post orthopaedic surgery. (Obstetrics & Gynecology)

Initial inpatient consultation for a 36-year-old male on orthopaedic service with complaint of localized dental pain. (Oral & Maxillofacial Surgery)

99252 Initial hospital consultation for a 45-year-old male, previously abstinent alcoholic, who relapsed and was admitted for management of gastritis. The patient readily accepts the need for further treatment. (Addiction Medicine)

Initial hospital consultation for a 35-year-old dialysis patient with episodic oral ulcerations. (Oral & Maxillofacial Surgery)

Initial inpatient preoperative consultation for a 43-year-old female with cholecystitis and well-controlled hypertension. (Cardiology)

Initial inpatient consultation for recommendation of antibiotic prophylaxis for a patient with a synthetic heart valve who will undergo urologic surgery. (Internal Medicine)

Initial inpatient consultation for possible drug induced skin eruption in 50-year-old male. (Dermatology)

Preoperative inpatient consultation for evaluation of hypertension in a 60-year-old male who will undergo a cholecystectomy. Patient had a normal annual check-up in your office four months ago. (Internal Medicine)

Initial inpatient consultation for 66-year-old patient with wrist and hand pain and finger numbness, secondary to carpal tunnel syndrome. (Orthopaedic Surgery/Plastic Surgery)

Initial inpatient consultation for a 66-year-old male smoker referred for pain management immediately status post-biliary tract surgery done via sub-costal incision. (Anesthesiology/Pain Medicine)

99253 Initial hospital consultation for a 50-year-old female with incapacitating knee pain due to generalized rheumatoid arthritis. (Orthopaedic Surgery)

Initial hospital consultation for a 60-year-old male with avascular necrosis of the left femoral heel with increasing pain. (Orthopaedic Surgery)

Initial hospital consultation for a 45-year-old female with compound mandibular fracture and concurrent head, abdominal and/or orthopaedic injuries. (Oral & Maxillofacial Surgery)

Initial hospital consultation for a 22-year-old female, paraplegic, to evaluate wrist and hand pain. (Orthopaedic Surgery)

Initial hospital consultation for a 40-year-old male with 10-day history of incapacitating unilateral sciatica, unable to walk now, not improved by bed rest. (Neurosurgery)

Initial hospital consultation, requested by pediatrician, for treatment recommendations for a patient admitted with persistent inability to walk following soft tissue injury to ankle. (Physiatry)

Initial hospital consultation for a 27-year-old previously healthy male who vomited during IV sedation and may have aspirated gastric contents. (Anesthesiology)

Initial hospital consultation for a 33-year-old female, post-abdominal surgery, who now has a fever. (Internal Medicine)

Initial inpatient consultation for a 57-year-old male, post lower endoscopy, for evaluation of abdominal pain and fever. (General Surgery)

Initial inpatient consultation for rehabilitation of a 73-year-old female one week after surgical management of a hip fracture. (Physical Medicine & Rehabilitation)

Initial inpatient consultation for diagnosis/management of fever following abdominal surgery. (Internal Medicine)

Initial inpatient consultation for a 35-year-old female with a fever and pulmonary infiltrate following cesarean section. (Pulmonary Medicine)

Initial inpatient consultation for a 42-year-old nondiabetic patient, postop cholecystectomy, now with an acute urinary tract infection. (Nephrology)

Initial inpatient consultation for 53-year-old female with moderate uncomplicated pancreatitis. (Gastroenterology)

Initial inpatient consultation for 45-year-old patient with chronic neck pain with radicular pain of the left arm. (Orthopaedic Surgery)

Initial inpatient consultation for 8-year-old patient with new onset of seizures who has a normal examination and previous history. (Neurology)

99254 Initial hospital consultation for a 15-year-old patient with painless swelling of proximal humerus with lytic lesion by X ray. (Orthopaedic Surgery)

Initial hospital consultation for evaluation of a 29-year-old female with a diffusely positive medical review of systems and history of multiple surgeries. (Psychiatry)

Initial hospital consultation for a 70-year-old diabetic female with gangrene of the foot. (Orthopaedic Surgery)

Initial inpatient consultation for a 47-year-old female with progressive pulmonary infiltrate, hypoxemia, and diminished urine output. (Anesthesiology)

Initial hospital consultation for a 13-month-old with spasmodic cough, respiratory distress, and fever. (Allergy & Immunology)

Initial hospital consultation for a patient with failed total hip replacement with loosening and pain upon walking. (Orthopaedic Surgery)

Initial hospital consultation for a 62-year-old female with metastatic breast cancer to the femoral neck and thoracic vertebra. (Orthopaedic Surgery)

Initial hospital consultation for a 39-year-old female with nephrolithiasis requiring extensive opioid analgesics, whose vital signs are now elevated. She initially denied any drug use, but today gives history of multiple substance abuse, including opioids and prior treatment for a personality disorder. (Psychiatry)

Initial hospital consultation for a 70-year-old female without previous psychiatric history, who is now experiencing nocturnal confusion and visual hallucinations following hip replacement surgery. (Psychiatry)

Initial inpatient consultation for evaluation of a 63-year-old in the ICU with diabetes and chronic renal failure who develops acute respiratory distress syndrome 36 hours after a mitral valve replacement. (Anesthesiology)

Initial inpatient consultation for a 66-year-old female with enlarged supraclavicular lymph nodes, found on biopsy to be malignant. (Hematology/Oncology)

Initial inpatient consultation for a 43-year-old female for evaluation of sudden painful visual loss, optic neuritis and episodic paresthesia. (Ophthalmology)

Initial inpatient consultation for evaluation of a 71-year-old male with hyponatremia (serum sodium 114) who was admitted to the hospital with pneumonia. (Nephrology)

Initial inpatient consultation for a 72-year-old male with emergency admission for possible bowel obstruction. (Internal Medicine/General Surgery)

Initial inpatient consultation for a 35-year-old female with fever, swollen joints, and rash of one-week duration. (Rheumatology)

99255 Initial inpatient consultation for a 76-year-old female with massive, life-threatening gastrointestinal hemorrhage and chest pain. (Gastroenterology)

Initial inpatient consultation for a 75-year-old female, admitted to intensive care with acute respiratory distress syndrome, who is hypersensitive, has a moderate metabolic acidosis, and a rising serum creatinine. (Nephrology)

Initial hospital consultation for patient with a history of complicated low back pain and neck problems with previous multiple failed back surgeries. (Orthopaedic Surgery/Neurosurgery)

Initial hospital consultation for a 66-year-old female, two days post-abdominal aneurysm repair, with oliguria and hypertension of one-day duration. (Nephrology/Internal Medicine)

Initial hospital consultation for a patient with shotgun wound to face with massive facial trauma and airway obstruction. (Oral & Maxillofacial Surgery)

Initial hospital consultation for patient with severe pancreatitis complicated by respiratory insufficiency, acute renal failure, and abscess formation. (General Surgery/Colon & Rectal Surgery)

Initial hospital consultation for a 35-year-old multiple-trauma male patient with complex pelvic fractures to evaluate and formulate management plan. (Orthopaedic Surgery)

Initial inpatient consultation for adolescent patient with fractured femur and pelvis who pulled out IVs and disconnected traction in attempt to elope from hospital. (Psychiatry)

Initial hospital consultation for a 16-year-old primigravida at 32-weeks gestation requested by a family practitioner for evaluation of severe hypertension, thrombocytopenia, and headache. (Obstetrics & Gynecology)

Initial hospital consultation for a 58-year-old insulin-dependent diabetic with multiple antibiotic allergies, now with multiple fascial plane abscesses and airway obstruction. (Oral & Maxillofacial Surgery)

Initial inpatient consultation for a 55-year-old male with known cirrhosis and ascites, now with jaundice, encephalopathy, and massive hematemesis. (Gastroenterology)

Initial hospital consultation for a 25-year-old male, seen in emergency room with severe, closed head injury. (Neurosurgery)

Initial hospital consultation for a 2-day-old male with single ventricle physiology and subaortic obstruction. Family counseling following evaluation for multiple, staged surgical procedures. (Thoracic Surgery)

Initial hospital consultation for a 45-year-old male admitted with subarachnoid hemorrhage and intracranial aneurysm on angiogram. (Neurosurgery)

Initial inpatient consultation for myxedematous patient who is hypoventilating and obtunded. (Endocrinology)

Initial hospital consultation for a 45-year-old patient with widely metastatic lung carcinoma, intractable back pain, and a history that includes substance dependence, NSAID allergy, and two prior laminectomies with fusion for low back pain. (Pain Medicine)

Initial hospital consultation for evaluation of treatment options in a 50-year-old patient with cirrhosis, known peptic ulcer disease, hypotension, encephalopathy, and massive acute upper gastrointestinal bleeding which cannot be localized by endoscopy. (Interventional Radiology)

Initial inpatient consultation in the ICU for a 70-year-old male who experienced a cardiac arrest during surgery and was resuscitated. (Cardiology)

Initial inpatient consultation for a patient with severe pancreatitis complicated by respiratory insufficiency, acute renal failure and abscess formation. (Gastroenterology)

Initial inpatient consultation for a 70-year-old cirrhotic male admitted with ascites, jaundice, encephalopathy, and massive hematemesis. (Gastroenterology)

Initial inpatient consultation in the ICU for a 51-year-old patient who is on a ventilator and has a fever two weeks after a renal transplantation. (Infectious Disease)

Initial inpatient consultation for evaluation and formulation of plan for management of multiple trauma patient with complex pelvic fracture, 35-year-old male. (General Surgery/Orthopaedic Surgery)

Initial inpatient consultation for a 50-year-old male with a history of previous myocardial infarction, now with acute pulmonary edema and hypotension. (Cardiology)

Initial inpatient consultation for 45-year-old male with recent, acute subarachnoid hemorrhage, hesitant speech, mildly confused, drowsy. High risk group for HIV+ status. (Neurosurgery)

Initial inpatient consultation for 36-year-old female referred by her internist to evaluate a patient being followed for abdominal pain and fever. The patient has developed diffuse abdominal pain, guarding, rigidity and increased fever. (Obstetrics & Gynecology)

Emergency Department Services

New or Established Patient

99281 Emergency department visit for a patient for removal of sutures from a well-healed, uncomplicated laceration. (Emergency Medicine)

Emergency department visit for a patient for tetanus toxoid immunization. (Emergency Medicine)

Emergency department visit for a patient with several uncomplicated insect bites. (Emergency Medicine)

99282 Emergency department visit for a 20-year-old student who presents with a painful sunburn with blister formation on the back. (Emergency Medicine)

Emergency department visit for a child presenting with impetigo localized to the face. (Emergency Medicine)

Emergency department visit for a patient with a minor traumatic injury of an extremity with localized pain, swelling, and bruising. (Emergency Medicine)

Emergency department visit for an otherwise healthy patient whose chief complaint is a red, swollen cystic lesion on his/her back. (Emergency Medicine)

Emergency department visit for a patient presenting with a rash on both legs after exposure to poison ivy. (Emergency Medicine)

Emergency department visit for a young adult patient with infected sclera and purulent discharge from both eyes without pain, visual disturbance or history of foreign body in either eye. (Emergency Medicine)

99283 Emergency department visit for a sexually active female complaining of vaginal discharge who is afebrile and denies experiencing abdominal or back pain. (Emergency Medicine)

Emergency department visit for a well-appearing 8-year-old who has a fever, diarrhea, and abdominal cramps, is tolerating oral fluids and is not vomiting. (Emergency Medicine)

Emergency department visit for a patient with an inversion ankle injury, who is unable to bear weight on the injured foot and ankle. (Emergency Medicine)

Emergency department visit for a patient who has a complaint of acute pain associated with a suspected foreign body in the painful eye. (Emergency Medicine)

Emergency department visit for a healthy, young adult patient who sustained a blunt head injury with local swelling and bruising without subsequent confusion, loss of consciousness or memory deficit. (Emergency Medicine)

99284 Emergency department visit for a 4-year-old who fell off a bike sustaining a head injury with brief loss of consciousness. (Emergency Medicine)

Emergency department visit for an elderly female who has fallen and is now complaining of pain in her right hip and is unable to walk. (Emergency Medicine)

Emergency department visit for a patient with flank pain and hematuria. (Emergency Medicine)

Emergency department visit for a female presenting with lower abdominal pain and a vaginal discharge. (Emergency Medicine)

99285 Emergency department visit for a patient with a complicated overdose requiring aggressive management to prevent side effects from the ingested materials. (Emergency Medicine)

Emergency department visit for a patient with a new onset of rapid heart rate requiring IV drugs. (Emergency Medicine)

Emergency department visit for a patient exhibiting active, upper gastrointestinal bleeding. (Emergency Medicine)

Emergency department visit for a previously healthy young adult patient who is injured in an automobile accident and is brought to the emergency department immobilized and has symptoms compatible with intra-abdominal injuries or multiple extremity injuries. (Emergency Medicine)

Emergency department visit for a patient with an acute onset of chest pain compatible with symptoms of cardiac ischemia and/or pulmonary embolus. (Emergency Medicine)

Emergency department visit for a patient who presents with a sudden onset of "the worst headache of her life," and complains of a stiff neck, nausea, and inability to concentrate. (Emergency Medicine)

Emergency department visit for a patient with a new onset of a cerebral vascular accident. (Emergency Medicine)

Emergency department visit for acute febrile illness in an adult, associated with shortness of breath and an altered level of alertness. (Emergency Medicine)

Critical Care Services

99291 First hour of critical care of a 65-year-old male with septic shock following relief of ureteral obstruction caused by a stone.

First hour of critical care of a 15-year-old with acute respiratory failure from asthma.

First hour of critical care of a 45-year-old who sustained a liver laceration, cerebral hematoma, flailed chest, and pulmonary contusion after being struck by an automobile.

First hour of critical care of a 65-year-old female who, following a hysterectomy, suffered a cardiac arrest associated with a pulmonary embolus.

First hour of critical care of a 6-month-old with hypovolemic shock secondary to diarrhea and dehydration.

First hour of critical care of a 3-year-old with respiratory failure secondary to pneumocystis carinii pneumonia.

Prolonged Services

Prolonged Physician Service With Direct (Face-to-Face) Patient Contact

Office or Other Outpatient

99354/ 99355 A 20-year-old female with history of asthma presents with acute bronchospasm and moderate respiratory distress. Initial evaluation shows respiratory rate 30, labored breathing and wheezing heard in all lung fields. Office treatment is initiated, which includes intermittent bronchial dilation and subcutaneous epinephrine. Requires intermittent physician face-to-face time with patient over a period of 2 to 3 hours. (Family Medicine/Internal Medicine)

Inpatient

99356 A 34-year-old primigravida presents to hospital in early labor. Admission history and physical reveals severe preeclampsia. Physician supervises management of preeclampsia, IV magnesium initiation and maintenance, labor augmentation with pitocin, and close maternal-fetal monitoring. Physician face-to-face involvement includes 40 minutes of continuous bedside care until the patient is stable, then is intermittent over several hours until the delivery. (Family Medicine/Internal Medicine/Obstetrics & Gynecology)

Prolonged Physician Service Without Direct Patient (Face-to-Face) Contact

99358/ 99359 A 65-year-old new patient with multiple problems is seen and evaluated. After the visit, the physician requires extensive time to talk with the patient's daughter, to review complex, detailed medical records transferred from previous physicians and to complete a comprehensive treatment plan. This plan also requires the physician to personally initiate and coordinate the care plan with a local home health agency and a dietician. (Family Medicine/Internal Medicine)

Physician Standby Services

99360 A 24-year-old patient is admitted to OB unit attempting VBAC. Fetal monitoring shows increasing fetal distress. Patient's blood pressure is rising and labor progressing slowly. A primary care physician is requested by the OB/GYN to standby in the unit for possible cesarean delivery and neonatal resuscitation. (Family Medicine/Internal Medicine)

Care Plan Oversight Services

99375 First month of care plan oversight for terminal care of a 58-year-old female with advanced intraabdominal ovarian cancer. Care plan includes home oxygen, diuretics IV for edema and ascites control and pain control management involving IV morphine infusion when progressive ileus occurred. Physician phone contacts with nurse, family, and MSW. Discussion with MSW concerning plans to withdraw supportive measures per patient wishes. Documentation includes review and modification of care plan and certifications from nursing, MSW, pharmacy, and DME. (Family Medicine/Internal Medicine)

Appendix D

Summary of CPT Add-on Codes

This listing is a summary of CPT add-on codes for *CPT 2009*. The codes listed below are identified in *CPT 2009* with a ✚ symbol.

01953
01968
01969
11001
11008
11101
11201
11732
11922
13102
13122
13133
13153
15003
15005
15101
15111
15116
15121
15131
15136
15151
15152
15156
15157
15171
15176
15201
15221
15241
15261
15301
15321
15331
15336
15341
15361
15366
15401
15421
15431
15787
15847
16036
17003
17312
17314
17315
19001
19126
19291
19295
19297
20930
20931
20936
20937
20938
20985
22103
22116
22208
22216
22226
22328
22522
22525
22527
22534
22585
22614
22632
22840
22841
22842
22843
22844
22845
22846
22847
22848
22851
26125
26861
26863
27358
27692
31620
31632
31633
31637
32501
33141
33225
33257
33258
33259
33508
33517
33518
33519
33521
33522
33523
33530
33572
33768
33884
33924
33961
34806
34808
34813
34826
35306
35390
35400
35500
35572
35600
35681
35682
35683
35685
35686
35697
35700
36218
36248
36476
36479
37185
37186
37206
37208
37250
37251
38102
38746
38747
43273
43635
44015
44121
44128
44139
44203
44213
44701
44955
47001
47550
48400
49326
49435
49568
49905
51797
56606
57267
58110
58611
59525
60512
61316
61517
61609
61610
61611
61612
61641
61642
61795
61797
61799
61800
61864
61868
62148
62160
63035
63043
63044
63048
63057
63066
63076
63078
63082
63086
63088
63091
63103
63295
63308
63621
64472
64476
64480
64484
64623
64627
64727
64778
64783
64787
64832
64837
64859
64872
64874
64876
64901
64902
65757
66990
67225
67320
67331
67332
67334
67335
67340
69990
74301
75774
75946
75964
75968
75993
75996
76125
76802
76810
76812
76814
76937
77001
77051
77052
78020
78478
78480
78496
78730
83901
87187
87904
88155
88185
88311
88312
88313
88314
90466
90468
90472
90474
92547
92608
92627
92973
92974
92978
92979
92981
92984
92996
92998
93320
93321
93325
93352
93571
93572
93609
93613
93621
93622
93623
93662
94645
95873
95874
95920
95962
95967
95973
95975
95979
96361
96366

96367
96368
96370
96371
96375
96376
96411
96415
96417
96423
96570
96571
97546
97811
97814
99100
99116
99135
99140
99145
99150
99292
99354
99355
99356
99357
99358
99359
99467
99602
99607
0054T
0055T
0063T
0076T
0079T
0081T
0092T
0095T
0098T
0151T
0159T
0163T
0164T
0165T
0172T
0173T
0174T
0189T
0190T
0196T

Appendix E

Summary of CPT Codes Exempt from Modifier 51

This listing is a summary of CPT codes that are exempt from the use of modifier 51. Procedures on this list are typically performed with another procedure but may be a stand alone procedure and not always be performed with other specified procedures. For add-on codes see Appendix D. This is not an exhaustive list of procedures that are typically exempt from multiple procedure reductions. The codes listed below are identified in *CPT 2009* with a ⊘ symbol.

17004

20697

20974

20975

31500

36620

44500

61107

93503

93539

93540

93544

93545

93555

93556

93600

93602

93603

93610

93612

93615

93616

93618

93631

94610

95900

95903

95904

95992

99143

99144

Appendix F

Summary of CPT Codes Exempt from Modifier 63

The listing is a summary of CPT codes that are exempt from the use of modifier 63. The codes listed below are additionally identified in *CPT 2009* with the parenthetical instruction "(Do not report modifier 63 in conjunction with...)".

30540	36660	63700
30545	39503	63702
31520	43313	63704
33401	43314	63706
33403	43520	65820
33470	43831	
33472	44055	
33502	44126	
33503	44127	
33505	44128	
33506	46070	
33610	46705	
33611	46715	
33619	46716	
33647	46730	
33670	46735	
33690	46740	
33694	46742	
33730	46744	
33732	47700	
33735	47701	
33736	49215	
33750	49491	
33755	49492	
33762	49495	
33778	49496	
33786	49600	
33922	49605	
33960	49606	
33961	49610	
36415	49611	
36420	53025	
36450	54000	
36460	54150	
36510	54160	

Appendix G

Summary of CPT Codes That Include Moderate (Conscious) Sedation

The following list of procedures includes conscious sedation as an inherent part of providing the procedure. These codes are identified in the CPT codebook with a ⊙ symbol.

Since these services include moderate sedation, it is not appropriate for the same physician to report both the service and the sedation codes 99143-99145. It is expected that if conscious sedation is provided to the patient as part of one of these services, it is provided by the same physician who is providing the service.

In the unusual event when a second physician other than the health care professional performing the diagnostic or therapeutic services provides moderate sedation in the facility setting (eg, hospital, outpatient hospital/ambulatory surgery center, skilled nursing facility) for the procedures listed in Appendix G, the second physician can report 99148-99150. However, for the circumstance in which these services are performed by the second physician in the nonfacility setting (eg, physician office, freestanding imaging center), codes 99148-99150 would not be reported. Moderate sedation does not include minimal sedation (anxiolysis), deep sedation, or monitored anesthesia care (00100-01999).

The inclusion of a procedure on this list does not prevent separate reporting of an associated anesthesia procedure/service (CPT codes 00100-01999) when performed by a physician other than the health care professional performing the diagnostic or therapeutic procedure. In such cases the person providing anesthesia services shall be present for the purpose of continuously monitoring the patient and shall not act as a surgical assistant. When clinical conditions of the patient require such anesthesia services, or in the circumstances when the patient does not require sedation, the operating physician is not required to report the procedure as a reduced service using modifier 52.

19298	**31624**	**31725**	**33208**
20982	**31625**	**32201**	**33210**
22526	**31628**	**32550**	**33211**
22527	**31629**	**32551**	**33212**
31615	**31635**	**33010**	**33213**
31620	**31645**	**33011**	**33214**
31622	**31646**	**33206**	**33216**
31623	**31656**	**33207**	**33217**

33218	**43202**	**43453**
33220	**43204**	**43456**
33222	**43205**	**43458**
33223	**43215**	**44360**
33233	**43216**	**44361**
33234	**43217**	**44363**
33235	**43219**	**44364**
33240	**43220**	**44365**
33241	**43226**	**44366**
33244	**43227**	**44369**
33249	**43228**	**44370**
35470	**43231**	**44372**
35471	**43232**	**44373**
35472	**43234**	**44376**
35473	**43235**	**44377**
35474	**43236**	**44378**
35475	**43237**	**44379**
35476	**43238**	**44380**
36555	**43239**	**44382**
36557	**43240**	**44383**
36558	**43241**	**44385**
36560	**43242**	**44386**
36561	**43243**	**44388**
36563	**43244**	**44389**
36565	**43245**	**44390**
36566	**43246**	**44391**
36568	**43247**	**44392**
36570	**43248**	**44393**
36571	**43249**	**44394**
36576	**43250**	**44397**
36578	**43251**	**44500**
36581	**43255**	**44901**
36582	**43256**	**45303**
36583	**43257**	**45305**
36585	**43258**	**45307**
36590	**43259**	**45308**
36870	**43260**	**45309**
37184	**43261**	**45315**
37185	**43262**	**45317**
37186	**43263**	**45320**
37187	**43264**	**45321**
37188	**43265**	**45327**
37203	**43267**	**45332**
37210	**43268**	**45333**
37215	**43269**	**45334**
37216	**43271**	**45335**
43200	**43272**	**45337**
43201	**43273**	**45338**

45339
45340
45341
45342
45345
45355
45378
45379
45380
45381
45382
45383
45384
45385
45386
45387
45391
45392
47011
48511
49021
49041
49061
49440
49441
49442
49446
50021
50382
50384
50385
50386
50387
50592
50593
58823
66720
69300
77600
77605
77610
77615
92953
92960
92961
92973
92974
92975
92978
92979
92980
92981
92982
92984
92986
92987
92995
92996
93312
93313
93314
93315
93316
93317
93318
93501
93505
93508
93510
93511
93514
93524
93526
93527
93528
93529
93530
93539
93540
93541
93542
93543
93544
93545
93555
93556
93561
93562
93571
93572
93609
93613
93615
93616
93618
93619
93620
93621
93622
93624
93640
93641
93642
93650
93651
93652

Appendix H

Alphabetic Index of Performance Measures by Clinical Condition or Topic

Appendix H is an alphabetical listing of **clinical conditions and topics** with which the measures and codes are associated. It provides an overview of the performance measures, a listing of the CPT Category II codes that may be used with each measure, as well as any applicable reporting instructions. It is intended to be used as a crosswalk to the Category II code section allowing users an overview of the measures and the Category II codes that should be used with each measure, linking the Category II codes to the specific measures and measure sets from which these codes were derived. The clinical conditions or topics are listed in alphabetical order within this appendix to allow rapid access to the conditions/topics currently included in the CPT codebook. For the latest Appendix H information, visit the AMA website at www.ama-assn.org/go/cpt.

In order for a patient to be included in the numerator for a particular performance measure, a patient must meet the denominator inclusion criteria for that measure. Prior to coding, users must review (1) the complete description of the code in the Category II section of the CPT codebook and web site and (2) the specification documents of its associated performance measure as found on the measure developer's website. The superscripted numbers that follow the specific title for the performance measure direct users to footnotes at the bottom of each page of this appendix. The footnotes identify the measure developer and the developer's Web address.

►Only modifiers 1P, 2P, 3P, and 8P can be used with Category II codes. Other modifiers **cannot** be used with Category II codes.◄ In addition, the modifiers included within the Category II code section and Appendix H are only intended to be used when parenthetical notes, guidelines, or reporting language specifically allow their use.

Performance Measure Exclusionary Modifiers

Performance measurement exclusion modifiers may be used to indicate that a service specified by a performance measure was considered but, due to either medical, patient, or systems reason(s) documented in the medical record, the service was not provided. These modifiers serve as denominator exclusions from the performance measure. *Not all listed measures provide for exclusions.* The modifiers currently available include the noted listing:

1P Performance measure exclusion modifier due to medical reasons

Includes:

- Not indicated (absence of organ/limb, already received/performed, other)
- Contraindicated (patient allergic history, potential adverse drug interaction, other)
- Other medical reasons

2P Performance measure exclusion modifier due to patient reasons

Includes:

- Patient declined
- Economic, social, or religious reasons
- Other patient reasons

3P Performance measure exclusion modifier due to system reasons

Includes:

- Resources to perform the services not available (eg, equipment, supplies)
- Insurance coverage or payer-related limitations
- Other reasons attributable to health care delivery system

Reporting Modifier

Modifier 8P is intended to be used as a "reporting modifier" to allow the reporting of circumstances when an action described in a measure's numerator is not performed and the reason is not otherwise specified.

8P Performance measure reporting modifier—action not performed, reason not otherwise specified

[1]Physician Consortium for Performance Improvement: www.physicianconsortium.org
[2]National Committee on Quality Assurance (NCQA): Health Employer Data Information Set (HEDIS®), www.ncqa.org
[3]Joint Commission on Accreditation of Healthcare Organizations (JCAHO), ORYX Initiative Performance Measures: www.jcaho.org/pms
[4]National Diabetes Quality Improvement Alliance: www.nationaldiabetesalliance.org
[5]Joint measure from the Physician Consortium for Performance Improvement, www.physicianconsortium.org, and National Committee on Quality Assurance (NCQA), www.ncqa.org
[6]The Society of Thoracic Surgeons, www.sts.org, National Quality Forum, www.qualityforum.org

Brief Description of Performance Measure & Source and Reporting Instructions	CPT Category II Code(s)	Code Descriptor
►Acute Bronchitis (A-BRONCH)◄		
►Avoidance of (Inappropriate) Antibiotic Treatment in Adults with Acute Bronchitis[2]—To assess the percentage of adults 18-64 years of age with a diagnosis of acute bronchitis who were not dispensed an antibiotic prescription on or within 3 days after the date of service **Numerator:** Patients who were dispensed an antibiotic prescription on or 3 days after the episode date **Denominator:** All patients aged 18-64 years of age with a diagnosis of acute bronchitis **Exclusion(s):** Documentation of medical reasons for prescribing or dispensing an antibiotic **Percentage** of adults 18-64 years of age with a diagnosis of acute bronchitis who were not dispensed an antibiotic prescription on or 3 days after the episode date **Reporting Instructions:** Report one of these codes code for a patient identified in the eligible population. For patient with appropriate medical exclusion criteria report 4120F with modifier 1P. There are no exclusions for 4124F◄	**►4120F** **4124F◄**	►Antibiotic prescribed or dispensed Antibiotic neither prescribed nor dispensed◄
►Acute Otitis Externa/Otitis Media with Effusion (AOE/OME)◄		
►Acute Otitis Externa: Topical Therapy[1]—Whether or not the patient aged 2 years and older with a diagnosis of AOE was prescribed topical preparations **Numerator:** Patients who were prescribed topical preparations **Denominator:** All patients aged 2 years and older with a diagnosis of AOE **Exclusion(s):** Documentation of medical reason(s) for not prescribing topical preparations Documentation of patient reason(s) for not prescribing topical preparations **Percentage** of patients aged 2 years and older with a diagnosis of AOE who were prescribed topical preparations **Reporting Instructions:** For patient with appropriate exclusion criteria, report 4130F with modifier 1P or 2P◄	**►4130F◄**	►Topical preparations (including OTC) prescribed for acute otitis externa◄
►Acute Otitis Externa: Pain Assessment[1]—Patient visits for those patients aged 2 years and older with a diagnosis of AOE with assessment for auricular or periauricular pain **Numerator:** Patient visits with assessment for auricular or periauricular pain **Denominator:** All patient visits for those patients aged 2 years and older with a diagnosis of AOE **Exclusion(s):** Documentation of medical reason(s) for not assessing auricular or periauricular pain **Percentage** of patient visits for those patients aged 2 years and older with a diagnosis of AOE with assessment for auricular or periauricular pain **Reporting Instructions:** Report at each encounter for AOE. For patient with appropriate exclusion criteria report 1116F with modifier 1P◄	**►1116F◄**	►Auricular or periauricular pain assessed◄
►Systemic Antimicrobial Therapy: Avoidance of Inappropriate Use[1]—Whether or not the patient aged 2 years and older with a diagnosis of AOE was **not** prescribed systemic antimicrobial therapy **Numerator:** Patients who were **not** prescribed systemic antimicrobial therapy (continued)	**►4131F** **4132F◄**	►Systemic antimicrobial therapy prescribed Systemic antimicrobial therapy not prescribed◄

[1]Physician Consortium for Performance Improvement: www.physicianconsortium.org
[2]National Committee on Quality Assurance (NCQA): Health Employer Data Information Set (HEDIS®), www.ncqa.org
[3]Joint Commission on Accreditation of Healthcare Organizations (JCAHO), ORYX Initiative Performance Measures: www.jcaho.org/pms
[4]National Diabetes Quality Improvement Alliance: www.nationaldiabetesalliance.org
[5]Joint measure from the Physician Consortium for Performance Improvement, www.physicianconsortium.org, and National Committee on Quality Assurance (NCQA), www.ncqa.org
[6]The Society of Thoracic Surgeons, www.sts.org, National Quality Forum, www.qualityforum.org

Brief Description of Performance Measure & Source and Reporting Instructions	CPT Category II Code(s)	Code Descriptor
►Acute Otitis Externa/Otitis Media with Effusion (AOE/OME)◄ cont'd		
Denominator: All patients aged 2 years and older with a diagnosis of AOE **Exclusion(s):** Documentation of medical reason(s) for prescribing systemic antimicrobial therapy **Percentage** of patients aged 2 years and older with a diagnosis of AOE who were **not** prescribed systemic antimicrobial therapy **Reporting Instructions:** Report 4131F or 4132F for each patient. If there is a valid medical reason for prescribing systemic antimicrobial therapy, report 4131F with modifier 1P. There are no performance exclusions for code 4132F. Do not report modifiers 1P, 2P, or 3P with this code ◄		
►Diagnostic Evaluation: Assessment of Tympanic Membrane Mobility[1]—Patient visits for those patients aged 2 months through 12 years with a diagnosis of OME with assessment of tympanic membrane mobility with pneumatic otoscopy or tympanometry **Numerator:** Patient visits with assessment of tympanic membrane mobility with pneumatic otoscopy or tympanometry **Denominator:** All patient visits for those patients aged 2 months through 12 years with a diagnosis of OME **Exclusion(s):** Documentation of medical reason(s) for not assessing tympanic membrane mobility with pneumatic otoscopy or tympanometry Documentation of patient reason(s) for not assessing tympanic membrane mobility with pneumatic otoscopy or tympanometry **Percentage** of patient visits for those patients aged 2 months through 12 years with a diagnosis of OME with assessment of tympanic membrane mobility with pneumatic otoscopy or tympanometry **Reporting Instructions:** Report at each encounter for OME. For patient with appropriate exclusion criteria report 2035F with modifier 1P or 2P◄	**►2035F◄**	►Tympanic membrane mobility assessed with pneumatic otoscopy or tympanometry◄
►Otitis Media with Effusion: Hearing Testing[1]—Whether or not the patient aged 2 months through 12 years with a diagnosis of OME who received tympanostomy tube insertion had a hearing test performed within 6 months prior to tympanostomy tube insertion **Numerator:** Patients who had a hearing test performed within 6 months prior to tympanostomy tube insertion **Denominator:** All patients aged 2 months through 12 years with a diagnosis of OME who received tympanostomy tube insertion **Exclusion(s):** Documentation of medical reason(s) for not performing a hearing test within 6 months prior to tympanostomy tube insertion Documentation of system reason(s) for not performing a hearing test within 6 months prior to tympanostomy tube insertion **Percentage** of patients aged 2 months through 12 years with a diagnosis of OME who received tympanostomy tube insertion who had a hearing test performed within 6 months prior to tympanostomy tube insertion **Reporting Instructions:** Report at time of tympanostomy tube insertion procedure. Documentation should include that hearing test was performed AND the actual results of the hearing test are documented in the chart. Hearing test may have been performed by reporting physician or other provider. For patient with appropriate exclusion criteria, report 3230F with modifier 1P or 3P◄	**►3230F◄**	►Documentation that hearing test was performed within 6 months prior to tympanostomy tube insertion◄

[1]Physician Consortium for Performance Improvement: www.physicianconsortium.org
[2]National Committee on Quality Assurance (NCQA): Health Employer Data Information Set (HEDIS®), www.ncqa.org
[3]Joint Commission on Accreditation of Healthcare Organizations (JCAHO), ORYX Initiative Performance Measures: www.jcaho.org/pms
[4]National Diabetes Quality Improvement Alliance: www.nationaldiabetesalliance.org
[5]Joint measure from the Physician Consortium for Performance Improvement, www.physicianconsortium.org, and National Committee on Quality Assurance (NCQA), www.ncqa.org
[6]The Society of Thoracic Surgeons, www.sts.org, National Quality Forum, www.qualityforum.org

Brief Description of Performance Measure & Source and Reporting Instructions	CPT Category II Code(s)	Code Descriptor
►Acute Otitis Externa/Otitis Media with Effusion (AOE/OME)◄cont'd		
►Otitis Media with Effusion Antihistamines or Decongestants: Avoidance of Inappropriate Use[1]—Whether or not the parent/caregiver of the patient aged 2 months through 12 years with a diagnosis of OME was not prescribed or recommended to receive antihistamines or decongestants **Numerator:** Patients who were not prescribed or recommended to receive antihistamines or decongestants **Denominator:** All patients aged 2 months through 12 years with a diagnosis of OME **Exclusion(s):** Documentation of medical reason(s) for prescribing or recommending to receive antihistamines or decongestants **Percentage** of patients aged 2 months through 12 years with a diagnosis of OME were not prescribed or recommended to receive antihistamines or decongestants **Reporting Instructions:** Report 4133F or 4134F for each patient. If there is a valid medical reason for prescribing or recommending to receive antihistamines or decongestants, report 4133F with modifier 1P. There are no performance exclusions for code 4134F. Do not report modifiers 1P, 2P, or 3P with this code◄	**►4133F** **4134F◄**	►Antihistamines or decongestants prescribed or recommended Antihistamines or decongestants neither prescribed nor recommended◄
►Systemic Antimicrobials: Avoidance of Inappropriate Use[1]—Whether or not the patient aged 2 months through 12 years with a diagnosis of OME was **not** prescribed systemic antimicrobials **Numerator:** Patients who were **not** prescribed systemic antimicrobials **Denominator:** All patients aged 2 months through 12 years with a diagnosis of OME **Exclusion(s):** Documentation of medical reason(s) for prescribing systemic antimicrobials **Percentage** of patients aged 2 months through 12 years with a diagnosis of OME who were **not** prescribed systemic antimicrobials **Reporting Instructions:** If there is a valid medical reason for prescribing systemic antimicrobials, report 4131F with modifier 1P. There are no performance exclusions for code 4132F. Do not report modifiers 1P, 2P, or 3P with this code◄	**►4131F** **4132F◄**	►Systemic antimicrobial therapy prescribed Systemic antimicrobial therapy not prescribed◄
►Otitis Media with Effusion Systemic Steroids: Avoidance of Inappropriate Use[1]—Whether or not the patient aged 2 months through 12 years with a diagnosis of OME was **not** prescribed systemic corticosteroids **Numerator:** Patients who were **not** prescribed systemic corticosteroids **Denominator:** All patients aged 2 months through 12 years with a diagnosis of OME **Exclusion(s):** Documentation of medical reason(s) for prescribing systemic corticosteroids **Percentage** of patients aged 2 months through 12 years with a diagnosis of OME who were **not** prescribed systemic corticosteroids **Reporting Instructions:** Report 4135F or 4136F for each patient. If there is a valid medical reason **for prescribing** systemic corticosteroids, report 4135F with modifier 1P. There are no performance exclusions for code 4136F. Do not report modifiers 1P, 2P, or 3P with this code◄	**►4135F** **4136F◄**	►Systemic corticosteroids prescribed Systemic corticosteroids not prescribed◄

[1]Physician Consortium for Performance Improvement: www.physicianconsortium.org
[2]National Committee on Quality Assurance (NCQA): Health Employer Data Information Set (HEDIS®), www.ncqa.org
[3]Joint Commission on Accreditation of Healthcare Organizations (JCAHO), ORYX Initiative Performance Measures: www.jcaho.org/pms
[4]National Diabetes Quality Improvement Alliance: www.nationaldiabetesalliance.org
[5]Joint measure from the Physician Consortium for Performance Improvement, www.physicianconsortium.org, and National Committee on Quality Assurance (NCQA), www.ncqa.org
[6]The Society of Thoracic Surgeons, www.sts.org, National Quality Forum, www.qualityforum.org

Brief Description of Performance Measure & Source and Reporting Instructions	CPT Category II Code(s)	Code Descriptor
►Anesthesiology/Critical Care (CRIT)◄		
►Prevention of Ventilator-Associated Pneumonia: Head Elevation[1]—Whether or not the patient aged 18 years and older receiving care in the ICU who received mechanical ventilation had an order on the first ventilator day for head of bed elevation (30-45 degrees) **Numerator:** Patients who had an order on the first ventilator day for head of bed elevation (30-45 degrees) **Denominator:** All patients aged 18 years and older receiving care in the ICU who receive mechanical ventilation **Exclusion(s):** Documentation of medical reason(s) for not ordering head of bed elevation (30-45 degrees) on the first ventilator day **Percentage** of ICU patients aged 18 years and older who receive mechanical ventilation and who had an order on the first ventilator day for head of bed elevation (30-45 degrees) **Reporting Instructions:** Report 4168F or 4169F for each patient receiving critical care services (99291). If 4168F and patient has an order for head of bed elevation (30-45 degrees) on first ventilator day report 4167F. For patients with appropriate exclusion criteria use 4167F with modifier 1P◄	**►4167F** **Denominator Codes:** **4168F** **4169F◄**	►Head of bed elevation (30-45 degrees) on first ventilator day ordered◄ ►Patient receiving care in the intensive care unit (ICU) and receiving mechanical ventilation, 24 hours or less◄ ►Patient either not receiving care in the intensive care unit (ICU) OR *not* receiving mechanical ventilation OR receiving mechanical ventilation greater than 24 hours◄
►Prevention of Catheter-Related Bloodstream Infections (CRBSI)–Central Venous Catheter Insertion Protocol[1]—Whether or not patient who has undergone central venous catheter (CVC) insertion had all elements of maximal sterile barrier technique (cap AND mask AND sterile gown AND sterile gloves AND a large sterile sheet AND hand hygiene AND 2% chlorhexidine for cutaneous antisepsis) followed **Numerator:** Patients for whom central venous catheter (CVC) was inserted with all elements of maximal sterile barrier technique (cap AND mask AND sterile gown AND sterile gloves AND a large sterile sheet AND hand hygiene AND 2% chlorhexidine for cutaneous antisepsis) followed **Denominator:** All patients who undergo CVC insertion **See technical specifications for types of CVC's included in denominator.** **Exclusion(s):** Documentation of medical reason(s) for not following all elements of maximal sterile barrier technique during CVC insertion (including CVC insertion performed on emergency basis) **Percentage** of patients who undergo CVC insertion for whom a CVC was inserted with all elements of maximal sterile barrier technique (cap AND mask AND sterile gown AND sterile gloves AND a large sterile sheet AND hand hygiene AND 2% chlorhexidine for cutaneous antisepsis) followed **Reporting Instructions:** Report 6030F for patient for whom CVC was inserted with all elements of maximal sterile barrier technique followed. For patient with appropriate exclusion criteria, report 6030F with modifier 1P◄	**►6030F◄**	►All elements of maximal sterile barrier technique including: cap AND mask AND sterile gown AND sterile gloves AND a large sterile sheet AND hand hygiene AND 2% chlorhexidine for cutaneous antisepsis, followed◄

[1]Physician Consortium for Performance Improvement: www.physicianconsortium.org
[2]National Committee on Quality Assurance (NCQA): Health Employer Data Information Set (HEDIS®), www.ncqa.org
[3]Joint Commission on Accreditation of Healthcare Organizations (JCAHO), ORYX Initiative Performance Measures: www.jcaho.org/pms
[4]National Diabetes Quality Improvement Alliance: www.nationaldiabetesalliance.org
[5]Joint measure from the Physician Consortium for Performance Improvement, www.physicianconsortium.org, and National Committee on Quality Assurance (NCQA), www.ncqa.org
[6]The Society of Thoracic Surgeons, www.sts.org, National Quality Forum, www.qualityforum.org

Brief Description of Performance Measure & Source and Reporting Instructions	CPT Category II Code(s)	Code Descriptor
►Anesthesiology/Critical Care (CRIT)◄, cont'd		
►Anesthesiology/Critical Care (CRIT) Perioperative Temperature Management for Surgical Procedures Under General Anesthesia[1]—Whether or not the patients, regardless of age, undergoing a surgical or therapeutic procedure under general or neuraxial anesthesia of 60 minutes duration or longer had *either* active warming used intraoperatively for the purpose of maintaining normothermia, OR at least one body temperature equal to or greater than 36 degrees Centigrade (or 96.8 degrees Fahrenheit) recorded within the 30 minutes immediately before or the 30 minutes immediately after anesthesia end time **Numerator:** Patients for whom *either:* • Active warming was used intraoperatively for the purpose of maintaining normothermia, OR • At least one body temperature equal to or greater than 36 degrees Centigrade (or 96.8 degrees Fahrenheit) was recorded within the 30 minutes immediately before or the 30 minutes immediately after anesthesia end time **For purposes of this measure, active warming is limited to the following modalities only: forced-air warming, warm water garments** **Denominator:** All patients, regardless of age, undergoing surgical or therapeutic procedures under general or neuraxial anesthesia of 60 minutes duration or longer **Exclusion(s):** Documentation of one of the following medical reason(s) for not using active warming intraoperatively for the purpose of maintaining normothermia OR achieving at least one body temperature equal to or greater than 36 degrees Centigrade (or 96.8 degrees Fahrenheit) recorded within the 30 minutes immediately before or the 30 minutes immediately after anesthesia end time: • Intentional hypothermia • Not indicated due to anesthetic technique: peripheral nerve block without general anesthesia, OR monitored anesthesia care **Percentage** of patients, regardless of age, undergoing surgical or therapeutic procedures under general or neuraxial anesthesia of 60 minutes duration or longer for whom *either* active warming was used intraoperatively for the purpose of maintaining normothermia, OR at least one body temperature equal to or greater than 36 degrees Centigrade (or 96.8 degrees Fahrenheit) was recorded within the 30 minutes immediately before or the 30 minutes immediately after anesthesia end time **Reporting Instructions:** For patient with appropriate exclusion criteria, report 4250F with modifier 1P◄	**►4250F◄**	►Active warming used intraoperatively for the purpose of maintaining normothermia, OR at least one body temperature equal to or greater than 36 degrees Centigrade (or 96.8 degrees Fahrenheit) recorded within the 30 minutes immediately before or the 30 minutes immediately after anesthesia end time◄
►Annual Monitoring (AM)◄		
►Annual monitoring for patients on angiotensin converting enzyme (ACE) inhibitors or angiotensin receptor blockers (ARB)[2]— Annual monitoring for patients on digoxin Annual monitoring for patients on diuretics Annual monitoring for patients on anticonvulsants (continued)	**►4188F**	►Appropriate angiotensin converting enzyme (ACE) or angiotensin receptor blockers (ARB) therapeutic monitoring test ordered or performed

[1]Physician Consortium for Performance Improvement: www.physicianconsortium.org
[2]National Committee on Quality Assurance (NCQA): Health Employer Data Information Set (HEDIS®), www.ncqa.org
[3]Joint Commission on Accreditation of Healthcare Organizations (JCAHO), ORYX Initiative Performance Measures: www.jcaho.org/pms
[4]National Diabetes Quality Improvement Alliance: www.nationaldiabetesalliance.org
[5]Joint measure from the Physician Consortium for Performance Improvement, www.physicianconsortium.org, and National Committee on Quality Assurance (NCQA), www.ncqa.org
[6]The Society of Thoracic Surgeons, www.sts.org, National Quality Forum, www.qualityforum.org

Brief Description of Performance Measure & Source and Reporting Instructions	CPT Category II Code(s)	Code Descriptor
►Annual Monitoring (AM)◄, cont'd		
Percentage of patients 18 years of age and older who received at least a 180-days supply of ambulatory medication therapy for a select therapeutic agent during the measurement year and at least one therapeutic monitoring event for the therapeutic agent in the measurement year.	**4189F**	Appropriate digoxin therapeutic monitoring test ordered or performed
• Annual monitoring for patients on angiotensin converting enzyme (ACE) inhibitors or angiotensin receptor blockers (ARB) • Annual monitoring for patients on digoxin • Annual monitoring for patients on diuretics • Annual monitoring for patients on anticonvulsants	**4190F**	Appropriate diuretic therapeutic monitoring test ordered or performed
Numerator: Patients have received the annual appropriate therapeutic monitoring event for the therapeutic agent. Patients who are prescribed a medication in the following drug classes for at least 180-day supply and who have received the appropriate therapeutic monitoring event for the therapeutic agent.	**4191F**	Appropriate anticonvulsant therapeutic monitoring test ordered or performed
Appropriate annual monitoring for patients taking the following includes: • ACE/ARB: • at least one serum potassium and either a serum creatinine • or a blood urea nitrogen therapeutic monitoring test in the measurement year.	**Denominator Codes:**	
• Digoxin: • at least one serum potassium and either a serum creatinine • or a blood urea nitrogen therapeutic monitoring test in the measurement year. • Diuretic: • at least one serum potassium and either a serum creatinine • or a blood urea nitrogen therapeutic monitoring test in the measurement year.	**4210F**	Angiotensin converting enzyme (ACE) or angiotensin receptor blockers (ARB) medication therapy for 6 months or more.
• Anticonvulsant: • at least one drug serum concentration level monitoring test for the prescribed drug in the measurement year.	**4220F**	Digoxin medication therapy for 6 months or more
Denominator: All patients 18 years and older who are prescribed at least 180-day supply (6 months) of medication in the following drug classes: • angiotensin converting enzyme (ACE) inhibitors or angiotensin receptor blockers (ARB)	**4221F**	Diuretic medication therapy for 6 months or more
• digoxin • diuretics • anticonvulsants **Exclusion(s):** Medical reasons for not receiving the appropriate annual therapeutic monitoring **Percentage** of patients 18 years and older who received at least a 180-days supply of ambulatory medication therapy for a select therapeutic agent and are receiving the appropriate annual therapeutic monitoring **Reporting instructions:** Report this code for a patient at least once during the measurement year for patients identified in the eligible population. For patient with appropriate exclusion criteria report 4188F, 4189F, 4190F, or 4191F with modifier 1P. Measure requirements will be met when the appropriate documentation is present in administrative claims or internal databases◄	**4230F◄**	Anticonvulsant medication therapy for 6 months or more◄

[1]Physician Consortium for Performance Improvement: www.physicianconsortium.org
[2]National Committee on Quality Assurance (NCQA): Health Employer Data Information Set (HEDIS®), www.ncqa.org
[3]Joint Commission on Accreditation of Healthcare Organizations (JCAHO), ORYX Initiative Performance Measures: www.jcaho.org/pms
[4]National Diabetes Quality Improvement Alliance: www.nationaldiabetesalliance.org
[5]Joint measure from the Physician Consortium for Performance Improvement, www.physicianconsortium.org, and National Committee on Quality Assurance (NCQA), www.ncqa.org
[6]The Society of Thoracic Surgeons, www.sts.org, National Quality Forum, www.qualityforum.org

Brief Description of Performance Measure & Source and Reporting Instructions	CPT Category II Code(s)	Code Descriptor
Asthma		
Asthma Assessment[1]—Whether or not patient was evaluated during at least one office visit during the reporting year for the frequency (numeric) of daytime and nocturnal asthma symptoms **Numerator:** Patients who were evaluated during at least one office visit during the reporting year for the frequency (numeric) of daytime and nocturnal asthma symptoms **Denominator:** All patients aged 5-40 years with asthma **Exclusion(s):** None **Percentage** of patients aged 5-40 years with asthma who were evaluated during at least one office visit during the reporting year for the frequency (numeric) of daytime and nocturnal asthma symptoms **Reporting Instructions:** To be counted in calculations of this measure, symptom frequency must be numerically quantified. Measure may also be met by physician documentation or patient completion of an asthma assessment tool/survey/questionnaire. Assessment tool may include the Quality Metric Asthma Control Test™, National Asthma Education & Prevention Program (NAEPP) Asthma Symptoms and Peak Flow Diary. There are no exclusions for this measure; modifiers 1P, 2P, and 3P may not be used	**1005F**	Asthma symptoms evaluated (includes physician documentation of numeric frequency of symptoms or patient completion of an asthma assessment tool/survey/ questionnaire)
Asthma Pharmacologic Therapy[1]—Whether or not patient with mild, moderate, or severe **persistent** asthma was prescribed **either** the preferred long-term control medication (inhaled corticosteroid) or an acceptable alternative treatment **Numerator:** Patients who were prescribed **either** the preferred[a] long-term control medication (inhaled corticosteroids) or an acceptable alternative treatment[b] (cromolyn sodium, leukotriene modifier, nedocromil, OR sustained release theophylline) **Denominator:** All patients aged 5-40 years with mild, moderate or severe persistent asthma **Exclusion(s):** Documentation of patient reason(s) (eg economic, social, religious) for not prescribing either the preferred long-term control medication (inhaled corticosteroids) or an acceptable alternative treatment. (There are no medical exclusion criteria.) **Percentage** of all patients with mild, moderate, or severe **persistent** asthma who were prescribed **either** the preferred long-term control medication (inhaled corticosteroids) or an acceptable alternative treatment **Reporting Instructions:** Report 1038F or 1039F for each asthma patient. If long-term control medication (or acceptable alternative treatment) prescribed, report 4015F. Report 4015F with 1038F. Report modifier 2P for patient who meets exclusion criteria. Modifier 1P may not be reported with 4015F. [a,b]Refer to complete description of measure developer's Web site for list of medications, treatment recommendations, dosages	**4015F** **Denominator Codes:** **1038F** **1039F**	Persistent asthma, preferred long term control medication or acceptable alternative treatment, prescribed Persistant asthma (mild, moderate or severe) Intermittent asthma
►Back Pain (BkP)◄		
►Initial Visit for Back Pain[2]—Whether or not a patient with a diagnosis of back pain during the initial visit for the episode of back pain had back pain and function assessed* **Numerator:** Patients who had **all** five of the following components assessed*: • Pain assessment • Functional status • Patient history, including notation of presence or absence of warning signs • Assessment of prior treatment and response **and** • Employment status (continued)	**►1130F**	►Back pain and function assessed, including all of the following: Pain assessment AND functional status AND patient history, including notation of presence or absence of "red flags" (warning signs) AND assessment of prior treatment and response, AND employment status

[1]Physician Consortium for Performance Improvement: www.physicianconsortium.org
[2]National Committee on Quality Assurance (NCQA): Health Employer Data Information Set (HEDIS®), www.ncqa.org
[3]Joint Commission on Accreditation of Healthcare Organizations (JCAHO), ORYX Initiative Performance Measures: www.jcaho.org/pms
[4]National Diabetes Quality Improvement Alliance: www.nationaldiabetesalliance.org
[5]Joint measure from the Physician Consortium for Performance Improvement, www.physicianconsortium.org, and National Committee on Quality Assurance (NCQA), www.ncqa.org
[6]The Society of Thoracic Surgeons, www.sts.org, National Quality Forum, www.qualityforum.org

Brief Description of Performance Measure & Source and Reporting Instructions	CPT Category II Code(s)	Code Descriptor
►Back Pain (BkP)◄, cont'd		
Denominator: All patients with diagnosis of back pain at the initial visit of the episode **Exclusion(s):** None "Red flags" (warning signs) include: • History of cancer or - Unexplained weight loss • Current infection or - Immunosuppression • Fracture or suspected fracture - Motor vehicle accident or industrial injury with suspicion of fracture - Major fall with suspicion of fracture • Cauda equine syndrome or progressive neurologic deficit - Saddle anesthesia - Recent onset bladder dysfunction (urine retention, increased frequency, overflow incontinence) - Recent onset fecal incontinence (loss of bowel control) - Major motor weakness **Percentage** of patients with a diagnosis of back pain during the initial visit for the episode of back pain had back pain and function assessed **Reporting Instructions:** Report 0525F or 0526F for each patient. Use 0525F to indicate the initial visit and 0526F to indicate a subsequent visit during the episode of back pain. Report 1130F for all patients for whom, during the initial visit of the episode of back pain, pain assessment, functional status, patient history, assessment of prior treatment and response, **and** employment status was assessed There are no performance exclusions for this measure; modifiers 1P, 2P and 3P may not be used *Note: Measure specifications should be referred to in order to determine criteria to meet any of the required assessments◄	**Denominator Codes:** **0525F** **0526F◄**	 Initial visit for episode Subsequent visit for episode◄
►Physical Exam after Back Pain Onset[2]—Whether or not a patient with a diagnosis of back pain received a physical examination during the initial visit for the episode of back pain **Numerator:** Patients who had a physical exam on the date of the initial visit for back pain* • For patients **with** radicular symptoms, documentation of physical exam must include the following (at a minimum): - Indication of straight leg raise test, **and** - Notation of completion of neurovascular exam (a neurovascular exam must include ankle and knee reflexes; quadriceps, ankle and great toe dorsiflexion strength; plantar flexion; muscle strength; motor testing; pulses in lower extremities; and sensory exam) • For patients **without** radicular symptoms, documentation of physical exam must include the following: - Documentation of straight leg raise or neurovascular exam or clear notation of absence or presence of neurologic deficits **Denominator:** All patients with diagnosis of back pain at the initial visit of the episode (continued)	**►2040F** **Denominator Codes:** **0525F** **0526F◄**	►Physical examination on the date of the initial visit for low back performed, in accordance with specifications Initial visit for episode Subsequent visit for episode◄

[1]Physician Consortium for Performance Improvement: www.physicianconsortium.org
[2]National Committee on Quality Assurance (NCQA): Health Employer Data Information Set (HEDIS®), www.ncqa.org
[3]Joint Commission on Accreditation of Healthcare Organizations (JCAHO), ORYX Initiative Performance Measures: www.jcaho.org/pms
[4]National Diabetes Quality Improvement Alliance: www.nationaldiabetesalliance.org
[5]Joint measure from the Physician Consortium for Performance Improvement, www.physicianconsortium.org, and National Committee on Quality Assurance (NCQA), www.ncqa.org
[6]The Society of Thoracic Surgeons, www.sts.org, National Quality Forum, www.qualityforum.org

Brief Description of Performance Measure & Source and Reporting Instructions	CPT Category II Code(s)	Code Descriptor
►Back Pain (BkP)◄, cont'd		
Exclusion(s): Medical exclusion for not receiving a physical examination (ie, patients with bilateral lower extremity amputations) **Percentage** of patients with a diagnosis of back pain who received a physical examination on the date of the initial visit **Reporting Instructions:** Report 0525F or 0526F for each patient. Use code 0525F to indicate the initial visit and 0526F to indicate a subsequent visit during the episode of low back pain. Only initial visits (0508F) will be included in the numerator. Report 2040F if a physical exam occurred as specified. There are no performance exclusions for this measure; modifiers 1P, 2P and 3P may not be used *Note: Measure specifications should be referred to in order to determine criteria to meet any of the required assessments◄		
►**Mental Health Assessment after Back Pain Onset**[2]—Whether or not a patient with a diagnosis of back pain received a mental health assessment. Specifically a patient must have documentation of a mental health assessment present in the medical record prior to intervention (back surgery or epidural steroid injection) *or* when pain lasts longer than six weeks. **Numerator:** Patients with documentation of at least one mental health assessment prior to intervention or for patients with back pain lasting longer than six weeks* **Denominator:** All patients undergoing back surgery or epidural steroid injection (see technical specifications for list of procedures) or who have had back pain lasting longer than six weeks **Exclusion(s):** None **Percentage** of patients with a diagnosis of back pain for whom documentation of a mental health assessment is present in the medical record prior to intervention or when pain lasts longer than six weeks after the initial visit **Reporting Instructions:** If reporting at the time of procedure, it is not necessary to report one of the denominator codes. If reporting at time of E/M visit, use denominator codes to indicate duration of pain. If a mental health assessment occurred as specified, report code 2044F. Report this measure only once during an episode of back pain. There are no performance exclusions for this measure; modifiers 1P, 2P and 3P may not be used * Note: Measure specifications should be referred to in order to determine criteria to meet the mental health assessment requirement	**►2044F** **Denominator Codes:** **1134F** **1135F◄**	►Documentation of mental health assessment prior to intervention (back surgery or epidural steroid injection) or for back pain episode lasting longer than six weeks Episode of back pain lasting six weeks or less Episode of back pain lasting longer than six weeks◄

►**Appropriate Imaging for Acute Back Pain**[2]—Whether or not a patient with a diagnosis of back pain has a report of an imaging study performed during the six weeks after pain onset or order for an imaging study during the six weeks after pain onset, in the absence of "red flags" (warning signs - signs or symptoms that would warrant imaging) (*overuse measure, lower performance is better*)
"Red flags" (warning signs) include:
• History of cancer or
  - Unexplained weight loss
• Current infection or
  - Immunosuppression
(continued)
	►3330F
	
	3331F
	
	Denominator Codes:
	
	1134F
		►Imaging study ordered
		
		Imaging study not ordered
		
		Episode of back pain lasting six weeks or less

[1]Physician Consortium for Performance Improvement: www.physicianconsortium.org
[2]National Committee on Quality Assurance (NCQA): Health Employer Data Information Set (HEDIS®), www.ncqa.org
[3]Joint Commission on Accreditation of Healthcare Organizations (JCAHO), ORYX Initiative Performance Measures: www.jcaho.org/pms
[4]National Diabetes Quality Improvement Alliance: www.nationaldiabetesalliance.org
[5]Joint measure from the Physician Consortium for Performance Improvement, www.physicianconsortium.org, and National Committee on Quality Assurance (NCQA), www.ncqa.org
[6]The Society of Thoracic Surgeons, www.sts.org, National Quality Forum, www.qualityforum.org

Brief Description of Performance Measure & Source and Reporting Instructions	CPT Category II Code(s)	Code Descriptor
►Back Pain (BkP)◄, cont'd		
• Fracture or suspected fracture - Motor vehicle accident or industrial injury with suspicion of fracture - Major fall with suspicion of fracture • Cauda equine syndrome or progressive neurologic deficit - Saddle anesthesia - Recent onset bladder dysfunction (urine retention, increased frequency, overflow incontinence) - Recent onset fecal incontinence (loss of bowel control) - Major motor weakness **Numerator:** Patients with an order for an imaging study Note: Evidence of a report of an imaging study related to this episode is considered evidence of an order. See technical specifications for listing of applicable imaging studies. Include only those orders generated by the reporting physician or practice. **Denominator:** All patients with back pain lasting six weeks or less **Exclusion(s):** Documentation of medical reason(s) for ordering or performing an imaging study, which include: • History of cancer • Current infection • Fracture or suspected fracture • Cauda equina syndrome or progressive neurologic deficit **Percentage** of patients with a diagnosis of back pain for whom the physician ordered imaging studies during the six weeks after pain onset, in the absence of "red flags" (warning signs) (overuse measure, lower performance is better) **Reporting Instructions:** Two codes must be reported for this measure. Report either 1134F or 1135F for each patient. If the duration of back pain is less than six weeks (1134F) and an imaging study **was** ordered, report 3330F; if an imaging study **was not** ordered, report 3331F. Evidence of an imaging study report for the back pain episode should be included as evidence of an order for an imaging study. If there is a valid medical reason to order an imaging study for patients with back pain lasting less than six weeks, report 1P with 3330F◄	**1135F◄**	Episode of back pain lasting longer than six weeks◄
►Advice for Normal Activities for Back Pain Patients[2] Whether or not a patient during the initial visit for an episode of back pain was counseled (advised) to maintain or resume normal activities* **Numerator:** Patients with documentation on the date of the initial visit with the physician of advice to maintain or resume normal activities* **Denominator:** All patients with diagnosis of back pain at the initial visit of the episode **Exclusion(s):** None **Percentage** of patients whose physician advised them to maintain or resume normal activities. **Reporting Instructions:** Report 0525F or 0526F for each patient. Use 0525F to indicate the initial visit and 0526F to indicate a subsequent visit during the episode of back pain. Only initial visits (0525F) will be included in the numerator. There are no performance exclusions for this measure; modifiers 1P, 2P and 3P may not be used. * This advice must be tempered by consideration of the patient's usual job or life demands. Heavy lifting, trunk twisting and bodily vibrations should be avoided in the acute phase◄	**►4245F** **Denominator Codes:** **0525F** **0526F◄**	►Patient counseled during the initial visit to maintain or resume normal activities Initial visit for episode Subsequent visit for episode◄

[1]Physician Consortium for Performance Improvement: www.physicianconsortium.org
[2]National Committee on Quality Assurance (NCQA): Health Employer Data Information Set (HEDIS®), www.ncqa.org
[3]Joint Commission on Accreditation of Healthcare Organizations (JCAHO), ORYX Initiative Performance Measures: www.jcaho.org/pms
[4]National Diabetes Quality Improvement Alliance: www.nationaldiabetesalliance.org
[5]Joint measure from the Physician Consortium for Performance Improvement, www.physicianconsortium.org, and National Committee on Quality Assurance (NCQA), www.ncqa.org
[6]The Society of Thoracic Surgeons, www.sts.org, National Quality Forum, www.qualityforum.org

Brief Description of Performance Measure & Source and Reporting Instructions	CPT Category II Code(s)	Code Descriptor
►**Back Pain (BkP)**◄**, cont'd**		
►**Advice Against Bed Rest for Back Pain Patients**[2]—Whether or not a patient with an episode of back pain was counseled against bed rest lasting 4 days or longer during the initial visit **Numerator:** Patients with medical record documentation that a physician advised them against bed rest lasting four days or longer during the initial visit for back pain **Denominator:** All patients with diagnosis of back pain at the initial visit of the episode **Exclusion(s):** None **Percentage** of patients with an episode of back pain who received advice against bed rest lasting four days or longer during initial visit with the physician **Reporting Instructions:** Report 0525F or 0526F for each patient. Use 0525F to indicate the initial visit and 0526F to indicate a subsequent visit during the episode of back pain. Only initial visits (0525F) will be included in the numerator. There are no performance exclusions for this measure; modifiers 1P, 2P, and 3P may not be used◄	►**4248F** **Denominator Codes:** **0525F** **0526F**◄	►Patient counseled during the initial visit for an episode of back pain against bed rest lasting 4 days or longer Initial visit for episode Subsequent visit for episode◄
►**Recommendation for Exercise for Back Pain Patients**[2]—Whether or not a patient during an episode of back pain lasting longer than 12 weeks received instructions for therapeutic exercise with follow up by physician **or** was counseled to perform supervised exercise **Numerator:** Patients who were recommended a supervised exercise program *or* Patients who were provided instructions for therapeutic exercise with follow-up by the physician **Denominator:** All patients with back pain lasting longer than 12 weeks **Exclusion(s):** None **Percentage** of patients who were recommended a supervised exercise program or who were provided instructions for therapeutic exercise with follow-up by the physician during an episode of back pain lasting longer than 12 weeks **Reporting Instructions:** Report either 1136F or 1137F for each patient. Report 4240F if instructions for therapeutic exercise with follow-up by the physician at the point of follow-up or after follow-up. If counseling for supervised exercise program was provided, report 4242F. There are no performance exclusions for this measure; modifiers 1P, 2P, and 3P may not be used◄	►**4240F** **4242F** **Denominator Codes:** **1136F** **1137F**◄	►Instruction in therapeutic exercise with follow-up by the physician provided to patients during episode of back pain lasting longer than 12 weeks Counseling for supervised exercise program provided to patients during episode of back pain lasting longer than 12 weeks Episode of back pain lasting 12 weeks or less Episode of back pain lasting longer than 12 weeks◄
►**Chronic Kidney Disease (CKD)**◄		
►**Blood Pressure Management**[1]—Number of visits with blood pressure measurement <130/80 mmHG OR ≥130/80 mmHG with a documented plan of care for the patient aged 18 years and older with the diagnosis of advanced CKD (stage 4 or 5, not receiving Renal Replacement Therapy [RRT]) **Numerator:** Patient visits with blood pressure <130/80 mmHG OR ≥130/80 mmHG with a documented plan of care* (continued)	►**0513F** **2000F** **3074F**	►Elevated blood pressure plan of care documented Blood pressure measured Most recent systolic blood Pressure, less than 130 mm Hg

[1]Physician Consortium for Performance Improvement: www.physicianconsortium.org
[2]National Committee on Quality Assurance (NCQA): Health Employer Data Information Set (HEDIS®), www.ncqa.org
[3]Joint Commission on Accreditation of Healthcare Organizations (JCAHO), ORYX Initiative Performance Measures: www.jcaho.org/pms
[4]National Diabetes Quality Improvement Alliance: www.nationaldiabetesalliance.org
[5]Joint measure from the Physician Consortium for Performance Improvement, www.physicianconsortium.org, and National Committee on Quality Assurance (NCQA), www.ncqa.org
[6]The Society of Thoracic Surgeons, www.sts.org, National Quality Forum, www.qualityforum.org

Brief Description of Performance Measure & Source and Reporting Instructions	CPT Category II Code(s)	Code Descriptor
►Chronic Kidney Disease (CKD)◄, cont'd		
A documented plan of care should include one or more of the following: recheck blood pressure at specified future date; initiate or alter pharmacologic therapy; documented review of patient's home blood pressure log which indicates that patient's blood pressure is or is not well controlled. If multiple blood pressure measurements are taken at a single visit, use the most recent measurement taken at that visit **Denominator:** All visits for patients aged 18 years and older with the diagnosis of advanced CKD (stage 4 or 5, not receiving RRT) **Exclusion(s):** None **Percentage** of visits for patients aged 18 years and older with the diagnosis of advanced CKD (stage 4 or 5, not receiving RRT), with a blood pressure <130/80 mmHg OR blood pressure ≥130/80 with a documented plan of care **Reporting Instructions:** For the systolic blood pressure value, report one of the three systolic codes; for the diastolic blood pressure value, report one of the three diastolic codes. If 3075F, 3077F, 3079F or 3080F are reported and there is a documented plan of care for elevated BP during the visit, also report 0513F. There are no performance exclusions for this measure; modifiers 1P, 2P, or 3P may not be used◄	**3075F** **3077F** **3078F** **3079F** **3080F◄**	Most recent systolic blood Pressure, 130 to 139 mm Hg Most recent systolic blood Pressure, greater than or equal to 140 mm Hg Most recent diastolic blood Pressure, less than 80 mm Hg Most recent diastolic blood Pressure, 80-89 mm Hg Most recent diastolic blood Pressure, greater than or equal to 90 mm Hg◄
►ACE Inhibitor (ACE) or Angiotensin Receptor Blocker (ARB) Therapy[1]—Whether or not the patient aged 18 years and older with the diagnosis of advanced CKD (stage 4 or 5, not receiving Renal Replacement Therapy [RRT]) and hypertension and proteinuria was prescribed ACE inhibitor or ARB therapy during the 12 month reporting period **Numerator:** Patients who were prescribed ACE inhibitor or ARB therapy during the 12 month reporting period **Denominator:** All patients aged 18 years and older with a diagnosis of advanced CKD (stage 4 or 5, not RRT) and hypertension and proteinuria **Exclusion(s):** Documentation of medical reason(s) for not prescribing ACE inhibitor or ARB therapy. Documentation of patient reason(s) for not prescribing ACE inhibitor or ARB therapy **Percentage** of patients aged 18 years and older with a diagnosis of advanced CKD (stage 4 or 5, not receiving RRT), and hypertension and proteinuria who were prescribed ACE inhibitor or ARB therapy during the 12 month reporting period **Reporting Instructions:** In order to qualify for the denominator, three ICD-9 codes must be reported: one for each of the following conditions: CKD (stage 4 or 5), and Hypertension and Proteinuria. For patient with appropriate exclusion criteria, report 4009F with modifier 1P or 2P◄	**►4009F◄**	►Angiotensin converting enzyme (ACE) inhibitor or Angiotensin Receptor Blocker (ARB) therapy prescribed◄
►Laboratory Testing (Calcium, Phosphorus, and Intact Parathyroid Hormone (PTH), and Lipid Profile)[1]—Whether or not the patient aged 18 years and older with the diagnosis of advanced CKD (stage 4 or 5, not receiving Renal Replacement Therapy [RRT]) had the following laboratory testing ordered at least once during the 12 month reporting period: serum levels of calcium, phosphorus and intact PTH, and lipid profile **Numerator:** Patients who had the following laboratory testing ordered at least once during the 12 month reporting period: serum levels of calcium, phosphorus and intact PTH, and lipid profile (continued)	**►3278F◄**	►Serum levels of calcium, phosphorus, intact Parathyroid Hormone (iPTH) and lipid profile ordered◄

[1]Physician Consortium for Performance Improvement: www.physicianconsortium.org
[2]National Committee on Quality Assurance (NCQA): Health Employer Data Information Set (HEDIS®), www.ncqa.org
[3]Joint Commission on Accreditation of Healthcare Organizations (JCAHO), ORYX Initiative Performance Measures: www.jcaho.org/pms
[4]National Diabetes Quality Improvement Alliance: www.nationaldiabetesalliance.org
[5]Joint measure from the Physician Consortium for Performance Improvement, www.physicianconsortium.org, and National Committee on Quality Assurance (NCQA), www.ncqa.org
[6]The Society of Thoracic Surgeons, www.sts.org, National Quality Forum, www.qualityforum.org

Brief Description of Performance Measure & Source and Reporting Instructions	CPT Category II Code(s)	Code Descriptor
►Chronic Kidney Disease (CKD)◄, cont'd		
Denominator: All patients aged 18 years and older with the diagnosis of advanced CKD (stage 4 or 5, not receiving RRT) **Exclusion(s):** Documentation of medical reason(s) for not ordering serum levels of calcium, phosphorus, intact PTH, and/or lipid profile Documentation of patient reason(s) for not ordering serum levels of calcium, phosphorus, intact PTH, and/or lipid profile **Percentage** of patients aged 18 years and older with the diagnosis of advanced CKD (stage 4 or 5, not receiving RRT), who had the following laboratory testing ordered at least once during the 12 month reporting period: serum levels of calcium, phosphorus and intact PTH, and lipid profile **Reporting Instructions:** For patient with appropriate exclusion criteria, report 3278F with modifier 1P or 2P◄		
►Plan of Care: Elevated Hemoglobin for Patients Receiving Erythropoiesis-Stimulating Agents (ESA)[1]—Number of calendar months during which a patient aged 18 years and older with the diagnosis of advanced CKD (stage 4 or 5, not receiving Renal Replacement Therapy [RRT]), receiving ESA therapy, and has a hemoglobin level < 13 g/dL OR has a hemoglobin level ≥ 13 g/dL with a documented plan of care for elevated hemoglobin level **Numerator:** Number of calendar months during which patient's hemoglobin level is < 13 g/dL OR patient's hemoglobin level is ≥ 13 g/dL with a documented plan of care for elevated hemoglobin level A documented plan of care should include reducing the ESA dose and repeating hemoglobin at a specified future date **Denominator:** Calendar months for all patients aged 18 years and older with the diagnosis of advanced CKD (stage 4 or 5, not receiving RRT), receiving ESA therapy **Exclusion(s):** None **Percentage** of calendar months during the 12 month reporting period during which patients aged 18 years and older with the diagnosis of advanced CKD (stage 4 or 5, not receiving RRT), receiving ESA therapy, have a hemoglobin level < 13 g/dL OR whose hemoglobin level is ≥ 13 g/dL with a documented plan of care for elevated hemoglobin level **Reporting Instructions:** Report this measure once during each calendar month that the patient receives professional services (see technical specifications). Report 4171F or 4172F for each patient. If patient is receiving ESA therapy, report the code that corresponds to the hemoglobin level using 3279F or 3280F or 3281F. If patient is receiving ESA therapy and hemoglobin level is ≥ 13 g/dL and plan of care for elevated hemoglobin level is documented, also report 0514F. There are no performance exclusions for this measure; modifiers 1P, 2P, or 3P may not be used◄	**►0514F** **3279F** **3280F** **3281F** **Denominator Codes:** **4171F** **4172F◄**	►Plan of care for elevated hemoglobin level documented for patient receiving Erythropoiesis-Stimulating Agent (ESA) therapy Hemoglobin level greater than or equal to 13 g/dL Hemoglobin level 11 g/dL to 12.9 g/dL Hemoglobin level less than 11 g/dL Patient receiving Erythropoiesis-Stimulating Agent (ESA) therapy Patient not receiving Erythropoiesis-Stimulating Agent (ESA) therapy◄
►Influenza Immunization[1]—Whether or not the patient aged 18 years and older with the diagnosis of advanced CKD (stage 4 or 5, not receiving Renal Replacement Therapy [RRT]) received the influenza immunization during the flu season (September through February) **Numerator:** Patients who received the influenza immunization during the flu season (September through February) (continued)	**►4037F◄**	►Influenza immunization ordered or administered◄

[1]Physician Consortium for Performance Improvement: www.physicianconsortium.org
[2]National Committee on Quality Assurance (NCQA): Health Employer Data Information Set (HEDIS®), www.ncqa.org
[3]Joint Commission on Accreditation of Healthcare Organizations (JCAHO), ORYX Initiative Performance Measures: www.jcaho.org/pms
[4]National Diabetes Quality Improvement Alliance: www.nationaldiabetesalliance.org
[5]Joint measure from the Physician Consortium for Performance Improvement, www.physicianconsortium.org, and National Committee on Quality Assurance (NCQA), www.ncqa.org
[6]The Society of Thoracic Surgeons, www.sts.org, National Quality Forum, www.qualityforum.org

Brief Description of Performance Measure & Source and Reporting Instructions	CPT Category II Code(s)	Code Descriptor
►Chronic Kidney Disease (CKD)◄, cont'd		
Denominator: All patients aged 18 years and older with the diagnosis of advanced CKD (stage 4 or 5, not receiving RRT **Exclusion(s):** Documentation of medical reason(s) for patient not receiving the influenza immunization. Documentation of patient reason(s) for patient not receiving the influenza immunization. Documentation of system reason(s) for patient not receiving the influenza immunization **Percentage** of patients aged 18 years and older with the diagnosis of advanced CKD (stage 4 or 5, not receiving RRT), who received the influenza immunization during the flu season (September through February) **Reporting Instructions:** For patient with appropriate exclusion criteria, report 4037F with modifier 1P, 2P, or 3P◄		
►Referral for AV Fistula[1]—Whether or not the patient aged 18 years and older with the diagnosis of advanced CKD (stage 4 or 5, not receiving Renal Replacement Therapy [RRT]) was referred for AV fistula at least once during the 12 month reporting period **Numerator:** Patients who were referred for AV fistula at least once during the 12 month reporting period **Denominator:** All patients aged 18 years and older with the diagnosis of advanced CKD (stage 4 or 5, not receiving RRT) **Exclusion(s):** Documentation of medical reason(s) for not referring for an AV fistula. Documentation of patient reason(s) for not referring for an AV fistula **Percentage** of patients aged 18 years and older with the diagnosis of advanced CKD (stage 4 or 5, not receiving RRT) who were referred for AV fistula at least once during the 12 month reporting period **Reporting Instructions:** For patient with appropriate exclusion criteria, report 4051F with modifier 1P or 2P◄	**►4051F◄**	►Referred for an arteriovenous (AV) fistula◄
Chronic Obstructive Pulmonary Disease (COPD)		
Smoking Assessment[1]—Whether or not patient with COPD was queried about smoking **Numerator:** All patients who were queried about smoking during one or more office visits each year **Denominator:** All patients with the diagnosis of COPD **Percentage** of patients who were queried about smoking at least annually **Reporting Instructions:** When reporting 1000F, it is required to report 1034F, and/or 1035F, or 1036F There are no exclusions for this measure; modifiers 1P, 2P, and 3P may not be used	**1000F** **1034F** **1035F** **1036F**	Tobacco use assessed Current tobacco smoker Current smokeless tobacco user (eg, chew, snuff) Current tobacco non-user
Assessment of Symptoms[1]—Whether or not patient had COPD symptoms assessed at least annually **Numerator:** All patients with COPD symptoms assessed during one or more office visits each year **Denominator:** All patients with the diagnosis of COPD **Percentage** of patients who were assessed for COPD symptoms at least annually There are no exclusions for this measure; modifiers 1P, 2P, and 3P may not be used	**1015F**	Chronic obstructive pulmonary disease (COPD) symptoms assessed (Includes assessment of at least one of the following: dyspnea, cough/sputum, wheezing), or respiratory symptom assessment tool completed

[1]Physician Consortium for Performance Improvement: www.physicianconsortium.org
[2]National Committee on Quality Assurance (NCQA): Health Employer Data Information Set (HEDIS®), www.ncqa.org
[3]Joint Commission on Accreditation of Healthcare Organizations (JCAHO), ORYX Initiative Performance Measures: www.jcaho.org/pms
[4]National Diabetes Quality Improvement Alliance: www.nationaldiabetesalliance.org
[5]Joint measure from the Physician Consortium for Performance Improvement, www.physicianconsortium.org, and National Committee on Quality Assurance (NCQA), www.ncqa.org
[6]The Society of Thoracic Surgeons, www.sts.org, National Quality Forum, www.qualityforum.org

Brief Description of Performance Measure & Source and Reporting Instructions	CPT Category II Code(s)	Code Descriptor
Chronic Obstructive Pulmonary Disease (COPD), cont'd		
Spirometry Evaluation[1]—Whether or not patient spirometry results were documented **Numerator:** All patients with documented spirometry results on the medical record **Denominator:** All patients with the diagnosis of COPD **Exclusion(s):** Documentation of medical, patient, or system reason(s) for no spirometry evaluation **Percentage** of patients with COPD who had a spirometry evaluation documented **Reporting Instructions:** For patients with appropriate exclusion criteria, report 3023F with modifier 1P, 2P, or 3P	**3023F**	Spirometry results documented and reviewed
Smoking Cessation Intervention[1]—Whether or not the patient who is a smoker received a smoking cessation intervention **Numerator:** All smokers who received a smoking cessation intervention during one or more office visits each year **Denominator:** All patients with the diagnosis of COPD identified as smokers **Exclusion(s):** None **Percentage** of smokers with COPD who received a smoking cessation intervention at least annually **Reporting Instructions:** Report 1034F for each cigarette smoker. Report either 1034F, 1035F, or 1036 for each patient. If patient is a smoker and received cessation intervention, report 4000F or 4001F, or both. Report 4000F or 4001F only if 1034F has been reported There are no exclusions for this measure; modifiers 1P, 2P, and 3P may not be used	**4000F** **4001F** **Denominator Codes:** **1034F** **1035F** **1036F**	Tobacco use cessation intervention, counseling Tobacco use cessation intervention, pharmacologic therapy Current tobacco smoker Current smokeless tobacco user (eg, chew, snuff) Current tobacco non-user
Inhaled Bronchodilator[1]—Whether or not the symptomatic patient was prescribed an inhaled bronchodilator **Numerator:** All symptomatic patients who were prescribed an inhaled bronchodilator **Denominator:** All patients with the diagnosis of COPD who have an $FEV_1/FVC < 70$ % and have symptoms **Denominator Inclusions:** Documentation of COPD symptoms; Documentation of $FEV_1/FVC < 70\%$ **Exclusion(s):** Documentation of medical, patient, or system reason(s) for not prescribing an inhaled bronchodilator **Percentage** of symptomatic patients with COPD who were prescribed an inhaled bronchodilator **Reporting Instructions:** Report either 3025F or 3027F for all COPD patients. For patients with appropriate exclusion criteria, report 4025F with modifier 1P, 2P, or 3P.	**4025F** **Denominator Codes:** **3025F** **3027F**	Inhaled bronchodilator prescribed Spirometry test results demonstrate $FEV_1/FVC < 70\%$ with COPD symptoms (eg, dyspnea, cough/sputum, wheezing) Spirometry test results demonstrate $FEV_1/FVC \geq 70\%$ or patient does not have COPD symptoms
Assessment of Oxygen Saturation[1]—Whether or not oxygen saturation was assessed at least annually **Numerator:** All patients with oxygen saturation assessed and documented **Denominator:** All patients with the diagnosis of COPD and a $FEV_1 < 40\%$ of predicted value (continued)	**3028F**	Oxygen saturation results documented and reviewed (Includes assessment through pulse oximetry or arterial blood gas measurement)

[1]Physician Consortium for Performance Improvement: www.physicianconsortium.org
[2]National Committee on Quality Assurance (NCQA): Health Employer Data Information Set (HEDIS®), www.ncqa.org
[3]Joint Commission on Accreditation of Healthcare Organizations (JCAHO), ORYX Initiative Performance Measures: www.jcaho.org/pms
[4]National Diabetes Quality Improvement Alliance: www.nationaldiabetesalliance.org
[5]Joint measure from the Physician Consortium for Performance Improvement, www.physicianconsortium.org, and National Committee on Quality Assurance (NCQA), www.ncqa.org
[6]The Society of Thoracic Surgeons, www.sts.org, National Quality Forum, www.qualityforum.org

Brief Description of Performance Measure & Source and Reporting Instructions	CPT Category II Code(s)	Code Descriptor
Chronic Obstructive Pulmonary Disease (COPD), cont'd		
Denominator Inclusion: Documentation of FEV_1 < 40% of predicted value **Exclusion(s):** Documentation of medical, patient, or system reason(s) for not assessing oxygen saturation **Percentage** of COPD patients with oxygen saturation assessed at least annually **Reporting Instructions:** Report 3040F or 3042F for all COPD patients. If oxygen saturation assessed, also report 3028F. For patients with appropriate exclusion criteria, report 3028F with modifier 1P, 2P, or 3P	**Denominator Codes** **3040F** **3042F**	 Functional expiratory volume (FEV_1) < 40% of predicted value Functional expiratory volume (FEV_1) ≥ 40% of predicted value
Long-Term Oxygen Therapy[1]—Whether or not patient with COPD was prescribed long-term oxygen therapy **Numerator:** All patients who were prescribed long term oxygen therapy **Denominator:** All patients with a diagnosis of COPD and an oxygen saturation ≤ 88% or a PaO_2 ≤ 55 mm Hg **Denominator Inclusion:** PaO_2 ≤ 55 mm Hg or oxygen saturation ≤ 88% **Exclusion(s):** Documentation of medical, patient, or system reason(s) for not prescribing long term oxygen therapy **Percentage** of patients with COPD that were prescribed long term oxygen therapy **Reporting Instructions:** Report 3035F or 3037F for all COPD patients. Report 4030F with 3035F if long term oxygen therapy prescribed For patients with appropriate exclusion criteria, report 4030F with modifier 1P, 2P, or 3P	**4030F** **Denominator Codes:** **3035F** **3037F**	Long term oxygen therapy prescribed (more than fifteen hours per day) Oxygen saturation ≤ 88% or a PaO_2 ≤ 55 mm Hg Oxygen saturation > 88% or PaO_2 > 55 mmHg
►**Recommendation of Influenza Immunization**[1]—Whether or not the patient aged 18 years and older with a diagnosis of COPD was recommended to receive an influenza immunization annually **Numerator:** Patients who were recommended to receive an influenza immunization annually **Denominator:** All patients age 18 years and older with a diagnosis of COPD **Exclusion(s):** Documentation of medical (eg, documentation of immunization previously given during the current flu season *) or system reason(s) for not recommending an influenza immunization ***Current flu season is defined as September-February** **Percentage** of patients aged 18 years and older with a diagnosis of COPD who were recommended to receive an influenza immunization annually **Reporting Instructions:** Report either code 4035F for patients who have been recommended an influenza immunization or 4037F for patients for whom an influenza immunization was ordered or administered◄ For patients with appropriate exclusion criteria, report 4035F with modifier 1P or 3P	**4035F** **4037F**	Influenza immunization recommended Influenza immunization ordered or administered
►**Influenza Immunization Administered**[1]—Whether or not the patient aged 18 years and older with a diagnosis of COPD received an influenza immunization during the current flu season **Numerator:** Patients who are administered an influenza immunization during the visit or who have already received an influenza immunization during the current flu season* *Current flu season is defined as September through February. **Denominator:** All patients aged 18 years and older with a diagnosis of COPD seen during the flu season (continued)	**4037F**	Influenza immunization ordered or administered

[1]Physician Consortium for Performance Improvement: www.physicianconsortium.org
[2]National Committee on Quality Assurance (NCQA): Health Employer Data Information Set (HEDIS®), www.ncqa.org
[3]Joint Commission on Accreditation of Healthcare Organizations (JCAHO), ORYX Initiative Performance Measures: www.jcaho.org/pms
[4]National Diabetes Quality Improvement Alliance: www.nationaldiabetesalliance.org
[5]Joint measure from the Physician Consortium for Performance Improvement, www.physicianconsortium.org, and National Committee on Quality Assurance (NCQA), www.ncqa.org
[6]The Society of Thoracic Surgeons, www.sts.org, National Quality Forum, www.qualityforum.org

Brief Description of Performance Measure & Source and Reporting Instructions	CPT Category II Code(s)	Code Descriptor
Chronic Obstructive Pulmonary Disease (COPD), cont'd		
Exclusion(s): Documentation of medical, patient, or system reason(s) for not administering the influenza immunization **Percentage** of patients aged 18 years and older with a diagnosis of COPD who received an influenza immunization during the current flu season **Reporting Instructions:** Report 4037F for patients for whom an influenza immunization was ordered or administered. For patient with appropriate exclusion criteria report 4037F with modifier 1P, 2P, or 3P◄		
►**Assessment of Pneumococcus Immunization Status**[1]—Whether or not the patient aged 18 year and older with a diagnosis of COPD was assessed for pneumococcus immunization status **Numerator:** Patients who were assessed for pneumococcus immunization status **Denominator:** All patients aged 18 years and older with the diagnosis of COPD **Exclusion(s):** Documentation of medical (eg documentation that pneumococcus immunization was not indicated), patient, or system reason(s) for not assessing pneumococcus immunization status **Percentage** of patients aged 18 years and older with a diagnosis of COPD who were assessed for pneumococcus immunization status **Reporting Instructions:** For patients with appropriate criteria, report 1022F with modifier 1P, 2P, or 3P◄	**1022F**	Pneumococcus immunization status assessed
►**Pneumococcus Immunization Administered**[1]—Whether or not the patient aged 18 years and older with a diagnosis of COPD received a pneumococcus immunization **Numerator:** Patients who are administered a pneumococcus immunization during a visit or who have already received a pneumoccus immunization status **Denominator:** All patients aged 18 years and older with the diagnosis of COPD **Exclusion(s):** Documentation of medical, patient, system (eg, pneumococcus immunization recommended, but not administered reason(s) for not administering the pneumococcus immunization **Percentage** of patients aged 18 years and older with a diagnosis of COPD who received a pneumcoccus immunization◄ **Reporting Instructions:** For patients with appropriate exclusion criteria, report 4040F with modifier 1P, 2P, or 3P	**4040F**	Pneumococcal immunization ordered or administered
Pulmonary Rehabilitation: Exercise Training Recommended[1]—Whether or not patient exercise training was recommended **Numerator:** All patients for whom exercise training was recommended **Denominator:** All patients with the diagnosis of COPD and dyspnea Documentation of dyspnea (1019F) **Exclusion(s):** Documentation of medical or system reason(s) for not recommending exercise training **Percentage** of patients for whom exercise training was recommended **Reporting Instructions:** Report 1018F or 1019F for all COPD patients. For patients with appropriate exclusion criteria, report 4033F with modifier 1P or 3P. Report 4033F with 1019F	**4033F** **Denominator Codes:** **1018F** **1019F**	Pulmonary rehabilitation exercise training recommended Dyspnea assessed, not present Dyspnea assessed, present

[1]Physician Consortium for Performance Improvement: www.physicianconsortium.org
[2]National Committee on Quality Assurance (NCQA): Health Employer Data Information Set (HEDIS®), www.ncqa.org
[3]Joint Commission on Accreditation of Healthcare Organizations (JCAHO), ORYX Initiative Performance Measures: www.jcaho.org/pms
[4]National Diabetes Quality Improvement Alliance: www.nationaldiabetesalliance.org
[5]Joint measure from the Physician Consortium for Performance Improvement, www.physicianconsortium.org, and National Committee on Quality Assurance (NCQA), www.ncqa.org
[6]The Society of Thoracic Surgeons, www.sts.org, National Quality Forum, www.qualityforum.org

Brief Description of Performance Measure & Source and Reporting Instructions	CPT Category II Code(s)	Code Descriptor
Community-Acquired Bacterial Pneumonia (CAP)		
Chest Radiograph[1]—Whether or not patient had a chest X-ray performed **Numerator:** All patients with a chest X-ray performed **Denominator:** All patients with the diagnosis of community-acquired bacterial pneumonia **Exclusion(s):** Documentation of medical, patient, or system reason(s) for not performing a chest X-ray **Percentage** of community-acquired bacterial pneumonia patients ≥ 18 years of age with a chest X-ray performed **Reporting Instructions:** For patients with appropriate exclusion criteria, report 3006F with modifier 1P, 2P, or 3P	**3006F**	Chest X-ray results documented and reviewed
Composite Code: Community-Acquired Bacterial Pneumonia Assessment— See individual measures listed below for (includes all of the following components): Co-morbid conditions assessed (1026F) Vital signs recorded (2010F) Mental status assessed (2014F) Hydration status assessed (2018F)	**0012F**	Community-acquired bacterial pneumonia assessment
Assessment of Comorbid Conditions[1]—Whether or not patient was assessed for comorbid conditions **Numerator:** All patients assessed for history of comorbid conditions **Denominator:** All patients with the diagnosis of community-acquired bacterial pneumonia **Exclusion(s):** None **Percentage** of patients ≥ 18 years of age with community-acquired bacterial pneumonia who were assessed for comorbid conditions **Reporting Instructions:** There are no exclusions for this measure; modifiers 1P, 2P, and 3P may not be used	**1026F**	Co-morbid conditions assessed (eg, includes assessment for presence or absence of: malignancy, liver disease, congestive heart failure, cerebrovascular disease, renal disease, chronic obstructive pulmonary disease, asthma, diabetes, other co-morbid conditions)
Vital Signs[1]—Whether or not patient had vital signs recorded **Numerator:** All patients with vital signs recorded **Denominator:** All patients with the diagnosis of community-acquired bacterial pneumonia **Exclusion(s):** None **Percentage** of community-acquired bacterial pneumonia patients ≥ 18 years of age with vital signs recorded **Reporting Instructions:** There are no exclusions for this measure; modifiers 1P, 2P, and 3P may not be used	**2010F**	Vital signs recorded (includes at minimum: temperature, pulse, respiration, and blood pressure)
Assessment of Oxygen Saturation[1]—Whether or not patient had oxygen saturation assessed **Numerator:** All patients with oxygen saturation assessed **Denominator:** All patients with the diagnosis of community-acquired bacterial pneumonia (continued)	**3028F**	Oxygen saturation results documented and reviewed (Includes assessment through pulse oximetry or arterial blood gas measurement)

[1]Physician Consortium for Performance Improvement: www.physicianconsortium.org
[2]National Committee on Quality Assurance (NCQA): Health Employer Data Information Set (HEDIS®), www.ncqa.org
[3]Joint Commission on Accreditation of Healthcare Organizations (JCAHO), ORYX Initiative Performance Measures: www.jcaho.org/pms
[4]National Diabetes Quality Improvement Alliance: www.nationaldiabetesalliance.org
[5]Joint measure from the Physician Consortium for Performance Improvement, www.physicianconsortium.org, and National Committee on Quality Assurance (NCQA), www.ncqa.org
[6]The Society of Thoracic Surgeons, www.sts.org, National Quality Forum, www.qualityforum.org

Brief Description of Performance Measure & Source and Reporting Instructions	CPT Category II Code(s)	Code Descriptor
Community-Acquired Bacterial Pneumonia (CAP), cont'd		
Exclusion(s): Documentation of medical, patient, or system reason(s) for not assessing oxygen saturation **Percentage** of patients ≥ 18 years of age with community-acquired bacterial pneumonia with oxygen saturation assessed **Reporting Instructions:** For patients with appropriate exclusion criteria, report 3028F with modifier 1P, 2P, or 3P		
Assessment of Mental Status[1]—Whether or not patient had mental status assessed **Numerator:** All patients with mental status assessed **Denominator:** All patients with the diagnosis of community-acquired bacterial pneumonia **Exclusion(s):** None **Percentage** of community-acquired bacterial pneumonia patients age ≥ 18 years of age with mental status assessed **Reporting Instructions:** There are no exclusions for this measure; modifiers 1P, 2P, and 3P may not be used	**2014F**	Mental status assessed (normal/mildly impaired/severely impaired)
Assessment of Hydration Status[1]—Whether or not the patient had hydration status assessed **Numerator:** All patients with hydration status assessed **Denominator:** All patients with the diagnosis of community-acquired bacterial pneumonia **Exclusion(s):** None **Percentage** of community-acquired bacterial pneumonia patients age ≥ 18 years of age with hydration status assessed **Reporting Instructions:** There are no exclusions for this measure; modifiers 1P, 2P, and 3P may not be used	**2018F**	Hydration status assessed (normal/mildly dehydrated/ severely dehydrated)
Level of Care Rationale[1]—Whether or not an assessment was made to determine the level of care **Numerator:** All patients with documented rationale for level of care **Denominator:** All patients with the diagnosis of community-acquired bacterial pneumonia **Percentage** of community-acquired bacterial pneumonia patients ≥ 18 years of age who had a documented rationale for level of care based on severity of illness and safety of home care **Reporting Instructions:**There are no exclusions for this measure; modifiers 1P, 2P, and 3P may not be used	**6005F**	Rationale (eg, severity of illness and safety) for level of care (eg, home, hospital) documented
Empiric Antibiotic[1]—Whether or not patient was prescribed an appropriate empiric antibiotic **Numerator:** All patients with an appropriate empiric antibiotic prescribed **Denominator:** All patients with the diagnosis of community-acquired bacterial pneumonia **Exclusion(s):** Documentation of medical, patient, or system reason(s) for not prescribing an antibiotic **Percentage** of community-acquired bacterial pneumonia patients ≥ 18 years of age who were prescribed an appropriate empiric antibiotic **Reporting Instructions:** For patients with appropriate exclusion criteria, report 4045F with modifier 1P, 2P, or 3P	**4045F**	Appropriate empiric antibiotic prescribed (See measure developer's Web site for definition of appropriate antibiotic)

[1]Physician Consortium for Performance Improvement: www.physicianconsortium.org
[2]National Committee on Quality Assurance (NCQA): Health Employer Data Information Set (HEDIS®), www.ncqa.org
[3]Joint Commission on Accreditation of Healthcare Organizations (JCAHO), ORYX Initiative Performance Measures: www.jcaho.org/pms
[4]National Diabetes Quality Improvement Alliance: www.nationaldiabetesalliance.org
[5]Joint measure from the Physician Consortium for Performance Improvement, www.physicianconsortium.org, and National Committee on Quality Assurance (NCQA), www.ncqa.org
[6]The Society of Thoracic Surgeons, www.sts.org, National Quality Forum, www.qualityforum.org

Brief Description of Performance Measure & Source and Reporting Instructions	CPT Category II Code(s)	Code Descriptor
Community-Acquired Bacterial Pneumonia (CAP), cont'd		
Smoking Assessment[1]—Whether or not patient was queried about smoking **Numerator:** All patients who were queried about smoking **Denominator:** All patients with the diagnosis of community-acquired bacterial pneumonia **Exclusion(s):** None **Percentage** of patients with community-acquired bacterial pneumonia who were queried about smoking **Reporting Instructions:** When reporting 1000F, it is required to report 1034F, and/or 1035F, or 1036F. There are no exclusions for this measure; modifiers 1P, 2P, and 3P may not be used	**1000F** **1034F** **1035F** **1036F**	Tobacco use assessed Current tobacco smoker Current smokeless tobacco user (eg, chew, snuff) Current tobacco non-user
Smoking Cessation Intervention[1]—Whether or not patient received a smoking cessation intervention **Numerator:** All patients who received a smoking cessation intervention **Denominator:** All patients with the diagnosis with community-acquired bacterial pneumonia identified as smokers **Exclusion(s):** None **Percentage** of patients ≥ 18 years of age with community-acquired bacterial pneumonia who received a smoking cessation intervention **Reporting Instructions:** Report 1034F for each cigarette smoker. Report either 1034F, 1035F, or 1036F for each patient. If patient is a smoker and received cessation intervention, report 4000F or 4001F, or both. Report 4000F or 4001F only if 1034F has been reported	**4000F** **4001F** **Denominator Codes:** **1034F** **1035F** **1036F**	Tobacco use cessation intervention, counseling Tobacco use cessation intervention, pharmacologic therapy Current tobacco smoker Current smokeless tobacco user (eg, chew, snuff) Current tobacco non-user
►**Assessment of Influenza Immunization Status**[1,2]—Whether or not patient aged 18 years and older with a diagnosis of community-acquired bacterial pneumonia was assessed for influenza immunization status **Numerator:** Patients who were assessed for influenza immunization status **Denominator:** All patients aged 18 years and older with the diagnosis of community-acquired bacterial pneumonia **Exclusion(s):** Documentation of medical reason(s) for not assessing influenza immunization status (eg, documentation that immunization was not indicated) **Percentage** of patients age 18 years age and older with a diagnosis of community-acquired bacterial pneumonia who were assessed for influenza immunization status◄ **Reporting Instructions:** For patients with appropriate exclusion criteria, report 1030F with modifier 1P	**1030F**	Influenza immunization status assessed
►**Assessment of Pneumococcus Immunization Status**[1,2]—Whether or not patient aged 18 years and older with a diagnosis of community-acquired bacterial pneumonia was assessed for pneumococcus immunization status **Numerator:** Patients who were assessed for pneumococcus immunization status **Denominator:** All patients aged 18 years and older with a diagnosis of community-acquired bacterial pneumonia **Exclusion(s):** Documentation of medical reason(s) for not assessing pneumococcus immunization status (eg, documentation that immunization was not indicated) **Percentage** of patients 18 years and older with a diagnosis of community-acquired bacterial pneumonia who were assessed for pneumococcus immunization status◄ **Reporting Instructions:** For patient with appropriate exclusion criteria, report 1022F with modifier 1P	**1022F**	Pneumococcus immunization status assessed

[1]Physician Consortium for Performance Improvement: www.physicianconsortium.org
[2]National Committee on Quality Assurance (NCQA): Health Employer Data Information Set (HEDIS®), www.ncqa.org
[3]Joint Commission on Accreditation of Healthcare Organizations (JCAHO), ORYX Initiative Performance Measures: www.jcaho.org/pms
[4]National Diabetes Quality Improvement Alliance: www.nationaldiabetesalliance.org
[5]Joint measure from the Physician Consortium for Performance Improvement, www.physicianconsortium.org, and National Committee on Quality Assurance (NCQA), www.ncqa.org
[6]The Society of Thoracic Surgeons, www.sts.org, National Quality Forum, www.qualityforum.org

Brief Description of Performance Measure & Source and Reporting Instructions	CPT Category II Code(s)	Code Descriptor
Coronary Artery Bypass Graft (CABG)		
Use of Internal Mammary Artery (IMA) Graft in Primary, Isolated Coronary Artery Bypass Graft (CABG) Surgery[6]—Whether or not a patient received an IMA graft in the performance of a primary, isolated CABG procedure. **Numerator:** All patients who received an IMA graft in isolated CABG procedures **Denominator:** All patients who received a primary isolated CABG procedure **Exclusion(s):** Medical reasons for not receiving an IMA graft in the performance of a primary, isolated CABG procedure **Reporting Instructions:** This measure is not intended for use with repeat CABG procedures. For patients with documented medical reasons for not receiving an IMA graft in the performance of a primary, isolated CABG procedure, report modifier 1P with code 4110F	**4110F**	Internal mammary artery graft performed for primary, isolated coronary artery bypass graft procedure
Use of Beta Blocker in Isolated Coronary Artery Bypass Graft (CABG) Surgery[6] Whether or not a patient was administered beta blocker within 24 hours prior to surgical incision for isolated CABG surgery **Numerator:** Patients who were administered beta blocker within 24 hours prior to surgical incision **Denominator:** All patients undergoing isolated CABG surgery **Exclusion(s):** Medical reasons for not administering beta blocker within 24 hours prior to surgical incision for isolated CABG surgery **Percentage** of patients who were administered beta blocker within 24 hours prior to surgical incision for isolated CABG surgery **Reporting Instructions:** For patients with medical reasons for not administering beta blocker within 24 hours prior to surgical incision for isolated CABG surgery, report modifier 1P with code 4115F	**4115F**	Beta blocker administered within 24 hours prior to surgical incision
Coronary Artery Disease (CAD)		
Smoking Cessation Evaluation[1]—Whether or not patient with CAD was queried one or more times about cigarette smoking **Numerator:** Patients who were queried one or more times about cigarette smoking **Denominator:** All patients with CAD **Exclusion(s):** None **Percentage** of patients who were queried one or more times about cigarette smoking **Reporting Instructions:** When reporting 1000F, it is required to report 1034F, and/or 1035F, or 1036F There are no exclusions for this measure; modifiers 1P, 2P, and 3P may not be used	**1000F** **1034F** **1035F** **1036F**	Tobacco use assessed Current tobacco smoker Current smokeless tobacco user (eg, chew, snuff) Current tobacco non-user
Smoking Cessation Intervention[1]—Whether or not patient identified as a cigarette smoker received intervention for smoking cessation **Numerator:** Patients who were received smoking cessation intervention **Denominator:** All patients with CAD identified as cigarette smokers **Exclusion(s):** None **Percentage** of patients identified as cigarette smokers who received intervention for smoking cessation **Reporting Instructions:** Report 1034F for each cigarette smoker. Report either 1034F, 1035F, or 1036F for each patient. If patient is a smoker and received cessation intervention, report 4000F or 4001F, or both. Report 4000F or 4001F only if 1034F has been reported There are no exclusions for this measure; modifiers 1P, 2P, and 3P may not be used	**4000F** **4001F** **Denominator Codes:** **1034F** **1035F** **1036F**	Tobacco use cessation intervention, counseling Tobacco use cessation intervention, pharmacologic therapy Current tobacco smoker Current smokeless tobacco user (eg, chew, snuff) Current tobacco non-user

[1]Physician Consortium for Performance Improvement: www.physicianconsortium.org
[2]National Committee on Quality Assurance (NCQA): Health Employer Data Information Set (HEDIS®), www.ncqa.org
[3]Joint Commission on Accreditation of Healthcare Organizations (JCAHO), ORYX Initiative Performance Measures: www.jcaho.org/pms
[4]National Diabetes Quality Improvement Alliance: www.nationaldiabetesalliance.org
[5]Joint measure from the Physician Consortium for Performance Improvement, www.physicianconsortium.org, and National Committee on Quality Assurance (NCQA), www.ncqa.org
[6]The Society of Thoracic Surgeons, www.sts.org, National Quality Forum, www.qualityforum.org

Brief Description of Performance Measure & Source and Reporting Instructions	CPT Category II Code(s)	Code Descriptor
Coronary Artery Disease (CAD), cont'd		
Symptom & Activity Assessment[1]—Whether or not patient's level of activity and anginal symptoms were evaluated during office visit **Numerator:** Patients evaluated for both level of activity and anginal symptoms during one or more office visits **Denominator:** All patients with CAD **Exclusion(s):** None **Percentage** of patients who were evaluated for both level of activity and anginal symptoms during one or more office visits **Reporting Instructions:** There are no exclusions for this measure; modifiers 1P, 2P, and 3P may not be used	**1002F**	Anginal symptoms and level of activity assessed
Blood Pressure Measurement[1]—Most recent systolic and diastolic blood pressure measurement **Numerator:** Patients who had a blood pressure measurement during the last office visit **Denominator:** All patients with CAD **Exclusion(s):** None **Percentage** of patients who had a blood pressure measurement during the last office visit **Reporting Instructions:** There are no exclusions for this measure; modifiers 1P, 2P, and 3P may not be used	**2000F**	Blood pressure measured
Lipid Profile[1]—Whether or not a lipid profile was obtained **Numerator:** Patients who received at least one lipid profile (or ALL component tests) **Denominator:** All patients with CAD **Exclusion(s):** None **Percentage** of patients who received at least one lipid profile (or ALL component tests)	**3011F**	Lipid panel results documented and reviewed (must include total cholesterol, HDL-C, triglycerides and calculated LDL-C)
Drug Therapy for Lowering LDL-Cholesterol[1]—Whether or not patient was prescribed lipid-lowering therapy **Numerator:** Patients who were prescribed lipid-lowering therapy **Denominator:** All patients with CAD **Exclusion(s):** Documentation of medical, patient, or system reason(s) for not prescribing lipid-lowering therapy **Percentage** of patients who were prescribed a lipid-lowering therapy (based on current ACC/AHA guidelines) **Reporting Instructions:** For patients with appropriate exclusion criteria, report code 4002F with modifier 1P, 2P, or 3P	**4002F**	Statin therapy prescribed
Beta-Blocker Therapy- Prior Myocardial Infarction (MI)[1]—Whether or not CAD patient with prior MI at any time was prescribed beta-blocker therapy **Numerator:** Patients who were prescribed beta-blocker therapy **Denominator:** All patients with CAD who also have a prior MI at any time **Exclusion(s):** Documentation of medical, patient reason(s) for not prescribing beta-blocker therapy, or system reason **Percentage** of CAD patients who also have prior MI at any time who were prescribed beta-blocker therapy **Reporting Instructions:** For patients with appropriate exclusion criteria, report code 4006F with modifier 1P, 2P, or 3P	**4006F**	Beta-blocker therapy prescribed

[1]Physician Consortium for Performance Improvement: www.physicianconsortium.org
[2]National Committee on Quality Assurance (NCQA): Health Employer Data Information Set (HEDIS®), www.ncqa.org
[3]Joint Commission on Accreditation of Healthcare Organizations (JCAHO), ORYX Initiative Performance Measures: www.jcaho.org/pms
[4]National Diabetes Quality Improvement Alliance: www.nationaldiabetesalliance.org
[5]Joint measure from the Physician Consortium for Performance Improvement, www.physicianconsortium.org, and National Committee on Quality Assurance (NCQA), www.ncqa.org
[6]The Society of Thoracic Surgeons, www.sts.org, National Quality Forum, www.qualityforum.org

Brief Description of Performance Measure & Source and Reporting Instructions	CPT Category II Code(s)	Code Descriptor
Coronary Artery Disease (CAD), cont'd		
Angiotensin Converting Enzyme (ACE) Inhibitor or Angiotensin Receptor Blocker (ARB) Therapy[1]—Whether or not CAD patient with diabetes and/or left ventricular systolic dysfunction (LVSD) was prescribed ACE inhibitor or ARB therapy **Numerator:** Patients who were prescribed ACE inhibitor or ARB therapy **Denominator:** All CAD patients aged ≥ 18 years of age with diabetes and/or left ventricular ejection fraction (LVEF) < 40% or moderately or severely depressed left ventricular systolic function **Exclusion(s):** Documentation of medical, patient, or system reason(s) for not prescribing ACE or ARB therapy **Percentage** of CAD patients who also have diabetes and/or left ventricular systolic dysfunction (LVSD) who were prescribed ACE inhibitor or ARB therapy **Reporting Instructions:** Report either 3021F or 3022F or corresponding ICD-9 diagnosis code for diabetes for each CAD patient. For patient with appropriate exclusion criteria, report 4009F with modifier 1P, 2P, or 3P	**4009F** **Denominator Codes** **3021F** **3022F**	Angiotensin converting enzyme (ACE) inhibitor or Angiotensin Receptor Blocker (ARB) therapy prescribed Left ventricular ejection fraction (LVEF) < 40% or documentation of moderately or severely depressed left ventricular systolic function Left ventricular ejection fraction (LVEF) ≥ 40% or documentation as normal or mildly depressed left ventricular systolic function
Antiplatelet Therapy[1]—Whether or not patient was prescribed antiplatelet therapy **Numerator:** Patients who were prescribed antiplatelet therapy **Denominator:** All patients with CAD **Exclusion(s):** Documentation of medical, patient, or system reason(s) for not prescribing antiplatelet therapy **Percentage** of patients who were prescribed antiplatelet therapy **Reporting Instructions:** For patients with appropriate exclusion criteria, report code 4011F with modifier 1P, 2P, or 3P	**4011F**	Oral antiplatelet therapy prescribed (eg, aspirin, clopidogrel/Plavix, or combination of aspirin and dipyridamole/ Aggrenox)
For Critical Care, see Anesthesiology/Critical Care (CRIT)		
Diabetes		
A1c Management[4]—Whether or not patient received one or more A1c test(s) **Numerator:** Patients who received one or more A1c test(s) **Denominator:** Patients with diagnosed diabetes 18-75 years of age **Exclusion(s):** None **Percentage** of patients with diagnosed diabetes aged 18-75 years with one or more A1c test(s) **Reporting Instructions:** In order to meet this measure, the date of test when it was performed and the corresponding result are required. For this reason, report one of the two Category II codes listed and use the date of service as the date of the test, not the date of the reporting of the category II code. The measure may also be met by reporting the Category I code, 83036 Hemoglobin; by copper sulfate method, non-automated, glycated, when performed ►To report most recent hemoglobin A1c level ≥ 9.0%, see codes 3044F-3045F◄ To report most recent hemoglobin A1c level ≤ 9.0%, see codes 3044F-3045F	**3044F** **3045F** **3046F**	Most recent hemoglobin A1c HbA1c level < 7.0% Most recent hemoglobin A1c (HbA1c) level 7.0% to 9.0% Most recent hemoglobin A1c level > 9.0%
A1c Management[4]—Whether or not patient's most recent A1c level > 9.0% (poor control) **Numerator:** Patients with most recent A1c level > 9.0% (poor control) **Denominator:** Patients diagnosed with diabetes 18-75 years of age **Exclusion(s):** None (continued)	**3044F** **3045F**	Most recent hemoglobin A1c HbA1c level < 7.0% Most recent hemoglobin A1c (HbA1c) level 7.0% to 9.0%

[1]Physician Consortium for Performance Improvement: www.physicianconsortium.org
[2]National Committee on Quality Assurance (NCQA): Health Employer Data Information Set (HEDIS®), www.ncqa.org
[3]Joint Commission on Accreditation of Healthcare Organizations (JCAHO), ORYX Initiative Performance Measures: www.jcaho.org/pms
[4]National Diabetes Quality Improvement Alliance: www.nationaldiabetesalliance.org
[5]Joint measure from the Physician Consortium for Performance Improvement, www.physicianconsortium.org, and National Committee on Quality Assurance (NCQA), www.ncqa.org
[6]The Society of Thoracic Surgeons, www.sts.org, National Quality Forum, www.qualityforum.org

Brief Description of Performance Measure & Source and Reporting Instructions	CPT Category II Code(s)	Code Descriptor
Diabetes, cont'd		
Percentage of patients with most recent A1c level > 9.0% (poor control) **Reporting Instructions:** In order to meet this measure, the date of test when it was performed and the corresponding result are required. For this reason, report one of the two Category II codes listed and use the date of service as the date of the test, not the date of the reporting of the Category II code To report most recent hemoglobin A1c level < 9.0%, see codes 3044F-3045F	**3046F**	Most recent hemoglobin A1c level > 9.0%
A1c Management[2]—Whether or not patient's most recent A1c level < 7.0% (tight control) **Numerator:** Patients with most recent A1c level < 7.0% (tight control) **Denominator:** Patients diagnosed with diabetes 18-75 years of age **Exclusion(s):** Documentation of medical reasons for not pursuing tight control of A1c level Percentage of patients with most recent A1c level < 7.0% (tight control) **Reporting Instructions:** In order to meet this measure, the date of test when it was performed and the corresponding result are required. For this reason, report one of the three Category II codes listed and use the date of service as the date of the test, not the date of the reporting of the Category II code. For patients with appropriate exclusion criteria report 3044F, 3045F or 3046F with 1P. To report most recent hemoglobin A1c level ≤9.0%, see codes 3044F-3045F	**3044F** **3045F** **3046F**	Most recent hemoglobin HbA1c level < 7.0% Most recent hemoglobin HbA1c level 7.0% to 9.0% Most recent hemoglobin A1c level > 9.0%
Lipid Management[4]—Whether or not patient received at least one LDL-C test **Numerator:** Patients who received at least one LDL-C test **Denominator:** Patients diagnosed with diabetes 18-75 years of age **Exclusion(s):** None **Percentage** of patients diagnosed with diabetes aged 18-75 years with at least one LDL-C test **Reporting Instructions:** In order to meet this measure, the date of test when it was performed and the corresponding result are required. For this reason, report one of the three Category II codes listed and use the date of service as the date of the test, not the date of the reporting of the Category II code. The measure may also be met by reporting the listed lipid test Category I codes, when performed There are no exclusions for this measure; modifiers 1P, 2P, and 3P may not be used	**3048F** **3049F** **3050F**	Most recent LDL-C < 100 mg/dL Most recent LDL-C 100-129 mg/dL Most recent LDL-C ≥ 130 mg/dL
Lipid Management[4]—Whether or not patient's most recent LDL-C < 130 mg/dL **Numerator:** Patients with most recent LDL-C < 130 mg/dL **Denominator:** Patients diagnosed with diabetes 18-75 years of age **Exclusion(s):** None **Percentage** of patients diagnosed with diabetes aged 18-75 years with most recent LDL-C < 130 mg/dL **Reporting Instructions:** In order to meet this measure, the date of test when it was performed and the corresponding result are required. For this reason, report one of the three Category II codes listed and use the date of service as the date of the test, not the date of the reporting of the Category II code. There are no performance exclusions for this measure; modifiers 1P, 2P, and 3P may not be used	**3048F** **3049F** **3050F**	Most recent LDL-C < 100 mg/dL Most recent LDL-C 100-129 mg/dL Most recent LDL-C ≥ 130 mg/dL

[1]Physician Consortium for Performance Improvement: www.physicianconsortium.org
[2]National Committee on Quality Assurance (NCQA): Health Employer Data Information Set (HEDIS®), www.ncqa.org
[3]Joint Commission on Accreditation of Healthcare Organizations (JCAHO), ORYX Initiative Performance Measures: www.jcaho.org/pms
[4]National Diabetes Quality Improvement Alliance: www.nationaldiabetesalliance.org
[5]Joint measure from the Physician Consortium for Performance Improvement, www.physicianconsortium.org, and National Committee on Quality Assurance (NCQA), www.ncqa.org
[6]The Society of Thoracic Surgeons, www.sts.org, National Quality Forum, www.qualityforum.org

Brief Description of Performance Measure & Source and Reporting Instructions	CPT Category II Code(s)	Code Descriptor
Diabetes, cont'd		
Lipid Management[4]—Whether or not patient's most recent LDL-C < 100 mg/dL **Numerator:** Patients with most recent LDL-C < 100 mg/dL **Denominator:** Patients diagnosed with diabetes 18-75 years of age **Exclusion(s):** None **Percentage** of patients diagnosed with diabetes aged 18-75 years with most recent LDL-C < 100 mg/dL **Reporting Instructions:** In order to meet this measure, the date of test, when it was performed and the corresponding result are required. For this reason, report one of the three Category II codes listed and use the date of service as the date of the test, not the date of the reporting of the Category II code.	**3048F** **3049F** **3050F**	Most recent LDL-C < 100 mg/dL Most recent LDL-C 100-129 mg/dL Most recent LDL-C ≥ 130 mg/dL
Urine Protein Screening[4]—Whether or not a patient received at least one test for microalbumin during the measurement year **or** had evidence of medical attention for existing nephropathy **or** has documentation of microalbuminuria or albuminuria **or** is on an angiotensin converting enzyme (ACE) inhibitor or angiotensin receptor blocker (ARB) **Numerator:** Patients with at least one test for microalbumin during the measurement year; or who had evidence of medical attention for existing nephropathy or documentation of microalbuminuria or albuminuria or are on an ACE inhibitor or ARB therapy **Denominator:** Patients diagnosed with diabetes 18-75 years of age **Exclusion(s):** None **Percentage** of patients diagnosed with diabetes 18-75 years of age with at least one test for microalbumin during the measurement year; or who had evidence of medical attention for existing nephropathy or documentation of microalbuminuria or albuminuria or are on an ACE inhibitor or ARB therapy **Reporting Instructions:** Report any one of the codes listed using the following: 1. Codes 3060F, 3061F, and 3062F may be used to indicate that a patient received at least one test for microabluminuria 2. Code 3066F may be used if there is evidence of nephropathy **or** if there was a patient visit to a nephrologist 3. Code 3062F may be used to indicate that a patient had documentation of microalbuminuria or albuminuria 4. Code 4009F may be used if patient is on an ACE inhibitor or ARB therapy 5. Any CPT Category I code and corresponding result, when performed, and reported with any of the following ICD-9-CM diagnosis or procedure codes found in specifications: ICD-9-CM codes: 39.27, 39.42, 39.43, 39.53, 39.93-39.95, 54.98, 55.4-55.6, 250.4, 403, 404, 405.01, 405.11, 405.91, 581.81, 582.9, 583.81, 584-586, 588, 753.0, 753.1, 791.0; V codes: V42.0, V45.1, V56 6. CPT Category I codes for microalbumin measurement or quantitative timed urine albumin measurement and corresponding result as follows: 82042, 82043, 82044,83518, 84156 or (84160, 84165, 84166) with code 81050	**3060F** **3061F** **3062F** **3066F** **4009F**	Positive microalbuminuria test result documented and reviewed Negative microalbuminuria test result documented and reviewed Positive macroalbuminuria test result documented and reviewed Documentation of treatment for nephropathy (eg, patient receiving dialysis, patient being treated for ESRD, CRF, ARF, or renal insufficiency, any visit to a nephrologist) Angiotensin converting enzyme (ACE) inhibitor or Angiotensin Receptor Blocker (ARB) therapy prescribed

[1]Physician Consortium for Performance Improvement: www.physicianconsortium.org
[2]National Committee on Quality Assurance (NCQA): Health Employer Data Information Set (HEDIS®), www.ncqa.org
[3]Joint Commission on Accreditation of Healthcare Organizations (JCAHO), ORYX Initiative Performance Measures: www.jcaho.org/pms
[4]National Diabetes Quality Improvement Alliance: www.nationaldiabetesalliance.org
[5]Joint measure from the Physician Consortium for Performance Improvement, www.physicianconsortium.org, and National Committee on Quality Assurance (NCQA), www.ncqa.org
[6]The Society of Thoracic Surgeons, www.sts.org, National Quality Forum, www.qualityforum.org

Brief Description of Performance Measure & Source and Reporting Instructions	CPT Category II Code(s)	Code Descriptor
Diabetes, cont'd		
►Urine Protein Screening (Medical Attention for Nephropathy)[2,4] To assess the percentage of patients aged 18-75 years of age with diabetes (type 1 and type 2) who received urine protein screening or medical attention for nephropathy. **Numerator:** Patients who have a nephropathy screening during one or more office visits within 12 months. This measure is looking for a nephropathy screening test or evidence of nephropathy. **Denominator:** All patients aged 18-75 years of age with the diagnosis of diabetes **Exclusion(s)/Modifiers:** None ***Describe what the measure results are:*** The percentage of patients aged 18-75 years of age with diabetes (type 1 and type 2) who received urine protein screening or medical attention for nephropathy. **Reporting Instructions:** Report one or more of these codes for urine protein screening or medical attention to nephropathy at least once per reporting period◄	**►3060F** **3061F** **3062F** **3066F** **4009F◄**	►Positive microalbuminuria test result documented and reviewed Negative microalbuminuria test result documented and reviewed Positive macroalbuminuria test result documented and reviewed Documentation of treatment for nephropathy (eg, patient receiving dialysis, patient being treated for ESRD, CRF, ARF, or renal insufficiency, any visit to a nephrologist) Angiotensin converting enzyme (ACE) inhibitor or Angiotensin Receptor Blocker (ARB) therapy prescribed◄
Eye Examination[4]—Whether or not patient received a dilated eye exam or seven standard field stereoscopic photos with interpretation by an ophthalmologist or optometrist or imaging validated to match diagnosis from these photos during the reporting year or during the prior year if the patient is at low risk* for retinopathy **Numerator:** Patients who received a dilated eye exam or seven standard field stereoscopic photos with interpretation by an ophthalmologist or optometrist or imaging validated to match diagnosis from these photos during the reporting year, or during the prior year, if patient is at low risk* for retinopathy **Denominator:** Patients with diagnosed diabetes 18-75 years of age; Low risk patient (defined as a patient who had no evidence of retinopathy in the prior year) must have had an evaluation in the prior year **Exclusion(s):** None **Percentage** of patients who received a dilated eye exam or seven standard field stereoscopic photos with interpretation by an ophthalmologist or optometrist or imaging validated to match diagnosis from these photos during the reporting year **Reporting Instructions:** Only one of these codes should be reported *A patient is considered low risk if the following criterion is met: has no evidence of retinopathy on one of the accepted examinations in the prior year	**2022F** **2024F** **2026F** **OR** **3072F**	Dilated retinal eye exam with interpretation by an ophthalmologist or optometrist documented and reviewed OR Seven standard field stereoscopic photos with interpretation by an ophthalmologist or optometrist documented and reviewed OR Eye imaging validated to match diagnosis from seven standard field stereoscopic photos results documented and reviewed OR Low risk for retinopathy (no evidence of retinopathy in the prior year)
Foot Examination[4]—Whether or not patient received at least one foot exam, defined in any manner **Numerator:** Patients who received at least one foot exam, defined in any manner **Denominator:** Patients diagnosed with diabetes 18-75 years of age **Exclusion(s):** Patients with bilateral foot/leg amputation **Percentage** of patients diagnosed with diabetes 18-75 years of age receiving at least one foot exam, defined in any manner **Reporting Instructions:** Report 2028F with modifier 1P for patients with bilateral foot/leg amputation	**2028F**	Foot examination performed (includes examination through visual inspection, sensory exam with monofilament, and pulse exam - report when any of the three components are completed)

[1]Physician Consortium for Performance Improvement: www.physicianconsortium.org
[2]National Committee on Quality Assurance (NCQA): Health Employer Data Information Set (HEDIS®), www.ncqa.org
[3]Joint Commission on Accreditation of Healthcare Organizations (JCAHO), ORYX Initiative Performance Measures: www.jcaho.org/pms
[4]National Diabetes Quality Improvement Alliance: www.nationaldiabetesalliance.org
[5]Joint measure from the Physician Consortium for Performance Improvement, www.physicianconsortium.org, and National Committee on Quality Assurance (NCQA), www.ncqa.org
[6]The Society of Thoracic Surgeons, www.sts.org, National Quality Forum, www.qualityforum.org

Brief Description of Performance Measure & Source and Reporting Instructions	CPT Category II Code(s)	Code Descriptor
Diabetes, cont'd		
Blood Pressure Management[2]—Whether or not patient's most recent blood pressure is < 130 mm Hg systolic and < 80 mm Hg diastolic **Numerator:** Patients whose most recent blood pressure is < 130 mm Hg systolic and < 80 mm Hg diastolic. **Denominator:** Patients diagnosed with diabetes 18-75 years of age **Exclusion(s):** Documentation of medical reasons that diastolic < 80 is not medically indicated. Documentation of medical reasons that systolic < 130 is not medically indicated. Percentage of patients diagnosed with diabetes 18-75 years of age with most recent blood pressure < 130 mm Hg systolic and < 80 mm Hg diastolic. **Reporting Instructions:** Two codes must be reported here. For the systolic blood pressure value, report one of the three systolic codes; for the diastolic blood pressure value, report one of the three diastolic codes. For patients in whom a goal of 130/80 is not medically indicated, report codes 3075F, 3077F, 3078F, 3079F, 3080F with modifier 1P. ►*Code 2000F has been included with the Diabetes measure set to reflect potential use in the Physician Quality Reporting Initiative (PQRI) to identify non-performance of a blood pressure check. To identify non-performance of a blood pressure check report code 2000F with modifier 8P. 2000F is not valid for another use in this measure◄	**►2000F◄** **3074F** **3075F** **3077F** **3078F** **3079F** **3080F**	►Blood pressure measured◄ Most recent systolic blood pressure < 130 mm Hg Most recent systolic blood pressure 130 to 139 mm Hg Most recent systolic blood pressure ≥ 140 mm Hg Most recent diastolic blood pressure < 80 mm Hg Most recent diastolic blood pressure 80-89 mm Hg Most recent diastolic blood pressure ≥ 90 mm Hg
Blood Pressure Management[4] (Measure #2)—Whether or not patient's most recent blood pressure is < 140/80 mm Hg **Numerator:** Patients whose most recent blood pressure < 140/80 mm Hg **Denominator:** Patients diagnosed with diabetes 18-75 years of age **►Exclusion(s):** None◄ **Percentage** of patients diagnosed with diabetes 18-75 years of age with most recent blood pressure < 140/80 mm Hg **Reporting Instructions:** Two codes must be reported here. For the systolic blood pressure value, report one of the two systolic codes; for the diastolic blood pressure value, report one of the three diastolic codes To report most recent recent systolic blood pressure <140 mm Hg, see codes 3074F-3075F. ►There are no exclusions for this measure; modifiers 1P, 2P, and 3P may not be used◄	**Systolic Codes:** **3074F** **3075F** **3077F** **Diastolic Codes:** **3078F** **3079F** **3080F**	 Most recent systolic blood pressure < 130 mm Hg Most recent systolic blood pressure 130 to 139 mm Hg Most recent systolic blood pressure ≥ 140 mm Hg Most recent diastolic blood pressure < 80 mm Hg Most recent diastolic blood pressure 80-89 mm Hg Most recent diastolic blood pressure ≥ 90 mm Hg
Smoking Cessation[4]—Whether or not patient's smoking status was ascertained and documented **Numerator:** Patients whose smoking status was ascertained and documented **Denominator:** Patients diagnosed with diabetes 18-75 years of age **►Exclusion(s):** None◄ **Percentage** of patients diagnosed with diabetes 18-75 years of age whose smoking status was ascertained and documented **Reporting Instructions:** Report 1034F for each cigarette smoker. Report either 1034F, 1035F, or 1036F for each patient. If patient is a smoker and received cessation intervention, report 4000F or 4001F, or both. Report 4000F or 4001F only if 1034F has been reported There are no exclusions for this measure; modifiers 1P, 2P, and 3P may not be used	**4000F** **4001F** **Denominator Codes:** **1034F** **1035F** **1036F**	Tobacco use cessation intervention, counseling Tobacco use cessation intervention, pharmacologic therapy Current tobacco smoker Smokeless tobacco user Current tobacco non-user

[1] Physician Consortium for Performance Improvement: www.physicianconsortium.org
[2] National Committee on Quality Assurance (NCQA): Health Employer Data Information Set (HEDIS®), www.ncqa.org
[3] Joint Commission on Accreditation of Healthcare Organizations (JCAHO), ORYX Initiative Performance Measures: www.jcaho.org/pms
[4] National Diabetes Quality Improvement Alliance: www.nationaldiabetesalliance.org
[5] Joint measure from the Physician Consortium for Performance Improvement, www.physicianconsortium.org, and National Committee on Quality Assurance (NCQA), www.ncqa.org
[6] The Society of Thoracic Surgeons, www.sts.org, National Quality Forum, www.qualityforum.org

Brief Description of Performance Measure & Source and Reporting Instructions	CPT Category II Code(s)	Code Descriptor
Diabetes, cont'd		
►**Appropriate Eye Exam for People with Diabetes** [2]—Whether or not patients aged 18-75 years of age with diabetes (type 1 and type 2) had a dilated eye exam. **Numerator:** Patients who have an eye exam for diabetic retinal disease at least once **Denominator:** All patients aged 18-75 years of age with the diagnosis of diabetes **Exclusion(s): None** **Percentage** of patients aged 18-75 years of age with diabetes (type 1 and type 2) who had a dilated eye exam. **Reporting Instructions:** Report either code 2022F or 2024F or 2026F or 3072F for each patient at least once during the measurement year. There are no exclusions for this measure; modifiers 1P, 2P, and 3P may not be used◄	►2022F	►Dilated retinal eye exam with interpretation by an ophthalmologist or optometrist documented and reviewed
	2024F	Seven standard field stereoscopic photos with interpretation by an ophthalmologist or optometrist documented and reviewed
	2026F	Eye imaging validated to match diagnosis from seven standard field stereoscopic photos results documented and reviewed
	3072F◄	Low risk for retinopathy (no evidence of retinopathy in the prior year)◄
Emergency Medicine (EM)		
Electrocardiogram Performed for Non-Traumatic Chest Pain[5]—Whether or not the patient aged 40 years and older with an emergency department discharge diagnosis of non-traumatic chest pain had an ECG performed **Numerator:** Patients who had an ECG performed **Denominator:** All patients aged 40 years and older with an emergency department discharge diagnosis of non-traumatic chest pain **Exclusion(s):** Documentation of medical reason(s) for not performing an ECG; documentation of patient reason(s) for not performing an ECG **Percentage** of patients aged 40 years and older with an emergency department discharge diagnosis of non-traumatic chest pain who had an ECG performed **Reporting Intructions:** For patient with appropriate exclusion criteria, report 3120F with modifier 1P or 2P	3120F	12-Lead ECG performed
Aspirin at Arrival for Acute Myocardial Infarction (AMI)[5]—Whether or not the patient with an emergency department discharge diagnosis of AMI had documentation of receiving aspirin within 24 hours before emergency department arrival or during emergency department stay **Numerator:** Patients who had documentation of receiving aspirin within 24 hours before emergency department arrival or during emergency department stay **Denominator:** All patients with an emergency department discharge diagnosis of acute myocardial infarction **Exclusion(s):** Documentation of medical reason(s) for not receiving aspirin within 24 hours before emergency department arrival or during emergency department stay; documentation of patient reason(s) for not receiving aspirin within 24 hours before emergency department arrival or during emergency department stay **Percentage** of patients with AMI who had documentation of receiving aspirin within 24 hours before or after hospital arrival **Reporting Instructions:** For patient with appropriate exclusion criteria, report 4084F with modifier 1P or 2P	4084F	Aspirin received within 24 hours before emergency department arrival or during emergency department stay

[1]Physician Consortium for Performance Improvement: www.physicianconsortium.org
[2]National Committee on Quality Assurance (NCQA): Health Employer Data Information Set (HEDIS®), www.ncqa.org
[3]Joint Commission on Accreditation of Healthcare Organizations (JCAHO), ORYX Initiative Performance Measures: www.jcaho.org/pms
[4]National Diabetes Quality Improvement Alliance: www.nationaldiabetesalliance.org
[5]Joint measure from the Physician Consortium for Performance Improvement, www.physicianconsortium.org, and National Committee on Quality Assurance (NCQA), www.ncqa.org
[6]The Society of Thoracic Surgeons, www.sts.org, National Quality Forum, www.qualityforum.org

Brief Description of Performance Measure & Source and Reporting Instructions	CPT Category II Code(s)	Code Descriptor
Emergency Medicine (EM), cont'd		
Electrocardiogram Performed for Syncope[5]—Whether or not the patient aged 60 years and older with an emergency department discharge diagnosis of syncope had an ECG performed **Numerator:** Patients who had an ECG performed **Denominator:** All patients aged 60 years and older with an emergency department discharge diagnosis of syncope **Exclusion(s):** Documentation of medical reason(s) for not performing an ECG; documentation of patient reason(s) for not performing an ECG **Percentage** of patients aged 60 years and older with an emergency department discharge diagnosis of syncope who had an ECG performed **Reporting Instructions:** For patient with appropriate exclusion criteria, report 3120F with modifier 1P or 2P	**3120F**	12-Lead ECG performed
Vital Signs for Community-Acquired Bacterial Pneumonia[5]—Whether or not the patient aged 18 years and older with the diagnosis of community-acquired pneumonia had vital signs documented and reviewed **Numerator:** Patients with vital signs (temperature, pulse, respiratory rate, and blood pressure) documented and reviewed **Denominator:** All patients aged 18 years and older with the diagnosis of community-acquired bacterial pneumonia **Exclusion(s):** None **Percentage** of patients aged 18 years and older with the diagnosis of community-acquired bacterial pneumonia with vital signs documented and reviewed **Reporting Instructions:** There are no exclusions for this measure; modifiers 1P, 2P and 3P may not be used	**2010F**	Vital signs (temperature, pulse, respiratory rate, and blood pressure) documented and reviewed
Assessment of Oxygen Saturation for Community-Acquired Bacterial Pneumonia[5]—Whether or not the patient aged 18 years and older with the diagnosis of community-acquired bacterial pneumonia had oxygen saturation documented and reviewed **Numerator:** Patients with oxygen saturation documented and reviewed **Denominator:** All patients aged 18 years and older with the diagnosis of community-acquired bacterial pneumonia ►**Exclusion(s):** Documentation of physician reason(s) for not documented and reviewed oxygen saturation; documentation of patient reason(s) for not assessing documented and reviewed oxygen saturation; documentation of system reason(s) for not documented and reviewed oxygen saturation◄ **Percentage** of patients aged 18 years and older with the diagnosis of community-acquired bacterial pneumonia with oxygen saturation documented and reviewed **Reporting Instructions:** For patients with appropriate exclusion criteria, report 3028F with modifier 1P, 2P, or 3P	**3028F**	Oxygen saturation results documented and reviewed
Assessment of Mental Status for Community-Acquired Bacterial Pneumonia[5] (Measure #6)—Whether or not the patient aged 18 years and older with the diagnosis of community-acquired bacterial pneumonia had mental status assessed **Numerator:** Patients with mental status assessed **Denominator:** All patients aged 18 years and older with the diagnosis of community-acquired bacterial pneumonia with mental status assessed. (continued)	**2014F**	Mental status assessed

[1]Physician Consortium for Performance Improvement: www.physicianconsortium.org
[2]National Committee on Quality Assurance (NCQA): Health Employer Data Information Set (HEDIS®), www.ncqa.org
[3]Joint Commission on Accreditation of Healthcare Organizations (JCAHO), ORYX Initiative Performance Measures: www.jcaho.org/pms
[4]National Diabetes Quality Improvement Alliance: www.nationaldiabetesalliance.org
[5]Joint measure from the Physician Consortium for Performance Improvement, www.physicianconsortium.org, and National Committee on Quality Assurance (NCQA), www.ncqa.org
[6]The Society of Thoracic Surgeons, www.sts.org, National Quality Forum, www.qualityforum.org

Brief Description of Performance Measure & Source and Reporting Instructions	CPT Category II Code(s)	Code Descriptor
Emergency Medicine (EM), cont'd		
Exclusions: None **Percentage** of patients aged 18 years and older with the diagnosis of community-acquired bacterial pneumonia with mental status assessed **Reporting Instructions:** There are no exclusions for this measure; modifiers 1P, 2P, and 3P may not be used		
Empiric Antibiotic for Community-Acquired Bacterial Pneumonia[5]—Whether or not the patient aged 18 years and older with a diagnosis of community-acquired bacterial pneumonia had an appropriate empiric antibiotic prescribed **Numerator:** Patients with an appropriate empiric antibiotic prescribed Appropriate empiric antibiotic for treatment of community-acquired bacterial pneumonia (CAP) should include any medication from one of the following four drug classes: Fluoroquinolones, Macrolides, Doxycycline, Beta Lactam with Macrolide or Doxycycline (as defined by current ATS/IDSA guidelines). **Denominator:** All patients 18 years and older with the diagnosis of community-acquired bacterial pneumonia **Exclusion(s):** Documentation of physician reason(s) for not prescribing an antibiotic; documentation of patient reason(s) for not prescribing an antibiotic; documentation of system reason(s) for not prescribing an antibiotic **Percentage** of patients aged 18 years and older with the diagnosis of community-acquired bacterial pneumonia with an appropriate empiric antibiotic prescribed **Reporting Instructions:** For patients with appropriate exclusion criteria, report 4045F with modifier 1P, 2P, or 3P	**4045F**	Appropriate empiric antibiotic prescribed
End Stage Renal Disease (ESRD)		
►**Plan of Care for Inadequate Hemodialysis**[1]—Number of calendar months during which a patient aged 18 years and older with a diagnosis of ESRD receiving hemodialysis has Kt/V ≥1.2 OR has Kt/V <1.2 with a documented plan of care **Numerator:** Number of calendar months during which patients aged 18 years and older with a diagnosis of ESRD receiving hemodialysis have Kt/V ≥1.2 OR have Kt/V < 1.2 with a documented plan of care A documented plan of care may include checking for adequacy of the AV access, increasing the blood flow, increasing the dialyzer size, increasing the time of dialysis sessions, adjusting dialysis prescription, or documenting residual renal function. **Denominator:** Calendar months for all patients aged 18 years and older with a diagnosis of ESRD who are receiving hemodialysis **Exclusion(s):** None **Percentage** of calendar months during the 12 month reporting period in which patients aged 18 years and older with a diagnosis of ESRD receiving hemodialysis have a Kt/V ≥ 1.2 OR have a Kt/V < 1.2 with a documented plan of care **Reporting Instructions:** Report this measure during each calendar month a patient is receiving hemodialysis. Report 4052F or 4053F or 4054F for each patient. Report 3082F or 3083F or 3084F for the corresponding Kt/V measurement. If Kt/V < 1.2 (3082F) and patient has a plan of care for inadequate hemodialysis, also report 0505F. There are no performance exclusions for this measure; modifiers 1P, 2P, or 3P may not be used◄	►**0505F** **3082F** **3083F** **3084F** **Denominator Codes:** **4052F** **4053F** **4054F**◄	►Hemodialysis plan of care documented Kt/V less than 1.2 (Clearance of urea [Kt]/volume [V]) Kt/V equal to or greater than 1.2 and less than 1.7 (Clearance of urea [Kt]/volume [V]) Kt/V greater than or equal to 1.7 (Clearance of urea [Kt]/volume [V]) Hemodialysis via functioning arterio-venous (AV) fistula Hemodialysis via functioning arterio-venous (AV) graft Hemodialysis via catheter◄

[1]Physician Consortium for Performance Improvement: www.physicianconsortium.org
[2]National Committee on Quality Assurance (NCQA): Health Employer Data Information Set (HEDIS®), www.ncqa.org
[3]Joint Commission on Accreditation of Healthcare Organizations (JCAHO), ORYX Initiative Performance Measures: www.jcaho.org/pms
[4]National Diabetes Quality Improvement Alliance: www.nationaldiabetesalliance.org
[5]Joint measure from the Physician Consortium for Performance Improvement, www.physicianconsortium.org, and National Committee on Quality Assurance (NCQA), www.ncqa.org
[6]The Society of Thoracic Surgeons, www.sts.org, National Quality Forum, www.qualityforum.org

Brief Description of Performance Measure & Source and Reporting Instructions	CPT Category II Code(s)	Code Descriptor
End Stage Renal Disease (ESRD), cont'd		
►**Plan of Care for Inadequate Peritoneal Dialysis**[1]—Whether or not a patient aged 18 years and older with a diagnosis of ESRD receiving peritoneal dialysis has a Kt/V $\geq$ 1.7 OR has a Kt/V < 1.7 with a documented plan of care at least three times during the 12 month reporting period **Numerator:** Patients who have a Kt/V $\geq$ 1.7 OR have a Kt/V < 1.7 with a documented plan of at least three times during the 12 month reporting period A documented plan of care may include assessing for non-adherence with the peritoneal prescription, sampling, and collection; assessing for error in the peritoneal dialysis prescription and/or inadequate monitoring of the delivered dose; performing peritoneal equilibrium testing; assessing for inadequate patient education; increasing the exchange volume; increasing the number of exchanges per 24 hours; assessing for modality (continuous ambulatory peritoneal dialysis (CAPD) or continuous cyclic peritoneal dialysis (CCPD). **Denominator:** All patients aged 18 years and older with a diagnosis of ESRD receiving peritoneal dialysis **Exclusion(s):** None **Percentage** of patients aged 18 years and older with a diagnosis of ESRD receiving peritoneal dialysis who have a Kt/V $\geq$ 1.7 OR have a Kt/V < 1.7 with a documented plan of care at least three times during the 12 month reporting period **Reporting Instructions:** Report 3082F or 3083F or 3084F for the corresponding Kt/V measurement during the calendar month when patient is receiving peritoneal dialysis. If Kt/V < 1.7 (3082F or 3083F), and patient has a plan of care, also report 0507F. There are no performance exclusions for this measure; modifiers 1P, 2P, or 3P may not be used◄	►**0507F** **3082F** **3083F** **3084F**◄	►Peritoneal dialysis plan of care documented Kt/V < 1.2 (Clearance of urea [Kt]/volume [V]) Kt/V equal to or greater than 1.2 and less than 1.7 (Clearance of urea [Kt]/volume [V]) Kt/V $\geq$ 1.7 (Clearance of urea [Kt]/volume [V]) ◄
►**Influenza Immunization**[1]—Whether or not the patient aged 18 years and older with a diagnosis of ESRD and receiving dialysis received the influenza immunization during the flu season (September through February) **Numerator:** Patients who received the influenza immunization during the flu season (September through February) **Denominator:** All patients aged 18 years and older with a diagnosis of ESRD and receiving dialysis **Exclusion(s):** Documentation of medical, patient, or system reason(s) for patient not receiving the influenza immunization during the flu season (September through February) **Percentage** of patients aged 18 years and older with a diagnosis of ESRD and receiving dialysis who received the influenza immunization during flu season (September through February) **Reporting Instructions:** For patient with appropriate exclusion criteria use 4037F with modifier 1P, 2P, or 3P◄	►**4037F**◄	►Influenza immunization ordered or administered◄
►**Vascular Access-Patients Receiving Hemodialysis**[1]—Whether or not the patient aged 18 years and older with a diagnosis of ESRD and receiving hemodialysis has a functioning AV fistula or is referred for an AV fistula at least once during the 12 month reporting period **Numerator:** Patients who have a functioning AV fistula OR patients who are referred for AV fistula at least once during the 12 month reporting period (continued)	►**4051F** **4052F**	►Referred for an arterio-venous (AV) fistula Hemodialysis via functioning arterio-venous (AV) fistula

[1]Physician Consortium for Performance Improvement: www.physicianconsortium.org
[2]National Committee on Quality Assurance (NCQA): Health Employer Data Information Set (HEDIS®), www.ncqa.org
[3]Joint Commission on Accreditation of Healthcare Organizations (JCAHO), ORYX Initiative Performance Measures: www.jcaho.org/pms
[4]National Diabetes Quality Improvement Alliance: www.nationaldiabetesalliance.org
[5]Joint measure from the Physician Consortium for Performance Improvement, www.physicianconsortium.org, and National Committee on Quality Assurance (NCQA), www.ncqa.org
[6]The Society of Thoracic Surgeons, www.sts.org, National Quality Forum, www.qualityforum.org

Brief Description of Performance Measure & Source and Reporting Instructions	CPT Category II Code(s)	Code Descriptor
End Stage Renal Disease (ESRD), cont'd		
Denominator: All patients aged 18 years and older with a diagnosis of ESRD and receiving hemodialysis **Exclusion(s):** Documentation of medical or patient reason(s) for not having a functioning AV fistula or being referred for an AV fistula (eg, documentation of a functioning AV graft) **Percentage** of patients aged 18 years and older with a diagnosis of ESRD and receiving hemodialysis who have a functioning AV fistula OR patients who are referred for an AV fistula at least once during the 12 month reporting period **Reporting Instructions:** Report 4052F or 4053F or 4054F or 4055F to specify the type of access for each patient receiving hemodialysis If patient is receiving hemodialysis via functioning AV fistula, report 4052F only once; additional codes do not need to be reported. For patient receiving hemodialysis via a catheter, report 4051F if referred for an AV fistula For patient receiving hemodialysis via AV graft, reporting 4053F will exclude patient from measure; 1P or 2P is not required For patient with appropriate exclusion criteria, report 4051F with modifier 1P or 2P◄	**Denominator Codes:** **4052F** **4053F** **4054F** **4055F◄**	 Hemodialysis via functioning arterio-venous (AV) fistula Hemodialysis via functioning arterio-venous (AV) graft Hemodialysis via catheter Patient receiving peritoneal dialysis◄
►Vascular Access-Patients Receiving Hemodialysis with a Permanent Catheter[1]—Whether or not the patient aged 18 years and older with a diagnosis of ESRD receiving hemodialysis with a permanent catheter is referred for evaluation for AV fistula at least once during the 12 month reporting period **Numerator:** Patients who are referred for evaluation for AV fistula at least once during the 12 month reporting period **Denominator:** All patients aged 18 years and older with a diagnosis of ESRD receiving hemodialysis with a permanent catheter **Exclusion(s):** Documentation of medical reason(s) for not being referred for evaluation for AV fistula (eg, documentation of a functioning AV graft, documentation that patient is enrolled in Hospice) Documentation of patient reason(s) for not being referred for evaluation for AV fistula **Percentage** of patients aged 18 years and older with a diagnosis of ESRD receiving hemodialysis with a permanent catheter who are referred for evaluation for AV fistula at least once during the 12 month reporting period **Reporting Instructions:** Report 4052F or 4053F or 4054F or 4055F for each patient. If patient has a permanent catheter (4054F) and has been referred for evaluation for AV fistula, also report 4051F. For patient with appropriate exclusion criteria, report 4051F with modifier 1P or 2P. For patient receiving hemodialysis via AV graft, reporting 4053F alone will exclude patient from measure; 1P or 2P is not required◄	**►4051F** **Denominator Codes:** **4052F** **4053F** **4054F** **4055F◄**	►Referred for an arterio-venous (AV) fistula Hemodialysis via functioning arterio-venous (AV) fistula Hemodialysis via functioning arterio-venous (AV) graft Hemodialysis via catheter Patient receiving peritoneal dialysis◄
►Plan of Care for Anemia[1]—Number of calendar months during which a patient with a diagnosis of ESRD receiving dialysis had a hemoglobin (Hgb) ≥ 11 g/dL OR had a Hgb < 11 g/dL with a documented plan of care **Numerator:** Number of calendar months during which patients have a Hgb ≥ 11 g/dL OR have a Hgb < 11 with a documented plan of care (continued)	**►3279F** **3280F**	►Hemoglobin level greater than or equal to 13 g/dL Hemoglobin level 11 g/dL to 12.9 g/dL

[1]Physician Consortium for Performance Improvement: www.physicianconsortium.org
[2]National Committee on Quality Assurance (NCQA): Health Employer Data Information Set (HEDIS®), www.ncqa.org
[3]Joint Commission on Accreditation of Healthcare Organizations (JCAHO), ORYX Initiative Performance Measures: www.jcaho.org/pms
[4]National Diabetes Quality Improvement Alliance: www.nationaldiabetesalliance.org
[5]Joint measure from the Physician Consortium for Performance Improvement, www.physicianconsortium.org, and National Committee on Quality Assurance (NCQA), www.ncqa.org
[6]The Society of Thoracic Surgeons, www.sts.org, National Quality Forum, www.qualityforum.org

Brief Description of Performance Measure & Source and Reporting Instructions	CPT Category II Code(s)	Code Descriptor
End Stage Renal Disease (ESRD), cont'd		
Denominator: Calendar months during which all patients aged 18 years and older with a diagnosis of ESRD are receiving dialysis **Exclusion(s):** None Percentage of calendar months during the 12 month reporting period in which patients aged 18 years and older with a diagnosis of ESRD who are receiving dialysis have a Hgb ≥ 11 g/dL OR have a Hgb < 11 g/dL with a documented plan of care **Reporting Instructions:** Report this measure for each calendar month a patient is receiving dialysis Report the code that corresponds to the hemoglobin value. If hemoglobin < 11 g/dL (3281F) and patient has a documented plan of care, also report 0516F. There are no performance exclusions for this measure; modifiers 1P, 2P, or 3P may not be used◄	**3281F** **0516F◄**	Hemoglobin level less than 11 g/dL Anemia plan of care documented◄
Eye Care (EC)		
Primary Open-Angle Glaucoma: Optic Nerve Evaluation[5]—Whether or not the patient aged 18 years and older with a diagnosis of primary open-angle glaucoma had an optic nerve head evaluation during one or more office visits within 12 months **Numerator:** Patients who have an optic nerve head evaluation during one or more office visits within 12 months **Denominator:** All patients aged 18 years and older with a diagnosis of primary open-angle glaucoma **Exclusion(s):** Documentation of medical reason(s) for not performing an optic nerve head evaluation **Percentage** of patients aged 18 years and older with a diagnosis of primary open-angle glaucoma who have an optic nerve head evaluation during one or more office visits within 12 months **Reporting Instructions:** For patients with appropriate exclusion criteria, report 2027F with modifier 1P Modifier 1P may also be used if physician is asked to report on this measure but is not the physician providing the primary management of primary open angle glaucoma	**2027F**	Optic nerve head evaluation performed
►Primary Open-Angle Glaucoma: Reduction of Intraocular Pressure (IOP) by 15% OR Documentation of a Plan of Care[5]—Whether or not the patient aged 18 years and older with a diagnosis of primary open-angle glaucoma whose glaucoma treatment has not failed (the most recent IOP was reduced by at least 15% from the pre-intervention level) OR if the most recent IOP was not reduced by at least 15% from the pre-intervention level a plan of care was documented within 12 months **Numerator:** Patients whose glaucoma treatment has not failed (the most recent IOP was reduced by at least 15% from the pre-intervention level) OR if the most recent IOP was not reduced by at least 15% from the pre-intervention level a plan of care was documented within 12 months Plan of care may include: recheck of IOP at specified time, change in therapy, perform additional diagnostic evaluations, monitoring per patient decisions or unable to achieve due to health system reasons, and/or referral to a specialist (continued)	**►0517F** **3284F** **3285F◄**	►Glaucoma plan of care documented Intraocular pressure (IOP) reduced by a value of greater than or equal to 15% from the pre-intervention level Intraocular pressure (IOP) reduced by a value less than 15% from the pre-intervention level◄

[1]Physician Consortium for Performance Improvement: www.physicianconsortium.org
[2]National Committee on Quality Assurance (NCQA): Health Employer Data Information Set (HEDIS®), www.ncqa.org
[3]Joint Commission on Accreditation of Healthcare Organizations (JCAHO), ORYX Initiative Performance Measures: www.jcaho.org/pms
[4]National Diabetes Quality Improvement Alliance: www.nationaldiabetesalliance.org
[5]Joint measure from the Physician Consortium for Performance Improvement, www.physicianconsortium.org, and National Committee on Quality Assurance (NCQA), www.ncqa.org
[6]The Society of Thoracic Surgeons, www.sts.org, National Quality Forum, www.qualityforum.org

Brief Description of Performance Measure & Source and Reporting Instructions	CPT Category II Code(s)	Code Descriptor
Eye Care (EC), cont'd		
Denominator: All patients aged 18 years and older with a diagnosis of primary open-angle glaucoma **Exclusion(s):** Documentation of system reason(s) for not reducing the IOP by at least 15% from the pre-intervention level or documenting a plan of care Percentage of patients aged 18 years and older with a diagnosis of primary open-angle glaucoma whose glaucoma treatment has not failed (the most recent IOP was reduced by at least 15% from the pre-intervention level) OR if the most recent IOP was not reduced by at least 15% from the pre-intervention level a plan of care was documented within 12 months **Reporting Instructions:** Report 3284F or 3285F for each patient. If Intraocular pressure (IOP) is reduced by a value less than 15% from the pre-intervention level and there is a plan of care documented, also report 0517F For patient with appropriate exclusion criteria, report 0517F with modifier 3P. The system reason exclusion may be used if a physician is asked to report on this measure but is not the ophthalmologist or optometrist providing the primary management for primary open-angle glaucoma◄		
Age-Related Eye Disease Study (AREDS): AREDS Formulation Prescribed/Recommended[5]—Whether or not the patient aged 50 years and older with a diagnosis of age-related macular degeneration had the AREDS formulation prescribed/recommended within 12 months **Numerator:** Patients who had the AREDS formulation prescribed/recommended within 12 months **Denominator:** All patients aged 50 years and older with a diagnosis of age-related macular degeneration **Exclusion(s):** Documentation of medical reason(s) for not prescribing/recommending antioxidant vitamin or mineral supplements the AREDS formulation (eg, mild AMD, patient smokes, patient does not meet criteria for antioxidant vitamin or mineral supplements as outlined in the Age-Related Eye Disease Study) **Percentage** of patients aged 50 years and older with a diagnosis of age-related macular degeneration who had the AREDS formulation prescribed/recommended within 12 months **Reporting Instructions:** For patients with appropriate exclusion criteria, report 4007F with modifier 1P Report 4007F with 1P modifier for patient with mild AMD Modifier 1P may be used if physician is asked to report on this measure but is not the physician providing the primary management of AMD	**4007F**	Age-Related Eye Disease Study (AREDS) formulation prescribed or recommended
Age-Related Macular Degeneration: Dilated Macular Examination[5]—Whether or not the patient aged 50 years and older with a diagnosis of age-related macular degeneration had a dilated macular examination performed which included documentation of the presence or absence of macular thickening or hemorrhage AND the level of macular degeneration severity during one or more office visits within 12 months **Numerator:** Patients who had a dilated macular examination performed which included documentation of the presence or absence of macular thickening or hemorrhage AND the level of macular degeneration severity during one or more office visits within 12 months (continued)	**2019F**	Dilated macular exam performed, including documentation of the presence or absence of macular thickening or hemorrhage AND the level of macular degeneration severity

[1]Physician Consortium for Performance Improvement: www.physicianconsortium.org
[2]National Committee on Quality Assurance (NCQA): Health Employer Data Information Set (HEDIS®), www.ncqa.org
[3]Joint Commission on Accreditation of Healthcare Organizations (JCAHO), ORYX Initiative Performance Measures: www.jcaho.org/pms
[4]National Diabetes Quality Improvement Alliance: www.nationaldiabetesalliance.org
[5]Joint measure from the Physician Consortium for Performance Improvement, www.physicianconsortium.org, and National Committee on Quality Assurance (NCQA), www.ncqa.org
[6]The Society of Thoracic Surgeons, www.sts.org, National Quality Forum, www.qualityforum.org

Brief Description of Performance Measure & Source and Reporting Instructions	CPT Category II Code(s)	Code Descriptor
Eye Care (EC), cont'd		
Denominator: All patients aged 50 years and older with a diagnosis of age-related macular degeneration **Exclusion(s):** Documentation of medical or patient reason(s) for not performing a dilated macular examination **Percentage** of patients aged 50 years and older with a diagnosis of age-related macular degeneration who had a dilated macular examination performed which included documentation of the presence or absence of macular thickening or hemorrhage AND the level of macular degeneration severity during one or more office visits within 12 months **Reporting Instructions:** For patient with appropriate exclusion criteria, report 2019F with modifier 1P or 2P Modifier 1P may also be used if physician is asked to report on this measure but is not the physician providing the primary management of AMD		
Cataracts: Assessment of Visual Functional Status[5]—Whether or not the patient aged 18 years and older with a diagnosis of cataract(s) was assessed for visual functional status during one or more office visits within 12 months **Numerator:** Patients who were assessed for visual functional status during one or more office visits within 12 months Medical record must include: Documentation that patient is operating well with vision or not operating well with vision based on discussion with the patient OR Documentation of use of a standardized scale or completion of an assessment questionnaire [eg, VF-14, ADVS (Activities of Daily Vision Scale), or VFQ (Visual Function Questionnaire)] **Denominator:** All patients aged 18 years and older with a diagnosis of cataract(s) **Exclusion(s):** Documentation of medical reason(s) for not assessing for visual functional status **Percentage** of patients aged 18 years and older with a diagnosis of cataract(s) who were assessed for visual functional status during one or more office visits within 12 months **Reporting Instructions:** For patient with appropriate exclusion criteria, report 1055F with modifier 1P Modifier 1P may be used if physician is asked to report on this measure but is not the physician providing the primary management for cataract(s)	**1055F**	Visual functional status assessed
Cataracts: Documentation of Pre-Surgical Axial Length, Corneal Power Measurement and Method of Intraocular Lens Power Calculation[5]—Whether or not the patient aged 18 years and older who had cataract surgery had documentation of pre-surgical axial length, corneal power measurement and method of intraocular lens power calculation performed and documented within six months prior to the procedure **Numerator:** Patients who had the pre-surgical axial length, corneal power measurement and method of intraocular lens power calculation performed and documented within six months prior to the procedure **Denominator:** All patients aged 18 years and older who had cataract surgery (continued)	**3073F**	Pre-surgical (cataract) axial length, corneal power measurement and method of intraocular lens power calculation documented (must be performed within six months prior to surgery)

[1]Physician Consortium for Performance Improvement: www.physicianconsortium.org
[2]National Committee on Quality Assurance (NCQA): Health Employer Data Information Set (HEDIS®), www.ncqa.org
[3]Joint Commission on Accreditation of Healthcare Organizations (JCAHO), ORYX Initiative Performance Measures: www.jcaho.org/pms
[4]National Diabetes Quality Improvement Alliance: www.nationaldiabetesalliance.org
[5]Joint measure from the Physician Consortium for Performance Improvement, www.physicianconsortium.org, and National Committee on Quality Assurance (NCQA), www.ncqa.org
[6]The Society of Thoracic Surgeons, www.sts.org, National Quality Forum, www.qualityforum.org

Brief Description of Performance Measure & Source and Reporting Instructions	CPT Category II Code(s)	Code Descriptor
Eye Care (EC), cont'd		
Exclusion(s): Documentation of medical reason(s) for not performing the pre-surgical axial length, corneal power measurement and method of intraocular lens power calculation **Percentage** of patients aged 18 years and older who had cataract surgery who had documentation of pre-surgical axial length, corneal power measurement and method of intraocular lens power calculation performed and documented within six months prior to the procedure **Reporting Instructions:** For patients with appropriate exclusion criteria, report 3073F with modifier 1P		
Diabetic Retinopathy: Documentation of Presence or Absence of Macular Edema and Level of Severity of Retinopathy[5]—Whether or not the patient aged 18 years and older with a diagnosis of diabetic retinopathy had a dilated macular or fundus exam performed which included documentation of the level of severity of retinopathy AND the presence or absence of macular edema during one or more office visits within 12 months **Numerator:** Patients who had a dilated macular or fundus exam performed which included documentation of the level of severity of retinopathy AND the presence or absence of macular edema during one or more office visits within 12 months Medical record must include: Documentation of the level of severity of retinopathy (eg, background diabetic retinopathy, proliferative diabetic retinopathy, nonproliferative diabetic retinopathy) AND Documentation of whether macular edema was present or absent **Denominator:** All patients aged 18 years and older with a diagnosis of diabetic retinopathy **Exclusion(s):** Documentation of medical or patient reason(s) for not receiving a dilated macular or fundus examination **Percentage** of patients aged 18 years and older with a diagnosis of diabetic retinopathy who had a dilated macular or fundus exam performed which included documentation of the level of severity of retinopathy AND the presence or absence of macular edema during one or more office visits within 12 months **Reporting Instructions:** For patients with appropriate exclusion criteria, report 2021F with modifier 1P or 2P Modifier 1P may be used if physician is asked to report on this measure but is not the physician providing the primary management of diabetic retinopathy	**2021F**	Dilated macular or fundus exam performed, including documentation of the presence or absence of macular edema AND level of severity of retinopathy
Diabetic Retinopathy: Communication with the Physician Managing Ongoing Diabetes Care[5]—Whether or not the patient aged 18 years and older with a diagnosis of diabetic retinopathy who had a dilated macular or fundus exam performed had documented communication to the physician who manages the ongoing care of the patient with diabetes regarding the findings of the dilated macular or fundus exam at least once within 12 months (continued)	**5010F**	Findings of dilated macular or fundus exam communicated to the physician managing the diabetes care

[1]Physician Consortium for Performance Improvement: www.physicianconsortium.org
[2]National Committee on Quality Assurance (NCQA): Health Employer Data Information Set (HEDIS®), www.ncqa.org
[3]Joint Commission on Accreditation of Healthcare Organizations (JCAHO), ORYX Initiative Performance Measures: www.jcaho.org/pms
[4]National Diabetes Quality Improvement Alliance: www.nationaldiabetesalliance.org
[5]Joint measure from the Physician Consortium for Performance Improvement, www.physicianconsortium.org, and National Committee on Quality Assurance (NCQA), www.ncqa.org
[6]The Society of Thoracic Surgeons, www.sts.org, National Quality Forum, www.qualityforum.org

Brief Description of Performance Measure & Source and Reporting Instructions	CPT Category II Code(s)	Code Descriptor
Eye Care (EC), cont'd		
Numerator: Patients with documentation, at least once within 12 months, of communication of the findings of the dilated macular or fundus exam to the physician who manages the patient's diabetic care Documentation in the medical record indicating that the results of the macular or fundus exam were communicated (eg, verbally, or by letter) with the physician managing the patient's diabetic care OR A copy of a letter in the medical record to the physician managing the patient's diabetic care outlining the findings of the dilated macular or fundus exam. **Denominator:** All patients aged 18 years and older with a diagnosis of diabetic retinopathy who had a dilated macular or fundus exam performed **Exclusion(s):** Documentation of medical reason(s) for not communicating the findings of the macular or fundus exam to the physician who manages the ongoing care of the patient with diabetes Documentation of patient reason(s) for not communicating the findings of the macular or fundus exam to the physician who manages the ongoing care of the patient with diabetes **Percentage** of patients aged 18 years and older with a diagnosis of diabetic retinopathy who had a dilated macular or fundus exam performed with documented communication to the physician who manages the ongoing care of the patient with diabetes regarding the findings of the dilated macular or fundus exam at least once within 12 months **Reporting Instructions:** • Report 2021F for each patient who had a dilated macular or fundus exam performed meeting the denominator inclusion. Do not report 5010F without a modifier unless reporting 2021F. Also report 5010F where findings of dilated macular or fundus exam communicated to the physician managing the diabetes care; for patients with appropriate exclusion criteria, report 5010F with modifier 1P or 2P • Modifier 1P may be used if physician is asked to report on this measure but is not the physician providing the primary management of diabetic retinopathy	**Denominator Code:** **2021F**	Dilated macular or fundus exam performed, including documentation of the presence or absence of macular edema AND level of severity of retinopathy
►**Primary Open-Angle Glaucoma: Counseling on Glaucoma**[5]—Whether or not the patient aged 18 years and older with a diagnosis of primary open-angle glaucoma or his/her caregiver(s) were counseled within 12 months about (1) the potential impact of glaucoma on visual functioning and quality of life, and (2) the importance of treatment adherence **Numerator:** Patients or their caregiver(s) who were counseled within 12 months about (1) the potential impact of glaucoma on their visual functioning and quality of life and (2) the importance of treatment adherence **Denominator:** All patients aged 18 years and older with a diagnosis of primary open-angle glaucoma **Exclusion(s):** Documentation of medical reason(s) for not providing counseling to the patient or caregiver(s) (eg, patient has impaired mental status and no caregiver) Documentation of system reason(s) for not providing counseling to the patient or caregiver(s) (continued)	**►4174F◄**	►Counseling about the potential impact of glaucoma on visual functioning and quality of life, and importance of treatment adherence provided to patient and/or caregiver(s)◄

[1]Physician Consortium for Performance Improvement: www.physicianconsortium.org
[2]National Committee on Quality Assurance (NCQA): Health Employer Data Information Set (HEDIS®), www.ncqa.org
[3]Joint Commission on Accreditation of Healthcare Organizations (JCAHO), ORYX Initiative Performance Measures: www.jcaho.org/pms
[4]National Diabetes Quality Improvement Alliance: www.nationaldiabetesalliance.org
[5]Joint measure from the Physician Consortium for Performance Improvement, www.physicianconsortium.org, and National Committee on Quality Assurance (NCQA), www.ncqa.org
[6]The Society of Thoracic Surgeons, www.sts.org, National Quality Forum, www.qualityforum.org

Brief Description of Performance Measure & Source and Reporting Instructions	CPT Category II Code(s)	Code Descriptor
Eye Care (EC), cont'd		
Percentage of patients aged 18 years and older with a diagnosis of primary open-angle glaucoma or their caregiver(s) who were counseled within 12 months about 1) the potential impact of glaucoma on visual functioning and quality of life, and 2) the importance of treatment adherence **Reporting Instructions:** For patient with appropriate exclusion criteria, report 4174F with modifier 1P or 3P. The system reason exclusion may be used if a physician is asked to report on this measure but is not the physician providing the primary management for primary open-angle glaucoma◄		
►**Cataracts: 20/40 or Better Visual Acuity within 90 Days Following Cataract Surgery**[5]—Whether or not the patient aged 18 years and older who had cataract surgery and no significant ocular conditions impacting the visual outcome of surgery had best-corrected visual acuity of 20/40 or better (distance or near) achieved within 90 days following the cataract surgery **Numerator:** Patients who had best-corrected visual acuity of 20/40 or better (distance or near) achieved within 90 days following cataract surgery **Denominator:** All patients aged 18 years and older who had cataract surgery and no significant pre-operative ocular conditions impacting the visual outcome of surgery **Exclusion(s):** Patients with comorbid conditions that impact the visual outcome of surgery (see measure technical specifications for a detailed list of conditions) **Percentage** of patients aged 18 years and older who had cataract surgery and no significant pre-operative ocular conditions impacting the visual outcome of surgery and had best-corrected visual acuity of 20/40 or better (distance or near) achieved within 90 days following the cataract surgery **Reporting Instructions:** Performance exclusions for this measure are obtained using ICD-9 diagnosis codes (see measure technical specifications for detailed list of qualifying conditions); modifiers 1P, 2P, or 3P may not be used◄	**►4175F◄**	►Best-corrected visual acuity of 20/40 or better (distance or near) achieved within the 90 days following cataract surgery◄
►**Cataracts: Comprehensive Pre-operative Assessment for Cataract Surgery with Intraocular Lens (IOL) Placement**[5]—Whether or not the patient aged 18 years and older who had cataract surgery with intraocular lens (IOL) placement received a comprehensive preoperative assessment of (1) dilated fundus exam, (2) axial length, corneal keratometry measurement and method of IOL power calculation; and (3) functional or medical indication(s) for surgery prior to the cataract surgery with IOL placement within 12 months prior to cataract surgery **Numerator:** Patients who received a comprehensive preoperative assessment of (1) dilated fundus exam, (2) axial length, corneal keratometry measurement and method of IOL power calculation; and (3) functional or medical indication(s) for surgery prior to the cataract surgery with IOL placement within 12 months prior to cataract surgery **Denominator:** All patients aged 18 years and older who had cataract surgery with IOL placement (continued)	**►0014F** **2020F** **3073F**	►Comprehensive preoperative assessment performed for cataract surgery with intraocular lens (IOL) placement Dilated fundus evaluation performed within 12 months prior to cataract surgery Pre-surgical (cataract) axial length, corneal power measurement and method of intraocular lens power calculation documented (must be performed within 12 months prior to surgery)

[1]Physician Consortium for Performance Improvement: www.physicianconsortium.org
[2]National Committee on Quality Assurance (NCQA): Health Employer Data Information Set (HEDIS®), www.ncqa.org
[3]Joint Commission on Accreditation of Healthcare Organizations (JCAHO), ORYX Initiative Performance Measures: www.jcaho.org/pms
[4]National Diabetes Quality Improvement Alliance: www.nationaldiabetesalliance.org
[5]Joint measure from the Physician Consortium for Performance Improvement, www.physicianconsortium.org, and National Committee on Quality Assurance (NCQA), www.ncqa.org
[6]The Society of Thoracic Surgeons, www.sts.org, National Quality Forum, www.qualityforum.org

Brief Description of Performance Measure & Source and Reporting Instructions	CPT Category II Code(s)	Code Descriptor
Eye Care (EC), cont'd		
Exclusion(s): None **Percentage** of patients aged 18 years and older with a procedure of cataract surgery with IOL placement who received a comprehensive preoperative assessment of 1) dilated fundus exam, 2) axial length, corneal keratometry measurement, and method of IOL power calculation; and 3) functional or medical indication(s) for surgery prior to the cataract surgery with IOL placement within 12 months prior to cataract surgery **Reporting Instructions:** If all three components of the numerator are performed, report composite code 0014F for this measure If fewer than all three components are performed, report only the code(s) for the components that have been performed There are no performance exclusions for this measure; modifiers 1P, 2P, or 3P may not be used◄	**3325F◄**	Preoperative assessment of functional or medical indication(s) for surgery prior to the cataract surgery with intraocular lens placement (must be performed within twelve months prior to cataract surgery)◄
►**Age-Related Macular Degeneration (AMD): Counseling on Antioxidant Supplement**[5]—Whether or not the patient aged 50 years and older with a diagnosis of age-related macular degeneration (AMD) and/or his/her caregiver(s) were counseled within 12 months on the benefits and/or risks of the Age-Related Eye Disease Study (AREDS) formulation for preventing progression of AMD **Numerator:** Patients and/or their caregiver(s) who were counseled within 12 months on the benefits and/or risks of the AREDS formulation for preventing progression of AMD **Denominator:** All patients aged 50 years and older with a diagnosis of age-related macular degeneration **Exclusion(s):** Documentation of system reason(s) for not counseling the patient and/or caregiver(s) on the benefits and/or risks of the AREDS formulation **Percentage** of patients aged 50 years and older with a diagnosis of age-related macular degeneration and/or their caregiver(s) who were counseled within 12 months on the benefits and/or risks of the AREDS formulation for preventing progression of AMD **Reporting Instructions:** For patient with appropriate exclusion criteria, report 4177F with modifier 3P. The system reason exclusion may be used if a physician is asked to report on this measure but is not the physician providing the primary management for age-related macular degeneration◄	**►4177F◄**	►Counseling about the benefits and/or risks of the Age-Related Eye Disease Study (AREDS) formulation for preventing progression of age-related macular degeneration (AMD) provided to patient and/or caregiver(s)◄
Gastroesophageal Reflux Disease (GERD)		
Assessment for Alarm Symptoms[5]—Whether or not the patient aged 18 years and older with diagnosis of GERD, seen for an initial evaluation, was assessed for the presence or absence of the following alarm symptoms: involuntary weight loss, dysphagia, and GI bleeding **Numerator:** Patients who were assessed for the presence or absence of the following alarm symptoms: involuntary weight loss, dysphagia, and GI bleeding **Denominator:** All patients aged 18 years and older with the diagnosis of GERD, seen for an initial evaluation **Exclusion(s):** Documentation of medical reason(s) for not assessing for alarm symptoms. **Percentage** of patients aged 18 years and older with a diagnosis of GERD, seen for an initial evaluation, who were assessed for the presence or absence of the following alarm symptoms: involuntary weight loss, dysphagia, and GI bleeding **Reporting Instructions:** Report either 1070F or 1071F when alarm symptoms assessed. For patient with appropriate exclusion criteria, report 1070F with modifier 1P	**1070F** **1071F**	Alarm symptoms (involuntary weight loss, dysphagia, or gastrointestinal bleeding) assessed; none present Alarm symptoms (involuntary weight loss, dysphagia, or gastrointestinal bleeding) assessed; one or more present

[1]Physician Consortium for Performance Improvement: www.physicianconsortium.org
[2]National Committee on Quality Assurance (NCQA): Health Employer Data Information Set (HEDIS®), www.ncqa.org
[3]Joint Commission on Accreditation of Healthcare Organizations (JCAHO), ORYX Initiative Performance Measures: www.jcaho.org/pms
[4]National Diabetes Quality Improvement Alliance: www.nationaldiabetesalliance.org
[5]Joint measure from the Physician Consortium for Performance Improvement, www.physicianconsortium.org, and National Committee on Quality Assurance (NCQA), www.ncqa.org
[6]The Society of Thoracic Surgeons, www.sts.org, National Quality Forum, www.qualityforum.org

Brief Description of Performance Measure & Source and Reporting Instructions	CPT Category II Code(s)	Code Descriptor
Gastroesophageal Reflux Disease (GERD), cont'd		
Upper Endoscopy for Patients with Alarm Symptoms[5]—Whether or not the patient aged 18 years and older with a diagnosis of GERD, seen for an initial evaluation, with documentation of at least one alarm symptom was either referred for upper endoscopy or had an upper endoscopy performed **Numerator:** Patients who were either referred for an upper endoscopy or had an upper endoscopy performed **Denominator:** All patients aged 18 years and older with a diagnosis of GERD, seen for an initial evaluation, with documentation of at least one alarm symptom **(involuntary weight loss, dysphagia, or GI bleeding)** **Exclusion(s):** Documentation of medical, patient, or system reason(s) for not referring for or not performing an upper endoscopy **Percentage** of patients aged 18 years and older with a diagnosis of GERD, seen for an initial evaluation, with at least one alarm symptom, who were either referred for an upper endoscopy or had an upper endoscopy performed **Reporting Instructions:** Report 1070F or 1071F for each patient. If patient had documentation of at least one GERD alarm symptom and had upper endoscopy performed, report 3130F or the corresponding Category I code. If patient had documentation of at least one GERD alarm symptom and was referred for upper endoscopy, report 3132F. For patient with appropriate exclusion criteria, report either 3130F or 3132F with modifier 1P, 2P, or 3P	**3130F** **3132F** **Denominator Codes:** **1070F** **1071F**	Upper gastrointestinal endoscopy performed Documentation of referral for upper gastrointestinal endoscopy Alarm symptoms (involuntary weight loss, dysphagia, or gastrointestinal bleeding) assessed; none present Alarm symptoms (involuntary weight loss, dysphagia, or gastrointestinal bleeding) assessed; one or more present
Biopsy for Barrett's Esophagus[5]—Whether or not the patient aged 18 years and older with a diagnosis of GERD or heartburn whose endoscopy report indicates a suspicion of Barrett's esophagus had a forceps esophageal biopsy performed **Numerator:** Patients who had a forceps esophageal biopsy performed **Denominator:** All patients aged 18 years and older with a diagnosis of GERD or heartburn whose endoscopy report indicates a suspicion of Barrett's esophagus **Exclusion(s):** Documentation of medical reason(s) for not performing a forceps esophageal biopsy **Percentage** of patients aged 18 years and older with a diagnosis of GERD or heartburn whose endoscopy report indicates a suspicion of Barrett's esophagus who had a forceps esophageal biopsy performed **Reporting Instructions:** This measure should be reported by the physician performing the endoscopy Report 3140F or 3141F for each patient If endoscopy report included documentation that Barrett's esophagus was suspected, also report 3150F if patient had esophageal biopsy performed. For patient with appropriate exclusion criteria, report 3150F with modifier 1P	**3150F** **Denominator Codes:** **3140F** **3141F**	Forceps esophageal biopsy performed Upper gastrointestinal endoscopy report indicates suspicion of Barrett's esophagus Upper gastrointestinal endoscopy report indicates no suspicion of Barrett's esophagus
Barium Swallow–Inappropriate Use[5]—Whether or not the patient aged 18 years and older seen for an initial evaluation of GERD did not have a Barium swallow test ordered **Numerator:** Patients who did not have Barium swallow test ordered **Denominator:** All patients aged 18 years and older seen for an initial evaluation of GERD **Exclusion(s):** Documentation of medical reason(s) for ordering a Barium swallow test **Percentage**of patients aged 18 years and older seen for an initial evaluation of GERD who did not have a Barium swallow test ordered (continued)	**3142F** **3200F**	Barium swallow test ordered Barium swallow test not ordered

[1]Physician Consortium for Performance Improvement: www.physicianconsortium.org
[2]National Committee on Quality Assurance (NCQA): Health Employer Data Information Set (HEDIS®), www.ncqa.org
[3]Joint Commission on Accreditation of Healthcare Organizations (JCAHO), ORYX Initiative Performance Measures: www.jcaho.org/pms
[4]National Diabetes Quality Improvement Alliance: www.nationaldiabetesalliance.org
[5]Joint measure from the Physician Consortium for Performance Improvement, www.physicianconsortium.org, and National Committee on Quality Assurance (NCQA), www.ncqa.org
[6]The Society of Thoracic Surgeons, www.sts.org, National Quality Forum, www.qualityforum.org

Brief Description of Performance Measure & Source and Reporting Instructions	CPT Category II Code(s)	Code Descriptor
Gastroesophageal Reflux Disease (GERD) , cont'd		
Reporting Instructions: If barium swallow test was ordered at initial evaluation for GERD, report 3142F. If barium swallow was not ordered at initial evaluation, report 3200F. If there is documentation that supports the reason for ordering a barium swallow, report 3142F with modifier 1P		
►Gastroesophageal Reflux Disease (GERD) Continuous Medication Therapy - Assessment of GERD Symptoms[5]—Whether or not the patient aged 18 years and older with a diagnosis of GERD who has been prescribed continuous proton pump inhibitor (PPI) or histamine H2 receptor antagonist (H2RA) therapy had an annual assessment of his/her GERD symptoms after 12 months of therapy **Numerator:** Patients who had an annual assessment of their GERD symptoms after 12 months of therapy **Denominator:** All patients aged 18 years and older with a diagnosis of GERD who have been prescribed continuous proton pump inhibitor (PPI) or histamine H2 receptor antagonist (H2RA) therapy* ***Continuous therapy is defined as proton pump inhibitor (PPI) or histamine H2 receptor antagonist (H2RA) therapy lasting twelve months or more to treat GERD** **Exclusion(s):** Documentation of medical reason(s) for not assessing GERD symptoms **Percentage** of patients aged 18 years and older with the diagnosis of GERD who have been prescribed continuous proton pump inhibitor (PPI) or histamine H2 receptor antagonist (H2RA) therapy who received an annual assessment of their GERD symptoms after 12 months of therapy **Reporting Instructions:** Report 4185F or 4186F for each patient. If patient is receiving continuous (12-months) proton pump inhibitor (PPI) or histamine H2 receptor antagonist (H2RA) therapy and has had GERD symptoms assessed annually after 12 months of therapy, report 1118F. For patient with appropriate exclusion criteria use 1118F with modifier 1P◄	**►1118F** **Denominator Codes:** **4185F** **4186F◄**	►GERD symptoms assessed after 12 months of therapy Continuous (12-months) therapy with proton pump inhibitor (PPI) or histamine H2 receptor antagonist (H2RA) received No continuous (12-months) therapy with either proton pump inhibitor (PPI) or histamine H2 receptor antagonist (H2RA) received◄
Geriatrics (GER)		
Medication Reconciliation[5]—Whether or not the patient aged 65 years and older discharged from any inpatient facility (eg, hospital, skilled nursing facility, or rehabilitation facility) and seen within 60 days following discharge in the office by the physician providing on-going care had a reconciliation of the discharge medications with the current medication list in the outpatient medical record documented **Numerator:** Patients who had a reconciliation of the discharge medications with the current medication list in the outpatient medical record documented **Denominator:** All patients aged 65 years and older discharged from any inpatient facility (eg, hospital, skilled nursing facility, or rehabilitation facility) and seen within 60 days following discharge in the office by the physician providing on-going care **Exclusion(s):** None **Percentage** of patients aged 65 years and older discharged from any inpatient facility (eg, hospital, skilled nursing facility, or rehabilitation facility) and seen within 60 days following discharge in the office by the physician providing on-going care who had a reconciliation of the discharge medications with the current medication list in the medical record documented (continued)	**1111F** **Denominator Code** **1110F**	Discharge medications reconciled with the current medication list in outpatient medical record Patient discharged from an inpatient facility (eg hospital, skilled nursing facility, or rehabilitation facility) within the last 60 days

[1]Physician Consortium for Performance Improvement: www.physicianconsortium.org
[2]National Committee on Quality Assurance (NCQA): Health Employer Data Information Set (HEDIS®), www.ncqa.org
[3]Joint Commission on Accreditation of Healthcare Organizations (JCAHO), ORYX Initiative Performance Measures: www.jcaho.org/pms
[4]National Diabetes Quality Improvement Alliance: www.nationaldiabetesalliance.org
[5]Joint measure from the Physician Consortium for Performance Improvement, www.physicianconsortium.org, and National Committee on Quality Assurance (NCQA), www.ncqa.org
[6]The Society of Thoracic Surgeons, www.sts.org, National Quality Forum, www.qualityforum.org

Brief Description of Performance Measure & Source and Reporting Instructions	CPT Category II Code(s)	Code Descriptor
Geriatrics (GER), cont'd		
Reporting Instructions: Report only for patients who were discharged from an inpatient facility (eg hospital, skilled nursing facility, or rehabilitation facility) within the last 60 days If there is documentation of reconcilation of discharge medications with the current medication list, report 1111F. There are no exclusions; modifiers 1P, 2P and 3P may not be used		
►**Advance Care Plan**[5]—Whether or not the patient aged 65 years and older has an advance care plan or surrogate decision maker documented in the medical record or documentation in the medical record that an advance care plan was discussed but patient did not wish or was not able to name a surrogate decision maker or provide an advance care plan **Numerator:** Patients who have an advance care plan or surrogate decision maker documented in the medical record or documentation in the medical record that an advance care plan was discussed but patient did not wish or was not able to name a surrogate decision maker or provide an advance care plan **Definition: For the purposes of this measure, "documentation that patient did not wish or was not able to name a surrogate decision or provide an advance care plan" may also include, as appropriate, the following:** That the patient's cultural and/or spiritual beliefs preclude a discussion of advance care planning, as it would be viewed as harmful to the patient's beliefs and thus harmful to the physician-patient relationship **Denominator:** All patients aged 65 years and older **Exclusion(s):** None **Percentage** of patients aged 65 years and older who have an advance care plan or surrogate decision maker documented in the medical record or documentation in the medical record that an advance care plan was discussed but patient did not wish or was not able to name a surrogate decision maker or provide an advance care plan **Reporting Instructions:** Report 1123F or 1124F for each patient. If patient's cultural and/or spiritual beliefs preclude a discussion of advance care planning, report 1124F. There are no performance exclusions for this measure; modifiers 1P, 2P or 3P may not be used. The reporting physician does not need to be the physician who documented or discussed advance care planning with the patient but it must be in the medical record at the time of reporting **Note: This measure applies to all healthcare settings (eg, inpatient, nursing home, ambulatory). For each of these settings, there should be documentation in the medical record(s) that advance care planning was discussed or documented◄**	►**1123F** **1124F◄**	►Advance Care Planning discussed and documented, advance care plan or surrogate decision maker documented in the medical record Advance Care Planning discussed and documented in the medical record, patient did not wish or was not able to name a surrogate decision maker or provide an advance care plan◄
Assessment of Presence or Absence of Urinary Incontinence in Women Aged 65 Years and Older[5]—Whether or not the female patient aged 65 years and older was assessed for the presence or absence of urinary incontinence within 12 months **Numerator:** Patients who were assessed for the presence or absence of urinary incontinence within 12 months Urinary incontinence is defined as any involuntary leakage of urine **Denominator:** All female patients aged 65 years and older **Exclusion(s):** Documentation of medical reason(s) for not assessing for the presence or absence of urinary incontinence (continued)	**1090F**	Presence or absence of urinary incontinence assessed

[1]Physician Consortium for Performance Improvement: www.physicianconsortium.org
[2]National Committee on Quality Assurance (NCQA): Health Employer Data Information Set (HEDIS®), www.ncqa.org
[3]Joint Commission on Accreditation of Healthcare Organizations (JCAHO), ORYX Initiative Performance Measures: www.jcaho.org/pms
[4]National Diabetes Quality Improvement Alliance: www.nationaldiabetesalliance.org
[5]Joint measure from the Physician Consortium for Performance Improvement, www.physicianconsortium.org, and National Committee on Quality Assurance (NCQA), www.ncqa.org
[6]The Society of Thoracic Surgeons, www.sts.org, National Quality Forum, www.qualityforum.org

Brief Description of Performance Measure & Source and Reporting Instructions	CPT Category II Code(s)	Code Descriptor
Geriatrics (GER), cont'd		
Percentage of female patients aged 65 years and older who were assessed for the presence or absence of urinary incontinence within 12 months **Reporting Instructions:** For patient with appropriate exclusion criteria, report 1090F with modifier 1P		
Characterization of Urinary Incontinence in Women Aged 65 Years and Older[5]—Whether or not the female patient aged 65 years and older with a diagnosis of urinary incontinence whose urinary incontinence was characterized at least once within 12 months **Numerator:** Patients whose urinary incontinence was characterized (may include one or more of the following: frequency, volume, timing, type of symptoms or how bothersome to the patient) at least once within 12 months **Denominator:** All female patients aged 65 years and older with a diagnosis of urinary incontinence **Exclusion(s):** None **Percentage** of female patients aged 65 years and older with a diagnosis of urinary incontinence whose urinary incontinence was characterized at least once within 12 months **Reporting Instructions:** There are no exclusions for this measure; modifiers 1P, 2P, and 3P may not be used	**1091F**	Urinary incontinence characterized (eg frequency, volume, timing, type of symptoms, how bothersome)
Plan of Care for Urinary Incontinence in Women Aged 65 Years and Older[5]—Whether or not the female patient aged 65 years and older with a diagnosis of urinary incontinence had a documented plan of care for urinary incontinence at least once within 12 months **Numerator:** Patients with a documented plan of care for urinary incontinence at least once within 12 months **Definition:** Plan of care may include behavioral interventions (eg, bladder training, pelvic floor muscle training, prompted voiding), referral to specialist, surgical treatment, reassess at follow-up visit, lifestyle interventions, addressing co-morbid factors, modifications or discontinuation of medications contributing to urinary incontinence, or pharmacologic therapy **Denominator:** All female patients aged 65 years and older with a diagnosis of urinary incontinence **Exclusion(s):** None **Percentage** of female patients aged 65 years and older with a diagnosis of urinary incontinence with a documented plan of care for urinary incontinence at least once within 12 months **Reporting Instructions:** There are no exclusions for this measure. Modifiers 1P, 2P, and 3P may not be used	**0509F**	Urinary incontinence plan of care documented

[1]Physician Consortium for Performance Improvement: www.physicianconsortium.org
[2]National Committee on Quality Assurance (NCQA): Health Employer Data Information Set (HEDIS®), www.ncqa.org
[3]Joint Commission on Accreditation of Healthcare Organizations (JCAHO), ORYX Initiative Performance Measures: www.jcaho.org/pms
[4]National Diabetes Quality Improvement Alliance: www.nationaldiabetesalliance.org
[5]Joint measure from the Physician Consortium for Performance Improvement, www.physicianconsortium.org, and National Committee on Quality Assurance (NCQA), www.ncqa.org
[6]The Society of Thoracic Surgeons, www.sts.org, National Quality Forum, www.qualityforum.org

Brief Description of Performance Measure & Source and Reporting Instructions	CPT Category II Code(s)	Code Descriptor
Geriatrics (GER), cont'd		
Screening for Future Fall Risk[5]—Whether or not the patient aged 65 years and older was screened for future fall risk (2 or more falls in the past year or any fall with injury in the past year) at least once within 12 months **Numerator:** Patients who were screened for future fall risk (patients are considered at risk for future falls if they have had 2 or more falls in the past year or any fall with injury in the past year) at least once within 12 months **Denominator:** All patients aged 65 years and older **Exclusion(s):** Documentation of medical reason(s) for not screening for future fall risk (eg, patient is not ambulatory) **Percentage** of patients aged 65 years and older who were screened for future fall risk at least once within 12 months **Reporting Instructions:** For patient with appropriate exclusion criteria, report either 1100F or 1101F with modifier 1P	**1100F** **1101F**	Patient screened for future fall risk; documentation of two or more falls in the past year or any fall with injury in the past year Patient screened for future fall risk; documentation of no falls in the past year or only one fall without injury in the past year
►**Risk Assessment for Falls**[5]—Whether or not the patient aged 65 years and older with a history of falls had a risk assessment for falls completed within 12 months **Numerator:** Patients who had a risk assessment for falls completed within 12 months *Risk assessment is comprised of: • Balance/gait AND one or more of the following: • Postural blood pressure • Vision • Home fall hazards • Documentation on whether medications are a contributing factor or not to falls within the past 12 months (Note: all components do not need to be completed during one patient visit) **Definition:** A fall is defined as a sudden, unintentional change in position causing an individual to land at a lower level, on an object, the floor, or the ground, other than as a consequence of sudden onset of paralysis, epileptic seizure, or overwhelming external force. **See technical specifications for detailed requirements for each component** **Denominator:** All patients aged 65 years and older with a history of falls (history of falls is defined as 2 or more falls in the past year or any fall with injury in the past year) **Exclusion(s):** Documentation of medical reason(s) for not completing a risk assessment for falls **Percentage** of patients aged 65 years and older with a history of falls who had a risk assessment for falls completed within 12 months **Reporting Instructions:** Report 1100F or 1101F for each patient. If patient has a history of falls (1100F) and there is a risk assessment for falls, also report 3288F. For patient with appropriate exclusion criteria, report 3288F with modifier 1P◄	►**3288F** **Denominator Codes:** **1100F** **1101F**◄	►Falls risk assessment documented Patient screened for future fall risk; documentation of two or more falls in the past year or any fall with injury in the past year Documentation of no falls in the past year or only one fall without injury in the past year◄
►**Plan of Care for Falls**[5]—Whether or not the patient aged 65 years and older with a history of falls had a plan of care for falls documented within 12 months **Numerator:** Patients with a plan of care for falls documented within 12 months *Plan of care must include: • consideration of appropriate assistance device AND • balance, strength, and gait training (continued)	►**0518F** **Denominator Codes:** **1100F**	►Falls plan of care documented Patient screened for future fall risk; documentation of two or more falls in the past year or any fall with injury in the past year

[1]Physician Consortium for Performance Improvement: www.physicianconsortium.org
[2]National Committee on Quality Assurance (NCQA): Health Employer Data Information Set (HEDIS®), www.ncqa.org
[3]Joint Commission on Accreditation of Healthcare Organizations (JCAHO), ORYX Initiative Performance Measures: www.jcaho.org/pms
[4]National Diabetes Quality Improvement Alliance: www.nationaldiabetesalliance.org
[5]Joint measure from the Physician Consortium for Performance Improvement, www.physicianconsortium.org, and National Committee on Quality Assurance (NCQA), www.ncqa.org
[6]The Society of Thoracic Surgeons, www.sts.org, National Quality Forum, www.qualityforum.org

Brief Description of Performance Measure & Source and Reporting Instructions	CPT Category II Code(s)	Code Descriptor
Geriatrics (GER), cont'd		
Definition: A fall is defined as a sudden, unintentional change in position causing an individual to land at a lower level, on an object, the floor, or the ground, other than as a consequence of sudden onset of paralysis, epileptic seizure, or overwhelming external force **Denominator:** All patients aged 65 years and older with a history of falls (history of falls is defined as 2 or more falls in the past year or any fall with injury in the past year) **Exclusion(s):** Documentation of medical reason(s) why a plan of care is not documented **Percentage** of patients aged 65 years and older with a history of falls who had a plan of care for falls documented within 12 months **Reporting Instructions:** Report 1100F or 1101F for each patient. If patient has a history of falls (1100F) and there is a plan of care for falls documented, also report 0518F. For patient with appropriate exclusion criteria, report 0518F with modifier 1P◄	**1101F◄**	Patient screened for future fall risk; documentation of no falls in the past year or only one fall without injury in the past year◄
Heart Failure (HF)		
Composite Measure: Heart Failure Assessment[1] See individual measures listed below for the following: Level of activity assessed (1003F) Clinical symptoms of volume overload (excess) assessed (1004F) Blood pressure measured (2000F) Weight recorded (2001F) Clinical signs of volume overload (excess) assessed (2002F)	**0001F**	Heart failure assessed
Assessment of Activity Level[1]—Number of visits with assessment of activity level per number of visits **Numerator:** Patient visits with assessment of current level of activity OR documentation of standardized scale OR completion of assessment tool (May include use of New York Heart Association Functional Classification of Congestive Heart Failure, Kansas City Cardiomyopathy Questionnaire; Minnesota™ Living with Heart Failure Questionnaire, or Guyatt's Chronic Heart Failure Questionnaire) **Denominator:** All patient visits for patients aged ≥ 18 years with heart failure **Exclusion(s):** None **Percentage** of patient visits with assessment of activity level **Reporting Instructions:**There are no exclusions for this measure; modifiers 1P, 2P, and 3P may not be used	**1003F**	Level of activity assessed
Assessment of Clinical Symptoms of Volume Overload (Excess)[1]—Number of patient visits with assessment of clinical symptoms of volume overload (excess) per number of visits **Numerator:** Patient visits with assessment of clinical *symptoms* of volume overload (excess) Assessment for absence or presence of symptoms of volume overload must include dyspnea, orthopnea, or documentation of standardized scale or completion of assessment tool (may include New York Heart Association Functional Classification of Congestive Heart Failure, Kansas City Cardiomyopathy Questionnaire; Minnesota™ Living with Heart Failure Questionnaire, or Guyatt's Chronic Heart Failure Questionnaire) **Denominator:** All patient visits for patients aged ≥ 18 years with heart failure (continued)	**1004F**	Clinical symptoms of volume overload (excess) assessed

[1]Physician Consortium for Performance Improvement: www.physicianconsortium.org
[2]National Committee on Quality Assurance (NCQA): Health Employer Data Information Set (HEDIS®), www.ncqa.org
[3]Joint Commission on Accreditation of Healthcare Organizations (JCAHO), ORYX Initiative Performance Measures: www.jcaho.org/pms
[4]National Diabetes Quality Improvement Alliance: www.nationaldiabetesalliance.org
[5]Joint measure from the Physician Consortium for Performance Improvement, www.physicianconsortium.org, and National Committee on Quality Assurance (NCQA), www.ncqa.org
[6]The Society of Thoracic Surgeons, www.sts.org, National Quality Forum, www.qualityforum.org

Brief Description of Performance Measure & Source and Reporting Instructions	CPT Category II Code(s)	Code Descriptor
Heart Failure (HF), cont'd		
Percentage of patient visits with assessment of clinical symptoms of volume overload (excess) **Reporting Instructions:** There are no exclusions for this measure; modifiers 1P, 2P, and 3P may not be used		
Blood Pressure Measurement[1]—Number of visits with blood pressure measurement recorded per number of visits **Numerator:** Patient visits with blood pressure measurement recorded **Denominator:** All patient visits for patients aged ≥ 18 years with HF **Exclusion(s):** None **Percentage** of patient visits with a blood pressure measurement recorded **Reporting Instructions:** There are no exclusions for this measure; modifiers 1P, 2P, and 3P may not be used	**2000F**	Blood pressure measure
Weight Measurement[1]—Number of visits with weight measurement recorded per number of visits **Numerator:** Patient visits with weight measurement recorded **Denominator:** All patient visits for patients aged ≥ 18 years with heart failure **Exclusion(s):** None **Percentage** of patient visits with weight measurement recorded **Reporting Instructions:** There are no exclusions for this measure; modifiers 1P, 2P, and 3P may not be used	**2001F**	Weight recorded
Assessment of Clinical Signs of Volume Overload (Excess)[1]—Number of visits with assessment of clinical signs of volume overload (excess) per number of visits **Numerator:** Patient visits with assessment of clinical *signs* of volume overload (excess) Assessment for presence or absence of signs of volume overload must include: peripheral edema OR Rales OR Hepatomegaly OR Ascites OR Assessment of jugular venous pressure OR S3 or S4 gallop **Denominator:** All patient visits for patients aged ≥ 18 years with heart failure **Exclusion(s):** None **Percentage** of patient visits with assessment of clinical signs of volume overload (excess) **Reporting Instructions:** There are no exclusions for this measure; modifiers 1P, 2P, and 3P may not be used	**2002F**	Clinical signs volume overload (excess) assessed
Left Ventricular Function (LVF) Assessment[1]—Whether or not patient has quantitative or qualitative results of LVF assessment recorded **Numerator:** Patients with quantitative or qualitative results of LVF assessment recorded **Denominator:** All patients aged ≥ 18 years with heart failure **Exclusion(s):** None **Percentage** of patients with quantitative or qualitative results of LVF assessment recorded **Reporting Instructions:** There are no exclusions for this measure; modifiers 1P, 2P, and 3P may not be used	**3020F**	Left ventricular function (LVF) assessment (eg, echocardiography, nuclear test, or ventriculography) documented in the medical record (Includes: Quantitative or qualitative assessment results)

[1]Physician Consortium for Performance Improvement: www.physicianconsortium.org
[2]National Committee on Quality Assurance (NCQA): Health Employer Data Information Set (HEDIS®), www.ncqa.org
[3]Joint Commission on Accreditation of Healthcare Organizations (JCAHO), ORYX Initiative Performance Measures: www.jcaho.org/pms
[4]National Diabetes Quality Improvement Alliance: www.nationaldiabetesalliance.org
[5]Joint measure from the Physician Consortium for Performance Improvement, www.physicianconsortium.org, and National Committee on Quality Assurance (NCQA), www.ncqa.org
[6]The Society of Thoracic Surgeons, www.sts.org, National Quality Forum, www.qualityforum.org

Brief Description of Performance Measure & Source and Reporting Instructions	CPT Category II Code(s)	Code Descriptor
Heart Failure (HF), cont'd		
Patient Education[1]—Whether or not patient education was provided **Numerator:** Patients provided with patient education at one or more visit(s). Patient education should include one or more of the following: weight monitoring; diet (sodium restriction); symptom management; physical activity; smoking cessation; medication instruction; minimizing or avoiding use of NSAIDs; referral for visiting nurse; referral for specific educational or management programs; or prognosis/end-of-life issues **Denominator:** All patients aged ≥ 18 years with heart failure and with one or more visit(s) **Denominator Inclusion(s):** Patients with one or more visit(s) **Percentage** of heart failure patients who were provided with patient education on disease management and health behavior changes during one or more visit(s) **Reporting Instructions:**There are no exclusions for this measure; modifiers 1P, 2P, and 3P may not be used	**4003F**	Patient education, written/oral, appropriate for patients with heart failure performed
Beta-Blocker Therapy[1]—Whether or not HF patient with LVSD was prescribed beta-blocker therapy **Numerator:** Patients who were prescribed beta-blocker therapy **Denominator:** All heart failure patients ≥ 18 years of age with left ventricular ejection fraction (LVEF) < 40% or with moderately or severely depressed left ventricular systolic function **Denominator Inclusion(s):** Patients with heart failure and left ventricular systolic dysfunction (LVSD) (LVEF < 40% or with moderately or severely depressed left ventricular systolic function) **Exclusion(s):** Documentation of medical, patient, or system reason(s) for not prescribing beta-blocker therapy. **Percentage** of heart failure patients with LVSD who were prescribed beta-blocker therapy **Reporting Instructions:** Report either 3021F or 3022F for each heart failure patient. For patient with appropriate exclusion criteria, report 4006F with modifier 1P, 2P, or 3P	**4006F** **Denominator Codes:** **3021F** **3022F**	Beta-blocker therapy prescribed Left ventricular ejection fraction (LVEF) < 40% or documentation of moderately or severely depressed left ventricular systolic function Left ventricular ejection fraction (LVEF) ≥ 40% or documentation as normal or mildly depressed left ventricular systolic function
Angiotensin Converting Enzyme (ACE) Inhibitor or Angiotensin Receptor Blocker (ARB) Therapy for Left Ventricular Systolic Dysfunction (LVSD)[1]—Whether or not heart failure patients who also have LVSD were prescribed ACE inhibitor or ARB therapy **Numerator:** Patients who were prescribed ACE inhibitor or ARB therapy **Denominator Inclusion:** All heart failure patients aged ≥ 18 years with left ventricular ejection fraction (LVEF <40% or with moderately or severely depressed left ventricular systolic function) **Exclusion(s):** Documentation of medical, patient, or system reasons for not prescribing ACE inhibitor or ARB therapy **Percentage** of heart failure patients who also have LVSD and who were prescribed ACE or ARB inhibitor **Reporting Instructions:** Report either 3021F or 3022F for each heart failure patient. For patients with appropriate exclusion criteria, report 4009F with modifier 1P, 2P, or 3P	**4009F** **Denominator Codes:** **3021F** **3022F**	Angiotensin converting enzyme (ACE) inhibitor or Angiotensin Receptor Blocker (ARB) therapy prescribed Left ventricular ejection fraction (LVEF) < 40% or documentation of moderately or severely depressed left ventricular systolic function Left ventricular ejection fraction (LVEF) ≥ 40% or documentation as normal or mildly depressed left ventricular systolic function

[1]Physician Consortium for Performance Improvement: www.physicianconsortium.org
[2]National Committee on Quality Assurance (NCQA): Health Employer Data Information Set (HEDIS®), www.ncqa.org
[3]Joint Commission on Accreditation of Healthcare Organizations (JCAHO), ORYX Initiative Performance Measures: www.jcaho.org/pms
[4]National Diabetes Quality Improvement Alliance: www.nationaldiabetesalliance.org
[5]Joint measure from the Physician Consortium for Performance Improvement, www.physicianconsortium.org, and National Committee on Quality Assurance (NCQA), www.ncqa.org
[6]The Society of Thoracic Surgeons, www.sts.org, National Quality Forum, www.qualityforum.org

Brief Description of Performance Measure & Source and Reporting Instructions	CPT Category II Code(s)	Code Descriptor
Heart Failure (HF), cont'd		
Warfarin Therapy for Patients With Atrial Fibrillation[1]—Whether or not heart failure patient who also has paroxysmal or chronic atrial fibrillation was prescribed warfarin therapy **Numerator:** Patients who were prescribed warfarin therapy **Denominator:** All heart failure patients aged ≥ 18 years with paroxysmal or chronic atrial fibrillation **Denominator Inclusion:** Patients with heart failure and paroxysmal or chronic atrial fibrillation **Exclusion(s):** Documentation of medical, patient, or system reason(s) for not prescribing warfarin therapy **Percentage** of heart failure patients who also have paroxysmal or chronic atrial fibrillation who were prescribed warfarin therapy **Reporting Instructions:** For patients with appropriate exclusion criteria, report 4012F with modifier 1P, 2P, or 3P	**4012F**	Warfarin therapy prescribed
Heart Failure Discharge Instructions[3] **Numerator:** Heart failure patients with documentation that they or their caregivers were given written discharge instructions or other educational material addressing all of the following: activity level, diet, discharge medications, follow-up appointment, weight monitoring, what to do if symptoms worsen **Denominator:** Heart failure patients discharged home **Exclusion(s):** Patients less than 18 years of age **Percentage** of hospitalized heart failure patients in the denominator who received written discharge instructions	**4014F**	Written discharge instructions provided to heart failure patients discharged home. (Instructions include all of the following components: activity level, diet, discharge medications, follow-up appointment, weight monitoring, what to do if symptoms worsen)[3] (Excludes patients < 18 years of age)
►Hematology (HEM)◄		
►Myelodysplastic Syndrome (MDS) and Acute Leukemias-Baseline Cytogenetic Testing Performed on Bone Marrow[1]—Whether or not the patient aged 18 years and older with a diagnosis of MDS or an acute leukemia had baseline cytogenetic testing performed on bone marrow **Numerator:** Patients who had baseline cytogenetic testing performed on bone marrow Baseline refers to testing that is performed at time of diagnosis or prior to initiating treatment (eg, transfusion, growth factors or anti-neoplastic therapy) for that diagnosis **Denominator:** All patients aged 18 years and older with a diagnosis of MDS or an acute leukemia **Exclusion(s):** Documentation of medical reason(s) for not performing baseline cytogenetic testing; Documentation of patient reason(s) for not performing baseline cytogenetic testing; Documentation of system reason(s) for not performing baseline cytogenetic testing **Percentage** of patients aged 18 years and older with a diagnosis of MDS or an acute leukemia who had baseline cytogenetic testing performed on bone marrow **Reporting Instructions:** Treatment may include transfusion, growth factors or anti-neoplastic therapy For patients with a medical reason for not performing cytogenetic testing (eg, no liquid bone marrow or fibrotic marrow), report 3155F with modifier 1P (continued)	**►3155F◄**	►Cytogenetic testing performed on bone marrow at time of diagnosis or prior to initiating treatment◄

[1]Physician Consortium for Performance Improvement: www.physicianconsortium.org
[2]National Committee on Quality Assurance (NCQA): Health Employer Data Information Set (HEDIS®), www.ncqa.org
[3]Joint Commission on Accreditation of Healthcare Organizations (JCAHO), ORYX Initiative Performance Measures: www.jcaho.org/pms
[4]National Diabetes Quality Improvement Alliance: www.nationaldiabetesalliance.org
[5]Joint measure from the Physician Consortium for Performance Improvement, www.physicianconsortium.org, and National Committee on Quality Assurance (NCQA), www.ncqa.org
[6]The Society of Thoracic Surgeons, www.sts.org, National Quality Forum, www.qualityforum.org

Brief Description of Performance Measure & Source and Reporting Instructions	CPT Category II Code(s)	Code Descriptor
►Hematology (HEM)◄, cont'd		
For patients with a patient reason for not performing cytogenetic testing (eg, at time of diagnosis receiving palliative care or not receiving treatment as defined above), report 3155F with modifier 2P For patients with a system reason for not performing cytogenetic testing (eg, patient previously treated by another physician at the time cytogenetic testing performed), report 3155F with modifier 3P◄		
►Myelodysplastic Syndrome (MDS)-Documentation of Iron Stores in Patients Receiving Erythropoietin Therapy[1]—Whether or not the patient aged 18 years and older with a diagnosis of MDS who is receiving erythropoietin therapy had documentation of iron stores prior to initiating erythropoietin therapy **Numerator:** Patients with documentation of iron stores prior to initiating erythropoietin therapy Documentation includes either: Bone marrow examination including iron stain OR Serum iron measurement by ferritin or serum iron and total iron binding capacity (TIBC) **Denominator:** All patients aged 18 years and older with a diagnosis of MDS who are receiving erythropoietin therapy **Exclusion(s):** Documentation of system reason(s) for not documenting iron stores prior to initiating erythropoietin therapy **Percentage** of patients aged 18 years and older with a diagnosis of MDS who are receiving erythropoietin therapy with documentation of iron stores prior to initiating erythropoietin therapy **Reporting Instructions:** If using CPT II codes to report the denominator, report either 4090F or 4095F for each patient. Otherwise report the appropriate drug administration code and the appropriate drug code for the erythropoietin. If patient is receiving erythropoietin therapy and iron stores were documented prior to initiating erythropoietin therapy, also report 3160F. If patient was started on erythropoietin therapy under the care of another physician, is responding to erythropoietin therapy, and there is no documentation of iron stores, report 3160F with modifier 3P◄	**►3160F** **Denominator Codes:** **4090F** **4095F◄**	►Documentation of iron stores prior to initiating erythropoietin therapy Patient receiving erythropoietin therapy Patient not receiving erythropoietin therapy◄
►Multiple Myeloma: Treatment with Bisphosphonates[1]—Whether or not the patient aged 18 years and older with a diagnosis of multiple myeloma, not in remission, was prescribed or is receiving intravenous bisphosphonate therapy within the 12 month reporting period **Numerator:** Patients who were prescribed or received intravenous bisphosphonate therapy within the 12 month reporting period (For a listing of intravenous bisphosphonates that qualify for reporting 4100F please see the measure technical specifications.) **Denominator:** All patients aged 18 years and older with a diagnosis of multiple myeloma, not in remission **Exclusion(s):** Documentation of medical reason(s) for not prescribing bisphosphonates; Documentation of patient reason(s) for not prescribing bisphosphonates **Percentage** of patients aged 18 years and older with a diagnosis of multiple myeloma, not in remission, who were prescribed or received intravenous bisphosphonate therapy within the 12 month reporting period **Reporting Instructions:** For patient with appropriate exclusion criteria, report 4100F with modifier 1P or 2P◄	**►4100F◄**	►Bisphosphonate therapy, intravenous, ordered or received◄

[1]Physician Consortium for Performance Improvement: www.physicianconsortium.org
[2]National Committee on Quality Assurance (NCQA): Health Employer Data Information Set (HEDIS®), www.ncqa.org
[3]Joint Commission on Accreditation of Healthcare Organizations (JCAHO), ORYX Initiative Performance Measures: www.jcaho.org/pms
[4]National Diabetes Quality Improvement Alliance: www.nationaldiabetesalliance.org
[5]Joint measure from the Physician Consortium for Performance Improvement, www.physicianconsortium.org, and National Committee on Quality Assurance (NCQA), www.ncqa.org
[6]The Society of Thoracic Surgeons, www.sts.org, National Quality Forum, www.qualityforum.org

Brief Description of Performance Measure & Source and Reporting Instructions	CPT Category II Code(s)	Code Descriptor
►Hematology (HEM)◄, cont'd		
►Chronic Lymphocytic Leukemia (CLL)-Baseline Flow Cytometry[1]—Whether or not the patient aged 18 years and older with a diagnosis of CLL had baseline flow cytometry studies performed **Numerator:** Patients who had baseline flow cytometry studies performed Baseline refers to testing that is performed at time of diagnosis or prior to initiating treatment (ie, antineoplastic therapy) for that diagnosis **Denominator:** All patients aged 18 years and older with a diagnosis of CLL **Exclusion(s):** Documentation of medical, patient, or system reason(s) for not performing baseline flow cytometry studies **Percentage** of patients aged 18 years and older with a diagnosis of CLL who had baseline flow cytometry studies performed **Reporting Instructions:** Treatment may include antineoplastic therapy. For patients with a medical reason for not performing baseline flow cytometry studies, report 3170F with modifier 1P For patients with a patient reason for not performing cytogenetic testing (eg, receiving palliative care or not receiving treatment as defined above), report 3170F with modifier 2P For patients with a system reason for not performing cytogenetic testing (eg, patient previously treated by another physician at the time baseline flow cytometry studies were performed), report 3170F with modifier 3P◄	**►3170F◄**	►Flow cytometry studies performed at time of diagnosis or prior to initiating treatment◄
Hepatitis C (HEP C)		
►Testing for Chronic Hepatitis C: Confirmation of Hepatitis C Viremia (HCV)[1]—Whether or not the patient aged 18 years and older with a diagnosis of Hepatitis C seen for an initial evaluation had HCV RNA testing ordered or previously performed **Numerator:** Patients for whom HCV RNA testing was ordered or previously performed **Denominator:** All patients aged 18 years and older with a diagnosis of Hepatitis C seen for initial evaluation **Exclusion(s):** Documentation of medical reason(s) for not ordering or performing HCV RNA Documentation of patient reason(s) for not ordering or performing HCV RNA **Percentage** of patients aged 18 years and older with a diagnosis of Hepatitis C seen for an initial evaluation who had HCV RNA testing ordered or previously performed **Reporting Instructions:** If this measure is reported on the same claim as an E/M service for "new patient" (99201-99205), the denominator code (1119F or 1121F) does not need to be reported If reporting an established patient code or consultation code, (99212-99215 or 99241-99245), the reporting physician should use 1119F to report initial evaluation for condition or 1121F to denote a subsequent evaluation If 1119F is reported and RNA testing for Hepatitis C viremia is ordered or was previously performed and results are documented, also report 3265F. For patients with appropriate exclusion criteria report 3265F with modifier 1P or 2P◄	**►3265F** **Denominator Codes:** **1119F** **1121F◄**	►Ribonucleic acid (RNA) testing for Hepatitis C viremia ordered or results documented Initial evaluation for condition Subsequent evaluation for condition◄

[1]Physician Consortium for Performance Improvement: www.physicianconsortium.org
[2]National Committee on Quality Assurance (NCQA): Health Employer Data Information Set (HEDIS®), www.ncqa.org
[3]Joint Commission on Accreditation of Healthcare Organizations (JCAHO), ORYX Initiative Performance Measures: www.jcaho.org/pms
[4]National Diabetes Quality Improvement Alliance: www.nationaldiabetesalliance.org
[5]Joint measure from the Physician Consortium for Performance Improvement, www.physicianconsortium.org, and National Committee on Quality Assurance (NCQA), www.ncqa.org
[6]The Society of Thoracic Surgeons, www.sts.org, National Quality Forum, www.qualityforum.org

Brief Description of Performance Measure & Source and Reporting Instructions	CPT Category II Code(s)	Code Descriptor
Hepatitis C (HEP C), cont'd		
►Hepatitis C Ribonucleic Acid (RNA) Testing Before Initiating Therapy—Whether or not the patient aged 18 years and older with a diagnosis of chronic Hepatitis C who is receiving antiviral treatment had quantitative HCV RNA testing performed within 6 months prior to initiation of treatment **Numerator:** Patients for whom quantitative HCV RNA testing was performed within 6 months prior to initiation of treatment **Denominator:** All patients aged 18 years and older with a diagnosis of chronic Hepatitis C who are receiving antiviral treatment **Exclusion(s):** Documentation of medical reason(s) for not performing HCV RNA within 6 months prior to treatment **Percentage** of patients aged 18 years and older with a diagnosis of chronic Hepatitis C who are receiving antiviral treatment for whom a quantitative HCV RNA testing was performed within 6 months prior to initiation of treatment **Reporting Instructions:** Report 4150F or 4151F for each patient. If patient is receiving antiviral therapy and received RNA test for Hepatitis C within 6 months prior to initiation of antiviral treatment, also report 3218F. Report this measure only once. For patient with appropriate exclusion criteria report 3218F with modifier 1P. If patient is first seen by physician after initiation of treatment, report 3218F with modifier 1P◄	**►3218F** **Denominator Codes:** **4150F** **4151F◄**	►RNA testing for Hepatitis C documented as performed within six months prior to initiation of antiviral treatment for Hepatitis C Patient receiving antiviral treatment for Hepatitis C Patient not receiving antiviral treatment for Hepatitis C◄
►HCV Genotype Testing Prior to Therapy[1]—Whether or not the patient aged 18 years and older with a diagnosis of chronic Hepatitis C who is receiving antiviral treatment had HCV genotype testing performed prior to initiation of treatment **Numerator:** Patients for whom HCV genotype testing was performed prior to initiation of treatment **Denominator:** All patients aged 18 years and older with a diagnosis of chronic hepatitis C who are receiving antiviral treatment **Exclusion(s):** None **Percentage** of patients aged 18 years and older with a diagnosis of chronic hepatitis C who are receiving antiviral treatment for whom HCV genotype testing was performed prior to initiation of treatment **Reporting Instructions:** Report 4150F or 4151F for each patient. If patient is receiving antiviral therapy and had Hepatitis C genotype testing performed prior to initiation of antiviral treatment, also report 3266F. Report this measure only once. There are no performance exclusions for this measure; modifiers 1P, 2P, or 3P may not be used◄	**►3266F** **Denominator Codes:** **4150F** **4151F◄**	►Hepatitis C genotype testing documented as performed prior to initiation of antiviral treatment for Hepatitis C Patient receiving antiviral treatment for Hepatitis C Patient not receiving antiviral treatment for Hepatitis C◄
►Consideration for Antiviral Therapy[1]—Whether or not the patient aged 18 years and older with a diagnosis of chronic Hepatitis C was considered for peginterferon and ribavirin therapy within the 12 month reporting period **Numerator:** Patients who were considered for peginterferon and ribavirin therapy within the 12 month reporting period **Denominator:** All patients aged 18 years and older with a diagnosis of chronic Hepatitis C **Exclusion(s):** None **Percentage** of patients aged 18 years and older with a diagnosis of chronic Hepatitis C who were considered for peginterferon and ribavirin therapy within the 12 month reporting period **Reporting Instructions:** Therapy is considered if both peginterferon and ribavirin therapy are prescribed or there are documented reasons for the patient not to receive this therapy therefore there are no exclusions for this measure. If combination therapy is prescribed report 4153F. Modifier 1P, 2P, or 3P may not be used◄	**►4152F** **4153F◄**	►Documentation that combination peginterferon and ribavirin therapy considered Combination peginterferon and ribavirin therapy prescribed◄

[1]Physician Consortium for Performance Improvement: www.physicianconsortium.org
[2]National Committee on Quality Assurance (NCQA): Health Employer Data Information Set (HEDIS®), www.ncqa.org
[3]Joint Commission on Accreditation of Healthcare Organizations (JCAHO), ORYX Initiative Performance Measures: www.jcaho.org/pms
[4]National Diabetes Quality Improvement Alliance: www.nationaldiabetesalliance.org
[5]Joint measure from the Physician Consortium for Performance Improvement, www.physicianconsortium.org, and National Committee on Quality Assurance (NCQA), www.ncqa.org
[6]The Society of Thoracic Surgeons, www.sts.org, National Quality Forum, www.qualityforum.org

Brief Description of Performance Measure & Source and Reporting Instructions	CPT Category II Code(s)	Code Descriptor
Hepatitis C (HEP C), cont'd		
►**Combination Antiviral Therapy**[1]—Whether or not the patient aged 18 years and older with a diagnosis of chronic Hepatitis C who is receiving antiviral treatment was prescribed peginterferon and ribavirin therapy within the 12 month reporting period **Numerator:** Patients who were prescribed peginterferon and ribavirin therapy within the 12 month reporting period **Denominator:** All patients aged 18 years and older with a diagnosis of chronic Hepatitis C who are receiving antiviral treatment **Exclusion(s):** Documentation of medical reason(s) for not prescribing peginterferon and ribavirin therapy Documentation of patient reason(s) for not prescribing peginterferon and ribavirin therapy Documentation of system reason(s) for not prescribing peginterferon and ribavirin therapy **Percentage** of aged 18 years and older with a diagnosis of chronic Hepatitis C who are receiving antiviral treatment who were prescribed peginterferon and ribavirin therapy within the 12 month reporting period **Reporting Instructions:** Report 4150F or 4151F for each patient. If patient was prescribed peginterferon and ribavirin therapy, also report 4153F. For patient with appropriate exclusion criteria, report 4153F with modifier 1P, 2P, or 3P◄	►**4153F** **Denominator Codes:** **4150F** **4151F◄**	►Combination peginterferon and ribavirin therapy prescribed Patient receiving antiviral treatment for Hepatitis C Patient not receiving antiviral treatment for Hepatitis C◄
►**HCV Quantitative RNA Testing at Week 12 of Therapy**[1]—Whether or not the patient aged 18 years and older with a diagnosis of chronic Hepatitis C who is receiving antiviral treatment had quantitative HCV RNA testing performed at 12 weeks from the initiation of antiviral treatment **Numerator:** Patients for whom quantitative HCV RNA testing was performed at 12 weeks from the initiation of antiviral treatment **Denominator:** All patients aged 18 years and older with a diagnosis of chronic Hepatitis C who are receiving antiviral treatment **Exclusion(s):** Documentation of medical reason(s) for not performing quantitative HCV RNA at 12 weeks Documentation of patient reason(s) for not performing quantitative HCV RNA at 12 weeks **Percentage** of patients aged 18 years and older with a diagnosis of chronic Hepatitis C who are receiving antiviral treatment for whom quantitative HCV RNA testing was performed at 12 weeks from the initiation of antiviral treatment **Reporting Instructions:** Report 4150F or 4151F for each patient. If patient is receiving treatment for Hepatitis C at week 12 and patient received quantitative HCV RNA testing during the 12th week of treatment, also report 3220F. Also report date of test that corresponds to week 12 treatment. For patient with appropriate exclusion criteria, report 3220F with modifier 1P **Note: Technical specifications for this measure will include testing completed within 11-13 weeks of treatment◄**	►**3220F** **Denominator Codes:** **4150F** **4151F◄**	►Hepatitis C quantitative RNA testing documented as performed at 12 weeks from initiation of antiviral treatment Patient receiving antiviral treatment for Hepatitis C Patient not receiving antiviral treatment for Hepatitis C◄
►**Hepatitis A Vaccination**[1]—Whether or not the patient aged 18 years and older with a diagnosis of Hepatitis C was offered or received Hepatitis A vaccination, or who has documented immunity **Numerator:** Patients who were recommended to receive or who have received hepatitis A vaccination, or who have documented immunity **Denominator:** All patients aged 18 years and older with a diagnosis of Hepatitis C (continued)	►**4154F** **4155F**	►Hepatitis A vaccine series recommended Hepatitis A vaccine series previously received

[1]Physician Consortium for Performance Improvement: www.physicianconsortium.org
[2]National Committee on Quality Assurance (NCQA): Health Employer Data Information Set (HEDIS®), www.ncqa.org
[3]Joint Commission on Accreditation of Healthcare Organizations (JCAHO), ORYX Initiative Performance Measures: www.jcaho.org/pms
[4]National Diabetes Quality Improvement Alliance: www.nationaldiabetesalliance.org
[5]Joint measure from the Physician Consortium for Performance Improvement, www.physicianconsortium.org, and National Committee on Quality Assurance (NCQA), www.ncqa.org
[6]The Society of Thoracic Surgeons, www.sts.org, National Quality Forum, www.qualityforum.org

Brief Description of Performance Measure & Source and Reporting Instructions	CPT Category II Code(s)	Code Descriptor
Hepatitis C (HEP C), cont'd		
Exclusion(s): Documentation of medical reason(s) for not recommending or administering Hepatitis A vaccine series **Percentage** of patients aged 18 years and older with a diagnosis of Hepatitis C who were recommended to receive or have received Hepatitis A vaccination, or who have documented immunity **Reporting Instructions:** For patient with appropriate exclusion criteria, report 4154F or 4155F or 3215F with modifier 1P◄	**3215F◄**	Patient has documented immunity to Hepatitis A◄
►**Hepatitis B Vaccination**[1]—Whether or not the patient aged 18 years and older with a diagnosis of Hepatitis C was offered or received Hepatitis B vaccination, or who has documented immunity **Numerator:** Patients who were recommended to receive or who have received Hepatitis B vaccination, or who have documented immunity **Denominator:** All patients aged 18 years and older with a diagnosis of Hepatitis C **Exclusion(s):** Documentation of medical reason(s) for not recommending or administering Hepatitis B vaccination **Percentage** of patients aged 18 years and older with a diagnosis of Hepatitis C who were recommended to receive or have received Hepatitis B vaccination, or who have documented immunity **Reporting Instructions:** For patient with appropriate exclusion criteria report either 4156F or 4157F or 3216F with modifier 1P◄	**►4156F** **4157F** **3216F◄**	►Hepatitis B vaccine series recommended Hepatitis B vaccine series previously received Patient has documented immunity to Hepatitis B◄
►**Education Regarding Risk of Alcohol Consumption**[1]—Whether or not the patient aged 18 years and older with a diagnosis of Hepatitis C received education regarding the risk of alcohol consumption at least once within the 12 month reporting period **Numerator:** Patients who received education regarding the risk of alcohol consumption at least once within the 12 month reporting period **Denominator:** All patients aged 18 years and older with a diagnosis of Hepatitis C **Exclusion(s):** None **Percentage** of patients aged 18 years and older with a diagnosis of Hepatitis C who received education regarding the risk of alcohol consumption at least once within the 12 month reporting period **Reporting Instructions:** Report 4158F if patient education regarding risk of alcohol consumption was performed. There are no performance exclusions; modifiers 1P, 2P, or 3P may not be used◄	**►4158F◄**	►Patient education regarding risk of alcohol consumption performed◄
►**Counseling Regarding Use of Contraception Prior to Antiviral Therapy**[1]—Whether or not the female patient aged 18 to 44 years and all men aged 18 years and older with a diagnosis of chronic Hepatitis C who are receiving antiviral treatment received counseling regarding contraception prior to the initiation of treatment **Numerator:** Patients who were counseled regarding contraception prior to the initiation of treatment **Denominator:** All women aged 18 to 44 years and all men aged 18 years and older with a diagnosis of chronic Hepatitis C who are receiving antiviral treatment **Exclusion(s):** Documentation of medical reason(s) for not counseling patient regarding contraception (continued)	**►4159F** **Denominator Codes:** **4150F** **4151F◄**	►Counseling regarding contraception received prior to initiation of antiviral treatment Patient receiving antiviral treatment for Hepatitis C Patient not receiving antiviral treatment for Hepatitis C◄

[1]Physician Consortium for Performance Improvement: www.physicianconsortium.org
[2]National Committee on Quality Assurance (NCQA): Health Employer Data Information Set (HEDIS®), www.ncqa.org
[3]Joint Commission on Accreditation of Healthcare Organizations (JCAHO), ORYX Initiative Performance Measures: www.jcaho.org/pms
[4]National Diabetes Quality Improvement Alliance: www.nationaldiabetesalliance.org
[5]Joint measure from the Physician Consortium for Performance Improvement, www.physicianconsortium.org, and National Committee on Quality Assurance (NCQA), www.ncqa.org
[6]The Society of Thoracic Surgeons, www.sts.org, National Quality Forum, www.qualityforum.org

Brief Description of Performance Measure & Source and Reporting Instructions	CPT Category II Code(s)	Code Descriptor
Hepatitis C (HEP C), cont'd		
Percentage of female patients aged 18 to 44 years and all men aged 18 years and older with a diagnosis of chronic Hepatitis C who are receiving antiviral treatment who were counseled regarding contraception prior to the initiation of treatment **Reporting Instructions:** Report 4150F or 4151F for each patient. If patient is receiving antiviral treatment for Hepatitis C and patient received counseling regarding contraception, also report 4159F. For patient with appropriate exclusion criteria, report 4159F with modifier 1P. If patient is first seen by physician after initiation of treatment, report 3218F with modifier 1P◄		
Hypertension (HTN)		
Blood Pressure Measurement[1]—Number of visits with blood pressure measurement recorded per number of visits **Numerator:** Patient visits with blood pressure measurement recorded **Denominator:** All patient visits for patients aged ≥ 18 years with hypertension **Percentage** of patient visits with blood pressure recorded for patients aged ≥ 18 years **Reporting Instructions:** There are no exclusions for this measure; modifiers 1P, 2P, and 3P may not be used	**2000F**	Blood pressure measure
Plan of Care[1]—Number of visits with documented plan of care for hypertension per number of visits during which either systolic blood pressure ≥ 140 mm Hg or diastolic blood pressure ≥ 90 mm Hg **Numerator:** Patient visits with documented plan of care for hypertension Plan of care should include one or more of the following: Recheck blood pressure at specified future date, initiate or alter pharmacologic therapy, initiate or alter non-pharmacologic therapy **Denominator:** All patient visits during which patients ≥18 years of age diagnosed with hypertension have either systolic blood pressure ≥ 140 mm Hg or diastolic blood pressure ≥ 90 mm Hg **Percentage** of patient visits during which either systolic blood pressure ≥ 140 mm Hg or diastolic blood pressure ≥ 90 mm Hg, with documented plan of care for hypertension **Reporting Instructions:** For this measure to be met, three codes must be reported: one code for systolic blood pressure, one code for diastolic blood pressure, and the code for hypertension plan of care (4050F). If no documentation of plan of care, or patient does not have elevated blood pressure at the visit, report only two codes for corresponding systolic and diastolic blood pressure values ►To report most recent systolic blood pressure < 140 mmHg, see codes 3074F-3075F. There are no exclusions for this measure; modifiers 1P, 2P, and 3P may not be used.◄	**4050F**	Hypertension plan of care documented as appropriate
	Denominator Codes:	
	Systolic Codes:	
	3074F	Most recent systolic blood pressure < 130 mm Hg
	3075F	Most recent systolic blood pressure 130 to 139 mm Hg
	3077F	Most recent systolic blood pressure ≥ 140 mm HG
	Diastolic Codes:	
	3078F	Most recent diastolic blood pressure < 80 mm Hg
	3079F	Most recent diastolic blood pressure 80 - 89 mm Hg
	3080F	Most recent diastolic blood pressure ≥ 90 mm Hg

[1]Physician Consortium for Performance Improvement: www.physicianconsortium.org
[2]National Committee on Quality Assurance (NCQA): Health Employer Data Information Set (HEDIS®), www.ncqa.org
[3]Joint Commission on Accreditation of Healthcare Organizations (JCAHO), ORYX Initiative Performance Measures: www.jcaho.org/pms
[4]National Diabetes Quality Improvement Alliance: www.nationaldiabetesalliance.org
[5]Joint measure from the Physician Consortium for Performance Improvement, www.physicianconsortium.org, and National Committee on Quality Assurance (NCQA), www.ncqa.org
[6]The Society of Thoracic Surgeons, www.sts.org, National Quality Forum, www.qualityforum.org

Brief Description of Performance Measure & Source and Reporting Instructions	CPT Category II Code(s)	Code Descriptor
Major Depressive Disorder (MDD)		
►Depression Screening and Assessment in High Risk Patients SUP[2]—Whether or not a patient who is 18 years and older and is identified in a high risk category (ie, age or condition) who has a documented result from a depression screen or assessment during the measurement year. **Numerator:** Documented results of depression screen or assessment during the measurement year. Note: Patients who are screened positive for depressive symptoms who do not receive further assessment of depressive symptoms with a standardized tool do not count toward the numerator. Documentation of any one of the following counts toward this measure: • Negative screen for depressive symptoms using a standardized tool** • No significant depressive symptoms using a standardized tool** • Mild to moderate depressive symptoms using a standardized tool** • Clinically significant depressive symptoms using a standardized tool** * Note: Measure specifications should be referred to determine criteria to meet any of the listed risk categories (ie, the denominators) **Note: Measure specifications should be referred to identify acceptable standardized tools for screening and assessment **Denominator:** Adults, 18 years and older, who have been identified in one or more of following the high risk categories (ie, age or condition)*: • Patients with diabetes • Patients with cardiovascular disease including acute myocardial infraction (AMI), coronary artery bypass graft (CABG) or percutaneous transluminal coronary angioplasty (PTCA) ○ Two methods can be used to identify the eligible population: (1) a cardiac event or (2) an ischemic vascular disease (IVD) diagnosis. For the cardiac event (AMI, CABG, or PTCA) the look back is from January 1 through November 1 of the year prior to the measurement year; for the IVD diagnosis the look back is the measurement and the year prior to the measurement year. • Patients with persistent asthma • Patients with chronic obstructive pulmonary disease (COPD) • Patients with low back pain • Patients who are 65 years and older **Exclusion(s):** None **Reporting Instructions:** Report code 3351F, 3352F, 3353F, or 3354F for patients identified as high risk when acceptable screening or assessment has been documented. There are no performance exclusions for this measure; modifiers 1P, 2P, and 3P may not be used **Note: Measure specifications should be referred to identify acceptable standardized tools for screening and assessment◄	**►3351F** **3352F** **3353F** **3354F◄**	►Negative screen for depressive symptoms as categorized by using a standardized depression screening/assessment tool No significant depressive symptoms as categorized by using a standardized depression assessment tool Mild to moderate depressive symptoms as categorized by using a standardized depression screening/assessment tool Clinically significant depressive symptoms as categorized by using a standardized depression screening/assessment tool◄

[1]Physician Consortium for Performance Improvement: www.physicianconsortium.org
[2]National Committee on Quality Assurance (NCQA): Health Employer Data Information Set (HEDIS®), www.ncqa.org
[3]Joint Commission on Accreditation of Healthcare Organizations (JCAHO), ORYX Initiative Performance Measures: www.jcaho.org/pms
[4]National Diabetes Quality Improvement Alliance: www.nationaldiabetesalliance.org
[5]Joint measure from the Physician Consortium for Performance Improvement, www.physicianconsortium.org, and National Committee on Quality Assurance (NCQA), www.ncqa.org
[6]The Society of Thoracic Surgeons, www.sts.org, National Quality Forum, www.qualityforum.org

Brief Description of Performance Measure & Source and Reporting Instructions	CPT Category II Code(s)	Code Descriptor
Major Depressive Disorder (MDD), cont'd		
►**Major Depressive Disorder: Diagnostic Evaluation**[1]—Whether or not a patient aged 18 years and older with a new diagnosis or recurrent episode of MDD met the DSM-IV™ criteria during the visit in which the new diagnosis or recurrent episode was identified during the reporting year **Numerator:** Patients with documented evidence that they met the DSM-IV™ criteria* [At least 5 elements (must include: (1) depressed mood or (2) loss of interest or pleasure) with symptom duration of two weeks or longer] during the visit in which the new diagnosis of an initial or recurrent episode was identified during the reporting year *DSM-IV™ criteria includes presence of depressed mood, marked diminished interest/pleasure, significant weight loss or weight gain, insomnia or hypersomnia, psychomotor agitation or retardation, fatigue or loss of energy, feelings of worthlessness, diminished ability to concentrate and recurrent suicidal ideation **Denominator:** Patients aged 18 years and older with a new diagnosis or recurrent episode of MDD **Exclusion(s):** None **Percentage** of patients aged 18 years and older with a new diagnosis or recurrent episode of MDD with documented evidence of having met DSM-IV™ criteria during the visit in which the new diagnosis or recurrent episode was identified during the reporting year **Reporting Instructions:** Report 3093F for each patient with a new diagnosis of an initial or recurrent episode of MDD. Report 1040F where DSM- IV™ criteria documented There are no performance exclusions for this measure; modifiers 1P, 2P, and 3P may not be used◄	**►1040F** **Denominator Codes:** **3093F◄**	►DSM-IV™ criteria for major depressive disorder documented at the initial evaluation Documentation of new diagnosis of initial or recurrent episode of major depressive disorder◄
Suicide Risk Assessment[1]—Whether or not a patient aged 18 years and older with a new diagnosis or recurrent episode of MDD was assessed for suicide risk at each visit during the reporting year **Numerator:** Patients who had a suicide risk assessment at each visit during the reporting year **Denominator:** Patients aged 18 years and older with a new diagnosis of an initial or recurrent episode of MDD **Exclusion:** Documentation that patient is in remission (no longer meeting DSM-IV™ criteria) **Percentage** of patients aged 18 years and older with a new diagnosis or recurrent episode of MDD who had a suicide risk assessment completed at each visit during the reporting year **Reporting Instructions:** Report 3093F for each patient with a new, confirmed diagnosis of MDD. Report 3085F for assessment of suicide risk. For patient with appropriate exclusion criteria, report 3092F	**3085F** **Denominator Codes:** **3093F** **Exclusion Code:** **3092F**	Suicide risk assessed Documentation of new diagnosis of initial or recurrent episode of major depressive disorder Major depressive disorder, in remission
Severity Classification at Initial Visit[1]—Whether or not a patient aged 18 years and older was classified for severity of his/her MDD during the visit in which the new diagnosis or recurrent episode was identified during the reporting year **Numerator:** Patients whose severity of MDD was classified during the visit in which the new diagnosis or recurrent episode was identified during the reporting year (continued)	**Severity Classification Codes:** **3088F**	Major depressive disorder, mild

[1]Physician Consortium for Performance Improvement: www.physicianconsortium.org
[2]National Committee on Quality Assurance (NCQA): Health Employer Data Information Set (HEDIS®), www.ncqa.org
[3]Joint Commission on Accreditation of Healthcare Organizations (JCAHO), ORYX Initiative Performance Measures: www.jcaho.org/pms
[4]National Diabetes Quality Improvement Alliance: www.nationaldiabetesalliance.org
[5]Joint measure from the Physician Consortium for Performance Improvement, www.physicianconsortium.org, and National Committee on Quality Assurance (NCQA), www.ncqa.org
[6]The Society of Thoracic Surgeons, www.sts.org, National Quality Forum, www.qualityforum.org

Brief Description of Performance Measure & Source and Reporting Instructions	CPT Category II Code(s)	Code Descriptor
Major Depressive Disorder (MDD), cont'd		
Denominator: All patients aged 18 years and older with a new diagnosis of an initial or recurrent episode of MDD **Exclusion(s):** None **Percentage** of patients aged 18 years and older with a new diagnosis or recurrent episode of MDD whose severity of MDD was classified during the visit in which the new diagnosis or recurrent episode was identified during the reporting year **Reporting Instructions:** Report 3093F for each patient with a new diagnosis of an initial or recurrent episode of MDD during the reporting year. Also report 3088F or 3089F or 3090F or 3091F or 3092F for the corresponding severity classification There are no exclusions for this measure; modifiers 1P, 2P, and 3P may not be used	**3089F** **3090F** **3091F** **3092F** **Denominator Code:** **3093F**	Major depressive disorder, moderate Major depressive disorder, severe without psychotic features Major depressive disorder, severe with psychotic features Major depressive disorder, in remission Documentation of new diagnosis of initial or recurrent episode of major depressive disorder
Treatment: Psychotherapy, Medication Management, and/or Electroconvulsive Therapy (ECT)[1]—Whether or not the patient aged 18 years and older with a new diagnosis or recurrent episode of MDD received therapy appropriate to his/her classification during the reporting year **Numerator:** Patients who received therapy appropriate to their classification during the reporting year *Appropriate treatment for corresponding severity classification:* **Mild MDD:** Psychotherapy OR Antidepressant medication **Moderate MDD:** Psychotherapy OR Antidepressant medication OR Psychotherapy and antidepressant medication **Severe MDD without psychotic features:** Antidepressant medications OR Psychotherapy and antidepressant medications **Severe MDD with psychotic features:** Antidepressant medication and antipsychotic medication OR ECT **Denominator:** All patients aged 18 years and older with a new diagnosis of an initial or recurrent episode of MDD **Exclusion(s):** Documentation of medical, patient, or system reason(s) for not prescribing treatment. **Percentage** of patients aged 18 years and older with a new diagnosis or recurrent episode of MDD who received therapy appropriate to their severity classification during the reporting year (continued)	**Treatment Codes:** **4060F** **4062F** **4064F** **4065F** **4066F** **4067F** **90870**	 Psychotherapy services provided Patient referral for psychotherapy documented Antidepressant pharmacotherapy prescribed Antipsychotic pharmacotherapy prescribed Electroconvulsive Therapy (ECT) provided Patient referral for electroconvulsive therapy (ECT) documented Electroconvulsive therapy

[1]Physician Consortium for Performance Improvement: www.physicianconsortium.org
[2]National Committee on Quality Assurance (NCQA): Health Employer Data Information Set (HEDIS®), www.ncqa.org
[3]Joint Commission on Accreditation of Healthcare Organizations (JCAHO), ORYX Initiative Performance Measures: www.jcaho.org/pms
[4]National Diabetes Quality Improvement Alliance: www.nationaldiabetesalliance.org
[5]Joint measure from the Physician Consortium for Performance Improvement, www.physicianconsortium.org, and National Committee on Quality Assurance (NCQA), www.ncqa.org
[6]The Society of Thoracic Surgeons, www.sts.org, National Quality Forum, www.qualityforum.org

Brief Description of Performance Measure & Source and Reporting Instructions	CPT Category II Code(s)	Code Descriptor
Major Depressive Disorder (MDD), cont'd		
Reporting Instructions: Report 3093F for each patient with a new diagnosis of an initial or recurrent episode of MDD. Report one code from severity classification codes for each patient. Report all treatment codes that apply. For patient with appropriate exclusion criteria, report an appropriate treatment code with modifier 1P, 2P, or 3P **Mild MDD: Report 3088F and:** (a) Psychotherapy- 4060F or 4062F (b) Antidepressant medication- 4064F **Moderate MDD: Report 3089F and:** (c) Psychotherapy- 4060F or 4062F (d) Antidepressant medication- 4064F (e) Psychotherapy and antidepressant medication-4060F or 4062F AND 4064F **Severe MDD without psychotic features: Report 3090F and:** (f) Antidepressant medications - 4064F (g) Psychotherapy and antidepressant medications- 4060F or 4062F AND 4064F **Severe MDD with psychotic features: Report 3091F and:** (h) Antidepressant medication and antipsychotic medication-4064F and 4065F (i) ECT- 4066F or 4067F or 90870	**Severity Classification Codes:** **3088F** **3089F** **3090F** **3091F** **3092F** **Denominator Code:** **3093F**	 Major depressive disorder, mild Major depressive disorder, moderate Major depressive disorder, severe without psychotic features Major depressive disorder, severe with psychotic features Major depressive disorder, in remission Documentation of new diagnosis of initial or recurrent episode of major depressive disorder
Melanoma (ML)		
►Melanoma Follow Up Measures[5] Whether or not the patient with a new diagnosis of melanoma or a history of melanoma received all of the following aspects of care within the 12 month reporting period: (1) Patient was asked specifically if he/she had any new and changing moles **AND** (2) A complete physical skin examination was performed and the morphology, size, and location of new or changing pigmented lesions were noted **AND** (3) Patient was counseled to perform a monthly self skin examination **Numerator:** Patients who received all of the following aspects of care at least once within the 12 month reporting period: (1) Patient was asked specifically if he/she had any new or changing moles **AND** (2) A complete physical skin examination* was performed and the morphology, size, and location of new or changing pigmented lesions were noted **AND** (3) Patient was counseled to perform a monthly self skin examination ***A complete physical skin exam includes: head (including the face), neck, chest (including the axillae), abdomen, back, and extremities. The genitalia (including the groin and buttocks) may also be examined (optional)** **Denominator:** All patients with a new diagnosis of melanoma or a history of melanoma. **Exclusion(s):** Documentation of system reason(s) for not performing the follow up service (eg, another physician performed the service) (continued)	**►0015F** **1050F** **2029F** **5005F◄**	►Melanoma follow up completed History obtained regarding new or changing moles Complete physical skin exam performed Patient counseled to perform a monthly self skin examination◄

[1]Physician Consortium for Performance Improvement: www.physicianconsortium.org
[2]National Committee on Quality Assurance (NCQA): Health Employer Data Information Set (HEDIS®), www.ncqa.org
[3]Joint Commission on Accreditation of Healthcare Organizations (JCAHO), ORYX Initiative Performance Measures: www.jcaho.org/pms
[4]National Diabetes Quality Improvement Alliance: www.nationaldiabetesalliance.org
[5]Joint measure from the Physician Consortium for Performance Improvement, www.physicianconsortium.org, and National Committee on Quality Assurance (NCQA), www.ncqa.org
[6]The Society of Thoracic Surgeons, www.sts.org, National Quality Forum, www.qualityforum.org

Brief Description of Performance Measure & Source and Reporting Instructions	CPT Category II Code(s)	Code Descriptor
Melanoma (ML), cont'd		
Percentage of patients with a new diagnosis of melanoma or a history of melanoma who received all of the following aspects of care within the 12 month reporting period: (1) Patient was asked specifically if he/she had any new and changing moles **AND** (2) A complete physical skin examination was performed and the morphology, size, and location of new or changing pigmented lesions were noted **AND** (3) Patient was counseled to perform a monthly self skin examination **Reporting Instructions:** If all three components of the numerator are performed, report composite code 0015F for this measure If fewer than the three components are performed, report only the code(s) for the components that have been performed If there is a valid system reason(s) for not performing one or more of the components of the numerator, report the corresponding code(s) with modifier 3P◄		
►**Melanoma Continuity of Care**[5]—Whether or not the patient with a current diagnosis of melanoma or a history of melanoma had information entered into a recall system with the target date for the next complete physical skin exam specified, at least once within the 12 month reporting period **Numerator:** Patients whose information was entered into a recall system* with the target date for the next complete physical skin exam specified, at least once within the 12 month reporting period ***The recall system should be linked to a process for notifying patients when their next physical exam is due and should include the following elements at a minimum: patient identifier, patient contact information, cancer diagnosis(es), dates(s) of initial cancer diagnosis (if known), and the target date for the next complete physical skin exam** **Denominator:** All patients with a current diagnosis of melanoma or a history of melanoma **Exclusion(s):** Documentation of system reason for not entering patient's information into a recall system (eg, melanoma being monitored by another physician provider) **Percentage** of patients with a current diagnosis of melanoma or a history of melanoma whose information was entered into a recall system with the target date for the next complete physical skin exam specified, at least once within the 12 month reporting period **Reporting Instructions:** For patient with appropriate exclusion criteria, report 7010F with modifier 3P◄	**►7010F◄**	►Patient information entered into a recall system with the target date for the next exam specified◄
►**Melanoma Coordination of Care**[5]—Whether or not the patient diagnosed with a new episode of melanoma has a treatment plan documented in the chart that was communicated to the physician(s) providing continuing care within one month of diagnosis **Numerator:** Patients who have a treatment plan documented in the chart that was communicated to the physician(s) providing continuing care within one month of diagnosis ***A treatment plan should include the following elements: diagnosis, tumor thickness, and plan for surgery or alternate care** **Denominator:** All patients diagnosed with a new episode of melanoma (continued)	**►5050F** **Denominator Codes:** **1127F** **1128F◄**	►Treatment plan communicated to provider(s) managing continuing care within one month of diagnosis New episode for condition Subsequent episode for condition◄

[1]Physician Consortium for Performance Improvement: www.physicianconsortium.org
[2]National Committee on Quality Assurance (NCQA): Health Employer Data Information Set (HEDIS®), www.ncqa.org
[3]Joint Commission on Accreditation of Healthcare Organizations (JCAHO), ORYX Initiative Performance Measures: www.jcaho.org/pms
[4]National Diabetes Quality Improvement Alliance: www.nationaldiabetesalliance.org
[5]Joint measure from the Physician Consortium for Performance Improvement, www.physicianconsortium.org, and National Committee on Quality Assurance (NCQA), www.ncqa.org
[6]The Society of Thoracic Surgeons, www.sts.org, National Quality Forum, www.qualityforum.org

Brief Description of Performance Measure & Source and Reporting Instructions	CPT Category II Code(s)	Code Descriptor
Melanoma (ML), cont'd		
Exclusion(s): Documentation of patient reason(s) for not communicating treatment plan (eg, patient asks that treatment plan not be communicated to physician[s] providing continuing care) Documentation of system reason(s) for not communicating treatment plan (eg, patient does not have a primary care physician or referring physician) **Percentage** of patients diagnosed with a new episode of melanoma who have a treatment plan documented in the chart that was communicated to the physician(s) providing continuing care within one month of diagnosis **Reporting Instructions:** Report 1127F or 1128F for each patient. If 1127F and patient has a treatment plan communicated to physician(s) managing continuing care, also report 5050F For patient with appropriate exclusion criteria, also report 5050F with modifier 2P or 3P◄		
►**Over Utilization of Imaging Studies in Stage 0-IA Melanoma**[5]—Whether or not the patient with American Joint Committee on Cancer (AJCC) Stage 0 or IA melanoma, without signs or symptoms, did not have imaging studies ordered **Numerator:** Patients with stage 0 or IA melanoma, without signs or symptoms, for whom no diagnostic imaging studies were ordered (ie, chest x-ray [CXR], computed tomography [CT], Ultrasound, magnetic resonance imaging [MRI], positron emission tomography [PET], or nuclear medicine scans) **Denominator:** All patients with Stage 0 or IA melanoma **Exclusion(s):** Documentation of medical reason(s) for ordering diagnostic imaging studies (eg, patient has signs or symptoms that justify imaging studies) Documentation of system reason(s) for ordering diagnostic imaging studies (eg, requirement for clinical trial enrollment, ordered by another provider) **Percentage** of patients with stage 0 or IA melanoma, without signs or symptoms, for whom no imaging studies were ordered **Reporting Instructions:** Report an appropriate code from the 3302F-3312F series for American Joint Committee on Cancer (AJCC) cancer stage for each patient. For patient with Stage 0 or 1A (3302F or 3303F), also report 3319F or 3320F. If patient has a valid medical or system reason for ordering diagnostic imaging studies, report 3319F with modifier 1P or 3P; do not report modifiers with 3320F◄	**►3319F**	►One of the following diagnostic imaging studies ordered: chest X-ray, CT, Ultrasound, MRI, PET, or nuclear medicine scans
	3320F	None of the following diagnostic imaging studies ordered: chest X-ray, CT, Ultrasound, MRI, PET, and nuclear medicine scans
	Denominator Codes:	
	3302F	AJCC Cancer Stage 0, documented
	3303F	AJCC Cancer Stage IA, documented
	3304F	AJCC Cancer Stage IB, documented
	3305F	AJCC Cancer Stage IC, documented
	3306F	AJCC Cancer Stage IIA, documented
	3307F	AJCC Cancer Stage IIB, documented
	3308F	AJCC Cancer Stage IIC, documented
	3309F	AJCC Cancer Stage IIIA, documented
	3310F	AJCC Cancer Stage IIIB, documented
	3311F	AJCC Cancer Stage IIIC, documented
	3312F◄	AJCC Cancer Stage IV, documented◄

[1]Physician Consortium for Performance Improvement: www.physicianconsortium.org
[2]National Committee on Quality Assurance (NCQA): Health Employer Data Information Set (HEDIS®), www.ncqa.org
[3]Joint Commission on Accreditation of Healthcare Organizations (JCAHO), ORYX Initiative Performance Measures: www.jcaho.org/pms
[4]National Diabetes Quality Improvement Alliance: www.nationaldiabetesalliance.org
[5]Joint measure from the Physician Consortium for Performance Improvement, www.physicianconsortium.org, and National Committee on Quality Assurance (NCQA), www.ncqa.org
[6]The Society of Thoracic Surgeons, www.sts.org, National Quality Forum, www.qualityforum.org

Brief Description of Performance Measure & Source and Reporting Instructions	CPT Category II Code(s)	Code Descriptor
Oncology (ONC)		
►**Cancer Stage Documented**[1]—Whether or not the patient with a diagnosis of breast, colon, or rectal cancer who is receiving chemotherapy or radiation therapy had either a baseline American Joint Committee on Cancer (AJCC) cancer stage or documentation that the cancer is metastatic in the medical record **Numerator:** Patients who have a baseline AJCC cancer stage or documentation that the cancer is metastatic in the medical record at least once during the 12 month reporting period Cancer stage refers to stage at diagnosis **Denominator:** All patients with a diagnosis of breast, colon, or rectal cancer seen in the ambulatory setting **Exclusion(s):** None **Percentage** of patients with a diagnosis of breast, colon, or rectal cancer seen in the ambulatory setting who have a baseline AJCC cancer stage or documentation that the cancer is metastatic in the medical record at least once during the 12 month reporting **Reporting Instructions:** Report 3300F if American Joint Committee on Cancer (AJCC) stage is documented and reviewed or 3301F if cancer stage is documented in the medical record as metastatic and reviewed There are no performance exclusions for this measure; modifiers 1P, 2P, or 3P may not be used◄	**►3300F** **3301F◄**	►American Joint Committee on Cancer (AJCC) stage documented and reviewed Cancer stage documented in medical record as metastatic and reviewed◄
►**Hormonal Therapy for Stage IC-IIIC, ER/PR Positive Breast Cancer**[1]—Whether or not the female patient aged 18 years and older with Stage IC through Stage IIIC, estrogen receptor (ER) or progesterone receptor (PR) positive breast cancer was prescribed tamoxifen or an aromatase inhibitor (AI) within the 12 month reporting period **Numerator:** Patients who were prescribed tamoxifen or an aromatase inhibitor (AI) within the 12 month reporting period **Denominator:** All female patients aged 18 years and older with Stage IC through Stage IIIC, estrogen receptor (ER) or progesterone receptor (PR) positive breast cancer **Exclusion(s):** Documentation of medical reason(s) for not prescribing tamoxifen or an aromatase inhibitor (eg, patient's disease has progressed to metastatic; patient is receiving a gonadotropin-releasing hormone analogue, patient has received oophorectomy, patient is receiving radiation or chemotherapy, patient diagnosis date was ≥ 5 years from reporting date) Documentation of patient reason(s) for not prescribing tamoxifen or an aromatase inhibitor (eg, patient refusal) Documentation of system reason(s) for not prescribing tamoxifen or an aromatase inhibitor (eg, patient is currently enrolled in a clinical trial) **Percentage** of female patients aged 18 years and older with Stage IC through Stage IIIC, estrogen receptor (ER) or progesterone receptor (PR) positive breast cancer who were prescribed tamoxifen or an aromatase inhibitor (AI) within the 12 month reporting period **Reporting Instructions:** Report an appropriate code from the 3302F - 3312F series for AJCC cancer stage for each patient. For patients with Stage IC through Stage IIIC (3305F-3311F) also report 3315F or 3316F. If patient with Stage IC through Stage IIIC is estrogen receptor (ER) or progesterone receptor (PR) positive (3315F), and tamoxifen or an aromatase inhibitor (AI) is prescribed, also report 4179F For patient with appropriate exclusion criteria, report 4179F with modifier 1P, 2P, or 3P (continued)	**►4179F** **Denominator Codes:** **3302F** **3303F** **3304F** **3305F** **3306F** **3307F** **3308F** **3309F** **3310F** **3311F** **3312F**	►Tamoxifen or aromatase inhibitor (AI) prescribed AJCC Cancer Stage 0, documented AJCC Cancer Stage IA, documented AJCC Cancer Stage IB, documented AJCC Cancer Stage IC, documented AJCC Cancer Stage IIA, documented AJCC Cancer Stage IIB, documented AJCC Cancer Stage IIC, documented AJCC Cancer Stage IIIA, documented AJCC Cancer Stage IIIB, documented AJCC Cancer Stage IIIC, documented AJCC Cancer Stage IV, documented

[1]Physician Consortium for Performance Improvement: www.physicianconsortium.org
[2]National Committee on Quality Assurance (NCQA): Health Employer Data Information Set (HEDIS®), www.ncqa.org
[3]Joint Commission on Accreditation of Healthcare Organizations (JCAHO), ORYX Initiative Performance Measures: www.jcaho.org/pms
[4]National Diabetes Quality Improvement Alliance: www.nationaldiabetesalliance.org
[5]Joint measure from the Physician Consortium for Performance Improvement, www.physicianconsortium.org, and National Committee on Quality Assurance (NCQA), www.ncqa.org
[6]The Society of Thoracic Surgeons, www.sts.org, National Quality Forum, www.qualityforum.org

Brief Description of Performance Measure & Source and Reporting Instructions	CPT Category II Code(s)	Code Descriptor
Oncology (ONC), cont'd		
If reporting exclusion and initial stage or ER/PR status unknown, it is not required to report one of the codes for AJCC Cancer Stage◄	**3315F** **3316F◄**	Estrogen receptor (ER) or progesterone receptor (PR) positive breast cancer Estrogen receptor (ER) and progesterone receptor (PR) negative breast cancer◄
►Adjuvant Chemotherapy for Stage IIIA Through Stage IIIC Colon Cancer Patients[1]—Whether or not the patient aged 18 years and older with Stage IIIA through Stage IIIC colon cancer was prescribed or previously received adjuvant chemotherapy within the 12 month reporting period **Numerator:** Patients who are prescribed or who have previously received adjuvant chemotherapy* within the 12 month reporting period *According to current NCCN guidelines, the following therapies are recommended: 5-fluorouracil/leucovorin or capecitabine, or 5-fluorouracil/leucovorin/oxaliplatin **Denominator:** All patients aged 18 years and older with Stage IIIA through Stage IIIC colon cancer **Exclusion(s):**Documentation of medical reason(s) for not prescribing adjuvant chemotherapy (eg, medical comorbidities, diagnosis date more than 5 years prior to the current visit date; patient's cancer has metastasized; medical contraindication/allergy, poor performance status) Documentation of patient reason(s) for not prescribing adjuvant chemotherapy (eg, patient refusal) Documentation of system reason(s) for not prescribing adjuvant chemotherapy (eg, patient is currently enrolled in a clinical trial that precludes prescription of chemotherapy) **Percentage** of patients aged 18 years and older with Stage IIIA through Stage IIIC colon cancer who are prescribed or who have previously received adjuvant chemotherapy within the 12 month reporting period **Reporting Instructions:** Report an appropriate code from the 3302F - 3312F series for AJCC cancer stage for each patient. For patient with 3309F or 3310F or 3311F, also report 4180F if patient was prescribed or previously received adjuvant chemotherapy. For patient with appropriate exclusion criteria, report 4180F with modifier 1P, 2P, or 3P. If reporting exclusion, it is not required to report one of the codes for AJCC Cancer Stage◄	**►4180F**	Adjuvant chemotherapy prescribed or previously received for Stage IIIA through Stage IIIC colon cancer
	Denominator Codes:	
	3302F	AJCC Cancer Stage 0, documented
	3303F	AJCC Cancer Stage IA, documented
	3304F	AJCC Cancer Stage IB, documented
	3305F	AJCC Cancer Stage IC, documented
	3306F	AJCC Cancer Stage IIA, documented
	3307F	AJCC Cancer Stage IIB, documented
	3308F	AJCC Cancer Stage IIC, documented
	3309F	AJCC Cancer Stage IIIA, documented
	3310F	AJCC Cancer Stage IIIB, documented
	3311F	AJCC Cancer Stage IIIC, documented
	3312F◄	AJCC Cancer Stage IV, documented
►Plan for Chemotherapy Documented Before Chemotherapy Administered[1]—Whether or not the patient with a diagnosis of breast, colon, or rectal cancer who is receiving intravenous chemotherapy had a planned chemotherapy regimen (which includes, at a minimum: drug[s] prescribed, dose, and duration) documented prior to the initiation of a new treatment regimen **Numerator:** Patients for whom the planned chemotherapy regimen (which includes, at a minimum: drug(s) prescribed, dose, and duration) is documented prior to initiation of a new treatment regimen (continued)	**►0519F◄**	►Planned chemotherapy regimen, including at a minimum: drug(s) prescribed, dose, and duration, documented prior to initiation of a new treatment regimen◄

[1]Physician Consortium for Performance Improvement: www.physicianconsortium.org
[2]National Committee on Quality Assurance (NCQA): Health Employer Data Information Set (HEDIS®), www.ncqa.org
[3]Joint Commission on Accreditation of Healthcare Organizations (JCAHO), ORYX Initiative Performance Measures: www.jcaho.org/pms
[4]National Diabetes Quality Improvement Alliance: www.nationaldiabetesalliance.org
[5]Joint measure from the Physician Consortium for Performance Improvement, www.physicianconsortium.org, and National Committee on Quality Assurance (NCQA), www.ncqa.org
[6]The Society of Thoracic Surgeons, www.sts.org, National Quality Forum, www.qualityforum.org

Brief Description of Performance Measure & Source and Reporting Instructions	CPT Category II Code(s)	Code Descriptor
Oncology (ONC), cont'd		
Denominator: All patients with a diagnosis of breast, colon, or rectal cancer who are receiving intravenous chemotherapy **Exclusion(s):** None **Percentage** of patients with a diagnosis of breast, colon, or rectal cancer who are receiving intravenous chemotherapy for whom the planned chemotherapy regimen (which includes, at a minimum: drug(s) prescribed, dose, and duration) is documented prior to the initiation of a new treatment regimen **Reporting Instructions:** There are no performance exclusions for this measure; modifiers 1P, 2P, or 3P may not be used◄		
►**Treatment Summary Communication–Radiation Oncology**[1]—Whether or not the patient with a diagnosis of cancer who has undergone radiation therapy has a treatment summary report in the chart that was communicated to the physician(s) providing continuing care within one month of completing treatment **Numerator:** Patients who have a treatment summary* report in the chart that was communicated to the physician(s) providing continuing care within one month of completing treatment ***Treatment Summary definition - a report that includes mention of all of the following components: (1) dose delivered; (2) relevant assessment of tolerance to and progress towards the treatment goals; and (3) subsequent care plans** **Denominator:** All patients with a diagnosis of cancer who have undergone brachytherapy or external beam radiation therapy **Exclusion(s):** Documentation of a patient reason(s) for not communicating the treatment summary report to the physician(s) providing continuing care (eg, patient requests that report not be sent) Documentation of a system reason(s) for not communicating the treatment summary report to the physician(s) providing continuing care (eg, patient does not have any physician responsible for providing continuing care) **Percentage** of patients with a diagnosis of cancer who have undergone brachytherapy or external beam radiation therapy who have a treatment summary* report in the chart that was communicated to the physician(s) providing continuing care within one month of completing treatment **Reporting Instructions:** This measure is reported once at the conclusion of each course of radiation treatment For patient with appropriate exclusion criteria, report 5020F with modifier 2P or 3P◄	**►5020F◄**	►Treatment summary report communicated to physician(s) managing continuing care within one month of completing treatment◄
►**Normal Tissue Dose Constraints Specified**[1]—Whether or not the patient with a diagnosis of cancer receiving 3D conformal radiation therapy had documentation in medical record that normal tissue dose constraints were established within 5 treatment days from the initiation of a course of conformal radiation for a minimum of one tissue **Numerator:** Patients who had documentation in medical record that normal tissue dose constraints were established within five treatment days from the initiation of a course of 3D conformal radiation for a minimum of one tissue **Denominator:** All patients with a diagnosis of cancer who receive 3D conformal radiation therapy **Exclusion(s):** None (continued)	**►0520F◄**	►Normal tissue dose constraints established within five treatment days from the initiation of a course of 3D conformal radiation for a minimum of one tissue/organ◄

[1]Physician Consortium for Performance Improvement: www.physicianconsortium.org
[2]National Committee on Quality Assurance (NCQA): Health Employer Data Information Set (HEDIS®), www.ncqa.org
[3]Joint Commission on Accreditation of Healthcare Organizations (JCAHO), ORYX Initiative Performance Measures: www.jcaho.org/pms
[4]National Diabetes Quality Improvement Alliance: www.nationaldiabetesalliance.org
[5]Joint measure from the Physician Consortium for Performance Improvement, www.physicianconsortium.org, and National Committee on Quality Assurance (NCQA), www.ncqa.org
[6]The Society of Thoracic Surgeons, www.sts.org, National Quality Forum, www.qualityforum.org

Brief Description of Performance Measure & Source and Reporting Instructions	CPT Category II Code(s)	Code Descriptor
Oncology (ONC), cont'd		
Percentage of patients with a diagnosis of cancer receiving 3D conformal radiation therapy with documentation in the medical record that normal tissue dose constraints were established within 5 treatment days from the initiation of a course of conformal radiation for a minimum of one tissue **Reporting Instructions:** There are no performance exclusions for this measure; modifiers 1P, 2P, or 3P may not be used◄		
►**Pain Intensity Quantified-Medical Oncology and Radiation Oncology**[1]—Visits for the patient with a diagnosis of cancer currently receiving chemotherapy or radiation therapy in which pain intensity is quantified **Numerator:** Number of patient visits in which pain intensity is quantified* *Pain severity can by quantified using a standard instrument, such as a 0-10 numerical rating scale, a categorical scale, or the pictorial scale **Denominator:** All visits for patients with a diagnosis of cancer currently receiving chemotherapy or radiation therapy **Exclusion(s):** None **Percentage** of visits for patients with a diagnosis of cancer currently receiving chemotherapy or radiation therapy in which pain intensity is quantified **Reporting Instructions:** Report 1126F if pain severity is quantified and no pain is present, or report 1125F if pain severity is quantified and pain is present There are no performance exclusions for this measure; modifiers 1P, 2P, or 3P may not be used◄	**►1125F** **1126F◄**	►Pain severity quantified; pain present Pain severity quantified; no pain present◄
►**Plan of Care for Pain–Medical Oncology and Radiation Oncology**[1]—Visits for the patient with a diagnosis of cancer currently receiving chemotherapy or radiation therapy who reports having pain and has a documented plan of care to address pain **Numerator:** Visits that included a documented plan of care* to address pain *A documented plan of care may include: use of opioids, a bowel regimen, nonopioid analgesics, psychological support, patient and/or family education, or reassessment of pain **Denominator:** All visits for patients with a diagnosis of cancer currently receiving chemotherapy or radiation therapy who report having pain **Exclusion(s):** None **Percentage** of visits for patients with a diagnosis of cancer currently receiving chemotherapy or radiation therapy who report having pain with a documented plan of care to address pain **Reporting Instructions:** Report 1125F or 1126F for each patient. If 1125F and a plan of care to address pain is documented, also report 0521F There are no performance exclusions for this measure; modifiers 1P, 2P, or 3P may not be used◄	**►0521F** **Denominator Codes:** **1125F** **1126F◄**	►Plan of care to address pain documented Pain severity quantified; pain present Pain severity quantified; no pain present◄
►**Pathology Report–Medical Oncology and Radiation Oncology**[1]—Whether or not the patient with a diagnosis of cancer receiving chemotherapy has a pathology report in the medical record that confirms malignancy prior to the initiation of therapy **Numerator:** Patients with a pathology report in the medical record that confirms malignancy prior to the initiation of therapy (continued)	**►3317F**	►Pathology report confirming malignancy documented in the medical record and reviewed prior to the initiation of chemotherapy

[1]Physician Consortium for Performance Improvement: www.physicianconsortium.org
[2]National Committee on Quality Assurance (NCQA): Health Employer Data Information Set (HEDIS®), www.ncqa.org
[3]Joint Commission on Accreditation of Healthcare Organizations (JCAHO), ORYX Initiative Performance Measures: www.jcaho.org/pms
[4]National Diabetes Quality Improvement Alliance: www.nationaldiabetesalliance.org
[5]Joint measure from the Physician Consortium for Performance Improvement, www.physicianconsortium.org, and National Committee on Quality Assurance (NCQA), www.ncqa.org
[6]The Society of Thoracic Surgeons, www.sts.org, National Quality Forum, www.qualityforum.org

Brief Description of Performance Measure & Source and Reporting Instructions	CPT Category II Code(s)	Code Descriptor
Oncology (ONC), cont'd		
Denominator: All patients with a diagnosis of cancer receiving chemotherapy or radiation therapy **Exclusion(s):** Documentation of a medical reason(s) for not having a pathology report in the medical record confirming malignancy prior to the initiation of therapy (eg, palliative treatment for metastatic illness) **Percentage** of patients with a diagnosis of cancer receiving chemotherapy with a pathology report in the medical record that confirms malignancy prior to the initiation of therapy **Reporting Instructions:** This measure is to be reported once at the beginning of treatment. Report 3317F for patient receiving chemotherapy or 3318F for patient receiving radiation therapy For patient with appropriate exclusion criteria, report 3317F or 3318F with modifier 1P. If patient is first seen by the reporting physician after the treatment has been initiated, the pathology report should be documented before the reporting physician continues treatment. The physician continuing the treatment(s) should report as if treatment is being initiated◄	**3318F◄**	Pathology report confirming malignancy documented in the medical record and reviewed prior to the initiation of radiation therapy◄
Osteoarthritis (Adult)		
Composite Measure: Osteoarthritis Assessment—See individual measures listed below for: Osteoarthritis symptoms and functional status assessed (1006F) Use of anti-inflammatory or over-the-counter (OTC) analgesic medications assessed (1007F) Initial examination of the involved joint(s) (includes visual inspection, palpation, range of motion) (2004F)	**0005F**	Osteoarthritis **assessed**
Symptom and Functional Assessment[1]—Patient visits with assessment for function and pain/number of visits **Numerator:** Patient visits with assessment for level of function and pain documented during the reporting year **Denominator:** All visits for patients aged ≥ 21 years with osteoarthritis **Exclusion:** None **Percentage** of osteoarthritis patient visits with assessment for function and pain during the reporting year **Reporting Instructions:** Use when osteoarthritis is addressed during the patient encounter There are no exclusions for this measure; modifiers 1P, 2P, and 3P may not be used	**1006F**	Osteoarthritis symptoms and functional status assessed (may include the use of a standardized scale or the completion of an assessment questionnaire, such as the SF-36, AAOS Hip & Knee Questionnaire)
Assessment for Use of Anti-Inflammatory or Analgesic OTC Medications[1]—Patient visits with assessment for use of anti-inflammatory or analgesic OTC medications per number of visits during the reporting year **Numerator:** Patient visits with assessment for use of anti-inflammatory or analgesic OTC medications **Denominator:** All patient visits for patients aged ≥ 21 years with osteoarthritis **Percentage** of osteoarthritis patient visits with assessment for use of anti-inflammatory or analgesic over-the-counter (OTC) medications (continued)	**1007F**	Use of anti-inflammatory or analgesic over-the-counter (OTC) medications for symptom relief assessed

[1]Physician Consortium for Performance Improvement: www.physicianconsortium.org
[2]National Committee on Quality Assurance (NCQA): Health Employer Data Information Set (HEDIS®), www.ncqa.org
[3]Joint Commission on Accreditation of Healthcare Organizations (JCAHO), ORYX Initiative Performance Measures: www.jcaho.org/pms
[4]National Diabetes Quality Improvement Alliance: www.nationaldiabetesalliance.org
[5]Joint measure from the Physician Consortium for Performance Improvement, www.physicianconsortium.org, and National Committee on Quality Assurance (NCQA), www.ncqa.org
[6]The Society of Thoracic Surgeons, www.sts.org, National Quality Forum, www.qualityforum.org

Brief Description of Performance Measure & Source and Reporting Instructions	CPT Category II Code(s)	Code Descriptor
Osteoarthritis (Adult), cont'd		
Reporting Instructions: Use when osteoarthritis is addressed during the patient encounter There are no exclusions for this measure; modifiers 1P, 2P, and 3P may not be used		
Nonsteroidal Anti-inflammatory Drug (NSAID) Risk Assessment[1]—Whether or not patient on prescribed or OTC NSAIDs was assessed for GI/renal risk factors during the reporting year **Numerator:** Patients who were assessed for *all* of the following GI and Renal risk factors during the reporting year: • GI bleed • History of peptic ulcer disease (PUD) • Concomitant use of glucocorticoids or anticoagulants • Smoking • Significant alcohol use • Age > 65 years • Renal disease (Cr > 2.0 mg/dl) • Hypertension • Heart failure • Concomitant use of diuretic or angiotensin-converting enzyme (ACE) inhibitor **Denominator:** All patients ≥ 21 years of age with osteoarthritis on a prescribed or OTC NSAID **Percentage** of patients ≥ 21 years of age with osteoarthritis on prescribed or OTC NSAIDs who were assessed for gastrointestinal and renal risk factors during the reporting year **Reporting Instructions:** There are no exclusions for this measure; modifiers 1P, 2P, and 3P may not be used	**1008F**	Gastrointestinal and renal risk factors assessed for patients on prescribed or OTC non-steroidal anti-inflammatory drug (NSAID)
Physical Examination of the Involved Joint[1]—Whether or not a physical examination of the involved joint was performed during the initial visit during the reporting year **Numerator:** Patients for whom a physical examination of the involved joint was performed during the initial visit during the reporting year **Denominator:** All patients aged ≥ 21 years of age with osteoarthritis **Percentage** of patients > 21 years of age with osteoarthritis for whom a physical examination of the involved joint was performed during the initial visit during the reporting year **Reporting Instructions:** Use only for initial osteoarthritis visit or for visits for new joint involvement There are no exclusions for this measure; modifiers 1P, 2P, and 3P may not be used	**2004F**	Initial examination of the involved joint(s) (includes visual inspection, palpation, range of motion)
Anti-inflammatory/Analgesic Therapy[1]—Patient visits during which an anti-inflammatory agent or analgesic was considered/Number of visits during the reporting year **Numerator:** Patient visits during which an anti-inflammatory agent or analgesic was considered during the reporting year **Denominator:** All patient visits for patients aged ≥ 21 years of age with osteoarthritis (continued)	**4016F**	Anti-inflammatory/analgesic agent prescribed

[1]Physician Consortium for Performance Improvement: www.physicianconsortium.org
[2]National Committee on Quality Assurance (NCQA): Health Employer Data Information Set (HEDIS®), www.ncqa.org
[3]Joint Commission on Accreditation of Healthcare Organizations (JCAHO), ORYX Initiative Performance Measures: www.jcaho.org/pms
[4]National Diabetes Quality Improvement Alliance: www.nationaldiabetesalliance.org
[5]Joint measure from the Physician Consortium for Performance Improvement, www.physicianconsortium.org, and National Committee on Quality Assurance (NCQA), www.ncqa.org
[6]The Society of Thoracic Surgeons, www.sts.org, National Quality Forum, www.qualityforum.org

Brief Description of Performance Measure & Source and Reporting Instructions	CPT Category II Code(s)	Code Descriptor
Osteoarthritis (Adult), cont'd		
Numerator Inclusion(s): Documentation that an anti-inflammatory agent or analgesic was prescribed; Documentation of medical or patient reasons(s) for not prescribing an anti-inflammatory agent or analgesic **Percentage** of visits for patients ≥21 years of age with osteoarthritis during which an anti-inflammatory agent or analgesic was considered during the reporting year **Reporting Instructions:** Report 4016F alone or with modifier (1P if medical reason for not prescribing an anti-inflammatory or analgesic was documented or 2P modifier if patient reason for not prescribing an anti-inflammatory or analgesic was documented.) For this measure, the modifiers do not act as denominator exclusions, but rather demonstrate that therapy was considered and are included in the numerator when calculating the measure		
Gastrointestinal Prophylaxis[1]—Patient visits during which GI prophylaxis was considered/Number of visits during the reporting year **Numerator:** Patient visits during which GI prophylaxis was considered during the reporting year **Denominator:** All visits for patients aged ≥ 21 years of age with osteoarthritis on a prescribed or OTC NSAID **Numerator Inclusion(s):** Documentation that GI prophylaxis was prescribed; documentation of medical or patient reason(s) for not prescribing GI prophylaxis **Percentage** of visits for patients aged ≥ 21 years of age with osteoarthritis during which GI prophylaxis was considered during the reporting year **Reporting Instructions:** Report 4017F alone or with modifier (1P if medical reason for not prescribing GI prophylaxis was documented or 2P modifier if patient reason for not prescribing GI prophylaxis was documented). For this measure, the modifiers do not act as denominator exclusions, but rather demonstrate that therapy was considered and are included in the numerator when calculating the measure	**4017F**	Gastrointestinal prophylaxis for NSAID use prescribed
Therapeutic Exercise for the Involved Joint[1]—Patient visits during which therapeutic exercise for the hip or knee was considered/Number of visits during the reporting year **Numerator:** Patient visits during which therapeutic exercise for the knee or hip was considered during the reporting year **Denominator:** All patient visits for patients ≥ 21 years of age with osteoarthritis of the hip or knee **Numerator Inclusion(s):** Documentation of medical or patient reason(s) for not instructing therapeutic exercise or prescribing physical therapy for the hip or knee; documentation that therapeutic exercise for the hip or knee was instructed; documentation that physical therapy for the hip or knee was prescribed **Percentage** of visits for patients ≥ 21 years of age with osteoarthritis of the hip or knee during which therapeutic exercise for the hip or knee (therapeutic exercise instructed or physical therapy prescribed) was considered during the reporting year **Reporting Instructions:** Report 4018F alone or or with modifier (1P if medical reason for not instructing therapeutic exercise or prescribing physical therapy was documented; 2P if patient reason for not instructing therapeutic exercise or prescribing physical therapy was documented.) For this measure, the modifiers do not act as denominator exclusions, but rather demonstrate that therapy was considered and are included in the numerator when calculating the measure	**4018F**	Therapeutic exercise for the involved joint(s) instructed or physical or occupational therapy prescribed

[1]Physician Consortium for Performance Improvement: www.physicianconsortium.org
[2]National Committee on Quality Assurance (NCQA): Health Employer Data Information Set (HEDIS®), www.ncqa.org
[3]Joint Commission on Accreditation of Healthcare Organizations (JCAHO), ORYX Initiative Performance Measures: www.jcaho.org/pms
[4]National Diabetes Quality Improvement Alliance: www.nationaldiabetesalliance.org
[5]Joint measure from the Physician Consortium for Performance Improvement, www.physicianconsortium.org, and National Committee on Quality Assurance (NCQA), www.ncqa.org
[6]The Society of Thoracic Surgeons, www.sts.org, National Quality Forum, www.qualityforum.org

Brief Description of Performance Measure & Source and Reporting Instructions	CPT Category II Code(s)	Code Descriptor
Osteoporosis (OP)		
Communication with the Physician Managing On-going Care Post Fracture[5] (Measure #1)—Whether or not the patient aged 50 years and older treated for a hip, spine or distal radial fracture had documentation of communication to the physician managing the patient's on-going care that a fracture occurred and that the patient was or should be tested or treated for osteoporosis **Numerator:** Patients with documentation of communication with the physician managing the patient's on-going care that a fracture occurred and that the patient was or should be tested or treated for osteoporosis Communication may include: Documentation in the medical record indicating that the physician treating the fracture communicated (eg, verbally, by letter, DEXA report was sent with the physician managing the patient's on-going care OR A copy of a letter in the medical record outlining whether the patient was or should be treated for osteoporosis. **Denominator:** All patients aged 50 years and older treated for hip, spine or distal radial fracture **Exclusion(s):** Documentation of medical or patient reason(s) for not communicating with the physician managing the patient's on-going care that a fracture occurred and that the patient was or should be tested or treated for osteoporosis **Percentage** of patients aged 50 years and older treated for a hip, spine or distal radial fracture with documentation of communication with the physician managing the patient's on-going care that a fracture occurred and that the patient was or should be tested or treated for osteoporosis **Reporting Instructions:** -If the physician treating the fracture is the same physician who is providing the ongoing care, report 5015F -For patient with appropriate exclusion criteria report 5015F with modifier 1P or 2P -Communication to the physician managing the ongoing care of the patient must should occur within 3 months of treatment for the fracture to allow reporting of 5015F	**5015F**	Documentation of communication that a fracture occurred and that the patient was or should be tested or treated for osteoporosis Osteoporosis (OP)
Osteoporosis (OP) Screening or Therapy for Women Aged 65 Years and Older[5]—Whether or not the female patient aged 65 years and older who had a central DXA measurement ordered or performed at least once since age 60 or pharmacologic therapy prescribed within 12 months **Numerator:** Patients who had a central DXA measurement ordered or results documented at least once since age 60 or pharmacologic therapy prescribed within 12 months **Denominator:** All female patients aged 65 years and older **Exclusion(s):** Documentation of medical, patient, or system reason(s) for not ordering or performing a central DXA measurement or not prescribing pharmacologic therapy **Percentage** of female patients aged 65 years and older who have a central DXA measurement ordered or results documented at least once since age 60 or pharmacologic therapy prescribed within 12 months (continued)	**3095F** **3096F** **4005F**	Central Dual-energy X-Ray Absorptiometry (DXA) results documented Central Dual-energy X-Ray Absorptiometry (DXA) ordered Pharmacologic therapy (other than minerals/vitamins) for osteoporosis prescribed

[1]Physician Consortium for Performance Improvement: www.physicianconsortium.org
[2]National Committee on Quality Assurance (NCQA): Health Employer Data Information Set (HEDIS®), www.ncqa.org
[3]Joint Commission on Accreditation of Healthcare Organizations (JCAHO), ORYX Initiative Performance Measures: www.jcaho.org/pms
[4]National Diabetes Quality Improvement Alliance: www.nationaldiabetesalliance.org
[5]Joint measure from the Physician Consortium for Performance Improvement, www.physicianconsortium.org, and National Committee on Quality Assurance (NCQA), www.ncqa.org
[6]The Society of Thoracic Surgeons, www.sts.org, National Quality Forum, www.qualityforum.org

Brief Description of Performance Measure & Source and Reporting Instructions	CPT Category II Code(s)	Code Descriptor
Osteoporosis (OP), cont'd		
Reporting Instructions: -Report 3095F if patient has documentation of being tested since age 60 -Report 3096F If Central DXA was ordered -Report 4005F if patient was treated using pharmacologic agents for osteoporosis -For patient with appropriate exclusion criteria report either 3095F, 3096F, or 4005F with modifier 1P, 2P, or 3P.		
Osteoporosis (OP) Management Following Fracture[5]—Whether or not the patient aged 50 years and older with a fracture of the hip, spine or distal radius had a central DXA measurement ordered or results documented or pharmacologic therapy prescribed **Numerator:** Patients who had a central DXA measurement ordered or results documented or pharmacologic therapy prescribed **Denominator:** All patients aged 50 years and older with a fracture of the hip, spine or distal radius **Exclusion(s):** Documentation of medical, patient, or system reason(s) for not ordering or performing a central DXA measurement or not prescribing pharmacologic therapy **Percentage** of patients aged 50 years and older with a fracture of the hip, spine or distal radius who had a central DXA measurement ordered or performed or pharmacologic therapy prescribed **Reporting Instructions:** -Report either 3095F or 4005F if patient has documentation of being tested or treated for osteoporosis -Report 3096F if Central DXA was ordered -For patient with appropriate exclusion criteria report either 3095F, 3096F or 4005F with modifier 1P, 2P, or 3P -The management (DXA ordered or performed or pharmacologic therapy prescribe) should occur within 3 months of notification of the fracture from the physician treating the fracture	**3095F** **3096F** **4005F** **76075**	Central Dual-energy X-Ray Absorptiometry (DXA) results documented Central Dual-energy X-Ray Absorptiometry (DXA) ordered Pharmacologic therapy (other than minerals/vitamins) for osteoporosis prescribed Dual energy X-ray absorptiometry (DXA), bone density study, one or more sites; axial skeleton (eg, hips, pelvis, spine)
Pharmacologic Therapy[5]—Whether or not the patient aged 50 years and older with a diagnosis of osteoporosis was prescribed pharmacologic therapy within 12 months **Numerator:** Patients who were prescribed pharmacologic therapy* within 12 months *U.S. Food and Drug Administration approved pharmacologic options for osteoporosis prevention and/or treatment of postmenopausal osteoporosis include, in alphabetical order: bisphosphonates (alendronate, ibandronate, and risedronate), calcitonin, estrogens (estrogens and/or hormone therapy), parathyroid hormone [PTH (1-34), teriparatide], and selective estrogen receptor modules or SERMS (raloxifene). **Denominator:** All patients aged 50 years and older with the diagnosis of osteoporosis **Exclusion(s):** Documentation of medical, patient, or system reason(s) for not prescribing pharmacologic therapy **Percentage** of patients aged 50 years and older with a diagnosis of osteoporosis who were prescribed pharmacologic therapy within 12 months **Reporting Instructions:** For patient with appropriate exclusion criteria report 4005F with modifier 1P, 2P, or 3P	**4005F**	Pharmacologic therapy (other than minerals/vitamins) for osteoporosis prescribed

[1]Physician Consortium for Performance Improvement: www.physicianconsortium.org
[2]National Committee on Quality Assurance (NCQA): Health Employer Data Information Set (HEDIS®), www.ncqa.org
[3]Joint Commission on Accreditation of Healthcare Organizations (JCAHO), ORYX Initiative Performance Measures: www.jcaho.org/pms
[4]National Diabetes Quality Improvement Alliance: www.nationaldiabetesalliance.org
[5]Joint measure from the Physician Consortium for Performance Improvement, www.physicianconsortium.org, and National Committee on Quality Assurance (NCQA), www.ncqa.org
[6]The Society of Thoracic Surgeons, www.sts.org, National Quality Forum, www.qualityforum.org

Brief Description of Performance Measure & Source and Reporting Instructions	CPT Category II Code(s)	Code Descriptor
Osteoporosis (OP), cont'd		
Osteoporosis (OP) Counseling for Vitamin D and Calcium Intake and Exercise[5]—Whether or not the patient, regardless of age, with a diagnosis of osteoporosis is either receiving both calcium and vitamin D or had documented counseling regarding both calcium and vitamin D intake, and exercise at least once within 12 months **Numerator:** Patients who are either receiving both calcium and vitamin D or have been counseled regarding both calcium and vitamin D intake, and exercise at least once within 12 months **Denominator:** All patients, regardless of age, with the diagnosis of osteoporosis **Exclusion(s):** Documentation of medical reason(s) for patient not receiving both calcium and vitamin D and not needing counseling regarding both calcium and vitamin D intake, and exercise (eg, patient has dementia and is unable to receive counseling) **Percentage** of patients, regardless of age, with a diagnosis of osteoporosis who either received both calcium and vitamin D or had documented counseling regarding both calcium and vitamin D intake, and exercise at least once within 12 months **Reporting Instructions:** -Report 4019F if there is documentation that patient is either receiving both calcium and vitamin D or was counseled regarding calcium and vitamin D use; and also counseled on exercise within 12 months -For patient with appropriate exclusion criteria report 4019F with modifier 1P	**4019F**	Documentation of receipt of counseling on exercise AND either both calcium and vitamin D use or counseling regarding both calcium and vitamin D use
►Pathology (PATH)◄		
►Breast Cancer Resection Pathology Reporting-pT Category (Primary Tumor) and pN (Regional Lymph Nodes) with Histologic Grade[1]—Whether or not the breast cancer pathology report included the pT category, the pN category and the histologic grade **Numerator:** Reports that include the pT category, the pN category and the histologic grade **Denominator:** All breast cancer resection pathology reports (excluding biopsies) **Exclusion(s):** Documentation of medical reason(s) for not including the pT category, the pN category or the histologic grade (eg, re-excision without residual tumor; non-carcinomas) **Percentage** of breast cancer resection pathology reports that include the pT category (primary tumor), the pN category (regional lymph nodes) and the histologic grade **Reporting Instructions:** Report this measure each time a breast cancer resection pathology report is prepared. For breast cancer resection pathology report with appropriate exclusion criteria report 3260F with modifier 1P◄	**►3260F◄**	►pT category (primary tumor) and pN category (regional lymph nodes) and histologic grade documented in pathology report◄
►Colorectal Cancer Resection Pathology Reporting-pT Category (Primary Tumor) and pN Category (Regional Lymph Node) with Histologic Grade[1]—Whether or not the colorectal cancer resection pathology report includes the pT category, the pN category and the histologic grade **Numerator:** Reports that include the pT category, the pN category and the histologic grade **Denominator:** All colon and rectum cancer resection pathology reports (continued)	**►3260F◄**	►pT category (primary tumor) and pN category (regional lymph nodes) and histologic grade documented in pathology report◄

[1]Physician Consortium for Performance Improvement: www.physicianconsortium.org
[2]National Committee on Quality Assurance (NCQA): Health Employer Data Information Set (HEDIS®), www.ncqa.org
[3]Joint Commission on Accreditation of Healthcare Organizations (JCAHO), ORYX Initiative Performance Measures: www.jcaho.org/pms
[4]National Diabetes Quality Improvement Alliance: www.nationaldiabetesalliance.org
[5]Joint measure from the Physician Consortium for Performance Improvement, www.physicianconsortium.org, and National Committee on Quality Assurance (NCQA), www.ncqa.org
[6]The Society of Thoracic Surgeons, www.sts.org, National Quality Forum, www.qualityforum.org

Brief Description of Performance Measure & Source and Reporting Instructions	CPT Category II Code(s)	Code Descriptor
►Pathology (PATH)◄, cont'd		
Exclusion(s): Documentation of medical reason(s) for not including the pT category, the pN category or the histologic grade (eg, non-carcinomas; anal canal) **Percentage** of colon and rectum cancer resection pathology reports that include the pT category (primary tumor), the pN (lymph nodes) category and the histologic grade **Reporting Instructions:** Report this measure each time a colorectal cancer resection pathology report is prepared. For colon and rectum cancer resection pathology report with appropriate exclusion criteria report 3260F with modifier 1P◄		
Pediatric Acute Gastroenteritis (PAG)		
Documentation of Hydration Status[1]—Whether or not a patient 1 month through 5 years of age with a diagnosis of acute gastroenteritis had a documented hydration status **Numerator:** Patients with documented hydration status **Denominator:** Patients 1 month through 5 years of age with the diagnosis of acute gastroenteritis **Exclusion(s):** None **Percentage** of patients 1 month through 5 years of age with a diagnosis of acute gastroenteritis who had hydration status documented **Report Instructions:** There are no exclusions for this measure; modifiers 1P, 2P, and 3P may not be used	**2030F** **2031F**	Hydration status documented, normally hydrated Hydration status documented, dehydrated
Weight Measurement[1]—Whether or not patient 1 month through 5 years of age with a diagnosis of acute gastroenteritis had weight measurement recorded **Numerator:** Patients who had their weight measurement recorded **Denominator:** Patients 1 month through 5 years of age with a diagnosis of acute gastroenteritis **Exclusion(s):** None **Percentage** of patients 1 month through 5 years of age with a diagnosis of acute gastroenteritis who had weight measurement recorded **Reporting Instructions:** There are no exclusions for this measure; modifiers 1P, 2P, and 3P may not be used	**2001F**	Weight recorded
Recommendation of Appropriate Oral Rehydration Solution[1]—Whether or not an appropriate oral rehydration solution was recommended for the patient 1 month through 5 years of age with a diagnosis of acute gastroenteritis **Numerator:** Patients for whom an appropriate oral rehydration solution was recommended **Denominator:** Patients 1 month through 5 years of age with the diagnosis of acute gastroenteritis, treated in ambulatory settings (eg, physician office or treated in the emergency department and discharged to home) **Exclusion(s):** None **Percentage** of patients 1 month through 5 years of age with the diagnosis of acute gastroenteritis for whom an appropriate oral rehydration solution was recommended **Reporting Instructions:** Report 2030F or 2031F for all patients. Report 4056F with 2031F	**4056F** **Denominator Codes:** **2030F** **2031F**	Appropriate oral rehydration solution recommended Hydration status documented, normally hydrated Hydration status documented, dehydrated

[1]Physician Consortium for Performance Improvement: www.physicianconsortium.org
[2]National Committee on Quality Assurance (NCQA): Health Employer Data Information Set (HEDIS®), www.ncqa.org
[3]Joint Commission on Accreditation of Healthcare Organizations (JCAHO), ORYX Initiative Performance Measures: www.jcaho.org/pms
[4]National Diabetes Quality Improvement Alliance: www.nationaldiabetesalliance.org
[5]Joint measure from the Physician Consortium for Performance Improvement, www.physicianconsortium.org, and National Committee on Quality Assurance (NCQA), www.ncqa.org
[6]The Society of Thoracic Surgeons, www.sts.org, National Quality Forum, www.qualityforum.org

Brief Description of Performance Measure & Source and Reporting Instructions	CPT Category II Code(s)	Code Descriptor
Pediatric Acute Gastroenteritis (PAG), cont'd		
Education[1]—Whether or not a patient's caregiver received education on diet and on when to contact the physician for a patient 1 month through 5 years of age with a diagnosis of acute gastroenteritis **Numerator:** Patients whose caregiver received education regarding diet and when to contact the physician **Denominator:** All patients 1month through 5 years of age with the diagnosis of acute gastroenteritis, treated in ambulatory settings (physician office or treated in the emergency room and discharged to home **Exclusion(s):** None **Percentage** of patients 1 month through 5 years of age with a diagnosis of acute gastroenteritis whose caregiver received education regarding diet and on when to contact the physician **Reporting Instructions:** There are no exclusions for this measure; modifiers 1P, 2P, and 3P may not be used	**4058F**	Pediatric Gastroenteritis Education provided to caregiver
Pediatric Pharyngitis (PHAR)		
Appropriate Testing for Children with Pharyngitis[2]—Whether or not children 2-18 years of age (inclusive) who were diagnosed with pharyngitis and dispensed or prescribed an antibiotic received a group A strep test. **Numerator:** Patients who received a group A streptococcus (strep) test **Denominator:** All patients aged 2-18 years with the diagnosis of pharyngitis who were dispensed or prescribed antibiotic treatment **Exclusion(s):** Medical or patient reasons for not performing Group A Strep Tests. **Percentage** of children 2-18 years of age (inclusive) diagnosed with pharyngitis and dispensed or prescribed an antibiotic who received a group A strep test for the visit. **Reporting Instructions:** Note: Because this measure is being specified for physician reporting, the instructions request physicians to report prescribing or dispensing of medication. For Medical or patient reasons for not performing a Group A Strep Test, report code 3210F with modifier 1P or 2P There are no performance measure exclusions for codes 4120F and 4124F for children with pharyngitis. Do not report modifiers 1P, 2P, or 3P with these codes for this condition	**3210F** **Denominator Codes:** **4120F** **4124F**	 Antibiotic prescribed or dispensed Antibiotic neither prescribed nor dispensed
Perioperative Care 2 (PERI 2)		
Timing of Prophylactic Antibiotics–Ordering Physician[5]—Whether or not the surgical patient aged 18 years and older undergoing a procedure with the indications for prophylactic parenteral antibiotics had an order for an antibiotic to be given within one hour (if vancomycin, two hours) prior to the surgical incision (or start of procedure when no incision is required) **Numerator:** Surgical patients who have an order for an antibiotic to be given within one hour (if vancomycin, two hours) prior to the surgical incision (or start of procedure when no incision is required) **Denominator:** All surgical patients aged 18 years and older undergoing procedures with the indications for prophylactic parenteral antibiotics (List of procedures is available in measure specifications) (continued)	**4047F** **4048F**	Documentation of order for prophylactic antibiotics to be given within one hour (if fluoroquinolone or vancomycin, two hours) prior to surgical incision (or start of procedure when no incision is required) Documentation that prophylactic antibiotic was given within one hour (if fluoroquinolone or vancomycin, two hours) prior to surgical incision (or start of procedure when no incision is required)

[1]Physician Consortium for Performance Improvement: www.physicianconsortium.org
[2]National Committee on Quality Assurance (NCQA): Health Employer Data Information Set (HEDIS®), www.ncqa.org
[3]Joint Commission on Accreditation of Healthcare Organizations (JCAHO), ORYX Initiative Performance Measures: www.jcaho.org/pms
[4]National Diabetes Quality Improvement Alliance: www.nationaldiabetesalliance.org
[5]Joint measure from the Physician Consortium for Performance Improvement, www.physicianconsortium.org, and National Committee on Quality Assurance (NCQA), www.ncqa.org
[6]The Society of Thoracic Surgeons, www.sts.org, National Quality Forum, www.qualityforum.org

Brief Description of Performance Measure & Source and Reporting Instructions	CPT Category II Code(s)	Code Descriptor
Perioperative Care 2 (PERI 2), cont'd		
Exclusion(s): Documentation of medical reason(s) for not ordering an antibiotic to be given within one hour (if vancomycin, two hours) prior to the surgical incision (or start of procedure when no incision is required) **Percentage** of surgical patients aged 18 years and older undergoing procedures with the indications for prophylactic parenteral antibiotics who have an order for an antibiotic to be given within one hour (if vancomycin, two hours) prior to the surgical incision (or start of procedure when no incision is required) **Reporting Instructions:** It is anticipated that this measure will be reported by the physician performing the procedure • There must be documentation of an order (written, verbal or standing order/protocol) specifying that antibiotic is to be given within the specified timeframe OR documentation that antibiotic has been given within the specified timeframe • Report 4047F if prophylactic antibiotic was ordered or 4048F if antibiotic has been given. • For patient meeting exclusion criteria, report 4047F with modifier 1P		
Timing of Prophylactic Antibiotics–Administering Physician[5]—Whether or not administration of prophylactic parenteral antibiotic was initiated within one hour (if fluoroquinolone or vancomycin, two hours) prior to the surgical incision (or start of procedure when no incision is required) for the surgical patient aged 18 years and older who had an order for a prophylactic parenteral antibiotic to be given within one hour (if fluoroquinolone or vancomycin, two hours) prior to the surgical incision (or start of procedure when no incision is required) **Numerator:** Surgical patients for whom administration of a prophylactic antibiotic has been initiated within one hour (if fluoroquinolone or vancomycin, two hours) prior to the surgical incision (or start of procedure when no incision is required) **Denominator:** All surgical patients aged 18 years and older who have an order for a parenteral antibiotic to be given within one hour (if fluoroquinolone or vancomycin, two hours) prior to the surgical incision (or start of procedure when no incision is required) **Exclusion(s):** None **Percentage** of surgical patients aged 18 years and older who have an order for a parenteral antibiotic to be given within one hour (if fluoroquinolone or vancomycin, two hours) prior to the surgical incision (or start of procedure when no incision is required) for whom administration of a prophylactic antibiotic has been initiated within one hour (if fluoroquinolone or vancomycin, two hours) prior to the surgical incision (or start of procedure when no incision is required) **Reporting Instructions:** • It is anticipated that the physician administering or responsible for the administering the prophylactic antibiotic will report this measure. The identification of patients for the denominator of this measure is exclusively dependent on the presence of an order for prophylactic antibiotics to be given. A surgical procedure list is not used to identify these patients • There must be documentation of an order (written, verbal or standing order/protocol) specifying that antibiotic is to be given within the specified timeframe • Report 4047F where there is documentation of an order for prophylactic antibiotics to be given within one hour of surgical incision. If antibiotics were not given within the appropriate timeframe as ordered, report only 4047F • Also report 4048F when prophylactic antibiotic was given within the specified timeframe There are no exclusions for this measure; modifiers 1P, 2P, and 3P may not be used	**4048F** **Denominator Code:** **4047F**	Documentation that prophylactic antibiotic was given within one hour (if fluoroquinolone or vancomycin, two hours) prior to surgical incision (or start of procedure when no incision is required) Documentation of order for prophylactic antibiotic to be given within one hour (if fluoroquinolone or vancomycin, two hours) prior to surgical incision (or start of procedure when no incision is required)

[1]Physician Consortium for Performance Improvement: www.physicianconsortium.org

[2]National Committee on Quality Assurance (NCQA): Health Employer Data Information Set (HEDIS®), www.ncqa.org

[3]Joint Commission on Accreditation of Healthcare Organizations (JCAHO), ORYX Initiative Performance Measures: www.jcaho.org/pms

[4]National Diabetes Quality Improvement Alliance: www.nationaldiabetesalliance.org

[5]Joint measure from the Physician Consortium for Performance Improvement, www.physicianconsortium.org, and National Committee on Quality Assurance (NCQA), www.ncqa.org

[6]The Society of Thoracic Surgeons, www.sts.org, National Quality Forum, www.qualityforum.org

Brief Description of Performance Measure & Source and Reporting Instructions	CPT Category II Code(s)	Code Descriptor
Perioperative Care 2 (PERI 2), cont'd		
Selection of Prophylactic Antibiotic–First OR Second Generation Cephalosporin[5]—Whether or not the surgical patient aged 18 years and older undergoing a procedure with the indications for a first OR second generation cephalosporin had an order for cefazolin OR cefuroxime for antimicrobial prophylaxis **Numerator:** Surgical patients who had an order for cefazolin OR cefuroxime for antimicrobial prophylaxis **Denominator:** All surgical patients aged 18 years and older undergoing procedures with the indications for a first OR second generation cephalosporin prophylactic antibiotic (List of procedures is available in measure specifications) **Exclusion(s):** Documentation of medical reason(s) for not ordering cefazolin OR cefuroxime for antimicrobial prophylaxis **Percentage** of surgical patients aged 18 years and older undergoing procedures with the indications for a first OR second generation cephalosporin prophylactic antibiotic who had an order for cefazolin OR cefuroxime for antimicrobial prophylaxis **Reporting Instructions:** • It is anticipated that this measure will be reported by the physician performing the procedure • There must be documentation of an *order* (written, verbal or standing order/protocol) for cefazolin or cefuroxime for antimicrobial prophylaxis OR documentation that cefazolin or cefuroxime was *given* • Report 4041F if cefazolin or cefuroxime was ordered • If either cefazolin or cefuroxime was administered, there is a presumption that an order existed for that administration. In this case, 4041F should be reported • For patient with appropriate exclusion criteria report 4041F with modifier 1P	**4041F**	Documentation of order for cefazolin OR cefuroxime for antimicrobial prophylaxis
Discontinuation of Prophylactic Antibiotics (Non-Cardiac Procedures)[5]—Whether or not the non-cardiac surgical patient aged 18 years and older undergoing a procedure with the indications for prophylactic antibiotics AND who received a prophylactic antibiotic, has an order for discontinuation of prophylactic antibiotics within 24 hours of surgical end time **Numerator:** Non-cardiac surgical patients who have an order for discontinuation of prophylactic antibiotics within 24 hours of surgical end time **Denominator:** All non-cardiac surgical patients 18 years and older undergoing procedures with the indications for prophylactic antibiotics AND who received a prophylactic antibiotic (List of procedures is available in measure specifications) **Exclusion(s):** Documentation of medical reason(s) for not discontinuing prophylactic antibiotics within 24 hours of surgical end time **Percentage** of non-cardiac surgical patients aged 18 years and older undergoing procedures with the indications for prophylactic antibiotics AND who received a prophylactic antibiotic, who have an order for discontinuation of prophylactic antibiotics within 24 hours of surgical end time (continued)	**4049F** **Denominator Codes:** **4046F** **4042F**	Documentation that order was given to discontinue prophylactic antibiotics within 24 hours of surgical end time, non-cardiac procedure Documentation that prophylactic antibiotics were given within 4 hours prior to surgical incision or given intraoperatively Documentation that prophylactic antibiotics were neither given within 4 hours prior to surgical incision nor given intraoperatively

[1]Physician Consortium for Performance Improvement: www.physicianconsortium.org
[2]National Committee on Quality Assurance (NCQA): Health Employer Data Information Set (HEDIS®), www.ncqa.org
[3]Joint Commission on Accreditation of Healthcare Organizations (JCAHO), ORYX Initiative Performance Measures: www.jcaho.org/pms
[4]National Diabetes Quality Improvement Alliance: www.nationaldiabetesalliance.org
[5]Joint measure from the Physician Consortium for Performance Improvement, www.physicianconsortium.org, and National Committee on Quality Assurance (NCQA), www.ncqa.org
[6]The Society of Thoracic Surgeons, www.sts.org, National Quality Forum, www.qualityforum.org

Brief Description of Performance Measure & Source and Reporting Instructions	CPT Category II Code(s)	Code Descriptor
Perioperative Care 2 (PERI 2), cont'd		
Reporting Instructions: • It is anticipated that this measure will be reported by the physician performing the procedure • Patients may be counted as having "received a prophylactic antibiotic" if the antibiotic was received within 4 hours prior to the surgical incision (or start of procedure when no incision is required) or intraoperatively • There must be documentation of an *order* (written, verbal or standing order/protocol) specifying that prophylactic antibiotic is to be discontinued within 24 hours of surgical end time **OR** specifying a course of antibiotic administration limited to that 24-hour period (eg, to be given every 8 hours for three doses) **OR** documentation that prophylactic antibiotic *was* discontinued within 24 hours of surgical end time • Report either 4046F or 4042F for each patient. If patient received prophylactic antibiotics and there was an order for discontinuation within 24 hours after surgical end time, also report 4049F. For patient with appropriate exclusion criteria, report 4049F with modifier 1P		
Discontinuation of Prophylactic Antibiotics (Cardiac Procedures)[5]—Whether or not the cardiac surgical patient aged 18 years and older undergoing a procedure with the indications for prophylactic antibiotics AND who received prophylactic antibiotics, has an order for discontinuation of prophylactic antibiotics within 48 hours of surgical end time **Numerator:** Cardiac surgical patients who have an order for discontinuation of prophylactic antibiotics within 48 hours of surgical end time **Denominator:** All cardiac surgical patients 18 years and older undergoing procedures with the indications for prophylactic antibiotics AND who received a prophylactic antibiotic (List of procedures available in measure specifications) **Exclusion(s):** Documentation of medical reason(s) for not discontinuing prophylactic antibiotics within 48 hours of surgical end time **Percentage** of cardiac surgical patients aged 18 years and older undergoing procedures with the indications for prophylactic antibiotics AND who received a prophylactic antibiotic, who have an order for discontinuation of prophylactic antibiotics within 48 hours of surgical end time **Reporting Instructions:** • It is anticipated that this measure will be reported by the physician performing the procedure -Patients may be counted as having "received a prophylactic antibiotic" if the antibiotic was received within 4 hours prior to the surgical incision (or start of procedure when no incision is required) or intraoperatively • There must be documentation of an **order** (written, verbal or standing order/protocol) specifying that prophylactic antibiotic is to be discontinued within 48 hours of surgical end time **OR** specifying a course of antibiotic administration limited to that 48-hour period (eg, to be given every 8 hours for three doses) **OR** documentation that prophylactic antibiotic *was* discontinued within 48 hours of surgical end time • Report either 4046F or 4042F for each patient. If patient received prophylactic antibiotics and there was an order for discontinuation within 48 hours after surgical end time, also report 4043F. For patient with appropriate exclusion criteria, report 4043F with modifier 1P	**4043F** **Denominator Codes:** **4046F** **4042F**	Documentation that an order was given to discontinue prophylactic antibiotics within 48 hours of surgical end time, cardiac procedure Documentation that prophylactic antibiotics were given within 4 hours prior to surgical incision or given intraoperatively Documentation that prophylactic antibiotics were neither given within 4 hours prior to surgical incision nor given intraoperatively

[1]Physician Consortium for Performance Improvement: www.physicianconsortium.org
[2]National Committee on Quality Assurance (NCQA): Health Employer Data Information Set (HEDIS®), www.ncqa.org
[3]Joint Commission on Accreditation of Healthcare Organizations (JCAHO), ORYX Initiative Performance Measures: www.jcaho.org/pms
[4]National Diabetes Quality Improvement Alliance: www.nationaldiabetesalliance.org
[5]Joint measure from the Physician Consortium for Performance Improvement, www.physicianconsortium.org, and National Committee on Quality Assurance (NCQA), www.ncqa.org
[6]The Society of Thoracic Surgeons, www.sts.org, National Quality Forum, www.qualityforum.org

Brief Description of Performance Measure & Source and Reporting Instructions	CPT Category II Code(s)	Code Descriptor
Perioperative Care 2 (PERI 2), cont'd		
Venous Thromboembolism (VTE) Prophylaxis[5]—Whether or not the surgical patient aged 18 years and older undergoing a procedure for which VTE prophylaxis is indicated in all patients had an order for LMWH, LDUH, adjusted-dose warfarin, fondaparinux, or mechanical prophylaxis to be given within 24 hours prior to incision time or within 24 hours after surgery end time **LMWH-**Low molecular weight heparin **LDUH-**Low-dose unfractionated heparin **Numerator:** Surgical patients who had an order for LMWH, LDUH, adjusted-dose warfarin, fondaparinux or mechanical prophylaxis to be given within 24 hours prior to incision time or within 24 hours after surgery end time **Denominator:** All surgical patients aged 18 years and older undergoing procedures for which VTE prophylaxis is indicated in all patients (List of procedures available in measure specifications) **Exclusion(s):** Documentation of medical reason(s) for patient not receiving LMWH, LDUH, adjusted-dose warfarin, fondaparinux, or mechanical prophylaxis within 24 hours prior to incision time or 24 hours after surgery end time **Percentage** of surgical patients aged 18 years and older undergoing procedures for which VTE prophylaxis is indicated in all patients who had an order for LMWH, LDUH, adjusted-dose warfarin, fondaparinux or mechanical prophylaxis to be given within 24 hours prior to incision time or within 24 hours after surgery end time **Reporting Instructions:** • There must be documentation of an order (written, verbal or standing order/protocol) for VTE prophylaxis OR documentation that VTE prophylaxis was received • Report 4044F where there is documentation of an order for VTE prophylaxis or where it was given within the specified timeframe • For patient with appropriate exclusion criteria, report 4044F with modifier 1P	**4044F**	Documentation that an order was given for venous thromboembolism (VTE) prophylaxis to be given within 24 hrs prior to incision time or 24 hours after surgery end time
►Prenatal Care (PRENATAL)◄		
►Anti-D Immune Globulin[1]—Whether or not the D (Rh) negative and unsensitized patient who gave birth during the 12-month period, who was seen for continuing prenatal care, received anti-D immune globulin at 26-30 weeks gestation **Numerator:** Patients who received anti-D immune globulin at 26-30 weeks gestation **Denominator:** All patients who are D (Rh) negative and unsensitized who gave birth during the 12-month period, seen for continuing prenatal care **Exclusion(s):** Documentation of medical reason(s) for patient not receiving anti-D immune globulin at 26-30 weeks gestation Documentation of patient reason(s) for patient not receiving anti-D immune globulin at 26-30 weeks gestation Documentation of system reason(s) for patient not receiving anti-D immune globulin at 26-30 weeks gestation **Percentage** of D (Rh) negative, unsensitized patients who gave birth during the 12-month period who received anti-D immune globulin at 26-30 weeks gestation **Reporting Instructions:** Report 3290F or 3291F for each patient. If patient is D (Rh) negative and unsensitized (3290F) and patient was administered Anti-D immune globulin between 26 and 30 weeks gestation, also report 4178F For patients with appropriate exclusion criteria use 4178F with modifier 1P, 2P, or 3P◄	**►4178F** **Denominator Codes:** **3290F** **3291F◄**	►Anti-D immune globulin received between 26 and 30 weeks gestation Patient is D (Rh) negative and unsensitized Patient is D (Rh) positive or sensitized◄

[1]Physician Consortium for Performance Improvement: www.physicianconsortium.org
[2]National Committee on Quality Assurance (NCQA): Health Employer Data Information Set (HEDIS®), www.ncqa.org
[3]Joint Commission on Accreditation of Healthcare Organizations (JCAHO), ORYX Initiative Performance Measures: www.jcaho.org/pms
[4]National Diabetes Quality Improvement Alliance: www.nationaldiabetesalliance.org
[5]Joint measure from the Physician Consortium for Performance Improvement, www.physicianconsortium.org, and National Committee on Quality Assurance (NCQA), www.ncqa.org
[6]The Society of Thoracic Surgeons, www.sts.org, National Quality Forum, www.qualityforum.org

Brief Description of Performance Measure & Source and Reporting Instructions	CPT Category II Code(s)	Code Descriptor
►Prenatal Care (PRENATAL)◄, cont'd		
►Screening for Human Immunodeficiency Virus (HIV)[1]—Whether or not the patient who gave birth during the 12-month period, who was seen for continuing prenatal care, was screened for HIV infection during the first or second prenatal care visit **Numerator:** Patients who were screened for HIV infection during the first or second prenatal care visit **Denominator:** All patients who gave birth during the 12-month period, seen for continuing prenatal care **Exclusion(s):** Documentation of medical reason(s) for not screening for HIV during the first or second prenatal care visit (eg, patient has known HIV) Documentation of patient reason(s) for not screening for HIV during the first or second prenatal care visit **Percentage** of patients who gave birth during the 12-month period who were screened for HIV infection during the first or second prenatal care visit **Reporting Instructions:** For patient with appropriate exclusion criteria, report 3292F with modifier 1P or 2P◄	**►3292F◄**	►HIV testing ordered or documented and reviewed during the first or second prenatal visit◄
Prenatal-Postpartum Care		
Timeliness of Prenatal Care[2] **Numerator:** Number of women who received a prenatal care visit as a member of the managed care organization (MCO) in the first trimester or within 42 days of enrollment in the MCO **Denominator:** Women who had live births between November 6th of the year prior to the measurement year and November 5th of the measurement year, who were continuously enrolled at least 43 days prior to delivery through 56 days after delivery **Exclusion(s):** None **Percentage** of patients in the denominator who received prenatal care **Reporting Instructions:** There are no exclusions for this measure; modifiers 1P, 2P, and 3P may not be used	**0500F**	Initial prenatal care visit (report at first prenatal encounter with health care professional providing obstetrical care. Report also date of visit and, in a separate field, the date of the last menstrual period - LMP)
Prenatal Flow Sheet[1]—Whether or not patient has a prenatal flowsheet in use by the date of the first physician visit **Numerator:** Number of patients with a flow sheet in use by the date of the first physician visit, which contains at a minimum: blood pressure, weight, urine protein, uterine size, fetal heart tones, and estimated date of delivery **Denominator:** Pregnant women seen for prenatal care **Exclusion(s):** Patients seen for consultation only, not for continuing care **Percentage** of patients in the denominator with a prenatal flow sheet in use by the first physician visit **Reporting Instructions:** There are no exclusions for this measure; modifiers 1P, 2P, and 3P may not be used	**0501F**	Prenatal flow sheet documented in medical record by first prenatal visit (documentation includes at mininum blood pressure, weight, urine protein, uterine size, fetal heart tones, and estimated date of delivery). Report also: date of visit and, in a separate field, the date of the last menstrual period - LMP (Note: If reporting 0501F Prenatal flow sheet, it is not necessary to report 0500F Initial prenatal care visit)

[1]Physician Consortium for Performance Improvement: www.physicianconsortium.org
[2]National Committee on Quality Assurance (NCQA): Health Employer Data Information Set (HEDIS®), www.ncqa.org
[3]Joint Commission on Accreditation of Healthcare Organizations (JCAHO), ORYX Initiative Performance Measures: www.jcaho.org/pms
[4]National Diabetes Quality Improvement Alliance: www.nationaldiabetesalliance.org
[5]Joint measure from the Physician Consortium for Performance Improvement, www.physicianconsortium.org, and National Committee on Quality Assurance (NCQA), www.ncqa.org
[6]The Society of Thoracic Surgeons, www.sts.org, National Quality Forum, www.qualityforum.org

Brief Description of Performance Measure & Source and Reporting Instructions	CPT Category II Code(s)	Code Descriptor
Prenatal-Postpartum Care, cont'd		
Frequency of Ongoing Prenatal Care[2] **Numerator:** Number of women in the denominator who had an unduplicated count of less than 21%, 21%-40%, 41%-60%, 61%-80%, or greater than or equal to 81% of the expected number of prenatal care visits, adjusted for the month of pregnancy at time of enrollment and gestational age **Denominator:** Women who had live births during the measurement year Exclusion(s): MCOs must exclude members for whom a prenatal visit is not indicated Percentage of patients in the denominator with expected number of prenatal visits **Reporting Instructions:** There are no exclusions for this measure; modifiers 1P, 2P, and 3P may not be used	**0502F**	Subsequent prenatal care visit
Postpartum Care[2] **Numerator:** Number of women in the denominator who had a postpartum visit on or between 21 days and 56 days after delivery **Denominator:** Women who had live births between November 6th of the year prior to the measurement year and November 5th of the measurement year, who were continuously enrolled at least 43 days prior to delivery through 56 days after delivery **Percentage** of patients in the denominator who had a postpartum visit between 21 and 56 days after delivery **Reporting Instructions:** There are no exclusions for this measure; modifiers 1P, 2P, and 3P may not be used	**0503F**	Postpartum care visit
Preventive Care & Screening (PV)		
Adult Influenza Immunization[1]—Whether or not patient received an influenza immunization **Numerator:** Patients who received an influenza immunization **Denominator:** All patients greater than or equal to 50 years of age **Exclusion(s):** Documentation of medical, patient, or system reason(s) for declining immunization **Percentage** of patients who received an influenza immunization **Reporting Instructions:** For patients with appropriate exclusion criteria use 4037F with modifier 1P, 2P, or 3P. Use 4037F with modifier 1P if previously immunized for current season	**4037F**	Influenza immunization ordered or administered
►**Adult Colorectal Cancer Screening[1, 2]**—Whether or not patient was screened for colorectal cancer during the one-year measurement period◄ **Numerator:** Patients with any of the recommended colorectal cancer screening test(s) performed (fecal occult blood testing annually; flexible sigmoidoscopy every five years; annual fecal occult blood testing plus flexible sigmoidoscopy every five years; double contrast barium enema every five years; colonoscopy every ten years) **Denominator:** All patients aged greater than or equal to 50 years **Exclusion(s):** Documentation of medical, patient, or system reason(s) for not providing colorectal cancer screening **Percentage** of patients screened for colorectal cancer **Reporting Instructions:** For patients with appropriate exclusion criteria, report 3017F with modifier 1P, 2P, or 3P	**3017F**	Colorectal cancer screening results documented and reviewed

[1]Physician Consortium for Performance Improvement: www.physicianconsortium.org
[2]National Committee on Quality Assurance (NCQA): Health Employer Data Information Set (HEDIS®), www.ncqa.org
[3]Joint Commission on Accreditation of Healthcare Organizations (JCAHO), ORYX Initiative Performance Measures: www.jcaho.org/pms
[4]National Diabetes Quality Improvement Alliance: www.nationaldiabetesalliance.org
[5]Joint measure from the Physician Consortium for Performance Improvement, www.physicianconsortium.org, and National Committee on Quality Assurance (NCQA), www.ncqa.org
[6]The Society of Thoracic Surgeons, www.sts.org, National Quality Forum, www.qualityforum.org

Brief Description of Performance Measure & Source and Reporting Instructions	CPT Category II Code(s)	Code Descriptor
Preventive Care & Screening (PV), cont'd		
►**Colorectal Cancer Screening**[2]—To assess the precentage of patients 50-80 years of age who received the appropriate colorectal cancer screening **Numerator:** Patients who had at least one appropriate screening for colorectal cancer during the reporting period (See measure for list of appropriate screenings) **Denominator:** All patients 51-80 years of age **Exclusion(s):** Medical reasons for not providing a colorectal caner screening (*eg,* diagnosis of colorectal cancer, total colectomy) **Percentage** of patients 50-80 years of age who had the appropriate colorectal cancer screening **Reporting Instructions:** Report this code for a patient at least once during the measurement year for patients identified in the eligible population. For patients with appropriate exclusion criteria report 3017F with modifier 1P◄	►**3017F**◄	►Colorectal cancer screening results documented and reviewed ◄
Screening Mammography[1]—Whether or not female patient had a mammogram performed during the two-year measurement period **Numerator:** Female patients who had a mammogram performed **Denominator:** All female patients aged 50-69 years **Exclusion(s):** Documentation of medical, patient, or system reason(s) for declining or not performing screening mammography **Percentage** of female patients who had a mammogram performed during the two-year measurement period **Reporting Instructions:** For patients with appropriate exclusion criteria use 3014F with modifier 1P, 2P, 3P	**3014F**	Screening mammography results documented and reviewed
►**Breast Cancer Screening**[2]—To assess the percentage of women 40-69 years of age who had a mammogram to screen for breast cancer during the previous 24 months **Numerator:** Patients who had at least one mammogram within the last 24 months **Denominator:** All women 42-69 years of age **Exclusion(s):** Documentation of medical reasons for not performing a screening mammogram (eg, Women who had a bilateral mastectomy or two unilateral mastectomies) **Percentage** of women 40-69 years old who have had a mammogram to screen for breast cancer during the reporting period or the year prior to the reporting period (24 months) **Reporting Instructions:** Report this code for a patient at least once during the measurement year for patients identified in the eligible population. For patient with appropriate exclusion criteria report 3014F with modifier 1P◄	►**3014F**◄	►Screening mammography results documented and reviewed◄
►**Pneumococcal Vaccination for Patients 65 Years and Older**[2]—To assess the percentage of patients 65 years and older who have ever received a pneumococcal vaccine **Numerator:** Patients who have ever received a pneumococcal vaccination **Denominator:** All patients 65 years and older **Exclusion(s):** Medical reason for not providing a pneumococcal vaccination (eg, Patients with previous anaphylactic reaction to the vaccine or any of its components) **Percentage** of patients 65 years and older who have received the pneumococcal vaccination **Reporting Instructions:** Report this code for all patients in the denominator at least once during the measurement period◄	►**4040F**◄	►Pneumococcal vaccine administered or previously received◄

[1]Physician Consortium for Performance Improvement: www.physicianconsortium.org
[2]National Committee on Quality Assurance (NCQA): Health Employer Data Information Set (HEDIS®), www.ncqa.org
[3]Joint Commission on Accreditation of Healthcare Organizations (JCAHO), ORYX Initiative Performance Measures: www.jcaho.org/pms
[4]National Diabetes Quality Improvement Alliance: www.nationaldiabetesalliance.org
[5]Joint measure from the Physician Consortium for Performance Improvement, www.physicianconsortium.org, and National Committee on Quality Assurance (NCQA), www.ncqa.org
[6]The Society of Thoracic Surgeons, www.sts.org, National Quality Forum, www.qualityforum.org

Brief Description of Performance Measure & Source and Reporting Instructions	CPT Category II Code(s)	Code Descriptor
Preventive Care & Screening (PV), cont'd		
Tobacco Use[1]—Whether or not patient was queried about tobacco use one or more times **Numerator:** Patients who were queried about tobacco use one or more times **Denominator:** All patients aged ≥ 18 years at the beginning of the two-year measurement period **Percentage** of patients queried about tobacco use one or more times during the two-year measurement period **Reporting Instructions:** When reporting 1000F, it is required to report 1034F, and/or 1035F, or 1036F	**1000F** **1034F** **1035F** **1036F**	Tobacco use, smoking, assess Current tobacco smoker Smokeless tobacco user Tobacco non-user
Tobacco Use Intervention[1]—Whether or not patient identified as a tobacco user received cessation intervention **Numerator:** Patients identified as tobacco users who received cessation intervention **Denominator:** All patients ≥ 18 years at the beginning of the two-year measurement period identified as tobacco users **Percentage** of patients identified as tobacco users who received cessation intervention during the two year measurement period **Reporting Instructions:** Report 1034F, 1035F or 1036F for each patient. If patient is a tobacco user (1034F or 1035F) and received cessation intervention, report 4000F or 4001F or both There are no exclusions for this measure; modifiers 1P, 2P, and 3P may not be used	**4000F** **4001F** **Denominator Codes:** **1034F** **1035F** **1036F**	Tobacco use cessation intervention, counseling Tobacco use cessation intervention, pharmacologic therapy Current tobacco smoker Smokeless tobacco user Tobacco non-user
►**Advising Smokers to Quit[2]**—To assess the percentage of patients who have received advice to quit smoking from a doctor or other health provider during the reporting period. **Numerator:** Patients identified as current tobacco smokers and advised (cessation intervention or counseling) to quit smoking. **Denominator:** All patients aged 18 years and older. **Exclusion(s):** None **Percentage** of patients who are current tobacco smokers who have been advised to quit smoking. **Reporting Instructions:** Report 1034F or 1036F or 1034F AND 4000F or 4001F for all patients in the denominator at least once during the reporting period. For patient identified as smokers who did not receive cessation intervention or counseling report 4000F with modifier 8P There are no performance exclusions for this measure; modifiers 1P, 2P, and 3P may not be used◄	►**1034F** **1036F** **1035F** **4000F** **4001F**◄	►Current tobacco smoker Tobacco non-user Current smokeless tobacco user (eg, chew) Tobacco use cessation intervention, counseling Tobacco use cessation intervension, pharmacologic therapy◄
Prostate Cancer (PRCA)		
►**Initial Evaluation[1]**—Whether or not a patient with prostate cancer receiving interstitial prostate brachytherapy, OR external beam radiotherapy to the prostate, OR radical prostatectomy, OR cryotherapy had documented evaluation of prostate-specific antigen (PSA), AND primary tumor (T) stage, AND Gleason score (continued)	►**3268F**◄	►Prostate-specific antigen (PSA), AND primary tumor (T) stage, AND Gleason score documented prior to initiation of treatment◄

[1]Physician Consortium for Performance Improvement: www.physicianconsortium.org
[2]National Committee on Quality Assurance (NCQA): Health Employer Data Information Set (HEDIS®), www.ncqa.org
[3]Joint Commission on Accreditation of Healthcare Organizations (JCAHO), ORYX Initiative Performance Measures: www.jcaho.org/pms
[4]National Diabetes Quality Improvement Alliance: www.nationaldiabetesalliance.org
[5]Joint measure from the Physician Consortium for Performance Improvement, www.physicianconsortium.org, and National Committee on Quality Assurance (NCQA), www.ncqa.org
[6]The Society of Thoracic Surgeons, www.sts.org, National Quality Forum, www.qualityforum.org

Brief Description of Performance Measure & Source and Reporting Instructions	CPT Category II Code(s)	Code Descriptor
Prostate Cancer (PRCA), cont'd		
Numerator: Patients with documented evaluation of prostate-specific antigen (PSA), AND primary tumor (T) stage, AND Gleason score **Denominator:** All patients with prostate cancer receiving interstitial prostate brachytherapy, OR external beam radiotherapy to the prostate, OR radical prostatectomy, OR cryotherapy **Exclusion(s):** Documentation of medical reason(s) for not evaluating prostate-specific antigen (PSA), OR primary tumor (T) stage, OR Gleason score **Percentage** of patients with prostate cancer receiving interstitial prostate brachytherapy, OR external beam radiotherapy to the prostate, OR radical prostatectomy, OR cryotherapy with documented evaluation of prostate-specific antigen (PSA), AND primary tumor (T) stage, AND Gleason score **Reporting Instructions:** Report 3268F if Prostate-specific antigen (PSA), AND primary tumor (T) stage, AND Gleason score are documented as performed prior to initiation of therapy. For patient with appropriate exclusion criteria, report 3268F with modifier 1P◄		
►Overuse Measure–Bone Scan for Staging Low-Risk Patients[1]—Whether or not a patient with a diagnosis of prostate cancer at low risk of recurrence receiving interstitial prostate brachytherapy, OR external beam radiotherapy to the prostate, OR radical prostatectomy, OR cryotherapy did **not** have a bone scan performed at any time since diagnosis of prostate cancer **Numerator:** Patients who did not have a bone scan performed at any time since diagnosis of prostate cancer **Denominator:** All patients with a diagnosis of prostate cancer at low risk of recurrence receiving interstitial prostate brachytherapy, OR external beam radiotherapy to the prostate, OR radical prostatectomy, OR cryotherapy See technical specifications for definitions of low risk, intermediate risk, and high risk for recurrence of prostate cancer **Exclusion(s):** Documentation of medical reason(s) for **having** a bone scan performed (including documented pain, salvage therapy, other medical reasons) Salvage therapy is defined as treatment given to a patient with clinically localized prostate cancer who has not responded to, or can not tolerate other treatments, or any treatment given after recurrence of a tumor Documentation of system reason(s) for **having** a bone scan performed (including bone scan ordered by someone other than reporting physician) **Percentage** of patients with a diagnosis of prostate cancer at low risk of recurrence receiving interstitial prostate brachytherapy, OR external beam radiotherapy to the prostate, OR radical prostatectomy, OR cryotherapy who did **not** have a bone scan performed at any time since diagnosis of prostate cancer **Reporting Instructions:** Report 3271F or 3272F or 3273F or 3274F for each patient. If the patient is classified as low risk (3271F) and did not have a bone scan performed at any time since diagnosis of prostate cancer, report 3270F If there is a valid medical or system reason for performing a bone scan, report 3269F with modifier 1P or 3P; do not report modifiers with 3270F If a patient is receiving salvage therapy, report 3269F with modifier 1P◄	**►3269F** **3270F** **Denominator Codes:** **3271F** **3272F** **3273F** **3274F◄**	►Bone scan performed prior to initiation of treatment or at any time since diagnosis of prostate cancer Bone scan not performed prior to initiation of treatment nor at any time since diagnosis of prostate cancer Low risk of recurrence, prostate cancer Intermediate risk of recurrence, prostate cancer High risk of recurrence, prostate cancer Prostate cancer risk of recurrence not determined or neither low, intermediate nor high◄

[1]Physician Consortium for Performance Improvement: www.physicianconsortium.org
[2]National Committee on Quality Assurance (NCQA): Health Employer Data Information Set (HEDIS®), www.ncqa.org
[3]Joint Commission on Accreditation of Healthcare Organizations (JCAHO), ORYX Initiative Performance Measures: www.jcaho.org/pms
[4]National Diabetes Quality Improvement Alliance: www.nationaldiabetesalliance.org
[5]Joint measure from the Physician Consortium for Performance Improvement, www.physicianconsortium.org, and National Committee on Quality Assurance (NCQA), www.ncqa.org
[6]The Society of Thoracic Surgeons, www.sts.org, National Quality Forum, www.qualityforum.org

Brief Description of Performance Measure & Source and Reporting Instructions	CPT Category II Code(s)	Code Descriptor
Prostate Cancer (PRCA), cont'd		
►**Treatment Options for Patients with Clinically Localized Disease**[1]—Whether or not patient with clinically localized prostate cancer receiving interstitial prostate brachytherapy, OR external beam radiotherapy to the prostate, OR radical prostatectomy, OR cryotherapy received counseling on, at a minimum, the following treatment options for clinically localized disease: active surveillance, AND interstitial prostate brachytherapy, AND external beam radiotherapy, AND radical prostatectomy **Numerator:** Patients who received counseling on, at a minimum, the following treatment options for clinically localized disease: active surveillance, AND interstitial prostate brachytherapy, AND external beam radiotherapy, AND radical prostatectomy **Denominator:** All patients with clinically localized prostate cancer AND receiving interstitial prostate brachytherapy, OR external beam radiotherapy to the prostate, OR radical prostatectomy, OR cryotherapy **Exclusion(s):** Documentation of medical reason for not counseling patient on, at a minimum, the following treatment options for clinically localized disease: active surveillance, AND interstitial prostate brachytherapy, AND external beam radiotherapy, AND radical prostatectomy (ie, salvage therapy**) ** Salvage therapy is defined as treatment given to a patient with clinically localized prostate cancer who has not responded to, or can not tolerate other treatments, or any treatment given after recurrence of a tumor. **Percentage** of patients with clinically localized prostate cancer AND receiving interstitial prostate brachytherapy, OR external beam radiotherapy to the prostate, OR radical prostatectomy, OR cryotherapy who received counseling on, at a minimum, the following treatment options for clinically localized disease: active surveillance, AND interstitial prostate brachytherapy, AND external beam radiotherapy, AND radical prostatectomy **Reporting Instructions:** For patient with appropriate exclusion criteria, report 4163F with modifier 1P◄	**►4163F◄**	►Patient counseling at a minimum on all of the following treatment options for clinically localized prostate cancer: active surveillance, AND interstitial prostate brachytherapy, AND external beam radiotherapy, AND radical prostatectomy, provided prior to initiation of treatment◄
►**Adjuvant Hormonal Therapy for High-Risk Patients**[1]—Whether or not patient with a diagnosis of prostate cancer at high risk of recurrence receiving external beam radiotherapy to the prostate was prescribed adjuvant hormonal therapy (GnRH [gonadotropin-releasing hormone] agonist or antagonist) **Numerator:** Patients who were prescribed adjuvant hormonal therapy (GnRH [gonadotropin-releasing hormone] agonist or antagonist) **Denominator:** All patients with a diagnosis of prostate cancer at high risk of recurrence receiving external beam radiotherapy to the prostate See technical specifications for definitions of low risk, intermediate risk, and high risk for recurrence of prostate cancer, and for list of medications **Exclusion(s):** Documentation of medical reason(s) for not prescribing adjuvant hormonal therapy (GnRH agonist or antagonist) Documentation of patient reason(s) for not prescribing adjuvant hormonal therapy (GnRH agonist or antagonist) **Percentage** of patients with a diagnosis of prostate cancer at high risk of recurrence receiving external beam radiotherapy to the prostate who were prescribed adjuvant hormonal therapy (GnRH agonist or antagonist) **Reporting Instructions:** Report 3271F or 3272F or 3273F or 3274F for each patient. If the patient is classified as high risk (3273F) and was prescribed adjuvant hormonal therapy (GnRH [gonadotropin-releasing hormone] agonist or antagonist), report 4164F For patients with appropriate exclusion criteria use 4164F with modifier 1P or 2P◄	**►4164F** **Denominator Codes:** **3271F** **3272F** **3273F** **3274F◄**	►Adjuvant (ie, in combination with external beam radiotherapy to the prostate for prostate cancer) hormonal therapy (GnRH [gonadotropin-releasing hormone] agonist or antagonist) prescribed/administered Low risk of recurrence, prostate cancer Intermediate risk of recurrence, prostate cancer High risk of recurrence, prostate cancer Prostate cancer risk of recurrence not determined or neither low, intermediate nor high◄

[1]Physician Consortium for Performance Improvement: www.physicianconsortium.org
[2]National Committee on Quality Assurance (NCQA): Health Employer Data Information Set (HEDIS®), www.ncqa.org
[3]Joint Commission on Accreditation of Healthcare Organizations (JCAHO), ORYX Initiative Performance Measures: www.jcaho.org/pms
[4]National Diabetes Quality Improvement Alliance: www.nationaldiabetesalliance.org
[5]Joint measure from the Physician Consortium for Performance Improvement, www.physicianconsortium.org, and National Committee on Quality Assurance (NCQA), www.ncqa.org
[6]The Society of Thoracic Surgeons, www.sts.org, National Quality Forum, www.qualityforum.org

Brief Description of Performance Measure & Source and Reporting Instructions	CPT Category II Code(s)	Code Descriptor
Prostate Cancer (PRCA), cont'd		
►Three-Dimensional Radiotherapy[1]—Whether or not a patient with prostate cancer receiving external beam radiotherapy to the prostate only (no metastases) received three-dimensional conformal radiotherapy (3D-CRT) or intensity modulated radiation therapy (IMRT) **Numerator:** Patients who receive three-dimensional conformal radiotherapy (3D-CRT) or intensity modulated radiation therapy (IMRT) **Denominator:**All patients with prostate cancer receiving external beam radiotherapy to the prostate only (no metastases) **Exclusion(s):** None **Percentage** of patients with prostate cancer receiving external beam radiotherapy to the prostate only (no metastases) who receive 3D-CRT or IMRT **Reporting Instructions:** Report 4200F or 4201F for each patient. If 4200F is reported and patient received 3D-CRT or IMRT, also report 4165F There are no performance exclusions for this measure; modifiers 1P, 2P, or 3P may not be used◄	**►4165F** **Denominator Codes:** **4200F** **4201F◄**	►Three-dimensional conformal radiotherapy (3D-CRT) or intensity modulated radiation therapy (IMRT) received External beam radiotherapy to prostate only External beam radiotherapy for prostate cancer to region(s) other than prostate only◄
►Radiology (RAD)◄		
►Stenosis Measurement in Carotid Imaging Reports [5]—Whether or not the patient had a final report for carotid imaging studies (neck MR angiography [MRA], neck CT angiography [CTA], neck duplex ultrasound, carotid angiogram) performed that included direct or indirect reference to measurements of distal internal carotid diameter as the denominator for stenosis measurement **Numerator:** Final carotid imaging study reports that include direct or indirect reference to measurements of distal internal carotid diameter as the denominator for stenosis measurement **Definition: "Direct or indirect reference to measurements of distal internal carotid diameter as the denominator for stenosis measurement" includes direct angiographic stenosis calculation based on the distal lumen as the denominator for stenosis measurement OR an equivalent validated method referenced to the above method (eg, for duplex ultrasound studies, velocity parameters that correlate the residual internal carotid lumen with methods based on the distal internal carotid lumen)** **Denominator:** All final reports for carotid imaging studies (neck MR angiography [MRA], neck CT angiography [CTA], neck duplex ultrasound, carotid angiogram) performed **Exclusion(s):** None **Percentage** of final reports for carotid imaging studies (neck MR angiography [MRA], neck CT angiography [CTA], neck duplex ultrasound, carotid angiogram) performed that include direct or indirect reference to measurements of distal internal carotid diameter as the denominator for stenosis measurement **Reporting Instructions:** There are no performance exclusions for this measure; modifiers 1P, 2P, or 3P may not be used◄	**►3100F◄**	►Carotid image study report includes direct or indirect reference to measurements of distal internal carotid diameter as the denominator for stenosis measurement◄
►Mammography Assessment Category Data Collection[5]—Whether or not the patient undergoing a screening mammogram has an assessment category [eg, Mammography Quality Standards Act (MQSA), Breast Imaging Reporting and Data System (BI-RADS®), or FDA approved equivalent categories] entered into an internal database that will, at a minimum, allow analysis of abnormal interpretation (recall) rate (continued)		

[1]Physician Consortium for Performance Improvement: www.physicianconsortium.org
[2]National Committee on Quality Assurance (NCQA): Health Employer Data Information Set (HEDIS®), www.ncqa.org
[3]Joint Commission on Accreditation of Healthcare Organizations (JCAHO), ORYX Initiative Performance Measures: www.jcaho.org/pms
[4]National Diabetes Quality Improvement Alliance: www.nationaldiabetesalliance.org
[5]Joint measure from the Physician Consortium for Performance Improvement, www.physicianconsortium.org, and National Committee on Quality Assurance (NCQA), www.ncqa.org
[6]The Society of Thoracic Surgeons, www.sts.org, National Quality Forum, www.qualityforum.org

Brief Description of Performance Measure & Source and Reporting Instructions	CPT Category II Code(s)	Code Descriptor
►Radiology (RAD)◄, cont'd		
Numerator: Patients whose assessment category [eg, Mammography Quality Standards Act (MQSA), Breast Imaging Reporting and Data System (BI-RADS®), or FDA approved equivalent categories] is entered into an internal database that will, at a minimum, allow analysis of abnormal interpretation (recall) rate Definition of abnormal interpretation (recall): Any screening mammograms that receives an MQSA assessment category of incomplete, probably benign, suspicious, or highly suggestive of malignancy; BI-RADS® category 0, 3, 4, or 5; or FDA-approved equivalent assessment categories (see technical specifications for a list of equivalent categories) **Denominator:** All patients undergoing screening mammograms **Exclusion(s):** None **Percentage** of patients undergoing screening mammograms whose assessment category [eg, Mammography Quality Standards Act (MQSA), Breast Imaging Reporting and Data System (BI-RADS®), or FDA approved equivalent categories] is entered into an internal database that will, at a minimum, allow analysis of abnormal interpretation (recall) rate **Reporting Instructions:** There are no performance exclusions for this measure; modifiers 1P, 2P, or 3P may not be used◄	►7020F◄	►Mammogram assessment category [eg, Mammography Quality Standards Act (MQSA), Breast Imaging Reporting and Data System (BI-RADS®), or FDA approved equivalent categories] entered into an internal database to allow for analysis of abnormal interpretation (recall) rate◄
►Inappropriate Use of "Probably Benign" Assessment Category in Mammography Screening[5]—Whether or not the patient had a final report for a screening mammograms that was classified as "probably benign" **Numerator:** Final reports classified as "probably benign" Definition of "probably benign" classification: MQSA assessment category of "probably benign"; BI-RADS® category 3; or FDA-approved equivalent assessment category (see technical specifications for a list of equivalent categories) **Denominator:** All final reports for screening mammograms **Exclusion(s):** None **Percentage** of final reports for screening mammograms that are classified as "probably benign" **Reporting Instructions:** Report an appropriate code from the 3340F -3350F series for a mammogram assessment category for each patient. There are no performance exclusions for this measure; modifiers 1P, 2P, or 3P may not be used◄	►3340F	►Mammogram assessment category of "incomplete: need additional imaging evaluation", documented
	3341F	Mammogram assessment category of "negative", documented
	3342F	Mammogram assessment category of "benign", documented
	3343F	Mammogram assessment category of "probably benign", documented
	3344F	Mammogram assessment category of "suspicious", documented
	3345F	Mammogram assessment category of "highly suggestive of malignancy", documented
	3350F◄	Mammogram assessment category of "known biopsy proven malignancy", documented◄

[1]Physician Consortium for Performance Improvement: www.physicianconsortium.org
[2]National Committee on Quality Assurance (NCQA): Health Employer Data Information Set (HEDIS®), www.ncqa.org
[3]Joint Commission on Accreditation of Healthcare Organizations (JCAHO), ORYX Initiative Performance Measures: www.jcaho.org/pms
[4]National Diabetes Quality Improvement Alliance: www.nationaldiabetesalliance.org
[5]Joint measure from the Physician Consortium for Performance Improvement, www.physicianconsortium.org, and National Committee on Quality Assurance (NCQA), www.ncqa.org
[6]The Society of Thoracic Surgeons, www.sts.org, National Quality Forum, www.qualityforum.org

Brief Description of Performance Measure & Source and Reporting Instructions	CPT Category II Code(s)	Code Descriptor
►Radiology (RAD)◄, cont'd		
►Communication of Suspicious Findings From the Diagnostic Mammogram to the Practice Managing Ongoing Care[5]—Whether or not the patient undergoing a diagnostic mammogram classified as "suspicious" or "highly suggestive of malignancy" has documentation of direct communication of findings from the diagnostic mammogram to the practice within 3 business days of exam interpretation **Numerator:** Patients with documentation of direct communication of findings from the diagnostic mammogram to the practice that manages the patient's on-going care within 3 business days of exam interpretation Direct communication is defined as communication by the diagnostic imager or a designee to the treating or referring physician or his/her representative with confirmed receipt of the findings (either by fax confirmation, verbal communication, or certified letter) **Denominator:** All patients undergoing diagnostic mammograms that are classified as "suspicious" or "highly suggestive of malignancy" Definition of "suspicious" or "highly suggestive of malignancy" classification: MQSA final assessment category of "suspicious" or "highly suggestive of malignancy"; BI-RADS® category 4 or 5; or FDA-approved equivalent assessment categories (see technical specifications for a list of equivalent categories) **Exclusion(s):** Documentation of system reason(s) for not directly communicating the findings from the diagnostic mammogram to the practice that manages the patient's on-going care within 3 business days of exam interpretation (eg, patient is self-referred, no healthcare provider named) **Percentage** of patients undergoing diagnostic mammograms that are classified as "suspicious" or "highly suggestive of malignancy" with documentation of direct communication of findings from the diagnostic mammogram to the practice that manages the patient's on-going care within 3 business days of exam interpretation **Reporting Instructions:** Report an appropriate code from the 3340F -3350F series for a mammogram assessment category for each patient. If patient received a final mammogram assessment category of "suspicous" or "highly likely of malignancy" (3344F or 3345F), and there is documentation of direct communication of findings, also report 5060F.This measure is intended for use by the physician interpreting the mammogram◄	**►5060F** **Denominator Codes:** **3340F** **3341F** **3342F** **3343F** **3344F** **3345F** **3350F◄**	►Findings from diagnostic mammogram communicated to practice managing patient's on-going care within 3 business days of exam interpretation Mammogram assessment category of "incomplete: need additional imaging evaluation", documented Mammogram assessment category of "negative", documented Mammogram assessment category of "benign", documented Mammogram assessment category of "probably benign", documented Mammogram assessment category of "suspicious", documented Mammogram assessment category of "highly suggestive of malignancy", documented Mammogram assessment category of "known biopsy proven malignancy", documented◄
►Communication of Suspicious Findings From the Diagnostic Mammogram to the Patient[5]—Whether or not the patient undergoing a diagnostic mammogram classified as "suspicious" or "highly suggestive of malignancy" has documentation of direct communication of findings from the diagnostic mammogram to the patient within 5 business days of exam interpretation **Numerator:** Patients with documentation of direct communication of findings from the diagnostic mammogram to the patient within 5 business days of exam interpretation Direct communication is defined as communication by the diagnostic imager or a designee to the patient with confirmed receipt of the findings (either by fax confirmation, verbal communication, or certified letter) (continued)	**►5062F**	►Findings from diagnostic mammogram communicated to patient within 5 business days of exam interpretation

[1]Physician Consortium for Performance Improvement: www.physicianconsortium.org
[2]National Committee on Quality Assurance (NCQA): Health Employer Data Information Set (HEDIS®), www.ncqa.org
[3]Joint Commission on Accreditation of Healthcare Organizations (JCAHO), ORYX Initiative Performance Measures: www.jcaho.org/pms
[4]National Diabetes Quality Improvement Alliance: www.nationaldiabetesalliance.org
[5]Joint measure from the Physician Consortium for Performance Improvement, www.physicianconsortium.org, and National Committee on Quality Assurance (NCQA), www.ncqa.org
[6]The Society of Thoracic Surgeons, www.sts.org, National Quality Forum, www.qualityforum.org

Brief Description of Performance Measure & Source and Reporting Instructions	CPT Category II Code(s)	Code Descriptor
►Radiology (RAD)◄, cont'd		
Denominator: All patients undergoing diagnostic mammograms that are classified as "suspicious" or "highly suggestive of malignancy" Definition of "suspicious" or "highly suggestive of malignancy" classification: MQSA final assessment category of "suspicious" or "highly suggestive of malignancy"; BI-RADS® category 4 or 5; or FDA-approved equivalent assessment categories (see technical specifications for a list of equivalent categories) **Exclusion(s):** None **Percentage** of patients undergoing diagnostic mammograms that are classified as "suspicious" or "highly suggestive of malignancy" with documentation of direct communication of findings from the diagnostic mammogram to the patient within 5 business days of exam interpretation **Reporting Instructions:** Report an appropriate code from the 3340F -3350F series for a mammogram assessment category for each patient. If patient received a final mammogram assessment category of "suspicous" or "highly suggestive of malignancy" (3344F or 3345F), and there is documentation of direct communication of findings to the patient, also report 5062F. This measure is intended for use by the physician interpreting the mammogram◄	**Denominator Codes:** **3340F**	Mammogram assessment category of "incomplete: need additional imaging evaluation", documented
	3341F	Mammogram assessment category of "negative", documented
	3342F	Mammogram assessment category of "benign", documented
	3343F	Mammogram assessment category of "probably benign", documented
	3344F	Mammogram assessment category of "suspicious", documented
	3345F	Mammogram assessment category of "highly suggestive of malignancy", documented
	3350F◄	Mammogram assessment category of "known biopsy proven malignancy", documented◄
►**Reminder system for mammograms**[5]—Whether or not the patient aged 40 years and older undergoing a screening mammogram has information entered into a reminder system* with a target due date for the next mammogram **Numerator:** Patients whose information is entered into a reminder system* with a target due date for the next mammogram *The reminder system should be linked to a process for notifying patients when their next mammogram is due and should include the following elements at a minimum: patient identifier, patient contact information, dates(s) of prior screening mammogram(s) (if known), and the target due date for the next screening mammogram **Denominator:** All patients aged 40 years and older undergoing a screening mammogram **Exclusion(s)**: None **Percentage** of patients aged 40 years and older undergoing a screening mammogram whose information is entered into a reminder system* with a target due date for the next mammogram **Reporting Instructions:** There are no performance exclusions for this measure; modifiers 1P, 2P, or 3P may not be used◄	**►7025F◄**	►Patient information entered into a reminder system with a target due date for the next mammogram◄

[1]Physician Consortium for Performance Improvement: www.physicianconsortium.org
[2]National Committee on Quality Assurance (NCQA): Health Employer Data Information Set (HEDIS®), www.ncqa.org
[3]Joint Commission on Accreditation of Healthcare Organizations (JCAHO), ORYX Initiative Performance Measures: www.jcaho.org/pms
[4]National Diabetes Quality Improvement Alliance: www.nationaldiabetesalliance.org
[5]Joint measure from the Physician Consortium for Performance Improvement, www.physicianconsortium.org, and National Committee on Quality Assurance (NCQA), www.ncqa.org
[6]The Society of Thoracic Surgeons, www.sts.org, National Quality Forum, www.qualityforum.org

Brief Description of Performance Measure & Source and Reporting Instructions	CPT Category II Code(s)	Code Descriptor
►Radiology (RAD)◄, cont'd		
►CT Radiation Dose Reduction[5]—Whether or not the patient has final reports for CT examinations performed with documentation of use of appropriate radiation dose reduction devices OR manual techniques for appropriate moderation of exposure **Numerator:** Final reports for CT examinations that include documentation of use of appropriate radiation dose reduction devices OR manual techniques for appropriate moderation of exposure **Denominator:** All final reports for CT examinations performed **Exclusion(s):** None **Percentage** of final reports for CT examinations performed with documentation of use of appropriate radiation dose reduction devices OR manual techniques for appropriate moderation of exposure **Reporting Instructions:** There are no performance exclusions for this measure; modifiers 1P, 2P, or 3P may not be used◄	**►6040F◄**	**►Use of appropriate radiation dose reduction devices OR manual techniques for appropriate moderation of exposure, documented◄**
►Exposure Time Reported for Procedures Using Fluoroscopy[5]—Whether or not the patient has final reports for procedures using fluoroscopy that include documentation of radiation exposure or exposure time **Numerator:** Final reports for procedures using fluoroscopy that include documentation of radiation exposure or exposure time **Denominator:** All final reports for procedures using fluoroscopy **Exclusion(s):** None **Percentage** of final reports for procedures using fluoroscopy that include documentation of radiation exposure or exposure time **Reporting Instructions:** Typically, fluoroscopy is not reported separately for surgical services when performed by the same physician. Visit the measure developer's website for technical specifications regarding use of code 6045F There are no performance exclusions for this measure; modifiers 1P, 2P, or 3P may not be used◄	**►6045F◄**	►Radiation exposure or exposure time in final report for procedure using fluoroscopy, documented◄
Rheumatoid Arthritis (RA)		
►Disease Modifying Anti-Rheumatic Drug Therapy in Rheumatoid Arthritis[2]—Whether or not patients who were diagnosed with rheumatoid arthritis were dispensed, administered or prescribed at least one ambulatory prescription for a disease modifying anti-rheumatic drug (DMARD) during the measurement year. **Numerator:** Patients with at least one prescription or dispension for a disease modifying anti-rheumatic drug (DMARD). Dispensed encompasses administered DMARD therapy. **Denominator:** All patients aged 18 years and older with a diagnosis of rheumatoid arthritis. **Exclusion(s):** Documentation of medical reasons (patient diagnosed with HIV, members who have diagnosis for pregnancy during the reporting period) for not dispensing or dispersing a disease modifying anti-rheumatic drug therapy. **Percentage** of patients who were diagnosed with rheumatoid arthritis and who were dispensed at least one ambulatory prescription for a disease modifying anti-rheumatic drug (DMARD) during the reporting year (continued)	**►4187F◄**	►Disease modifying anti-rheumatic drug therapy prescribed or, dispensed, or administered◄

[1]Physician Consortium for Performance Improvement: www.physicianconsortium.org
[2]National Committee on Quality Assurance (NCQA): Health Employer Data Information Set (HEDIS®), www.ncqa.org
[3]Joint Commission on Accreditation of Healthcare Organizations (JCAHO), ORYX Initiative Performance Measures: www.jcaho.org/pms
[4]National Diabetes Quality Improvement Alliance: www.nationaldiabetesalliance.org
[5]Joint measure from the Physician Consortium for Performance Improvement, www.physicianconsortium.org, and National Committee on Quality Assurance (NCQA), www.ncqa.org
[6]The Society of Thoracic Surgeons, www.sts.org, National Quality Forum, www.qualityforum.org

Brief Description of Performance Measure & Source and Reporting Instructions	CPT Category II Code(s)	Code Descriptor
Rheumatoid Arthritis (RA), cont'd		
Reporting Instructions: Report this code for a patient at least once during the measurement year for patients identified in the eligible population. For patient with appropriate exclusion criteria report 4187F with modifier 1P◄		
Stroke and Stroke Rehabilitation (STR)		
Deep Vein Thrombosis Prophylaxis (DVT) for Ischemic Stroke or Intracranial Hemorrhage[5]—Whether or not the patient aged 18 years and older with the diagnosis of ischemic stroke OR intracranial hemorrhage received DVT prophylaxis by end of hospital day 2 **Numerator:** Patients who received Deep Vein Thrombosis (DVT) prophylaxis by end of hospital day 2 **Definition:** For purposes of this measure, DVT prophylaxis can include Low Molecular Weight Heparin (LMWH), Low-Dose Unfractionated Heparin (LDUH), intravenous heparin, low-dose subcutaneous heparin, or intermittent pneumatic compression devices **Denominator:** All patients aged 18 years and older with the diagnosis of ischemic stroke OR intracranial hemorrhage **Exclusion(s):** Documentation of medical reason(s) (including physician documentation that patient is ambulatory) for not receiving DVT prophylaxis by end of hospital day 2; documentation of patient reason(s) for not receiving DVT prophylaxis by end of hospital day 2 **Percentage** of patients aged 18 years and older with the diagnosis of ischemic stroke OR intracranial hemorrhage who received DVT prophylaxis by end of hospital day 2 **Reporting Instructions:** For patient with appropriate exclusion criteria report 4070F with modifier 1P or 2P	**4070F**	Deep Vein Thrombosis (DVT) prophylaxis received by end of hospital day 2
Discharged on Antiplatelet Therapy[5]—Whether or not the patient aged 18 years and older with the diagnosis of ischemic stroke or TIA was prescribed antiplatelet therapy at discharge **Numerator:** Patients who were prescribed antiplatelet therapy at discharge Definition: Antiplatelet therapy: aspirin, combination of aspirin and extended-release dipyridamole, clopidogrel, ticlopidine **Denominator:** All patients aged 18 years and older with a diagnosis of ischemic stroke or TIA **Exclusion(s):** Documentation of medical reason(s) (including documentation that patient is on anticoagulation therapy) for not prescribing antiplatelet therapy at discharge; documentation of patient reason(s) for not prescribing antiplatelet therapy at discharge **Percentage** of patients aged 18 years and older with a diagnosis of ischemic stroke or TIA who were prescribed antiplatelet therapy at discharge **Reporting Instructions:** For patient with appropriate exclusion criteria report 4073F with modifier 1P or 2P	**4073F**	Oral antiplatelet therapy prescribed at discharge
Anticoagulant Therapy Prescribed for Atrial Fibrillation at Discharge[5]—Whether or not the patient aged 18 years and older with the diagnosis of ischemic stroke or TIA with documented permanent, persistent, or paroxysmal atrial fibrillation was prescribed an anticoagulant at discharge (continued)	**4075F**	Anticoagulant therapy prescribed at discharge

[1]Physician Consortium for Performance Improvement: www.physicianconsortium.org
[2]National Committee on Quality Assurance (NCQA): Health Employer Data Information Set (HEDIS®), www.ncqa.org
[3]Joint Commission on Accreditation of Healthcare Organizations (JCAHO), ORYX Initiative Performance Measures: www.jcaho.org/pms
[4]National Diabetes Quality Improvement Alliance: www.nationaldiabetesalliance.org
[5]Joint measure from the Physician Consortium for Performance Improvement, www.physicianconsortium.org, and National Committee on Quality Assurance (NCQA), www.ncqa.org
[6]The Society of Thoracic Surgeons, www.sts.org, National Quality Forum, www.qualityforum.org

Brief Description of Performance Measure & Source and Reporting Instructions	CPT Category II Code(s)	Code Descriptor
Stroke and Stroke Rehabilitation (STR), cont'd		
Numerator: Patients who were prescribed an anticoagulant at discharge **Denominator:** All patients aged 18 years and older with the diagnosis of ischemic stroke or TIA with documented permanent, persistent, or paroxysmal atrial fibrillation **Exclusion(s):** Documentation of medical reason(s) for not prescribing an anticoagulant at discharge; documentation of patient reason(s) for not prescribing an anticoagulant at discharge **Percentage** of patients aged 18 years and older with the diagnosis of ischemic stroke or TIA with documented permanent, persistent, or paroxysmal atrial fibrillation who were prescribed an anticoagulant at discharge **Reporting Instructions:** Report 1060F or 1061F for each patient. If anticoagulant therapy prescribed at discharge, also report 4075F. For patient with appropriate exclusion criteria report 4075F with modifier 1P or 2P	**Denominator Codes:** **1060F** **1061F**	 Documentation of permanent OR persistent OR paroxysmal atrial fibrillation Documentation of absence of permanent AND persistent AND paroxysmal atrial fibrillation
Tissue Plasminogen Activator (t-PA) Considered[5]—Whether or not the patient aged 18 years and older with the diagnosis of ischemic stroke whose time from symptom onset to arrival is less than 3 hours was considered for t-PA administration **Numerator:** Patients who were considered for t-PA administration(given t-PA or documented reasons for patient not being a candidate for therapy) **Denominator:** All patients aged 18 years and older with the diagnosis of ischemic stroke whose time from symptom onset to arrival is less than 3 hours **Exclusion(s):** None **Percentage** of patients aged 18 years and older with the diagnosis of ischemic stroke whose time from symptom onset to arrival is less than 3 hours who were considered for t-PA administration **Reporting Instructions:** Report either 1065F or 1066F for each patient. If time from symptom onset to arrival is less than 3 hours, and t-PA was considered, also report 4077F	**4077F** **Denominator Codes:** **1065F** **1066F**	Documentation that tissue plasminogen activator (t-PA) administration was considered Ischemic stroke symptom onset of less than 3 hours prior to arrival Ischemic stroke symptom onset greater than or equal to 3 hours prior to arrival
Screening for Dysphagia[5]—Whether or not the patient aged 18 years and older with the diagnosis of ischemic stroke or intracranial hemorrhage underwent a dysphagia screening process before taking any foods, fluids or medication by mouth **Numerator:** Patients who underwent a dysphagia screening process before taking any foods, fluids or medication by mouth **Denominator:** All patients aged 18 years and older with the diagnosis of ischemic stroke or intracranial hemorrhage who receive any food, fluids or medication by mouth **Exclusion(s):** Documentation of medical reason(s) for not screening for dysphagia before taking any foods, fluids or medication by mouth **Percentage** of patients aged 18 years and older with the diagnosis of ischemic stroke or intracranial hemorrhage who underwent a dysphagia screening process before taking any foods, fluids or medication by mouth **Reporting Instructions:** • Report 6015F or 6020F for each patient. • If dysphagia screening was conducted prior to receiving food, fluid or medication by mouth or prior to ordering food, fluid, or medication by mouth, also report 6010F. • If patient is NPO, only report 6020F. For patient with appropriate exclusion criteria, report 6010F with modifier 1P	**6010F** **Denominator Codes:** **6015F** **6020F**	Dysphagia screening conducted prior to order for or receipt of any foods, fluids or medication by mouth Patient receiving or eligible to receive food, fluids or medication by mouth NPO (nothing by mouth) ordered

[1]Physician Consortium for Performance Improvement: www.physicianconsortium.org
[2]National Committee on Quality Assurance (NCQA): Health Employer Data Information Set (HEDIS®), www.ncqa.org
[3]Joint Commission on Accreditation of Healthcare Organizations (JCAHO), ORYX Initiative Performance Measures: www.jcaho.org/pms
[4]National Diabetes Quality Improvement Alliance: www.nationaldiabetesalliance.org
[5]Joint measure from the Physician Consortium for Performance Improvement, www.physicianconsortium.org, and National Committee on Quality Assurance (NCQA), www.ncqa.org
[6]The Society of Thoracic Surgeons, www.sts.org, National Quality Forum, www.qualityforum.org

Brief Description of Performance Measure & Source and Reporting Instructions	CPT Category II Code(s)	Code Descriptor
Stroke and Stroke Rehabilitation (STR), cont'd		
Consideration of Rehabilitation Services[5]—Whether or not consideration of rehabilitation services is documented for patients aged 18 years and older with the diagnosis of ischemic stroke or intracranial hemorrhage **Numerator:** Patients for whom consideration of rehabilitation services (ordered rehabilitation or documented that rehabilitation was not indicated) is documented **Denominator:** All patients aged 18 years and older with the diagnosis of ischemic stroke or intracranial hemorrhage **Exclusion(s):** None **Percentage** of patients aged 18 years and older with the diagnosis of ischemic stroke or intracranial hemorrhage for whom consideration of rehabilitation services is documented **Reporting Instructions:** Report 4079F if rehabilitation services considered (ordered or not indicated with documented reasons). There are no exclusions; modifiers may not be used with this measure. When 4079F is not reported it indicates rehabilitation services were not considered	**4079F**	Documentation that rehabilitation services were considered
Carotid Imaging Reports[5]—Whether or not the final report of a carotid imaging study (neck MR angiography [MRA], neck CT angiography [CTA], neck duplex ultrasound, carotid angiogram) for a patient aged 18 years and older with a diagnosis of *ischemic stroke* or *TIA* includes direct or indirect reference to measurements of distal internal carotid diameter as the denominator for stenosis measurement **Numerator:** Final carotid imaging study reports that include direct or indirect reference to measurements of distal internal carotid diameter as the denominator for stenosis measurement **Definition:** "Direct or indirect reference to measurements of distal internal carotid diameter as the denominator for stenosis measurement" includes direct angiographic stenosis calculations based on the distal lumen as the denominator for stenosis measurement OR an equivalent validated method referenced to the above method (eg, for duplex ultrasound studies, velocity parameters that correlate the *residual* internal carotid lumen with methods based on the *distal* internal carotid lumen) **Denominator:** All final reports for carotid imaging studies (neck MR angiography [MRA], neck CT angiography [CTA], neck duplex ultrasound, carotid angiogram) performed for patients aged 18 years and older with a diagnosis of ischemic stroke or TIA **Exclusion(s):** Documentation of medical reason(s) for not including direct or indirect reference to measurements of distal internal carotid diameter **Percentage** of final reports for carotid imaging studies (neck MR angiography [MRA], neck CT angiography [CTA], neck duplex ultrasound, carotid angiogram) performed for patients aged 18 years and older with the diagnosis of ischemic stroke or TIA that include direct or indirect reference to measurements of distal internal carotid diameter as the denominator for stenosis measurement **Reporting Instructions:** For patient with appropriate exclusion criteria report 3100F with modifier 1P	**3100F**	Carotid image study report includes direct or indirect reference to measurements of distal internal carotid diameter as the denominator for stenosis measurement

[1]Physician Consortium for Performance Improvement: www.physicianconsortium.org
[2]National Committee on Quality Assurance (NCQA): Health Employer Data Information Set (HEDIS®), www.ncqa.org
[3]Joint Commission on Accreditation of Healthcare Organizations (JCAHO), ORYX Initiative Performance Measures: www.jcaho.org/pms
[4]National Diabetes Quality Improvement Alliance: www.nationaldiabetesalliance.org
[5]Joint measure from the Physician Consortium for Performance Improvement, www.physicianconsortium.org, and National Committee on Quality Assurance (NCQA), www.ncqa.org
[6]The Society of Thoracic Surgeons, www.sts.org, National Quality Forum, www.qualityforum.org

Brief Description of Performance Measure & Source and Reporting Instructions	CPT Category II Code(s)	Code Descriptor
Stroke and Stroke Rehabilitation (STR), cont'd		
Computed Tomography (CT) or Magnetic Resonance Imaging (MRI) Reports—Whether or not the final report of a CT or MRI study of the brain performed within 24 hours of arrival to the hospital for a patient aged 18 years and older with a diagnosis of ischemic stroke or TIA or intracranial hemorrhage includes documentation of the presence or absence of each of the following: hemorrhage and mass lesion and acute infarction **Numerator:** Final reports of the initial CT or MRI that include documentation of the presence or absence of each of the following: hemorrhage and mass lesion and acute infarction **Denominator:** All final reports for CT or MRI studies of the brain performed within 24 hours of arrival to the hospital for patients aged 18 years and older with an admitting diagnosis of ischemic stroke or TIA or intracranial hemorrhage **Exclusion(s):** None **Percentage** of final reports for CT or MRI studies of the brain performed within 24 hours of arrival to the hospital for patients aged 18 years and older with the diagnosis of ischemic stroke or TIA or intracranial hemorrhage that include documentation of the presence or absence of each of the following: hemorrhage and mass lesion and acute infarction **Reporting Instructions:** It is intended that this measure be reported during an inpatient stay for ischemic stroke, TIA or intracranial hemorrhage. Report 3111F or 3112F for each patient If CT or MRI of brain was performed within 24 hours of arrival to the hospital and final CT or MRI report included documentation of presence or absence of hemorrhage and mass lesion and acute infarction, also report 3110F There are no exclusions; modifiers 1P, 2P, and 3P may not be used	**3110F** **Denominator Codes:** **3111F** **3112F**	Presence or absence of hemorrhage and mass lesion and acute infarction documented in final CT or MRI report CT or MRI of the brain performed within 24 hours of arrival to the hospital CT or MRI of the brain performed greater than 24 hours after arrival to the hospital
Upper Respiratory Infection in Children (URI)		
Appropriate Treatment for Children with Upper Respiratory Infection—Whether or not children 3 months to 18 years of age (inclusive) who were seen for a visit with a diagnosis of only upper respiratory infection (URI) were appropriately NOT prescribed or dispensed an antibiotic. **Numerator:** Patients who were not prescribed or dispensed an antibiotic on the visit. **Denominator:** All patients aged 3 months to 18 years (inclusive) with only a diagnosis of upper respiratory infection **Exclusion(s):** Documentation of Medical Reason(s) for prescribing antibiotic. **Percentage** of children 3 months to 18 years of age (inclusive) who were seen for a visit with a diagnosis of only upper respiratory infection (URI) and were appropriately not prescribed or dispensed an antibiotic. **Reporting Instructions:** Measure note: **This measure is being specified for physician reporting. Antibiotic dispensing from claims data is not the denominator criteria (see NCQA HEDIS® 2007 health plan measure) • For URI patients with documented medical reasons for prescribing or dispensing an antibiotic, report modifier 1P with code 4124F. • There are no performance measure exclusions for 4120F. Do not report modifiers 1P, 2P, or 3P with this code.	**4120F** **4124F**	Antibiotic prescribed or dispensed Antibiotic neither prescribed nor dispensed

[1]Physician Consortium for Performance Improvement: www.physicianconsortium.org
[2]National Committee on Quality Assurance (NCQA): Health Employer Data Information Set (HEDIS®), www.ncqa.org
[3]Joint Commission on Accreditation of Healthcare Organizations (JCAHO), ORYX Initiative Performance Measures: www.jcaho.org/pms
[4]National Diabetes Quality Improvement Alliance: www.nationaldiabetesalliance.org
[5]Joint measure from the Physician Consortium for Performance Improvement, www.physicianconsortium.org, and National Committee on Quality Assurance (NCQA), www.ncqa.org
[6]The Society of Thoracic Surgeons, www.sts.org, National Quality Forum, www.qualityforum.org

Appendix I

Genetic Testing Code Modifiers

This listing of modifiers is intended for reporting with molecular laboratory procedures related to genetic testing. Genetic testing modifiers should be used in conjunction with CPT and HCPCS codes to provide diagnostic granularity of service to enable providers to submit complete and precise genetic testing information without altering test descriptors. These two-character modifiers are categorized by mutation. The first (numeric) character indicates the disease category and the second (alpha) character denotes gene type. Introductory guidelines in the molecular diagnostic and molecular cytogenetic code sections of the CPT codebook provide further guidance in interpretation and application of genetic testing modifiers.

Neoplasia (Solid Tumor, Excluding Sarcoma and Lymphoma)

0A BRCA1 (hereditary breast/ovarian cancer)

0B BRCA2 (hereditary breast cancer)

0C Neurofibromin (neurofibromatosis, type 1)

0D Merlin (neurofibromatosis, type 2)

0E c-RET (multiple endocrine neoplasia, types 2A/B, familial medullary thyroid carcinoma)

0F VHL (Von Hippel Lindau disease, renal carcinoma)

0G SDHD (hereditary paraganglioma)

0H SDHB (hereditary paraganglioma)

0I ERRB2, commonly called Her-2/neu

0J MLH1 (HNPCC, mismatch repair genes)

0K MSH2, MSH6, or PMS2 (HNPCC, mismatch repair genes)

0L APC (hereditary polyposis coli)

0M Rb (retinoblastoma)

0N TP53, commonly called p53

0O PTEN (Cowden's syndrome)

0P KIT, also called CD117 (gastrointestinal stromal tumor)

0Z Solid tumor gene, not otherwise specified

Neoplasia (Sarcoma)

1A WT1 or WT2 (Wilm's tumor)

1B PAX3, PAX7, or FOXO1A (alveolar rhabdomyosarcoma)

1C FLI1, ERG, ETV1, or EWSR1 (Ewing's sarcoma, desmoplastic round cell)

1D DDIT3 or FUS (myxoid liposarcoma)

1E NR4A3, RBF56, or TCF12 (myxoid chondrosarcoma)

1F SSX1, SSX2, or SYT (synovial sarcoma)

1G MYCN (neuroblastoma)

1H COL1A1 or PDGFB (dermatofibrosarcoma protruberans)

1I TFE3 or ASPSCR1 (alveolar soft parts sarcoma)

1J JAZF1 or JJAZ1 (endometrial stromal sarcoma)

1Z Sarcoma gene, not otherwise specified

Neoplasia (Lymphoid/Hematopoietic)

2A RUNX1 or CBFA2T1, commonly called AML1 or ETO, genes associated with t(8;21) AML1—also ETO (acute myelogenous leukemia)

2B BCR or ABL1, genes associated with t(9;22) (chronic myelogenous or acute leukemia) BCR—also ABL (chronic myeloid, acute lymphoid leukemia)

2C PBX1 or TCF3, genes associated with t(1;19) (acute lymphoblastic leukemia) CGF1

2D CBFB or MYH11, genes associated with inv 16 (acute myelogenous leukemia) CBF beta (leukemia)

2E MLL (acute leukemia)

2F PML or RARA, genes associated with t(15;17) (acute promyelocytic leukemia) PML/RAR alpha (promyelocytic leukemia)

2G ETV6, commonly called TEL, gene associated with t(12;21) (acute leukemia) TEL (Leukemia)

2H BCL2 (B cell lymphoma, follicle center cell origin) bcl-2 (Lymphoma)

2I CCND1, commonly called BCL1, cyclin D1 (Mantle cell lymphoma, myeloma) bcl-1 (lymphoma)

2J MYC (Burkitt lymphoma) c-myc (lymphoma)

2K IgH (lymphoma/leukemia)

2L IGK (lymphoma/leukemia)

2M TRB, T cell receptor beta (lymphoma/leukemia)

2N TRG, T cell receptor gamma (lymphoma/leukemia)

2O SIL or TAL1 (T cell leukemia)

2T BCL6 (B cell lymphoma)

2Q API1 or MALT1 (MALT lymphoma)

2R NPM or ALK, genes associated with t(2;5) (anaplastic large cell lymphoma)

2S FLT3 (Acute myelogenous leukemia)

2Z Lymphoid/hematopoietic neoplasia, not otherwise specified

Non-Neoplastic Hematology/Coagulation

3A F5, commonly called Factor V (Leiden, others) (hypercoagulable state)

3B FACC (Fanconi anemia)

3C FACD (Fanconi anemia)

3D HBB, beta globin (thalassemia, sickle cell anemia, other hemoglobinopathies)

3E HBA, commonly called alpha globin (thalassemia)

3F MTHFR (elevated homocystinemia)

3G F2, commonly called prothrombin (20210, others) (hypercoagulable state) prothrombin (factor II, 20210A) (hypercoagulable state)

3H F8, commonly called factor VIII (hemophilia A/VWF)

3I F9, commonly called factor IX (hemophilia B)

3K F13, commonly called factor XIII (bleeding or hypercoagulable state) beta globin

3Z Non-neoplastic hematology/coagulation, not otherwise specified

Histocompatiblity/Blood Typing/Identity/Microsatellite

4A HLA-A

4B HLA-B

4C HLA-C

4D HLA-D

4E HLA-DR

4F HLA-DQ

4G HLA-DP

4H Kell

4I Fingerprint for engraftment (post allogeneic progenitor cell transplant)

4J Fingerprint for donor allelotype (allogeneic transplant)

4K Fingerprint for recipient allelotype (allogeneic transplant)

4L Fingerprint for leukocyte chimerism (allogeneic solid organ transplant)

4M Fingerprint for maternal versus fetal origin

4N Microsatellite instability

4O Microsatellite loss (loss of heterozygosity)

4Z Histocompatiblity/blood typing, not otherwise specified

Neurologic, Non-Neoplastic

5A ASPA, commonly called Aspartoacylase A (Canavan disease)

5B FMR-1 (fragile X, FRAXA, syndrome)

5C FRDA, commonly called Frataxin (Freidreich ataxia)

5D HD, commonly called Huntington (Huntington's disease)

5E GABRA5, NIPA1, UBE3A, or ANCR GABRA (Prader Willi-Angelman syndrome)

5F GJB2, commonly called Connexin-26 (hereditary hearing loss) Connexin-32 (GJB2) (hereditary deafness)

5G GJB1, commonly called Connexin-32 (X-linked Charcot-Marie-Tooth disease)

5H SNRPN (Prader Willi-Angelman syndrome)

5I SCA1, commonly called Ataxin-1 (spinocerebellar ataxia, type 1)

5J SCA2, commonly called Ataxin-2 (spinocerebellar ataxia, type 2)

5K MJD, commonly called Ataxin-3 (spinocerebellar ataxia, type 3, Machado-Joseph disease)

5L CACNA1A (spinocerebellar ataxia, type 6)

5M ATXN7 Ataxin-7 (spinocerebellar ataxia, type 7)

5N PMP-22 (Charcot-Marie-Tooth disease, type 1A)

5O MECP2 (Rett syndrome)

5Z Neurologic, non-neoplastic, not otherwise specified

Muscular, Non-Neoplastic

6A DMD, commonly called dystrophin (Duchenne/Becker muscular dystrophy)

6B DMPK (myotonic dystrophy, type 1)

6C ZNF-9 (myotonic dystrophy, type 2)

6D SMN1/SMN2 (autosomal recessive spinal muscular atrophy)

6E MTTK, commonly called tRNAlys (myotonic epilepsy, MERRF)

6F MTTL1, commonly called tRNAleu (mitochondrial encephalomyopathy, MELAS)

6Z Muscular, not otherwise specified

Metabolic, Other

7A APOE, commonly called apolipoprotein E (cardiovascular disease or Alzheimer's disease)

7B NPC1 or NPC2, commonly called sphingomyelin phosphodiesterase (Nieman-Pick disease)

7C GBA, commonly called acid beta glucosidase (Gaucher disease)

7D HFE (hemochromatosis)

7E HEXA, commonly called hexosaminidase A (Tay-Sachs disease)

7F ACADM (medium chain acyl CoA dehydrogenase deficiency)

7Z Metabolic, other, not otherwise specified

Metabolic, Transport

8A CFTR (cystic fibrosis)

8B PRSS1 (hereditary pancreatitis)

8C Long QT syndrome, KCN (Jervell and Lange-Nielsen syndromes, types 1, 2, 5, and 6) and SCN (Brugada syndrome, SIDS and type 3)

8Z Metabolic, transport, not otherwise specified

Metabolic-Pharmacogenetics

9A TPMT, commonly called (thiopurine methyltransferase) (patients on antimetabolite therapy)

9B CYP2 genes, commonly called cytochrome p450 (drug metabolism)

9C ABCB1, commonly called MDR1 or p-glycoprotein (drug transport)

9D NAT2 (drug metabolism)

9L Metabolic-pharmacogenetics, not otherwise specified

Dysmorphology

9M FGFR1 (Pfeiffer and Kallman syndromes)

9N FGFR2 (Crouzon, Jackson-Weiss, Apert, Saethre-Chotzen syndromes)

9O FGFR3 (achondroplasia, hypochondroplasia, thanatophoric dysplasia, types I and II, Crouzon syndrome with acanthosis nigricans, Muencke syndromes)

9P TWIST (Saethre-Chotzen syndrome)

9Q DGCR, commonly called CATCH-22 (DiGeorge and 22q11 deletion syndromes)

9Z Dysmorphology, not otherwise specified

Appendix J

Electrodiagnostic Medicine Listing of Sensory, Motor, and Mixed Nerves

This summary assigns each sensory, motor, and mixed nerve with its appropriate nerve conduction study code in order to enhance accurate reporting of codes 95900, 95903, and 95904. Each nerve constitutes one unit of service.

Motor Nerves Assigned to Codes 95900 and 95903

I. Upper extremity, cervical plexus, and brachial plexus motor nerves
   A. Axillary motor nerve to the deltoid
   B. Long thoracic motor nerve to the serratus anterior
   C. Median nerve
      1. Median motor nerve to the abductor pollicis brevis
      2. Median motor nerve, anterior interosseous branch, to the flexor pollicis longus
      3. Median motor nerve, anterior interosseous branch, to the pronator quadratus
      4. Median motor nerve to the first lumbrical
      5. Median motor nerve to the second lumbrical
   D. Musculocutaneous motor nerve to the biceps brachii
   E. Radial nerve
      1. Radial motor nerve to the extensor carpi ulnaris
      2. Radial motor nerve to the extensor digitorum communis
      3. Radial motor nerve to the extensor indicis proprius
      4. Radial motor nerve to the brachioradialis
   F. Suprascapular nerve
      1. Suprascapular motor nerve to the supraspinatus
      2. Suprascapular motor nerve to the infraspinatus
   G. Thoracodorsal motor nerve to the latissimus dorsi
   H. Ulnar nerve
      1. Ulnar motor nerve to the abductor digiti minimi
      2. Ulnar motor nerve to the palmar interosseous
      3. Ulnar motor nerve to the first dorsal interosseous
      4. Ulnar motor nerve to the flexor carpi ulnaris
   I. Other

II. Lower extremity motor nerves
   A. Femoral motor nerve to the quadriceps
      1. Femoral motor nerve to vastus medialis
      2. Femoral motor nerve to vastus lateralis
      3. Femoral motor nerve to vastus intermedialis
      4. Femoral motor nerve to rectus femoris
   B. Ilioinguinal motor nerve
   C. Peroneal (fibular) nerve
      1. Peroneal motor nerve to the extensor digitorum brevis
      2. Peroneal motor nerve to the peroneus brevis
      3. Peroneal motor nerve to the peroneus longus
      4. Peroneal motor nerve to the tibialis anterior
   D. Plantar motor nerve
   E. Sciatic nerve
   F. Tibial nerve
      1. Tibial motor nerve, inferior calcaneal branch, to the abductor digiti minimi
      2. Tibial motor nerve, medial plantar branch, to the abductor hallucis
      3. Tibial motor nerve, lateral plantar branch, to the flexor digiti minimi brevis
   G. Other

III. Cranial nerves and trunk
- A. Cranial nerve VII (facial motor nerve)
  - 1. Facial nerve to the frontalis
  - 2. Facial nerve to the nasalis
  - 3. Facial nerve to the orbicularis oculi
  - 4. Facial nerve to the orbicularis oris
- B. Cranial nerve XI (spinal accessory motor nerve)
- C. Cranial nerve XII (hypoglossal motor nerve)
- D. Intercostal motor nerve
- E. Phrenic motor nerve to the diaphragm
- F. Recurrent laryngeal nerve
- G. Other

IV. Nerve Roots
- A. Cervical nerve root stimulation
  - 1. Cervical level 5 (CT)
  - 2. Cervical level 6 (C6)
  - 3. Cervical level 7 (C7)
  - 4. Cervical level 8 (C8)
- B. Thoracic nerve root stimulation
  - 1. Thoracic level 1 (T1)
  - 2. Thoracic level 2 (T2)
  - 3. Thoracic level 3 (T3)
  - 4. Thoracic level 4 (T4)
  - 5. Thoracic level 5 (T5)
  - 6. Thoracic level 6 (T6)
  - 7. Thoracic level 7 (T7)
  - 8. Thoracic level 8 (T8)
  - 9. Thoracic level 9 (T9)
  - 10. Thoracic level 10 (T10)
  - 11. Thoracic level 11 (T11)
  - 12. Thoracic level 12 (T12)
- C. Lumbar nerve root stimulation
  - 1. Lumbar level 1 (L1)
  - 2. Lumbar level 2 (L2)
  - 3. Lumbar level 3 (L3)
  - 4. Lumbar level 4 (L4)
  - 5. Lumbar level 5 (L5)
- D. Sacral nerve root stimulation
  - 1. Sacral level 1 (S1)
  - 2. Sacral level 2 (S2)
  - 3. Sacral level 3 (S3)
  - 4. Sacral level 4 (S4)

Sensory and Mixed Nerves Assigned to Code 95904

I. Upper extremity sensory and mixed nerves
- A. Lateral antebrachial cutaneous sensory nerve
- B. Medial antebrachial cutaneous sensory nerve
- C. Medial brachial cutaneous sensory nerve
- D. Median nerve
  - 1. Median sensory nerve to the first digit
  - 2. Median sensory nerve to the second digit
  - 3. Median sensory nerve to the third digit
  - 4. Median sensory nerve to the fourth digit
  - 5. Median palmar cutaneous sensory nerve
  - 6. Median palmar mixed nerve
- E. Posterior antebrachial cutaneous sensory nerve
- F. Radial sensory nerve
  - 1. Radial sensory nerve to the base of the thumb
  - 2. Radial sensory nerve to digit 1

- G. Ulnar nerve
  1. Ulnar dorsal cutaneous sensory nerve
  2. Ulnar sensory nerve to the fourth digit
  3. Ulnar sensory nerve to the fifth digit
  4. Ulnar palmar mixed nerve
- H. Intercostal sensory nerve
- I. Other

II. Lower extremity sensory and mixed nerves

- A. Lateral femoral cutaneous sensory nerve
- B. Medial calcaneal sensory nerve
- C. Medial femoral cutaneous sensory nerve
- D. Peroneal nerve
  1. Deep peroneal sensory nerve
  2. Superficial peroneal sensory nerve, medial dorsal cutaneous branch
  3. Superficial peroneal sensory nerve, intermediate dorsal cutaneous branch
- E. Posterior femoral cutaneous sensory nerve
- F. Saphenous nerve
  1. Saphenous sensory nerve (distal technique)
  2. Saphenous sensory nerve (proximal technique)
- G. Sural nerve
  1. Sural sensory nerve, lateral dorsal cutaneous branch
  2. Sural sensory nerve
- H. Tibial sensory nerve (digital nerve to toe 1)
- I. Tibial sensory nerve (medial plantar nerve)
- J. Tibial sensory nerve (lateral plantar nerve)
- K. Other

III. Head and trunk sensory nerves

- A. Dorsal nerve of the penis
- B. Greater auricular nerve
- C. Ophthalmic branch of the trigeminal nerve
- D. Pudendal sensory nerve
- E. Suprascapular sensory nerves
- F. Other

The following table provides a reasonable maximum number of studies performed per diagnostic category necessary for a physician to arrive at a diagnosis in 90% of patients with that final diagnosis. The numbers in each column represent the number of studies recommended. The appropriate number of studies to be performed is based upon the physician's discretion.

Indication	Type of Study/Maximum Number of Studies				
		Nerve Conduction Studies (95900, 95903, 95904)		Other EMG Studies (95934, 95936, 95937)	
	Needle EMG (95860-95864, 95867-95870)	Motor NCS With and/or Without F wave	Sensory NCS	H-Reflex	Neuromuscular Junction Testing (Repetitive Stimulation)
Carpal Tunnel (Unilateral)	1	3	4	—	—
Carpal Tunnel (Bilateral)	2	4	6	—	—
Radiculopathy	2	3	2	2	—
Mononeuropathy	1	3	3	2	—
Polyneuropathy/Mononeuropathy Multiplex	3	4	4	2	—
Myopathy	2	2	2	—	2
Motor Neuronopathy (eg, ALS)	4	4	2	—	2
Plexopathy	2	4	6	2	—
Neuromuscular Junction	2	2	2	—	3
Tarsal Tunnel Syndrome (Unilateral)	1	4	4	—	—
Tarsal Tunnel Syndrome (Bilateral)	2	5	6	—	—
Weakness, Fatigue, Cramps, or Twitching (Focal)	2	3	4	—	2
Weakness, Fatigue, Cramps, or Twitching (General)	4	4	4	—	2
Pain, Numbness, or Tingling (Unilateral)	1	3	4	2	—
Pain, Numbness, or Tingling (Bilateral)	2	4	6	2	—

Appendix K

Product Pending FDA Approval

Some vaccine products have been assigned a CPT Category I code in anticipation of future approval from the Food and Drug Administration (FDA). Following is a list of the vaccine product codes pending FDA approval status that are identified in the CPT codebook with the (✗) symbol. Upon revision of the approval status by the FDA, notation of this revision will be provided via the AMA CPT "Category I Vaccine Codes" Internet listing (www.ama-assn.org/ama/pub/category/10902.html) and in subsequent publications of the CPT codebook.

90650

90661

90662

90663

90696

90738

Appendix L

Vascular Families

Assignment of branches to first, second, and third order in this table makes the assumption that the starting point is catheterization of the aorta. This categorization would not be accurate, for instance, if a femoral or carotid artery were catheterized directly in an antegrade direction. Arteries highlighted in bold are those more commonly reported during arteriographic procedures.

First Order → **Second Order Branch** → **Third Order Branch** → **Beyond Third Order Branches**

- **Innominate**
  - **R. common carotid**
    - **R. internal carotid**
      - R. ophthalmic
      - R. p. communicating
      - R. middle cerebral
      - R. a. cerebral
    - **R. external carotid**
      - R. superior thyroid
      - R. ascending pharyngeal
      - R. facial
      - R. lingual
      - R. occipital
      - R. p. auricular
      - R. superficial temporal
      - R. internal maxillary
      - R. middle meningeal
  - **R. subclavian & axillary**
    - **R. vertebral** — Basilar
    - R. internal thoracic (internal mammary)
    - R. thyrocervical trunk
      - R. inferior thyroid
      - R. suprascapular
      - R. transverse cervical
    - R. costocervical trunk
      - R. highest intercostal
      - R. deep cervical
    - R. lateral thoracic
    - R. thoracoacromial
    - R. humeral circumflex (A/P)
    - R. subscapular — R. circumflex scapular
    - **R. brachial**
    - R. deep brachial
      - R. ulnar
      - R. radial
      - R. interosseous
      - R. deep palmar arch
      - R. superficial palmar arch
      - R. metacarpals and digitals
- **L. common carotid**
  - **L. internal carotid**
    - L. ophthalmic
    - L. p. communicating
    - L. middle cerebral
    - L. a. cerebral
  - **L. external carotid**
    - L. superior thyroid
    - L. ascending pharyngeal
    - L. facial
    - L. lingual
    - L. occipital
    - L. p. auricular
    - L. superficial temporal
    - L. internal maxillary — L. middle meningeal

R = right, L = left, A = anterior, P = posterior

First Order	Second Order Branch	Third Order Branch	Beyond Third Order Branches
L. subclavian & axillary	**L. vertebral**		
	L. internal thoracic (internal mammary)		
	L. thyrocervical trunk	L. inferior thyroid	
		L. suprascapular	
		L. transverse cervical	
	L. costocervical trunk	L. highest intercostal	
		L. deep cervical	
	L. lateral thoracic		
	L. thoracoacromial		
	L. humeral circumflex (A/P)		
	L. subscapular	L. circumflex scapular	
	L. brachial		
		L. ulnar	
		L. radial	
	L. deep brachial		
		L. interosseous	L. deep palmar arch
			L. superficial palmar arch
			L. metacarpals and digitals
Intercostals			
Bronchials			
Recurrent esophageal			
Inferior phrenic	Superior suprarenal		
Celiac trunk	L. gastric	Esophageal branch	
	Splenic	Dorsal pancreatic	Inferior transverse pancreatic
		Great pancreatic	
		Caudal pancreatic	
		Gastroepiploic	
		Short gastrics	
	Common hepatic	Gastroduodenal	P. superior pancreaticoduodenal
			A. superior pancreaticoduodenal
		Proper Hepatic	L. hepatic
			R. hepatic
			Cystic
			Gastroepiploic
			Supraduodenal
			Intermediate hepatic
Middle suprarenal			
Superior mesenteric	Middle colic		
	Inferior pancreaticoduodenal	P. inferior pancreaticoduodenal	
		A. inferior pancreaticoduodenal	
	Jejunal		
	Ileocolic		
	Appendicular		
	P. cecal		
	A. cecal		
	Marginal		
	R. colic		

R = right, L = left, A = anterior, P = posterior

First Order	Second Order Branch	Third Order Branch	Beyond Third Order Branches
Renal	Inferior suprarenal		
Testicular / Ovarian			
Lumbar			
Inferior mesenteric	L. colic		
	Sigmoid	Rectosigmoid Superior rectal	
Middle sacral			
Common Iliac	**Internal iliac**	Iliolumbar Lateral sacral Superior gluteal Umbilical Superior vesical Obturator Inferior vesical Middle rectal Inferior rectal Internal pudendal Inferior gluteal	
	External iliac	Inferior epigastric	Cremasteric Pubic
		Deep circumflex iliac	Ascending deep circumflex iliac
	Common femoral	**Profunda femoris**	Medial descending Perforating branches Lateral descending Lateral circumflex
		Deep external pudendal Superficial external pudendal Ascending lateral circumflex femoral Descending lateral circumflex femoral Transverse lateral circumflex femoral	
		Superficial femoral	Geniculate **Popliteal** **A. tibial** **Peroneal** **P. tibial**
R. & L. main pulmonary arteries (venous selective)			

Reference: Kadir S. *Atlas of Normal and Variant Angiographic Anatomy.* Philadephia, Pa: WB Saunders Co; 1991.
R = right, L = left, A = anterior, P = posterior

Appendix M

Summary of Crosswalked Deleted CPT Codes

This listing is a summary of the deleted *CPT 2008* codes and descriptors that are able to be crosswalked to *CPT 2009* codes.

Deleted CPT 2008 Code	CPT 2009 Code	CPT 2008 Code Descriptor
99289	99466	Critical care services delivered by a physician, face-to-face, during an interfacility transport of critically ill or critically injured pediatric patient, 24 months of age or less; first 30-74 minutes of hands on care during transport
99290	99467	Critical care services delivered by a physician, face-to-face, during an interfacility transport of critically ill or critically injured pediatric patient, 24 months of age or less; each additional 30 minutes (List separately in addition to code for primary service)
99293	99471	Initial inpatient pediatric critical care, per day, for the evaluation and management of a critically ill infant or young child, 29 days through 24 months of age
99294	99472	Subsequent inpatient pediatric critical care, per day, for the evaluation and management of a critically ill infant or young child, 29 days through 24 months of age
99295	99468	Initial inpatient neonatal critical care, per day, for the evaluation and management of a critically ill neonate, 28 days of age or less
99296	99469	Subsequent inpatient neonatal critical care, per day, for the evaluation and management of a critically ill neonate, 28 days of age or less
99298	99478	Subsequent intensive care, per day, for the evaluation and management of the recovering very low birth weight infant (present body weight less than 1500 g)
99299	99479	Subsequent intensive care, per day, for the evaluation and management of the recovering low birth weight infant (present body weight of 1500-2500 g)
99300	99480	Subsequent intensive care, per day, for the evaluation and management of the recovering infant (present body weight of 2501-5000 g)
99431	99460	History and examination of the normal newborn infant, initiation of diagnostic and treatment programs and preparation of hospital records. (This code should also be used for birthing room deliveries.)
99432	99461	Normal newborn care in other than hospital or birthing room setting, including physical examination of baby and conference(s) with parent(s)
99433	99462	Subsequent hospital care, for the evaluation and management of a normal newborn, per day
99435	99463	History and examination of the normal newborn infant, including the preparation of medical records. (This code should only be used for newborns assessed and discharged from the hospital or birthing room on the same date.)
99436	99464	Attendance at delivery (when requested by delivering physician) and initial stabilization of newborn
99440	99465	Newborn resuscitation: provision of positive pressure ventilation and/or chest compressions in the presence of acute inadequate ventilation and/or cardiac output
20986	0054T, 0055T	Computer-assisted surgical navigational procedure for musculoskeletal procedures; with image guidance based on intraoperatively obtained images (eg, fluoroscopy, ultrasound) (List separately in addition to code for primary procedure)
20987	0054T, 0055T	Computer-assisted surgical navigational procedure for musculoskeletal procedures; with image guidance based on preoperative images (List separately in addition to code for primary procedure)
52606	52214	Transurethral fulguration for postoperative bleeding occurring after the usual follow-up time
52612	52601	Transurethral resection of prostate; first stage of two-stage resection (partial resection)

Deleted CPT 2008 Code	CPT 2009 Code	CPT 2008 Code Descriptor
52614	52601	Transurethral resection of prostate; second stage of two-stage resection (resection completed)
52620	52630	Transurethral resection; of residual obstructive tissue after 90 days postoperative
61793	61796-61800, 63620, 63621	Stereotactic radiosurgery (particle beam, gamma ray or linear accelerator), one or more sessions
77781	77785, 77786	Remote afterloading high intensity brachytherapy; 1-4 source positions or catheters
77782	77785-77787	Remote afterloading high intensity brachytherapy; 5-8 source positions or catheters
77783	77785-77787	Remote afterloading high intensity brachytherapy; 9-12 source positions or catheters
77784	77785-77787	Remote afterloading high intensity brachytherapy; over 12 source positions or catheters
88400	88720	Bilirubin, total, transcutaneous
90760	96360	Intravenous infusion, hydration; initial, 31 minutes to 1 hour
90761	96361	Intravenous infusion, hydration; each additional hour (List separately in addition to code for primary procedure)
90765	96365	Intravenous infusion, for therapy, prophylaxis, or diagnosis (specify substance or drug); initial, up to 1 hour
90766	96366	Intravenous infusion, for therapy, prophylaxis, or diagnosis (specify substance or drug); each additional hour (List separately in addition to code for primary procedure)
90767	96367	Intravenous infusion, for therapy, prophylaxis, or diagnosis (specify substance or drug); additional sequential infusion, up to 1 hour (List separately in addition to code for primary procedure)
90768	96368	Intravenous infusion, for therapy, prophylaxis, or diagnosis (specify substance or drug); concurrent infusion (List separately in addition to code for primary procedure)
90769	96369	Subcutaneous infusion for therapy or prophylaxis (specify substance or drug); initial, up to one hour, including pump set-up and establishment of subcutaneous infusion site(s)
90770	96370	Subcutaneous infusion for therapy or prophylaxis (specify substance or drug); each additional hour (List separately in addition to code for primary procedure)
90771	96371	Subcutaneous infusion for therapy or prophylaxis (specify substance or drug); additional pump set-up with establishment of new subcutaneous infusion site(s) (List separately in addition to code for primary procedure)
90772	96372	Therapeutic, prophylactic or diagnostic injection (specify substance or drug); subcutaneous or intramuscular
90773	96373	Therapeutic, prophylactic or diagnostic injection (specify substance or drug); intra-arterial
90774	96374	Therapeutic, prophylactic or diagnostic injection (specify substance or drug); intravenous push, single or initial substance/drug
90775	96375	Therapeutic, prophylactic or diagnostic injection (specify substance or drug); each additional sequential intravenous push of a new substance/drug (List separately in addition to code for primary procedure)
90776	96376	Therapeutic, prophylactic or diagnostic injection (specify substance or drug); each additional sequential intravenous push of the same substance/drug provided in a facility (List separately in addition to code for primary procedure)
90779	96379	Unlisted therapeutic, prophylactic or diagnostic intravenous or intra-arterial injection or infusion
90918	90951-90953, 90963, 90967	End-stage renal disease (ESRD) related services per full month; for patients younger than two years of age to include monitoring for the adequacy of nutrition, assessment of growth and development, and counseling of parents
90919	90954-90956, 90964, 90968	End-stage renal disease (ESRD) related services per full month; for patients between two and eleven years of age to include monitoring for the adequacy of nutrition, assessment of growth and development, and counseling of parents

Deleted CPT 2008 Code	CPT 2009 Code	CPT 2008 Code Descriptor
90920	90957-90959, 90965, 90969	End-stage renal disease (ESRD) related services per full month; for patients between twelve and nineteen years of age to include monitoring for the adequacy of nutrition, assessment of growth and development, and counseling of parents
90921	90960-90962, 90966, 90970	End-stage renal disease (ESRD) related services per full month for patients twenty years of age and older
90922	90951-90953, 90963, 90967	End-stage renal disease (ESRD) related services (less than full month), per day; for patients younger than two years of age
90923	90954-90956, 90964, 90968	End-stage renal disease (ESRD) related services (less than full month), per day; for patients between two and eleven years of age
90924	90957-90959, 90965, 90969	End-stage renal disease (ESRD) related services (less than full month), per day; for patients between twelve and nineteen years of age
90925	90960-90962, 90966, 90970	End-stage renal disease (ESRD) related services (less than full month), per day; for patients twenty years of age and older
93727	93285, 93291, 93298	Electronic analysis of implantable loop recorder (ILR) system (includes retrieval of recorded and stored ECG data, physician review and interpretation of retrieved ECG data and reprogramming)
93731	93280, 93288, 93294	Electronic analysis of dual-chamber pacemaker system (includes evaluation of programmable parameters at rest and during activity where applicable, using electrocardiographic recording and interpretation of recordings at rest and during exercise, analysis of event markers and device response); without reprogramming
93732	93280, 93288, 93294	Electronic analysis of dual-chamber pacemaker system (includes evaluation of programmable parameters at rest and during activity where applicable, using electrocardiographic recording and interpretation of recordings at rest and during exercise, analysis of event markers and device response); with reprogramming
93733	93293	Electronic analysis of dual chamber internal pacemaker system (may include rate, pulse amplitude and duration, configuration of wave form, and/or testing of sensory function of pacemaker), telephonic analysis
93734	93279, 93288, 93294	Electronic analysis of single chamber pacemaker system (includes evaluation of programmable parameters at rest and during activity where applicable, using electrocardiographic recording and interpretation of recordings at rest and during exercise, analysis of event markers and device response); without reprogramming
93735	93279, 93288, 93294	Electronic analysis of single chamber pacemaker system (includes evaluation of programmable parameters at rest and during activity where applicable, using electrocardiographic recording and interpretation of recordings at rest and during exercise, analysis of event markers and device response); with reprogramming
93736	93293	Electronic analysis of single chamber internal pacemaker system (may include rate, pulse amplitude and duration, configuration of wave form, and/or testing of sensory function of pacemaker), telephonic analysis
93741	93282, 93289, 93292, 93295	Electronic analysis of pacing cardioverter-defibrillator (includes interrogation, evaluation of pulse generator status, evaluation of programmable parameters at rest and during activity where applicable, using electrocardiographic recording and interpretation of recordings at rest and during exercise, analysis of event markers and device response); single chamber or wearable cardioverter-defibrillator system, without reprogramming
93742	93282, 93289, 93292, 93295	Electronic analysis of pacing cardioverter-defibrillator (includes interrogation, evaluation of pulse generator status, evaluation of programmable parameters at rest and during activity where applicable, using electrocardiographic recording and interpretation of recordings at rest and during exercise, analysis of event markers and device response); single chamber or wearable cardioverter-defibrillator system, with reprogramming
93743	93283, 93289, 93295	Electronic analysis of pacing cardioverter-defibrillator (includes interrogation, evaluation of pulse generator status, evaluation of programmable parameters at rest and during activity where applicable, using electrocardiographic recording and interpretation of recordings at rest and during exercise, analysis of event markers and device response); dual chamber, without reprogramming

Deleted CPT 2008 Code	CPT 2009 Code	CPT 2008 Code Descriptor
93744	93283, 93289, 93295	Electronic analysis of pacing cardioverter-defibrillator (includes interrogation, evaluation of pulse generator status, evaluation of programmable parameters at rest and during activity where applicable, using electrocardiographic recording and interpretation of recordings at rest and during exercise, analysis of event markers and device response); dual chamber, with reprogramming
1080F	1123F, 1124F	Surrogate decision maker or advance care plan documented in the medical record
4007F	4177F	Age-Related Eye Disease Study (AREDS) formulation prescribed or recommended
0058T	89240	Cryopreservation; reproductive tissue, ovarian
0059T	89240	Cryopreservation; reproductive tissue, oocyte(s)
0088T	41530	Submucosal radiofrequency tissue volume reduction of tongue base, one or more sites, per session (ie, for treatment of obstructive sleep apnea syndrome)
0089T	95803	Actigraphy testing, recording, analysis and interpretation (minimum of three-day recording)
0090T	22856	Total disc arthroplasty (artificial disc), anterior approach, including discectomy to prepare interspace (other than for decompression) cervical; single interspace
0093T	22864	Removal of total disc arthroplasty, anterior approach cervical; single interspace
0096T	22861	Revision of total disc arthroplasty, anterior approach cervical; single interspace
0137T	55706	Biopsy, prostate, needle, saturation sampling for prostate mapping
0162T	95980-95982	Electronic analysis and programming, reprogramming of gastric neurostimulator (ie, morbid obesity)

Index

Instructions for the Use of the CPT Index

Main Terms

The index is organized by main terms. Each main term can stand alone, or be followed by up to three modifying terms. There are four primary classes of main entries:

1. Procedure or service.
   For example: Endoscopy; Anastomosis; Splint
2. Organ or other anatomic site.
   For example: Tibia; Colon; Salivary Gland
3. Condition.
   For example: Abscess; Entropion; Tetralogy of Fallot
4. Synonyms, Eponyms, and Abbreviations.
   For example: EEG; Bricker Operation; Clagett Procedure

Modifying Terms

A main term may be followed by a series of up to three indented terms that modify the main term. When modifying terms appear, one should review the list, as these subterms do have an effect on the selection of the appropriate code for the procedure.

Code Ranges

Whenever more than one code applies to a given index entry, a code range is listed. If several non-sequential codes apply, they will be separated by a comma. For example:

Esophagus
    Reconstruction 43300, 43310, 43313

If two or more sequential codes apply, they will be separated by a hyphen. For example:

Debridement
    Burns 01951-01953, 16020-16030

Conventions

As a space saving convention, certain words infer some meaning. This convention is primarily used when a procedure or service is listed as a subterm. For example:

Knee
    Incision (of)

In this example, the word in parentheses (of) does not appear in the index, but it is inferred. As another example:

Pancreas
    Anesthesia (for procedures on)

In this example, as there is no such entity as pancreas anesthesia, the words in parentheses are inferred. That is, anesthesia for procedures on the pancreas.

The alphabetic index is NOT a substitute for the main text of the CPT codebook. Even if only one code appears, the user must refer to the main text to ensure that the code selection is accurate.

A

A Vitamin
See Vitamin, A

A-II
See Angiotensin II

Abbe-Estlander Procedure
See Reconstruction; Repair, Cleft Lip

Abdomen
Abdominal Aorta
  Angiography 75635
Abdominal Wall
  Removal
    Mesh 11008
    Prosthesis 11008
  Repair
    Hernia 49491-49496, 49501, 49507, 49521, 49590
  Tumor
    Excision 22900
  Unlisted Services and Procedures 22999
Abscess
  Incision and Drainage 49020, 49040
    Open 49040
    Percutaneous 49021
Angiography 74175, 75635
Artery
  Ligation 37617
Biopsy 49000
Bypass Graft 35907
Cannula/Catheter
  Removal 49422
Celiotomy
  for Staging 49220
CT Scan 74150-74175, 75635
Cyst
  Destruction/Excision 49203-49205
Drainage
  Fluid 49080-49081
Ectopic Pregnancy 59130
Endometrioma
  Destruction/Excision 49203-49205
Exploration 49000-49002
  Blood Vessel 35840
  Staging 58960
Incision 49000
  Staging 58960
Incision and Drainage
  Pancreatitis 48000
Infraumbilical Panniculectomy 15830
Injection
  Air 49400
  Contrast Material 49400
Insertion
  Catheter 49419-49421, 49324
  Venous Shunt 49425
Intraperitoneal
  Catheter Exit Site 49436
  Catheter Insertion 49324, 49435
  Catheter Removal 49422
  Catheter Revision 49325
  Shunt
    Ligation 49428
    Removal 49429
Laparotomy
  Staging 49220
Magnetic Resonance Imaging (MRI) 74181-74183
Needle Biopsy
  Mass 49180
Peritoneocentesis 49080-49081
Radical Resection 51597
Repair
  Blood Vessel 35221
    with Other Graft 35281
    with Vein Graft 35251
  Hernia 49491-49525, 49560-49587
  Suture 49900
Revision
  Venous Shunt 49426
Suture 49900
Tumor
  Destruction/Excision 49203-49205
Ultrasound 76700-76705
Unlisted Services and Procedures 49999
Wound Exploration
  Penetrating 20102
X-ray 74000-74022

Abdominal
Aorta
  See Abdomen, Abdominal Aorta; Aorta, Abdominal
Aortic Aneurysm
  See Aorta, Abdominal, Aneurysm
Deliveries
  See Caesarean Delivery
Hysterectomy
  See Hysterectomy, Abdominal
Lymphangiogram
  See Lymphangiography, Abdomen
Paracentesis
  See Abdomen, Drainage
Radiographies
  See Abdomen, X-ray
Wall
  See Abdomen, Abdominal Wall
  Debridement
    Infected 11005-11006
  Reconstruction 49905
  Removal
    Mesh 11008
    Prosthesis 11008
  Surgery 22999
  Tumor
    Excision 22900

Abdominohysterectomy
See Hysterectomy, Abdominal

Abdominopelvic Amputation
See Amputation, Interpelviabdominal

Abdominoplasty
See Panniculectomy
Excision 15830, 15847

Ablation
Anal
  Polyp 46615
  Tumor 46615
Bone
  Tumor 20982
Colon
  Tumor 45339
Cryosurgical
  Fibroadenoma 19105
  Renal Mass 50250
  Renal Tumor
    Percutaneous 50593
CT Scan Guidance 77013
Endometrial 58353-58356, 58563
Endometrium
  Ultrasound Guidance 58356
Heart
  Arrhythmogenic Focus 93650-93652
    See Cardiology; Diagnostic, Intracardiac Pacing and Mapping
  Atrioventricular Node Function 93650
Liver
  Tumor
    Laparoscopic 47370-47371
    Open 47380-47382
Lung
  Tumor
    Radiofrequency 32998
Magnetic Resonance Guidance 77022
Parenchymal Tissue
  CT Scan Guidance 77013
Prostate 55873
Pulmonary Tumor 32998
Radiofrequency 32998
Renal Cyst 50541
Renal Mass 50542
  Radiofrequency 50592
Renal Tumor
  Cryotherapy
    Percutaneous 50593
Tongue Base
  Radiofrequency 41530
Turbinate Mucosa 30801-30802
Ultrasound
  Guidance 76940
  Uterine Tumor 0071T-0072T
Uterine Tumor
  Ultrasound, Focused 0071T-0072T
Vein
  Endovenous 36475-36479

Abortion
See Obstetrical Care
Incomplete 59812
Induced
  by Dilation and Curettage 59840
  by Dilation and Evacuation 59841
  by Saline 59850-59851
  by Vaginal Suppositories 59855-59856
  with Hysterectomy 59100, 59852, 59857
Missed
  First Trimester 59820
  Second Trimester 59821
Septic 59830
Spontaneous 59812
Therapeutic
  by Saline 59850
    with Dilation and Curettage 59851
    with Hysterectomy 59852

Abrasion
Skin
  Chemical Peel 15788-15793

Absorption Spectrophotometry, Atomic
See Atomic Absorption Spectroscopy

Accessory Nerve, Spinal
See Nerves, Spinal Accessory

Accessory, Toes
See Polydactyly, Toes

ACE
See Angiotensin Converting Enzyme (ACE), Performance Measures

Acetabuloplasty 27120-27122

Acetabulum
Fracture
  Closed Treatment 27220-27222
  Open Treatment 27226-27228
  with Manipulation 27222
  without Manipulation 27220
Reconstruction 27120
  with Resection, Femoral Head 27122
Tumor
  Excision 27076

Acetaldehyde
Blood 82000

Acetaminophen
Urine 82003

Acetic Anhydrides 84600

Acetone
Blood or Urine 82009-82010

Acetone Body 82009-82010

Acetylcholinesterase
Blood or Urine 82013

AcG
See Clotting Factor

Achilles Tendon
Incision 27605-27606
Lengthening 27612
Repair 27650-27654

Achillotomy
See Tenotomy, Achilles Tendon

Acid
Gastric 82926-82928

Acid Diethylamide, Lysergic
See Lysergic Acid Diethylamide

Acid Fast Bacilli (AFB)
Culture 87116

Acid Fast Bacillus Culture
See Culture, Acid Fast Bacilli

Acid Fast Stain 88312

Acid Perfusion Test
Esophagus 91012, 91030

Acid Phosphatase 84060-84066

Acid Probes, Nucleic
See Nucleic Acid Probe

Acid Reflux Test
Esophagus 91034-91038

Acid, Adenylic
See Adenosine Monophosphate (AMP)

Acid, Aminolevulinic
See Aminolevulinic Acid (ALA)

Acid, Ascorbic
See Ascorbic Acid

Acid, Deoxyribonucleic
See Deoxyribonucleic Acid

Acid, Folic
See Folic Acid

Acid, Glycocholic
See Cholylglycine

Acid, Lactic
See Lactic Acid

Acid, N-Acetylneuraminic
See Sialic Acid

Acid, Phenylethylbarbituric
See Phenobarbital

Acid, Uric
See Uric Acid

Acidity/Alkalinity
See pH

Acids, Amino
See Amino Acids

Acids, Bile
See Bile Acids

Acids, Fatty
See Fatty Acid

Acids, Guanylic
See Guanosine Monophosphate

Acids, N-Acetylneuraminic
See Sialic Acid

Acne Surgery
Incision and Drainage
  Abscess 10060-10061
  Comedones 10040
  Cyst 10040
  Milia, Multiple 10040
  Pustules 10040

Acne Treatment
Abrasion 15786-15787
Chemical Peel 15788-15793
Cryotherapy 17340
Dermabrasion 15780-15783
Exfoliation
  Chemical 17360

Acoustic Evoked Brain Stem Potential
See Evoked Potential, Auditory Brainstem

Acoustic Neuroma
See Brain, Tumor, Excision; Brainstem; Mesencephalon; Skull Base Surgery

Acoustic Recording
Heart Sounds
  with Computer Analysis 0068T-0070T

Acromioclavicular Joint
Arthrocentesis 20605
Arthrotomy 23044
  with Biopsy 23101
Dislocation 23540-23552
  Open Treatment 23550-23552
X-ray 73050

Acromion
Excision
  Shoulder 23130

Acromionectomy
Partial 23130

Acromioplasty 23415-23420
Partial 23130

ACTH
See Adrenocorticotropic Hormone (ACTH)

ACTH Releasing Factor
See Corticotropic Releasing Hormone (CRH)

Actigraphy
Sleep Study 95803

Actinomyces
Antibody 86602

Actinomycosis 86000

Actinomycotic Infection
See Actinomycosis

Actinotherapy 0168T, 96900
See Dermatology

Activated Factor X
See Thrombokinase

Activated Partial Thromboplastin Time
See Thromboplastin, Partial, Time

Activation, Lymphocyte
See Blastogenesis

Activities of Daily Living
See Physical Medicine/Therapy/Occupational Therapy

Activity, Glomerular Procoagulant
See Thromboplastin

Acupuncture
with Electrical Stimulation 97813-97814
without Electrical Stimulation 97810-97811

Acute Poliomyelitis
See Polio

Acylcarnitines 82016-82017

Adamantinoma, Pituitary
See Craniopharyngioma

Addam Operation
See Dupuytren's Contracture

Adductor Tenotomy of Hip
See Tenotomy, Hip, Adductor

Adenoidectomy
See Adenoids, Excision

Adenoids
Excision 42830-42836
  with Tonsils 42820-42821
Unlisted Services and Procedures 42999

Adenoma
Pancreas
  Excision 48120
Parathyroid
  Localization
    Injection Procedure 78808
Thyroid Gland Excision 60200

Adenosine 3'5' Monophosphate
See Cyclic AMP

Adenosine Diphosphate
Blood 82030

Adenosine Monophosphate (AMP)
Blood 82030

Adenovirus
Antibody 86603
Antigen Detection
  Enzyme Immunoassay 87301
  Immunofluorescense 87260

Adenovirus Vaccine
See Vaccines

Adenylic Acid
See Adenosine Monophosphate (AMP)

ADH
See Antidiuretic Hormone

Adhesions
Epidural 62263-62264
Eye
  Corneovitreal 65880
  Incision
    Anterior Segment 65860-65870
    Posterior Segment 65875
Intermarginal
  Construction 67880
    Transposition of Tarsal Plate 67882
Intestinal
  Enterolysis 44005
    Laparoscopic 44180
Intracranial
  Lysis 62161
Intrauterine
  Lysis 58559
Labial
  Lysis 56441
Lungs
  Lysis 32124
Pelvic
  Lysis 58660, 58662, 58740
Penile
  Lysis
    Post-circumcision 54162
Preputial
  Lysis 54450
Urethral
  Lysis 53500

Adipectomy
See Lipectomy

ADL
See Activities of Daily Living

Administration
Immunization
  Each Additional Vaccine/Toxoid 90472, 90474
    with Counseling 90466, 90468
  One Vaccine/Toxoid 90471, 90473
    with Counseling 90465, 90467

ADP
See Adenosine Diphosphate

ADP Phosphocreatine Phosphotransferase
See CPK

Adrenal Cortex Hormone
See Corticosteroids

Adrenal Gland
Biopsy 60540-60545
Excision
  Laparoscopy 60650
  Retroperitoneal Tumor 60545
Exploration 60540-60545
Nuclear Medicine
  Imaging 78075

Adrenal Medulla
See Medulla

Adrenalectomy 60540
Anesthesia 00866
Laparoscopic 50545

Adrenalin
See Catecholamines
Blood 82383
Urine 82384

Adrenaline-Noradrenaline
Testing 82382-82384

Adrenocorticotropic Hormone (ACTH) 80400-80406, 80412, 80418, 82024
Blood or Urine 82024
Stimulation Panel 80400-80406

Adrenogenital Syndrome 56805, 57335

Adult TCell Leukemia Lymphoma Virus I
See HTLV I

Advanced Life Support
See Emergency Department Services
Physician Direction 99288

Advancement
Genioglossus 21199
Tendon
  Foot 28238

Advancement Flap
See Skin, Adjacent Tissue Transfer

Aerosol Inhalation
See Pulmonology, Therapeutic
Pentamidine 94642

AFB
See Acid Fast Bacilli (AFB)

Afferent Nerve
See Sensory Nerve

AFP
See Alpha-Fetoprotein

After Hours Medical Services 99050

Agents, Anticoagulant
See Clotting Inhibitors

Agglutinin
Cold 86156-86157
Febrile 86000

Aggregation
Platelet 85576

AHG
See Clotting Factor

AICD (Pacing Cardioverter-Defibrillator)
See Defibrillator, Heart; Pacemaker, Heart

Aid, Hearing
See Hearing Aid

AIDS Antibodies
See Antibody, HIV

AIDS Virus
See HIV-1

Akin Operation
See Bunion Repair

ALA
See Aminolevulinic Acid (ALA)

Alanine 2 Oxoglutarate Aminotransferase
See Transaminase, Glutamic Pyruvic

Alanine Amino (ALT) 84460

Alanine Transaminase
See Transaminase, Glutamic Pyruvic

Albarran Test
See Water Load Test

Albumin
Ischemia modified 82045
Serum, Plasma or Whole Blood 82040
Urine 82042-82044

Alcohol
Breath 82075
Ethyl
  Blood 82055
  Urine 82055
Ethylene Glycol 82693

Alcohol Dehydrogenase
See Antidiuretic Hormone

Alcohol, Isopropyl
See Isopropyl Alcohol

Alcohol, Methyl
See Methanol

Aldolase
Blood 82085

Aldosterone
Blood 82088
Suppression Evaluation 80408
Urine 82088

Alimentary Canal
See Gastrointestinal Tract

Alkaline Phosphatase 84075-84080
Leukocyte 85540
WBC 85540

Alkaloids
See Specific Drug
Urine 82101

Allergen Bronchial Provocation Tests
See Allergy Tests; Bronchial Challenge Test

Allergen Challenge, Endobronchial
See Bronchial Challenge Test

Allergen Immunotherapy
Allergen
  Prescription/Supply/Injection 95120-95125
  with Extract Supply 95144
    Injection 95115-95117
Antigens 95144
IgE 86003-86005
IgG 86001
Insect Venom
  Prescription/Supply 95145-95149
  Prescription/Supply/Injection 95130-95134
Prescription/Supply 95165
  Insect, Whole Body 95170
Rapid Desensitization 95180

Allergy Services/Procedures
See Office and/or Other Outpatient Services; Allergen and Immunotherapy
Education and Counseling 99201-99215
Unlisted Services and Procedures 95199

Allergy Tests
Challenge Test
  Bronchial 95070-95071
  Ingestion 95075
Eye Allergy 95060
Food Allergy 95075
Intradermal
  Allergen Extract 95024-95028
  Biologicals 95015
  Drugs 95015
  Incremental 95027
  Venoms 95015
Nasal Mucous Membrane Test 95065
Nose Allergy 95065
Patch
  Application Tests 95044
  Photo Patch 95052
Photosensitivity 95056
Provocative Testing 95078
Skin Tests
  Allergen Extract 95004, 95024, 95027
  Biologicals 95010
  Drugs 95010
  Venoms 95010

Allogeneic Donor
Lymphocyte Infusion 38242

Allogeneic Transplantation
See Homograft

Allograft
Aortic Valve 33406, 33413
Bone
  Structural 20931
Cartilage
  Knee 27415
Lung Transplant 32850
Skin 15300-15336
Spine Surgery
  Morselized 20930
  Structural 20931

Allograft Preparation
Cornea 65757
Heart 33933, 33944
Intestines 44715-44721
Kidney 50323-50329
Liver 47143-47147
Lung 32855-32856, 33933
Pancreas 48551-48552
Renal 50323-50329

Allotransplantation
Intestines 44135-44136
Renal 50360-50365
  Removal 50370

Almen Test
See Blood, Feces

Alpha-1 Antitrypsin 82103-82104

Alpha-2 Antiplasmin 85410

Alpha-Fetoprotein
Amniotic Fluid 82106
Serum 82105, 82107

Alphatocopherol 84446

ALT
See Transaminase, Glutamic Pyruvic

Altemeier Procedure
See Anus; Rectum, Prolapse, Excision

Aluminum
Blood 82108

Alveola
Fracture
  Closed Treatment 21421
  Open Treatment 21422-21423

Alveolar Cleft
Ungrafted Bilateral 21147
Ungrafted Unilateral 21146

Alveolar Nerve
Avulsion 64738
Incision 64738
Transection 64738

Alveolar Ridge
Fracture
  Closed Treatment 21440
  Open Treatment 21445

Alveolectomy 41830

Alveoloplasty 41874

Alveolus
Excision 41830

Amide, Procaine
See Procainamide

Amikacin
Assay 80150

Amine
Vaginal Fluid 82120

Amino Acids 82127-82139

Aminolevulinic Acid (ALA)
Blood or Urine 82135

Aminotransferase
See Transaminase

Aminotransferase, Alanine
See Transaminase, Glutamic Pyruvic

Aminotransferase, Aspartate
See Transaminase, Glutamic Oxaloacetic

Amitriptyline
Assay 80152

Ammonia
Blood 82140
Urine 82140

Amniocenteses
See Amniocentesis

Amniocentesis 59000
See Chromosome Analysis
Induced Abortion 59850
  with Dilation and Curettage 59851
  with Dilation and Evacuation 59851
  with Hysterectomy 59852
Urine
  with Amniotic Fluid Reduction 59001

Amnioinfusion
Transabdominal 59070

Amnion
Amniocentesis 59000
  with Amniotic Fluid Reduction 59001
Amnioinfusion
  Transabdominal 59070

Amniotic Fluid
Alpha-Fetoprotein 82106
Scan 82143
Testing 83661, 83663-83664

Amniotic Membrane
See Amnion

Amobarbital 82205

AMP
See Adenosine Monophosphate (AMP)

AMP, Cyclic
See Cyclic AMP

Amphetamine
Blood or Urine 82145

Amputation
See Radical Resection; Replantation
Ankle 27888
Arm, Lower 25900-25905, 25915
  Revision 25907-25909
Arm, Upper 24900-24920
  and Shoulder 23900-23921
  Revision 24925-24930
  with Implant 24931-24935
Cervix
  Total 57530
Ear
  Partial 69110
  Total 69120
Finger 26910-26952
Foot 28800-28805
Hand at Metacarpal 25927
  at Wrist 25920
    Revision 25922
  Revision 25924, 25929-25931
Interpelviabdominal 27290
Interthoracoscapular 23900
Leg, Lower 27598, 27880-27882
  Revision 27884-27886
Leg, Upper 27590-27592
  at Hip 27290-27295
  Revision 27594-27596
Metacarpal 26910
Metatarsal 28810
Penis
  Partial 54120
  Radical 54130-54135
  Total 54125
Thumb 26910-26952
Toe 28810-28825
Tuft of Distal Phalanx 11752
Upper Extremity 24940
  Cineplasty 24940

Amputation through Hand
See Hand, Amputation

Amputation, Nose
See Resection, Nose

Amylase
Blood 82150
Urine 82150

ANA
See Antinuclear Antibodies (ANA)

Anabolic Steroid
See Androstenedione

Anal Abscess
See Abscess, Anal

Anal Bleeding
See Anus, Hemorrhage

Anal Fistula
See Fistula, Anal

Anal Fistulectomy
See Excision, Fistula, Anal

Anal Fistulotomy
See Fistulotomy, Anal

Anal Sphincter
Dilation 45905
Incision 46080

Anal Ulceration
See Anus, Fissure

Analgesia
See Anesthesia; Sedation

Analgesic Cutaneous Electrostimulation
See Application, Neurostimulation

Analysis
Computer Data 99090
  Cardiovascular Monitoring 93290, 93297, 93299
  Cardioverter-defibrillator 93289, 93295-93296
  Loop Recorder 93291, 93298-93299
  Multivariate Probability Assessment 0185T
  Pacemaker 93288, 93293-93294
Electroencephalogram
  Digital 95957
Electronic
  Drug Infusion Pump 62367-62368
  Pacing Cardioverter-Defibrillator
    Data Analysis 93289, 93295-93296
    Evaluation of Programming 93282-93284, 93287, 93641-93642
    Initial Evaluation 93640
    See Pacemaker, Heart
  Pulse Generator 95970-95971, 95980-95982
Physiologic Data, Remote 99091
Protein
  Tissue
    Western Blot 88372
Semen 89320-89322
  Sperm Isolation 89260-89261

Analysis, Spectrum
See Spectrophotometry

Anaspadias
See Epispadias

Anastomosis
Arteriovenous Fistula
  Direct 36821
  with Bypass Graft 35686
  with Graft 36825-36830, 36832
Artery
  to Aorta 33606
  to Artery
    Cranial 61711
Bile Duct
  to Bile Duct 47800
  to Intestines 47760, 47780
Bile Duct to Gastrointestinal 47785
Broncho-Bronchial 32486
Caval to Mesenteric 37160
Cavopulmonary 33768
Colorectal 44620
Epididymis
  to Vas Deferens
    Bilateral 54901
    Unilateral 54900
Excision
  Trachea 31780-31781
Fallopian Tube 58750
Gallbladder to Intestines 47720-47740
Hepatic Duct to Intestines 47765, 47802
Ileo-Anal 45113
Intestine to Intestine 44130
Intestines
  Colo-anal 45119
  Cystectomy 51590
  Enterocystoplasty 51960
  Ileoanal 44157-44158
  Resection
    Laparoscopic 44202-44205
Intrahepatic Portosystemic 37182-37183
Jejunum 43825
Microvascular
  Free Transfer
    Jejunum 43496
Nerve
  Facial to Hypoglossal 64868
  Facial to Phrenic 64870
Oviduct 58750
Pancreas to Intestines 48520-48540, 48548
Portocaval 37140
Pulmonary 33606
Renoportal 37145
Splenorenal 37180-37181
Stomach 43825
  to Duodenum 43810, 43855
    Revision 43850
  to Jejunum 43820, 43860-43865
Tubotubal 58750
Ureter
  to Bladder 50780-50785
  to Colon 50810-50815
    Removal 50830
  to Intestine 50800, 50820-50825
    Removal 50830
  to Kidney 50727-50750
  to Ureter 50727, 50760-50770
Vein
  Saphenopopliteal 34530
Vein to Vein 37140-37160, 37182-37183

Anastomosis of Lacrimal Sac to Conjunctival Sac
See Conjunctivorhinostomy

Anastomosis of Pancreas
See Pancreas, Anastomosis

Anastomosis, Aorta-Pulmonary Artery
See Aorta, Anastomosis, to Pulmonary Artery

Anastomosis, Bladder, to Intestine
See Enterocystoplasty

Anastomosis, Hepatic Duct
See Hepatic Duct, Anastomosis

Anderson Tibial Lengthening 27715
See Ankle; Tibia, Osteoplasty, Lengthening

Androstanediol Glucuronide 82154

Anesthesia Local

Aneurysm Repair

Angel Dust

Angina Assessment

Angiocardiographies

Angiography

Angioma

Angioplasties, Coronary Balloon

Angioplasty

Angioscopy
Non-Coronary Vessels 35400

Angiotensin Converting Enzyme (ACE) 82164
See Performance Measures

Angiotensin Forming Enzyme
See Renin

Angiotensin I 84244
Riboflavin 84252

Angiotensin II
Blood or Urine 82163

Angle Deformity
Reconstruction
  Toe 28313

Anhydride, Carbonic
See Carbon Dioxide

Anhydrides, Acetic
See Acetic Anhydrides

Animal Inoculation 87001-87003, 87250

Ankle
See Fibula; Leg, Lower; Tibia; Tibiofibular Joint
Abscess
  Incision and Drainage 27603
Amputation 27888
Arthrocentesis 20605
Arthrodesis 27870
Arthrography 73615
Arthroplasty 27700-27703
Arthroscopy
  Surgical 29891-29899
Arthrotomy 27610-27612, 27620-27626
Biopsy 27613-27614, 27620
Bursa
  Incision and Drainage 27604
Disarticulation 27889
Dislocation
  Closed Treatment 27840-27842
  Open Treatment 27846-27848
Exploration 27610, 27620
Fracture
  Bimalleolar 27808-27814
  Lateral 27786-27814, 27792
  Medial 27760-27766, 27808-27814
  Posterior 27767-27769, 27808-27814
  Trimalleolar 27816-27823
Fusion 27870
Hematoma
  Incision and Drainage 27603
Incision 27607
Injection
  Radiologic 27648
Lesion
  Excision 27630
Magnetic Resonance Imaging (MRI) 73721-73723
Manipulation 27860
Removal
  Foreign Body 27610, 27620
  Implant 27704
  Loose Body 27620
Repair
  Achilles Tendon 27650-27654
  Ligament 27695-27698
  Tendon 27612, 27680-27687
Strapping 29540
Synovium
  Excision 27625-27626
Tenotomy 27605-27606
Tumor
  Excision 27615-27619
Unlisted Services and Procedures 27899
X-ray 73600-73610
  with Contrast 73615

Ankylosis (Surgical)
See Arthrodesis

Annuloplasty
Percutaneous, Intradiscal 0062T, 0063T, 22526-22527

Anogenital Region
See Perineum

Anoplasty
Stricture 46700-46705

Anorectal
Biofeedback 90911
Repair
  Fistula 0170T, 46706

Anorectal Exam (Surgical) 45990

Anorectal Myectomy
See Myomectomy, Anorectal

Anorectovaginoplasty 46744-46746

Anoscopy
Ablation
  Polyp 46615
  Tumor 46615
Biopsy 46606
Dilation 46604
Exploration 46600
Hemorrhage 46614
Removal
  Foreign Body 46608
  Polyp 46610-46612
  Tumor 46610-46612

Antebrachium
See Forearm

Antecedent, Plasma Thromboplastin
See Plasma Thromboplastin, Antecedent

Antepartum Care
Cesarean Delivery 59510
  Previous 59610, 59618
Vaginal Delivery 59425-59426

Anterior Ramus of Thoracic Nerve
See Intercostal Nerve

Anthrax Vaccine
See Vaccines

Anthrogon
See Follicle Stimulating Hormone (FSH)

Anti Australia Antigens
See Antibody, Hepatitis B

Anti D Immunoglobulin
See Immune Globulins, Rho (D)

Anti-Human Globulin Consumption Test
See Coombs Test

Anti-Phospholipid Antibody
See Antibody, Phospholipid

Antiactivator, Plasmin
See Alpha-2 Antiplasmin

Antibiotic Administration
Injection 96372-96379
Prescribed or Dispensed 4120F-4124F

Antibiotic Sensitivity 87181-87184, 87188
Enzyme Detection 87185
Minimum Bactericidal Concentration 87187
Minimum Inhibitory Concentration 87186

Antibodies, Thyroid-Stimulating
See Immunoglobulin, Thyroid Stimulating

Antibodies, Viral
See Viral Antibodies

Antibody
See Antibody Identification; Microsomal Antibody
Actinomyces 86602
Adenovirus 86603
Antinuclear 86038-86039
Antiphosphatidylserine (Phospholipid) 86148
Antiprothrombin 0030T
Antistreptolysin O 86060-86063
Aspergillus 86606
Bacterium 86609
Bartonella 86611
Beta 2 Glycoprotein I 86146
Blastomyces 86612
Blood Crossmatch 86920-86923
Bordetella 86615
Borrelia 86618-86619
Brucella 86622
Campylobacter 86625
Candida 86628
Cardiolipin 86147
Chlamydia 86631-86632
Coccidioides 86635
Coxiella Burnetii 86638
Cryptococcus 86641
Cyclic Citrullinated Peptide (CCP) 86200
Cytomegalovirus 86644-86645
Cytotoxic Screen 86807-86808
Deoxyribonuclease 86215
Deoxyribonucleic Acid (DNA) 86225-86226
Diphtheria 86648
Ehrlichia 86666
Encephalitis 86651-86654
Enterovirus 86658
Epstein-Barr Virus 86663-86665
Fluorescent 86255-86256
Francisella Tularensis 86668
Fungus 86671
Giardia Lamblia 86674
Growth Hormone 86277

Antiplatelet Therapy
See Performance Measures

Antiprotease, Alpha 1
See Alpha-1 Antitrypsin

Antiprothrombin Antibody 0030T

Antistreptococcal Antibody 86215

Antistreptokinase Titer 86590

Antistreptolysin O 86060-86063

Antithrombin III 85300-85301

Antithrombin VI
See Fibrin Degradation Products

Antitoxin Assay 87230

Antiviral Antibody
See Viral Antibodies

Antrostomy
Sinus
  Maxillary 31256-31267

Antrotomy
Sinus
  Maxillary 31020-31032
Transmastoid 69501

Antrum of Highmore
See Sinus, Maxillary

Antrum Puncture
Sinus
  Maxillary 31000
  Sphenoid 31002

Anus
See Hemorrhoids; Rectum
Ablation 46615
Abscess
  Incision and Drainage 46045-46050
Biofeedback 90911
Biopsy
  Endoscopy 46606
Crypt
  Excision 46210-46211
Dilation
  Endoscopy 46604
Endoscopy
  Biopsy 46606
  Dilation 46604
  Exploration 46600
  Hemorrhage 46614
  Removal
    Foreign Body 46608
    Polyp 46610, 46612
    Tumor 46610, 46612
Excision
  Tag 46220, 46230
Exploration
  Endoscopy 46600
  Surgical 45990
Fissure
  Destruction 46940-46942
  Excision 46200
Fistula
  Excision 46270-46285
  Repair 0170T, 46706
Hemorrhage
  Endoscopic Control 46614
Hemorrhoids
  Clot Excision 46320
  Destruction 46930
  Excision 46250-46262
  Injection 46500
  Ligation 46221, 46945-46946
  Stapling 46947
  Suture 46945-46946
Imperforated
  Repair 46715-46742
Incision
  Septum 46070
Lesion
  Destruction 46900-46917, 46924
  Excision 45108, 46922
Manometry 91122
Placement
  Seton 46020
Reconstruction 46742
  Congenital Absence 46730-46740
  Sphincter 46750-46751, 46760-46762
  with Graft 46753
  with Implant 46762
Removal
  Foreign Body 46608
  Seton 46030
  Suture 46754
  Wire 46754
Repair
  Anovaginal Fistula 46715-46716
  Cloacal Anomaly 46748
  Fistula 0170T, 46706
  Stricture 46700-46705
Sphincter
  Chemodenervation 46505
  Electromyography 51784-51785
  Needle 51785
Unlisted Services and Procedures 46999

Aorta
Abdominal
  Aneurysm 0078T, 0079T, 0080T, 0081T, 34800-34805, 34825-34832, 35081-35103, 75952-75953
  Thromboendarterectomy 35331
Anastomosis
  to Pulmonary Artery 33606
Angiogram
  Radiologic Injection 93544
    See Cardiac Catheterization, Injection
Angioplasty 35452
Aortography 75600-75630
Ascending
  Graft 33864
Balloon 33967, 33970
Catheterization
  Catheter 36200
  Intracatheter/Needle 36160
Circulation Assist 33967, 33970
Conduit to Heart 33404
Excision
  Coarctation 33840-33851
Insertion
  Balloon Device 33967
  Graft 33330-33335, 33864
  Intracatheter/Needle 36160
Removal
  Balloon Assist Device 33968, 33971
Repair 33320-33322, 33802-33803
  Coarctation 33840-33851
  Graft 33860-33877
    Ascending 33864
  Hypoplastic or Interrupted Aortic Arch 33852-33853
  Sinus of Valsalva 33702-33720
Suspension 33800
Suture 33320-33322
Thoracic
  Repair 75956-75959
    Endovascular 33880-33891
Valve
  Incision 33415
  Repair 33400-33403
    Left Ventricle 33414
    Supravalvular Stenosis 33417
  Replacement 33405-33413
X-ray with Contrast 75600-75630

Aorta-Pulmonary ART Transposition
See Transposition, Great Arteries

Aortic Sinus
See Sinus of Valsalva

Aortic Stenosis
Repair 33415
  Supravalvular 33417

Aortic Valve
See Heart, Aortic Valve

Aortic Valve Replacement
See Replacement, Aortic Valve

Aortocoronary Bypass
See Coronary Artery Bypass Graft (CABG)

Aortocoronary Bypass for Heart Revascularization
See Artery, Coronary, Bypass

Aortography ... 75600-75605, 75630, 93544
See Angiography
Serial 75625
with Iliofemoral Artery 75630

Aortoiliac
Embolectomy 34151-34201
Thrombectomy 34151-34201

Aortopexy 33800

Aortoplasty
Supravalvular Stenosis 33417

AP
See Voiding Pressure Studies

Apert-Gallais Syndrome
See Adrenogenital Syndrome

Aphasia Testing 96105
See Neurology, Diagnostic

Apheresis
Therapeutic 36511-36516

Apical-Aortic Conduit 33404

Apicectomy
- with Mastoidectomy ... 69605
  - Petrous ... 69530

Apoaminotransferase, Aspartate
See Transaminase, Glutamic Oxaloacetic

Apolipoprotein
- Blood or Urine ... 82172

Appendectomy ... 44950-44960
- Laparoscopic ... 44970

Appendiceal Abscess
See Abscess, Appendix

Appendico-Vesicostomy
- Cutaneous ... 50845

Appendix
- Abscess
  - Incision and Drainage
    - Open ... 44900
    - Percutaneous ... 44901
- Excision ... 44950-44960

Application
- Allergy Tests ... 95044
- Bone Fixation Device
  - Multiplane ... 20692
    - Stereotactic Computer Assisted ... 20696-20697
  - Uniplane ... 20690
- Caliper ... 20660
- Cranial Tongs ... 20660
- Fixation Device
  - Shoulder ... 23700
- Halo
  - Cranial ... 20661
    - Thin Skull Osteology ... 20664
  - Femoral ... 20663
  - Maxillofacial Fixation ... 21100
  - Pelvic ... 20662
- Interdental Fixation Device ... 21110
- Intervertebral Device ... 22851
- Neurostimulation ... 64550
- Radioelement ... 77761-77778
  - Surface ... 77789
  - with Ultrasound ... 76965
- Stereotactic Frame ... 20660
  - Headframe ... 61800

Application of External Fixation Device
See Fixation Device, Application, External

APPT
See Thromboplastin, Partial, Time

Aquatic Therapy
See Physical Medicine/Therapy/Occupational Therapy

Aqueous Shunt
- to Extraocular Reservoir ... 66180
  - Revision ... 66185

Arch, Zygomatic
See Zygomatic Arch

Arm
See Radius; Ulna; Wrist
- Lower
  - Abscess ... 25028
  - Amputation ... 24900-24920, 25900-25905, 25915
    - Cineplasty ... 24940
    - Revision ... 25907-25909
  - Angiography ... 73206
  - Artery
    - Ligation ... 37618
  - Biopsy ... 25065-25066
  - Bursa
    - Incision and Drainage ... 25031
  - Bypass Graft ... 35903
  - Cast ... 29075
  - CT Scan ... 73200-73206
  - Decompression ... 25020-25025
  - Exploration
    - Blood Vessel ... 35860
  - Fasciotomy ... 24495, 25020-25025
  - Hematoma ... 25028
  - Lesion, Tendon Sheath
    - Excision ... 25110
  - Magnetic Resonance Imaging (MRI) ... 73218-73220, 73223
  - Reconstruction
    - Ulna ... 25337
  - Removal
    - Foreign Body ... 25248
  - Repair
    - Blood Vessel with Other Graft ... 35266
    - Blood Vessel with Vein Graft ... 35236
    - Decompression ... 24495
    - Muscle ... 25260-25263, 25270
      - Secondary ... 25265
    - Secondary
      - Muscle ... 25272-25274
      - Tendon ... 25272-25274
    - Tendon ... 25260-25263, 25270, 25280-25295, 25310-25316
      - Secondary ... 25265
    - Tendon Sheath ... 25275
  - Replantation ... 20805
  - Splint ... 29125-29126
  - Tendon
    - Excision ... 25109
  - Tenotomy ... 25290
  - Tumor
    - Excision ... 25075-25077
  - Ultrasound ... 76880
  - Unlisted Services and Procedures ... 25999
  - X-ray ... 73090
    - with Upper Arm ... 73092
- Removal
  - Foreign Body
    - Forearm or Wrist ... 25248
- Repair
  - Muscle ... 24341
  - Tendon ... 24341
- Upper
  - Abscess
    - Incision and Drainage ... 23930
      - *See* Elbow; Humerus
  - Amputation ... 23900-23921, 24900-24920
    - Cineplasty ... 24940
    - Revision ... 24925-24930
    - with Implant ... 24931-24935
  - Anesthesia ... 00400, 01710-01782
  - Angiography ... 73206
  - Artery
    - Ligation ... 37618
  - Biopsy ... 24065-24066
  - Bypass Graft ... 35903
  - Cast ... 29065
  - CT Scan ... 73200-73206
  - Exploration
    - Blood Vessel ... 35860
  - Hematoma
    - Incision and Drainage ... 23930
  - Magnetic Resonance Imaging (MRI) ... 73218-73220, 73223
  - Muscle Revision ... 24330-24331
  - Removal
    - Cast ... 29705
    - Foreign Body ... 24200-24201
  - Repair
    - Blood Vessel with Other Graft ... 35266
    - Blood Vessel with Vein Graft ... 35236
    - Muscle Transfer ... 24301, 24320
    - Tendon ... 24332
    - Tendon Lengthening ... 24305
    - Tendon Revision ... 24320
    - Tendon Transfer ... 24301
    - Tenotomy ... 24310
  - Replantation ... 20802
  - Splint ... 29105
  - Tumor
    - Excision ... 24075-24077
  - Ultrasound ... 76880
  - Unlisted Services and Procedures ... 24999
  - Wound Exploration
    - Penetrating ... 20103
- X-ray
  - with Lower Arm
    - Infant ... 73092

Arnold-Chiari Malformation Repair
See Decompression, Skull

Arrest, Epiphyseal
See Epiphyseal Arrest

Arrhythmogenic Focus
- Heart
  - Catheter Ablation ... 93650-93652
  - Destruction ... 33250-33251, 33261

Arsenic ... 83015
- Blood or Urine ... 82175

ART
See Syphilis Test

Arterial Catheterization
See Cannulation, Arterial

Arterial Dilatation, Transluminal
See Angioplasty, Transluminal

Arterial Grafting for Coronary Artery Bypass
See Bypass Graft, Coronary Artery, Arterial

Arterial Pressure
See Blood Pressure

Arterial Puncture ... 36600

Arteriography, Aorta
See Aortography

Artery Catheterization, Pulmonary

Arthrectomy

Arthrocentesis

Arthrodeses

Arthrodesis

Attachment
See Fixation

Atticotomy 69631, 69635

Audiologic Function Tests
See Ear, Nose and Throat; Hearing Evaluation
Acoustic Reflex 92568
Acoustic Reflex Decay 92569
Audiometry
  Bekesy 92560-92561
  Comprehensive 92557
  Conditioning Play..................92582
  Groups 92559
  Pure Tone 92552-92553
  Select Picture 92583
  Speech 92555-92556
  Visual Reinforcement 92579
Central Auditory Function 92620-92621
Diagnostic Analysis
  Auditory Brainstem Implant 92640
Electrocochleography..................92584
Evoked Otoacoustic Emission 92587-92588
Filtered Speech 92571
Loudness Balance 92562
Screening 92551
Sensorineural Acuity 92575
Short Increment Sensitivity Index 92564
Staggered Spondaic Word Test 92572
Stenger Test 92565, 92577
Synthetic Sentence Test 92576
Tinnitus Assessment 92625
Tone Decay 92563

Audiometry
Bekesy 92560-92561
Brainstem Evoked Response 92585-92586
Comprehensive 92557
Conditioning Play 92582
Groups 92559
  See Ear, Nose and Throat
Pure Tone 92552-92553
Select Picture 92583
Speech 92555-92556
Tympanometry 92567

Auditory Brain Stem Evoked Response
See Evoked Potential, Auditory Brainstem

Auditory Canal
Decompression 61591
External
  Abscess
    Incision and Drainage 69020
  Biopsy 69105
  Lesion
    Excision 69140-69155
  Reconstruction
    for Congenital Atresia 69320
    for Stenosis 69310
  Removal
    Cerumen 69210
    Ear Wax 69210
    Foreign Body 69200-69205
Internal
  Decompression 69960

Auditory Canal Atresia, External
See Atresia, Congenital, Auditory Canal, External

Auditory Evoked Otoacoustic Emission 92587-92588

Auditory Evoked Potentials 92585-92586
See Audiologic Function Tests

Auditory Labyrinth
See Ear, Inner

Auditory Meatus
X-ray 70134

Auditory Tube
See Eustachian Tube

Augmentation
Chin 21120, 21123
Malar 21270
Mandibular Body
  with Bone Graft 21127
  with Prosthesis 21125
Osteoplasty
  Facial Bones 21208
Percutaneous
  Spine 22523-22525

Augmentation Mammoplasty
See Breast, Augmentation

Augmented Histamine Test 91052
See Gastric Analysis Test

Aural Rehabilitation 92626-92633

Auricle (Heart)
See Atria

Auricular Fibrillation
See Fibrillation, Atrial

Auricular Prosthesis 21086

Australia Antigen
See Hepatitis Antigen, B Surface

Autograft
Bone
  Local 20936
  Morselized 20937
  Structural 20938
Chondrocytes
  Knee 27412
for Spine Surgery
  Local 20936
  Morselized 20937
  Structural 20938
Osteochondral
  Knee 27416
  Talus 28446
Skin
  Dermal 15130-15136
  Epidermal 15110-15116, 15150-15157
  Harvesting
    for Tissue Culture 15040

Autologous Blood Transfusion
See Autotransfusion

Autologous Transplantation
See Autograft

Autonomic Nervous System Function
See Neurology, Diagnostic; Neurophysiologic Testing

Autoprothrombin C
See Thrombokinase

Autoprothrombin I
See Proconvertin

Autoprothrombin II
See Christmas Factor

Autoprothrombin III
See Stuart-Prower Factor

Autopsy
Coroner's Exam 88045
Forensic Exam 88040
Gross and Micro Exam 88020-88029
Gross Exam 88000-88016
Organ 88037
Regional 88036
Unlisted Services and Procedures 88099

Autotransfusion
Blood 86890-86891

Autotransplant
See Autograft

Autotransplantation
Renal 50380

AV Fistula
See Arteriovenous Fistula

AV Shunt
See Arteriovenous Shunt

Avulsion
Nails 11730-11732
Nerve 64732-64772

Axillary Arteries
See Artery, Axillary

Axillary Nerve
Injection
  Anesthetic 64417

Axis, Dens
See Odontoid Process

B

B Antibodies, Hepatitis
See Antibody, Hepatitis B

B Antigens, Hepatitis
See Hepatitis Antigen, B

B Complex Vitamins
B-12 Absorption 78270-78272

B-Cells
Count 86355

B-DNA
See Deoxyribonucleic Acid

b-Hexosaminidase 83080

B-1 Vitamin
See Thiamine

B-6 Vitamin
See Vitamin, B-6

B-12 Vitamin
See Cyanocobalamin

Bacillus Calmette Guerin Vaccine
See BCG Vaccine

Back/Flank
Biopsy 21920-21925
Repair
  Hernia 49540
Strapping 29220
Tumor
  Excision 21930
  Radical Resection 21935
Wound Exploration
  Penetrating 20102

Backbone
See Spine

Bacteria Culture
Additional Methods 87077
Aerobic 87040-87071
Anaerobic 87073-87076
Blood 87040
Other Source 87070-87075
Screening 87081
Stool 87045-87046
Urine 87086-87088

Bacterial Endotoxins 87176

Bacterial Overgrowth Breath Test 91065

Bactericidal Titer, Serum 87197

Bacterium
Antibody 86609

BAER
See Evoked Potential, Auditory Brainstem

Baker Tube
Intestine Decompression 44021

Baker's Cyst 27345

Balanoplasty
See Penis, Repair

Balkan Grippe
See Q Fever

Balloon Angioplasties, Coronary
See Percutaneous Transluminal Angioplasty

Balloon Angioplasty
See Angioplasty

Balloon Assisted Device
Aorta 33967-33974

Band, Pulmonary Artery
See Banding, Artery, Pulmonary

Banding
Artery
  Fistula 37607
  Pulmonary 33690

Bank, Blood
See Blood Banking

Bankart Procedure
See Capsulorrhaphy, Anterior

Barany Caloric Test
See Caloric Vestibular Test

Barbiturates
Blood or Urine 82205

Bardenheurer Operation
See Ligation, Artery, Chest

Bariatric Surgery 43644-43645, 43770-43774, 43842-43848, 43886-43888

Barium 83015

Barium Enema 74270-74280

Barker Operation
See Talus, Excision

Barr Bodies 88130

Barr Procedure
See Tendon, Transfer, Leg, Lower

Bartholin's Gland
Abscess
  Incision and Drainage 56420
Cyst
  Repair 56440
Excision 56740
Marsupialization 56440

Bartonella
Antibody 86611

Bartonella Detection 87470-87472

Basic Life Services 99450

Basic Proteins, Myelin
See Myelin Basic Protein

Basilar Arteries
See Artery, Basilar

Batch-Spittler-McFaddin Operation
See Disarticulation, Knee

BCG Vaccine 90585-90586
See Vaccines

Be Antigens, Hepatitis
See Hepatitis Antigen, Be

Bed Sores
See Debridement; Pressure Ulcer (Decubitus); Skin Graft and Flap

Bekesy Audiometry
See Audiometry, Bekesy

Belsey IV Procedure
See Fundoplasty

Bender-Gestalt Test 96101-96103

Benedict Test for Urea
See Urinalysis, Qualitative

Benign Cystic Mucinous Tumor
See Ganglion

Benign Neoplasm of Cranial Nerves
See Cranial Nerve

Bennett Fracture
See Phalanx; Thumb, Fracture

Bennett Procedure
See Repair, Leg, Upper, Muscle; Revision

Benzidine Test
See Blood, Feces

Benzodiazepine
Assay 80154

Benzoyl Cholinesterase
See Cholinesterase

Bernstein Test
See Acid Perfusion Test, Esophagus

Beryllium 83015

Beta 2 Glycoprotein I Antibody 86146

Beta Blocker Therapy
See Performance Measures

Beta Glucosidase 82963

Beta Hypophamine
See Antidiuretic Hormone

Beta Lipoproteins
See Lipoprotein, LDL

Beta Test
See Psychiatric Diagnosis

Beta-2-Microglobulin
Blood 82232
Urine 82232

Beta-hydroxydehydrogenase ..80406

Bethesda System 88164-88167

Bicarbonate 82374

Biceps Tendon
Insertion 24342

Bichloride, Methylene
See Dichloromethane

Bicuspid Valve
See Mitral Valve

Bifrontal Craniotomy 61557

Bilaminate Skin Substitute/Neodermis
See Tissue
Repair
See Tissue, Culture Repair; Tissue, Culture, Skin Grafts

Bile Acids 82239
Blood 82240

Bile Duct
See Gallbladder
Anastomosis
with Intestines 47760, 47780-47785
Biopsy
Endoscopy 47553
Catheterization 75982
Change Catheter Tube 75984
Cyst
Excision 47715
Destruction
Calculi (Stone) 43265
Dilation
Endoscopy 43271, 47555-47556
Drainage
Transhepatic 75980
Endoscopy
Biopsy 47553
Cannulation 43273
Destruction
Calculi (Stone) 43265
Tumor 43272
Dilation 43271, 47555-47556
Exploration 47552
Intraoperative 47550
Removal
Calculi (Stone) 43264, 47554
Foreign Body 43269
Stent 43269
Specimen Collection 43260
Sphincter Pressure 43263
Sphincterotomy 43262
Tube Placement 43267-43268
Exploration
Atresia 47700
Endoscopy 47552
Incision
Sphincter 43262, 47460
Incision and Drainage 47420-47425
Insertion
Catheter 47510, 47525, 75982
Revision 47530
Stent 47511, 47801
Nuclear Medicine
Imaging 78223
Reconstruction
Anastomosis 47800
Removal
Calculi (Stone) 43264, 47420-47425
Percutaneous 47630
Foreign Body 43269
Stent 43269
Repair 47701
Gastrointestinal Tract 47785
with Intestines 47760, 47780
Tube Placement
Nasobiliary 43267
Stent 43268
Tumor
Destruction 43271
Excision 47711-47712
Unlisted Services and Procedures 47999
X-ray
Guide Dilation 74360
with Contrast 74300-74320
Calculus Removal 74327
Guide Catheter 74328, 74330

Bile Duct, Common, Cystic Dilatation
See Cyst, Choledochal

Bilirubin
Blood 82247-82248
Feces 82252
Total
Direct 82247-82248
Transcutaneous 88720

Billroth I or II
See Gastrectomy, Partial

Bilobectomy 32482

Bimone
See Testosterone

Binding Globulin, Testosterone-Estradiol
See Globulin, Sex Hormone Binding

Binet Test 96101-96103

Binet-Simon Test 96101-96103

Binocular Microscopy 92504

Biofeedback
See Training, Biofeedback
Anorectal 90911
Psychiatric Treatment 90875-90876

Biofeedback Training
See Training, Biofeedback

Bioimpedance
Thorax 93701

Biological Skin Grafts
See Allograft, Skin

Biometry
Eye 76516-76519, 92136

Biopsies, Needle
See Needle Biopsy

Biopsy
See Brush Biopsy; Needle Biopsy
Abdomen 49000
Adrenal Gland 60540-60545
Anal
Endoscopy 46606
Ankle 27613-27614, 27620
Arm, Lower 25065-25066
Arm, Upper 24065-24066
Artery
Temporal 37609
Auditory Canal, External 69105
Back/Flank 21920-21925
Bile Duct
Endoscopy 47553
Bladder 52354
Cystourethroscope 52204
Cystourethroscopy 52224, 52250
Blood Vessel
Transcatheter 75970
Bone 20220-20245
Bone Marrow 38221
Brain 61140
Stereotactic 61750-61751
Brainstem 61575-61576
Breast 19100-19103
Stereotactic Localization 77031
Bronchi
Catheterization 31717
Endoscopic 31625-31629, 31632-31633
Brush
Bronchi 31717
Renal Pelvis 52007
Ureter 52007
with Cystourethroscopy 52204
Carpometacarpal Joint
Synovium 26100
Cervix 57454-57455, 57460, 57500, 57520
Chorionic Villus 59015
Colon 44025, 44100
Endoscopy 44389, 45380, 45391-45392
Multiple
with Colostomy, Cecostomy 44322
Colon-Sigmoid
Endoscopy 45305, 45331
Conjunctiva 68100
Cornea 65410
Duodenum 44010
Ear
External 69100
Elbow 24065-24066, 24101
Synovium 24100
Embryo Blastomere 89290-89291
Endometrium 58100-58110, 58558
Epididymis 54800, 54865
Esophagus
Endoscopy 43202
Forceps 3150F
Eye Muscle 67346
Eyelid 67810
Forearm
Soft Tissue 25065-25066
Gallbladder
Endoscopy 43261
Gastrointestinal, Upper
Endoscopy 43239
Hand Joint
Synovium 26100
Heart 93505
Hip 27040-27041
Joint 27052
Hypopharynx 42802
Ileum
Endoscopy 44382
Interphalangeal Joint
Finger 26110
Toe 28054
Intertarsal Joint
Toe 28050
Intestines, Small 44020, 44100
Endoscopy 44361, 44377

Biopsy, Skin

Biopsy, Vein

Biostatistics

Biosterol

Birthing Room

Bischof Procedure

Bizzozero's Corpuscle/Cell

Bladder

Repair
  Diverticulum 52305
  Exstrophy 51940
  Fistula 44660-44661, 45800-45805, 51880-51925
  Neck 51845
  Wound 51860-51865
Resection 52500
Sphincter Surgery 52277
Suspension 51990
Suture
  Fistula 44660-44661, 45800-45805, 51880-51925
  Wound 51860-51865
Tumor
  Excision 51530
Unlisted Services and Procedures 53899
Urethrocystography 74450-74455
Urethrotomy 52270-52276
Urinary Incontinence Procedures
  Laparoscopy 51990-51992
  Plan of Care Documented 0509F
X-ray 74430
  with Contrast 74450-74455

Bladder Voiding Pressure Studies 51795

Blalock-Hanlon Procedure 33735-33737
See Septostomy, Atrial

Blalock-Taussig Procedure
See Shunt, Great Vessel

Blast Cells
See Stem Cell

Blast Transformation
See Blastogenesis

Blastocyst Implantation
See Implantation

Blastocyst Transfer
See Embryo Transfer

Blastogenesis 86353

Blastomyces
Antibody 86612

Blastomycosis, European
See Cryptococcus

Bleeding
See Hemorrhage
Anal
  See Anus, Hemorrhage
Disorder
  See Coagulopathy
Time 85002
Tube
  Passage and Placement 91100
Uterine
  See Hemorrhage, Uterus
Vaginal
  See Hemorrhage, Vaginal

Blepharoplasty 15820-15823
See Canthoplasty
Anesthesia 00103

Blepharoptosis
Repair 67901-67909
  Frontalis Muscle Technique 67901
    with Fascial Sling 67902
  Superior Rectus Technique with Fascial Sling 67906
  Tarso Levator Resection/Advancement
    External Approach 67904
    Internal Approach 67903

Blepharorrhaphy
See Tarsorrhaphy

Blepharospasm
Chemodenervation 64612

Blepharotomy 67700

Blister
See Bulla

Blom-Singer Prosthesis 31611

Blood
See Blood Cell Count, Complete Blood Count
Bleeding Time 85002
Blood Clot
  Assay 85396
    Activity 85397
    ADAMTS-13 85397
  Coagulation Time 85345-85348
  Clotting
    Factor 85250-85293
    Factor Test 85210-85244
    Inhibitors 85300-85302, 85305, 85307
  Lysis Time 85175
  Retraction 85170
  Thrombolytic Agents
    Tissue Plasminogen Activator (tPA) 4077F
Collection, for Autotransfusion
  Intraoperative 86891
  Preoperative 86890
Feces 82270, 82272
  by Hemoglobin Immunoassay 82274
Gastric Contents 82273
Hemoglobin A1c (HbA1c) Level 3044F-3045F
Hemoglobin
  Concentration 85046
  Quantitative 88740
  Transcutaneous
    Carboxyhemoglobin 88740
    Methemoglobin 88741
Nuclear Medicine
  Flow Imaging 78445
  Red Cell 78140
  Red Cell Survival 78130-78135
Osmolality 83930
Other Source 82273
Plasma
  Exchange 36514-36516
Platelet
  Aggregation 85576
  Automated Count 85049
  Count 85008
  Manual Count 85032
Stem Cell
  Count 86367
  Donor Search 38204
  Erythropoietin Therapy 3160F, 4090F-4095F
  Harvesting 38205-38206
  Transplantation 38240-38242
    Cell Concentration 38215
    Cryopreservation 38207, 88240
    Plasma Depletion 38214
    Platelet Depletion 38213
    Red Blood Cell Depletion 38212
    T-cell Depletion 38210
    Thawing 38208-38209, 88241
    Tumor Cell Depletion 38211
    Washing 38209
Trancutaneous
  Carboxyhemoglobin 88740
  Methemoglobin 88741
Transfusion 36430
  Exchange 36455
    Newborn 36450
  Fetal 36460
  Push
    Infant 36440
Unlisted Services and Procedures 85999
Urine 83491
Viscosity 85810

Blood Banking
Frozen Blood Preparation 86930-86932
Frozen Plasma Preparation 86927
Physician Services 86077-86079

Blood Cell
CD4 and CD8
  Including Ratio 86360
Enzyme Activity 82657
Exchange 36511-36513
Sedimentation Rate
  Automated 85652
  Manual 85651

Blood Cell Count
Automated 85049
B-Cells 86355
Blood Smear 85007-85008
Differential WBC Count 85004-85007, 85009
Hematocrit 85014
Hemoglobin 85018
Hemogram
  Added Indices 85025-85027
  Automated 85025-85027
  Manual 85032
Microhematocrit 85013
Natural Killer (NK) Cells 86357
Red Blood Cells 85032-85041
Reticulocyte 85044-85046
Stem Cells 86367
T-Cells 86359-86361
White Blood Cells 85032, 85048, 89055

Blood Cell Count, Red
See Red Blood Cell (RBC), Count

Blood Cell Count, White
See White Blood Cell, Count

Blood Cell, Red
See Red Blood Cell (RBC)

Blood Cell, White
See Leukocyte

Heinz
  See Heinz Bodies
Inclusion
  See Inclusion Bodies
Ketone
  See Ketone Body

Body Cast
Halo ... 29000
Removal ... 29700, 29710-29715
Repair ... 29720
Risser Jacket ... 29010-29015
Turnbuckle Jacket ... 29020-29025
Upper Body and Head ... 29040
Upper Body and Legs ... 29046
Upper Body and One Leg ... 29044
Upper Body Only ... 29035

Body Fluid
Crystal Identification ... 89060

Body of Vertebra
See Vertebral Body

Body Section
X-ray ... 76100
  Motion ... 76101-76102

Body System, Neurologic
See Nervous System

Boil
See Furuncle

Boil, Vulva
See Abscess, Vulva

Bone
See Specific Bone
Ablation
  Tumor ... 20982
Biopsy ... 20220-20245
Carpal
  See Carpal Bone
Cheek
  See Cheekbone
CT Scan
  Density Study ... 77078-77079
Cyst
  Drainage ... 20615
  Injection ... 20615
Dual Energy X-ray Absorptiometry ... 77080-77081
Excision
  Epyphyseal Bar ... 20150
  Facial Bones ... 21026
  Mandible ... 21025
Facial
  See Facial Bone
Fixation
  Caliper ... 20660
  Cranial Tong ... 20660
  Halo ... 20661-20663, 21100
  Interdental ... 21110
  Multiplane ... 20692
    Stereotactic Computer Assisted ... 20696-20697
  Pin/Wire ... 20650
  Skeletal
    Humeral Epicondyle
      Percutaneous ... 24566
  Stereotactic Frame ... 20660
  Uniplane ... 20690
Fracture
  Osteoporosis Screening ... 5015F
Hyoid
  See Hyoid Bone
Insertion
  Needle ... 36680
  Osseointegrated Implant
    for External Speech Processor/ Cochlear Stimulator ... 69714-69718
Marrow
  Cytogenic Testing ... 3155F
Metatarsal
  See Metatarsal Bone
Nasal
  See Nasal Bone
Navicular
  See Navicular
Nuclear Medicine
  Density Study ... 78350-78351
  Imaging ... 78300-78320
  SPECT ... 78320
  Unlisted Services and Procedures ... 78399
Osteoporosis
  Pharmacologic Therapy ... 4005F
Protein ... 83937
Removal
  Fixation Device ... 20670-20680
Replacement
  Osseointegrated Implant
    for External Speech Processor/ Cochlear Stimulator ... 69717-69718
Scan
  See Bone, Nuclear Medicine; Nuclear Medicine Imaging
Semilunar
  See Lunate
Sesamoid
  See Sesamoid Bone
Spur
  See Exostosis
Tarsal
  See Ankle Bone
Temporal
  See Temporal Bone
X-ray
  Age Study ... 77072
  Dual Energy Absorptiometry ... 77080-77081
  Length Study ... 77073
  Osseous Survey ... 77074-77077

Bone 4-Carboxyglutamic Protein
See Osteocalcin

Bone Conduction Hearing Device, Electromagnetic
Implantation/Replacement ... 69710
Removal/Repair ... 69711

Bone Density Study
Appendicular Skeleton ... 77079, 77081
Axial Skeleton ... 77078, 77080
Ultrasound ... 76977
Vertebral Fracture Assessment ... 77082

Bone Graft
Any Donor Area ... 20900-20902
Augmentation
  Mandibular Body ... 21127
Femur ... 27170
Fracture
  Orbit ... 21408
Harvesting ... 20900-20902
Malar Area ... 21210
Mandible ... 21215
Mandibular Ramus ... 21194
Maxilla ... 21210
Microvascular Anastomosis
  Fibula ... 20955
  Other ... 20962
Nasal Area ... 21210
Nasomaxillary Complex Fracture ... 21348
Open Treatment
  Craniofacial Separation ... 21436
Osteocutaneous Flap ... 20969-20973
Reconstruction
  Mandibular Rami ... 21194
  Midface ... 21145-21160
Skull ... 61316
  Excision ... 62148
Spine Surgery
  Allograft
    Morselized ... 20930
    Structural ... 20931
  Autograft
    Local ... 20936
    Morselized ... 20937
    Structural ... 20938
Vascular Pedicle ... 25430

Bone Healing
Electrical Stimulation
  Invasive ... 20975
  Noninvasive ... 20974
Ultrasound Stimulation ... 20979

Bone Infection
See Osteomyelitis

Bone Marrow
Aspiration ... 38220
Harvesting ... 38230
Magnetic Resonance Imaging (MRI) ... 77084
Needle Biopsy ... 38221
Nuclear Medicine
  Imaging ... 78102-78104
Smear ... 85097
T-Cell Transplantation ... 38240-38242
Trocar Biopsy ... 38221

Bone Plate
Mandible ... 21244

Bone Wedge Reversal
Osteotomy ... 21122

Bordetella
Antibody ... 86615
Antigen Detection
  Direct Fluorescence ... 87265

Borrelia
Antibody ... 86618-86619

Borrelia burgdorferi ab
See Antibody, Lyme Disease

Brainstem
See Brain
Biopsy 61575-61576
Decompression 61575-61576
Evoked Potentials 92585-92586
Lesion
Excision 61575-61576

Branchial Cleft
Cyst
Excision 42810-42815

Branchioma
See Branchial Cleft, Cyst

Breast
Ablation
Cryosurgery 19105
Abscess
Incision and Drainage 19020
Augmentation 19324-19325
Biopsy 19100-19103
Catheter Placement
for Interstitial Radioelement
Application 19296-19298; 20555, 41019
Cyst
Puncture Aspiration 19000-19001
Excision
Biopsy 19100-19103
Capsules 19371
Chest Wall Tumor 19260-19272
Cyst 19120
Lactiferous Duct Fistula 19112
Lesion 19120-19126, 19301
by Needle Localization 19125-19126
Mastectomy 19300-19307
Nipple Exploration 19110
Exploration 19020
Implants
Insertion 19340-19342
Preparation of Moulage 19396
Removal 19328-19330
Supply 19396
Incision
Capsules 19370
Injection
Radiologic 19030
Magnetic Resonance Imaging
(MRI) 77058-77059
with Computer-aided Detection 0159T
Mammoplasty
Augmentation 19324-19325
Reduction 19318
Mastopexy 19316
Metallic Localization Clip Placement 19295
Needle Biopsy 19100
Needle Wire Placement 19290-19291
Periprosthetic Capsulectomy 19371
Periprosthetic Capsulotomy 19370
Reconstruction 19357-19369
Augmentation 19324-19325
Mammoplasty 19318-19325
Nipple 19350-19355
Areola 19350
Revision 19380
with Free Flap 19364
with Latissimus Dorsi Flap 19361
with Other Techniques 19366
with Tissue Expander 19357
with Transverse Rectus Abdominis
Myocutaneous Flap 19367-19369
Reduction 19318
Removal
Capsules 19371
Modified Radical 19307
Partial 19300-19302
Radical 19305-19306
Simple, Complete 19303
Subcutaneous 19304
Repair
Suspension 19316
Stereotactic Localization 77031
Ultrasound 76645
Unlisted Services and Procedures 19499
X-ray 77055-77057
Localization Nodule 77032
with Computer-aided
Detection 77051-77052

Breath Odor Alcohol
See Alcohol, Breath

Breath Test
Alcohol, Ethyl 82075
Heart Transplant Rejection Detection 0085T
Helicobacter Pylori ...78267-78268, 83013-83014
Hydrogen 91065

Breathing, Inspiratory Positive-Pressure
See Intermittent Positive Pressure Breathing (IPPB)

Bricker Procedure
Intestines Anastomosis 50820

Bristow Procedure
See Capsulorrhaphy, Anterior

Brock Operation
See Valvotomy, Pulmonary Valve

Broken, Nose
See Fracture, Nasal Bone

Bronchi
Aspiration
Endoscopic 31645-31646
Biopsy
Endoscopic 31625-31629, 31632-31633
Catheterization
with Bronchial Brush Biopsy 31717
Endoscopy
Aspiration 31645-31646
Biopsy 31625-31629, 31632-31633
Destruction
Tumor 31641
Dilation 31630-31631, 31636-31638
Excision
Lesion 31640
Exploration 31622
Foreign Body Removal 31635
Fracture 31630
Injection 31656
Lesion 31640-31641
Stenosis 31641
Tumor 31640-31641
Ultrasound 31620
Exploration
Endoscopic 31622
Fracture
Endoscopy 31630
Injection
X-ray 31656-31715
Needle Biopsy 31629, 31633
Reconstruction 31770
Graft Repair 31770
Stenosis 31775
Removal
Foreign Body 31635
Repair
Fistula 32815
Stenosis
Endoscopic Treatment 31641
Stent
Placement 31636-31637
Revision 31638
Tumor
Excision 31640
Ultrasound 31620
Unlisted Services and Procedures 31899
X-ray
with Contrast 71040-71060

Bronchial Allergen Challenge
See Bronchial Challenge Test

Bronchial Alveolar Lavage 31624

Bronchial Brush Biopsy
with Catheterization 31717

Bronchial Brushings/Protected Brushing 31623

Bronchial Challenge Test
See Allergy Tests
with Antigens, Gases 95070
with Chemicals 95071

Bronchial Provocation Tests
See Bronchial Challenge Test

Bronchioalveolar Lavage
See Lung, Lavage

Broncho-Bronchial Anastomosis 32486

Bronchoalveolar Lavage
See Lung, Lavage

Bronchography 71040-71060
Injection
Transtracheal 31715
Segmental
Injection 31656

Bronchoplasty 32501
See Reconstruction, Bronchi
Excision Stenosis and Anastomosis 31775
Graft Repair 31770

Bronchopneumonia, Hiberno-Vernal
See Q Fever

Bronchopulmonary Lavage
See Lung, Lavage

Bronchoscopy
Alveolar Lavage 31624

Revascularization
Extremity 35903
Neck 35901
Thorax 35905
Revision
Lower Extremity
Femoral Artery 35883-35884
with Angioplasty 35879
with Vein Interposition 35881
Secondary Repair 35870
Splenic Artery 35536, 35636
Subclavian Artery ...35506, 35511-35516, 35526, 35606-35616, 35626, 35645
Thrombectomy 37184-37186
Other than Hemodialysis Graft or Fistula 35875-35876
Tibial Artery ..35566-35571, 35623, 35666-35671
Tibial/Peroneal Trunk-Tibial
Venous Graft 35570
Tibial-Tibial
Venous Graft 35570
Vertebral Artery 35508, 35515, 35642-35645
with Composite Graft 35681

Bypass In-Situ
Femoral Artery 35583-35585
Peroneal Artery 35585-35587
Popliteal Artery 35583, 35587
Tibial Artery 35585-35587
Ventricular Restoration 33548

Bypass, Cardiopulmonary
See Cardiopulmonary Bypass

C

C-13
Urea Breath Test 83013-83014
Urease Activity 83013-83014

C-14
Urea Breath Test 78267-78268
Urease Activity 83013-83014

C-Peptide 80432, 84681

C-Reactive Protein 86140-86141

C-Section
See Cesarean Delivery

C Vitamin
See Ascorbic Acid

CABG
See Coronary Artery Bypass Graft (CABG)

Cadmium
Urine 82300

Caffeine Halothane Contracture Test (CHCT) 89049

Calcaneal Spur
See Heel Spur

Calcaneus
Craterization 28120
Cyst
Excision 28100-28103
Diaphysectomy 28120
Excision 28118-28120
Fracture
Open Treatment 28415-28420
Percutaneous Fixation 28406
with Manipulation 28405-28406
without Manipulation 28400
Repair
Osteotomy 28300
Saucerization 28120
Tumor
Excision 27647, 28100-28103
X-ray 73650

Calcareous Deposits
Subdeltoid
Removal 23000

Calcifediol
Blood or Urine 82306

Calcifediol Assay
See Calciferol

Calciferol
Blood or Urine 82307

Calcification
See Calcium, Deposits

Calciol
See Vitamin, D-3

Calcitonin
Blood or Urine 82308
Stimulation Panel 80410

Calcium
Blood
Infusion Test 82331
Deposits
See Removal, Calculi (Stone); Removal, Foreign Bodies
Ionized 82330
Total 82310
Urine 82340

Calcium-Binding Protein, Vitamin K-Dependent
See Osteocalcin

Calcium-Pentagastrin Stimulation 80410

Calculus
Analysis 82355-82370
Destruction
Bile Duct 43265
Pancreatic Duct 43265
Removal
Bile Duct 43264, 47554, 74327
Bladder 51050, 52310-52318, 52352
Kidney 50060-50081, 50130, 50561, 50580, 52352
Pancreatic Duct 43264
Ureter 50610-50630, 50961, 50980, 51060-51065, 52320-52325, 52352
Urethra 52310-52315, 52352

Calculus of Kidney
See Calculus, Removal, Kidney

Caldwell-Luc Procedure
See Sinus/Sinuses, Maxillary; Sinusotomy; Sternum, Fracture
Orbital Floor Blowout Fracture 21385
Sinusotomy 31030-31032

Caliper
Application/Removal 20660

Callander Knee Disarticulation
See Disarticulation, Knee

Callosum, Corpus
See Corpus Callosum

Calmette Guerin Bacillus Vaccine
See BCG Vaccine

Caloric Vestibular Test 92533

Calprotectin
Fecal 83993

Calycoplasty 50405

Camey Enterocystoplasty 50825

CAMP
See Cyclic AMP

Campbell Procedure 27422

Campylobacter
Antibody 86625

Campylobacter Pylori
See Helicobacter Pylori

Canal, Ear
See Auditory Canal

Canal, Semicircular
See Semicircular Canal

Canalith Repositioning 95992

Canaloplasty 69631, 69635

Candida
Antibody 86628
Skin Test 86485

Cannulation 36821
Arterial 36620-36625
Endoscopic
Common Bile Duct 43273
Pancreatic Duct 43273
Sinus
Maxillary 31000
Sphenoid 31002
Thoracic Duct 38794

Cannulation, Renoportal
See Anastomosis, Renoportal

Cannulization
See Catheterization
Arteriovenous 36145, 36810-36815

Declotting 36593, 36860-36861
ECMO 36822
External
  Declotting 36860-36861
Vas Deferens 55200
Vein to Vein 36800

Canthocystostomy
See Conjunctivorhinostomy

Canthopexy
Lateral 21282
Medial 21280

Canthoplasty 67950

Canthorrhaphy 67880-67882

Canthotomy 67715

Canthus
Reconstruction 67950

Cap, Cervical
See Cervical Cap

Capsule
See Capsulodesis
Elbow
  Arthrotomy 24006
  Excision 24006
Foot 28264
Interphalangeal Joint
  Excision 26525
  Incision 26525
Knee 27435
Metacarpophalangeal Joint
  Excision 26520
  Incision 26520
Metatarsophalangeal Joint
  Release 28289
Shoulder
  Incision 23020
Wrist
  Excision 25320

Capsulectomy
Breast
  Periprosthetic 19371

Capsulodesis
Metacarpophalangeal Joint 26516-26518

Capsulorrhaphy
Anterior 23450-23462
Multi-Directional Instability 23466
Posterior 23465
Wrist 25320

Capsulotomy
Breast
  Periprosthetic 19370
Foot 28260-28262
Hip
  with Release, Flexor Muscles 27036
Interphalangeal Joint 28272
Knee 27435
Metacarpophalangeal Joint 26520
Metatarsophalangeal Joint 28270
Toe 28270-28272
Wrist 25085

Captopril 80416-80417

Carbamazepine
Assay 80156-80157

Carbazepin
See Carbamazepine

Carbinol
See Methanol

Carbohydrate Deficient Transferrin 82373

Carbon Dioxide
Blood or Urine 82374

Carbon Tetrachloride 84600

Carboxycathepsin
See Angiotensin Converting Enzyme (ACE)

Carboxyhemoglobin 82375-82376, 88740

Carbuncle
Incision and Drainage 10060-10061

Carcinoembryonal Antigen
See Antigen, Carcinoembryonic

Carcinoembryonic Antigen 82378

Cardiac
See Coronary
Muscle
  See Myocardium
Neoplasm
  See Heart, Tumor
Pacemaker
  See Heart, Pacemaker
Septal Defect
  See Septal Defect

Cardiac Arrhythmia, Tachycardia
See Tachycardia

Cardiac Atria
See Atria

Cardiac Catheterization
Combined Left and Right Heart 93526-93529
Combined Right and Retrograde Left
  Congenital Cardiac Anomalies 93531
Combined Right and Transseptal Left
  Congenital Cardiac Anomalies ..93532-93533
for Angiography 93508, 93541-93543
for Biopsy 93505
for Dilution Studies 93561-93562
Imaging 93555-93556
Injection 93539-93545
  See Catheterization, Cardiac
Left Heart 93510-93524
Pacemaker 33210
Right
  Congenital Cardiac Anomalies 93530
Right Heart 93501-93503

Cardiac Electroversion
See Cardioversion

Cardiac Event Recorder
Implantation 33282
Removal 33284

Cardiac Magnetic Resonance Imaging (CMRI)
Complete Study 75554
Limited Study 75555
Morphology 75553
Velocity Flow Mapping 75556

Cardiac Massage
Thoracotomy 32160

Cardiac Output
Indicator Dilution 93561-93562
Inert Gas Rebreathing 0104T-0105T

Cardiac Rehabilitation 93797-93798

Cardiac Transplantation
See Heart, Transplantation

Cardiectomy
Donor 33930, 33940

Cardioassist 92970-92971

Cardiolipin Antibody 86147

Cardiology
See Defibrillator, Heart; Electrocardiography; Pacemaker, Heart
Diagnostic
  Acoustic Recording with ComputerAnalysis
    Heart Sounds 0068T-0069T, 0070T
  Atrial Electrogram
    Esophageal Recording 93615-93616
  Cardiovascular Monitor, Implantable
    Data Analysis 93290, 93297, 93299
  Cardioverter-Defibrillator, Implantable
    Data Analysis 93289, 93295-93296
    Evaluation of Programming ..93282-93284, 93287, 93640-93642
  Echocardiography
    Doppler 93303-93321, 93662
    Intracardiac 93662
    Transesophageal 93318
    Transthoracic ..93303-93317, 93350-93352
  Electrocardiogram
    Evaluation 93000, 93010, 93014, 93660, 0178T-0180T
    Microvolt T-wave Alternans 93025
    Monitoring 93224-93237
    Patient-Activated 93268-93272
    Rhythm 93040-93042
    Tracing 93005
    Transmission 93012
  Ergonovine Provocation Test 93024
  Hemodynamic Monitoring
  Non-invasive 0086T
  Intracardiac Pacing and Mapping 93631
    3-D Mapping 93613
    Follow-up Study 93624
    Stimulation and Pacing 93623
  Intracardiac Pacing and Recording
    Arrhythmia Induction 93618-93624
    Bundle of His 93600, 93619-93620
    Comprehensive 93619-93622
    Intra-Atrial 93602, 93610

Right Ventricle 93603
Tachycardia Sites 93609
Ventricular 93612
Intravascular Ultrasound 92978-92979
Left Ventricular Pressure
Measurement 0086T
Loop Recorder, Implantable
Data Analysis 93291, 93298-93299
Evaluation of Programming 93285
Pacemaker Testing 93642
Antitachycardia System 93724
Data Analysis 93288, 93293-93294
Evaluation of Device
Programming 93279-93281, 93286
Perfusion Imaging 78460-78461
See Nuclear Medicine
Stress Tests
Cardiovascular 93015-93018
Drug Induced 93024
Multiple Gated Acquisition (MUGA) .78473
Tilt Table Evaluation 93660
Therapeutic
Cardioverter-Defibrillator, Implantable
Data Analysis 93289, 93295-93296
Evaluation of Programming ..93282-93284, 93287
Initial Set-up and Programming 93745
Cardioassist 92970-92971
Cardioversion 92960-92961
Intravascular Ultrasound 92978-92979
Pacing
Transcutaneous, Temporary 92953
Thrombolysis 92975-92977
Thrombolysis, Coronary 92977
Valvuloplasty
Percutaneous 92986-92990

Cardiomyotomy
See Esophagomyotomy

Cardioplasty 43320

Cardiopulmonary Bypass 33926
See Heart; Lung, Transplantation

Cardiopulmonary Resuscitation 92950

Cardiotomy 33310-33315

Cardiovascular Stress Test
See Exercise Stress Tests

Cardioversion 92960-92961

Care
Custodial
See Nursing Facility Services
Intensive
See Intensive Care
Neonatal Intensive
See Intensive Care, Neonatal
Self
See Self Care

Care Plan Oversight Services
See Physician Services

Carneous Mole
See Abortion

Carnitine 82379

Carotene 82380

Caroticum, Glomus
See Carotid Body

Carotid Artery
Aneurysm Repair
Vascular Malformation or Carotid-Cavernous
Fistula 61710
Excision 60605
Ligation 37600-37606
Stenosis Imaging 3100F
Stent, Transcatheter Placement 0075T-0076T
Transection
with Skull Base Surgery 61609

Carotid Body
Lesion
Carotid Artery 60605
Excision 60600

Carpal Bone
See Wrist
Arthroplasty
with Implant 25443
Cyst
Excision 25130-25136
Dislocation
Closed Treatment 25690
Open Treatment 25695
Excision 25210-25215
Partial 25145
Fracture
Closed Treatment 25622, 25630
Open Treatment 25628, 25645
with Manipulation 25624, 25635
without Manipulation 25630
Incision and Drainage 26034
Insertion
Vascular Pedicle 25430
Osteoplasty 25394
Repair 25431-25440
Scaphoid (Navicular) Fracture 25628
Sequestrectomy 25145
Tumor
Excision 25130-25136

Carpal Tunnel
Injection
Therapeutic 20526

Carpal Tunnel Syndrome
Decompression 64721

Carpals
Incision and Drainage 25035

Carpectomy 25210-25215

Carpometacarpal Joint
Arthrodesis
Hand 26843-26844
Thumb 26841-26842
Arthrotomy 26070
Biopsy
Synovium 26100
Dislocation
Closed Treatment 26670
with Manipulation 26675-26676
Open Treatment 26685-26686
Exploration 26070
Fusion
Hand 26843-26844
Thumb 26841-26842
Removal
Foreign Body 26070
Repair 25447
Synovectomy 26130

Cartilage Graft
Costochondral 20910
Ear to Face 21235
Harvesting 20910-20912
Nasal Septum 20912
Rib to Face 21230

Cartilage, Arytenoid
See Arytenoid

Cartilage, Ear
See Ear Cartilage

Cartilaginous Exostoses
See Exostosis

Case Management Services
Anticoagulant Management 99363-99364
Team Conferences 99366-99368
Telephone Calls 98966-98968

Cast
See Brace; Splint
Body
Risser Jacket 29010-29015
Body Cast
Halo 29000
Turnbuckle Jacket 29020-29025
Upper Body and Head 29040
Upper Body and Legs 29046
Upper Body and One Leg 29044
Upper Body Only 29035
Clubfoot 29450
Cylinder 29365
Finger 29086
Hand 29085
Hip 29305-29325
Leg
Rigid Total Contact 29445
Long Arm 29065
Long Leg 29345-29355, 29365, 29450
Long Leg Brace 29358
Patellar Tendon Bearing (PTB) 29435
Removal 29700-29715
Repair 29720
Short Arm 29075
Short Leg 29405-29435, 29450
Shoulder 29049-29058
Walking 29355, 29425
Revision 29440
Wedging 29740-29750
Windowing 29730
Wrist 29085

Casting
Unlisted Services and Procedures 29799

Castration
See Orchiectomy

Castration, Female
See Oophorectomy

CAT Scan
See CT Scan

Cataract
Excision 66830
Dilated Fundus Evaluation 2021F
Incision 66820-66821
Laser 66821
Stab Incision 66820
Removal/Extraction
Extracapsular 66982, 66984
Intracapsular 66983
Presurgical Measurement and Calculations 3073F

Catecholamines 80424, 82382-82384
Blood 82383
Urine 82382

Cathepsin-D 82387

Catheter
See Cannulization; Venipuncture
Aspiration
Nasotracheal 31720
Tracheobronchial 31725
Bladder 51701-51703
Irrigation 51700
Declotting 36593
Exchange
Intravascular 37209, 75900
Peritoneal 49423
Intracatheter
Irrigation 99507
Obstruction Clearance 36596
Pericatheter
Obstruction
Clearance 36595
Placement
Brain
Stereotactic 0169T
Breast
for Interstitial Radioelement Application ...19296-19298, 20555, 41019
Bronchus
for Intracavitary Radioelement Application 31643
Removal
Central Venous 36589
Peritoneum 49422
Spinal Cord 62355
Repair
Central Venous 36575
Replacement
Central Venous 36580-36581, 36584
Repositioning 36597

Catheterization
See Catheter
Abdomen 49420-49421
Abdominal Artery 36245-36248
Aorta 36160-36215
Arterial
Cutdown 36625
Intracatheter/Needle 36100-36140
Percutaneous 36620
Arteriovenous Shunt 36145
Bile Duct 47530
Change 47525
Percutaneous 47510
Bladder 51010, 51045
Brachiocephalic Artery 36215-36218
Brain 61210
Replacement 62160, 62194, 62225
Stereotactic 0169T
Bronchography 31710
Cardiac
Combined Left and Right Heart 93526-93529
Combined Right and Retrograde Left for Congenital Cardiac Anomalies 93531
Combined Right and Transseptal Left for Congenital Cardiac Anomalies 93532-93533
Flow Directed 93503
for Biopsy 93505
for Dilution Studies 93561-93562
Imaging 93555-93556
Injection 93539-93545
Left Heart 93510-93524
Pacemaker 33210
Right Heart 36013, 93501
for Congenital Cardiac Anomalies 93530
Central 36555-36566
Cerebral Artery 36215
Cystourethroscopy
Ejaculatory Duct 52010
Ureteral 52005
Ear, Middle 69405
Eustachian Tube 69405
Fallopian Tube 58345, 74742
Intracardiac
Ablation 93650-93652
Jejunum
for Enteral 44015
Kidney
Drainage 50392
with Ureter 50393
Legs 36245-36248
Nasotracheal 31720
Newborn
Umbilical Vein 36510
Pelvic Artery 36245-36248
Peripheral 36568-36571
Placement
Arterial Coronary Conduit without Concomitant Left Heart Catheterization 93508
Coronary Artery without Concomitant Left Heart Catheterization 93508
Venous Coronary Bypass Graft without Concomitant Left Heart Catheterization 93508
Pleural Cavity 32550
Portal Vein 36481
Pulmonary Artery 36013-36015
Radioelement Application 55875
Removal
Fractured Catheter 75961
Obstructive Material
Intracatheter 36596
Pericatheter 36595
Salivary Duct 42660
Skull 61107
Spinal Cord 62350-62351
Thoracic Artery 36215-36218
Tracheobronchi 31725
Umbilical Artery 36660
Umbilical Vein 36510
Ureter
Endoscopic 50553, 50572, 50953, 50972, 52005
Injection 50394, 50684
Manometric Studies 50396, 50686
Uterus
Radiology 58340
Vena Cava 36010
Venous
Central Line 36555-36556, 36568-36569, 36580, 36584
First Order 36011
Intracatheter/Needle 36000
Organ Blood 36500
Second Order 36012
Umbilical Vein 36510
Ventricular 61020-61026, 61210-61215

Cauda Equina
See Spinal Cord
Decompression 63005-63011, 63017, 63047-63048, 63055-63057, 63087-63091
Exploration 63005-63011, 63017

Cauterization
Anal Fissure 46940-46942
Cervix 57522
Cryocautery 57511
Electro or Thermal 57510
Laser Ablation 57513
Chemical
Granulation Tissue 17250
Everted Punctum 68705
Nasopharyngeal Hemorrhage 42970
Nose
Hemorrhage 30901-30906
Skin Lesion 11055-11057, 17000-17004
Skin Tags 11200-11201
Turbinate Mucosa 30801-30802

Cavernitides, Fibrous
See Peyronie Disease

Cavernosography
Corpora 54230

Cavernosometry 54231

Cavities, Pleural
See Pleural Cavity

Cavus Foot Correction 28309

CBC
See Blood Cell Count; Complete Blood Count (CBC)

CCL4
See Carbon Tetrachloride

CCU Visit
See Critical Care Services

CD142 Antigens
See Thromboplastin

CD143 Antigens
See Angiotensin Converting Enzyme (ACE)

CD4 86360

CD8 86360

CEA
See Carcinoembryonic Antigen

Cecil Repair
See Urethroplasty

Cecostomy 44300
Contrast 49465
Insertion of Tube 49442
Laparoscopic 44188
Obstructive Material Removal 49460
Radiological Evaluation of Tube 49465
Tube Replacement 49450

Celiac Plexus
Destruction 64680
Injection
  Anesthetic 64530
  Neurolytic 64680

Celiac Trunk Artery
See Artery, Celiac

Celioscopy
See Endoscopy, Peritoneum

Celiotomy 49000
Abdomen
  for Staging 49220

Cell Count
Body Fluid 89050-89051

Cell, Blood
See Blood Cell

Cell, Islet
See Islet Cell

Cell, Mother
See Stem Cell

Cell-Stimulating Hormone, Interstitial
See Luteinizing Hormone (LH)

Cellobiase
See Beta Glucosidase

Cellular Inclusion
See Inclusion Bodies

Central Shunt 33764

Central Venous Catheter Placement
Insertion
  Central 36555-36558
  Peripheral 36568-36569
Repair 36575
Replacement 36580-36585
Repositioning 36597

Central Venous Catheter Removal 36589

Cephalic Version
of Fetus
  External 59412

Cephalocele
See Encephalocele

Cephalogram, Orthodontic
See Orthodontic Cephalogram

Cerclage
Cervix 57700
  Abdominal 59325
  Removal Under Anesthesia 59871
  Vaginal 59320

Cerebellopontine Angle Tumor
See Brain, Tumor, Excision; Brainstem; Mesencephalon; Skull Base Surgery

Cerebral Cortex Decortication
See Decortication

Cerebral Death
See Brain Death

Cerebral Hernia
See Encephalocele

Cerebral Perfusion Analysis 0042T

Cerebral Thermography
See Thermogram, Cephalic

Cerebral Ventriculographies
See Ventriculography

Cerebral Vessels
Angioplasty 61630
Dilation
  Intracranial Vasospasm 61640-61642
Occlusion 61623
Placement
  Stent 61635

Cerebrose
See Galactose

Cerebrospinal Fluid 86325
Nuclear Imaging 78630-78650

Cerebrospinal Fluid Leak 63744
Brain
  Repair 61618-61619, 62100
Nasal/Sinus Endoscopy
  Repair 31290-31291
Spinal Cord
  Repair 63707-63709

Cerebrospinal Fluid Shunt 63740, 63746
Creation 62180-62192, 62200-62223
Irrigation 62194
Removal 62256-62258
Replacement 62160, 62194, 62225-62230
Reprogramming 62252

Ceruloplasmin 82390

Cerumen
Removal 69210

Cervical Cap 57170

Cervical Lymphadenectomy 38720-38724

Cervical Mucus Penetration Test 89330

Cervical Plexus
Injection
  Anesthetic 64413

Cervical Pregnancy 59140

Cervical Puncture 61050-61055

Cervical Smears 88141, 88155, 88164-88167, 88174-88175
See Cytopathology

Cervical Spine
See Vertebra, Cervical

Cervical Sympathectomy
See Sympathectomy, Cervical

Cervicectomy 57530

Cervicoplasty 15819

Cervicothoracic Ganglia
See Stellate Ganglion

Cervix
See Cytopathology
Amputation
  Total 57530
Biopsy 57500, 57520
  Colposcopy 57454-57455, 57460
Cauterization 57522
  Cryocautery 57511
  Electro or Thermal 57510
  Laser Ablation 57513
Cerclage 57700
  Abdominal 59325
  Removal Under Anesthesia 59871
  Vaginal 59320
Colposcopy 57452-57461
Conization 57461, 57520-57522
Curettage
  Endocervical 57454, 57456, 57505
Dilation
  Canal 57800
  Stump 57558
    and Curettage 57558
Ectopic Pregnancy 59140
Excision
  Radical 57531
  Stump
    Abdominal Approach 57540-57545
    Vaginal Approach 57550-57556
  Total 57530
Exploration
  Endoscopy 57452
Insertion
  Dilation 59200
  Laminaria 59200
  Prostaglandin 59200
Repair
  Cerclage 57700
    Abdominal 59325
    Suture 57720
    Vaginal 59320
Unlisted Services and Procedures 58999

Cesarean Delivery
Antepartum Care 59610, 59618
Delivery
  after Attempted Vaginal Delivery 59618
    Delivery Only 59620
    Postpartum Care 59622
    Routine Care 59610, 59618
Delivery Only 59514

Chloride, Methylene
See Dichloromethane

Chlorinated Hydrocarbons 82441

Chlorohydrocarbon
See Chlorinated Hydrocarbons

Chlorpromazine 84022

Choanal Atresia
Repair 30540-30545

Cholangiography
Injection 47500-47505
Intraoperative 74300-74301
Percutaneous 74320
  with Laparoscopy 47560-47561
Postoperative 74305
Repair
  with Bile Duct Exploration 47700
  with Cholecystectomy ..47563, 47605, 47620

Cholangiopancreatography 43260
See Bile Duct; Pancreatic Duct
Repair
  See Bile Duct; Pancreatic Duct
  with Biopsy 43261
  with Surgery 43262-43267, 43269

Cholangiostomy
See Hepaticostomy

Cholangiotomy
See Hepaticostomy

Cholecalciferol
See Vitamin, D-3

Cholecystectomy 47562-47564, 47600-47620
Any Method 47562-47564
  with Cholangiography ..47563, 47605, 47620
  with Exploration Common Duct .47564, 47610

Cholecystenterostomy 47570, 47720-47741

Cholecystography 74290-74291

Cholecystotomy 47480, 48001
Percutaneous 47490

Choledochoplasty
See Bile Duct, Repair

Choledochoscopy 47550

Choledochostomy 47420-47425

Choledochotomy 47420-47425

Choledochus, Cyst
See Cyst, Choledochal

Cholera Vaccine
Injectable 90725

Cholesterol
Measurement 83721
Serum 82465
Testing 83718-83719

Choline Esterase I
See Acetylcholinesterase

Choline Esterase II
See Cholinesterase

Cholinesterase
Blood 82480-82482

Cholylglycine
Blood 82240

Chondroitin Sulfate 82485

Chondromalacia Patella
Repair 27418

Chondropathia Patellae
See Chondromalacia Patella

Chondrosteoma
See Exostosis

Chopart Procedure 28800-28805
See Amputation, Foot; Radical Resection; Replantation

Chordotomies
See Cordotomy

Chorioangioma
See Lesion, Skin

Choriogonadotropin
See Chorionic Gonadotropin

Choriomeningitides, Lymphocytic
See Lymphocytic Choriomeningitis

Chorionic Gonadotropin 80414, 84702-84703
Stimulation 80414-80415

Chorionic Growth Hormone
See Lactogen, Human Placental

Chorionic Tumor
See Hydatidiform Mole

Chorionic Villi
See Biopsy, Chorionic Villus

Chorionic Villus
Biopsy 59015

Choroid
Destruction
  Lesion 0016T, 67220-67225

Choroid Plexus
Excision 61544

Christmas Factor 85250

Chromaffinoma, Medullary
See Pheochromocytoma

Chromatin, Sex
See Barr Bodies

Chromatography
Column/Mass Spectrometry 82541-82544
Gas Liquid or HPLC 82486, 82491-82492
Paper 82487-82488
Thin-Layer 82489

Chromium 82495

Chromogenic Substrate Assay .85130

Chromosome Analysis
See Amniocentesis
Added Study 88280-88289
Amniotic Fluid 88267-88269
  Culture 88235
Biopsy Culture
  Tissue 88233
Bone Marrow Culture 88237
Chorionic Villus 88267
  5 Cells 88261
  15-20 Cells 88262
  20-25 Cells 88264
  45 Cells 88263
  Culture 88235
for Breakage Syndromes 88245-88249
Fragile-X 88248
Lymphocyte Culture 88230
Pregnancy Associated Plasma Protein-A ...84163
Skin Culture
  Tissue 88233
Tissue Culture 88239
Unlisted Services and Procedures 88299

Chromotubation 58350
Oviduct 58350

Chronic Erection
See Priapism

Chronic Interstitial Cystitides
See Cystitis, Interstitial

Ciliary Body
Cyst
  Destruction
    Cryotherapy 66720
    Cyclodialysis 66740
    Cyclophotocoagulation 66710-66711
    Diathermy 66700
    Nonexcisional 66770
Destruction
  Cyclophotocoagulation 66710-66711
  Endoscopic 66711
Lesion
  Destruction 66770
Repair 66680

Cimino Type Procedure 36821

Cinefluorographies
See Cineradiography

Cineplasty
Arm, Lower or Upper 24940

Cineradiography
Esophagus 74230
Pharynx 70371, 74230
Speech Evaluation 70371
Swallowing Evaluation 74230
Unlisted Services and Procedures ..76120-76125

Circulation Assist
Aortic 33967, 33970
Balloon 33967, 33970
External 33960-33961

Circulation, Extracorporeal
See Extracorporeal Circulation

Circulatory Assist
See Circulation Assist

Circumcision
Repair 54163
Surgical Excision 54161
  Newborn 54150, 54160

Cisternal Puncture 61050-61055

Cisternography 70015
Nuclear 78630

Citrate
Blood or Urine 82507

Clagett Procedure
See Chest Wall, Repair, Closure

Clavicle
Craterization 23180
Cyst
  Excision 23140
    with Allograft 23146
    with Autograft 23145
Diaphysectomy 23180
Dislocation
  Acromioclavicular Joint
    Closed Treatment 23540-23545
    Open Treatment 23550-23552
  Sternoclavicular Joint
    Closed Treatment 23520-23525
    Open Treatment 23530-23532
  without Manipulation 23540
Excision 23170
  Partial 23120, 23180
  Total 23125
Fracture
  Closed Treatment
    with Manipulation 23505
    without Manipulation 23500
  Open Treatment 23515
Pinning, Wiring 23490
Prophylactic Treatment 23490
Repair Osteotomy 23480-23485
Saucerization 23180
Sequestrectomy 23170
Tumor
  Excision 23140, 23146, 23200
    with Autograft 23145
  Radical Resection 23200
X-ray 73000

Clavicula
See Clavicle

Claviculectomy
Partial 23120
Total 23125

Claw Finger Repair 26499

Cleft Cyst, Branchial
See Branchial Cleft, Cyst

Cleft Foot
Reconstruction 28360

Cleft Hand
Repair 26580

Cleft Lip
Repair 40700-40761
Rhinoplasty 30460-30462

Cleft Palate
Repair 42200-42225
Rhinoplasty 30460-30462

Cleft, Branchial
See Branchial Cleft

Clinical Act of Insertion
See Insertion

Clinical Chemistry Test
See Chemistry Tests, Clinical

Clinical Investigation
FDA-approved Drugs
  Single Patient
    by Pharmacist 0130T

Clinical Pathology
See Pathology, Clinical

Clitoroplasty
Intersex State 56805

Closed [Transurethral] Biopsy of Bladder
See Biopsy, Bladder, Cystourethroscopy

Clostridial Tetanus
See Tetanus

Clostridium Botulinum Toxin
See Chemodenervation

Clostridium Difficile
Antigen Detection
  Enzyme Immunoassay 87324
by Immunoassay
  with Direct Optical Observation 87803

Clostridium Tetani ab
See Antibody, Tetanus

Closure 12001-13160
Anal Fistula 46288
Atrioventricular Valve 33600
Cystostomy 51880
Enterostomy 44625-44626
  Laparoscopic 44227
Lacrimal Fistula 68770
Lacrimal Punctum
  Plug 68761
  Thermocauterization, Ligation or Laser Surgery 68760
Rectovaginal Fistula 57300-57308
Semilunar Valve 33602
Septal Defect 33615
  Ventricular 33675-33677, 0166T-0167T, 93581
Sternotomy 21750
Ventricular Tunnel 33722

Closure of Esophagostomy
See Esophagostomy, Closure

Closure of Gastrostomy
See Gastrostomy, Closure

Closure, Atrial Septal Defect
See Heart, Repair, Atrial Septum

Closure, Cranial Sutures, Premature
See Craniosynostosis

Closure, Fistula, Vesicouterine
See Fistula, Vesicouterine, Closure

Closure, Meningocele Spinal
See Meningocele Repair

Closure, Vagina
See Vagina, Closure

Clot 34401-34490, 35875-35876, 50230
See Thrombectomy; Thromboendarterectomy

Clot Lysis Time 85175

Clot Retraction 85170

Clotting Disorder
See Coagulopathy

Clotting Factor 85210-85293

Clotting Inhibitors 85300-85305, 85307

Clotting Operation
See Excision, Nail Fold

Clotting Test
Protein C 85303, 85307
Protein S 85306

Clotting Time
See Coagulation Time

Clubfoot Cast 29450
Wedging 29750

CMG
See Cystometrogram

CMRI
See Cardiac Magnetic Resonance Imaging

CMV
See Cytomegalovirus

CNPB
See Continuous Negative Pressure Breathing (CNPB); Pulmonology, Therapeutic

Co-Factor I, Heparin
See Antithrombin III

CO_2
See Carbon Dioxide

Coagulation
Unlisted Services and Procedures 85999

Coagulation Defect
See Coagulopathy

Coagulation Factor
See Clotting Factor
Factor I
  See Fibrinogen

Factor II
See Prothrombin
Factor III
See Thromboplastin
Factor IV
See Calcium
Factor VII
See Proconvertin
Factor VIII
See Clotting Factor
Factor IX
See Christmas Factor
Factor X
See Stuart-Prower Factor
Factor Xa
See Thrombokinase
Factor XI
See PlasmaThromboplastin, Antecedent
Factor XII
See Hageman Factor
Factor XIII
See Fibrin Stabilizing Factor

Coagulation Time 85345-85348

Coagulation, Blood
See Blood Clot

Coagulation, Light
See Photocoagulation

Coagulin
See Thromboplastin

Coagulopathy 85390
Assay 85130

Cocaine
Blood or Urine 82520
Screen 82486

Coccidioides
Antibody 86635

Coccidioidin Test
See Streptokinase, Antibody

Coccidioidomycosis
Skin Test 86490

Coccygeal Spine Fracture
See Coccyx, Fracture

Coccygectomy 15920-15922, 27080

Coccyx
Excision 27080
Fracture
Closed Treatment 27200
Open Treatment 27202
Tumor
Excision 49215
X-ray 72220

Cochlear Device
Insertion 69930
Programming 92601-92604

Codeine
Alkaloid Screening 82101

Codeine Screen 82486

Cofactor Protein S
See Protein S

Coffey Operation
See Uterus, Repair, Suspension

Cognitive Function Tests .. 96101-96120
See Neurology, Diagnostic

Cognitive Skills Development .97532
See Physical Medicine/Therapy/Occupational Therapy

Cold Agglutinin 86156-86157

Cold Pack Treatment 97010

Cold Preservation
See Cryopreservation

Cold Therapies
See Cryotherapy

Colectomy
Partial 44140
Laparoscopic 44213
with Anastomosis 44140
Laparoscopic 44204, 44207-44208
with Coloproctostomy 44145-44146
with Colostomy 44141-44144
Laparoscopic 44206, 44208
with Ileocolostomy
Laparoscopic 44205
with Ileostomy 44144
with Ileum Removal 44160
with Transcanal Approach 44147
Total
Laparoscopic 44210-44212
with Proctectomy and Ileostomy 44210-44212
without Proctectomy 44210
Open
with Complete Proctectomy 45121
with Ileostomy 44150-44151
with Proctectomy 44155-44158

Collagen Cross Links 82523

Collagen Injection 11950-11954

Collar Bone
See Clavicle

Collateral Ligament
Ankle
Repair 27695-27698
Interphalangeal Joint 26545
Knee Joint
Repair 27409
Knee Repair 27405
Metacarpophalangeal Joint 26540-26542
Repair
Ankle 27695-27698

Collection and Processing
Allogenic Blood
Harvesting of Stem Cells 38205
Autologous Blood
Harvesting of Stem Cells 38206
Intraoperative 86891
Preoperative 86890

Specimen
Capillary Blood 36416
Venous Access Device 36591
Venous Blood 36415, 36591-36592
Venous Catheter 36592
Washings
Esophagus 91000
Stomach 91055

Colles Fracture 25600-25605

Colles Fracture Reversed
See Smith Fracture

Collins Syndrome, Treacher
See Treacher-Collins Syndrome

Collis Procedure
See Gastroplasty with Esophagogastric Fundoplasty

Colon
See Colon-Sigmoid
Biopsy 44025, 44100, 44322
Endoscopic 44389, 45380, 45391-45392
Colostomy
Revision 44340-44346
Colotomy 44322
Colostomy 44320
CT Scan
Colonography 0066T, 0067T
Virtual Colonoscopy 0066T, 0067T
Destruction
Lesion 44393, 45383
Tumor 44393, 45383
Endoscopy
Biopsy 44389, 45380, 45391-45392
Destruction
Lesion 44393
Tumor 44393, 45383
Dilation 45386
Exploration 44388, 45378, 45381, 45386
Hemorrhage 44391, 45382
Injection, Submucosal 45381
Placement
Stent 45387
Removal
Foreign Body 44390, 45379
Polyp 44392, 45384-45385
Tumor 45384-45385
Specimen Collection 45380
Ultrasound 45391-45392
via Colotomy 45355
via Stoma 44388-44397
Virtual 0066T, 0067T
Excision
Partial 44140-44147, 44160
Laparoscopic 44204-44208
Total 44150-44158
Laparoscopic 44210-44212
Exploration 44025
Endoscopy 44388, 45378, 45381, 45386
Hemorrhage
Endoscopic Control 44391, 45382
Hernia 44050
Incision
Creation
Stoma 44320-44322
Exploration 44025

Combined Heart-Lung Transplantation
See Transplantation, Heart-Lung

Combined Right and Left Heart Cardiac Catheterization
See Cardiac Catheterization, Combined Left and Right Heart

Comedones
Removal 10040

Commissurotomy
Right Ventricle 33476-33478

Common Sensory Nerve
Repair/Suture 64834

Common Truncus
See Truncus Arteriosus

Communication Device
Non-Speech-Generating 92605-92606
Speech-Generating 92606-92609

Community/Work Reintegration
Training 97537
  See Physical Medicine/Therapy/Occupational Therapy

Compatibility Test
Blood 86920, 86923

Complement
Antigen 86160
Fixation Test 86171
Functional Activity 86161
Hemolytic
  Total 86162
Total 86162

Complete Blood Count (CBC) 85025-85027
See Blood Cell Count

Complete Colectomy
See Colectomy, Total

Complete Pneumonectomy
See Pneumonectomy, Completion

Complete Transposition of Great Vessels
See Transposition, Great Arteries

Complex, Factor IX
See Christmas Factor

Complex, Vitamin B
See B Complex Vitamins

Component Removal, Blood
See Apheresis

Composite Graft 15760-15770, 35681-35683

Compound B
See Corticosterone

Compound F
See Cortisol

Compression, Nerve, Median
See Carpal Tunnel Syndrome

Computed Tomographic Scintigraphy
See Emission Computerized Tomography

Computed Tomography (CT)
See CT Scan; Specific Anatomic Site

Computer Analysis
Acoustic Recording
  Heart Sounds
    with Computer Analysis 0068T-0069T, 0070T
Probability Assessment 0185T

Computer-Aided Detection
Chest X-ray 0152T
Lesion
  Chest Radiograph 0174T-0175T
Mammography 77051-77052
  Magnetic Resonance Imaging (MRI) 0159T

Computer-Assisted Navigation 0054T-0055T, 20985

Computer-Assisted Testing 96103
Neuropsychological 96120
Psychological 96103

Computer Data Analysis 99090

Computerized Emission Tomography
See Emission Computerized Tomography

Concentration of Specimen 87015

Concentration, Hydrogen-Ion
See pH

Concentration, Minimum Inhibitory
See Minimum Inhibitory Concentration

Concentric Procedure 28296

Concha Bullosa Resection
with Nasal/Sinus Endoscopy 31240

Conchae Nasale
See Nasal Turbinate

Conduction, Nerve
See Nerve Conduction

Conduit, Ileal
See Ileal Conduit

Condyle
Humerus
  Fracture
    Closed Treatment 24576-24577
    Open Treatment 24579
    Percutaneous 24582
Metatarsal
  Excision 28288
Phalanges
  Toe
    Excision 28126

Condyle, Mandibular
See Mandibular Condyle

Condylectomy
Temporomandibular Joint 21050
with Skull Base Surgery 61596-61597

Condyloma
Destruction 54050-54065

Conference
Medical
  with Interdisciplinary Team 99366-99368

Confirmation
Drug 80102

Congenital Arteriovenous Malformation
See Arteriovenous Malformation

Congenital Elevation of Scapula
See Sprengel's Deformity

Congenital Heart Septum Defect
See Septal Defect

Congenital Kidney Abnormality
Nephrolithotomy 50070
Pyeloplasty 50405
Pyelotomy 50135

Congenital Laryngocele
See Laryngocele

Congenital Vascular Anomaly
See Vascular Malformation

Conisation
See Cervix, Conization

Conization
Cervix 57461, 57520-57522

Conjoint Psychotherapy 90847
See Psychiatric Treatment, Family

Conjunctiva
Biopsy 68100
Cyst
  Incision and Drainage 68020
Fistulize for Drainage
  with Tube 68750
  without Tube 68745
Graft 65782
  Harvesting 68371
Harvesting 68371
Incision 0124T
Lesion
  Destruction 68135
  Excision 68110-68130
    More than 1 cm 68115
    with Adjacent Sclera 68130
Reconstruction 68320-68335
  Symblepharon
    with Graft 68335
  with Flap
    Bridge or Partial 68360
    Total 68362
Repair
  Symblepharon
    Division 68340
    with Graft 68335
    without Graft 68330

Coronary Angioplasty, Transluminal Balloon
See Percutaneous Transluminal Angioplasty

Coronary Artery
CT Scan 0146T-0149T
Insertion
  Stent 92980-92981
Ligation 33502
Placement
  Radiation Delivery Device 92974
Repair 33500-33507

Coronary Artery Bypass Graft (CABG) 33503-33505, 33510-33516
Arterial 33533-33536
Arterial Graft 33548
Arterial-Venous 33517-33523
Beta Blocker Administered 4115F
Harvest
  Upper Extremity Artery 35600
Internal Mammary Artery Graft 4110F
Reoperation 33530
Venous 33510-33516

Coronary Endarterectomy 33572

Coroner's Exam 88045

Coronoidectomy
Temporomandibular Joint 21070

Corpectomy 63101-63103

Corpora Cavernosa
Corpus Spongiosum Shunt 54430
Glans Penis Fistulization 54435
Injection 54235
Irrigation
  Priapism 54220
Saphenous Vein Shunt 54420
X-ray with Contrast 74445

Corpora Cavernosa, Plastic Induration
See Peyronie Disease

Corpora Cavernosography 74445

Corpus Callosum
Transection 61541

Corpus Vertebrae (Vertebrale)
See Vertebral Body

Correction of Cleft Palate
See Cleft Palate, Repair

Correction of Lid Retraction
See Repair, Eyelid, Retraction

Correction of Malrotation of Duodenum
See Ladd Procedure

Correction of Syndactyly
See Syndactyly, Repair

Correction of Ureteropelvic Junction
See Pyeloplasty

Cortex Decortication, Cerebral
See Decortication

Cortical Mapping
Transection
  by Electric Stimulation 95961-95962

Corticoids
See Corticosteroids

Corticoliberin
See Corticotropic Releasing Hormone (CRH)

Corticosteroid Binding Globulin
See Transcortin

Corticosteroid Binding Protein
See Transcortin

Corticosteroids
Blood 83491
Urine 83491

Corticosterone
Blood or Urine 82528

Corticotropic Releasing Hormone (CRH) 80412

Cortisol 80400-80406, 80418-80420, 80436, 82530
Stimulation 80412
Total 82533

Cortisol Binding Globulin 84449

Costectomy
See Resection, Ribs

Costen Syndrome
See Temporomandibular Joint (TMJ)

Costotransversectomy 21610

Cothromboplastin
See Proconvertin

Cotte Operation 58400-58410
See Repair, Uterus, Suspension; Revision

Cotton Procedure
Bohler Procedure 28405

Counseling
See Preventive Medicine
Smoking and Tobacco Use
Cessation 99406-99407

Counseling and/or Risk Factor Reduction Intervention, Preventive Medicine, Individual Counseling
See Preventive Medicine, Counseling and/or Risk Factor Reduction Intervention, Individual Counseling

Count
Blood Cell
  See Blood Cell Count
Blood Platelet
  See Blood, Platelet, Count
Cell
  See Cell Count
Complete Blood
  See Complete Blood Count (CBC)
Erythrocyte
  See Red Blood Cell (RBC), Count
Leukocyte
  See White Blood Cell, Count
Reticulocyte
  See Reticulocyte, Count

Counterimmuno-electrophoresis 86185

Counters, Cell
See Cell Count

Countershock, Electric
See Cardioversion

Coventry Tibial Wedge Osteotomy
See Osteotomy, Tibia

Cowper's Gland
Excision 53250

Coxa
See Hip

Coxiella Burnetii
Antibody 86638

Coxsackie
Antibody 86658

CPAP
See Continuous Positive Airway Pressure

CPK
Blood 82550-82552

CPR (Cardiopulmonary Resuscitation) 92950

Cranial Bone
Halo
  Thin Skull Osteology 20664
Reconstruction
  Extracranial 21181-21184
Tumor
  Excision 61563-61564

Cranial Halo 20661

Cranial Nerve
Avulsion 64732-64760, 64771
Cranial Nerve II
  See Optic Nerve
Cranial Nerve V
  See Trigeminal Nerve
Cranial Nerve VII
  See Facial Nerve
Cranial Nerve X
  See Vagus Nerve
Cranial Nerve XI
  See Accessory Nerve
Cranial Nerve XII
  See Hypoglossal Nerve
Decompression 61458, 64716
Implantation
  Electrode 64553, 64573
Incision 64732-64752, 64760, 65771
Injection
  Anesthetic 64400-64408, 64412
  Neurolytic 64600-64610
Insertion
  Electrode 64553, 64573

Neuroplasty 64716
Release 64716
Repair
Suture, with or without Graft ... 64864-64865
Section 61460
Transection 64732-64760, 64771
Transposition 64716

Cranial Tongs
Application/Removal 20660
Removal 20665

Craniectomy 61501
See Craniotomy
Anesthesia 00211
Decompression 61322-61323, 61340-61343
Exploratory 61304-61305
Extensive, for Multiple Suture
Craniosynostosis 61558-61559
for Electrode 61860-61875
Release Stenosis 61550-61552
Surgical 61312-61315, 61320-61323, 61440-61480, 61500-61516, 61518-61522

Craniofacial Procedures
Unlisted Services and Procedures 21299

Craniofacial Separation
Closed Treatment 21431
Open Treatment 21432-21436
Wire Fixation 21431

Craniomegalic Skull
Reduction 62115-62117

Craniopharyngioma
Excision 61545

Cranioplasty 62120
Encephalocele Repair 62120
for Defect 62140-62141, 62145
with Autograft 62146-62147
with Bone Graft 61316, 62146-62147

Craniostenosis
See Craniosynostosis

Craniosynostosis
Bifrontal Craniotomy 61557
Extensive Craniectomy 61558-61559

Craniotomy
See Burr Hole; Craniectomy; Drill Hole; Puncture
Anesthesia 00211
Bifrontal 61557
Decompression 61322-61323
Exploratory 61304-61305
for Craniosynostosis 61556-61557
for Encephalocele 62121
for Implant of Neurostimulators 61850-61875
Frontal 61556
Parietal 61556
Surgery 61312-61315, 61320-61323, 61440, 61490, 61546, 61570-61571, 61582-61583, 61590, 61592, 61760, 62120
with Bone Flap 61510-61516, 61526-61530, 61533-61545, 61566-61567

Cranium
See Skull

Craterization
Calcaneus 28120
Clavicle 23180
Femur 27070-27071, 27360
Fibula 27360, 27641
Hip 27070
Humerus 23184, 24140
Ileum 27070
Metacarpal 26230
Metatarsal 28122
Olecranon Process 24147
Phalanges
Finger 26235-26236
Toe 28124
Pubis 27070
Radius 24145, 25151
Scapula 23182
Talus 28120
Tarsal 28122
Tibia 27360, 27640
Ulna 24147, 25150

Creatine 82553-82554
Blood or Urine 82540

Creatine Kinase
Total 82550

Creatine Phosphokinase
Blood 82552
Total 82550

Creatinine
Blood 82565
Clearance 82575
Other Source 82570
Urine 82570-82575

Creation
Arteriovenous
Fistula/Autogenous Graft 36825
Catheter Exit Site 49436
Colonic Reservoir 45119
Complete Heart Block 93650
Defect 40720
Ileal Reservoir 44158, 45113
Lesion 61790, 63600
Mucofistula 44144
Pericardial Window 32659
Recipient Site 15002-15005
Shunt
Cerebrospinal Fluid 62200
Subarachnoid
Lumbar-Peritoneal 63740
Subarachnoid-Subdural 62190
Ventriculo 62220
Sigmoid Bladder 50810
Speech Prosthesis 31611
Stoma
Bladder 51980
Kidney 50395
Renal Pelvis 50395
Tympanic Membrane 69433-69436
Ureter 50860
Ventral Hernia 39503

CRF
See Corticotropic Releasing Hormone (CRH)

CRH
See Corticotropic Releasing Hormone (CRH)

Cricoid Cartilage Split
Larynx 31587

Cricothyroid Membrane
Incision 31605

Cristobalite
See Silica

Critical Care Services 99291-99292
See Emergency Department Services; Prolonged Attendance
Evaluation and Management 99291-99292
Gastric Intubation 91105
Interfacility Transport 99466-99467
Ipecac Administration for Poison 99175
Neonatal
Initial 99468
Low Birth Weight Infant 99478-99479
Subsequent 99469
Pediatric
Initial 99471, 99475
Interfacility Transport 99466-99467
Subsequent 99472, 99476
Remote
Video-Conferenced Evaluation and
Management 0188T, 0189T

Cross Finger Flap 15574

Crossmatch 86920-86923

Crossmatching, Tissue
See Tissue Typing

Cruciate Ligament
Arthroscopic Repair 29888-29889
Repair 27407-27409
Knee
with Collateral Ligament 27409

Cryoablation
See Cryosurgery

Cryofibrinogen 82585

Cryofixation
See Cryopreservation

Cryoglobulin 82595

Cryopreservation
Cells 38207-38209, 88240-88241
Embryo 89258
for Transplantation .32850, 33930, 33940, 44132, 47133, 47140, 48550, 50300-50320, 50547
Freezing and Storage 38207, 88240
Sperm 89259
Testes 89335
Thawing
Embryo 89352
Oocytes 89353
Reproductive Tissue 89354
Sperm 89356

Cryosurgery 17000-17286, 47371, 47381
See Cryotherapy; Destruction
Fibroadenoma 0120T
Breast 19105

Labyrinthotomy 69801
Lesion
  Kidney 50250
  Mouth 40820
  Penis 54056, 54065
  Vagina 57061-57065
  Vulva 56501-56515

Cryotherapy
Ablation
  Renal Tumor 50593
Acne 17340
Destruction
  Ciliary Body 66720
Lesion
  Cornea 65450
  Retina 67208, 67227
Retinal Detachment
  Prophylaxis 67141
  Repair 67101, 67113
Trichiasis
  Correction 67825

Cryptectomy 46210-46211

Cryptococcus
Antibody 86641
Antigen Detection
  Enzyme Immunoassay 87327

Cryptococcus Neoformans
Antigen Detection
  Enzyme Immunoassay 87327

Cryptorchism
See Testis, Undescended

Cryptosporidium
Antigen Detection
  Direct Fluorescence 87272
  Enzyme Immunoassay 87328

Crystal Identification
Any Body Fluid 89060
Tissue 89060

CSF
See Cerebrospinal Fluid Leak

CT Angiography
Coronary Arteries 0146T, 0148T
  Coronary Calcium Evaluation 0147T, 0149T

CT Scan
3D Rendering 76376-76377
Bone
  Density Study 77078-77079
Brain 3111F-3112F
Drainage 75989
Follow-up Study 76380
Guidance
  Localization 77011
  Needle Placement 77012
  Parenchymal Tissue Ablation 77013
  Radiation Therapy 77014
  Vertebroplasty 72292
  Visceral Tissue Ablation 76362
Heart
  Hemorrhage Documented 3110F
  Infarction Documented 3110F
  Lesion Documented 3110F
Unlisted Services and Procedures 76497
with Contrast 70460
  Abdomen 74160
  Arm 73201
  Brain 0042T, 70460
  Cerebral Blood Flow/Volume 0042T
  Ear 70481
  Face 70487
  Head 70460
  Leg 73701
  Maxilla 70487
  Neck 70491
  Orbit 70481
  Pelvis 72193
  Sella Turcica 70481
  Spine
    Cervical 72126
    Lumbar 72132
    Thoracic 72129
  Thorax 71260
without and with Contrast
  Abdomen 74170-74175, 75635
  Arm 73202-73206
  Brain 70470, 70496
  Chest 71275
  Ear 70482
  Face 70488
  Head 70470, 70496
  Heart
    3D Rendering 0145T, 0146T, 0147T, 0148T, 0149T, 0150T-0151T
    Coronary Calcium Evaluation 0147T, 0149T
    Functional Evaluation 0151T
    Morphology 0145T, 0148T, 0149T, 0150T
  Leg 73702-73706, 75635
  Maxilla 70488
  Neck 70492, 70498
  Orbit 70482
  Pelvis 72191, 72194
  Sella Turcica 70482
  Spine
    Cervical 72127
    Lumbar 72133
    Thoracic 72130
  Thorax 71270-71275
without Contrast 70450
  Abdomen 74150
  Arm 73200
  Brain 70450
  Colon
    Colonography 0066T, 0067T
    Virtual Colonoscopy 0066T, 0067T
  Ear 70480
  Face 70486
  Head 70450
  Heart
    3D Rendering 0144T
    Coronary Calcium Evaluation 0144T
  Leg 73700
  Maxilla 70486
  Neck 70490
  Orbit 70480
  Pelvis 72192
  Sella Turcica 70480
  Spine
    Cervical 72125
    Lumbar 72131
    Thoracic 72128
  Thorax 71250

CT Scan, Radionuclide
See Emission Computerized Tomography

Cuff, Rotator
See Rotator Cuff

Culdocentesis
See Colpocentesis

Culture
Acid Fast Bacilli 87116
Amniotic Fluid
  Chromosome Analysis 88235
Bacteria
  Additional Methods 87077
  Aerobic 87040-87070
  Anaerobic 87073-87076
  Blood 87040
  Other 87070-87073
  Screening 87081
  Stool 87045-87046
  Urine 87086-87088
Bone Marrow
  Chromosome Analysis 88237
Chlamydia 87110
Chorionic Villus
  Chromosome Analysis 88235
Fertilized Oocytes
  for In Vitro Fertilization 89250
    Co-Culture of Embryo 89251
Fungus
  Blood 87103
  Hair 87101
  Identification 87106
  Nail 87101
  Other 87102
  Skin 87101
Lymphocyte
  Chromosome Analysis 88230
Mold 87107
Mycobacteria 87116-87118
Mycoplasma 87109
Oocyte/Embryo 89250
  Co-Culture of Oocyte/Embryo 89251
  Extended Culture 89272
Pathogen
  by Kit 87084
Skin
  Chromosome Analysis 88233
Tissue
  Toxin/Antitoxin 87230
  Virus 87252-87253
Tubercle Bacilli 87116
Typing 87140-87158
Unlisted Services and Procedures 87999
Yeast 87106

Curettage
See Dilation and Curettage
Cervix
  Endocervical 57454, 57456, 57505
Cornea 65435-65436
  Chelating Agent 65436
Hydatidiform Mole 59870
Postpartum 59160

Curettage and Dilatation
See Dilation and Curettage

Curettage, Uterus
See Uterus, Curettage

Curettement
Skin Lesion 11055-11057, 17004, 17110, 17270, 17280

Curietherapy
See Brachytherapy

Custodial Care
See Domiciliary Services; Nursing Facility Services

Cutaneolipectomy
See Lipectomy

Cutaneous Electrostimulation, Analgesic
See Application, Neurostimulation

Cutaneous Tag
See Skin, Tags

Cutaneous Tissue
See Integumentary System

Cutaneous-Vesicostomy
See Vesicostomy, Cutaneous

CVS
See Biopsy, Chorionic Villus

Cyanacobalamin
See Cyanocobalamin

Cyanide
Blood 82600
Tissue 82600

Cyanocobalamin 82607-82608

Cyclic AMP 82030

Cyclic GMP 83008

Cyclic Somatostatin
See Somatostatin

Cyclocryotherapy
See Cryotherapy, Destruction, Ciliary Body

Cyclodialysis
Destruction
  Ciliary Body 66740

Cyclophotocoagulation
Destruction
  Ciliary Body 66710-66711

Cyclosporine
Assay 80158

Cyst
Abdomen
  Destruction/Excision 49203-49205
Ankle
  Capsule 27630
  Tendon Sheath 27630
Bartholin's Gland
  Excision 56740
  Repair 56440
Bile Duct 47715
Bladder
  Excision 51500
Bone
  Drainage 20615
  Injection 20615
Brain
  Drainage 61150-61151, 61156, 62161-62162
  Excision 61516, 61524, 62162
Branchial Cleft
  Excision 42810-42815
Breast
  Incision and Drainage 19020
  Puncture Aspiration 19000-19001
Calcaneus 28100-28103
Carpal 25130-25136
Choledochal 47715
Ciliary Body
  Destruction 66770
Clavicle
  Excision 23140-23146
Conjunctiva 68020
Dermoid
  Nose
    Excision 30124-30125
Drainage
  Contrast Injection 49424
    with X-ray 76080
Excision
  Cheekbone 21030
  Clavicle 23140
    with Allograft 23146
    with Autograft 23145
  Femur 27355-27358
  Ganglion
    See Ganglion
  Humerus
    with Allograft 23156
    with Autograft 23155
  Hydatid
    See Echinococcosis
  Lymphatic
    See Lymphocele
  Maxilla 21030
  Mediastinum 32662
  Olecranon Process
    with Allograft 24126
    with Autograft 24125
  Pericardial 32661
  Pilonidal 11770-11772
  Radius
    with Allograft 24126
    with Autograft 24125
  Scapula 23140
    with Allograft 23146
    with Autograft 23145
  Ulna
    with Allograft 24126
    with Autograft 24125
  Zygoma 21030
Facial Bones
  Excision 21030
Femur 27065-27067
Fibula 27635-27638
Ganglion
  Aspiration/Injection 20612
Gums
  Incision and Drainage 41800
Hip 27065-27067
Humerus
  Excision 23150-23156, 24110
    with Allograft 24116
    with Autograft 24115
Ileum 27065-27067
Incision and Drainage 10060-10061
  Pilonidal 10080-10081
Iris
  Destruction 66770
Kidney
  Ablation 50541
  Aspiration 50390
  Excision 50280-50290
  Injection 50390
  X-ray 74470
Knee
  Baker's 27345
  Excision 27347
Leg, Lower
  Capsule 27630
  Tendon Sheath 27630
Liver 47010
  Drainage 47010
    Open 47010
  Repair 47300
Lung
  Incision and Drainage 32200
  Removal 32140
Lymph Node
  Axillary/Cervical
    Excision 38550-38555
Mandible
  Excision 21040, 21046-21047
Maxilla
  Excision 21030, 21048-21049
Mediastinal
  Excision 39200
Metacarpal 26200-26205
Metatarsal 28104-28107
Mouth 41005-41009, 41015-41018
  Incision and Drainage 40800-40801
Mullerian Duct
  Excision 55680
Nose
  Excision 30124-30125
Olecranon 24120
Ovarian
  Excision 58925
  Incision and Drainage 58800-58805
Pancreas 48500
  Anastomosis 48520-48540
  Excision 48120
Pelvis
  Aspiration 50390
  Injection 50390
Pericardial
  Excision 33050
Phalanges
  Finger 26210-26215
  Toe 28108
Pilonidal
  Excision 11770-11772
  Incision and Drainage 10080-10081
Pubis 27065-27067
Radius 24120, 25120-25126

Rathke's Pouch
See Craniopharyngioma
Removal
Skin 10040
Retroperitoneal
Destruction/Excision 49203-49205
Salivary Gland Creation
Destruction/Excision
Drainage 42409
Excision 42408
Scapula
Excision 23140-23146
Seminal Vesicle
Excision 55680
Skin
Puncture Aspiration 10160
Spinal Cord
Aspiration 62268
Incision and Drainage 63172-63173
Sublingual Gland Drainage 42409
Excision 42408
Talus 28100-28103
Tarsal 28104-28107
Thyroglossal Duct
Excision 60280-60281
Incision and Drainage 60000
Thyroid Gland Aspiration 60300
Excision 60200
Injection 60300
Tibia 27635-27638
Tongue 41000-41006, 41015
Ulna 24120, 25120-25126
Urachal
Bladder
Excision 51500
Vaginal
Excision 57135
Wrist 25130-25136
Excision 25111-25112
Zygoma
Excision 21030

Cyst, Ovary
See Ovary, Cyst

Cystatin C
Blood 82610

Cystatins, Kininogen
See Kininogen

Cystectomy
Complete 51570
with Bilateral Pelvic
Lymphadenectomy 51575, 51585, 51595
with Continent Diversion 51596
with Ureteroileal Conduit 51590
with Ureterosigmoidostomy 51580
Ovarian 58925
Laparoscopic 58661
Partial
Complicated 51555
Reimplantation of Ureters 51565
Simple 51550

Cystic Hygroma
See Hygroma

Cystine
Urine 82615

Cystitis
Interstitial 52260-52265

Cystography 74430
Injection 52281
Radiologic 51600

Cystolithotomy 51050

Cystometrogram 51725-51726

Cystoplasty 51800

Cystorrhaphy 51860-51865

Cystoscopy 52000

Cystoscopy, with Biopsy
See Biopsy, Bladder, Cystourethroscopy

Cystostomy
Change Tube 51705-51710
Closure 51880
Home Visit 99505
with Fulguration 51020
with Insertion Radioactive Material 51020
with Urethrectomy
Female 53210
Male 53215

Cystotomy
Excision
Bladder Diverticulum 51525
Bladder Tumor 51530
Repair of Ureterocele 51535
Vesical Neck 51520
Repair Ureterocele 51535
with Calculus Basket Extraction 51065
with Destruction Intravesical Lesion 51030
with Drainage 51040
with Fulguration 51020
with Insertion
Radioactive Material 51020
Ureteral Catheter 51045
with Removal Calculus 51050, 51065

Cystourethrogram, Retrograde
See Urethrocystography, Retrograde

Cystourethropexy
See Vesicourethropexy

Cystourethroplasty 51800-51820
Radiofrequency Micro-Remodeling 0193T

Cystourethroscopy .52000, 52351, 52601, 52647-52648, 53500
Biopsy 52204, 52354
Brush 52007
Calibration and/or Dilation Urethral Stricture or Stenosis 52281
Catheterization
Ejaculatory Duct 52010
Ureteral 52005
Destruction
Lesion 52400
Dilation
Bladder 52260-52265
Intra-Renal Stricture 52343, 52346
Ureter 52341-52342, 52344-52345
Urethra 52281
Evacuation
Clot 52001
Female Urethral Syndrome 52285
Incision
Ejaculatory Duct 52402
Injection of Implant Material 52327
Insertion
Indwelling Ureteral Stent 50947, 52332
Radioactive Substance 52250
Ureteral Guide Wire 52334
Urethral Stent 52282
Lithotripsy 52353
Manipulation of Ureteral Calculus 52330
Meatotomy
Ureteral 52290-52305
Removal
Calculus . .52310-52315, 52320-52325, 52352
Foreign Body 52310-52315
Urethral Stent 52310-52315
Resection
Ejaculatory Duct 52402
External Sphincter 52277
Tumor 52355
Urethral Syndrome 52285
Vasectomy
Transurethral 52402
Vasotomy
Transurethral 52402
with Direct Vision Internal Urethrotomy 52276
with Ejaculatory Duct Catheterization 52010
with Fulguration 52214, 52354
Lesion 52224
Tumor 52234-52240
with Internal Urethrotomy
Female 52270
Male 52275
with Steroid Injection 52283
with Ureteral Catheterization 52005
with Ureteral Meatotomy 52290-52305

Cytochrome Reductase, Lactic
See Lactic Dehydrogenase

Cytogenetic Study
Bone Marrow 3155F
Molecular
DNA Probe 88271-88275, 88291, 88365
Unlisted Services and Procedures 88299

Cytomegalovirus
Antibody 86644-86645
Antigen Detection
Direct Fluorescence 87271
Enzyme Immunoassay 87332
Nucleic Acid 87495-87497

Cytometries, Flow
See Flow Cytometry

Cytopathology
Cervical or Vaginal
Requiring Interpretation by Physician 88141
Thin Layer Prep 88142-88143, 88174-88175
Concentration Technique 88108
See Saccomonno Technique
Evaluation 88172
Fluids, Washings, Brushings 88104-88108
Forensic 88125
Other Source 88160-88162

Selective Cellular Enhancement Technique ... 88112
Smears
Cervical or Vaginal ... 88141-88167, 88174-88175
Unlisted Services and Procedures ... 88199

Cytoscopy
See Bladder, Endoscopy

Cytosol Aminopeptidase
See Leucine Aminopeptidase

Cytotoxic Screen
Lymphocyte ... 86805-86806
Percent Reactive Antibody (PRA) ... 86807-86808
Serum Antibodies ... 86807-86808

D

D & C Yellow No. 7
See Fluorescein

D-2, Vitamin
See Calciferol

D and C
See Dilation and Curettage

D and E
See Dilation and Evacuation

D Galactose
See Galactose

D Glucose
See Glucose

D Vitamin
See Vitamin, D

D-Xylose Absorption Test ... 84620

Dacryoadenectomy
Partial ... 68505
Total ... 68500

Dacryocystectomy ... 68520

Dacryocystogram
See Dacryocystography

Dacryocystography ... 68850, 70170
Nuclear Imaging ... 78660

Dacryocystorhinostomy ... 68720
Total
with Nasal/Sinus Endoscopy ... 31239

Dacryocystostomies
See Dacryocystotomy

Dacryocystotomy ... 68420

Daily Living Activities
See Activities of Daily Living

Damus-Kaye-Stansel Procedure
See Anastomosis, Pulmonary

Dana Operation
See Rhizotomy

Dandy Operation
See Ventriculocisternostomy

Dark Adaptation Examination ... 92284

Dark Field Examination ... 87164-87166

Darkroom Test
See Glaucoma, Provocative Test

Darrach Procedure
See Excision, Ulna, Partial

David Procedure
See Aorta, Ascending, Graft

Day Test
See Blood, Feces

de Quervain's Disease Treatment ... 25000

Death, Brain
See Brain Death

Debridement
Brain ... 62010
Burns ... 01951-01953, 16020-16030
Mastoid Cavity
Complex ... 69222
Simple ... 69220
Metatarsophalangeal Joint ... 28289
Muscle
Infected ... 11004-11006
Nails ... 11720-11721
Nose
Endoscopic ... 31237
Pancreatic Tissue ... 48105
Skin
Eczematous ... 11000-11001
Excision ... 15920-15999
Full Thickness ... 11041
Infected ... 11000-11006
Partial Thickness ... 11040
Subcutaneous Tissue ... 11042-11044
Infected ... 11004-11006
with Open Fracture and/or Dislocation ... 11010-11012
Sternum ... 21627
Wound
Non-Selective ... 97602
Selective ... 97597-97598

Debulking Procedure
Ovary/Pelvis ... 58952-58958

Decompression
See Section
Arm, Lower ... 24495, 25020-25025
Auditory Canal, Internal ... 69960
Brainstem ... 61575-61576
Cauda Equina ... 63011, 63017, 63047-63048, 63056-63057, 63087-63091
Cranial Nerve ... 61458
Esophagogastric Varices ... 37181
Facial Nerve ... 61590
Intratemporal
Lateral to Geniculate Ganglion ... 69720, 69740
Medial to Geniculate Ganglion ... 69725, 69745
Total ... 69955
Fasciotomy
Pelvic/Buttock ... 27027
with Debridement ... 27057
Finger ... 26035
Gasserian Ganglion
Sensory Root ... 61450
Hand ... 26035-26037
Intestines
Small ... 44021
Jejunostomy
Laparoscopic ... 44186
Leg
Fasciotomy ... 27600-27602
Nerve ... 64702-64727
Root ... 63020-63048, 63055-63103
Nucleus of Disc
Lumbar ... 62287
Optic Nerve ... 67570
Orbit ... 61330
Removal of Bone ... 67414, 67445
Pelvis/Buttock
Fasciotomy ... 27027
with Debridement ... 27057
Skull ... 61322-61323, 61340-61345
Spinal Cord ... 63001-63017, 63045-63103
Cauda Equina ... 63005
Osteophytectomy ... 22856
Tarsal Tunnel Release ... 28035
Volvulus ... 45321, 45337
with Nasal/Sinus Endoscopy
Optic Nerve ... 31294
Orbit Wall ... 31292-31293
Wrist ... 25020-25025

Decortication
Lung
Endoscopic ... 32651-32652
Partial ... 32225
Total ... 32220
with Parietal Pleurectomy ... 32320

Decubiti
See Pressure Ulcer (Decubitus)

Decubitus Ulcers
See Debridement; Pressure Ulcer (Decubitus); Skin Graft and Flap

Deetjeen's Body
See Blood, Platelet

Defect, Coagulation
See Coagulopathy

Defect, Heart Septal
See Septal Defect

Defect, Septal Closure, Atrial
See Heart, Repair, Atrial Septum

Deferens, Ductus
See Vas Deferens

Defibrillation
See Cardioversion

Defibrillator, Heart
See Pacemaker, Heart
Cardioverter-Defibrillator, Implantable
  Data Analysis 93289, 93295-93296
  Evaluation of Programming 93282-93284, 93287, 93640-93642
Insertion Single/Dual Chamber
  Electrodes 33216-33217, 33224-33225, 33249
  Pulse Generator 33240
Removal Single/Dual Chamber
  Electrodes 33243-33244
  Pulse Generator 33241
Repair 33218-33220
Repositioning Single/Dual Chamber
  Electrodes 33215, 33226
Revise Pocket Chest 33223
Wearable Device 93745

Deformity, Boutonniere
See Boutonniere Deformity

Deformity, Sprengel's
See Sprengel's Deformity

Degenerative, Articular Cartilage, Patella
See Chondromalacia Patella

Degradation Products, Fibrin
See Fibrin Degradation Products

Dehydroepiandrosterone 82626

Dehydroepiandrosterone Sulfate 82627

Dehydrogenase, 6-Phosphogluconate
See Phosphogluconate-6, Dehydrogenase

Dehydrogenase, Alcohol
See Antidiuretic Hormone

Dehydrogenase, Glucose-6-Phosphate
See Glucose-6-Phosphate, Dehydrogenase

Dehydrogenase, Glutamate
See Glutamate Dehydrogenase

Dehydrogenase, Isocitrate
See Isocitric Dehydrogenase

Dehydrogenase, Lactate
See Lactic Dehydrogenase

Dehydrogenase, Malate
See Malate Dehydrogenase

Dehydroisoandrosterone Sulfate
See Dehydroepiandrosterone Sulfate

Delay of Flap
Skin Graft 15600-15630

Deligation
Ureter 50940

Deliveries, Abdominal
See Cesarean Delivery

Delivery
See Cesarean Delivery; Vaginal Delivery

Delorme Operation
See Pericardiectomy

Denervation
Hip
  Femoral 27035
  Obturator 27035
  Sciatic 27035

Denervation, Sympathetic
See Excision, Nerve, Sympathetic

Denis-Browne Splint 29590

Dens Axis
See Odontoid Process

Denver Developmental Screening Test 96101-96103

Denver Krupic Procedure
See Aqueous Shunt, to Extraocular Reservoir

Denver Shunt
Patency Test 78291

Denver-Krupin Procedure 66180

Deoxycorticosterone
See Desoxycorticosterone

Deoxycortisol 80436, 82634

Deoxyephedrine
See Methamphetamine

Deoxyribonuclease
Antibody 86215

Deoxyribonuclease I
See DNAse

Deoxyribonucleic Acid
Antibody 86225-86226
Extraction 83890-83891

Depilation
See Removal, Hair

Depletion
Plasma 38214
Platelet 38213
T-Cell 38210
Tumor Cell 38211

Deposit Calcium
See Calcium, Deposits

Depth Electrode
Insertion 61760

Derma-Fat-Fascia Graft 15770

Dermabrasion 15780-15783

Dermatology
Actinotherapy 96900
Examination of Hair
  Microscopic 96902
Ultraviolet A Treatment 96912
Ultraviolet B Treatment 96910
Ultraviolet Light Treatment 96900, 96913
Unlisted Services and Procedures 96999

Dermatoplasty
Septal 30620

Dermoid
See Cyst, Dermoid

Derrick-Burnet Disease
See Q Fever

Descending Abdominal Aorta
See Aorta, Abdominal

Desipramine
Assay 80160

Desmotomy
See Ligament, Release

Desoxycorticosterone 82633

Desoxycortone
See Desoxycorticosterone

Desoxyephedrine
See Methamphetamine

Desoxynorephedrin
See Amphetamine

Desoxyphenobarbital
See Primidone

Desquamation
See Exfoliation

Destruction
Acne 17340-17360
  Cryotherapy 17340
Arrhythmogenic Focus
  Heart...............33250-33251, 33261
Bladder 51020, 52214-52224, 52354
Calculus
  Bile Duct 43265
  Kidney 50590
  Pancreatic Duct 43265
Chemical Cauterization
  Granulation Tissue 17250
Chemosurgery 17110-17111
Ciliary Body
  Cryotherapy 66720
  Cyclodialysis 66740
  Cyclophotocoagulation 66710-66711
  Diathermy 66700
  Endoscopic 66711
Cryosurgery 17110-17111
Curettement 17110-17111
Cyst
  Abdomen 49203-49205
  Ciliary Body 66770
  Iris 66770
Electrosurgery 17110-17111
Endometrial Ablation 58356
Endometriomas
  Abdomen 49203-49205
Fissure
  Anal 46940-46942
Hemorrhoids
  Thermal 46930
Kidney 52354
  Endoscopic 50557, 50576
Laser Surgery 17110-17111

Diaphragm
Repair
for Eventration 39545
Hernia 39502-39541
Laceration 39501
Resection 39560-39561
Unlisted Procedures 39599
Vagina
Fitting 57170

Diaphragm Contraception
See Contraception, Diaphragm

Diaphysectomy
Calcaneus 28120
Clavicle 23180
Femur 27360
Fibula 27360, 27641
Humerus 23184, 24140
Metacarpal 26230
Metatarsal 28122
Olecranon Process 24147
Phalanges
Finger 26235-26236
Toe 28124
Radius 24145, 25151
Scapula 23182
Talus 28120
Tarsal 28122
Tibia 27360, 27640
Ulna 24147, 25150

Diastase
See Amylase

Diastasis
See Separation

Diathermy 97024
See Physical Medicine/Therapy/Occupational Therapy
Destruction
Ciliary Body 66700
Lesion
Retina 67208, 67227
Retinal Detachment
Prophylaxis 67141
Repair 67101

Diathermy, Surgical
See Electrocautery

Dibucaine Number 82638

Dichloride, Methylene
See Dichloromethane

Dichlorides, Ethylene
See Dichloroethane

Dichloroethane 84600

Dichloromethane 84600

Diethylamide, Lysergic Acid
See Lysergic Acid Diethylamide

Diethylether 84600

Differential Count
See White Blood Cell Count

Differentiation Reversal Factor
See Prothrombin

Diffusion Test, Gel
See Immunodiffusion

Digestive Tract
See Gastrointestinal Tract

Digit
See Finger; Toe
Destruction 64632
Injection 64455
Replantation 20816-20822

Digital Artery Sympathectomy 64820

Digital Slit-Beam Radiograph
See Scanogram

Digits
Pinch Graft 15050

Digoxin
Assay 80162

Dihydrocodeinone 82646

Dihydrocodeinone Screen 82486

Dihydroepitestosterone
See Dihydrotestosterone

Dihydrohydroxycodeinone
See Oxycodinone

Dihydromorphinone 82486, 82649

Dihydrotestosterone 82651

Dihydroxyethanes
See Ethylene Glycol

Dihydroxyvitamin D 82652

Dilatation, Transluminal Arterial
See Angioplasty, Transluminal

Dilation
See Dilation and Curettage
Anal
Endoscopy 46604
Sphincter 45905
Bile Duct
Endoscopy 43271, 47555-47556
Stricture 74363
Bladder
Cystourethroscopy 52260-52265
Bronchi
Endoscopy 31630, 31636-31638
Cerebral Vessels
Intracranial Vasospasm 61640-61642
Cervix
Canal 57800
Stump 57558
Colon
Endoscopy 45386
Colon-Sigmoid
Endoscopy 45340
Esophagus 43450-43458
Balloon 43220, 43249
Endoscopy 43220-43226, 43249
Surgical 43510
Intestines, Small
Endoscopy 44370
Kidney 50395
Intra-Renal Stricture 52343, 52346
Lacrimal Punctum 68801
Larynx
Endoscopy 31528-31529
Nasolacrimal Duct
Balloon Catheter 68816
Pancreatic Duct
Endoscopy 43271
Rectum
Endoscopy 45303
Sphincter 45910
Salivary Duct 42650-42660
Trachea
Endoscopy 31630-31631, 31636-31638
Transluminal
Aqueous Outflow Canal 0176T-0177T
Ureter 50395, 52341-52342, 52344-52345
Endoscopy 50553, 50572, 50953, 50972
Urethra 52260-52265
General 53665
Suppository and/or Instillation 53660-53661
Urethral
Stenosis 52281
Stricture 52281, 53600-53621
Vagina 57400

Dilation and Curettage 59840
See Curettage; Dilation
Cervical Stump 57558
Cervix 57558, 57800
Corpus Uteri 58120
Hysteroscopy 58558
Postpartum 59160
with Amniotic Injections 59851
with Vaginal Suppositories 59856

Dilation and Evacuation 59841
with Amniotic Injections 59851

Dimethadione 82654

Dioxide, Carbon
See Carbon Dioxide

Dioxide, Silicon
See Silica

Dipeptidyl Peptidase A
See Angiotensin Converting Enzyme (ACE)

Diphenylhydantoin
See Phenytoin

Diphosphate, Adenosine
See Adenosine Diphosphate

Diphtheria
See Vaccines
Antibody 86648

Dipropylacetic Acid
Assay 80164

Direct Pedicle Flap
Formation 15570-15576

Disability Evaluation Services
Basic Life and/or Disability Evaluation 99450
Work-Related or Medical Disability Evaluation 99455-99456

with Fracture 26645
Open Treatment 26665
Percutaneous Fixation 26650
with Manipulation 26641-26650
Tibiofibular Joint
Closed Treatment 27830-27831
Open Treatment 27832
Vertebra
Additional Segment
Open Treatment 22328
Cervical
Open Treatment 22326
Closed Treatment 22305
with Manipulation, Casting and/or Bracing 22315
without Manipulation 22310
Lumbar
Open Treatment 22325
Thoracic
Open Treatment 22327
Wrist
Closed Treatment 25660, 25675, 25680
Intercarpal 25660
Open Treatment 25670
Open Treatment 25670, 25685
Percutaneous Fixation 25671
Radiocarpal 25660
Open Treatment 25670
Radioulnar
Closed Treatment 25675
Open Treatment 25676
Percutaneous Fixation 25671
with Fracture
Closed Treatment 25680
Open Treatment 25685
with Manipulation 25660, 25675, 25680

Dislocation, Radiocarpal Joint
See Radiocarpal Joint, Dislocation

Disorder
Blood Coagulation
See Coagulopathy
Penis
See Penis
Retinal
See Retina

Displacement Therapy
Nose 30210

Dissection
Hygroma, Cystic
Axillary/Cervical 38550-38555
Lymph Nodes 38542

Dissection, Neck, Radical
See Radical Neck Dissection

Distention
See Dilation

Diverticula, Meckel's
See Diverticulum, Meckel's

Diverticulectomy 44800
Esophagus 43130-43135

Diverticulectomy, Meckel's
See Meckel's Diverticulum, Excision

Diverticulum
Bladder
See Bladder, Diverticulum
Meckel's
Excision 44800
Repair
Urethra 53400-53405

Division
Muscle
Foot 28250
Plantar Fascia
Foot 28250

Division, Isthmus, Horseshoe Kidney
See Symphysiotomy, Horseshoe Kidney

Division, Scalenus Anticus Muscle
See Muscle Division, Scalenus Anticus

Dl-Amphetamine
See Amphetamine

DMO
See Dimethadione

DNA
Antibody 86225-86226

DNA Endonuclease
See DNAse

DNA Probe
See Cytogenetics Studies; Nucleic Acid Probe

DNAse
Antibody 86215

Domiciliary Services
See Nursing Facility Services
Assisted Living 99339-99340
Discharge Services 99315-99316
Established Patient 99334-99337
New Patient 99324-99328

Donor Procedures
Conjunctival Graft 68371
Heart Excision 33940
Heart/Lung Excision 33930
Liver Segment 47140-47142
Stem Cells
Donor Search 38204

Dopamine
See Catecholamines
Blood 82383-82384
Urine 82382, 82384

Doppler Echocardiography 76827-76828, 93306-93308, 93320-93350
Extracranial 93875
Intracardiac 93662
Transesophageal 93318
Transthoracic 93303-93317

Doppler Scan
Arterial Studies
Extremities 93922-93924
Fetal
Middle Cerebral Artery 76821
Umbilical Artery 76820
Extremities 93965
Intracranial Arteries 93886-93893

Dorsal Vertebra
See Vertebra, Thoracic

Dose Plan
See Dosimetry

Dosimetry
Radiation Therapy 77300, 77331
Brachytherapy 77326-77328
Intensity Modulation 77301
Teletherapy 77305-77321

Double-Stranded DNA
See Deoxyribonucleic Acid

Doxepin
Assay 80166

DPH
See Phenytoin

Drainage
See Excision; Incision; Incision and Drainage; Paracentesis
Abdomen
Abdomen Fluid 49080-49081
Abscess
Appendix 44900-44901
Percutaneous 44901
Brain 61150-61151
Eyelid 67700
Liver 47010-47011
Ovary
Percutaneous 58823
Pelvic
Percutaneous 58823
Pericolic
Percutaneous 58823
Perirenal or Renal 50020-50021
Percutaneous 50021
Prostate 52700
Retroperitoneal 49060-49061
Percutaneous 49061
Subdiaphragmatic or Subphrenic 49040-49041
Percutaneous 49040-49041
with X-ray 75989
Amniotic Fluid
Diagnostic Aspiration 59000
Therapeutic Aspiration 59001
Bile Duct
Transhepatic 75980
Brain Fluid 61070
Bursa 20600-20610
Cerebrospinal Fluid 61000-61020, 61050, 61070, 62272
Cervical Fluid 61050
Cisternal Fluid 61050
Cyst
Bone 20615
Brain 61150-61151, 62161-62162
Breast 19000-19001
Ganglion 20612
Liver 47010-47011
Percutaneous 47011
Salivary Gland 42409
Sublingual Gland 42409

Duodenum
Biopsy 44010
Exclusion 48547
Exploration 44010
Incision 44010
Motility Study 91022
Removal
Foreign Body 44010
X-ray 74260

Duplex Scan
See Vascular Studies
Arterial Studies
Aorta 93978-93979
Extracranial 93880-93882
Lower Extremity 93925-93926
Penile 93980-93981
Upper Extremity 93930-93931
Visceral 93975-93979
Hemodialysis Access 93990
Venous Studies
Extremity 93970-93971
Penile 93980-93981

Dupuy-Dutemp Operation
See Reconstruction, Eyelid; Revision

Dupuytren's Contracture .. 26040-26045

Durand-Nicolas-Favre Disease
See Lymphogranuloma Venereum

Dust, Angel
See Phencyclidine

Duvries Operation
See Tenoplasty

Dwyer Procedure
See Osteotomy, Calcaneus

DXA
See Dual X-ray Absorptiometry (DXA)

Dynamometry
See Osteotomy, Calcaneus
Venous Studies
See Osteotomy, Calcaneus
with Ophthalmoscopy 92260

E

E Antigens
See Hepatitis Antigen, Be

E B Virus
See Epstein-Barr Virus

E Vitamin
See Tocopherol

E1
See Estrone

E2
See Estradiol

E3
See Estriol

Ear
Collection of Blood 36415-36416
Drum 69420-69421, 69433-69436, 69450, 69610-69620
See Tympanic Membrane
External
Abscess Incision and Drainage
Complicated 69005
Simple 69000
Biopsy 69100
Excision
Partial 69110
Total 69120
Hematoma
Incision and Drainage 69000-69005
Reconstruction 69300
Unlisted Services and Procedures 69399
Inner
CT Scan 70480-70482
Excision
Labyrinth 69905-69910
Exploration
Endolymphatic Sac 69805-69806
Incision 69820
Labyrinth 69801-69802
Semicircular Canal 69840
Insertion
Cochlear Device 69930
Semicircular Canal 69820
Unlisted Services and Procedures 69949
Vertigo
See Canalith Repositioning
Middle
Catheterization 69405
CT Scan 70480-70482
Exploration 69440
Inflation
with Catheterization 69400
without Catheterization 69401
Insertion
Catheter 69405
Lesion
Excision 69540
Reconstruction
Tympanoplasty with Antrotomy or Mastoidotomy 69635-69637
Tympanoplasty with Mastoidectomy 69641-69646
Tympanoplasty without Mastoidectomy 69631-69633
Removal
Ventilating Tube 69424
Repair
Oval Window 69666
Round Window 69667
Revision
Stapes 69662
Tumor
Excision 69550-69554
Unlisted Services and Procedures 69799
Outer
CT Scan 70480-70482

Ear Canal
See Auditory Canal

Ear Cartilage
Graft
to Face 21235

Ear Lobes
Pierce 69090

Ear Protector Attenuation 92596
See Hearing Aid Services

Ear Wax
See Cerumen

Ear, Nose, and Throat
See Hearing Aid Services; Otorhinolaryngology, Diagnostic
Audiologic Function Tests
Acoustic Reflex 92568
Acoustic Reflex Decay 92569
Audiometry
Bekesy 92560-92561
Comprehensive 92557
Conditioning Play 92582
Evoked Response 92585-92586
Groups 92559
Pure Tone 92552-92553
Select Picture 92583
Speech 92555-92556
Brainstem Evoked Response 92585-92586
Central Auditory Function 92620-92621
Ear Protector Evaluation 92596
Electrocochleography 92584
Filtered Speech 92571
Hearing Aid Evaluation 92590-92595
Loudness Balance 92562
Screening Test 92551
Sensorineural Acuity 92575
Short Increment Sensitivity Index (SISI) 92564
Staggered Spondaic Word Test 92572
Stenger Test 92565, 92577
Synthetic Sentence Test 92576
Tone Decay 92563
Tympanometry 92567
Audiometry
Evoked Otoacoustic Emissions .. 92587-92588
Visual Reinforcement 92579
Binocular Microscopy 92504
Diagnostic Analysis
Auditory Brainstem Implant 92640
Facial Nerve Function Study 92516
Hearing, Language and Speech Evaluation .92506
Laryngeal Function Study 92520
Nasal Function Study 92512
Nasopharyngoscopy 92511
Vestibular Function Tests
Additional Electrodes 92547
Caloric Tests 92533, 92543
Nystagmus
Optokinetic 92534, 92544
Positional 92532, 92542
Spontaneous 92531, 92541
Posturography 92548
Torsion Swing Test 92546
Tracking Tests 92545

Ebstein Anomaly Repair 33468

Eccrine Glands
Chemodenervation
Axillae 64650
Feet 64999

Electric Stimulation
See Electrical Stimulation

Electric Stimulation, Transcutaneous
See Application, Neurostimulation

Electrical Stimulation
Bone Healing
  Invasive 20975
  Noninvasive 20974
Brain Surface 95961-95962
Gastric
  Electrode Implantation 0155T, 0157T
  Electrode Removal 0156T, 0158T
  Electrode Replacement 0155T, 0157T
  Electrode Revision 0156T, 0158T
Guidance
  for Chemodenervation 95873
Physical Therapy
  Attended, Manual 97032
  Unattended 97014

Electro-Hydraulic Procedure 52325

Electro-Oculography 92270

Electroanalgesia
See Application, Neurostimulation

Electrocardiography
12 Lead 3120F
24-Hour Monitoring 93224-93237
Evaluation 93000, 93010, 93014, 93660
Rhythm
  Evaluation 93042
  Microvolt T-wave Alternans 93025
  Tracing 93041
  Tracing and Evaluation 93040
Signal Averaged 93278
Transmission 93012
Wearable Patient-Activated Recording
  Transmission and Evaluation . . .93268, 93270
    Interpretation 93272
    Monitoring 93271

Electrocautery 17000-17286
See Destruction

Electrochemistry
See Electrolysis

Electroconvulsive Therapy 90870

Electrocorticogram
Intraoperative 95829

Electrode, Depth
See Depth Electrode
Electrode Array Intracranial 61850-61868, 61885-61886
Peripheral Nerve 64555, 64575
Retinal 0100T
Spinal 63650-63655

Electrodesiccation 17000-17286
Lesion
  Penis 54055

Electroejaculation 55870

Electroencephalography (EEG) 95816
Brain Death 95824
Coma 95822
Digital Analysis 95957
Electrode Placement 95830
Intraoperative 95955
Monitoring . . .95812-95813, 95950-95953, 95956
  with Drug Activation 95954
  with Physical Activation 95954
  with WADA Activation 95958
Sleep 95822, 95827
Standard 95819

Electrogastrography 91132-91133

Electrogram, Atrial
Esophageal Recording 93615-93616

Electrolysis 17380

Electromyographs
See Electromyography, Needle

Electromyography
Anorectal with Biofeedback 90911
Fine Wire
  Dynamic 96004
Needle
  Extremities 95861-95864
  Extremity 95860
  Face and Neck Muscles 95867-95868
  Guidance
    for Chemodenervation 95874
  Hemidiaphragm 95866
  Larynx 95865
  Ocular 92265
  Other than Thoracic Paraspinal 95870
  Single Fiber Electrode 95872
  Thoracic Paraspinal Muscles 95869
Sphincter Muscles
  Anus 51784-51785
    Needle 51785
  Urethra 51784-51785
    Needle 51785
Surface
  Dynamic 96002-96004

Electron Microscopy 88348-88349

Electronic Analysis
Cardioverter-Defibrillator, Implantable
  Data Analysis 93289, 93295-93296
  Evaluation of Programming 93282-93284, 93287, 93640, 93642
Drug Infusion Pump 62367-62368
Neurostimulator Pulse Generator . . .95970-95982
Loop Recorder, Implantable
  Data Analysis 93291, 93298-93299
  Evaluation of Programming 93285

Electrophoresis
Counterimmuno- 86185
Immuno- 86320-86327
Immunofixation 86334-86335
Protein 84165-84166
Unlisted Services and Procedures 82664

Electrophysiology Procedure 93600-93660

Electroretinogram
See Electroretinography

Electroretinography 92275

Electrostimulation, Analgesic Cutaneous
See Application, Neurostimulation

Electrosurgery
Benign Lesions 17110-17111
Trichiasis
  Correction 67825

Electroversion, Cardiac
See Cardioversion

Elevation, Scapula, Congenital
See Sprengel's Deformity

Elliot Operation
See Excision, Lesion, Sclera

Eloesser Procedure
See Thoracostomy, Empyema

Eloesser Thoracoplasty
See Thoracoplasty

Embolectomy
Aortoiliac Artery 34151-34201
Axillary Artery 34101
Brachial Artery 34101
Carotid Artery 34001
Celiac Artery 34151
Femoral 34201
Iliac 34151-34201
Innominate Artery 34001-34101
Mesentery Artery 34151
Peroneal Artery 34203
Popliteal Artery 34203
Pulmonary Artery 33910-33916
Radial Artery 34111
Renal Artery 34151
Subclavian Artery 34001-34101
Tibial Artery 34203
Ulnar Artery 34111

Embolization
Leiomyomata 37210

Embryo
Biopsy 89290-89291
Cryopreservation 89258
Cryopreserved
  Preparation
    Thawing 89352
Culture 89250
  with Co-Culture Oocyte 89251
Hatching
  Assisted
    Microtechnique 89253
Preparation
  for Transfer 89255
Storage 89342

Embryo Implantation
See Implantation

Embryo Transfer
In Vitro Fertilization 58974-58976
  Intrafallopian Transfer 58976
  Intrauterine Transfer 58974

Epinephrine
See Catecholamines
Blood 82383-82384
Urine 82384

Epiphyseal Arrest
Femur 20150, 27185, 27475, 27479-27485, 27742
Fibula 20150, 27477-27485, 27730-27742
Radius 20150, 25450-25455
Tibia . . 20150, 27477-27485, 27730, 27734-27742
Ulna 20150, 25450-25455

Epiphyseal Separation
Radius
Closed Treatment 25600
Open Treatment 25607-25609

Epiphysiodesis
See Epiphyseal Arrest

Epiphysis
See Bone; Specific Bone

Epiploectomy 49255

Episiotomy 59300

Epispadias
Penis
Reconstruction 54385
Repair 54380-54390
with Exstrophy of Bladder 54390
with Incontinence 54380-54390

Epistaxis 30901-30906
with Nasal/Sinus Endoscopy 31238

EPO
See Erythropoietin

Epstein-Barr Virus
Antibody 86663-86665

Equina, Cauda
See Cauda Equina

ERCP
See Bile Duct; Cholangiopancreatography; Pancreatic Duct

ERG
See Electroretinography

Ergocalciferol
See Calciferol

Ergocalciferols
See Calciferol

Ergonovine Provocation Test . . . 93024

Erythrocyte
See Red Blood Cell (RBC)

Erythrocyte ab
See Antibody, Red Blood Cell

Erythrocyte Count
See Red Blood Cell (RBC), Count

Erythropoietin 82668

Escharotomy
Burns 16035-16036

Escherichia coli 0157
Antigen Detection
Enzyme Immunoassay 87335

ESD
See Endoscopy, Gastrointestinal, Upper

Esophageal Acid Infusion Test
See Acid Perfusion Test

Esophageal Polyp
See Polyp, Esophagus

Esophageal Tumor
See Tumor, Esophagus

Esophageal Varices
Ligation 43205, 43400
Transection/Repair 43401

Esophagectomy
Partial 43116-43124
Total 43107-43113, 43124

Esophagoenterostomy
with Total Gastrectomy 43620

Esophagogastroduodenoscopies
See Endoscopy, Gastrointestinal, Upper

Esophagogastromyotomy
See Esophagomyotomy

Esophagogastrostomy 43320

Esophagojejunostomy 43340-43341

Esophagomyotomy . . 32665, 43330-43331
with Fundoplasty 43279

Esophagorrhaphy
See Esophagus, Suture

Esophagoscopies
See Endoscopy, Esophagus

Esophagostomy 43350-43352
Closure 43420-43425

Esophagotomy 43020, 43045

Esophagotracheal Fistula
See Fistula, Tracheoesophageal

Esophagus
Acid Perfusion Test 91030
Acid Reflux Tests 91034-91038
Balloon Distension
Provocation Study 91040
Biopsy
Endoscopy 43202
Forceps 3150F
Cineradiography 74230
Dilation 43450-43458
Endoscopic 43220-43226, 43248-43249
Surgical 43510
Endoscopy
Biopsy 43202
Dilation 43220-43226
Exploration 43200
Hemorrhage 43227
Injection 43201, 43204
Insertion Stent 43219
Needle Biopsy 43232
Removal
Foreign Body 43215
Polyp 43216-43217, 43228
Tumor 43216, 43228
Ultrasound 43231-43232
Vein Ligation 43205
Excision
Diverticula 43130-43135
Partial 43116-43124
Total 43107-43113, 43124
Exploration
Endoscopy 43200
Hemorrhage 43227
Incision 43020, 43045
Muscle 43030
Injection
Sclerosing Agent 43204
Submucosal 43201
Insertion
Stent 43219
Tamponade 43460
Tube 43510
Intubation with Specimen Collection 91000
Lesion
Excision 43100-43101
Ligation 43405
Motility Study 78258, 91010-91012
Needle Biopsy
Endoscopy 43232
Nuclear Medicine
Imaging (Motility) 78258
Reflux Study 78262
Reconstruction 43300, 43310, 43313
Creation
Stoma 43350-43352
Esophagostomy 43350
Fistula 43305, 43312, 43314
Gastrointestinal 43360-43361
Removal
Foreign Bodies . . 43020, 43045, 43215, 74235
Lesion 43216
Polyp 43216-43217, 43228
Repair 43300, 43310, 43313
Esophagogastric Fundoplasty . . 43324-43325
Laparoscopic 43280
Esophagogastrostomy 43320
Esophagojejunostomy 43340-43341
Fistula . . . 43305, 43312, 43314, 43420-43425
Muscle 43330-43331
Pre-existing Perforation 43405
Varices 43401
Wound 43410-43415
Suture 43405
Wound 43410-43415
Ultrasound
Endoscopy 43231-43232
Unlisted Services and Procedures . . 43289, 43499
Vein
Ligation 43205, 43400
Video 74230
X-ray 74220

Esophagus Neoplasm
See Tumor, Esophagus

Esophagus, Varix
See Esophageal Varices

Evoked Potential

See Audiologic Function Tests
Auditory Brainstem 92585-92586
Central Motor
  Transcranial Motor Stimulation .95928-95929
Somatosensory Testing 95925-95927
Visual, CNS 95930

Evoked Potential, Auditory

See Auditory Evoked Potentials

Ewart Procedure

See Palate, Reconstruction, Lengthening

Excavatum, Pectus

See Pectus Excavatum

Exchange

Drainage Catheter
  Under Radiologic Guidance 49423
Intraocular Lens 66986
Intravascular Catheter 37209, 75900

Exchange Transfusion

See Blood, Transfusion, Exchange

Excision

See Debridement; Destruction
Abscess
  Brain 61514, 61522
  Olecranon Process 24138
  Radius 24136
  Ulna 24138
Acromion
  Shoulder 23130
Adenoids 42830-42836
Adenoma
  Thyroid Gland 60200
Adrenal Gland 60540
  Laparoscopic 60650
  with Excision Retroperitoneal Tumor ..60545
Alveolus 41830
Anal Crypt 46210-46211
Anal Fissure 46200
Anal Tag 46220, 46230
Aorta
  Coarctation 33840-33851
Appendix 44950-44960
Arteriovenous Malformation
  Spinal 63250-63252
Arytenoid Cartilage 31400
  Endoscopic 31560-31561
Atrial Septum 33735-33737
Bartholin's Gland 56740
Bladder
  Diverticulum 51525
  Neck 51520
  Partial 51550-51565
  Total 51570, 51580, 51590-51597
    with Nodes 51575, 51585, 51595
  Transurethral 52640
  Tumor 51530
Bladder Neck Contracture
  Postoperative 52640
Bone
  Facial 21026
  Mandible 21025
  Postoperative
    Femur 20150
    Fibula 20150
    Radius 20150
    Tibia 20150
    Ulna 20150
Bone Abscess
  Facial 21026
  Mandible 21025
Brain
  Amygdala 61566
  Epileptogenic Focus 61536
  Hemisphere 61542-61543
  Hippocampus 61566
  Other Lobe 61323, 61539-61540
  Temporal Lobe 61537-61538
Brain Lobe
  See Lobectomy, Brain
Breast
  Biopsy 19100-19103
  Chest Wall Tumor 19260-19272
  Cyst 19120-19126
  Lactiferous Duct Fistula 19112
  Lesion 19120-19126
    by Needle Localization 19125-19126
  Mastectomy 19300-19307
  Nipple Exploration 19110
Bulbourethral Gland 53250
Bullae
  Lung 32141
    Endoscopic 32655
Burns 01951-01953, 15002-15005
Bursa
  Elbow 24105
  Femur 27062
  Ischial 27060
  Knee 27340
  Wrist 25115-25116
Bypass Graft 35901-35907
Calcaneus 28118-28120
Calculi (Stone)
  Parotid Gland 42330, 42340
  Salivary Gland 42330-42340
  Sublingual Gland 42330
  Submandibular Gland 42330-42335
Carotid Artery 60605
Carpal 25145, 25210-25215
Cartilage
  Knee Joint 27332-27333
  Shoulder Joint 23101
  Temporomandibular Joint 21060
  Wrist 25107
Caruncle
  Urethra 53265
Cataract
  Secondary 66830
Cervix
  Radical 57531
  Stump
    Abdominal Approach 57540-57545
    Vaginal Approach 57550-57556
  Total 57530
Chalazion
  Multiple
    Different Lids 67805
    Same Lid 67801
  Single 67800
  with Anesthesia 67808
Chest Wall
  Tumor 19260-19272
Choroid Plexus 61544
Clavicle
  Partial 23120, 23180
  Sequestrectomy 23170
  Total 23125
  Tumor
    Radical Resection 23200
Coccyx 27080
Colon
  Excision
    Partial 44140-44147, 44160
      with Anastomosis 44140
    Total 44150-44158
  Laparoscopic
    with Anastomosis 44204, 44207-44208
    with Colostomy 44206, 44208
    with Ileocolostomy 44205
Condyle
  Temporomandibular Joint 21050
Constricting Ring
  Finger 26596
Cornea
  Epithelium 65435
    with Chelating Agent 65436
  Scraping 65430
Coronoidectomy 21070
Cowper's Gland 53250
Cranial Bone
  Tumor 61563-61564
Cyst
  See Ganglion Cyst
  Bile Duct 47715
  Bladder 51500
  Brain 61516, 61524, 62162
  Branchial 42810-42815
  Calcaneus 28100-28103
  Carpal 25130-25136
  Cheekbone 21030
  Clavicle 23140
    with Allograft 23146
    with Autograft 23145
  Facial Bones 21030
  Femur 27065-27067, 27355-27358
  Fibula 27635-27638
  Finger 26160
  Foot 28090
  Hand 26160
  Hip 27065-27067
  Humerus 23150, 24110
    with Allograft 23156, 24116
    with Autograft 23155, 24115
  Ileum 27065-27067
  Kidney 50280-50290
  Knee 27345-27347
  Lung 32140
  Mandible 21040, 21046-21047
  Maxilla 21030, 21048-21049
  Mediastinal 39200
  Mediastinum 32662
  Metacarpal 26200-26205
  Metatarsal 28104-28107
  Mullerian Duct 55680
  Nose 30124-30125
  Olecranon 24120
  Olecranon Process
    with Allograft 24126
    with Autograft 24125
  Ovarian 58925
    See Cystectomy, Ovarian

Intraspinal 63265-63273
Knee 27347
Larynx
Endoscopic 31545-31546
Leg, Lower 27630
Meniscus 27347
Mesentery 44820
Mouth 40810-40816, 41116
Nerve 64774-64792
Neuroma 64778
Nose
Intranasal 30117-30118
Orbit 61333
Lateral Approach 67420
Removal 67412
Palate 42104-42120
Pancreas 48120
Penis 54060
Surgical Excision Penile
Plaque 54110-54112
Pharynx 42808
Rectum 45108
Sclera 66130
Skin
Benign 11400-11471
Malignant 11600-11646
Skull 61500, 61615-61616
Spermatic Cord 55520
Spinal Cord 63300-63308
Stomach 43611
Talus
Arthroscopic 29891
Testis 54512
Tibia
Arthroscopic 29891
Toe 28092
Tongue 41110-41114
Urethra 52224, 53265
Uterus 59100
Leiomyomata .58140, 58545-58546, 58561
Uvula 42104-42107
Wrist Tendon 25110
Lesion, Arthroscopic
Ankle 29891
Talus 29891
Tibia 29891
Lesion, Tendon Sheath
Arm, Lower 25110
Lip 40500-40530
Frenum 40819
Liver
Extensive 47122
Lobectomy 47125-47130
Partial ...47120, 47125-47130, 47140-47142
Total 47133
Lung
Bronchus Resection 32486
Bullae
Endoscopic 32655
Completion 32488
Emphysematous 32491
Lobe 32480-32482
Segment 32484
Total 32440-32445
Tumor, Apical Tumor
with Reconstruction 32504
with Resection 32503
Wedge Resection 32500
Endoscopic 32657
Lung/Heart
Donor 33930
Lymph Nodes 38500, 38510-38530
Abdominal 38747
Inguinofemoral 38760-38765
Limited, for Staging
Para-Aortic 38562
Pelvic 38562
Retroperitoneal 38564
Pelvic 38770
Radical
Axillary 38740-38745
Cervical 38720-38724
Suprahyoid 38700
Retroperitoneal Transabdominal 38780
Thoracic 38746
Mandibular
Exostosis 21031
Mastoid
Complete 69502
Radical 69511
Modified 69505
Petrous Apicectomy 69530
Simple 69501
Maxilla
Exostosis 21032
Maxillary Torus Palatinus 21032
Meningioma
Brain 61512, 61519
Meniscectomy
Temporomandibular Joint 21060
Metacarpal 26230
Metatarsal 28110-28114, 28122, 28140
Condyle 28288
Mouth
Frenum 40819
Mucosa
Gums 41828
Mouth 40818
Nail Fold 11765
Nails 11750-11752
Nerve
Foot 28055
Leg, Lower 27326
Leg, Upper 27325
Sympathetic 64802-64818
Neurofibroma 64788-64790
Neurolemmoma 64788-64792
Neuroma 64774-64786
Nose
Dermoid Cyst
Complex 30125
Simple 30124
Polyp 30110-30115
Rhinectomy 30150-30160
Skin 30120
Submucous Resection
Nasal Septum 30520
Turbinate 30140
Turbinate 30130-30140
Odontoid Process 22548
Olecranon Process 24147
Omentum 49255
Ovary 58720
Partial
Oophorectomy 58940
Ovarian Malignancy 58943
Peritoneal Malignancy 58943
Tubal Malignancy 58943
Wedge Resection 58920
Total 58940-58943
Oviduct 58720
Palate 42120, 42145
Pancreas
Ampulla of Vater 48148
Duct 48148
Partial ..48140-48146, 48150, 48153-48154, 48160
Peripancreatic Tissue 48105
Total 48155-48160
Parathyroid Gland 60500-60502
Parotid Gland 42340
Partial 42410-42415
Total 42420-42426
Patella 27350
See Patellectomy
Penile Adhesions
Post-circumcision 54162
Penis
Frenulum 54164
Partial 54120
Prepuce 54150-54161, 54163
Radical 54130-54135
Total 54125
Pericardium 33030-33031
Endoscopic 32659
Petrous Temporal
Apex 69530
Phalanges
Finger 26235-26236
Toe 28124-28126, 28150-28160
Pharynx 42145
Partial 42890
Resection 42892-42894
with Larynx 31390-31395
Pituitary Gland 61546-61548
Pleura 32310-32320
Endoscopic 32656
Polyp
Intestines 43250
Nose
Extensive 30115
Simple 30110
Sinus 31032
Urethra 53260
Pressure Ulcers 15920-15999
See Skin Graft and Flap
Prostate
Abdominoperineal 45119
Partial 55801, 55821-55831
Perineal 55801-55815
Radical 55810-55815, 55840-55845
Regrowth 52630
Residual Obstructive Tissue 52630
Retropubic 55831-55845
Suprapubic 55821
Transurethral 52601, 52630
Pterygium
with Graft 65426
Pubis
Partial 27070-27071
Radical Synovium Wrist 25115-25116
Radius 24130, 24136, 24145, 24152-24153, 25145
Styloid Process 25230
Rectum
Partial 45111, 45113-45116, 45123
Prolapse 45130-45135

Neck 21555-21557
Olecranon Process 24120
with Allograft 24126
with Autograft 24125
Parotid Gland 42410-42426
Pelvis 27047-27049
Pericardial 33050
Pericardium 32661
Phalanges 26210-26215, 26260-26262
Toe 26215, 28108, 28175
Pituitary Gland 61546-61548, 62165
Presacral 49215
Pubis 27065-27067
Radius 24120-24125, 25120-25126, 25170
Rectum 45160-45170
Transanal Endoscopic 0184T
Sacrococcygeal 49215
Scapula 23140
with Allograft 23146
with Autograft 23145
Shoulder 23075-23077
Skull 61500
Spermatocele
See Spermatocele, Excision
Spinal Cord 63275-63290
Spleen, Total
See Splenectomy, Total
Sternum 21630
Stomach 43610
Talus 27647, 28100-28103
Tarsal 28104-28107, 28171
Thorax 21555-21557
Thyroid 60200
Tibia 27635-27638, 27645-27646
Trachea
Cervical 31785
Thoracic 31786
Ulna 24120-24125, 25120-25126, 25170
Ureter 52355
Urethra 52234-52240, 52355, 53220
Uterus
Abdominal Approach 58140, 58146
Vaginal Approach 58145
Vagina 57135
Vertebra, Lumbar 22102
Vertebra, Thoracic 22101
Wrist 25075-25077
Zygoma 21030, 21034
Turbinate 30130-30140
Tympanic Nerve 69676
Ulcer
Stomach 43610
Ulna 24147, 25145
Complete 25240
Partial 25150-25151, 25240
Umbilicus 49250
Ureter
See Ureterectomy
Ureterocele 51535
Urethra
Diverticulum 53230-53235
Prolapse 53275
Total
Female 53210
Male 53215
Uterus
Laparoscopic 58541-58544, 58550
Leiomyomata 58546
Partial 58180
Radical 58210, 58285
Laparoscopic 58548
Removal Tubes and/or
Ovaries 58262-58263, 58291, 58552, 58554
with Colpectomy 58275-58280
with Colpo-Urethrocystopexy 58267, 58293
with Repair of Enterocele 58270, 58292, 58294
Total 58150-58152, 58200
Vaginal 58260, 58290-58294, 58550, 58553
Uvula 42140-42145
Vagina
Closure 57120
Complete
with Removal of Paravaginal Tissue .57111
with Removal of Paravaginal Tissue
with Lymphadenectomy 57112
with Removal of Vaginal Wall 57110
Partial
with Removal of Paravaginal Tissue .57107
with Removal of Paravaginal Tissue
with Lymphadenectomy 57109
with Removal of Vaginal Wall 57106
Septum 57130
Total 57110
with Hysterectomy 58275-58280
Repair of Enterocele 58280
Varicocele
Spermatic Cord 55530-55540
Abdominal Approach 55535
Hernia Repair 55540
Vas Deferens 55250
Vascular Malformation
Finger 26115
Hand 26115
Vein
Varicose 37765-37766
Vertebra
Additional Segment 22103, 22116
Cervical 22110
for Tumor 22100, 22110
Lumbar 22102
for Tumor 22114
Thoracic 22112
for Tumor 22101
Vertebral Body
Decompression 63081-63103
Lesion 63300-63308
Vitreous 67039
Total
Applicator Placement 0190T
Pars Plana Approach 67036, 67041-67043
Vulva
Radical
Complete 56633-56640
Partial 56630-56632
Simple
Complete 56625
Partial 56620
Wrist Tendon 25109

Exclusion
Duodenum 48547
Small Intestine 44700

Exenteration
Eye
Removal Orbital Contents 65110
Therapeutic Removal of Bone 65112
with Muscle or Myocutaneous Flap 65114
Pelvis 45126, 58240

Exercise Stress Tests 93015-93018

Exercise Test
See Electromyography, Needle
Ischemic Limb 95875

Exercise Therapy 97110-97113
See Physical Medicine/Therapy/Occupational Therapy

Exfoliation
Chemical 17360

Exocrine, Pancreas
See Pancreas

Exomphalos
See Omphalocele

Exostectomy 28288, 28290

Exostoses
See Exostosis

Exostoses, Cartilaginous
See Exostosis

Exostosis
Excision 69140

Expander, Skin, Inflatable
See Tissue, Expander

Expired Gas Analysis 94680-94690, 94770
See Pulmonology, Diagnostic
Nitric Oxide 95012
Spectroscopic 0064T

Exploration
Abdomen 49000-49002
Penetrating Wound 20102
Staging 58960
Adrenal Gland 60540-60545
Anal
Endoscopy 46600
Ankle 27610, 27620
Anus
Surgical 45990
Arm, Lower 25248
Artery
Brachial 24495
Carotid 35701
Femoral 35721
Other 35761
Popliteal 35741
Back
Penetrating Wound 20102
Bile Duct
Atresia 47700
Endoscopy 47552-47553
Blood Vessel
Abdomen 35840
Chest 35820
Extremity 35860
Neck 35800

Farnsworth-Munsell Color Test
See Color Vision Examination

Farr Test
See Gammaglobulin, Blood

Fasanella-Servat Procedure ...67908

Fascia Graft 15840

Fascia Lata Graft
Harvesting 20920-20922

Fascial Defect
Repair 50728

Fascial Graft
Free
Microvascular Anastomosis 15758
Open Treatment
Sternoclavicular Dislocation 23532

Fasciectomy
Foot 28060
Radical 28060-28062
Palm 26121-26125

Fasciocutaneous Flaps ...15731-15738

Fasciotomy
Arm, Lower 24495, 25020-25025
Buttock
Decompression 27027
with Debridement 27057
Foot 28008
Hand Decompression 26037
Hip 27025
Knee 27305, 27496-27499
Leg, Lower 27600-27602, 27892-27894
Leg, Upper ...27305, 27496-27499, 27892-27894
Palm 26040-26045
Pelvis
Decompression 27027
with Debridement 27057
Plantar
Endoscopic 29893
Thigh 27025
Toe 28008
Wrist 25020-25025

FAST
See Allergen Immunotherapy

Fat
Feces 82705-82715
Removal
Lipectomy 15876-15879

Fat Stain
Feces 89125
Respiratory Secretions 89125
Sputum 89125
Urine 89125

Fatty Acid
Blood 82725
Long-Chain Omega-3
Red Blood Cell (RBC) Membranes 0111T
Very Long Chain 82726

Favre-Durand Disease
See Lymphogranuloma Venereum

FC Receptor 86243

FDP
See Fibrin Degradation Products

Feedback, Psychophysiologic
See Biofeedback; Training, Biofeedback

Female Castration
See Oophorectomy

Female Gonad
See Ovary

Femoral Arteries
See Artery, Femoral

Femoral Nerve
Injection
Anesthetic 64447-64448

Femoral Stem Prosthesis
See Arthroplasty, Hip

Femoral Vein
See Vein, Femoral

Femur
See Hip; Knee; Leg, Upper
Abscess
Incision 27303
Bursa
Excision 27062
Craterization 27070, 27360
Cyst
Excision 27065-27067, 27355-27358
Diaphysectomy 27360
Drainage 27303
Excision 27070, 27360
Epiphyseal Bar 20150
Neurectomy
Hamstring 27325
Popliteal 27326
Fracture 27244
Closed Treatment 27501-27503, 27267-27268
Distal 27508, 27510, 27514
Distal, Medial or Lateral Condyle 27509
Open Treatment 27514
Epiphysis 27516-27519
Open Treatment 27519
Intertrochanteric 27244
Closed Treatment 27238
Treatment with Implant 27244
with Implant 27245
with Manipulation 27240
Neck
Closed Treatment 27230-27232
Open Treatment 27236
Percutaneous Fixation 27235
Open Treatment .27245, 27269, 27506-27507, 27511-27513
Percutaneous Fixation 27509
Peritrochanteric 27244
Closed Treatment 27238, 27267, 27268
Open Treatment 27269
Treatment with Implant 27244
with Implant 27245
with Manipulation 27240
Proximal End, Head
Closed Treatment 27267-27268
Shaft 27500, 27502, 27506-27507
Subtrochanteric 27244
Closed Treatment 27238
Treatment with Implant 27244
with Implant 27245
with Manipulation 27240
Supracondylar 27501-27503, 27509, 27511-27513
Open Treatment 27511, 27513
Transcondylar 27501-27503, 27509, 27511-27513
Open Treatment 27511, 27513
Trochanteric
Closed Treatment 27246
Open Treatment 27248
with Manipulation 27503
without Manipulation 27501
Halo 20663
Lesion
Excision 27062
Osteoplasty
Lengthening 27466-27468
Shortening 27465, 27468
Osteotomy
without Fixation 27448
Prophylactic Treatment 27187, 27495
Realignment 27454
Reconstruction 27468
at Knee 27442-27443, 27446
Lengthening 27466-27468
Shortening 27465, 27468
Repair 27470-27472
Epiphysis 27181, 27475, 27742
Arrest 27185
Muscle Transfer 27110
Osteotomy 27140, 27151-27156, 27161-27165, 27450-27454
with Graft 27170
Saucerization 27070, 27360
Tumor
Excision ..27065-27067, 27355-27358, 27365
X-ray 73550

Fenestration Procedure
Semicircular Canal 69820
Revision 69840
Tracheostomy 31610

Fenestration, Pericardium
See Pericardiostomy

Fern Test 89060
See Smear and Stain, Wet Mount

Ferric Chloride
Urine 81005

Ferrihemoglobin
See Methemoglobin

Ferritin
Blood or Urine 82728

Ferroxidase
See Ceruloplasmin

Fertility Control
See Contraception

Splint 29130-29131
Strapping 29280
Tendon Sheath
　Excision 26145
　Incision 26055
　Incision and Drainage 26020
Tenotomy 26060, 26460
　Flexor 26455
Tumor
　Excision 26115-26117
Unlisted Services and Procedures 26989
X-ray 73140

Finger Flap
Tissue Transfer 14350

Finger Joint
See Intercarpal Joint

Finney Operation
See Gastroduodenostomy

FISH
See Fluorescent In Situ Hybridization

Fissure in Ano
See Anus, Fissure

Fissurectomy 46200

Fissurectomy, Anal
See Anus, Fissure, Excision

Fistula
Anal
　Repair 0170T, 46288, 46708
Autogenous Graft 36825
Bronchi
　Repair 32815
Carotid-Cavernous
　Repair 61710
Chest Wall
　Repair 32906
Conjunctiva
　with Tube or Stent 68750
　without Tube 68745
Enterovesical
　Closure 44660-44661
Ileoanal Pouch
　Repair 46710-46712
Kidney 50520-50526
Lacrimal Gland Closure 68770
　Dacryocystorhinostomy 68720
Nose
　Repair 30580-30600
Oval Window 69666
Postauricular 69700
Rectovaginal
　Abdominal Approach 57305
　Transperineal Approach 57308
　with Concomitant Colostomy 57307
Round Window 69667
Sclera
　Iridencleisis or Iridotasis 66165
　Sclerectomy with Punch or Scissors
　with Iridectomy 66160
　Thermocauterization with Iridectomy 66155
　Trabeculectomy ab Externo in Absence
　Previous Surgery 66170
　Trabeculectomy ab Externo with
　Scarring 66172
　Trephination with Iridectomy 66150
Suture
　Kidney 50520-50526
　Ureter 50920-50930
Trachea 31755
Tracheoesophageal
　Repair 43305, 43312, 43314
　Speech Prosthesis 31611
Ureter 50920-50930
Urethra 53400-53405
Urethrovaginal 57310
　with Bulbocavernosus Transplant 57311
Vesicouterine
　Closure 51920-51925
Vesicovaginal
　Closure 51900
　Transvesical and Vaginal Approach 57330
　Vaginal Approach 57320
X-ray 76080

Fistula Arteriovenous
See Arteriovenous Fistula

Fistulectomy
Anal 46060, 46270-46285
　See Hemorrhoids

Fistulization
Conjunction
　to Nasal Cavity 68745
Esophagus 43350-43352
Intestines 44300-44346
Lacrimal Sac
　to Nasal Cavity 68720
Penis 54435
Pharynx 42955
Sclera
　for Glaucoma 0123T
Tracheopharyngeal 31755

Fistulization, Interatrial
See Septostomy, Atrial

Fistulotomy
Anal 46270, 46280

Fitting
Cervical Cap 57170
Contact Lens 92070, 92310-92313
　See Contact Lens Services
Diaphragm 57170
Low Vision Aid 92354-92355
　See Spectacle Services
Spectacle Prosthesis 92352-92353
Spectacles 92340-92342

Fitzgerald Factor 85293

Fixation
Interdental
　without Fracture 21497

Fixation (Device)
See Application; Bone, Fixation; Spinal Instrumentation
Application
　External 20690-20692, 20696-20697
Pelvic
　Insertion 22848
Removal
　External 20694
　Internal 20670-20680
Sacrospinous Ligament
　Vaginal Prolapse 57282
Shoulder 23700
Skeletal
　Humeral Epycondyle
　　Percutaneous 24566
Spinal
　Insertion 22841-22847
　Prosthetic 22851
　Reinsertion 22849

Fixation Test, Complement
See Complement, Fixation Test

Fixation, External
See External Fixation

Fixation, Kidney
See Nephropexy

Fixation, Rectum
See Proctopexy

Fixation, Tongue
See Tongue, Fixation

Flank
See Back/Flank

Flap
See Skin Graft and Flap
Free
　Breast Reconstruction 19364
Grafts 15570-15738, 15842
Latissimus Dorsi
　Breast Reconstruction 19361
Omentum 49905
　Free
　　with Microvascular Anastomosis 49906
Transverse Rectus Abdominis Myocutaneous
　Breast Reconstruction 19367-19369

Flatfoot Correction 28735

Flea Typhus
See Murine Typhus

Fletcher Factor 85292

Flow Cytometry 88182-88189
Diagnostic/Pretreatment 3170F

Flow-Volume Loop
See Pulmonology, Diagnostic
Pulmonary 94375

Flu Vaccines 90645-90648, 90655-90663

Fluid Collection
Incision and Drainage
　Skin 10140

Fluid, Amniotic
See Amniotic Fluid

Fluid, Body
See Body Fluid

Fluid, Cerebrospinal
See Cerebrospinal Fluid

Fluorescein
Angiography, Ocular 92287
Intravenous Injection
  Vascular Flow Check, Graft 15860

Fluorescein Angiography
See Angiography, Fluorescein

Fluorescent In Situ Hybridization 88365

Fluoride
Blood 82735
Urine 82735

Fluoroscopy
Bile Duct
  Calculus Removal 74327
  Guide Catheter 74328, 74330
Chest
  Bronchoscopy 31622-31640
  Complete (Four Views) 71034
  Partial (Two Views) 71023
Drain Abscess 75989
GI Tract
  Guide Intubation 74340
Hourly 76000-76001
Introduction
  GI Tube 74340
Larynx 70370
Nasogastric 43752
Needle Biopsy 77002
Orogastric 43752
Pancreatic Duct
  Guide Catheter 74329-74330
Pharynx 70370
Renal
  Guide Catheter 74475
Spine/Paraspinous
  Guide Catheter/Needle 77003
Unlisted Services and Procedures 76496
Ureter
  Guide Catheter 74480
Venous Access Device 36598, 77001
Vertebra
  Osteoplasty 77291

Flurazepam
Blood or Urine 82742

Flush Aortogram 75722-75724

FNA
See Fine Needle Aspiration

Foam Stability Test 83662

Fold, Vocal
See Vocal Cords

Foley Operation Pyeloplasty
See Pyeloplasty

Foley Y-Pyeloplasty 50400-50405

Folic Acid 82747
Blood 82746

Follicle Stimulating Hormone (FSH) 80418, 80426, 83001

Folliculin
See Estrone

Follitropin
See Follicle Stimulating Hormone (FSH)

Follow-up Inpatient Consultations
See Consultation, Follow-up Inpatient

Follow-up Services
See Hospital Services; Office and/or Other Outpatient Services
Post-Op 99024

Fontan Procedure
See Repair, Heart, Anomaly; Revision

Food Allergy Test 95075
See Allergy Tests

Foot
See Metatarsal; Tarsal
Amputation 28800-28805
Bursa
  Incision and Drainage 28001
Capsulotomy 28260-28264
Cast 29450
Fasciectomy 28060
  Radical 28060-28062
Fasciotomy 28008
  Endoscopic 29893
Incision 28002-28005
Joint
  See Talotarsal Joint; Tarsometatarsal Joint
  Magnetic Resonance Imaging (MRI) 73721-73723
Lesion
  Excision 28080, 28090
Magnetic Resonance Imaging (MRI) 73718-73720
Nerve
  Destruction
    Neurolytic 64632
  Excision 28055
  Incision 28035
Neurectomy 28055
Neuroma
  Excision 28080
  Injection of Anesthetic or Steroid 64455
  Morton's
    Destruction 64632
    Injection 64455
Reconstruction
  Cleft Foot 28360
Removal
  Foreign Body 28190-28193
Repair
  Muscle 28250
  Tendon 28200-28230, 28234-28238
Replantation 20838
Sesamoid
  Excision 28315
Splint 29590
Strapping 29540, 29590
Suture
  Tendon 28200-28210
Tendon Sheath
  Excision 28086-28088
Tenotomy 28230, 28234
Tumor
  Excision 28043-28046
Unlisted Services and Procedures 28899
X-ray 73620-73630

Foot Abscess
See Abscess, Foot

Foot Navicular Bone
See Navicular

Forearm 20805
See Arm, Lower

Forehead
Flap 15731
Reconstruction 21179-21180, 21182-21184
  Midface 21159-21160
Reduction 21137-21139

Forehead and Orbital Rim
Reconstruction 21172-21180

Foreign Body Removal
Peritoneal Cavity 49402
Pharynx 42809
Shoulder 23331

Forensic Exam 88040
Cytopathology 88125
Phosphatase, Acid 84061

Foreskin of Penis
See Penis, Prepuce

Formycin Diphosphate
See Fibrin Degradation Products

Fournier's Gangrene
See Debridement, Skin, Subcutaneous Tissue, Infected

Fowler-Stephens Orchiopexy
See Orchiopexy

Fowler-Stephens Procedure 54650

Fraction, Factor IX
See Christmas Factor

Fracture
Acetabulum
  Closed Treatment 27220-27222
  Open Treatment 27226-27228
  with Manipulation 27222
  without Manipulation 27220
Alveola
  Closed Treatment 21421
  Open Treatment 21422-21423
Alveolar Ridge
  Closed Treatment 21440
  Open Treatment 21445
Ankle
  Bimalleolar 27808-27814
  Closed 27816-27818
  Lateral 27786-27814, 27792
  Medial 27760-27766, 27808-27814
  Posterior 27767-27769, 27808-27814
  Trimalleolar 27816-27823
  with Manipulation 27818
  without Manipulation 27816

Ankle Bone
Medial 27760-27762
Bennett's
See Thumb, Fracture
Bronchi
Endoscopy 31630
Calcaneus
Closed Treatment 28400-28405
Open Treatment 28415-28420
Percutaneous Fixation 28436
with Manipulation 28405-28406
without Manipulation 28400
Carpal
Closed Treatment
with Manipulation 25624, 25635
without Manipulation 25622, 25630
Open Treatment 25628, 25645
Carpal Scaphoid
Closed Treatment 25622
Open Treatment 25628
Cheekbone
Open Treatment 21360-21366
with Manipulation 21355
Clavicle
Closed Treatment
with Manipulation 23505
without Manipulation 23500
Open Treatment 23515
Closed Treatment 27520
Coccyx
Closed Treatment 27200
Open Treatment 27202
Colles
See Colles Fracture
Colles-Reversed
See Smith Fracture
Elbow
Monteggia
Closed Treatment 24620
Open Treatment 24635
Open Treatment 24586-24587
Femur
Closed Treatment 27230, 27238-27240, 27246, 27267-27268, 27500-27503, 27508, 27510, 27516-27517
with Manipulation 27232
without Manipulation 27267
Open Treatment 27269
Distal 27508, 27510, 27514
Epiphysis 27516-27519
Intertrochanteric
Closed Treatment 27238
Intramedullary Implant 27245
Plate/Screw Implant 27244
Treatment with Implant 27244-27245
with Manipulation 27240
Neck
Closed Treatment 27230
Open Treatment 27236
Percutaneous Fixation 27235
with Manipulation 27232
Open Treatment 27245, 27248, 27506-27507, 27511-27514, 27519
Percutaneous Fixation 27235, 27509
Peritrochanteric
Closed Treatment 27238
Intramedullary Implant Shaft 27245, 27500, 27502, 27506-27507
Open Treatment 27244-27245
with Manipulation 27240
Proximal
Closed Treatment 27267-27268
Open Treatment 27269
Subtrochanteric
Closed Treatment 27238
Intramedullary Implant 27245
Open Treatment 27244-27245
with Manipulation 27240
Supracondylar 27501-27503, 27509, 27511-27513
Transcondylar 27501-27503, 27509, 27511-27513
Trochanteric
Closed Treatment 27246
Open Treatment 27248
with Manipulation . . . 27232, 27502-27503, 27510
without Manipulation 27230, 27238, 27246, 27500-27501, 27508, 27516-27517, 27520
Fibula
Bimalleolar
Closed Treatment 27808-27810
Open Treatment 27814
Closed Treatment 27780-27781, 27786-27788, 27808-27810
Malleolus 27786-27814
Open Treatment 27784, 27792, 27814
Shaft 27780-27786, 27808
Open Treatment 27784
with Manipulation 27788, 27810
without Manipulation 27780-27781
Frontal Sinus
Open Treatment 21343-21344
Great Toe
Closed Treatment 28490
without Manipulation 28490
Heel
Open Treatment 28415-28420
with Manipulation 28405-28406
without Manipulation 28400
Humerus
Closed Treatment 24500-24505
with Manipulation 23605
without Manipulation 23600
Condyle
Closed Treatment 24576-24577
Open Treatment 24579
Percutaneous 24582
Epicondyle
Closed Treatment 24560-24565
Open Treatment 24575
Skeletal Fixation
Percutaneous 24566
Greater Tuberosity Fracture
Closed Treatment with Manipulation 23625
Closed Treatment without Manipulation 23620
Open Treatment 23630
Open Treatment 23615-23616
Shaft 24500-24505, 24516
Open Treatment 24515
Supracondylar
Closed Treatment 24530-24535
Open Treatment 24545-24546
Percutaneous Fixation 24538
Transcondylar
Closed Treatment 24530-24535
Open Treatment 24545-24546
Percutaneous Fixation 24538
with Dislocation
Closed Treatment 23665
Open Treatment 23670
with Shoulder Dislocation
Closed Treatment 23675
Open Treatment 23680
Hyoid Bone
Open Treatment 21495
Ilium
Open Treatment 27215, 27218
Percutaneous Fixation 27216
Knee 27520
Arthroscopic Treatment 29850-29851
Open Treatment 27524
Larynx
Open Treatment 31584
Malar Area
Open Treatment 21360-21366
with Bone Graft 21366
with Manipulation 21355
Mandible
Closed Treatment
Interdental Fixation 21453
with Manipulation 21451
without Manipulation 21450
Open Treatment 21454-21470
External Fixation 21454
with Interdental Fixation 21462
without Interdental Fixation 21461
Percutaneous Treatment 21452
Maxilla
Closed Treatment 21421
Open Treatment 21422-21423
Metacarpal
Closed Treatment 26600-26605
with Fixation 26607
Open Treatment 26615
Percutaneous Fixation 26608
with Manipulation 26605-26607
without Manipulation 26600
Metatarsal
Closed Treatment 28470-28475
Open Treatment 28485
Percutaneous Fixation 28476
with Manipulation 28475-28476
without Manipulation 28450, 28470
Monteggia
See Fracture, Ulna; Monteggia Fracture
Nasal Bone
Closed Treatment 21310-21320
Open Treatment 21325-21335
with Manipulation 21315-21320
without Manipulation 21310
Nasal Septum
Closed Treatment 21337
Open Treatment 21336
Nasal Turbinate
Therapeutic 30930
Nasoethmoid
Open Treatment 21338-21339
Percutaneous Treatment 21340
with Fixation 21340
Nasomaxillary
Closed Treatment 21345
Open Treatment 21346-21348

Fragile-X
Chromosome Analysis 88248

Fragility
Red Blood Cell
Mechanical 85547
Osmotic 85555-85557

Frames, Stereotactic
See Stereotactic Frame

Francisella 86000
Antibody 86668

Fredet-Ramstedt Procedure 43520

Free E3
See Estriol

Free Skin Graft
See Skin, Grafts, Free

Free T4
See Thyroxine, Free

Frei Disease
See Lymphogranuloma Venereum

Frenectomy 40819, 41115

Frenectomy, Lingual
See Excision, Tongue, Frenum

Frenotomy 40806, 41010

Frenulectomy 40819

Frenuloplasty 41520

Frenum
Lip
Incision 40806
See Lip

Frenumectomy 40819

Frickman Operation
See Proctopexy

Frontal Craniotomy 61556

Frontal Sinus
See Sinus, Frontal

Frontal Sinusotomy
See Exploration, Sinus, Frontal

Frost Suture 67875

Frozen Blood Preparation 86930-86932

Fructose 84375
Semen 82757

Fructose Intolerance Breath Test 91065

Fruit Sugar
See Fructose

FSF 85290-85291

FSH
See Follicle Stimulating Hormone (FSH)

FSP
See Fibrin Degradation Products

FT-4 84439

Fulguration
See Destruction
Bladder 51020
Cystourethroscopy with 52214
Lesion 52224
Tumor 52234-52240
Ureter 50957, 50976
Ureterocele
Ectopic 52301
Orthotopic 52300

Fulguration, Endocavitary
See Electrocautery

Full Thickness Graft 15200-15261

Function Test, Lung
See Pulmonology, Diagnostic

Function Test, Vestibular
See Vestibular Function Tests

Function, Study, Nasal
See Nasal Function Study

Functional Ability
See Activities of Daily Living

Fundoplasty
Esophagogastric 43324-43325
Laparoscopic 43279, 43280
with Gastroplasty 43326
Esophagomyotomy
Laparoscopic 43279

Fundoplication
See Fundoplasty, Esophagogastric

Fungus
Antibody 86671
Culture
Blood 87103
Hair 87101
Identification 87106
Nail 87101
Other 87102
Skin 87101
Tissue Exam 87220

Funnel Chest
See Pectus Excavatum

Furuncle
Incision and Drainage 10060-10061

Furuncle, Vulva
See Abscess, Vulva

Fusion
See Arthrodesis
Pleural Cavity 32560
Thumb
in Opposition 26820

Fusion, Epiphyseal-Diaphyseal
See Epiphyseal Arrest

Fusion, Joint
See Arthrodesis

Fusion, Joint, Ankle
See Ankle, Arthrodesis

Fusion, Joint, Interphalangeal, Finger
See Arthrodesis, Finger Joint, Interphalangeal

G

Gait Training 97116
See Physical Medicine/Therapy/Occupational Therapy

Galactogram 77053-77054
Injection 19030

Galactokinase
Blood 82759

Galactose
Blood 82760
Urine 82760

Galactose-1-Phosphate
Uridyl Transferase 82775-82776

Galeazzi Fracture/ Dislocation 25525-25526

Gall Bladder
See Gallbladder

Gallbladder
See Bile Duct
Anastomosis
with Intestines 47720-47741
Excision 47562-47564, 47600-47620
Exploration 47480
Incision 47490
Incision and Drainage 47480
Nuclear Medicine
Imaging 78223
Removal
Calculi (Stone) 47480
Repair
with Gastroenterostomy 47741
with Intestines 47720-47740
Unlisted Services and Procedures 47999
X-ray with Contrast 74290-74291

Galvanocautery
See Electrocautery

Galvanoionization
See Iontophoresis

Gamete Intrafallopian Transfer (GIFT) 58976

Gamete Transfer
In Vitro Fertilization 58976

Gamma Camera Imaging
See Nuclear Medicine

Gamma Glutamyl Transferase 82977

Kidney
  See Kidney, Transplantation
Liver
  See Liver, Transplantation
Lung
  See Lung, Transplantation
Muscle
  Cheek 15841-15845
Nail Bed
  Reconstruction 11762
Nerve 64885-64907
Oral Mucosa 40818
Organ
  See Transplantation
Pancreas
  See Pancreas, Transplantation
Skin
  Biological
    See Allograft, Skin
  Blood Flow Check, Graft 15860
    See Skin Graft and Flap
  Harvesting
    for Tissue Culture 15040
  Vascular Flow Check, Graft 15860
Tendon
  Finger 26392
  Hand 26392
  Harvesting 20924
Tissue
  Harvesting 20926
Vein
  Cross-Over 34520

Grain Alcohol
See Alcohol, Ethyl

Granulation Tissue
Cauterization, Chemical 17250

Gravi, Myasthenia
See Myasthenia Gravis

Gravities, Specific
See Specific Gravity

Great Toe
Free Osteocutaneous Flap with Microvascular Anastomosis 20973

Great Vessels
Shunt
  Aorta to Pulmonary Artery
    Ascending 33755
    Descending 33762
  Central 33764
  Subclavian to Pulmonary Artery 33750
  Vena Cava to Pulmonary Artery .33766-33767
Unlisted Services and Procedures 33999

Great Vessels Transposition
See Transposition, Great Arteries

Greater Tuberosity Fracture
with Shoulder Dislocation
  Closed Treatment 23665
  Open Treatment 23670

Greater Vestibular Gland
See Bartholin's Gland

Green Operation
See Scapulopexy

Gridley Stain 88312

Grippe, Balkan
See Q Fever

Gritti Operation
See Amputation, Leg, Upper; Radical Resection; Replantation

Groin Area
Repair
  Hernia 49550-49557

Group Health Education ..98961-98962, 99078

Grouping, Blood
See Blood Typing

Growth Factors, Insulin-Like
See Somatomedin

Growth Hormone 83003
Human 80418, 80428-80430, 86277

Growth Hormone Release Inhibiting Factor
See Somatostatin

GTT
See Hydatidiform Mole

Guaiac Test
See Blood, Feces

Guanosine Monophosphate 83008

Guanosine Monophosphate, Cyclic
See Cyclic GMP

Guanylic Acids
See Guanosine Monophosphate

Guard Stain 88313

Gullet
See Esophagus

Gums
Abscess
  Incision and Drainage 41800
Alveolus
  Excision 41830
Cyst
  Incision and Drainage 41800
Excision
  Gingiva 41820
  Operculum 41821
Graft
  Mucosa 41870
Hematoma
  Incision and Drainage 41800
Lesion
  Destruction 41850
  Excision 41822-41828
Mucosa
  Excision 41828
Reconstruction
  Alveolus 41874
  Gingiva 41872
Removal
  Foreign Body 41805
Tumor
  Excision 41825-41827
Unlisted Services and Procedures 41899

Gunning-Lieben Test
See Acetone, Blood or Urine

Guthrie Test 84030

H

H Flu
See Hemophilus Influenza

H-Reflex Study 95934-95936

HAA (Hepatitis Associated Antigen)
See Hepatitis Antigen, B Surface

HAAb
See Antibody, Hepatitis

Haemoglobin F
See Fetal Hemoglobin

Haemorrhage
See Hemorrhage

Haemorrhage Rectum
See Hemorrhage, Rectum

Hageman Factor 85280

HAI Test
See Hemagglutination Inhibition Test

Hair
Electrolysis 17380
KOH Examination 87220
Microscopic Evaluation 96902
Transplant
  Punch Graft 15775-15776
  Strip Graft 15220-15221

Hair Removal
See Removal, Hair

Hallux
See Great Toe

Halo
Body Cast 29000
Cranial 20661
  for Thin Skull Osteology 20664
Femur 20663
Maxillofacial 21100
Pelvic 20662
Removal 20665

Haloperidol
Assay 80173

Halstead-Reitan Neurospychological Battery ..96118

Halsted Mastectomy
See Mastectomy, Radical

Halsted Repair
See Hernia, Repair, Inguinal

Ham Test
See Hemolysins

Hammertoe Repair 28285-28286

Hamster Penetration Test 89329

Hand
See Carpometacarpal Joint; Intercarpal Joint
Amputation
at Metacarpal 25927
at Wrist 25920
Revision 25922
Revision 25924, 25929-25931
Arthrodesis
Carpometacarpal Joint 26843-26844
Intercarpal Joint 25820-25825
Bone
Incision and Drainage 26034
Cast 29085
Decompression 26035-26037
Fracture
Carpometacarpal 26641-26650
Interphalangeal 26740-26746
Metacarpal 26600-26615
Metacarpophalangeal 26740-26746
Phalangeal 26720-26735, 26750-26765
Insertion
Tendon Graft 26392
Magnetic Resonance Imaging (MRI) 73218-73223
Reconstruction
Tendon Pulley 26500-26502
Removal
Implantation 26320
Tube/Rod 26390-26392, 26416
Repair
Blood Vessel 35207
Cleft Hand 26580
Muscle 26591-26593
Tendon
Extensor 26410-26416, 26426-26428, 26433-26437
Flexor 26350-26358, 26440
Profundus 26370-26373
Replantation 20808
Strapping 29280
Tendon
Excision 26390
Extensor 26415
Tenotomy 26450, 26460
Tumor
Excision 26115-26117
Unlisted Services and Procedures 26989
X-ray 73120-73130

Hand Abscess
See Abscess, Hand

Hand Phalange
See Finger, Bone

Hand(s) Dupuytrens Contracture(s)
See Dupuytren's Contracture

Handling
Device 99002
Radioelement 77790
Specimen 99000-99001

Hanganutziu Deicher Antibodies
See Antibody, Heterophile

Haptoglobin 83010-83012

Hard Palate
See Palate

Harelip Operation
See Cleft Lip, Repair

Harii Procedure 25430

Harrington Rod
Insertion 22840
Removal 22850

Hartmann Procedure
Laparoscopic 44206
Open 44143

Harvest of Upper Extremity Artery for Coronary Artery Bypass 35600

Harvesting
Bone Graft 20900-20902
Bone Marrow 38230
Cartilage Graft 20910-20912
Conjunctival Graft 68371
Eggs
In Vitro Fertilization 58970
Endoscopic
Vein for Bypass Graft 33508
Fascia Lata Graft 20920-20922
Intestines 44132-44133
Kidney 50300-50320, 50547
Liver 47133, 47140-47142
Lower Extremity Vein
for Vascular Reconstruction 35572
Skin
for Tissue Culture 15040
Stem Cell 38205-38206
Tendon Graft 20924
Tissue Grafts 20926
Upper Extremity Artery
for Coronary Artery Bypass Graft 35600
Upper Extremity Vein
for Bypass Graft 35500

Hauser Procedure 27420

Hayem's Elementary Corpuscle
See Blood, Platelet

Haygroves Procedure
See Reconstruction, Acetabulum; Revision

HBcAb
See Antibody, Hepatitis

HBeAb
See Antibody, Hepatitis

HBeAg
See Hepatitis Antigen, Be

HBsAb
See Antibody, Hepatitis

HBsAg (Hepatitis B Surface Antigen)
See Hepatitis Antigen, B Surface

HCG
See Chorionic Gonadotropin

HCO3
See Bicarbonate

HCV Antibodies
See Antibody, Hepatitis C

HDL
See Lipoprotein

Head
Angiography 70496, 70544-70546
CT Scan 70450-70470, 70496
Excision 21015-21070
Fracture and/or Dislocation 21310-21497
Incision 21010, 61316, 62148
Introduction or Removal 21076-21116
Lipectomy, Suction Assisted 15876
Magnetic Resonance Angiography (MRA) 70544-70546
Nerve
Graft 64885-64886
Other Procedures 21299, 21499
Repair/Revision and/or Reconstruction 21120-21296
Ultrasound Exam 76506, 76536
Unlisted Services and Procedures 21499
X-ray 70350

Head Rings, Stereotactic
See Stereotactic Frame

Headbrace
Application 21100
Application/Removal 20661

Heaf Test
See TB Test

Health Behavior
See Evaluation and Management, Health Behavior

Health Risk Assessment Instrument
See Preventive Medicine

Hearing Aid
Bone Conduction
Implantation 69710
Removal 69711
Repair 69711
Replacement 69710

Hearing Aid Check 92592-92593

Hearing Aid Services
Electroacoustic Test 92594-92595
Examination 92590-92591

Hearing Tests
See Audiologic Function Tests; Hearing Evaluation

Hearing Therapy 92507-92508, 92601-92604

Heart
Ablation 33250-33266
Allograft Preparation 33933

Hepatitis B Virus Surface ab
See Antibody, Hepatitis B, Surface

Hepatorrhaphy
See Liver, Repair

Hepatotomy
Abscess 47010-47011
Percutaneous 47011
Cyst 47010-47011
Percutaneous 47011

Hernia Repair
Abdominal 49590
Incisional 49560
Recurrent 49565
Diaphragmatic 39502-39541
Epigastric 49570
Incarcerated 49572
Laparoscopic 49652-49653
Femoral 49550
Incarcerated 49553
Recurrent 49555
Recurrent Incarcerated 49557
Incisional
Incarcerated 49561
Laparoscopic 49654-49657
Inguinal 49491, 49495-49500, 49505
Incarcerated ..49492, 49496, 49501, 49507, 49521
Laparoscopic 49650-49651
Recurrent 49520
Sliding 49525
Strangulated 49492
Lumbar 49540
Lung 32800
Orchiopexy 54640
Recurrent Incisional
Incarcerated 49566
Reducible 49565
Umbilicus
Incarcerated 49582, 49587
Laparoscopic 49652-49653
Reducible 49580, 49585
with Spermatic Cord 55540
Spigelian 49590
Laparoscopic 49652-49653
Ventral
Laparoscopic 49652-49653

Hernia, Cerebral
See Encephalocele

Hernia, Rectovaginal
See Rectocele

Hernia, Umbilical
See Omphalocele

Heroin Screen 82486

Heroin, Alkaloid Screening 82101

Herpes Simplex
Antibody 86696
Antigen Detection
Immunofluorescence 87273-87274
Nucleic Acid 87528-87530
Identification
Smear and Stain 87207

Herpes Smear and Stain 87207

Herpes Virus-4 (Gamma), Human
See Epstein-Barr Virus

Herpes Virus-6 Detection .87531-87533

Herpetic Vesicle
Destruction 54050-54065

Heteroantibodies
See Antibody, Heterophile

Heterograft
Skin 15400-15421

Heterologous Transplant
See Xenograft

Heterologous Transplantation
See Heterograft

Heterophile Antibody 86308-86310

Heterotropia
See Strabismus

Hex B
See b-Hexosaminidase

Hexadecadrol
See Dexamethasone

Hexosephosphate Isomerase
See Phosphohexose Isomerase

Heyman Procedure 27179, 28264

Hg Factor
See Glucagon

HGB
See Hemoglobin, Concentration

HGH
See Growth Hormone, Human

HHV-4
See Epstein-Barr Virus

HIAA
See Hydroxyindolacetic Acid, Urine

Hib Vaccine
4 Dose Schedule
HbOC 90645
PRP-T 90648
PRP-D
Booster 90646
PRP-OMP
3 Dose Schedule 90647

Hibb Operation
See Spinal Cord; Spine, Fusion; Vertebra; Vertebral Body; Vertebral Process

Hidradenitis
See Sweat Gland
Excision 11450-11471
Suppurative
Incision and Drainage 10060-10061

High Altitude Simulation Test 94452-94453

High Density Lipoprotein
See Lipoprotein

High Molecular Weight Kininogen
See Fitzgerald Factor

Highly Selective Vagotomy
See Vagotomy, Highly Selective

Highmore Antrum
See Sinus/Sinuses, Maxillary

Hill Procedure 43324
Laparoscopic 43280

Hinton Positive
See RPR

Hip
See Femur; Pelvis
Abscess
Incision and Drainage 26990
Arthrocentesis 20610
Arthrodesis 27284-27286
Arthrography 73525
Arthroplasty 27130-27132
Arthroscopy 29860-29863
Arthrotomy 27030-27033
Biopsy 27040-27041
Bone
Drainage 26992
Bursa
Incision and Drainage 26991
Capsulectomy
with Release, Flexor Muscles 27036
Cast 29305-29325
Craterization 27070
Cyst
Excision 27065-27067
Denervation 27035
Echography
Infant 76885-76886
Endoprosthesis
See Prosthesis, Hip
Excision 27070
Exploration 27033
Fasciotomy 27025
Fusion 27284-27286
Hematoma
Incision and Drainage 26990
Injection
Radiologic 27093-27096
Reconstruction
Total Replacement 27130
Removal
Cast 29710
Foreign Body 27033, 27086-27087
Arthroscopic 29861
Loose Body
Arthroscopic 29861
Prosthesis 27090-27091
Repair
Muscle Transfer 27100-27105, 27111
Osteotomy 27146-27156
Tendon 27097
Saucerization 27070
Stem Prostheses
See Arthroplasty, Hip
Strapping 29520

Tenotomy
Abductor Tendon 27006
Adductor Tendon 27000-27003
Iliopsoas 27005
Total Replacement 27130-27132
Tumor
Excision 27047-27049, 27065-27067
Radical 27075-27076
Ultrasound
Infant 76885-76886
X-ray 73500-73520, 73540
Intraoperative 73530
with Contrast 73525

Hip Joint
Arthroplasty 27132
Revision 27134-27138
Arthrotomy 27052
Biopsy 27052
Capsulotomy
with Release, Flexor Muscles 27036
Dislocation 27250-27252
Congenital 27256-27259
Open Treatment 27253-27254
without Trauma 27265-27266
Manipulation 27275
Reconstruction
Revision 27134-27138
Synovium
Excision 27054
Arthroscopic 29863
Total Replacement 27132

Hip Stem Prostheses
See Arthroplasty, Hip

Hippocampus
Excision 61566

Histamine 83088

Histamine Release Test 86343

Histochemistry 88318-88319

Histocompatibility Testing
See Tissue Typing

Histoplasma
Antibody 86698
Antigen 87385

Histoplasma capsulatum
Antigen Detection
Enzyme Immunoassay 87385

Histoplasmin Test
See Histoplasmosis, Skin Test

Histoplasmoses
See Histoplasmosis

Histoplasmosis
Skin Test 86510

History and Physical
See Evaluation and Management, Office and/or Other Outpatient Services
Pelvic Exam 57410

HIV
Antibody 86701-86703
Confirmation Test 86689

HIV-1
Antigen Detection
Enzyme Immunoassay 87390

HIV-2
Antigen Detection
Enzyme Immunoassay 87391

HK3 Kallikrein
See Antigen, Prostate Specific

HLA Typing 86812-86817

HMRK
See Fitzgerald Factor

HMW Kininogen
See Fitzgerald Factor

Hoffman Apparatus 20690

Hofmeister Operation
See Gastrectomy, Total

Holotranscobalamin 0103T

Holten Test
See Creatinine, Urine, Clearance

Home Services
Activities of Daily Living 99509
Anticoagulant Management 99363-99364
Apnea Monitoring 94774-94777
Catheter Care 99507
Enema Administration 99511
Established Patient 99347-99350
Hemodialysis 99512
Home Infusion Procedures 99601-99602
Individual or Family Counseling 99510
Intramuscular Injections 99506
Mechanical Ventilation 99504
New Patient 99341-99345
Newborn Care 99502
Postnatal Assessment 99501
Prenatal Monitoring 99500
Respiratory Therapy 99503
Sleep Studies 95805-95811
Actigraphy Testing 95803
Stoma Care 99505
Unlisted Services and Procedures 99600
Ventilation Assist 94005

Home Visit
See House Calls

Homocyst(e)ine 83090
Urine 82615

Homogenization, Tissue 87176

Homograft
Skin 15300-15336

Homologous Grafts
See Graft

Homologous Transplantation
See Homograft

Homovanillic Acid
Urine 83150

Hormone Assay
ACTH 82024
Aldosterone
Blood or Urine 82088
Androstenedione
Blood or Urine 82157
Androsterone
Blood or Urine 82160
Angiotensin II 82163
Corticosterone 82528
Cortisol
Total 82533
Dehydroepiandrosterone 82626
Dihydroelestosterone 82651
Dihydrotestosterone 82651
Epiandrosterone 82666
Estradiol 82670
Estriol 82677
Estrogen 82671-82672
Estrone 82679
Follicle Stimulating Hormone 83001
Growth Hormone 83003
Hydroxyprogesterone 83498-83499
Luteinizing Hormone 83002
Somatotropin 83003
Testosterone 84403
Vasopressin 84588

Hormone Pellet Implantation 11980

Hormone, Adrenocorticotrophic
See Adrenocorticotropic Hormone (ACTH)

Hormone, Corticotropin-Releasing
See Corticotropic Releasing Hormone (CRH)

Hormone, Growth
See Growth Hormone

Hormone, Human Growth
See Growth Hormone, Human

Hormone, Interstitial Cell-Stimulating
See Luteinizing Hormone (LH)

Hormone, Parathyroid
See Parathormone

Hormone, Pituitary Lactogenic
See Prolactin

Hormone, Placental Lactogen
See Lactogen, Human Placental

Hormone, Somatotropin Release-Inhibiting
See Somatostatin

Hormone, Thyroid-Stimulating
See Thyroid Stimulating Hormone (TSH)

Hormone-Binding Globulin, Sex
See Globulin, Sex Hormone Binding

Hormones, Adrenal Cortex
See Corticosteroids

Hormones, Antidiuretic
See Antidiuretic Hormone

Hospital Discharge Services
See Discharge Services, Hospital

Hospital Services
Inpatient Services 99238-99239
Discharge Services 99238-99239, 1110F-1111F
Initial Care
New or Established Patient ..99221-99233
Initial Hospital Care 99221-99223
Newborn 99460-99462, 99477
Prolonged Services 99356-99357
Subsequent Hospital Care 99231-99233
Observation
Discharge Services 99234-99236
Initial Care 99218-99220
New or Established Patient ..99218-99220
Same Day Admission
Discharge Services 99234-99236
Subsequent Newborn Care 99462

Hot Pack Treatment 97010
See Physical Medicine and Rehabilitation

House Calls 99341-99350

HPL
See Lactogen, Human Placental

HTLV I
Antibody
Confirmatory Test 86689
Detection 86687

HTLV II
Antibody 86688

HTLV III
See HIV

HTLV III Antibodies
See Antibody, HIV

HTLV IV
See HIV-2

Hubbard Tank Therapy 97036
See Physical Medicine/Therapy/Occupational Therapy

Hue Test 92283

Huggin Operation
See Orchiectomy, Simple

Huhner Test 89300, 89320

Human Chorionic Gonadotropin
See Chorionic Gonadotropin

Human Chorionic Somatomammotropin
See Lactogen, Human Placental

Human Cytomegalovirus Group
See Cytomegalovirus

Human Growth Hormone (HGH) 80418, 80428-80430

Human Herpes Virus 4
See Epstein-Barr Virus

Human Immunodeficiency Virus
See HIV

Human Immunodeficiency Virus 1
See HIV-1

Human Immunodeficiency Virus 2
See HIV-2

Human Papillomavirus
See Vaccine

Human Papillomavirus Detection 87620-87622

Human Placental Lactogen
See Lactogen, Human Placental

Human T Cell Leukemia Virus I
See HTLV I

Human T Cell Leukemia Virus I Antibodies
See Antibody, HTLV I

Human T Cell Leukemia Virus II
See HTLV II

Human T Cell Leukemia Virus II Antibodies
See Antibody, HTLV II

Humeral Epicondylitides, Lateral
See Tennis Elbow

Humeral Fracture
See Fracture, Humerus

Humerus
See Arm, Upper; Shoulder
Abscess
Incision and Drainage 23935
Craterization 23184, 24140
Cyst
Excision 23150, 24110
with Allograft 23156, 24116
with Autograft 23155, 24115
Diaphysectomy 23184, 24140
Excision 23174, 23184, 23195, 24134, 24140, 24150-24151
Fracture
Closed Treatment 24500-24505
with Manipulation 23605
without Manipulation 23600
Condyle
Closed Treatment 24576-24577
Open Treatment 24579
Percutaneous Fixation 24582
Epicondyle
Closed Treatment 24560-24565
Open Treatment 24575
Skeletal Fixation
Percutaneous 24566
Greater Tuberosity Fracture
Closed Treatment with Manipulation 23625
Closed Treatment without Manipulation 23620
Open Treatment 23630
Open Treatment 23615-23616
Shaft 24500-24505, 24516
Open Treatment 24515
Supracondylar
Closed Treatment 24530-24535
Open Treatment 24545-24546
Percutaneous Fixation 24538
Transcondylar
Closed Treatment 24530-24535
Open Treatment 24545-24546
Percutaneous Fixation 24538
with Dislocation 23665-23670
Osteomyelitis 24134
Pinning, Wiring 23491, 24498
Prophylactic Treatment 23491, 24498
Radical Resection 23220-23222
Repair 24430
Nonunion, Malunion 24430-24435
Osteoplasty 24420
Osteotomy 24400-24410
with Graft 24435
Resection Head 23195
Saucerization 23184, 24140
Sequestrectomy 23174, 24134
Tumor
Excision 23150, 23220-23222, 24110
with Allograft 23156, 24116
with Autograft 23155, 24115
X-ray 73060

Hummelshein Operation
See Strabismus, Repair

Humor Shunt, Aqueous
See Aqueous Shunt

HVA
See Homovanillic Acid

Hyaluron Binding Assay 0087T

Hybridization Probes, DNA
See Nucleic Acid Probe

Hydatid Disease
See Echinococcosis

Hydatid Mole
See Hydatidiform Mole

Hydatidiform Mole
Evacuation and Curettage 59870
Excision 59100

Hydration 96360-96361
Rehydration Oral Solution 4056F
Status 2030F-2031F

Hydrocarbons, Chlorinated
See Chlorinated Hydrocarbons

Hydrocele
Aspiration 55000
Excision
Bilateral
Tunica Vaginalis 55041
Unilateral
Spermatic Cord 55500
Tunica Vaginalis 55040
Repair 55060

Hydrochloric Acid, Gastric
See Acid, Gastric

Hydrochloride, Vancomycin
See Vancomycin

Hydrocodon
See Dihydrocodeinone

Hydrogen Ion Concentration
See pH

Hydrolase, Acetylcholine
See Acetylcholinesterase

Hydrolase, Triacylglycerol
See Lipase

Hydrolases, Phosphoric Monoester
See Phosphatase

Hydrotherapy (Hubbard Tank) . . 97036
See Physical Medicine/Therapy/Occupational Therapy

Hydrotubation 58350

Hydroxyacetanilide
See Acetaminophen

Hydroxycorticosteroid 83491

Hydroxyindolacetic Acid 83497
Urine 83497

Hydroxypregnenolone 80406, 84143

Hydroxyprogesterone 80402-80406, 83498-83499

Hydroxyproline 83500-83505

Hydroxytyramine
See Dopamine

Hygroma
Cystic
  Axillary/Cervical
    Excision 38550-38555

Hymen
Excision 56700
Incision 56442

Hymenal Ring
Revision 56700

Hymenectomy 56700

Hymenotomy 56442

Hyoid
Bone
  Fracture
    Open Treatment 21495
Muscle
  Incision and Suspension 21685

Hyperbaric Oxygen Pressurization 99183

Hypercycloidal X-ray 76101-76102

Hyperdactylies
See Supernumerary Digit

Hyperglycemic Glycogenolytic Factor
See Glucagon

Hyperhidrosis 64650-64653

Hypertelorism of Orbit
See Orbital Hypertelorism

Hyperthermia Therapy
See Thermotherapy

Hyperthermia Treatment . . 77600-77620

Hypnotherapy 90880

Hypodermis
See Subcutaneous Tissue

Hypogastric Plexus
Destruction 64681
Injection
  Anesthetic 64517
  Neurolytic 64681

Hypoglossal Nerve
Anastomosis
  to Facial Nerve 64868

Hypoglossal-Facial Anastomosis
See Anastomosis, Nerve, Facial to Hypoglossal

Hypopharynges
See Hypopharynx

Hypopharynx
Biopsy 42802

Hypophysectomy 61546-61548, 62165

Hypophysis
See Pituitary Gland

Hypopyrexia
See Hypothermia

Hypospadias
Repair 54300, 54352
  Complications 54340-54348
  First Stage 54304
    Proximal Penile or Penoscrotal 54332
  One Stage
    Meatal Advancement 54322
    Perineal 54336
  Urethroplasty
    Local Skin Flaps 54324
    Local Skin Flaps and Mobilization of Urethra 54326
    Local Skin Flaps, Skin Graft Patch and/or Island Flap 54328
  Urethroplasty for Second Stage . 54308-54316
    Free Skin Graft 54316
  Urethroplasty for Third Stage 54318

Hypothermia 99185-99186

Hypoxia
Breathing Response 94450
High Altitude Simulation Test 94452-94453

Hysterectomy
Abdominal
  Radical 58210
  Resection of Ovarian Malignancy 58951, 58953-58956
  Supracervical 58180
  Total 58150, 58200, 58956
    with Colpo-Urethrocystopexy 58152
    with Omentectomy 58956
    with Partial Vaginectomy 58200
Cesarean
  after Cesarean Delivery 59525
  with Closure of Vesicouterine Fistula . . 51925
Laparoscopic 58541-58544
  Radical 58548
  Total 58570-58573
Removal
  Lesion 59100
Supracervical
  Laparoscopic 58541-58544
Vaginal 58260-58270, 58290-58294, 58550-58554
  Laparoscopic 58550, 58570-58573
  Radical 58285
  Removal Tubes/Ovaries 58262-58263, 58291-58292, 58552, 58554
    Repair of Enterocele . 58263, 58292, 58294
  with Colpectomy 58275-58280
  with Colpo-Urethrocystopexy . . 58267, 58293

Hysterolysis
See Lysis, Adhesions, Uterus

Hysteroplasty 58540

Hysterorrhaphy 58520, 59350

Hysterosalpingography 74740
Catheterization 58345
Injection Procedure 58340

Hysterosalpingostomy
See Implantation, Tubouterine

Hysteroscopy
Ablation
  Endometrial 58563
Diagnostic 58555
Lysis
  Adhesions 58559
Placement
  Fallopian Tube Implants 58565
Removal
  Impacted Foreign Body 58562
  Leiomyomata 58561
Resection
  of Intrauterine Septum 58560
Surgical with Biopsy 58558
Unlisted Services and Procedures . . 58578-58579

Hysterosonography
See Ultrasound; Sonohysterography

Hysterotomy 59100
See Ligation, Uterus
Induced Abortion
  with Amniotic Injections 59852
  with Vaginal Suppositories 59857

Hysterotrachelectomy
See Amputation, Cervix

I

I Antibodies, HTLV
See Antibody, HTLV-I

Implant, Orbital
See Orbital Implant

Implant, Penile
See Penile Prosthesis

Implant, Penile Prosthesis, Inflatable
See Penile Prosthesis, Insertion, Inflatable

Implant, Subperiosteal
See Subperiosteal Implant

Implant, Ureters into, Bladder
See Anastomosis, Ureter, to Bladder

Implantation
Artificial Heart
  Intracorporeal 0051T
Bone
  for External Speech Processor/ Cochlear Stimulator 69714-69718
Brain
  Chemotherapy 61517
  Thermal Perfusion Probe 0077T
Cardiac Event Recorder 33282
Contraceptive Capsules 11975, 11977
Drug Delivery Device 11981, 11983, 61517
Electrode
  Brain 61850-61875
  Gastric 43647, 43648
  Nerve 64553-64581
  Spinal Cord 63650-63655
  Stomach 0155T, 0157T
Eye
  Anterior Segment 65920
  Aqueous Shunt to Extraocular Placement or Replacement of Pegs 65125
  Corneal Ring Segments 0099T
  Posterior Segment
    Extraocular 67120
    Intraocular 67121
  Reservoir 66180
  Vitreous
    Drug Delivery System 67027
Fallopian Tube 58565
Hearing Aid Hormone Pellet(s)
  Bone Conduction 69710
Hip Prosthesis
  See Arthroplasty, Hip
Hormone Pellet 11980
Intraocular Lens
  See Insertion, Intraocular Lens
Joint
  See Arthroplasty
Mesh
  Debridement Closure 49568
  Hernia Repair 49568, 49652-49657
  Vaginal Repair 57267
Nerve
  into Bone 64787
  into Muscle 64787
Neurostimulators
  Gastric 95980-95982
  Pulse Generator 61885
  Receiver 61886
Ovum 58976
Pulse Generator
  Brain 61885-61886
  Spinal Cord Electrode Array 63685
Receiver
  Brain 61885-61886
  Spinal Cord 63685
Removal 20670-20680
  Elbow 24164
  Radius 24164
Reservoir Vascular Access Device
  Declotting 36593
Retinal Electrode Array 0100T
Total Replacement Heart System
  Intracorporeal 0051T
Tubouterine 58752
Ventricular Assist Device 33976
  Extracorporeal 0048T
  Intracorporeal 33979

Impression, Maxillofacial
Auricular Prosthesis 21086
Definitive Obturator Prosthesis 21080
Facial Prosthesis 21088
Interim Obturator 21079
Mandibular Resection Prosthesis 21081
Nasal Prosthesis 21087
Oral Surgical Splint 21085
Orbital Prosthesis 21077
Palatal Augmentation Prosthesis 21082
Palatal Lift Prosthesis 21083
Speech Aid Prosthesis 21084
Surgical Obturator 21076

IMT
See Intima-Media Thickness Study

In Situ Hybridization
See Nucleic Acid Probe, Cytogenetic Studies, Morphometric Analysis

In Vitro Fertilization 58321-58322

In Vivo NMR Spectroscopy
See Magnetic Resonance Spectroscopy

Incision
See Incision and Drainage
Abdomen 49000
  Exploration 58960
Abscess
  Soft Tissue 20000-20005
Accessory Nerve 63191
Anal
  Fistula 46270, 46280
  Septum 46070
  Sphincter 46080
Ankle 27607
  Tendon 27605-27606
Anus
  See Anus, Incision
Aortic Valve
  for Stenosis 33415
Artery
  Nose 30915-30920
Atrial Septum 33735-33737
Bile Duct
  Sphincter 43262, 47460
Bladder
  Catheterization 51045
  with Destruction 51020-51030
  with Radiotracer 51020
Bladder Diverticulum 52305
Brachial Artery
  Exposure 34834
Brain
  Amygdalohippocampectomy 61566
  Subpial 61567
Breast
  Capsules 19370
Burn Scab 16035-16036
Buttock 27027, 27057
Cataract
  Secondary
    Laser Surgery 66821
    Stab Incision Technique 66820
Chest
  Biopsy 32095-32100
Colon
  Exploration 44025
  Stoma
    Creation 44320-44322
    Revision 44340-44346
Cornea
  for Astigmatism 65772
Corpus Callosum 61541
Cricothyroid Membrane 31605
Dentate Ligament 63180-63182
Duodenum 44010
Ear, Inner
  Labyrinth
    with Mastoidectomy 69802
    with or without Cryosurgery 69801
Elbow 24000
Esophagus 43020, 43045
  Muscle 43030
Exploration
  Heart 33310-33315
  Kidney 50010
Eye
  Adhesions 65880
    Anterior Segment 65860-65865
    Anterior Synechiae 65870
    Corneovitreal 65880
    Posterior 65875
  Anterior Chamber 65820
  Conjunctiva 0124T
  Trabeculae 65850
Eyelid
  Canthus 67715
  Sutures 67710
Femoral Artery
  Exposure 34812-34813
Fibula 27607
Finger
  Decompression 26035
  Tendon 26060, 26455-26460
  Tendon Sheath 26055
Foot 28005
  Capsule 28260-28264
  Fasciotomy 28008
  for Infection 28002-28003
  Tendon 28230, 28234
Frontal Lobe 61490
Gallbladder 47490
Hand Decompression 26035-26037
  Tendon 26450, 26460
Heart
  Exploration 33310-33315
Hemorrhoids
  External 46083

Incision and Drainage

Abscess
  Abdomen 49020, 49040
    Open 49040
    Percutaneous 49021
  Anal 46045-46050
  Ankle 27603
  Appendix 44900
    Open 44900
    Percutaneous 44901
  Arm, Lower 25028
  Arm, Upper 23930-23931
  Auditory Canal, External 69020
  Bartholin's Gland 56420
  Bladder 51080
  Brain 61320-61321
  Breast 19020
  Ear, External
    Complicated 69005
    Simple 69000
  Elbow 23930
  Epididymis 54700
  Eyelid 67700
  Finger 26010-26011
  Gums 41800
  Hip 26990
  Kidney 50020
    Open 50020
    Percutaneous 50021
  Knee 27301
  Leg, Lower 27603
  Leg, Upper 27301
  Liver 47010
    Open 47010
    Percutaneous 47011
  Lung 32200
    Percutaneous 32201
  Lymph Node 38300-38305
  Mouth 40800-40801, 41005-41009, 41015-41018
  Nasal Septum 30020
  Neck 21501-21502
  Nose 30000-30020
  Ovary 58820-58822
    Abdominal Approach 58822
  Palate 42000
  Paraurethral Gland 53060
  Parotid Gland 42300-42305
  Pelvis 26990, 45000
  Perineum 56405
  Peritoneum 49020
    Percutaneous 49021
  Prostate 55720-55725
  Rectum ..45005-45020, 46040, 46050-46060
  Retroperitoneal 49060
    Open 49060
  Salivary Gland 42300-42320
  Scrotum 54700, 55100
  Skene's Gland 53060
  Skin 10060-10061
  Subdiaphragmatic
    Percutaneous 49040-49041
  Sublingual Gland 42310-42320
  Submaxillary Gland 42310-42320
  Subphrenic
    Percutaneous 49040-49041
  Testis 54700
  Thorax 21501-21502
  Throat 42700-42725
  Tongue 41000-41006, 41015
  Tonsil 42700
  Urethra 53040
  Uvula 42000
  Vagina 57010
  Vulva 56405
  Wrist 25028
Ankle 27610
Bile Duct 47420-47425
Bladder 51040
Bulla
  Skin
    Puncture Aspiration 10160
Bursa
  Ankle 27604
  Arm, Lower 25031
  Elbow 23931
  Foot 28001
  Hip 26991
  Knee 27301
  Leg, Lower 27604
  Leg, Upper 27301
  Palm 26025-26030
  Pelvis 26991
  Wrist 25031
Carbuncle
  Skin 10060-10061
Carpals 25035, 26034
Comedones
  Skin 10040
Cyst
  Conjunctiva 68020
  Gums 41800
  Liver
    Open 47010
    Percutaneous 47011
  Lung 32200
    Percutaneous 32201
  Mouth 40800-40801, 41005-41009, 41015-41018
  Ovarian 58800-58805
  Skin 10040, 10060-10061
    Pilonidal 10080-10081
    Puncture Aspiration 10160
  Spinal Cord 63172-63173
  Thyroid Gland 60000
  Tongue 41000-41006, 41015, 60000
Elbow
  Abscess 23935
  Arthrotomy 24000
Femur 27303
Fluid Collection
  Skin 10140
Foreign Body
  Skin 10120-10121
Furuncle 10060-10061
Gallbladder 47480
Hematoma
  Ankle 27603
  Arm, Lower 25028
  Arm, Upper 23930
  Brain 61312-61315
  Ear, External
    Complicated 69005
    Simple 69000
  Elbow 23930
  Epididymis 54700
  Gums 41800
  Hip 26990
  Knee 27301
  Leg, Lower 27603
  Leg, Upper 27301
  Mouth 40800-40801, 41005-41009, 41015-41018
  Nasal Septum 30020
  Neck 21501-21502
  Nose 30000-30020
  Pelvis 26990
  Scrotum 54700
  Skin 10140
    Puncture Aspiration 10160
  Skull 61312-61315
  Testis 54700
  Thorax 21501-21502
  Tongue 41000-41006, 41015
  Vagina 57022-57023
  Wrist 25028
Hepatic Duct 47400
Hip
  Bone 26992, 27030
Humerus
  Abscess 23935
Interphalangeal Joint
  Toe 28024
Intertarsal Joint 28020
Kidney 50040, 50125
Knee 27303, 27310
Lacrimal Gland 68400
Lacrimal Sac 68420
Liver
  Abscess or Cyst 47010-47011
    Percutaneous 47011
Mediastinum 39000-39010
Metatarsophalangeal Joint 28022
Milia, Multiple 10040
Onychia 10060-10061
Orbit 67405, 67440
Paronychia 10060-10061
Pelvic
  Bone 26992
Penis 54015
Pericardium 33025
Phalanges
  Finger 26034
Pilonidal Cyst 10080-10081
Pustules
  Skin 10040
Radius 25035
Seroma
  Skin 10140
Shoulder
  Abscess 23030
  Arthrotomy
    Acromioclavicular Joint 23044
    Sternoclavicular Joint 23044
  Bursa 23031
  Hematoma 23030
Shoulder Joint
  Arthrotomy
    Glenohumeral Joint 23040
Spine
  Abscess 22010-22015
Tarsometatarsal Joint 28020
Tendon Sheath
  Finger 26020
  Palm 26020

Influenza Virus
Antibody 86710
by Immunoassay
with Direct Optical Observation 87804

Infraorbital Nerve
Avulsion 64734
Incision 64734
Transection 64734

Infrared Light Treatment 97026
See Physical Medicine/Therapy/Occupational Therapy

Infratentorial Craniectomy 61520-61521

Infusion
Amnion
Transabdominal 59072
Cerebral
Intravenous
for Thrombolysis 37195
Intra-Arterial 96373
Unlisted 96379
Intraosseous 36680
Intravenous Unlisted 96379
Diagnostic/Prophylactic/
Therapeutic 96365-96368, 96379
Hydration 96360-96361
Radioelement 77750
Subcutaneous 96369-96371
Transcatheter Therapy 37201-37202

Infusion Pump
Electronic Analysis
Spinal Cord 62367-62368
Insertion
Intra-Arterial 36260
Intra-Arterial
Removal 36262
Revision 36261
Intravenous
Insertion 36563
Repair 36576
Replacement 36583
Maintenance 95990-95991, 96521-96522
See Chemotherapy, Pump Services
Spinal Cord 62361-62362
Ventricular Catheter 61215

Infusion Therapy 62350-62351, 62360-62362
See Injection, Chemotherapy
Arterial Catheterization 36640
Chemotherapy 96401-96542, 96545, 96549
Home Infusion Procedures 99601-99602
Intravenous 96365-96368, 96379
Pain 62360-62362, 62367-62368
Subcutaneous 96369-96371, 96379
Transcatheter Therapy 75896

Ingestion Challenge Test 95075
See Allergy Tests

Inguinal Hernia Repair
See Hernia, Repair, Inguinal

INH
See Drug Assay

Inhalation
Pentamidine 94642

Inhalation Provocation Tests
See Bronchial Challenge Test

Inhalation Treatment 94640, 94644-94645, 94664, 99503
See Pulmonology, Therapeutic

Inhibin A 86336

Inhibition Test, Hemagglutination
See Hemagglutination Inhibition Test

Inhibition, Fertilization
See Contraception

Inhibitor, Alpha 1-Protease
See Alpha-1 Antitrypsin

Inhibitor, Alpha 2-Plasmin
See Alpha-2 Antiplasmin

Inhibitory Concentration, Minimum
See Minimum Inhibitory Concentration

Initial Inpatient Consultations
See Consultation, Initial Inpatient

Injection
See Allergen Immunotherapy; Infusion
Abdomen
Air 49400
Contrast Material 49400
Angiography
Pulmonary 75746
Ankle
Radial 27648
Antibiotic
See AntibioticAdministration
Antigen (Allergen) 95115-95125
Aorta (Aortography)
Radiologic 93544
Aponeurosis 20550
Bladder
Radiologic 51600-51610
Brain Canal 61070
Bronchography
Segmental 31656
Bursa 20600-20610
Cardiac Catheterization 93539-93545
Carpal Tunnel
Therapeutic 20526
Chemotherapy 96401-96542, 96545, 96549
Cistern
Medication or Other 61055
Contrast 49465
via Catheter 36598, 49424
Corpora Cavernosa 54235
Cyst
Bone 20615
Kidney 50390
Pelvis 50390
Thyroid 60300
Diagnostic
Additional Sequential, Each Push 96376
Elbow
Arthrography
Radiologic 24220
Epidural
See Epidural, Injection
Esophageal Varices
Endoscopy 43243
Esophagus
Sclerosing Agent 43204
Submucosal 43201
Extremity
Pseudoaneurysm 36002
Eye
Air 66020
Medication 66030
Eyelid
Subconjunctional 68200
Foot
Nerve 64455
Ganglion
Anesthetic 64505, 64510
Ganglion Cyst 20612
Gastric Secretion Stimulant 91052
Gastric Varices
Endoscopy 43243
Heart Vessels
Cardiac Catheterization 93539-93545
See Catheterization, Cardiac
Radiologic 93545
Hemorrhoids
Sclerosing Solution 46500
Hip
Radiologic 27093-27095
Insect Venom 95130-95134
Intervertebral Disc
Chemonucleolysis Agent 62292
Radiological 62290-62291
Intra-Amniotic 59852
Intra-Arterial 96373, 96379
Thrombolytic 37184-37186
Intradermal
for Tattooing 11920-11922
Intralesional
Skin 11900-11901
Intramuscular 96372
Therapeutic 96372, 99506
Intravenous 96379
Nuclear Diagnostic Localization 78808
Thrombolytic 37187-37188
Unlisted 96379
Vascular Flow Check, Graft 15860
Intravenous Push 96374-96376
Joint 20600-20610
Kidney
Drugs 50391
Radiologic 50394
Knee
Radiologic 27370
Lacrimal Gland
Radiologic 68850
Left Heart
Radiologic 93543
Lesion
Skin 11900-11901
Ligament 20550
Liver 47015
Radiologic 47500-47505
Mammary Ductogram/Galactogram 19030
Muscle Endplate
Extremity 64614
Facial 64612

Inner Ear

Innominate

Innominate Arteries

Inorganic Sulfates

Inpatient Consultations

INR Test Review

Insemination

Insertion

Graft
Aorta 33330-33335
Heart Vessel 33330-33335
Guide
Kidney Pelvis 50395
Guide Wire
Endoscopy 43248
Esophagoscopy 43248
with Dilation 43226
Heyman Capsule
Uterus
for Brachytherapy 58346
Iliac Artery
Occlusion Device 34808
Implant
Bone
for External Speech Processor/
Cochlear Stimulator 69714-69718
Infusion Pump
Intra-Arterial 36260
Intravenous 36563
Spinal Cord 62361-62362
Intracatheter/Needle
Aorta 36160
Arteriovenous Shunt 36145
Intra-Arterial 36100-36140
Intravenous 36000
Kidney 50392
Intraocular Lens 66983
Manual or Mechanical
Technique 66982, 66984
Not Associated with Concurrent Cataract
Removal 66985
Intrauterine Device (IUD) 58300
IVC Filter 75940
Jejunostomy Tube
Endoscopy 44372
Percutaneous 49441
Keel
Laryngoplasty 31580
Laminaria 59200
Mesh
Pelvic Floor 57267
Nasobiliary Tube
Endoscopy 43267
Nasopancreatic Tube
Endoscopy 43267
Needle
Bone 36680
Intraosseous 36680
Prostate 55875-55876
Needle Wire
Trachea 31730
Neurostimulator
Pulse Generator 64590
Receiver 64590
Nose
Septal Prosthesis 30220
Obturator
Larynx 31527
Ocular Implant
in Scleral Shell 65130
Muscles, Attached 65140
Muscles, Not Attached 65135
with Foreign Material 65155
with/without Conjunctival Graft 65150
Orbital Transplant 67550
Oviduct
Chromotubation 58350
Hydrotubation 58350
Ovoid
Vagina
for Brachytherapy 57155
Pacemaker
Fluoroscopy/Radiography 71090
Heart 33206-33208, 33212-33213
Pacing Cardio-Defibrillator
Leads 33216-33220,
33224-33225, 33243-33244
Pulse Generator Only 33240-33241
Packing
Vagina 57180
Penile Prosthesis, Inflatable
See Penile Prosthesis, Insertion, Inflatable
Pessary
Vagina 57160
Pin
Skeletal Traction 20650
Probe
Brain 61770
Prostaglandin 59200
Prostate
Radioactive Substance 55860
Prosthesis
Knee 27438, 27445
Nasal Septal 30220
Palate 42281
Pelvic Floor 57267
Penis
Inflatable 54401-54405
Noninflatable 54400
Speech 31611
Testis 54660
Urethral Sphincter 53444-53445
Pulse Generator
Brain 61885-61886
Heart 33212-33213
Spinal Cord 63685
Radioactive Material
Bladder 51020
Cystourethroscopy 52250
Receiver
Brain 61885-61886
Spinal Cord 63685
Reservoir
Brain 61210-61215
Spinal Cord 62360
Subcutaneous 49419
Shunt 36835
Abdomen
Vein 49425
Venous 49426
Intrahepatic Portosystemic 37182
Spinal Instrument 22849
Spinous Process 0171T-0172T, 22841
Spinal Instrumentation
Anterior 22845-22847
Internal Spinal Fixation 22841
Pelvic Fixation 22848
Posterior Nonsegmental
Harrington Rod Technique 22840
Posterior Segmental 22842-22844
Prosthetic Device 22851
Stent
Bile Duct 43268, 47801
Percutaneous 47511
Bladder 51045
Conjunctiva 68750
Coronary 92980-92981
Esophagus 43219
Gastrointestinal, Upper 43256
Ileum 44383
Indwelling 50605
Lacrimal Duct 68815
Pancreatic Duct 43268
Small Intestines 44370, 44379
Ureter 50688
Ureter via Kidney 50393
Ureteral 50947, 52332
Urethral 0084T, 52282
Tamponade
Esophagus 43460
Tandem
Uterus
for Brachytherapy 57155
Tendon Graft
Finger 26392
Hand 26392
Testicular Prosthesis
See Prosthesis, Testicular, Insertion
Tissue Expanders
Skin 11960-11971
Tube
Bile Duct 43268
Esophagus 43510
Gastrointestinal, Upper 43241
Ileum 44383
Kidney 50398
Pancreatic Duct 43268
Small Intestines 44379
Trachea 31730
Ureter 50688
Ureteral Guide Wire 52334
Vascular Pedicle
Carpal Bone 25430
Venous Access Device
Central 36560-36566
Peripheral 36570-36571
Ventilating Tube 69433
Ventricular Assist Device 33975
Wire
Skeletal Traction 20650

Inspiratory Positive Pressure Breathing

See Intermittent Positive Pressure Breathing (IPPB)

Instillation

Contrast Material
Drugs
Bladder 51720
Kidney 50391
Ureter 50391

Instillation, Bladder

See Bladder, Instillation

Instrumentation

See Application; Bone, Fixation; Spinal Instrumentation

Intersex State
Clitoroplasty 56805
Vaginoplasty 57335

Intersex Surgery
Female to Male 55980
Male to Female 55970

Interstitial Cell Stimulating Hormone
See Luteinizing Hormone (LH)

Interstitial Cystitides, Chronic
See Cystitis, Interstitial

Interstitial Cystitis
See Cystitis, Interstitial

Interstitial Fluid Pressure
Monitoring 20950

Interstitial Cell Stimulating Hormone
See Luteinizing Hormone (LH)

Intertarsal Joint
Arthrotomy 28020, 28050
Exploration 28020
Removal
  Foreign Body 28020
  Loose Body 28020
Synovial
  Biopsy 28050
  Excision 28070

Interthoracoscapular Amputation
See Amputation, Interthoracoscapular

Intertrochanteric Femur Fracture
See Femur, Fracture, Intertrochanteric

Intervertebral Chemonucleolysis
See Chemonucleolysis

Intervertebral Disc
Annuloplasty 22526-22527
Arthroplasty 0092T, 0163T, 22856, 22857
Discography
  Cervical 72285
  Lumbar 72295
  Thoracic 72285
Excision
  Decompression 63075-63078
  Herniated 63020-63044, 63055-63066
Injection
  Chemonucleolysis Agent 62292
  X-ray 62290-62291
Removal 0095T, 0164T, 22864, 22865
Revision 0098T, 0165T, 22861, 22862

Intestinal Anastomosis
See Anastomosis, Intestines

Intestinal Invagination
See Intussusception

Intestinal Peptide, Vasoactive
See Vasoactive Intestinal Peptide

Intestine
Biopsy 44100
Lesion
  Excision 44110-44111
Unlisted Services and Procedures 44238, 44799

Intestines
Allotransplantation 44135-44136
  Removal 44137
Anastomosis 44625-44626
  Laparoscopic 44227
Bleeding Tube 91100
Closure
  Enterostomy
    Large or Small 44625-44626
  Stoma 44620-44625
Excision
  Donor 44132-44133
Exclusion 44700
Laparoscopic Resection
  with Anastomosis 44202-44208
Lysis of Adhesions
  Laparoscopic 44180
Nuclear Medicine
  Imaging 78290
Reconstruction
  Bladder 50820
  Colonic Reservoir 45119
Repair
  Diverticula 44605
  Obstruction 44615
  Ulcer 44605
  Wound 44605
Resection
  Laparoscopic 44227
Suture
  Diverticula 44605
  Stoma 44620-44625
  Ulcer 44605
  Wound 44605
Transplantation
  Allograft Preparation 44715-44721
  Donor Enterectomy 44132-44133
  Removal of Allograft 44137

Intestines, Large
See Anus; Colon; Rectum

Intestines, Small
Anastomosis 43845, 44130
Biopsy 44020
  Endoscopy 44361
Catheterization
  Jejunum 44015
Decompression 44021
Destruction
  Lesion 44369
  Tumor 44369
Endoscopy 44364
  Biopsy 44361, 44377
  Control of Bleeding 44366, 44378
    via Stoma 44382
  Destruction
    Lesion 44369
    Tumor 44369
  Diagnostic 44376
  Exploration 44360
  Hemorrhage 44366
  Insertion
    Stent 44370, 44379
    Tube 44379
  Pelvic Pouch 44385-44386
  Removal
    Foreign Body 44363
    Lesion 44365
    Polyp 44364-44365
    Tumor 44364-44365
  Tube Placement 44372
  Tube Revision 44373
  via Stoma 44380
Enterostomy 44300
Excision 44120-44128
  Partial with Anastomosis 44140
Exclusion 44700
Exploration 44020
Gastrostomy Tube 44373
Hemorrhage 44378
Hemorrhage Control 44366
Ileostomy 44310-44314, 45136
  Continent 44316
Incision 44020
  Creation
    Pouch 44316
    Stoma 44300-44310, 44314
  Decompression 44021
  Exploration 44020
  Revision
    Stoma 44312
    Stoma Closure 44620-44626
Insertion
  Catheter 44015
  Duodenostomy Tube 49441
  Jejunostomy Tube 44372, 49441
Jejunostomy 44310
Lysis
  Adhesions 44005
Removal
  Foreign Body 44020, 44363
Repair
  Diverticula 44602-44603
  Enterocele
    Abdominal Approach 57270
    Vaginal Approach 57268
  Fistula 44640-44661
  Hernia 44050
  Malrotation 44055
  Obstruction 44050
  Ulcer 44602-44603
  Volvulus 44050
  Wound 44602-44603
Revision
  Jejunostomy Tube 44373, 49451-49452
Specimen Collection 89100-89105
Suture
  Diverticula 44602-44603
  Fistula 44640-44661
  Plication 44680
  Ulcer 44602-44603
  Wound 44602-44603
X-ray 74245, 74249-74251
  Guide Intubation 74355

Intestinovesical Fistula
See Fistula, Enterovesical

Intima-Media Thickness (IMT) Study
Artery
  Carotid, Common 0126T

Intimectomy
See Endarterectomy

Intra Arterial Injections
See Injection, Intraarterial

Intra-Abdominal Voiding Pressure Studies 51797

Intra-Osseous Infusion
See Infusion, Intraosseous

Intracapsular Extraction of Lens
See Extraction, Lens, Intracapsular

Intracardiac Echocardiography 93662

Intracranial
Biopsy 61140
Extracranial 61623
Microdissection 69990

Intracranial Arterial Perfusion
Thrombolysis 61624

Intracranial Neoplasm, Acoustic Neuroma
See Brain, Tumor, Excision

Intracranial Neoplasm, Craniopharyngioma
See Craniopharyngioma

Intracranial Neoplasm, Meningioma
See Meningioma

Intrafallopian Transfer, Gamete
See GIFT

Intraluminal Angioplasty
See Angioplasty

Intramuscular Injection
See Injection, Intramuscular

Intraocular Lens
Exchange 66986
Insertion 66983
  Manual or Mechanical Technique 66982, 66984
  Not Associated with Concurrent Cataract Removal 66985

Intratracheal Intubation
See Insertion, Endotracheal Tube

Intrauterine Contraceptive Device
See Intrauterine Device (IUD)

Intrauterine Device (IUD)
Insertion 58300
Removal 58301

Intrauterine Synechiae
See Adhesions, Intrauterine

Intravascular Sensor
Pressure
  Complete Study 93982

Intravascular Stent
See Transcatheter, Placement, Intravascular Stents
X-ray 75960

Intravascular Ultrasound
Intraoperative 37250-37251

Intravenous Infusion
Diagnosis 96365-96368
Hydration 96360-96361
  Status Documented 2030F-2031F

Intravenous Injection
See Injection, Intravenous

Intravenous Pyelogram
See Urography, Intravenous

Intravenous Therapy
See Injection, Chemotherapy
Pain Management 96365-96379

Intravesical Instillation
See Bladder, Instillation

Intravitreal Injection
Pharmacologic Agent 67028

Intrinsic Factor 83528
Antibody 86340

Introduction
Breast
  Metallic Localization Clip Placement 19295
  Preoperative Placement, Needle 19290-19291
Contraceptive Capsules
  Implantable 11975-11977
Drug Delivery Implant 11981, 11983
Gastrointestinal Tube 44500
  with Fluoroscopic Guidance 74340
Tissue Expanders
  Skin 11960-11971

Intubation
See Insertion
Endotracheal Tube 31500
Eustachian Tube
  See Catheterization, Eustachian Tube
Gastric 89130-89141, 91105
Specimen Collection
  Esophagus 91000
  Stomach 91055

Intubation Tube
See Endotracheal Tube

Intussusception
Barium Enema 74283
Reduction
  Laparotomy 44050

Invagination, Intestinal
See Intussusception

Inversion, Nipple
See Nipples, Inverted

Iodide Test
See Nuclear Medicine, Thyroid, Uptake

Iodine Test
See Starch Granules, Feces

Ionization, Medical
See Iontophoresis

Iontophoreses
See Iontophoresis

Iontophoresis 97033
Sweat Collection 89230

IP
See Allergen Immunotherapy

Ipecac Administration 99175

IPPB
See Intermittent Positive Pressure Breathing; Pulmonology, Therapeutic

Iridectomy
by Laser Surgery 66761
Peripheral for Glaucoma 66625
with Corneoscleral or Corneal Section 66600
with Sclerectomy with Punch or Scissors 66160
with Thermocauterization 66155
with Transfixion as for Iris Bombe 66605
with Trephination 66150

Iridencleisis 66165

Iridodialysis 66680

Iridoplasty 66762

Iridotasis 66165

Iridotomy
by Laser Surgery 66761
by Stab Incision 66500
Excision
  Optical 66635
  Peripheral 66625
  with Corneoscleral or Corneal Section 66600
  with Cyclectomy 66605
Incision
  Stab 66500
  with Transfixion as for Iris Bombe 66505
Optical 66635
Peripheral 66625
Sector 66630

Iris
Cyst
  Destruction 66770
Excision
  Iridectomy
    Optical 66635
    Peripheral 66625
    Sector 66630
    with Corneoscleral or Corneal Section 66600
    with Cyclectomy 66605
Incision
  Iridotomy
    Stab 66500
    with Transfixion as for Iris Bombe 66505

Lesion
  Destruction 66770
Repair
  with Ciliary Body 66680
    Suture 66682
Revision
  Laser Surgery 66761
  Photocoagulation 66762
Suture
  with Ciliary Body 66682

Iron 83540

Iron Binding Capacity 83550

Iron Hematoxylin Stain 88312

Iron Stain 85536, 88313

Irradiation
Blood Products 86945

Irrigation
Bladder 51700
Catheter
  Brain 62194, 62225
Corpora Cavernosa
  Priapism 54220
Penis
  Priapism 54220
Peritoneal
  See Peritoneal Lavage
Rectum
  for Fecal Impaction 91123
Shunt
  Spinal Cord 63744
Sinus
  Maxillary 31000
  Sphenoid 31002
Vagina 57150
Venous Access Device 96523

Irving Sterilization
See Ligation, Fallopian Tube, Oviduct

Ischemic Stroke
Onset 1065F-1066F
Tissue Plasminogen Activator (tPA)
  Documentation That Administration
  Was Considered 4077F

Ischial
Bursa
  Excision 27060
Tumor
  Excision 27078-27079

Ischiectomy 15941

Island Pedicle Flaps 15740

Islands of Langerhans
See Islet Cell

Islet Cell
Antibody 86341
Transplantation 0141T-0143T

Isocitrate Dehydrogenase
See Isocitric Dehydrogenase

Isocitric Dehydrogenase
Blood 83570

Isolation
Sperm 89260-89261

Isomerase, Glucose 6 Phosphate
See Phosphohexose Isomerase

Isopropanol
See Isopropyl Alcohol

Isopropyl Alcohol 84600

Isthmusectomy
Thyroid Gland 60210-60225

IUD
See Intrauterine Device (IUD)

IV
See Injection, Chemotherapy; Intravenous Therapy

IV Infusion Therapy
See Allergen Immunotherapy; Chemotherapy; Infusion; Injection, Chemotherapy

IV Injection
See Injection, Intravenous

IV, Coagulation Factor
See Calcium

IVC Filter
Placement 75940

IVF
See Artificial Insemination; In Vitro Fertilization

Ivy Bleeding Time 85002

IX Complex, Factor
See Christmas Factor

J

Jaboulay Operation
See Gastroduodenostomy

Jaboulay Operation Gastroduodenostomy
See Gastroduodenostomy

Jannetta Procedure
See Decompression, Cranial Nerve; Section

Japanese Encephalitis Virus
See Vaccine

Japanese, River Fever
See Scrub Typhus

Jatene Type 33770-33781

Jaw Joint
See Facial Bones; Mandible; Maxilla

Jaws
Muscle Reduction 21295-21296
X-ray
  for Orthodontics 70355

Jejunostomy
Catheterization 44015
Contrast 49465
Insertion
  Catheter 44015
  Percutaneous 49441
Laparoscopic 44186-44187
Non-Tube 44187, 44310
Obstructive Material Removal 49460
Replacement 49451
with Pancreatic Drain 48001

Jejunum
Creation
  Stoma
Laparoscopic 44186
Transfer
  with Microvascular Anastomosis
    Free 43496

Johannsen Procedure 53400

Joint
See Specific Joint
Acromioclavicular
  See Acromioclavicular Joint
Arthrocentesis 20600-20610
Aspiration 20600-20610
Dislocation
  See Dislocation
Drainage 20600-20610
Finger
  See Intercarpal Joint
Fixation (Surgical)
  See Arthrodesis
Foot
  See Foot, Joint
Hip
  See Hip Joint
Injection 20600-20610
Intertarsal
  See Intertarsal Joint
Knee
  See Knee Joint
Ligament
  See Ligament
Metacarpophalangeal
  See Metacarpophalangeal Joint
Metatarsophalangeal
  See Metatarsophalangeal Joint
Nuclear Medicine
  Imaging 78300, 78315
Radiology
  Stress Views 77071
Sacroiliac
  See Sacroiliac Joint
Shoulder
  See Glenohumeral Joint
Sternoclavicular
  See Sternoclavicular Joint
Survey 77077
Temporomandibular
  See Temporomandibular Joint (TMJ)
  Dislocation Temporomandibular
    See Dislocation, Temporomandibular Joint
  Implant
    See Prosthesis, Temporomandibular Joint
Wrist
  See Radiocarpal Joint

Kloramfenikol
See Chloramphenicol

Knee
See Femur; Fibula; Patella; Tibia
Abscess ... 27301
Arthrocentesis ... 20610
Arthrodesis ... 27580
Arthroplasty ... 27440-27445, 27447
  Revision ... 27486-27487
Arthroscopy
  Diagnostic ... 29870
  Surgical ... 29866-29868, 29871-29889
Arthrotomy ... 27310, 27330-27335, 27403
Autogaft, Osteochondral, Open ... 27416
Biopsy ... 27323-27324, 27330-27331
  Synovium ... 27330
Bone
  Drainage ... 27303
Bursa ... 27301
  Excision ... 27340
Cyst
  Excision ... 27345-27347
Disarticulation ... 27598
Dislocation ... 27550-27552, 27560-27562
  Open Treatment ... 27556-27558, 27566
Drainage ... 27310
Excision
  Cartilage ... 27332-27333
  Ganglion ... 27347
  Lesion ... 27347
  Synovium ... 27334-27335
Exploration ... 27310, 27331
Fasciotomy ... 27305, 27496-27499
Fracture ... 27520-27524
  Arthroscopic Treatment ... 29850-29851
Fusion ... 27580
Hematoma ... 27301
Incision
  Capsule ... 27435
Injection
  X-ray ... 27370
Magnetic Resonance Imaging (MRI) ... 73721-73723
Manipulation ... 27570
Meniscectomy ... 27332-27333
Reconstruction ... 27437-27438
  Ligament ... 27427-27429
  with Prosthesis ... 27445
Removal
  Foreign Body ... 27310, 27331, 27372
  Loose Body ... 27331
  Prosthesis ... 27488
Repair
  Ligament ... 27405-27409
    Collateral ... 27405
    Collateral and Cruciate ... 27409
    Cruciate ... 27407-27409
  Meniscus ... 27403
  Tendon ... 27380-27381
Replacement ... 27447
Retinacular
  Release ... 27425
Strapping ... 29530
Suture
  Tendon ... 27380-27381
Transplantation
  Chondrocytes ... 27412
  Meniscus ... 29868
  Osteochondral
    Allograft ... 27415, 29867
    Autograft ... 27412, 29866
Tumor
  Excision ... 27327-27329, 27365
Unlisted Services and Procedures ... 27599
X-ray ... 73560-73564
  Arthrography ... 73580
  Bilateral ... 73565
X-ray with Contrast
  Arthrography ... 73580

Knee Joint
Arthroplasty ... 27446

Knee Prosthesis
See Prosthesis, Knee

Kneecap
Excision ... 27350
Repair
  Instability ... 27420-27424

Knock-Knee Repair ... 27455-27457

Kocher Operation ... 23650-23680
See Clavicle; Scapula; Shoulder, Dislocation, Closed Treatment

Kocher Pylorectomy
See Gastrectomy, Partial

Kock Pouch ... 44316
Formation ... 50825

Kock Procedure ... 44316

KOH
See Hair, Nails, Tissue, Examination for Fungi

Kraske Procedure ... 45116

Kroenlein Procedure ... 67420

Krukenberg Procedure ... 25915

Kuhlmann Test ... 96101-96103

Kyphectomy
More than Two Segments ... 22819
Up to Two Segments ... 22818

Kyphoplasty ... 22523-22525

L

L Ascorbic Acid
See Ascorbic Acid

L Aspartate 2 Oxoglutarate Aminotransferase
See Transaminase, Glutamic Oxaloacetic

L Glutamine
See Glutamine

L-Alanine
See Aminolevulinic Acid (ALA)

L-Leucylnaphthylamidase
See Leucine Aminopeptidase

L/S Ratio
Amniotic Fluid ... 83661

Labial Adhesions
Lysis ... 56441

Labyrinth
See Ear, Inner

Labyrinthectomy ... 69905
with Mastoidectomy ... 69910
with Skull Base Surgery ... 61596

Labyrinthotomy
with Mastoidectomy ... 69802
with/without Cryosurgery ... 69801

Laceration Repair
See Specific Site

Lacrimal Duct
Balloon ... 68816
Canaliculi
  Repair ... 68700
Dilation ... 68816
Exploration ... 68810
  Canaliculi ... 68840
  Stent ... 68815
  with Anesthesia ... 68811
Insertion
  Stent ... 68815
Nasolacrimal Duct Probing ... 68816
Removal
  Dacryolith ... 68530
  Foreign Body ... 68530
X-ray with Contrast ... 70170

Lacrimal Gland
Biopsy ... 68510
Close Fistula ... 68770
Excision
  Partial ... 68505
  Total ... 68500
Fistulization ... 68720
Incision and Drainage ... 68400
Injection
  X-ray ... 68850
Nuclear Medicine
  Tear Flow ... 78660
Removal
  Dacryolith ... 68530
  Foreign Body ... 68530
Repair
  Fistula ... 68770
Tumor
  Excision
    Frontal Approach ... 68540
    with Osteotomy ... 68550
X-ray ... 70170

Lacrimal Punctum
Closure
  by Plug ... 68761
  by Thermocauterization, Ligation or Laser Surgery ... 68760
Dilation ... 68801
Incision ... 68440
Repair ... 68705

Gastric Restrictive Procedures .43770-43774, 43848, 43886-43888
Gastroenterostomy 43644-43645
Roux-En-Y 43644
Transplantation
Islet Cell 0143T
Unlisted Services and Procedures .38129, 38589, 43289, 43659, 44238, 44979, 45499, 47379, 47579, 49329, 49659, 50549, 50949, 51999, 54699, 55559, 58578-58579, 58679, 59898
Ureterolithotomy 50945
Ureteroneocystostomy 50947-50948
Urethral Suspension 51990
Vaginal Hysterectomy 58550-58554
Vaginal Suspension 57425
Vagus Nerves
Transection 43651-43652
with X-ray 47560

Laparotomy
Electrode Implantation
Gastric 43881, 0157T
Electrode Removal
Gastric 43882, 0158T
Electrode Replacement
Gastric 43881, 0157T
Electrode Revision
Gastric 43882, 0158T
Exploration 47015, 49000-49002
Hemorrhage Control 49002
Second Look 58960
Staging 49220, 58960
with Biopsy 49000

Laparotomy, Exploratory
See Abdomen, Exploration

Lapidus Procedure 28297

Large Bowel
See Anus; Rectum

Laroyenne Operation
See Vagina, Abscess, Incision and Drainage

Laryngeal Function Study 92520

Laryngeal Sensory Testing 92614-92617

Laryngectomy 31360-31382
Partial 31367-31382
Subtotal 31367-31368

Laryngocele
Removal 31300

Laryngofissure 31300

Laryngography 70373
Instillation

Laryngopharyngectomy
See Excision, Larynx, with Pharynx

Laryngopharynx
See Hypopharynx

Laryngoplasty
Burns 31588
Cricoid Split 31587
Laryngeal Stenosis 31582
Laryngeal Web 31580
Open Reduction of Fracture 31584

Laryngoscopy
Diagnostic 31505
Direct 31515-31571
Exploration 31505, 31520-31526, 31575
Fiberoptic 31575-31579
with Stroboscopy 31579
Indirect 31505-31513
Newborn 31520
Operative 31530-31561

Laryngotomy 31300
Diagnostic 31320

Larynx
Aspiration
Endoscopy 31515
Biopsy
Endoscopy 31510, 31535-31536, 31576
Dilation
Endoscopic 31528-31529
Electromyography
Needle 95865
Endoscopy
Direct 31515-31571
Excision 31545-31546
Exploration 31505, 31520-31526, 31575
Fiberoptic 31575-31579
with Stroboscopy 31579
Indirect 31505-31513
Operative 31530-31561
Excision
Lesion 31512, 31578
Endoscopic 31545-31546
Partial 31367-31382
Total 31360-31365
with Pharynx 31390-31395
Exploration
Endoscopic 31505, 31520-31526, 31575
Fracture 31584
Insertion
Obturator 31527
Nerve
Destruction 31595
Reconstruction
Burns 31588
Cricoid Split 31587
Other 31588
Stenosis 31582
Web 31580
Removal
Foreign Body
Endoscopic ...31511, 31530-31531, 31577
Lesion
Endoscopic ...31512, 31545-31546, 31578
Repair
Reinnervation Neuromuscular Pedicle .31590
Stroboscopy 31579
Tumor
Excision 31300
Endoscopic 31540-31541
Unlisted Services and Procedures 31599
Vocal Cord(s)
Injection 31513, 31570-31571
X-ray 70370
with Contrast 70373

Laser Surgery
Anus 46614, 46917
Cautery
Esophagus 43227
Hemorrhoids 46930
Lacrimal Punctum 68760
Lens, Posterior 66821
Lesion
Mouth 40820
Nose 30117-30118
Penis 54057
Skin 17000-17111, 17260-17286
Myocardium 33140-33141
Prostate 52647-52648
Spine
Discectomy 62287
Tumors
Urethra and Bladder 52234
Urethra and Bladder 52214

Laser Treatment 17000-17286, 96920-96922
See Destruction

Lateral Epicondylitis
See Tennis Elbow

Latex Fixation 86403-86406

LATS
See Thyrotropin Releasing Hormone (TRH)

Latzko Operation
See Repair, Vagina, Fistula; Revision

LAV
See HIV

LAV Antibodies
See Antibody, HIV

LAV-2
See HIV-2

Lavage
Colon 44701
Lung
Bronchial 31624
Total 32997
Peritoneal 49080

LCM
See Lymphocytic Choriomeningitis

LD
See Lactate Dehydrogenase

LDH 83615-83625

LDL
See Lipoprotein, LDL

Lead 83655

Leadbetter Procedure 53431

Lecithin-Sphingomyelin Ratio .83661

Lecithinase C
See Tissue Typing

Lee and White Test 85345

LEEP Procedure 57460

LeFort Procedure
Vagina 57120

LeFort I Procedure
Midface Reconstruction 21141-21147, 21155, 21160
Palatal or Maxillary Fracture 21421-21423

LeFort II Procedure
Midface Reconstruction 21150-21151
Nasomaxillary Complex Fracture 21345-21348

LeFort III Procedure
Craniofacial Separation 21431-21436
Midface Reconstruction 21154-21159

Left Atrioventricular Valve
See Mitral Valve

Left Heart Cardiac Catheterization
See Cardiac Catheterization, Left Heart

Leg
Cast
  Rigid Total Contact 29445
Lower
  See Ankle; Fibula;Knee; Tibia
  Abscess
    Incision and Drainage 27603
  Amputation 27598, 27880-27882
    Revision 27884-27886
  Angiography 73706
  Artery
    Ligation 37618
  Biopsy 27613-27614
  Bursa
    Incision and Drainage 27604
  Bypass Graft 35903
  Cast 29405-29435, 29450
  CT Scan 73700-73706
  Decompression 27600-27602
  Exploration
    Blood Vessel 35860
  Fasciotomy 27600-27602, 27892-27894
  Hematoma
    Incision and Drainage 27603
  Lesion
    Excision 27630
  Magnetic Resonance Imaging (MRI) 73718-73720
  Neurectomy 27325-27326
  Repair
    Blood Vessel 35226
    Blood Vessel with Other Graft 35286
    Blood Vessel with Vein Graft 35256
    Fascia 27656
    Tendon 27658-27692
  Splint 29515
  Strapping 29580
  Suture
    Tendon 27658-27665
  Tumor
    Excision 27615-27619
  Ultrasound 76880
  Unlisted Services and Procedures 27899
  Unna Boot 29580
  X-ray 73592
Upper
  See Femur
  Abscess 27301
  Amputation 27590-27592
    at Hip 27290-27295
    Revision 27594-27596
  Angiography 73706, 75635
  Artery
    Ligation 37618
  Biopsy 27323-27324
  Bursa 27301
  Bypass Graft 35903
  Cast 29345-29355, 29365, 29450
  Cast Brace 29358
  CT Scan 73700-73706, 75635
  Exploration
    Blood Vessel 35860
  Fasciotomy 27305, 27496-27499, 27892-27894
  Halo Application 20663
  Hematoma 27301
  Magnetic Resonance Imaging (MRI) 73718-73720
  Neurectomy 27325-27326
  Removal
    Cast 29705
    Foreign Body 27372
  Repair
    Blood Vessel with Other Graft 35286
    Blood Vessel with Vein Graft 35256
    Muscle 27385-27386, 27400, 27430
    Tendon 27393-27400
  Splint 29505
  Strapping 29580
  Suture
    Muscle 27385-27386
  Tenotomy 27306-27307, 27390-27392
  Tumor
    Excision 27327-27329
  Ultrasound 76880
  Unlisted Services and Procedures 27599
  Unna Boot 29580
  X-ray 73592
Wound Exploration
  Penetrating 20103

Leg Length Measurement X-ray
See Scanogram

Legionella
Antibody 86713
Antigen 87277-87278, 87540-87542

Legionella Micdadei
Antigen Detection
  Immunofluorescence 87277

Legionella Pneumophila
Antigen Detection
  Direct Fluorescence 87278

Leiomyomata
Embolization 37210
Removal 58140, 58545-58546, 58561

Leishmania
Antibody 86717

Lengthening, Tendon
See Tendon, Lengthening

Lens
Extracapsular 66940
Incision 66821
  Laser 66821
Intracapsular 66920
  Dislocated 66930
Intraocular
  Exchange 66986
  Reposition 66825
Prosthesis
  Insertion 66983
    Manual or Mechanical Technique 66982, 66984
    Not Associated with Concurrent Cataract Removal 66985
Removal
  Lens Material
    Aspiration Technique 66840
    Extracapsular 66940
    Intracapsular 66920-66930
    Pars Plana Approach 66852
    Phacofragmentation Technique 66850

Lens Material
Aspiration Technique 66840
Pars Plana Approach 66852
Phacofragmentation Technique 66850

Leptomeningioma
See Meningioma

Leptospira
Antibody 86720

Leriche Operation 64809
See Sympathectomy, Thoracolumbar

Lesion
See Tumor
Anal
  Destruction 46900-46917, 46924
  Excision 45108, 46922
Ankle
  Tendon Sheath 27630
Arm, Lower
  Tendon Sheath
    Excision 25110
Auditory Canal, External
  Excision
    Exostosis 69140
    Radical with Neck Dissection 69155
    Radical without Neck Dissection 69150
    Soft Tissue 69145
Bladder
  Destruction 51030
Brain
  Excision 61534, 61536, 61600-61608, 61615-61616
Brainstem
  Excision 61575-61576
Breast
  Excision 19120-19126
Carotid Body
  Excision 60600-60605
Chemotherapy 96405-96406
  Destruction 67220-67225
Choroid
  Destruction 0016T
Ciliary Body
  Destruction 66770

Colon
Destruction 44393, 45383
Excision 44110-44111
Conjunctiva
Destruction 68135
Excision 68110-68130
Over 1cm 68115
with Adjacent Sclera 68130
Expression 68040
Cornea
Destruction 65450
Excision 65400
of Pterygium 65420-65426
Cranium 77432
Destruction
Ureter ...52341-52342, 52344-52345, 52354
Ear, Middle
Excision 69540
Epididymis
Excision 54830
Esophagus
Ablation 43228
Excision 43100-43101
Removal 43216
Excision 59100
Bladder 52224
Urethra 52224, 53265
Eye
Excision 65900
Eyelid
Destruction 67850
Excision
Multiple, Different Lids 67805
Multiple, Same Lid 67801
Single 67800
Under Anesthesia 67808
without Closure 67840
Facial
Destruction 17000-17004, 17280-17286
Femur
Excision 27062
Finger
Tendon Sheath 26160
Foot
Excision 28080, 28090
Gums
Destruction 41850
Excision 41822-41828
Hand Tendon Sheath 26160
Intestines
Excision 44110
Intestines, Small
Destruction 44369
Excision 44111
Iris
Destruction 66770
Larynx
Excision 31545-31546
Leg, Lower
Tendon Sheath 27630
Lymph Node
Incision and Drainage 38300-38305
Mesentery
Excision 44820
Mouth
Destruction 40820
Excision 40810-40816, 41116
Vestibule
Destruction 40820
Repair 40830
Nerve
Excision 64774-64792
Nose
Intranasal
External Approach 30118
Internal Approach 30117
Orbit
Excision 61333, 67412
Palate
Destruction 42160
Excision 42104-42120
Pancreas
Excision 48120
Pelvis
Destruction 58662
Penis
Destruction
Cryosurgery 54056
Electrodesiccation 54055
Extensive 54065
Laser Surgery 54057
Simple 54050-54060
Surgical Excision 54060
Excision 54060
Penile Plague 54110-54112
Pharynx
Destruction 42808
Excision 42808
Radiosurgery
Cranial 61796-61800
Rectum
Excision 45108
Removal
Larynx 31512, 31578
Resection 52354
Retina
Destruction
Extensive 67227-67228
Localized 0017T, 67208-67210
Radiation by Implantation of Source...67218
Sciatic Nerve
Excision 64786
Sclera
Excision 66130
Skin
Abrasion 15786-15787
Biopsy 11100-11101
Destruction
Benign 17110-17111, 17250
Malignant 17260-17286
by Photodynamic Therapy 96567
Premalignant 17000-17004
Excision
Benign 11400-11471
Malignant 11600-11646
Injection 11900-11901
Paring or Curettement 11055-11057
Shaving 11300-11313
Skin Tags
Removal 11200-11201
Skull
Excision ..61500, 61600-61608, 61615-61616
Spermatic Cord
Excision 55520
Spinal Cord
Destruction 62280-62282
Excision 63265-63273
Stomach
Excision 43611
Testis
Excision 54512
Toe
Excision 28092
Tongue
Excision 41110-41114
Uvula
Destruction 42145
Excision 42104-42107
Vagina
Destruction 57061-57065
Vulva
Destruction
Extensive 56515
Simple 56501
Wrist Tendon
Excision 25110

Leu 2 Antigens
See CD8

Leucine Aminopeptidase 83670

Leukemia Lymphoma Virus I Antibodies, Human T Cell
See Antibody, HTLV-I

Leukemia Lymphoma Virus I, Adult T Cell
See HTLV I

Leukemia Lymphoma Virus II Antibodies, Human T Cell
See Antibody, HTLV-II

Leukemia Virus II, Hairy Cell Associated, Human T Cell
See HTLV II

Leukoagglutinins 86021

Leukocyte
See White Blood Cell
Alkaline Phosphatase 85540
Antibody 86021
Count 85032, 85048, 89055
Histamine Release Test 86343
Phagocytosis 86344
Transfusion 86950

Levarterenol
See Noradrenalin

Levator Muscle Repair
See Blepharoptosis, Repair

LeVeen Shunt
Insertion 49425
Patency Test 78291
Revision 49426

Levulose
See Fructose

LGV
See Lymphogranuloma Venereum

LH
See Luteinizing Hormone (LH)

LHR
See Leukocyte Histamine Release Test

Lid Suture
See Blepharoptosis, Repair

Lidocaine
Assay 80176

Lift, Face
See Face Lift

Ligament
See Specific Site
Collateral
  Repair
    Knee
      with Cruciate Ligament 27409
Dentate
  Section 63180-63182
Injection 20550
Release
  Coracoacromial 23415
  Transverse Carpal 29848
Repair
  Elbow 24343-24346
  Knee Joint 27405-27409

Ligation
Artery
  Abdomen 37617
  Carotid 37600-37606
  Chest 37616
  Coronary 33502
  Ethmoidal 30915
  Extremity 37618
  Fistula 37607
  Maxillary 30920
  Neck 37615
  Temporal 37609
Esophageal Varices 43204, 43400
Fallopian Tube
  Oviduct 58600-58611, 58670
Gastroesophageal 43405
Hemorrhoids 46945-46946
Oviducts 59100
Salivary Duct 42665
Shunt
  Aorta
    Pulmonary 33924
  Peritoneal
    Venous 49428
Thoracic Duct 38380
  Abdominal Approach 38382
  Thoracic Approach 38381
Vas Deferens 55450
Vein
  Clusters 37785
  Esophagus 43205, 43244, 43400
  Femoral 37650
  Gastric 43244
  Iliac 37660
  Jugular, Internal 37565
  Perforate 37760
  Saphenous 37700-37735, 37780
  Vena Cava 37620

Ligature Strangulation
Skin Tags 11200-11201

Light Coagulation
See Photocoagulation

Light Scattering Measurement
See Nephelometry

Light Therapy, UV
See Actinotherapy

Limb
See Extremity

Limited Lymphadenectomy for Staging
See Lymphadenectomy, Limited, for Staging

Limited Neck Dissection
with Thyroidectomy 60252

Limited Resection Mastectomies
See Breast, Excision, Lesion

Lindholm Operation
See Tenoplasty

Lingual Bone
See Hyoid Bone

Lingual Frenectomy
See Excision, Tongue, Frenum

Lingual Nerve
Avulsion 64740
Incision 64740
Transection 64740

Lingual Tonsil
See Tonsils, Lingual

Linton Procedure 37760

Lip
Biopsy 40490
Excision 40500-40530
  Frenum 40819
Incision
  Frenum 40806
Reconstruction 40525-40527
Repair 40650-40654
  Cleft Lip 40700-40761
  Fistula 42260
Unlisted Services and Procedures 40799

Lip, Cleft
See Cleft Lip

Lipase 83690

Lipectomy
Excision 15830-15839
Suction Assisted 15876-15879

Lipectomy, Aspiration
See Liposuction

Lipids
Feces 82705-82710

Lipo-Lutin
See Progesterone

Lipolysis, Aspiration
See Liposuction

Lipophosphodiesterase I
See Tissue Typing

Lipoprotein
(a) 83695
Blood 83695, 83700-83721
LDL 83700-83704, 83721
Phospholipase A2 83698

Lipoprotein, Alpha
See Lipoprotein

Lipoprotein, Pre-Beta
See Lipoprotein, Blood

Liposuction 15876-15879

Lisfranc Operation
See Amputation, Foot; Radical Resection; Replantation

Listeria Monocytogenes
Antibody 86723

Lithium
Assay 80178

Litholapaxy 52317-52318

Lithotripsy
See Extracorporeal Shock Wave Therapy
Bile Duct Calculi (Stone)
  Endoscopy 43265
Bladder 52353
Kidney 50590, 52353
Pancreatic Duct Calculi (Stone)
  Endoscopy 43265
Ureter 52353
Urethra 52353
with Cystourethroscopy 52353

Lithotrity
See Litholapaxy

Liver
See Hepatic Duct
Ablation
  Tumor 47380-47382
    Laparoscopic 47370-47371
Abscess
  Aspiration 47015
  Incision and Drainage
    Open 47010
    Percutaneous 47011
  Injection 47015
Aspiration 47015
Biopsy 47100
Cyst
  Aspiration 47015
  Incision and Drainage
    Open 47010
    Percutaneous 47011
Excision
  Extensive 47122
  Partial 47120, 47125-47130, 47140-47142
  Total 47133
Injection 47015
  Radiologic 47505
  X-ray 47500

Lobectomy 47125-47130
  Partial 47120
Needle Biopsy 47000-47001
Nuclear Medicine
  Function Study 78220
  Imaging 78201-78216
  Vascular Flow 78206
Repair
  Abscess 47300
  Cyst 47300
  Wound 47350-47362
Suture
  Wound 47350-47362
Transplantation 47135-47136
  Allograft Preparation 47143-47147
Trisegmentectomy 47122
Unlisted Services and Procedures . .47379, 47399

Living Activities, Daily
See Activities of Daily Living

Lobectomy
Brain 61323, 61537-61540
Contralateral Subtotal
  Thyroid Gland 60212, 60225
Liver 47120-47130
Lung 32480-32482
  Sleeve 32486
Parotid Gland 42410-42415
Segmental 32663
Sleeve 32486
Temporal Lobe 61537-61538
Thyroid Gland Partial 60210-60212
  Total 60220-60225
Total 32663

Lobotomy
Frontal 61490

Local Excision Mastectomies
See Breast, Excision, Lesion

Local Excision of Lesion or Tissue of Femur
See Excision, Lesion, Femur

Localization of Nodule
Radiographic
  Breast 77032

Log Hydrogen Ion Concentration
See pH

Long Acting Thyroid Stimulator
See Thyrotropin Releasing Hormone (TRH)

Long-Term Care Facility Visits
See Nursing Facility Services

Longmire Operation
See Anastomosis, Hepatic Duct to Intestines

Loopogram
See Urography, Antegrade

Loose Body
Removal
  Ankle 27620
  Carpometacarpal Joint 26070
  Elbow 24101
  Interphalangeal Joint 28020
    Toe 28024
  Knee Joint 27331
  Metatarsophalangeal Joint 28022
  Tarsometatarsal Joint 28020
  Toe 28022
  Wrist 25101

Lord Procedure
See Anal Sphincter, Dilation

Louis Bar Syndrome
See Ataxia Telangiectasia

Low Birth Weight Intensive Care Services 99478-99480

Low Density Lipoprotein
See Lipoprotein, LDL

Low Frequency Ultrasound 0183T

Low Vision Aids
See Spectacle Services
Fitting 92354-92355

Lower Extremities
See Extremity, Lower

Lower GI Series
See Barium Enema

LRH
See Luteinizing Releasing Factor

LSD
See Lysergic Acid Diethylamide

LTH
See Prolactin

Lumbar
See Spine
Decompression, Disc Percutaneous 62287

Lumbar Plexus
Decompression 64714
Injection
  Anesthetic 64449
Neuroplasty 64714
Release 64714
Repair/Suture 64862

Lumbar Puncture
See Spinal Tap

Lumbar Spine Fracture
See Fracture, Vertebra, Lumbar

Lumbar Sympathectomy
See Sympathectomy, Lumbar

Lumbar Vertebra
See Vertebra, Lumbar

Lumen Dilation 74360

Lumpectomy 19301-19302

Lunate
Arthroplasty
  with Implant 25444
Dislocation
  Closed Treatment 25690
  Open Treatment 25695

Lung
Ablation 32998
Abscess
  Incision and Drainage
    Open 32200
    Percutaneous 32200-32201
Aspiration 32420
Biopsy 32095-32100
Bullae
  Excision 32141
    Endoscopic 32655
Cyst
  Incision and Drainage
    Open 32200
  Removal 32140
Decortication
  Endoscopic 32651-32652
  Partial 32225
  Total 32220
  with Parietal Pleurectomy 32320
Empyema
  Excision 32540
Excision
  Bronchus Resection 32486
  Completion 32488
  Donor
    Heart-Lung 33930
    Lung 32850
  Emphysematous 32491
  Empyema 32540
  Lobe 32480-32482
  Segment 32484
  Total 32440-32445
  Tumor 32503-32504
  Wedge Resection 32500
    Endoscopic 32657
Foreign Body
  Removal 32151
Hemorrhage 32110
Lavage
  Bronchial 31624
  Total 32997
Lysis
  Adhesions 32124
Needle Biopsy 32405
Nuclear Medicine
  Imaging, Perfusion 78580-78585
  Imaging, Ventilation 78586-78594
  Unlisted Services and Procedures 78599
Pneumocentesis 32420
Pneumolysis 32940
Pneumothorax 32960
Puncture 32420
Removal
  Bronchoplasty 32501
  Completion Pneumonectomy 32488
  Extrapleural 32445
  Single Lobe 32480
  Single Segment 32484
  Sleeve Lobectomy 32486
  Sleeve Pneumonectomy 32442
  Total Pneumonectomy 32440-32445
  Two Lobes 32482
  Volume Reduction 32491
  Wedge Resection 32500
Repair
  Hernia 32800
Segmentectomy 32484

Fallopian Tube 58740
Foreskin 54450
Intestinal 44005
Labial 56441
Lung 32124
Nose 30560
Ovary 58740
Oviduct 58740
Penile
Post-Circumcision 54162
Ureter 50715-50725
Urethra 53500
Uterus 58559
Euglobulin 85360
Labial
Adhesions 56441
Nose
Intranasal Synechia 30560

Lysozyme 85549

M

Macrodactylia
Repair 26590

Magnesium 83735

Magnet Operation
See Ciliary Body; Cornea; Eye, Removal, Foreign Body; Iris; Lens; Retina; Sclera; Vitreous

Magnetic Resonance
Unlisted Services and Procedures 76498

Magnetic Resonance Angiography (MRA)
Abdomen 74185
Arm 73225
Chest 71555
Head 70544-70546
Leg 73725
Neck 70547-70549
Pelvis 72198
Spine 72159

Magnetic Resonance Imaging (MRI)
3D Rendering 76376-76377
Abdomen 74181-74183
Ankle 73721-73723
Arm 73218-73220, 73223
Bone Marrow Study 77084
Brain 70551-70555
Intraoperative 70557-70559
Breast 77058-77059
with Computer-aided Detection 0159T
Chest 71550-71552
Elbow 73221
Face 70540-70543
Finger Joint 73221
Foot 73718-73719
Foot Joints 73721-73723
Guidance
Needle Placement 77021
Parenchymal Tissue Ablation 77022
Hand 73218-73220, 73223
Heart 75557-75564
Joint
Lower Extremity 73721-73723
Upper Extremity 73221-73223
Knee 73721-73723
Leg 73718-73720
Neck 70540-70543
Orbit 70540-70543
Pelvis 72195-72197
Spectroscopy 76390
Spine
Cervical 72141-72142, 72156-72158
Lumbar 72148-72158
Thoracic 72146-72147, 72156-72158
Temporomandibular Joint (TMJ) 70336
Toe 73721-73723
Unlisted 76498
Wrist 73221

Magnetic Resonance Spectroscopy 76390

Magnetic Stimulation
Transcranial 0160T, 0161T

Magnetoencephalography (MEG) 95965-95967

Magnuson Procedure 23450

MAGPI Operation 54322

MAGPI Procedure
See Hypospadias, Repair

Major Vestibular Gland
See Bartholin's Gland

Malar Area
Augmentation 21270
Bone Graft 21210
Fracture
Open Treatment 21360-21366
with Bone Graft 21366
with Manipulation 21355
Reconstruction 21270

Malar Bone
See Cheekbone

Malaria Antibody 86750

Malaria Smear 87207

Malate Dehydrogenase 83775

Maldescent, Testis
See Testis, Undescended

Male Circumcision
See Circumcision

Malformation, Arteriovenous
See Arteriovenous Malformation

Malic Dehydrogenase
See Malate Dehydrogenase

Malignant Hyperthermia Susceptibility
Caffeine Halothane Contracture Test (CHCT) 89049

Malleolus
See Ankle; Fibula; Leg, Lower; Tibia; Tibiofibular Joint

Mallet Finger Repair 26432

Maltose
Tolerance Test 82951-82952

Malunion Repair
Femur
with Graft 27472
without Graft 27470
Metatarsal 28322
Tarsal Joint 28320

Mammalian Oviduct
See Fallopian Tube

Mammaplasty
See Breast, Reconstruction; Mammoplasty

Mammary Abscess
See Abscess, Breast

Mammary Arteries
See Artery, Mammary

Mammary Duct
X-ray with Contrast 77053-77054

Mammary Ductogram
Injection 19030

Mammary Stimulating Hormone
See Prolactin

Mammillaplasty
See Nipples, Reconstruction

Mammogram
Breast
Localization Nodule 77032

Mammography 77055-77057
Magnetic Resonance Imaging (MRI)
with Computer-Aided Detection 0159T
Screening 77057
with Computer-Aided Detection 77051-77052

Mammoplasty
Augmentation 19324-19325
Reduction 19318

Mammotomy
See Incision, Breast; Incision and Drainage, Breast; Mastotomy

Mammotropic Hormone, Pituitary
See Prolactin

Mammotropic Hormone, Placental
See Lactogen, Human Placental

Mammotropin
See Prolactin

Mandated Services
On Call Services 99027

Repair
by Excision 69601-69603
Fistula 69700
with Apicectomy 69605
with Tympanoplasty 69604

Mastoid Cavity
Debridement 69220-69222

Mastoidectomy
Osseointegrated Implant
for External Speech Processor/
Cochlear Stimulator 69715, 69718
with Apicectomy 69605
with Skull Base Surgery 61590, 61597
Decompression 61595
Facial Nerve 61595
with Tympanoplasty 69604, 69641-69646
Cochlear Device Implantation 69930
Complete 69502
Revision 69601
Ossicular Chain Reconstruction 69605
Radical 69511
Modified 69505
Revision 69602-69603
Simple 69501
with Labyrinthectomy 69910
with Labyrinthotomy 69802
with Petrous Apicectomy 69530

Mastoidotomy 69635-69637
with Tympanoplasty 69635
Ossicular Chain Reconstruction 69636
and Synthetic Prosthesis 69636

Mastoids
Polytomography 76101-76102
X-ray 70120-70130

Mastopexy 19316

Mastotomy 19020

Maternity Care
See Abortion; Cesarean Delivery; Ectopic Pregnancy; Obstetrical Care

Maternity Care and Delivery 59612-59622, 59898

Maxilla
See Facial Bones; Mandible
Bone Graft 21210
CT Scan 70486-70488
Cyst
Excision 21048-21049
Excision 21030, 21032-21034
Fracture
Closed Treatment 21345, 21421
Open Treatment .21346-21348, 21422-21423
with Fixation 21345-21347
Osteotomy 21206
Reconstruction
with Implant 21245-21246, 21248-21249
Tumor
Excision 21048-21049

Maxillary Arteries
See Artery, Maxillary

Maxillary Sinus
See Sinus/Sinuses, Maxillary

Maxillary Torus Palatinus
Tumor Excision 21032

Maxillectomy 31225-31230

Maxillofacial Fixation
Application
Halo Type Appliance 21100

Maxillofacial Impressions
Auricular Prosthesis 21086
Definitive Obturator Prosthesis 21080
Facial Prosthesis 21088
Interim Obturator Prosthesis 21079
Mandibular Resection Prosthesis 21081
Nasal Prosthesis 21087
Oral Surgical Splint 21085
Orbital Prosthesis 21077
Palatal Augmentation Prosthesis 21082
Palatal Lift Prosthesis 21083
Speech Aid Prosthesis 21084
Surgical Obturator Prosthesis 21076

Maxillofacial Procedures
Unlisted Services and Procedures 21299

Maxillofacial Prosthetics 21076-21089
Unlisted Services and Procedures 21089

Maydl Operation 45563, 50810
See Colostomy

Mayo Hernia Repair
See Hernia, Repair, Umbilicus

Mayo Procedure 28292

Maze Procedure
Endoscopic 33265-33266
Open 33254-33256

McBride Procedure 28292

McBurney Operation
See Hernia, Repair, Inguinal

McCannel Procedure 66682

McKissock Surgery
See Breast, Reduction

McVay Operation
See Hernia, Repair, Inguinal

Measles Uncomplicated
See Rubeola

Measles Vaccine
See Vaccines

Measles, German
See Rubella

Meat Fibers
Feces 89160

Meatoplasty 69310

Meatotomy 53020-53025
Cystourethroscopy 52281
Infant 53025
Prostate
Laser Coagulation 52647
Laser Vaporization 52648
Transurethral Electrosurgical Resection
Prostate 52601
Ureter 52290
Ureteral
Cystourethroscopy 52290-52305

Meckel's Diverticulum
Excision 44800
Unlisted Services and Procedures 44899

Median Nerve
Decompression 64721
Neuroplasty 64721
Release 64721
Repair/Suture
Motor Thenar 64835
Transposition 64721

Median Nerve Compression
See Carpal Tunnel Syndrome

Mediastinal Cyst
See Cyst, Mediastinal; Mediastinum, Cyst

Mediastinoscopy 39400

Mediastinotomy
Cervical Approach 39000
Transthoracic Approach 39010

Mediastinum
See Chest; Thorax
Cyst
Excision 32662, 39200
Endoscopy
Biopsy 39400
Exploration 39400
Exploration 39000-39010
Incision and Drainage 39000-39010
Needle Biopsy 32405
Removal
Foreign Body 39000-39010
Tumor
Excision 32662, 39220
Unlisted Procedures 39499

Medical Disability Evaluation Services 99455-99456

Medical Genetics 96040
Genetic Counseling 96040

Medical Team Conference 99366-99368

Medical Testimony 99075

Medication Therapy Management
Pharmacist Provided 99605-99607

Medicine, Preventive
See Preventive Medicine

Medicine, Pulmonary
See Pulmonology

Medulla
Tractotomy 61470

Medullary Tract
Incision 61470
Section 61470

Meibomian Cyst
See Chalazion

Membrane Oxygenation, Extracorporeal
See Extracorporeal Membrane Oxygenation

Membrane, Mucous
See Mucosa

Membrane, Tympanic
See Ear, Drum

Meninges
Tumor
  Excision 61512, 61519

Meningioma
Excision 61512, 61519
Tumor
  Excision 61512, 61519

Meningitis, Lymphocytic Benign
See Lymphocytic Choriomeningitis

Meningocele Repair 63700-63702

Meningococcal
See Vaccines

Meningococcal Vaccine
See Vaccines

Meningococcus
See Neisseria Meningitidis

Meningomyelocele
See Myelomeningocele

Meniscectomy
Knee Joint 27332-27333
Temporomandibular Joint 21060

Meniscus
Knee
  Excision 27332-27333
  Repair 27403
  Transplantation 29868

Mental Nerve
Avulsion 64736
Incision 64736
Transection 64736

Meprobamate 83805

Mercury 83015, 83825

Mesencephalic Tract
Incision 61480
Section 61480

Mesencephalon
Tractotomy 61480

Mesenteric Arteries
See Artery, Mesenteric

Mesentery
Lesion
  Excision 44820
Repair 44850
Suture 44850
Unlisted Services and Procedures 44899

Mesh
Implantation
  Hernia 49568, 49652-49657
Insertion
  Pelvic Floor 57267
Removal
  Abdominal Infected 11008

Metabisulfite Test
See Red Blood Cell (RBC), Sickling

Metabolite 82520

Metacarpal
Amputation 26910
Craterization 26230
Cyst
  Excision 26200-26205
Diaphysectomy 26230
Excision 26230
  Radical
    for Tumor 26250-26255
Fracture
  Closed Treatment 26605
    with Fixation 26607
  Open Treatment 26615
  Percutaneous Fixation 26608
  with Manipulation 26605-26607
  without Manipulation 26600
Ostectomy
  Radical
    for Tumor 26250-26255
Repair
  Lengthening 26568
  Nonunion 26546
  Osteotomy 26565
Saucerization 26230
Tumor
  Excision 26200-26205

Metacarpophalangeal Joint
Arthrodesis 26850-26852
Arthroplasty 26530-26531
Arthroscopy
  Diagnostic 29900
  Surgical 29901-29902
Arthrotomy 26075
Biopsy
  Synovium 26105
Capsule
  Excision 26520
  Incision 26520
Capsulodesis 26516-26518
Dislocation
  Closed Treatment 26700
  Open Treatment 26715
  Percutaneous Fixation 26705-26706
  with Manipulation 26340
Exploration 26075
Fracture
  Closed Treatment 26740
  Open Treatment 26746
  with Manipulation 26742
Fusion 26516-26518, 26850-26852
Removal of Foreign Body 26075
Repair
  Collateral Ligament 26540-26542
Synovectomy 26135

Metadrenaline
See Metanephrines

Metals, Heavy
See Heavy Metal

Metamfetamine
See Methamphetamine

Metanephrines 83835

Metatarsal
See Foot
Amputation 28810
Condyle
  Excision 28288
Craterization 28122
Cyst
  Excision 28104-28107
Diaphysectomy 28122
Excision 28110-28114, 28122, 28140
Fracture
  Closed Treatment
    with Manipulation 28475-28476
    without Manipulation 28470
  Open Treatment 28485
  Percutaneous Fixation 28476
Free Osteocutaneous Flap with Microvascular Anastomosis 20972
Repair 28322
  Lengthening 28306-28307
  Osteotomy 28306-28309
Saucerization 28122
Tumor
  Excision 28104-28107, 28173

Metatarsectomy 28140

Metatarsophalangeal Joint
Arthrotomy 28022, 28052
Cheilectomy 28289
Dislocation 28630-28635, 28645
  Open Treatment 28645
  Percutaneous Fixation 28636
Exploration 28022
Great Toe
  Arthrodesis 28750
  Fusion 28750
Removal
  of Foreign Body 28022
  of Loose Body 28022
Repair
  Hallux Rigidus 28289
Synovial
  Biopsy 28052
  Excision 28072
Toe 28270

Methadone 83840

Methaemoglobin
See Methemoglobin

Methamphetamine
Blood or Urine 82145

Methanol 84600

Methbipyranone
See Metyrapone

Methemalbumin 83857

Methemoglobin 83045-83050

Methenamine Silver Stain 88312

Methopyrapone
See Metyrapone

Methoxyhydroxymandelic Acid
See Vanillylmandelic Acid

Methsuximide 83858

Methyl Alcohol
See Methanol

Methylamphetamine
See Methamphetamine

Methylene Bichloride
See Dichloromethane

Methylfluorprednisolone
See Dexamethasone

Methylmorphine
See Codeine

Metroplasty
See Hysteroplasty

Metyrapone 80436

MIC
See Minimum Inhibitory Concentration

Micro-Ophthalmia
Orbit Reconstruction 21256

Microalbumin
Urine 82043-82044

Microbiology 87001-87999

Microdissection 88380-88381

Microfluorometries, Flow
See Flow Cytometry

Microglobulin, Beta 2
Blood 82232
Urine 82232

Micrographic Surgery
Mohs Technique 17311-17315

Micrographic Surgery, Mohs
See Mohs Micrographic Surgery

Micropigmentation
Correction 11920-11922

Microscope, Surgical
See Operating Microscope

Microscopic Evaluation
Hair 96902

Microscopies, Electron
See Electron Microscopy

Microscopy
Ear Exam 92504

Microsomal Antibody 86376

Microsomia, Hemifacial
See Hemifacial Microsomia

Microsurgery
Operating Microscope 69990

Microvascular Anastomosis
Bone Graft
  Fibula 20955
  Other 20962
Fascial Flap, Free 15758
Muscle Flap, Free 15756
Osteocutaneous Flap with 20969-20973
Skin Flap, Free 15757

Microvite A
See Vitamin, A

Microwave Therapy 97024
See Physical Medicine/Therapy/Occupational Therapy

Midbrain
See Brain; Brainstem; Mesencephalon; Skull Base Surgery

Midcarpal Medioccipital Joint
Arthrotomy 25040

Middle Cerebral Artery Velocimetry 76821

Middle Ear
See Ear, Middle

Midface
Reconstruction
  Forehead Advancement 21159-21160
  with Bone Graft 21145-21160, 21188
  without Bone Graft 21141-21143

Migration Inhibitory Factor (MIF) 86378

Mile Operation
See Colectomy, Total, with Proctectomy

Milia, Multiple
Removal 10040

Miller Procedure 28737

Miller-Abbott Intubation .44500, 74340

Minerva Cast 29035
Removal 29710

Minimum Inhibitory Concentration 87186

Minimum Lethal Concentration 87187

Minnesota Multiphasic Personality Inventory
See MMPI

Miscarriage
Incomplete Abortion 59812
Missed Abortion
  First Trimester 59820
  Second Trimester 59821
Septic Abortion 59830

Missed Abortion
See Abortion

Mitchell Procedure 28296

Mitogen Blastogenesis 86353

Mitral Valve
Incision 33420-33422
Repair 33420-33427
  Incision 33420-33422
Replacement 33430

Mitrofanoff Operation 50845
See Appendico-Vesicostomy

Miyagawanella
See Chlamydia

MLC
See Lymphocyte, Culture

MMPI 96101-96103
Computer-Assisted 96103

MMR Shots 90707
See Vaccines

Mobilization
Splenic Flexure 44139
  Laparoscopic 44213
Stapes 69650

Moderate Sedation
See Sedation

Modified Radical Mastectomy
See Mastectomy, Modified Radical

Mohs Micrographic Surgery 17311-17315

Molar Pregnancy
See Hydatidiform Mole

Mold
Culture 87107

Mole, Carneous
See Abortion

Mole, Hydatid
See Hydatidiform Mole

Molecular Cytogenetics ..88271-88275
Interpretation and Report 88291

Molecular Diagnostics ...83890-83914
Amplification 83898-83901, 83908
Cell Lysis 83907
Dot/Slot Production 83893
Enzymatic Digestion 83892
Extraction 83890-83891
Interpretation 83912
Molecular Isolation (Extraction) 83890
Mutation Identification 83904-83906
  Enzymatic Ligation 83914
Mutation Scanning 83903
Nucleic Acid Amplification ..83900-83901, 83908
Nucleic Acid Extraction 83890-83891, 83907
Nucleic Acid Probe 83896
Nucleic Acid Transfer 83897
Polymerase Reaction Chain 83898

Excision
  Sphenoid Sinus 31288
Lid Margin
  Correction of Trichiasis 67835
  Nasal Test 95065
  Ophthalmic Test 95060
Rectum
  Proctoplasty for Prolapse 45505

Mucus Cyst
See Mucous Cyst

MUGA (Multiple Gated Acquisition) 78472-78478, 78483

Muller Procedure
See Sleep Study

Multifetal Pregnancy Reduction 59866

Multiple Sleep Latency Testing (MSLT) 95805

Multiple Valve Procedures
See Valvuloplasty

Mumford Operation
See Claviculectomy, Partial

Mumford Procedure 29824

Mumps
Antibody 86735
Immunization 90704, 90707, 90710
Vaccine 90704
  MMR 90707
  MMRV 90710

Muramidase 85549

Murine Typhus 86000

Muscle
See Specific Muscle
Abdomen
  See Abdominal Wall
Biopsy 20200-20206
Debridement
  Infected 11004-11006
  Nonviable 27057
Heart
  See Myocardium
Neck
  See Neck Muscle
Removal
  Foreign Body 20520-20525
Repair
  Extraocular 67346
  Forearm 25260-25274
  Wrist 25260-25274
Revision
  Arm, Upper 24330-24331
Transfer
  Arm, Upper 24301, 24320
  Elbow 24301
  Femur 27110
  Hip 27100-27105, 27111
  Shoulder 23395-23397, 24301, 24320

Muscle Compartment Syndrome
Detection 20950

Muscle Denervation
See Denervation

Muscle Division
Scalenus Anticus 21700-21705
Sternocleidomastoid 21720-21725

Muscle Flaps 15731-15738
Free 15756

Muscle Grafts 15841-15845

Muscle Testing
Dynamometry, Eye 92260
Extraocular Multiple Muscles 92265
Manual 95831-95834

Muscle, Oculomotor
See Eye Muscles

Muscles
Repair
  Extraocular 65290, 67346

Musculo-Skeletal System
See Musculoskeletal System

Musculoplasty
See Muscle, Repair

Musculoskeletal System
Computer-Assisted Surgical Navigation 0054T-0055T, 20985
Unlisted Services and Procedures 20999, 24999, 25999, 26989, 27299, 27599, 27899
Unlisted Services and Procedures, Head ...21499

Musculotendinous (Rotator) Cuff
Repair 23410-23412

Mustard Procedure
See Repair, Great Arteries; Revision

Myasthenia Gravis
Tensilon Test.........................95857

Myasthenic, Gravis
See Myasthenia Gravis

Mycobacteria
Culture 87116
  Identification 87118
Detection 87550-87562
Sensitivity Studies 87190

Mycoplasma
Antibody 86738
Culture 87109
Detection 87580-87582

Mycota
See Fungus

Myectomy, Anorectal
See Myomectomy, Anorectal

Myelencephalon
See Medulla

Myelin Basic Protein
Cerebrospinal Fluid 83873

Myelography
Brain 70010
Spine
  Cervical 72240
  Lumbosacral 72265
  Thoracic 72255
  Total 72270

Myelomeningocele
Repair 63704-63706

Myeloperoxidase (MPO) 83876

Myelotomy 63170

Myocardial
Perfusion Imaging ...78460-78465, 78478-78480
  See Nuclear Medicine
Positron Emission Tomography (PET) 78459

Myocardial Imaging 78466-78469
Positron Emission Tomography
  Perfusion Study 78491-78492
Repair
  Postinfarction 33542

Myocutaneous Flaps 15731-15738, 15756

Myofascial Pain Dysfunction Syndrome
See Temporomandibular Joint (TMJ)

Myofibroma
See Leiomyomata

Myoglobin 83874

Myomectomy
Anorectal 45108
Uterus 58140-58146, 58545-58546

Myoplasty
See Muscle, Repair

Myotomy
Esophagus 43030
Hyoid 21685

Myringoplasty 69620

Myringostomy
See Myringotomy

Myringotomy 69420-69421

Myxoid Cyst
See Ganglion

N

N. Meningitidis
See Neisseria Meningitidis

Naffziger Operation
See Decompression, Orbit; Section

Nagel Test
See Color Vision Examination

Retroperitoneal Mass ... 49180
Salivary Gland ... 42400
Spinal Cord ... 62269
Testis ... 54500
Thyroid Gland ... 60100
Transbronchial ... 31629, 31633

Needle Localization
Breast
- Placement ... 19290-19291
- with Lesion Excision ... 19125-19126

Magnetic Resonance Guidance ... 77021

Needle Manometer Technique ... 20950

Needle Wire
Introduction
- Trachea ... 31730

Placement
- Breast ... 19290-19291

Neer Procedure ... 23470

Neisseria Gonorrheae ... 87590-87592, 87850

Neisseria Meningitidis
Antibody ... 86741

Neobladder
Construction ... 51596

Neonatal Critical Care
See Newborn Care
Initial ... 99468
Subsequent ... 99469

Neoplasm
Cancer Photoradiation Therapy
- *See* Photochemotherapy

Cardiac
- *See* Heart, Tumor

Colon
- *See* Colon, Tumor

Esophageal
- *See* Tumor, Esophagus

Spinal Cord
- *See* Spinal Cord, Neoplasm

Unspecified Nature of Brain
- *See* Brain, Tumor

Neoplastic Growth
See Tumor

Nephelometry ... 83883

Nephrectomy
Donor ... 50300-50320, 50547
Laparoscopic ... 50545-50548
Partial ... 50240
- Laparoscopic ... 50543

Recipient ... 50340
with Ureters ... 50220-50236, 50546, 50548

Nephrolith
See Calculus, Removal, Kidney

Nephrolithotomy ... 50060-50075

Nephropexy ... 50400-50405

Nephroplasty
See Kidney, Repair

Nephropyeloplasty
See Pyeloplasty

Nephrorrhaphy ... 50500

Nephroscopy
See Endoscopy, Kidney

Nephrostogram ... 50394

Nephrostolithotomy
Percutaneous ... 50080-50081

Nephrostomy ... 50040
Change Tube ... 50398
Endoscopic ... 50562-50570
Percutaneous ... 52334
with Drainage ... 50040
X-ray with Contrast
- Guide Dilation ... 74485

Nephrostomy Tract
Establishment ... 50395

Nephrotomogram
See Nephrotomography

Nephrotomography ... 74415

Nephrotomy ... 50040-50045
with Exploration ... 50045

Nerve
Cranial
- *See* Cranial Nerve

Facial
- *See* Facial Nerve

Intercostal
- *See* Intercostal Nerve

Lingual
- *See* Lingual Nerve

Median
- *See* Median Nerve

Obturator
- *See* Obturator Nerve

Peripheral
- *See* Peripheral Nerve

Phrenic
- *See* Phrenic Nerve

Sciatic
- *See* Sciatic Nerve

Spinal
- *See* Spinal Nerve

Tibial
- *See* Tibial Nerve

Ulnar
- *See* Ulnar Nerve

Vestibular
- *See* Vestibular Nerve

Nerve Conduction
Motor Nerve ... 95900-95903
Sensory Nerve or Mixed ... 95904

Nerve Root
See Cauda Equina; Spinal Cord
Decompression ... 22856, 63020-63048, 63055-63103
Incision ... 63185-63190
Section ... 63185-63190

Nerve Stimulation, Transcutaneous
See Application, Neurostimulation

Nerve Teasing ... 88362

Nerve II, Cranial
See Optic Nerve

Nerve V, Cranial
See Trigeminal Nerve

Nerve VII, Cranial
See Facial Nerve

Nerve X, Cranial
See Vagus Nerve

Nerve XI, Cranial
See Accessory Nerve

Nerve XII, Cranial
See Hypoglossal Nerve

Nerves
Anastomosis
- Facial to Hypoglossal ... 64868
- Facial to Phrenic ... 64870
- Facial to Spinal Accessory ... 64866

Avulsion ... 64732-64772
Biopsy ... 64795
Decompression ... 64702-64727
Destruction ... 64600-64681
- Laryngeal, Recurrent ... 31595

Foot
- Excision ... 28055
- Incision ... 28035

Graft ... 64885-64907
Implantation
- Electrode ... 64553-64581
- to Bone ... 64787
- to Muscle ... 64787

Incision ... 43640-43641, 64732-64772
Injection
- Anesthetic ... 01991-01992, 64400-64530
- Neurolytic Agent ... 64600-64681

Insertion
- Electrode ... 64553-64581

Lesion
- Excision ... 64774-64792

Neurofibroma
- Excision ... 64788-64792

Neurolemmoma
- Excision ... 64788-64792

Neurolytic
- Internal ... 64727

Neuroma
- Destruction ... 64632
- Excision ... 64774-64786
- Injection ... 64455

Neuroplasty ... 64702-64721
Removal
- Electrode ... 64585

Repair
- Graft ... 64885-64911
- Microdissection ... 69990
- Suture ... 64831-64876

Spinal Accessory
- Incision ... 63191
- Section ... 63191

Suture ... 64831-64876

Hospital Observation Services 99217-99220
Initial Office Visit 99201-99205
See Evaluation and Management; Office and Other Outpatient
Inpatient Consultations 99251-99255
Office and/or Other Outpatient Consultations 99241-99245

Newborn Care 99460-99465, 99502
Attendance at Delivery 99464
Birthing Room 99460
Blood Transfusion 36450
See Neonatal Intensive Care
Circumcision
Clamp or Other Device 54150
Surgical Excision 54160
History and Examination 99460, 99463
Laryngoscopy 31520
Normal 99460-99463
Prepuce Slitting 54000
Preventive
Office 99432
Resuscitation 99465
Standby for Cesarean Delivery 99360
Subsequent Hospital Care 99462
Umbilical Artery Catheterization 36660

Nickel 83885

Nicolas-Durand-Favre Disease
See Lymphogranuloma Venereum

Nicotine 83887

Nidation
See Implantation

Nipples
See Breast
Inverted 19355
Reconstruction 19350

Nissen Operation
See Fundoplasty, Esophagogastric

Nissen Procedure 43324
Laparoscopic 43280

Nitrate Reduction Test
See Urinalysis

Nitric Oxide 95012

Nitroblue Tetrazolium Dye Test 86384

Nitrogen, Blood Urea
See Blood Urea Nitrogen

NMR Imaging
See Magnetic Resonance Imaging (MRI)

NMR Spectroscopies
See Magnetic Resonance Spectroscopy

No Man's Land
Tendon Repair 26356-26358

Noble Procedure
See Repair; Suture

Nocardia
Antibody 86744

Nocturnal Penile Rigidity Test 54250

Nocturnal Penile Tumescence Test 54250

Node Dissection, Lymph
See Dissection, Lymph Nodes

Node, Lymph
See Lymph Nodes

Nodes
See Lymph Nodes

Non-Invasive Vascular Imaging
See Vascular Studies

Non-Office Medical Services ..99056
Emergency Care 99060

Non-Stress Test, Fetal 59025

Nonunion Repair
Femur
with Graft 27472
without Graft 27470
Metatarsal 28322
Tarsal Joint 28320

Noradrenalin
Blood 82383-82384
Urine 82384

Norchlorimipramine
See Imipramine

Norepinephrine
See Catecholamines
Blood 82383-82384
Urine 82384

Nortriptyline
Assay 80182

Norwood Procedure 33611-33612, 33619
See Repair, Heart, Ventricle; Revision

Nose
Abscess
Incision and Drainage 30000-30020
Actinotherapy
Intranasal 0168T
Artery
Incision 30915-30920
Biopsy
Intranasal 30100
Dermoid Cyst
Excision
Complex 30125
Simple 30124
Displacement Therapy 30210
Endoscopy
Diagnostic 31231-31235
Surgical 31237-31294
Excision
Rhinectomy 30150-30160
Fracture
Closed Treatment 21345
Open Treatment 21325-21336, 21338-21339, 21346-21347
Percutaneous Treatment 21340
with Fixation 21330, 21340, 21345-21347
Hematoma
Incision and Drainage 30000-30020
Hemorrhage
Cauterization 30901-30906
Insertion
Septal Prosthesis 30220
Intranasal
Actinotherapy 0168T
Lesion
External Approach 30118
Internal Approach 30117
Phototherapy 0168T
Lysis of Adhesions 30560
Phototherapy
Intranasal 0168T
Polyp
Excision
Extensive 30115
Simple 30110
Reconstruction
Cleft Lip/Cleft Palate 30460-30462
Dermatoplasty 30620
Primary 30400, 30420
Secondary 30430-30450
Septum 30520
Removal
Foreign Body 30300
Anesthesia 30310
Lateral Rhinotomy 30320
Repair
Adhesions 30560
Cleft Lip 40700-40761
Fistula 30580-30600, 42260
Rhinophyma 30120
Septum 30540-30545, 30630
Synechia 30560
Vestibular Stenosis 30465
Skin
Excision 30120
Surgical Planing 30120
Submucous Resection Turbinate
Excision 30140
Turbinate
Excision 30130-30140
Fracture 30930
Injection 30200
Turbinate Mucosa
Cauterization 30801-30802
Unlisted Services and Procedures 30999

Nose Bleed 30901-30906
See Hemorrhage, Nasal

NTD 86384
See Nitroblue Tetrazolium Dye Test

Nuclear Antigen
Antibody 86235

Nuclear Imaging
See Nuclear Medicine

Nuclear Magnetic Resonance Imaging
See Magnetic Resonance Imaging (MRI)

Nuclear Magnetic Resonance Spectroscopy

Nuclear Medicine

Nucleases, DNA

Nucleic Acid Probe 83896

Gardnerella Vaginalis .87512
Hepatitis B Virus .87517
Hepatitis C .87522
Hepatitis G .87527
Herpes Simplex Virus .87530
Herpes Virus-6 .87533
HIV-1 .87536
HIV-2 .87539
Legionella Pneumophila .87542
Mycobacteria Avium-Intracellulare .87562
Mycobacteria Species .87552
Mycobacteria Tuberculosis .87557
Mycoplasma Pneumoniae .87582
Neisseria Gonorrheae .87592
Not Otherwise Specified .87799
Papillomavirus, Human .87622
Streptococcus, Group A .87652

Nucleolysis, Intervertebral Disc
See Chemonucleolysis

Nucleotidase .83915

Nursemaid Elbow .24640

Nursing Facility Discharge Services
See Discharge Services, Nursing Facility

Nursing Facility Services
Annual Assessment .99318
Care Plan Oversight Services .99379-99380
Comprehensive Assessments
Discharge Services .99315-99316, 1110F-1111F
Initial Care .99304-99306
Subsequent Care .99307-99310

Nuss Procedure
with Thoracoscopy .21743
without Thoracoscopy .21742

Nutrition Therapy
Group .97804
Home Infusion .99601-99602
Initial Assessment .97802
Reassessment .97803

Nystagmus Tests
See Vestibular Function Tests
Optokinetic .92534, 92544
Positional .92532, 92542
Spontaneous .92531, 92541

O

O_2 Saturation
See Oxygen Saturation

Ober-Yount Procedure .27025
See Fasciotomy, Hip

Obliteration
Mastoid .69670
Vagina
Total .57110-57112
Vault .57120

Oblongata, Medulla
See Medulla

Observation .99234-99236
See Evaluation and Management; Hospital Services

Obstetrical Care
Abortion
Induced
by Amniocentesis Injection .59850-59852
See Abortion; Cesarean Delivery; Ectopic Pregnancy
by Dilation and Curettage .59840
by Dilation and Evaluation .59841
Missed
First Trimester .59820
Second Trimester .59821
Spontaneous .59812
Therapeutic .59840-59852
Antepartum Care .59425-59426
Cesarean Delivery .59618-59622
Only .59514
Postpartum Care .59515
Routine .59510
with Hysterectomy .59525
Curettage
Hydatidiform Mole .59870
Evacuation
Hydatidiform Mole .59870
External Cephalic Version .59412
Miscarriage
Surgical Completion .59812-59821
Placenta Delivery .59414
Postpartum Care .59430, 59514
Septic Abortion .59830
Total (Global) .59400, 59610, 59618
Unlisted Services and Procedures .59898-59899
Vaginal
after Cesarean .59610-59614
Vaginal Delivery .59409-59410
Delivery after Cesarean .59610-59614

Obstruction
See Occlusion

Obstruction Clearance
Venous Access Device .36595-36596

Obstruction Colon
See Colon, Obstruction

Obturator Nerve
Avulsion .64763-64766
Incision .64763-64766
Transection .64763-64766

Obturator Prosthesis .21076
Definitive .21080
Insertion
Larynx .31527
Interim .21079

Occipital Nerve, Greater
Avulsion .64744
Incision .64744
Injection
Anesthetic .64405
Transection .64744

Occlusion
Extracranial
Intracranial .61623
Fallopian Tube
Oviduct .58565, 58615
Penis
Vein .37790
Umbilical Cord .59072

Occlusive Disease of Artery
See Repair, Artery; Revision

Occult Blood .82270-82272
by Hemoglobin Immunoassay .82274

Occupational Therapy
Evaluation .97003-97004

Ocular Implant
See Orbital Implant
Insertion
in Scleral Shell .65130
Muscles, Attached .65140
Muscles, Not Attached .65135
Modification .65125
Reinsertion .65150
with Foreign Material .65155
Removal .65175

Ocular Muscle
See Eye Muscles

Ocular Orbit
See Orbit

Ocular Photoscreening .99174

Ocular Prostheses
See Prosthesis, Ocular

Oculomotor Muscle
See Eye Muscles

Oddi Sphincter
See Sphincter of Oddi

Odontoid Dislocation
Open Treatment/Reduction .22318
with Grafting .22319

Odontoid Fracture
Open Treatment/Reduction .22318
with Grafting .22319

Odontoid Process
Excision .22548

Oesophageal Neoplasm
See Tumor, Esophagus

Oesophageal Varices
See Esophageal Varices

Oesophagus
See Esophagus

Oestradiol
See Estradiol

Office and/or Other Outpatient Services
See History and Physical Consultation

Tonometry
Serial 92100
Ultrasound 76511-76529
Visual Acuity Screen 99172-99173
Visual Field Exam 92081-92083
Visual Function Screen 99172, 99174

Ophthalmoscopy 92225-92226
See Ophthalmology, Diagnostic

Opiates 83925

Optic Nerve
Decompression 67570
with Nasal/Sinus Endoscopy 31294
Head Evaluation 2027F

Optokinetic Nystagmus Test
See Nystagmus Tests, Optokinetic

Oral Lactose Tolerance Test 82951-82953
See Glucose, Tolerance Test

Oral Mucosa
See Mouth, Mucosa

Oral Surgical Splint 21085

Orbit
See Orbital Contents; Orbital Floor; Periorbital Region
Biopsy 61332
Exploration 67450
Fine Needle Aspiration or Orbital Contents 67415
Orbitotomy without Bone Flap 67400
CT Scan 70480-70482
Decompression 61330
Bone Removal 67414, 67445
Exploration 61332, 67400, 67450
Lesion
Excision 61333
Fracture
Closed Treatment
with Manipulation 21401
without Manipulation 21400
Open Treatment 21406-21408
Blowout Fracture 21385-21395
Incision and Drainage 67405, 67440
Injection
Retrobulbar 67500-67505
Tenon's Capsule 67515
Insertion
Implant 67550
Lesion
Excision 67412, 67420
Magnetic Resonance Imaging (MRI) 70540-70543
Removal
Decompression 67445
Exploration 61334
Foreign Body 61334, 67413, 67430
Implant 67560
Sella Turcica 70482
Unlisted Services and Procedures 67599
X-ray 70190-70200

Orbit Area
Reconstruction
Secondary 21275

Orbit Wall
Decompression
with Nasal/Sinus Endoscopy 31292-31293

Orbital Contents
Aspiration 67415

Orbital Floor
See Orbit; Periorbital Region
Fracture
Blow Out 21385-21395

Orbital Hypertelorism
Osteotomy
Periorbital 21260-21263

Orbital Implant
See Ocular Implant
Insertion 67550
Removal 67560

Orbital Prosthesis 21077

Orbital Rim and Forehead
Reconstruction 21172-21180

Orbital Rims
Reconstruction 21182-21184

Orbital Transplant 67560

Orbital Walls
Reconstruction 21182-21184

Orbitocraniofacial Reconstruction
Secondary 21275

Orbitotomy
with Bone Flap
for Exploration 67450
Lateral Approach 67420
with Drainage 67440
with Removal Foreign Body 67430
with Removal of Bone for Decompression 67445
with Removal Foreign Body 67413
with Removal of Bone for Decompression 67414
without Bone Flap
for Exploration 67400
with Drainage Only 67405
with Removal Lesion 67412

Orchidectomies
See Excision, Testis

Orchidopexy
See Orchiopexy

Orchidoplasty
See Repair, Testis

Orchiectomy
Laparoscopic 54690
Partial 54522
Radical
Abdominal Exploration 54535
Inguinal Approach 54530
Simple 54520

Orchiopexy
Abdominal Approach 54650
Inguinal Approach 54640
Intra-Abdominal Testis 54692

Orchioplasty
See Repair, Testis

Organ Grafting
See Transplantation

Organ or Disease-Oriented Panel
Electrolyte 80051
General Health Panel 80050
Hepatic Function Panel 80076
Hepatitis Panel 80074
Lipid Panel 80061
Metabolic
Basic 80047, 80048
Comprehensive 80053
Obstetric Panel 80055
Renal Function 80069

Organ System, Neurologic
See Nervous System

Organic Acids 83918-83921

Ormond Disease
See Retroperitoneal Fibrosis

Orogastric Tube
Placement 43752

Oropharynx
Biopsy 42800

Orthodontic Cephalogram 70350

Orthomyxoviridae
See Influenza Virus

Orthomyxovirus
See Influenza Virus

Orthopantogram 70355

Orthopedic Cast
See Cast

Orthopedic Surgery
Computer Assisted Navigation 20985-20987
Stereotaxis
Computer Assisted 20985-20987

Orthoptic Training 92065

Orthoroentgenogram 77073

Orthosis
See Orthotics

Orthotics
Check-Out 97762
Management and Training 97760

Os Calcis Fracture
See Calcaneus, Fracture

Osmolality
Blood 83930
Urine 83935

Osseous Survey 77074-77076

Osseous Tissue
See Bone

Ovariectomies
See Oophorectomy

Ovariolysis 58740

Ovary
Abscess
Incision and Drainage 58820-58822
Abdominal Approach 58822
Biopsy 58900
Cyst
Incision and Drainage 58800-58805
Excision 58662, 58720
Cyst 58925
Partial
Oophorectomy 58661, 58940
Ovarian Malignancy 58943
Peritoneal Malignancy 58943
Tubal Malignancy 58943
Wedge Resection 58920
Total 58940-58943
Laparoscopy 58660-58662, 58679
Lysis
Adhesions 58660, 58740
Radical Resection 58950-58952
Transposition 58825
Tumor
Resection 58950-58958
Unlisted Services and Procedures ..58679, 58999
Wedge Resection 58920

Oviduct
Anastomosis 58750
Chromotubation 58350
Ectopic Pregnancy 59120-59121
Excision 58700-58720
Fulguration
Laparoscopic 58670
Hysterosalpingography 74740
Laparoscopy 58679
Ligation 58600-58611
Lysis
Adhesions 58740
Occlusion 58615
Laparoscopic 58671
Repair 58752
Anastomosis 58750
Create Stoma 58770
Unlisted Services and Procedures ..58679, 58999
X-ray with Contrast 74740

Ovocyte
See Oocyte

Ovulation Tests 84830

Ovum Implantation
See Implantation

Ovum Transfer Surgery
See Gamete Intrafallopian Transfer

Oxalate 83945

Oxidase, Ceruloplasmin
See Ceruloplasmin

Oxidoreductase, Alcohol-Nad+
See Antidiuretic Hormone

Oximetry (Noninvasive)
See Pulmonology, Diagnostic
Blood O_2 Saturation
Ear or Pulse 94760-94762

Oxoisomerase
See Phosphohexose Isomerase

Oxosteroids
See Ketosteroids

Oxycodinone 80102-80103, 83925

Oxygen Saturation 82805-82810

Oxygenation, Extracorporeal Membrane
See Extracorporeal Membrane Oxygenation

Oxyproline
See Hydroxyproline

Oxytocin Stress Test, Fetal 59020

P

P & P
See Proconvertin

P B Antibodies
See Antibody, Heterophile

P-Acetamidophenol
See Acetaminophen

Pacemaker, Heart
See Cardiology; Defibrillator, Heart; Electrocardiography
Conversion 33214
Data Analysis 93288, 93293-93294
Electronic Analysis
Antitachycardia System 93724
Leads 93640-93641
Wearable Device 93288
Evaluation and Programming 93286
Dual Lead 93280
Multiple Lead 93281
Single Lead 93279
Insertion 33206-33208
Electrode 33210-33211, 33216-33217, 33224-33225
Pulse Generator Only 33212-33213
Removal 33233-33237
via Thoracotomy 33236-33237
Repair
Electrode 33218-33220
Replacement
Catheter 33210
Electrode 33210-33211
Insertion 33206-33208
Pulse Generator 33212-33213
Repositioning
Electrode 33215, 33226
Revise Pocket
Chest 33222
Telephonic Analysis 93293
Upgrade 33214

Pachymetry
Eye 76514

Packing
Nasal Hemorrhage 30901-30906

Pain Management
Epidural/Intrathecal 62350-62351, 62360-62362, 99601-99602
Intravenous Therapy .96365-96368, 96374-96379

Palate
Abscess
Incision and Drainage 42000
Biopsy 42100
Excision 42120, 42145
Fracture
Closed Treatment 21421
Open Treatment 21422-21423
Lesion
Destruction 42160
Excision 42104-42120
Prosthesis
Augmentation 21082
Impression 42280
Insertion 42281
Lift 21083
Reconstruction
Lengthening 42226-42227
Repair
Cleft Palate 42200-42225
Laceration 42180-42182
Vomer Flap 42235
Unlisted Services and Procedures 42299

Palate, Cleft
See Cleft Palate

Palatoplasty 42200-42225

Palatoschisis
See Cleft Palate

Palm
Bursa
Incision and Drainage 26025-26030
Fasciectomy 26121-26125
Fasciotomy 26040-26045
Tendon
Excision 26170
Tendon Sheath
Excision 26145
Incision and Drainage 26020

Palsy, Seventh Nerve
See Facial Nerve Paralysis

Pancreas
Anastomosis
with Intestines 48520-48540, 48548
Anesthesia 00794
Biopsy 48100
Needle Biopsy 48102

Paronychia
Incision and Drainage 10060-10061

Parotid Duct
Diversion 42507-42510
Reconstruction 42507-42510

Parotid Gland
Abscess
  Incision and Drainage 42300-42305
Calculi (Stone)
  Excision 42330, 42340
Excision
  Partial 42410-42415
  Total 42420-42426
Tumor
  Excision 42410-42426

Parotitides, Epidemic
See Mumps

Pars Abdominalis Aortae
See Aorta, Abdominal

Partial
Colectomy
  See Colectomy, Partial
Cystectomy
  See Cystectomy, Partial
Esophagectomy
  See Esophagectomy, Partial
Gastrectomy
  See Excision, Stomach, Partial
Glossectomy
  See Excision, Tongue, Partial
Hepatectomy
  See Excision, Liver, Partial
Mastectomy
  See Breast, Excision, Lesion
Nephrectomy
  See Excision, Kidney, Partial
Pancreatectomy
  See Pancreatectomy, Partial
Splenectomy
  See Splenectomy, Partial
Thromboplastin Time
  See Thromboplastin, Partial Time
Ureterectomy
  See Ureterectomy, Partial

Particle Agglutination 86403-86406

Parvovirus
Antibody 86747

Patch
Allergy Tests 95044
  See Allergy Tests

Patella
See Knee
Dislocation 27560-27566
Excision 27350
  with Reconstruction 27424
Fracture 27520-27524
Reconstruction 27437-27438
Repair
  Chondromalacia 27418
  Instability 27420-27424

Patella, Chondromalacia
See Chondromalacia Patella

Patellar Tendon Bearing (PTB) Cast 29435

Patellectomy
with Reconstruction 27424

Paternity Testing 86910-86911

Patey's Operation
See Mastectomy, Radical

Pathologic Dilatation
See Dilation

Pathology
Clinical
  Consultation 80500-80502
Surgical 88355
  Consultation 88321-88325
    Intraoperative 88329-88334
  Decalcification Procedure 88311
  Electron Microscopy 88348-88349
  Gross and Micro Exam
    Level II 88302
    Level III 88304
    Level IV 88305
    Level V 88307
    Level VI 88309
  Gross Exam
    Level I 88300
  Histochemistry 88318-88319
  Immunocytochemistry 88342
  Immunofluorescent Study 88346-88347
  Morphometry
    Nerve 88356
    Skeletal Muscle 88355
    Tumor 88358-88361
  Nerve Teasing 88362
  Special Stain 88312-88314
  Staining 88312-88314
  Tissue Hybridization 88365
  Unlisted Services and Procedures 88399, 89240

PBG
See Porphobilinogen

PCP
See Phencyclidine

PCR
See Polymerase Chain Reaction

Peans' Operation
See Amputation, Leg, Upper, at Hip; Radical Resection; Replantation

Pectoral Cavity
See Chest Cavity

Pectus Carinatum
Reconstructive Repair 21740-21742
  with Thoracoscopy 21743

Pectus Excavatum
Reconstructive Repair 21740-21742
  with Thoracoscopy 21743

Pediatric Critical Care 99471-99472

Pediatric Intensive Care 99478

Pedicle Fixation
Insertion 22842-22844

Pedicle Flap
Formation 15570-15576
Island 15740
Neurovascular 15750
Transfer 15650

PEEP
See Pressure Breathing, Positive

Pelvi-Ureteroplasty
See Pyeloplasty

Pelvic Adhesions
See Adhesions, Pelvic

Pelvic Exam 57410

Pelvic Exenteration 51597

Pelvic Fixation
Insertion 22848

Pelvic Lymphadenectomy 58210, 58958

Pelvimetry 74710

Pelviolithotomy 50130

Pelvis
See Hip
Abscess
  Incision and Drainage 26990, 45000
Angiography 72191
Biopsy 27040-27041
Bone
  Drainage 26992
Brace Application 20662
Bursa
  Incision and Drainage 26991
CT Scan 72191-72194
Cyst
  Aspiration 50390
  Injection 50390
Destruction
  Lesion 58662
Endoscopy
  Destruction of Lesion 58662
  Lysis of Adhesions 58660
  Oviduct Surgery 58670-58671
Exclusion
  Small Intestine 44700
Exenteration 45126, 58240
Fasciotomy
  Decompression 27027
    with Debridement 27057
Halo 20662
Hematoma
  Incision and Drainage 26990
Lysis
  Adhesions 58660
Magnetic Resonance Angiography 72198
Magnetic Resonance Imaging (MRI) 72195-72197
Removal
  Foreign Body 27086-27087

Performance Test

Perfusion

Perfusion Pump

Perfusion, Intracranial Arterial

Pericardectomies

Pericardial Cyst

Pericardial Sac

Pericardial Window

Pericardial Window Technic

Pericardiectomy

Pericardiocentesis 33010-33011
Ultrasound Guidance 76930

Pericardiostomy
Tube 33015

Pericardiotomy
Removal
Clot 33020
Foreign Body 33020

Pericardium
Cyst
Excision 32661, 33050
Excision 32659, 33030-33031
Incision
Removal
Clot 33020
Foreign Body 33020
with Tube 33015
Incision and Drainage 33025
Puncture Aspiration 33010-33011
Removal
Clot
Endoscopic 32658
Foreign Body
Endoscopic 32658
Tumor
Excision 32661, 33050

Peridural Anesthesia
See Anesthesia, Epidural

Peridural Injection
See Epidural, Injection

Perineal Prostatectomy
See Prostatectomy, Perineal

Perineoplasty 56810

Perineorrhaphy
Repair
Rectocele 57250

Perineum
Abscess
Incision and Drainage 56405
Colposcopy 99170
Debridement
Infected 11004, 11006
Removal
Prosthesis 53442
Repair 56810
X-ray with Contrast 74775

Perionychia
See Paronychia

Periorbital Region
Reconstruction
Osteotomy with Graft 21267-21268
Repair-Osteotomy 21260-21263

Peripheral Artery Disease (PAD) Rehabilitation 93668

Peripheral Nerve
Repair/Suture
Major 64856, 64859

Periprosthetic Capsulectomy
Breast 19371

Peristaltic Pumps
See Infusion Pump

Peritoneal Dialysis ..90945-90947, 4055F
Kt/V Level 3082F-3084F

Peritoneal Free Air
See Pneumoperitoneum

Peritoneal Lavage 49080

Peritoneocentesis 49080-49081

Peritoneoscopy
See Peritoneum, Endoscopy

Peritoneum
Abscess
Incision and Drainage 49020
Percutaneous 49021
Chemotherapy Administration 96445
See Chemotherapy
Endoscopy
Biopsy 47561
Diagnostic 49320
Drainage
Lymphocele 49323
X-ray 47560
Exchange
Drainage Catheter 49423
Injection
Contrast
via Catheter 49424
Ligation
Shunt 49428
Removal
Cannula/Catheter 49422
Foreign Body 49402
Shunt 49429
Tumor
Resection 58950-58958
Unlisted Services and Procedures 49999
Venous Shunt
Injection 49427
X-ray 74190

Persistent Truncus Arteriosus
See Truncus Arteriosus

Persistent, Omphalomesenteric Duct
See Diverticulum, Meckel's

Personal Care
See Self Care

Personality Test 96101-96103
Computer-Assisted 96103

Pessary
Insertion 57160

Pesticides
Chlorinated Hydrocarbons 82441

PET
See Positron Emission Tomography

Petrous Temporal
Excision
Apex 69530

Peyronie Disease
Injection 54200
Surgical Exposure 54205
with Graft 54110-54112

pH
See Blood
Exhaled Breath Condensate 0140T
Other Fluid 83986
Urine 83986

Phacoemulsification
Removal
Extracapsular Cataract 66982, 66984
Secondary Membranous Cataract 66850

Phagocytosis
White Blood Cells 86344

Phalangectomy
Toe 28150
Partial 28160

Phalanges (Hand)
See Finger, Bone

Phalanx, Finger
Craterization 26235-26236
Cyst
Excision 26210-26215
Diaphysectomy 26235-26236
Excision 26235-26236
Radical
for Tumor 26260-26262
Fracture
Articular
Closed Treatment 26740
Open Treatment 26746
with Manipulation 26742
Distal 26755-26756
Closed Treatment 26750
Open Treatment 26765
Percutaneous Fixation 26756
Open Treatment 26735
Distal 26765
Shaft 26720-26727
Open Treatment 26735
Incision and Drainage 26034
Ostectomy
Radical
for Tumor 26260-26262
Repair
Lengthening 26568
Nonunion 26546
Osteotomy 26567
Saucerization 26235-26236
Thumb
Fracture
Shaft 26720-26727
Tumor
Excision 26210-26215

Phalanx, Great Toe
See Phalanx, Toe
Fracture 28490
Open Treatment 28505
with Manipulation 28495-28496

Photopheresis
- Extracorporeal ... 36522
- Photopheresis
  - *See* Actinotherapy; Photochemotherapy

Photoradiation Therapies
- *See* Actinotherapy

Photoscreen, Ocular ... 99174

Photosensitivity Testing ... 95056
- *See* Allergy Tests

Phototherapies
- *See* Actinotherapy

Phototherapy, Ultraviolet
- *See* Actinotherapy

Phrenic Nerve
- Anastomosis
  - to Facial Nerve ... 64870
- Avulsion ... 64746
- Incision ... 64746
- Injection
  - Anesthetic ... 64410
- Transection ... 64746

Physical Medicine/Therapy/Occupational Therapy
- *See* Neurology, Diagnostic
- Activities of Daily Living ... 97535, 99509
- Aquatic Therapy
  - with Exercises ... 97113
- Athletic Training
  - Evaluation ... 97005
  - Re-Evaluation ... 97006
- Check-Out
  - Orthotic/Prosthetic ... 97762
- Cognitive Skills Development ... 97532
- Community/Work Reintegration ... 97537
- Evaluation ... 97001-97002
- Kinetic Therapy ... 97530
- Manual Therapy ... 97140
- Modalities
  - Contrast Baths ... 97034
  - Diathermy Treatment ... 97024
  - Electric Stimulation
    - Attended, Manual ... 97032
    - Unattended ... 97014
  - Hot or Cold Pack ... 97010
  - Hydrotherapy (Hubbard Tank) ... 97036
  - Infrared Light Treatment ... 97026
  - Iontophoresis ... 97033
  - Microwave Therapy ... 97024
  - Paraffin Bath ... 97018
  - Traction ... 97012
  - Ultrasound ... 97035
  - Ultraviolet Light ... 97028
  - Unlisted Services and Procedures ... 97039
  - Vasopneumatic Device ... 97016
  - Whirlpool Therapy ... 97022
- Orthotics Training ... 97760
- Osteopathic Manipulation ... 98925-98929
- Procedures
  - Aquatic Therapy ... 97113
  - Direct ... 97032-97039
  - Gait Training ... 97116
  - Group Therapeutic ... 97150
  - Massage Therapy ... 97124
  - Neuromuscular Reeducation ... 97112
  - Physical Performance Test ... 97750
  - Supervised ... 97010-97028
  - Therapeutic Exercises ... 97110
  - Traction Therapy ... 97140
  - Work Hardening ... 97545-97546
- Prosthetic Training ... 97761
- Sensory Integration ... 97533
- Therapeutic Activities ... 97530
- Unlisted Services and Procedures ... 97139, 97799
- Wheelchair Management ... 97542
- Work Reintegration ... 97537

Physical Therapy
- *See* Physical Medicine/Therapy/Occupational Therapy

Physician Services
- Care Plan Oversight Services ... 99339-99340, 99374-99380
  - Domiciliary Facility ... 99339-99340
  - Home Health Agency Care ... 99374
  - Home or Rest Home Care ... 99339-99340
  - Hospice ... 99377-99378
  - Nursing Facility ... 99379-99380
- Case Management Services ... 99366-99368
- Direction, Advanced Life Support ... 99288
- Online ... 99444
- Prolonged
  - with Direct Patient Contact ... 99354-99357
    - Outpatient/Office ... 99354-99355
  - with Direct Patient Services
    - Inpatient ... 99356-99357
  - without Direct Patient Contact ... 99358-99359
- Standby ... 99360
- Supervision, Care Plan Oversight
  - Services ... 99339-99340, 99374-99380
- Team Conference ... 99367
  - Telephone ... 99441-99443

Piercing of Ear Lobe ... 69090

Piles
- *See* Hemorrhoids

Pilonidal Cyst
- Excision ... 11770-11772
- Incision and Drainage ... 10080-10081

Pin
- *See* Wire
- Insertion/Removal
  - Skeletal Traction ... 20650
- Prophylactic Treatment
  - Femur ... 27187
  - Humerus ... 24498
  - Shoulder ... 23490-23491

Pinch Graft ... 15050

Pinna
- *See* Ear, External

Pinworms
- Examination ... 87172

Pirogoff Procedure ... 27888

Pituitary Epidermoid Tumor
- *See* Craniopharyngioma

Pituitary Gland
- Excision ... 61546-61548
- Tumor
  - Excision ... 61546-61548, 62165

Pituitary Growth Hormone
- *See* Growth Hormone

Pituitary Lactogenic Hormone
- *See* Prolactin

Pituitectomy
- *See* Excision, Pituitary Gland

PKU
- *See* Phenylalanine

Placement
- Adjustable Gastric Restrictive Device ... 43770
- Broncheal Stent ... 31636-31637
- Catheter
  - Aneurysm Sac
    - Pressure Sensor ... 34806
      - Complete Study ... 93982
  - Brain
    - for Chemotherapy ... 0169T
  - Breast
    - for Interstitial Radioelement Application ... 19296-19298, 20555, 41019
  - Bronchus
    - for Intracavitary Radioelement Application ... 31643
      - *See* Catheterization
  - Head
    - Interstitial Radioelement Application ... 41019
  - Neck
    - Interstitial Radioelement Application ... 41019
  - Pelvic Organs
    - Interstitial Radioelement Application ... 55920
  - Prostate ... 55875
- Catheter, Cardiac ... 93503
  - *See* Catheterization, Cardiac
- Cecostomy Tube ... 44300, 49442
- Colonic Stent ... 44397, 45327, 45345, 45387
- Dosimeter
  - Prostate ... 55876
- Drainage
  - Pancreas ... 48001
- Duodenostomy Tube ... 49441
- Endovascular Prosthesis
  - Aorta ... 33883-33886
- Enterostomy Tube ... 44300
- Fiducial Markers
  - Prostate ... 55876
- Gastostomy Tube ... 43246, 49440
- Guidance
  - Catheter
    - Abscess ... 75989
    - Bile ... 75982
    - Specimen ... 75989
  - Prosthesis
    - Thoracic Aorta ... 75958-75959
- Interstitial Device
  - Prostate ... 55876
- Intravascular Stent
  - Coronary ... 92980-92981
  - Intracranial ... 61635

Pneumogram
Pediatric 94772

Pneumolysis 32940

Pneumonectomy 32440-32500
Completion 32488
Donor 32850, 33930
Sleeve 32442
Total 32440-32445

Pneumonology
See Pulmonology

Pneumonolysis 32940
Intrapleural 32652
Open Intrapleural 32124

Pneumonostomy 32200-32201

Pneumonotomy
See Incision, Lung

Pneumoperitoneum 49400

Pneumoplethysmography
Ocular 93875

Pneumothorax
Chemical Pleurodesis 32560
Pleural Scarification for Repeat 32215
Therapeutic
  Injection Intrapleural Air 32960
Thoracentesis with Tube Insertion 32422

Polio
Antibody 86658
Vaccine 90712-90713

Poliovirus Vaccine
See Vaccines

Pollicization
Digit 26550

Polya Gastrectomy
See Gastrectomy, Partial

Polydactylism
See Polydactyly; Supernumerary Digit

Polydactyly
Digit
  Reconstruction 26587
  Repair 26587
Toe 28344

Polymerase Chain Reaction 83898

Polyp
Antrochoanal
  Removal 31032
Esophagus
  Ablation 43228
Nose
  Excision
    Endoscopic 31237-31240
    Extensive 30115
    Simple 30110
Sphenoid Sinus
  Removal 31051
Urethra
  Excision 53260

Polypectomy
Nose
  Endoscopic 31237
Uterus 58558

Polypeptide, Vasoactive Intestinal
See Vasoactive Intestinal Peptide

Polysomnography 95808-95811

Polyuria Test
See Water Load Test

Pomeroy's Operation
See Tubal Ligation

Pooling
Blood Products 86965

Popliteal Arteries
See Artery, Popliteal

Popliteal Synovial Cyst
See Baker's Cyst

Poradenitistras
See Lymphogranuloma Venereum

PORP (Partial Ossicular Replacement Prosthesis) .69633, 69637

Porphobilinogen
Urine 84106-84110

Porphyrin Precursors 82135

Porphyrins
Feces 84126-84127
Urine 84119-84120

Port Film 77417

Portal Vein
See Vein, Hepatic Portal

Portoenterostomies, Hepatic
See Hepaticoenterostomy

Portoenterostomy 47701

Positional Nystagmus Test
See Nystagmus Tests, Positional

Positive End Expiratory Pressure
See Pressure Breathing, Positive

Positive-Pressure Breathing, Inspiratory
See Intermittent Positive Pressure Breathing (IPPB)

Positron Emission Tomography (PET)
Brain 78608-78609
Heart 78459
Myocardial Imaging
  Perfusion Study 78491-78492

Post-Op Visit 99024

Postauricular Fistula
See Fistula, Postauricular

Postcaval Ureter
See Retrocaval Ureter

Postmortem
See Autopsy

Postop Vas Reconstruction
See Vasovasorrhaphy

Postoperative Wound Infection
Incision and Drainage 10180

Postpartum Care
Cesarean Delivery 59515
  after Attempted Vaginal Delivery 59622
  Previous 59610, 59614-59618, 59622
Vaginal Delivery 59430
  after Previous Cesarean Delivery 59614

Potassium 84132
Urine 84133

Potential, Auditory Evoked
See Auditory Evoked Potentials

Potential, Evoked
See Evoked Potential

Potts-Smith Procedure 33762

Pouch, Kock
See Kock Pouch

PPP
See Fibrin Degradation Products

PRA
See Cytotoxic Screen

Prealbumin 84134

Prebeta Lipoproteins
See Lipoprotein, Blood

Pregnancy
Abortion
  Induced 59855-59857
    by Amniocentesis Injection ..59850-59852
    by Dilation and Curettage 59840
    by Dilation and Evaluation 59841
  Septic 59830
  Therapeutic
    by Dilation and Curettage 59851
    by Hysterectomy 59852
    by Saline 59850
Cesarean Delivery 59618-59622
  Only 59514
  Postpartum Care 59514-59515
  Routine Care 59510
  Vaginal Birth After 59610-59614
  with Hysterectomy 59525
Ectopic
  Abdominal 59130
  Cervix 59140
  Interstitial
    Partial Resection Uterus 59136
    Total Hysterectomy 59135
  Laparoscopy
    with Salpingectomy and/or Oophorectomy 59151
    without Salpingectomy and/or Oophorectomy 59150
  Tubal 59121
    with Salpingectomy and/or Oophorectomy 59120

Ptosis
See Blepharoptosis; Procidentia

PTT
See Thromboplastin, Partial, Time

Ptyalectasis
See Dilation, Salivary Duct

Pubic Symphysis 27282

Pubis
Craterization 27070
Cyst
  Excision 27065-27067
Excision 27070
Saucerization 27070
Tumor
  Excision 27065-27067

Pudendal Nerve
Avulsion 64761
Destruction 64630
Incision 64761
Injection
  Anesthetic 64430
  Neurolytic 64630
Transection 64761

Puestow Procedure 48548

Pulled Elbow
See Nursemaid Elbow

Pulmonary Artery
Banding 33690
Catheterization 36013-36015
Embolism 33910-33916
  Excision 33910-33916
Percutaneous Transluminal
Angioplasty 92997-92998
Reimplantation 33788
Repair 33690, 33917-33920
  Reimplantation 33788
Shunt
  from Aorta 33755-33762, 33924
  from Vena Cava 33766-33767
  Subclavian 33750
Transection 33922

Pulmonary Function Test
See Pulmonology, Diagnostic

Pulmonary Haemorrhage
See Hemorrhage, Lung

Pulmonary Perfusion Imaging
Nuclear Medicine 78588

Pulmonary Valve
Incision 33470-33474
Repair 33470-33474
Replacement 33475

Pulmonary Vein
Repair
  Complete 33730
  Partial 33724
  Stenosis 33726
Stenosis
  Repair 33726

Pulmonology
Diagnostic
  Airway Closing Volume 94370
  Apnea Monitoring
    Pediatric 94774-94777
  Bronchodilation 94664
  Carbon Dioxide Response Curve 94400
  Carbon Monoxide Diffusion Capacity .. 94720
  Expired Gas Analysis
    CO_2 94770
    NO 95012
    O_2 and CO_2 94681
    O_2 Update, Direct 94680
    O_2 Uptake, Indirect 94690
    Quantitative 94250
    Spectroscopy 0064T
  Flow-Volume Loop 94375
  Function Study 78596
  Functional Residual Capacity 94240
  Hemoglobin O_2 Affinity 82820
  High Altitude Simulation
  Test (HAST) 94452-94453
  Hypoxia Response Curve 94450
  Inhalation Treatment 94640
  Maldistribution of Inspired Air 94350
  Maximum Breathing Capacity 94200
  Maximum Voluntary Ventilation 94200
  Membrane Compliance 94750
  Membrane Diffusion Capacity 94725
  Nitrogen Washout Curve 94350
  Oximetry
    Ear or Pulse 94760-94762
  Resistance to Airflow 94360
  Spectroscopy 0064T
  Spirometry 94010-94070
    Evaluation 94010-94070
    Patient Initiated with
    Bronchospasm 94014-94016
  Sputum Mobilization with Inhalants ... 94664
  Stress Test 94621
  Stress Test, Pulmonary 94620
  Thoracic Gas Volume 94260
Therapeutic
  Expired Gas Analysis 94250
  Inhalation
    Pentamidine 94642
  Inhalation Treatment ... 94640, 94644-94645, 94664, 99503
  Intrapulmonary Surfactant
  Administration 94610
  Manipulation of Chest Wall 94667-94668
  Pressure Ventilation
    Negative CNPB 94662
    Positive CPAP 94660
  Unlisted Services and Procedures 94799
  Ventilation Assist 94002-94005, 99504
Unlisted Services and Procedures 94799

Pulse Generator
Electronic Analysis .. 95970-95971, 95980-95982
Heart
  Insertion/Replacement 33212-33213

Pulse Rate Increased
See Tachycardia

Pump
See Chemotherapy, Pump Services; Infusion Pump

Pump Services
Oxygenator/Heat Exchanger 99190-99192

Pump Stomach for Poison 91105

Pump, Infusion
See Infusion Pump

Punch Graft 15775-15776

Puncture
Artery 36600
Chest
  Drainage 32421-32422
Cisternal
  See Cisternal Puncture
Lumbar
  See Spinal Tap
Lung 32420
Pericardium 33010-33011
Pleural Cavity
  Drainage 32421-32422
Skull
  Drain Fluid 61000-61020
    Cistern 61050
  Inject Cistern 61055
  Inject Ventricle 61026
  Shunt
    Drain Fluid 61070
    Injection 61070
Spinal Cord
  Diagnostic 62270
  Drain Fluid 62272
  Lumbar 62270
Tracheal
  Aspiration and/or Injection 31612

Puncture Aspiration
Abscess
  Skin 10160
Bulla 10160
Cyst
  Breast 19000-19001
  Skin 10160
Hematoma 10160

Puncturing
See Puncture

Pure-Tone Audiometry
See Audiometry, Pure Tone

Pustules
Removal 10040

Putti-Platt Procedure 23450

PUVA
See Dermatology; Photochemotherapy; Ultraviolet Light Therapy

Pyelogram
See Urography, Intravenous; Urography, Retrograde

Pyelography 74400, 74425
Injection 50394

Pyelolithotomy 50130
Anatrophic 50075
Coagulum 50130

Peritoneal Tumor
  Bilateral Salpingo-Oophorectomy-Omentectomy 58952-58956
  with Radical Dissection for Debulking 58952-58954
Phalanges
  Finger 26260-26262
  Toe 28175
Radius 25170
Scalp 21015
Scapula 23210
Shoulder 23077
Sternum 21630-21632
Talus
  Tumor 27647
Tarsal 28171
Tibia 27645
Tonsil 42842-42845
Tumor
  Back/Flank 21935
  Femur 27365
  Knee 27329, 27365
  Leg, Upper 27329
  Neck 21557
  Thorax 21557
Ulna 25170
Wrist 25077

Radical Vaginal Hysterectomy
See Hysterectomy, Vaginal, Radical

Radical Vulvectomy
See Vulvectomy, Radical

Radio-Cobalt B-12 Schilling Test
See Vitamin, B-12, Absorption Study

Radioactive Colloid Therapy 79300

Radioactive Substance
Insertion
  Prostate 55860

Radiocarpal Joint
Arthrotomy 25040
Dislocation
  Closed Treatment 25660

Radiocinematographies
See Cineradiography

Radioelement
Application 77761-77778
  Surface 77789
  with Ultrasound 76965
Handling 77790
Infusion 77750

Radioelement Substance
Catheter Placement
  Breast 19296-19298
  Bronchus 31643
  Muscle 20555
  Prostate 55875
  Soft Tissue 20555
Needle Placement
  Muscle 20555
  Prostate 55875-55876
  Soft Tissue 20555

Radiography
See Radiology, Diagnostic; X-ray

Radioimmunosorbent Test
See Gammaglobulin, Blood

Radioisotope Brachytherapy
See Brachytherapy

Radioisotope Scan
See Nuclear Medicine

Radiological Marker
Preoperative Placement
  Excision of Breast Lesion 19125-19126

Radiology
See Nuclear Medicine, Radiation Therapy, X-ray, Ultrasound
Diagnostic
  Unlisted Services and Procedures 76499
Stress Views 77071

Radionuclide CT Scan
See Emission Computerized Tomography

Radionuclide Imaging
See Nuclear Medicine

Radionuclide Therapy
See Radiopharmaceutical Therapy

Radionuclide Tomography, Single-Photon Emission-Computed
See SPECT

Radiopharmaceutical Localization
Inflammatory Process 78805
Injection 78808

Radiopharmaceutical Therapy
Interstitial 79300
Intra-Arterial 79445
Intra-Articular 79440
Intracavitary 79200
Intravenous 79101, 79403
Oral 79005
Unlisted Services and Procedures 79999

Radiotherapeutic
See Radiation Therapy

Radiotherapies
See Irradiation

Radiotherapy, Surface
See Application, Radioelement, Surface

Radioulnar Joint
Arthrodesis
  with Resection of Ulna 25830
Dislocation
  Closed Treatment 25525, 25675
  Open Treatment 25676
  Percutaneous Fixation 25671

Radius
See Arm, Lower; Elbow; Ulna
Arthroplasty 24365
  with Implant 24366, 25441
Craterization 24145, 25151
Cyst
  Excision 24125-24126, 25120-25126
Diaphysectomy 24145, 25151
Dislocation
  Partial 24640
  Subluxate 24640
  with Fracture
    Closed Treatment 24620
    Open Treatment 24635
Excision 24130, 24136, 24145, 24152-24153
  Epiphyseal Bar 20150
  Partial 25145
  Styloid Process 25230
Fracture 25605
  Closed Treatment 25500-25505, 25520, 25600-25605
    with Manipulation 25605
    without Manipulation 25600
  Colles 25600
  Distal 25600-25609
    Closed Treatment 25600-25605
    Open Treatment 25607-25609
  Head/Neck
    Closed Treatment 24650-24655
    Open Treatment 24665-24666
  Open Treatment 25515, 25525-25526, 25574
  Percutaneous Fixation 25606
  Shaft 25500-25526
    Open Treatment 25515, 25574-25575
  Smith 25600
  with Ulna 25560-25565
    Open Treatment 25575
Implant
  Removal 24164
Incision and Drainage 25035
Osteomyelitis 24136, 24145
Osteoplasty 25390-25393
Prophylactic Treatment 25490, 25492
Repair
  Epiphyseal Arrest 25450-25455
  Epiphyseal Separation
    Closed 25600
    Closed with Manipulation 25605
    Open Treatment 25607-25609
    Percutaneous Fixation 25606
  Malunion or Nonunion 25400, 25415
  Osteotomy 25350-25355, 25370-25375
    and Ulna 25365
  with Graft 25405, 25420-25426
Saucerization 24145, 25151
Sequestrectomy 24136, 25145
Tumor
  Cyst 24120
  Excision 24125-24126, 25120-25126, 25170

Ramstedt Operation
See Pyloromyotomy

Ramus Anterior, Nervus Thoracicus
See Intercostal Nerve

Range of Motion Test
Extremities or Trunk 95851
Eye 92018-92019
Hand 95852

Rapid Heart Rate
See Tachycardia

Rapid Plasma Reagin Test 86592-86593

Mandibular Rami
with Bone Graft 21194
with Internal Rigid Fixation 21196
without Bone Graft 21193
without Internal Rigid Fixation 21195
Maxilla
with Implant 21245-21246, 21248-21249
Metacarpophalangeal Joint 26530-26531
Midface
Forehead Advancement 21159-21160
with Bone Graft 21145-21160, 21188
without Bone Graft 21141-21143
Mouth 40840-40845
Nail Bed 11762
Nasoethmoid Complex 21182-21184
Navicular 25443
Nose
Cleft Lip/Cleft Palate 30460-30462
Dermatoplasty 30620
Primary 30400-30420
Secondary 30430-30450
Septum 30520
Orbit 21256
Orbit Area
Secondary 21275
Orbit with Bone Grafting 21182-21184
Orbital Rim 21172-21180
Orbital Rims 21182-21184
Orbital Walls 21182-21184
Orbitocraniofacial
Secondary Revision 21275
Oviduct
Fimbrioplasty 58760
Palate
Cleft Palate 42200-42225
Lengthening 42226-42227
Parotid Duct
Diversion 42507-42510
Patella 27437-27438
Instability 27420-27424
Penis
Angulation 54360
Chordee 54300-54304
Complications 54340-54348
Epispadias 54380-54390
Hypospadias 54332, 54352
One Stage Distal with
Urethroplasty 54324-54328
One Stage Perineal 54336
Periorbital Region
Osteotomy with Graft 21267-21268
Pharynx 42950
Pyloric Sphincter 43800
Radius 24365, 25390-25393, 25441
Arthroplasty
with Implant 24366
Shoulder Joint
with Implant 23470-23472
Skull 21172-21180
Defect 62140-62141, 62145
Spinal Elements 63051, 63295
Sternum 21740-21742
with Thoracoscopy 21743
Stomach
for Obesity 43644-43645, 43845-43848
Gastric Bypass 43644-43645, 43846
Roux-En-Y 43644, 43846
with Duodenum . 43810, 43850-43855, 43865
with Jejunum 43820-43825, 43860
Superior-Lateral Orbital Rim and
Forehead 21172-21175
Supraorbital Rim and Forehead 21179-21180
Symblepharon 68335
Temporomandibular Joint
Arthroplasty 21240-21243
Throat 42950
Thumb
from Finger 26550
Opponensplasty 26490-26496
Tibia
Lengthening 27715
Tubercle 27418
Toe
Angle Deformity 28313
Extra Toes 28344
Hammertoe 28285-28286
Macrodactyly 28340-28341
Polydactylous 26587
Syndactyly 28345
Webbed Toe 28345
Tongue
Frenum 41520
Trachea
Carina 31766
Cervical 31750
Fistula 31755
Intrathoracic 31760
Trapezium 25445
Tympanic Membrane 69620
Ulna 25390-25393, 25442
Radioulnar 25337
Ureter 50700
with Intestines 50840
Urethra 53410-53440, 53445
Complications 54340-54348
Hypospadias
One Stage Distal with Meatal
Advancement 54322
One Stage Distal with
Urethroplasty 54324-54328
Suture to Bladder 51840-51841
Urethroplasty for Second Stage 54308-54316
Urethroplasty for Third Stage 54318
Uterus 58540
Vas Deferens
See Vasovasorrhaphy
Vena Cava 34502
with Resection 37799
Wound Repair 13100-13160
Wrist 25332
Capsulectomy 25320
Capsulorrhaphy 25320
Realign 25335
Zygomatic Arch 21255

Rectal Bleeding

See Hemorrhage, Rectum

Rectal Prolapse

See Procidentia, Rectum

Rectal Sphincter

Dilation 45910

Rectocele

Repair 45560

Rectopexy

See Proctopexy

Rectoplasty

See Proctoplasty

Rectorrhaphy

See Rectum, Suture

Rectovaginal Fistula

See Fistula, Rectovaginal

Rectovaginal Hernia

See Rectocele

Rectum

See Anus
Abscess
Incision and Drainage 45005-45020, 46040, 46060
Biopsy 45100
Dilation
Endoscopy 45303
Endoscopy
Destruction
Tumor 45320
Dilation 45303
Exploration 45300
Hemorrhage 45317
Removal
Foreign Body 45307
Polyp 45308-45315
Tumor 45308-45315
Volvulus 45321
Excision
Partial 45111, 45113-45116, 45123
Total 45110, 45112, 45119-45120
with Colon 45121
Exploration
Endoscopic 45300
Surgical 45990
Hemorrhage
Endoscopic 45317
Injection
Sclerosing Solution 45520
Laparoscopy 45499
Lesion
Excision 45108
Manometry 91122
Prolapse
Excision 45130-45135
Pulsed Irrigation
Fecal Impaction 91123
Removal
Fecal Impaction 45915
by Pulsed Irrigation 91123
Foreign Body 45307, 45915
Repair
Fistula 0170T, 45800-45825
Injury 45562-45563
Prolapse 45505-45541, 45900
Rectocele 45560
Stenosis 45500
with Sigmoid Excision 45550
Sensation, Tone, and Compliance Test 91120
Stricture
Excision 45150

Eye
Bone 67414, 67445
Ocular Contents
with Implant 65093
without Implant 65091
Orbital Contents Only 65110
with Bone 65112
with Implant
Muscles Attached 65105
Muscles, Not Attached 65103
with Muscle or Myocutaneous Flap . . . 65114
without Implant 65101
Fallopian Tube
Laparoscopy 58661
with Hysterectomy . . . 58542, 58544, 58548
Fat
Lipectomy 15876-15879
Fecal Impaction
Rectum 45915
Fibrin Deposit 32150
Fixation Device 20670-20680
Foreign Body 65205-65265
Anal 46608
Ankle Joint 27610, 27620
Arm
Lower 25248
Upper 24200-24201
Auditory Canal, External 69200
with Anesthesia 69205
Bile Duct 43269
Bladder 52310-52315
Brain 61570, 62163
Bronchi 31635
Colon 44025, 44390, 45379
Colon-Sigmoid 45332
Conjunctival Embedded 65210
Cornea
with Slit Lamp 65222
without Slit Lamp 65220
Duodenum 44010
Elbow 24000, 24101, 24200-24201
Esophagus 43020, 43045, 43215, 74235
External Eye 65205
Eyelid 67938
Finger 26075-26080
Foot 28190-28193
Gastrointestinal, Upper 43247
Gum 41805
Hand 26070
Hip 27033, 27086-27087
Hysteroscopy 58562
Interphalangeal Joint
Toe 28024
Intertarsal Joint 28020
Intestines, Small 44020, 44363
Intraocular 65235
Kidney 50561, 50580
Knee Joint 27310, 27331, 27372
Lacrimal Duct 68530
Lacrimal Gland 68530
Larynx 31511, 31530-31531, 31577
Leg, Upper 27372
Lung 32151
Mandible 41806
Mediastinum 39000-39010
Metatarsophalangeal Joint 28022
Mouth 40804-40805
Muscle 20520-20525
Nose 30300
Anesthesia 30310
Lateral Rhinotomy 30320
Orbit 61334, 67413, 67430
with Bone Flap 67430
without Bone Flap 67413
Pancreatic Duct 43269
Patella
See Patellectomy
Pelvis 27086-27087
Penile Tissue 54115
Penis 54115
Pericardium 33020
Endoscopic 32658
Peritoneum 49402
Pharynx 42809
Pleura 32150-32151
Endoscopic 32653
Posterior Segment
Magnetic Extraction 65260
Nonmagnetic Extraction 65265
Rectum 45307, 45915
Scrotum 55120
Shoulder 23040-23044
Complicated 23332
Deep 23331
Subcutaneous 23330
Skin
with Debridement 11010-11012
Stomach 43500
Subcutaneous Tissue 10120-10121
with Debridement 11010-11012
Tarsometatarsal Joint 28020
Tendon Sheath 20520-20525
Toe 28022
Ureter 50961, 50980
Urethra 52310-52315
Uterus 58562
Vagina 57415
Wrist 25040, 25101, 25248
Hair
Electrolysis 17380
Halo 20665
Hearing Aid
Bone Conduction 69711
Hematoma
Brain 61312-61315
Implantation 20670-20680
Ankle 27704
Contraceptive Capsules 11976-11977
Disc 22865
Elbow 24160
Eye 67120-67121
Finger 26320
Hand 26320
Radius 24164
Wrist 25449
Infusion Pump
Intra-Arterial 36262
Intravenous 36590
Spinal Cord 62365
Intra-Aortic Balloon 33974
Assist Device 33968, 33971
Intrauterine Device (IUD) 58301
Keel
Laryngoplasty 31580
Lacrimal Gland
Partial 68505
Total 68500
Lacrimal Sac
Excision 68520
Laryngocele 31300
Leiomyomata 58545-58546, 58561
Lens 66920-66940
Lens Material 66840-66852
Lesion
Conjunctiva 68040
Larynx 31512, 31578
Endoscopic 31545-31546
Loose Body
Ankle 27620
Carpometacarpal Joint 26070
Elbow 24101
Interphalangeal Joint
Toe 28024
Intertarsal Joint 28020
Knee Joint 27331
Metatarsophalangeal Joint 28022
Tarsometatarsal Joint 28020
Toe 28022
Wrist 25101
Lung
Apical Tumor 32503-32504
Bronchoplasty 32501
Completion Pneumonectomy 32488
Cyst 32140
Extrapleural 32445
Single Lobe 32480
Single Segment 32484
Sleeve Lobectomy 32486
Sleeve Pneumonectomy 32442
Total Pneumonectomy 32440-32445
Two Lobes 32482
Volume Reduction 32491
Wedge Resection 32500
Lymph Nodes
Abdominal 38747
Inguinofemoral 38760-38765
Pelvic 38770
Retroperitoneal
Transabdominal 38780
Thoracic 38746
Mammary Implant 19328-19330
Mastoid
Air Cells 69670
Mesh
Abdominal Wall 11008
Milia, Multiple 10040
Nails 11730-11732, 11750-11752
Neurostimulators
Pulse Generator 64595
Receiver 64595
Ocular Implant 65175, 65920
Orbital Implant 67560
Ovary
Laparoscopy 58661
with Hysterectomy . . . 58542, 58544, 58548
Pacemaker
Heart 33233-33237
Patella, Complete 27424
Plate
Skull 62142

Renal Pelvis 50400-50405
Wound 50500
Knee
Cartilage 27403
Instability 27420
Ligament 27405-27409
Collateral 27405
Collateral and Cruciate 27409
Cruciate 27407-27409
Meniscus 27403
Tendon 27380-27381
Larynx
Fracture 31584
Reinnervation
Neuromuscular Pedicle 31590
Leg
Lower
Fascia 27656
Tendon 27658-27692
Upper
Muscle 27385-27386, 27400, 27430
Tendon 27393-27400
Ligament
See Ligament, Repair
Lip 40650-40654
Cleft Lip 40700-40761
Fistula 42260
Liver
Abscess 47300
Cyst 47300
Wound 47350-47361
Lung
Hernia 32800
Pneumolysis 32940
Tear 32110
Mastoidectomy
Complete 69601
Modified Radical 69602
Radical 69603
with Apicectomy 69605
with Tympanoplasty 69604
Maxilla
Osteotomy 21206
Mesentery 44850
Metacarpal
Lengthening 26568
Nonunion 26546
Osteotomy 26565
Metacarpophalangeal Joint
Capsulodesis 26516-26518
Collateral Ligament 26540-26542
Fusion 26516-26518
Metatarsal 28322
Osteotomy 28306-28309
Microsurgery 69990
Mitral Valve 33420-33427
Mouth
Laceration 40830-40831
Vestibule of 40830-40845
Musculotendinous Cuff 23410-23412
Nail Bed 11760
Nasal Deformity
Cleft Lip 40700-40761
Nasal Septum 30630
Navicular 25440
Neck Muscles
Scalenus Anticus 21700-21705
Sternocleidomastoid 21720-21725
Nerve 64876
Graft 64885-64911
Microrepair 69990
Suture 64831-64876
Nose
Adhesions 30560
Fistula 30580-30600, 42260
Rhinophyma 30120
Septum 30540-30545, 30630
Synechia 30560
Vestibular Stenosis 30465
Omphalocele 49600-49611
Osteotomy
Femoral Neck 27161
Radius
and Ulna 25365
Ulna
and Radius 25365
Vertebra
Additional Segment 22216, 22226
Cervical 22210, 22220
Lumbar 22214, 22224
Thoracic 22212, 22222
Oviduct 58752
Create Stoma 58770
Pacemaker
Heart
Electrode 33218-33220
Palate
Laceration 42180-42182
Vomer Flap 42235
Pancreas
Cyst 48500
Pseudocyst 48510-48511
Percutaneous 48511
Paravaginal Defect 57284-57285, 57423
Pectus Carinatum 21740-21742
with Thoracoscopy 21743
Pectus Excavatum 21740-21742
with Thoracoscopy 21743
Pelvic Floor
Prosthetic Insertion 57267
Pelvis
Osteotomy 27158
Tendon 27098
Penis
Fistulization 54435
Injury 54440
Priapism 54420-54435
Shunt 54420-54430
Perineum 56810
Periorbital Region
Osteotomy 21260-21263
Phalanx
Finger
Lengthening 26568
Osteotomy 26567
Nonunion 26546
Toe
Osteotomy 28310-28312
Pharynx
with Esophagus 42953
Pleura 32215
Prosthesis
Penis 54408
Pulmonary Artery 33917-33920, 33925-33926
Reimplantation 33788
Pulmonary Valve 33470-33474
Pulmonary Venous Return 33724
Pulmonary Venous Stenosis 33726
Quadriceps
See Quadriceps, Repair
Radius
Epiphyseal 25450-25455
Malunion or Nonunion 25400, 25415
Osteotomy 25350-25355, 25370-25375
with Graft 25405, 25420-25426
Rectocele
See Rectocele, Repair
Rectovaginal Fistula 57308
Rectum
Fistula 0170T, 45800-45825
Injury 45562-45563
Prolapse 45505-45541, 45900
Rectocele 45560
Stenosis 45500
with Sigmoid Excision 45550
Retinal Detachment with Diathermy
See Diathermy, Retinal Detachment, Repair
Rotator Cuff
See Rotator Cuff, Repair
Salivary Duct 42500-42505
Fistula 42600
Scapula
Fixation 23400
Scapulopexy 23400
Sclera
See Sclera, Repair
Scrotum 55175-55180
Septal Defect 33813-33814
Shoulder
Capsule 23450-23466
Cuff 23410-23412
Ligament Release 23415
Muscle Transfer 23395-23397
Musculotendinous Rotator
Cuff 23415-23420
Tendon 23410-23412, 23430-23440
Tenomyotomy 23405-23406
Simple, Integumentary System
See Integumentary System, Repair, Simple
Sinus
Ethmoid
Cerebrospinal Fluid Leak 31290
Sphenoid
Cerebrospinal Fluid Leak 31291
Sinus of Valsalva 33702-33722
Skin
Wound
Complex 13100-13160
Intermediate 12031-12057
Simple 12020-12021
Skull
Cerebrospinal Fluid Leak 62100
Encephalocele 62120
Spica Cast 29720
Spinal Cord 63700
Cerebrospinal Fluid Leak 63707-63709
Meningocele 63700-63702
Myelomeningocele 63704-63706
Spinal Meningocele
See Meningocele, Repair
Spine
Lumbar Vertebra 22524-22525
Osteotomy 22210-22226
Thoracic Vertebra 22523, 22525

Repeat Surgeries

Replacement

Prosthesis
Skull 62143
Urethral Sphincter 53448
Pulmonary Valve 33475
Pulse Generator
Brain 61885
Peripheral Nerve 64590
Spinal Cord 63685
Receiver
Brain 61885
Peripheral Nerve 64590
Spinal Cord 63685
Skin
Acellular Dermal Matrix 15170-15176
Skull Plate 62143
Spinal Cord
Reservoir 62360
Stent
Ureteral 50382, 50387
Subcutaneous Port
for Gastric Restrictive Procedure 43888
Tissue Expanders
Skin 11970
Total Replacement
See Hip, Total Replacement
Total Replacement Heart System
Intracorporeal 0052T, 0053T
Tricuspid Valve 33465
Ureter
with Intestines 50840
Venous Access Device 36582-36583, 36585
Catheter 36578
Venous Catheter
Central 36580-36581, 36584

Replantation
Arm, Upper 20802
Digit 20816-20822
Foot 20838
Forearm 20805
Hand 20808
Thumb 20824-20827

Report Preparation
Extended, Medical 99080
Psychiatric 90889

Reposition
Toe to Hand 26551-26556

Repositioning
Central Venous Catheter 36597
Electrode
Heart 33215-33217, 33226
Gastrostomy Tube 43761
Heart
Defibrillator
Leads 33215-33216, 33226, 33249
Intraocular Lens 66825
Tricuspid Valve 33468

Reproductive Tissue
Cryopreserved
Preparation
Thawing 89354
Storage 89344

Reprogramming
Shunt
Brain 62252

Reptilase Test 85635

Reptilase Time
See Thrombin Time

Resection
Aortic Valve
Stenosis 33415
Bladder Diverticulum 52305
Bladder Neck
Transurethral 52500
Brain Lobe
See Lobectomy, Brain
Chest Wall 19260-19272
Diaphragm 39560-39561
Endaural
See Ear, Inner, Excision
Humeral Head 23195
Intestines, Small
Laparoscopic 44202-44203
Lung 32503-32504
Mouth
with Tongue Excision 41153
Myocardium
Aneurysm 33542
Septal Defect 33545
Nasal Septum Submucous
See Nasal Septum, Submucous Resection
Nose
Septum 30520
Ovary, Wedge
See Ovary, Wedge Resection
Palate 42120
Phalangeal Head
Toe 28153
Prostate Transurethral
See Prostatectomy, Transurethral
Radical
Arm, Upper 24077
Elbow 24077
with Contracture Release 24149
Foot 28046
Humerus 24150-24151
Radius 24152-24153
Tumor
Ankle 27615
Calcaneus or Talus 27647
Clavicle 23200
Femur 27365
Fibula 27646
Humerus 23220
Humerus with Autograft 23221
Humerus with Prosthetic Replacement 23222
Knee 27329, 27365
Leg, Lower 27615
Leg, Upper 27329
Metatarsal 28173
Phalanx, Toe 28175
Scapula 23210
Tarsal 28171
Tibia 27645
Ribs 19260-19272, 32900
Synovial Membrane
See Synovectomy
Temporal Bone 69535
Tumor
Fallopian Tube 58957-58958
Ovary 58957-58958
Peritoneum 58957-58958
Ulna
Arthrosedis
Radioulnar Joint 25830
Ureterocele
Ectopic 52301
Orthotopic 52300
Vena Cava
with Reconstruction 37799

Resonance Spectroscopy, Magnetic
See Magnetic Resonance Spectroscopy

Respiration, Positive-Pressure
See Pressure Breathing, Positive

Respiratory Pattern Recording
Preventive
Infant 94772

Respiratory Syncytial Virus
Antibody 86756
Antigen Detection
Direct Fluorescence 87280
Direct Optical Observation 87807
Enzyme Immunoassay 87420

Respiratory Syncytial Virus Immune Globulin
See Immune Globulins
Antigen Detection
See Immune Globulins, Respiratory Syncytial Virus

Response, Auditory Evoked
See Auditory Evoked Potentials

Rest Home Visit
See Domiciliary Services

Resuscitation
Cardiac
See Cardiac Massage
Cardio-Pulmonary
See Cardio-Pulmonary Resuscitation
Newborn 99465

Reticulocyte
Count 85044-85045

Retina
Incision
Encircling Material 67115
Lesion
Extensive
Destruction 67227-67228
Localized
Destruction 0017T, 67208-67218
Macular/Fundus Exam, Dilated 2019F-2021F
Findings Communicated for Diabetes Management 5010F
Repair
Detachment 67113
by Scleral Buckling 67112
Cryotherapy or Diathermy 67101
Injection of Air 67110
Photocoagulation 67105

Fracture
  Closed Treatment 21800
  External Fixation 21810
  Open Treatment 21805
Graft
  to Face 21230
Resection 19260-19272, 32900
X-ray 71100-71111

Riboflavin 84252

Richardson Operation Hysterectomy
See Hysterectomy, Abdominal, Total

Richardson Procedure 53460

Rickettsia
Antibody 86757

Ridell Operation
See Sinusotomy, Frontal

Ridge, Alveolar
See Alveolar Ridge

Right Atrioventricular Valve
See Tricuspid Valve

Right Heart Cardiac Catheterization
See Cardiac Catheterization, Right Heart

Ripstein Operation
See Proctopexy

Risk Factor Reduction Intervention
See Performance Measures, Preventive Medicine

Risser Jacket 29010-29015
Removal 29710

Rocky Mountain Spotted Fever 86000

Roentgen Rays
See X-ray

Roentgenographic
See X-ray

Roentgenography
See Radiology, Diagnostic

Ropes Test 83872

Rorschach Test 96101

Ross Information Processing Assessment 96125

Ross Procedure 33413

Rotation Flap
See Skin, Adjacent Tissue Transfer

Rotator Cuff
Repair 23410-23420

Rotavirus
Antibody 86759
Antigen Detection
  Enzyme Immunoassay 87425

Rotavirus Vaccine
3 Dose 90680
2 Dose 90681

Round Window
Repair Fistula 69667

Round Window Fistula
See Fistula, Round Window

Roux-En-Y Procedure 43621, 43633-43634, 43644, 43846, 47740-47741, 47780-47785, 48540

RPR 86592-86593

RSV
See Immune Globulins; Respiratory Syncytial Virus

RT3
See Triiodothyronine, Reverse

Rubbing Alcohol
See Isopropyl Alcohol

Rubella
Antibody 86762
Vaccine 90706-90710

Rubella HI Test
See Hemagglutination Inhibition Test

Rubella/Mumps
See Vaccines

Rubeola
Antibody 86765
Antigen Detection
  Immunofluorescence 87283

Rubeolla
See Rubeola

Russell Viper Venom Time 85612-85613

S

Sac, Endolymphatic
See Endolymphatic Sac

Saccomanno Technique 88108

Sacral Nerve
Implantation
  Electrode 64561, 64581
Insertion
  Electrode 64561, 64581

Sacroiliac Joint
Arthrodesis 27280
Arthrotomy 27050
Biopsy 27050
Dislocation
  Open Treatment 27218
Fusion 27280
Injection for Arthrography 27096
X-ray 72200-72202, 73542

Sacrum
Tumor
  Excision 49215
X-ray 72220

Sahli Test
See Gastroenterology, Diagnostic, Stomach

Salicylate
Assay 80196

Saline-Solution Abortion
See Abortion, Induced, by Saline

Salivary Duct
Catheterization 42660
Dilation 42650-42660
Ligation 42665
Repair 42500-42505
  Fistula 42600

Salivary Gland Virus
See Cytomegalovirus

Salivary Glands
Abscess
  Incision and Drainage 42310-42320
Biopsy 42405
Calculi (Stone)
  Excision 42330-42340
Cyst
  Drainage 42409
  Excision 42408
Injection
  X-ray 42550
Needle Biopsy 42400
Nuclear Medicine
  Function Study 78232
  Imaging 78230-78231
Parotid
  Abscess 42300-42305
Unlisted Services and Procedures 42699
X-ray 70380-70390
  with Contrast 70390

Salmonella
Antibody 86768

Salpingectomy 58262-58263, 58291-58292, 58552, 58554, 58661, 58700
Ectopic Pregnancy
  Laparoscopic Treatment 59151
  Surgical Treatment 59120
Oophorectomy 58943

Salpingo-Oophorectomy 58720
Resection Ovarian Malignancy 58950-58958
Resection Peritoneal Malignancy 58950-58958
Resection Tubal Malignancy 58950-58958

Salpingohysterostomy
See Implantation, Tubouterine

Salpingolysis 58740

Salpingoneostomy 58673, 58770

Sclerotomy
See Incision, Sclera

Screening, Drug
See Drug Screen
Alcohol and/or Substance Abuse . . .99408-99409

Scribner Cannulization 36810

Scrotal Varices
See Varicocele

Scrotoplasty 55175-55180

Scrotum
Abscess
Incision and Drainage 54700, 55100
Excision 55150
Exploration 55110
Hematoma
Incision and Drainage 54700
Removal
Foreign Body .55120
Repair 55175-55180
Ultrasound 76870
Unlisted Services and Procedures 55899

Scrub Typhus 86000

Second Look Surgery
See Reoperation

Section
See Decompression
Cesarean
See Cesarean Delivery
Cranial Nerve 61460
Spinal Access .63191
Dentate Ligament 63180-63182
Gasserian Ganglion
Sensory Root .61450
Medullary Tract 61470
Mesencephalic Tract 61480
Nerve Root .63185-63190
Spinal Accessory Nerve 63191
Spinal Cord Tract 63194-63199
Tentorium Cerebelli 61440
Vestibular Nerve
Transcranial Approach 69950
Translabyrinthine Approach 69915

Sedation
Moderate .99143-99150
with Independent Observation . .99143-99145

Seddon-Brookes Procedure . . .24320

Sedimentation Rate
Blood Cell
Automated 85652
Manual 85651

Segmentectomy
Breast 19301-19302
Lung 32484

Seidlitz Powder Test
See X-ray, with Contrast

Selective Cellular Enhancement Technique 88112

Selenium 84255

Self Care
See Physical Medicine/Therapy/Occupational Therapy
Training 97535, 98960-98962, 99509

Sella Turcica
CT Scan 70480-70482
X-ray 70240

Semen
See Sperm

Semen Analysis 89300-89322
Sperm Analysis 89331
Antibodies 89325
with Sperm Isolation 89260-89261

Semenogelase
See Antigen, Prostate Specific

Semicircular Canal
Incision
Fenestration 69820
Revised 69840

Semilunar
Bone
See Lunate
Ganglion
See Gasserian Ganglion

Seminal Vesicle
Cyst
Excision 55680
Excision 55650
Incision 55600-55605
Mullerian Duct
Excision 55680
Unlisted Services and Procedures 55899

Seminal Vesicles
Vesiculography 74440
X-ray with Contrast 74440

Seminin
See Antigen, Prostate Specific

Semiquantitative 81005

Sengstaken Tamponade
Esophagus 43460

Senning Procedure 33774-33777
See Repair, Great Arteries; Revision

Senning Type 33774-33777

Sensitivity Study
Antibiotic
Agar 87181
Disc 87184
Enzyme Detection 87185
Macrobroth 87188
MIC 87186
Microtiter 87186
MLC 87187
Mycobacteria .87190
Antiviral Drugs
HIV-1
Tissue Culture 87904

Sensor, Transcatheter Placement 34806

Sensorimotor Exam 92060

Sensory Nerve
Common
Repair/Suture .64834

Sentinel Node
Injection Procedure 38792

Separation
Craniofacial
Closed Treatment 21431
Open Treatment 21432-21436

Septal Defect
Repair 33813-33814
Ventricular
Closure .33675-33688
Open 33675-33688
Percutaneous 93581
Transmyocardial 0166T-0167T

Septectomy
Atrial 33735-33737
Balloon (Rashkind Type) 92992
Blade Method (Park) 92993
Closed
See Septostomy, Atrial
Submucous Nasal
See Nasal Septum, Submucous Resection

Septic Abortion
See Abortion, Septic

Septoplasty 30520

Septostomy
Atrial 33735-33737
Balloon (Rashkind Type) 92992
Blade Method (Park) 92993

Septum, Nasal
See Nasal Septum

Sequestrectomy
Carpal 25145
Clavicle 23170
Humeral Head 23174
Humerus 24134
Olecranon Process 24138
Radius 24136, 25145
Scapula 23172
Skull 61501
Ulna 24138, 25145

Serialography
Aorta 75625

Serodiagnosis, Syphilis
See Serologic Test for Syphilis

Serologic Test for Syphilis 86592-86593

Seroma
Incision and Drainage
Skin 10140

Serotonin 84260

Peritoneal
 Venous
  Injection 49427
  Ligation 49428
  Removal 49429
 X-ray 75809
Pulmonary Artery
 See Pulmonary Artery, Shunt
Revision
 Arteriovenous 36832
Spinal Cord
 Creation 63740-63741
 Irrigation 63744
 Removal 63746
 Replacement 63744
Superior Mesenteric-Caval
 See Anastomosis, Caval to Mesenteric
Ureter to Colon 50815
Ventriculocisternal with Valve
 See Ventriculocisternostomy

Shuntogram 75809

Sialic Acid 84275

Sialodochoplasty 42500-42505

Sialogram
See Sialography

Sialography 70390

Sickling
Electrophoresis 83020

Siderocytes 85536

Siderophilin
See Transferrin

Sigmoid
See Colon-Sigmoid

Sigmoid Bladder
Cystectomy 51590

Sigmoidoscopy
Ablation
 Polyp 45339
 Tumor 45339
Biopsy 45331
Collection
 Specimen 45331
Exploration 45330, 45335
Hemorrhage Control 45334
Injection
 Submucosal 45335
Needle Biopsy 45342
Placement
 Stent 45345
Removal
 Foreign Body 45332
 Polyp 45333, 45338
 Tumor 45333, 45338
Repair
 Volvulus 45337
Ultrasound 45341-45342

Signal-Averaged Electrocardiography
See Electrocardiogram

Silica 84285

Silicon Dioxide
See Silica

Silicone
Contouring Injections 11950-11954

Silver Operation
See Keller Procedure

Silver Procedure 28290

Simple Mastectomies
See Mastectomy

Single Photon Absorptiometry
See Absorptiometry, Single Photon

Single Photon Emission Computed Tomography
See SPECT

Sinu, Sphenoid
See Sinus/Sinuses, Sphenoid

Sinus/Sinuses
Ethmoid
 Excision 31200-31205
  with Nasal/Sinus Endoscopy 31254-31255
 Repair of Cerebrospinal Leak 31290
Ethmoidectomy
 Excision 31254
Frontal
 Destruction 31080-31085
 Exploration 31070-31075
  with Nasal/Sinus Endoscopy 31276
 Fracture
  Open Treatment 21343-21344
 Incision 31070-31087
Injection 20500
 Diagnostic 20501
Maxillary
 Antrostomy 31256-31267
 Excision 31225-31230
 Exploration 31020-31032
  with Nasal/Sinus Endoscopy 31233
 Incision 31020-31032, 31256-31267
 Irrigation 31000
 Skull Base 61581
 Surgery 61581
Multiple
 Incision 31090
 Paranasal
  Incision 31090
Pilonidal
 See Cyst, Pilonidal
Sinus of Valsalva
 Repair 33702-33722
Sinus Venosus
 Repair 33645
Sphenoid
 Biopsy 31050-31051
 Exploration 31050-31051
  with Nasal/Sinus Endoscopy 31235
 Incision 31050-31051
  with Nasal/Sinus Endoscopy 31287-31288
 Irrigation 31002
 Repair of Cerebrospinal Leak 31291
 Sinusotomy 31050-31051
 Skull Base Surgery 61580-61581
Unlisted Services and Procedures 31299
X-ray 70210-70220

Sinusectomy, Ethmoid
See Sinus/Sinuses; Ethmoidectomy

Sinusoidal Rotational Testing
See Ear, Nose and Throat

Sinusoscopy
Sinus
 Maxillary 31233
 Sphenoid 31235

Sinusotomy
See Sinus/Sinuses, Multiple
Combined 31090
Frontal Sinus
 Exploratory 31070-31075
 Nonobliterative 31086-31087
 Obliterative 31080-31085
Maxillary 31020-31032
Multiple
 Paranasal 31090
Sphenoid Sinus 31050-31051

Sirolimus
Drug Assay 80195

SISI Test 92564

Sistrunk Operation
See Cyst, Thyroid Gland, Excision

Six Minute Walk Test 94620

Size Reduction, Breast
See Breast, Reduction

Skeletal Fixation
Humeral Epicondyle
 Percutaneous 24566

Skeletal Traction
Insertion/Removal
 Pin/Wire 20650

Skene's Gland
Abscess
 Incision and Drainage 53060
Destruction 53270
Excision 53270

Skilled Nursing Facilities (SNFs)
See Nursing Facility Services

Skin
Abrasion 15786-15787
 Chemical Peel 15788-15793
 Dermabrasion 15780-15783
Abscess
 See Abscess, Skin
Adjacent Tissue Transfer 14000-14350
Allogenic Substitute 15340-15341
 Dermal 15360-15366
Allografts
 See Allograft, Skin
Biopsy 11100-11101
Chemical Exfoliation 17360
Complete Physical Examination 2029F

Skin Graft and Flap

Skull

Skull Base Surgery
Anterior Cranial Fossa
Bicoronal Approach 61586
Craniofacial Approach 61580-61583
Extradural 61600-61601
LeFort I Osteotomy Approach 61586
Orbitocranial Approach 61584-61585
Transzygomatic Approach 61586
Carotid Aneurysm 61613
Carotid Artery 61610
Transection/Ligation 61609-61612
Craniotomy 62121
Dura
Repair of Cerebrospinal Fluid Leak 61618-61619
Middle Cranial Fossa
Extradural 61605, 61607
Infratemporal Approach 61590-61591
Intradural 61606, 61608
Orbitocranial Zygomatic Approach 61592
Posterior Cranial Fossa
Extradural 61615
Intradural 61616
Transcondylar Approach 61596-61597
Transpetrosal Approach 61598
Transtemporal Approach 61595

Sleep Study 95806-95807
Actigraphy 95803

Sliding Inlay Graft, Tibia
See Ankle; Tibia, Repair

Sling Operation
Incontinence 53440
Removal 53442
Stress Incontinence 51992, 57287
Vagina 57287-57288

Small Bowel
See Intestines, Small
Neoplasm
See Tumor, Intestines, Small

SMAS Flap 15829

Smear
Cervical
See Cervical Smears
Papanicolaou
See Pap Smears

Smear and Stain
See Cytopathology, Smears
Cornea 65430
Fluorescent 87206
Gram or Giesma 87205
Ova/Parasites 87177, 87209
Parasites 87207-87209
Wet Mount 87210

Smith Fracture 25600-25605

Smith-Robinson Operation
See Arthrodesis, Vertebra

Smoking and Tobacco Use Cessation
Counseling 99406-99407

SO_4
See Sulfate

Soave Procedure 45120

Sodium 84295, 84302
Urine 84300

Sodium Glycinate, Theophylline
See Theophylline

Sofield Procedure 24410

Soft Tissue
See Tissue, Soft

Solar Plexus
See Celiac Plexus

Solitary Cyst
See Bone, Cyst

Somatomammotropin, Chorionic 83632

Somatomedin 84305

Somatosensory Testing
Lower Limbs 95926
Trunk or Head 95927
Upper Limbs 95925

Somatostatin 84307

Somatotropin 83003

Somatotropin Release Inhibiting Hormone
See Somatostatin

Somatropin
See Growth Hormone, Human

Somnographies
See Polysomnography

Somophyllin T
See Theophylline

Sonography
See Echography

Sonohysterography 76831
Saline Infusion
Injection Procedure 58340

Sore, Bed
See Pressure Ulcer (Decubitus)

Spasm Eyelid
See Blepharospasm

Special Services
After Hours Medical Services 99050
Analysis
Remote Physiologic Data 99091
Computer Data Analysis 99090
Device Handling 99002
Emergency Care In Office 99058
Emergency Care Out of Office 99060
Extended Hours Medical Services 99051-99053
Group Education 99078
Self-Management 98961-98962
Hyperbaric Oxygen 99183
Hypothermia 99185-99186
Individual Education
Self-management 98960
Medical Testimony 99075
Non-Office Medical Services 99056
On Call Services 99026-99027
Phlebotomy 99199
Post-Op Visit 99024
Pump Services 99190-99192
Reports and Forms
Medical, Extended 99080
Psychiatric 90889
Specimen Handling 99000-99001
Supply of Materials 99070
Educational 99071
Unlisted Services and Procedures 99199
Unusual Travel 99082

Specific Gravity
Body Fluid 84315

Specimen Collection
Intestines 89100-89105
Stomach 89130-89141

Specimen Concentration 87015

Specimen Handling 99000-99001

SPECT 78607
See Emission Computerized Tomography
Abscess Localization 78807
Bone 78320
Cerebrospinal Fluid 78647
Heart
Multiple 78465
Single 78464
Kidney 78710
Liver 78205
Tumor Localization 78803

Spectacle Services
Fitting
Low Vision Aid 92354-92355
Spectacle Prosthesis 92352-92353
Spectacles 92340-92342
Repair 92370-92371

Spectrometry
Mass
Analyte
Qualitative 83788
Quantitative 83789

Spectrophotometry 84311
Atomic Absorption
See Atomic Absorption Spectroscopy

Spectroscopy
Atomic Absorption 82190
Expired Breath Analysis 0064T
Magnetic Resonance 76390

Spectrum Analyses
See Spectrophotometry

Speech Evaluation 92506
Cine 70371
for Prosthesis 92597, 92607-92608
Video 70371

Spinal Nerve
Avulsion 64772
Transection 64772

Spinal Tap
See Cervical Puncture; Cisternal Puncture; Subdural Tap; Ventricular Puncture
Drainage Fluid 62272
Lumbar 62270

Spine
See Intervertebral Disc; Spinal Cord; Vertebra; Vertebral Body; Vertebral Process
Allograft
  Morselized 20930
  Structural 20931
Arthroplasty
  Lumbar 22856-22865
Aspiration 62267
Augmentation
  Lumbar Vertebra 22524-22525
  Thoracic Vertebra 22523, 22525
Autograft
  Local 20936
  Morselized 20937
  Structural 20938
Biopsy 20250-20251
CT Scan
  Cervical 72125-72127
  Lumbar 72131-72133
  Thoracic 72128-72130
Decompression 62287
Fixation 22842
Fusion
  Anterior 22808-22812
  Anterior Approach 22548-22585, 22812
  Exploration 22830
  Lateral Extracavitary 22532-22534
  Posterior Approach 22590-22802
Incision and Drainage
  Abscess 22010-22015
Insertion
  Instrumentation 22840-22848, 22851
Kyphectomy 22818-22819
Magnetic Resonance Angiography 72159
Magnetic Resonance Imaging
  Cervical 72141-72142, 72156-72158
  Lumbar 72148-72158
  Thoracic 72146-72147, 72156-72158
Manipulation
  with Anesthesia 22505
Myelography
  Cervical 72240
  Lumbosacral 72265
  Thoracic 72255
  Total 72270
Radiosurgery
  Stereotactic 63620-63621
Reconstruction
  Dorsal Spine Elements 63295
Reinsertion
  Instrumentation 22849
Removal
  Instrumentation 22850, 22852-22855
Repair, Osteotomy
  Anterior 22220-22226
  Posterior 22210-22214
    Cervical Laminoplasty 63050-63051
    Posterolateral 22216
Ultrasound 76800
Unlisted Services and Procedures, Surgery 22899
X-ray 72020, 72090
  Absorptiometry 77080-77082
  Cervical 72040-72052
  Lumbosacral 72100-72120
  Standing 72069
  Thoracic 72070-72074
  Thoracolumbar 72080
  Total 72010
  with Contrast
    Cervical 72240
    Lumbosacral 72265
    Thoracic 72255
    Total 72270

Spine Chemotherapy
Administration 96450
  See Chemotherapy

Spirometry 94010-94070
See Pulmonology, Diagnostic
Patient Initiated 94014-94016

Splanchnicectomy
See Nerves, Sympathectomy, Excision

Spleen
Excision 38100-38102
  Laparoscopic 38120
Injection
  Radiologic 38200
Nuclear Medicine
  Imaging 78185, 78215-78216
Repair 38115

Splenectomy
Laparoscopic 38120
Partial 38101
Partial with Repair, Ruptured Spleen 38115
Total 38100
  En bloc 38102

Splenoplasty
See Repair, Spleen

Splenoportography 75810
Injection Procedures 38200

Splenorrhaphy 38115

Splint
See Casting; Strapping
Arm
  Long 29105
  Short 29125-29126
Finger 29130-29131
Foot 29590
Leg
  Long 29505
  Short 29515
Oral Surgical 21085
Ureteral
  See Ureteral Splinting

Split Grafts 15100-15101, 15120-15121

Split Renal Function Test
See Cystourethroscopy, Catheterization, Ureteral

Splitting
Blood Products 86985

Spontaneous Abortion
See Abortion

Sprengel's Deformity 23400

Spring Water Cyst
See Cyst, Pericardial

Spur, Bone
See Exostosis
Calcaneal
  See Heel Spur

Sputum Analysis 89220

SRIH
See Somatostatin

Ssabanejew-Frank Operation
See Incision, Stomach, Creation, Stoma; Incision and Drainage

Stabilizing Factor, Fibrin
See Fibrin Stabilizing Factor

Stable Factor 85230

Stallard Procedure
See Conjunctivorhinostomy

Stamey Procedure 51845
See Repair, Bladder, Neck

Standby Services
Physician 99360

Stanford-Binet Test
See Psychiatric Diagnosis

Stanftan
See Binet Test

Stapedectomy
Revision 69662
with Footplate Drill Out 69661
without Foreign Material 69660

Stapedotomy
Revision 69662
with Footplate Drill Out 69661
without Foreign Material 69660

Stapes
Excision
  with Footplate Drill Out 69661
  without Foreign Material 69660
Mobilization
  See Mobilization, Stapes
Release 69650
Revision 69662

Staphyloma
Sclera
  Repair
    with Graft 66225
    without Graft 66220

Starch Granules
Feces 89225

Stoffel Operation
See Rhizotomy

Stoma
Creation
Bladder 51980
Kidney 50551-50561
Stomach
Neonatal 43831
Temporary 43830-43831
Ureter 50860
Ureter
Endoscopy via 50951-50961

Stomach
Anastomosis
with Duodenum 43810, 43850-43855
with Jejunum ...43820-43825, 43860-43865
Biopsy 43600-43605
Creation
Stoma
Temporary 43830-43831
Temporary Stoma
Laparoscopic 43653
Electrode
Removal 0156T, 0158T, 43882
Electrogastrography 91132-91133
Excision
Partial 43631-43635, 43845
Total 43620-43622
Exploration 43500
Gastric Bypass 43644-43645, 43846
Revision 43848
Gastric Restrictive Procedures 43770-43774, 43848, 43886-43888
Implantation
Electrodes 0155T, 0157T, 43647, 43881
Incision 43830-43832
Exploration 43500
Pyloric Sphincter 43520
Removal
Foreign Body 43500
Intubation with Specimen Prep 91055
Laparoscopy 0155T-0156T, 43647-43648
Nuclear Medicine
Blood Loss Study 78278
Emptying Study 78264
Imaging 78261
Protein Loss Study 78282
Reflux Study 78262
Vitamin B-12 Absorption 78270-78272
Reconstruction
for Obesity 43644-43645, 43842-43847
Roux-En-Y 43644, 43846
Removal
Foreign Body 43500
Repair 48547
Fistula 43880
Fundoplasty 43324-43325
Laparoscopic 43280
Laceration 43501-43502
Stoma 43870
Ulcer 43501
Replacement
Electrodes 0155T, 0157T, 43647, 43881
Specimen Collection 89130-89141
Stimulation of Secretion 91052
Suture
Fistula 43880
for Obesity 43842-43843
Stoma 43870
Ulcer 43840
Wound 43840
Tumor
Excision 43610-43611
Ulcer
Excision 43610
Unlisted Services and Procedures ..43659, 43999

Stomatoplasty
See Mouth, Repair

Stone, Kidney
See Calculus, Removal, Kidney

Stookey-Scarff Procedure
See Ventriculocisternostomy

Stool Blood
See Blood, Feces

Storage
Embryo 89342
Oocyte 89346
Reproductive Tissue 89344
Sperm 89343

Strabismus
Chemodenervation 67345
Repair
Adjustable Sutures 67335
Extraocular Muscles 67340
One Horizontal Muscle 67311
One Vertical Muscle 67314
Posterior Fixation Suture Technique ..67334-67335
Previous Surgery, Not Involving Extraocular Muscles 67331
Release Extensive Scar Tissue 67343
Superior Oblique Muscle 67318
Transposition 67320
Two Horizontal Muscles 67312
Two or More Vertical Muscles 67316

Strapping
See Cast; Splint
Ankle 29540
Back 29220
Chest 29200
Elbow 29260
Finger 29280
Foot 29540, 29590
Hand 29280
Hip 29520
Knee 29530
Shoulder 29240
Thorax 29200
Toes 29550
Unlisted Services and Procedures 29799
Unna Boot 29580
Wrist 29260

Strassman Procedure 58540

Strayer Procedure
Leg, Lower 27687

Streptococcus pneumoniae Vaccine
See Vaccines

Streptococcus, Group A
Antigen Detection
Enzyme Immunoassay 87430
Nucleic Acid 87650-87652
Direct Optical Observation 87880

Streptococcus, Group B
by Immunoassay
with Direct Optical Observation 87802

Streptokinase, Antibody 86590

Stress Tests
Cardiovascular 93015-93024
Multiple Gated Acquisition (MUGA) 78472-78473
Myocardial Perfusion Imaging 78460-78465
Pulmonary 94620-94621
See Pulmonology, Diagnostic

Stricture
Repair
Urethra 53400-53405
Urethra
See Urethral Stenosis

Stricturoplasty
Intestines 44615

Stroboscopy
Larynx 31579

STS 86592-86593
See Syphilis Test

Stuart-Prower Factor 85260

Study, Color Vision
See Color Vision Examination

Sturmdorf Procedure 57520

Styloid Process
Radial
Excision 25230

Styloidectomy
Radial 25230

Stypven Time
See Russell Viper Venom Time

Subacromial Bursa
Arthrocentesis 20610

Subclavian Arteries
See Artery, Subclavian

Subcutaneous Infusion
See Infusion, Subcutaneous

Subcutaneous Injection
See Injection, Subcutaneous

Subcutaneous Mastectomies
See Mastectomy, Subcutaneous

Subcutaneous Tissue
Excision 15830-15839, 15847

Colon
Diverticula ... 44604-44605
Fistula ... 44650-44661
Plication ... 44680
Stoma ... 44620-44625
Ulcer ... 44604-44605
Wound ... 44604-44605
Esophagus
Wound ... 43410-43415
Eyelid ... 67880
Closure of ... 67875
with Transposition of Tarsal Plate ... 67882
Wound
Full Thickness ... 67935
Partial Thickness ... 67930
Facial Nerve
Intratemporal
Lateral to Geniculate Ganglion ... 69740
Medial to Geniculate Ganglion ... 69745
Foot
Tendon ... 28200-28210
Gastroesophageal ... 43405
Great Vessel ... 33320-33322
Hemorrhoids ... 46945-46946
Hepatic Duct
See Hepatic Duct, Repair
Intestine
Large
Diverticula ... 44605
Ulcer ... 44605
Wound ... 44605
Intestines
Large
Diverticula ... 44604
Ulcer ... 44604
Wound ... 44604
Small
Diverticula ... 44602-44603
Fistula ... 44640-44661
Plication ... 44680
Ulcer ... 44602-44603
Wound ... 44602-44603
Stoma ... 44620-44625
Iris
with Ciliary Body ... 66682
Kidney
Fistula ... 50520-50526
Horseshoe ... 50540
Wound ... 50500
Leg, Lower
Tendon ... 27658-27665
Leg, Upper
Muscle ... 27385-27386
Liver
Wound ... 47350-47361
Mesentery ... 44850
Nerve ... 64831-64876
Pancreas ... 48545
Pharynx
Wound ... 42900
Rectum
Fistula ... 45800-45825
Prolapse ... 45540-45541
Removal
Anesthesia ... 15850-15851
Spleen
See Splenorrhapy
Stomach
Fistula ... 43880
Laceration ... 43501-43502
Stoma ... 43870
Ulcer ... 43501, 43840
Wound ... 43840
Tendon
Foot ... 28200-28210
Knee ... 27380-27381
Testis
Injury ... 54670
Suspension ... 54620-54640
Thoracic Duct
Abdominal Approach ... 38382
Cervical Approach ... 38380
Thoracic Approach ... 38381
Throat
Wound ... 42900
Tongue
Base Suspension ... 41512
to Lip ... 41510
Trachea
Fistula
with Plastic Repair ... 31825
without Plastic Repair ... 31820
Stoma
with Plastic Repair ... 31825
without Plastic Repair ... 31820
Wound
Cervical ... 31800
Intrathoracic ... 31805
Ulcer ... 44604-44605
Ureter ... 50900
Deligation ... 50940
Fistula ... 50920-50930
Urethra
Fistula ... 45820-45825, 53520
Stoma ... 53520
to Bladder ... 51840-51841
Wound ... 53502-53515
Uterus
Fistula ... 51920-51925
Rupture ... 58520, 59350
Suspension ... 58400-58410
Vagina
Cystocele ... 57240, 57260
Enterocele ... 57265
Fistula
Rectovaginal ... 57300-57307
Transvesical and Vaginal Approach ... 57330
Urethrovaginal ... 57310-57311
Vesicovaginal ... 51900, 57320-57330
Rectocele ... 57250-57260
Suspension ... 57280, 57283
Wound ... 57200-57210
Vas Deferens ... 55400
Vein
Femoral ... 37650
Iliac ... 37660
Vena Cava ... 37620
Wound ... 44604-44605

Swallowing
Evaluation ... 92610-92613, 92616-92617
Imaging ... 74230
Treatment ... 92526

Swanson Procedure ... 28309

Sweat Collection
Iontophoresis ... 89230

Sweat Glands
Excision
Axillary ... 11450-11451
Inguinal ... 11462-11463
Perianal ... 11470-11471
Perineal ... 11470-11471
Umbilical ... 11470-11471

Sweat Test ... 82435
See Chloride, Blood

Swenson Procedure ... 45120

Syme Procedure ... 27888

Sympathectomy
Artery
Digital ... 64820
Radial ... 64821
Superficial Palmar Arch ... 64823
Ulnar ... 64822
Cervical ... 64802
Cervicothoracic ... 64804
Digital Artery
with Magnification ... 64820
Lumbar ... 64818
Presacral ... 58410
Thoracic ... 32664
Thoracolumbar ... 64809
with Rib Excision ... 21616

Sympathetic Nerve
Excision ... 64802-64818
Injection
Anesthetic ... 64508, 64520-64530

Sympathins
See Catecholamines

Symphysiotomy
Horseshoe Kidney ... 50540

Symphysis, Pubic
See Pubic Symphysis

Syncytial Virus, Respiratory
See Respiratory Syncytial Virus

Syndactylism, Toes
See Webbed, Toe

Syndactyly
Repair ... 26560-26562

Syndesmotomy
See Ligament, Release

Syndrome
Adrenogenital
See Adrenogenital Syndrome
Ataxia-Telangiectasia
See Ataxia Telangiectasia
Bloom
See Bloom Syndrome
Carpal Tunnel
See Carpal Tunnel Syndrome
Costen's
See Temporomandibular Joint (TMJ)

Erb-Goldflam
See Myasthenia Gravis
Ovarian Vein
See Ovarian Vein Syndrome
Synechiae, Intrauterine
See Adhesions, Intrauterine
Treacher Collins
See Treacher-Collins Syndrome
Urethral
See Urethral Syndrome

Syngesterone
See Progesterone

Synostosis (Cranial)
See Craniosynostosis

Synovectomy
Arthrotomy with
Glenohumeral Joint 23105
Sternoclavicular Joint 23106
Elbow 24102
Excision
Carpometacarpal Joint 26130
Finger Joint 26135-26140
Hip Joint 27054
Interphalangeal Joint 26140
Knee Joint 27334-27335
Metacarpophalangeal Joint 26135
Palm 26145
Wrist 25105, 25118-25119
Radical 25115-25116

Synovial
Bursa
See Bursa
Cyst
See Ganglion
Membrane
See Synovium
Popliteal Space
See Baker's Cyst

Synovium
Biopsy
Carpometacarpal Joint 26100
Interphalangeal Joint 26110
Knee Joint 27330
Metacarpophalangeal Joint
with Synovial Biopsy 26105
Excision
Carpometacarpal Joint 26130
Finger Joint 26135-26140
Hip Joint 27054
Interphalangeal Joint 26140
Knee Joint 27334-27335

Syphilis ab
See Antibody, Treponema Pallidum

Syphilis Test 86592-86593

Syrinx
Spinal Cord
Aspiration 62268

System
Endocrine
See Endocrine System
Hemic
See Hemic System
Lymphatic
See Lymphatic System
Musculoskeletal
See Musculoskeletal System
Nervous
See Nervous System

T

T Cell Leukemia Virus I Antibodies, Adult
See Antibody, HTLV-I

T Cell Leukemia Virus I, Human
See HTLV I

T Cell Leukemia Virus II Antibodies, Human
See Antibody, HTLV-II

T Cell Leukemia Virus II, Human
See HTLV II

T-Cells
CD4
Absolute 86361
Count 86359
Ratio 86360

T Lymphotropic Virus Type III Antibodies, Human
See Antibody, HIV

T-3
See Triiodothyronine

T3 Free
See Triiodothyronine, Free

T-4 .... 84436-84439, 86360

T4 Molecule
See CD4

T4 Total
See Thyroxine, Total

T-7 Index
See Thyroxine, Total

T-8
See CD8; T-Cells, Ratio

T-Cell T8 Antigens
See CD8

T-Phyl
See Theophylline

Taarnhoj Procedure
See Decompression, Gasserian Ganglion, Sensory Root; Section

Tachycardia
Heart
Recording 93609

Tacrolimus
Drug Assay 80197

Tag, Skin
See Skin, Tags

Tail Bone
Excision 27080
Fracture 27200-27202

Takeuchi Procedure 33505

Talectomy
See Astragalectomy

Talotarsal Joint
Dislocation 28570-28575, 28585
Percutaneous Fixation 28576

Talus
Arthrodesis
Pantalar 28705
Subtalar 28725
Triple 28715
Arthroscopy
Surgical 29891-29892
Subtalar 29904-29907
Autograft, Osteochondral 28446
Craterization 28120
Cyst
Excision 28100-28103
Diaphysectomy 28120
Excision 28120, 28130
Fracture
Open Treatment 28445
Percutaneous Fixation 28436
with Manipulation 28435-28436
without Manipulation 28430
Repair
Osteochondritis Dissecans 29892
Osteotomy 28302
Saucerization 28120
Tumor
Excision 27647, 28100-28103

Tap
Cisternal
See Cisternal Puncture
Lumbar Diagnostic
See Spinal Tap

Tarsal
Fracture
Percutaneous Fixation 28456

Tarsal Bone
See Ankle Bone

Tarsal Joint
See Foot
Arthrodesis 28730-28735, 28740
with Advancement 28737
with Lengthening 28737
Craterization 28122
Cyst
Excision 28104-28107
Diaphysectomy 28122
Dislocation 28540-28545, 28555
Percutaneous Fixation 28545-28546
Excision 28116, 28122

Fracture
  Open Treatment 28465
  with Manipulation 28455-28456
  without Manipulation 28450
Fusion 28730-28735, 28740
  with Advancement 28737
  with Lengthening 28737
Repair 28320
  Osteotomy 28304-28305
Saucerization 28122
Tumor
  Excision 28104-28107, 28171

Tarsal Strip Procedure 67917-67924

Tarsal Tunnel Release 28035

Tarsal Wedge Procedure .67916, 67923

Tarsometatarsal Joint
Arthrodesis 28730-28735, 28740
Arthrotomy 28020, 28050
Dislocation 28600-28605, 28615
  Percutaneous Fixation 28606
Exploration 28020
Fusion 28730-28735, 28740
Removal
  Foreign Body 28020
  Loose Body 28020
Synovial
  Biopsy 28050
  Excision 28070

Tarsorrhaphy 67875
Median 67880
Severing 67710
  with Transposition of Tarsal Plate 67882

Tattoo
Cornea 65600
Skin 11920-11922

TB Test
Antigen Response 86480
Skin Test 86580

TBG
See Thyroxine Binding Globulin

TBS
See Bethesda System

TCT
See Thrombin Time

Td Shots
See Tetanus Immunization; Vaccines

Team Conference
Case Management Services 99366-99368

Tear Duct
See Lacrimal Duct

Tear Gland
See Lacrimal Gland

Technique
Pericardial Window
  See Pericardiostomy
Projective
  See Projective Test

Teeth
X-ray 70300-70320

Telangiectasia
Chromosome Analysis 88248
Injection 36468

Telangiectasia, Cerebello-Oculocutaneous
See Ataxia Telangiectasia

Telephone
Evaluation and Management
  Nonphysician 98966-98968
  Physician 99441-99443
Pacemaker Analysis 93293
Transmission of ECG 93012

Teletherapy
Dose Plan 77305-77321

Temperature Gradient Studies .93740

Temporal Arteries
See Artery, Temporal

Temporal Bone
Electromagnetic Bone Conduction Hearing Device
  Implantation/Replacement 69710
  Removal/Repair 69711
Excision 69535
Resection 69535
Tumor
  Removal 69970
Unlisted Services and Procedures 69979

Temporal, Petrous
Excision
  Apex 69530

Temporomandibular Joint (TMJ)
Arthrocentesis 20605
Arthrography 70328-70332
  Injection 21116
Arthroplasty 21240-21243
Arthroscopy
  Diagnostic 29800
  Surgical 29804
Arthrotomy 21010
Cartilage
  Excision 21060
Condylectomy 21050
Coronoidectomy 21070
Dislocation
  Closed Treatment 21480-21485
  Open Treatment 21490
Injection
  Radiologic 21116
Magnetic Resonance Imaging (MRI) 70336
Manipulation 21073
Meniscectomy 21060
Prostheses
  See Prosthesis, Temporomandibular Joint
Reconstruction
  See Reconstruction, Temporomandibular Joint
X-ray with Contrast 70328-70332

Tenago Procedure 53431

Tendinosuture
See Suture, Tendon

Tendon
Achilles
  See Achilles Tendon
Arm, Upper
  Revision 24320
Excision
  Finger 26180
  Forearm 25109
  Palm 26170
  Wrist 25109
Finger
  Excision 26180
Forearm
  Excision 25109
  Repair 25260-25274
Graft
  Harvesting 20924
Insertion
  Biceps Tendon 24342
Lengthening
  Ankle 27685-27686
  Arm, Upper 24305
  Elbow 24305
  Finger 26476, 26478
  Forearm 25280
  Hand 26476, 26478
  Leg, Lower 27685-27686
  Leg, Upper 27393-27395
  Toe 28240
  Wrist 25280
Palm
  Excision 26170
Release
  Arm, Lower 25295
  Arm, Upper 24332
  Wrist 25295
Shortening
  Ankle 27685-27686
  Finger 26477, 26479
  Hand 26477, 26479
  Leg, Lower 27685-27686
Transfer
  Arm, Lower 25310-25312, 25316
  Arm, Upper 24301
  Elbow 24301
  Finger 26497-26498
  Hand 26480-26489
  Leg, Lower 27690-27692
  Leg, Upper 27400
  Pelvis 27098
  Thumb 26490-26492, 26510
  Wrist 25310-25312, 25316
Transplant
  Leg, Upper 27396-27397
Wrist
  Excision 25109
  Repair 25260-25274

Tendon Origin
Insertion
  Injection 20551

Tendon Pulley Reconstruction of Hand
See Hand, Reconstruction, Tendon Pulley

Repair
Injury 54670
Suspension 54620-54640
Torsion 54600
Suture
Injury 54670
Suspension 54620-54640
Transplantation
to Thigh 54680
Tumor
Excision 54530-54535
Undescended
Exploration 54550-54560
Unlisted Services and Procedures ..54699, 55899

Testosterone 84402
Response 80414
Stimulation 80414-80415
Total 84403

Testosterone Estradiol Binding Globulin
See Globulin, Sex Hormone Binding

Tetanus 86280
Antibody 86774
Immunoglobulin 90389
Vaccine 90703

Tetrachloride, Carbon
See Carbon Tetrachloride

Tetralogy of Fallot ...33692-33697, 33924

Thal-Nissen Procedure 43325

Thawing
See Frozen Blood Preparation
Cryopreserved
Embryo 89352
Oocytes 89356
Reproductive Tissue 89354
Sperm 89353
Previously Frozen Cells 38208-38209

Thawing and Expansion
of Frozen Cell 88241

THBR
See Thyroid Hormone Binding Ratio

Theleplasty
See Nipples, Reconstruction

Theophylline
Assay 80198

Therapeutic
Abortion
See Abortion, Therapeutic
Apheresis
See Apheresis, Therapeutic
Drug Assay
See Drug Assay
Mobilization
See Mobilization
Photopheresis
See Photopheresis
Radiology
See Radiology, Therapeutic

Therapies
Cold
See Cryotherapy
Exercise
See Exercise Therapy
Family
See Psychotherapy, Family
Language
See Language Therapy
Milieu
See Environmental Intervention
Occupational
See Occupational Therapy
Photodynamic
See Photochemotherapy
Photoradiation
See Actinotherapy
Physical
See Physical Medicine/Therapy/Occupational Therapy
Speech
See Speech Therapy
Tocolytic
See Tocolysis
Ultraviolet
See Actinotherapy

Therapy
ACE Inhibitor Therapy
See Performance Measures
Beta Blocker Therapy
See Performance Measures
Desensitization
See Allergen Immunotherapy
Hemodialysis
See Hemodialysis
Hot Pack
See Hot Pack Treatment
Pharmacologic; for Cessation of Tobacco Use
See Performance Measures
Radiation
Brachytherapy 0182T
See Irradiation
Speech
See Speech Therapy
Statin Therapy, Prescribed
See Performance Measures

Thermocauterization
Ectropion
Repair 67922
Lesion
Cornea 65450

Thermocoagulation
See Electrocautery

Thermotherapy
Prostate 53850-53852
Microwave 53850
Radiofrequency 53852

Thiamine 84425

Thiersch Operation 15050
See Pinch Graft

Thiersch Procedure 46753

Thigh
Fasciotomy 27025
See Femur; Leg, Upper

Thin Layer Chromatographies
See Chromatography, Thin-Layer

Thiocyanate 84430

Third Disease
See Rubella

Thompson Procedure 27430

Thoracectomy
See Thoracoplasty

Thoracentesis 32421-32422

Thoracic
Anterior Ramus
See Intercostal Nerve
Arteries
See Artery, Thoracic
Cavity
See Chest Cavity
Duct
See Lymphatics
Cannulation 38794
Ligation 38380
Abdominal Approach 38382
Thoracic Approach 38381
Suture
Abdominal Approach 38382
Cervical Approach 38380
Thoracic Approach 38381
Empyema
See Abscess, Thorax
Surgery
Video-Assisted
See Thoracoscopy
Vertebra
See Vertebra, Thoracic
Wall
See Chest Wall

Thoracocentesis
See Thoracentesis

Thoracoplasty 32905
with Closure Bronchopleural Fistula 32906

Thoracoscopy
Diagnostic 32601-32606
with Biopsy 32602, 32604, 32606
without Biopsy 32601, 32603, 32605
Surgical 32650-32665
with Control Traumatic Hemorrhage ...32654
with Creation Pericardial Window 32659
with Esophagomyotomy 32665
with Excision Mediastinal Cyst, Tumor and/or Mass 32662
with Excision Pericardial Cyst, Tumor and/or Mass 32661
with Excision-Plication of Bullae 32655
with Lobectomy 32663
with Parietal Pleurectomy 32656

Transfer
Adjacent
Eyelids 67961
Skin 14000-14350
Facial Muscles 15845
Finger Flap 14350
Toe Flap 14350
Typing
HLA Antibodies 86812-86817
Lymphocyte Culture 86821-86822

Tissue Culture
from Skin Harvest 15040
Skin Grafts 15150-15157, 15340-15366

Tissue Factor
See Thromboplastin

TLC
See Chromatography, Thin-Layer
Screen 84375

TMJ
See Temporomandibular Joint (TMJ)
Manipulation, Therapeutic
See Manipulation, Temporomandibular Joint
Prostheses
See Prosthesis, Temporomandibular Joint

Tobacco
See Performance Measures

Tobramycin
Assay 80200

Tocolysis 59412

Tocopherol 84446

Toe
See Interphalangeal Joint, Toe; Metatarsophalangeal Joint; Phalanx
Amputation 28810-28825
Capsulotomy 28270-28272
Fasciotomy 28008
Fracture
See Fracture, Phalanges, Toe
Lesion
Excision 28092
Reconstruction
Angle Deformity 28313
Extra Toes 28344
Hammertoe 28285-28286
Macrodactyly 28340-28341
Syndactyly 28345
Webbed Toe 28345
Repair
Bunion 28290-28299
Muscle 28240
Tendon 28232-28234, 28240
Webbed 28280
Webbed Toe 28345
Tenotomy 28010-28011, 28232-28234
Unlisted Services and Procedures 28899

Toe Flap
Tissue Transfer 14350

Toes
Arthrocentesis 20600
Dislocation
See Specific Joint
Magnetic Resonance Imaging (MRI) 73721-73723
Reconstruction
Extra Digit 26587
Repair
Extra Digit 26587
Macrodactylia 26590
Reposition to Hand 26551-26556
Strapping 29550
X-ray 73660

Tolbutamide Tolerance Test 82953

Tolerance Test
Glucagon 82946
Glucose 82951-82952
with Tolbutamide 82953
Heparin-Protamine 85530
Insulin 80434-80435
Maltose 82951-82952
Tolbutamide 82953

Tomodensitometries
See CT Scan

Tomographic Scintigraphy, Computed
See Emission Computerized Tomography

Tomographic SPECT
Myocardial Imaging 78469

Tomographies, Computed X-ray
See CT Scan

Tomography, Computerized Axial
Abdomen
See Abdomen, CT Scan
Head
See Head, CT Scan

Tomography, Emission Computed
See Positron Emission Tomography
Single Photon
See SPECT

Tompkins Metroplasty 58540
See Uterus, Reconstruction

Tongue
Abscess
Incision and Drainage ..41000-41006, 41015
Base Suspension 41512
Biopsy 41100-41105
Cyst
Incision and Drainage 41000-41006, 41015, 60000
Excision
Complete 41140-41155
Frenum 41115
Partial 41120-41135
with Mouth Resection 41150-41153
with Radical Neck 41135, 41145, 41153-41155
Fixation 41500
Hematoma
Incision and Drainage ..41000-41006, 41015
Incision
Frenum 41010
Lesion
Excision 41110-41114
Reconstruction
Frenum 41520
Repair
See Repair, Tongue
Laceration 41250-41252
Suture 41510
Suture 41510
Unlisted Services and Procedures 41599

Tonography 92120
with Provocation 92130

Tonometry, Serial 92100

Tonsil, Pharyngeal
See Adenoids

Tonsillectomy 42820-42826

Tonsils
Abscess
Incision and Drainage 42700
Excision 42825-42826
Lingual 42870
Radical 42842-42845
Tag 42860
with Adenoids 42820-42821
Lingual
Destruction 42870
Unlisted Services and Procedures 42999

Topiramate
Assay 80201

Torek Procedure
See Orchiopexy

Torkildsen Procedure 62180

TORP (Total Ossicular Replacement Prosthesis) 69633, 69637

Torsion Swing Test 92546

Torula
See Cryptococcus

Torus Mandibularis
Tumor Excision 21031

Total
Abdominal Hysterectomy
See Hysterectomy, Abdominal, Total
Bilirubin Level
See Bilirubin, Total
Catecholamines
See Catecholamines, Urine
Cystectomy
See Bladder, Excision, Total
Dacryoadenectomy
See Dacryoadenectomy, Total
Elbow Replacement
See Replacement, Elbow, Total
Esophagectomy
See Esophagectomy, Total

Gastrectomy
  See Excision, Stomach, Total
Hemolytic Complement
  See Complement, Hemolytic, Total
Hip Arthroplasty
  See Hip, Total Replacement
Knee Arthroplasty
  See Prosthesis, Knee
Mastectomies
  See Mastectomy
Ostectomy of Patella
  See Patellectomy
Splenectomy
  See Splenectomy, Total

Touroff Operation 37615
See Ligation, Artery, Neck

Toxicology Screen 80100-80103

Toxin Assay 87230

Toxin, Botulinum
See Chemodenervation

Toxoplasma
Antibody 86777-86778

Trabeculectomies
See Trabeculoplasty

Trabeculectomy ab Externo
in Absence of Previous Surgery 66170
with Scarring Previous Surgery 66172

Trabeculoplasty
by Laser Surgery 65855

Trabeculotomy ab Externo
Eye 65850

Trachea
Aspiration 31720
  Catheter 31720-31725
Dilation 31630-31631, 31636-31638
Endoscopy
  via Tracheostomy 31615
Excision
  Stenosis 31780-31781
Fistula
  with Plastic Repair 31825
  without Plastic Repair 31820
Fracture
  Endoscopy 31630
Incision
  Emergency 31603-31605
  Planned 31600-31601
  with Flaps 31610
Introduction
  Needle Wire 31730
Puncture
  Aspiration and/or Injection 31612
Reconstruction
  Carina 31766
  Cervical 31750
  Fistula 31755
  Intrathoracic 31760
Repair
  Cervical 31750
  Fistula 31755
  Intrathoracic 31760
  Stoma 31613-31614
Revision
  Stoma
    Scars 31830
Scar
  Revision 31830
Stenosis
  Excision 31780-31781
  Repair 31780-31781
Stoma
  Repair
    with Plastic Repair 31825
    without Plastic Repair 31820
  Revision
    Scars 31830
Tumor
  Excision
    Cervical 31785
    Thoracic 31786
Unlisted Services and Procedures
  Bronchi 31899
Wound
  Suture
    Cervical 31800
    Intrathoracic 31805

Tracheal
Stent
  Placement 31631
Tubes
  See Endotracheal Tube

Trachelectomy 57530
Radical 57531

Tracheloplasty
See Cervicoplasty

Trachelorrhaphy 57720

Tracheo-Esophageal Fistula
See Fistula, Tracheoesophageal

Tracheobronchoscopy
through Tracheostomy 31615

Tracheoplasty
Cervical 31750
Intrathoracic 31760
Tracheopharyngeal Fistulization 31755

Tracheostoma
Revision 31613-31614

Tracheostomy
Emergency 31603-31605
Planned 31600-31601
Revision
  Scar 31830
Surgical Closure
  with Plastic Repair 31825
  without Plastic Repair 31820
Tracheobronchoscopy through 31615
with Flaps 31610

Tracheotomy
Tube Change 31502

Tracking Tests (Ocular) 92545
See Ear, Nose and Throat

Tract, Urinary
See Urinary Tract

Traction Therapy
See Physical Medicine/Therapy/Occupational Therapy
Manual 97140
Mechanical 97012

Tractotomy
Medulla 61470
Mesencephalon 61480

Training
Activities of Daily Living 97535, 99509
Biofeedback 90901-90911
Cognitive Skills 97532
Community/Work Reintegration 97537
Home Management 97535, 99509
Orthoptic/Pleoptic 92065
Orthotics 97760
Prosthetics 97761
Self Care 97535, 98960-98962, 99509
Sensory Integration 97533
Walking (Physical Therapy) 97116
Wheelchair Management 97542

TRAM Flap
Breast Reconstruction 19367-19369

Trans-Scaphoperilunar
Fracture/Dislocation
  Closed Treatment 25680
  Open Treatment 25685

Transaminase
Glutamic Oxaloacetic 84450
Glutamic Pyruvic 84460

Transanal Endoscopic Microsurgery (TEMS)
See Bladder, Neck

Transcatheter
Biopsy 37200
Closure
  Percutaneous
    Heart 93580-93581
  Transmyocardial
    Heart 0166T, 0167T
Embolization
  Percutaneous 37204
    Cranial 61624-61626
Occlusion
  Percutaneous 37204
    Cranial 61624-61626
Placement
  Intravascular Stents 0075T-0076T, 37205-37208, 37215-37216
  Sensor, Aneurysmal Sac 34806
Therapy
  Embolization 75894
  Infusion 37201-37202, 75896-75898
  Perfusion
    Cranial 61624-61626
  Retrieval 75961

Transcatheter Foreign Body
Retrieval 37203

Transcortin 84449

Transurethral Procedure
See Specific Procedure
Prostate
Incision 52450
Resection 52630
Thermotherapy 53850-53852
Microwave 53850
Radiofrequency 53852

Trapezium
Arthroplasty
with Implant 25445

Travel, Unusual 99082

Treacher-Collins Syndrome
Midface Reconstruction 21150-21151

Treatment, Tocolytic
See Tocolysis

Trendelenburg Operation
See Varicose Vein, Removal, Secondary Varicosity

Trephine Procedure
Sinusotomy
Frontal 31070

Treponema Pallidum
Antibody
Confirmation Test 86781
Antigen Detection
Direct Fluorescence 87285

TRH
See Thyrotropin Releasing Hormone (TRH)

Triacylglycerol
See Triglycerides

Triacylglycerol Hydrolase
See Lipase

Tributyrinase
See Lipase

Trichiasis
Repair 67825
Epilation, by Forceps 67820
Epilation, by Other than Forceps 67825
Incision of Lid Margin 67830
with Free Mucous Membrane Graft 67835

Trichina
See Trichinella

Trichinella
Antibody 86784
Trichogram 96902

Trichomonas Vaginalis
Antigen Detection
Nucleic Acid 87660
by Immunoassay with Direct Optical Observation 87808

Trichrome Stain 88313

Tricuspid Valve
Excision 33460
Repair 33463-33465
Replacement 33465
Repositioning 33468

Tridymite
See Silica

Trigeminal Ganglia
See Gasserian Ganglion

Trigeminal Nerve
Destruction 64600-64610
Injection
Anesthetic 64400
Neurolytic 64600-64610

Trigeminal Tract
Stereotactic
Create Lesion 61791

Trigger Finger Repair 26055

Trigger Point
Injection
One or Two Muscles 20552
Two or More Muscles 20553

Triglyceridase
See Lipase

Triglyceride Lipase
See Lipase

Triglycerides 84478

Trigonocephaly 21175

Triiodothyronine
Free 84481
Reverse 84482
Total 84480
True 84480

Triolean Hydrolase
See Lipase

Trioxopurine
See Uric Acid

Tripcellim
See Trypsin

Trisegmentectomy 47122

Trocar Biopsy
Bone Marrow 38221

Trochanteric Femur Fracture
See Femur, Fracture, Trochanteric

Trophoblastic Tumor GTT
See Hydatidiform Mole

Troponin 84484
Qualitative 84512
Quantitative 84484

Truncal Vagotomies
See Vagotomy, Truncal

Truncus Arteriosus
Repair 33786

Truncus Brachiocephalicus
See Artery, Brachiocephalic

Trunk, Brachiocephalic
See Artery, Brachiocephalic

Trypanosomiases
See Trypanosomiasis

Trypanosomiasis 86171, 86280

Trypsin
Duodenum 84485
Feces 84488-84490

Trypsin Inhibitor, Alpha 1-Antitrypsin
See Alpha-1 Antitrypsin

Trypure
See Trypsin

Tsalicylate Intoxication
See Salicylate

TSH
See Thyroid Stimulating Hormone

TSI
See Thyroid Stimulating Immunoglobulin

Tsutsugamushi Disease
See Scrub Typhus

TT
See Thrombin Time

TT-3
See Triiodothyronine, True

TT-4
See Thyroxine, True

Tuba Auditoria (Auditiva)
See Eustachian Tube

Tubal Embryo Stage Transfer
See Embryo Transfer

Tubal Ligation 58600
Laparoscopic 58670
with Cesarean Delivery 58611

Tubal Occlusion
See Fallopian Tube, Occlusion; Occlusion
Create Lesion

Tubal Pregnancy 59121
with Salpingectomy and/or Oophorectomy 59120

Tube Change
Colonic 49450
Duodenostomy 49451
Gastro-Jejeunostomy 49452
Gastrostomy 43760, 49446
Jejunostomy 49451
Tracheostomy 31502

Tube Placement
Cecostomy Tube 44300, 49442
Duodenostomy Tube 49441

U

UDP Galactose Pyrophosphorylase
See Galactose-1-Phosphate, Uridyl Transferase

UFR
See Uroflowmetry

Ulcer
Anal
See Anus, Fissure
Decubitus
See Debridement; Pressure Ulcer (Decubitus); Skin Graft and Flap
Pinch Graft 15050
Pressure 15920-15999
Stomach
Excision 43610

Ulcerative, Cystitis
See Cystitis, Interstitial

Ulna
See Arm, Lower; Elbow; Humerus; Radius
Arthrodesis
Radioulnar Joint
with Resection 25830
Arthroplasty
with Implant 25442
Centralization or Wrist 25335
Craterization 24147, 25150-25151
Cyst
Excision 24125-24126, 25120-25126
Diaphysectomy 24147, 25150-25151
Excision 24147
Abscess 24138
Complete 25240
Epiphyseal Bar 20150
Partial 25145-25151, 25240
Fracture
Closed Treatment 25530-25535
Olecranon 24670-24675
Open Treatment 24685, 25545
Shaft 25530-25545
Open Treatment 25574
Styloid
Closed Treatment 25650
Open Treatment 25652
Percutaneous Fixation 25651
with Dislocation
Closed Treatment 24620
Open Treatment 24635
with Manipulation 25535
with Radius 25560-25565
Open Treatment 25575
without Manipulation 25530
Incision and Drainage 25035
Osteoplasty 25390-25393
Prophylactic Treatment 25491-25492
Reconstruction
Radioulnar 25337
Repair
Epiphyseal Arrest 25450-25455
Malunion or Nonunion 25400, 25415
Osteotomy 25360, 25370-25375
and Radius 25365
with Graft 25405, 25420-25426
Saucerization 24147, 25150-25151
Sequestrectomy 24138, 25145
Tumor
Cyst 24120
Excision 24125-24126, 25120-25126, 25170

Ulnar Arteries
See Artery, Ulnar

Ulnar Nerve
Decompression 64718
Neuroplasty 64718-64719
Reconstruction 64718-64719
Release 64718-64719
Repair/Suture
Motor 64836
Transposition 64718-64719

Ultrasonic
See Ultrasound

Ultrasonic Cardiography
See Echocardiography

Ultrasonic Procedure 52325

Ultrasonography
See Echography

Ultrasound
See Echocardiography; Echography
3D Rendering 76376-76377
Abdomen 76700-76705
Arm 76880
Artery
Intracranial 93886-93893
Middle Cerebral 76821
Umbilical 76820
Bladder 51798
Bone Density Study 76977
Breast 76645
Bronchi
Endoscopy 31620
Chest 76604
Colon
Endoscopic 45391-45392
Colon-Sigmoid
Endoscopic 45341-45342
Computer-Assisted Surgical Navigation
Intraoperative 20986
Preoperative 20987
Drainage
Abscess 75989
Echoencephalography
See Echoencephalography
Esophagus
Endoscopy 43231-43232
Eye 76510-76513
Arteries 93875
Biometry 76516-76519
Foreign Body 76529
Pachymetry 76514
Fetus 76818-76828
Follow-Up 76970
for Physical Therapy 97035
Gastrointestinal 76975
Gastrointestinal, Upper
Endoscopic 43237-43238, 43242, 43259
Guidance
Amniocentesis 59001, 76946
Amnioinfusion 59070
Arteriovenous Fistulae 76936
Chorionic Villus Sampling 76945
Cryosurgery 55873
Drainage
Fetal Fluid 59074
Endometrial Ablation 58356
Fetal Cordocentesis 76941
Fetal Transfusion 76941
Heart Biopsy 76932
Needle Biopsy 43232, 43238, 43242, 45342, 45392, 76942
Occlusion
Umbilical Cord 59072
Ova Retrieval 76948
Pericardiocentesis 76930
Pseudoaneurysm 76936
Radiation Therapy 76950
Radioelement 76965
Shunt Placement
Fetal 59076
Thoracentesis 76942
Tissue Ablation 76940
Vascular Access 76937
Head 76506, 76536
Heart
Fetal 76825
Hips
Infant 76885-76886
Hysterosonography 76831
Intraoperative 76998
Intravascular
Intraoperative 37250-37251
Kidney 76770-76776
Leg 76880, 0183T
Neck 76536
Needle or Catheter Placement 20555
Non-Coronary
Intravascular 75945-75946
Pelvis 76856-76857
Pregnant Uterus 76801-76817
Prostate 76873
Rectal 76872-76873
Retroperitoneal 76770-76775
Scrotum 76870
Sonohysterography 76831
Spine 76800
Stimulation to Aid Bone Healing 20979
Umbilical Artery 76820
Unlisted Services and Procedures 76999
Uterus
Tumor Ablation 0071T-0072T
Vagina 76830

Ultraviolet Light Therapy
Dermatology
Ultraviolet A 96912
Ultraviolet B 96910
for Dermatology 96900
for Physical Medicine 97028
for Respiratory Medicine 0168T

Umbilectomy ... 49250

Umbilical
Artery Ultrasound ... 76820
Hernia
See Omphalocele
Vein Catheterization
See Catheterization, Umbilical Vein

Umbilical Cord
Occlusion ... 59072

Umbilicus
Excision ... 49250
Repair
Hernia ... 49580-49587
Omphalocele ... 49600-49611

Undescended Testicle
See Testis, Undescended

Unfertilized Egg
See Ova

Unguis
See Nails

Unilateral Simple Mastectomy
See Mastectomy

Unlisted Services and Procedures ... 99499, 99600
Abdomen ... 22999, 49329, 49999
Allergy/Immunology ... 95199
Anal ... 46999
Anesthesia ... 01999
Arm ... 25999
Arthroscopy ... 29999
Autopsy ... 88099
Bile Duct ... 47999
Bladder ... 51999
Brachytherapy ... 77799
Breast ... 19499
Bronchi ... 31899
Cardiac ... 33999
Cardiovascular Studies ... 93799
Casting ... 29799
Cervix ... 58999
Chemistry Procedure ... 84999
Chemotherapy ... 96549
Chest ... 32999
Coagulation ... 85999
Colon ... 44799
Conjunctiva Surgery ... 68399
Craniofacial ... 21299
CT Scan ... 76497
Cytogenetic Study ... 88299
Cytopathology ... 88199
Dermatology ... 96999
Dialysis ... 90999
Diaphragm ... 39599
Ear
External ... 69399
Inner ... 69949
Middle ... 69799
Endocrine System ... 60699
Epididymis ... 55899
Esophagus ... 43289, 43499
Evaluation and Management Services ... 99499
Eye Muscle ... 67399
Eye Surgery
Anterior Segment ... 66999
Posterior Segment ... 67299
Eyelid ... 67999
Fluoroscopy ... 76496
Forearm ... 25999
Gallbladder ... 47999
Gastroenterology Test ... 91299
Gum ... 41899
Hand ... 26989
Hemic System ... 38999
Hepatic Duct ... 47999
Hip Joint ... 27299
Home Services ... 99600
Hysteroscopy ... 58579
Immunization ... 90749
Immunology ... 86849
Infusion ... 96379
Injection ... 96379
Injection of Medication ... 96379
Intestine ... 44238, 44799
Kidney ... 49659
Lacrimal System ... 68899
Laparoscopy ... 38129, 38589, 43289, 43659, 44238, 44979, 47379, 47579, 49329, 49659, 50549, 50949, 54699, 55559, 58578, 58679, 59898, 60659
Larynx ... 31599
Lip ... 40799
Liver ... 47379, 47399
Lungs ... 32999
Lymphatic System ... 38999
Magnetic Resonance ... 76498
Maxillofacial ... 21299
Maxillofacial Prosthetics ... 21089
Meckel's Diverticulum ... 44899
Mediastinum ... 39499
Mesentery Surgery ... 44899
Microbiology ... 87999
Mouth ... 40899, 41599
Musculoskeletal ... 25999, 26989
Musculoskeletal Surgery
Abdominal Wall ... 22999
Neck ... 21899
Spine ... 22899
Thorax ... 21899
Musculoskeletal System ... 20999
Ankle ... 27899
Arm, Upper ... 24999
Elbow ... 24999
Head ... 21499
Knee ... 27599
Leg, Lower ... 27899
Leg, Upper ... 27599
Necropsy ... 88099
Nervous System Surgery ... 64999
Neurology/Neuromuscular Testing ... 95999
Nose ... 30999
Nuclear Medicine ... 78999
Blood ... 78199
Bone ... 78399
Endocrine System ... 78099
Genitourinary System ... 78799
Heart ... 78499
Hematopoietic System ... 78199
Lymphatic System ... 78199
Musculoskeletal System ... 78399
Nervous System ... 78699
Therapeutic ... 79999
Obstetrical Care ... 59898-59899
Omentum ... 49329, 49999
Ophthalmology ... 92499
Orbit ... 67599
Otorhinolaryngology ... 92700
Ovary ... 58679, 58999
Oviduct ... 58679, 58999
Palate ... 42299
Pancreas Surgery ... 48999
Pathology ... 89240
Pelvis ... 27299
Penis ... 55899
Peritoneum ... 49329, 49999
Pharynx ... 42999
Physical Therapy ... 97039, 97139, 97799
Pleura ... 32999
Pressure Ulcer ... 15999
Preventive Medicine ... 99429
Prostate ... 55899
Psychiatric ... 90899
Pulmonology ... 94799
Radiation Physics ... 77399
Radiation Therapy ... 77499
Planning ... 77299
Radiology, Diagnostic ... 76499
Radionuclide Therapy ... 79999
Radiopharmaceutical Therapy ... 79999
Rectum ... 45499, 45999
Salivary Gland ... 42699
Scrotum ... 55899
Seminal Vesicle ... 55899
Shoulder Surgery ... 23929
Sinuses ... 31299
Skin ... 17999
Special Services and Reports ... 99199
Spine ... 22899
Stomach ... 43659, 43999
Strapping ... 29799
Surgical Pathology ... 88399
Temporal Bone ... 69979
Testis ... 54699, 55899
Throat ... 42999
Tongue ... 41599
Tonsil/Adenoid ... 42999
Toxoid ... 90749
Trachea ... 31899
Transfusion ... 86999
Ultrasound ... 76999
Ureter ... 50949
Urinary System ... 53899
Uterus ... 58578-58579, 58999
Uvula ... 42299
Vaccine ... 90749
Vagina ... 58999
Vas Deferens ... 55899
Vascular ... 37799
Vascular Endoscopy ... 37501
Vascular Injection ... 36299
Vascular Studies ... 93799
Wrist ... 25999

Unna Paste Boot ... 29580
Removal ... 29700

UPP
See Urethra Pressure Profile

Ureterostomy Stent
Change 50688

Ureterostomy Tube
Change 50688

Ureterotomy 50600
Insertion Indwelling Stent 50605

Ureteroureterostomy 50760-50770, 50830

Urethra
Abscess
  Incision and Drainage 53040
Adhesions
  Lysis 53500
Artificial Sphincter
  Repair 53449
Biopsy 52204, 53200
Destruction 52214-52224
Dilation 52260-52265, 53600-53621
  General 53665
  Suppository and/or Instillation 53660-53661
Diverticulum
  See Urethral Diverticulum
Drainage
  Extravasation 53080-53085
Endoscopy 52000
  Biopsy 52204, 52354
  Catheterization 52010
  Destruction 52354, 52400
  Evacuation
    Clot 52001
  Excision
    Tumor 52355
  Exploration 52351
  Incision
    Ejaculatory Duct 52402
  Injection of Implant Material 51715
  Lithotripsy 52353
  Removal
    Calculus 52352
  Resection
    Ejaculatory Duct 52402
  Vasectomy 52402
  Vasotomy 52402
Excision
  Diverticulum 53230-53235
  Total
    Female 53210
    Male 53215
Incision 53000-53010
  Meatus 53020-53025
Incision and Drainage 53060
Insertion
  Stent 0084T, 52282
Lesion
  Destruction 53265
  Excision 53260
Paraurethral Gland
  Incision and Drainage 53060
Polyp
  Destruction 53260
  Excision 53260
Pressure Profile 51772
Prolapse
  Destruction 53275
  Excision 53275
  Repair 53275
Radiotracer 52250
Reconstruction 53410-53440, 53445
  and Bladder 51800-51820
    Radiofrequency Micro-Remodeling 0193T
  Complications 54340-54348
  Hypospadias
    One Stage 54322-54328
    Second Stage 54308-54316
    Third Stage 54318
  Meatus 53450-53460
Removal
  Calculus 52310-52315
  Foreign Body 52310-52315
  Sling 53442
  Urethral Stent 52310-52315
Repair
  Diverticulum 53240, 53400-53405
  Fistula 45820-45825, 53400-53405, 53520
  Sphincter 57220
  Stricture 53400-53405
  Urethrocele 57230
  Wound 53502-53515
Skene's Gland
  Incision and Drainage 53060
Sphincter 52277
  Electromyography 51784-51785
    Needle 51785
  Insertion
    Prosthesis 53444
  Reconstruction 53445
  Removal
    Prosthesis 53446-53447
  Repair
    Prosthesis 53449
  Replacement
    Prosthesis 53448
Suture
  Fistula 45820-45825, 53520
  to Bladder 51840-51841
  Wound 53502-53515
Tumor
  Destruction 53220
  Excision 53220
Unlisted Services and Procedures 53899
Urethrocystography 74450-74455
Urethrotomy 52270-52276
X-ray with Contrast 74450-74455

Urethral
Diverticulum
  Marsupialization 53240
Meatus, Dorsal
  See Epispadias
Sphincter
  Biofeedback Training 90911
  Insertion
    Prosthesis 53444
  Removal
    Prosthesis 53446-53447
  Replacement
    Prosthesis 53448
Stenosis
  Dilation 52281
Stent
  Insertion 0084T, 52282
  Removal
    Bladder 52310-52315
    Urethra 52310-52315
Stricture
  Dilation 52281, 53600-53621
  Injection
    Steroids 52283
Syndrome
  Cystourethroscopy 52285

Urethrectomy
Total
  Female 53210
  Male 53215

Urethrocele
See Urethra, Prolapse

Urethrocystography 74450-74455
Contrast and/or Chain 51605
Retrograde 51610
Voiding 51600

Urethrocystopexy
See Vesicourethropexy

Urethromeatoplasty 53450-53460

Urethropexy 51840-51841

Urethroplasty 46744-46746
First Stage 53400
One Stage
  Hypospadias 54322-54328
Reconstruction
  Female Urethra 53430
  Male Anterior Urethra 53410
  Prostatic/Membranous Urethra
    First Stage 53420
    One Stage 53415
    Second Stage 53425
Second Stage 53405
  Hypospadias 54308-54316
Third Stage
  Hypospadias 54318

Urethrorrhaphy 53502-53515

Urethroscopy
See Endoscopy, Urethra

Urethrostomy 53000-53010

Urethrotomy 53000-53010
Direct Vision
  with Cystourethroscopy 52276
Internal 52601, 52647-52648
with Cystourethroscopy
  Female 52270
  Male 52275

Uric Acid
Blood 84550
Other Source 84560
Urine 84560

Uridyltransferase, Galactose-1-Phosphate
See Galactose-1-Phosphate, Uridyl Transferase

V

Cholera
Injectable 90725
Diphtheria and Tetanus (Td) 90714, 90718
Diphtheria Toxoid 90719
Diphtheria, Tetanus (DT) 90702
Diphtheria, Tetanus, Acellular Pertussis (DTaP) 90700
Diphtheria, Tetanus, Acellular Pertussis and Hemophilus Influenza B (Hib) (DTaP-Hib) . . . 90721
Diphtheria, Tetanus, Acellular Pertussis, Haemophilus Influenza Type B, and Inactivated Poliovirus (DTaP-Hib-IPV) 90698
Diphtheria, Tetanus, Acellular Pertussis, and Inactivated Poliovirus (DTaP-IPV) 90696
Diphtheria, Tetanus, Acellular Pertussis, Hepatitis B, and Inactivated Poliovirus (DTaP-HepB-IPV) 90723
Diphtheria, Tetanus, and Acellular Pertussis (TdaP) 90715
Diphtheria, Tetanus, Whole Cell Pertussis (DTP) 90701
Diphtheria, Tetanus, Whole Cell Pertussis and Hemophilus Influenza B (Hib) (DTP-Hib) 90720
Encephalitis, Japanese 90735
Inactivated 90738
Hemophilus Influenza B 90645-90648
Hepatitis A 90632-90634
Hepatitis A and Hepatitis B 90636
Hepatitis B 90740-90747
Hepatitis B and Hemophilus Influenza B (HepB-Hib) 90748
Human Papilloma Virus (HPV) 90649, 90650
Influenza 90655-90663
Lyme Disease 90665
Measles 90705
Measles and Rubella 90708
Measles, Mumps and Rubella (MMR) 90707
Measles, Mumps, Rubella and Varicella (MMRV) 90710
Meningococcal 90733-90734
Mumps 90704
Plague 90727
Pneumococcal 90669, 90732
Poliovirus, Inactivated
Intramuscular 90713
Subcutaneous 90713
Poliovirus, Live
Oral 90712
Rabies 90675-90676
Rotavirus 90680, 90681
Rubella 90706
Tetanus and Diphtheria 90714, 90718
Tetanus Toxoid 90703
Tetanus, Diphtheria, and Acellular Pertussis (TdaP) 90715
Tuberculosis (BCG) 90585-90586
Typhoid 90690-90693
Unlisted Vaccine/Toxoid 90749
Varicella (Chicken Pox) 90716
Yellow Fever 90717
Zoster (Shingles) 90736

Vagina

Abscess
Incision and Drainage 57010
Amines Test 82120
Biopsy
Colposcopy 57421
Endocervical 57454
Extensive 57105
Simple 57100
Closure 57120
Colposcopy . . . 57420-57421, 57455-57456, 57461
Construction
with Graft 57292
without Graft 57291
Cyst
Excision 57135
Dilation 57400
Endocervical
Biopsy 57454
Exploration 57452
Excision
Closure 57120
Complete
with Removal of Paravaginal Tissue 57111, 57112
with Removal of Vaginal Wall 57110
Partial
with Removal of Paravaginal Tissue . 57107
with Removal of Paravaginal Tissue with Lymphadenectomy 57109
with Removal of Vaginal Wall 57106
Total 57110
with Hysterectomy 58275-58280
with Repair of Enterocele 58280
Exploration
Endocervical 57452
Incision 57000
Fluid
Sialidase Activity 87905
Hematoma
Incision and Drainage 57022-57023
Hemorrhage 57180
Hysterectomy 58290, 58550-58554
Incision and Drainage 57020
Insertion
Ovoid
for Brachytherapy 57155
Packing for Bleeding 57180
Pessary 57160
Irrigation 57150
Lesion
Destruction 57061-57065
Extensive 57065
Simple 57061
Prolapse
Sacrospinous Ligament Fixation 57282
Removal
Foreign Body 57415
Prosthetic Graft 57295-57296
Sling
Stress Incontinence 57287
Repair 56800
Cystocele 57240, 57260
Combined Anteroposterior . . . 57260-57265
Posterior 57240
Enterocele 57265
Fistula 51900
Rectovaginal 57300-57308
Transvesical and Vaginal Approach . . 57330
Urethrovaginal 57310-57311
Vesicovaginal 51900, 57320-57330
Hysterectomy 58267, 58293
Incontinence 57284-57285, 57288
Obstetric 59300
Paravaginal Defect 57284-57285, 57423
Pereyra Procedure 57289
Prolapse 57282-57285, 57423
Prosthesis Insertion 57267
Rectocele
Combined Anteroposterior . . . 57260-57265
Posterior 57250
Suspension 57280-57283
Laparoscopic 57425
Urethral Sphincter 57220
Wound 57200-57210
Colpoperineorrhaphy 57210
Colporrhaphy 57200
Revision
Prosthetic Graft 57295-57296
Sling
Stress Incontinence 57287
Septum
Excision 57130
Suspension 57280-57283
Laparoscopic 57425
Suture
Cystocele 57240, 57260
Enterocele 57265
Fistula 51900, 57300-57330
Rectocele 57250-57260
Wound 57200-57210
Tumor
Excision 57135
Ultrasound 76830
Unlisted Services and Procedures 58999
X-ray with Contrast 74775

Vaginal Delivery 59400, 59610-59614

after Previous Cesarean Delivery . . . 59610-59612
Attempted 59618-59622
Antepartum Care 59400
Cesarean Delivery after Attempted 59618
Delivery Only 59620
Postpartum Care 59622
Delivery after Previous Vaginal Delivery Only
Postpartum Care 59614
Delivery Only 59409
External Cephalic Version 59412
Placenta 59414
Postpartum Care 59410
Routine Care 59400

Vaginal Hysterectomy 58552-58554

Vaginal Smear

See Pap Smears

Vaginal Suppositories

Induced Abortion 59855
with Dilation and Curettage 59856
with Hysterectomy 59857

Vaginectomy

See Colpectomy

Vaginoplasty

Intersex State 57335

Vaginorrhaphy

See Colporrhaphy

Vestibule of Mouth
See Mouth, Vestibule of

Vestibuloplasty 40840-40845

Vidal Procedure
See Varicocele, Spermatic Cord, Excision

Video
Esophagus 74230
Pharynx 70371, 74230
Speech Evaluation 70371
Swallowing Evaluation 74230

Video-Assisted Thoracoscopic Surgery
See Thoracoscopy

Videoradiography
Unlisted Services and Procedures .. 76120-76125

VII, Coagulation Factor
See Proconvertin

VII, Cranial Nerve
See Facial Nerve

VIII, Coagulation Factor
See Clotting Factor

Villus, Chorionic
See Chorionic Villus

Villusectomy
See Synovectomy

VIP
See Vasoactive Intestinal Peptide

Viral Antibodies 86280

Viral Warts
See Warts

Virtual Colonoscopy
Diagnostic 0067T
Screening 0066T

Virus
AIDS
See HIV-1
Burkitt Lymphoma
See Epstein-Barr Virus
Human Immunodeficiency
See HIV
Influenza
See Influenza Virus
Respiratory Syncytial
See Respiratory Syncytial Virus
Salivary Gland
See Cytomegalovirus

Virus Identification
Immunofluorescence 87254

Virus Isolation 87250-87255

Visceral Larval Migrans 86280

Viscosities, Blood
See Blood, Viscosity

Visit, Home
See House Calls

Visual Acuity Screen 99172-99173

Visual Field Exam 92081-92083

Visual Function Screen ... 1055F, 99172

Visual Reinforcement Audiometry 92579
See Audiologic Function Tests

Visualization
Ileal Conduit 50690

Vital Capacity Measurement ... 94150

Vitamin 84591
A 84590
B Complex
See B Complex Vitamins
B-1 84425
B-12 82607-82608
Absorption Study 78270-78272
Holotranscobalamin 0103T
B-2 84252
B-6 84207
B-6 Measurement
See Pyridoxal Phosphate
BC
See Folic Acid
C 82180
D 82307, 82652, 4019F
D, 25-Hydroxy Measurement
See Calcifediol
D-2
See Calciferol
D-3 82306
E 84446
K 84597
K Dependent Bone Protein
See Osteocalcin
K-Dependent Protein S
See Protein S

Vitelline Duct
See Omphalomesenteric Duct

Vitrectomy
Anterior Approach
Partial 67005
for Retinal Detachment 67112-67113
Monitoring of Intraocular Pressure 0173T
Drainage Device 0191T, 0192T
Pars Plana Approach 67036-67043
Subtotal 67010
with Endolaser Panretinal Photocoagulation 67040
with Focal Endolaser Photocoagulation 67039
with Implantation or Replacement
Drug Delivery System 67027

Vitreous
Aspiration 67015
Excision
Pars Plana Approach ... 67036, 67041-67043
with Focal Endolaser Photocoagulation 67039
Implantation
Drug Delivery System 67027
Incision
Strands 67030-67031
Injection
Fluid Substitute 67025
Pharmacologic Agent 67028
Placement
Radiation Source 0190T
Removal
Anterior Approach 67005
Subtotal 67010
Replacement
Drug Delivery System 67027
Strands
Discission 67030
Severing 67031
Subtotal 67010

VLDL
See Lipoprotein, Blood

VMA
See Vanillylmandelic Acid

Vocal Cords
Injection
Endoscopy 31513
Therapeutic 31570-31571

Voice Box
See Larynx

Voice Button 31611

Voiding Pressure Studies
Abdominal 51797
Bladder 51795
Rectum 51797

Volatiles 84600

Volhard's Test
See Water Load Test

Volkman Contracture 25315-25316

Volume Reduction
Blood Products 86960

Volume Reduction, Lung
See Lung Volume Reduction

Von Kraske Proctectomy
See Proctectomy, Partial

VP
See Voiding Pressure Studies

Vulva
Abscess
Incision and Drainage 56405
Colposcopy 56820
Biopsy 56821
Excision
Complete 56625, 56633-56640
Partial 56620, 56630-56632
Radical 56630-56631, 56633-56640
Complete 56633-56640
Partial 56630-56632
Simple
Complete 56625
Partial 56620
Lesion
Destruction 56501-56515

W

Exploration
  Penetrating
    Abdomen/Flank/Back 20102
    Chest 20101
    Extremity 20103
    Neck 20100
  Penetrating Trauma 20100-20103
Infection
  Incision and Drainage
    Postoperative 10180
Negative Pressure Therapy 97605-97606
Repair
  Complex 13100-13160
  Intermediate 12031-12057
  Simple 12001-12021
  Urethra 53502-53515
Suture
  Bladder 51860-51865
  Kidney 50500
  Trachea
    Cervical 31800
    Intrathoracic 31805
  Urethra 53502-53515
Vagina
  Repair 57200-57210

Wrist

See Arm, Lower; Carpal Bone
Abscess 25028
Arthrocentesis 20605
Arthrodesis 25800
  with Graft 25810
  with Sliding Graft 25805
Arthrography 73115
Arthroplasty 25332, 25443, 25447
  Revision 25449
  Total Replacement 25446
  with Implant 25441-25442, 25444-25445
Arthroscopy
  Diagnostic 29840
  Surgical 29843-29848
Arthrotomy 25040, 25100-25105
  for Repair 25107
Biopsy 25065-25066, 25100-25101
Bursa
  Excision 25115-25116
  Incision and Drainage 25031
Capsule
  Incision 25085
Cast 29085
Cyst 25130-25136
Decompression 25020-25025
Disarticulation 25920
  Reamputation 25924
  Revision 25922
Dislocation
  Closed Treatment 25660
  Intercarpal 25660
    Open Treatment 25670
  Open Treatment 25670, 25676
  Percutaneous Fixation 25671
  Radiocarpal 25660
    Open Treatment 25670
  Radioulnar
    Closed Treatment 25675
    Percutaneous Fixation 25671
  with Fracture
    Closed Treatment 25680
    Open Treatment 25685
  with Manipulation 25259, 25660, 25675
Excision
  Carpal 25210-25215
  Cartilage 25107
Exploration 25040, 25101
Fasciotomy 25020-25025
Fracture 25645
  Closed Treatment 25622, 25630
  Open Treatment 25628
  with Dislocation 25680-25685
  with Manipulation 25259, 25624, 25635
Ganglion Cyst
  Excision 25111-25112
Hematoma 25028
Incision 25040, 25100-25105
  Tendon Sheath 25000-25001
Injection
  Carpal Tunnel
    Therapeutic 20526
  X-ray 25246
Joint
  See Radiocarpal Joint
Lesion, Tendon Sheath
  Excision 25110
Magnetic Resonance Imaging (MRI) 73221
Reconstruction
  Capsulectomy 25320
  Capsulorrhaphy 25320
  Carpal Bone 25394, 25430
  Realign 25335
Removal
  Foreign Body 25040, 25101, 25248
  Implant 25449
  Loose Body 25101
  Prosthesis 25250-25251
Repair 25447
  Bone 25440
  Carpal Bone 25431
  Muscle 25260, 25270
    Secondary 25263-25265, 25272-25274
  Tendon 25260, 25270, 25280-25316
    Secondary 25263-25265, 25272-25274
  Tendon Sheath 25275
Strapping 29260
Synovium
  Excision 25105, 25115-25119
Tendon
  Excision 25109
Tendon Sheath
  Excision 25115-25116
Tenodesis 25300-25301
Tenotomy 25290
Tumor 25130-25136
  Excision 25075-25077
Unlisted Services and Procedures 25999
X-ray 73100-73110
  with Contrast 73115

X

X, Coagulation Factor

See Stuart-Prower Factor

X, Cranial Nerve

See Vagus Nerve

X-Linked Ichthyoses

See Syphilis Test

X-ray

Abdomen 74000-74022
Abscess 76080
Acromioclavicular Joint 73050
Ankle 73600-73610
Arm, Lower 73090
Arm, Upper 73092
Artery
  Atherectomy 75992-75996
Auditory Meatus 70134
Barium Swallow Test 3142F, 3200F
Bile Duct
  Guide Dilation 74360
Body Section 76100
  Motion 76101-76102
Bone
  Age Study 77072
  Dual Energy Absorptiometry ...77080-77081
  Length Study 77073
  Osseous Survey 77074-77077
  Ultrasound 76977
Breast 77055-77057
  Localization Nodule 77032
  with Computer-aided
    Detection 77051-77052
Calcaneus 73650
Chest 71010-71035
  Complete (Four Views)
    with Fluoroscopy 71034
  Insert Pacemaker 71090
  Partial (Two Views)
    with Fluoroscopy 71023
  Stereo 71015
  with Computer-Aided
    Detection 0174T-0175T
  with Fluoroscopy 71090
Clavicle 73000
Coccyx 72220
Consultation 76140
Duodenum 74260
Elbow 73070-73080
Esophagus 74220
Eye 70030
Facial Bones 70140-70150
Fallopian Tube 74742
Femur 73550
Fibula 73590
Finger 73140
Fistula 76080
Foot 73620-73630
Gastrointestinal Tract 74240-74245
  Guide Dilation 74360
  Guide Intubation 74340
  Upper 3142F, 3200F

Y

Yacoub Procedure
See Ascending Aorta Graft

Yeast
Culture 87106

Yellow Fever Vaccine 90717

Yersinia
Antibody 86793

YHrium-Aluminum-Garnet (YAG) Laser
See Eye, Incision

Z

Ziegler Procedure
Discission Secondary Membranous Cataract 66820

Zinc 84630

Zinc Manganese Leucine Aminopeptidase
See Leucine Aminopeptidase

Zygoma
See Cheekbone

Zygomatic Arch
Fracture
Open Treatment 21356-21366
with Manipulation 21355

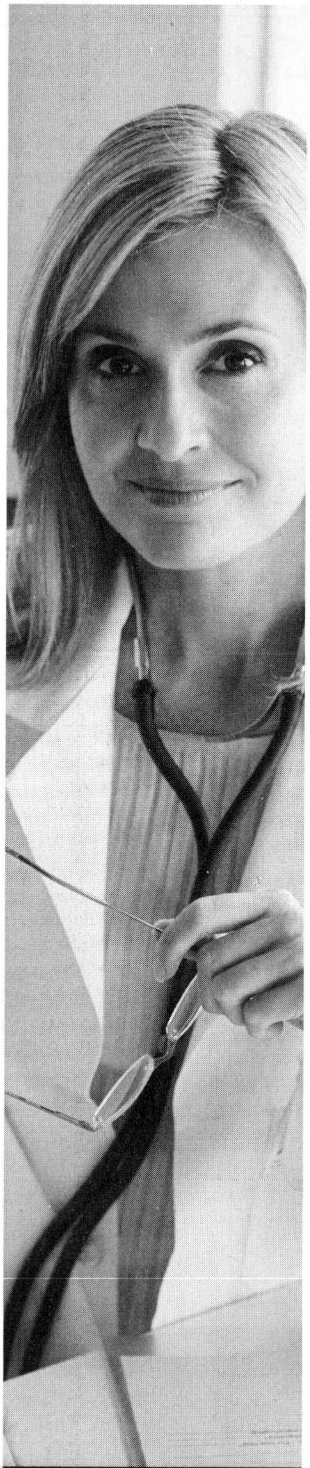